# Library and Book Trade Almanac™

formerly **The Bowker Annual**

2009 | 54th Edition

# Library and Book Trade Almanac™

## formerly The Bowker Annual

### 2009 | 54th Edition

**Editor** Dave Bogart
**Consultant** Julia C. Blixrud

 Information Today, Inc.

Published by Information Today, Inc.
Copyright © 2009 Information Today, Inc.
All rights reserved

International Standard Book Number  978-1-57387-349-9
International Standard Serial Number  0068-0540
Library of Congress Catalog Card Number  55-12434

Information Today, Inc.
143 Old Marlton Pike
Medford, NJ   08055-8750
Phone:    800-300-9868 (customer service)
          800-409-4929 (editorial queries)
Fax:      609-654-4309
E-mail (orders): custserv@infotoday.com
Web Site: http://www.infotoday.com

Printed and bound in the United States of America

US $209
ISBN 13: 978-1-57387-349-9
20900

9 781573 873499

# Contents

## International Reports

# Part 2
# Legislation, Funding, and Grants

## Legislation

## Funding Programs and Grant-Making Agencies

# Part 3
# Library/Information Science Education, Placement, and Salaries

# Part 4
# Research and Statistics

# Part 5
# Reference Information

# Distinguished Books

# Part 6
# Directory of Organizations

## Directory of Library and Related Organizations

## Directory of Book Trade and Related Organizations

# Preface

This 54th edition of the *Library and Book Trade Almanac* (formerly the *Bowker Annual Library and Book Trade Almanac*) once again incorporates practical information and informed analysis of interest to librarians, publishers, and others in the rapidly evolving information world.

The past year has seen many changes, from a new administration in Washington to a deepening national and world financial crisis. There are new challenges—and fresh opportunities—around every corner, and the demand for reliable and accurate information continually grows. Our aim is to help answer that demand.

This edition's Special Reports focus on five areas of interest.

- William C. Welburn and Janice Welburn examine the strides made by libraries in dealing with a diverse public and in making sure diversity is a major consideration in acquisition of resources and in staffing and training practices.

- Edward Valauskas and Nancy John review major developments in scholarly publishing, particularly in the changing balance between author and publisher.

- M. Sue Baughman looks at organization development in libraries, commenting that "The development of the capacity of a library to deal effectively with change is critical for maintaining its position with its customers and community."

- Sarah K. Wiant details important developments in the ever-changing realm of copyright.

- Julie Beth Todaro analyzes the particular needs of community colleges as they design information programs, resources, and services to match student requirements.

Part 1 continues with reports on the activities of federal libraries, federal agencies, and national and international library and publishing organizations.

Recent and current legislation affecting libraries and publishing is covered in Part 2, along with the programs and activities of major grant-making agencies.

Part 3 offers a wealth of professional information for librarians, including salary studies, job-seeking advice, and a full list of the year's library scholarship and award winners.

Part 4 contains our growing statistics and research section, which offers detailed data on many aspects of the library and publishing worlds, from trends in school library media resource funding to an examination of U.S. world trade in books.

Reference information fills Part 5, including a roster of major literary prize winners and lists of notable books and other resources for all ages.

Part 6 is our directory of library and publishing organizations at the state, national, and international levels, and also includes a calendar of major upcoming events.

The *Library and Book Trade Almanac* is the work of many hands. We are grateful to everyone who supplied reports, assembled statistics, and responded to our many requests for information. Special gratitude is due to Consultant Editor Julia C. Blixrud and Contributing Editor Catherine Barr, and to Christine McNaull for her invaluable assistance in making it all come together.

We believe you will find this 54th edition a valuable resource to which you will often turn, and, as always, we welcome your comments and suggestions for future editions.

Dave Bogart
Editor

# Part 1
# Reports from the Field

# Special Reports

## The Promise of Diversity in the Library Community

William C. Welburn and Janice Welburn

*Dedication:*
The authors dedicate this report to Virginia Lacy Jones,
Arnulfo Duenes Trejo, and E. J. Josey, who pioneered efforts
to bring diversity to libraries and librarianship.

In recent decades, libraries, library associations, and library and information science (LIS) educators have created important partnerships to promote diversity as a core value in education and practice. As a result of the collaborations among library and information professionals and educators, substantial gains have been made in building inclusive communities in libraries, archives, and information centers, reflecting the ideas and actions of staff and decision-makers on outreach and service, acquiring information resources, and preserving and providing access to the cultural heritage of diverse communities.

The synergy created in the library community* to recruit library and information professionals from diverse communities is also reflective of a renewed commitment to workplace diversity. What remains for the library community to consider is the extent to which changing institutional and professional practices to achieve diversity will be driven by broader social transformations, given the consistency of reportage on the speed of demographic and cultural change in large and mid-sized cities, small towns, and rural communities (Roberts, 2008), along with the limitations placed on geopolitical boundaries as a way of defining the meaning of *community*. To "think globally, act locally" is far too narrow a world view in an increasingly networked, diverse society. The challenges posed to LIS environments by such social transformations are substantially reflected in how diversity is understood in concept and in practice. Specifically, how is diver-

---

*By "library community" the authors refer to a broad membership that includes libraries, archives, and information centers, library and information professionals, and degree programs in library and information science.

William Welburn has served as Associate Dean of the Graduate College at the University of Illinois at Urbana-Champaign since 2006. He writes on a range of library issues, including diversity, libraries and graduate education, and documenting African American cultures and communities. Janice Welburn has been Dean of the Raynor Memorial Libraries at Marquette University since 1996. She has published on issues in management and diversity and is co-editor with Beth McNeil of *Human Resource Management in Today's Academic Library* (Libraries Unlimited, 2004) and of a forthcoming collection of essays on advocacy and academic libraries.

sity defined to meet the challenges of the first decades of the 21st century? How does diversity in practice play out in different communities and libraries? If diversity is accepted as a core professional value, then what strategies are available to transform both profession and workplace in libraries? And what evidence must we have to determine the efficacy of diversity in practice?

## Definition of Diversity

There is no shortage of examples of how diversity is embraced among associations in the library community. Within the American Library Association (ALA), diversity has been listed as a key action area since 1998, when ALA Council designated diversity as "a fundamental value of the association and its members . . . reflected in its commitment to recruiting people of color and people with disabilities to the profession and to the promotion and development of library collections and services for all people" (American Library Association, 2007). The Society of American Archivists (SAA) has identified diversity as a "significant and ongoing concern of the SAA membership and the archival profession" (Society of American Archivists, 2002). Among ALA divisions, the Association of College and Research Libraries (ACRL) has provided space for sections and discussion groups focusing on information resources in diverse areas of studies and has issued reports and white papers on racial and ethnic diversity in the academic library work force (Neely and Peterson, 2007). ACRL has also had in existence for nearly two decades a standing Racial and Ethnic Diversity Committee, with a charge to "initiate, advise and mobilize support for appropriate action related to issues of racial and ethnic diversity in academic librarianship including recruitment, advancement and retention of under-represented groups to academic librarianship and the promotion of quality academic library and information services for members of racial and ethnic groups." (Association of College and Research Libraries, 2006). ALA has also encouraged diversity initiatives through roundtables and discussion groups, such as the longstanding Social Responsibilities Round Table (SRRT); the Gay, Lesbian, Bisexual, and Transgendered Round Table (GLBTRT); and the Diversity Officers Discussion Group of its Library Leadership and Management Association (LLAMA). Moreover, the list of ALA-affiliated organizations—among them REFORMA, the American Indian Library Association, the Black Caucus of ALA, and the Asian/Pacific American Librarians Association—continues to mature, offering focal points for organizing racialized and ethnic communities outside of the organization proper.

However, defining the meaning of diversity is more elusive in the library community, as it has been for corporations, higher education, and for government and nonprofit organizations. The efforts of associations described earlier are trend-driven, created in response to or in consideration of significant changes in demography and in cultural norms. The term *diversity* takes on different meaning as discussion deepens on how to recruit new library and information professionals or on developing programs that effectively reach various communities. In practice, diversity is more of a world view or perception of the ways in which different groups associate with one another than it is a mix of characteristics of individual people. As organizational behaviorists Daan van Knippenberg and Michaéla C. Schippers observed:

> Our review of the field [of diversity] suggests that four issues in this respect warrant attention: first, the possibility to better understand the effects of diversity by distinguishing between different types of diversity; second, the potential added value of moving beyond the study of demographic and functional diversity; third, the potential added value of conceptualizations of diversity that move beyond simple dispersion; and fourth, the notion that diversity's effects may be better understood if the influence of different dimensions of diversity is studied in interactions rather than as additive effects (van Knippenberg and Schippers, 2008).

In other words, these observations advise us to think about *diversity* as an all-encompassing word that not only takes into consideration such demographic characteristics as race, ethnicity, gender, and sexual identity, but also less apparent dimensions, including class, educational background, and cognitive differences. The utility of diversity requires managers to "define the motive(s) behind their interest in diversity and identify the specific ways diversity will benefit their organizations" (Kreitz, 2008). Not only does the meaning of *diversity* entail association or social interaction between two or more different groups; it does not exclude or privilege any single group, and serves to countervail a sense of isolation felt by one group in relation to others, especially under conditions of social inequity.

## Diversity as Characteristics of Community

Much of the focus of diversity in libraries has been aimed at population trends and changes reflected in such indicators as migration and immigration, social mobility, economic class, linguistic isolation, age, and physical disability. Regardless of type of institution, libraries, archives, and information centers are key agencies for communicating information across various communities of users, no matter how they are distinguished from one another by these indicators. In the United States substantial changes continue to be experienced in the racial and ethnic composition of communities, as evidenced by recent reports from the U.S. Census Bureau. While these changes are part of historical patterns of U.S. immigration and migration, today racialized and ethnic communities are emerging across small-town America as well as in the nation's cities, and dramatic social change is particularly evident in the numbers of households where languages other than English are spoken (Roberts, 2008).

Beyond race and ethnicity, diversity has come to signify growing challenges to the status quo on fundamental civil and human rights. This is also evident in the responses of lesbian, gay, bisexual, and transgendered communities seeking to secure fundamental civil rights and the removal of social barriers that affect state laws and the practices of government and private sector organizations on a broad range of issues, from health care to marriage.

The social milieu of communities rapidly changes not through the presence of distinct groups, but by their association with one another in shared spaces. Rather than focus our attention on the existence of individual cultural groups as a point of reference for designing services, we need to look at such changes as migration and how marginalized communities efforts to assert their rights alter the way in which groups associate with one another. This association also defines the ways in which libraries and library and information professionals work with those communities on issues ranging from outreach and service to hiring practices and equity in the workplace.

## Diversity as Interaction Between Groups

The association between different populations—rather than the dispersion of groups—provides a clearer pathway to manage diversity in library communities. Diversity then becomes a dynamic construct reflecting both social interactions between disparate groups and deeper-level associations beyond important demographic characteristics that include cognitive, interpersonal, and intercultural differences. Libraries and library and information professionals can further develop strategies for managing diversity by identifying points of intersection between communities or demographic groups where people share common ground, whether by necessity or by choice (Blackwell, Kwoh, and Pastor, 2002), or conversely where people from one group are substantially isolated from other groups because of cultural barriers. A remarkable example of the capacity of libraries to create opportunities in shared spaces is described by Robert Putnam and Lewis Feldstein in *Better Together: Restoring the American Community* (Putnam and Feldstein, 2004). They observed the coexistence of different groups in a branch of the Chicago Public Library as a form of social benefit to the broader community. They characterized the branch library—resting between communities that were socioeconomically and culturally different from one another—as a third place that fosters social engagement away from home, school, and work. In this example, library services are affected, if not consciously reformed, by planning that takes into consideration the common interests of diverse communities in a contact zone for reading and resolving information needs (Elmborg, 2006).

## Diversity and Social Inequality

A third aspect of diversity has received renewed interest (Kalev, Dobbin, and Kelly, 2006), that of the effect of long-term social inequality on underlying structures of organizations and societies. Social inequality establishes a basis for looking at imbalances and inequities that undermine even the most earnest approaches to promoting diversity in organizations and communities. Unfortunately, social inequalities are hard to eradicate. Sociologist Charles Tilly defined these durable inequalities as ". . . those that last from one social interaction to the next . . ." and respond to categorical rather than individual differences that separate whole classes or groups from one another (Tilly, 1999).

Social inequality represents the greatest challenge to diversity in library communities. It affects the allocation of resources for outreach programming and services; available funding to strengthen library collections; and hiring, team building, and promotion practices. It weathers leadership changes and economic fluctuations, and it survives well-intended diversity training and programming

(Kalev, Dobbin, and Kelly, 2006). Leadership from frontline librarians and administrators alike is required to shift priorities, alter organizational practices, and ensure enduring changes that mirror, if not outpace, broader societal transformations.

## Diversity in Libraries: Advocacy in Practice

If managing diversity means a focus on the way that groups of people connect with one another, and if the real challenge presented by diversity is to eradicate social inequality, then progress on diversity in libraries should be looked at on the basis of specific steps taken by the library community. In the past two decades, several important strides toward building an inclusive and diverse community have been taken by librarians, archivists, and other information professionals; these have involved partnerships or collaborative activity between institutions, working professionals, and professional associations, with extraordinary support from governmental and private sector institutions and foundations. Efforts toward diversity in libraries have assumed the strategic practices of advocacy (Todaro, 2007) to achieve change in three important areas: education of the next generations of librarians and information professionals, the development of librarians from diverse backgrounds who seek to advance their careers through professional growth opportunities, and redefining and restructuring outreach and services to diverse communities.

## Preparing Coming Generations

Think of diversity as a continuum; not a linear path where everything follows in proper sequence, but a river much like that depicted by William Bowen and Derek Bok in the opening pages of *The Shape of the River*—a process like "nurturing talent" that entails "moving down a winding river, with rock-strewn rapids and slow channels, muddy at times and clear at others." It is no coincidence that the authors go on to write, "Particularly when race is involved, there is nothing simple, smooth, or highly predictable about the education of young people." (Bowen and Bok, 1998).

Whether young in age or career, the source of the river—the "cradle" of diversity—lies in recruiting and preparing new library and information professionals through programs in library and information science, perhaps in collaboration with libraries, information centers, archives, and other organizations. Yet the process of recruiting students to master's programs poses several significant challenges. According to the 2004 annual statistical report of the Association for Library and Information Science Education (ALISE, 2005), 12.3 percent of the 16,878 students enrolling in ALA-accredited master's degree programs in fall 2003 were age 24 or younger, approximating students from a traditional undergraduate-to-graduate population making library and information science their first post-baccalaureate career choice. A considerably larger number—22.8 percent—were students in the 25–29 age bracket. These data suggest that a twofold recruiting and marketing strategy continues to be needed to attract master's students in LIS programs in order to increase the proportion of students recruited directly from baccalaureate degree programs while also preserving the appeal of the master's degree to returning, nontraditional, and second-career students and to individuals recruited directly from the ranks of library staffs.

There are challenges in both groups that are especially pronounced when working with diverse communities defined by race and ethnicity, gender, sexual identity, class, and disability; challenges that are further highlighted by deep-level diversities of cognitive and social behaviors. For instance, students from racialized and ethnic communities who are also traditional-aged undergraduate students are likely to consider library and information science among an array of academic and professional options that on the surface appear to be more lucrative or ensure higher professional status—among them disciplines in which women were historically under-represented, such as the sciences and engineering. These disciplines have become substantially more aggressive in changing their gender compositions, and this competition adversely affects the chances of attracting women to information technology positions. As a result, recruiting students from diverse communities has become a more severely competitive endeavor that requires an increased investment in marketing and more rigorous recruiting.

Returning students must also weigh the benefits of an advanced degree against an array of costs, including tuition, suspending income, and personal and family obligations. The cost of graduate education has increased greatly in recent years. Especially hard hit are racial and ethnic minority students and students from low-income families for whom graduate education may appear to be financially prohibitive (Redd, 2006). The challenge, then, for LIS educators and for professional associations is to simultaneously market opportunities and options and create financial safety nets for those who opt to pursue degrees.

Several important initiatives have been introduced by LIS programs, libraries, and professional associations that serve as creative responses to the challenge of attracting and building diverse communities of students. Many present-day programs are rooted in the initiatives of previous generations, particularly in the work of Virginia Lacy Jones and E. J. Josey, in the Graduate Library Institute for Spanish-speaking Americans (GLISSA) created in 1975 by Arnulfo Duenes Trejo, and in a series of institutes created by Lorene B. Brown at Atlanta University in the late 1970s and early 1980s. These early initiatives provide an important context for observing the accomplishments of the current generation of programs centered in LIS programs and libraries. The LIS Access Midwest Program (LAMP) centered at the University of Illinois at Urbana-Champaign brings together LIS programs and libraries throughout the Midwest to "encourage undergraduate students from under-represented populations to consider graduate work in LIS" (GSLIS Alumni Magazine, 2008) combining mentoring and financial support to create an opportunity for undergraduate students to select library and information science as a first-choice career option.

At the University of Arizona, the Knowledge River program has drawn students from Hispanic and Native American communities to the School of Information Resources and Library Science. The program not only provides financial incentives but support from cohort groups, cultural fluency, and opportunity for engagement in communities through library and related internships. The Indiana State Library has created a program, "Librarians Leading in Diversity" (LLID), that provides networking and mentoring opportunities to students from various racial and ethnic communities across the state who agree to work for Indiana's libraries for at least two years. The Dallas Public Library, in an effort to increase the number of Spanish-speaking library professionals in the metropolitan Dallas area, has funding to create opportunities for staff to pursue master's degrees. These initiatives have a common source of external funding—the Institute for Museum and Library Services' Laura Bush 21st Century Librarian grant program, which has proven critical to inaugurating an array of creative solutions to diversifying the community of library and information professionals.

Associations have also developed important initiatives that provide financial support, leadership and mentoring, and programmatic involvement for students from culturally diverse communities. For instance, membership in ALA and its divisions has supported minority scholarship programs since the mid-1970s. Each year since the early 1990s, ALA's Library and Information Technology Association (LITA) has awarded two scholarships, the LITA/OCLC Minority Scholarship and the LITA/LSSI Minority Scholarship, to encourage diversity in careers in library and information technology. In 1993 SAA established the Harold T. Pinkett Minority Student Award "to encourage exceptional minority students to consider careers in the archival profession and, in turn, increase minority participation in SAA by exposing minority students to the experience of attending national meetings and encouraging them to join the organization" (Society of American Archivists, 2008). More recently, the efforts of ALA (the Spectrum Scholarship Program), ARL (Recruiting a Diverse Work Force), SAA (the Mosaic Scholarship Program), the Special Libraries Association (the Affirmative Action Scholarship), the American Association of Law Librarians (the George A. Strait Minority Scholarship), and the inclusion of library science in the Gates Millennium Scholarship Program have not only financed students' LIS educations but also offered leadership opportunities and socialization into professional life.

Finally, key support for LIS students also comes from scholarships awarded by the Black Caucus of the American Library Association, REFORMA, the Asian/Pacific American Library Association, and the American Indian Library Association. These organizations are also crucial to agenda-setting on the full range of diversity issues inside ALA by providing forums to recruit and sustain librarians from their respective groups and to advocate for social and cultural change within the LIS profession at large.

## Residency Programs: Launching Careers

In addition to creating new opportunities to support efforts to recruit culturally diverse communities of students to LIS programs and, specifically, to offset funding obstacles, libraries and associations have worked collaboratively to form residency programs. Although the concept is not new (Brewer, 1997) and is congruent with the goals of internship programs developed in many federal libraries, many new programs developed in the past two decades have had a specific focus on diversity. As Raquel V. Cogell noted in the introduction to a collection of essays on residency programs as a strategy for advocating diversity, "In spite of the assault on affirmative action across the country, the number of programs designed to increase the presence of librarians from the four major under-represented groups seems to be increasing rather than diminishing. There are close to 20 active minority-based residency programs, more than half of which were established between 1995–2000." (Cogell and Grunwell, 2001).

The function of residencies, according to ALISE, is to provide "postdegree work experiences designed as entry-level programs for professionals who have recently received an MLS," which is distinguished from internships for current LIS students and fellowships for midcareer librarians (Brewer, 1997). Residents often serve from one to two years either in rotation in a library or within an area of specialization to gain exposure to career and professional development requirements. In some instances, where there is a critical mass, residents form a professional community. In others, individual mentoring with experienced librarians is crucial, often leading to presentations, publications, and involvement in professional organizations.

Interest has not diminished, although residency programs appear to be concentrated in academic and research libraries. In November 2008 ACRL approved a Residency Interest Group formed from the Library Residency Working Group. The purpose of this new interest group is to provide "a central location for information about program availability; the creation of core competencies, evaluation and assessment standards; and the overall advancement of the quality of resident education" (Association of College and Research Libraries, 2008).

## Diversifying Library Leadership

Not only are residencies designed to launch careers, there is some expectation that libraries, archives, and information centers are preparing the next generation of leaders. Several associations and individual libraries and LIS programs have initiated programs designed to do this. The Spectrum Scholarship Program mentioned above and the Dallas Public Library "Grow Your Own Librarian" program are both designed to develop leadership skills among participants. In addition, several important career-development programs have been created by leading library organizations since the mid-1990s. The Special Libraries Association (SLA) has a long history of efforts to encourage participation by under-represented minorities through its Committee on Positive Action Programs for Minority Groups, formed in 1973 and now called the Diversity Leadership Development Program Committee. The program provides mentoring opportunities for a population of early-career librarians who are "traditionally under-represented in the Association's membership by mentoring them for more leadership opportunities within SLA" (Special Libraries Association, 2008). The Association of Research Libraries (ARL) Leadership and Career Development Program, for the past dozen years, has selected a group of participants from under-represented populations for mentoring and professional development through attendance at national meetings and two institutes, mentoring and coaching by an ARL library director, and related activities. Many of their alumni have accepted positions of higher responsibility, including posts as library directors in college and university libraries (Offord, 2006). Finally, the American Association of Law Librarians established its Minority Leadership Development Award in 2001 to "nurture leaders for the future and to introduce minority law librarians to leadership opportunities within the association" (American Association of Law Librarians, n.d.).

## Reaching Diverse Communities

Although a substantial amount of attention has been focused on diversity in the library workplace, important advances have been made in addressing environments and cultures of communities served by libraries. Understanding the growing diversity of community life in large and moderately sized cities, small towns, and rural communities throughout the United States is key to understanding how libraries, archives, and related organizations are reaching diverse communities. Examples include efforts to better serve bilingual and multilingual communities, to work with students on college campuses, or to meet the changing needs of scholarship in historical and cultural studies.

One important avenue to assess the impact of diversity in communities is to examine library and information services through historical lenses. This provides an opportunity to examine the historical sociology of association among libraries, archives, and related institutions with community growth, social movements, and migration and changing populations. There is a significant body of research looking at issues and events in historical context by a number of researchers, including Dorothy Porter, Billie Walker (Walker, 2005), John Mark Tucker (Tucker, 1998) Cheryl Knott Malone (Malone, 1999, 2000, 2007), Michael Fultz (Fultz, 2006) and Salvador Güereña and Edward Erazo (Güereña and Erazo, 2000) who have looked at the development of services in segregated environments, libraries caught in the milieu of social change, and the efforts of individual librarians to create opportunities to serve diverse communities.

Looking at the past in association with the present can give added insight into the ways in which libraries have dealt with important social processes and conditions. Much of the cited historical research has focused on services to segregated and assimilating racialized populations and the assurance of fundamental civil rights. These historical lenses are especially useful in understanding a vast array of contemporary issues regarding populations of library users that are not only culturally diverse but differ along linguistic and economic dimensions or by physical or mental ability to use resources, services, technologies, or buildings, and that can include populations that are underserved by a full range of community and social services.

Two important yet radically different examples of our understanding of the ways in which we reach diverse communities at present involve issues of access based on disability and language. Regarding the challenges of disability as a part of the broader discussion of diversity, the question of fundamental civil rights governs much of the current focus on removing obstacles and thinking in terms of accessibility to facilities, services, resources, and technologies. According to the U.S. Census Bureau, by 2005 nearly 1 in 5 Americans (more than 50 percent of them aged 65 or older) reported having a disability (Brault, 2008). ALA's Association of Specialized and Cooperative Library Agencies (ASCLA) has been especially resourceful in providing guidance on legal, behavioral, and technical issues and support for removing access barriers (American Library Association, online tutorial, "Accessibility Basics for Librarians"). Additionally, some individual libraries have given consideration to the cultures of disabilities. For instance, Rochester Institute of Technology Libraries has assembled resources on deaf culture, broken down by race and ethnicity, that provide more insight into the cultural dimensions within the disabled population (Rochester Institute of Technology Libraries, n.d.).

Service to non-English-speakers has been a part of library services in communities that have historically served as ports of entry for immigrants; however, U.S. Census data clearly supports a broader perception that language diversity is substantially more prevalent today in small to medium-sized cities and towns and rural communities. According to the Census Bureau, more than 47 million Americans (18 percent of the population) speak a language other than English at home. This represents a substantial increase from previous decades, up from 14 percent in 1990 and 11 percent in 1980 (Shin and Bruno, 2003). Despite the angst expressed in political and media debates over immigration and English-only laws, the demand for services and resources is significant. Surveys by OCLC indicate a demand for non-English-language materials by library users that transcends public, school, and community and four-year colleges (OCLC, 2008). A major study issued in 2008 by the ALA Office for Research and Statistics also found that the trends among public libraries serving populations of non-English-speakers mirror census reports, in that an increasing number of libraries in communities with fewer than 100,000 residents are serving increasing numbers of non-English-speakers. Moreover, literacy as indicated by reading and library habits is crucial to considering services to linguistically isolated communities. The marriage of population trends and evidence from recent library reports suggests that more libraries—school, public, and academic alike—are challenged to design services, provide access to information resources, and employ technologies that are increasingly sensitive to linguistic isolation and multilingualism.

## Suggestions for Future Development

A review of diversity as practiced among librarians, archivists, and other information professionals, and by libraries and professional associations, gives a clear indication of an evolution in diversity as a core value. There is, however, a need to develop a better understanding of how the library community in general can improve its efforts on diversity as it addresses long-term inequality in social processes of hiring and advancement for working professionals, agenda-setting for associations, and institutional change in response to multiple publics served by libraries, archives, and other information agencies. To further our understanding of diversity and its implications at the end of the first decade of the 21st century, two needs emerge.

First, there is a paucity of research on diversity as it relates to both workplace development and association with broader community and social change (Kalev, Dobbin, and Kelly, 2006) (Winston, 2001). The use of historical, ethnographic, and other qualitative methodologies by LIS researchers may be increasingly important to observe and analyze societal transformations that affect the library community and, in turn, the effectiveness of what the library community itself has done to affect broader social change. Second, equally important, is our opportunity to review and assess the best practices of libraries and librarians across the United States and in other countries. As Patricia Kreitz observed, there is utility in examining best practices in the absence of other research; however, best practices can also benefit from "systematic and careful reflection on hard-won practical experience" (Kreitz, 2008) and careful assessment of observations.

## References

ALISE, 2005. *Library and Information Science Statistical Report: 2004–2005.*

American Association of Law Librarians. http://www.aallnet.org/about/award_mlda.asp (accessed January 6, 2009).

American Library Association. *Accessibility Basics for Librarians.* http://www.ala.org/ala/aboutala/offices/oitp/emailtutorials/accessibilitya/accessibility.cfm (accessed January 7, 2009).

———. *Key Action Areas.* April 19, 2007. http://www.ala.org/ala/aboutala/missionhistory/keyactionareas/index.cfm (accessed January 8, 2009).

———. "Non-English Speakers." March 25, 2008. http://www.ala.org/ala/aboutala/offices/olos/nonenglishspeakers/index.cfm (accessed January 8, 2009).

Association of College and Research Libraries. "ACRL Racial and Ethnic Diversity Committee." http://www.ala.org/ala/mgrps/divs/acrl/about/committees/acrlracialethnic.cfm (accessed January 9, 2009).

———. "ACRL Launches Interest Groups." November 2008. http://www.ala.org/ala/newspresscenter/news/pressreleases2008/november2008/acrlinterest.cfm (accessed January 15, 2009).

Blackwell, Angela Glover, Stewart Kwoh, and Manuel Pastor. *Searching for the Uncommon Common Ground: New Dimensions on Race in America* (Norton, 2002).

Bowen, William G., and Derek Bok. *The Shape of the River: Long-Term Consequences of Considering Race in College and University Admissions* (Princeton University, 1998).

Brault, Matthew W. "Americans with Disabilities: 2005." Current Population Reports, pp. 70–117, U.S. Bureau of Census, 2008.

Brewer, Julie. "Post-Master's Residency Programs: Enhancing the Development of New Professionals and Minority Recruitment in Academic and Research Libraries." *College and Research Libraries* 58(6) (November 1997): 528–537.

Cogell, Raquel V., and Cindy A. Grunwell. *Diversity in Libraries: Academic Residency Programs* (Greenwood, 2001).

Elmborg, James. "Libraries in the Contact Zone: On the Creation of Educational Space." *Reference & User Services Quarterly* 46 (1) (2006): 56–64.

Fultz, Michael. "Black Public Libraries in the South in the Era of De Jure Segregation." *Libraries & the Cultural Record* 41(3) (Summer 2006): 337–359.

GSLIS Alumni Magazine (University of Illinois Graduate School of Library and Information Science). "Expanding Minority Recruitment and Retention." 2008: 16.

Güereña, Salvador, and Edward Erazo. "Latinos and Librarianship." *Library Trends* 49(1) (Summer 2000): 138–181.

Kalev, Alexandra, Frank Dobbin, and Erin Kelly. "Best Practices or Best Guesses? Assessing the Efficacy of Corporate Affirmative Action and Diversity Policies." *American Sociological Review* 71 (August 2006): 589–617.

Kreitz, Patricia A. "Best Practices for Managing Organizational Diversity." *Journal of Academic Librarianship* 2008: 101–120.

Library Residency Working Group. http://libraryresidents.wordpress.com/ residents). (accessed January 5, 2009).

Malone, Cheryl Knott. "Autonomy and Accommodation: Houston's Colored Carnegie Library, 1907–1922." *Libraries & Culture* 34(2) (1999): 95–114.

———. "Toward a Multicultural American Public Library History." *Libraries & Culture* 35(1) (Winter 2000): 77–86.

———. "Unannounced and Unexpected: The Desegregation of Houston Public Library in the Early 1950s." *Library Trends* 55(3) (Winter 2007): 665–674.

Neely, Teresa Y, and Lorna Peterson. *Achieving Racial and Ethnic Diversity Among Academic and Research Librarians: The Recruitment, Retention, and Advancement of Librarians of Color.* White paper, ACRL, 2007.

OCLC. "Surveys Measure Demand for Non-English Materials." October 14, 2008. http://www.oclc.org/news/announcements/announcement303.htm (accessed January 7, 2009).

Offord, Jerome, Jr. "Recruiting a Diverse Research Library Workforce." ARL, December 2006: 8–9.

Putnam, Robert D., and Lewis Feldstein. *Better Together: Restoring the American Community* (Simon & Schuster, 2004).

Redd, Ken. "Financing Graduate Education: Current Trends, Future Concerns." Council of Graduate Schools. December 2006. http://www.cgsnet.org/ portals/0/pdf/mtg_am06Redd.pdf (accessed December 7, 2008).

Roberts, Sam. "In Biggest U.S. Cities, Minorities Are at 50%." December 9, 2008. http://www.nytimes.com (accessed December 9, 2008).

Rochester Institute of Technology Libraries. Deaf Culture, Diversity, and Sociology. http://library.rit.edu/directory/739 (accessed January 7, 2009).

Shin, Hyon, and Rosalind Bruno. "Language Use and English-Speaking Ability: 2000." U.S. Bureau of the Census, 2003. http://www.census.gov/prod/ 2003pubs/c2kbr-29.pdf (accessed January 7, 2009).

Society of American Archivists. Harold T. Pinkett Minority Student Award. 2008. http://www.archivists.org/governance/handbook/section12-pinkett.asp (accessed January 8, 2009).

————. Resolution on Diversity. August 2002. http://www.archivists.org/statements/res-diversity.asp (accessed December 9, 2008).

Special Libraries Association. Diversity Leadership Development Program. 2008. http://www.sla.org/DLDP (accessed January 6, 2009).

Tilly, Charles. *Durable Inequality.* University of California Press, 1999.

Todaro, Julie. "Recruitment, Retention, Diversity—Cornerstones of Future Success." *C&RL News,* September 2007: 504–510.

Tucker, John Mark, ed. *Untold Stories: Civil Rights, Libraries, and Black Librarianship.* Graduate School of Library and Information Science, University of Illinois, 1998.

van Knippenberg, Daan, and Michaéla Schippers. "Work Group Diversity." *Annual Review of Psychology,* 2008: 515–541.

Walker, Billie E. "Daniel Alexander Payne Murray (1852–1925), Forgotten Librarian, Bibliographer, and Historian." *Libraries & Culture* 40(1) (2005): 25–37.

Winston, Mark. "The Importance of Leadership Diversity: The Relationship Between Diversity and Organizational Success in the Academic Environment." *College and Research Libraries,* November 2001: 517–526.

# Scholarly Publishing in 2008—
# The Year of the Author

Edward J. Valauskas

Graduate School of Library and Information Science, Dominican University
Chief Editor, *First Monday* (http://firstmonday.org)

Nancy R. John

Associate Professor Emerita, University of Illinois at Chicago

Silvia Toccoli

Ph.D. student, University of Trento, Trento, Italy

In a 2008 article, "Agreements Between 12 Publishers and the Authors Subject to the NIH Public Access Policy," Ben Grillot writes:

> Authors and publishers have long negotiated the ownership of copyright in scholarly works. However, with the rise of electronic publishing and a growing trend towards open and public access models, traditional author-publisher agreements are changing.[1]

Indeed, these two sentences hint at the major development in scholarly publishing in 2008. While a gradual shift had been in the works for some time, it was in 2008 that we could really see a change in the balance between the author and publisher, tilting clearly in the direction of the author. For this reason, we are dubbing 2008 "The Year of the Author." From policies designed to increase access to authors' writings, to improved grant rules to allow support of open access publication, to mandates for open access to publicly funded research findings, to payment to authors for use of their works—the author seemed to be at the center of many 2008 developments.

## Firmer NIH Public Access Policy

Since May 2005 NIH-funded researchers had been encouraged to make the published results of their research available *openly* within a year of publication. Despite considerable enthusiasm for this idea in theory, the practical outcome of the policy was disappointing. Because the deposit of articles was voluntary, only a few authors and publishers made articles available. Since January 11, 2008, when the policy became mandatory, the number of authors submitting their papers has grown sevenfold (see Table 1).[2] However, this increase is far from full compliance. This significant increase—a positive sign—notwithstanding, many issues are yet to be settled, including who pays for open access, what a fair price for access might be, and whether all of this will make a difference in the scholarly community.

The Wellcome Trust has had a mandatory open access policy in place since the end of 2006 for its funded projects. A 2008 survey found the disappointing result that only 27 percent of papers were freely available within six months.[3] It will be interesting to see the long-term effects of policies such as that of NIH and the Wellcome Trust.

**Table 1 / Monthly Aggregate Submission Statistics from NIH Manuscript Submission System**
Total manuscripts

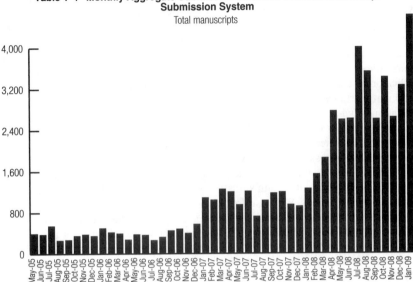

Source: NIH Public Access NIHMS Statistics http://www.nihms.nih.gov/stats/index.html (accessed February 16, 2009).

## More Journals Allow Self-Archiving

In a March 2008 article in *Serials Review,* Harnad et al.[4] write: "In response to the research community's expressed desire for OA [open access], the latest JISC/RoMEO survey of more than 10,000 journals indicates that over 90 percent are already "green"; that is, they have given their official green light to author self-archiving (http://romeo.eprints.org/stats.php)."

Data at the JISC/RoMEO site[5] indicate that 65 percent of the 497 publishers listed at RoMEO support some sort of self-archiving (possibly at a cost to the author); the actual breakdown is this: 154 (31 percent) allow archiving of pre- and post-prints; 107 (22 percent) allow archiving of post-prints, 60 (12 percent) allow archiving of pre-prints, and 176 (35 percent) do not yet formally support archiving by the authors. This is good news for authors interested in seeing their work being read and used. If the author has the financial means or the intellectual perspicacity or the firm commitment to open access, there is often a way.

## Citation No Longer the Gold Standard?

For many authors, the ultimate impact of their works is measured in who cites them, where they are cited, and how often they are cited. Two interesting articles published in 2008 took a critical look at the impact that electronic access is having on citation patterns. Many scholars believed that electronic access to publications would bring about a democratizing leveling of the playing field, resulting in more and more use of publications to bolster one's ideas.

James Evans[6] in *Science* found that, contrary to this belief, electronic access was actually resulting in narrower citation patterns and fewer citations. Tenopir and King[7] substantiated this finding, but also discovered that the number of articles being read was increasing at the same time. So while authors browse more, because of electronic access, they ultimately were more selective in choosing items to cite in their works. This suggests that citations are no longer an absolute indicator of whether an article is being read, and further that while authors may read many articles, the list in their papers may be a somewhat abbreviated representation of what they consulted in preparing their papers.

In an "attention economy"[8] scholarly authors seek publication outlets for their research where they will reach the largest audiences. Increasingly, Web-based, openly accessible scholarly journals provide a diverse and global readership. Indeed, these journals provide proof of this "attention" in the form of Web use logs, readily available with statistics on the specific number of downloads of each published paper.[9] Web use log statistics are proving their value to academics in the promotion and tenure process, giving committees further evidence on the use of published scholarship. For example, suppose we select a paper from the December 2005 issue of *First Monday*. Aaron Delwiche would like to know how many times that specific paper was examined between its publication and the end of 2007. The logs from the *First Monday* server reveal that the paper was downloaded on 829 occasions in December 2005 (published exactly on the first Monday of the month), 10,709 times in 2006, and 6,758 times in 2007, for a total of 18,296 for the period 2005–2007.

Since promotion and tenure committees, award judges, grant juries, and others continue to consider the impact of a scholar's works, it is important to understand what indicators are available and just what they represent. These two studies raise questions about time-worn assumptions. What will the future be for citation studies? It's still too early to tell. But the work of Evans and of Tenopir and King suggests that there is a lot more to learn about the impact that electronic availability of scholarly works is having on the world of scholarship.

## Rebirth of the Public Domain?

While the Creative Commons license offers authors the choice to place their work into the public domain, very little discussion of the value of such a choice has been evident in the literature; 2008 saw the start of a discussion that might show that the public domain is not just about government works and expired copyrights.

The public domain figured prominently in 2008. First a new book, published late in the year, James Boyle's *The Public Domain: Enclosing the Commons of the Mind* (Yale University Press), takes a fascinating look at the "range wars of the information age." Boyle's book summarizes much of his research on the public domain, even giving us an intellectual property equivalent of the Miranda Warning—the Jefferson Warning. Boyle writes, "So Jefferson gives us a classic set of cautions, cautions that we should be required to repeat, as police officers repeat the Miranda Warning to a suspect. In this case, they should be repeated before we rush off into the world of intellectual property policy rather than before we talk to the police without our lawyers present."[10]

Public Domain Day—January 1—was celebrated in a variety of ways. The first day of 2008 saw a variety of works enter the public domain (depending on local conditions for copyright protection—"life plus 50 years" vs. "life plus 70 years"). The writings of authors as diverse as Nikos Kazantzakis, Jean de Brunhoff, and Edith Wharton[11] came out into the open. The first day of 2009 witnessed the release of LibriVox's 2,000th public domain audiobook online, none other than Edward Gibbon's *The History of the Decline and Fall of the Roman Empire*.[12] LibriVox uses volunteers to record public domain audiobooks that are then made freely available via their Web site (http://librivox.org).

## Google Book Search and the Publishing Community

In the spirit of developing a healthy and robust public domain—perhaps—Google finally settled with a variety of publishers over its book-scanning activities.[13] This "agreement" did not really resolve the issue of digital fair use, nor invent entirely new models for handling rights in large-scale content projects. Indeed, the Book Rights Registry established by this settlement is somewhat akin to other organizations negotiating rights such as ASCAP—but with a big difference since the Book Rights Registry is a private, not public, body funded with a tidy $34.5 million from Google.[14] The settlement will certainly give Google the green light to continue its efforts with Book Search. In October 2008 Google had 7 million books available with 1 million identified as public domain works.[15] In any case, authors are the clear winners in the decision, with the Book Rights Registry providing one avenue for authors to deal with their digital rights and secure some portion of royalties for the use of their work. However, a number of other questions remain unsettled, such as the fate of orphan works.

## Orphan Works

Digital projects, such as Google Book Search and the hundreds of new projects undertaken by libraries around the world in 2008, are increasingly encountering orphan works, copyrighted material for which it is difficult or impossible to track down the rights holders. The U.S. Congress has repeatedly attempted to resolve this matter, with legislation proposed in 2003 and 2005, but these bills all died. In 2006 the Copyright Office at the Library of Congress released a report on orphan works with recommendations for legislative remedies. In the Senate, the Shawn Bentley Orphan Works Act of 2008, introduced by Sens. Patrick Leahy (D-Vt.) and Orrin Hatch (R-Utah) attempted to address the issue. This legislation was supported by the Copyright Office as well as a variety of library organizations; some 70 organizations, largely representing illustrators and photographers, were opposed to the act.[16] Passed by the Senate, the act spent the rest of 2008 in the House Committee on the Judiciary.[17] Given the dire need for a resolution of the orphan works question, a congressional resolution of some sort seemed likely to be passed sometime in 2009. This legislative solution is needed because the courts will not provide an answer; the U.S. Supreme Court refused in 2008 to hear an appeal of *Kahle* v. *Ashcroft.*[18]

## Textbooks

Textbooks have always been an interesting area of scholarly publishing. Nearly every scholar has thought about writing one, and the halls of academe are rife with stories of professors whose works have financed significantly improved lifestyles. The cost of textbooks was the subject of lively debate during the summer of 2008. Amid reports of the spiraling prices, articles dealing with the resulting boycotts and market for pirated copies appeared in major news publications. Congress acted on the issue by passing the Higher Education Opportunity Act of 2008, signed into law on August 14, containing provisions dealing directly with university textbooks.

By July 1, 2010, publishers are required to provide information about the differences between editions and pricing of textbooks, especially bundled packages, and universities must inform students of the costs of textbooks before they register for a course. While that date is still more than a year away, many universities began to comply with the general approach of the provisions in the fall 2008 semester.[19]

Given the high costs of textbooks—totaling more than 25 percent of tuition and related fees, according to a Government Accountability Office study[20]—students should be able to plan their budgets better and consider options. Students in turn are responding by organizing their own alternatives, including faculty support for open textbooks.[21] A variety of open textbook projects have emerged, including the Open Book Project (http://openbookproject.net), California Open Source Textbook Project (http://www.opensourcetext.org), and Free High School Science Texts (http://www.fhsst.org). These efforts will continue to multiply and grow in 2009.

## HathiTrust Project Moves Ahead

The HathiTrust (http://www.hathitrust.org) is a collaborative digital repository of the 13 universities of the Committee on Institutional Cooperation along with the University of California system. Many of these digitized items were originally part of the Google Book Search and Open Content Alliance Projects in which the Hathi members participated. But in this changing world of electronic access, these universities have decided to band together to provide perpetual access to the large number of holdings they have digitized. To date, 2,607,638 volumes (equivalent to 97 terabytes) have been digitized, of which 15 percent is in the public domain.

## Open Access in Europe

It would be wrong to give the impression that changes in the world of scholarly publishing occur only in the United States. Far from being U.S.-centric, changes in scholarly publishing are occurring on a swifter and more coordinated timeline in Europe. The Europeans may have improved opportunities in the infrastructure of the European Commission (EU), but their progress is largely due to the widespread engagement of scholars, funders, and politicians in the debate about the future of scholarly publishing.

At a 2007 conference,[22] a group of European scientific organizations[23] initiated a petition,[24] directed to the EU, advocating for guaranteed public access to publicly funded research results. The petition specifically supported the implementation of open access in the scientific publishing sector and called on the EU to intensify its efforts to promote open access publications. In 2008 many individuals and institutions signed the petition. On January 11, 2008, the Scientific Council of the European Research Council (ERC) released its long-awaited open access policy. It requires all ERC-funded research to be made available openly within six months of publication. Additionally, primary data collected in the course of ERC-funded research also must appear in publicly accessible, open databases within six months. Given that the council provides billions of euros to hundreds of researchers, this mandate is especially significant. As another consequence, in an April 2008 document,[25] the EU supported open access by recommending ten points[26] that member states should undertake to promote the broad dissemination of knowledge created with public funds.

Additionally, the EU launched a pilot project in summer 2008 to ensure that at least one-fifth of its funded research will be openly available. Funding in the EU's Seventh Research Framework Programme amounts to more than 50 billion euros.[27]

Elsewhere in Europe, in January 2009 the European Organization for Nuclear Research (CERN) began an initiative that aims to convert all high energy physics literature to open access. This new project, called SCOAP3[28] (Sponsoring Consortium for Open Access Publishing in Particle Physics), proposes a new model and no doubt it will reinforce the position of the high energy physics community as the first community widely supporting open archives and repositories.

In April 2008 SPARC Europe (the Scholarly Publishing and Academic Resources Coalition's European ally) and the Directory of Open Access Journals (DOAJ) introduced a new SPARC Europe Seal for Open Access Journals.[29] To be eligible, journals must use a Creative Commons Attribution license (CC-BY) in accordance with the Open Knowledge Definition[30] and the ethos of the Budapest Open Access Initiative.[31] In addition, this seal means that these journals provide interoperable metadata for all their articles to DOAJ, which makes the metadata OAI-compliant, thereby increasing the access to these journals by researchers.

There is certainly an overwhelming hunger on the part of European researchers for digital information. Europe's digital library, Europeana, was overwhelmed on its first day of use in November. Expecting five million hits per hour, the site saw three times as many. Even with expanded server capacity, Europeana was pulled until it could handle its enormous popularity.[32] No doubt other future megaprojects will also discover that demand for their riches outstrips their technology.

## Conclusion

Overall, 2008 was quite an active year for issues relating to scholarly publishing and open access. Given the state of the economy, these will certainly grow in significance in 2009 and beyond. If access to scholarly information can continue to become more author-centric, the world of scholarship will profit.

## Notes

1. Ben Grillot, "PubMed Central Deposit and Author Rights: Agreements Between 12 Publishers and the Authors Subject to the NIH Public Access Policy," *ARL: A Bimonthly Report on Research Library Issues and Actions from ARL, CNI, and SPARC,* no. 259 (August 2008): p. 1.

2. "NIH PubMed Central Submission Rates Soar" (Association of Research Libraries, SPARC), at http://www.arl.org/sparc/advocacy/nih/index.shtml (accessed February 12, 2009).

3. Zoë Corbyn, 2008, "Low Compliance with Open-Access Rule Criticized," *Times Higher Education Supplement* (February 21), at http://www.timeshighereducation.co.uk/story. asp?storyCode=400678&sectioncode=26.

4. Stevan Harnad, Tim Brody, François Vallières, Les Carr, Steve Hitchcock, Yves Gingras, Charles Oppenheim, Chawki Hajjem, Eberhard R. Hilf, "The Access/Impact Problem and the Green and Gold Roads to Open Access: An Update," *Serials Review,* vol. 34, no. 1, March 2008, pp. 36–40, ISSN 0098-7913, DOI: 10.1016/j.serrev.2007.12.005 (http://www. sciencedirect.com/science/article/B6W63-4S0HC0P-1/2/273ce267efe063d9e089fef26cd0bb16).

5. http://www.sherpa.ac.uk/romeo.php?stats=yes.

6. James A. Evans, "Electronic Publication and the Narrowing of Science and Scholarship," *Science* 321, no. 5887 (2008), pp. 395–399.

7. Carol Tenopir and Donald W. King, "Electronic Journals and Changes in Scholarly Article Seeking and Reading Patterns," *D-Lib Magazine,* vol. 14, no. 11/12 (November/December 2008).

8. Michael H. Goldhaber, 1997, "The Attention Economy and the Net," *First Monday,* vol. 2, no. 4 (April), at http://journals.uic.edu/fm/article/view/519/440; Michael H. Goldhaber, 2006, "The Value of Openness in an Attention Economy," *First Monday,* vol. 11, no. 6 (June), at http://journals.uic.edu/fm/article/view/1334/1254.

9. Kate Marek and Edward J. Valauskas, 2002, "Web Logs as Indices of Electronic Journal Use: Tools for Identifying a 'Classic' Article," *Libri,* vol. 52, no. 4, pp. 220–230, and at http://librijournal.org/pdf/2002-4pp.220-230.pdf; David Nicholas, Paul Huntington, Hamid R. Jamali, and Anthony Watkinson, 2006, "The Information Seeking Behaviour of the Users of Digital Scholarly Journals," *Information Processing and Management,* vol. 42, no. 5 (September), pp. 1345–1365.

10. James Boyle, *The Public Domain: Enclosing the Commons of the Mind,* p. 21 and at http://yupnet.org/boyle/archives/41.

11. John Mark Ockerbloom, 2008, "Public Domain Day Gifts" (January 1), at http://everybodyslibraries.com/2008/01/01/public-domain-day-gifts.

12. http://librivox.org/2008/12/31/librivox-reaches-2000.

13. See the settlement documents at http://books.google.com/booksrightsholders/agreement.html.

14. See the perceptive comments by Sherwin Siy on the agreement at http://www.publicknowledge.org/node/1828.

15. http://en.wikipedia.org/wiki/Google_Book_Search.

16. See http://www.owoh.org.

17. See http://judiciary.house.gov/issues/issues_orphan.html.

18. Andrew Albanese, 2008, "Supreme Court Declines to Hear Orphan Works Case," *Library Journal* (January 16), at http://www.libraryjournal.com/article/CA6523163.html; Wendy Davis, "Copyright Protection Stymies Online Archive," *Online Media Daily* January 9, 2008.

19. See the American Council on Education Textbook Forum at http://www.solutionsforourfuture.org/site/PageServer?pagename=heoa_home

20. "College Textbooks: Enhanced Offerings Appear to Drive Recent Price Increases," GAO-05-806 (July 29, 2005), at http://www.gao.gov/products/GAO-05-806.

21. Marissa Graziadio, 2008, "Online Textbook Alternative Garners Faculty Support," at http://www.dailytargum.com/2.4985/1.493133-1.493133.

22. See http://oa.mpg.de/openaccess-berlin/berlindeclaration.html.

23. For a list of the signatories, see http://oa.mpg.de/openaccess-berlin/signatories.html.

24. See http://www.ec-petition.eu.

25. See Brussels, 10.4.2008, C(2008)1329, *Commission Recommendation on the Management of Intellectual Property in Knowledge Transfer Activities and Code of Practice for Universities and Other Public Research Organizations,* at http://ec.europa.eu/invest-in-research/pdf/ip_recommendation_en.pdf.

26. See pp. 3–4 of http://ec.europa.eu/invest-in-research/pdf/ip_recommendation_en.pdf.

27. See http://www.sparceurope.org/news/european-commission-launches-open-access-pilot.

28. See http://www.scoap3.org/files/Scoap3ExecutiveSummary.pdf and http://www.edri.org/edri-gram/number7.1/open-access-hep.

29. See https://mx2.arl.org/Lists/SPARC-OAForum/Message/4329.html.

30. See http://opendefinition.org.

31. See http://www.soros.org/openaccess.

32. "Europeana Website Overwhelmed on Its First Day by Interest of Millions of Users," at http://dev.europeana.eu/press_releases.php.

# Organization Development in Libraries

M. Sue Baughman

Assistant Dean for Organizational Development
University of Maryland Libraries

Libraries often must deal with change. How libraries prepare themselves for an accelerated rate of change determines how successful they will be at any given time, and the development of a capacity to deal effectively with change is critical for maintaining a library's position with its customers and community.

Capacity building can occur in a variety of ways. Organization development (OD) is one of the capacity builders, and increasing numbers of libraries are turning to the theory and practice of OD to enhance their change efforts. This article seeks to report on the status of OD in libraries and examine why developing skills to deal with change—whether on the individual or organizational level—is critical for libraries' survival. The reader will learn how many types of activities in which libraries engage fall within the rubric of OD, and that it is important that libraries evaluate OD strategies and share this knowledge with the wider library community.

## Libraries and Change

Libraries, now more than ever, must be able to adapt to their changing environments. Change occurs when priorities shift or when the needs of customers warrant a new approach to service. Technology has at times advanced so quickly that libraries struggle to keep up, not only with the development of faster and cheaper technology but also in their ability to support the skills that staff must have to successfully navigate new technologies. Another critical driver of change is an uncertain financial climate libraries now face. As budgets rise and fall, libraries must make adjustments in order to cope with new financial realities.

Throughout this dynamic environment, one thing remains constant. Charles Lowry defines this important constant as the core mission of libraries. He states that libraries' core mission is "delivering access to the world of scholarly information to support learning in the classroom and the discovery of new knowledge and invention. That is the foundation on which we should build organizational strategy."[1] He further stresses the importance of keeping in touch with customers' needs; by not doing so, libraries risk losing their value to their customers. In addition, Lowry points out the critical need to keep in touch with employees; otherwise organizations "lose the opportunity to meet and solve challenges."[2] Lowry made these comments eight years ago when a number of large libraries, academic libraries in particular, were beginning to consider the notion of OD. More and more libraries were beginning to consider the critical need to engage staff in different ways to manage change.

All types of organizations that are nimble and able to adapt to environmental factors, whether internal or external, are better equipped to deal with situations as they occur. Libraries that develop staff skills and flexibility and use innovative approaches to address problems will be more successful in meeting the challenges they must confront.

Another reason libraries are discussing and engaging in the theories and practices of OD is the desire to improve the "health" of the organization, building on the notion that organizations are "no longer stand-alone entities that can operate autonomously in a relatively stable environment. They are part of a system of relationships and interactions that is in a constantly dynamic state."[3] The profile of a healthy organization coming from the behavioral sciences arena includes the following characteristics. The healthy organization: (a) defines itself as a system transforming needs and materials into goods and services; (b) maintains a strong sense of purpose; (c) operates in a "form follows function" mode—the work to be done determines the organizational structures; (d) employs team management as the dominant mode; (e) respects customer service, both inside and outside the organization; (f) receives, processes, and widely shares information; (g) encourages decisions to be made at the level closest to the customer; (h) keeps communication open in all directions; (i) continuously values learning at all levels; (j) recognizes innovation and creativity; (k) respects the need to help staff create balance between work and life needs; (l) keeps a social agenda such as community citizenship and protecting the environment; and (m) pays attention to efficiency, quality, and safety awareness in operations.[4]

These characteristics offer a road map for achieving a healthy organization. Libraries may argue that keeping a social agenda is not apropos, but more and more libraries are making strides to become more environmentally conscious and adopting "green" strategies. Creating a healthy organization can be greatly supported with the application of OD theories and practices.

## Organization Development

The field of OD has evolved since the late 1950s and early 1960s with its foundation in behavioral sciences such as psychology, sociology, organizational behavior, and management. Leaders in this field of study linked theory and practice, arguing that if organizations better understood how they functioned, then improvements in organization could be made. Theorists and practitioners of OD espouse a number of definitions that share many of the same characteristics. One appropriate definition follows:

> Organization development is an effort (1) planned, (2) organization-wide, and (3) managed from the top, to (4) increase organization effectiveness and health through (5) planned interventions in the organization's "processes," using behavioral-science knowledge.[5]

Richard Beckhard's explanation of each of these elements can help an organization understand what an OD program should entail. A planned effort is a strategic process that includes a diagnosis of the organization plus a plan for improvement. Resources, including staff, finances, and time, must be available to carry out the plan. Change efforts can be small or large and both will have an impact on the total organization. Top management of the organization must be invested in the OD program for the program to be successful. This must be evident in both word and deed. Incorporating a wide range of OD activities focusing on skill development—decision making, problem solving, and values clarification, to name a few—builds the capacity of individuals, groups, and the organization itself. Increasing the effectiveness of the organization and its health will be best realized when the organization keeps a vision of the end results in mind.

## Engagement of Libraries in OD

Understanding of the theories and practice of OD in libraries is developing in a number of ways. Participation in the American Library Association's Library Leadership and Management Association's Organization Development Discussion Group has grown steadily since the group was formed in 2001. Participants include library staff with responsibility for OD in a variety of capacities, through human resources, staff development, OD, or some other administrative position. Participants also include library staff interested in the application of OD and how it is being used in libraries. There are a number of articles in the library literature that describe the depth and breadth of OD activities. Two fundamental pieces are Maureen Sullivan's review of the history of OD in libraries that appears in a 2004 issue of *Library Administration & Management* and the entire issue of the summer 2004 *Library Trends,* which covers current trends and applications of OD in all types of libraries.[6] A number of articles in the literature also describe libraries' involvement in teams, assessment activities used to measure change, and learning organizations, all of which incorporate some element of OD.

Several research projects are under way that are studying the application of OD in libraries. One project being conducted by the author and Janet Parsch of the University of Arkansas is the study of how Association of Research Libraries (ARL) member libraries are implementing OD. The goals of this research project are to understand if and how libraries are applying OD activities, defining the activities being conducted and whether the implementation of these activities has had an impact on services, funding of the library, or the position of the library in its community. Two surveys were administered in 2008 addressing these issues; one was sent to deans of the libraries and one to staff responsible for implementing OD activities and interventions. Preliminary review of the data so far indicates that libraries are implementing a wide range of activities that fall under the domain of OD even though the activities may not be named as such. One of the activities used most often is strategic planning. Of particular interest are the comments about the impact OD has had on libraries. This is most commonly associated with improved customer service.

A second ongoing research project is the development of a survey called ClimateQUAL—Organizational Climate and Diversity Assessment. This tool measures library staff perceptions concerning their library's commitment to organizational policies and procedures, principles of diversity, and staff attitudes. The survey addresses a number of climate issues, such as diversity, teamwork, learning, and fairness, as well as current managerial practices and staff attitudes and beliefs. This collaborative project—led by the University of Maryland Libraries, the University of Maryland Industrial/Organizational Psychology Program, and

ARL—has five goals: (1) develop a tool that assesses the "health" of the library; (2) develop a database of norms to help libraries interpret their results; (3) develop an active community of libraries charged with sharing experiences and strategies that improved library effectiveness; (4) track changes in libraries over time to permit objective feedback regarding effectiveness of the attempted practices and strategies; and (5) build empirical validation of the "healthy organization" theory. Current activities include testing the survey instrument with academic libraries and developing ways to report results to participating libraries.

As noted, one of the goals of the ClimateQUAL—Organizational Climate and Diversity Assessment project is to create an understanding of a healthy organization, which in this case is slightly different from the definition presented earlier. Here the healthy organization is defined as "an organization in which employees feel empowered. It is one in which employees believe that management values them and treats them fairly. It is an organization in which the policies, practices, and procedures are administered consistently and these practices work in concert to facilitate the attainment of one or more organizational goals (e.g., productivity, efficiency, safety). Finally, it is an organization in which the connection with its environment is not forgotten."[7] In addition, the "healthy organization sends two kinds of complementary messages to their employees (i.e., concern for employees and concern for customers). The 'concern for employees' message is sent when organizational practices, policies, and procedures strongly indicate that things like teamwork, diversity, and justice are valued. The 'concern for customers' message is created when the organizational practices, policies, and procedures strongly indicate that customers are valued and meeting their needs is essential."[8] As this project evolves, the researchers seek to map the various scales of the survey to organizational systems (such as communication, compensation, structure, and so forth) and to identify the OD activities that could have the most impact in addressing changes needed to improve the library's health.

## OD Activities and Interventions

OD activities and interventions can address a variety of situations that will lead to organizational change. Jennerich and Baughman discuss the range and scope of OD interventions that are used to address a particular need. Before determining what intervention might be most effective, it is important to fully understand the current philosophy of the organization, the motivation for change, and the attitudes of the participants about change. Understanding these and other basic parameters of the organization will ensure that the most appropriate tool is selected, increasing the likelihood that the end result will be successful. Table 1 illustrates the various categories of OD activities or interventions.[9]

The use of OD activities or interventions (sometimes called improvement strategies) can and should occur on multiple levels: individual, between employees, within a group or team, or organization-wide. At the individual level, activities are geared to support the growth and expansion of skills of the library staff member. Enhancing the staff member's capacity to participate effectively in a team or group has only positive effects on the organization. The same holds true

Table 1 / OD Interventions by Category

| Categories | Activities and Interventions |
| --- | --- |
| Diagnostic | Activities are designed to ascertain the state of a system and can include interviews, questionnaires, surveys, and so forth. |
| Team Building | Activities focus on enhancing the operation of teams and can include role and task clarity, ground rules, interpersonal dynamics, and so forth. |
| Intergroup | These activities are designed to improve the effectiveness between groups that must work together to accomplish a goal and can include activities that help them understand how to do this. |
| Education and Training | These activities improve an individual's skills, abilities, and knowledge. They can be geared toward task or interpersonal competencies and include such things as decision making, problem solving, goal setting, and so forth. |
| Process Consultation | This is an approach that is used to help the "client" gain insight into what is happening within the organization and develop the skills to diagnose and manage what is occurring. The focus is on processes such as leadership, authority, communication, problem solving, and decision making. |
| Planning and Goal Setting | Activities focus on the theory and practice of setting goals and using problem solving models. |
| Strategic Management | Activities that direct attention to the organization's mission and goals as well as environmental factors such as strengths, weaknesses, threats, and opportunities are effective for planning short- or long-term efforts. |
| Organizational Transformation | Activities that involve large-scale change—paying attention to systems such as rewards, values, culture, structure, management philosophy, and so forth—can lead to lasting transformation. |

for the interactions between employees. Activities at this level could be between two staff members or between a supervisor and an employee. The more effectively groups—whether organized into teams, units, or departments—work together to carry out responsibilities, the more positive results will be recognized not only at the individual level but also at the organizational level. Finally, development at the organizational level focuses on its vision, mission, goals, and most likely its structure. Here it is also important to pay attention to the various systems at play, including rewards, values, compensation, and evaluation of the change efforts. Table 2 provides a variety of examples of interventions on the four levels.[10]

When libraries identify the need to implement activities or interventions, consideration of several issues is important. Having a clear outcome in mind at the beginning of the process, one that has been shared widely with those affected, will ensure participation and buy-in. Relevance of the activity or intervention to the change effort helps establish a context for library staff. If staff have the opportunity to integrate what they are learning with tasks or processes, the change effort has a better chance of lasting. Another critical consideration is how the effectiveness of the change effort will be measured. Thinking about evaluation at the beginning of the change process is beneficial on two levels, helping with mid-course corrections if they are needed and celebrating the completion and successful execution of the change. Selecting the most effective activity or intervention is important, as is consideration of who will lead the change efforts.

Table 2 / OD Interventions by Level

| Individual | Between Employees | Teams or Groups | Entire Organization |
| --- | --- | --- | --- |
| • Job redesign<br>• Training and management development<br>• Career development<br>• Individual observation and feedback<br>• Individual skill coaching<br>• Serving as a sounding board for decisions | • Values clarification<br>• Conflict resolution<br>• Norm setting<br>• Role clarification and negotiation<br>• Improving communication ability<br>• Decision making<br>• Problem solving<br>• Project planning and implementation | • Values clarification<br>• Conflict resolution<br>• Consensus building<br>• Norm setting<br>• Role clarification and negotiation<br>• Improving communication ability<br>• Decision making<br>• Problem solving<br>• Process improvement<br>• Project planning and implementation | • Vision, mission, and values development<br>• Goal setting<br>• Strategic planning<br>• Organization restructure and redesign<br>• Change management<br>• Commitment to new programs<br>• Commitment to new ways of managing |

## Roles in OD

The implementation of OD in a library requires a variety of resources (people and funds) and time. Leadership for these change efforts will ensure a stronger likelihood of success. Top management, while identified as critical supporters, cannot always lead the implementation of change. External consultants can play a large role in helping libraries through change efforts, but they can be expensive, which may limit libraries' abilities to use them. In fact, an increasing number of libraries are turning to internal staff to lead change efforts. These internal experts may appear as part of human resources or be based in a staff-development program or possibly in a planning program. Based on the number of activities in which libraries might engage to address the individual or organizational needs, multiple people may be assigned to lead different elements of change efforts.

A combination of roles might be employed, depending on the goals of the libraries for their OD efforts. Examples include the following:

*Process expert/facilitator.* This role recommends and/or guides a process that will lead to a change. The person filling this role is not a content expert, but is well versed in tools and techniques that help staff reach their goal. The process expert/facilitator remains objective and neutral throughout the activities.

*Content expert.* This role requires someone with specific content expertise or experience who can define the problems and objectives for change. An example of this might occur in the area of information technology. This expert could guide a library through evaluation of its operations and practices.

*Trainer.* The trainer designs, leads, and evaluates learning experiences within the change efforts. This role could be external or internal and work with the individual, teams/groups, and the organization as a whole.

*Fact finder.* This role identifies, gathers, and possibly assimilates information, data, and other resources that inform the change effort. This role might be filled internally or externally. An internal example is the person with responsibility for collecting statistics for the library.

*Process counselor.* This person observes, diagnoses, and facilitates interpersonal relationships within the organization.

*Objective observer/reflector.* This is the most non-directive role and is someone who observes, mirrors, and reports on what is seen. This role is not involved in any decision making about possible strategies for change.[11]

In addition to determining who has responsibility for managing OD activities in libraries, an issue currently being debated is where the OD leader should be placed within the organization. In some existing situations, this person reports directly to the dean or director of the library; in other cases, he or she is positioned within human resources. There is no right or wrong answer. Preliminary data from the Baughman and Parsch research project indicates that the OD leader can sit almost equally between the two possibilities. Based on qualitative commentary in the project surveys, it appears that the placement of the OD leader depends on the goals of the libraries' change efforts and the importance of the change to the libraries. Of note as well is that position titles are distributed across a wide range of possibilities. It is clear that OD activities and interventions are occurring in libraries and that someone other than the dean or director is leading the effort. What is less clear from this research project is how OD will continue to play a critical role in helping libraries deal with change.

## Strengthening the Value of OD in Libraries

Libraries that are engaged in OD describe their successes and even their challenges, but why are more libraries not taking advantage of the powerful role OD can play? There are several possible answers to this question. One is that while some libraries have been utilizing OD for some time, it is still a relatively new concept for libraries. Another answer perhaps comes from the OD definition mentioned earlier, that change efforts must be planned. Diagnosis of a situation and planning a change effort takes time. Libraries may not feel they can take the time needed to do this. In addition, not all libraries have the staff resources available to assign such work. However, there are small steps that libraries of all types can effectively take to implement OD activities and interventions.

The editors of the Summer 2004 issue of *Library Trends* offered their insights on the values of organizational issues, change, and leadership. These insights also speak to the benefits of engaging in OD. The insights are summarized below.

1 *Library employees are an underutilized (and often undervalued) resource.* Each person working in a library can make a unique contribution to the success of the library. This requires a commitment to the library's mission. Often employees' skills go untapped. More and more staff want to be engaged in the goals of the library.

2 *Group processes in libraries can be improved.* The recent trend in libraries to accomplish work in teams, groups, or committees requires attention to how people work together to do this. Often staff have not

been trained to manage collaborative work as they are used to completing tasks or roles individually.

**3** *Libraries as organizations can be structured and operated more effectively.* Libraries can have quite complex organizational structures, which can result in competition for resources or even competing goals. Form following function might help reduce this complexity. The traditional boundaries around the work being done in libraries are becoming less meaningful, but letting go of traditions can be challenging.

**4** *Leadership is critical in libraries, and all employees should be seen (and developed) as leaders.* The value of every employee as a leader in the library is a relatively new concept. Moving away from the more hierarchical leadership models and training and encouraging employees to be more accountable for the success of the library will only strengthen the library's ability to adapt to change.

**5** *Positive and empowering approaches to managing and leading libraries are more effective than some traditional approaches.* Utilizing tools, activities, or interventions that expand the capacity of library staff to make decisions, solve problems, improve work flow processes, and so forth can lead to positive results. Letting positive change feed on itself can lead to continued positive change.

**6** *Change in libraries can be anticipated, planned, and implemented in better ways.* Change is inevitable and may need to happen rapidly. Developing the organizational capacity to understand, assess, and address the ever-changing needs of customers could position the library to be more effective.

**7** *Ideas and tools for improving libraries as organizations usually originate from disciplines outside library and information science.* Libraries have adopted and used the research of disciplines including business, sociology, and psychology. Applying different models and approaches to do the work of libraries is a key to adapting strategies that have worked well in other types of organizations.[12]

These perspectives on how libraries can better position themselves to successfully manage change fit nicely within the framework of organization development. OD has not only evolved over time in its theoretical descriptions of what OD is but also in how OD is practiced and the benefits that result from OD activities and interventions. To expand on the critical relationship between libraries and OD, and OD's potential value to libraries, a recent article on OD in the 21st century articulates five historical themes. These themes illustrate how libraries have incorporated OD:

- OD has always been about developing organizations; it is oriented to improving organization effectiveness in the broadest terms through the application of the behavioral and social sciences.
- OD has always been concerned with transferring knowledge and skills so that the system builds the capacity to manage change in the future.

Assessment, reflection, and feedback are key to this learning, and participation and involvement are the strategy.

- OD has always been concerned with the values underlying its practice . . .
The original values of human potential, participation, and development
have broadened to include financial performance and customer satisfaction . . .

- OD has always been concerned with the integration of process and content
. . . the way OD practitioners add value is through crafting processes of
change, of challenging personal processes and assumptions, and of understanding interpersonal relationships and group dynamics in an effort to
make work designs, reward systems, or organization structures more
effective.

- OD has traditionally been concerned with the measurement and evaluation
of change processes and their effectiveness . . . More recently, there has
been emphasis on action and the development of interventions . . . evaluation and research have become less emphasized.[13]

These five themes can be applied to libraries and their efforts to deal more
effectively with change. In the past ten years, change has been occurring more
frequently and requiring libraries to adapt more quickly. Within the broader field
of organization development, which can also be directed at libraries, there is a
call to do more about evaluating change processes, understanding the impact that
has been realized as a result of the changes and what has been learned from the
process itself. For libraries, in particular, it is imperative that this information be
shared as widely as possible through additional research, publication of articles
in the library literature, and continued discussions in informal and formal venues.

## Conclusion

Strengthening the abilities of library staff and libraries to deal with change is
critical. This must be a continuous process, not just when a perceived need is
acknowledged. OD is already playing an important role in libraries for building
the capacity to deal with change. This is occurring on a number of levels within
the organization. There are several clear tenets that must be adhered to in order to
be successful. Change efforts are led and supported by top management. It does
not matter what the activities or interventions used to support change are called.
It is most important that the ability to be flexible and ready to adapt to change is
developed and fostered throughout the entire organization.

## Sources

1. Charles B. Lowry, "The More Things Change . . ." *portal: Libraries and the Academy* 1, 4
(2001), pp. vii.

2. Ibid, viii.

3. Richard Beckhard, "The Healthy Organization" in *Organization Development,* ed. by Joan
V. Gallos (Jossey-Bass, 2006), 951.

4. Ibid, 951–952.

5. Richard Beckhard, "What Is Organization Development?" in *Organization Development,* ed. by Joan V. Gallos (Jossey-Bass, 2006), 3.

6. Maureen Sullivan, "Organization Development in Libraries," *Library Administration & Management* 18, 4 (2004); *Library Trends* 53, 1 (2004), ed. by Keith Russell and Denise Stephens.

7. Paul J. Hanges, Juliet P. Aiken, and Xiafang Chen, "Climate for Diversity and Customer Service: The Healthy Organization." Paper accepted for presentation at the 2008 American Psychological Association Conference, Boston, Massachusetts, p. 5, http://www.lib.umd. edu/ocda/hanges_libraryapa.pdf (accessed January 29, 2009). See also the Association of Research Libraries information on ClimateQUAL at http://www.lib.umd.edu/ocda (accessed January 29, 2009).

8. Ibid, 5.

9. Elaine Jennerich and M. Sue Baughman, "Creating Smooth Sailing" in *The Expert Library: Staffing, Sustaining, and Advancing the Academic Library in the 21st Century.* American Library Association, Association of College and Research Libraries (in press).

10. Rima Shaffer, "Principles of Organization Development." Info-Line: The How-To Reference Tool for Training and Performance Professionals. ASTD, Revised 1999, pp. 6–7.

11. Ibid, 13–14.

12. Keith Russell and Denise Stephens, "Organizational Development, Leadership, Change, and the Future of Libraries." *Library Trends* 53, 1 (Summer 2004), pp. 239–241.

13. Ann E. Feyerherm and Christopher G. Worley, "Forward to the Past: Reclaiming OD's Influence in the World." *OD Practitioner* 40, 4 (2008), p. 3.

# Digital Concerns Again Top Developments in Copyright

Sarah K. Wiant

Law Librarian and Professor of Law, Washington and Lee University

Librarians are affected by a broad span of copyright concerns. Finding a balance between the rights of users and those of content owners, particularly in the digital environment, is essential to the development of new works and the free flow of information. Events during 2008 show there remains a need to update copyright law to provide the protection needed by libraries and archives to carry out their missions.

## Google Books Settlement

In 2004, when Google began its Book Search book-digitization program, five research libraries agreed to permit the scanning of the books within their collections. Google digitized approximately 7 million books; 1 million were out of copyright, and another million were covered by an agreement to allow "peer view," so the case focused on the remaining 5 million. Four years later, Google settled with the Association of American Publishers (AAP), which had sued for copyright infringement on behalf of its members.

This is a huge and complex case with repercussions for users, content owners, the publishing industries, libraries, and others. Under the settlement,[1] the Authors Guild and AAP agreed not to sue for copyright infringement and Google agreed to pay $125 million.

It was unclear what "fair use" meant in determining how much of a book Google could display before paying royalties to authors and publishers. Under the terms of the settlement, Google may display 20 percent of a book without payment. But "fair use" is still undefinable.

Copyright is critical to creators, who must be vigilant in protecting their work from those who believe that because something is on the Internet it is free from copyright. But copyright owners must find a new business model rather than suing users who continue to find new ways to access online content.

As part of the settlement, Google agreed to create a not-for-profit book rights registry for which it will pay itself $35 million of the $125 million settlement. The registry will address some of the issues associated with "orphan works," books (or other content) still protected by copyright but whose authors or owners are difficult to locate; Congress has been unable to pass legislation to address orphan works as proposed by the U.S. Copyright Office in 2006. As Lawrence Lessig, a Harvard Law professor (formerly at Stanford), commented, "Establishing who owns what is real progress."

The registry will allow content owners to control uses and accrue royalties for their out-of-print works. It is a good and important advance, but it should be independent and run on an opt-in basis rather than an opt-out basis. Authors should not be required to opt-out in order to choose to make their works either available freely or under another license. Under the terms of the settlement, the registry must offer Google better terms than it would give to a competitor using data or resources that Google provides to the registry.

A possible competitor, Microsoft, abandoned its book-scanning venture in 2008. Google leads Yahoo's open content alliance (OCA) in scanning, and OCA likely could not compete because of the price protections afforded Google. The European digital library also might be a competitor. It matters greatly who owns the registry; it is an extension of the search. The registry contains two parts with one part used by authors to register their works and the other operated on behalf of Google.

The court appointed class counsel to represent the two subclasses: authors of books and other writings and their heirs and assigns; and publishers of books and periodicals. A copyright holder must opt out of the settlement to maintain the right to sue Google individually for copyright infringement. A fairness hearing was scheduled for June 11, 2009.

It is now clear that book scanning will be a lucrative business for Google, but the settlement also means that public libraries will be permitted to offer online viewing at a single terminal within the library (additional terminals will require a fee). Printing will require a per-page fee. Even works published before 1923, generally in the public domain, now will be accessed only through Google, as the gatekeeper, via its proprietary search. Libraries that open their collection to Google will have copies of their scanned works.

Some are questioning whether higher education is surrendering its information and technology goals to the private corporation. Stay tuned.

## DMCA Tenth Anniversary

On the tenth anniversary of the Digital Millennium Copyright Act (DMCA) in October 2008, the act's benefits and disadvantages were discussed in Washington. The act prohibits the circumvention of technology that controls access to protected works. It also prohibits the manufacture and sale of products and services that are primarily designed for circumvention of technological measures to protect copyright works. DMCA requires a triennial review of "persons . . . adversely affected by" certain access or copying prohibitions.[2] The Copyright Office allows exemptions to DMCA (a total of six).

During the first round of rulemaking, two classes of works were exempted: (1) compilations of Web sites blocked by filtering software, and (2) works—including computer programs—that do not permit access because of malfunction, damage, or obsolescence. The second triennial review established four classes of exempted works: (1) compilations that blocked Web sites that operate to prevent e-mail, (2) computer programs protected by privacy devices (dongles) that prevent access due to malfunction or damage and that are obsolete, (3) video games that require the original hardware to access, and (4) e-books with access controls that prevent the read-aloud function. The third round exempted cell phone locks.

Among the proposals in the 2009 round of comments and hearings during the fourth triennial inquiry to determine DMCA exemptions is a request from the Electronic Freedom Foundation for a DMCA exemption for "jail breaking" by iPhone owners. One of Apple's "software locks" limits iPhone owners to Apple-approved applications.

Among the more controversial uses of DMCA is the demand for takedowns of YouTube videos despite claims of fair use of the copyrighted materials within the posted videos. Often the video contains only a few seconds of a news broadcast or music.

For example, Fox Broadcasting objected recently to the use of three short videos posted on YouTube to support political commentary and invoked the takedown provisions of the DMCA.[3] Fox claims that bloggers can link to the broadcaster's Web site. Bloggers claim this would hamper the political debate and, in this case, would be impossible because Fox never posted the video to its Web site. Even if it had been posted, a blogger should be allowed a fair use to view a small portion without viewing an entire program. The controversy adds to the debate over the need to amend DMCA.

## Georgia State Suit for Infringement

Oxford University Press, Cambridge University Press, and SAGE Publications sued Georgia State University (GSU) alleging that the university distributed unauthorized copies of course reading materials published by the plaintiffs through the GSU electronic course reserve system, its Blackboard/WebCT course management system, and departmental Web pages.[4] The suit seeks injunction relief rather than monetary damages.[5]

A significant difference between the early copy shop cases of Kinko's[6] and Michigan Document Services[7] is that the readings are provided by the GSU library through its electronic reserve system rather than by a copy shop.

The publishers believe that providing excerpts of copyrighted materials requires a license and that the university is infringing their copyrights by providing copies without paying royalties.

The complaint provides remarkably specific examples of some of the alleged infringing uses. The copying, in some cases, presses the outer limits of what is generally viewed as fair use. Notably, two of the plaintiffs are nonprofit university presses.

For some time, AAP has threatened college and universities over electronic reserve practices. A few years ago, Cornell University and AAP reached an agreement under the threat of litigation and released joint guidelines. This is the first lawsuit publishers have filed over e-reserve practices.

The university had posted on its Web page a policy drafted by Georgia law professor Ray Patterson that provided an expansive view of fair use. Some would say that it set out what fair use ought to be rather than what courts have held it to be.

In June 2008 Georgia State admitted that it was distributing materials to students, but it asserted that the online distribution of course materials fell within the fair use exemption.[8] The university also argued that it was protected by sovereign immunity under the 11th Amendment to the Constitution.

Colleges and universities are closely following the suit. For years, publishers and the academy have argued over how much copying is required for the use to be "systematic" and "widespread" and thus not "fair." Settlement is possible. The suit carries risks for publishers in suing customers. A settlement would resolve the dispute between these two parties. A settlement might also have the effect of curbing copying that might or might not be fair use.

## Music Industry

The Recording Industry Association of America (RIAA) announced a change in its litigation strategy. It will no longer sue individuals (mostly students) for alleged music piracy. In January 2009 RIAA dumped MediaSentry as its enforcement technology in favor of DtecNet, the Danish investigation technology. If this company can prove real downloading occurred, litigation may still follow. This is perhaps RIAA's response to those courts that did not accept "making available" as a theory of liability for music infringement.

Instead of suing students for music piracy, the recording industry proposes taxing students. Warner Music Group is talking with several major universities about blanket licenses similar to models for music performed on radio and TV.[9] Colleges and universities would collect the money and the recording industry would distribute it to authors, composers, and the public. For the "voluntary blanket licensing" to work, all colleges and universities would have to sign on. Some view this proposal as "join—or else."

RIAA announced that it will rely on cooperation with major Internet service providers (ISPs); when it finds a customer making music available online, the ISP will notify the customer that they might be uploading music illegally.[10]

Unlike the majority of the thousands sued by RIAA for unauthorized downloading of music, Joel Tenenbaum, a Boston University graduate student, chose to fight back. When representing himself became too difficult, he sought assistance from Harvard Law School professor Charles Nesson and his CyberOne class.[11] Nesson asserts that because the statute seeks to punish violators with penalties far in excess of actual damages (the statute provides for a minimum of $750 to a maximum of $150,000 for willful infringement), the statute is unconstitutional. The market value of an iTunes song is 99 cents. RIAA is seeking $1 million in damages. In January 2009 the plaintiffs subpoenaed Arthur and Judith Tenenbaum (Joel's parents) to produce their home computer to have it imaged. This equipment is not the equipment on which the downloading allegedly took place, nor is it the machine owned by Joel's parents when he resided with them. Nesson and his students decided to litigate in the court of public opinion. Time will tell how successful this strategy will be.

In February 2009 Ruckus Network abruptly shut down its "online jukebox," which provided a free and legal alternative to unauthorized file sharing.[12] Last year Total Music, created by Sony/BMG Music Entertainment and Universal Music Group bought Ruckus. Total Music was working on a music store to compete with iTunes, Amazon, and other online music providers. This initiative is dead. The music service was supported by ad revenue that declined dramatically in the latter half of the year. More than 200 colleges and universities, pressed by the recording industry to do something about music piracy, found Ruckus an easy way to comply.

In 2008 Congress renewed the Higher Education Act, which mandates that colleges and universities offer alternatives to illegal downloading, but what exactly that requirement means is unclear. Perhaps the next step will be collective licensing. The U.S. Department of Education has begun drafting regulations "to effectively combat piracy violations."

## Open Access

In February 2008 Harvard Arts and Science faculty voted to publish their scholarly articles online. The faculty will retain copyright on their articles and works, giving the open access movement a significant boost.[13] Harvard Law School faculty followed suit and voted unanimously in May 2008 to make faculty articles freely available in an online repository. Faculty may also post articles on their own Web sites and others may copy them as long as the copies are not used for profit.[14] Each faculty member grants to the university president a non-exclusive irrevocable worldwide license to exercise the copyrights in these articles.

## OCLC License

A new policy promulgated by the Online Computer Library Center (OCLC) recommends principles of shared data creation in its Policy for Use and Transfer of WorldCat Records to govern its members' uses of OCLC bibliographic records.[15] In 1998 the European Union created a database right that does not exist in the United States. OCLC sought to protect its database under copyright for a compilation of factual entries. Uncertain about the extent of the protection, OCLC proposes a new license to govern certain uses. Under the proposal there are some questions whether libraries would be able to share the content of their libraries with other groups. For example, millions of Web sites are crawled by the Google search engine without negotiation between Google and the library. Currently, OCLC shares the 125 million records in WorldCat with Google. A Google algorithm determines whether or not a WorldCat record appears in the search results.

Libraries expressed concern because of the possibilities in the license that might restrict downstream use of metadata. Controversy has arisen over its breach provisions, noncompliance penalties, choice of forum clause, and retrospective application provisions. Members have discussed the extent to which OCLC might use its compilation copyright to control further uses of the records.

In light of the members' concern, the OCLC Review Board of Shared Data Creation and Stewardship is seeking feedback from the global library community regarding the revised policy. OCLC intended to implement the revised policy in the third quarter of 2009.

## Best Practices in Media Literacy Education

The issue of the application of fair use has always been complex and confusing, even more so when applied to the use of media by educators. A new guide[16]— created by Pat Aufderheide, Center for Social Media; Peter Jaszi, professor of law at American University's Washington College of Law; and Renee Hobbs of Temple Media Education Lab—offers advice to clarify the issues. The document is designed to provide guidance to educators who make use of clips from television shows or other popular works in their classrooms. Jaszi argues that fair use is more permissive than many educators think.

The code sets out five principles of consensus developed as a result of meetings with representative of many associations, including the national Association for Media Literacy Education and the National Council of Teachers of English.

In consultation with the Center for Social Media in the School of Communication at American University and the Washington College of Law, the Association of Independent Video and Filmmakers developed a statement of what documentary filmmakers regard as a reasonable application of fair use.[17]

## Copyright Labs

The Copyright Clearance Center (http://www.copyright.com) launched Copyright Labs (http://www.copyrightlabs.com) as a Web-based testing ground for new services.[18] Three applications are available for public use. The first, Google Scholar Firefox Extension, is an add-on to the Firefox browser that allows users to seek copyright permission at www.copyright.com, linking them to permissions information unique to the specific item. Four types of search results are supported: a normal result, a book, a citation, and a U.S. patent.

Another plug-in is Copyright.com Open Search, a copyright permission utility. This add-on aids in licensing content located online.

The third application, ACAP Validator, aids in implementing the Automated Content Access Protocol (ACAP) standard for communicating access rules to search engines. The Validator has not been widely accepted. ACAP permits publishers to direct search engines as to how long an article remains in the search engine index, unlike the robots.txt system that only allows publishers to determine whether a spider can access a Web site.[19]

These newer open source applications recognize the need to post articles in the marketplace.

## Section 108 Report

For several years the library community has worked with the Copyright Office and interested parties to develop a consensus for legislation that would permit libraries to digitize "orphan works." These are works whose copyright holders cannot be located despite extensive and costly efforts. The risk of potential legal action generally intimidates users from making use of these works following an unsuccessful search to locate the lawful owner. Many of these materials have great cultural and historical significance.

The planning of the National Digital Information Infrastructure and Preservation Program (NDIIPP) and the work of the U.S. Copyright Office indicated that the digital world is changing the ways in which libraries and archives carry out their missions. A 19-member study group was appointed to re-examine Section 108 of the Copyright Act and to recommend amendments to address concerns of copyright holders as well as libraries and archives. The study group developed recommendations on a consensus basis and presented its finds in March 2008.[20] Among the recommendations was a proposal to address orphan works.

Following the Section 108 study, the Copyright Office proposed legislation that would limit liability for infringement to reasonable compensation if the owner appeared. Most content owners and users endorsed the proposed legislation, but it stalled when photographers and visual artists expressed concerns. There is interest in pursuing legislation to address this vexing problem.[21]

## Copyright Czar

During fall 2008 Congress approved the creation of a cabinet-level position as part of the Pro IP Act, previously called the Enforcement of Intellectual Property Rights Act.[22] The legislation initially included a controversial measure granting the Department of Justice the authority to sue copyright infringers on behalf of the movie and music industries. The section was removed when the White House lobbied against having the department assume those responsibilities. Traditionally, it has been the responsibility of copyright owners to enforce their own copyrights.

The legislation requires Senate confirmation of a newly created executive-level Intellectual Property Enforcement Coordinator. The coordinator and the office are to develop plans to combat piracy and report to Congress. Hollywood, unions, RIAA, and the U.S. Chamber of Commerce supported the establishment of the copyright czar's office to oversee the government crackdown on intellectual property enforcement. The proposal called for the czar to be aided by an FBI piracy unit.[23]

## Cases

*Greenberg* v. *National Geographic Society*
On December 8, 2008, the U.S. Supreme Court denied a request to review Greenberg's appeal of the 11th Circuit's *en banc* ruling that a CD-ROM collection of *National Geographic* magazine was a protected revision.[24] The revision of the print publication under 17 U.S.C. § 201(c) is precisely the kind that the Supreme Court recognized in *Tasini.*[25]

The library community supported the National Geographic Society's position, arguing that libraries would incur huge costs if the court were to find in favor of the photographer, Greenberg. Libraries were pleased with the court's denial of review. National Geographic did not infringe a photographer's copyrights that were originally published in the print editions of the magazine. The court on remand found that introductory sequence was not privileged.[26]

*Virgin Records of America* v. *Thomas*
In *Virgin Records of America* v. *Thomas*[27] the jury was the first to hold liable the copyright infringer for making songs available for distribution. The single mother who offered to share 24 songs on the Kazaa online file-sharing network was liable for $222,000.[28] Record companies did not have to prove actual distribution

to prove infringement. Judge Michael J. Davis subsequently reversed himself, declaring that his instructions were wrong. He now holds that dissemination through online peer-to-peer file sharing is required to establish distribution. The judge implored Congress to amend the act to preclude such excessive awards.

*Warner Bros. Entertainment, Inc.* v. *RDR Books*
The U.S. District Court for the Southern District of New York declined to protect under fair use a lexicon based on the Harry Potter books.[29] The *Harry Potter Lexicon,* written by Steven Vander Ark, a former library media specialist, is a guide to creatures, characters, objects, events, and places that exist in the world of Harry Potter. The entries are followed by citations to locations in the Harry Potter books. Vander Ark also maintains a popular fan-based Harry Potter Web site. RDR Books sought to publish Vander Ark's 400-page book, which contains 2,437 entries substantially similar to descriptions in the original text. The plaintiff argued that Vander Ark's work not only violated Harry Potter author J. K. Rowling's right of reproduction but also her right to control derivatives. Although the court found substantial similarities, it also found the work was not a derivative, and found it unprotected because there was no transformative purpose.

The case has implications for the production of reference and secondary works. So long as the copying is not extensive, it will be permissible. Book reviews are generally not derivatives. Vander Ark intends to release a revised version in 2009; meanwhile, Rowling intends to produce her own Harry Potter encyclopedia.

## Notes

1. http://www.googlebooksettlement.com/r/view_settlement_agreement.
2. 17 U.S.C. § 1201(a)(c).
3. http://www.citizen.org/pressroom/release.cfm?ID=2796.
4. "Publishers Sue Georgia State on Digital Reading Matter." *New York Times,* April 16, 2008, c2.
5. http://www.publishers.org/main/PressCenter/documents/GSUlawsuitcomplaint.pdf.
6. *Basic Books* v. *Kinko's,* 758 F. Supp.1522 (S.D.N.Y.1991).
7. *Princeton University Press* v. *Michigan Document Services,* 99 F.3d 1381 (6th Cir.1997).
8. Andrea L. Foster, "In Lawsuit, University Asserts That Downloading Copyrighted Texts Is Fair Use." *Chronicle of Higher Education,* June 27, 2008.
9. "Recording Industry Proposes Taxing Students Instead of Suing Them." *Chronicle of Higher Education,* December 8, 2008.
10. http://blogs.wsj.com/law/2008/12/19/recording-industry-to-end-litigation-strategy-thanks-judge-davis.
11. "Nesson, CyberOne, and the RIAA." Berkman Center for Internet and Society at Harvard University (http://cyber.law.harvard.edu/node/4837).
12. Jeffrey R. Young, "What a Music Service Demise Says About Campus Downloading." *Chronicle of Higher Education,* February 12, 2009 (http://chronicle.com/daily/2009/02/11410n.htm).
13. "Harvard Faculty Adopts Open-Access Requirement." *Chronicle of Higher Education,* February 12, 2008 (http://chronicle.com/news/article/3943/Harvard-faculty-adopts-open-access-requirement).

14. http://www.oclc.org/us/en/worldcat/catalog/policy/recordusepolicy.pdf.

15. http://www.law.harvard.edu/news/2008/05/07_openaccess.php.

16. http://www.centerforsocialmedia.org/resources/publications/code_for_media_literacy_ education.

17. *Documentary Filmmakers Statement of Best Practices in Fair Use* (http://www.centerforsocialmedia.org/rock/backgrounddocs/bestpractices.pdf).

18. Michael LoPresti, "CCC Seeks a New Formula with Launch of Copyright Labs" (http://newsbreaks.infotoday.com/nbReader.asp?articleid=40443).

19. Ibid.

20. *Section 108 Study Group Report,* March 2008 (http://www.section108.gov/docs/ Sec108StudyGroupReport.pdf).

21. Library Copyright Alliance, "The Pro-Library Copyright Agenda." December 2008 (http://aallnet.org/aallwash/LCATransition2008.pdf).

22. Prioritizing Resources and Organization for Intellectual Property Act of 2008, Pub. L. No. 110-403, 122 Stat. 4256.

23. David Kravets, "Senate Passes Bill Creating 'Copyright Czar.'" *Wired* (http://blog.wired. com/27bstroke6/2008/09/senate-passes-b.html).

24. Cert. denied. 77 U.S.L.W. 3344.

25. *New York Times Co., Inc.* v. *Tasini,* 533 U.S. 483 (2001).

26. 533 F.3d 1244 (11th Cir. 2008).

27. 2007 WL 2826645 (C.Minn.2007).

28. *Capitol Records, Inc.* v. *Thomas,* 579 F. Supp. 2d 1210 (D.Minn.2008).

29. 575 F. Supp. 2d 513 (S.D.N.Y. 2008).

# Designing Community College Information Resources

Julie Beth Todaro

Community colleges, a presence in higher education since the early 20th century, now enroll more than a third of America's college students. The community college librarian is an active partner in the teaching and learning experience.

Founded to offer broader opportunities to those seeking general education and work force training, public and private community colleges have long played an important local role in transitioning individuals from high school to higher education; community economic development through general and customized work force education and training; career retraining and refocusing; and recreational and lifelong learning experiences through credit, noncredit, and continuing education opportunities. Community colleges have been committed to open-door admissions policies and to providing opportunities close to home, smaller classroom venues, teaching that supports diverse learning styles, self-directed learning and self-paced content, and diverse formats of content to support the breadth of student needs.

Community colleges have also excelled at offering their students extensive general and specialized higher education support services including counseling, advising and placement, tutoring, multiple opportunities for testing in secure environments, and multiple formats of primary and secondary curriculum content. Community colleges offer a broad range of learning venues and library services, choices of hardware and software, information literacy integrated into the curriculum, point-of-use assistance at reference desks, information and help desks, and quiet and small group study environments that support active learning and the design and creation of multiple formats of print and media content for classroom assignments.

In addition to both community and classroom teaching and learning venues, many community colleges are committed to extracurricular activities such as student clubs, athletics, and music (band and orchestra) and to internal college and service learning experiences such as student newspapers, student government, and theater.

When all enrollments are estimated, community colleges serve nearly 25 million individuals. In more than 2,300 institutions with more than 3,000 campuses—ranging from hundreds to thousands of students per campus—community colleges provide open access to higher education, prepare students to advance to four-year institutions, are often the mainstay of work force development and skills training, and provide continuing education and other noncredit education that reaches into every corner of the community.

Julie Beth Todaro, Dean of Library Services for Austin Community College in Austin, Texas, has worked in academic, public, and school libraries for more than 35 years and in library education at the University of Michigan, Texas Woman's University, the University of Texas at Austin, and for the 15-school WISE Consortium. She holds an MLIS from the University of Texas at Austin and a Ph.D. from Columbia University. She is a consultant in the areas of management and organizational development, advocacy, information literacy, 21st-century librarianship, and customer service, and is a past president of the Association of College and Research Libraries.

Twenty-first-century community colleges are affordable, have an average student age of 29 and classes made up of more than 35 percent minorities and nearly 40 percent first-generation higher education enrollees coming from a wide range of backgrounds and lifestyles—including 8 percent non-U.S. citizens and nearly 20 percent single parents. Community colleges are at the forefront of educating healthcare workers (nurses, emergency medical technicians, physical therapists, and so forth) and first responders (80 percent of fire and police personnel), and in the provision of basic and advanced skills training for the general work force.

These educational institutions, long known for recognizing and supporting the broadest spectrum of learning needs, lead in distributed or distance and electronic learning and offer digital campuses; partial and complete degrees, certificates, and coursework; and online learning in general and work force education. Colleges strive for "anytime" support for learning and to provide a seamless delivery of higher education in general and specifically the higher education hybrid experience where students move easily from the classroom to a community learning environment to the digital landscape and back again.

## Overarching Issues

While the issues today's community colleges face obviously vary from community to community, many overarching national issues affect all community colleges. Broadly, today's issues include the following:

*Assessment*—Higher education in general is being asked at the local, state, and national level—as well as from the fund-raising/development arena—to increase levels of assessment and to articulate levels of student success, specifically in the areas of learning and educational growth.

Assessment isn't a new phenomenon in higher education and especially in community colleges involved in general education or work force education. However, increasingly detailed data and documentation is being required, especially in work force areas such as health sciences (with expanded and increased evidence-based education). Examples of contemporary assessment questions include: How are we determining what students need to learn? What are we *promising* that students learn? How effective is teaching? Did the students learn what we said they would? Are modes and methods identical in delivering content; are in-person learning opportunities identical to online learning opportunities? Is learning delivered equally across formats (in-person versus digital) and equally, across locations such as campuses, branch campuses, centers, and sites? How effective are all college offices and support services? Are colleges planning strategically for today's operations and for the next few years? Is planning proactive and reactive? Are decisions made appropriately? Are decisions data-driven? Are decisions made at all?

*E-Anything*—Technology drives so much of teaching and learning today, and community colleges struggle to focus on the student and the match of appropriate teaching and learning—no matter the mode, method, or delivery—to the student. Technology challenges are at the root of many discussions in the higher education arena. Is pedagogy infused with technology appropriately? Are e-classes and e-curriculum identical to curriculum delivered in person? Can institutions keep up with rapidly changing technologies? Are dollars available for sustaining today's technology (hardware and software) and for the commitment to cutting-edge discovery so critical to teaching and learning? Can the e-curriculum keep up with the local and global workplace? Can institutions provide technology and appropriate training to students, faculty, and staff? Are facilities "tech ready"? Are e-curriculum delivery models successful business plans for education?

*Teaching and Learning*—One can argue that students don't change through the decades but that the world around them does; however, the reality is that the ways in which students learn, their learning needs, and the critical competencies necessary—most importantly the match of teaching to learning—do change. Today's students may well be different from students in previous years in terms of new learning preferences, shortened attention spans, and diminished under-standing of "how" to learn. They often arrive at college with less-than-desired breadth and depth in K–12 education, a lack of critical thinking and active learning abilities, and gaps in important disciplines such as science and math. Colleges are challenged with

- Finding out on admission (through standardized and unique testing) the status of today's students' knowledge before offering appropriate advising and design of their educational program
- Identifying necessary core curricula for successful programs in both general education and work force training
- Providing diverse remediation pathways to make students successful as appropriately and quickly as possible
- Ensuring access to professional development for faculty to ensure knowledge of pedagogy for today's students
- Commitment to diverse faculty to match a diverse student body

Related issues include the cost of course management software, and monitoring of student behaviors such as plagiarism in general and electronic plagiarism in particular.

*Funding*—An obvious issue is uncertain funding for today's and tomorrow's higher education environments. In moderately hard times, many institutions raise tuition, implement or increase fees including technology fees, and ramp up grant-seeking and fund-raising groups. Projections for the economy point to a near if not full-blown recession. During significant downturns, people tend to go back to school—often to affordable community colleges—and shrinking or failing funding sources and fewer available federal, state, and local dollars mean that colleges can easily end up with more enrollments and/or more students to educate for the same or fewer dollars.

Educational environments tend to offer relatively safe employment in economic downturns, but these institutions are not immune to reduced services with worst-case scenarios of abandoned programs, closed campuses, and employee furloughs and layoffs. In general, funding problems hit technology and building projects. Projections in some states are dire for the end of fiscal year (FY) 2009 and FY 2010, and others predict hard times in 2010 and even harder in 2011.

*Additional Issues*—A myriad of other issues are being addressed by community colleges: safety and security; the needs of honors and accelerated students; sustainability; maintaining a cutting-edge curriculum; educating as many professionals (such as nurses and emergency medical technicians) as needed; succession planning; and continuous professional development (for example, in management and leadership training).

## Community College Libraries

Whether we call them "libraries," "learning resources," "learning resource centers," or something else, community college library environments excel at supporting their students. Community college librarians are creative in offering traditional and nontraditional library services on campuses, branch campuses, extension centers, and other sites and through online environments, and—like all good academic librarians—they design programs, resources, and services to match student requirements. Community college librarians must look to the institution as a whole when tailoring library resources and services to match course offerings and student needs.

### Assessment

Libraries are striving to assess their resources and services in meaningful ways for accreditation processes, to evaluate their role in the "lives" of students, and to provide institutions with material illustrating the critical role that librarians and libraries play in community colleges. Librarians are applying national standards for information literacy—both general and discipline-specific—to their local programs, and are exploring the use of such interactive techniques as "clickers" that provide classroom student feedback, national customer service surveys, and organizational culture surveys. They are pushing to expand the library's role in providing support services in course management software, striving to expand analysis of use of the library's electronic resources, and working to assess the impact of library resources and services.

The library's assessment questions are often based on the institution's assessment questions, and include: How are we determining what students need to learn for information literacy? Are institutions promising that students will learn information literacy competencies? Which ones? Are libraries involved in the design and delivery of this curriculum? How effective are library presentations? Did students learn what the library said they would learn? Are different modes and methods identical in delivering information literacy content? Is information literacy delivered equally across formats (in-person and digital)? What library services supporting curriculum assignments, and specifically information literacy assignments, are provided at campuses, branch campuses, centers, and sites? Are libraries included in broader institutional planning? How can library services become included in national assessment opportunities? Is the library making data-driven decisions? Is the library planning proactively as well as being responsive—based on assessment and data—to student, faculty, and staff needs?

## E-Anything

Community college libraries struggle—given space constraints and limited funding and numbers of staff—to balance traditional, modern, and cutting-edge library resources and services. These libraries typically do not have the money to provide sufficient depth and breadth of electronic resources, and they rely heavily on consortial opportunities. As with assessment, the broader questions of the institution mirror those of the library. Are in-person information literacy offerings identical to electronic information literacy offerings? Can libraries provide technology and appropriate training to students and library staff? Are libraries "tech ready"? Are library technical resources organized and accessible? With whom should libraries partner to expand technology offered to students? Can information technology/library partnerships be formed?

## Teaching and Learning

Just as students in today's classrooms are different, students in libraries are different. Contemporary students need both basic library skills and advanced information literacy for in-depth research. Libraries are challenged with

- Determining students' information literacy skill levels
- Identifying necessary information literacy for general education and the work force
- Commitment to diverse library staff to match a diverse student body

One additional major role librarians play in today's community colleges is in the identification and prevention of plagiarism, a problem exacerbated by the world of electronic resources. Librarians are taking a leadership role in teaching appropriate rules and regulations regarding citing information and research, and in teaching faculty techniques for determining evidence of plagiarism and preventing plagiarism.

## Funding

It follows that funding issues in today's community colleges are funding issues in today's community college libraries. As typically non-revenue-generating areas of institutions, libraries fight for space as well as for operating and capital dollars. Some libraries do profit—either completely or partially—from the institution's technology fees, but in general library budgets rise and fall with the institution's overall budget.

Moderate to significant cutbacks can mean fewer dollars for electronic resources and print materials as well as reduced hours, fewer staff through layoffs and lost positions, a lack of new hardware, and postponement of renovation and new building to create tech-ready physical structures that will engage students and serve as in-person and digital destinations.

Additional issues for community college libraries include reduced funding for consortial relationships at regional and state levels, resulting in even fewer electronic resources; safety and security for in-person facilities and resources as well as for digital library environments; finding dollars to continue to support critical accreditation standards for work force and general education as well as for new work force and general education programs; succession planning; and continuous professional development (such as 2.0 teaching and learning activities and design of digital instructional resources).

Also of concern are:

- Redesigning libraries to engage students and faculty by providing individual leisure/learning environments, active learning opportunities, and workstations for creating print and electronic content for classroom assignments
- Convincing administrators that libraries should expand at the rate of college enrollments and advocating expansion for physical facilities and library employees
- Finding opportunities to integrate information literacy into credit, non-credit, and continuing education curriculum
- Identifying outcomes for student learning that takes place through the library-designed information literacy curriculum
- Choosing techniques for 2.0 point-of-use reference and instruction including synchronous and asynchronous chats/discussions, Twitter, and so forth
- Identifying methods and finding funding for software tools to manage, organize, and increase accessibility to online resources
- Outsourcing library functions and services
- Marketing library resources and services
- Identifying critical needs for training and development of library professionals and paraprofessionals
- Providing equity of access to technology, determining who teaches students basic technology and computer skills and establishing checkout of library hardware policies and procedures
- Identifying, educating, and expanding internal partnerships with faculty, advisory boards, and so forth

There are many similarities among the varied higher education environments that serve—with great commitment—tens of thousands of students around the clock, both in-person and through virtual destinations. Community college libraries, however, provide fewer in-depth research materials and more diverse formats and reading levels; offer less deep-research information literacy and more developmental or remedial and basic and work force information literacy; and offer extensive online information literacy to support distributed and online learning opportunities.

## Resources

"AACC Position Statement on Information Literacy." American Association of Community Colleges, May 4, 2008. (accessed 1 February 2009) http://www. aacc.nche.edu/About/Positions/Pages/ps05052008.aspx.

"AACC Position Statement on Library and Learning Resource Center Programs." American Association of Community Colleges, January 6, 2003. (accessed 18 January 2009) http://www.aacc.nche.edu/About/Positions/Pages/ ps01062003.aspx.

"About Community Colleges." American Association of Community Colleges. (accessed 15 January 2009) http://www.aacc.nche.edu/AboutCC/Pages/ default.aspx.

Association of College and Research Libraries. (accessed 20 February 2009) http://www.ala.org/ala/mgrps/divs/acrl/index.cfm

"CCSSE Information Literacy Items." Community and Junior Colleges Library Section Wiki. Association of College and Research Libraries. (accessed 19 February 2009) http://wikis.ala.org/acrl/index.php/CCSSE_Information_ Literacy_Items.

"CJCLS." Association of College and Research Libraries. (accessed 20 February 2009). http://wikis.ala.org/acrl/index.php/Cjcls.

"Community and Junior Colleges Library Section." Association of College and Research Libraries. (accessed 21 February 2009) http://www.ala.org/ala/ mgrps/divs/acrl/about/sections/cjcls/index.cfm.

"Position Statement on Student Services and Library and Learning Resource Center Program Support for Distance Learning." American Association of Community Colleges. (accessed 3 February 2009) http://www.aacc.nche. edu/About/Positions/Pages/ps02102005.aspx.

# Federal Agency and Federal Library Reports

## Library of Congress

10 First St. S.E., Washington, DC 20540
202-707-5000, World Wide Web http://www.loc.gov

James H. Billington
Librarian of Congress

Founded in 1800, the Library of Congress is the nation's oldest federal cultural institution and the largest library in the world, with more than 141 million items in various languages, disciplines, and formats. The library's mission is to make its resources available and useful to Congress and the American people and to sustain and preserve a universal collection of knowledge and creativity for future generations. The library serves Congress and the nation both on-site in its reading rooms on Capitol Hill and through global access to its resources via its award-winning Web site, http://www.loc.gov.

### Legislative Support to Congress

Serving Congress is the library's highest priority, particularly in the area of legislative support. During the past year, the library provided Congress with current, objective research and analysis relevant to funding for the wars in Iraq and Afghanistan, foreign aid reform, nuclear nonproliferation, the financial and housing market crises, tax laws, climate change, aviation policy, energy prices and supply, higher education, and unemployment compensation. The rights of children, the disabled, and returning service members and veterans were also issues for which the Congressional Research Service (CRS) provided legislative support to Congress.

CRS responded to more than 870,000 research requests from members of Congress and committees during the year. The Legislative Information System (LIS), developed solely for use by Congress and congressional staff members, continued to provide access to information on past and current legislation through all facets of the lawmaking process. Work continued to upgrade the system, which celebrated its tenth year of operation.

Report compiled by Audrey Fischer, Public Affairs Specialist, Library of Congress.

The Law Library—the world's largest, holding 2.6 million items—provided comprehensive international, comparative, and foreign law research to Congress. During the year, Law Library staff wrote 596 legal research reports, special studies, and memoranda in response to congressional inquiries.

The *Global Legal Monitor* was transformed from a monthly pdf file into a continually updated online publication accessible on the Law Library's Web site. The searchable publication covers legal news and developments worldwide. The Global Legal Information Network (GLIN), which gives Congress access to the laws of 35 member nations, was upgraded in November 2008. The most significant enhancement was the application of digital signatures to each full-text document in the GLIN database for security purposes. Other new features include a simplified Chinese Web interface and direct access to information on the acts of the British Parliament.

The Copyright Office provided policy advice and technical assistance to Congress on important copyright laws and related issues. The Register of Copyrights testified before Congress on the matter of orphan works (works still protected by copyright but for which an owner cannot be identified or located). During the year, the Shawn Bentley Orphan Works Act of 2008 passed the Senate and was referred to the House, but no action had been taken by year's end.

In March 2008, after several years of analysis, the Section 108 Study Group issued its final report. The report, which is accessible at http://www.section108. gov, makes recommendations for reforming the section of the Copyright Act (known as the "library exception") that provides limited exceptions for libraries and archives so that they may make copies to replace copyrighted works in their collections when necessary, preserve them for the long term, and make them available to users.

Section 109 of the Satellite Home Viewer Extension and Reauthorization Act (SHVERA) of 2004 required the Copyright Office to examine and compare the statutory licensing systems for the cable and satellite television industries under Sections 111, 119, and 122 of the Copyright Act and make recommendations. The Copyright Office sought comment from the affected industries, copyright owners, and other interested parties and held three days of hearings in July 2007. The principal recommendation of the report, issued on June 30, 2008, was for Congress to move toward abolishing Section 111 and Section 119 of the act inasmuch as the cable and satellite industries are established entities with substantial market power, able to negotiate agreements with copyright owners for programming carried on distant broadcast signals. A copy of the report is accessible on the Copyright Office Web site at http://www.copyright.gov.

## Security

With support from Congress, the library developed further its security program for staff, patrons, facilities, and collections. The year's focus was enhancing the emergency preparedness program, improving security at the library's outlying facilities, and expanding staff security awareness. In coordination with other agencies on Capitol Hill and elsewhere, the library continued upgrading its emergency preparedness capabilities, facilities security, and internal controls safeguarding its collections. Improvements were made in the area of communications between Library of Congress Police and the U.S. Capitol Police regarding situations that affect the Capitol complex.

In June 2008 the Office of Security and Emergency Preparedness conducted the first library-wide shelter-in-place drills in the library's three buildings on Capitol Hill. In August the library's new emergency public address system was installed. Emergency preparedness measures were implemented at all five of the library's outlying annexes. Increased physical security measures were implemented at the library's Packard Campus for Audio-Visual Conservation in Culpeper, Virginia, and the book-storage facility in Fort Meade, Maryland. Plans were also put in place to safeguard staff and visitors traversing the tunnel connecting the library's Thomas Jefferson Building and the Capitol Visitor Center, which opened in December 2008.

The Information Technology (IT) Security Program became fully functional in 2008, ensuring that the library's mission-critical systems are reliable and secure and that the technology infrastructure that supports these systems is uncompromised. The library's technology infrastructure includes three data centers, more than 350 servers, 225 library-wide business enterprise applications, 9,500 voice connections, 14,000 data network connections, 5,000 workstations, and 1,000 local printers. IT security directives were revised to incorporate "best practices" across industry and government. Library staff completed the mandatory annual IT security awareness training.

## Budget

During fiscal year (FY) 2008, the library operated with a congressional appropriation of $613,496,414, including authority to spend up to $50,447,565 in offsetting collections.

## Development

The library's fund-raising activities during FY 2008 brought in a total of $23.6 million, representing 936 gifts from 711 donors. Those gifts from individuals, foundations, corporations, trusts, associations, councils, and societies represented a 77 percent increase in private sector gifts compared with the previous year. Gifts, including $4.2 million received through the library's planned giving program, were made to 76 different library funds. The library forged partnerships with 283 first-time donors, who gave $5.6 million, or 24 percent of the gifts received during the year. A new donations Web site at http://www.loc.gov/donate, launched in July 2008, facilitates public support for the library through online giving.

Nineteen new gift and trust funds were established, including the Mary Wolfskill Trust Fund in memory of a former Manuscript Division staff member. The fund supports an internship program that fosters interest in archival work among undergraduate and graduate students and assists visiting archivists attending the Modern Archives Institute.

The James Madison Council—the library's first private sector advisory group—continued to provide substantial support for a number of initiatives. Gifts from Madison Council members in FY 2008 totaled $8 million, bringing the council's total support since 1990 to $188 million. Private gifts supported a variety of new and continuing initiatives, including exhibitions, acquisitions, and symposia and other scholarly programs. Private donors gave more than $1.4 million to support the 2008 National Book Festival and $4.1 million to develop the new Library of Congress Experience (bringing the total to $20.2 million in private funding for the new Experience).

## Collections

The size of the library's collections grew to 141.8 million items during the year, an increase of more than 3 million over the previous year. This figure included more than 32 million cataloged books and other print materials, 62 million manuscripts, 16 million microforms, 5.3 million maps, 5.6 million pieces of sheet music, 14 million visual materials (photographs, posters, moving images, prints, and drawings), 3 million audio materials, and more than 1 million items in miscellaneous formats.

### Cataloging

During 2008 the library cataloged 350,631 bibliographic volumes. Production of full- and core-level original cataloging totaled 208,321 bibliographic records. With the library serving as the secretariat for the international Program for Cooperative Cataloging (PCC), member institutions created 200,858 new name authorities and 3,116 new subject authorities. In addition, the library contributed 91,016 new name authorities and 35,748 new subject headings.

During the year the library completed a project to implement online cataloging of materials in Arabic, Hebrew, Persian, and East Asian languages, and scripts directly in its integrated library management system, the LC ILS. As a result, library staff can create online catalog records for materials published in the JACKPHY languages (Japanese, Arabic, Chinese, Korean, Persian, Hebrew, and Yiddish).

In January 2008 a Working Group on the Future of Bibliographic Control (convened by the library to examine the future of bibliographic description in the 21st century) issued its final report. Chaired jointly by José-Marie Griffiths, dean of the School of Information and Library Science at the University of North Carolina at Chapel Hill, and Olivia Madison, dean of libraries at Iowa State University, the group included representatives of libraries, library associations, and the information technology community.

The report recommended the following:

• Increase the efficiency of bibliographic production for all libraries through cooperation and sharing of bibliographic records and through use of data produced in the overall supply chain.

- Transfer effort into high-value activity. In particular, provide greater value for knowledge creation through leveraging access to unique materials that are currently hidden and underused.
- Position technology by recognizing that the World Wide Web is libraries' technology platform as well as the appropriate platform for standards. Recognize that users are not only people but also applications that interact with library data.
- Position the library community for the future by adding evaluative, qualitative, and quantitative analyses of resources. Work to realize the potential provided by the Functional Requirements for Bibliographic Records (FRBR) framework.
- Strengthen the library and information science profession through education and through development of metrics that will inform decision making now and in the future.

The report, and the library's response to its recommendations, can be found at http://www.loc.gov/bibliographic-future.

Effective October 1, 2008, a reorganization of the Acquisitions and Bibliographic Access Division resulted in the merger of acquisitions and cataloging functions. The reorganization ends an older "industrial" model of work, in which an incoming book moved slowly along an "assembly line" of acquisitions and processing units. As a result of the merger, a book acquired as a copyright deposit, purchase, gift, or exchange will go to one division, instead of several, for centralized "processing." That term encompasses ordering, cataloging, shelflisting, barcoding, and all the other activities that enable the library's users to find one particular book among more than 20 million unique titles.

### Important New Acquisitions

The library receives millions of items each year from copyright deposits, federal agencies, and purchases, exchanges, and gifts. Significant acquisitions made possible by the Madison Council included an 1820 hand-colored map of the United States by John Melish (1771–1822).

During the year, the library also acquired the following significant items and collections:

- A 54-volume manuscript of *Genji Monogatari*, or *The Tale of Genji*, a Japanese work held to be the world's first novel, written in the early 11th century by Murasaki Shikibu
- Four richly illuminated 15th-century Armenian ecclesiastical manuscripts
- The papers of civil rights activist James Forman, American composer Charles Strouse, and Frank Stanton, president of the Columbia Broadcasting System (CBS) from 1946 to 1971
- The original artwork by Steve Ditko for Marvel Comics' "Amazing Fantasy #15," the comic book that introduced Spider-Man in August 1962

- More than 150 black-and-white photographs of the 1963 March on Washington, a highlight of the civil rights movement
- More than 500 color photographs of the library's Thomas Jefferson, John Adams, and James Madison buildings by photographer Carol Highsmith

## Reference Services

In addition to serving Congress, the library provides reference services to the public in its reading rooms and through its Web site. During the year the library's staff handled more than 545,000 reference requests that were received in person, on the telephone, and through written and electronic correspondence. Library staff also responded to reference questions received from other libraries around the globe through an online system known as QuestionPoint and directly from patrons through Ask a Librarian at http://www.loc.gov/rr/askalib. More than 1.1 million items were circulated for use within the library.

To expand access to knowledge and to spark the creativity of future generations, the library lowered from 18 to 16 the minimum age for use of its Main Reading Room for research purposes, effective April 24 (the library's anniversary).

## Online Resources

Through its National Digital Library Program and digitization efforts by various divisions, the library has been adding high-quality digital content to its award-winning Web site, http://www.loc.gov.

The Web site gives users access to the institution's unparalleled resources, such as its online catalog, selected collections in various formats, copyright and legislative information, library exhibitions, and Webcasts and podcasts of library events, among other resources. Consistently recognized as one of the top federal sites, the Web site recorded more than 85 million visits and 610 million page views in FY 2008.

In conjunction with the opening of the new Library of Congress Experience in April 2008, the library launched a "personalized" Web site at http://myLOC.gov. The site allows visitors to take a virtual tour of the exhibitions that compose the new Experience. Library exhibitions are accessible online at http://www.loc.gov/exhibits, and the exhibitions Web site was redesigned in conjunction with the launch of myLOC.gov.

Improvements in the Integrated Library System increased the availability of the Online Public Access Catalog to external users. The public legislative information system, THOMAS (http://www.thomas.gov), and the Global Legal Information Network (http://www.glin.gov) continued to track legislative issues and provide legal information.

As a portal to the library's millions of online resources, the Wise Guide (http://www.loc.gov/wiseguide) continued to introduce users to the library's Web site. The site is updated monthly with a series of articles containing links to the library's online resources.

Several new presentations were added to the American Memory Web site (http://memory.loc.gov), which offers access to more than 135 American history collections (15.3 million digital files).

Special presentations were dedicated to the various heritage months celebrating the achievements of African Americans, Hispanics, Jews, Asians, and women. These sites were produced in collaboration with other federal agencies in order to provide a single place from which to access these important historic materials in the custody of the federal government.

Included among the more than 5,500 individual recollections accessible on the Veterans History Project (VHP) site at http://www.loc.gov/vets are new presentations added in 2008. Special presentations added to the site during the year honored veterans of World War I and the contributions of African American, Asian, Jewish, Hispanic, and woman veterans. VHP also commemorated the 60th anniversary of the racial integration of the U.S. armed forces with online interviews.

The library continued its use of Web 2.0 concepts to increase access to its resources. These concepts include social networking, photo- and video-sharing sites, wikis, and blogs. In its first year of implementation, the library's blog kept readers informed about library initiatives and milestones and provided related links to its resources.

By subscribing to the library's RSS (Really Simple Syndication) feeds and e-mail update service, users can stay up to date about areas of the library's site that interest them. To sign up, visit http://www.loc.gov/rss.

The library continued to promote its activities by producing and making accessible podcasts on its Web site at http://www.loc.gov/podcasts. The podcasts include interviews conducted with authors participating in the National Book Festival. Webcasts of selected lectures, readings, conferences, and symposia held at the library were also added to the Web site at http://www.loc.gov/webcasts.

In January 2008 the library undertook a pilot project with Flickr, a photo-sharing Web site (http:/www.flickr.com) that allows users to describe their own and other photographs through the practice of "tagging"—describing individual items with one or more descriptive terms. The library contributed more than 3,100 digital photographs from two popular collections housed in its Prints and Photographs Division for which no copyright restrictions are known to exist. The goals of the pilot were to provide wider access to the collections to a broader audience and to explore new ways to acquire the best possible information about these collections for the benefit of researchers and posterity. By the end of the first day, according to Flickr's blog, users had added more than 4,000 unique tags across the collection. About 19,000 tags were added in total. By the end of the year, the library's photographs had garnered more than 10 million views, 7,166 comments, and more than 67,000 tags.

## Global Access

The Library of Congress provides access to global resources through cooperative agreements and exchanges with other nations, as well as its overseas offices. The overseas offices (http://www.loc.gov/acq/ovop) collect and catalog materials from 86 countries—in some 150 languages and 25 scripts—in Africa, Asia, Latin America, and the Middle East.

### World Digital Library

The World Digital Library (WDL), first proposed to UNESCO by the Librarian of Congress in 2005, aims to make available on the Internet, free of charge and in multilingual format, significant primary materials from cultures around the world, including manuscripts, maps, rare books, music scores, recordings, films, prints, photographs, architectural drawings, and other significant cultural materials.

In October 2007 the Library of Congress and five partner institutions (the Bibliotheca Alexandrina, the National Library of Brazil, the National Library and Archives of Egypt, the National Library of Russia, and the Russian State Library) presented the prototype of the future WDL at the UNESCO General Conference in Paris. The public launch of WDL in cooperation with UNESCO was scheduled for April 2009. Its Internet address is http://www.worlddigitallibrary.org.

To further its goal of building digital library capabilities in the developing world, the WDL project provided to the Iraqi National Library and Archives, on long-term loan, digitization equipment and training for staff that will enable Iraq to participate in the project.

In 2008 libraries in China, Israel, Japan, Morocco, the Netherlands, Qatar, Serbia, Slovakia, and Sweden, and the Columbus Memorial Library of the Organization of American States agreed to include content from their collections in WDL. The library signed an agreement with the King Abdullah University of Science and Technology (KAUST) of Saudi Arabia establishing a partnership to digitize items pertaining to the history of science in the Arab and Islamic worlds and make them available on WDL.

Several U.S. institutions also joined the WDL project. These included the National Archives and Records Administration, the John Carter Brown Library at Brown University, and Yale University.

## Preservation

During 2008 the library assessed the preservation needs of more than 374,000 items from its general and special collections, including books, photographs, maps, audiovisual materials, and other formats. During the year, more than 8 million items were repaired, mass-deacidified, and microfilmed or otherwise reformatted. Notable items treated during the year included Benjamin Franklin's copy of the First Continental Congress's 1774 Petition to the King, and George Washington's December 23, 1783, letter to Congress regarding his resignation from the Army. Conservators also treated approximately 20 volumes from Thomas Jefferson's personal library, which went on display in April 2008, and items from the Jay I. Kislak Collection that were on display in the library's Exploring the Early Americas exhibition.

To meet the challenges of preserving traditional and new media, the library hired four preservation research scientists as part of a multifaceted preservation research initiative. Housed in the Preservation Research and Testing Division of the library's Preservation Directorate, the initiative will include the opening of two "green" energy-efficient laboratories—a chemical and mechanical properties laboratory and an optical properties laboratory. The initiative will also include a new center to safeguard and make accessible the library's rare and valuable preservation-science reference collection.

In the wake of natural disasters such as hurricanes, tornadoes, floods, and forest fires, the Preservation Directorate developed an emergency-preparedness Web site that addresses collections-care issues. On August 29, 2008, to mark the third anniversary of Hurricane Katrina, the library announced a new Web page on the site titled "Learning from Katrina" (http://www.loc.gov/preserv/emergprep/katrinarespond.html). Visitors to the site can hear seven interviews with professional conservators who helped salvage collections affected by the August 2005 storm. During 2008 the site was updated with resources on fire response and recovery.

The library continued to play a leadership role in the preservation of materials in a variety of formats, including books, photographs, newspapers, films, and sound recordings. It also played an outreach role in the preservation of the nation's heritage through several oral history projects. Highlights appear below.

## Books

The library continued to fill new units at its book-storage facility at Fort Meade, Maryland. Construction of high-density storage modules 3 and 4, which began in October 2006, was scheduled for completion in April 2009. During 2008 a total of 377,744 items were accessioned and transferred to the facility, bringing the total to 2.7 million items stored there. The retrieval rate—within 12 business hours or less—was 100 percent.

With a $2 million grant from the Alfred P. Sloan Foundation, the library is digitizing more than 25,000 public domain works. The project, titled Digitizing American Imprints, was first announced on January 31, 2007, with a focus on at-risk "brittle books" from the library's special collections.

During 2008 ten Scribe book scanners were installed in the library's Adams Building under a contract with the nonprofit Internet Archive. Work began in the new Federal Scan Center to digitize high-demand General Collections materials in the areas of American history, local history, and genealogy. The digitized books will eventually be accessible through the library's Online Public Access Catalog. Presently the scanned materials are accessible on the Internet Archive's Web site at http://www.internetarchive.org. As of early 2009, the project had digitized more than 25,000 books totaling 8.5 million images.

During FY 2008 the library's Federal Library and Information Center Committee (FLICC) established an agreement with the Internet Archive to provide on-site scanning services for other federal agencies under a program to be called FEDScan.

## Newspapers

The Library of Congress has long preserved newspapers from around the world. With funding from the National Endowment for the Humanities (NEH), the library participated in the U.S. Newspaper Program, a 23-year effort that culminated in 2007 with a total of 72 million endangered newspaper pages microfilmed since the project's inception.

Continuing its commitment to newspaper preservation, NEH is funding the National Digital Newspaper Program, an initiative to digitize and provide free and public access to historic American newspapers that are in the public domain. The Library of Congress is making the materials accessible on the Chronicling America Web site, which was launched in March 2007. In 2008 the site grew to 2.7 million digital items, comprising more than 680,000 newspaper pages published between 1880 and 1910 and representing 94 newspapers in 9 states and the District of Columbia. Also accessible on the site is a downloadable listing of all digitized titles with links to available issues and other information. The system also offers a weekly RSS feed and an e-mail subscription service. The site is at http://www.loc.gov/chroniclingamerica.

## Maps

In collaboration with the National Institute for Standards and Technology (NIST) and the Alcoa Foundation, the library's Preservation Directorate and the Geography and Map Division created a permanent, oxygen-free aluminum housing for the world map drawn in 1507 by Martin Waldseemüller that shows the name "America" for the first time. Housed in the encasement, the map is on display as part of "Exploring the Early Americas: The Jay I. Kislak Collection at the Library of Congress," which opened in December 2007. The knowledge obtained through the process of designing and installing this case has been documented and shared with the national and international preservation community on the Preservation Directorate's Web site.

## Audiovisual Collections

Opened in July 2007, the library's Packard Campus for Audio-Visual Conservation in Culpeper, Virginia, consolidates its audiovisual collections—the world's largest and most comprehensive—previously housed in Library of Congress buildings in four states and the District of Columbia.

Philanthropist David Woodley Packard and the Packard Humanities Institute donated the state-of-the-art facility to the American people, the largest-ever private gift to the legislative branch of the U.S. government. The $155 million facility was financed jointly by the gift from Packard and appropriations from Congress totaling $82.1 million.

The Packard Campus comprises a collections building, where 5.7 million items (1.2 million moving images, nearly 3 million sound recordings, and 1.5 million related items, such as manuscripts, posters, and screenplays) are housed under ideal conditions; a conservation building, where the collections are acquired, managed, and preserved; and a separate facility with 124 vaults, where nitrate films can be stored safely.

In FY 2008, its initial year of operation, the first phase of building the sound and video preservation laboratories was completed and a robotic system called SAMMA (System for the Automated Migration of Media Assets) began to create preservation-quality digital files from cassette-based media. Construction of the film laboratory was completed and new preservation and technology staff were hired.

Researchers in the library's related reading rooms on Capitol Hill are able to see or hear derivative copies of the digital files through high-speed fiber-optic connections with Culpeper. The Packard Campus also boasts an on-site facility for scholars and a new theater. Opened in September 2008, the 200-seat Mount Pony Theater was inaugurated with a film series featuring titles named to the library's National Film Registry. The art deco-style theater is one of only five theaters in the country equipped to show original classic film prints on nitrate film stock as they would have been screened in theaters prior to 1950. The theater also features a custom-built organ that will provide live music accompaniment for silent movies.

## Films

The library continued its commitment to preserving the nation's film heritage. The 25 films listed below were named to the National Film Registry in 2008, bringing the total to 500. The library works to ensure that the films listed on the registry are preserved, either through its motion picture preservation program at the Packard Campus or through collaborative ventures with other archives, motion picture studios, and independent filmmakers.

*The Asphalt Jungle* (1950)
*Deliverance* (1972)
*Disneyland Dream* (1956)
*A Face in the Crowd* (1957)
*Flower Drum Song* (1961)
*Foolish Wives* (1922)
*Free Radicals* (1979)
*Hallelujah* (1929)
*In Cold Blood* (1967)
*The Invisible Man* (1933)
*Johnny Guitar* (1954)
*The Killers* (1946)
*The March* (1964)
*No Lies* (1973)
*On the Bowery* (1957)
*One Week* (1920)
*The Pawnbroker* (1965)
*The Perils of Pauline* (1914)
*Sergeant York* (1941)
*The 7th Voyage of Sinbad* (1958)
*So's Your Old Man* (1926)

*George Stevens WW2 Footage* (1943–1946)

*The Terminator* (1984)

*Water and Power* (1989)

*White Fawn's Devotion* (1910)

### Sound Recordings

The library is conducting a study on the state of audio preservation, which will be published in FY 2009. The results will inform a comprehensive plan for a national audio preservation program, the first of its kind, as directed by Congress in the National Recording Preservation Act of 2000.

Under the terms of the act, the Librarian of Congress is also responsible for selecting recordings annually that are "culturally, historically, or aesthetically significant." In May 2008 the librarian announced the following additions to the National Recording Registry, bringing the total to 250.

The First Trans-Atlantic Broadcast (March 14, 1925)

"Allons a Lafayette," Joseph Falcon (1928)

"Casta Diva," from Bellini's "Norma"; Rosa Ponselle, accompanied by the Metropolitan Opera Orchestra and Chorus, conducted by Giulio Setti (1928 and 1929)

"If I Could Hear My Mother Pray Again," Thomas A. Dorsey (1934)

"Sweet Lorraine," Art Tatum (1940)

"Fibber's Closet Opens for the First Time," from the "Fibber McGee and Molly" radio program (1940)

"Wings Over Jordan," Wings Over Jordan choir (1941)

New York Mayor Fiorello LaGuardia reading newspaper comics (1945)

"Call It Stormy Monday but Tuesday Is Just As Bad," T-Bone Walker (1947)

Harry S Truman's acceptance speech at the 1948 Democratic National Convention (1948)

"The Jazz Scene," various artists (1949)

"It Wasn't God Who Made Honky Tonk Angels," Kitty Wells (1952)

"My Fair Lady," original cast recording (1956)

Navajo Shootingway Ceremony Field Recordings, recorded by David McAllester (1957–1958)

" 'Freight Train' and Other North Carolina Folk Songs and Tunes," Elizabeth Cotten (1959)

Marine Band Concert Album to Help Benefit the National Cultural Center (1963)

"Oh, Pretty Woman," Roy Orbison (1964)

"Tracks of My Tears," Smokey Robinson and the Miracles (1965)

"You'll Sing a Song and I'll Sing a Song," Ella Jenkins (1966)

"Music from the Morning of the World," various artists; recorded by David Lewiston (1966)

"For the Roses," Joni Mitchell (1972)

"Headhunters," Herbie Hancock (1973)

Ronald Reagan Radio Broadcasts (1976–1979)

"The Sounds of Earth," disc prepared for the Voyager spacecraft (1977)

"Thriller," Michael Jackson (1982)

### Oral History

The library's American Folklife Center continued its mandate to "preserve and present American folklife" through a number of outreach and oral history programs such as the Veterans History Project (VHP), StoryCorps, and the National Visionary Leadership Project.

VHP was established by Congress in 2000 to record and preserve first-person accounts of armed services veterans who served during wartime. In November 2008 Congress demonstrated its continued support of the project with a bipartisan resolution establishing Veterans History Project Week to coincide with Veterans Day.

In the project's eighth year, the VHP collection grew to more than 60,000 individual audiotaped and videotaped submissions containing interviews, correspondence, diaries, memoirs, photographs, scrapbooks, films, maps, and other artifacts. At year's end more than 5,500 collections were accessible on the project's Web site at http://www.loc.gov/folklife/vets.

The StoryCorps project was conceived by David Isay of Sound Portraits Productions, who was inspired by the library's collection of oral history records made by the Works Progress Administration (WPA) during the late 1930s and early 1940s. Like the WPA recordings, the interviews being collected by Story-Corps will be housed in the American Folklife Center. At year's end the StoryCorp archive included more than 15,000 stories. In addition to weekly broadcasts on National Public Radio's "Morning Edition," StoryCorps stories are available as downloadable podcasts.

During FY 2008 the National Visionary Leadership Project (NVLP) donated more than 200 original videotaped interviews with prominent African Americans to the Library of Congress. These oral histories are the seed of a collection that will be housed in the American Folklife Center. Ray Charles, Dorothy Height, Gordon Parks, John Hope Franklin, and Coretta Scott King are a few of the prominent African Americans whose oral interviews were conducted by project cofounders Renee Poussaint, a former network television correspondent and documentary filmmaker, and Camille O. Cosby, an educator and producer.

## Digital Preservation

In December 2000 Congress asked the library to lead a collaborative project to develop a national strategy for preserving digital content for future generations. Through the project known as the National Digital Information Infrastructure and Preservation Program (NDIIPP), the library is working with 130 partners from universities, libraries, archives, federal agencies, and the private sector to preserve items that are "born digital." Its Web site is at http://www.digitalpreservation.gov.

## Preserving Creative America

The Preserving Creative America Project was launched in 2007 to target preservation issues broadly—from digital photographs, cartoons, and motion pictures to sound recordings and video games. In August 2007 the library awarded contracts totaling $2.15 million to eight private partners to preserve creative works in digital format: the Academy of Motion Picture Arts and Sciences; the American Society of Media Photographers; ARTstor; BMS/Chace; the Film and Television Archive of the University of California, Los Angeles; the Society of American Archivists; Universal Press Syndicate; and the University of Illinois at Urbana-Champaign. Work began in 2008 to establish standards, select content, and begin transferring content to the Library of Congress.

## State Records

States face formidable challenges in caring for digital records with long-term legal and historical value. During 2008 a total of 23 states, working in four consortia, joined the library in an initiative to preserve important state government information in digital form. The projects will collect several categories of digital information, such as geospatial data, legislative records, court case files, Web-based publications, and executive agency records. Each project will also work to share tools, services, and best practices to help every state manage its digital heritage.

## Electronic Journals

The library has historically received print publications through the copyright deposit system. Electronic scholarly journals, which increasingly have no print equivalents, are widely considered to be at risk of loss. The library is working with external organizations to provide a new service, eDeposit, that will allow copyright owners to electronically deposit their publications into a digital archive maintained by the library.

In 2008 agreements were reached with major publishers and third parties to transfer content to the library. Tools, services, and processes for acquiring and transferring e-journal content into the library's production environment and archival storage systems were developed and transfer of electronic content began.

## Web Capture

Since 2000 the library's Web Capture Team has preserved content on the Web pertaining to a variety of specific topics. These are accessible at http://www. loc.gov/webcapture. In August 2008 the Library of Congress, California Digital Library, University of North Texas Libraries, Internet Archive, and the U.S. Government Printing Office announced a collaborative project to preserve public U.S. government Web sites at the end of the George W. Bush administration on January 19, 2009. The project is intended to document federal agencies' online archive during the transition of government and to enhance the existing collections of the five partner institutions. Congressional Web sites, which the library has been preserving on a monthly basis since December 2003, will also be part of the project.

# Copyright

The collections of the Library of Congress have been created largely through the copyright system. The library's Copyright Office annually handles about 1 million deposit copies in all formats. In 2008 the Copyright Office forwarded 526,000 copies of works with a net worth of approximately $23.8 million to the library. Approximately half of these items were received from publishers under the mandatory-deposit provisions of the copyright law.

During the year the Copyright Office received about 560,000 new claims to copyright, which covered more than 1 million works. It registered about 233,000 of those claims. The reduction in the number of registrations from the previous year's figures was due in part to implementation of the new IT system for electronic copyright registration (eCO) through the Internet. The new system accommodates traditional formats as well as items that are "born digital."

The Copyright Royalty and Distribution Reform Act of 2004 (Public Law 108-419) replaced the Copyright Arbitration Royalty Panels with an entity comprising three copyright royalty judges and their staff. The Librarian of Congress swore the judges into office in January 2006. In their third year of operation, the judges set rates and terms for various statutory licenses and distributed royalty fees collected by the Copyright Office. The total distributions made in fiscal 2008 were $204,663,712.65 from eight funds, which represents a decrease of $75,267,195.25 from fiscal 2007.

# National Library Service for the Blind and Physically Handicapped

Established in 1931 when President Herbert Hoover signed the Pratt-Smoot Act into law, the National Library Service for the Blind and Physically Handicapped (NLS) circulates more than 22 million copies of braille and recorded books and magazines to some 500,000 readers through a network of 131 cooperating libraries. NLS also provides a free service known as the 102 Talking-Book Club to more than 3,700 patrons who are 100 years of age or older.

During 2008 NLS continued its work toward the next generation of audio technology, digital talking books. The project calls for phasing in playback machines and media for digital talking books and phasing out analog cassettes and equipment. In June the library awarded contracts for critical elements of the project. Shinano-Kenshi Corporation Ltd./Plextor-LLC will produce digital talking book players and LC Industries will produce digital talking book cartridge-mailing containers. In August a contract was awarded to Northstar Systems to produce USB flash-memory cartridges for recorded audiobooks to be distributed to patrons of the talking book program.

NLS launched a pilot project in 2006 to make audio books available as downloadable files over the Internet. In 2008 the project was renamed BARD (Braille and Audio Reading Download) to reflect plans to include digital braille, which is currently accessible through NLS's Web-Braille program. By the end of the year, 3,798 patrons and 69 network libraries had signed up to use NLS BARD, which offers more than 11,000 titles.

## John W. Kluge Center

The John W. Kluge Center was established in 2000 with a gift of $60 million from John W. Kluge, Metromedia president and founding chairman of the James Madison Council, the library's private sector advisory group. Located within the library's Office of Scholarly Programs, the center's goal is to bring the world's top scholars to the library where they can use the institution's unparalleled resources and interact with public policymakers in Washington. The center also administers the Kluge Prize, which rewards lifetime achievement in the study of humanity for disciplines not recognized by Nobel prizes; the 2008 winner of the prize is listed below under "Honors and Awards."

During 2008 the Kluge Center continued to draw outstanding senior scholars and postdoctoral fellows. Through their work, scholars, researchers, literary enthusiasts, and the general public deepened their understanding of the cultural, historical, philosophical, scientific, and creative dimensions of human experience.

The Kluge Center sponsored symposia, lectures, book talks, and conferences, as well as a series of talks by fellows and scholars on their particular areas of research. In June 2008 new media and pop culture expert Douglas Rushkof delivered the fourth lecture in the Digital Natives lecture series. Derrick De Kerckhove, holder of the Harissios Papamarkou Chair in Education at the Kluge Center, coordinates the lecture series, focusing on the impact on society of the generation that has been raised with the computer as a natural part of their lives.

In July 2008 historian Dane Kennedy lectured on three waves of European decolonization. The Kluge Center also sponsored a four-week summer institute for college and university teachers titled "Rethinking America in a Global Perspective," funded by the National Endowment for the Humanities.

For more information about the Kluge Center, visit http://www.loc.gov/kluge.

## Publications

Each year the library publishes books, calendars, and other printed products featuring its vast content, many in cooperation with trade publishers.

Major works published in 2008 that featured the library and its collections included *On These Walls: Inscriptions and Quotations in the Library of Congress* (an updated version featuring images of the library by Carol M. Highsmith) and *The Naming of America: Martin Waldseemüller's 1507 World Map and the Cosmographiae Introductio.*

The first three volumes in a new series titled Field of Vision showcase the work of Depression-era photographers Russell Lee, Ben Shahn, and Marion Post Wolcott.

Two titles were added to the Norton/Library of Congress Visual Sourcebook in Architecture, Design, and Engineering Series: *Public Markets* and *Eero Saarinen: Buildings from the Balthazar Korab Archive.*

# Exhibitions

On April 12, 2008—111 years after the Thomas Jefferson Building first opened to the public—the library invited visitors to experience the grandeur of the building and the resources housed within it using digital interactive technologies.

The new Library of Congress Experience is aimed at increasing public awareness of the library's creative and intellectual resources, collections, and unique treasures. The Experience capitalizes on the construction of the Capitol Visitor Center and the tunnel that opened in December 2008 connecting the Capitol with the library's Thomas Jefferson Building. The creation of this new passageway was among the motivations for the library to design new interactive displays, which are aimed in part at students and teachers.

Working with the Architect of the Capitol, library offices, and outside contractors, and drawing on the expertise of the library's curators, the Interpretive Programs Office developed four new features that compose the Library of Congress Experience: "Exploring the Early Americas: The Jay I. Kislak Collection at the Library of Congress," "Creating the United States," "Thomas Jefferson's Library," and "The Art and Architecture of the Thomas Jefferson Building." Interactive kiosks in the Great Hall allow visitors to zoom in on details of the space and explore in detail a display of two of the library's most prized objects, the Gutenberg Bible and the Giant Bible of Mainz. Visitors can take a virtual tour of these exhibitions at myLOC.gov.

The second phase of the Experience was implemented on December 11. Visitors now receive a "passport to knowledge" that enables them to personalize their visits while exploring the library's collections, educational content, and related materials on-site and, later, online.

The passport also invites visitors to participate in Knowledge Quest, an educational adventure in which players investigate artifacts from the library's buildings and exhibitions.

# Special Events

During the year the library presented more than 570 special events including poetry and literary programs, concerts, lectures, and symposia, many of which were broadcast live or archived on the library's Web site. A list of upcoming events is posted at http://www.loc.gov/loc/events.

### Literary Events

Since its inception in 2001, the library's National Book Festival has become an anticipated annual event. The 2008 book festival was held on September 27 on the National Mall. Hosted once again by First Lady Laura Bush, with support from the Target store chain and other private donors, the festival drew more than 120,000 book lovers.

During the year, the library's Poetry and Literature Center sponsored a number of programs featuring new and renowned poets reading from their works.

Yugoslavia-born poet Charles Simic served as the library's Poet Laureate Consultant in Poetry for the 2007–2008 literary season. Simic and 19 other noted poets were featured in the winter 2008 season of "The Poet and the Poem from the Library of Congress," a radio series available to broadcast by National Public Radio. Simic closed the poetry series on May 8, 2008, with a lecture on poetry and translation.

The fall 2008 Poetry at Noon readings at the library featured poets laureate from Kentucky and Indiana and other poets from those states. For more information on the library's poetry programs, visit http://www.loc.gov/poetry.

The library sponsored numerous book talks, many offered as part of the Center for the Book's "Books and Beyond" lecture series, which focuses on the importance of books and reading. [For more on the activities of the Center of the Book, see the following article—*Ed.*]

### Concerts

Since 1925 the library's Coolidge Auditorium has been a venue for world-class performers and world premieres of commissioned works. Sponsored by the Music Division, the library's annual concert series reflects the diversity of music in America and features many genres—classical, jazz, musical theater, dance, pop, and rock. The 2007–2008 season included tribute concerts honoring composer Leonard Bernstein on the 50th anniversary of West Side Story and the dance legacy of tap dancer Bill "Bojangles" Robinson.

The American Folklife Center continued to sponsor its outdoor concert series "Homegrown: The Music of America" with diverse musical traditions including blues and gospel.

In 2008 the "Concerts from the Library of Congress" radio series, which ran from the 1930s through the 1990s, returned to the air nationwide after more than a decade. Produced jointly by the library, CD Syndications, and the Washington, D.C., NPR station WETA-FM, the 13-part series invited listeners to enter the library's concert hall and sample its vast music collections with hour-long programs accompanied by companion Web packages.

### Symposia and Lectures

During the year various library divisions sponsored hundreds of programs and lectures on a wide range of topics. In March 2008 the American Folklife Center presented a symposium titled "Art, Culture, and Government: The New Deal at 75" to examine the multifaceted social, cultural, and fiscal-recovery programs launched by the Franklin D. Roosevelt administration in 1933.

## Outreach

The library continued to share its treasures both nationally and internationally on its Web site, through its Learning Page for teachers, traveling exhibitions, and other programs.

In the fall of 2008 it launched an educational "road show," "National Treasures, Local Treasures: The Library of Congress at Your Fingertips." The program brought the riches of the library to five cities across the country. Each event began with a screening of a special feature available with the DVD of "National Treasure 2: Book of Secrets," filmed in part in the library's Jefferson Building. Participating libraries received a copy of the DVD, the 2008 edition of *On These Walls: Inscriptions and Quotations of the Library of Congress,* and a facsimile of a historic map of their local area from the library's collections. The library's Educational Outreach Office demonstrated the new interactive Library of Congress Experience Web site, myLOC.gov, to students and teachers at each venue.

## Honors and Awards

### Kluge Prize

Historians Peter Robert Lamont Brown and Romila Thapar received the 2008 Kluge Prize for Lifetime Achievement in the Study of Humanity in a ceremony held December 10 at the library. They are the sixth and seventh recipients since the inception of the prize in 2003. Brown is a historian whose interdisciplinary and multilingual approach has led to new understandings of the Middle East and Europe between 100 and 1000 A.D. Thapar is a scholar of the early history of India whose rigorous studies have challenged old ideas and brought to life the richness and diversity of the subcontinent. Endowed by Library of Congress benefactor John W. Kluge, the prize is unique among international prizes at the $1 million level in rewarding a wide range of disciplines including history, philosophy, politics, anthropology, sociology, religion, criticism in the arts and humanities, and linguistics, as well as a variety of cultural perspectives.

### Living Legend Award

For achievements that the Librarian of Congress described as "distinguished, sustained and remarkable," seven people were designated "living legends" by the library at the opening-day ceremonies for the new Library of Congress Experience on April 12, 2008. Mickey Hart, musicologist and former percussionist for the Grateful Dead, presided over the awards ceremony. The honorees were race-car driver Mario Andretti, civil rights activist Julian Bond, jazz pianist and composer Herbie Hancock, historian David McCullough, journalists Cokie Roberts and Bob Schieffer, and major league baseball outfielder and manager Frank Robinson. In recognition of her contributions to literacy and support of the National Book Festival since its inception in 2000, First Lady Laura Bush received a special Living Legend medallion at the National Book Festival evening gala on September 26.

### Poet Laureate Consultant in Poetry

In July Kay Ryan was appointed the library's Poet Laureate Consultant in Poetry for 2008–2009. She opened the literary season on October 16 with a reading from her works.

**Billington Receives Presidential Medal**

On December 10, President George W. Bush presented Librarian of Congress James H. Billington with the Presidential Citizens Medal in honor of "his stewardship of the Library of Congress and his dedication to strengthening the cultural life of our nation." The Presidential Citizens Medal was established in 1969 to recognize U.S. citizens "who have performed exemplary deeds of service for the nation."

[For book-related awards, see "Literary Prizes, 2008" in Part 5—*Ed.*]

## Additional Sources of Information

Library of Congress telephone numbers for public information:

| | |
|---|---|
| Main switchboard (with menu) | 202-707-5000 |
| Reading room hours and locations | 202-707-6400 |
| General reference | 202-707-3399 |
| | TTY 202-707-4210 |
| Visitor information | 202-707-8000 |
| | TTY 202-707-6200 |
| Exhibition hours | 202-707-4604 |
| Reference assistance | 202-707-6500 |
| Copyright information | 202-707-3000 |
| Copyright hotline (to order forms) | 202-707-9100 |
| Sales shop (credit card orders) | 888-682-3557 |

# Center for the Book

Library of Congress, Washington, DC 20540
World Wide Web http://www.loc.gov/cf

John Y. Cole
Director

With its network of affiliated centers in 50 states and the District of Columbia and more than 80 organizations serving as its national reading promotion partners, the Center for the Book is one of the Library of Congress's most dynamic and visible educational outreach programs. It was established by Congress in 1977 (P.L. 95-129) to use the resources and prestige of the Library of Congress to stimulate public interest in books and reading. A secondary but important purpose was to increase public understanding of the role of the Library of Congress and its collections in preserving and advancing the nation's cultural heritage.

Today the center promotes books, reading, literacy, and libraries and encourages the study of books, reading, and the printed word—nationally and internationally.

The Center for the Book is a successful public-private partnership. It has always relied entirely on outside funding to support all of its activities; only its four staff positions are paid through appropriated funds.

## Highlights of 2008

During 2008 the Center for the Book

- Took the lead in organizing "National Treasures, Local Treasures: The Library of Congress at Your Fingertips," a pilot educational program presented through state Centers for the Book at five major public libraries in 2008
- Organized the author and reading promotion programs at the 2008 National Book Festival, held on the National Mall on September 27
- Received the Mystery Writers of America's Raven Award in recognition of its dedication to reading promotion, literacy education, and the crucial role it has played in the National Book Festival since its origin in 2001
- Cosponsored the publication of two books, *On These Walls: Inscriptions and Quotations in the Library of Congress* (Scala) and *Library: The Drama Within* (Bunker Hill)

## Looking to the Center's Future

In March 2008 Natalie Cole Furner, former director of the California Center for the Book, completed her "Study of the Future of the Center for the Book," which was commissioned in 2007. Based on research and interviews with Library of Congress administrators, state center coordinators, and nonprofit partner organizations, Furner recommended that the center should: continue to develop resources that "make it easier" for the Library of Congress as a whole to benefit from its activities; improve communication with its two principal partnership networks (state centers and national reading promotion organizational partners); increase its use of technology to further its mission; enhance its fund-raising strategies and activities; and continue its recent focus on young readers.

## Promoting Young Readers

In partnership with the Children's Book Council, the Center for the Book stimulated dozens of events that featured distinguished children's author Jon Scieszka in his capacity as the first National Ambassador for Young People's Literature. Scieszka was appointed to his two-year term on January 3, 2008, by Librarian of Congress James H. Billington. During 2008 he traveled throughout the country promoting books and reading for young people, reaching out in particular to children considered to be reluctant readers. His major appearances were at the official launching of Children's Book Week in May and the National Book Festival in September.

A total of 150 young readers across the country were honored with state and national awards for their achievements in the center's Letters About Literature (LAL) reading promotion and writing contest. Six national winners received cash awards and also earned for their school or community library a $10,000 LAL reading promotion grant. The national LAL program, with financial support provided by Target Stores, challenges young readers to write a personal letter to an author describing how that author's work somehow changed their view of the world or of themselves. In 2008 more than 59,000 children and young adults in grades 4 through 12 participated in the program, which the Center for the Book initiated in the mid-1980s. Nearly all of the state Centers for the Book administer LAL awards at the local level.

For the past 13 years the Center for the Book has cosponsored River of Words, an annual environmental poetry and art competition for students ages 5–19. The national winners and finalists were honored at the Library of Congress on May 12, 2008, in a ceremony moderated by project co-founder Robert Hass, U.S. Poet Laureate 1995–1997. A colorful new book was introduced at the ceremony: *River of Words: Young Poets and Artists on the Nature of Things* (Milkweed). Many of the state Centers for the Book participate in the project at the state level. In 2008, for the first time, young poets and artists from River of Words were featured in the Teens Pavilion at the National Book Festival.

During 2008 the Center for the Book began working with the library's Public Affairs Office and the Ad Council to improve and make more useful the Lifelong Literacy Web site at http://www.literacy.gov. The Ad Council, interested in targeting young readers, looks to the center—through such efforts as the National Ambassador for Young People's Literature program—for new ways of attracting young people to the site in ways that are more interactive and participatory. The overall theme of the current advertising for the Web site is "Explore New Worlds—Read," which was the Center for the Book's national reading promotion theme in 1992.

A significant partnership was formed in 2008 with the Read It Loud! Foundation, cosponsoring a campaign to encourage 5 million parents and caregivers to make a commitment to read each day to a child. This is a five-year campaign.

Planning started for the opening in 2009 of the Library of Congress Young Readers Center, a showcase for projects that encourage reading and literacy among young people. The center's immediate focus will be on providing personal and family reading-aloud experiences, supplemented by demonstrations of the library's online educational projects aimed at younger audiences.

## Celebrating Citizens of the World of Books

Louis L'Amour (1908–1988), one of the most prolific and bestselling authors of all time, was honored by the Center for the Book at the Library of Congress on March 10, 2008. Librarian of Congress Billington named L'Amour the center's inaugural "Champion of the Book," a designation reserved for those who have made an especially important contribution to the world of books. The event celebrated the centennial of L'Amour's birth and his continuing legacy.

The center was the principal organizer of the library's September 10 celebration of the life and achievements of 93-year-old novelist Herman Wouk, who was honored with the first Library of Congress Lifetime Achievement Award for the Writing of Fiction. Supreme Court Justice Ruth Bader Ginsburg, Martha Raddatz of ABC News, and *New York Times* columnist William Safire read excerpts from Wouk's works *The Caine Mutiny* (1951), *War and Remembrance* (1978), and *Inside, Outside* (1985). Singer-songwriter Jimmy Buffet sang a medley of songs from the musical inspired by Wouk's story of island escapism, *Don't Stop the Carnival* (1965). Buffet had persuaded Wouk to collaborate with him on the musical in 1997.

On November 3 the Center for the Book and the library's African and Middle Eastern Division marked the 50th anniversary of the publication of Nigerian author Chinua Achebe's celebrated novel *Things Fall Apart* with a symposium, book talk, and informal birthday party for the author.

## State Centers for the Book

Since 1984 the Center for the Book has established centers in the 50 states and the District of Columbia, a network that leverages the resources of the center in the Library of Congress as well as those of the state centers.

The center's annual Idea Exchange Day is one way in which representatives from the state centers can convene to hear about the innovative methods the individual state centers use to promote reading and literacy. Participants come away with new ideas and adopt them in their own state centers. The 2008 Idea Exchange Day was held May 13 at the Library of Congress. Coordinators from 38 states and the District of Columbia attended and discussed projects such as Letters About Literature, River of Words, "one book" and Big Read reading initiatives, as well as the Pavilion of States at the National Book Festival. Ideas also were exchanged about fund raising, board development, and other administrative matters. Novelist Brad Meltzer, who participated in the 2008 National Book

Festival, was a guest speaker at the luncheon and evening reception. Follow-up meetings on specific topics were held the following morning.

The Boorstin awards for innovative reading promotion efforts were presented. The Kansas, Ohio, and Rhode Island state centers each received a $1,000 award, donated to the Center for the Book by Ruth Boorstin, widow of Librarian of Congress Daniel J. Boorstin (1975–1987), who established the Center for the Book in 1977.

## Reading Promotion Partners

More than 80 civic, educational, and governmental organizations are "reading promotion partners" of the Center for the Book, working with it to promote books, reading, literacy, and libraries in ways that are compatible with their own organizational goals. In addition, the center is part of several reading, education, and literacy promotion networks. On March 12, 2008, more than 40 partners gathered at the Library of Congress to display project materials, share ideas, and report on their reading and literacy promotion programs. New organizational partners during 2008 included the Read It Loud! Foundation, My Own Book, and Masterpiece WGBH, the book-based television mystery series on WGBH, the Boston Public Broadcasting System affiliate. During the year the center cohosted reading promotion events at the Library of Congress with several of its partners, including the National Literary Society of the Deaf, the Writers in the Schools project of the PEN/Faulkner Foundation, Library of America, and the National Coalition for Literacy.

## Events and Projects

For the eighth year, the Center for the Book played a key role in the 2008 National Book Festival, which is organized and sponsored by the Library of Congress and was again hosted by First Lady Laura Bush. The center develops, coordinates, and oversees arrangements for the presentations by the festival's authors, illustrators, and poets and manages the festival's Pavilion of the States. Held on the National Mall on September 27, the festival attracted a crowd of more than 120,000. Seventy popular authors, illustrators, and poets made presentations and signed books. The Pavilion of the States featured reading, literacy, and library promotion programs from all 50 states, the District of Columbia, American Samoa, Guam, Puerto Rico, and the U.S. Virgin Islands.

Center for the Book Director John Cole introduced three programs in the "Teens and Children" pavilion: speaker Jon Scieszka, the National Ambassador for Young People's Literature; writers Pamela Michael and David Gewanter, who presented students from the River of Words project; and writer and illustrator Mary Brigid Barrett, president of the National Children's Book and Literacy Alliance and editor of *Our White House: Looking In, Looking Out,* a new anthology that promotes reading and historical literacy.

During the year the center hosted 19 book talks at the Library of Congress, many of them in its "Books and Beyond" author series. Most featured the author or authors of a newly published book that was based on the library's collections or related to a specific Library of Congress program. Speakers in 2008 included Pulitzer Prize-winning book critic Michael Dirda, novelist Stephen King and his wife Tabitha and son Owen, former Secretary of State Madeleine Albright, and environmentalist Bill McKibben. All of the talks can be seen as Webcasts on the center's Web site.

## Outreach and Publications

The Library of Congress issued 34 press releases about Center for the Book activities during 2008. Director Cole, an associate member of the Standing Committee on Literacy and Reading of the International Federation of Library Associations and Institutions (IFLA), edited two issues of the IFLA *Section on Literacy and Reading Newsletter,* which were produced and distributed by the Center for the Book.

In collaboration with the Library of Congress Publishing Office and Scala Publications, Cole revised the text for a new edition of his *On These Walls: Inscriptions and Quotations in the Library of Congress,* which was published in September. The new version features more than 100 color photographs by Carol M. Highsmith. In October Bunker Hill Publishing produced a new edition of *Library: The Drama Within,* a book of photographs by Diane Asséo Griliches. The new edition features "For the Love of Libraries," an introductory essay by Cole.

# National Agricultural Library

U.S. Department of Agriculture, Abraham Lincoln Bldg.
10301 Baltimore Ave., Beltsville, MD 20705-2351
E-mail agref@nal.usda.gov
World Wide Web http://www.nal.usda.gov

Gary McCone
Associate Director

The U.S. Department of Agriculture's National Agricultural Library (NAL) is the world's largest and most accessible agricultural research library, offering service directly to the public and via its Web site, http://www.nal.usda.gov. The library was created with the U.S. Department of Agriculture (USDA) in 1862 and established as a national library by Congress (7 USCS § 3125a) as the primary agricultural information resource of the United States.

Congress assigned to the library the responsibilities to

- Acquire, preserve, and manage information resources relating to agriculture and allied sciences
- Organize agricultural information products and services and provide them within the United States and internationally
- Plan, coordinate, and evaluate information and library needs relating to agricultural research and education
- Cooperate with and coordinate efforts toward development of a comprehensive agricultural library and information network
- Coordinate the development of specialized subject information services among the agricultural and library information communities

NAL is the only library in the United States with the mandate to carry out these national and international responsibilities for the agricultural community. The library's vision is "advancing access to global information for agriculture."

The library is located in Beltsville, Maryland, near Washington, D.C., on the grounds of USDA's Henry A. Wallace Beltsville Agricultural Research Center. Its 15-story Abraham Lincoln Building is named in honor of the president who created the Department of Agriculture and signed many of the major U.S. laws affecting agriculture.

NAL employs about 165 librarians, information specialists, computer specialists, administrators, and clerical personnel, supplemented by about 80 contract staff, as well as volunteers and cooperators from NAL partnering organizations.

The library's expert staff, leadership in delivering information services, collaborations with other U.S. and international agricultural research and information organizations, extensive collection of agricultural information, AGRICOLA bibliographic database of citations to the agricultural literature, and advanced information technology infrastructure contribute to NAL's reputation as one of the world's foremost agricultural libraries.

## The Collection

The NAL collection dates to the congressionally approved 1839 purchase of books for the Agricultural Division of the Patent Office, predating the 1862 establishment of USDA itself. Today, NAL provides access to billions of pages of agricultural information—an immense collection of scientific books, journals, audiovisuals, reports, theses, software, laser discs, artifacts, and images in agriculture—and to a widening array of digital media, as well as databases and other information resources germane to the broad reach of agriculture-related sciences.

The library's collection contains nearly 3.6 million items dating from the 16th century to the present, including the most complete repository of USDA publications and the world's most extensive set of materials on the history of agriculture in the United States. The collection covers all aspects of agriculture and related sciences and is a comprehensive resource for agricultural scientists, policy makers, regulators, and scholars.

## Networks of Cooperation

The NAL collection and information resources are supplemented by networks of cooperation with other institutions, including arrangements with agricultural libraries at U.S. land-grant universities, other U.S. national libraries, agricultural libraries in other countries, and libraries of the United Nations and other international organizations.

### AgNIC

NAL serves as the secretariat for the Agriculture Network Information Center (AgNIC) Alliance, a voluntary, collaborative partnership that hosts a distributed network of discipline-specific agricultural information Web sites (http://www.agnic.org). In 2008 the combined AgNIC partner Web statistics totaled more than 130 million Web hits. AgNIC provides access to high-quality agricultural information selected by AgNIC partners, including land-grant universities, NAL, and other institutions globally. AgNIC welcomed three new institutions during 2007–2008: the International Food Policy Research Institute (IFPRI), Oklahoma State University's William E. Brock Memorial Library, and Colorado Water Resources Research Institute (CWRRI). AgNIC's 60 member institutions offer 59 subject-specific sites, and additional sites and resources are being developed. During 2008 partners continued to build full-text content through a variety of projects such as metadata harvesting. This service uses the Open Archives Initiative (OAI) protocols to harvest metadata for full-text resources from targeted institutional repositories and collections for a single point of access.

### AGLINET

As the U.S. node of an international agricultural information system, NAL also serves as a gateway to U.S. agricultural libraries and resources. NAL cooperates with other libraries, information centers, and consortia via several reciprocal

agreements. It is part of the Agricultural Libraries Network (AGLINET) administered by the Food and Agriculture Organization (FAO) of the United Nations.
AGLINET is a worldwide voluntary network of agricultural libraries with strong
regional/country coverage and other collections of specialized subject resources.

### Animal Science Image Gallery

NAL and the American Society of Animal Science are collaborators on the
online Animal Science Image Gallery. The gallery's images, animations, and
videos, which have accompanying text, are intended for classroom and educational outreach. Originally funded through a USDA Higher Education Challenge
Grant, the gallery will be hosted in perpetuity by NAL. Gallery editors, reviewers, and submitters come from the membership of the American Society of
Animal Science, the American Dairy Science Association, the Poultry Science
Association, the Equine Science Society, the American Society for Nutrition, the
Society for the Study of Reproduction, and the American College of Therio-
genologists.

## Building the NAL Collection

NAL annually acquires approximately 17,000 serial titles, including more than
7,000 digital journals. More than 1,500 of those digital journals in agriculture
and related sciences are purchased with permanent data-storage rights.

The library has primary responsibility for collecting and retaining all publications of USDA and its agencies, and is the only U.S. national library with a
legislative mandate to collect comprehensively in the following disciplines: animal sciences, plant sciences, agricultural economics and statistics, agricultural
products, agricultural chemistry and engineering, agronomy and soil conservation, forestry and forest products, rural sociology and rural life, food sciences,
and nutrition. In addition to these core subjects, the NAL collection contains
extensive materials in such related subjects as biology, natural history, wildlife
ecology, pollution, genetics, natural resources, meteorology, and fisheries.

Since the mid-1800s NAL has carried out a strong global program to acquire
publications through international exchange. The types of publications received
on exchange are often difficult to acquire through established subscription vendors, and constitute a valuable body of "gray literature" that is not widely available in other U.S. libraries. Over the last decade, the move from paper to digital
publishing has significantly reduced the number of exchange opportunities.
Nonetheless, NAL initiates and coordinates these exchanges with more than
2,500 partners worldwide. In general, NAL's acquisition program and collection
development policy are based upon its responsibility to provide service to the
staff of the Department of Agriculture, U.S. land-grant universities, and the general public in all subjects pertaining to agriculture. The NAL Collection Development Policy (http://www.nal.usda.gov/about/policy/coll_dev_toc.shtml) outlines
the scope of subjects collected and the degree of coverage for each subject. This
policy is regularly revised to include emerging subject areas and incorporate
guidelines for collecting new formats, especially digital formats. NAL collection

policies reflect and differentiate the collecting responsibilities of the National Library of Medicine and the Library of Congress. The three national libraries have developed cooperative collection development policy statements for three subject areas: biotechnology, human nutrition and food, and veterinary sciences.

## National Digital Library for Agriculture

Since the mid-1990s NAL has continually revised its collection development strategies to emphasize digital formats and World Wide Web resources. This has been accompanied by expansion of the amount of agricultural information collected and distributed in digital formats, as the library makes a transition toward a future National Digital Library for Agriculture.

In January 2007 NAL released a design concept Web site for the digital library and invited public comment. Comments received discussed federated search of NAL collections, the e-Answer service of the American Distance Education Coalition, Library of Congress Web sites, the FAO document repository, the Germplasm Resources Information Network database, and Science.gov.

## Special Collections

The NAL special collections program emphasizes access to and preservation of rare and unique materials documenting the history of agriculture and related sciences. Items in the library's special collections include rare books, manuscripts, nursery and seed trade catalogs, posters and photographs, and other rare or unique materials documenting agricultural subjects. Materials date from the 1500s to the late 1900s and include many international sources.

Detailed information about NAL special collections is available on the NAL Web site at http://www.nal.usda.gov/speccoll.

NAL special collections of note include the following:

- The U.S. Department of Agriculture History Collection (http://www.nal.usda.gov/speccoll/collect/history.html), assembled over 80 years by USDA historians, includes letters, memoranda, reports, and papers of USDA officials, as well as photographs, oral histories, and clippings covering the activities of the department from its founding through the early 1990s. A guide to this collection is viewable via the NAL Web site.
- The U.S. Department of Agriculture Pomological Watercolor Collection (http://www.nal.usda.gov/speccoll/collect/pomology.html) includes more than 7,000 expertly detailed, botanically accurate watercolor illustrations of fruits and nuts representing newly introduced varieties, healthy and diseased fruits, and depictions of various stages of development. Created between 1880 and 1915, the watercolor illustrations served as official documentation of the work of the Office of the Pomologist and were used for creation of chromolithographs in publications distributed widely by the department. Although created for scientific accuracy, the works in this collection are artistic treasures in their own right.

- The Henry G. Gilbert Nursery and Seed Trade Catalog Collection (http://www.nal.usda.gov/speccoll/collect/nursery.html) is a rich collection of historic catalogs of the nursery and seed trade. Started in 1904 by USDA economic botanist Percy L. Ricker, the collection is used by researchers to document the introduction of plants to the United States, study economic trends, and illustrate early developments in American landscape design. The earliest catalogs document the trade to the mid-1700s. NAL continues to collect nursery and seed catalogs.

- The Rare Book Collection (http://www.nal.usda.gov/speccoll/collect/rarebook.html) highlights agriculture's printed historical record and covers a wide variety of subjects. The collection, international in scope, documents early agricultural practices in Britain and Europe as well as the Americas. NAL holdings of Carl Linnaeus, "father of taxonomy," include more than 300 books by or about Linnaeus, among them a rare first edition of his 1735 work *Systema Naturae*.

- NAL offers access to more than 300 manuscript collections (http://www.nal.usda.gov/speccoll/collectionsguide/mssindextemp.shtml) documenting the story of American agriculture and its influence on the world.

In recent years, the library has enhanced access to its special collections by putting digitized images on its Web site. NAL provides in-house research and reference services for its special collections, and offers fee-based duplication services. Detailed indexes to the content of many manuscript collections are available in print as well as on the Web. AGRICOLA—NAL's catalog and index to its collections—includes bibliographic entries for special collection items, manuscripts, and rare books.

## Preservation

NAL is committed to the preservation of its print and nonprint collections. The library continues to monitor and improve the environmental quality of stacks to extend the longevity of all materials in the collection. The long-term strategy is to ensure that the growing body of agricultural information is systematically identified, preserved, and archived.

The library's program of digital conversion of print material has resulted in a growing collection of USDA publications, including *Home and Garden Bulletin, Agriculture Information Bulletin, Agricultural Economic Report, Journal of Agricultural Research, Yearbook of the United States Department of Agriculture,* and several Agricultural Marketing Service series. Other historical USDA publications include *Report of the Commissioner of Agriculture,* published from 1862 to 1888, continued by *Report of the Secretary of Agriculture,* published from 1889 to 1893. *Century of Service: The First 100 Years of the United States Department of Agriculture,* published in 1963, explores the history of the department from its establishment in 1862 through the Kennedy administration. NAL also has completed digitizing the popular Agriculture Handbook series and has begun to digitize the Technical Bulletin series. The library provides online access to these and other full-text publications, including many non-USDA historical materials not restricted by copyright, via the NAL digital repository, known as AgSpace.

## AgSpace

The digital repository AgSpace is a combination of several efforts within NAL under various stages of development and implementation. Among them are the following:

- The library has undertaken several projects to digitize, store, and provide online access to historic print documents. The majority of the nearly 500,000 pages currently available online are USDA documents. The full text of these materials and more information about these digitization projects can be found at http://naldr.nal.usda.gov.
- NAL is developing procedures to collect, store, and make publicly available the current research publications of USDA scientists and employees. As of the end of 2008, more than 20,000 articles had been added to the repository. AgSpace does not yet hold all appropriate research publications, but NAL is working to acquire them. Eventually, AgSpace will be the primary source and first resort to identify and use all USDA publications, research and otherwise.

Long-range plans include collecting, maintaining, and providing access to a broad range of agricultural information in a wide variety of digital formats. The end result will be a perpetual, reliable, publicly accessible repository of digital documents, datasets, images, audiovisual files, and so forth relating to agriculture.

## AGRICOLA

AGRICOLA (AGRICultural On-Line Access) is the catalog and index to NAL collections, as well as a primary public source offering worldwide access to agricultural information. AGRICOLA is searchable on the Web (http://agricola. nal.usda.gov), but can also be accessed on a fee basis through several commercial vendors, both online and on CD-ROM. Users can also subscribe to the complete AGRICOLA file on a fee basis from the National Technical Information Service, part of the U.S. Department of Commerce.

The AGRICOLA database covers materials in all formats, including printed works from the 15th century onward. The records describe publications and resources encompassing all aspects of agriculture and allied disciplines. Thousands of AGRICOLA records contain links to networked Web resources. The AGRICOLA database is organized into two components, updated with newly catalogcd and indexed materials, searchable separately or together:

- NAL Public Access Catalog, containing citations to books, audiovisual materials, serial titles, and other materials in the NAL collection (AGRI-

COLA also contains some bibliographic records for items cataloged by other libraries but not held in the NAL collection)
- NAL Article Citation Database, which includes citations to serial articles, book chapters, reports, and reprints

In 2007 NAL implemented a rescoped AGRICOLA Index to offer more links to full-text articles and avoid duplication with other abstracting and indexing services. To be considered for indexing in AGRICOLA, publications must meet at least one of the following criteria:

- Be a U.S. Department of Agriculture publication, or contain articles or chapters authored by USDA personnel
- Support NAL Information Centers
- Contain articles or chapters on core agricultural topics, written in English
- Not be indexed by other abstracting and indexing services

The 2008 list of publications indexed in AGRICOLA can be found at http://riley.nal.usda.gov/nal_display/index.php?info_center=8&tax_level=2&tax_subject=157&topic_id=2010. The rescoped AGRICOLA index continues to serve as the search tool to access NAL collections.

## Information Management and Information Technology

Over the past quarter century, NAL has applied information technology to support managing and providing access to a diverse array of agricultural information. Technological developments spearheaded by the library date back to the 1940s and 1950s, when NAL Director Ralph Shaw invented "electronic machines" such as the photo charger, rapid selector, and photo clerk. NAL has made numerous technological improvements since.

NAL has fully implemented the Voyager integrated library management system (produced by Endeavor Information Systems, now known as the Ex Libris Group). The system supports ordering, receiving, and invoice processing for purchases; creating and maintaining indexing and cataloging records for AGRICOLA; circulation and the Online Public Access Catalog. The Voyager system has also been integrated with the Relais (Relais International, Inc.) system for supporting NAL interlibrary loan and document delivery services.

### NALT Agricultural Thesaurus

NAL is known for its expertise in developing and using a thesaurus, or controlled vocabulary, a critical component of effective digital information systems. The NAL Agricultural Thesaurus (NALT) (http://agclass.nal.usda.gov/agt/agt.shtml) is a hierarchical vocabulary of agricultural and biological terms. Updated annually, NALT broadly defines the subject scope of agriculture, organized according to 17 subject categories and with 2,574 definitions. Biological nomenclature comprises most terms in the thesaurus, although it also includes terminology in the supporting biological, physical, and social sciences. Suggestions for new terms or definitions can be sent by e-mail to NAL at thesaurus@ars.usda.gov.

Originally prepared to meet the needs of Agricultural Research Service (ARS) scientists, NALT is now extensively used to aid retrieval in agricultural information systems within USDA and elsewhere. NALT is the indexing vocabulary for NAL's bibliographic database of 4 million article citations to agricultural resources included in the AGRICOLA database.

NAL released the eighth edition of NALT, containing approximately 73,000 terms, in January 2009. Terminology associated with herbicides, forestry, and fire science was expanded in this edition. The taxonomic classification of fungi was realigned based on the 2007 international collaborative work published by D. S. Hibbett in *Mycological Research,* "A Higher-Level Phylogenetic Classification of the Fungi." The common and scientific names of many insects and mites were added this edition.

### Spanish-Language Version

The NAL Glossary is a collection of definitions of agricultural terms developed in conjunction with the creation of NALT. The 2007 edition contains more than 2,500 terms ranging across agriculture and its many ancillary subjects, most composed by the NALT staff.

The library publishes Spanish-language versions of its NALT and Glossary of Agricultural Terms, which carry the names "Tesauro Agrícola" and "Glosario," respectively. The NALT and Glossary in Spanish support increased Spanish-language access to agricultural information throughout the United States and the world, accommodating the complexity of the Spanish language from a Western Hemisphere perspective.

In 2008 the Inter-American Institute for Cooperation on Agriculture (IICA) and NAL expanded their existing collaboration to include the Spanish- and English-language versions of the thesaurus and glossary. IICA and NAL, with the aid of Latin American experts, cooperatively develop and maintain these terminology tools to support the advancement of agricultural information in the Americas.

The Spanish-language version of NALT is updated concurrently with the annual release of the English version. The 2009 edition contains more than 69,000 terms and 2,500 definitions. The thesaurus Web site is bilingual, available in both Spanish and English interfaces.

Although these compilations are primarily intended for indexers, computer programmers working with Web search engines, and others who gather and organize information, the glossary and thesaurus are also suitable for students, teachers, writers, translators, and people who work in agriculture. Users can download all four publications from the Web site in a variety of formats (pdf, XML, MARC 21, and RDF-SKOS) from http://agclass.nal.usda.gov/download.shtml.

## Library Services

NAL serves the agricultural information needs of customers through a combination of Web-based and traditional library services including reference, document delivery, and information center services. The NAL Web site (http://www.nal.usda.gov) offers access to a wide variety of full-text resources as well as online access to reference and document delivery services. During 2008 the library delivered more than 90 million direct customer services throughout the world via its Web site and other Internet-based services.

The main reading room in the library's Beltsville facility features a walk-up service desk, access to an array of digital information resources, including full-text scientific journals, a current periodicals collection and on-site request service for materials from NAL's print collection. NAL also operates a walk-in reference and digital services center at USDA headquarters in downtown Washington, D.C. Services at both facilities are available 8:30 to 4:30 Monday through Friday, except federal holidays.

NAL's information centers are reliable sources of comprehensive science-based information on key aspects of U.S. agriculture, providing timely, accurate, and in-depth coverage of their specialized subject areas. Their staff offer extensive Web-based information resources and advanced reference services. Each NAL information center has its own Web site and is a partner in the Agriculture Network Information Center (AgNIC), http://www.agnic.org. Presently, NAL has seven information centers:

- The Alternative Farming Systems Information Center (AFSIC) (http://afsic.nal.usda.gov) specializes in farming methods that maintain the health and productivity of the entire farming enterprise, including the natural resource base.

- The Animal Welfare Information Center (AWIC) (http://awic.nal.usda.gov) provides scientific information and referrals to help ensure the proper care and treatment of animals used in biomedical research, in teaching, in exhibition, and by animal dealers.

- The Food and Nutrition Information Center (FNIC) (http://fnic.nal.usda.gov), a leader in food and human nutrition information dissemination since 1971, provides credible, accurate, and practical resources for nutrition and health professionals, educators, government personnel, and consumers. FNIC maintains a staff of expert information specialists with training in food science and human nutrition and can assist in answering customer questions on food and human nutrition.

- The Food Safety Information Center (FSIC) (http://foodsafety.nal.usda.gov) provides links to consumer, educator, and research information on a variety of food safety topics. During 2008 a new search interface was released for its Research Projects Database to include the addition of more than 1,000 projects funded by foreign governments.

- The National Invasive Species Information Center (NISIC) (http://www.invasivespeciesinfo.gov) is a gateway to invasive species information, covering federal, state, local, and international sources. In 2008 NISIC launched the http://www.itap.gov Web site to support the Federal Interagency Committee on Invasive Terrestrial Animals and Pathogens (ITAP).

- In collaboration with other USDA agencies, NAL operates the popular Nutrition.gov (http://www.nutrition.gov) Web site to provide vetted, science-based nutrition information for the general consumer and highlight the latest in nutrition news and tools from across government agencies. A team of dietitians and nutrition information specialists at NAL's Food and Nutrition Information Center maintain Nutrition.gov and provide reference services to answer customer questions on food and nutrition issues. The site is an important tool for developing food- and exercise-based strategies for weight management, and for disseminating the work of multiple federal agencies in a national obesity prevention effort. Nutrition.gov includes databases, recipes, interactive tools, and specialized information for infants and children, adult men and women, and seniors. The site links to information on the USDA food pyramid, dietary guidelines, dietary supplements, fitness, and food safety. It provides a comprehensive source of information on nutrition and dietary guidance from multiple federal agencies.

- The Rural Information Center (http://ric.nal.usda.gov) provides information and referral services on community economic development, small business development, healthcare access and financing, housing, environment, quality of life, community leadership, and education to organizations and individuals working to maintain the vitality of the nation's communities.
- The Water Quality Information Center (WQIC) (http://www.nal.usda.gov/wqic) collects, organizes, and communicates scientific findings, educational methodologies, and public policy issues relating to water resources and agriculture.

Agricultural interest in renewable fuels remained high throughout 2008. As part of the USDA Strategic Energy Science Plan for Research, Education, and Extension, NAL continued to build a foundation for a potential information center focused on the issues of renewable resources, bioenergy, and bioproducts.

## Web-Based Products and Services

During 2008 the NAL Web site received an average of more than 7 million hits each month from people seeking agricultural information. The library anticipates that Web site usage will increase in response to the site's user-friendly design, enhanced searching capabilities, and continual improvement in content.

In addition to creating an around-the-clock Web site for its external customers, in 2008 NAL introduced an internal Web site for staff, increasing overall productivity by creating "one-stop shopping" for employees. This intranet reduced the need for employees to search elsewhere for job-related tools, training materials, and human resources and financial information, and provided work-related social activities such as bulletin boards; photo galleries of employee luncheons, farewells, and retirements; and after-work fitness groups. The intranet brings together employees from all library divisions, forming a cohesive working unit, improved relations, and raised employee morale.

"InfoFarm: The NAL Blog" (http://weblogs.nal.usda.gov/infofarm) has been active for more than a year and is becoming increasingly popular. Its purpose is to give NAL a "human" voice, give NAL customers a fresh glimpse into what NAL does, and give NAL a chance to converse with its customers. The Special Libraries Association wrote: "InfoFarm is written in an engaging style with lots of links to great Web sites and is certain to interest anyone who eats food."

## DigiTop

DigiTop, the USDA's Digital Desktop Library, provides online access to thousands of journals in full text, 13 citation databases, hundreds of newspapers from around the world, significant additional digital reference resources, and an array of personalized services. DigiTop is available to the entire USDA work force worldwide—more than 100,000 people—24 hours a day. NAL staff provides help desk services and continuous user education and training.

During fiscal year 2008 nearly 1.1 million articles were downloaded from DigiTop. The monetized value of viewed content is yielding significant return on government investment, generates unprecedented cost efficiencies, and demonstrates the high value of the program to USDA users.

### Document Delivery Services

NAL's document delivery operation responds to requests received from around the world for agricultural information materials. For USDA employees, NAL acquires needed information materials that are not otherwise available from NAL collections.

NAL uses the Relais Enterprise document request system, integrated with its Voyager integrated library system, to support document delivery. This means NAL customers can both request and receive materials digitally and check on the status of their requests via the World Wide Web. NAL no longer accepts document requests submitted via e-mail, ARIEL (Agricultural Research Information Express Loan), fax, or mail. Documents must be requested via the Web, using AGRICOLA or blank request forms. NAL also accepts requests via OCLC (NAL's symbol is AGL) and DOCLINE (NAL's libid is MDUNAL).

To deliver documents, NAL uses an array of methods as requested by its customers. Library staff, contractors, and cooperators work together to fill document delivery and interlibrary loan requests and deliver them to customers via the Internet through ARIEL, fax, mail, courier, and other means.

# National Library of Medicine

8600 Rockville Pike, Bethesda, MD 20894
301-496-6308, 888-346-3656, fax 301-496-4450
E-mail publicinfo@nlm.nih.gov, World Wide Web http://www.nlm.nih.gov

Kathleen Cravedi, Director

Melanie Modlin, Deputy Director

Office of Communications and Public Liaison

The National Library of Medicine (NLM), in Bethesda, Maryland, is the world's largest library of the health sciences and a part of the National Institutes of Health, U.S. Department of Health and Human Services (HHS). Since its founding in 1836 NLM has played a pivotal role in translating biomedical research into practice. It is the developer of electronic information services that deliver trillions of bytes of data to millions of users daily. Scientists, health professionals, and the public in the United States and around the world search the library's online information resources more than 1 billion times each year; by one recent estimate, they glean more than 5 terabytes of information per day, which is comparable to downloading the entire print holdings of the Library of Congress every week.

In today's increasingly digital world, NLM carries out its mission of enabling biomedical research, supporting health care and public health, and promoting healthy behavior by

- Acquiring, organizing, and preserving the world's scholarly biomedical literature
- Providing access to biomedical and health information across the nation, in partnership with the 5,600-member National Network of Libraries of Medicine (NN/LM)
- Via its National Center for Biotechnology Information (NCBI), serving as a leading global resource for building, curating, and providing sophisticated access to molecular biology and genomic information, including material from the Human Genome Project and Genome-Wide Association Studies
- Creating high-quality information services relevant to toxicology and environmental health, health services research, and public health
- Conducting research and development on biomedical communications systems, methods, technologies, and networks, and information dissemination and utilization among health professionals, patients, and the public
- Funding advanced biomedical informatics research and serving as the primary supporter of pre- and post-doctoral research training in biomedical informatics at 18 U.S. universities

The library is open to all and has many services and resources, for scientists, health professionals, historians, and the public. NLM has nearly 12 million books, journals, manuscripts, audiovisuals, and other forms of medical information—in more than 150 languages—on its shelves, making it the largest health science library in the world. Patrons can also have access to a vast collection of books, manuscripts, and art relating to the history of the health sciences. Used not only by scholars, these materials are frequently integrated into fascinating exhibitions and displays for visitors. Traveling versions of NLM exhibitions attract crowds across the country.

NLM continues to focus on the goals of its 2006–2016 long-range plan, including key activities in support of interoperable electronic health records, more effective disaster and emergency response, and development of a robust knowledge base for personalized health care.

## Information Services for the Public

NLM has extensive information resources to serve the general public, from elementary school children to senior citizens.

### MedlinePlus

The library's main portal for consumer health information is MedlinePlus (http://www.medlineplus.gov), available in English and Spanish. Much of this material is based on research done or sponsored by the NIH Institutes and there are thousands of links to reliable health information that has been reviewed by medical librarians for suitability. MedlinePlus, introduced in 1998, receives approximately 11 million unique visitors and 80 million page views each month. MedlinePlus en Español accounts for about one-third of that total.

MedlinePlus has 780 "health topics." Each topic points the user to reliable information on all aspects of a disease or health condition, clinical trials, complementary and alternative medicine, prevention, management, therapies, current research, and the latest news from the print media. In addition to the health topics, there are medical dictionaries, a medical encyclopedia, directories of hospitals and providers, and links to the scientific literature. There is also a series of surgical videos that show actual operations involving common surgical procedures.

MedlinePlus recently introduced a multilingual feature, providing access to high-quality health information in languages other than English and Spanish. This service helps not only the public but also the information professionals and health care providers who serve them. The collection contains links to health information in more than 40 languages, from Amharic to Vietnamese, on more than 260 topics.

The MedlinePlus service known as Go Local links users to medical and social services in their community that are related to their interest. With six new sites added in 2008, Go Local now covers 42 percent of the U.S. population.

One section of MedlinePlus, Interactive Health Tutorials, relates especially to the long-range goal of providing information services that specifically promote health literacy and reduce health disparities. The user will find more than 170 interactive programs featuring color images and sound that explain medical tests, procedures, and conditions in easy-to-read language. Users can also listen as the script of the tutorial is read.

## NIH MedlinePlus

In partnership with the National Institutes of Health and the Friends of the National Library of Medicine, the library provides editorial guidance for a free quarterly magazine, *NIH MedlinePlus,* which gives consumers an extensive range of authoritative health information. Launched in May 2006, it is distributed nationwide through doctors' offices, health centers, clinics and hospitals, medical libraries, congressional offices, and an expanding list of individual subscribers. It has a readership of approximately 2.5 million nationwide. *NIH MedlinePlus Salud,* a Spanish/English version of the publication, will debut in 2009.

For more information on *NIH MedlinePlus* or to subscribe, visit http://www.nlm.nih.gov/medlineplus/magazine/index.html.

## ClinicalTrials.gov

ClinicalTrials.gov, launched in 2000, provides comprehensive information about all types of clinical research studies. The Web site (http://www.ClinicalTrials.gov) has more than 63,000 protocol records sponsored by the U.S. government, the pharmaceutical industry, and academic and international organizations from all 50 states and 158 countries. ClinicalTrials.gov receives more than 52 million page views a month and approximately 800,000 unique visitors a month.

In 2008 ClinicalTrials.gov researched, designed, tested, and implemented a results database. Required by law, this first-of-its-kind resource includes results information on primary and secondary outcomes of registered trials as well as information on the patient populations studied. When fully implemented, the registry and results database will become a resource for scientific and clinical information that can assist in providing more comprehensive information about ongoing and completed research for patients, healthcare providers, and researchers.

## Genetics Home Reference

Genetics Home Reference (GHR) (http://ghr.nlm.nih.gov) offers basic information about genetic conditions and the genes and chromosomes related to those conditions, providing a bridge between the public's questions about human genetics and the rich technical data that has emerged from the Human Genome Project and other genomic research. The site, created in 2003, now includes summaries of more than 325 genetic conditions, more than 500 genes, all the human chromosomes, and information about disorders caused by mutations in mitochondrial DNA. Usage of the GHR Web site increased nearly 50 percent in the past year, and it continues to be recognized as an important health resource.

## Historical Exhibitions and Programs

NLM exhibitions, designed to appeal to the public as well as the specialist, highlight the library's historical resources and expand its audience—most of the shows also travel to libraries and other institutions around the nation. The current exhibition, "Against the Odds: Making a Difference in Global Health," looks at the revolution in health taking place in locations around the world. The interactive display on the Bethesda, Maryland, campus of NIH also includes an informative Web site (http://apps.nlm.nih.gov/againsttheodds/index.cfm) with lesson plans for middle school and high school teachers. Free traveling versions of NLM exhibitions explore topics as diverse as Harry Potter and America's women physicians. The History of Medicine Division's Exhibition Program coordinates these events.

### NIHSeniorHealth

Another information resource for the public is NIHSeniorHealth.gov (http://www.nihseniorhealth.gov), which is maintained by the library in collaboration with the National Institute on Aging and other NIH Institutes and Centers. In June 2008 NLM released a redesigned NIHSeniorHealth Web site, featuring a home page with improved navigation and content organized by categories as well as alphabetically. NIHSeniorHealth.gov contains information in a format that is especially tailored to seniors' needs—large type, for example. It also has a "talking" function that allows users to listen as the text is read to them.

## Information Services for the Scientific and Medical Communities

### MEDLINE/PubMed

The most frequently consulted online scientific medical resource in the world is MEDLINE/PubMed (http://www.pubmed.gov), a publicly available database of references and abstracts for medical journal articles from 1948 to the present. During 2008 PubMed saw 4.1 billion page views.

PubMed contains more than 18 million citations from more than 20,300 journals. Links to full-text journals indexed in PubMed increased from 5,880 in July 2007 to 6,324 in July 2008.

### PubMed Central

Another important part of NLM's online holdings is PubMed Central (PMC) (http://www.pubmedcentral.gov), a Web-based repository of biomedical journal literature providing free, unrestricted access to the full text of articles. As of July 2008 more than 1.5 million articles were available from the PMC journal archive, a 50 percent increase over the previous year. A growing number of articles by NIH-funded researchers are now being deposited and made available to the public via PMC in response to the NIH Public Access Policy.

### GenBank

Last year marked the 25th anniversary of GenBank (http://www.ncbi.nlm.nih.gov/Genbank), the NIH genetic sequence database. This widely used resource began modestly, as a collection of 600 DNA sequences for the entire year 1982. Today, this annotated collection of all publicly available DNA sequences includes approximately 130 million sequences from 300,000 species.

Integrated retrieval tools allow seamless searching of the sequence data housed in GenBank and related resources, including literature and curated reference gene and genome databases. These resources are essential tools in the analysis of gene function, the identification of disease genes, and the development of new hypotheses about potential therapies. NLM's National Center for Biotechnology Information (NCBI) is responsible for all phases of GenBank production, support, and distribution.

## Genome-Wide Association Studies

NCBI also has a prominent role in the important new Genome-Wide Association Studies project, an area that figured prominently in the deliberations of NLM's long-range planners as they discussed the promise of new research correlating genotype, phenotype, and environmental data. The Genome-Wide Association Studies (GWAS) program is a major NIH-wide initiative directed at understanding the genetic factors underlying human disease. GWAS involves linking genotype data with phenotype information in order to identify the genetic factors that influence health, disease, and response to treatment. NCBI is building the databases that will incorporate the clinical and genetic data, link them to the molecular and bibliographic resources at NCBI, and, for the first time, make these data available to the scientific and clinical research community.

## Database of Genotype and Phenotype (dbGaP)

When dbGaP was launched in 2006, only two studies on its subject matter had been published. As of June 2008 a total of 23 studies had been released, on both public summary-level data and individual level phenotype/genotype data. The Framingham Heart Study was updated and other studies covered such disease areas as psoriasis, schizophrenia, bipolar disorder, and Parkinson's disease. DbGaP (http://www.ncbi.nlm.nih.gov/sites/entrez?Db=gap) and related NCBI databases are important elements in providing a powerful discovery system in which users will be able to glean information from many areas of genetics from a single online search.

# Areas of Special Interest

## Disaster Information Management

NLM has been involved in disaster response and management since the late 1960s, when its Specialized Information Services Division was established as the U.S. government focal point for information on toxic substances and environmental health. NLM is now working with the Pan American Health Organization and other Central American institutions as partners in the Central American Network for Disaster and Health Information (CANDHI). This consortium helps health professionals in the most natural-disaster-prone areas on earth, Latin America and the Caribbean, get information before disasters strike.

Closer to home, NLM has created the Disaster Information Management Research Center (DIMRC), providing a platform for demonstrating how libraries and librarians can be active in answering the need for preparedness for man-made and natural disasters. One aspect of this effort is the development of a curriculum for a new library science specialty, Disaster Information Specialist.

Users can download NLM's Wireless Information System for Emergency Responders (WISER) to their hand-held devices. Another version of WISER is in development that will facilitate early detection of post-traumatic stress disorder and traumatic brain injury.

### Standards for Personal Health Records

A Personal Health Record (PHR) is an electronic medical record whose contents are controlled and managed by the person whose data it carries. This challenge has attracted much press attention in recent years, and the U.S. information technology industry, health industry, and federal government envision the PHR as a possible solution to the information-sharing and efficiency problems in health care.

NLM has embarked on the development and deployment of a PHR in order to study and improve the utility of such devices, reduce barriers to their adoption, identify best practices, and provide a platform and test bed for advanced PHR applications. The development of the NLM PHR is based on a set of existing health care message and vocabulary standards that have either been developed by, or are supported by, NLM and for the most part are also fall under the accepted standards of the Secretary of Health and Human Services.

## Administration

The director of the Library, Donald A. B. Lindberg, M.D., is guided in matters of policy by a Board of Regents consisting of 10 appointed and 11 ex officio members.

### Table 1 / Selected NLM Statistics*

| Library Operation | Volume |
| --- | --- |
| Collection (book and nonbook) | 11,890,964 |
| Items cataloged | 21,507 |
| Serial titles received | 20,901 |
| Articles indexed for MEDLINE | 671,904 |
| Circulation requests processed | 405,475 |
| For interlibrary loan | 234,020 |
| For on-site users | 171,455 |
| Computerized searches (MEDLINE/PubMed) | 775,504,557 |
| Budget authority | $323,387,000 |
| Staff | 699 |

*For the year ending September 30, 2008

# United States Government Printing Office

732 North Capitol St. N.W., Washington, DC 20401
202-512-1957, e-mail gsomerset@gpo.gov
World Wide Web http://www.gpo.gov

Gary Somerset

Media and Public Relations Manager

The U.S. Government Printing Office (GPO) is the federal government's primary centralized resource for gathering, cataloging, producing, providing, and preserving published information in all its forms. Since its inception, GPO has offered Congress, the courts, and government agencies a set of centralized services, enabling them to produce printed documents easily and cost effectively according to a uniform set of federal government specifications. In addition, GPO has offered these publications for sale to the public and made them widely available at no cost through the Federal Depository Library Program (FDLP).

Today GPO is at the epicenter of technological change as it embraces its historic mission while looking to the digital future.

GPO is part of the legislative branch of the federal government and operates under the authority of the public printing and documents chapters of Title 44 of the U.S. Code. In addition to Congress, all three branches of the federal government rely on GPO's services. Congressional documents, Supreme Court decisions, federal regulations and reports, IRS tax forms, and U.S. passports all are produced by or through GPO.

GPO's headquarters, which includes a bookstore, is located in Washington, D.C. Nationwide, GPO maintains 15 field locations and two major distribution facilities, in Pueblo, Colorado, and Laurel, Maryland.

GPO's information dissemination activities include FDLP, which disseminates information products from the three branches of government to nearly 1,250 libraries nationwide; GPO Access, which provides online access to titles on GPO servers as well as links to titles on other federal Web sites; and a program that sells government publications to the public. GPO also administers the Cataloging and Indexing Program, the By-Law Program, and the distribution component of the International Exchange Program of the Library of Congress. To achieve its mission to provide timely, permanent, no-fee public access to federal government publications, GPO coordinates a network of libraries that assist the public in using government information resources, maintains tools such as the Catalog of Government Publications (CGP) to identify, describe, locate, and obtain publications, and maintains a permanent collection of government publications.

Together, these activities disseminate one of the world's largest volumes of published information. This report focuses on GPO's role as the disseminator of government information in print and electronic formats.

Amanda Colvin, Carrie Gibb, and Kelly Quest, U.S. Government Printing Office, prepared this report.

## Federal Digital System

GPO's Federal Digital System (FDsys), when fully deployed, will manage, preserve, provide version control and access to, and disseminate authentic U.S. government information. FDsys will include all known federal government documents within the scope of GPO's FDLP and other information dissemination programs. The system design is based on the Reference Model for an Open Archival Information System (OAIS) (ISO 14721:2003).

FDsys will allow federal content creators to create and submit content to be preserved, authenticated, managed, and delivered upon request. Content entered into the system will be cataloged according to GPO metadata and document creation standards. This content will be available for Web searching, Internet viewing, downloading and printing, and as document masters for conventional and on-demand printing or other dissemination methods. Content may include text and associated graphics, including print, digital, video, audio, or other forms that may emerge.

FDsys capabilities will be deployed in a series of releases. The first release launched as a public beta in January 2009. This release provides advanced searching and browsing capabilities, greatly enhancing the current capabilities of GPO Access. FDsys will contain eight collections at launch; completion of migration of the GPO Access content to FDsys is expected in mid-2009. FDsys will replace GPO Access after all content within GPO Access is migrated into FDsys.

The new Office of the Federal Register (OFR) publication *Daily Compilation of Presidential Documents* was specifically engineered for FDsys. This publication contains information released by the White House Press Office regarding orders, statements, and remarks made by the president. This new daily online publication replaces the printed *Weekly Compilation of Presidential Documents.* It can be accessed at http://fdsys.gpo.gov/fdsys/browse/collection.action?collectionCode=CPD.

For more information on FDsys, go to http://www.gpo.gov/fdsys.htm. To use the FDsys public beta, visit http://fdsys.gpo.gov.

### Authentication

As more government information becomes available electronically, data integrity and nonrepudiation of information become more critical. In furthering its mission to provide permanent public access to authentic U.S. government publications, GPO is working to afford users further assurance that files electronically disseminated through GPO Access remain unchanged since GPO first authenticated them, and to provide security for and safeguard federal government publications within the scope of FDLP.

In late January 2008 GPO implemented an Automated pdf Signing System (APS), allowing GPO to authenticate documents in bulk while continuing to ensure the integrity and authenticity of those documents. This has enabled application of digital signatures in a more timely, efficient, and cost-effective manner than can be achieved manually.

The new APS system was used to digitally sign and certify the fiscal year (FY) 2009 federal budget, released in February 2008. The digitally signed and certified pdf files within this application contain GPO's seal of authenticity, notifying users that a document has not been altered since it was authenticated and disseminated by GPO.

Additionally, in March 2008 GPO's beta Public and Private Laws authenticated database for the 110th Congress was launched as a permanent online application on GPO Access. In January 2009 GPO authenticated a third application, Congressional Bills, which includes all versions introduced since the beginning of the 110th Congress.

GPO's authentication initiative is slated to continue, with more authenticated online applications to come. For more information, visit http://www.gpoaccess.gov/authentication.

## Online Training

As part of its education and outreach mission, GPO has presented several programs on topics relating to FDLP through Online Programming for All Libraries (OPAL), a Web conferencing service. In February 2008 GPO opened its OPAL room to members of the depository library community so that they can present additional educational and training sessions for the community's benefit. In FY 2009 GPO staff and members of the depository community continue to present educational sessions in OPAL, and these sessions will remain available as an archive on the OPAL Web site, which can be accessed at http://www.opal-online.org/archiveGPO.htm.

## Federal Bulletin Board Migration

The year 2008 was a time of change for the Federal Bulletin Board (FBB) as GPO staff continued work to ensure the safety and security of online applications. Efforts were coordinated to update the infrastructure of FBB, following a recommendation from GPO's Information Technology department to migrate content to a Web-hosted ftp server that includes 500 gigabytes of space. Testing with internal and external FBB users helped to confirm that the proposed site fit customers' needs, and, most importantly, provided similar capabilities of the old FBB while ensuring a more stable system. Recommendations were provided to the vendor, and final migration occurred in August 2008. A total of 228 directories were migrated to the replacement ftp site, and FBB content will remain available to the public in perpetuity. FBB can be accessed at http://fedbbs.access.gpo.gov.

# Federal Depository Library Program

## Integrated Library System

The overall goal of the implementation of GPO's Integrated Library System (ILS) is the provision of access to bibliographic records of federal government publications, many containing links to the electronic version of the publication, to depositories and the public. The ILS system's power and capabilities can be utilized to provide needed services. The goal is also to streamline workflow and internal activities in support of FDLP and to reduce the use of and dependency on legacy systems.

The enhanced online Catalog of Government Publications (CGP) is an index of public documents from all three branches of the federal government, currently covering 1976 forward. In the online information environment, CGP is essential to GPO's core mission of ensuring that the public has access to federal government information. From its launch in March 2006 through November 2008, nearly 51 million successful requests were made of CGP, an average of 51,000 successful requests per day. The enhanced CGP is a component of a modernization plan to replace older legacy systems with GPO's state-of-the-art ILS. CGP can be found at http://catalog.gpo.gov.

New services of CGP released in 2008 included the Federal Depository Library Directory (FDLD), an administrative interface enabling depository libraries to update their directory information and post notes for the public's information; and a public interface to FDLD that enables searching and retrieving depository library contact and location information.

Future enhancements to GPO's ILS will include implementing the MetaLib federated searching product (multi-database searching capability) available from the CGP as well as enhancements to FDLD.

### Automated Metadata Extraction Project

In FY 2008 GPO entered into an Interagency Agreement with the Defense Technical Information Center (DTIC) in collaboration with Old Dominion University to develop cataloging records using the automated metadata extraction software tools and processes that DTIC currently uses. Project completion is expected in October 2009. The Automated Metadata Extraction agreement is being conducted in two phases over two years.

The first phase of the agreement, focused on GPO Environmental Protection Agency (EPA) harvested documents, is nearly finished. GPO will begin final evaluation of the extracted metadata from phase one and determine the feasibility of automated metadata extraction being used for EPA harvested documents. For the second phase of the agreement, GPO has identified and provided 1,000 FDLP in-scope congressional pdf files to Old Dominion for analysis. Upon completion of the extensive analysis of these documents and final evaluation analysis of both types of documents, GPO will determine the ultimate feasibility of software developed through this project being used in its library services operations.

### Digitization Efforts

GPO has been working with the library community, other federal agencies, and the public on a national digitization project with the goal of digitizing all retrospective federal publications back to the earliest days of the federal government. GPO envisions a cooperative, mutually beneficial relationship with one or more private or public sector participants in which the uncompressed, unaltered files created as a result of the conversion process are delivered to GPO at no cost to the government. This content will be made available online, free of charge, from GPO. To help meet this challenge, a statement of work was created, and a request for proposals was posted to the government Web site Federal Business Opportunities (https://www.fbo.gov). The review of the proposals was nearly complete in early 2008. Once GPO makes a decision for award, the Joint Committee on Printing (JCP) must approve that potential selection before work can begin.

GPO has coordinated efforts with staff at the Library of Congress on two key digitization projects, the bound *Congressional Record* from the 43rd Congress through the 105th Congress, and the *United States Statutes at Large*. For these projects, the Library of Congress digitizes the material to meet GPO's specifications for converted content for preservation masters. The digitized material is expected to be ingested into FDsys.

GPO has begun negotiations with the National Oceanic and Atmospheric Administration (NOAA) Coastal Service Center to incorporate the Coastal Zone Information Center Digital Collection into FDsys for preservation purposes and provide public access to an already digitized collection.

During 2008 GPO staff continued to work with other agencies on the National Digital Standards Advisory Board's Federal Agencies Still Image Digitization Working Group. This project fosters the establishment of common standards, methods, practices, and guidelines for the digitization of visual material (not including motion picture images). The creation of common standards for digitization encourages the exchange of research ideas and results, promotes collaboration among federal agencies and institutions, gives the public a product of uniform quality, and sets a benchmark for providers of digitization services.

### Registry of U.S. Government Publications Digitization Projects

GPO relaunched an enhanced Registry of U.S. Government Publication Digitization Projects (http://registry.fdlp.gov) in June 2008. The new registry is powered by a platform that provides better functionality for contributors, users, and GPO staff.

The enhanced registry allows

- Viewing digitization projects by category or alphabetically by title
- Searching the entire registry, as well as searching by category or field
- Viewing a list of new or recently updated projects
- Adding new projects to the registry
- Adding the GPO RSS feed to an individual's reader to deliver notice of new listings
- Viewing of listings by contributor

The registry currently lists more than 120 federal government digitization projects from institutions throughout the United States. Additional information about GPO's digitization and preservation initiatives can be found at http://www.gpoaccess.gov/legacy/index.html.

### FDLP Partnerships

GPO currently maintains 16 partnerships with federal depository libraries and federal agencies, and is continuing its efforts to increase the number of its partnerships so as to ensure permanent public access to digitized government content and material contained within databases.

During FY 2008 GPO entered into three new partnerships. The first, with the Naval Postgraduate School, allows depository libraries to gain access to the Homeland Security Digital Library (HSDL), a database containing U.S. policy documents, presidential directives, and national strategy documents, as well as other specialized resources relating to the study of homeland security. The second partnership is with the University of Illinois at Chicago and other participating federal depository libraries to promote the Government Information Online: Ask a Librarian (GIO) service. GIO is a free Web-based virtual reference service that focuses on responding to government information-related questions. The third partnership is with the Government Accountability Office (GAO) to provide permanent public access to the GAO Reports and GAO Comptroller General Decisions databases available on the GAO Web site.

### Depository Library Administration and Public Access Assessments

Federal depository libraries follow both the FDLP requirements found in Title 44, U.S. Code, Chapter 19 and those prescribed by GPO. These requirements, as well as guidance to help depository library personnel understand the requirements, are found in the *Federal Depository Library Handbook.* The handbook and periodic updates are disseminated via the FDLP Desktop, a Web resource for depository library personnel.

GPO also reviews how each individual depository library applies the requirements and guidance, as it has the responsibility to ensure that libraries receiving federal government publications paid for by taxpayers are fulfilling the responsibility of making the publications freely available to the public. This is accomplished primarily through the Public Access Assessments program, a review of conditions at each individual depository library. The program emphasizes how federal depository libraries serve the public's federal government information needs by reviewing how each library provides access to, and services for, U.S. government information resources. Public Access Assessments also offer the opportunity for GPO and individual libraries to share information to increase the efficiency and effectiveness of FDLP.

### FDLP Marketing Plan

Launched in summer 2008, the FDLP marketing plan is designed to market the services of federal depository libraries to the widest audience possible, as well as to provide depositories with the tools necessary to market their own services, both to the general public and non-federal depository libraries.

The marketing plan provides methods depositories can use to promote FDLP to non-depositories and the general public. In October 2008 new "Easy as FDL" promotional products became available to depositories free of charge, and

FDLP's first promotional video was launched on FDLP Desktop. The full FDLP marketing plan and description of the "Easy as FDL" marketing campaign can be found on the FDLP Desktop at http://fdlp.gov/outreach/promotionalresources/98-fdlpmarketingplan.

### Regional Depository Libraries Study

During FY 2008 GPO was directed by the Joint Committee on Printing (JCP) to conduct a study of the condition of regional depository libraries. The purpose of the study was to evaluate the extent to which public access to federal depository resources may be impaired by current or projected organizational, financial, technological, or other conditions.

After consultation with and input from depository libraries, in June 2008 GPO released a draft report and made it available for depository comment. All comments were reviewed, and a final report of findings was created. This report, "Regional Depository Libraries in the 21st Century: A Preliminary Assessment," was submitted to JCP in January 2009. The report is available at http://www.fdlp.gov/home/about/209-studyofregionals.

### LSCM Year in Review

At the fall Depository Library Council Conference and Meeting in October 2008, GPO unveiled its first annual *Library Services and Content Management (LSCM) Year in Review*. This document, covering FY 2008, recounts LSCM's major accomplishments in support of FDLP, the Cataloging and Indexing Program, the International Exchange Service, and the By-Law Program. A copy of the report was distributed to every federal depository library. This document will be released annually in October. The *Year in Review* is archived on the FDLP Desktop at http://fdlp.gov/component/content/article/108.

### Pre-1976 Shelflist Conversion Project

During FY 2008 GPO contracted with Progressive Technology Federal Systems, Inc. (PTFS) to acquire bibliographic metadata transcription services for the estimated 600,000 non-OCLC cataloging cards in its million-card historic shelflist. These cards contain brief bibliographic metadata captured as part of the cataloging activities of the Cataloging and Indexing Program and FDLP from the 1870s through October 1992. GPO is working with PTFS to convert the bibliographic metadata on these cards into machine-readable records in MARC 21 format so they can be loaded into GPO's ILS and made accessible to the public through the Catalog of Government Publications. GPO and PTFS have developed the workflow necessary for the conversion and will begin work on the first set of shelflist cards in FY 2009.

### Community Outreach

GPO continues to provide outreach to the depository library community. Efforts include travel by GPO staff, public access assessments, partnerships, online training, and GPO-sponsored meetings.

In FY 2008 GPO outreach activities included participation in the Universal Access Digital Library Summit in Boston; a conference for Partnerships for Indian Education hosted by the U.S. Department of Education in Rapid City, South Dakota; the 2008 meeting of the International Association for Social Science Information Services and Technology (IASSIST) in Stanford, California; the Alabama Federal Depository Libraries meeting in Tuscaloosa, Alabama; and a videoconference with the Western Pennsylvania FDLP Regional Group. GPO expects outreach in 2009 to include an equally diverse range of interests and venues.

GPO representatives regularly participate in library association and other professional meetings, local regional meetings, and various workshops. Additionally, in 2009 GPO will hold two Depository Library Council meetings and the Federal Depository Library Conference, convene the Interagency Depository Seminar, and continue to support depository anniversary celebrations. Under the newly established public access assessment program, GPO librarians will work with depository libraries to assure free public access to federal government information and consult on best practices.

### Distribution and Other Statistics

During FY 2008 GPO distributed a total of 3,482,507 tangible copies of 7,084 titles (this includes print, microfiche, CDs, and DVDs). During the fiscal year, 19,900 titles were cataloged, up from 18,812 in FY 2007. Also during FY 2008, 17,410 "persistent URLs" (PURLs) were created, up from 11,909 in FY 2007. The number of titles available on GPO Access for FY 2008 rose to 377,366, up from 322,571 titles in FY 2007.

## GPO Access

Under the mandate of Public Law 103-40, GPO is required to maintain an electronic directory of federal electronic information, provide a system of online access to the *Congressional Record*, the *Federal Register*, and other appropriate publications, and operate an electronic storage facility for federal electronic information. GPO's response to this mandate was the launch of GPO Access in 1994. GPO Access began with three databases; today GPO Access allows worldwide access to more than 4,000 databases and 120 applications. GPO also has a firm commitment to permanent public access. Once federal information has been placed on GPO Access, this information will be archived indefinitely.

Since its inception, GPO Access has experienced a continuous and steady usage increase. There were more than 336,624,700 GPO Access retrievals in FY 2008.

With 377,366 available titles, GPO Access contains a wide variety of applications, ranging from congressional and legislative information to federal regulations and presidential materials. GPO also hosts 22 federal Web sites, including that of the Supreme Court, as well as a reference suite of services for finding federal government information.

## Ben's Guide to U.S. Government

Ben's Guide to U.S. Government (http://bensguide.gpo.gov), the educational component of GPO Access, strives to introduce and explain for school-age audiences the workings of the three branches of the federal government. Through the use of primary source materials, grade-appropriate explanations, and a stimulating site design, Ben's Guide not only increases the public's access to and knowledge of the federal government, but makes learning fun.

The site is divided into four grade levels (K–2, 3–5, 6–8, and 9–12) and also provides an area for parents and educators. The material in each of these sections is tailored specifically for its intended audience. Ben's Guide includes historical documents and information on legislative and regulatory processes, elections, and citizenship. The site also features learning activities and a list of federal Web sites designed for students, parents, and educators.

# New and on the Horizon

### FDLP Desktop

The beta release of the FDLP Desktop provided an opportunity to learn how the federal depository library community uses the Web and utilizes content about FDLP disseminated online. During 2008 GPO worked to leverage Web standards, user expectations, and evolving Web features and functionality to create not only a single point of access for FDLP-related news and information but also to create an interconnected community that can network instantly via the Web.

As part of this learning process, GPO released FDLP Community. This site is designed to create an online, interactive venue to enhance the world of government documents. All members of the federal depository library community can share their knowledge, experiences, and resources while benefiting from the expertise of other library professionals from around the country.

The final version of FDLP Desktop was launched in January 2009. The final launch allows GPO to streamline its information dissemination and allows users to access FDLP-related information via their Web browser, RSS feeds, e-mail, and SMS alerts. FDLP Desktop is available at http://www.fdlp.gov.

### Publications

*History of the Capitol*—House Document No. 108-240, *Glenn Brown's History of the United States Capitol,* which examines the preservation of the Capitol building, was made available in January 2008 at http://www.gpoaccess.gov/serialset/cdocuments/hd108-240/index.html.

*Statutes at Large*—*United States Statutes at Large* (Volume 119, 109th Congress, 1st Session) was made available in February 2008; and Volume 120, 109th Congress, 2nd Session was made available in June 2008 at http://www.gpoaccess.gov/statutes/index.html. *United States Statutes at Large* is the permanent collection of all laws and resolutions enacted during each session of Congress. Every public and private law passed by Congress is published in *Statutes at Large* in order of the date it was enacted into law. The laws are arranged by public law number and are cited by volume and page number. Also included are concurrent resolutions, proclamations by the president, proposed and ratified amendments to the Constitution, and reorganization plans.

*Black Americans in Congress*—House Document No. 108-224, *Black Americans in Congress 1870–2007* offers comprehensive historical information on the 121 African Americans who have served in Congress. It was made available in October 2008 at http://www.gpoaccess.gov/serialset/cdocuments/hd108-224/index.html.

*Plum Book—United States Government Policy and Supporting Positions (Plum Book)*, 2008 edition, was made available in November 2008 at http://www. gpoaccess.gov/plumbook/index.html. The *Plum Book* is published by the Senate Committee on Governmental Affairs and the House Committee on Government Reform, alternately, after each presidential election. It lists more than 7,000 federal civil service leadership and support positions in the legislative and executive branches nationwide that may be subject to non-competitive appointment.

*New Member Pictorial Directory*—The directory for the 111th Congress was made available in November 2008 at http://www.gpoaccess.gov/pictorial/111th/newmems.html. Published by the Joint Committee on Printing, in its printed form it is a pocket-sized compilation of color photographs of all of the men and women of the 111th Congress, including the Senate and House leadership, officers, and appointed delegates and the resident commissioner. It also includes photos of the president, vice president, and other Capitol officials and contains information on length of service, political party affiliation, and congressional district. A "party division" page lists the total numbers of Republicans, Democrats, and Independents in the Senate and the House and an alphabetical list of senators and representatives.

## Selling Government Publications

GPO's Sales Program currently offers for sale approximately 5,500 individual government titles on a broad array of subjects. These are sold principally via the Internet, e-mail, telephone, fax, and mail. The program operates on a cost-recovery basis. Publications for sale include books, forms, posters, pamphlets, microfiche, CD-ROMs, computer diskettes, and magnetic tapes. Subscription services for both dated periodicals and basic-and-supplement services (involving an initial volume and supplemental issues) also are offered.

GPO's U.S. Government Online Bookstore (http://bookstore.gpo.gov) is the public's prime source of information on GPO's sales inventory. The online bookstore includes a searchable database of all in-print publications, as well as an extensive archive of recently out of print titles. It also includes a broad spectrum of special publication collections featuring new and popular titles and key product lines. GPO uses Pay.gov (https://www.pay.gov/paygov), a secure government-wide financial management transaction portal available around the clock. The online bookstore also provides customers with the option of expedited shipping, new and improved shopping cart and order confirmation e-mails, and expanded ordering options for international customers.

Express service, which includes priority handling and expedited delivery, is available for orders placed by telephone for domestic delivery. Orders placed before noon eastern time for in-stock publications and single-copy subscriptions will be delivered within two working days. The toll-free telephone number is 866-512-1800 (or 202-512-1800 within the Washington, D.C., area).

Consumer-oriented publications also are either sold or distributed at no charge through the Federal Citizen Information Center in Pueblo, Colorado, which GPO operates on behalf of the General Services Administration.

Members of the public can register free of charge to receive e-mail updates when new publications become available for sale through GPO's New Titles by Topic E-mail Alert Service. This service can be accessed at http://bookstore.gpo.gov/alertservice.jsp.

Standing order service is available to ensure automatic receipt of many GPO recurring and series publications. Standing order customers receive each new edition automatically as soon as it is published. This service can be set up using a major credit card or a Superintendent of Documents Deposit Account. For more information on how to set up a standing order for recurring or series publications, call 866-512-1800 (or 202-512-1800 within the Washington, D.C., area) or e-mail contactcenter@gpo.gov.

The GPO sales program has begun using print-on-demand technology to increase the long-term availability of publications and is testing the capabilities of a number of vendors. The program also has brought its bibliographic practices more in line with those of the commercial publishing sector by utilizing ONIX (Online Information Exchange), a standard electronic format for sharing product data with wholesale and retail booksellers, other publishers, and anyone else involved in the sale of books. ONIX enables GPO to have government publications listed, promoted, and sold by commercial book dealers worldwide. GPO sales titles are listed on Amazon.com, Barnesandnoble.com and other online commercial book selling sites.

# National Technical Information Service

U.S. Department of Commerce, Springfield, VA 22161
800-553-NTIS (6847) or 703-605-6000
World Wide Web http://www.ntis.gov

Linda Davis
Marketing Communications

The National Technical Information Service (NTIS) is the nation's largest and most comprehensive source of government-funded scientific, technical, engineering, and business information produced or sponsored by U.S. and international government sources. NTIS is a federal agency within the U.S. Department of Commerce.

Since 1945 the NTIS mission has been to operate a central U.S. government access point for scientific and technical information useful to American industry and government. NTIS maintains a permanent archive of this declassified information for researchers, businesses, and the public to access quickly and easily. Release of the information is intended to promote U.S. economic growth and development and to increase U.S. competitiveness in the world market.

The NTIS collection of more than 2 million titles contains products available in various formats. Such information includes reports describing research conducted or sponsored by federal agencies and their contractors; statistical and business information; U.S. military publications; multimedia training programs; databases developed by federal agencies; and technical reports prepared by research organizations worldwide. NTIS maintains a permanent repository of its information products.

More than 200 U.S. government agencies contribute to the NTIS collection, including the National Aeronautics and Space Administration; Environmental Protection Agency; the departments of Agriculture, Commerce, Defense, Energy, Health and Human Services, Homeland Security, Interior, Labor, Treasury, Veterans Affairs, Housing and Urban Development, Education, and Transportation; and numerous other agencies. International contributors include Canada, Japan, Britain, and several European countries.

## NTIS on the Web

NTIS offers Web-based access to the latest government scientific and technical research information products. Visitors to http://www.ntis.gov can search the entire collection dating back to 1964 free of charge. NTIS also provides downloading capability for many technical reports, and purchase of the publications on CD as well as paper copies.

## National Technical Reports Library

New at NTIS is the National Technical Reports Library (NTRL), which delivers high-quality government technical content in all subject areas directly and seamlessly to the user's desktop. The NTRL service gives access to more than 2 million NTIS bibliographic records and more than 500,000 full-text documents in pdf format. For more information, visit http://www.ntis.gov/products/ntrl.aspx.

## NTIS Database

The NTIS Database (listings of information products acquired by NTIS since 1964) offers unparalleled bibliographic coverage of U.S. government and worldwide government-sponsored research. Its contents represent hundreds of billions of research dollars and cover a range of important topics including agriculture, biotechnology, business, communication, energy, engineering, the environment, health and safety, medicine, research and development, science, space, technology, and transportation.

Most records include abstracts. Database summaries describe technical reports, datafiles, multimedia/training programs, and software. These titles are often unique to NTIS and generally are difficult to locate from any other source. The complete NTIS Database provides instant access to more than 2 million records.

Free 30-day trials of the NTIS Database are available through the GOV. Research_Center (http://grc.ntis.gov). The NTIS Database can be leased directly from NTIS and can also be accessed through several commercial services. For an updated list of organizations offering NTIS Database products, see http://www.ntis.gov/products/commercial.aspx.

To lease the NTIS Database directly from NTIS, contact the NTIS Subscriptions Department at 800-363-2068 or 703-605-6060. For more information, see http://www.ntis.gov/products/ntisdb.aspx.

## Other Databases Available from NTIS

NTIS offers several valuable research-oriented database products. To find out more about accessing the databases, visit http://www.ntis.gov/products/types/databases/data.asp.

### FEDRIP

The Federal Research in Progress Database (FEDRIP) provides access to information about ongoing federally funded projects in the fields of the physical sciences, engineering, and life sciences. The ongoing research announced in FEDRIP is an important component of the technology transfer process in the United States; FEDRIP's uniqueness lies in its structure as a nonbibliographic information source of research in progress. Project descriptions generally include project title, keywords, start date, estimated completion date, principal investigator, performing and sponsoring organizations, summary, and progress report. Record content varies depending on the source agency.

There are many reasons to search FEDRIP. Among these are to avoid research duplication, locate sources of support, identify leads in the literature, stimulate ideas for planning, identify gaps in areas of investigation, and locate individuals with expertise. To access an updated list of organizations offering FEDRIP Database products, see http://www.ntis.gov/products/fedrip.aspx.

## AGRICOLA

As one of the most comprehensive sources of U.S. agricultural and life sciences information, the Agricultural Online Access Database (AGRICOLA) contains bibliographic records for documents acquired by the National Agricultural Library (NAL) of the U.S. Department of Agriculture. The complete database dates from 1970 and contains more than 4 million citations to journal articles, monographs, theses, patents, software, audiovisual materials, and technical reports relating to agriculture.

AGRICOLA serves as the document locator and bibliographic control system for the NAL collection. The extensive file provides comprehensive coverage of newly acquired worldwide publications in agriculture and related fields. AGRI-COLA covers the field of agriculture in the broadest sense. Subjects include Agricultural Economics, Agricultural Education, Agricultural Products, Animal Science, Aquaculture, Biotechnology, Botany, Cytology, Energy, Engineering, Feed Science, Fertilizers, Fibers and Textiles, Food and Nutrition, Forestry, Horticulture, Human Ecology, Human Nutrition, Hydrology, Hydroponics, Microbiology, Natural Resources, Pesticides, Physiology, Plant and Animal, Plant Sciences, Public Health, Rural Sociology, Soil Sciences, Veterinary Medicine, and Water Quality. To access an updated list of organizations offering AGRICOLA Database products, see http://www.ntis.gov/products/agricola.aspx.

## AGRIS

The International Information System for the Agricultural Science and Technology (AGRIS) Database is a cooperative system for collecting and disseminating information on the world's agricultural literature in which more than 100 national and multinational centers take part. References to citations for U.S. publications given coverage in the AGRICOLA Database are not included in AGRIS. A large number of citations in AGRIS are not found in any other database. References to nonconventional literature (documents not commercially available) contain a note explaining where a copy can be obtained. AGRIS can be used to find citations to agricultural information from around the world. Much of this information includes government documents, technical reports, and nonconventional literature that have their source in both developed and developing countries and that can be found nowhere else. To access an updated list of organizations offering AGRIS Database products, see http://www.ntis.gov/products/agris.aspx.

### Energy Science and Technology

The Energy Science and Technology Database (EDB) is a multidisciplinary file containing worldwide references to basic and applied scientific and technical research literature. The information is collected for use by government managers, researchers at national laboratories, and other research efforts sponsored by the U.S. Department of Energy, and the results of this research are transferred to the public. Abstracts are included for records from 1976 to the present. EDB also contains the Nuclear Science Abstracts, a comprehensive abstract and index collection to the international nuclear science and technology literature for the period 1948–1976. Included are scientific and technical reports of the U.S. Atomic Energy Commission, U.S. Energy Research and Development Administration and its contractors, other agencies, universities, and industrial and research organizations. Approximately 25 percent of the records in the file contain abstracts. Nuclear Science Abstracts contains more than 900,000 bibliographic records. The entire EDB contains more than 3 million bibliographic records. To access an updated list of organizations offering EDB products, visit http://www.ntis.gov/products/engsci.aspx.

## Specialized Online Subscriptions

Those wishing to expand their access to subject-specific resources through use of the Internet are likely to benefit from the NTIS online options highlighted below. Online subscriptions offer quick, convenient online access to the most current information available.

### World News Connection

World News Connection (WNC) is an NTIS online news service accessible only via the World Wide Web. WNC makes available English-language translations of time-sensitive news and information from thousands of non-U.S. media. Particularly effective in its coverage of local media, WNC provides the power to identify what is happening in a specific country or region. The information is obtained from speeches, television and radio broadcasts, newspaper articles, periodicals, and books. The subject matter focuses on socioeconomic, political, scientific, technical, and environmental issues and events.

The information in WNC is provided to NTIS by the Foreign Broadcast Information Service (FBIS), a U.S. government agency. For more than 60 years, analysts from FBIS's domestic and overseas bureaus have monitored timely and pertinent open source material, including gray literature. Uniquely, WNC allows subscribers to take advantage of the intelligence-gathering experience of FBIS.

WNC is updated every government business day. Generally, new information is available within 24 to 72 hours of the time of original publication or broadcast.

Subscribers can conduct unlimited interactive searches and have the ability to set up automated searches known as profiles. When a profile is created, a search is run against WNC's latest news feed to identify articles relevant to a subscriber's topic of interest. The results are automatically sent to the subscriber's e-mail address.

Access to WNC is available through Dialog Corporation. To use the service, complete the WNC form at http://www.dialog.com/contacts/forms/wnc.shtml.

### U.S. Export Administration Regulations

U.S. Export Administration Regulations (EAR) provides the latest rules controlling the export of U.S. dual-use commodities, technology, and software. Step by step, EAR explains when an export license is necessary and when it is not, how to obtain an export license, policy changes as they are issued, new restrictions on exports to certain countries and of certain types of items, and where to obtain further help.

This information is now available through NTIS in looseleaf form, on CD-ROM, and online. An e-mail update notification service is also available.

For more information, see https://bxa.ntis.gov.

## Special Subscription Services

### NTIS Alerts

More than 1,000 new titles are added to the NTIS collection every week. NTIS Alerts were developed in response to requests from customers to search and tap into this newly obtained information. NTIS prepares a list of search criteria that is run against all new studies and research and development reports in 16 subject areas. An NTIS Alert provides a twice-monthly information briefing service covering a wide range of technology topics.

An NTIS Alert provides numerous benefits: efficient, economical, and timely access to the latest U.S. government technical studies; concise, easy-to-read summaries; information not readily available from any other source; contributions from more than 100 countries; and subheadings within each issue designed to identify essential information quickly.

For more information, call the NTIS Subscriptions Department at 703-605-6060 or see http://www.ntis.gov/products/alerts.aspx.

### SRIM

Selected Research in Microfiche (SRIM) is an inexpensive, tailored information service that delivers full-text microfiche copies of technical reports based on a customer's needs. Customers choose between Standard SRIM Service (selecting one or more of the 320 existing subject areas) or Custom SRIM Service, which creates a new subject area to meet their particular needs. Custom SRIM Service requires a one-time fee to cover the cost of strategy development and computer programming to set up a profile. Except for this fee, the cost of Custom SRIM is the same as the Standard SRIM. Through this ongoing subscription service, customers receive microfiche copies of new reports pertaining to their field(s) of interest, as NTIS obtains the reports.

For more information, see http://www.ntis.gov/products/srim.aspx. To place an order, call 800-363-2068 or 703-605-6060.

The SRIM service is also available in CD-ROM format—Science and Technology on CD. Documents are digitized and stored in pdf format that can easily be viewed using free Adobe Acrobat Reader software. With Science and Technology on CD, NTIS can provide more publications—those that cannot be rendered on microfiche, such as colorized illustrations or oversized formats.

For more information, see http://www.ntis.gov/products/STonCD.aspx. To place an order, call 800-363-2068 or 703-605-6060.

# NTIS Customer Service

NTIS's automated systems keep it at the forefront when it comes to customer service. Shopping online at NTIS is safe and secure; its secure socket layer (SSL) software is among the best available today.

Electronic document storage is fully integrated with NTIS's order-taking process, allowing it to provide rapid reproduction for the most recent additions to the NTIS document collection. Most orders for shipment are filled and delivered anywhere in the United States in five to seven business days. Rush service is available for an additional fee.

# Key NTIS Contacts for Ordering

### Order by Phone

Sales Desk                                                  800-553-6847 or 703-605-6000
8:30 A.M.–5:00 P.M. Eastern time, Monday–Friday

Subscriptions                                             800-363-2068 or 703-605-6060
8:30 A.M.–5:00 P.M. Eastern time, Monday–Friday

TDD (hearing impaired only)                                           703-487-4639
8:30 A.M.–5:00 P.M. Eastern time, Monday–Friday

### Order by Fax

24 hours a day, seven days a week                                     703-605-6900
To verify receipt of fax, call 703-605-6090, 7:00 A.M.–5:00 P.M. Eastern time Monday–Friday

### Order by Mail

National Technical Information Service
5285 Port Royal Road
Springfield, VA 22161

RUSH Service (available for an additional fee)    800-553-6847 or 703-605-6000
Note: If requesting RUSH Service, please do not mail your order

### Order Via World Wide Web

Direct and secure online ordering                               http://www.ntis.gov

### Order Via E-Mail

24 hours a day                                                    orders@ntis.gov
For Internet security, customers placing an order by e-mail can register their credit card in advance. To do so, call 703-605-6070 between 7:00 A.M. and 5:00 P.M. Eastern time, Monday–Friday.

# National Archives and Records Administration

8601 Adelphi Rd., College Park, MD 20740
301-837-2000, World Wide Web http://www.archives.gov

Susan M. Ashtianie

Director, Policy and Planning Staff

The National Archives and Records Administration (NARA), an independent federal agency, is the nation's record keeper. NARA safeguards and preserves the records of the federal government so that the people can discover, use, and learn from this documentary heritage. NARA ensures continuing access to the essential documentation of the rights of American citizens and the actions of their government.

NARA is singular among the world's archives as a unified federal institution that accessions and preserves materials from all three branches of government. It carries out its mission through a national network of archives and records services facilities, including presidential libraries that document administrations back to Herbert Hoover. NARA assists federal agencies in documenting their activities, administering records management programs, scheduling records, and retiring non-current records to federal records centers. The agency also assists the National Historical Publications and Records Commission in its grant program for state and local records and edited publications of the papers of prominent Americans; publishes the laws, regulations, presidential documents, and other official notices of the federal government through the *Federal Register*; and oversees classification and declassification policy in the federal government through the Information Security Oversight Office. NARA constituents include the federal government, educators and their students at all levels, a history-minded public, family historians, the media, the archival community, and a broad spectrum of professional associations and researchers in such fields as history, political science, law, library and information services, and genealogy.

The size and breadth of NARA's holdings are staggering. Together, NARA's facilities hold approximately 30.5 million cubic feet (equivalent to more than 76 billion pieces of paper) of original textual and nontextual materials from the executive, legislative, and judicial branches of the federal government.

NARA's multimedia collections include nearly 117,000 motion picture films; more than 8 million maps, charts, and architectural drawings; more than 250,000 sound and video recordings; more than 27 million aerial photographs; more than 14 million still pictures and posters; and more than 6 billion electronic records.

NARA employs approximately 3,250 people, of whom nearly 2,600 are full-time permanent staff members.

## Strategic Directions

NARA's strategic priorities are laid out in *Preserving the Past to Protect the Future: The Strategic Plan of the National Archives and Records Administration*

*2006–2016.* Success for the agency as envisioned in the plan centers on six strategic goals:

- As the nation's record keeper, NARA will ensure the continuity and effective operation of federal programs by expanding its leadership and services in managing the government's records.
- NARA will preserve and process records to ensure access by the public as soon as legally possible.
- NARA will address the challenges of electronic records in government to ensure success in fulfilling NARA's mission in the digital era.
- NARA will provide prompt, easy, and secure access to its holdings anywhere, anytime.
- NARA will increase access to its records in ways that further civic literacy in the United States through museums, public outreach, and education programs.
- NARA will be equipped to meet the changing needs of its customers.

The plan lays out strategies for reaching these goals, sets milestone targets for accomplishments through 2016, and identifies measurements for gauging progress. The targets and measurements are further delineated in NARA's Annual performance plans.

The strategic plan and annual performance plans, together with performance and accountability reports, are available on the NARA Web site at http://www. archives.gov/about/plans-reports or by calling 301-837-1850.

## Records and Access

### Internet

NARA's Web site, http://www.archives.gov, provides the most widely available means of electronic access to information about the agency and its services. Feedback from visitors to the Web site, and from visitors to the National Archives building in Washington, D.C., led to the creation of portals designed to support the particular needs of genealogists, veterans and their families, educators and students, researchers, the general public, records managers, journalists, information security specialists, members of Congress, and federal employees. The site includes directions on how to contact NARA and do research at its facilities; descriptions of its holdings in an online catalog (at http://www.archives. gov/research/arc); direct access to certain archival electronic records (at http:// www.archives.gov/aad); digital copies of selected archival documents; an Internet Web form (at http://www.archives.gov/contact/inquire-form.html) for customer questions, reference requests, comments, and complaints; electronic versions of Federal Register publications; online exhibits; and classroom resources for students and teachers. Other features include online tools, such as the interactive inquiry program at http://www.archives.gov/veterans/evetrecs that allows veterans and the next-of-kin of deceased veterans to complete and print, for mail-in submission, requests for their service records. At http://www.

archives.gov/presidential-libraries, visitors can link to individual presidential library Web sites to explore the nation's history through its leaders.

Copies of military pension records from the American Revolution through World War I, census pages, land files, court records, and microfilm publications can be ordered online as well as books, apparel, and accessories at http://www.archives.gov/order. Researchers can also submit reference questions about various research topics online.

Visitors to NARA's Web site can obtain Really Simple Syndication (RSS) feeds of the "Document for Today" feature, NARA news, and press releases. In spring 2008 the online National Archives Experience launched a new interactive Digital Vaults that features more than 1,200 records including documents, photographs, videos, and audio files. The interactive Digital Vaults allows visitors to create their own exhibit experience.

NARA celebrates its 75th anniversary in 2009 and has launched a Web site where visitors can view photographs of NARA through the decades, download desktop wallpapers and a screensaver, and submit personal stories about the National Archives. The site is at http://www.archives.gov/75th.

In cooperation with several federal agencies, NARA also has established a Web portal, http://www.regulations.gov, that provides access to federal rules and instructions for submitting comments on federal regulatory actions.

**Archival Research Catalog**

Using NARA's Archival Research Catalog (ARC), anyone with a computer connected to the Internet can search descriptions of NARA's nationwide holdings and view digital copies of some of its most popular documents. A significant piece of the electronic access strategy outlined in NARA's Strategic Plan, this online catalog of all NARA holdings nationwide allows the public to search for information about NARA's vast holdings, including those in the regional archives and presidential libraries, in a single online data system. Because of the vast amount of NARA holdings, it will take several years to fully populate ARC. At present, the catalog contains more than 2.4 million descriptions of archival holdings—more than 60 percent of NARA's total holdings—and more than 140,000 digital copies of high-interest documents. The documents available online include many of the holdings highlighted in the Public Vaults, NARA's permanent interactive exhibition. The catalog is found at http://www.archives.gov/research/arc.

**Digitization Projects**

NARA is working to digitize its traditional holdings to benefit their preservation and to provide greater access to the public. Although ARC gives users the ability to identify NARA's archival holdings via descriptions, NARA does not provide online access to the holdings themselves apart from the relatively small amount of material digitized and made available through ARC. Most of NARA's holdings currently are available only from the archival facility in which they are stored. By digitizing these holdings, NARA will vastly increase public access to them. During 2008 NARA created a strategy to deal with digitization efforts, which includes working with partners in the private sector to digitize its holdings. Currently more than 24,000 ARC descriptions link out to digital copies on partners' Web sites, and many thousands more will be made available in the future. For more information about NARA's digitization partnerships, visit http://www.archives.gov/digitization/index.html.

## Electronic Records Archives

NARA's Electronic Records Archives (ERA) is its strategic initiative to preserve and provide long-term access to valuable electronic records of the federal government, and to transition government-wide management of the lifecycle of all records into the realm of "e-government." The ERA Base system was put into production on June 27, 2008. The system currently standardizes the completion of lifecycle steps for all records, physical and electronic, NARA-wide, as well as supporting the transfer, virus scanning, verification, and bitstream-level preservation of electronic records. The ERA system will facilitate the achievement of NARA's mission well into the 21st century by enabling and automating major NARA processes.

After its official release in June, some 150 people were trained to use the ERA Base system, including NARA staff and records officers from four federal agencies selected to use the first release of the ERA system. As NARA evolves the infrastructure and architecture of the Base system to make it more flexible, the system will be opened to other agencies.

The ERA Base system currently allows for the creation, review, and approval of records schedules; requests to transfer records, as well as physical and legal custody of those records; the transfer, inspection, and archival storage of electronic records; and identification, communication, and resolution of transfer problems. Electronic records transfer can be done electronically or by sending media to NARA, and includes automatic scans for malware (malicious software) and sensitive content, verification of transferred files, and metadata extraction and management.

Although the current ERA systems are robust, development is a long way from complete. Features planned for the future include public access (slated for 2010), better long-term preservation solutions for e-records, the ability to redact sensitive content, support for Federal Records Centers, and exponential growth of storage solutions.

For more information about ERA, visit http://www.archives.gov/era.

## The National Archives Experience

The National Archives Experience, a set of interconnected resources made possible by a public-private partnership between NARA and the Foundation for the National Archives, provides a variety of ways of exploring the power and importance of the nation's records.

The Rotunda for the Charters of Freedom at the National Archives building in Washington, D.C., is the cornerstone of the National Archives Experience. On display are the Declaration of Independence, the Constitution, and the Bill of Rights, known collectively as the Charters of Freedom. The Public Vaults is a 9,000-square-foot permanent exhibition that conveys the feeling of going beyond the walls of the rotunda and into the stacks and vaults of the working archives.

Dozens of individual exhibits, many of them interactive, reveal the breadth and variety of NARA's holdings. Complementing the Public Vaults, the O'Brien Gallery hosts a changing array of topical exhibits based on National Archives records. The 290-seat McGowan Theater is a state-of-the-art showplace for NARA's extensive audiovisual holdings and serves as a forum for lectures and discussion. It also is home to the Charles Guggenheim Center for the Documentary Film at the National Archives. Inside the Boeing Learning Center, the ReSource Room is an access point for teachers and parents to explore documents found in the exhibits and to use NARA's records as teaching tools. The center's "Constitution-in-Action" Learning Lab is designed to provide a field trip adventure for middle and high school students that links to curriculum in the classroom.

A set of Web pages now makes the National Archives Experience available online, with an illustrated history of the Charters of Freedom and information on educational programs, special events, and exhibits currently at the National Archives. For more information, visit http://www.archives.gov/national-archives-experience.

### Building Research Center

At NARA's Robert M. Warner Research Center, researchers can consult with staff experts on records in the National Archives building and submit requests to examine original documents. The center houses approximately 275,000 rolls of microfilmed records, documenting military service prior to World War I, immigration into the United States, the federal census, Congress, federal courts in the District of Columbia, the Bureau of Indian Affairs, and the Freedmen's Bureau. The center also contains an extensive and expanding system of reference reports, helping researchers conduct research in federal documents.

### Archives Library Information Center

The Archives Library Information Center (ALIC) provides access to information on American history and government, archival administration, information management, and government documents. ALIC is physically located in two traditional libraries, in the National Archives building in Washington and at the National Archives at College Park, Maryland. Customers also can visit ALIC on the Internet at http://www.archives.gov/research/alic, where they will find "Reference at Your Desk" Internet links, staff-compiled bibliographies and publications, an online library catalog, and more. ALIC can be reached by phone at 202-357-5018 in Washington and at 301-837-3415 in College Park.

### Government Documents

Federal government publications are generally available to researchers at the 1,250 congressionally designated federal depository libraries throughout the United States. A record set of these publications also is part of NARA's archival holdings. "Publications of the U.S. Government" (Record Group 287) is a collection of selected publications of government agencies, arranged by the classification system (SuDoc System) devised by the Office of the Superintendent of Documents, Government Printing Office (GPO). The core of the collection is a library established in 1895 by GPO's Public Documents Division. By 1972, when NARA acquired the library, it included official publications dating from the early years of the federal government and selected publications produced for and by federal government agencies. Since 1972 the 25,000-cubic-foot collection has been augmented periodically with accessions of U.S. government publications selected by the Office of the Superintendent of Documents as a byproduct of its cataloging activity. As with the federal depository library collections, the holdings in NARA's Record Group 287 comprise only a portion of all publications published by the government.

### NARA Publications

NARA publishes guides and indexes to various portions of its archival holdings; catalogs of microfilmed records; informational leaflets and brochures; general interest books about NARA and its holdings that will appeal to anyone with an interest in U.S. history; more-specialized publications that will be useful to scholars, archivists, records managers, historians, researchers, and educators; facsimiles of certain documents; and *Prologue,* a scholarly journal published quarterly. Some publications are also available on NARA's Web site at http://www.archives.gov/publications/online.html. Many are available from NARA's Customer Service Center in College Park by telephoning 800-234-8861 or 866-272-6272 or faxing 301-837-0483 (or 301-837-2000 in the Washington area). The NARA Web site's publications home page, http://www.archives.gov/publications, provides detailed information about available publications and ordering.

### Federal Register

The *Federal Register* is the U.S. government's daily gazette, containing presidential documents, proposed and final federal regulations, and public notices of federal agencies. It is published by the Office of the Federal Register and printed and distributed by GPO. The two agencies collaborate in the same way to produce the annual revisions of the *Code of Federal Regulations* (*CFR*). Free access to the full text of the electronic version of the *Federal Register* and *CFR,* and to an unofficial, daily-updated electronic *CFR* (the *e-CFR*), is available through the GPO Access service at http://www.federalregister.gov. *Federal Register* documents scheduled for future publication are available for public inspection at the Office of the Federal Register (800 North Capitol St. N.W., Washington, DC 20001) or online at the electronic Public Inspection Desk (http://www.federalregister.gov). Access to rules published in the *Federal Register* and open for public comment, and a portal for submitting comments, are provided through the multi-agency Web site http://www.regulations.gov.

Access to the full texts of other Federal Register publications, including the *Compilation of Presidential Documents, Public Papers of the President,* slip laws, *U.S. Statutes at Large,* and the *United States Government Manual,* is available through the GPO Access service at http://www.federalregister.gov. Printed editions of these publications also are maintained at all federal depository libraries. The Public Law Electronic Notification Service (PENS) is a free subscription e-mail service available for notification of recently enacted public laws.

The Federal Register Table of Contents Service is a free e-mail service available for delivery of the daily table of contents from the *Federal Register* with direct links to documents.

The Office of the Federal Register also publishes information about its ministerial responsibilities associated with the operation of the Electoral College and ratification of constitutional amendments and provides access to related records. Publication information concerning laws, regulations, and presidential documents and services is available from the Office of the Federal Register (202-741-6000). Information about and additional finding aids for Federal Register publications, the Electoral College, and constitutional amendments also are available at http://www.archives.gov/federal-register.

Publications can be ordered by contacting GPO at http://bookstore.gpo.gov, and toll free at 866-512-1800. To submit orders by fax or by mail, visit http://bookstore.gpo.gov/help/index.jsp.

## Customer Service

Few records repositories serve as many customers as NARA. In fiscal year 2008 there were more than 140,000 researcher visits to NARA facilities nationwide, including archives, presidential libraries, and federal records centers. At the same time, more than 1.2 million customers requested information in writing. NARA also served the executive agencies of the federal government, the courts, and Congress by providing records storage, reference service, training, advice, and guidance on many issues relating to records management. Federal records centers replied to more than 8 million requests for information and records, including more than 1.2 million requests for information regarding military and civilian service records provided by the National Personnel Records Center in St. Louis, Missouri. NARA also provided informative public programs at its various facilities for more than 11,000 people. More than a million visited the National Archives Experience in Washington, and exhibits in the presidential library museums had more than 2 million visitors.

NARA knows it must understand who its customers are and what they need to ensure that people can discover, use, and learn from their documentary heritage in the National Archives. Customers are surveyed regularly to help NARA align its standards of performance with their expectations. By repeating surveys at frequent intervals, changes in performance are measured and appropriate actions taken to ensure that service levels reflect an appropriate balance between customer needs and NARA resources. NARA also maintains an Internet Web form (http://www.archives.gov/contact/inquire-form.html) to facilitate continuous feedback from customers about what is most important to them and what NARA might do better to meet their needs.

## Grants

The National Historical Publications and Records Commission (NHPRC) is the grant-making affiliate of NARA. The Archivist of the United States chairs the commission and makes grants on its recommendation. The commission's 14 other members represent the president of the United States (two appointees), the U.S. Supreme Court, the U.S. Senate and House of Representatives, the U.S. Departments of State and Defense, the Librarian of Congress, the American Association for State and Local History, the American Historical Association, the Association for Documentary Editing, the National Association of Government Archives and Records Administrators, the Organization of American Historians, and the Society of American Archivists.

The commission carries out a statutory mission to ensure understanding of the nation's past by promoting the preservation and use of essential historical documentation. The commission supports the creation and publication of documentary editions and research in the management and preservation of authentic electronic records, and it works in partnership with a national network of state archives and state historical records advisory boards to develop a national archival infrastructure. NHPRC grants help state and local governments, archives, universities, historical societies, professional organizations, and other nonprofit organizations establish or strengthen archival programs, improve training and techniques, preserve and process records collections, and provide access to them through finding aids, digitization of collections, and documentary editions of the papers of significant historical figures and movements in U.S. history. For more information about the commission, visit http://www.archives.gov/nhprc.

# Federal Library and Information Center Committee

101 Independence Ave. S.E., Washington, DC 20540-4935
202-707-4800, fax 202-707-4818, e-mail flicc@loc.gov

Roberta I. Shaffer

Executive Director

## Highlights of the Year

During fiscal year (FY) 2008, the Federal Library and Information Center Committee (FLICC) continued its mission to foster excellence in federal library and information services through interagency cooperation and to provide guidance and direction for FEDLINK.

FLICC quarterly membership meetings focused on a variety of broad federal information issues, including the future of bibliographic control, Internet Archive, federal library competencies, and future uses of library and information center physical space.

FLICC working groups completed an ambitious agenda. Notably, the Human Resources Working Group completed the "Federal Librarian Competencies" that define the knowledge, skills, and abilities (KSAs) needed to perform successfully. The competency document includes many suggestions and comments from colleagues and supporters in the federal information community and will be vetted through the Department of Defense (DoD) validation protocol and then presented to the Office of Personnel Management (OPM) for acceptance.

The Education Working Group presented a variety of seminars and workshops, including a week-long program for federal library technicians and a variety of other workshops, seminars, and institutes on data collection and program planning, talent mentoring, mining and management, writing for the Web, creating wikis and e-newsletters, and "Issues in Federal and Armed Forces Libraries."

The FLICC Awards Working Group announced its annual awards and launched plans for the next awards cycle, including a marketing campaign to raise awareness and highlight the importance of the various awards, the creation of a new category to recognize outstanding contributions to the field, and a redesign of the awards brochure.

The Preservation and Digitization Working Group (formerly the Preservation and Binding Working Group) planned and sponsored a workshop on preserving architectural drawing and a symposium on disaster planning. Because of the interest generated by the symposium and the mandate for federal agencies to have continuity of operations plans (COOPs), a new working group, Disaster Preparedness, was formed. This group is charged with overseeing Safety Net, a group of federal libraries in the Washington, D.C., metropolitan area that have agreed to aid each other in the event of a regional disaster. The Disaster Preparedness Working Group sponsored a symposium on COOPs incorporating the care of collections.

FLICC also continued its collaboration with the Library of Congress general counsel on a series of meetings between federal agency legal counsels and agency librarians. Now in their tenth year, these meetings grew out of the recognition that federal attorneys and librarians share many of the same concerns regarding issues relating to copyright law, privacy law, the Freedom of Information Act, and other laws in the electronic age, with regard both to using information within the agency and to publishing the agency's own information. These meetings have enhanced the relationship between agency attorneys and librarians and have helped them develop contacts with their counterparts at other agencies. This year's series featured discussions on legal issues relating to digitization of archival holdings and federal development of and use policies for Web 2.0 technologies.

FLICC released a redesign of its Web site in late summer. Now in full compliance with the Library of Congress Web guidelines and using the Office of Strategic Initiatives' "SWAN" templates, staff members managed, converted, supported, and updated the FLICC/FEDLINK Web site that comprises more than 3,000 pages of content, including video and resource links.

FEDLINK, FLICC's cooperative network, continued to enhance its fiscal operations while providing its members with $70.8 million in transfer-pay services, $5.4 million in direct-pay services, and an estimated $34.1 million in Direct Express services, saving federal agencies more than $14.6 million in vendor volume discounts and approximately $16.1 million more in cost avoidance.

To meet the requirements of the Fiscal Operations Improvement Act of 2000 (P.L. 106-481) that created new statutory authority for FEDLINK's fee-based activities, FEDLINK governing bodies and staff members confirmed that plans were on track for the third year of its rolling five-year business plan from FY 2006. They also began to explore the position of the FEDLINK program and its role in the federal sector of the commercial market. Budgeting efforts projected both costs and revenue, looking at private sector and historic costs with adjustments calculated based on vendor and Government Accountability Office (GAO) predictions. After examining program growth, realized savings through program management, and program reserves, FLICC/FEDLINK's oversight groups recommended a 1 percent fee reduction for transfer-pay services in FY 2009.

In winter 2007 FEDLINK released, via the Web, its annual survey directed at FLICC/FEDLINK leadership and members. FLICC/FEDLINK management and staff further integrated their planning and reporting into the new Library of Congress strategic plans and performance measurement for FY 2008 and FY 2009.

In FY 2008 FEDLINK continued to give federal agencies cost-effective access to an array of automated information retrieval services for online research, cataloging, and resource sharing. FEDLINK members also procured print serials, electronic journals, books and other publications, document delivery, and preservation services via Library of Congress/FEDLINK contracts with more than 130 major vendors. The program obtained further discounts for customers through consortia and enterprise-wide licenses for journals, aggregated information retrieval services, and electronic books. FEDLINK welcomed two new vendors to the program to meet FY 2008 requirements, including a new service area, digitization, and access for public domain documents. After working with Library of

Congress Library Services to begin to meet their needs, FEDLINK staff consulted with five agencies to use the new contract to digitize their public domain documents and provide access via the Internet Archive. They also consulted with 21 agencies to procure services to meet their specialized requirements in four categories: serials subscriptions, digitization, preservation and conservation, and cataloging and technical processing. They issued a revised request for proposals (RFP) for electronic retrieval services and awarded new contracts to 56 companies, including four new to the program.

In conjunction with the working groups, FLICC offered a total of 32 seminars, workshops, and lunchtime discussions to nearly 1,000 members of the federal library and information center community. Institutes and workshops looked at cataloging, taxonomy, preservation and disaster planning, project management, copyright, digital content management, Web 2.0, and career development. FLICC also collaborated with the Capital Consortium Library Network (CAP-CON) on educational events by co-promoting programs and opening events up to each other's members when additional registrations were available.

A new luncheon series, Learning @ Lunch, began in FY 2008 and featured a variety of topics and speakers. The series highlighted the Library of Congress Science, Technology, and Business Division; Washington Research Library Consortium; and the Defense Technical Information Center. Topics discussed included Managing Space and Earth Science Information in a Non-Bibliographic Environment; Employment Interviews; Librarian's Novelist: Life as a Lawyer, Librarian, and Novelist; Electronic Journals and Online Databases; and Future of the Peer-Reviewed Journal.

Staff members also served as principal speakers and leaders at a variety of national information community and professional association committees and conferences including the American Society for Information Science and Technology (ASIS&T), National Federation of Abstracting and Indexing Services (NFAIS), Military Librarians Workshop, Computers in Libraries (CIL), Internet Librarian, and FOSE, a conference and expo for military, government, and government contractors.

FEDLINK also negotiated discounted rates for several national conferences with Information Today, Inc. More than 335 attendees registered through FEDLINK to attend CIL 2008, saving the government approximately $80,000. More than 40 attendees registered through FEDLINK for WebSearch University, saving the government $10,000. Three FEDLINK members registered for the Internet Librarian conference for a savings of $1,000. FEDLINK also brokered member attendance at both the Joint Spring Workshop and the Special Libraries Association (SLA) annual conference, with 33 FEDLINK members registering through FEDLINK for the workshop, saving $1,000, and 8 attendees registering for the SLA annual conference through FEDLINK to take advantage of an extended early bird rate.

FEDLINK worked closely with its partner LC/ITS to complete the requirements documentation for the FEDLINK Customer Financial Management System (FEDLINK CFMS) that will significantly enhance the ability of vendors and member agencies to sell and buy information services online. FEDLINK CFMS will replace the program's Online IAG Customer Registration System that continues to operate while LC/ITS develops and tests the new system.

The FEDLINK Systems Office (FSO) also successfully released CCM Mercury, a document imaging and management system recommended by LC/ITS to replace the program's antiquated LAVA document system.

FEDLINK's financial management efforts also ensured that FEDLINK successfully passed the library's financial audit of FY 2007 transactions.

## Quarterly Membership Meetings

In addition to FLICC Working Group updates and reports from FLICC/FEDLINK staff members, each FLICC quarterly meeting included a special meeting focus on a variety of broad federal information issues including strategic planning for federal information organizations and libraries with a showcase from the Library of Congress, Government Printing Office, and the National Library of Medicine; the Library of Congress preservation strategy and disaster planning initiatives; skill sets and services for future federal librarians; and a variety of special reports on the National Agricultural Library, NASA Goddard Library, the Online Computer Library Center (OCLC), and a number of library association efforts.

## Executive Board

The FLICC Executive Board focused its efforts on a number of initiatives relating to the FLICC/FEDLINK Business Plan, the future of the Environmental Protection Agency and NASA libraries and other agency libraries, a federal library census, and FLICC's efforts with Safety Net and other preservation strategies and disaster planning.

## FLICC Working Groups

In addition to the activities outlined under "Highlights of the Year" above, FLICC working groups were involved in the following activities:

### Awards

To honor the innovative ways in which federal libraries, librarians, and library technicians fulfill the information demands of government, business, research, scholarly communities, and the American public, the Awards Working Group administered a series of national awards for federal librarianship.

The Federal Library/Information Center of the Year award, large library/information center category (for libraries with a staff of 11 or more federal and/or contract employees) went to the Combined Arms Research Library (CARL), U.S. Army Command and General Staff College, Fort Leavenworth, Kansas, which was recognized for its superior provision of a wide range of services to its 8,000 students, faculty, scholars, staff, and the Army community at large. In the small library/information center category (for libraries with a staff of ten or fewer federal and/or contract employees), the honors went to Landstuhl Regional Medical Center (LRMC) Library, Landstuhl, Germany, which is recognized for its world-class research facility that specializes in medical and dental medicine resources and serves numerous military medical facilities in Europe, Africa, and the Middle East.

The Federal Librarian of the Year award went to Thomas F. Lahr, deputy associate biologist for information, U.S. Geological Survey (USGS), Reston, Virginia, and the Federal Library Technician of the Year honors were awarded to Jill Golden, Marshall Center Research Library, Garmisch-Partenkirchen, Germany.

### Budget and Finance

In the spring quarter the Budget and Finance Working Group developed the FY 2009 FEDLINK budget and fee structure. The group produced an online budget questionnaire for FEDLINK members and used the results to verify assumptions for the FY 2009 budget. The final budget for FY 2009 reduced membership fees for transfer-pay customers 1 percent below FY 2008 levels—6.75 percent on accounts up to $300,000, 6 percent on amounts exceeding $300,000, and 5 percent on amounts exceeding $1,000,000. Direct-pay fees remained at FY 2008 levels, as did Direct Express fees of 0.75 percent for all participating commercial online information services vendors. Library of Congress officials approved the budget in September.

### Consortia and InterAgency Cooperative Activities

The mandate of the FLICC Consortia and InterAgency Cooperative Activities (CIC) Working Group is to look at consortial opportunities with publishers, in a given discipline, for consulting services and for purchases of library technology or integrated library systems. Formed in FY 2008, CIC further explored group purchases of selected services. It assisted FEDLINK staff and the FEDLINK Advisory Council in benchmarking a national plan for one major scientific publisher and recommended further discussions with another. It recommended establishing a temporary detail to FLICC/FEDLINK to help the program document and market existing consortia opportunities, establish more consortia discounts, and improve internal record-keeping and communication strategies for group discounts. The working group and the FEDLINK Advisory Council also cooperated in an examination of ways FLICC/FEDLINK can assist federal libraries that need to improve automation of in-house library functions.

### Education

During FY 2007 the Education Working Group, in concert with other FLICC working groups, sponsored a total of 32 seminars, workshops, and lunchtime discussions for members of the federal library and information center community. These programs focused on cataloging, taxonomy, preservation and disaster planning, project management, copyright, digital content management, Web 2.0, and career development.

### Libraries and Emerging Technologies

The Libraries and Emerging Technologies Working Group sponsored a program as part of the ALA Annual Conference with the ALA Federal and Armed Forces Libraries Round Table (FAFLRT) on Web 2.0 tools used in the federal government, and released the report *Leadership in Uncertain Times: Federal Librarians Envision Use of Physical Space Through 2020,* the product of a survey of librarians, a literature review on the related subject areas, and the collective experiences of the authors of the paper. The result is an extensive review of issues facing federal librarians as they plan for the provision of services and collections within their own agency or departments.

### Nominating

The Nominating Working Group oversaw the 2008 election process for FLICC rotating members, FLICC Executive Board members, the FEDLINK Advisory Council, and an OCLC Members Council Delegate. Librarians representing a variety of federal agencies agreed to place their names in nomination for these positions.

### Policy and Advocacy

The FLICC Marketing Subcommittee was tasked by the Policy and Advocacy Working Group to create materials for two audiences, federal librarians and federal managers (non-librarians) who must communicate the value of libraries and the role libraries play in federal agencies. In early 2008 the subcommittee delivered three important marketing products: marketing survey results regarding member marketing issues, best practices, benchmarking, and return on investment information; marketing exemplars from the federal community that are now housed on the FLICC Web site; and the final Marketing and Advocacy Resources Bibliography publication.

## Executive Director's Office

In addition to strategic planning and administrative efforts, FLICC responded to a call from the Department of Homeland Security (DHS) Library Program Office to conduct a research study to develop a strategy and change-management plan for establishing a library and information service to support the consolidation of the department's headquarters. FLICC collaborated with the Library of Congress Federal Research Service to conduct a comprehensive study and provide recommendations on the feasibility of functional integration of DHS library services, centralization of their collections, and co-location of their staff and functions.

FLICC also sponsored its first annual Career/Job Fair for Information Professionals in the Federal Government with nearly 150 attendees, 15 exhibiting organizations, and 24 organizational representatives from civilian and defense agencies. Follow-up surveys rated the fair as excellent and have sparked interested within the broader federal information community and academia.

Staff also participated in the annual Blacks in Government (BIG) conference and was active within the library's BIG chapter as well as the Diversity Advisory Council and the Cultural Observance Committee.

## Publications and Education Office

During FY 2008 FLICC continued its publication program as a digital communication provider and used the FEDLIB listserv to communicate critical advocacy and program information to more than 3,000 electronic subscribers.

It revised mission-critical materials and developed targeted resources to support the FEDLINK program, including revisions to the business plan, and two FEDLINK Information Alerts. FLICC also produced the minutes of the four FY 2008 FLICC Quarterly Meetings and six FLICC Executive Board meetings, and all FLICC Education Program promotional and support materials, including the FLICC Forum announcement, forum attendee and speaker badges, press advisories, speeches and speaker remarks, and forum collateral materials. FLICC produced 32 meeting announcements to promote FLICC education programs, FEDLINK membership and OCLC users' meetings, brown-bag discussion series and education institutes, and badges, programs, certificates of completion, and other supporting materials.

FY 2008 also saw the release of FLICC and FEDLINK's redesign of the program Web site. Now in full compliance with Library of Congress Web guidance, staff members managed, converted, supported, and updated the new Web site that includes more than 3,000 pages of content, video, and resource links.

FLICC staff members continued to convert all publications, announcements, alerts, member materials, meeting minutes, and working group resources into HTML and pdf formats. Staff also participated in the Federal Consortium on Second Life as part of ongoing efforts to influence federal agency use of Web 2.0 emerging technologies.

FLICC increased its distance-learning offerings by using Web conferencing software for a number of its free events, and incorporated electronic versions of PowerPoint and other presentation materials to enhance access to the resources available at educational programs.

To make the discussions and presentations at FLICC quarterly membership meetings available for members at remote locations, staff members recorded these sessions and distributed copies in DVD format. Staff members also tested several Web conferencing services to offer remote participants live and interactive attendance to these and other meetings.

In collaboration with FEDLINK Network Operations staff members, the publications staff continued to offer resources for the FEDLINK members/vendors forums, OCLC usage analysis reports, pricing data, and many other new documents, including the FY 2008 budget questionnaire and ballot, the FLICC/FEDLINK customer survey in support of the business plan, and a variety of training resources. Staff members also worked with Library of Congress contracts and gifts staff to make electronic versions of FEDLINK's Requests for Proposals available online for prospective vendors.

Publications staff members continued to support the member services unit and its online registration/online interagency agreement (IAG) system.

In conjunction with the working groups, FLICC offered a total of 32 seminars, workshops, and lunchtime discussions to 999 members of the federal library and information center community. Institutes and workshops looked at Web writing, preservation and disaster planning, project management, copyright, digital content management, Web 2.0, and career development.

FLICC continued its ongoing commitment to continuing education by hosting its popular institute for federal library technicians and its annual teleconference series "Soaring to . . . Excellence," produced by the College of DuPage. Federal and academic librarians also joined FLICC professionals to discuss various areas of librarianship, including peer-reviewed literature, taxonomies, acquisitions, cataloging, copyright laws, reference, and automation. The ongoing FLICC Great Escapes series returned in FY 2008 with library tours at the U.S. Department of the Interior Library, the Holocaust Museum Library, and the Brookings Institution.

FLICC provided organizational, promotional, and logistical support for FEDLINK meetings and events including the FEDLINK fall and spring membership meetings and 74 vendor presentations attended by 318 customers.

## FEDLINK

During FY 2008 FEDLINK (the Federal Library and Information Network) continued to give federal agencies cost-effective access to an array of automated information retrieval services for online research, cataloging, information management, and resource sharing. FEDLINK members also procured print serials, electronic journals, print and electronic books, sound recordings, audiovisual materials, document delivery, technical processing services, digitization, and preservation and conservation services via Library of Congress/FEDLINK contracts with approximately 130 major vendors. The program obtained further discounts for customers through consortia and enterprise-wide licenses for journals, aggregated information retrieval services, and books.

FEDLINK awarded new contracts for electronic retrieval services and competed requirements for serials subscription services for seven agencies under contracts with seven serial subscription agents. FEDLINK staff assisted seven agencies in using the preservation contracts to digitize and conserve special collections and create related metadata. Seven other agencies received help in procuring contract cataloging services.

The FEDLINK Advisory Council (FAC) met six times during the fiscal year. In addition to general oversight activities, the council provided insight into trends in the information industry.

The annual fall FEDLINK Membership meeting featured an overview of SERU (Serials E-Resources Understanding), an alternative to license agreements between libraries and information providers, with an analysis of how federal agencies might adapt it for their use. The afternoon vendor forum provided a forecast of trends in publishing. The spring FEDLINK membership meeting featured MaryBeth Dowdell, chair of the FLICC Budget and Finance Working Group, who presented the proposed budget for FY 2009, and a special "town meeting" on federal librarian competencies. The afternoon vendor forum presented a showcase of EbscoHost's Business Book Review product and a lesson on purpose alignment and positioning.

In support of outreach, FLICC/FEDLINK staff continued to support Web conferencing via the Elluminate application, and to produce a monthly electronic newsletter. They visited 20 federal agencies around the country to provide consultation on-site.

In the fall and spring, FEDLINK collaborated with CAPCON (now OCLC Eastern) to sponsor joint OCLC QuestionPoint Users Group meetings to help libraries share information about implementation and user training issues, and to provide updates on new functionality.

Eleanor Frierson, acting director of the National Agricultural Library, and Suzanne Ryder, chief librarian at the Naval Research Laboratory Library, represented FEDLINK on the OCLC Members Council where they added a federal perspective to the larger issues in librarianship and information science and contributed to plans that meet the cooperative needs of libraries and similar institutions.

FEDLINK staff highlighted services at national conferences, including those of the American Library Association and the Special Libraries Association (SLA), and the Government Accountability Office expo, presenting information about federal information needs.

At the North American Serials Interest Group (NASIG) conference, FEDLINK discussed federal libraries' needs in a discussion about increasing NASIG's relevancy to non-academic libraries.

Staff members also participated in additional national conferences, workshops, and meetings, including those of CENDI, the American Society for Information Science and Technology (ASIS&T), and the National Federation of Abstracting and Indexing Services (NFAIS), as well as SLA's Military Librarians Workshop, Computers in Libraries (CIL), Internet Librarian, and FOSE (the Federal Office Systems Exposition).

**FEDLINK Fiscal Operations**

FEDLINK continued to enhance its fiscal operations while providing its members with $70.8 million in transfer-pay services, $5.4 million in direct-pay services, and an estimated $34.1 million in Direct Express services, saving federal agencies more than $14.6 million in vendor volume discounts and approximately $16.1 million more in cost avoidance.

FLICC's governing bodies and FEDLINK staff members revisited the five-year business plan to support requirements of the Fiscal Operations Improvement Act of 2000 (P.L. 106-481) that created revolving fund statutory authority for FEDLINK's fee-based activities. The focus of the review was to assess performance in FY 2008 and update strategic initiatives and financial objectives for FY 2009 through FY 2013.

Staff members supported business plan goals for improving processes and expanding the market for product and services through the following initiatives: reducing fees one percentage point for transfer-pay customer procurements for FY 2009, implementing procedures for using pay.gov to for federal customer credit card purchases under $100,000 and vendor Direct Express payments to FEDLINK; streamlining invoicing and payment processes; and meeting with selected vendors to review requirements and acquire company data for electronic invoicing.

## Figure 1 / FLICC Educational Events for FY 2008

| Event | Attendees |
| --- | --- |
| Great Escape/LC Science, Technology and Business Division | 39 |
| Managing Space and Earth Science Information | 5 |
| Washington Research Library Consortium | 9 |
| Tough Questions—Good Answers: Taking Control of Any Interview | 15 |
| Planning for Results: Making Data Work for You | 24 |
| Soaring to Excellence Session 1 | 20 |
| Soaring to Excellence Session 2 | 20 |
| Soaring to Excellence Session 3 | 20 |
| Librarian's Novelist: Life as a Lawyer, Librarian, and Novelist | 10 |
| Great Escape: Brookings Institution Library | 28 |
| DTIC: 60 Years of Providing Defense Information for All | 10 |
| The Art of Strategic Persuasion: Essential Skills for Leaders | 5 |
| Demystifying the Latest Business Literature | 13 |
| Joint Spring Workshop 2008 | 148 |
| Talent Mentoring, Mining, and Management in the Federal Sector | 49 |
| Writing for the Web | 8 |
| Series: Electronic Journals Online Databases | 9 |
| Fall QuestionPoint Users Group Meeting | 41 |
| Spring QuestionPoint Users Group Meeting | 31 |
| Creating Wikis and E-Newsletters | 18 |
| Spring FEDLINK Membership Meeting | 70 |
| Purpose-Alignment-Positioning | 13 |
| Integrating Safety Net Tools into Your Agency's COOP | 61 |
| Future of the Peer-Reviewed Journal | 9 |
| Issues in Federal and Armed Forces Libraries | 34 |
| Institute for Federal Technicians | 57 |
| Great Escapes: The Holocaust Museum Library | 46 |
| Great Escapes: U.S. Naval Observatory | 20 |
| Great Escapes: Department of the Interior Library | 18 |
| FLICC Forum on Federal Information Policies | 109 |
| FEDScan Tours | 50 |
| Total | 999 |

### Direct Express Services

The FEDLINK Direct Express Program now includes nearly 70 vendors offering database retrieval services. The program provides procurement and payment options similar to those of the General Services Administration under which the vendors pay a quarterly service fee to FEDLINK based on customer billings for usage. The Direct Express program generated 59 percent of the fee revenue initially anticipated in the budget and the forecast for FY 2008.

### Budget and Revenue

During FY 2008 FEDLINK fee revenue from signed interagency agreements (IAGs) was approximately 0.2 percent, or $8,637 below FY 2007 levels, and was 3.2 percent, or $172,762, less than the FY 2008 budget. The FEDLINK fee revenue is expected to exceed FY 2008 expenditure obligations by $254,901. The program holds reserves for mandatory requirements of $1,498,597 for shutdown and bankruptcy risks and continuity of operations requirements of $980,000 for mission-essential systems and compliance risk mitigation initiatives.

### Financial Systems

The FEDLINK program began several initiatives to upgrade and restructure its customer support systems to meet the objectives of the FEDLINK business plan and to give customers a more secure and user-friendly environment to acquire FEDLINK services. FEDLINK worked to complete documentation for the FEDLINK Customer Financial Management System (FEDLINK CFMS), which will significantly enhance the ability of vendors and member agencies to perform online transactions for services. FEDLINK CFMS will replace the program's On-line IAG Customer Registration System, which continues to operate in the meantime.

### Financial Management, Reporting, and Control

FEDLINK successfully passed the Library of Congress Financial Audit for FY 2007 transactions and completed vulnerability assessments of program financial risks. As a follow-up requirement, staff members completed detail-control reviews of program financial operations.

# National Center for Education Statistics Library Statistics Program

U.S. Department of Education, Institute of Education Sciences
Elementary/Secondary and Libraries Studies Division
1990 K St. N.W., Washington, DC 20006

Adrienne Chute and Tai A. Phan

In an effort to collect and disseminate more-complete statistical information about libraries, the National Center for Education Statistics (NCES) initiated a formal library statistics program in 1989 that included surveys on academic libraries, school library media centers, public libraries, and state libraries. At the end of December 2007, the Public Libraries Survey and the State Library Agencies Survey were officially transferred to the Institute of Museum and Library Services' (IMLS's) Office of Library Programs. The Academic Libraries Survey (ALS) and the School Library Media Centers Survey (SLMCS) continue to be administered and funded by NCES, and are under the leadership of Tai A. Phan, program director, Library Statistics Program. [For detailed information on the surveys now being handled by IMLS, see "Institute of Museum and Library Services Library Programs" in Part 2—*Ed.*]

The library surveys conducted by NCES are designed to provide comprehensive nationwide data on the status of libraries. Federal, state, and local officials, professional associations, and local practitioners use these surveys for planning, evaluating, and making policy. These data are also available to researchers and educators.

The Library Statistics Program's Web site (http://nces.ed.gov/surveys/libraries) provides links to data search tools, data files, survey definitions, and survey designs for each survey. The two surveys still conducted by NCES—ALS and SLMCS—are described below.

## Academic Libraries

The Academic Libraries Survey provides descriptive statistics from approximately 3,600 academic libraries in the 50 states, the District of Columbia, and the outlying areas of the United States. NCES surveyed academic libraries on a three-year cycle between 1966 and 1988. From 1988 to 1998, the survey was a component of the Integrated Postsecondary Education Data System (IPEDS), and was on a two-year cycle. Beginning with fiscal year 2000, ALS is no longer a component of IPEDS, but it remains on a two-year cycle. IPEDS and ALS data can still be linked by the identification codes of the postsecondary education institutions. In aggregate, these data provide an overview of the status of academic libraries nationally and by state. ALS collects data on libraries in the entire universe of degree-granting postsecondary institutions, using a Web-based data collection system.

ALS has an established working group composed of representatives of the academic library community. Its mission is to improve data quality and the timeliness of data collection, processing, and release. NCES also works cooperatively with the American Library Association, the Association of Research Libraries, the Association of College and Research Libraries, and academic libraries in the collection of ALS data.

ALS collects data on the number of academic libraries, operating expenditures, full-time-equivalent library staff, service outlets, collection size, circulation, interlibrary loans, number of public service hours, library visits, reference transactions, consortia services, number of presentations, attendance at presentations, and electronic services. Academic libraries are also asked whether they provide reference services by e-mail or the Internet, technology for patrons with disabilities, and whether documents are digitized by library staff.

A First Look report, *Academic Libraries, 2006,* (NCES 2008-337) was released on the NCES Web site in July 2008. The final data file and documentation for the 2006 ALS public use data file were also released on the Web site in July 2008. NCES has developed a Web-based peer analysis tool for ALS called "Compare Academic Libraries," which currently uses the ALS 2006 data.

## School Library Media Centers

National surveys of school library media centers in elementary and secondary schools in the United States were conducted in 1958, 1962, 1974, 1978, 1986, 1993–1994, 1999–2000, and 2003–2004. Data collection for the 2007–2008 survey began during fall 2007 and ended in spring 2008. The 2007–2008 data will be available later in 2009.

NCES, with the assistance of the U.S. Bureau of the Census, conducts the School Library Media Centers Survey as part of the Schools and Staffing Survey (SASS). SASS is the nation's largest sample survey of teachers, schools, and principals in U.S. K–12 public and private schools. Data from the SLMCS questionnaire provide a national picture of school library staffing, collections, expenditures, technology, and services. Findings from the 2003–2004 survey can be found in *Characteristics of Schools, Districts, Teachers, Principals, and School Libraries in the United States: 2003–2004 Schools and Staffing Survey* (NCES 2006-313).

NCES also published a historical report about school libraries, *Fifty Years of Supporting Children's Learning: A History of Public School Libraries and Federal Legislation from 1953–2000.* Drawn from more than 50 sources, this report presents descriptive data about public school libraries since 1953. Along with key characteristics of school libraries, the report also presents national and regional standards, and federal legislation affecting school library media centers.

NCES has included library-oriented questions on the parent and the teacher instruments of its new Early Childhood Longitudinal Study (ECLS). For more information, visit http://nces.ed.gov/ecls. Library items also appear in National Household Education Survey (NHES) instruments. For more information about that survey, visit http://nces.ed.gov/nhes.

NCES also included a questionnaire about high school library media centers in the Education Longitudinal Study of 2002 (ELS: 2002). This survey collected data from tenth graders about their schools, their school library media centers, their communities, and their home life. The report *School Library Media*

*Centers: Selected Results from the Education Longitudinal Study of 2002* (ELS: 2002) (NCES 2005-302) is available on the NCES Web site. For additional information about this survey, visit http://nces.ed.gov/surveys/els2002.

Additional information on school library media center statistics and academic library statistics is available from Tai A. Phan, Elementary/Secondary and Libraries Studies Division, National Center for Education Statistics, Room 9026, 1990 K St. N.W., Washington, DC 20006, telephone 202-502-7431, e-mail tai. phan@ed.gov.

## How to Obtain Printed and Electronic Products

Reports are currently published in NCES's First Look format. First Look reports consist of a short collection of tables presenting state and national totals, a survey description, and data highlights. NCES also publishes separate, more in-depth studies analyzing these data.

### Internet Access

Many NCES publications (including out-of-print publications) and edited raw data files from the library surveys are available for viewing or downloading at no charge through the electronic catalog on the NCES Web site at http://nces.ed. gov/pubsearch.

### Ordering Printed Products

Many NCES publications are also available in printed format. To order one free copy of recent NCES reports, contact the Education Publications Center (ED Pubs) at http://www.edpubs.org, by e-mail at edpubs@edpubs.ed.gov, by toll-free telephone at 877-433-7827 (TTY/TDD 877-576-7734), by fax at 301-470-1244, or by mail at ED Pubs, P.O. Box 1398, Jessup, MD 20794-1398.

Many publications are available through the Education Resources Information Center (ERIC) system. For more information on services and products, visit http://www.eric.ed.gov. [For more information on the products available from ERIC, see "Education Resources Information Center" later in Part 1—*Ed.*]

Out-of-print publications and data files may be available through the NCES Electronic Catalog on the NCES Web site at http://nces.ed.gov/pubsearch or from the 1,250 federal depository libraries throughout the United States at http:// www.gpoaccess.gov/libraries.html. Use the NCES publication number included in the citations for publications and data files to quickly locate items in the NCES Electronic Catalog; use the GPO number to locate items in a federal depository library.

# Defense Technical Information Center

Fort Belvoir, VA 22060
703-767-8217
World Wide Web http://www.dtic.mil

Sandy Schwalb
Public Affairs Officer

The Defense Technical Information Center (DTIC) has served the information needs of the defense community for more than 60 years. DTIC is the central facility for the collection, storage, retrieval, and dissemination of scientific and technical information for the Department of Defense (DoD). DTIC is a DoD "field activity," which is an organization whose work reaches across all segments of DoD. In the office of the Under Secretary of Defense (Acquisition, Technology, and Logistics), DTIC reports to the Director, Defense Research and Engineering (DDR&E), and

- Provides controlled access to DoD information
- Is a vital link in the transfer of information among the defense-related government and civilian research and development communities
- Is a primary provider of Web services for organizations within DoD

DTIC is located in the Andrew T. McNamara Headquarters Complex Building at Fort Belvoir, Virginia, and has four regional offices, whose addresses appear at the end of this article.

## New 'DTIC Online'

In summer 2008 DTIC launched the new DTIC Online, a redesigned public Web site for DoD scientific and technical (S&T) information. This new site integrates three of DTIC's public Web sites: DTIC Search, DTIC Home, and its Public Scientific and Technical Information Network (STINET).

"This consolidation provides DTIC customers with a single point of entry to S&T information," DTIC Administrator R. Paul Ryan said. "While the new site includes users' favorite products and resources, enhancements have been made to improve navigation and provide access to more resources in one location."

DTIC's MultiSearch is enhanced in DTIC Online (http://multisearch.dtic.mil). This tool is a portal to the "deep" Web for government scientific and technical information, which searches content below the "surface" Web for information not accessible through commercial and government search engines. This search feature assists the DoD community in accessing S&T information over a wide range of DoD, federal, commercial, and international sources, which include DTIC collections, Science.gov, the Library of Congress, WorldWideScience.org, and Scitopia.org.

In addition, a new feature available in DTIC Online is Interest Area pages that provide links to pertinent information for specific S&T research communities.

## DoDTechipedia

DoDTechipedia, a DoD scientific and technical wiki, was launched in October 2008. DTIC developed and hosts DoDTechipedia, which offers an opportunity for the defense community to take advantage of wiki technology and share science and technology information more efficiently. It is designed to increase communication and collaboration among DoD scientists, engineers, program managers, and military personnel in the field.

## 2008 PEO Workshop

DTIC hosted its first event geared toward the defense acquisition community. Titled "Rapid Access to Technical Information Supporting Defense Acquisition," this acquisition and life cycle management symposium took place in Huntsville, Alabama, November 18–19. This meeting was geared toward Program Executive Officers (PEOs) and program managers.

Objectives of the workshop were to position DTIC as an agent of information excellence within DoD, to educate key stakeholders in the PEO community, and to provide an opportunity for networking and fostering relationships. Through this type of event, DTIC educates others in the DoD community as to how DTIC can help them do their jobs.

More than 100 attendees participated. Participants heard keynote addresses by Brig. Gen. R. Mark Brown, Commanding General, Soldier Systems Center, Natick, Massachusetts, and Randy Fowler, Assistant Deputy Under Secretary of Defense (Materiel Readiness). A highlight of the symposium was an interactive question-and-answer session between DTIC personnel and the audience, which provided DTIC with immediate feedback on how to better serve this community.

## Security of Information

While there is much publicly accessible material in the DTIC collection (in fact, nearly half of DoD's technical reports are publicly available the day they are published), some information is restricted by security classifications. The DoD's scientific and technical information is always categorized (or "marked," which is the term used in the defense community) by the office that originates the document. This marking determines how, and to whom, the information can be disseminated.

Some information is marked to protect national security. DTIC's databases contain such classified information, which may be marked "confidential" or "secret."

DTIC's databases also contain information that, although not classified, is still sensitive for various reasons. These documents are marked to show why the information is sensitive and with whom the document can be shared. Such documents are considered "unclassified, limited." Information in DTIC's databases that is neither classified nor limited can be released to the public and is referred to as "unclassified, unlimited."

The information in DTIC's collection is 51 percent "unclassified, unlimited," 40 percent "unclassified, limited," and 9 percent "classified."

## Resources

DTIC's holdings include technical reports on completed research; research summaries of planned, ongoing, and completed work; independent research and development summaries; defense technology transfer agreements; DoD planning documents; DoD directives and instructions; conference proceedings; security classification guides; command histories; and special collections that date back to World War II. DoD-funded researchers are required to search DTIC's collections to ensure that they do not "reinvent the wheel" and undertake unnecessary or redundant research.

The scope of DTIC's collection includes areas normally associated with defense research. DoD's interests are widespread, however; types of information found in DTIC include agriculture; atmospheric sciences; behavioral and social sciences; human factors engineering; "information warfare"; mathematic and computer sciences; nuclear science and technology; propulsion, engines, and fuels; radiation studies; and virtual reality.

## Registering for Services

DTIC offers its information services to a diverse population of the defense community. Due to the nature of the information that DTIC handles, users must qualify for services. In December 2008 DTIC had nearly 23,000 registered users. DTIC's customers include engineers, scientists, program managers, policy analysts, planners, and information specialists, working for DoD, other U.S. government agencies, and their contractors. DTIC's customers can be found in academia, the intelligence community, foreign governments (e.g., through negotiated agreements with Australia, Canada, France, Germany, the Netherlands, South Korea, and Britain) and also include military school students and taxpayers.

Registered users can order documents directly from DTIC. Individuals who are not eligible to register with DTIC can order "unclassified, unlimited" documents by contacting the National Technical Information Service (NTIS) at 800-553-NTIS (553-6847) or by visiting http://www.ntis.gov.

## DTIC's Primary Collections

The DTIC Technical Reports (TR) database contains more than 2 million reports in print, nonprint (CDs, DVDs, software, data files, databases and video recordings), and electronic formats conveying the results of defense-sponsored research, development, test, and evaluation efforts. It includes journal articles, DoD-sponsored patent applications, studies, analyses, open source literature from foreign countries, conference proceedings, and theses. Between 25,000 and 30,000 new documents are added each year.

The Research Summaries (RS) database contains descriptions of DoD research that provide information on technical content, responsible individuals and organizations, principal investigators, and funding sources at the work unit level. Available only to certain registered users, this collection is controlled by individual access restrictions. The collection consists of approximately 313,000 active and inactive summaries from 1965 to the present.

The Independent Research and Development (IR&D) database contains more than 172,000 descriptions (dating back to the mid-1970s) of research and development projects initiated and conducted by defense contractors independent of DoD control and without direct DoD funding. On average, almost $3 billion worth of IR&D projects are submitted to DTIC annually. The database includes basic and applied research, technology development efforts, and systems and concept formulation studies. Defense contractors and potential contractors are encouraged to submit project descriptions to the IR&D database. Accessible only to U.S. government organizations, the proprietary IR&D information is used to identify contractors with expertise in areas of interest to DoD and to avoid DoD duplication of industry R&D efforts.

## Information Sources

DTIC information is derived from many sources: DoD organizations (civilian and military) and DoD contractors; U.S. government organizations and their contractors; nonprofit organizations working on DoD scientific, research, and engineering activities; academia; and foreign governments. DTIC accepts information in print, nonprint (CDs and DVDs), and electronically via the Internet. DTIC gets information from the defense community, for the defense community, about defense and beyond. Having a full range of science and technology and research and development information within the DTIC collection ensures that technological innovations are linked to defense development and acquisition efforts. New research projects can begin with the highest level of information available. This avoids duplication of effort, maximizing the use of DoD project dollars.

## Training Opportunities

Free training is available to DTIC registered users at its Fort Belvoir, Virginia, headquarters and its four regional offices listed below. Training can be arranged off site if the instructor's travel costs are borne by the host organization/user. Customized courses can also be provided.

A three-day, hands-on class, "Searching DTIC Databases," covers methods for searching and retrieving scientific, research, and engineering information in the DTIC collection. The course provides additional information about a variety of Defense-related resources and services.

DTIC offers a three-day course designed to acquaint Scientific and Technical Information (STINFO) managers and other interested personnel with the requirements of the DoD Scientific and Technical Information Program. Marking documents and contract reporting requirements are covered. A one-day STINFO manager overview covers the highlights. A customized class that examines the rationale and mechanics of marking technical documents is available by arrangement with the instructor.

For additional training information, visit http://www.dtic.mil, click on DTIC A-Z, and select Training.

## Web Hosting Expertise

An early pioneer in Internet use for information dissemination, DTIC has designed and hosted more than 100 Web sites sponsored by components of the Office of the Secretary of Defense, military service headquarters organizations, and several defense agencies. DTIC also supports many DoD components in developing tools and processes that enhance the storage, retrieval, and use of information. An effective support program has been created for senior-level planners and other users of information resources. This shared infrastructure allows many organizations to obtain technologies and resources that no single organization could afford on its own.

Some of the many Web sites DTIC hosted in 2008 were

- The Federal Voting Assistance Program (FVAP), which provides absentee voting information to U.S. citizens who live outside the United States
- The Regional Air Movement Control Center, which provides support to flights over Iraq and Afghanistan
- The Defense Prisoner of War/Mission Personnel Office, which supports the recovery of Americans who are lost in a hostile environment

## Information Analysis Centers

Another facet of DTIC administrative activities is the management and funding of contractor-operated joint service-oriented Information Analysis Centers (IACs), which are research organizations. Chartered by DoD, IACs identify, analyze, and use scientific and technical information in specific technology areas. They also develop information and analysis products for the defense science and engineering communities. IACs are staffed by experienced technical area scientists, engineers, and information specialists who help users locate and analyze scientific and technical information in specific subject areas. They improve productivity in the defense research, development, and acquisition communities. For more information on IACs, visit http://iac.dtic.mil.

The DTIC-managed IACs as of January 2009 were AMMTIAC (Advanced Materials, Manufacturing, and Testing Information IAC); CBRNIAC (Chemical, Biological, Radiological, Nuclear Defense IAC); CPIAC (Chemical Propulsion IAC); DACS (Data and Analysis Center for Software); IATAC (Information Assurance Technology Analysis Center); MSIAC (Modeling and Simulation IAC); RIAC (Reliability IAC); SENSIAC (Sensors IAC); SURVIAC (Survivability IAC); and WSTIAC (Weapons Systems Technology IAC).

Many of the products and services produced by IACs are free of charge and include announcements of reports relevant to the particular IAC's field of interest, authoritative bibliographic search reports, the latest scientific and engineering information on specific technical subjects, consultation with or referral to world-recognized technical experts, and status of current technologies. The Total Electronic Migration System (TEMS), a gateway to the IAC collection, is available online. TEMS gives DTIC registered users the ability to perform full-text searches and retrieve mission-critical information.

## QuestionPoint

DTIC is a participating member of QuestionPoint, a virtual-reference service developed jointly by the Library of Congress and the Online Computer Library Center (OCLC) and supported by cooperating institutions worldwide. This collaborative digital reference service allows libraries and information centers to expand reference services with shared resources and subject specialists around the world. DTIC is part of the Global Reference Network, a worldwide group of libraries and institutions committed to digital reference, and the Defense Digital Library Research Service (DDLRS), an around-the-clock electronic reference assistance service for DoD libraries.

## Annual Conference

DTIC's 2008 Annual Conference, "Protecting While Sharing Defense Information," was held April 7–9 in Alexandria, Virginia. Attendees included scientists, engineers, and professionals in technology research and development, information science, and acquisition from the DoD, federal, and contractor communities. Government and commercial exhibitors demonstrated their latest information services and technologies. The more than 280 registrants included representatives from the Navy, Air Force, Army, DoD agencies, the contractor community, and academic institutions.

Topics included "Web 2.0 Initiatives and Collaboration in the Federal Government," "Export Control," "Homeland Security Research from A–Z," "DoD Lean Six Sigma Activities," "Journal Articles: Managing Preprints, Reprints and Copyright," and "International Cooperation and Collaboration." The luncheon speaker for the conference was Adrian Cronauer, the military DJ made famous by the movie "Good Morning Vietnam." He currently serves as the special assistant to the director of the Defense POW/Missing Personnel Office (DPMO).

DTIC's 2009 conference, "Defense Scientific and Technical Information: From Discovery to Access," was set for April 6–8, again in Alexandria.

## Outreach

DTIC customers can host, at their location, a briefing or demonstration of DTIC's products and services tailored to the organization's schedule and information needs. For more information, e-mail training@dtic.mil.

## DTIC Review

*DTIC Review* provides the full text of selected technical reports and a bibliography of other references of interest in one publication. Each volume provides a sampling of documents from the DTIC collection on a specific topic of current interest (see http://www.dtic.mil/dtic/prodsrvc/review/index.html). *DTIC Review* topics in 2008 included non-lethal weapons; intelligent autonomous vehicles; human, social, cultural, and behavior modeling; and introduction to Web 2.0.

## Cooperation and Collaboration

DTIC works with the information and library communities through many partnerships and affiliations. The following are among them:

- CENDI, an interagency working group of senior scientific and technical information managers from a number of U.S. federal agencies including the departments of Commerce, Energy, Interior, and Defense; the National Aeronautics and Space Administration; the Government Printing Office; and the Library of Congress (R. Paul Ryan, DTIC's administrator, served as CENDI's 2006–2008 chair)
- Science.gov, a collaboration of scientific and technical organizations in the federal government, a free gateway to more than 1,700 government information resources about science including technical reports, journal citations, databases, federal Web sites, and fact sheets
- US CODATA (Committee on Data for Science and Technology), whose goal is to improve the compilation, evaluation, storage, and retrieval of data of importance to science and technology
- NFAIS, the National Federation of Advanced Information Services (DTIC was a charter member of this organization, founded in 1958)
- FLICC, the Federal Library and Information Center Committee
- ASIDIC, the Association of Information and Dissemination Centers
- NISO, the National Information Standards Organization
- SLA, the Special Libraries Association

## Military Librarians Workshop

A number of DTIC staff members had leadership roles in planning for the Military Librarians Workshop (MLW) held in December. The conference theme was "Military Library 2.0: the Dawn of a New Revolution," which focused on how library staff, patrons, and facilities are interacting in an ever more digital, global, Web-social, and "usercentric" world. The conference was organized around three themes: Web 2.0 Technologies and Services, Digital Natives and Patron Expectations, and Digital Immigrants and 2.0 Staff Competencies.

DTIC librarians and information specialists were involved in conducting the MLW executive board and business meetings, registering attendees for the workshop, presenting the annual DTIC update, creating and providing the workshop's Web services, and hosting an exhibit table offering DTIC customers and prospective customers consultation and information on new and traditional DTIC products and services. The event is sponsored annually by the Military Librarians Division of SLA.

## DTIC Regional Offices

Midwestern Regional Office
Wright-Patterson Air Force Base, Ohio
Tel. 937-255-7905, fax 937-986-7002
E-mail dayton@dtic.mil

Northeastern Regional Office
Hanscom Air Force Base
Bedford, Massachusetts
Tel. 781-377-2413, fax 781-377-5627
E-mail boston@dtic.mil

Southwestern Regional Office
Kirtland Air Force Base, New Mexico
Tel. 505-846-6797, fax 505-846-6799
E-mail albuq@dtic.mil

Western Regional Office
El Segundo, California
Tel. 310-653-2483, fax 310-353-2159
E-mail losangel@dtic.mil

*Note:* DTIC and STINET are registered service marks of the Defense Technical Information Center.

# National Library of Education

Knowledge Utilization Division
National Center for Education Evaluation and Regional Assistance
Institute of Education Sciences, U.S. Department of Education
400 Maryland Ave. S.W., Washington, DC 20202
World Wide Web http://ies.ed.gov/ncee/projects/nat_ed_library.asp

## Christina Dunn

Director, National Library of Education
202-219-1012, e-mail christina.dunn@ed.gov

The U.S. Department of Education's National Library of Education (NLE) serves the information needs of the education community through two primary programs: the Education Resources Information Center, known as ERIC, and the Education Department Research Library/Reference Center. As part of the department's Institute of Education Sciences, NLE serves as the center for the collection, preservation, discovery, and retrieval of education information—especially information produced by and for the agency—and delivering it to millions of users, including teachers, scholars, students, parents, and others, around the globe.

Created under Public Law 103-227 (the Educational Research, Development, Dissemination, and Improvement Act of 1994) and reauthorized under Public Law 107-279 (the Education Sciences Reform Act of 2002), NLE reports to the Commissioner for Education Evaluation and Regional Assistance. It is required to operate under a director qualified in library science. The director—assisted by six federal staff including the ERIC director and contractors—carries out the four responsibilities stated in the law. The library

- Collects and archives information, including products and publications developed through, or supported by, the Institute of Education Sciences; and other relevant and useful education-related research, statistics, and evaluation materials and other information, projects, and publications that are consistent with scientifically valid research or the priorities and mission of the institute, and developed by the department and other federal agencies or entities

- Provides a central location within the federal government for information about education

- Provides comprehensive reference services on matters relating to education to employees of the Department of Education and its contractors and grantees, other federal employees, and members of the public

- Promotes greater cooperation and resource sharing among providers and repositories of education information in the United States

ERIC and NLE share these responsibilities. Collecting and archiving information, and providing a central location within the federal government for information about education, are primarily addressed through ERIC, while comprehensive reference service is the major focus of the library. Both NLE and

ERIC address promoting cooperation and resource sharing. ERIC, the major public program and outreach arm of NLE, is covered in the following separate article.

## ED Research Library

The Education Department (ED) Research Library/Reference Center—organized into Technical Services and Serials Management, and Reference and Document Delivery—operates with a staff of 13: five full-time federal staff and eight contract librarians. Both staffing and structure have to be flexible and able to respond to user needs, institutional initiatives, and changing technologies quickly and proficiently. To better describe its function as a research resource and to respond to popular demand, since the work of the organization has expanded well beyond traditional reference services, the ED Reference Center is now most often referred to as the ED Research Library. At least 95 percent of service delivery is technology-driven, with services provided to the 5,000 staff of the Department of Education located in Washington, D.C., and in ten regional offices ("education laboratories"), as well as to the agency's various boards, commissions, and contractors; other federal agencies; and the public.

Located at the department's Washington headquarters, the library collects and archives information on education issues, research, statistics, and policy, with a special emphasis on providing historical and current collections of agency documents, journals supporting the ERIC database, research reports supporting the What Works Clearinghouse, and resources supporting current and historical federal education legislation. The print collections now number nearly 93,000 titles.

During 2008 the library continued to develop initiatives begun in 2007, including improving communications and services to agency contractors by expanding virtual reference services. NLE works closely with other Institute of Education Science programs, including ERIC, the What Works Clearinghouse, the National Center for Education Statistics, and the ten regional education laboratories. For the latter, it provides a virtual reference desk service; for all programs, it provides document delivery, reference services, and citation analysis. During 2008 NLE became more active in promoting digital archiving as a solution for organizing documents that support special agency initiatives; it is currently organizing the National Mathematics Advisory Panel's working documents, as well as frequently asked questions from its own and the regional education laboratories' virtual reference desks.

An underlying factor in achieving these initiatives is better marketing of services and collections. In recent times the library has placed more emphasis on marketing and outreach within the agency, and it appears that these efforts are beginning to pay off. Use of the library has increased substantially, and requests for services by agency staff and contractors are up by almost 10 percent over 2006. As part of this effort, NLE has improved its collection and analysis of performance metrics, with findings on usability and user satisfaction driving changes in procedures, collection development and user services, and the overall marketing initiative.

In fiscal year (FY) 2008 the research library/reference center's budget was $1.5 million, the same as in FY 2007.

## Customers

During 2008 use of the center remained about the same as in 2007 at approximately 18,000 requests. Document delivery and interlibrary loan continued to grow, while requests for reference assistance declined. Although most information requests continue to come from the general public, most staff time (72 percent) continues to be devoted to responding to the information needs of Education Department staff and contractors. This group generated about 6,200 requests (34 percent of all requests received in 2008), with the agency's research offices and their contractors remaining the heaviest users. Continued promotion of the library's intranet portal to agency staff has resulted in increased usage, although growth has slowed from 2007 when use of the portal almost doubled. In 2008 agency staff accessed journal articles more frequently and conducted more database searches than in 2007. Also, staff seemed to access more services per visit than in the past.

In addition to staff and contractor use, another 4,500 requests (25 percent) came from other libraries, including those in government agencies; most were for interlibrary loan/document delivery services. The general public generated around 7,300 requests (41 percent), with most being for reference assistance. Of these, about 28 percent were referrals generated by the department's EDPubs service, the 1-800-USA-LEARN service, the Regional Education Laboratories Virtual Reference Desk, and the ERIC Help Desk.

Over the years, the characteristics of public users have changed little. More than 68 percent of the general public contacting the center in 2008 continued to be K–12 educators, students in institutions of higher education, or researchers; 29 percent were parents; and about 3 percent were unknown. As in 2007, the majority of these customers continued to access the library by telephone (59 percent) or e-mail (39 percent); only about 2 percent actually visited the facility.

## Collections

The library's collection focus remains the same: education issues (with an emphasis on research and policy) and related topics including law, public policy, economics, urban affairs, sociology, history, philosophy, psychology, cognitive development, and library and information science. During 2008 about 2,400 print monographs and 400 electronic publications, excluding agency documents, were added to the collection, but the number of paid journal subscriptions declined by 20. The total number of subscriptions increased from around 850 to 868, however, as several open access titles were added. About 74 percent of current journal subscriptions are delivered in electronic format, which is the preferred format due to the facility's limited storage capacity and customer demand for desktop accessibility to journal articles.

NLE maintains special collections of documents associated with its parent agency, having a complete collection of ERIC microfiche; research reports supporting the work of the What Works Clearinghouse and special panels, and current and historical publications of or relating to the agency, including a special collection of federal education legislation. Other historical collections include documents and archives of the former National Institute of Education and the former U.S. Office of Education, including reports, studies, manuals, statistical publications, speeches, and policy papers. Together, these collections represent a resource covering the history of the Department of Education and its predecessor agencies. The library also serves as a federal depository library under the U.S. Government Printing Office program.

With the digitization of the ERIC microfiche collection of about 340,000 documents, the library now has electronic access to the full text of all ERIC microfiche indexed between 1966 and 1992. In contrast, the ERIC Web site (http://www.ed.eric.gov) provides public access to those documents for which copyright clearance was obtained; as of December 2008, a total of 191,952 pdf files had been released on the site. All documents from the ERIC microfiche collection are available through interlibrary loan upon request.

## Services

The library's major role is to provide reference and other information services, including legislative reference and statistical information services, to the education community at large, as well as to provide document delivery services to department staff and contractors and interlibrary loan services to other libraries and federal agencies. Services to agency staff and contractors continue to grow, mostly because resources have been focused on this community over the last few years. With the recent availability of the digitized ERIC microfiche collection, the library is beginning to reach out to the education library community. While its service is more indirect, NLE also serves the broader education community through its involvement in the Regional Education Laboratories' Virtual Reference Desk, providing resources to researchers and end users alike.

Of the more than 7,000 inquiries from the general public received in 2008, most pertained to the same issues as in the previous several years: No Child Left Behind requirements, agency programs, student achievement and assessment, teacher quality and preparation, early childhood education, and national statistics. Other topics of public interest in 2008 included agency policy and budget; federal funding to states and local school districts; current education issues in the news such as charter schools, school choice, academic standards, failing schools, and preschool education; and teacher certification requirements. During 2008 inquiries from users in other countries also increased.

The library serves other libraries by lending books and other materials from its collection. During the past year it made available nearly 3,000 items, mostly agency documents, contractor reports, and recent research in the field of education. Most requests are from institutions of higher education, followed by federal and state agencies, and other libraries. Growth in this service line is probably due to a stronger collection of current education research reports, including those from other English-speaking countries, and of government documents, especially historical documents from the department.

Agency staff conducted more than 28,000 searches of the library's databases. Results of these searches coupled with contractor requests for specific titles generated requests for more than 6,000 journal articles and documents. Although more full-text journal articles are available to agency staff online, the number of requests for journal articles and other documents grew slightly over 2007, when there were 5,800 requests. NLE was able to fill about 46 percent of these requests from its own collections; the remaining 54 percent were filled from other sources—about 9 percent were borrowed from other libraries, 33 percent came from document delivery services, and 12 percent were purchased from book vendors and sponsoring organizations. More requests were filled from the library's collections than in past years probably because there has been a concerted effort over the last four years to fill gaps, especially in the journals collection, and to identify and acquire new publications more quickly.

The ED Research Library/Reference Center can be reached by e-mail at library@ed.gov or by telephone at 800-424-1616 (toll free), 202-205-5015, 202-205-5019 (reference desk), 202-205-7561 (TTY), or 202-401-0547 (fax). Located at the U.S. Department of Education Headquarters Building in Washington, D.C., it is open from 9 A.M. to 5 P.M. weekdays, except federal holidays.

# Education Resources Information Center

National Library of Education
National Center for Education Evaluation and Regional Assistance
Institute of Education Sciences, U.S. Department of Education
400 Maryland Ave. S.W., Washington, DC 20202
World Wide Web http://www.eric.ed.gov

## Luna Levinson

Director, ERIC Program
202-208-2321, e-mail Luna.Levinson@ed.gov

The Education Resources Information Center (ERIC), part of the National Library of Education, provides public access to the world's largest collection of education materials comprising more than 1.2 million bibliographic records and 214,000 full-text materials spanning the period 1966 to the present. All of the library functions are administered by the U.S. Department of Education's Institute of Education Sciences (IES).

## Mission and Activities

The mission of ERIC is to provide a comprehensive, easy-to-use, searchable, Internet-based bibliographic and, to the extent possible, full-text database of education research and information for educators, researchers, and the general public. The mission focus on electronic dissemination is a result of a modernization phase that began in 2003 leading to a consolidated digital library model, transitioning from a paper and microfiche collection built over a period of about 35 years by the 16 ERIC clearinghouses.

Activities that fulfill the ERIC mission are broadly categorized as collection development, content authorizations and agreements, acquisitions and processing, database and Web site operations, and communications. These five functions continue to evolve and improve as suggestions and guidance are received from a variety of sources including public comments and the ERIC Steering Committee and ERIC Content Experts. The steering committee and content experts are recognized authorities tasked with advising the ERIC contractor, Computer Sciences Corporation, on activities designed to ensure database quality.

ERIC is a centralized system that uses new technology to serve its primary audience, which includes K–12 teachers and early childhood educators, librarians, school and college administrators, education researchers, education policymakers, instructors and students in teacher preparation programs, parents, and the media and business communities.

## The ERIC Collection

In addition to being the world's largest education library, ERIC is one of the few collections to index non-journal materials as well as journal literature. The largest share of the collection (about 58 percent) consists of citations to journal articles, and a smaller portion (about 42 percent) consists of non-journal materials (gray literature), according to a 2001 estimate. In ERIC, the gray literature consists of research synthesis, dissertations, conference proceedings and selected papers such as keynote speeches, technical reports, policy papers, literature reviews, bibliographies, congressional hearings and reports, reports on federal and state standards, testing and regulations, U.S. Department of Education contractor reports (e.g., What Works Clearinghouse, and the National Center for Education Statistics), and working papers for established research and policy organizations. Providing access to this gray or fugitive literature is one of ERIC's signature strengths.

To support consistency and reliability in content coverage, most education journals are indexed comprehensively, including all articles in each issue. This was not always the policy in ERIC. Currently, ERIC indexes 834 journals comprehensively, whereas in 2003 (before modernization) it covered only 350 journals comprehensively. A small number of journals—66—are now indexed selectively in ERIC, whereas about 650 journals were indexed selectively in 2003. Articles from selectively covered journals are acquired by ERIC subject specialists who determine individual entries for the ERIC database according to the ERIC selection policy.

The broad selection standard provides that all materials added to the ERIC database are directly related to the field of education. The majority of the journals indexed in ERIC are peer-reviewed. The collection scope includes early childhood education through higher education, vocational education, and special education; it includes teacher education, education administration, assessment and evaluation, counseling, information technology, and the academic areas of reading, mathematics, science, environmental education, languages, and social studies. In addition, the collection includes resources addressing one of the three objectives identified in Section 172 of the Education Sciences Reform Act of 2002 (Public Law 107-279): closing the achievement gap, encouraging educational practices that improve academic achievement, and conducting education research.

Following that standard, there are three sets of specific criteria providing guidance for document selection. The quality criteria consist of five basic factors: completeness, integrity, objectivity, substantive merit, and utility/importance. Selection is further determined by sponsorship criteria; preference for inclusion in ERIC is given to those resources with identified sponsorship (for example, professional societies and government agencies). Detailed editorial criteria also provide factors for consideration, especially with regard to journals considered for comprehensive indexing.

All submissions considered for selection must be in digital format and are accompanied by author permission for dissemination. For individual document submissions, authors (copyright holders) register through the ERIC Web site feature My ERIC; follow the steps to enter bibliographic information, abstract, and document file; and submit the electronic document release form authorizing ERIC to disseminate the materials. Journal publishers, associations, and other entities with multiple documents also submit electronic content following guidance and instructions consistent with provider agreements from ERIC. Once publishers have signed an ERIC agreement, files can be submitted by e-mail or disk or by upload to ERIC's ftp site.

The complete list of journals indexed in ERIC, including the years of coverage and the number of articles indexed, is a tool on the ERIC Web site enabling users more easily to identify specific journal literature. Another convenience for users, designed to streamline the process of obtaining full text, is the Find in a Library feature, which leverages the Open URL Gateway and WorldCat to provide a link from ERIC records to electronic and print resources available in libraries. For all journals currently indexed in ERIC, there are links to publishers' Web sites so that users can purchase full-text articles.

Refinements to ERIC's technical architecture continue to improve system functionality and user satisfaction. Usability tests with participant groups including librarians, researchers, and students provide input on issues such as online submission, the Help section, and an extensive range of search operations. With all database enhancements, the development process contributes to increasing accessibility, efficiency, and quality.

Automated systems for acquisition and processing help to reduce the total time required to produce a database record, and most records are processed in less than 30 days. The ERIC bibliographic file is updated weekly on the ERIC Web site, and monthly totals of records published are displayed on the ERIC home page. During 2008 a total of 40,738 new records were published; of this number, 36,919 records represented journal articles and 3,822, non-journal documents. ERIC acquired 4,768 more records in 2008 than in 2007.

## Outreach and the Microfiche Digitization Project

ERIC outreach activities during 2008 included participation in major conventions for key audiences as well as dissemination meetings in the department and across other federal agencies. The American Library Association's Midwinter Meeting in Philadelphia provided an opportunity for ERIC to demonstrate the beta version of an audio tutorial on searching the digital library and to deliver an update on the effort to digitize the ERIC microfiche collection of about 340,000 documents. For other federal agencies involved in digitizing materials, including the Government Printing Office and the National Archives and Records Administration, ERIC provided a summary describing copyright diligence and technical specifications for the ERIC microfiche project. ERIC also exhibited at the American Education Research Association (AERA) annual meeting and conference, and promoted the use of the online submission system that allows authors to upload papers and abstracts electronically for submission to ERIC.

With final refinements following comments from audience groups, ERIC added a series of short, animated tutorials to help searchers use the database and all of its features from basic search functions to Boolean operators. Other tutorials include author search, citation management, combining descriptors, keyword versus descriptors search, phrase search, and truncating terms in a search. The Web site home page was updated to provide specific areas of interest and information to publishers, authors, librarians, and licensors; a news section offers a menu of recent developments such as the ERIC microfiche digitization project.

To increase public access to ERIC records, the department launched a major initiative in October 2006 to convert microfiche full-text documents published by

ERIC between 1966 and 1992 to digital format. The project scope is to digitize and archive microfiche full-text documents containing an estimated 43 million pages and to provide copyright due diligence by seeking permission from the copyright holders to make the electronic version available to users. The electronic images are stored in TIFF format for archival purposes and stored in pdf format for dissemination to users. The conversion and copyright tasks for this project are assigned to the National Archive Publishing Company in Ann Arbor, Michigan. The National Library of Education will retain a digital copy of the complete archive, scheduled for completion in 2009. As of December 2008 there were a total of 191,952 pdf files released to the public and available through the ERIC Web site. News about the ERIC digitization project has been announced on the ERIC Web site, at conferences, including the Federal Depository Library Program and the American Education Research Association, and in letters and posters distributed to university education libraries.

The ERIC digital library is accessible through the government-sponsored Web site as well as through Google, Google Scholar, Yahoo!, MSN, and commercial services such as Cambridge Scientific Abstracts, EBSCO, OCLC FirstSearch, and ProQuest. There were more than 105 million searches of ERIC in 2008.

# National Association and Organization Reports

## American Library Association

50 E. Huron St., Chicago, IL 60611
800-545-2433
World Wide Web http://www.ala.org

James Rettig
President

The American Library Association was founded in 1876 in Philadelphia and later chartered in the Commonwealth of Massachusetts; it is the oldest, largest, and most influential library association in the world. The association's membership of approximately 67,000 includes not only librarians but also library trustees, publishers, and other interested people from every state and many nations. The association serves public, state, school, and academic libraries, plus special libraries for people working in government, commerce and industry, the arts, and the armed services, or in hospitals, prisons, and other institutions.

ALA's mission is "to provide leadership for the development, promotion, and improvement of library and information services and the profession of librarianship in order to enhance learning and ensure access to information for all."

ALA is governed by an elected council—its policy-making body—and an executive board, which acts for the council in the administration of established policies and programs and is the body that manages within this context the affairs of the association, delegating management of the day-to-day operation to the association's executive director. ALA operations are implemented by staff through a structure of programmatic offices and support units. ALA also has 37 standing committees, designated as committees of the association or of its council.

ALA is home to 11 membership divisions, each focused on a type of library or library function. They are the American Association of School Librarians (AASL), the Association of College and Research Libraries (ACRL), the Association for Library Collections and Technical Services (ALCTS), the Association for Library Service to Children (ALSC), the Association of Library Trustees, Advocates, Friends, and Foundations (ALTAFF), the Association of Specialized and Cooperative Library Agencies (ASCLA), the Library and Information Technology Association (LITA), the Library Leadership and Management Association (LLAMA), the Public Library Association (PLA), the Reference and User Services Association (RUSA), and the Young Adult Library Services Association (YALSA).

ALA also hosts roundtables for members who share interests that do not fall within the scope of any of the divisions. A network of affiliates, chapters, and other organizations enables ALA to reach a broad audience.

Key action areas include diversity, equitable access to information and library services, education and lifelong learning, intellectual freedom, advocacy for libraries and the profession, literacy, and organizational excellence.

ALA offices are units of the association that address broad interests and issues of concern to ALA members; they track issues and provide information, services, and products for members and the general public. Current ALA offices are the Chapter Relations Office, the Development Office, the Governance Office, the International Relations Office, the Office for Accreditation, the Office for Diversity, the Office of Government Relations, the Office for Human Resource Development and Recruitment, the Office for Information Technology Policy, the Office for Intellectual Freedom (OIF), the Office for Library Advocacy (OLA), the Office for Literacy and Outreach Services (OLOS), the Office for Research and Statistics (ORS), the Public Information Office (PIO), the Public Programs Office (PPO), and the Washington (D.C.) Office.

ALA headquarters is in Chicago; the Office of Government Relations and Office for Information Technology Policy are housed at ALA's Washington Office. ALA also has an editorial office for *Choice,* a review journal for academic libraries, in Middletown, Connecticut.

ALA is a 501(c)(3) charitable and educational organization.

## Focusing on Connections

During his presidential year, 2008–2009 ALA President James Rettig focused on creating connections—connections among libraries; connections between the communities served and those who make funding and policy decisions; connections with prospective library workers, especially those in groups under-represented in the profession; and connections that allow ALA members to benefit from and contribute to their association and the profession in new ways.

At his inaugural banquet, Rettig, university librarian at the University of Richmond in Virginia, described libraries as "the only agency in American society that provides lifelong learning opportunities to every age group, to every economic group, to all. . . . We play many roles essential to the health and progress of our communities and the nation—proponents of freedom, defenders of access to information, custodians of the cultural record, educators."

Key initiatives addressed three critical issues: advocacy, diversity, and member participation. "I view our school, public, academic, and other types of libraries as parts of an integrated library ecosystem," he said. "If one part of the system is threatened or suffers, the entire system is threatened and suffers. We know that libraries offer incredible lifelong learning opportunities, yet no one type of library can deliver learning opportunities from cradle to grave. Through our library ecosystem, however, we offer these opportunities in abundance."

Work to support Rettig's key initiatives included enhancing advocacy programs and tools to help library workers and supporters at the grassroots level convey messages to decision-makers and the public at large; reaching out to library directors and career center directors at Chicago-area colleges with significant enrollment of students from under-represented groups to let to them know about available career opportunities and scholarship programs; and establishing a Craigslist-style network that members can use to find their place in the association.

## Highlights of the Year

### COPA Declared Unconstitutional

The Child Online Protection Act (COPA) was struck down for the third time in July when the Third Circuit Court of Appeals unanimously declared the act unconstitutional. The decision followed a decade of federal litigation and two decisions that were returned to lower courts by the Supreme Court. During the string of legal proceedings, ALA's Freedom to Read Foundation filed several friend-of-the-court briefs on behalf of the plaintiffs. Signed into law in 1998 but never enforced because of an injunction granted in February 1999, COPA mandated a $50,000-per-day fine and up to six months' incarceration for a Web site owner who posts a commercial online communication "that includes any material that is harmful to minors," unless the site keeps minors out through a digital age-verification gateway.

### Membership Hits New Record

ALA closed its 2008 fiscal year with a record 66,624 members, a 3 percent increase from fiscal 2007 and ahead of the previous largest year, 2005. Personal membership led with a 3.3 percent increase, to 62,998 individuals. Organizational and corporate membership was down slightly, with 3,361 and 265 members, respectively. Membership gains encompassed all personal member categories, including regular, student, and support staff. Retiree and continuing members were slightly ahead of the previous year, but did not show unusual or unexpected gains.

### Library Use Increases, But Not Funding

More and more people visited their public libraries in 2008 as the ranks of the unemployed swelled and job-related activities became a priority use of library computers and Internet services. A study showed that three-fourths of public libraries offered information technology training to their patrons, including how to conduct online job searches and how to use standard office software applications; and that one of the most critical roles public libraries play in hard economic times is helping patrons to access employment assistance.

The media—including network news and major newspapers—reported on this trend, but funders were for the most part strapped by shrinking revenues. Forecasts of modest library budget gains or moderate cuts for 2009 that prevailed early in 2008 became more pessimistic as the year drew to a close and the depth of the national economic morass became more clear. A survey of members of the Chief Officers of State Library Agencies at year's end revealed significant losses in state funding for public libraries in the year ahead—and anticipation of more cuts to come.

## EPA Libraries Reopen

In a victory for librarians and the public, the federal Environmental Protection Agency (EPA) announced in a March 2008 report to Congress that it would reopen by September 30 the four libraries closed in 2006 by a $2 million budget cut. EPA also noted that all libraries would be staffed by a librarian and assistants, and that $1 million in appropriations would help reestablish libraries, collections, and equipment. The report's release came about two weeks after a House of Representatives oversight committee hearing about the closures at which ALA President-Elect Rettig had testified. "The key issue to determine is whether or not the EPA's library plan is based on the end users' needs," Rettig said. "We think not."

## Grassroots Support for Library Media Centers

In a noteworthy show of community support, three mothers from Spokane, Washington, embarked on a grassroots effort to fight their school board's decision to close part of a $10.8 million deficit by halving the hours of the district's 10 full-time K–8 teacher-librarians. The women launched a campaign that ultimately gained almost $4 million for the 2008–2009 school year to maintain and improve library materials, collections, and services; in a further victory, a subsequently formed Basic Education Joint Task Force recommended in its final report that teacher-librarians be listed as "core teachers" rather than as support staff. ALA's OLA, PIO, and AASL worked to assist the grassroots effort.

## ALTA Approves New Name, Bylaws

In a special fall election, ALTA overwhelmingly approved revised bylaws and a new name, the Association for Library Trustees, Advocates, Friends, and Foundations (ALTAFF). The 293–31 vote by ALTA members was the latest step in a move to join ALTA with Friends of Libraries USA (FOLUSA) in an expanded, strengthened division. The revised bylaws, developed by a task force representing both ALA and FOLUSA, establish new sections for trustees, friends, foundations, and corporate friends within the expanded division.

## OIF Starts Conversation on Privacy

OIF launched an ambitious three-year campaign, the National Conversation on Privacy, to call attention to the value of privacy as the foundation for civil liberties and to highlight growing threats to privacy rights. Begun with a $350,000 seed grant from the Open Society Institute, the campaign calls on libraries and librarians to stand up as leaders and educators in communities nationwide, engaging the public and helping people understand their rights in the information age. Among its efforts, OIF is creating a toolkit that will provide librarians with ideas, examples, and support in carrying out the privacy initiative, as well as working to develop an interactive Web site, pursue additional funds, and coordinate further strategic initiatives.

## National Library Legislative Day

More than 400 librarians and library supporters converged on Washington, D.C., May 13–14, 2008, for the 34th annual National Library Legislative Day. An enthusiastic crowd of librarians from around the country brought the year's message—"Vote for Libraries!"—to their senators and representatives, discussing with them such issues as the USAPatriot Act, library funding, and the economic benefits of libraries. In addition, many other ALA members participated in Virtual Legislative Day, contacting their congressional offices by phone, e-mail, and fax to discuss the same critical federal issues facing libraries.

## Banned Books Week

The 27th celebration of Banned Books Week, OIF's long-running awareness campaign about challenges to library materials, followed up the huge success of the previous year's pirate theme with a "Closing Books Shuts Out Ideas" campaign that drew attention to three very popular challenged authors: Laura Ingalls Wilder, Judy Blume, and Stephen King. Posters used illustrations of their books along with text about the authors to reveal what's at stake when we consider removing books from a library. Also as part of the September 27–October 4 event, OIF hosted its fourth annual Read-Out! September 27, drawing an enthusiastic audience of about 1,000 to hear such authors as Blume, Stephen Chbosky, Lois Lowry, Luis Alberto Urrea, and Sara Paretsky read from their own or their favorite books that have been banned or challenged.

## Teen Read Week

Observed October 12–18, Teen Read Week 2008 used the theme "Books with Bite" to encourage teens to read a wide variety of books and graphic novels. This year's celebration included a special chat series, Night Bites, featuring several popular YA authors. The series was hosted by the Readergirlz, an online book community for teen girls. More than 8,000 teens voted on the Teens' Top Ten list, choosing Stephenie Meyer's *Eclipse* (Little, Brown) as the No. 1 popular young adult book from the previous year, and nearly 1,000 helped choose the 2009 theme, "Read Beyond Reality @ your library."

## PLA Approves New Bylaws

In May 2008 PLA members approved changes to its bylaws, effectively reshaping the structure of the organization. Major changes include reducing the size of the PLA board to facilitate decision making and provide greater member access to elected representatives; disbanding the executive committee, empowering the board to make binding decisions on its own; and replacing many committees with "communities of practice" (CoPs), virtual groups that are interest-focused and member-driven. PLA will transition to the new structure over two years, phasing out board members as terms expire.

## LAMA Adopts New Name: LLAMA

In the spring 2008 election, more than 90 percent of Library Leadership and Management Association members who cast ballots endorsed a new name for the division, formerly the Library Administration and Management Association. The new name, abbreviated as LLAMA rather than LAMA, became official September 1. It emphasizes the association's important role in developing present and future library leaders.

## ORS Studies Services for Non-English-Speakers

Made possible by a World Book Staff Award, an ORS study of library services and programs developed for non-English-speakers looked at effectiveness of services, barriers to library use, most frequently used services, and most successful library programs by language served. The published final report was released at PLA's 2008 conference, and the study was transferred to OLOS.

## ALA Boosts Use of Web 2.0 Tools

A number of ALA offices and divisions adopted Web 2.0 initiatives such as blogs, wikis, and social networking sites to increase visibility and connect with supporters. OIF's presence on Facebook and Second Life brought attention to events such as Banned Books Week and helped raise awareness about key supporters. ACRL launched presences on Facebook, Twitter, FriendFeed, and LinkedIn. The ALA Library added a Facebook page, a LinkedIn group, and a meebo chat link on the Professional Tips wiki. In April 2008 ALSC held three events on ALA Island in Second Life about El Día de los Niños/El Día de los Libros (Children's Day/Book Day) for members to discuss programming and celebration ideas. LITA enhanced its blog, adding podcasts from forum keynote presentations, Top Tech Trends, and presidents' programs. YALSA's Facebook fan page grew to more than 1,000 followers; YALSA also developed a FriendFeed account and a very popular Twitter, with more than 700 people following the latest division news on their cell phones and mobile devices.

## RUSA Redefines 'Reference'

To keep pace with the major changes in reference services in the last two decades, RUSA approved a new definition of "reference" in January. The result of seven years of investigation on the part of the Reference Services Section, this new definition is used as the basis for measuring and assessing reference services, and in its new form takes into account the broader range of activities that constitute reference in all types of libraries.

## Support Staff Certification Moves Ahead

With the help of library staff across the country, the Library Support Staff Certification Program continued to develop and solidify elements of the nine competency sets that academic and public library support staff should know. The project's advisory council next plans to determine the policies and procedures for the program and to do field testing through ALA divisions, library associations, and library technical assistant programs. ALA, in partnership with the Western Council of State Libraries, has been awarded $407,111 by the Institute of Museum and Library Services to develop the national voluntary certification program.

### ASCLA Tools Address Accessibility

To address the challenge of universal accessibility, ASCLA released two collections of accessibility guidelines. "Think Accessible Before You Buy" translates the technical lingo libraries encounter when evaluating and buying accessible electronic databases and resources, software for public use, or new Web site design or layout. This translation ultimately takes the form of a checklist and guidelines, supported with plenty of examples, to help libraries make informed purchasing decisions. "Library Accessibility—What You Need to Know" offers a springboard for libraries to create a culture among employees that patrons with disabilities are to be welcomed, not feared. The toolkit of 15 concise documents educates library staff about the challenges faced by disabled patrons and offers methods for delivering one-on-one library services to them.

### Campaign for America's Libraries

ALSC's Public Awareness Committee campaign began developing a second phase of its Kids! @ your library program, collecting input from librarians through a survey and from kids in grades 5–8 through a series of focus groups.

YALSA launched its @ your library toolkit at the 2008 Midwinter Meeting in Philadelphia, offering sample messages and tips for building partnerships. YALSA's advocacy committee followed up at the 2008 Annual Conference in Anaheim with training, including best practice examples, on how to use the toolkit.

### Campaign for the World's Libraries

The Pacific Island Association of Libraries and Archives joined as the newest member of the Campaign for the World's Libraries, developed by ALA and the International Federation of Library Associations and Institutions (IFLA) to showcase the unique and vital roles played by public, school, academic, and special libraries worldwide. To date, 34 countries have joined the campaign, and the @ your library brand has been translated into each country's language. New logos have also been developed to reflect the national colors of each member nation.

## Programs and Partners

### Campaign Partnerships

Thirty-four public libraries in 18 states received "The American Dream Starts @ your library" awards to add or expand literacy services for adult English-language learners. The one-time grants of $5,000, funded by the Dollar General Literacy Foundation and administered by OLOS, went to libraries that demonstrated the need to provide literacy services to adult immigrants in their community.

The Step Up to the Plate @ your library program, developed by ALA and the National Baseball Hall of Fame and Museum, kicked off its third season on April 4 in Mobile, Alabama, with Hall of Famer Ozzie Smith serving as spokesperson. Year three teamed up baseball and libraries to encourage fans of all ages to use the print and electronic resources at their libraries to answer a series of trivia questions. The program concluded with a drawing at the Hall of Fame in

Cooperstown, New York, where Smith and fellow Hall of Famers Robin Roberts and Phil Niekro chose 12-year-old Hannah Cavanaugh as the grand-prize winner.

Promoted in conjunction with the second season of Step Up to the Plate, Batting for Literacy @ your library recognized a librarian's use of baseball to enhance literacy or library services. Winner Al Smitley of the Northville (Michigan) District Library received a behind-the-scenes tour of the National Baseball Hall of Fame and tickets to attend the Hall of Fame game.

Continuing a seven-year partnership with the Campaign for America's Libraries, the March 2008 issue of *Woman's Day* magazine featured the four winners of its library initiative that asked readers how their library helped them start a business. Winners included the founder of I Love 2 Organize, a woman who started her own financial research group, a reader who used the Brooklyn Business Library's "Power Up!" contest to help fund her children's-clothing business, and a woman who became a self-publisher. The magazine also announced its next initiative, asking readers to submit stories on how they used their library to improve a family member's or their own mental, emotional, or physical health. Four of the submissions were featured in the magazine's March 2009 issue.

### Exhibitions on the Road

The Public Programs Office toured five exhibitions across the country— "Changing the Face of Medicine: Celebrating America's Women Physicians," "Alexander Hamilton: The Man Who Made Modern America," "Forever Free: Abraham Lincoln's Journey to Emancipation," "Lewis and Clark and the Indian Country," and "Benjamin Franklin: In Search of a Better World"—and announced two new traveling exhibitions that will tour public and academic libraries through 2012. "John Adams Unbound," based on a larger exhibition of the same name at the Boston Public Library, will visit 20 libraries, and 25 libraries will host "Pride and Passion: The African American Baseball Experience," which tells the story of black baseball players in the United States over the past century and a half.

The National Endowment for the Humanities (NEH) provided major funding to the Boston Public Library (BPL) for the John Adams exhibit, which explores Adams's personal library, a collection of 3,500 books held by BPL since 1894. NEH also provided major funding for "Pride and Passion," which is based on a permanent exhibition of the same name at the National Baseball Hall of Fame and Museum.

## Conferences and Workshops

### 2008 Annual Conference

Some 22,000 librarians, exhibitors, and library supporters attended the 2008 Annual Conference and Exhibition in Anaheim, California, June 26–July 2. The opening session featured political pundit Ron Reagan, son of late President Ronald Reagan, who brought the crowd to its feet with stinging observations about "what's going on in Washington."

At her ALA President's Program, Loriene Roy highlighted efforts to support Native American children's English and Native American language literacy and the creative work being done in Indian tribes across the nation. Hosted by Native American actor Wes Studi, the program included films by digital animation/claymation artist Roy Boney, Jr. and previews of "We Shall Remain," a five-part public television documentary.

More than 1,100 attendees celebrated winners Laura Amy Schlitz for the Newbery Medal-winning *Good Masters! Sweet Ladies! Voices from a Medieval Village* and Brian Selznick for the Caldecott Medal-winning *The Invention of Hugo Cabret*. The year's choices were groundbreaking: the Newbery winner was illustrated, and rather than a traditional picture book, the Caldecott winner was an illustrated novel of more than 500 pages.

Using computers on the exhibit floor, conference attendees—including special guest National Basketball Association Hall of Famer Kareem Abdul-Jabbar—e-mailed and faxed their members of Congress as part of ALA's Virtual Library Day on the Hill. More than 1,500 messages were sent to Congress about the importance of funding libraries, and library supporters from across the country also joined in the campaign to call attention to the value of today's libraries.

PPO presented the 14th annual LIVE! @ your library Reading Stage, with readings by Francesca Lia Block, Mark Doty, Firoozeh Dumas, Leif Enger, John Francis, Anya Ulinich, and other award-winning authors and poets.

The Disney Institute's Bruce Kimbrell shared the components of the successful Disney customer service model in a high-energy, fast-paced keynote presentation at the 2008 Empowerment Conference for library support staff, held June 28–29. More than 191 registrants attended the Empowerment Conference, whose 20-plus diverse programs supported the theme "Ride the Wave to Empowerment" with sessions on such topics as global trends affecting libraries, certification for library support staff, and extreme customer service.

In other offerings, OIF catapulted the issue of privacy into the news through its program "Privacy: Is It Time for a Revolution?" featuring author and Boing-Boing blogger Cory Doctorow; a Verizon-sponsored Open Gaming Night enticed more than 400 conference attendees and their families to play board and video games, mingle with friends and colleagues, and indulge in junk food; and actor and author Jamie Lee Curtis presented the keynote address at PLA's President's Program and Awards Presentation.

### 2009 Midwinter Meeting

Nearly 8,000 librarians and more than 2,300 exhibitors attended ALA's 2009 Midwinter Meeting January 23–28 in Denver.

Key themes of the annual planning meeting were the future role of libraries in tough economic times and the influence libraries will exert in the new administration of President Barack Obama.

In advance of the conference, ALA released a new Advocating in a Tough Economy Toolkit, aimed at helping members advocate more effectively for libraries in their communities. ALA President Rettig and 2004–2005 ALA President Carol Brey-Casiano moderated "Building Statewide Coalitions for All Libraries," a program focused on the value of building statewide coalitions during times of economic downturn. And the Financial Industry Regulatory Authority Investor Education Foundation and ALA announced $882,000 in grants to public libraries and library networks across the country through the Smart Investing @ your library initiative, which backs library efforts to provide patrons with effective, unbiased financial education resources.

An ALA Washington Office Update session addressed what to expect from the new administration, and a breakout session with Stephanie Vance of Advocacy Associates discussed effective techniques library advocates can use to communicate their messages to the new administration and Congress. Librarians and library advocates also worked on a direct message to President Obama in a special membership town hall meeting sponsored by ALA's Executive Board and Membership Meeting Committee.

Program speakers included Nobel Peace Prize winner and author Muhammad Yunus, who spoke at the ALA President's Program about how institutions such as libraries or those that provide loans to poverty-stricken individuals can transform and build the communities they serve. Pulitzer Prize-winning journalist Jim Sheeler, who has written movingly about the impact of the war in Iraq on the families of fallen soldiers, delivered the tenth annual Arthur Curley Memorial Lecture.

Attendees also had an opportunity to hear from ALA presidential candidates Roberta Stevens and Kent Oliver at the Presidential Candidates Forum and later at a joint reception where members could meet the candidates and share thoughts, interests, and concerns.

At the Youth Media Awards presentation honoring the best of the best in children's and young adult literature, the 2009 John Newbery Medal for the most distinguished contribution to children's literature went to Neil Gaiman, author of *The Graveyard Book,* illustrated by Dave McKean and published by HarperCollins. Beth Krommes, illustrator of *The House in the Night,* written by Susan Marie Swanson and published by Houghton Mifflin, won the 2009 Caldecott Medal for the most distinguished American picture book for children. The awards presentation was also broadcast through a live Webcast that attracted 9,000 registrants and through a Twitter feed.

### PLA National Conference

Almost 10,000 library staff, supporters, exhibitors, authors, and guests descended on Minneapolis March 25–29 for PLA's 12th National Conference. Workshops and discussions often drew standing-room-only crowds and focused on such key public library issues as technology; serving adults, youth, and new Americans; gaming in libraries; library design; and collection development. The conference opened with an address from philanthropist and author John Wood, founder of Room to Read, a nonprofit dedicated to helping children in the developing world through the power of education. Special programs included the Authors Readers Theatre (A.R.T.), featuring Avi, Pam Muñoz Ryan, Brian Selznick, and Sarah Weeks; and Best in Mystery Authors Revealed! which gave conference-goers a sneak peek into the plots written by today's premier mystery authors.

A first-ever PLA Virtual Conference allowed almost 200 off-site, online subscribers to join live, interactive Webcasts and workshops, online poster sessions, and special events such as Inside the Author's Studio, a daily chat with a well-known author.

**LITA National Forum**

The 11th Annual LITA National Forum, held October 16–19 in Cincinnati, offered preconferences, general sessions, and more than 30 concurrent sessions, vendor showcases, poster sessions, and managed discussions. Keynote speakers included Michael Porter, community product manager for WebJunction in Seattle, and R. David Lankes, director of the Information Institute of Syracuse University in New York. Two preconference workshops were offered: "Marketing the Value of the Library's IT Department," by Grace Sines and Gary McCone of the National Agricultural Library, and "Innovations in Next Generation Library Management Systems," with discussion of three interesting developments in open source library applications by Andrew Nagy, Villanova University; Tim Daniels, PINES program manager, Georgia Public Library Service; and Darrell R. Ulm, Stow-Munroe Falls (Ohio) Public Library.

# Publishing

### *American Libraries* Extends Electronic Offerings

The first double January/February Midwinter print issue of *American Libraries* (*AL*) appeared in January 2008; the shift to 10 print issues was a logical result of news and other content being made available in a variety of more frequent electronic formats. Reader Forum Online, a companion to the "Letters and Comments" section of the print magazine, also got under way, and the weekly e-newsletter *AL Direct,* in collaboration with ALA's Membership Development, launched a student edition with links to items of particular interest to LIS students.

Editor-in-Chief Leonard Kniffel had an exclusive interview with First Lady Laura Bush in the White House library in March 2008; a summary of the interview appeared in the May issue, and a videocast and transcript are available online. AL Focus, *AL*'s video site, celebrated its first anniversary in June with a selection of ten of the most popular videos, including a series of humorous videos for National Library Week in April, each viewed around 100,000 times.

### ALA Editions Offers 18 New Titles

Under the new editorial direction of Michael Jeffers, ALA Editions released 18 new titles in 2008, along with new Web extras for many publications and a new licensing deal with an Indian publisher/distributor. Among the titles published were *Sex, Brains, and Video Games: The Librarians' Guide to Teens in the Twenty-First Century* by Jennifer Burek Pierce; *Intellectual Property: Everything the Digital-Age Librarian Needs to Know* by Timothy Wherry; *Helping Home-schoolers in the Library* by Adrienne Furness; *The Quality Library: A Guide to Self-Driven Improvement, Better Efficiency, and Happier Customers* by Sarah Laughlin and Ray W. Wilson; *Teen Girls and Technology: What's the Problem, What's the Solution?* by Lesley Farmer; *Creating Your Library Brand: Communicating Your Relevance and Value to Your Patrons* by Elisabeth Doucett; and *The Small Public Library Survival Guide* by Herbert B. Landau.

### Electronic *Guide to Reference* Debuts

*Guide to Reference,* formerly *Guide to Reference Books,* has a long history in print as a core publication of librarianship in the United States. The new *Guide*—which opened in late August for trial subscriptions—is the first to be published electronically and the first to engage the Web as a medium for reference publishing and services. With its searchable, browsable, internally and externally linked database, the online *Guide* includes more than 16,000 trusted go-to sources and offers guidance in the form of introductory essays and annotations for entries. The *Guide*'s interactive features for lists and notes afford possibilities for LIS reference-course exercises, reference department activities such as collection weeding, and reference-desk training.

### Busy Year for ALA Graphics

Celebrities featured on ALA's popular READ posters included Common, Tim Gunn, Abigail Breslin, Eva Mendes, Rachael Ray, the Wayans family, and Kareem Abdul-Jabbar, who signed posters at the Annual Conference. A new "Get Smart" poster with Steve Carell was in great demand. Other posters and bookmarks spotlighted the Spiderwick Chronicles, Wonder Woman, Duck for President, Celebrate Black History @ your library, Babymouse, Kadir Nelson art for "Lift Every Voice and READ," Celebrate Latino Heritage @ your library, and ALA's youth media awards. In August ALA Graphics launched a READ CD blog, where four bloggers cover tips, tricks, examples of creative use, and technical assistance for the popular READ CD program. In conjunction with the blog, ALA Graphics started offering the opportunity to create free personalized electronic mini-READ posters that can be used on Web sites or blogs.

Program-related materials included those for Banned Books Week, Teen Read Week, National Library Week, El Día de los Niños/El Día de los Libros (Children's Day/Book Day), and Teen Tech Week. For National Library Workers Day, ALA Graphics partnered with the ALA-Allied Professional Association to produce "Libraries Work Because We Do" buttons, which proved to be a sell-out item.

### *Booklist* Expands Electronic Territory

Booklist Publications maintained the quality and depth of its print publications, with numerous features, articles, top-ten lists, read-alikes, listen-alikes, and more than 8,000 titles reviewed and recommended in adult, youth, media, and reference. But the buzz from Booklist Publications was largely electronic. *Booklist Online* started a new multi-voice blog, "Book Group Buzz," whose contributors include Kaite Mediatore Stover and Nick DiMartino, and in January launched the free e-newsletter *REaD ALERT.* Sent to about 75,000 readers on the same day that the latest issue of *Booklist* magazine is published online, *REaD ALERT* features quick links to a hand-picked selection of book reviews, features, and special Web-only content from *Booklist Online.*

### ALA TechSource Updates Website

The ALA TechSource blog migrated to the Drupal platform, the first step in a TechSource Web site update. Reflecting the pattern of how people now acquire information about the technologies that affect their daily work in libraries, *Library Technology Reports* went from six to eight issues a year starting in January, allowing for more topics to be covered more often. The editors continued to select hot-button topics, with issues including "Web 2.0 & Libraries: Part 2—Trends and Technologies," "Changing the Way We Work," "Gaming and Libraries: Broadening the Intersections," and "On the Move with the Mobile Web: Libraries and Mobile Technologies."

**ALA-APA Provides Resources on Salaries**

The ALA-Allied Professional Association: The Organization for the Advancement of Library Employees (ALA-APA) continued to publish and contribute to surveys reporting salaries of librarians and support staff. The 2008 ALA-APA Salary Survey: Librarian—Public and Academic had a greater response rate than previously, 29 percent, and revealed some gains and losses in librarian salaries; it also collected and reported data on library benefits, a five-year follow-up. ALA-APA also offers 30-day and annual subscriptions to the Library Salary Database, a tool for library human resources departments and directors as well as job-seekers. Subscribers can create reports of data by library type, region, and state from the 2006 through 2008 Salary Surveys. *Library Worklife: HR E-News for Today's Leaders,* the ALA-APA monthly online newsletter and ALA institutional member benefit, entered its fifth year of publication, with articles relating to human resources and career development.

## Leadership

James Rettig, university librarian at the University of Richmond in Virginia, was inaugurated as 2008–2009 ALA president at the 2008 Annual Conference in Anaheim.

Before joining the University of Richmond in 1998, Rettig had held administrative and public-service positions at the College of William and Mary, the University of Illinois at Chicago, the University of Dayton, and Murray State University. He served on the ALA Executive Board from 2003 to 2006 and was elected to three terms on the ALA Council.

Camila Alire, dean emerita at the University of New Mexico and Colorado State University, was named ALA president-elect in the 2008 election. Alire will serve as president-elect for the 2008–2009 term and will be inaugurated as ALA president at the 2009 Annual Conference in Chicago. Alire said she is looking forward to working with all ALA units and members to further advance the value of the nation's libraries and library workers.

Three new Executive Board members were elected by the ALA Council at the 2008 Midwinter Meeting. Starting three-year terms in June 2008 were Diane Chen, library information specialist at John F. Kennedy Middle School in Antioch, Tennessee; Joseph Eagan, manager of the Olney Library of the Montgomery County (Maryland) Public Libraries; and Em Claire Knowles, assistant dean for student administrative services at the Simmons Graduate School of Library and Information Science in Boston.

## Grants and Contributions

### Cultural Communities Fund Nears $1.4 Million

Wrapping up a campaign to raise matching funds for a challenge grant from the National Endowment for the Humanities (NEH), the Cultural Communities Fund (CCF) received more than $290,000 in gifts and pledges in 2008, bringing the total fund to just under $1.4 million. One of the year's notable contributions was a generous estate gift from Lee Allen Wheeler, a library enthusiast and frequent patron of the Oshkosh (Wisconsin) Public Library.

The Public and Cultural Programs Advisory Committee acted as a staunch advocate for CCF, supporting the fund-raising process by reaching out to potential donors on behalf of ALA and by helping the Public Programs Office reach yearly targets. More than 450 individual and corporate supporters have contributed to CCF, which is one of ALA's most successful endowment campaigns. Funding supports the creation of professional development opportunities for librarians, turnkey national model programs, and a wealth of program planning and presenting resources.

### Verizon Gives $1 Million for Gaming Initiative

In January 2008 the Verizon Foundation gave ALA a $1 million two-year Libraries, Literacy, and Gaming grant. First-year efforts focused on gathering resources, tools, lessons learned, and best practices from libraries currently offering organized programs featuring board, computer, and video games. Also as part of the initiative, which is administered by the Office for Literacy and Outreach Services, a panel of gaming experts from public, school, and academic libraries contributed, collected, and developed resources for "The Librarians Guide to Gaming: An online toolbox for gaming @ your library."

### Carnegie Funds 'I Love My Librarian' Award

Carnegie Corporation of New York awarded ALA $489,000 to support the Carnegie/New York Times I Love My Librarian Award, which was launched in 2008 and will continue annually through 2013. Administered by the Public Information Office and the Campaign for America's Libraries, the award encourages library users to recognize librarians' efforts to improve the lives of people in their communities. Up to ten public, school, and academic librarians will be selected each year. Each winner will receive a $5,000 cash award, a plaque, and a $500 travel stipend to attend the awards reception in New York.

### Dollar General Funds Disaster Relief

Dollar General awarded an additional $520,000 to continue Beyond Words: The Dollar General School Library Relief Program, which provides funding to rebuild and expand school library media programs in public schools affected by disasters. The grants can be used to defray the cost of replacing or supplementing books, media, and/or equipment. AASL administers the program in collaboration with the National Education Association.

## Major Awards and Honors

### Honorary Members

Pat Mora, Effie Lee Morris, and Peggy Sullivan were named as the 2008 ALA Honorary Members, the highest award bestowed by ALA in recognition of outstanding contributions of lasting importance to libraries and librarianship.

Mora, a Latina poet and author, was nominated in recognition of her work on behalf of bilingual reading for children, her establishment of El Día de los Niños/El Día de los Libros (Children's Day/Book Day), and her commitment to libraries and the promotion of reading and inclusiveness. Mora's books for children and adults have been recognized for their excellence by ALA, the Society of Children's Book Writers and Illustrators, and others. In 2002 the Texas Library Association named her as one of "100 Library Champions."

Morris, former coordinator of children's services at the San Francisco Public Library, was chosen for her vision, advocacy, and legacy to children's services in public libraries. She established the first Negro History Week celebration for children at the Cleveland Public Library and served as the first children's specialist for the blind at the New York Public Library.

Sullivan, a library consultant, was nominated in recognition of more than 50 years of dedicated librarianship during which she wrote the definitive scholarly history of the tenure of Carl Milam, who served as ALA secretary from 1920 to 1946 and saw ALA grow into an international organization. Her wide-ranging career includes serving as ALA executive director from 1992 to 1994; dean of the LIS program at Rosary College (now Dominican University), dean of the College of Professional Studies at Northern Illinois University, and numerous university teaching positions.

Honorary membership may be conferred upon a living citizen of any country whose contribution to librarianship or a closely related field is so outstanding that it is of lasting importance to the advancement of the whole field of library service. The designation is intended to reflect honor upon ALA as well as upon the individual. Honorary members are elected for life by vote of the ALA Council upon recommendation of the ALA Executive Board.

### James Madison Award

U.S. Sen. Russ Feingold (D-Wis.) was the recipient of the 2008 James Madison Award, which honors those who, at the national level, have championed, protected, and promoted public access to government information. Feingold supported the OPEN Government Act of 2007, which became law on December 31, 2007, and he has introduced or cosponsored several pieces of open-government legislation, including the National Security Letters Reform Act of 2007; the Lobbying, Ethics, and Earmarks Transparency and Accountability Act of 2007; and the Federal Agency Data Mining Reporting Act of 2007.

# Association of American Publishers

71 Fifth Ave., New York, NY 10010
212-255-0200, fax 212-255-7007

50 F St. N.W., Washington, DC 20001
202-347-3375, fax 202-347-3690

World Wide Web http://www.publishers.org

Judith Platt
Director, Communications/Public Affairs

The Association of American Publishers (AAP) is the national trade association of the U.S. book publishing industry. AAP was created in 1970 through the merger of the American Book Publishers Council, a trade publishing group, and the American Educational Publishers Institute, an organization of textbook publishers. AAP's more than 300 corporate members include most of the major commercial book publishers in the United States as well as smaller and medium-sized houses, not-for-profit publishers, university presses, and scholarly societies.

AAP members publish hardcover and paperback books in every field including general fiction and nonfiction; poetry; children's books; textbooks; Bibles and other religious works; reference works; scientific, medical, technical, professional, and scholarly books and journals; computer software; and a range of electronic products and services.

AAP policy is set by a board of directors, elected by the membership to four-year terms, under a chair who serves for two years. There is an executive committee composed of the chair, vice chair, secretary, and treasurer and a minimum of two at-large members. Management of the association, within the guidelines set by the board, is the responsibility of AAP's president and CEO. [Former Congresswoman Pat Schroeder held that post from June 1997 through May 1, 2009, when she was succeeded by another former member of Congress, Tom Allen—*Ed.*]

AAP maintains two offices, in New York and in Washington, D.C.

## Highlights of 2008

Among the highlights of the year in publishing:

- On October 28 AAP, the Authors Guild, and Google announced a settlement agreement resolving the copyright litigation initiated in 2005 over Google's Book Search program.
- The 2008 AAP Honors went to the National Book Critics Circle.
- The Miriam Bass Award for Creativity in Independent Publishing went to Archipelago Books.
- Richard Sarnoff began his second year as AAP chairman.

- AAP coordinated the filing of a lawsuit in federal court by three AAP member publishers to protest copyright infringement at Georgia State University.
- The R. R. Hawkins Award for the outstanding professional, scholarly, or reference work went to Princeton University Press for *The Dream of the Poem* by Peter Cole.
- AAP unveiled its *Handbook on Book Paper and the Environment.*
- A Cambodian literary project and its founder, Kho Tararith, received the 2008 Jeri Laber International Freedom to Publish Award.
- Year-end figures showed that net sales for U.S. publishers rose to $25 billion in 2007.
- Publishing industry veteran John Tagler joined AAP as vice president and executive director of its Professional and Scholarly Publishing (PSP) Division.
- AAP launched "Get Caught Listening," an audiobook extension of the Get Caught Reading program.
- "Book Editors Online and Unscripted," a pilot program bringing top editors together with an online audience of booksellers and media, was launched.
- AAP announced agreements with three universities—Hofstra, Syracuse, and Marquette—on new copyright guidelines for digitally delivered materials.
- The AAP School Division Fall Summit looked at technology trends in K–12 publishing.
- AAP medical publishers provided medical education resources to an obstetrics and gynecology residency program in Afghanistan.

## Government Affairs

AAP's Washington office is the industry's front line on matters of federal legislation and government policy. Washington keeps AAP members informed about developments on Capitol Hill and in the Executive Branch to enable the membership to develop consensus positions on national policy issues. AAP's government affairs professionals serve as the industry's voice in advocating the views and concerns of American publishers on questions of national policy.

A separate report details legislation and regulatory actions affecting book publishers in 2008. [See "Legislation and Regulations Affecting Publishing" in Part 2—*Ed.*]

## Communications/Public Affairs

The AAP Communications and Public Affairs program informs the trade press and other media, the AAP membership, and the general public about the association's work and serves as the industry's voice on a host of issues. Through the program's regular publications, press releases and advisories, op-ed pieces, and other means, AAP disseminates the publishing industry's views and provides up-to-the-minute information on subjects of concern to its members. The Communications/Public Affairs program has primary responsibility for the AAP Web site.

The association's public affairs activities include outreach and cooperative programs with such organizations as the Center for the Book in the Library of Congress, the Arts Advocacy Alliance (supporting the National Endowment for the Arts and other federal arts programs), PEN American Center and its International Freedom to Write Program, and a host of literacy and reading-promotion efforts including the early childhood literacy initiative Reach Out and Read.

In addition to the *AAP Monthly Report,* the association's regular newsletter, the communications program publishes a weekly electronic news bulletin for AAP members, the *Insider.*

## Get Caught Reading/Get Caught Listening

During 2008 AAP continued to promote its Get Caught Reading/¡Ajá, leyendo! literacy campaign. New Get Caught Reading celebrities for 2008 included Olivia the Pig, along with a number of National Basketball Association players who will help celebrate the program's tenth anniversary.

Recognizing the significant and growing impact of books in audio format, AAP announced the launch of a new audiobook extension to Get Caught Reading—Get Caught Listening, which celebrates the particular pleasures of listening to books in audiobook format. The campaign featured audiobook events at BookExpo America 2008 in Los Angeles and led into National Audiobooks Month in June.

A Get Caught Listening subcommittee—made up of leading trade audiobook publishers including BBC Audiobooks America, Hachette Book Group, Harper-Collins, Macmillan, Random House, and Simon & Schuster, along with representatives from the Audiobook Publishers Association—was created to spearhead the launch, development, and implementation of the new campaign.

The Get Caught Listening campaign incorporates prerecorded audio voice-overs by authors sharing their passion for audiobooks, complemented by a print campaign featuring those authors "getting caught" listening to their favorite book in audio format. XM Radio aired the voice-overs on "Sonic Theater" (now called Sirius XM Book Radio), XM's book and contemporary theater channel, and advertisements ran throughout the year in *Audiofile* magazine. Videos of selected participating authors are available for viewing on the Get Caught Reading Web site (http://www.getcaughtreading.org). Members of the American Booksellers Association's Book Sense program (now known as IndieBound) received posters and other materials to help them enlist the support of their local radio stations to run public service announcements promoting the Get Caught Reading program and to expand publicity for their stores.

Get Caught Reading exhibits were part of BookExpo America and the Brooklyn Book Fair.

Thousands of booksellers, teachers, and librarians continue to use http://www.getcaughtreading.org as a resource to initiate Get Caught Reading campaigns in their communities and to order artwork and send electronic cards. Newsletters highlighting educators' activities are written and distributed through AAP twice a year, and AAP continues its reading-promotion partnership with the American Booksellers Association.

A new committee will be formed in 2009 to explore the future of the campaign.

## Copyright

The AAP Copyright Committee coordinates efforts to protect and strengthen intellectual property rights and to enhance public awareness of the importance of copyright as an incentive to creativity. The committee monitors intellectual property legislation in the United States and abroad and serves as an advisory body to the AAP board in formulating policy on legislation and compliance activities, including litigation. The committee coordinates AAP's efforts to promote understanding and compliance with U.S. copyright law on college and university campuses. Carol Richman (SAGE Publications) chaired the committee in 2008. [For a detailed report on legislative issues that engaged the AAP Copyright Committee in 2008, see "Legislation and Regulations Affecting Publishing in 2008" in Part 2—*Ed.*]

Among its activities in 2008, the committee continued to monitor copyright issues relating to the Google Book Search program, including the lawsuit filed in federal court in the fall of 2005 by five major AAP members (McGraw-Hill, Pearson Education, Penguin Group USA, Simon & Schuster, and John Wiley & Sons) asserting that the Google Library Project's mass digitization of in-copyright books obtained from Google's library partners—without permission of the copyright owners—was not protected by fair use and represented massive copyright infringement. The case was settled in October with the announcement of an agreement that would expand online access to millions of in-copyright books and other written materials in the United States from the collections of a number of major U.S. libraries participating in Google Book Search. The agreement, reached after two years of negotiations, resolved the class-action lawsuit brought by book authors and the Authors Guild, as well as the separate publishers' lawsuit. The class action is subject to approval by the U.S. District Court for the Southern District of New York. The agreement promises to benefit readers and researchers, and enhance the ability of authors and publishers to distribute their content in digital form, by significantly expanding online access to works through Google Book Search, an ambitious effort to make millions of books searchable via the Web. A large number of domestic and international conference calls were conducted following the announcement, as AAP worked to educate the international publishing community about the settlement agreement. Publishers continued to work on establishing the Book Rights Registry specified by the settlement agreement, pending court approval of the settlement agreement anticipated for mid-2009. The committee also monitored a number of important court decisions in cases against Google, along with domestic and foreign news media coverage of Google's views and business transactions.

The committee continued to closely monitor issues arising from the "non-permissioned" use of copyrighted works in digital formats on college campuses, including library e-reserves. Following the agreement reached between AAP and Cornell University in 2006 on substantive guidelines for the use of such electronic course content, the committee turned its attention to identifying other schools to be contacted regarding copyright problems in policies and practices governing the use of electronic course content. AAP subsequently reached agreement with Syracuse University, Hofstra University, and Marquette University, and continued a dialogue with Duke University regarding electronic course content policies and practice. Although discussions continued about the implementation process, the school seems to have taken publishers' concerns seriously and addressed them through changes in institutional policies and procedures.

AAP coordinated the filing of a lawsuit by three AAP member publishers on April 15 in federal court in Atlanta to stop widespread copyright infringement at Georgia State University (GSU), one of three state universities that refused to engage with AAP in any dialogue regarding e-reserves policies and practices. The complaint, filed by Oxford University Press, Cambridge University Press, and SAGE Publications, charges that GSU officials are violating the law by systematically enabling professors to provide students with digital copies of copyrighted course readings published by the plaintiffs and numerous other publishers without those publishers' authorization. The lawsuit seeks injunctive relief to bring an end to such practices, but does not seek monetary damages. Since it remains unclear whether agreement with GSU on a settlement discussion process is feasible, the discovery process was continuing at the time this report was prepared. AAP will continue exploring contacts with other schools regarding their e-reserves policies and practices.

In March, AAP joined a friend-of-the-court (amicus) brief in support of the petition seeking review by the Supreme Court in the *Perfect 10* v. *Visa International* case. AAP had hoped that the Supreme Court would accept review of the Ninth Circuit's decision that rejected the applicability of secondary liability to credit card services that facilitate payments for access to infringing materials on Web sites. However, the court refused to review the case.

The Copyright Committee also approved AAP's participation in a friend-of-the-court brief in support of a request for rehearing or rehearing *en banc* in *Davis* v. *Blige,* a case in which the plaintiff had prevailed over the defendant-performer and the producers of her album on an infringement claim regarding two of the songs performed on the album. After the suit was filed, the plaintiff's co-author of the songs at issue had executed a transfer of ownership interest that was supposed to have retroactive effect and thus provide permission for the recording. However, the Second Circuit panel, which rejected the validity of the transfer in a ruling that would leave the defendant liable for infringement, rejected the request for rehearing and the full court rejected the request for rehearing *en banc.*

In late 2008 AAP joined one of four friend-of-the-court briefs filed by copyright advocates in *Cable Network News* v. *CSC Holdings,* considered as important to copyright-based industries as the *Sony, Grokster,* and *Tasini* cases, all of which were ultimately decided by the U.S. Supreme Court. Each of the briefs urged the Supreme Court to review a controversial decision by a Second Circuit panel that raised critical questions about the application of copyright law to automated computerized services through which copyrighted works are increasingly reproduced, distributed, and used by consumers. Reversing the district court, the appellate panel ruled that Cablevision does not violate the copyrights of motion picture and television studios by engaging in the unauthorized copying, storage, and transmission of their movies and other programming through "remote storage digital video recorder" services that are provided to its cable television system customers from its central facility. AAP joined in seeking reversal of the decision. AAP members are particularly interested in having the Supreme Court reject the Second Circuit panel's interpretation and application of the rulings in the *MDS* commercial copy shop decision.

AAP's Rights and Permissions Advisory Committee (RPAC), which operates under the aegis of the Copyright Committee, sponsors educational programs for rights and permissions professionals. Chaired by Bonnie Beacher (McGraw-Hill), RPAC sponsored a half-day seminar, "Your Questions Answered: Permissions Experts Tell All," featuring panel discussions involving veteran permissions professionals from a spectrum of specialized areas, including permissions seeking and granting, subsidiary rights, and music/film/non-print rights. In June 2008 RPAC hosted its annual conference in New York; more than 80 professionals took part in the day-long program. The conference featured sessions on copyright basics, accessibility issues, Section 108, copyright compliance on college campuses, fighting online infringements, and updates on pertinent legislation. RPAC maintains the AAP Imprints List, which can be found at http://www.publishers. org/main/Membership/member_03.htm. It provides contact information and information on various imprints for those seeking permissions. RPAC members are in the process of revising and updating the *Copyright Primer,* which was scheduled for release in mid-2009.

## Digital Series

AAP's Digital Issues Working Group, a forum for publishers to share information and learn about business opportunities and strategies in the digital world, held a series of meetings in 2008 featuring guest speakers on a range of subjects. Maja Thomas (Hachette Book Group) and Matt Shatz (Random House) served as co-chairs.

Meeting topics included the EPUB standard; digital chapter sales, personalized e-books, and other publisher initiatives; a proposal to investigate creating a national digital book archive for preservation; library uses of digital content and technologies; ISBN assignment issues relating to e-books and various consumer formats in which they may be available; and e-book platforms and applications for mobile phones.

## Diversity/Recruit and Retain

The association's Diversity/Recruit and Retain Committee (DRRC) continued to fulfill its mandate of attracting a talented and diverse work force to book publishing with its "Book Yourself a Career" campaign. The committee was chaired in

2008 by Bridget Marmion (Houghton Mifflin). College Outreach chair was Francine Rosado-Cruz (Penguin/Pearson).

The focus of the 2008 initiative was the production of multimedia promotions intended to acquaint recent college graduates with the various roles within the publishing industry. The video featured sound bites from "young to publishing" professionals and focused on several major themes, including "Why Book Publishing?" and "Diverse Backgrounds and Diverse Majors," and illustrated how careers in publishing embrace ethnic and professional diversity in such areas as sales, editorial, publicity, and graphic design. The video has also been posted on YouTube and the committee undertook an outreach initiative to market the profession in the digital environment. The committee and AAP members also use the video as a recruiting tool at college fairs.

DRRC's annual Introduction to Publishing Program—"From Cover to Cover"—highlighted young editors featured in the *Publishers Weekly* series "50 Under 40" and conveyed the upbeat message of success at an early age. In addition to offering an opportunity for networking, the program featured sessions on various facets of book publishing.

AAP continued to reach out to colleges, focusing on select schools in the Greater New York area and speaking about the industry on various programs and panels. Colleges and universities visited during the year included Rutgers, Baruch, City College of New York, Brooklyn College, and Queens College.

Now chaired by Ann Weinerman, manager of human resources at Random House, the group is addressing hiring practices in light of the economic downturn.

### Young to Publishing Group

The Young to Publishing Group (YPG), a subcommittee of DRRC, has a membership of more than 1,500 young industry professionals who have been in book publishing from one to five years. The group hosts monthly brown bag lunches featuring publishing industry leaders. Knopf Associate Art Director Chip Kidd, Bob Miller and Debbie Stier of HarperStudio, and editors from various trade houses including DC Comics, TWELVE, and Oxford University Press were among those who participated in 2008. The group hosts evening networking events, and in summer 2008 launched YPG-Link, an arm of YPG dedicated to connecting members with emerging literary agents through networking events. YPG also developed a Buddy Groups program, matching members with similar interests and forming small groups that meet socially outside YPG events. In 2009 the group planned to continue developing quality programming for members and building upon the newsletter and Web site http://www.youngtopublishing.com.

## Freedom to Read

The mandate of AAP's Freedom to Read Committee is to protect the free marketplace of ideas for American publishers. The committee serves as the industry's early warning system on issues such as libel, privacy, school and library censorship, reporter's privilege, Internet censorship, government regulation of protected speech, and third-party liability for protected speech. The committee coordinates

AAP participation in First Amendment court cases, sponsors educational programs, plays an active role in Media Coalition (a trade association of business-oriented groups concerned with censorship issues), and works with groups within and beyond the book community to advance common interests in the area of intellectual freedom. Elisabeth Sifton (Farrar, Straus & Giroux) chaired the committee in 2008.

## Libel Tourism

"Libel tourism," the use of plaintiff-friendly libel laws of other countries in attempts to silence U.S. authors and publishers, is an increasing concern for AAP members. "Libel tourists" bring lawsuits in other countries intended to intimidate U.S.-based authors writing on such sensitive subjects as the funding of terrorism. Even if they do not attempt to enforce the foreign libel judgment in the United States, the libel tourism movement's very existence can, and has, silenced the kind of reporting that U.S. law is designed to encourage and protect.

While several of the most recent high-profile examples of libel tourism involve judgments obtained in Britain, the threat is even wider and more insidious. The sale of books over the Internet exposes U.S. authors and publishers to the danger of being sued almost anywhere in the world, and libel tourism litigation remains a threat in any country where strong protections for freedom of speech are absent.

The threat posed by libel tourism has received increased attention as a result of the Rachel Ehrenfeld case. In 2004, soon after her book *Funding Evil: How Terrorism Is Financed—and How to Stop It* was published in the United States, Ehrenfeld, a New York-based author, was sued for libel by Saudi billionaire banker Khalid bin Mahfouz in a London court under Britain's libel laws. The fact that the book was never published in Britain and that a mere 23 copies were sold there via the Internet did not stop a British judge from issuing a default judgment against Ehrenfeld, awarding substantial monetary damages and costs, ordering a public apology, banning her book in Britain, and ordering the destruction of all unsold copies. Bin Mahfouz has successfully sued or silenced some 40 authors and publishers and boasts of these "victories" on his Web site (http://www.binmahfouz.info/en_index.html).

Ehrenfeld decided to fight back. Instead of taking part in the British proceedings, she countersued in federal court in New York seeking a declaration that the British judgment was unenforceable in the United States. A ruling by the New York Court of Appeals that New York's "long-arm statute" did not permit the exercise of personal jurisdiction over bin Mahfouz led to the dismissal of her suit but prompted swift action by the New York State Legislature in enacting the Libel Terrorism Protection Act. Nicknamed "Rachel's Law," it prohibits the enforcement of a foreign libel judgment unless a New York court determines that it does not violate the free speech and free press protections guaranteed by the First Amendment and the New York State Constitution, and it broadens the power of New York courts to exercise personal jurisdiction over non-residents who obtain foreign libel judgments against New York residents. It was signed into law by Governor David A. Paterson on April 30, 2008. A similar law was enacted and signed into law in Illinois in August.

Passage of the New York and Illinois legislation underscored the need for a federal statute to address the problem of libel tourism on a nationwide basis. Two versions were introduced in the House. H.R. 6146 prohibited U.S. courts from recognizing a foreign defamation judgment "based upon a publication concerning a public figure or a matter of public concern" unless the court determines that the foreign judgment is consistent with the free speech and free press protections guaranteed by the First Amendment. H.R. 5418, the Free Speech Protection Act, would have gone further, allowing the U.S. speaker to countersue in a U.S. court and to seek treble damages if the foreign plaintiff was shown to have engaged in a "scheme to suppress the First Amendment rights" of the U.S. speaker. The Free Speech Protection Act was also introduced in the Senate. In the closing days of the 110th Congress, the House passed H.R. 6146, but no further action was taken. Passage of effective legislation to fight libel tourism is a high priority for AAP in the 111th Congress.

The AAP Freedom to Read Committee and the Intellectual Freedom Committee of the American Library Association (ALA) joined in sponsoring a program at the ALA Annual Conference in June 2008. Titled "The Biggest Threat to Free Speech You May Never Have Heard Of," the program featured Rachel Ehrenfeld and Jonathan Bloom of Weil Gotshal & Manges, counsel to the AAP Freedom to Read Committee. The well-received program reinforced the commitment of the publishing and library communities to bring the issue of libel tourism to the widest possible audience.

### Plame v. McConnell

In February 2008 AAP, joined by 11 media and free speech groups, filed an amicus brief in the Second Circuit Court of Appeals urging it to reverse a ruling that forbids "outed" former CIA operative Valerie Plame Wilson from mentioning the dates of her CIA employment in her published memoir. The government's redactions were made despite the fact that Wilson had received an unclassified letter from a CIA benefits official clearly spelling out the dates of her employment and that this letter was introduced at House hearings, published in the *Congressional Record,* and is widely available on the Internet.

In May 2007, with publication of her memoir just months away, Wilson and her publisher, Simon & Schuster, sought a ruling from a federal district court in New York that the government was imposing an unlawful prior restraint in demanding that she remove from the book all mention of the dates of her CIA employment prior to 2002. The government filed a cross-motion for summary judgment, and in August 2007 the court granted the government's motion, finding that the information had been properly classified by the CIA, had never been declassified, and was not "officially acknowledged" by the agency. The book, *Fair Game: My Life as a Spy, My Betrayal by the White House,* was published in October 2007 with the redactions clearly shown, accompanied by a note from the publisher explaining what had been done. The book also contained an afterword by journalist Laura Rozen providing the historical context that Wilson was unable to include herself.

The amicus brief stated that as a result of the district court decision, "any member of the public can access and freely disseminate the pre-2002 dates of

Wilson's CIA employment, but Wilson herself cannot," a result that the brief calls "perverse." While not taking issue with the high level of deference ordinarily given to CIA classification decisions by the courts, the brief asserts that "the circumstances presented here—Wilson is seeking to publish under her own name autobiographical information that is readily accessible to the public—demand searching judicial scrutiny of [the government's] justifications," particularly in view of the strong constitutional presumption against prior restraints. The brief points out the irony that the case "involves the government's efforts to censor purportedly classified public domain information from a book that describes the wrongful disclosure to the media of classified information by senior government officials." The case continued in 2009.

## *VSDA* v. *Schwarzenegger*

In February 2008 AAP joined with other members of Media Coalition in filing an amicus brief urging the Ninth Circuit Court of Appeals to uphold a district court ruling in *VSDA* v. *Schwarzenegger* that struck down a California statute regulating the sale of violent video games. In August 2007 a U.S. District Court in California issued a permanent injunction barring enforcement of the statute, which would have banned the sale or rental of video games depicting violence in an "especially heinous, cruel or depraved" manner to anyone under 18, and would have required manufacturers and distributors to place warning labels on such games. The brief argues that the language of the statute is unconstitutionally vague and that the lower court was right in rejecting the state's attempt to regulate First Amendment-protected material on the basis of violent content.

## Legal Challenge to National Security Letters

AAP—along with ALA, the American Booksellers Foundation for Expression (ABFFE), the Freedom to Read Foundation, PEN American Center, and the American Association of University Professors—filed an amicus brief in March 2008 urging the U.S. Court of Appeals for the Second Circuit to uphold a lower court ruling that the National Security Letter (NSL) gag order is unconstitutional.

The brief was filed in support of a legal challenge brought by the American Civil Liberties Union (ACLU) and an unnamed "John Doe" Internet service provider, asserting that changes in the reauthorized USAPatriot Act did not correct constitutional flaws in its NSL provision. During the course of the litigation, the FBI withdrew the request for information under the NSL but left in place the accompanying permanent gag order.

In September 2007 U.S. District Court Judge Victor Marrero held the gag order to be a prior restraint of speech in violation of the First Amendment. Judge Marrero also found with respect to challenges to the gag order that the revised statute "impermissibly ties the judiciary's hands," depriving the courts of the ability to conduct a proper judicial review, in violation of the constitutional separation of powers.

The brief argues that under the amended NSL statute "the threat to bookstores and libraries remains." Although the revised statute purports to create an exemption for libraries, the brief stated, "it does nothing of the sort for the vast majority of libraries . . . To the extent that a library offers users the ability to send electronic communications—and virtually all libraries do—then the government may still 'seek records from libraries that many . . . fear will chill speech and use of these invaluable public institutions'."

## Journalist's Protection

Concern over the erosion of fundamental free press protections prompted the Freedom to Read Committee to continue to monitor and oppose coercive attempts to force journalists to reveal confidential sources.

One such case involved former *USA Today* reporter Toni Locy. On March 11, 2008, AAP joined in seeking an emergency ruling from the U.S. Court of Appeals for the District of Columbia to temporarily suspend payment of fines of up to $5,000 per day imposed on Locy for refusing to disclose sources for stories about the 2001 anthrax attacks. The fines were imposed by U.S. District Court Judge Reggie B. Walton in connection with a Privacy Act lawsuit brought against the government by former Army biological weapons expert Stephen Hatfill. In issuing the contempt citation against Locy, who now teaches journalism at West Virginia University, Walton refused to stay payment of the fines pending appeal and ordered Locy to "personally bear the responsibility" of paying the fines without assistance from *USA Today* or anyone else, a ruling the brief called "unwarranted, unprecedented, and overbroad." The following day the federal appellate court suspended payment of the fines pending Locy's appeal.

The appeal was argued in May, but no decision was handed down. Hatfill subsequently settled with the government for $5.8 million and the federal appeals court dismissed the appeal and vacated the district court's contempt order.

The Locy case highlighted the need for a federal shield law for journalists, and this continues to be a high legislative priority for AAP.

## *Powell's* v. *Myers*

AAP joined with six Oregon booksellers, the ACLU of Oregon, and other plaintiffs in challenging a new Oregon law that criminalizes the dissemination of sexually explicit material to anyone under the age of 13 or the dissemination to anyone under the age of 18 of any material with the intent to sexually arouse the recipient or the provider.

The lawsuit, filed April 25 in federal district court in Portland, sought an injunction barring enforcement of the statute, which it called unconstitutionally vague and overbroad and which it claimed burdens the exercise of free expression and creates a chilling effect on the sale, display, and dissemination of constitutionally protected speech. ABFFE, one of the plaintiffs, said that enforcement of the statute would be a "logistical nightmare" for Oregon booksellers.

In a ruling on December 12, a federal district judge refused to strike down the statute, which makes no provision for judging the material as a whole, or for considering its serious literary, artistic, or scientific value as required under the Supreme Court's *Miller* and *Ginsberg* rulings. In an approach he termed a "functional equivalency test" that relied heavily upon legislative history rather than the plain language of the statute, the judge concluded that nothing that is legal under the First Amendment would be illegal under the Oregon statute. The plaintiffs planned an appeal to the Ninth Circuit.

## *Big Hat Books* v. *Prosecutors*

In May 2008 AAP joined with booksellers, librarians, the Indianapolis Museum of Art, and civil liberties groups in challenging a new state law that trampled on the First Amendment rights of booksellers and other retailers in Indiana. The plaintiffs, including the Indiana ACLU and the Indianapolis Museum of Art, filed suit in federal district court in Indianapolis seeking an injunction barring enforcement of the statute.

The new law required any retailer that created a new establishment or relocated an existing one after July 1 and who sold or intended to sell any "sexually explicit material" to register with the Indiana Secretary of State as an "adult" business and to pay a $250 registration fee. Registration information would be passed along for monitoring by local governments, in effect creating a blacklist of "adult" retailers. The statutory language was so broad and ambiguous that bookstores carrying art and photography books, sex- and health-education materials, romance novels, and even classic fiction would be caught up in the "adult" business registry.

On July 1, the day the law was to go into effect, it was struck down by a federal judge in Indianapolis. Granting the plaintiffs' motion for summary judgment and holding the statute to be unconstitutionally vague and overbroad, U.S. District Court Judge Sarah Evans Barker pointed out that "A romance novel sold at a drugstore, a magazine offering sex advice in a grocery store checkout line, an R-rated DVD sold by a video rental shop, a collection of old *Playboy* magazines sold by a widow at a garage sale—all incidents of unquestionably lawful, non-obscene, non-pornographic material being sold to adults—would appear to necessitate registration under the statute." The state did not appeal the ruling.

## *Gorran* v. *Atkins Nutritionals*

More than a year after filing an amicus brief in *Gorran* v. *Atkins Nutritionals,* AAP welcomed a ruling by the U.S. Court of Appeals for the Second Circuit dismissing this trade practices suit, which had been brought by a former dieter against the bestselling Atkins diet book and Web site. AAP had taken the lead in an amicus brief in April 2007, urging the Second Circuit to reject arguments that the book, *Dr. Atkins' New Diet Revolution,* as well as portions of the Atkins Web site, were "commercial speech" because they promote the sale of Atkins-branded products, and are thus unprotected by the First Amendment and subject to state unfair competition laws. In its ruling, the Second Circuit held that the book and the Web site were not commercial speech but rather First Amendment-protected expression that sought to "communicate a particular view on health, diet, and nutrition, with an offer to purchase the message."

## *Trump* v. *O'Brien*

In the spring of 2007 AAP joined an amicus brief asking a New Jersey state appeals court to reject a lower court order compelling author Timothy O'Brien to turn over research material and identify confidential sources for his book *TrumpNation.* O'Brien and his publisher, Warner Books, were sued for defamation by Donald Trump, who claimed injury to his business reputation from the book's low estimation of his net worth. The trial court's order concluded that O'Brien's confidential sources were not entitled to state shield law protection since the book was "entertainment" not "news," notwithstanding the fact that as a financial reporter for the *New York Times* O'Brien had covered Trump's business dealings for years.

On October 24, the New Jersey Superior Court handed down a ruling reversing the trial court order, noting that books by investigative journalists are fully protected under state shield laws. The appellate court ruling made several references to AAP's amicus brief.

### Florida Rejects 'False Light' Claims

On October 23, 2008, the Florida Supreme Court ruled that "false light invasion of privacy" was not recognized as a cause of action under Florida law.

AAP and other media organizations had filed an amicus brief in *Rapp* v. *Jews for Jesus* after a lower state appellate court asked for a ruling on the viability of "false light" claims under Florida law. The case was argued in spring 2008, along with another false light case, *Anderson* v. *Gannett,* in which AAP had also filed an amicus brief.

"False light" claims, which are recognized in a number of states, allow plaintiffs to bring what are essentially defamation suits without having to surmount the substantive and procedural protections afforded defendants under defamation law. Such protections include placing the burden on the plaintiff to prove the speech false and intended to damage the plaintiff's reputation, and requiring that media defendants be given written notice and an opportunity to issue a correction or retraction before a suit is brought. The vague and ambiguous nature of the "false light" tort makes it a particularly serious threat to media defendants.

In its ruling, the Florida Supreme Court followed arguments made in AAP's brief, finding false light invasion of privacy to duplicate defamation without the First Amendment protections of defamation law, and finding the standard for false light (speech that is "highly offensive to a reasonable person") to be too vague to avoid chilling protected speech.

## Higher Education

AAP's Higher Education group serves the needs and interests of AAP members who publish for the postsecondary educational market. John Isley (Pearson Education) chaired the Higher Education Executive Committee in 2008.

During the year AAP continued to work at the federal and state levels with legislators and policy-makers, the National Association of College Stores and its members, the Text and Academic Authors Association, and students to address concerns about the price of course materials and to emphasize the range of choices and value of these educational resources.

AAP efforts included educating policy-makers and amending—or, if necessary, opposing—legislative initiatives that would limit the ability of textbook publishers to develop the best materials for faculties and students, restrict the sale of course materials and the release of new editions and technologies, and codify unworkable mandates for disclosing pricing and product information.

Textbook-related legislation was introduced in 29 states and was signed into law in eight: Arizona, Colorado, Florida, Iowa, Louisiana, Missouri, New Jersey, and New York. At the federal level, the Higher Education Opportunity Act, which included specific provisions relating to publishers, was also signed into law.

### Accessibility of Instructional Materials

In December 2008 AAP announced an agreement with the Alternative Media Access Center (AMAC), an initiative of the Georgia Board of Regents and the University System of Georgia, to develop and launch the AccessText Network, a comprehensive national online system that will make it easier and faster for students with print-related disabilities, such as blindness, to obtain the textbooks needed for their college courses.

The AccessText Network will improve the way electronic versions of print textbooks are delivered from publishers to campus-based disability services to students (DSS) offices and streamline the permission process for scanning copies of print textbooks when publisher files are unavailable, as well as for reusing alternate formats created by DSS offices. The service was using QuickBase, an online database powered by Intuit Inc., to enable publishers and colleges to effectively combine and share resources and expertise to meet students' needs.

The AccessText Network is the result of a multifaceted effort that included talks with disability service professionals, a nationwide review of current practices, exploration of existing distribution systems, and collaboration with the E-Text Solutions Group at the Association on Higher Education and Disability (AHEAD) and with AAP member publishers.

Funding for the development of AccessText was provided through donations by eight publishers: Cengage Learning, CQ Press, John Wiley & Sons, Macmillan, McGraw-Hill, Pearson, Reed Elsevier, and W. W. Norton.

### Critical Issues Task Force

The Higher Education Group's Critical Issues Task Force (CITF) guided the first stages of development of the AccessText Network. Members of CITF, who represent publishers of textbooks and other instructional materials for the postsecondary educational market in the United States, work exclusively on issues involving the provision of accessible instructional materials to students with print-related disabilities in postsecondary education.

CITF's efforts include responding to state legislative and policy initiatives and providing input to help shape accessibility provisions in draft legislation and implementation rules and guidelines.

CITF and publishers continued to maintain the Publisher Look-Up Service (http://www.publisherlookup.org), a site created by AAP to help DSS offices find the appropriate contacts at publishing houses to facilitate requests for electronic files or permissions to reproduce instructional materials in electronic form.

## International Copyright Protection

AAP's International Copyright Protection Committee (ICPC) works to combat international copyright piracy, to increase fair access to foreign markets, and to strengthen foreign intellectual property laws. The program continued to expand its reach in 2008, focusing not only on immediate policy and enforcement objectives but on projects with long-term benefits engaging nontraditional actors (especially education ministries and universities) in the piracy fight, and on efforts to quantify the costs of piracy to the publishing industry. Deborah Wiley (John Wiley & Sons) chaired the committee in 2008.

The People's Republic of China was once again a significant focus of AAP's efforts, with substantial work on market access and related policy issues, in addition to ongoing efforts on copyright protection. AAP supported several U.S. government China-related initiatives in 2008, including two cases in the World Trade Organization and bilateral discussions under the aegis of the Joint Commission on Commerce and Trade and the Strategic Economic Dialogue. These government-to-government engagements helped spotlight the significant cost to U.S. companies of China's restrictions on foreign investment in publishing-related activities and of rampant piracy.

AAP worked again with colleagues at Britain's Publishers Association (PA), continuing efforts to combat infringement of higher education textbooks at institutions of higher learning throughout China and intensifying their engagement with the Chinese government on Internet piracy. There was increasing evidence of widespread online piracy of journals and books in the academic sector, involving some of China's most prestigious universities. AAP and PA also worked to thwart the activities of one particularly active pirate of medical and scientific journals, using both the traditional Chinese enforcement system and working with member companies and publishing partners to focus political attention on the problem.

AAP also developed proposals for a government-industry partnership to deal with the growing number of on-campus infringement issues, including online piracy of academic materials and textbook reproduction, and the use and dissemination of illegal copies (hard copy and electronic) by academic and institutional libraries in China. AAP is developing strategies for 2009 focusing on the role of the university/library in ensuring conformity to national and international copyright standards.

AAP continued its textbook enforcement program in China, with actions against Zhejiang University in March and Shanghai Jiaotong University in September. These actions resulted in the seizure of more than 1,000 infringing copies and prompted punitive action by local authorities. AAP continued to press for active implementation of three notices issued by Chinese authorities in late 2006 forbidding Chinese universities to engage in illegal reproduction of textbooks.

Thailand became a major focus of AAP's enforcement program in 2008 in response to a serious problem involving the printing of illegal high-quality higher education textbooks for shipment to markets outside Thailand. In attacking the problem AAP collaborated with the Thai government, including investigative authorities, police, and intellectual property and customs authorities. U.S. government authorities are working directly with the Thai government.

Early in the year, AAP was part of an international effort in Japan to raise and publicize concerns over a proposed limitation to Japanese copyright law that would adversely affect scientific publishers. The effort was mobilized largely by the Japan Medical Publishers Association, in cooperation with other groups based in Japan and several international publishing associations. AAP worked with U.S. government officials to place the issue on agendas for government-to-government dialogue, and met with Japanese authorities during a trip to Tokyo in January. AAP welcomed indications that the Japanese government is advocating a market-based solution to the problem, which was the industry's objective.

Following negotiation of the Korea-U.S. Free Trade Agreement, AAP spent 2008 monitoring efforts by both the U.S. and South Korean governments to effect legislative approval of the agreement. Passage was still pending in both countries at the time this report was prepared. AAP supports the intellectual property provisions of the agreement, which contain not only key elements of legal protection against online piracy but also specific language addressing book piracy on university campuses. The language focuses on efforts by South Korea's Ministry of Education and individual universities to end on-campus reproduction and use of infringing materials, and AAP was working to see that these efforts are undertaken even before the Free Trade Agreement goes into effect. In addition, raids in March and September 2008 continued to target large-scale pirate operations and numerous photocopy shops found near university campuses. Prosecutions stemming from those raids are expected.

AAP continued to work in Taiwan through the Taiwan Book Publishers Association (TBPA), an alliance between AAP member companies and Taiwanese publishers. TBPA was active in 2008, cooperating with the Taiwan Intellectual Property Office and the Ministry of Education to put policies and programs in place to reduce on-campus piracy. AAP has also made sure that its member company representatives are aware of an important initiative to create and grow a reproduction-rights organization in Taiwan called the Chinese Oral and Literary Copyright Intermediary Association. AAP supported TBPA's efforts, working with local law enforcement authorities and the Ministry of Justice, to conduct raids in spring and fall 2008 to coincide with the start of the university terms. Especially notable were wide-scale fall raids throughout the island (including the cities of Taipei, Taichung, Tainan, HsinChu, I-Lan, HwaLian, and TaoYuan), resulting in seizures of nearly 1,000 pirated copies from 56 shops.

In Hong Kong, AAP's primary focus was an ongoing legislative process affecting foreign and local publishers, covering such issues as the scope of criminal liability for infringement of books and journals, exemptions from liability, and the application of copyright in the digital environment. AAP joined in enforcement activities with the Hong Kong Customs and Excise Department with a sharpened focus on ferreting out underground copy facilities. City-wide raids in January, June, September, and October 2008 were timed to coincide with the start of the university sessions.

AAP sought prosecutorial and judicial reform in the Philippines, raising awareness of the negative effects of the system's weaknesses on legitimate publishers and other intellectual property owners seeking to do business there. AAP worked closely with authorities including the Intellectual Property Office of the

Philippines and the National Book Development Board to ensure that publishers' voices were being heard with respect to policy development procedures within the two organizations on such subjects as fair use in an educational context and collective licensing for printed materials.

In cooperation with U.S. government officials who have taken great interest in the industry's issues, AAP continued engagement in India and Pakistan, including bilateral discussions and monitoring of enforcement, legislative, and educational issues in both countries.

AAP and its member companies were active in education, policy making, and related initiatives in Malaysia, Brazil, Singapore, Russia, Vietnam, Chile, Indonesia, Canada, and elsewhere. In February 2008 AAP, as a member of the International Intellectual Property Alliance, submitted specific recommendations regarding intellectual property protection in various foreign countries to the U.S. Trade Representative (USTR) as part of USTR's annual Special 301 review of intellectual property and market access problems worldwide. AAP members estimated annual losses of more than $500 million as a result of copyright piracy and related intellectual property theft.

## International Freedom to Publish

AAP's International Freedom to Publish Committee (IFTP) defends and promotes freedom of written communication worldwide. The committee monitors human rights issues and provides moral support and practical assistance to publishers and authors outside the United States who are denied basic freedoms. The committee carries on its work in close cooperation with other human rights groups, including the International Publishers Association's Freedom to Publish Committee, Human Rights Watch, and PEN American Center. Hal Fessenden (Viking Penguin) served as committee chairman in 2008.

In 2003 the committee established the Jeri Laber International Freedom to Publish Award, to be given annually to a book publisher outside the United States who has demonstrated courage in the face of political persecution. The award, which carries a cash prize, is named in honor of human rights activist Jeri Laber, one of IFTP's founding members, who continues to direct its work as an AAP consultant. The award has been given to publishers in Iran, Turkey, Indonesia, Egypt, and Cambodia.

The 2008 Laber award went to Kho Tararith and the Nou Hach Literary Project in Cambodia, which supports the development of modern Cambodian literature. Among other things, the group sponsors an annual writer's conference and workshop. The prize money will be used to pay for the group's annual publication in the Khmer language.

When the committee's candidate for the 2007 Jeri Laber Award, a prominent independent book publisher in Iran, declined the honor for fear of government reprisal, the committee decided to honor instead the entire beleaguered publishing community in Iran for its ongoing commitment to freedom of expression under extreme duress. Because it is not advisable to send U.S. funds into Iran, it was decided that the 2007 Laber Award would be used in the United States to help Iranian publishers traveling here. In 2008 the committee offered this award as a stipend to a courageous Iranian publisher planning to spend some months in the United States. However, at the last moment, Iranian authorities denied a visa to the publisher in question and, at the time this report was prepared, the visit had not taken place.

The committee continues to monitor developments in Iran and the situation of writers and publishers there. It has expressed its deep concern over "Procedural Guidelines for Publication" issued by the Iranian Ministry of Culture and Islamic Guidance. Intended to eliminate "unhealthy products" from books, the guidelines require a permit from the ministry for the distribution of all books.

IFTP also watches events in Turkey, including the ongoing harassment and persecution of writers, publishers, and journalists. Although Article 301 of the Turkish penal code was changed from "insulting Turkishness" to "insulting the state," setbacks continue to occur in Turkey.

IFTP members meet with writers, publishers, human rights activists, and others in areas where freedom of expression is seriously threatened. In 2008 committee members Hal Fessenden and Wendy Wolf, together with Larry Siems of PEN and several others, met in Cambodia with government officials, including the minster of education and the minister of information, with several non-governmental organizations, with children's book publishers, the Khmer Writers Association, and with the editor of a literary journal. Fessenden and Wolf conducted an all-day publishing seminar and Siems discussed the formation of a PEN chapter. The visiting committee members found that there is virtually no literature or independent publishing in Cambodia at present, and that censorship is deep and inbred.

The committee, together with the AAP president and CEO, sends letters of protest to government officials about violations of free expression in their countries. In 2008 letters were sent to three Azerbaijani officials about the prison sentence of Eynulla Fatullayev, an Azeri newspaper editor. Committee members in their individual capacities signed letters protesting the seizure in Russia of the files of the human rights organization Memorial and a letter in defense of Liu Xiaobo, a prominent human rights activist detained in China.

From time to time the committee makes small monetary contributions to free expression causes. In 2008 it approved a grant of $2,000 to pay for a shipment of the newspaper the *Zimbabwean,* published in South Africa and smuggled into Zimbabwe, and an additional grant of $500 to pay for a subscription to the newspaper that will go to a library in Zimbabwe.

During the year the committee hosted a number of speakers on various topics and from different parts of the world.

PEN American Center's Siems kept the committee informed about the situation of Iraqi translators being processed for entry into the United States; Joel Simon of the Committee to Protect Journalists (CPJ) kept the committee informed of the human rights situation in China at the time of the Olympics; Nina Ognianova spoke to the committee about freedom of expression in Russia "after" Putin; Nahid Mozaffari reported frequently on the situation of writers and publishers in Iran; Li Jianqiang, attorney and spokesperson for Chinese dissidents, spoke to the committee about dissent in China; Tom Rhodes of CPJ spoke to the committee about Zimbabwe; Elyse Lightman talked about Cambodia; Rachel Denber of Human Rights Watch spoke about the Russia-Georgia conflict over

South Ossetia; Carroll Bogert of Human Rights Watch described the human rights positions of presidential candidates John McCain and Barack Obama; Daniel Wilkinson of Human Rights Watch spoke about free expression in Venezuela; Joel Simon of CPJ spoke about climate change and the media; Rob Mahoney of CPJ spoke about the Global Network Initiative; and Steve Hubbell described the Open Society Institute's new fellowship program.

## Professional/Scholarly Publishing

AAP's Professional and Scholarly Publishing Division (PSP) is composed of association members who publish books, journals, loose-leaf, and electronic products in technology, science, medicine, business, law, humanities, the social and behavioral sciences, and scholarly reference. Professional societies and university presses, along with commercial organizations, play an important role in the division. Michael Hays (McGraw-Hill Higher Education) chaired the PSP Executive Council in 2008.

John Tagler, who has more than 35 years' experience in scientific, technical, and medical publishing, joined PSP in April 2008 as its vice president and executive director.

The 2008 PSP Annual Conference, "Interactivity 2008: Communities, Content, Connectivity," was held in Washington, D.C. Before the opening of the meeting, the PSP Electronic Information Committee sponsored a preconference seminar on "Cyberscholarship: Where Are Our Users Taking Us?" The conference had the highest registration level in more than five years.

The division sponsors an awards program, open only to AAP/PSP members, to acknowledge outstanding achievements in professional, scholarly, and reference publishing. In 2008 the R. R. Hawkins Award for the outstanding professional/scholarly work of the year went to *The Dream of the Poem* by Peter Cole, published by Princeton University Press. In addition, book awards were presented in more than 30 subject categories, in design and production, and in journal and electronic publishing. The PSP awards program donated more than 250 books to libraries in Washington, D.C. Each year, PSP donates scholarly works covering 30 different disciplines that have competed for PSP Awards on the basis of their contribution to research, innovation, and excellence.

A top priority for 2008 was development of a strategic plan for PSP. The project was launched in 2007 at a two-day meeting at which the PSP Executive Council and members of PSP committees convened to assess the current state of PSP, establish priorities, and recommend a path forward for the division. Based on the initial 2007 findings, the PSP Strategic Plan 2008–2010 was produced in July 2008. The plan calls for PSP to become the center of a robust and vibrant community engaging its member organizations, their individual constituencies, and the broader publishing community with an entrepreneurial and innovative spirit. This vision will be achieved through focusing in the areas of stimulating membership and educating the PSP publishing community as well as the other constituencies with which it interacts to better understand, appreciate, and support the continuing role of the publishing industry.

A key strategy to achieve these goals is establishment of a membership committee that will determine ways to expand and diversify PSP membership, improve member satisfaction, and increase communication with member organizations. Another is the formation of an education committee to expand the role of education and training and, in collaboration with existing PSP committees, develop advocacy and outreach programs to provide member organizations with better understanding of issues relevant to the PSP community. Looking beyond the professional and scholarly publishing community, the outreach effort seeks to communicate messages to external groups such as government administrators, academics, librarians, and grantmaking organizations to create a better understanding of the publisher's role in the scholarly communication process.

In pursuing a greater awareness among PSP members, *PSP . . . Links,* a periodic e-mail alerting service, was launched in mid-August. *PSP . . . Links* provides a quick, expedient, and inexpensive channel for communicating with the PSP community and raising awareness about a broad range of topics. It highlights new items on the PSP and AAP Web sites, announces educational seminars and conferences offered by PSP as well as other organizations with programs of interest, and points readers to articles, Web sites, and job postings of interest.

In a larger outreach to both members and external communities, a significantly revised pspcentral Web site (http://www.pspcentral.org) was launched in September. Led by the PSP Public Relations Committee, the site has a more contemporary look with many new features to make searching easier and more intuitive. A new section was launched on the site, "Publishing Facts: Learn More About Scholarly Information," providing a primer on the fundamentals of scholarly publishing.

In an effort to gain a better grasp on data relating to journals publishing in the professional and scholarly community, a concerted effort was made to maximize the response rate and usefulness of the AAP Annual Professional and Scholarly Journals Survey on 2007 journals publishing. The response rate improved considerably over the previous year's levels, with 19 publishers submitting data on 4,094 journals covering the years 2005–2007. Significantly, the journals in the sample published 595,926 articles in 2007, representing approximately 45 percent of the published scholarly and academic journal article output for that year. The information gathered in this most recent round of data collection provides a solid foundation for building a series of annual journal statistics reports that provide valuable insights into trends in professional and scholarly publishing.

Among the division's educational activities in 2008: the PSP American Medical Publishers Committee sponsored a Web seminar, "Publishing for the EHR 101," providing a multifaceted introduction to the world of electronic health records (EHRs) and its implications for medical publishers. The PSP Books Committee sponsored two one-day seminars, "Basics of Books Boot Camp," an entry-level overview of professional and scholarly book publishing, one in New York and a second in Chicago. The Books Committee also offered a one-day seminar for mid-level book publishers, "The Basics of E-Marketing." The PSP Journals Committee sponsored three seminars in the association's New York offices, "Making the Cut: How Librarians Apply Metrics and Other Factors in Evaluating Their Journals Collections," "Web Presence," and "Citation Analysis and Evaluating Research Performance: The Impact Factor, h-index and Beyond."

The PSP Public Issues Task Force has updated the PSP *Issues Glossary,* an online reference and research tool. This glossary is available through a new link on the home page of the PSP Web site: http://www.pspcentral.org/gloss/glossWelcome.cfm.

A new PSP membership brochure was produced for the first time in more than ten years. Titled *Building the Future of Professional and Scholarly Publishing,* the publication discusses the benefits of PSP membership and describes activities within the division as well as its committee structure and outreach efforts. The brochure is a cornerstone of a member-recruitment campaign under way in 2009.

AAP supported the Fair Copyright in Research Works Act, introduced on September 11, 2008, before the House Judiciary Subcommittee on Intellectual Property. AAP was active in organizing the publishing industry's submission of comments to the NIH Request for Information on the Public Access Policy during the two public comments periods, March 2008 and April-May 2008. Copies of AAP communications and comments as well as those from other publishing organizations can be found on pspcentral at http://www.pspcentral.org/commPublicAffairs/comPubAff-PubIss_001.cfm. [For more information, see "Legislation and Regulations Affecting Publishing in 2008" in Part 2—*Ed.*]

PSP supported or participated in a number of public service programs to provide medical information where it is needed throughout the world. PSP's American Medical Publishers' Committee (AMPC) collaborated with HOPE Worldwide to provide medical resources to obstetrics/gynecology fellows in residency programs in Afghanistan. More than 300 donated books will be used by physicians training in women's health at the Malalai Hospital at the Kabul University Medical School, the first-ever ob/gyn residency program in that country. AMPC was also active in answering a call from A. Hadi Al Khalili, M.D., cultural attaché to the Iraqi Embassy in Washington, D.C., to help relieve the acute shortage of quality medical references at Iraq's 20 medical schools. A core list of medical titles was compiled to serve medical students and residents and more than 3,000 books were received from 16 participating publishers. PSP continues to maintain active roles in Research4Life (a UN-coordinated global initiative for developing countries) and patientINFORM (a collaboration with four Virtual Health Organizations in the United States).

Internationally, PSP continues to cooperate with international publishing associations to find the right balance between fair use of intellectual property and rights holders' need to realize a fair return for their works. The division has worked with Britain's Publishing Association and the International Scientific, Technical, and Medical Association to gather information and produce reports on author/reader behavior and publishing trends in scholarly, professional, and academic research publishing.

## Resources for the Book Publishing Industry

### Compensation Reports

AAP continues to provide valuable aggregate data reports, including the annual *Survey on Compensation and Personnel Practices in the Book Publishing Indus-*

*try,* widely regarded as the most comprehensive and reliable source of data in this area. AAP's Compensation Committee, composed of senior compensation and human resources professionals, met throughout the year to create job descriptions and manage the survey process. Purchase of the report is available to participants in the survey.

Total Compensation Solutions, which produces the report for AAP, presented highlights of the 2008 report at AAP's Annual Human Resources Seminar, Compensation and Human Resources Practices in the Book Publishing Industry, in November.

The association also tracks holiday benefits for the publishing community and shares the data with a compensation committee of publishing industry professionals who independently oversee the holiday and vacation compensation for their respective houses.

**Annual Statistics**

AAP publishes industry statistics for all segments of book publishing, on a monthly and annual basis. Committees in the areas of consumer, trade, higher education, and professional publishing met throughout 2008 to revise the program and develop a strategy and implementation process for the dissemination of consumer and K–12 monthly reports. More than 80 publishers participate in AAP's monthly statistical reports, the only resource in publishing that aggregates revenue and compiles raw data on market size on a month-to-month basis, and provides year-to-date growth, based on participation by a cross section of the industry. In 2008 the organization also produced additional data points for the el-hi and international sales committees and directed a consumer outreach effort to journals publishers that resulted in a representation of 45 percent of total journal articles produced in the marketplace.

**Handbook on Book Paper and the Environment**

In February 2008 AAP unveiled its *Handbook on Book Paper and the Environment,* intended to assist publishers in navigating the confusing and often arcane issues relating to the development of environmental sustainability practices within the book publishing industry.

Developed by the AAP Paper Issues Working Group, the handbook is the first of its kind to address a range of environmental issues in the specific context of the book publishing industry, and reflects more than two years of extensive consultations and discussions with organizations representing a broad spectrum of interests, including environmental advocacy groups, forest certification and standards bodies, environmental industry consortiums and associations, economists, paper mills, and others, covering a host of governmental, commercial, and environmental issues as they relate to book paper production and the environment.

The handbook is intended to be an informational tool for book production professionals, their staff, and executive management interested in creating workable sustainability programs, providing up-to-date information to assist in efforts to balance economic and ecologic realities. Among the areas covered in the handbook are recycling (including pre- and post-consumer recycled fiber distinctions), forestry certification standards, "chain of custody" issues facing paper and recycling manufacturers, global practices and economic impacts, and green production efforts. The handbook also contains frequently asked questions, and organizational contact information.

The working group represents a broad cross section of the AAP membership. Its members include the American Chemical Society, Cambridge University Press, CQ Press, Hachette Book Group USA, Harcourt, HarperCollins USA, Harvest House Publishers, John Wiley & Sons, Keene Publishing, Lantern Books, Macmillan, McGraw-Hill, Pearson, Random House, Scholastic, Simon & Schuster, and W. W. Norton.

## School Division

During 2008 the AAP School Division again succeeded in its core mission of protecting funding for instructional materials and in serving as the national voice for the U.S. pre-K–12 school publishing industry. However, the School Division's successes early in the year were muted by the nation's economic downturn in the second half of the year. In 2008 net elementary and secondary (el-hi) sales increased by nearly 4 percent by June 30 only to tumble to -4.4 percent by December 31 as states and school districts began to cut budgets and slow spending.

### Public Policy

Under the direction and coordination of the School Division, school publishers achieved public policy victories in the 2008 legislative sessions that resulted in increased levels of funding for instructional materials.

*Florida*—Despite Florida's current budget crisis, funding for K–12 instructional materials fared well in the 2008 legislative session. AAP's advocacy efforts minimized cuts to instructional materials funding to 2.5 percent while most education budget lines were cut between 6 and 20 percent. The legislature funded instructional materials at $259,578,102, a reduction of $6,871,067.

*California*—The state's final budget for instructional materials provided $417.5 million—a slight cut of $2 million from the previous year. However, as a result of the state's economic crisis, it appeared that additional funds might be cut at mid-point in the fiscal year (early 2009).

*Texas*—AAP worked to ensure that "Proclamation 2010" for English, Language Arts, and Reading remains on track. The Texas legislature was not in session in 2008.

*Federal*—In November 2008 AAP and its members undertook an advocacy initiative for education spending in the federal economic stimulus package. AAP's efforts, along with those of many other national education organizations, succeeded in securing significant increases in education spending.

## Smaller and Independent Publishers

AAP's Smaller and Independent Publishing (SIP) Committee was created in 1998 to serve the special needs and interests of the association's small and independent publisher members. Gene Gollogley (Booklight, Inc.) continued to chair the committee in 2008.

In an effort to reach out to smaller and independent publishers on the West Coast, AAP experimented with hosting its annual SIP meeting in collaboration with BookExpo America in Los Angeles. Light BookExpo attendance prompted a decision to reschedule and relocate the meeting. It was held in November 2008 in New York, featuring an educational program titled "How to Navigate the Life Cycles of a Publishing House." The day-long program included sessions on successful start-ups, how to market on a small budget, and growth through organic means, plus seminars on acquisition, "going green" and copyright issues, and other topics. The meeting also featured presentation of the Miriam Bass Award for Creativity in Independent Publishing, which this year went to Archipelago Books, a Brooklyn-based not-for-profit literary press that specializes in world literature.

## Trade Publishing

AAP's Trade Publishing Group comprises publishers of fiction, general nonfiction, poetry, children's literature, religious, and reference publications, in hardcover, paperback, and electronic formats. Robert Miller (Hyperion) chaired the Trade Executive Committee for most of 2008, with Bridget Marmion (Houghton Mifflin Harcourt) succeeding him in the latter part of the year.

During the year the Trade Executive Committee undertook an initiative to provide information on forthcoming new titles via Web outreach through the launch of a pilot program, "Book Editors Online and Unscripted." The series of Webcasts that launched in September featured top editors previewing their winter 2009 book picks for an online audience of booksellers and the media. Over a two-week period, Book Editors Online and Unscripted featured two editors each day presenting upcoming winter titles, followed by a question-and-answer session moderated by then-*Publishers Weekly* editor-in-chief Sara Nelson. The half-hour presentations were Webcast live, allowing booksellers, librarians, the media, and other interested book professionals to follow them on the Internet, call in, and ask or type questions to participating editors immediately following the interview. The pilot program was created to respond to the cutbacks in space that newspapers are devoting to book reviews as well as cuts in reviewers' travel budgets. Until this pilot program got under way there had been no organized format that would give news media an opportunity to hear about winter 2009 titles from multiple publishers. Book Editors Online and Unscripted succeeded in engaging book media from coast to coast, allowing them to participate without leaving their desks.

Anticipating less-than-robust book sales for the holiday season, in late 2008 publishers and their authors collaborated to create a first-of-its-kind multimedia book campaign, BooksAreGreatGifts.com, offering a host of entertaining, funny, and thoughtful reasons why books make the perfect gift for every holiday throughout the year. An industry-wide effort facilitated by AAP, the campaign was created as a way of stimulating traffic to retail and online booksellers in the face of the economic downturn. The centerpiece of the campaign was a video produced by Random House featuring well-known public figures and authors from a number of AAP member houses, including Maya Angelou, Jonathan Lethem, Frank McCourt, Christopher Paolini, Jim Cramer, Alec Baldwin, and Barbara Walters. The BooksAreGreatGifts.com Web site also aggregated links to industry resources, including publisher sites that spotlight other creative content marketing books as great gifts, bestseller lists, Facebook pages, and reading group networks. The effort signified a collaborative "first" in trade publishing, bringing publishers and their authors together with the retail community. Participating publishers included Hachette Book Group, HarperCollins, Houghton Mifflin Harcourt, Hyperion, John Wiley & Sons, Penguin Group (USA), Random House, Simon & Schuster, St. Martin's, and W. W. Norton.

The video can be viewed through a link on the BooksAreGreatGifts.com Web site or streamed via YouTube. Retailers across the country shared the video with their customers. Expanded Books, a media distributor connecting publishers and booksellers to potential clients, agreed to distribute the author video to such major online resources as Yahoo! and MSN. Spanish-language television outlet Univision joined in the promotion and the video was featured on Amazon and Barnes & Noble sites. Serving as a springboard for promoting books as gifts year-round, the BooksAreGreatGifts.com campaign will feature video public service announcements with additional authors in 2009.

The Trade Group is responsible for the AAP Honors award program, identifying and selecting candidates from outside the publishing industry who have helped promote American books and authors. The honors are presented each year at the AAP Annual Meeting. In 2008 the AAP Honors went to the National Book Critics Circle for its unique contribution to America's literary life.

**Publishing Latino Voices of America**

AAP works to increase awareness of Latino books through its Publishing Latino Voices for America (PLVA) Task Force, and implemented several new programs in 2008. Prominent among them was the Las Comadres Borders National Book Club. Las Comadres, a national Latina organization, in cooperation with AAP and Borders, announced the launch of the Las Comadres and Friends National Latino Book Club at select Borders stores in Arizona, California, Florida, Illinois, Massachusetts, New Mexico, Texas, and Utah. Membership is open to anyone interested in reading English-language works written by Latina or Latino authors. Bestselling author Esmeralda Santiago served as the official spokesperson for the club, which grew out of a series of highly successful monthly teleconferences hosted by the Las Comadres network and featuring a book club-selected author.

During 2008 PLVA created a new *Latino Voices* brochure for the bookselling, library, and educational communities, and distributed it to schools and through book fairs and related events across the country. It was complemented by a recommended-reading list for May Latino Books Month. Focusing in particular on children's books, AAP created a new campaign to promote Día de los Niños/ Día de los Libros. Held each year held on April 30, it is a celebration of the written word for children of all cultural backgrounds created and produced by the Association for Library Service to Children, a division of the American Library Association (see http://www.ala.org/ala/dia). A list of recommended children's titles selected by ALSC was developed and promoted across the country, and the

list is available on ¡Ajá, leyendo!, AAP's Get Caught Reading Spanish component, at http://www.getcaughtreading.org.

### Adopt-A-School

AAP continued to match authors with schools throughout New York's five bor-
oughs as part of its Adopt-A-School program. Working with the New York City
Department of Education, the program, which launched in 2004, each year
matches 25 schools with authors to promote the joy of books and reading among
the city's children, ranging from pre-kindergarten through high school. Elementary, middle, and high schools were paired with publishers for author visits during Children's Book Week in November.

### Trade Libraries Committee

The association's Trade Libraries Committee, chaired by Talia Ross (Macmillan)
comprises representatives of major book publishing houses in partnership with
organizations including the American Library Association. The committee continued to focus its efforts in 2008 on promoting titles, hosting educational sessions for librarians at various trade conventions including BookExpo America,
the ALA Annual Conference, and the Texas Library Association meeting. The
committee hosted a second successful author dinner in Los Angeles at BookExpo
America 2008 featuring authors including Katherine Neville, David Fuller, Kate
Jacobs, Brad Meltzer, and Jennifer Haigh. The committee hosted a "book buzz"
program with marketing representatives as well as an educational session entitled
"What Librarians Wish Publishers Knew: What Makes Them Tick and What
Ticks Them Off."

## 2008 Annual Meeting

Some 200 publishing industry leaders and their guests gathered at the Yale Club in
New York City on March 5, 2008, for a dialogue on "The Future of Publishing."

Borders Group CEO George Jones (interviewed by Hachette Book Group
USA's David Young), Amazon.com's Steve Kessel (interviewed by AAP Chair-
man Richard Sarnoff), and the recently retired head of house of Simon &
Schuster, Jack Romanos (interviewed by bestselling author and Aspen Institute
President Walter Isaacson), shared what was, overall, an upbeat vision of the
industry and its ability to reinvent itself.

## FY 2008–2009 Budget Approved

The membership approved an operating budget of $9.5 million for fiscal year
2008–2009, with $6 million allocated to core activities; $1.1 million allocated to
Higher Education, and $2.4 million to the two divisions ($1.5 million for School
Division and $900,000 for PSP). A shortfall of $1.1 million will be drawn from
cash reserves.

# American Booksellers Association

200 White Plains Rd., Tarrytown, NY 10591
914-591-2665
World Wide Web http://www.BookWeb.org

Jill Perlstein
Director, Member Services

Founded in 1900, the American Booksellers Association (ABA) is a not-for-profit trade organization devoted to meeting the needs of its core members—independently owned bookstores with storefront locations—by providing advocacy, opportunities for peer interaction, education, support services, and new business models. ABA actively supports free speech, literacy, and programs that encourage reading. The association also hosts the annual ABA Convention in conjunction with the BookExpo America (BEA) conference and trade show.

## 2008 Highlights

In November 2007 then-ABA President Russ Lawrence announced in ABA's newsletter, *Bookselling This Week,* the creation of organizational Ends Statements, expressing the board's long-term goals. Ends Statements are an expression of what good ABA does, for whom, and at what cost or priority to the organization. The top-level Ends Statement that ABA adopted states: "ABA member bookstores will be professionally operated and profitable, and income derived from regular members' fees will be equal to, or less than, those of comparable trade associations." ABA CEO Avin Mark Domnitz is responsible for creating an annual strategic plan for the staff to follow in achieving these ends. Lawrence noted that this organizational change allows the ABA board to react more swiftly to shifts in membership priorities and other situations, thus positioning ABA to continue to lead in the bookselling industry.

Although ABA provides programs and services to a variety of industry professionals, its primary focus is on its core members. Independent booksellers are a profitable and growing force in a diverse marketplace, and are recognized as influential and vital links between authors, readers, publishers, and the community.

In 2008 ABA's members, like the rest of the retail world, continued to face rising rents, increases in costs, and a faltering economy. In addition, independent booksellers were confronted with growing competition for consumers' time and discretionary income from other media—including, increasingly, the Internet—as well as direct competition from a growing number of retail locations now selling books.

However, despite the challenges, independent bookstores continued to open in communities across the nation. A post-holiday season survey of independent retailers (including bookstores) conducted by the Institute for Local Self-Reliance found that the independent retailers were outperforming many chains at the end of 2008. Holiday sales at independent stores declined an average of 5 percent from the same time period in 2007, which compares favorably with the results of stores, open at least a year, of most competing chains. The survey also found that independent retailers in cities with active "buy local" campaigns reported much stronger holiday sales than those in cities without such campaigns. Independent retailers in these cities reported an average drop in sales of 3.2 percent, compared with a decline of 5.6 percent for those in cities without an active buy local initiative.

Although overall membership numbers have dropped, ABA remains strong as booksellers look to their association for education, products and services, advocacy, and networking opportunities. During 2008, despite the bleak economic landscape, ABA welcomed the openings of 69 new independent bookstores, four branch stores, and two online-only booksellers.

At the end of January 2008 ABA held its third annual Winter Institute in Louisville, Kentucky. The sold-out event, attended by more than 500 booksellers, began with a welcoming reception at Louisville's Muhammad Ali Center. The institute featured 24 education sessions over a two-day period, as well as a dozen "Rep Picks" presentations of notable upcoming titles and three keynote author events. Highlights included a roundtable discussion featuring authors Bill McKibben, Stacy Mitchell, and Michael Shuman, who talked about the role booksellers play in their communities, the buy local movement, and growing consumer awareness of the importance of locally owned independent businesses. ABA and publishers provided scholarships to a number of booksellers who otherwise might not have had the means to attend. The Winter Institute, which is free to ABA bookstore and provisional members, was repeated January 29–February 1, 2009, in Salt Lake City. Booksellers needed to pay only for their transportation and hotel room.

In March and April 2008 ABA senior staff and board members toured the country to hold bookseller forums in conjunction with regional bookseller association events. These annual member outreach meetings have no agenda and are designed to allow booksellers to have direct conversations with association staff and board members. In keeping with ABA's mission, education sessions were presented at each of the nine forums in eight states.

In fall 2008 ABA once again hosted educational programs at each of the regional booksellers' trade association shows, which take place every year beginning in September. ABA staff presented sessions ranging from "Green Retailing" and "Consumer Behavior Revealed" to fundamentals of budgeting and monitoring a store's financial operations.

### Convention and Expo

At the end of May 2008 ABA held its annual convention in conjunction with BookExpo America (BEA) at the Los Angeles Convention Center. ABA offered a full day of educational programming, highlighted by a variety of peer-to-peer and interactive opportunities at "Hotel ABA" in Hollywood. Hotel ABA is the exclusive bookseller-only hotel, where members receive group-rate rooms as well as other benefits, including publisher-sponsored receptions, welcome bags, and dedicated shuttle bus service. A "Welcome to Hollywood" pre-BEA event included walking tours, a trip to the Getty Museum, and a reception at the Egyptian Theatre.

The day of education began with an opening plenary session keynote address by actor and environmentalist Ed Begley, Jr. on the day-to-day realities of "living green." Other sessions included "Booksellers at the Tipping Point: Leveraging Localism and Independence to Promote Your Store," "Buying, Merchandising, and Selling Graphic Novels," "Building and Rewarding Customer Loyalty," "Green Retailing," "Print on Demand," "Give It Away to Get It Back: Using 'Thought Leadership' Marketing to Build Your Children's Business," "Renegotiating Your Lease," "Buying, Managing, and Selling Non-Book Items," "Creating Killer Events," "Managing Blockbuster Events: The Logistics of Events for 500 or More," "Loss Control: How to Stop Profits from Running Out the Front (and Back) Door," "Independent Retailing in 2008: A Report on the Shop Local Movement," "RFID: What You Need to Know," "Introduction to Co-op Advertising," and a budgeting and monitoring workshop.

As part of the luncheon programming, Amy Goodman—author and co-host of the radio and television news program "Democracy Now!"—spoke on the importance of individual conscience and action in a democracy and the role of booksellers in democratic society.

Also at BEA, in conjunction with ABA, the bookstore training and consulting group Paz & Associates conducted a bookseller's school aimed at prospective and new booksellers.

After an intense day of education, more than 900 people crowded into the Renaissance Hollywood Grand Ballroom for ABA's Celebration of Bookselling. Attendees heard acceptance speeches from the Book Sense Book of the Year Award winners, the *Publishers Weekly* Bookseller of the Year, the Pannell Award winners, and learned about the new ABA initiative IndieBound.

The winner of the Bookseller of the Year award was Vroman's Bookstore in Pasadena, California. The Lucile Micheels Pannell Award, sponsored by the Women's National Book Association, honors "the work of booksellers who stimulate, promote and encourage children's and young people's interest in books"; the 2009 recipients were (general bookstore) Kepler's Books and Magazines of Menlo Park, California, and (children's specialty bookstore) the Flying Pig Book Bookstore of Shelburne, Vermont. [For the Book Sense Book of the Year award winners, see "Literary Awards" in Part 5—*Ed.*]

### IndieBound Debuts

At the celebration, ABA CEO Domnitz introduced the attendees and the industry to the association's newest initiative, IndieBound. This innovative, community-oriented movement brings booksellers, readers, independent retailers, and local business alliances together. The mission of IndieBound is to enlighten consumers about the value of independent businesses, and to provide the means to help build—and sustain—healthy communities.

In the days following BEA, IndieBound's Literary Liberation Boxes—containing an IndieBound start-up kit, posters, bookmarks, buttons, staff shirts, decals, and more—began arriving at ABA member bookstores. A wide selection of IndieBound resources are available to members via ABA's Web site (http://www.BookWeb.org), to help booksellers adapt the materials for their own communities. All of ABA's former Book Sense programs were relaunched with an IndieBound-inspired look and energy. The Book Sense Picks List became the "Indie Next List—Great Reads from Booksellers You Trust." The Book Sense

Bestseller List was renamed the Indie Bestseller List. BookSense.com and the Book Sense Gift Card program were renamed the ABA E-Commerce Solution and the ABA Gift Card Program, respectively (both programs continue to offer bookstores cost-effective tools to meet the growing consumer demand in these areas).

In an effort to reach out to consumers and to build a new social network, IndieBound.org was launched. Book lovers can become fans of their favorite independent bookstores and other businesses, "friend" other members of the IndieBound community, add their favorite indie retailers to the site's searchable database, and build wish lists of book titles, with new functionality continually being added to the site.

One of the many IndieBound spirit-lines—"Eat, Sleep, Read"—has been spotted in windows, on doors, and on ceilings of bookstores all over the country. IndieGear is available, including T-shirts, sweatshirts, and even onesies for infants. Still in its early stages, IndieBound is evolving and capturing the imagination of a growing number of independent-minded people and businesses. "We're Indie Bound" decals are now seen in the windows of thousands of independent businesses.

IndieBound complements and supports buy local initiatives and has renewed enthusiasm for finding new ways for all independent businesses to work together to better their communities.

### Marketing Tools and Information

ABA continues to provide publishers and its Publisher Partners access to its membership via marketing tools including Advance Access, a biweekly e-mail to booksellers offering available advance reader copies (ARCs) and other materials. Publisher Partners also participate in the monthly Red and White Box mailings to stores. These mailings contain actionable marketing materials, ARCs, and promotional materials.

Providing members timely and essential information remains a key goal for ABA. The association's *Bookselling This Week* (*BTW*) offers weekly news dispatches e-mailed to more than 13,000 subscribers every Thursday. *BTW* features ABA and industry news, in-depth features, the latest association developments, and the Indie Bestsellers and Indie Next lists. *BTW* can also be accessed at http://news.bookweb.org, and readers have the ability to create their own easy-to-print editions of the newsletter. BTW Flashes alert readers to important developments on a variety of subjects.

The *ABA Book Buyer's Handbook,* available online as an exclusive benefit to ABA members, is the source for publishers' discount schedules, returns policies, trade terms, and more, including links to publishers' Web sites and e-mail addresses. Fully searchable and continually updated, it also lists the latest information on publishers' special offers. BookWeb.org continues to develop as a key information source for members, adding in 2008 a wide range of IndieBound material for members; increasing its content on the ABA members' blog, Omnibus; and responding to the needs of members' advocacy efforts with such things as news updates and suggested letters to legislators.

Regarding advocacy, ABA and its members continued to work actively nationwide on behalf of "e-fairness," the equitable collection of sales tax for online sales, and in April 2008 achieved a significant victory for independent retailers when the New York State Legislature adopted a budget that included an Internet sales tax provision requiring those online retailers with selling activities in the state—such as Amazon—to collect and remit sales tax on sales made to New York buyers. The provision, which went into effect on June 1, 2008, was challenged by Amazon, but the case was dismissed by a New York State judge in January 2009. In denying Amazon's argument, Judge Eileen Bransten wrote: "The neutral statute simply obligates out-of-state sellers to shoulder their fair share of the tax-collection burden when using New Yorkers to earn profit from other New Yorkers." [As of mid-February, Amazon continued to say it planned to appeal the decision—*Ed.*]

Several independent trade groups worked with ABA on the campaign for e-fairness, including the New Atlantic Independent Booksellers Association, the American Specialty Toy Retailing Association, the Coalition of Independent Music Stores, the Independent Florist Association, the National Association of College Stores, the North American Retailer Dealers Association, and the National Bicycle Dealers Association.

ABA hopes the initial outcome of the New York State e-fairness case will influence elected officials in other states to take the necessary steps to achieve e-fairness. In November ABA asked booksellers in 44 states that collect sales tax to write to their governors to urge that online retailers with in-state affiliates be required to collect and remit sales tax in accordance with existing laws. Eleven independent trade groups joined ABA in this effort. The groups stressed that, given the budget shortfalls that most states are facing, it is a state's obligation to ensure sales tax equity by requiring out-of-state retailers with nexus in the state to collect and remit sales tax. As an example, the groups pointed to New York State's Internet Sales Tax provision, which became law on June 1, 2008, and is expected to bring in $73 million in lost sales tax revenue in fiscal year 2009.

### Seeking 'Stimulus' Help

On December 23 ABA President Gayle Shanks wrote to President-Elect Barack Obama and his transition team to urge them to make the survival and long-range health of small business "a prominent part of [the] economic stimulus package."

Highlighting the "central challenge" to independent, locally owned businesses as "access to capital," Shanks called on the Obama administration to "work immediately to address the credit crisis that threatens U.S. small businesses by implementing steps . . . outlined during the campaign," specifically:

- Establishing a nationwide emergency lending facility for small businesses that can be run through the Small Business Administration's Disaster Loan Program
- Temporarily eliminating fees on the Small Business Administration's 7(a) and 504 loan guarantee programs for small businesses, to help increase private lending for small businesses

- Implementing a green economic stimulus package for small businesses focused on sensible steps to energy efficiency, which ABA believes would pay dividends on Main Streets across the country far beyond the cost of implementation

The letter also reminded the incoming administration that locally owned independent businesses "have a far greater economic impact on communities than larger, chain businesses; contribute more to local charities; and are largely responsible for our villages, towns, and cities retaining their unique characteristics." Shanks noted that "if the current downward economic spiral continues into 2009, the attendant losses of sales tax and other revenues will further widen the budget deficits of municipalities and states nationwide, which will only increase the demand for federal assistance in the face of spreading economic loss and pain."

**Other Activities**

With its partners in the Campaign for Reader Privacy, the association continued to play a leading role in the fight to restore safeguards for the privacy of bookstore and library records that were affected by the USAPatriot Act. ABA also worked with the American Booksellers Foundation for Free Expression (ABFFE) in the fight against censorship.

ABA is actively involved in the Book Industry Study Group (BISG), the book industry trade association for policy, standards, and research. Current BISG projects include developing standards to help publishers and booksellers sell digital books, working to improve the book industry's environmental impact, facilitating efficient electronic communication, and exploring ways to create growth and improve profitability throughout the industry.

In an effort to ensure that the needs of independent booksellers are understood by publishers creating electronic catalogs, ABA established an Electronic Catalog Task Force, which met in San Francisco in late August. The task force's recommendations were discussed with nine publishers in meetings the following month. ABA also shared information from the task force with Above the Treeline, a provider of collaboration-based business intelligence tools, which in October began field-testing Edelweiss, a new online, interactive catalog product.

Ongoing industry initiatives include working with publishers to improve distribution practices and facilitating meetings with booksellers and publishers to ensure a level playing field. In addition to the issues of e-fairness, ABA continued to monitor developments regarding the Small Employers Health Benefits Program Act of 2006 (S. 2510) and the Small Business Health Fairness Act (S. 406).

ABA's strong relationship with the Institute for Local Self-Reliance, the American Independent Business Alliance (AMIBA), the Business Alliance for Local Living Economies (BALLE), and Civic Economics has enabled these groups to work together in disseminating information about the importance of locally based independent businesses and their positive effect on communities.

In addition, the association supported the following industrywide observances: the Academy of American Poets' National Poetry Month, the American Library Association's Teen Read Week, the Association of American Publishers' "Get Caught Reading" Campaign and Latino Book Month; Banned Books Week;

the Children's Book Council's National Children's Book Week; the Lambda Literary Awards; the National Book Awards; and the Small Press Center's Small Press Month.

ABA continued to offer a suite of business management services to help bookstore owners to increase their bottom line, ranging from competitive rates for credit and debit card processing to discounted shipping services and supplies.

In support of future industry leaders, ABA continues to work with the Emerging Leaders Project, a group of young booksellers who network and discuss topics of interest throughout the year.

As independent booksellers face what is likely to be one of the most difficult retail environments in decades, ABA will continue to provide a stable support system, resources, and opportunities for independent businesses to thrive.

## American Booksellers Foundation for Free Expression

In 2008 the American Booksellers Foundation for Free Expression (ABFFE) spearheaded the creation of a statement signed by 19 organizations that called on Congress to pass the Free Speech Protection Act of 2008 (S. 2977). The act would help end "libel tourism," the effort to intimidate American authors and publishers by filing libel suits in other countries that do not offer the same protections for free speech as the United States.

The foundation also successfully challenged an Indiana law that would have forced booksellers and other retailers who sell a single "sexually explicit" item to register as an "adult" business and pay a $200 license fee.

The Kids' Right to Read Project, a joint initiative of ABFFE and the National Coalition Against Censorship, continued to fight book censorship at the local level. Since its launch in 2007, the project has opposed challenges to 64 titles in 23 states.

Continuing efforts to censor the Internet were also challenged by ABFFE, which was a plaintiff in the lawsuit against the Child Online Protection Act (COPA). The act was declared unconstitutional by the Third Circuit Court of Appeals in July.

More than 20 bookstores around the country hosted events at which reporters discussed the importance of protecting confidential news sources and issues relating to the growth of online journalism. The reporters' talks were cosponsored by ABFFE and MLRC Institute, a media education group. The McCormick Foundation provided the funding.

To promote Banned Books Week, the only national celebration of the freedom to read, ABFFE joined the American Library Association in launching a new Web site, http://www.bannedbooksweek.org, that provides a list of bookstores and libraries mounting displays and hosting Banned Books Week events.

ABFFE was founded by ABA in 1990. Its address is 275 Seventh Ave., Suite 1504, New York, NY 1000 (telephone 212-587-4025, World Wide Web http://www.abffe.org). Its president is Chris Finan.

# Association of Research Libraries

21 Dupont Circle N.W., Washington, DC 20036
202-296-2296, e-mail arlhq@arl.org
World Wide Web http://www.arl.org

Lee Anne George
Publications Program Officer

The Association of Research Libraries (ARL) represents 123 principal research libraries serving major research institutions in the United States and Canada. ARL influences the changing environment of scholarly communication and the public policies that affect research libraries and the diverse communities they serve. ARL pursues this mission by advancing the goals of its member research libraries, providing leadership in public and information policy to the scholarly and higher education communities, fostering the exchange of ideas and expertise, and shaping a future environment that leverages its interests with those of allied organizations.

In November 2004 the ARL Board of Directors approved a new strategic plan for 2005–2009 that focused ARL's mission and programs along three strategic directions: scholarly communication; public policies affecting research libraries; and the library's role in the transformation of research, teaching, and learning. In 2008 the strategic direction steering committees, task forces, and working groups continued the implementation of the strategic plan's goals. The following are highlights of the association's activities.

## Strategic Direction I: Scholarly Communication

*ARL will be a leader in the development of effective, extensible, sustainable, and economically viable models of scholarly communication that provide barrier-free access to quality information in support of teaching, learning, research, and service to the community.*

This strategic direction supports "new and enhanced models of scholarly communication that promote wide availability and enduring access."

### Implementing Public Access Policies

In February 2008 SPARC, Science Commons, and ARL jointly released a white paper to help university and medical school administrators ensure that their institutions comply with public access requirements that are a new condition of National Institutes of Health (NIH) funding. Effective April 7, 2008, investigators must deposit articles stemming from NIH funding into the agency's PubMed Central online archive, to be made publicly available no later than 12 months after publication in a journal. "Complying with the National Institutes of Health Public Access Policy: Copyright Considerations and Options" helps provosts, research administrators, and campus counsel understand their institution's copyright-related obligations and options under the new congressionally mandated policy, which replaces an earlier voluntary approach. The analysis was prepared by Michael W. Carroll, a lawyer, copyright expert, and faculty member at Villanova University law school. Carroll reviewed the policy and its background, explained the legal context, and presented six alternative copyright management strategies designed to help grantee institutions assure they reserve the necessary rights for articles to be made available in PubMed Central. The analysis is available at http://www.arl.org/sparc/advocacy/nih/copyright.html.

Also in February 2008 ARL released the guide "The NIH Public Access Policy: Guide for Research Universities" to focus on the implications of the new NIH policy for institutions as grantees. In addition to compliance concerns, the guide also considers the benefits of the new policy and institutions' opportunities to build on the policy requirements by seeking additional rights for using funded research to address local needs. The guide includes the following sections: Policy Overview, Institutional Responses, Retaining Rights, How to Deposit, and Resources. Reflecting the dynamic nature of campus implementation activities, the guide will be updated as more campuses release plans, resources, and tools that can serve as models for their peers. It is available at http://www.arl.org/sc/implement/nih/guide.

In March 2008 ARL and the National Association of State Universities and Land-Grant Colleges (NASULGC) presented a Webcast for vice presidents of research, administrators, and staff in funded research and grants offices to explore options for institutional responses to the NIH Public Access Policy. Presenters provided their perspectives on the new policy, particularly the issues around investigators' retaining the rights they need to deposit their articles in PubMed Central. The Webcast archive is available at http://www.arl.org/sc/models/models-resources/nih-pa/nih-webcast.

In the June issue of *ARL: A Bimonthly Report,* Duke University Scholarly Communications Officer Kevin L. Smith offered pragmatic strategies that authors and their institutions can use to manage authors' copyrights to fulfill the requirements of the NIH Public Access Policy. His article, "Managing Copyright for NIH Public Access: Strategies to Ensure Compliance," explored three strategic options for authors and institutions to retain and manage the rights needed to comply with the new policy. Although the three strategies are focused on meeting the NIH article deposit requirement, they could also be employed to accomplish a more comprehensive strategy for public dissemination of research. The article includes a sample letter that authors can use to notify publishers that an article they are submitting for consideration is based on NIH-funded research and therefore must be made accessible to the public under the NIH policy. The article is available at http://www.arl.org/resources/pubs/br/br258.shtml.

Drawing on a publicly maintained list of journal publishers' policies on author-rights management as they relate to the revised NIH Public Access Policy (http://oad.simmons.edu/oadwiki/Publisher_policies_on_NIH-funded_authors), in August Ben Grillot, a second-year student at George Washington University Law School and legal intern for ARL, developed an analysis of current options and trends based on a close examination of a set of 12 agreements. "PubMed Central Deposit and Author Rights: Agreements Between 12 Publishers and the Authors Subject to the NIH Public Access Policy" compared the policies with regard to the terms and procedures of deposit of the work, the length of any embargo period, and the rights of the author to use and share the work during the embargo period. The paper summarized terms for all 12 publishers and considered their implications for NIH-funded authors. The analysis is available at http://www.arl.org/bm~doc/grillot-pubmed.pdf.

## Library Publishing

In a March 2008 report, "Research Library Publishing Services: New Options for University Publishing," ARL explored the rapidly emerging role of research libraries as publishing service providers. Based on data from a survey of ARL members and interviews with program managers, the report describes current library publishing services and explores the environment in which they are emerging. The study looked at such service details as publishing software and business models as well as related institutional factors including partner relationships, related library services, and faculty engagement. The report provides valuable context for librarians and campus leaders considering the opportunities offered by this emerging library role. It is available at http://www.arl.org/resources/pubs/reports.

A small group of campus leaders met in August under the auspices of ARL, the Coalition for Networked Information (CNI), NASULGC, and the Association of American Universities (AAU) to discuss "The University's Role in Publishing Research and Scholarship." Attendees included provosts, chief research officers, chief information officers, press directors, and library directors. The conversation focused on the changing environment for making the products of faculty work available, and the changing role universities should play in ensuring that faculty work is disseminated as broadly as possible. A report including recommendations from the group will be released in 2009.

## New Model Publications

In spring 2008 ARL engaged Ithaka's Strategic Services Group to conduct an investigation into the range of online resources valued by scholars, paying special attention to those projects that are pushing beyond the boundaries of traditional formats and are considered innovative by the faculty who use them. An initial, field-study phase of the study engaged more than 300 librarian volunteers and partner librarians in structured conversations with faculty from a wide spectrum of disciplines at 46 academic institutions in North America. Between April 1 and June 15, the librarians interviewed faculty about the new kinds of scholarly works and communication practices that are currently contributing to their research and scholarship. Eighteen partner institutions volunteered to work with all of their liaison librarians, seeding cross-campus discussions of how communication practices of scholars and researchers have shifted. These conversations led to the contribution of more than 200 records describing new kinds of scholarly works to the study database.

The report authors evaluated each resource gathered by the field team and conducted interviews of project leaders of 11 representative resources. The report profiles eight genres of resources, including discussion of how and why the faculty members reported using the resources for their work, how content is selected for the site, and what financial sustainability strategies the resources are employing. In November 2008 ARL released the final report, "Current Models of Digital

Scholarly Communication," along with the database of exemplars that the study produced. The report is available at http://www.arl.org/bm~doc/current-models-report.pdf and the database can be searched at http://www.arl.org/sc/models/model-pubs/search-form.shtml.

### Institute on Scholarly Communication

The Orbis Cascade Alliance hosted the second regional ARL/Association of College and Research Libraries (ACRL) Institute on Scholarly Communication in December in Portland, Oregon. The institute used a competitive application process as seats were in high demand, and demonstrated organizational commitment was a prerequisite of participation.

ARL updated the FAIR (Freely Available Institute Resources) Web site, a component of the Institute on Scholarly Communication, which gathers outreach and program development tools created for institute events or developed by institute alumni. FAIR now offers four resource collections: outreach to faculty, program planning and development tools, staff development tools, and a collection of position descriptions with scholarly communication components. In addition, the collection of sample position descriptions has been significantly expanded with recent contributions from a range of academic institutions. Position titles range from Copyright Librarian to Digital Repository Coordinator, with many titles explicitly including the phrase "scholarly communication." All FAIR resources are available at http://www.arl.org/sc/institute/fair.

ARL's popular series of discussion guides for organizing library staff conversations on the changing scholarly communication system was revised and expanded in 2008. Nearly all of the original six guides in the Library Brown Bag Lunch Series on Issues in Scholarly Communication were updated and two new guides were added. Guides are now available on starting discussions of scholarly communication, talking with faculty, access to publicly funded research, author rights, institutional strategies for rights management, scholarly society roles, peer review, and new model publications. The guides, along with an overview for discussion leaders, are available at http://www.arl.org/sc/brownbag.

## Strategic Direction II: Public Policies Affecting Research Libraries

*ARL will influence information and other public policies, both nationally and internationally, that govern the way information is managed and made available.*

Part of the scope of this strategic direction is "influencing laws, public policies, regulations, and judicial decisions that are key to research libraries and their users." During 2008 ARL engaged in a variety of efforts to promote fair use in the digital environment, support public access to federally funded research, and protect the openness of the Internet.

### Copyright and Intellectual Property Policies

PRO IP Act

In January 2008, at the request of the House Judiciary Committee, the Copyright Office hosted a meeting on Section 104 of the Prioritizing Resources and Organization for Intellectual Property (PRO IP) Act. Provisions in the legislation sought to strengthen the civil and criminal laws relating to copyright and trademark infringement, establish a new office in the Office of the President that would coordinate national and international intellectual property enforcement initiatives, and establish a new intellectual property division within the Department of Justice. Meeting participants expressed extensive opposition to Section 104. Jonathan Band represented the Library Copyright Alliance (LCA) at the meeting and noted that Section 104 would exacerbate the orphan works situation with respect to compilations and derivative works. By greatly increasing the amount of statutory damages plaintiffs could recover for infringements of compilations and derivative works, Section 104 would make libraries and their patrons even more reluctant to use orphan works in support of research, teaching, and learning. LCA, with others in the public and private sectors, filed comments on the meeting. In late fall, the House and Senate passed a significantly changed bill. On October 13, President Bush signed the Enforcement of Intellectual Property Rights Act of 2008 into law. PL 110-403 created a new intellectual property "czar" in the administration and included provisions that expand the offenses for which civil forfeiture is a remedy and permit civil forfeiture of property used to facilitate infringement. The act contains other technical provisions concerning counterfeiting, criminal violations, and Justice Department programs, including funding five more International Intellectual Property Enforcement Coordinators in U.S. embassies. For additional information, see http://www.arl.org/pp/ppcopyright/copyleg.

## Harry Potter Lexicon and Fair Use Analysis

ARL and the American Library Association (ALA) released "How Fair Use Prevailed in the Harry Potter Case" by Jonathan Band. Band contends that, despite U.S. District Court Judge Robert Patterson's September 8, 2008, ruling that the print version of Steven Vander Ark's *Harry Potter Lexicon* infringed J. K. Rowling's copyright, "the big winner actually was fair use." Band drew three broad lessons from Judge Patterson's decision. First, fair use is alive and well—expression can be incorporated into transformative works, as long as the expression is reasonably necessary for achieving the transformative purpose. Second, the courts champion fair use, in contrast to historic and recently proposed legislation that continues to encroach on fair use and the public domain. Third, fair use is best defended when those being sued have the resources to take on plaintiffs with deep pockets backed by big industry. The *Lexicon*'s publisher was fortunate to have support from the Fair Use Project of Stanford Law School's Center for Internet and Society. Band notes that such public interest "law firms" play a critical role in leveling the copyright-litigation playing field. The analysis was published in the October issue of *ARL: A Bimonthly Report* and is available at http://www.arl.org/resources/pubs/br/br260.shtml.

## Google Library Project Settlement

In November ARL and ALA released "A Guide for the Perplexed: Libraries and the Google Library Project Settlement," by Jonathan Band. The guide is designed to help the library community better understand the terms and conditions of the recent settlement agreement between Google, the Authors Guild, and the Association of American Publishers (AAP) concerning Google's scanning of copyrighted works. Band notes that the settlement is extremely complex and presents significant challenges and opportunities to libraries. The guide outlines and simplifies the settlement's provisions, with special emphasis on the provisions that apply directly to libraries. The guide and related materials are available at http://www.arl.org/pp/ppcopyright/google.

Orphan Works

After many years of discussion and negotiations, the U.S. Senate and House introduced legislation in 2008 to address the thorny issues associated with the use of "orphan works"—works whose owners are difficult or impossible to locate. Orphan works legislation is intended to enable the use of copyrighted works without permission when the copyright owner cannot be found. The inability to locate copyright owners to clear the rights in their works prevents libraries from providing broad public access to the information in their collections, and prevents library patrons from making transformative uses of these works. ARL, as a member of LCA, wrote to members of the House and Senate expressing support for a well-crafted orphan works bill. The LCA letter notes that there are "remaining concerns . . . that need to be addressed for the legislation to be truly effective in solving the orphan works problem." These concerns are detailed in a position piece that LCA, AAU, and NASULGC developed.

ARL, through LCA, also provided suggested amendments on the orphan works legislation to the Senate and the House Committees. LCA's support of the legislation was predicated on the acceptance of these proposed changes to the legislation. Issues including state sovereign immunity, establishment of a "dark archive," development of "a best practice" by the Copyright Office, and others required change prior to endorsement. Higher education associations, including AAU and NASULGC, focused on state sovereign immunity issues and worked with Senate and House staff to ensure that the bill language was acceptable.

Just prior to the August congressional recess, the Senate tried to bring the Shawn Bentley Orphan Works Act of 2008 (S. 2913) to the floor for consideration. Several holds on the legislation derailed Senate passage at that time. Key issues remaining were inclusion of provisions concerning state sovereign immunity and concerns with bill language regarding "qualifying searches." The library and higher education communities offered language to resolve these remaining concerns but the recommended changes were not incorporated into the House and Senate legislation.

On September 26 the Senate approved the Shawn Bentley Orphan Works Act of 2008, which would enable the use of copyrighted works without permission when the owner cannot be found. Prior to passage, the Senate resolved several contentious issues, including concerns relating to state sovereign immunity and what constitutes a diligent search. The House failed to consider the Senate-passed bill. It was felt that the House and Senate might reintroduce orphan works legislation once the new Congress convened in 2009. For more information, see http://www.arl.org/pp/ppcopyright/orphan.

**Public Access Policies**

Access to Federally Funded Research

In March 2008 NIH conducted an open meeting to elicit further public comment on the revised NIH Public Access Policy, whereby investigators funded by NIH are required to submit their final manuscripts to PubMed Central where they will be publicly accessible within 12 months after publication. Presenters included librarians; institutional representatives; representatives of such associations as AAU, ARL, and NASULGC; commercial and not-for-profit publishers; and members of the public. Prudence Adler spoke on behalf of ARL. In addition, 451 comments were filed online.

In September the House Committee on the Judiciary conducted a hearing on issues surrounding the new NIH Public Access Policy. After the policy went into effect in April, deposit rates increased to more than 55 percent, a significant improvement from when the policy was voluntary. In addition, after January 2008 there was a steady increase in the number of publishers depositing either author manuscripts or published articles on behalf of the investigators. Despite the notable increase in deposits by investigators and publishers, some in the publishing community continued to oppose the NIH Public Access Policy. AAP raised concerns about how the NIH Public Access Policy affects copyright law and international treaty obligations. In response to these concerns, ARL and SPARC released an analysis showing how the NIH Public Access Policy does not affect U.S. copyright law. For more information, see http://www.arl.org/pp/access/accessfunded/nihaccess.shtml.

Other Public Access Policies

ARL, along with 19 other organizations, expressed serious concerns with the recent decision by the National Archives and Record Administration (NARA) to discontinue the capture and preservation of a "snapshot" of government Web pages at the end of the Bush administration. The signatories of the letter asked the Archivist of the United States to rescind the NARA decision. The groups noted that "not capturing federal Web sites now may mean losing millions of pages created during the Bush administration." In addition, they stated that "these records are essential components of our Nation's history. No other agency has both the public mandate and the public accountability necessary for protecting historical records."

ARL, with 24 other organizations, wrote in support of the Electronic Message Preservation Act (HR 5811), which directed the Archivist to establish standards for the capture, management, and preservation of White House e-mails and other electronic communications. The legislation also directed NARA to issue regulations requiring agencies to preserve electronic communications in an electronic format. The letters are available at http://www.arl.org/pp/access/accessresources.

Federal Depository Library Program

The U.S. Government Printing Office (GPO) released a draft report titled "Regional Depository Libraries in the 21st Century: A Time for Change?" In a letter to GPO, ARL expressed strong support for the proposed GPO recommendations included in the draft report in order ". . . to ensure that regional depository libraries are able to provide unimpaired access to government information dissemination products for future generations." GPO proposed that Chapter 19 of Title 44, which provides the statutory authority for the Federal Depository Library Program (FDLP), be revised to "allow a more flexible structure." GPO also recommended that the Kansas/Nebraska shared regional library proposal be approved and that other intrastate and multistate proposals be considered. ARL also noted that "while ARL believes that current law provides GPO with the needed authority to designate shared regionals and other designations as appropriate, we support the recommendation to affirm such authority in any revision to Title 44." In a memorandum to ARL, Anthony Zagami, retired general counsel emeritus of GPO and retired general counsel to the Joint Committee on Printing, identified changes needed to facilitate new regional models and the sharing of resources and collections in FDLP. ARL comments and Zagami's memo are available at http://www.arl.org/pp/access/fdlp.

**Telecommunications Policies**

ARL, with others in the public and private sectors, participated in a filing by the Center for Democracy and Technology opposing a Federal Communications Commission (FCC) proposal that would require certain service providers to block access to any text or video content that might harm a 5-year-old child in any way. The filing notes that the mandate is unconstitutional and raises significant First Amendment issues. Participants in the filing noted that "the Commission should step back from its proposed mandate and should—as directed by the Supreme Court in *Reno* v. *ACLU*—allow parents and individual Internet users to decide for themselves whether to use filtering technology and what filtering scheme to use." The filing is available at http://www.arl.org/pp/telecom.

**Privacy, Security, and Civil Liberties**

FISA Amendments Act

In February 2008 the U.S. Senate passed the Foreign Intelligence Surveillance Act (FISA) Amendments Act (S. 2248). The Senate bill lacked many of the important civil liberties provisions included in the House-passed bill, the RESTORE Act, and included retroactive immunity for telecommunications providers who participated in the Bush administration's warrantless surveillance program. ARL and ALA wrote in support of the RESTORE Act. Ultimately, Congress passed legislation closely resembling the bill as introduced in the Senate. For more information, see http://www.arl.org/pp/pscl.

Recommendations for the Obama Administration

ARL and ALA filed a joint statement for the September 16, 2008, hearing by the Subcommittee on the Constitution of the Senate Judiciary Committee on "Restoring the Rule of Law." The hearing record was designed to be a resource for the next president and Congress concerning privacy, civil liberties, and security issues. The statement focused on privacy and security issues such as National

Security Letters (NSLs), the USAPatriot Act, and FISA. The statement is available at http://www.arl.org/pp/pscl.

With a variety of different partners and organizations, ARL participated in numerous proposals for the incoming Obama administration concerning government information, transparency and accountability of government, privacy, and national security and secrecy. With the National Security Archive and others, ARL proposed restoring openness and effectiveness to the Freedom of Information Act, proposed changes to the classification and declassification system, and called for greater compliance with laws governing presidential records (see http://www.gwu.edu/~nsarchiv/news/20081112/index.htm). ARL joined with others in supporting many recommendations and proposals included in the Constitution Project's "Liberty and Security: Recommendations for the Next Administration and Congress" (http://2009transition.org/liberty-security). And, with others in the Right to Know community, ARL endorsed recommendations in the report "Moving Toward a 21st Century Right-to-Know Agenda: Recommendations to President-Elect Obama and Congress" (http://www.ombwatch.org/article/archive/551).

### Federal Funding

ARL and ALA filed a statement in support of an increase in the fiscal year (FY) 2009 budget request for the National Agricultural Library (NAL). The associations noted that "the President's FY 2009 budget request fails to provide the support needed to maintain current services at NAL and position the Library to serve our nation in the years ahead. At a minimum, restoration of the proposed reductions is critically important if NAL is to maintain its leadership in the provision of long-term preservation and access to agricultural information and literature." The joint statement is available at http://www.arl.org/pp/fedfund/Natl_Agri_Lib.shtml.

ARL and the Council on Library and Information Resources (CLIR) filed a statement in support of the FY 2009 budget request for the National Endowment for the Humanities (NEH). ARL and CLIR requested that the Subcommittee on Interior, Environment, and Related Agencies support a budget of $177 million for NEH in FY 2009, an increase of approximately $32 million above President Bush's request. In addition, ARL and ALA wrote in support of the NEH budget. The statements are available at http://www.arl.org/pp/fedfund/Ntl_Endowmnt_Humanities.shtml.

ARL, ALA, the Medical Library Association and the Special Libraries Association submitted a statement in support of the FY 2009 budget request for the U.S. Government Printing Office. The associations noted that "The investment in systems and services to provide the public with government publications will ensure that valuable electronic government information created today will be available and preserved for future generations." The statement is available at http://www.arl.org/pp/fedfund/GPO.shtml.

ARL, ALA, and the National Humanities Alliance (NHA) submitted a letter in support of the FY 2009 budget request of $645.8 million for the Library of Congress. Expressing concern about the impact of tight funding, the associations urged the Subcommittee on the Legislative Branch to "support full funding of this request as a necessary investment in one of the nation's greatest intellectual resources." In particular, ARL, ALA, and NHA supported an additional $6 million to strengthen the National Digital Information Infrastructure and Preservation Program (NDIIPP) network and continue technical collaborations that are essential to expanding the network over time. The associations expressed concerns that rising security costs and the weakness of the U.S. dollar may force reduction of Library of Congress support for overseas offices and non-U.S. acquisitions. They supported a $910,000 base increase for acquisitions in FY 2009 to help keep pace with increasing costs. The statement is available at http://www.arl.org/pp/fedfund/Library_of_Congress.shtml.

Prior to its recess in early October, Congress passed a continuing resolution to fund most federal agencies until early March 2009. The resolution provided most agencies with the previous year's appropriation levels.

## Strategic Direction III: The Library's Role in Research, Teaching, and Learning

*ARL will promote and facilitate new and expanding roles for ARL libraries to engage in the transformations affecting research and undergraduate and graduate education.*

### E-Science

The ARL Board of Directors enthusiastically accepted the final report of the ARL Task Force on Library Support for E-Science at the February 2008 board meeting. The report's recommendations formed the basis of the ARL e-science agenda for 2008. Included in the program plan is the development of resources to aid senior library leadership in understanding e-science concepts and in initiating discussion of library roles with campus leaders and other faculty. As part of this, the ARL e-science Web site was revised to include a range of useful resources. Other program emphases include offering relevant program sessions at ARL Membership Meetings and other venues and seeking opportunities to work with allied organizations and agencies to advance the research library's role in e-science. To carry out e-science activities, the report recommended the establishment of an E-Science Working Group. The report of the Task Force on Library Support for E-Science, "Agenda for Developing E-Science in Research Libraries," is available at http://www.arl.org/rtl/escience.

In October ARL and CNI sponsored the forum "Reinventing Science Librarianship: New Models for the Future" to explore the future of science librarianship. The program, planned and delivered by the ARL E-Science Working Group, was aimed at the leadership of libraries and enterprise-wide information technology (IT) services. Target audiences included directors or assistant directors of research libraries, campus IT services, science libraries, and health science libraries. The goal was to broaden the understanding of trends in scientific research and support leadership in applying these trends in planning for the development of new library roles. The program featured panels of speakers on e-science trends, data curation issues, supporting virtual organizations, the experience of health sciences libraries, and education for new roles. In addition, 15 libraries contributed 14 posters for display at the forum to showcase their organizations' work in science librarianship. Audio and slides from forum speakers and a description of the poster sessions are available at http://www.arl.org/resources/pubs/fallforumproceedings/forum08proceedings.shtml.

The ARL E-Science Working Group prepared the paper "E-Science Talking Points for ARL Deans and Directors" in conjunction with the forum. The paper provides brief commentaries on basic questions on the topic, as well as a short list of readings for additional information, and is available at http://www.arl.org/rtl/escience/eresource.shtml.

### Space and Facilities

The "ARL Learning Space Pre-Programming Tool Kit" was released in October. The tool kit enables library staff—without reliance on outside experts—to conduct pre-programming assessment in order to customize learning spaces to fit local circumstances. The kit includes an overview of the planning process for building a learning commons, as well as easy-to-use, one- to two-page guides to implementing a dozen different pre-programming assessment techniques. The techniques were tested in several libraries and consistently produced excellent data for developing informed building programs. The tool kit is available at http://www.arl.org/rtl/space.

In November Crit Stuart, ARL Program Director for Research, Teaching, and Learning, joined host Steve Worona in an EDUCAUSE Live! Web seminar to discuss "A Space of One's Own: Learning Environments Derived from User-Centered Discovery Techniques." This "Webinar" reviewed a number of user-centered programming assessment techniques for developing innovative learning spaces for students. The techniques are field-tested, easy to modify and extemporize on, and reliable in producing excellent data for constructing informed building programs. The Webcast archive is available at http://net.educause.edu/live0823.

Stuart also participated in a roundtable conversation recorded at the EDUCAUSE 2008 Annual Conference in December on the connection between space and learning. The podcast is available at http://connect.educause.edu/blog/gbayne/e08podcastinconversationl/47781?time=1228225473.

## Diversity Initiatives and Work Force Issues

ARL's Diversity Initiatives encapsulate a suite of efforts implemented across ARL's strategic directions that aid the association with defining and addressing diversity issues in ARL libraries while supporting activities that encourage broad participation in the library field. ARL Diversity Initiatives seek to encourage exploration of the rich gifts and talents that diverse individuals bring to the library. ARL staff work closely with a broad range of libraries, graduate library education programs, and other library associations to promote awareness of career opportunities in research libraries and support the academic success of students from groups currently under-represented in the profession.

### ARL Career Enhancement Program

The ARL Diversity Initiatives were awarded a $728,821 grant by the Institute of Museum and Library Services (IMLS) Laura Bush 21st-Century Librarian Program to create the ARL Career Enhancement Program. The program will partner with ARL libraries to provide 45 MLS (master's degree in library science) students from under-represented racial and ethnic groups with fellowships in research libraries. The program has four main components: a six- to twelve-week fellowship experience in a host library, a mentoring relationship with a professional librarian, participation in the annual ARL Leadership Institute, and career placement assistance from ARL staff. Using a fellowship-cohort model, this program seeks to address recruitment and retention of minority librarians by providing them with a close network of peers, while at the same time giving them practical learning experiences to complement their library school coursework. The fellowship host institutions are University at Albany, State University of New York; University of Arizona; University of California, San Diego; Columbia University; University of Kentucky; National Library of Medicine; North Carolina State University; and University of Washington. For more information, see http://www.arl.org/diversity/cep/index.shtml.

### Leadership and Career Development Program

The Leadership and Career Development Program (LCDP) prepares midcareer librarians from under-represented racial and ethnic groups to take on increasingly demanding leadership roles in ARL libraries. The 18-month program includes two four-day institutes, an opening and closing event held in conjunction with national professional meetings, a career-coaching relationship with an ARL library director or staff member, and a personalized visit to an ARL member library. In June ARL hosted the closing ceremony for the 2007–2008 LCDP Fellows. This ceremony commemorated the tenth anniversary of the first graduating class in 1998 and included a short program; an opportunity for the fellows to share their research findings; and networking opportunities for past fellows, current fellows, the ARL library community, and guests. The anniversary was also celebrated at the 153rd ARL Membership Meeting with a panel of speakers who addressed the positive impact of the program on individual careers, as well as on the libraries that sponsored and/or mentored participants. To date, 100 librarians have participated in LCDP. Eleven fellows were selected for the 2009–2010 class. See http://www.arl.org/diversity/lcdp/index.shtml.

### Initiative to Recruit a Diverse Work Force

The ARL Diversity Initiatives Working Group selected 17 MLS students from under-represented groups who are interested in careers in research libraries to participate in the 2008–2010 Initiative to Recruit a Diverse Work Force. These ARL Diversity Scholars will receive leadership development via ARL's annual Leadership Institute; a hosted visit to an ARL member library to learn more about the advanced operations of a research library; professional mentoring from an ARL librarian or an alumnus of either ARL's Leadership and Career Development Program or the Initiative to Recruit a Diverse Workforce; paid membership in a major professional association and in the American Library Association's five ethnic caucuses; and a stipend of $10,000 over two years to help defray the cost of graduate school. The initiative is funded by the Institute of Museum and Library Services (IMLS) and by voluntary contributions from 52 ARL member libraries. This funding reflects a commitment to create a diverse research library community that will better meet the new challenges of global competition and changing demographics. For more information about the initiative, see http://www.arl.org/diversity/init/index.shtml.

### Research Library Leadership Fellows

The second offering of the ARL Research Library Leadership Fellows (RLLF) Program was designed and sponsored by six ARL member libraries: University of California, Berkeley, and the California Digital Library; Harvard University; University of Minnesota; North Carolina State University; Pennsylvania State University; and the University of Toronto. Created in response to increasing demands for succession planning for research libraries, this executive leadership program offers a new approach to preparing the next generation of deans and directors who possess the unique skills to succeed in premier leadership positions in large, complex institutions. The 2007–2008 RLLF applicant pool was highly competitive and the selection committee, composed of the ARL directors sponsoring the program, chose 23 candidates representing a broad array of backgrounds and experiences from multiple ARL institutions.

The third and final institute for the 2007–2008 RLLF Program participants was hosted by the University of Minnesota March 31–April 5, 2008. The institute focused on how the library has been both responding to the university's restructuring and positioning itself based on its own planning. Other RLLF activities in 2008 included attendance at ARL and CNI meetings and site visits to the University of California, Berkeley, and Pennsylvania State University. See http://www.arl.org/leadership/rllf.

## Research, Statistics, and Measurement

The Statistics and Measurement Program seeks to describe and measure the performance of research libraries and their contributions to teaching, research, scholarship, and community service. As an enabling capability, the Statistics and Measurement Program identifies quantitative and qualitative metrics and assessment tools in support of ARL's mission and strategic objectives. The program expanded with the New Measures Initiative in the early 2000s and now hosts a suite of tools, projects, and services under the StatsQUAL (Statistics and Service Quality) brand. The StatsQUAL tools focus on developing new approaches for describing and evaluating library service effectiveness, return on investment, digital library services, the impact of networked electronic services, diversity, leadership, and organizational climate, among others. StatsQUAL hosts tools such as LibQUAL+, ClimateQUAL, MINES for Libraries, DigiQUAL, and ARL Statistics. More information is available at http://www.arl.org/stats.

LibQUAL+ is a widely popular assessment tool. In 2008 LibQUAL+ collected data from more than 167,000 users across 206 institutions. Welsh-,

Spanish-, and Japanese-language surveys were introduced and used by libraries in Wales, Mexico, and Japan. A group of academic libraries in France supported by the Ministry of Education also implemented the protocol successfully. Academic libraries from Belgium and Norway plan to join the effort in 2009. Highlights of the Session I 2008 survey are available at http://www.libqual.org/documents/admin/LibQUALHighlights2008_SessionI.pdf.

LibQUAL+ continues to offer training sessions in the United States and in Europe. The workshop "Using LibQUAL+ Effectively" was geared toward survey administrators and members of assessment groups/teams. It enables staff responsible for administering the LibQUAL+ survey to develop work plans that they can apply in their libraries to perform some simple analyses of the quantitative and qualitative results data, organize their colleagues and committees to work with LibQUAL+, present the results effectively to different stakeholders, utilize data to target areas for improvement, and develop a process of continuous assessment. For more information, see http://www.arl.org/news/pr/using-libqual-9may08.shtml.

The LibQUAL+ Lite pilot project was launched in April with six libraries testing whether randomly presented shortened surveys will produce higher numbers of responses. The pilot took place on a newly designed Web architecture and was expanded to include more libraries in the fall. There are plans to launch the new LibQUAL+ platform in 2009.

A LibQUAL+ interest group was formed to explore analyzing the qualitative comments collected by the survey, both in terms of locally relevant themes and in standardized themes across multiple libraries. The work done by Brown University's LibQUAL+ User Assessment Group, which used NVivo software to code user comments collected during the 2005 LibQUAL+ survey, was influential. The Brown research team developed a master list of common themes. Further research and follow-up steps are being planned to help libraries deal more effectively with the massive amount of qualitative data they receive through the LibQUAL+ survey (40 percent of survey respondents provide comments).

LibQUAL+ is not the only assessment protocol advocated by ARL member libraries. A recognition that assessment is multifaceted has led to the formation of a strong community of interest relating to assessment among ARL libraries. The first ARL Library Assessment Coordinators meeting was hosted by the University of Pennsylvania in Philadelphia in January 2008. The meeting was open to all those in ARL libraries who have responsibility for or work on assessment-related activities (not just assessment "coordinators") and was part of an ARL effort to support the community of assessment practice. It was designed not only to exchange information about assessment in libraries but also to help develop personal connections with counterparts at other institutions. Transcribed notes from these discussions are available on the Library Assessment Blog (http://libraryassessment.info/?p=107).

More than 50 academic, federal, special, and public librarians attended "Planning for Results: Making Data Work for You," cosponsored by ARL, OCLC CAPCON, SLA, and the Federal Library and Information Center Committee (FLICC) in February at the Cato Institute in Washington, D.C. The program examined the need for assessment, survey design issues, analysis and interpretation, communicating with stakeholders, and assessment as a public relations tool.

A second event on "The Art of Strategic Persuasion: Essential Skills for Leaders" took place in April. See http://www.arl.org/stats/statsevents.

A major event of the year was the 2008 Library Assessment Conference—Building Effective, Sustainable, Practical Assessment. Cosponsored by ARL, the University of Virginia Library, and the University of Washington Libraries, the conference convened in Seattle in August. The program offered more than 60 papers and panels presented in eight parallel sessions, more than 35 poster presentations, and six half-day workshops. The first Library Assessment Career Achievement awards were presented to three pioneers in the field—Amos Lakos, Shelley Phipps, and Duane Webster. Multiple post-conference workshops focused on such issues as visualization of data, usability, learning outcomes, and space planning. Conference presentations and related materials are available on the conference Web site http://libraryassessment.org.

ARL continues to enhance the assessment tool kit. ClimateQUAL is the newest tool in the StatsQUAL family, developed in partnership with the University of Maryland and supported by the ARL Statistics and Measurement Program. In 2007 a group of five ARL libraries completed a successful Phase I pilot implementing the organizational culture and diversity assessment survey that provides information on the climate for justice, service, and other dimensions critical for the delivery of excellent service. Phase II of the ClimateQUAL survey resulted in the collection of more than 1,500 surveys from library staff at ten university libraries as of spring 2008. The participating libraries were Arizona State, Cornell, Duke, Emory, Houston, Kansas State, Northwestern, NYU, Maryland, and Massachusetts–Amherst. A results meeting was held in conjunction with the ALA Annual Conference in Anaheim. For more information, see http://www.climatequal.org.

MINES for Libraries (MINES for "Measuring the Impact of Networked Electronic Services") is a methodology used by institutions to assess the value of their electronic resources. During 2008 a study was completed at the University of Macedonia in Thessaloniki, Greece. In the United States the methodology is currently being deployed by the University of Iowa for a second year and there are plans for a second implementation of this protocol with the Ontario Council of University Libraries (OCUL) libraries in 2009.

A meeting of the ARL survey coordinators and SPEC liaisons was held at the ALA Annual Conference in June and featured a discussion of the latest ARL Statistics data collection and the challenges and opportunities of the new way of accounting for serials. With ARL no longer asking libraries to count serial subscriptions, an ARL Task Force on Best Practices for Counting Serial Titles was formed to develop recommendations for methods for counting. The Task Force met for the first time at the ALA Annual Conference and again in August. A December Webcast reported on the findings of the task force and how the work of the group has informed changes in the ARL Statistics 2007–2008 survey. More than 150 representatives from ARL member libraries participated in the event. The Webcast is available at http://www.arl.org/stats/annualsurveys/arlstats/08statmail.shtml.

The Statistics and Measurement Program also provides data through a variety of electronic and print publications that describe salary compensation and collection, staffing, expenditure, and service trends for research libraries. The series includes the *ARL Annual Salary Survey, ARL Statistics, ARL Academic Law Library Statistics, ARL Academic Health Sciences Library Statistics,* and *ARL Preservation Statistics.* The ARL Interactive Statistics, hosted at the Geostat Center of the University of Virginia, continues to be a popular way of accessing the annual data collected by ARL. The ranked lists allow users to pick from more than 30 variables for data reports. This site is at http://fisher.lib.virginia.edu/arl/index.html.

The SPEC survey program gathers information on current research library operating practices and policies, and "hot topics," and publishes the SPEC Kit series as guides for libraries as they face ever-changing management issues. Six SPEC Kits were published in 2008: *SPEC Kit 304 Social Software in Libraries, SPEC Kit 305 Records Management, SPEC Kit 306 Promoting the Library, SPEC Kit 307 Manuscript Collections on the Web, SPEC Kit 308 Graduate Student and Faculty Spaces and Services,* and *SPEC Kit 309 Library Support for Study Abroad.* For a complete list of SPEC Kit titles, see http://www.arl.org/resources/pubs/spec/complete.shtml.

## Communications and Alliances

ARL's communications and alliances enabling capability is engaged in many activities that support ARL's strategic directions. These include acquainting ARL members with current, important developments of interest to research libraries; influencing policy- and decision-makers within the higher education, research, and scholarly communities; educating academic communities about issues relating to scholarly communication and research libraries; and providing the library community with information about activities in which research libraries are engaged. Using print and electronic media as well as direct outreach, the communications capability disseminates information about ARL to the higher education and scholarly communities, as well as to ARL member institutions, and publishes a full range of timely, accurate, and informative resources to assist library and higher education communities in their efforts to improve the delivery of scholarly communication. ARL makes most of its titles available electronically via the World Wide Web; some are available in excerpted form for preview before purchase and others are available in their entirety. See http://www.arl.org/resources/pubs. News about ARL activities and publications is available through the ARL-ANNOUNCE list, distributed widely to the library and higher education communities. To subscribe, visit http://www.arl.org/resources/emaillists.

## Governance and Membership Meetings

In April 2008 Jim Neal hosted a symposium at Columbia University's historic Low Library to celebrate the career of Duane Webster, who was retiring after 38 years at ARL, including the past 20 years as its executive director. Fifteen of Webster's colleagues gave presentations to the 150 guests about the many aspects of his leadership at ARL and his impact on the research library community. The presentations from the symposium, "Celebrating the Career of Duane Webster: A Symposium on the Association of Research Libraries History,

Accomplishments, Future Developments," is on the Columbia Web site at http://www.columbia.edu/cu/lweb/conferences/2008/arl-symposium.

At a reception saluting his career, ARL President Marianne Gaunt presented the ARL Distinguished Service Award to Webster in honor of his 38-year career as an advocate for research libraries. She also announced that the ARL Board of Directors had awarded him the honorary title executive director emeritus, a first in the 75-year history of the association. For more information, see http://www.arl.org/news/pr/webster-award-30may08.shtml.

Webster retired June 30 and was succeeded by Charles B. Lowry, who became executive director of ARL on July 1. Since 1996 Lowry had been the dean of libraries at the University of Maryland. Within ARL he has served on numerous committees and he was elected by the membership to serve on the ARL Board of Directors for 2005–2008. For more information, see http://www.arl.org/news/pr/lowry-executive-director-23apr08.shtml.

A total of 107 ARL member representatives attended the association's 152nd Membership Meeting in May 2008 at Coral Gables, Florida. The program opened with remarks by Peter McPherson, president of NASULGC, urging a focus on ensuring that public policy on intellectual property promotes progress. The business meeting featured updates from the board and key committees, including a report on implementing the new definition of "current serials" in the ARL Statistics. An overview of the program and discussion sessions, as well as speaker slides, is available at http://www.arl.org/resources/pubs/mmproceedings/152mm-proceedings.shtml.

ARL's 153rd Membership Meeting took place October 15–16 in Arlington, Virginia. The program featured remarks by two provosts, by ARL directors, and by other librarians who participated in ARL's leadership development programs: Leadership and Career Development Program and Research Library Leadership Fellows Program. The meeting sessions focused discussion around diversity in higher education, the future for the work of extended arguments, leadership roles in research libraries, and trends in e-science. Speakers' remarks and slides are available at http://www.arl.org/resources/pubs/mmproceedings/153mm-proceedings.shtml. At the business meeting, member library representatives ratified the ARL board's election of Brinley Franklin of the University of Connecticut as ARL vice president/president-elect and elected three new members of the board: Colleen Cook (Texas A&M), James Mullins (Purdue), and Sandra Yee (Wayne State). Tom Leonard of the University of California, Berkeley, began his term as ARL president.

# SPARC—The Scholarly Publishing and Academic Resources Coalition

21 Dupont Circle, Suite 800, Washington, DC 20036
202-296-2296, fax 202-872-0884, e-mail sparc@arl.org
World Wide Web http://www.arl.org/sparc

Heather Joseph
Executive Director

SPARC—the Scholarly Publishing and Academic Resources Coalition—is an international alliance of academic and research libraries working to correct imbalances in the scholarly publishing system. Its pragmatic focus is to stimulate the emergence of new scholarly communication models that expand the dissemination of scholarly research and reduce financial pressures on libraries. Action by SPARC in collaboration with stakeholders—including authors, publishers, and libraries—builds on the unprecedented opportunities created by the networked digital environment to advance the conduct of scholarship. It has become a catalyst for change.

SPARC works to promote expanded sharing of scholarship in the networked digital environment. It believes that faster and wider sharing of the outputs of the research process increases the impact of research, fuels the advancement of knowledge, and raises the return on research investments.

Developed by the Association of Research Libraries in 1997, SPARC was launched formally in 1998. It is now supported by a membership of 222 academic and research libraries and works in cooperation with its affiliates, SPARC Europe and SPARC Japan.

## Strategy

SPARC's strategy focuses on reducing barriers to the access, sharing, and use of scholarship. SPARC's highest priority is advancing the understanding and implementation of policies and practices that ensure open access to scholarly research outputs. While much of SPARC's focus to date has been on journal literature, its evolving strategy reflects an increasing focus on open access to research outputs and digital data of all kinds, in all subject areas. SPARC's role in stimulating change centers on three key program areas:

- Educating stakeholders about the problems facing scholarly communication and the opportunities for them to play a role in achieving positive change
- Advocating policy changes that advance scholarly communication and that explicitly recognize that dissemination of scholarship is an essential, inseparable component of the research process
- Incubating demonstrations of new publishing and sustainability models that benefit scholarship and academe

The organization's success has been a result of the interconnection of all three strategies.

## Developments in 2008

SPARC's 2008 actions were designed to advance the viability and acceptance of a more-open system of scholarship, with a primary focus on open access models for publishing and archiving the results of scholarly research. In particular, as interest in public access to the results of federally funded research continues to accelerate, SPARC worked to deploy a focused and disciplined advocacy strategy while remaining sufficiently agile to capitalize on emerging market opportunities that aligned with its objectives.

### Advocacy and Public Policy

The most highly visible public policy initiative for SPARC in 2008 was to continue to advance public access to the results of federally funded research. Working both legislatively and through the media, SPARC kept the issue front and center in its activities.

SPARC's major partners and allies in the public policy arena included the Open Access Working Group (OAWG), an alliance of leading organizations that support open access, and the Alliance for Taxpayer Access, a letterhead alliance that brings together the OAWG communities with patient-advocacy organizations, consumer groups, and other interested organizations. These groups were successful in securing the first-ever U.S. legislative mandate for public access, which ensures enhanced access to the results of research funded by the National Institutes of Health (NIH). President George W. Bush signed the Consolidated Appropriations Act of 2008 (H.R. 2764) on December 26, 2007, which included a provision directing NIH to provide the public with open online access to findings from its funded research. Effective April 7, 2008, NIH-funded researchers were required to deposit a copy of their final, peer-reviewed manuscripts into PubMed Central, NIH's digital archive of biomedical and life sciences journal literature, so that they could be made publicly available no later than 12 months after publication in a journal.

SPARC and its partners worked proactively in 2008 to identify and counter any activity opposing the NIH Public Access Policy. Efforts included coordinating grassroots and grasstops responses when necessary and defending the NIH policy against the potential introduction of any bill or regulation designed to overturn it. Anticipating a copyright challenge to the NIH policy, SPARC helped prepare a strategy to meet the challenge. This resulted in SPARC testifying at a House Judiciary Committee hearing on a bill opposing the NIH policy. SPARC also advocated for reintroduction of the Federal Research Public Access Act (FRPAA), which would expand the NIH policy to other agencies.

With allied organizations, SPARC also worked to support implementation of the first-ever Canadian policy on public access to federally funded research, at the Canadian Institutes for Health Research.

In the broader international arena, SPARC became an original signatory on the Cape Town Declaration for Open Education Resources, signaling a commitment to further pioneering open scholarship initiatives. SPARC continues to actively participate in national and international advisory committee meetings where public access policies are discussed, including the PubMed Central National Advisory Committee, the World Health Organization's Working Group on Access, WIPO (the World Intellectual Property Organization), CENDI (the interagency working group of senior scientific and technical information [STI] managers from 13 U.S. federal agencies), and other relevant groups. SPARC staff members often serve as a source for the media on the issue of public access.

## Open Access Day

SPARC, the Public Library of Science (PLoS), and Students for FreeCulture jointly sponsored the first international Open Access Day on October 14, 2008. Building on the worldwide momentum toward open access to publicly funded research, Open Access Day created an opportunity for the higher education community and the general public to understand more clearly the opportunities of wider access to and use of content. Researchers, educators, librarians, students, and the public participated in live worldwide broadcasts of events. More than 120 organizations signed up to participate in the day, originating from 27 countries. In North America, appearances featured Sir Richard Roberts, a joint winner of the 1993 Nobel Prize in Physiology or Medicine for discovering split genes and RNA splicing and one of 26 Nobel laureates to sign the Open Letter to U.S. Congress in support of taxpayer access to publicly funded research; and Philip E. Bourne, founding editor-in-chief of the open access journal *PLoS Computational Biology* and the author of the popular PLoS Computational Biology Ten Simple Rules Series. Bourne is a professor in the Skaggs School of Pharmacy and Pharmaceutical Sciences at the University of California, San Diego, associate director of the RCSB Protein Data Bank, senior advisor to the San Diego Supercomputer Center, adjunct professor at the Burnham Institute, and cofounder of the science Web 2.0 site SciVee.

The event also marked the launch of the Voices of Open Access Video Series. Key members of the research community, including a teacher, a librarian, a researcher, a student, a patient advocate, and a funder, presented their perspectives on the importance of open access to research across the higher education community and beyond and on why they personally are committed to open access. SPARC released the series of six one-minute videos in partnership with PLoS, on the occasion of the fifth anniversary of the launch of *PLoS Biology*, the flagship biology journal from the Public Library of Science. The series was created by filmmakers Karen Rustad and Matt Agnello.

Voices of Open Access defines open access as a fundamental component of a new system for exchanging scholarly research results, where health is transformed, research outputs are maximized to their fullest extent, efficiencies in the research process enable faster discoveries, the best science is made possible, young people are inspired, access transcends the wealth of the institution, cost savings are realized across the research process, and medical research conducted for the public good is made available to everyone who needs it. The series involves Barbara Stebbins, science teacher at Black Pine Circle School in Berkeley, California; Mark Walport, director of the Wellcome Trust in Britain; Sharon Terry, president and CEO of the Genetic Alliance, Washington, D.C.; Ida Sim, associate professor and a practicing physician at the University of California, San Francisco; Diane Graves, university librarian at Trinity University, San Antonio, Texas; and Andre Brown, Ph.D. student at the University of Pennsylvania.

The videos are publicly available to view, download, and repurpose under a CC-BY license at http://www.vimeo.com/oaday08. They are also available as a single file for viewing at events.

Open Access Day was inspired by the National Day of Action on February 15, 2007, led by Students for Free Culture with support from the Alliance for Taxpayer Access. In 2008 the same partners joined forces with PLoS, the open access scientific and medical Web publisher. The success of Open Access Day has led to plans for an Open Access Week in 2009. The event is set for October 19–23.

## Campus Education

Since its inception, SPARC has encouraged and aided grassroots scholarly communication advocacy efforts on college and university campuses. During 2008 SPARC staff members continued to deliver invited public presentations on SPARC's advocacy activities. These events were held both in person and, increasingly, as Webcasts and were hosted by library and publishing organizations in the United States and abroad.

Tools to support campus education programs have been a strong part of SPARC's programs and in 2008 SPARC published a timely guide defining options for institutions to comply with the copyright requirements of the NIH Public Access Policy. This joint SPARC/Science Commons/ARL white paper was written by Mike Carroll for policymaking staff in universities and other institutional recipients of NIH support responsible for ensuring compliance with the policy (see http://www.arl.org/sparc/publications/copyright.shtml). SPARC also published a guide for colleges and universities to advocate for institutional open access policies, which set out ten clear steps for policy development and adoption. Thinh Nguyen of Science Commons developed this paper, which discusses both the motivation and the process for establishing a binding institutional policy that automatically grants a copyright license from each faculty member to permit deposit of his or her peer-reviewed scholarly articles in institutional repositories, from which the works become available for others to read and cite. In addition, SPARC provided profiles highlighting steps by institutions to create open access publishing support funds (http://www.arl.org/sparc/publications/opendoors_v1.shtml).

In partnership with the Canadian Association of Research Libraries (CARL), SPARC launched a Canadian version of the popular Create Change Web site. Similar to the U.S. version, it provides additional resources for those working in a Canadian environment.

To keep the broader community informed about open access issues, SPARC administered a Wellcome Trust grant that supported the work of Peter Suber for his monthly *SPARC Open Access Newsletter* (http://www.arl.org/sparc/publications/soan/index.shtml) and Open Access News blog (http://www.earlham.edu/~peters/fos/fosblog.html). These resources regularly are cited as the most efficient means to keep abreast of open access activities around the world.

## SPARC Innovator Series

The SPARC Innovator program recognizes advances in scholarly communication realized by an individual, institution, or group. Typically, these advances exemplify SPARC principles by challenging the status quo in scholarly communication for the benefit of researchers, libraries, universities, and the public. The 2008 series identified two groups of individuals who had made significant contributions and successfully promoted positive change in scholarly communication.

The first recognition went to five student leaders. Hailed as "Agents of Change," these students point to the promise of a more open system for information sharing. Recognized were

- "The Technologist," Benjamin Mako Hill, graduate of the MIT Media Lab, current researcher at the Sloan School of Management at MIT, fellow in the MIT Center for Future Civic Media, and engineer of the 2007 "Overprice Tags" project at the MIT library
- "The Professional," Gavin Baker, political studies graduate of the University of Florida, open access director of Students for Free Culture, and co-mastermind of the National Day of Action for Open Access in February 2007
- "The Politician," Nick Shockey, current undergraduate and student senator at Trinity University in San Antonio and author of the second-ever student senate resolution in favor of public access to publicly funded research results
- "The Diplomat," Elizabeth Stark, student of law at Harvard, affiliate of the Berkman Center for Internet and Society, founder of Harvard Free Culture, and architect of one of the first student free thesis repositories
- "The Evangelist," Nelson Pavlosky, law student at George Mason University, cofounder of Students for Free Culture, and ally of the Student Global AIDS Campaign and Universities Allied for Essential Medicines

The second SPARC Innovator recognition went to the Faculty of Arts and Sciences (FAS) at Harvard for its unanimous vote in support of a policy that ensures open access to the faculty's published research results. A February 12, 2008, vote made the Harvard faculty the first in the United States to embrace an open access directive and the first to grant permission to the university to make their articles openly available. The policy, drafted by a ten-member provost's committee, was ratified by unanimous vote of a quorum of faculty members. The Harvard FAS vote and open access policy emerged at a time when there is growing concern among faculty that traditional publishing processes are not ensuring maximum access to their research.

## Student Campaign

SPARC expanded its program to partner with student groups and educate the next generation of academics on issues relating to scholarly communication. Successful working relationships have been established with student organizations including Student PIRGs (public interest research groups), Universities Allied for Essential Medicines, the American Medical Students Association, and Students for Free Culture.

Students were integral partners in the organization of Open Access Day (http://openaccessday.org) and generated a great deal of enthusiasm for continuing to raise awareness of scholarly communication issues.

SPARC sponsored the second annual SPARKY Awards contest, designed to help students articulate the characteristics that they value about the open Web and electronic communication using new media and technology. Cosponsors in 2008 included the Association of College and Research Libraries, the Association of Research Libraries, Penn Libraries at the University of Pennsylvania, Students for Free Culture, and the Student PIRGs. The 2008 contest theme was "MindMashup: The Value of Information Sharing." Well-suited for adoption as a college class assignment, the Sparky Awards invited contestants to submit videos of two minutes or less that imaginatively portray the benefits of the open, legal exchange of information. Mashup is an expression referring to a song, video, Web site, or software application that combines content from more than one source. To be eligible, submissions must be publicly available on the Internet—on a Web site or in a digital repository—and available for use under a Creative Commons License. For more on the awards, visit http:// www.sparkyawards.org.

Judges for the second annual Sparky Awards were Nicole Allen, director of the Student PIRGs' Make Textbooks Affordable campaign; Peter Decherney, assistant professor of cinema studies at the University of Pennsylvania; Barbara DeFelice, digital resources program director at Dartmouth College Library; Rick Johnson, SPARC's founding executive director and now a consultant and senior adviser to SPARC; Rich Jones, student and leader of the Boston University chapter of Students for Free Culture; Jennifer McLennan, SPARC's communications director; Kembrew McLeod, an independent documentary filmmaker and associate professor of communication studies at the University of Iowa; Jessica Reynoso of Campus MovieFest; Crit Stuart, director of research, teaching, and learning at the Association of Research Libraries; Anu Vedantham, director of the Weigle Information Commons at the University of Pennsylvania Libraries; and Mike Wesch, a cultural anthropologist at Kansas State University whose videos on technology, education, and information have been viewed more than 10 million times. The grand prize winner was "To Infinity and Beyond" by Danaya Panya, Sebastian Rivera, Hemanth Sirandas, Uriel Rotstein, and Jaymeni Patel, University of Illinois at Chicago Honors College (http://urliek.blogspot.com/2009/01/sparky-awards-entry.html).

Early in 2008 SPARC launched the "Right to Research" student-focused campaign in response to growing demand from the college student community for tools and resources to express their support for open access. It was developed by students and includes a Web site, brochure, and various leave-behinds (http://www.arl.org/sparc/students/index.shtml).

An internship program provides an opportunity for students to work with SPARC and two students were part of the program during 2008. The students are particularly helpful in identifying new technologies in support of SPARC's communication activities.

### Digital Repositories

SPARC continues to maintain and expand its content-rich resource on institutional repositories (http://www.arl.org/sparc/repositories).

The second SPARC digital repositories meeting was held in Baltimore in November 2008. More than 350 registrants attended the two-day event, held in cooperation with SPARC Europe and SPARC Japan (a Japan National Informatics Institute initiative), and examined how open online archives may be enhanced to further serve scholars, institutions, and the public. Librarians, researchers, funders, administrators, government officials, publishers, and technologists from around the world shared their experiences and best practices in building and supporting institutional and disciplinary digital repositories. The focus was on effective engagement with scholars and scientists to expand the sharing of research outputs via open repositories. The program, developed by a diverse and expert program committee, delved into four key areas: the Policy Environment, New Horizons, Campus Publishing Strategies, and Value-Added Services. Filling out the extensive program was a marketing practicum for repository advocates, an innovation fair, and keynote talks by John Wilbanks, vice president for science at Creative Commons and director of the Science Commons program; Bob Witeck, CEO and cofounder of Witeck-Combs Communications, a marketing communications and public relations agency in Washington, D.C.; and David Shulenburger, vice president for academic affairs at the National Association of State Universities and Land-Grant Colleges (NASULGC).

The meeting outcome site at http://www.arl.org/sparc/meetings/ir08/outcomes provides access to audio and select video files, presentations, and links to the wiki where the wider international repository community is invited to comment and build upon the Baltimore discussion. The next repository meeting is scheduled for November 2010.

SPARC also initiated a campaign in partnership with CARL focused on engaging faculty on the topic of digital repositories. A new brochure, *Greater Reach for Your Research,* provides information to faculty on the practical benefits of sharing their research.

To continue to advance the understanding of the role that data, and policies surrounding access to data, play in scholarly communications, SPARC supports the SPARC Open Data discussion list, moderated by Peter Murray-Rust (http://www.arl.org/sparc/opendata).

### Publisher Partnership Programs

SPARC supports and promotes useful examples of open access or other innovative publishing initiatives and participates in programs that highlight areas of common concern to libraries and not-for-profit publishers and where collaborative action can be beneficial.

During 2008 SPARC started work to redefine its Leading Edge and Alternative programs to begin to highlight alternative forms of widely available scholarship, with the aim of drawing attention to the importance of institutions that actively support/reward ventures that place a premium on the open accessibility of scholarship.

An analysis of active publishing ventures between university presses and libraries was conducted during the year. Raym Crow published a paper of current collaborative projects, and SPARC established Web resources in support of such collaborations (http://www.arl.org/sparc/media/09-0122.shtml). The guide is intended to help partnering organizations to

- Establish practical governance and administrative structures
- Identify funding models that accommodate the different financial objectives of libraries and presses
- Define objectives that advance the missions of both the library and of the press, without disrupting the broader objectives of either
- Demonstrate the value of collaboration to university administrators

SPARC has also participated in North American meetings to explore publisher transition strategies toward open access. SPARC has helped provide information about the SCOAP3 (Sponsoring Consortium for Open Access Publishing in Particle Physics) consortium, which is looking to facilitate open access publishing in high energy physics by redirecting subscription money.

SPARC is supporting efforts by the Stanford Encyclopedia of Philosophy (http://plato.stanford.edu) to build an endowment sufficient to sustain perpetual open access publication. That publication is now nearly 80 percent toward achieving its goal of self-sustainability. And SPARC continues to aid both BioOne (http://www.bioone.org) and Project Euclid (http://www.projecteuclid.org) in evolving sound, sustainable business practices needed to become leading platforms for digital dissemination of independent journals.

## Author Addendum and Author Rights Campaign

Publicity activities continue to promote the widespread adoption and use of the SPARC author copyright addendum. SPARC has partnered with Science Commons to launch a tool for authors to complete an addendum online (the Scholar's Copyright Addendum Engine). In addition, Science Commons and SPARC are working to collect and communicate data from authors and publishers on the use of the addendum. In collaboration with CARL, a Canadian version of the SPARC Author Addendum and brochure was published.

## International Activity

Change in scholarly communication models is needed on a global scale, and SPARC continued to intensify its impact in that arena by working in collaboration with international allies such as SPARC Europe, SPARC Japan, CARL, and various national and regional library associations.

SPARC partners with additional appropriate partners, including the Open Society Institute (OSI) and eIFL.net, a not-for-profit organization that supports and advocates for the wide availability of electronic resources by library users in transitional and developing countries.

To raise the profile of libraries as key stakeholders in policy decisions that affect the communication of research results, SPARC applied for and received observer status at the World Intellectual Property Organization (WIPO) and participated as an invited speaker in a session with delegates on WIPO's Copyright Committee.

### Business Consulting Services

SPARC provides ongoing consulting support to the library and publishing communities. Subsidized advisory services were made available to more than a dozen organizations and alternative publishing ventures in 2008.

### SPARC-ACRL Forum

A major component of SPARC's community outreach occurs twice a year at meetings of the American Library Association (ALA) when SPARC works with ALA's Association of College and Research Libraries (ACRL) and ACRL's scholarly communication committee to bring current issues to the attention of the community. The 2008 winter SPARC-ACRL Forum focused on "Working with the Facebook Generation: Engaging Student Views on Access to Scholarship" and featured Nelson Pavlosky, cofounder of Students for Free Culture; Stephanie Wang, graduate student in economics at Princeton University and former National Coordinating Committee member, Universities Allied for Essential Medicines; and Andre Brown, Ph.D. student in physics and astronomy at the University of Pennsylvania and co-blogger for Biocurious. The annual meeting addressed "Campus Open Access Policies: The Harvard Experience and How to Get There." Headlining the event was Stuart M. Shieber, professor of computer science at Harvard, director of the Center for Research on Computation and Society, faculty codirector of the Berkman Center for Internet and Society, and the key architect of the policy. He was joined by Catherine Candee, executive director, strategic publishing and broadcast initiatives, from the office of the president of the University of California (UC), who related similar activity in the UC system; and by Kevin L. Smith, scholarly communications officer at Duke University, who suggested legal considerations for institutions following the open access policy path.

### Governance

SPARC is guided by a Steering Committee. The 2009 committee chair is Ray English (Oberlin College). The other members are Larry Alford (Temple University), Sherrie Bergman (Bowdoin College), David Carlson (Southern Illinois University at Carbondale), Faye Chadwell (Oregon State University), Thomas Hickerson (University of Calgary), Paula Kaufman (University of Illinois at Urbana-Champaign), Jonathan Miller (Rollins College), Randy Olsen (Brigham Young University), Patricia Renfro (Columbia University), Bas Savenije (Utrecht University Library), Lee Van Orsdel (Grand Valley State University), and Vicki Williamson (University of Saskatchewan).

# Council on Library and Information Resources

1752 N St. N.W., Suite 800, Washington, DC 20036
202-939-4754, fax 202-939-4765
World Wide Web http://www.clir.org

Kathlin Smith
Director of Communications

The Council on Library and Information Resources (CLIR) is an independent, nonprofit organization that works at the intersection of libraries, scholarship, and technology. CLIR helps organize, structure, and sustain the collaborative effort needed to realize a new digital environment for research, teaching, and learning.

CLIR is supported by fees from sponsoring institutions, grants from public and private foundations, contracts with federal agencies, and donations from individuals. CLIR's Board of Directors establishes policy, oversees the investment of funds, sets goals, and approves strategies for their achievement. In November 2008 the CLIR board appointed as its newest members Stephen Rhind-Tutt, president of Alexander Street Press, and David Gift, vice provost for libraries, computing, and technology, and adjunct professor of radiology at Michigan State University. Their terms began in spring 2009. Also in November Stephen Nichols was elected chair of the CLIR board, succeeding Paula Kaufman, who had served as chair since 2006 and will continue to serve as a board member. Nichols is James M. Beall professor of French and humanities and chair of the Department of Romance Languages at Johns Hopkins University. A full listing of CLIR board members is available at http://www.clir.org/about/board.html.

In December CLIR President Charles Henry appointed G. Sayeed Choudhury as CLIR senior presidential fellow. Choudhury is associate dean for library digital programs and Hodson director of the Digital Research and Curation Center at the Sheridan Libraries, Johns Hopkins University. In 2009 he holds his fellowship concurrently with Michael Keller and Elliott Shore, who were appointed senior presidential fellows in 2007. Keller is university librarian at Stanford University, as well as director of academic information resources, founder and publisher of HighWire Press, and publisher of the Stanford University Press. Shore is chief information officer and Constance A. Jones director of libraries and professor of history at Bryn Mawr College.

In November 2008 CLIR moved its offices from 1755 Massachusetts Ave. N.W. to 1752 N St. N.W. in Washington, D.C.

During 2008 CLIR continued activity within the framework of the three-year agenda established in March 2007 (http://www.clir.org/activities/agenda.htm). The agenda deepens CLIR's traditional work in scholarly communications, preservation, leadership, and the emerging library, while also strengthening their interconnections. It integrates CLIR's work more tightly with efforts to develop a cyberinfrastructure that will promote, sustain, and advance research and teaching in the humanities and social sciences. The following pages describe these activities.

## Developments in 2008

### Cataloging Hidden Special Collections and Archives

Libraries, archives, and cultural institutions hold millions of items that have never been adequately described. These items are all but unknown to, and unused by, the scholars those organizations aim to serve. In March 2008 the Andrew W. Mellon Foundation awarded CLIR $4.27 million to create a national program to identify and catalog hidden special collections and archives. The program will award funds to institutions holding collections of high scholarly value that are difficult or impossible to locate through finding aids. Award recipients will create descriptive information for their hidden collections that will be linked to and interoperable with that of all other projects funded by this grant. In so doing, they will create a federated environment that can be built upon over time.

In December CLIR announced that 12 institutions and one collaborative project had been awarded grants under the new program. A list of recipients is available at http://www.clir.org/news/pressrelease/08hiddenpr3.html.

In conjunction with the hidden collections program, CLIR commissioned Lisa Spiro, director of the Digital Media Center at Rice University, to examine existing archival management systems and tools for creating and publishing encoded archival description (EAD) finding aids. Her report, available at http://www.clir.org/pubs/reports/spiro2009.html, provides a basis upon which to build from the experiences of institutions that receive grant funds. Spiro has also built a wiki that will support ongoing discussions and comment.

If funding for the hidden collections program is extended, CLIR will invite a second round of proposals in 2009.

In fall 2008 CLIR's work to create the hidden collections program was recognized by the Archivists Round Table of Metropolitan New York (ART), which selected CLIR to receive its 2008 Award for Outstanding Support of Archives.

### Promoting Digital Scholarship

In December 2007 the National Endowment for the Humanities (NEH) and CLIR launched a collaborative effort to develop a workshop to identify long-term research challenges at the intersection of humanities, social sciences, and computation. Increasingly, digital humanists face problems of organizing, engineering, and deploying the technologies they need to operate at a very large scale. To discuss these issues, CLIR invited some 30 leading scholars, technologists, and foundation representatives to the workshop, held in September 2008. To frame the discussions, CLIR commissioned a series of background papers illustrating the kinds of research projects that are possible and that point to future needs in areas such as archiving and preservation, data analysis, and semantic tools. CLIR was scheduled to publish these papers, along with a summary of workshop discussions, early in 2009.

### Blue Ribbon Task Force

Along with the Library of Congress, the National Archives and Records Administration, and the Joint Information Systems Committee of the United Kingdom,

CLIR is an institutional participant in the Blue Ribbon Task Force on Economically Sustainable Digital Preservation and Access. The 17-member task force, created in September 2007, is charged with developing recommendations for promoting the economic sustainability of digital information for the academic, public, and private sectors. It is funded by the National Science Foundation and the Andrew W. Mellon Foundation.

The group met periodically during 2008, and in December issued its interim report, available at http://brtf.sdsc.edu/biblio/BRTF_Interim_Report.pdf. The report, *Sustaining the Digital Investment: Issues and Challenges of Economically Sustainable Digital Preservation,* traces the contours of economically sustainable digital preservation, and identifies and explains the necessary conditions for achieving economic sustainability. The report also synthesizes current thinking on this topic, including testimony from 16 leading experts in digital preservation representing a variety of domains. In reviewing this synthesis, the task force identified a series of systemic challenges that create barriers to long-term, economically viable solutions.

The task force is continuing its work for a second and final year in 2009, and will issue its final report late in 2009 proposing practical recommendations for sustainable economic models to support access and preservation for digital data in the public interest. More information about the task force can be found at http://brtf.sdsc.edu.

### Support for NDIIPP

In 2008 CLIR continued to provide research and editing support for the Library of Congress's National Digital Information Infrastructure and Preservation Program (NDIIPP). This included editing early drafts of the Section 108-report, which addresses proposed revisions of the Digital Millennium Copyright Act to take into account the exceptions for libraries, archives, and museums in the context of networked, electronic information; a series of confidential interviews with key figures on the topics of e-journals, Web sites, broadcast television, and geographical information systems; and substantial support for the Blue Ribbon Task Force on Economically Sustainable Digital Preservation and Access.

### Reconceiving Research Libraries

In February 2008 CLIR convened 25 leading librarians, publishers, faculty members, and information technology (IT) specialists to consider how we should be rethinking the research library in a swiftly changing information landscape. Participants discussed the challenges and opportunities that libraries are likely to face in the next five to ten years, and how changes in scholarly communication will affect the future library. A key theme of the discussions was that the future of the research library cannot be considered apart from that of the academy as a whole. In August 2008 CLIR published a summary of the meeting, along with background essays written for the discussion (see Publications, below).

### Symposium on Scholarly Methods in the Humanities

In April 2008 CLIR and Brown University Libraries cosponsored a symposium on Scholarly Methods in the Humanities. The symposium was inspired by several questions, including:

- How has technology transformed teaching and learning?
- Given the tectonic shifts in every domain of scientific, technical, and artistic practice, what is legitimate scholarship?
- How is a scholar defined, and by whom, in this new environment?
- What is the role of the academic library in preserving and providing access to scholarship as well as in promoting the path to new scholarship?
- How has the academy changed, and how will it continue to change?

Speakers examined the role and impact of multimodal literacies on transforming the student's experience as scholar and lifelong learner. They also explored ways in which technology helps students think like scholars, how it helps students become digital scholars, and how their digital scholarship will ultimately change the definition of disciplines, as well as of scholarship and, ultimately, the academy itself.

### Upcoming Symposia

In September 2008 CLIR received $25,000 from the Samuel H. Kress Foundation to organize a series of symposia on scholarly methods and publication models in art history. CLIR will partner with Rice University Press to convene three symposia, held across the United States, that will focus on topics ranging from traditional aspects of art history to the adoption of new digital technologies and their implications. The proceedings of each symposium will be edited and published through Rice University Press and CLIR.

### Faculty Research Behavior Workshops

Early in 2007 CLIR piloted the first of its Faculty Research Behavior Workshops, which teach library and IT professionals ethnographic techniques that enable them to understand faculty members' work practices and how library and information services can address real faculty needs. Led by Nancy Foster, an anthropologist at the University of Rochester, the workshops have rapidly grown in popularity. In 2008 CLIR sponsored workshops at the University of California, Berkeley (February 20–21), George Washington University (April 28–29), and the University of Rochester (August 7–8).

### Frye Leadership Institute

The Frye Leadership Institute is designed to develop leaders who can guide and transform academic information services for higher education. The institute, which CLIR sponsors with EDUCAUSE and Emory University, is in its ninth year. It has trained some 400 librarians, faculty members, and IT experts.

The 2008 institute was held June 1–12 at Emory University in Atlanta. The 48 participants came from research universities, master's degree institutions, liberal arts colleges, and community colleges. Two participants came from universities abroad. Susan Perry, former CLIR interim president, and Brian Hawkins, former EDUCAUSE president, served as deans. The Frye Institute is supported with funds from the Robert W. Woodruff Foundation.

### Chief Information Officers

CLIR facilitates a semiannual forum that enables chief information officers (CIOs) of merged library and computing units in liberal arts colleges to discuss issues affecting teaching and learning on their campuses. At their May 2008 meeting the CLIR CIOs agreed to host a professional job exchange listserv that will allow their group, the Oberlin Group, the Associated Colleges of Appalachia, the Historically Black Colleges and Universities Library Alliance, and the American International Consortium of Academic Libraries to share expertise by making their needs known and exchanging staff. Exchange participants will work on discrete projects, such as digital asset management, open source software development, or new reference or technical service methods. They will not only share their knowledge with counterparts at the visiting institutions but also convey what they learned from their exchange experience to their colleagues upon returning to their home institutions.

## Awards

### Mellon Fellowships for Dissertation Research in Original Sources

In 2008 CLIR awarded Mellon Dissertation Fellowships to nine graduate students. The fellowships are intended to help graduate students in the humanities and related social science fields pursue original-source doctoral research and gain skill and creativity in using primary source materials in libraries, archives, museums, and related repositories. Established in 2001 and administered by CLIR, the program has awarded 10 to 15 annual fellowships of up to $20,000 each. In spring 2008 the Andrew W. Mellon Foundation awarded a grant that will allow CLIR to increase each fellowship to $25,000. CLIR will award the first round of these new fellowships—about 15 of them—in 2009.

### Postdoctoral Fellowship in Academic Libraries

CLIR created the Postdoctoral Fellowship in Academic Libraries for Humanists in response to changes in scholarly communication and the growing need to develop linkages among disciplinary scholarship, libraries, archives, and evolving digital tools.

In June 2008 five humanists were awarded new postdoctoral fellowships for 2008–2009; two fellows from the previous cohort are continuing their fellowships. In July 2008 the five new fellows spent two weeks at Bryn Mawr College, where, under the tutelage of CLIR senior presidential fellow Elliott Shore, they learned about the profession of academic librarianship. They met with several leaders in the library and information community to discuss issues affecting the profession. During two days of the seminar, they were joined by their supervisors and several former fellows.

In December 2007 CLIR received a planning grant from the Institute for Museum and Library Services (IMLS) to explore the possibility of giving institutions that have hosted postdoctoral fellows and are engaged in large-scale digitization projects a chance to develop a cohort of humanities and social sciences scholars who will work toward coordinating and linking the new large-scale initiatives that are being developed nationwide. CLIR convened two meetings—one in Washington, D.C., in March, and the other at the University of California, Los Angeles, in June—to develop a model that will build on this program by challenging fellows to solve problems of national as well as local concern.

### Rovelstad Scholarship in International Librarianship

Khue Duong, a master's degree candidate in the Information School at the University of Washington, was named the sixth recipient of the Rovelstad Scholarship in International Librarianship. The award provides travel funds for a student of library and information science to attend the annual meeting of the World Library and Information Congress of the International Federation of Library Associations and Institutions (IFLA). Duong's interest in international librarianship stems from his conviction that information issues "transcend cultural differences, geographical borders, and governmental policies." Duong has a bachelor of science degree in chemistry and English from the University of California, Los Angeles, and a master's degree in linguistics from the University of California, Santa Cruz.

### A. R. Zipf Fellowship in Information Management

Meredith Weiss, a doctoral student in information science at the University of North Carolina at Chapel Hill, was selected to receive the 2008 A. R. Zipf Fellowship in Information Management. Weiss's research focuses on higher education technology administration, organizational design, communications, and leadership; human/computer interaction; user-interface design; information system development and evaluation; and business intelligence systems. Her dissertation examines how chief information officers in institutions of higher education can best use academic evidence to ensure that the benefits of technology are fully realized. She holds master's degrees in information science and business administration from North Carolina Central University in Durham.

Named in honor of A. R. Zipf, a pioneer in information management systems, the $10,000 fellowship is awarded annually to a student who is enrolled in graduate school in the early stages of study and shows exceptional promise for leadership and technical achievement in information management.

## Publications

In November 2008 CLIR published *A Survey of Digital Humanities Centers in the United States* by information management consultant Diane Zorich. During 2008 Zorich surveyed some 30 U.S.-based digital humanities centers (DHCs)—

entities "where new media and technologies are used for humanities-based research, teaching, and intellectual engagement and experimentation." Her aim was to investigate the scope, financing, organizational structure, products, services, financing, and sustainability of DHCs, as well as the collaborative aspects of existing models. Completed in May 2008, the survey was used to inform Scholarly Communications Institute 6 (SCI 6), held in June at the University of Virginia. SCI 6 was devoted to assessing the needs, priorities, and challenges of national DHCs.

The report includes as an appendix a survey of digital humanities tools conducted by Lilly Nguyen and Katie Shilton, graduate students in the Department of Information Studies at the University of California, Los Angeles. Digital tools—software or computing products developed to provide access to, interpret, create, or communicate digital resources—are a critical part of the cyberinfrastructure that supports digital humanities research. Such tools are increasingly developed and supported by DHCs and the wider digital humanities community. However, the accessibility and clarity of these tools vary. If they are not visible, accessible, or understandable to researchers, they are less likely to be used broadly, less able to be built upon or extended, and ultimately less able to support the research for which they are intended. Nguyen and Shilton evaluated 39 tools developed by DHCs surveyed in Diane Zorich's report, paying special attention to the clarity of intentions and functions of the tools and the ease with which users can access them.

In August 2008 CLIR published *No Brief Candle: Reconceiving Research Libraries in the 21st Century.* The publication reports on a meeting held in February 2008 that invited leading librarians, publishers, faculty members, and information technology specialists to consider how we should be rethinking the research library in a swiftly changing information landscape. To inform the discussions, CLIR commissioned and circulated before the meeting essays from eight of the participants representing, variously, the perspectives of a provost, publisher, historian, foundation representative, librarians, and faculty members. *No Brief Candle* includes a meeting summary and background essays, and is available at http://www.clir.org/pubs/abstract/pub142abst.html.

In 2008 CLIR partnered with the Information Professionals Task Force of the American Society for Information Science and Technology (ASIS&T) to examine the status of information professional programs and related accreditation activities. With funds from CLIR, ASIS&T commissioned Samantha Becker and Bo Kinney, graduate students at the University of Washington's Information School, to conduct a preliminary analysis of accreditation programs training information professionals. The report, *Graduate Information Programs and Accreditation: Landscape Analysis and Survey,* was released in June 2008 and is available at http://www.asis.org/news.html. The report served as the basis for a September meeting at which representatives of information organizations discussed the establishment of a new accreditation process for the range of master's degree programs that educate information professionals.

In recent years, academic libraries have launched major initiatives to make their resources more easily available to users, but it is often difficult to know who is using these new resources and how well are they meeting users' needs. In April 2008 CLIR issued a report in which author Dawn Schmitz examines who is, or may be, using institutional repositories and mass-digitized collections. It outlines steps that academic and research libraries can take to learn more about such repositories, and suggests strategies that libraries may use to enhance the long-term planning and design of these projects. The report, *The Seamless Cyberinfrastructure: The Challenges of Studying Users of Mass Digitization and Institutional Repositories,* is available at http://www.clir.org/pubs/archives/schmitz.pdf.

*Many More than a Million: Building the Digital Environment for the Age of Abundance* was issued by CLIR in March 2008. It is a report of an invitational workshop held to discuss how very large digital collections are changing humanities research, and what infrastructure or systems are needed to provide services and materials to scholars who are dealing with collections on a new, and vastly expanded, scale. Attendees at the workshop, held in November 2007, included scholars in the digital humanities and representatives of research and funding agencies. The meeting report includes a summary of the discussions and identifies priorities for future work. It is available at http://www.clir.org/activities/digitalscholar/index.html.

In February 2008 CLIR published *Preservation in the Age of Large-Scale Digitization, A White Paper.* The report examines large-scale digital initiatives to identify issues that will influence the availability and usability, over time, of the digital books such projects create. Author Oya Rieger, associate university librarian for information technologies at Cornell University Library, describes four large-scale projects—Google Book Search, Microsoft Live Search Books (now defunct), Open Content Alliance, and the Million Book Project—and their digitization strategies. She then discusses a range of issues affecting the stewardship of the digital collections they create: selection, quality in content creation, technical infrastructure, and organizational infrastructure. The paper also attempts to foresee the likely impacts of large-scale digitization on book collections. *Preservation in the Age of Large-Scale Digitization* is available at http://www.clir.org/pubs/abstract/pub141abst.html.

# Digital Library Federation

1752 N St. N.W., Suite 800, Washington, DC 20036-2909
202-939-4761, fax 202-939-4765
World Wide Web http://www.diglib.org

Barrie Howard

Program Manager

The Digital Library Federation (DLF) is an international consortium of research libraries and related agencies that are furthering the development of electronic-information technologies for improved accessibility and usability of library collections and services. DLF provides leadership to libraries by identifying standards and best practices for building and providing access to digital collections, coordinating innovative digital library research and development, and incubating products and services that many libraries need but cannot develop individually.

DLF operates as a tax-exempt, nonprofit corporation through a small professional staff and is governed by a board of trustees on which each member institution is represented. Drawing from its 42 members and others in the scholarly, library, and computing communities, DLF brings together teams of experts to identify issues, and lead initiatives and special projects toward shared solutions.

## Organizational Leadership

DLF's leadership is composed of Executive Director Peter Brantley and an executive committee of officers elected by the board of trustees.

## Programmatic Activities

DLF pools effort, resources, and talent from its individual members for the advancement of the whole, and provides the following services:

- Coordination, facilitation, and support for collaborative research, standards development, and project start-ups
- Semiannual conferences for guiding the organization, reporting on new projects and updates, and sharing experiences in developing and managing electronic resources
- E-mail lists for exchanging information about developments within the membership and the broader digital library community and stimulating discussion
- A publicly accessible Web site for disseminating information about ongoing DLF activities, news, resources, and the organization itself
- Online and print publications, including conference proceedings, surveys, technical reports and specifications, white papers, and other information resources about digital library issues

## DLF Forums

DLF's semiannual conferences (forums) continue to catalyze initiatives, providing a platform for project progress reports, research paper presentations, proof-of-concept demonstrations, panel and roundtable discussions, and an opportunity for networking with colleagues to share information, create or renew cross-institutional collaboration, and recruit initiative participants. Forums are typically scheduled in spring and fall; the most recent took place in Minneapolis and Providence.

DLF continues to support a forum-related program providing travel awards to rising stars of the digital library community. The DLF Forum Fellowships for Librarians New to the Profession provide travel support for small groups of professionals to attend DLF forums to learn more about the library profession, see the results of digital projects from other institutions, and meet leaders in the profession. The success of the Forum Fellows program has resulted in many of the award winners returning to forums as presenters, participating in initiatives as key collaborators, or serving on the DLF Program Committee, which is responsible for some of the planning of future forums, and for peer review and selection of content for each forum program.

The last forum in 2008 saw the inaugural meeting of the DLF Project Managers' Group, which was created as a way for project managers to share their experiences, strategies, and challenges in managing digital library projects. The meeting was open to anyone who manages digital library projects, large or small, and more generally to anyone interested in the topic of digital library project management. Some topics of interest to the group included methods for prioritizing projects and work loads, managing expectations, learning from failure, and managing cultural differences among the project participants (IT staff vs. catalogers vs. content specialists). The first meeting featured lightning talks about various project management tools, and a case study "backstage" look at one digital library project.

## DLF Aquifer

DLF Aquifer models and develops network-based, scalable solutions to make a growing body of digital-library content easy to find and use across institutional boundaries.

In 2007 DLF received momentum for the aquifer initiative through an $816,000 grant from the Andrew W. Mellon Foundation for a two-year project, DLF Aquifer Development for Interoperability Across Scholarly Repositories: American Social History Online. Deliverables include implementation schemas, data models, and technologies that enable scholars to use digital collections as one in a variety of local environments.

Approaching the end of its second year, the Aquifer American Social History Online project boasts a Web site (http://www.dlfaquifer.org) designed for easy discovery of previously unknown digital library collections, as well as easy retrieval of known items. Using Zotero, a free, easy-to-use Firefox extension, scholars can gather and use online resources as well as annotate and share them.

To support the use of images, the American Social History Online Web site has integrated the Collectus and ImageViewer tools developed at the University of Virginia. These tools not only support saving and organizing items from image collections, but also enable slide-show creation so that images can be easily repurposed for classroom instruction.

American Social History Online has been developed using open source software and is currently available without fees or restrictions. The team is also developing integrations with the Sakai open source course management system.

With support from the Gladys Krieble Delmas Foundation, DLF Aquifer recently commissioned the report *Future Directions in Metadata Remediation for Metadata Aggregators* to identify and evaluate tools that could be used to tidy up and enhance metadata. Written by Greta de Groat, electronic media cataloger in the Metadata Development Unit of the Stanford University Libraries, the publication is available free of charge via the DLF Web site, or for sale through Amazon.com.

## ERMI 2

Following the success of the Electronic Resources Management Initiative (ERMI) launched in 2002, DLF has continued to foster rapid development of systems for managing electronic resources by providing a template for the detailed description of e-resource management problems and functional requirements and by promoting data standards. During the first phase of the initiative, the ERMI Steering Group realized that the environment, technologies, and business models relating to e-resources would continue to be highly dynamic. As a result, the work of the initiative would require ongoing review, assessment, and modification.

A second phase (ERMI 2), focused on further refinement of data standards-particularly those having to do with how license terms are summarized and interpreted and how usage data is transmitted and received—and made great progress through the completion of four sub-projects:

- Publication of the *White Paper on Interoperability Between Acquisitions Modules of Integrated Library Systems and Electronic Resource Management Systems,* which is a brief analysis of four case studies investigating the interoperability between the acquisitions modules of integrated library systems (ILSs) and electronic resource management systems (ERMs)
- Publication of the *Professional Training in License Term Mapping to ERM Systems* report, which encapsulates the curriculum of a series of professional training workshops in license term mapping to ERM systems sponsored by DLF and the Association of Research Libraries, including workshop handouts, an evaluative summary of the outcomes, and recommendations for future efforts in license education and mapping
- Approval of the Standardized Usage Statistics Harvesting Initiative (SUSHI) Protocol standard (ANSI/NISO Z39.39), which defines an automated request and response model for the harvesting of e-resource usage data utilizing a Web services framework that can replace user-mediated

collections of usage data reports, available at http://www.niso.org/workrooms/sushi

• Collaboration with the international standards group EDItEUR to create a specification for license term mapping to enable an ERMI subset to be extracted from another standard, ONIX for Licensing Terms

### Integrated Library Systems

In summer 2007 DLF convened the ILS-Discovery Interface Task Group for examining ILSs and their discovery systems, and exploring the development of a lightweight application programming interface (API) or computational framework that would permit the abstraction of the discovery layer away from an ILS, which often includes discovery via the Online Public Access Catalog (OPAC), in addition to cataloging, acquisition, and circulation functions.

As of the end of 2008, the ILS-DI Task Group had conducted a survey of libraries to gather information about existing and desired functionality between their ILSs and external systems, convened two meetings with ILS developers and vendors, authored the *DLF ILS Discovery Interface Task Group Technical Recommendation* and accompanying XML schema, and revised the recommendations and schema based on what was learned from the meetings. One of the task group members created a prototype to encourage implementation by commercial and open source developers. The recommendation document walks through several levels of discovery interface and ILS interoperability, with the baseline being Level 1, or the Basic Discovery Interface, which includes functions for exposing bibliographic records for harvesting, reporting the real-time availability of an item, and linking to detailed records or other service options such as placing an item on hold or initiating a recall. To achieve optimum interoperability, the task group has based the recommendation functionalities on standard Web technologies such as Dublin Core, OAI-PMH, and REST.

### METS

DLF continued support for the Metadata Encoding and Transmission Standard (METS), an XML schema for encoding descriptive, administrative, and structural metadata for digital resources. The standard is maintained by the Library of Congress and advanced through the work of the METS Editorial Board.

In 2008 the METS schema, schema documentation, and tutorial were translated into Chinese by Beijing Sinosoft. The tutorial was also translated into Spanish, and all these publications are available from http://www.loc.gov/standards/mets.

### Moving-Image Collections

With support from the Andrew W. Mellon Foundation, DLF published the conclusions of an environmental scan of traditional moving-image archives and of major public and university libraries, museums, and other cultural institutions such as U.S. public television broadcasters with significant film and video collections. The report summarizes which moving-image collections are potentially available for digitization, with an emphasis on open access to increase the volume of online content for teaching and learning.

The environmental scan was commissioned by a steering group called Lot 49, which initially convened in July 2007 to discuss digitization of moving-image archives with a focus on access for research, teaching, and learning. The group re-convened at the Library of Congress National Audio-visual Conservation Center in September 2008, extending participation beyond the initial group of moving-image experts to include such key cultural heritage federal agencies as the Library of Congress, the Institute of Museum and Library Services, and the National Endowment for the Humanities. A work plan was set with three main goals in mind:

- Compile a set of best practices for the moving-image community that will be gathered together from diverse topical areas, e.g., reformatting, preservation, and presentation, to be hosted from the DLF Web site
- Develop tools for video annotation and citation, including snippet citation, built on existing standards
- Advocate for the digitization of moving-image collections for access, as well as preservation

**Virtual Worlds**

The DLF Second Life (SL) initiative was launched in spring 2007 to explore the issues and opportunities presented by virtual worlds in the context of digital libraries and their roles in scholarship and publishing. In 2008 DLF's island Entropia relocated to http://slurl.com/secondlife/Entropia/147/127/22, and is now attached to the Alliance Library System Archipelago, west of Stanford University Libraries island and southwest of the San Jose State University School of Library and Information Science island.

In 2008 DLF added photos and links to 12 of its member institutions and to the Aquifer American Social History Online project Web site. Also, a meeting area with a screen was added for displaying slide show presentations and real-life (RL) live video feeds. This meeting area is currently being used to host year-long series of public seminars exploring the emerging field of digital humanities. The nine Mellon Seminars in Digital Humanities are taking place in RL at the University of California, Los Angeles (UCLA), and are broadcast via live feed to the Entropia meeting area. The RL participants will also see the SL audience in a seminar room on the UCLA campus. Another example of cross-world conferencing took place at a 2008 DLF Forum at which the SL initiative sponsored a panel of talks on the use of SL in an academic setting, with the panelists sharing their stories of teaching, learning, and research activities in SL. The efforts were well received by participants and audiences.

Finally, Entropia was featured in a "machinima"—an animated 3D real-time video capture used in virtual worlds—clip by HVX Silverstar, and in a slide show created by Bernadette Daly Swanson for presentation at the Bridging Worlds 2008 conference in Singapore. The machinima video, *I Am Library: Ode to Self-discovery and Collective Creativity in Second Life,* can be seen at http://www.youtube.com/watch?v=cM5ze9M3AJ4.

# Association for Library and Information Science Education

ALISE Headquarters, 65 East Wacker Place, Suite 1900, Chicago, IL 60601-7246
312-795-0996, fax 312-419-8950, e-mail contact@alise.org
World Wide Web http://www.alise.org

Michèle V. Cloonan
President 2008–2009

The Association for Library and Information Science Education (ALISE) is an independent, nonprofit professional association whose mission is to promote excellence in research, teaching, and service for library and information science (LIS) education through leadership, collaboration, advocacy, and dissemination of research.

The founders of the American Library Association (ALA) recognized the importance of formal library science education degree programs to the professionalization of librarians, supplementing the apprenticeships that were run under the auspices of libraries. In 1887 Melvil Dewey founded the first "School of Library Economy" in the United States at Columbia College. At least six other programs were established before the end of the century. In 1903 ALA's Committee on Library Training prepared a report on all library training programs. Subsequently, library school faculties formed the Round Table of Library School Instructors, which met for the first time in 1911 and four years later voted to become the Association of American Library Schools (AALS). This new organization was an independent, but ALA-affiliated, organization. In 1983 AALS changed its name to the current ALISE. As Connie Van Fleet, author of this report in last year's edition, noted, ALISE's "enduring purpose is to promote research that informs the scholarship of teaching and learning for library and information science, enabling members to integrate research into teaching and learning. The association provides a forum in which to share ideas, to discuss issues, to address challenges, and to shape the future of education for library and information science." ALISE continues to enjoy close ties with ALA as well as with other professional associations such as the American Society for Information Science and Technology (ASIS&T) and the International Federation of Library Associations and Institutions (IFLA). ALISE's mission, goals, and membership reflect its inclusive approach to the discipline and related professions.

Although AALS began as an association of "library school faculties," today ALISE is both an institutional and individual membership organization. Its membership has nearly doubled over the past five years from 348 members in 2003 to 620 personal and 27 institutional members in 2009. Most members—institutional and personal—are American and Canadian. ALISE has four categories of membership: personal members, institutional members, international affiliate members, and associate members. Institutional members include departments, programs, and schools that offer courses and programs intended to educate librarians, archivists, and other information professionals. Only personal membership, the largest category, will be described here.

Personal membership is open to any individual who has an interest in the objectives and programs of the association. Most members are full-time faculty, but doctoral students are an active and growing group. Their strong participation in ALISE is demonstrated by the Doctoral Special Interest Group (SIG)—one of the most active SIGs in ALISE—and the growth of the Doctoral Poster Research Session. The number of part-time and adjunct faculty members in library and information science programs is increasing, as is their membership in ALISE.

## Structure and Governance

The association's structure is designed to encourage effective use of ALISE's resources. The Medical Library Association manages the association under the leadership of Executive Director Kathleen Combs. The business of the association is carried out by a board of directors elected by the membership. The board establishes policy, sets goals and strategic directions, and provides oversight for the management of ALISE. It consists of a president, vice president/president-elect, past president, secretary/treasurer, and three directors elected on a rotating basis. The executive director is an ex officio, nonvoting board member. All elected board members serve three-year terms. The current officers are Linda C. Smith (University of Illinois at Urbana-Champaign), president; Lorna Peterson (University of Buffalo, State University of New York), vice president/president-elect; Michèle V. Cloonan (Simmons College), past president; and Jean Preer (Indiana University), secretary/treasurer. Directors are Andrew Wertheimer (University of Hawaii at Manoa), director for special interest groups; Susan Roman (Dominican University), director for external relations; and Melissa Gross (Florida State University), director for membership services.

Standing and special committees attend to general and specific areas of association concern. Standing committees that report directly to the board include Budget and Finance, Governance, Nominating, Recruitment, and the Membership Advisory Board. Development and Advancement is a subcommittee of Budget and Finance. Other standing committees are grouped and report through an appropriate coordinating committee: the Awards and Honors Coordinating Committee, which organizes and facilitates the work of committees that recognize service, teaching, and professional contribution; the Conference Program Planning Coordinating Committee, which organizes and facilitates work of all committees involved in conference program planning; the Publications Coordinating Committee, which attends to fiscal and operational matters relating to the association's publications program and facilitates the work of the publications advisory boards; and the Research Coordinating Committee, which organizes and facilitates the work of the research awards committees. Each coordinating committee has a designated board liaison. Committee chairs are appointed by the vice president/president-elect; in most cases, committee members are appointed by their respective chairs. Each committee is given an ongoing term of reference to guide its work, as well as the specific charges for the year. The president may appoint ad hoc committees or task forces to pursue special projects. In 2007 a task force was created to develop a code of ethics for library and information science educators, with a charge to present a recommendation at the 2009 ALISE annual conference. The task force requested a one-year extension, which the current board granted at its January 2009 meeting.

Special interest groups (SIGs) provide a less structured forum than committees. Their primary purpose is to provide a place for ALISE members to learn about current trends and practices in their areas of interest. Many of the SIGs sponsor panels at the annual conference; others hold roundtable discussions. The groups are distinct from the usual committee structure in that participation is voluntary rather than appointive, and no charges are assigned. The SIG structure is fairly flexible, and SIGs are created and dissolved depending on participation and interest. SIG conveners provide attendance figures to the director for special interest groups. If the numbers are consistently low, a SIG may be dissolved.

SIGs are currently organized into the following clusters (conveners are listed in parentheses):

*Roles and Responsibilities Cluster*—Assistant/Associate Deans and Directors (Rae-Anne Montague); Doctoral Students (Lauren Mandel); New Faculty (Jenny Bossaller); Part-time and Adjunct Faculty (Dan Fuller).

*Teaching and Learning Cluster*—Curriculum (Linda Lillard); Distance Education (Scott Klinger); Teaching Methods (David Walczyk).

*Topics and Courses Cluster*—Archival Records/Management Education (Mary Edsall Choquette); Gender Issues (Lesley Farmer); Historical Perspectives (Cindy Welch and Carol Tilley); Information Ethics (Toni Carbo); Information Policy (Mary Stansbury); International Library Education (Rebecca Miller); Multicultural, Ethnic, and Humanistic Concerns (Renate Chancellor and Shari Lee); Preservation Education (Mary Edsall Choquette); Research (Betsy Martens and Susan Burke); School Library Media (Allison G. Kaplan); Technical Services Education (Karen Snow and Gretchen Hoffman); Youth Services (Jamie Campbell Naidoo and Brian Sturm).

School representatives are a link between members and the board of directors. Each school or program designates a faculty member who is a current member of ALISE to serve as ALISE liaison. These representatives disseminate information from ALISE to members (and potential members) in their schools. They communicate ideas, information, and concerns to the ALISE director for membership services.

## Publications

ALISE has three primary avenues for promoting excellence in research, teaching, and service: a publications program, an annual conference, and a grants and awards program. There are four components to the ALISE publications program.

- The *Journal of Education for Library and Information Science* (*JELIS*) is a peer-reviewed quarterly journal edited by Michelle Kazmer and Kathleen Burnett of Florida State University. The journal presents refereed articles and columns relating to library and information science education. This year marks the publication's 50th anniversary.

- The ALISE *Directory of LIS Programs and Faculty in the United States and Canada* is an annual print volume. An online membership database, implemented in 2007, complements the print version.
- The *ALISE Library and Information Science Statistical Report* is published in cooperation with ALA's Committee on Accreditation. It is an annual compilation of statistical data on curriculum, faculty, students, income and expenditures, and continuing professional education. Upon the retirement of the long-serving editors Evelyn Daniel and Jerry Saye in 2007, the board, with extensive input from the membership, decided to rethink ALISE's approach to its gathering, manipulation, and presentation of data. Revisions to the process over the years had been minor, and the data-gathering was oriented to publication of the statistics in print. Also, rather than continuing to have a system of chapter and general editors, the board created a new position: ALISE Statistical Data Manager. In spring 2008 Danny P. Wallace, professor and EBSCO endowed chair of library service, School of Library and Information Studies at the University of Alabama, was selected for the post. He is working on implementing a database-driven environment for gathering, editing, and organizing the data.
- The fourth component of the publications program is the ALISE Web site. The site hosts the electronic *ALISE News,* which is published quarterly.

## Annual Conference

The ALISE Annual Conference, held immediately before the ALA Midwinter Meeting, is the major activity of the association. The conference serves scholarly, professional, career development, business, social, and networking purposes. There were 479 registrations for the 2009 conference, held in Denver January 20–23.

The conference theme was "Transforming LIS Education for the 21st Century: i-CREATE," which explored the complementary missions of libraries, museums, and archives. The program co-chairs, Tula Giannini and Paul Marty, solicited broad participation from inside and outside the association. The keynote speakers and the titles of their talks were Shirley Amore, "Transformation from the Inside Out: Developing Passionate Library Professionals Who Transform Communities"; Martín J. Gomez, "Building a Community of Practice"; and Joyce Ray, "The Digital Revolution: Developing Library Services for the Next Generation." Twenty-seven peer-reviewed papers (a 34 percent acceptance rate), were presented, along with eight juried panels (a 67 percent acceptance rate), and 14 SIG-sponsored programs.

Two poster sessions—Works-in-Progress and the ALISE/Jean Tague Sutcliffe Doctoral Student Research Poster Session—offered opportunities for intellectual engagement one-on-one and in groups. Birds-of-a-Feather brown-bag lunches allowed conference participants an informal forum to discuss shared areas of interest. In 2008 a Meet the Editors panel was added to the conference and proved so successful that it was offered again in 2009.

At the 2009 conference, the ALISE Academy was launched. This is a pre-conference professional development opportunity designed to inspire and guide LIS faculty (at all stages of their careers) and doctoral students in creating, building, and revising a research agenda, engaging in research activities, and maximizing the impact of their research efforts. At the inaugural academy, three concurrent sessions were held: "Launching the Research Agenda," "Retooling, Redirecting, and Revitalizing: Research After Tenure and Promotion," and "Capping a Research Career with Glory." The academy received generous support from the H. W. Wilson Foundation and Second-Hand Knowledge.

## Grants and Awards

ALISE grants and awards recognize individuals who have exhibited excellence in research, teaching, and in service to the profession and to ALISE. Two new awards were presented in 2009. The Norman Horrocks Leadership Award, which carries a plaque and monetary prize of $500, was created in 2008 to recognize a new ALISE member who has demonstrated outstanding leadership qualities in ALISE activities. Horrocks is professor emeritus, School of Information Management, Dalhousie University; his long and productive service to the association and the profession serves as a model for a new generation of library and information science educators. The inaugural Horrocks award was won by Linda Most.

Also established in 2009 was the Linworth Youth Services Paper Award, funded by Linworth Publishing. The winners were Shana Pribesh, Old Dominion University, and Karen Gavigan, University of North Carolina at Greensboro, for "Equal Opportunity? Poverty and Characteristics of School Library Media Centers."

[For a list of the winners of ALISE's 2008 awards, see "Library Scholarship and Award Recipients, 2008" in Part 3—Ed.]

## Membership Survey

A goal of the ALISE strategic plan for 2007–2010 is to deliver "relevant, high-quality services and [develop] strategic new initiatives to ensure membership growth to develop the association's unique purpose and vision." To learn more about which services ALISE members value, the board conducted a comprehensive Web-based survey in August 2008. The response rate was 22 percent (116 members). The answers will assist the board in improving services, future conferences, and the Web site. The full survey report is available to members on the ALISE Web site.

## Conclusion

ALISE is in sound financial shape and has created an operating reserve as well as an endowment fund to support its grants and awards program. Based on the feedback gleaned from the 2008 membership survey, new services are being created. The board is about to begin a new cycle of strategic planning, and ALISE is well poised to embrace new opportunities.

# International Reports

## International Federation of Library Associations and Institutions

P.O. Box 95312, 2509 CH The Hague, Netherlands
Tel. 31-70-314-0884, fax 31-70-383-4827, e-mail ifla@ifla.org
World Wide Web http://www.ifla.org

Beacher Wiggins
Director for Acquisitions and Bibliographic Access, Library of Congress
Library of Congress Representative to the Standing Committee
of the IFLA Section on Bibliography

The International Federation of Library Associations and Institutions (IFLA) is the preeminent international organization representing librarians, other information professionals, and library users. During 2008 IFLA protected the world's cultural and documentary heritage from the ravages of war and natural disaster; broadened participation in its activities by countries with developing economies; expanded the theory and practice of bibliographic control; and promoted equitable access to information without regard to barriers of poverty, handicap, or geographical isolation. Throughout the year, IFLA promoted an understanding of libraries as cultural heritage resources that are the patrimony of every nation.

## World Library and Information Congress

The World Library and Information Congress (WLIC) and 74th IFLA General Conference and Council attracted more than 3,280 participants from 150 countries to Quebec City August 10–14, 2008. Michaëlle Jean, Governor General of Canada, opened the congress with a speech in French; IFLA President Claudia Lux gave her presidential address in English, German, and French. The keynote speaker was Dany Laferrière, a Haitian-born resident of Montreal and Miami, Florida, whose latest novel, *Je Suis un Écrivain Japonais,* was published in 2008.

As 2008 was the 400th anniversary of the founding of Quebec City, the congress featured cultural events and entertainment recalling the interactions of English, French, and indigenous peoples in Canada, which reinforced the overall congress theme of "Libraries Without Borders: Navigating Towards Global Understanding."

Fourteen satellite meetings permitted intensive focus on special topics. These included "Rethinking Access to Information: Evolving Perspectives on Information Content and Delivery," held in Boston; "Disappearing Disciplinary Borders in the Social Science Library," at the University of Toronto; and "Multicultural to Intercultural: Libraries Connecting Communities," held in Vancouver. The remaining satellite meetings took place in Ottawa, Montreal, and Quebec City. The IFLA Cataloguing Section, with the Joint Steering Committee for Development of RDA, cosponsored a day-long satellite meeting on "RDA: Resource Description and Access," which introduced the new cataloging code that has been proposed to replace the Anglo-American Cataloguing Rules, 2nd Edition (AACR2).

The 2009 WLIC will take place in Milan August 23–27. The 2010 congress will be in Brisbane and the 2011 congress in San Juan.

## Conference of Directors of National Libraries

The Conference of Directors of National Libraries (CDNL) is an independent association that meets in conjunction with the IFLA WLIC to promote coopera- tion on matters of common interest to national libraries around the world. The CDNL president is Penny Carnaby, chief executive of the National Library of New Zealand, which hosts the CDNL Secretariat through 2009. Discussion at the CDNL meeting in Quebec City focused on the question "How can CDNL increase the strategic impact of national libraries?" with models of national libraries as global digital libraries.

## World Summit Follow-Up

The second World Summit on the Information Society (WSIS) was held in Tunis, Tunisia, November 16–18, 2005. WSIS is sponsored by the International Tele- communications Union, a United Nations organization separate from UNESCO. Thanks to IFLA's advocacy, the concluding document of WSIS, the "Tunis Agenda for the Information Society," recognized the role of libraries in providing equitable access to information and knowledge for all people and called on gov- ernments to support libraries in this role.

The IFLA leadership has worked to ensure a continued role for libraries in WSIS follow-up meetings and projects since 2005. IFLA was appointed modera- tor of the "Libraries and Archives" sub-theme of WSIS action line C3, "Access to information and knowledge," and of the "Heritage" sub-theme of action line C8, "Cultural diversity." An IFLA representative was also active in meetings of the WSIS-derived Global Alliance for ICT (Information and Communication Technologies) and Development and the UN Commission for Science and Tech- nology for Development. However, IFLA was still endeavoring to obtain full consultative status in the UN Economic and Social Council and to be represented in WSIS action line C7, "e-science." The IFLA Governing Board established an IFLA presidential committee on WSIS in 2007, which continued in 2008.

## Response to War and Natural Disaster

In 1996 IFLA was a founding member of the International Committee of the Blue Shield (ICBS) to protect cultural property in the event of natural and human disasters. Its current partners in ICBS are the International Council on Archives, the International Council on Monuments and Sites, the International Council of Museums, and the Coordinating Council of Audiovisual Archives Associations. In 2008 ICBS continued its concern for the preservation of cultural heritage in the ongoing war in Iraq and in natural disasters such as the massive earthquake in Bam, Iran, in 2003, the Asian tsunami of December 2004, and Hurricane Katrina in August 2005. The IFLA North American regional center for preservation and conservation, hosted at the Library of Congress, continued to develop a network of colleague institutions to provide a safety net for library collections during emergencies. Rescue work for Sri Lankan and other South Asian libraries in the wake of the 2004 tsunami will continue for years to come.

A milestone in 2008 was the establishment of the Association of National Committees of the Blue Shield (ANCBS), which held its founding conference in The Hague December 7–8 and established a permanent ANCBS coordination center in that city.

## Bibliographic Control

IFLA has worked steadily over the decades to improve bibliographic control, through practical workshops, support of the International Standard Bibliographic Description, and research that seeks to establish basic principles of bibliographic control and to identify areas where cataloging practice in different cultures can be harmonized to make library catalogs less expensive to produce and easier for patrons to use.

The IFLA Governing Board in 2003 joined with six national libraries—the British Library, the Deutsche Nationalbibliothek, the Library of Congress, the National Library of Australia, the Biblioteca Nacional de Portugal, and the Koninklijke Bibliotheek (Netherlands)—and the Conference of Directors of National Libraries (CDNL) to form the IFLA-CDNL Alliance for Bibliographic Standards (ICABS), now an IFLA core activity. In addition to general issues of bibliographic control, ICABS advanced the understanding of issues relating to long-term archiving of electronic resources. Beginning with the 2007 WLIC in Durban, South Africa, ICABS has shifted its focus to digital library developments. At the Quebec City congress, ICABS hosted sessions on digital objects as physical carriers of information and on preservation infrastructures.

Closely related to ICABS is the separate IFLA UNIMARC Core Activity (UCA), which maintains, develops, documents, and promotes the four UNIMARC formats for bibliographic, authority, classification, and holdings data. Since 2003, when it succeeded IFLA's former Universal Bibliographic Control and International MARC program, UCA has been hosted by the Biblioteca Nacional de Portugal. Under UCA, the Permanent UNIMARC Committee maintains the formats and also advises ICABS on matters relating to UNIMARC. In 2008 K. G. Saur published the third edition of the *UNIMARC Manual: Bibliographic Format,* edited by Permanent UNIMARC Committee Chair Alan Hopkinson of the United Kingdom.

Other ongoing projects under the IFLA Cataloguing Section included the Working Group on Functional Requirements and Numbering of Authority

Records (FRANAR) and the Working Group on Functional Requirements for Subject Authority Records (FRSAR). The IFLA Bibliography Section's Working Group on Electronic National Bibliographies issued guidelines for new bibliographies for worldwide review in 2008.

The Statement of International Cataloguing Principles was issued for worldwide review in 2008 and was scheduled for publication by K. G. Saur in 2009. The statement was the final product of the International Meeting of Experts on an International Cataloging Code (IME ICC), a series of five regional invitational conferences planned by the IFLA Cataloguing Section to explore similarities and differences in current national and regional cataloging rules, in an attempt to clarify where variations for languages and cultural differences may be needed and where rules might be the same. The first meeting was held in Frankfurt in 2003 for experts from Europe and North America; the second took place in Buenos Aires in conjunction with the 2004 WLIC and IFLA General Conference there. The third was held in Cairo in 2005. The fourth and fifth regional conferences took place in Seoul and in Pretoria in conjunction with the 2006 and 2007 WLICs. The goal of IME ICC was to increase the ability to share cataloging information worldwide by promoting standards for the content of bibliographic and authority records used in library catalogs.

## Copyright Issues

The IFLA Committee on Copyright and Other Legal Matters (CLM) works to ensure a proper balance between the claims of intellectual property rights holders and the needs of library users worldwide. With the Library Copyright Alliance, a coalition of five major U.S.-based library associations, CLM offered a joint statement at the second session of the World Intellectual Property Organization's (WIPO's) Committee on Development and Intellectual Property, held in Geneva July 7–11, 2008. The statement urged WIPO, a United Nations agency, to amend its convention to incorporate a development dimension to meet the needs of developing countries.

## Digital Libraries

IFLA's World Digital Library Working Group on Digital Library Guidelines, which began work in May 2007, issued recommendations and guidelines for content selection, metadata, technology, service, and organization of digital libraries in mid-2008. The working group is a contribution to the development of the World Digital Library, a digital repository of world culture cosponsored by UNESCO, the Library of Congress, national libraries in other countries, and IFLA.

## FAIFE

One of IFLA's core activities is Freedom of Access to Information and Freedom of Expression (FAIFE), which is defined in Article 19 of the United Nations Universal Declaration of Human Rights as a basic human right. Continuing the outreach mission to Israel and the Occupied Palestinian Territories that FAIFE began in 2007, IFLA President Claudia Lux attended the International Conference on Libraries from a Human Rights Perspective, held in Ramallah, West Bank, on March 31, 2008. At the urging of FAIFE, the Norwegian Library Association announced that it would provide financial support for the Palestinian Library Association to become a member of IFLA. In Quebec City, FAIFE and CLM hosted a discussion on barriers to access to government information, led by FAIFE Chairman Paul Sturges (University of Loughborough).

During 2008 FAIFE also compiled and publicized information resources needed to improve online public access to public health information, including information on HIV/AIDS. Under FAIFE's leadership, in December the IFLA Governing Board endorsed the IFLA Manifesto on Transparency, Good Government, and Corruption, which asserts that "libraries are in their very essence transparency institutions" that counter corruption and deceit in government, and the IFLA Statement on Access to Personally Identifiable Information in Historical Records. The latter strikes a balance between individual privacy rights and long-term preservation of and access to historical documents such as census records, military service records, and wills and testaments—the raw data of historical and biographical research.

## Grants and Awards

IFLA continues to collaborate with corporate partners and national libraries to maintain programs and opportunities that would otherwise not be possible, especially for librarians and libraries in developing countries. The Jay Jordan IFLA/OCLC Early Career Development Fellowships bring library and information science professionals from countries with developing economies who are in the early stages of their careers to OCLC headquarters in Dublin, Ohio, for four weeks of intensive experience in librarianship. In 2008 the five fellows were from India, Morocco, Nepal, South Africa, and Uganda. The six fellows for 2009 will be from Armenia, Kenya, Pakistan, Serbia, Uganda, and Zambia. The American Theological Library Association is the third sponsor of the program, and one of the fellows must be a theological librarian. Since its inception in 2001, the program has supported 44 librarians from 28 developing countries.

The Harry Campbell Conference Attendance Grant supports travel to the IFLA Conference from a developing country that has not had conference participants in recent years. The 2008 recipient was Volatiana Ranaivozafy, Centre Culturel Albert Camus, Antananarivo, Madagascar. The Dr. Shawky Salem Conference Grant supports conference attendance from an Arab country; it was won in 2008 by Mahmoud Khalifa of Cairo University.

The Frederic Thorpe Awards, established in 2003, are administered by the IFLA Libraries for the Blind Section and the Ulverscroft Foundation of Leicester, England, which Thorpe founded to support visually impaired people. The Ulverscroft Foundation renewed the program as the Ulverscroft/IFLA Best Practice Awards (Frederic Thorpe Awards) in 2006. The 2008 awards, announced in March 2008, were presented to Hélène Kudzia of the Médiathèque de l'Association Valentin Haüy, Paris, France, and Hosain Rohany Sadr of the National

Library and Archives of Iran; and to the Integrated Documentation System of the Cuyo National University, Mendoza, Argentina, and Centro para la Integracion y el Desarrollo del Invidente, Lima, Peru.

The Bill and Melinda Gates Foundation Access to Learning Award in 2008 was presented to the Vasconcelos Program in the state of Veracruz, Mexico. This annual award, managed by the Council on Library and Information Resources (CLIR), presents up to $1 million to libraries, library agencies, or comparable organizations outside the United States that have been innovative in providing free public access to information. Vasconcelos brings training for library skills and computer literacy to indigenous peoples of Veracruz, bringing trainers and equipment to rural areas using a fleet of all-terrain vehicles.

The IFLA International Marketing Award includes a stipend and travel to the annual IFLA Conference. The first-place winner in 2008 was Ros Dorsman of Central West Libraries, New South Wales, Australia, for an online classroom/ libraries partnership program. In 2002, 2003, and 2004, IFLA and 3M Library Systems cosponsored the marketing awards. After a hiatus in 2005, IFLA cosponsored the awards with SirsiDynix in 2006 and 2007. The Emerald Group sponsored the 2008 award.

## Membership and Finances

IFLA has approximately 1,700 members in 150 countries. Established at a conference in Edinburgh, Scotland, in 1927, it has been registered in the Netherlands since 1971 and has headquarters facilities at the Koninklijke Bibliotheek (Royal Library) in The Hague. Although IFLA did not hold a General Conference outside Europe and North America until 1980, there has since been steadily increasing participation from Asia, Africa, South America, and Australia. The federation now maintains regional offices for Africa (in Pretoria, South Africa); Asia and Oceania (in Singapore); and Latin America and the Caribbean (in Rio de Janeiro). The organization has seven official working languages—Arabic, Chinese, English, French, German, Russian, and Spanish—and offers a range of membership categories: international library associations, national library associations, other associations (generally regional or special library associations), institutions, institutional sub-units, one-person libraries, school libraries, personal affiliates, and student affiliates. Association and institution members have voting rights in the IFLA General Council and may nominate candidates for IFLA offices; personal affiliates have no voting rights but may run for any office. Except for personal and student affiliates, membership fees are keyed to the UNESCO Scale of Assessment and the United Nations List of Least Developed Countries, to encourage participation regardless of economic circumstances. The IFLA Core Activity Fund is supported by national libraries worldwide.

More than two dozen corporations in the information industry have formed a working relationship with IFLA as Corporate Partners, providing financial and in-kind support. Corporate Partners that contributed more than 3,000 euros in 2008 were OCLC, Inc.; SirsiDynix; software companies Infor and Tagsys; and publishers Brill, Elsevier, Emerald, K. G. Saur, ProQuest, and SAGE. In 2005 the IFLA Governing Board established the IFLA Fund, through which individuals and corporations can donate support for new initiatives, disaster relief, or the federation's operating budget. This was followed in 2007 by the establishment of the IFLA Foundation (Stichting IFLA).

UNESCO has given IFLA formal associate relations status, the highest level of relationship accorded to nongovernmental organizations by UNESCO. In addition, IFLA has observer status with the United Nations, WIPO, the International Council of Scientific Unions, the International Organization for Standardization, and the World Trade Organization.

## Personnel, Structure, and Governance

The secretary general of IFLA is Jennefer Nicholson, former executive director of the Australian Library and Information Association. Nicholson succeeds Peter Johan Lor, who retired in September 2008. Sjoerd M. J. Koopman is coordinator of professional activities, an IFLA headquarters position. The editor of the quarterly *IFLA Journal* is J. Stephen Parker. In 2008 IFLA hired Stuart Hamilton as its first senior policy advisor for advocacy, also a headquarters position.

The current president of IFLA is Claudia Lux, director general, Zentral- und Landesbibliothek Berlin, Germany. She began her two-year term in August 2007 with "Libraries on the Agenda" as her presidential theme. Lux obtained support from the German Foreign Ministry and the Goethe Institut to host three international conferences in Berlin during her term. The first took place January 18–19, 2007, with the theme "Free Access to Information." The second, held February 21–22, 2008, addressed "Free Access and Digital Divide: Challenges for Science and Society in the Digital Age." The third conference was held in February 2009, on the theme "Access to Knowledge Infrastructures: Networking through Libraries."

Alex Byrne, university librarian of the University of Technology, Sydney, Australia, was IFLA president from August 2005 until August 2007. The current president-elect is Ellen R. Tise, senior director for library and information services, University of Stellenbosch, South Africa. She will assume the presidency in 2009 at the close of the 75th WLIC in Milan. She began developing the theme of her presidency with a brainstorming session in Quebec City on the question "How can libraries and IFLA drive access to knowledge?"

The current treasurer of IFLA is Gunnar Sahlin, National Librarian of Sweden.

Under revised Statutes that took effect in 2001, IFLA's former Executive and Professional Boards were combined in a new Governing Board. The 21-member board (plus the secretary general, ex officio) is responsible for the federation's general policies, management and finance, and external communications. The current members, in addition to Lux, Tise, Sahlin, and Nicholson, are Helena Asamoah-Hassan (Ghana), Barbara J. Ford (United States), Bob McKee (Britain), Danielle Mincio (Switzerland), Pascal Sanz (France), Réjean Savard (Canada), Barbara Schleihagen (Germany), Joaquin Selgas Gutierrez (Spain), and Zhang Xiaolin (China), plus the chair and eight members of the Professional Committee, named below. In addition, Jesus Lau, Universidad Veracruzana, Mexico, and Sinikka Sipila, Finnish Library Association, were co-opted to the Governing Board in 2008.

The Governing Board delegates responsibility for overseeing the direction of IFLA between board meetings, within the policies established by the board, to the IFLA Executive Committee, which includes the president, president-elect, treasurer, chair of the Professional Committee, two members of the Governing Board (elected every two years by members of the board from among its elected members), and IFLA's secretary general, ex officio. The current elected Governing Board members of the Executive Committee are McKee and Savard.

The IFLA Professional Committee monitors the planning and programming of professional activities carried out by IFLA's two types of bodies: professional groups—8 divisions, 48 sections, and discussion groups—and core activities (formerly called core programs). The Professional Committee is composed of one elected officer from each division, plus a chair elected by the incoming members; the president or president-elect and the coordinator of professional activities, who serves as secretary; and two elected members of the Governing Board, currently Sanz and Zhang. Nancy E. Gwinn, director, Smithsonian Institution Libraries, chairs the Professional Committee.

The eight divisions of IFLA and their representatives on the Professional Committee are I: General Research Libraries (Ingrid Parent, Canada); II: Special Libraries (Steve Witt, United States); III: Libraries Serving the General Public (Torny Kjekstad, Norway); IV: Bibliographic Control (Patrice Landry, Switzerland); V: Collections and Services (Lynn F. Sipe, United States); VI: Management and Technology (Trine Kolderup Flaten, Norway); VII: Education and Research (Anna Maria Tammaro, Italy); and VIII: Regional Activities (Premila Gamage, Sri Lanka). Each division has interest sections such as Statistics and Evaluation, Library Theory and Research, and Management and Marketing; other sections focus on particular types of libraries or parts of the world.

The six core activities are Action for Development Through Libraries (ALP, formerly Advancement of Librarianship); Preservation and Conservation (PAC); IFLA-CDNL Alliance for Bibliographic Standards (ICABS); IFLA UNIMARC Core Activity, which maintains and develops the Universal MARC Format, UNIMARC; Free Access to Information and Freedom of Expression (FAIFE); and Copyright and Other Legal Matters (CLM). Two other longstanding IFLA projects are now considered core activities: the IFLA World Wide Web site IFLANET and the IFLA Voucher Scheme, which replaced the IFLA Office for International Lending. The Voucher Scheme enables libraries to pay for international interlibrary loan requests using vouchers purchased from IFLA rather than actual currency or credit accounts. By eliminating bank charges and invoices for each transaction, the voucher scheme reduces the administrative costs of international library loans and allows libraries to plan budgets with less regard to short-term fluctuations in the value of different national currencies. The Voucher Scheme has also encouraged participating libraries to voluntarily standardize their charges for loans at the rate of one voucher for up to 15 pages.

To ensure an arena within IFLA for discussion of new social, professional, or cultural issues, discussion groups are formed within divisions or sections, generally for a two-year period, with the approval of the Professional Committee. Discussion groups often evolve into permanent separate sections if the Professional Committee agrees that there is sufficient interest to warrant support from IFLA. There currently are discussion groups for Access to Information Network/

Africa; Agricultural Libraries; E-Learning; Libraries and Web 2.0; Library and Information Science Education in Developing Countries; New Professionals; and Women, Information, and Libraries.

## IFLA's Three Pillars: Society, Members, and Profession

In December 2004 the IFLA Governing Board endorsed a new operational model based on the three pillars of society, membership, and professional matters. A review of IFLA's core activities, conducted in 2003 and 2004, showed that all of the federation's core functions related to three strategic factors: the societal contexts in which libraries and information services operate, the membership of the federation, and the library profession.

Although the three pillars and the infrastructure of IFLA are interdependent, they can be roughly analyzed as follows: The Society Pillar focuses on the role and impact of libraries and information services in society. Activities supported by the Society Pillar include FAIFE, CLM, Blue Shield, IFLA's presence at the World Summit on the Information Society, and the new advocacy office at IFLA headquarters—all activities that preserve memory, feed development, enable education and research, and support international understanding and community well-being. The Profession Pillar focuses on IFLA's role as the global voice for libraries and information services through the work of its sections and divisions and its core activities ALP, ICABS, PAC, and UNIMARC. The Members Pillar includes IFLA's member services, conferences, and publications. The federation recognized a need to make IFLA more attractive to members around the world, and initiated the Global Library Association Development program (GLAD) to encourage membership from countries with developing economies.

IFLA's operational infrastructure, consisting of IFLA headquarters, the IFLANET Web site, and the IFLA governance structure, support and receive strategic direction from the three pillars. The three pillars enable IFLA to promote its four core values: freedom of access to information and expression, as stated in Article 19 of the Universal Declaration of Human Rights; the belief that such access must be universal and equitable access to support human well-being; delivery of high-quality library and information services in support of that access; and the commitment to enabling all members of IFLA to participate without regard to citizenship, disability, ethnic origin, gender, geographical location, political philosophy, race, or religion.

In 2007 and 2008 IFLA built further on the foundation of the three pillars with a new revision of the statutes and a restructuring that basically reassigns the various sections to new divisions. After Byrne drafted revised statutes in 2007, the IFLA Governing Board completed the revision in February 2008 and in March submitted the revised statutes to the membership, which decisively approved the revision by postal ballot in time for their endorsement at the Quebec City Congress. The new structure will take effect in August 2009 at the WLIC in Milan.

# Canadian Libraries in 2008:
# Spending, Copyright, Open Access Lead Year's News

Karen G. Adams

Director of Libraries, University of Manitoba

## Introduction

Canada's minority Conservative national government under Prime Minister Stephen Harper continued during 2008, with an election in October (the third in four years) that produced little change. On December 1, the three other parties in the Parliament—Liberals, New Democrats, and the Bloc Québécois—announced their intent to form a coalition government after voting the Conservatives out. On December 4 the prime minister was allowed by the governor general to suspend Parliament until late January 2009, thus avoiding the immediate challenge. In the interval, Michael Ignatieff became leader of the Liberal Party, the largest member of the potential coalition.

Canada's gross domestic product fell by 0.8 percent from November 2007 to November 2008, with the greatest losses in the manufacturing industries and wholesale trade. Sectors showing growth over this time period included education, health care, and public administration.[1] BookNet Canada data indicated that book sales were 6 percent higher in units and 2 percent higher in dollars in the last quarter of 2008 than they were in the last quarter of 2007.[2]

The Canadian dollar held strong during the first six months of the year, trading above the U.S. dollar in February and May. A minor decline in the 3rd quarter of the fiscal year was followed by a descent to 81 cents U.S. in the final quarter of the year. The strong Canadian dollar had for several years provided relief to the collections budgets of Canadian research libraries; the impact of the falling dollar varied, depending on the timing of individual institutions' serials invoices. The University of Alberta, the University of Manitoba, and Queen's University were among Canadian research libraries that put a moratorium on monograph acquisitions to manage the situation.

The trend to small increases or no change to provincial unconditional operating grants continued, with increases often tied to specific projects that supported the particular province's priorities. In Prince Edward Island, C$180,000 in new funding was allocated to support literacy materials and programming.[3] Similarly, New Brunswick invested C$100,000 in adult literacy collections in both official languages.[4] New Brunswick also increased the budget for its Provincial Archives by $ C$500,000.[5] Ontario announced a four-year commitment of C$40 million to hiring staff in school libraries[6] as well as making a commitment of C$15 million to the public library community to bridge the digital divide.[7] Ontario school libraries also received the first installment, totaling C$15 million, from a total four-year commitment of C$80 million made in 2007 to support the acquisition of books.[8] Knowledge Ontario, the province's multi-type library initiative, received an additional C$5 million to support the continuation of province-wide licensing of electronic databases and the development of collaborative services.[9]

The Toronto Reference Library, part of Toronto Public Library, received C$10 million from the province to support its expansion, designed to add a new event center, more gallery space, more study pods, Internet stations, and listening and learning labs.[10] In Manitoba, more than C$700,000 in new funding was allocated to public libraries: to improve access and technologies in rural and northern libraries, to establish new libraries for aboriginal (First Nations) communities and in the Rural Municipality of Springfield, and to update collections and technology at Winnipeg Public Library.[11] The government of Saskatchewan announced $C5.2 million over four years to implement a single integrated library system across the province's public library system.[12] In February the Alberta Library, the province's multi-type organization, announced provincial government funding to support digitization and the acquisition of a license for all public libraries in Alberta to language learning software to support immigrant Canadians.[13] On the west coast, the British Columbia government provided grants of up to C$10,000 to public libraries and other community organizations as part of its BC150 Celebration Grants program.[14] At the federal level, the budget of Library and Archives Canada (LAC) was C$157.6 million, up from C$114 million two years earlier, in part as recognition of the organization's new responsibility for the Portrait Gallery of Canada.[15]

## Copyright

The year began with the threat of a new copyright bill. When the House resumed sitting in late January, the budget became the priority. In the early months of the year, organizations on both sides of the debate took the opportunity to reinforce their positions publicly, with the news media fueling speculation about what would happen next; some 40,000 Canadians signed on to the Fair Copyright for Canada Facebook group. In February, despite the Conservative Party's support for and from the private sector, a coalition of businesses including Google, Yahoo!, Rogers, Telus, and the Canadian Association of Broadcasters formed the Business Coalition for Balanced Copyright, with the intent of seeking rights for consumers and businesses to use copyright materials that they buy.[16]

Also in February 2008 the U.S.-based International Intellectual Property Alliance indicated that Canada, Russia, and China were the biggest violators of U.S. copyright law.[17] And, in apparent anticipation of a bill, the Standing Committee on Heritage recommended that once the bill had been introduced and given first reading, it be referred to a special joint committee composed of members of the Standing Committee on Canadian Heritage and the Standing Committee on Industry, Science and Technology.[18]

In late April the chair of the Standing Committee on Industry announced that a bill would be introduced before the House broke for the summer in June.[19] Bill C-61 was released on June 12 with the government describing it as "a made-in-Canada" approach "that balances the interests of Canadians who use digital technology and those who create content."[20] Interested groups responded quickly. The Canadian Library Association (CLA) expressed disappointment that the bill took more away from users than it gave[21]; the Canadian Council on the Arts announced that the devil was in the details[22]; the Liberal opposition critic noted the lack of consultation in the creation of the bill[23]; the Canadian Association of University Teachers stated that the new legislation would restrict teachers' and students' access to electronic materials[24]; and the Canadian Association of Research Libraries said the bill required careful study.[25] The Canadian Music Creators Coalition saw the bill as an American-style approach.[26] On the other side, the Canadian Recording Industry Association and the Canadian Publishers Council applauded the bill.[27]

On September 7 Parliament was dissolved to make way for an October election, and once again a copyright reform bill died on the order paper.[28]

However, while the national plan to reform copyright fell through, Foreign Affairs and International Trade Canada continued its public consultations on the international Anti-Counterfeiting Trade Agreement (ACTA), intended to provide a new international standard for protection of intellectual property rights across countries such as the United States, Mexico, the European Union, Switzerland, Japan, and New Zealand.[29] Some Canadians objected to ACTA because of concerns over privacy[30]; others saw it as having a potential impact on copyright.[31]

The Board of Access Copyright, Canada's reprography collective, released its response to *Distribution of Royalties: Access Copyright* (the Friedland Report) in January 2008.[32] Access Copyright had commissioned the study in 2006 to undertake a review of the methodology of distributing royalties to publishers and authors. The board agreed to study further some of the report's recommendations, but declined to change either the distribution of royalties—which report author Martin Friedland had noted were based on 20-year-old data in some cases—or the size and composition of the board, which Friedland viewed as too large and too evenly divided between publishers and creators. In September the League of Canadian Poets convened a meeting of creators groups that supported changes to the distribution system, especially the amounts received by individual creators.[33]

A Copyright Board tariff on the sale of iPods slated to come into effect on January 1, 2008, was quashed by a ruling of the Federal Court of Appeal in early January. The tariff would have been as high as $75 per device.[34] Following up on a 2006 remission by the Federal Court of Appeal with respect to commercial radio station royalties (increased by 30 percent in 2005), the Copyright Board reaffirmed the tariffs set in October 2005, based on its view that the value of music to broadcasters had increased significantly since the tariff was first set in 1987.[35] In October the rates were extended to musical works communicated on the Internet.[36] On December 5 the board set private copying levies for 2008 and 2009. The private copying levy is a surcharge on blank media that consumers pay at the time of purchase with respect to the music to be copied on to the blanks, and the tariffs are then redistributed through the Canadian Private Copying Collective (CPCC) to authors, performers, and producers of recorded music. The rate for audiocassettes remained at 24 cents while the rate for CDs increased from 21 cents to 29 cents.[37]

The first Canadian to be convicted in Canada of copying a movie in the theater pleaded guilty in November 2008, was fined C$1,495, and was banned from movie houses for a year.

An Environics study of Canadian attitudes to intellectual property found three distinct groups: the 16 percent of Canadians who would never download from peer-to-peer sites, the 5 percent of Canadians who are unrepentant down-loaders, and the 25 percent who believe in both copyright and downloading. Eighty-three percent of Canadians supported the need for protection of copyright in music, videos, computer software, and books.[38]

## Access to Information

The federal government made two decisions that adversely affected the availability of government information. In order to save C$7 million, the Canadian Health Network, a user-friendly Web site that provided reliable health information to consumers, shut down on March 31, 2008, with the site being redirected to a much less user-friendly site hosted by the Public Health Agency of Canada.[39] On April 1 the Treasury Board authorized civil servants to stop filling out the Coordination of Access to Information Requests System (CAIRS), which tracked access to information requests filed with the federal government. It was publicly available and enabled researchers to keep track of requests and to find obscure documents using keyword searching.[40] The House of Commons Standing Committee on Access to Information, Privacy, and Ethics deplored the decision.[41]

On the open access front, the National Research Council, through its Canada Institute for Scientific and Technical Information (CISTI), and the Canadian Institutes of Health Research signed an agreement to establish an electronic repository, PubMed Central Canada (PMC Canada), of peer-reviewed health science research. The plan was to secure agreement from U.S. National Library of Medicine for PMC Canada to become part of the PubMed Central International network.[42] Also in support of open access, on February 28 the Canadian Association of Research Libraries (CARL) and the U.S.-based Scholarly Publishing and Academic Resources Coalition (SPARC) launched the Create Change Canada Web site in support of researcher sharing of data and knowledge.[43] The Canadian Library Association approved its first position statement on Open Access.[44] The first scholarly press created in Canada this century, Alberta's Athabasca University Press (AU Press), was also the first scholarly press in Canada to adopt open access principles and make its publications available for sale in print and freely available on the Web.[45] Another Alberta university, the University of Calgary, was the first Canadian university to establish an Authors Fund to cover Open Access author fees for faculty and graduate students.[46]

Industry Canada's Community Access Program, an initiative begun in 1994 as part of the federal government's strategy to address the digital divide, was initially scheduled to end on March 31, 2007, but pressure from the community caused the department to internally reallocate C$14.6 million for the program. The end date then became March 31, 2008. Again, program recipients—which included school and public libraries in rural and remote Canada—protested, with the result that a similar internal reallocation was made in the 2008–2009 fiscal year.[47, 48] Saskatchewan, one of Canada's least densely populated provinces, announced its own three-year plan to spend C$129 million to have high-speed Internet accessible everywhere.[49]

In April 2008 the Canadian Association of Internet Providers (CAIP) asked the regulatory agency Canadian Radio-Television and Telecommunications Commission (CRTC) to stop Bell Canada's practice of "throttling." Throttling involves slowing the transmission of data that consume high bandwidth. Because members of CAIP buy wholesale bandwidth from Bell, they were concerned about privacy, with data packets being opened by Bell, and by their loss of competitive advantage as independent service providers (ISPs). Their complaint also raised the emerging issue of net neutrality, the right of individuals to gain equitable access to the Internet content and applications of their choice.[50] CRTC denied the complaint on the grounds that Bell had demonstrated that it needed to be able to manage traffic on its network, and that the company applied the same practice to its own customers. The decision made no comment on the more general question of net neutrality, but did launch a proceeding to get public input into the question of how much control the phone companies should have over the bandwidth they sell to the smaller ISPs.[51] In December CRTC issued a decision that had the effect of requiring all of the large phone companies to offer the same Internet speeds to their wholesale customers as they offer to their retail customers.[52]

## Studies

Studies dealing with three aspects of books and reading were released in 2008. In late January Canadian Heritage issued "The Book Retail Sector in Canada." Its findings included a decline in market share by independent bookstores over the past decade, with domination by a single national chain and regional chains in Quebec. Use of nontraditional retailers and online sales were increasing. At the time of the study, the Canadian dollar was near the value of the U.S. dollar, which was creating problems with the price differentials that consumers could see on books, and making it cheaper for retailers to import books rather than buying them in Canada. And the 16,000 new titles produced annually in Canada were seen as exceeding consumer demand.[53] In February Statistics Canada's "Survey of Household Spending," using 2006 data, noted a 12 percent increase in spending on Internet access, a 38 percent increase in spending on new audio equipment, an 8 percent decrease in spending on movies, and a 5 percent decrease in spending on reading materials (with the exception of Alberta, where spending on reading materials increased 8 percent).[54] In July Statistics Canada released 2006 data on the book publishing industry, and identified a decrease from 12.1 percent in 2005 in the operating profit margin for the industry to 10.3 percent in 2006, and noted that the share of revenues going to foreign-controlled publishers had increased to 41.7 percent.[55]

In terms of reading, Ipsos-Reid conducted identical polls in the United States and Canada, and found that 73 percent of Americans had read a book in the past year, compared with 69 percent of Canadians.[56]

A Statistics Canada study of cultural workers, "Creative Input: The Role of Culture Occupations in the Economy During the 1990s," found that there were almost as many cultural workers employed in non-culture sectors as in designated cultural sectors, based on the analysis of data for 1991, 1996, and 2001. While the study found an overall increase in the number of cultural workers working outside the sector over the decade, the heritage occupations (librarians, archivists, and conservators) saw a decline in that same period. The major industries employing heritage workers were government service industries and educational service industries. The former saw a decline of 41 percent in the number of heritage workers and the latter saw a decline of 61 percent over the decade.[57]

Also looking at the cultural sector, the Conference Board of Canada released "Valuing Culture: Measuring and Understanding Canada's Creative Economy." Culture accounted for more than $43 billion (3.8 percent of Canada's GDP), with libraries accounting for $1.3 billion of that.[58]

The Canadian Internet Project (CIP) released the results of its second research undertaking on changing Internet habits and media consumption, using 2007 data; the first was based on 2004 data. At 78 percent, Canadians continued to be among the heaviest Internet users in the world. Ninety-six percent of 12- to 17-year-olds were on the Internet; at the other end of the age spectrum, more than half of Canadians over 60 use it regularly. Language was another element of the digital divide, with a 15 percent gap between English- and French-speakers, possibly due to English being the dominant language on the Internet. Fifty-four percent of Canadian homes had access to broadband, up 13 percent since the previous study. The study also documented multitasking, and found that 76 percent of Internet users were engaged in another activity while online. Talking on the phone was the most popular secondary activity. Forty percent of Canadian Internet users had visited a social networking site.[59]

## Censorship

The censorship front was relatively quiet in 2008. Early in the year, Calgary Catholic School District returned to their shelves *The Golden Compass* by Philip Pullman, which had been removed in 2007.[60] In Ontario, the Toronto District School Board pulled Barbara Coloroso's book *Extraordinary Evil: A Brief History of Genocide* following a complaint from the Turkish community about the inclusion of the Armenian genocide of 1915.[61]

The federal government stirred fears of censorship when it brought forward Bill C-10, an amendment to the Income Tax Act that passed the House of Commons in October and then moved on for Senate approval. The arts community, including the Canadian Library Association, protested the bill because it gave the minister the power to withhold funding from productions that he or she deemed to be contrary to public policy, as determined by the minister.[62] The bill had not received third reading in the Senate by the time the election was called in early September.

A journalist updated his complaint of censorship by the British Columbia government's information and privacy branch. The branch provided information to the complainant that was accompanied by reminders that the records were protected by crown copyright, and permission to use them would have to be sought and a royalty paid. As a result of the situation, a public inquiry was launched, but the journalist claimed that the province's attorney-general was trying to shut down the inquiry by challenging its jurisdiction.[63]

## Events

LAC's main site on Wellington Street in Ottawa had two incidents involving water damage in 2008. In May the building was closed for 48 hours when a broken pipe flooded two floors, causing damage to the book collection.[64] On June 1 another broken pipe caused a flood, but no books were damaged because they were still under protective coverings from the May flood.[65]

LAC closed the Canadian Book Exchange Centre at the end of June, thus saving C$500,000 annually. The 35-year-old program coordinated the transfer of surplus publications from one library to another, with libraries paying for shipping. LAC cited a decline in incoming volumes and libraries being less interested in acquiring materials through the program.[66]

In December the University of Toronto announced the largest gift for renewal of a Canadian library, C$10 million for the renewal of the Robarts humanities and social science library.[67] Also in Toronto, York University Libraries received a donation of C$1 million to endow the W. P. Scott Chair in E-Librarianship.[68] The government of Alberta awarded the University of Calgary's new library $25 million to match a donation of $25 million to the Taylor Family Digital Library project.[69] In British Columbia, Thompson Rivers University received provincial funding of C$29.3 million to construct a new library and First Nations learning center at its Kamloops campus.[70]

The Canadian Research Knowledge Network (CRKN), a partnership of Canadian universities dedicated to expanding digital content for the academic enterprise, moved out of the University of Ottawa, and into new facilities in April—a marker of the maturity of the organization. CRKN began in 1999 with federal funding of C$20 million as the Canadian National Site Licensing Project.[71] In 2008 CRKN also announced a C$47 million project to acquire digital scholarly content in social sciences and humanities disciplines, jointly funded by the federal government, eight provinces, and 67 universities.[72]

Having been in legal strike position since September 2007 over pay equity issues, in January 2008 unionized workers from the Greater Victoria Public Library (GVPL) walked off the job in a one-day protest over the suspension of a fellow worker. The suspension was triggered by a dispute over a "food for fines" program—under which nonperishable food items could be used to pay fines on delinquent bills and overdue books—and the authority to waive fines.[73] In February the GVPL library board locked out some 300 union[74] employees until agreement was reached to return to work at the beginning of April.[75]

Libraries in southern Ontario reported budget woes in 2008. At the Chatham-Kent Public Library, municipal councilors voted not to close three branch libraries to avoid a tax increase.[76] In Windsor, the library board initially refused to cut $800,000 from its budget,[77] and finally accepted a $400,000 cut, but by year's end was seeking restoration of $70,000 for new library materials.[78] In northern Ontario, Moosonee—a community with no library or bookstore—was the recipient of a Dolly Parton Imagination Library, which provided every preschooler with a free book.[79]

Canada's only "i-school," the University of Toronto's Faculty of Information Studies (FIS), became the Faculty of Information in July 2008; the new abbreviation will be the "iSchool."[80]

Toronto Public Library ended a long-standing policy tradition in June when it began to allow food and drink in most areas of its branches.[81] Also in 2008, renovations to its Dufferin/St. Clair Library revealed an art treasure: murals painted by prominent Canadian painter George Reid and two of his students between 1925 and 1932.[82]

The government of New Brunswick signed a memorandum of understanding as the first step in establishing a public library in the village of Cap-Pelé, the largest municipality without public library service in the province. The village will invest C$1 million in the facility, and the province will provide C$185,000 toward its collection, technology, and staffing.[83]

In October the Canadian library community participated in the first National Summit on Library Human Resources, convened to develop a national strategy to ensure an adequate supply of library and information professionals. Issues included professional development, recruiting to the profession, accessibility of library education programs, and leadership institutes.[84]

In November university library directors and university press directors held a landmark first meeting at the University of British Columbia (UBC) to discuss the scholarly publishing environment. Participants came from UBC, the University of Alberta, the University of Manitoba, the University of Toronto, McGill University, and Queen's University. While there was no consensus on such matters as Open Access, the group agreed to meet again.

North Vancouver (British Columbia) opened a new library in September. Halifax Regional Municipal Council approved in principle the construction of a new central library to replace the Spring Garden Road branch. Ottawa Public Library Board voted to ask the City of Ottawa to approve C$29 million in the library's 2009 capital budget to buy land for a new central library.[85]

## Initiatives

In 2008 two national digitization projects, AlouetteCanada and the Canadian Institute for Historical Microreproductions, merged to form Canadiana.org, a broadly based alliance of libraries, publishers, archives, museums, and other interested organizations.[86]

LAC's Initiative for Equitable Library Access (IELA) held consultations in Toronto, Vancouver, and Halifax on the creation of conditions for sustainable and equitable public library access for Canadians with print disabilities. IELA also announced three key activities: an Internet portal to serve as a gateway for information for and about people with print disabilities; service models, standards, and training materials; and an upgrade to the electronic clearinghouse for multiple format productions to make it easier for publishers to contribute electronic files to producers of multiple formats.[87] LAC also announced its participation in the Open Library Environment project, developing a design document for an open source integrated library system to support the needs of today's libraries.[88]

The Canadian National Institute for the Blind (CNIB) Library increased use of its collection by 25 percent in 2007–2008, following its first full year of using the DAISY technology and online collections.[89] DAISY enabled a book to be sent to a reader as a CD/DVD, a memory card, or over the Internet, and then read using refreshable braille display or screen reading software, printed as a braille book on paper, converted to a talking book using synthesized voice, printed on paper as a large-print book, or read as large-print text on a computer screen.[90]

The Canadian health library community completed phase 0 in its plan to create a Canadian Virtual Health Library (CVHL). The phase ended with the creation of an environmental scan, funded by Canada Health Infoway (CHI). The CVHL community then developed a proposal to CHI for resources to move to phase 1, the development of a detailed plan.[91]

The Canada Institute for Scientific and Technical Information hosted a national data management meeting in January 2008, and followed up by establishing a Research Data Strategy Working Group, to address the challenges of managing Canadian research data.[92]

Work by four of Canada's largest urban public libraries—Vancouver, Regina, Toronto, and Halifax—on understanding how to improve services to socially excluded individuals and communities culminated in the publication of the *Community-Led Libraries Toolkit.* The toolkit was mailed to every public library system in Canada and made available on the Web.[93]

Libraries in the Northwest Territories were weeded and updated. The Sir Alexander Mackenzie School Library in Inuvik launched a project to renew its library and eliminated dated material, including books that refer to the "Eskimo." New books to replace the old materials were received.[94] The Sam Hearne School Library had a similar project.[95]

British Columbia announced a new library federation for the Gulf Islands and Vancouver Island, IslandLink Library Federation, to support sharing resources and collaborative training across public libraries in Alert Bay, Greater Victoria, Powell River, and Salt Spring Island.[96]

Alberta announced a public consultation by three members of the Legislative Assembly on the future of public libraries, with meetings scheduled in September and October.[97]

The government of Saskatchewan announced a C$5.2 million project over four years to implement a single integrated library system across all 317 branches of its public library system.[98]

The Manitoba government announced the opening of the first independent public library on a First Nations community, Peguis First Nation Public Library, on October 16, supported by provincial funding.[99] Library services for Alberta's First Nations communities were also improved with the launch of the First Nations Information Connection (FNIC) on November 17. FNIC includes a Web-based portal that gives students at six First Nations colleges access to the holdings of the participating college libraries and electronic resources, as an offshoot of the Lois Hole Campus Alberta Digital Library.[100]

Ottawa Public Library used a C$30,000 donation to buy two arcade game machines for installation at the downtown and St. Laurent branches.[101]

The Bibliothèque et Archives Nationales du Québec (BAnQ) announced three collaborative projects. The first, a collaboration of public, college, and university libraries in Quebec, was a publicly searchable online catalog of participating library holdings, in May.[102] The second, in October, saw the provinces of Quebec and New Brunswick signing an agreement to share online services and collections between BAnQ and the New Brunswick Public Library Service. The third, also in October, was a partnership between BAnQ and the Bibliothèque Nationale de France (BnF) announcing a new French-language resource, the bibliography *Relations France-Québec Depuis 1760.*[103]

In Atlantic Canada, the University of Prince Edward Island became the first academic library in the world to run the open source product Evergreen/Island Pines as its integrated library system.[104] Novanet (the Nova Scotia academic library consortium) and the University of New Brunswick were the first library systems outside the United States to sign agreements to implement OCLC's WorldCat local for resource discovery and delivery.[105]

Still in Atlantic Canada, in commemoration of the 100th anniversary of the publication of L. M. Montgomery's *Anne of Green Gables,* Prince Edward Island's Provincial Library Service included 24 of Montgomery's titles in a special version of their "Book Club in a Bag," a tote bag containing ten copies of a book and a discussion guide that could be reserved online or in person at one of the 26 public libraries on the island.[106]

## Sources

1. http://freerangelibrarian.com/2009/02/02/a-dozen-from-ala-midwinter-2009.

2. http://www.booknetcanada.ca/mambo/index.php?option=com_content&task=view&id=397&Itemid=232.

3. http://www.gov.pe.ca/news/getrelease.php3?number=5708.

4. http://www.gnb.ca/cnb/news/pet/2008e1319pe.htm.

5. http://www.gnb.ca/cnb/news/ss/2008e0756ss.htm.

6. http://www.premier.gov.on.ca/news/Product.asp?ProductID=1952.

7. http://www.sols.org/ministryprojects/$15MillionInvestment/$15MConsultationRevised.pdf.

8. http://www.quillandquire.com/blog/index.php/2009/01/20/ontario-school-library-funding-comes-through.

9. http://www.knowledgeontario.ca/KO_News-p11.html.

10. http://www.culture.gov.on.ca/english/about/n270308.htm.

11. http://news.gov.mb.ca/news/index.html?archive=&item=3555.

12. http://www.gov.sk.ca/news?newsId=aa52a913-3305-412b-8323-c83c63c5c8c4.

13. TAL Tales, February 4, 2008.

14. http://www.bc150.ca/bc150.aspx?page=affiliation_pssg.

15. http://www.ccarts.ca/en/advocacy/bulletins/2008/3908.htm.

16. http://www.cbc.ca/technology/story/2008/02/13/tech-copyright.html.

17. http://www.cbc.ca/technology/story/2008/02/12/tech-copyright.html?ref=rss.

18. http://www2.parl.gc.ca/HousePublications/Publication.aspx?DocId=3285022&Language=E&Mode=1&Parl=39&Ses=2.

19. http://www.cpac.ca/forms/index.asp?dsp=template&act=view3&pagetype=vod&lang=e&clipID=1522.

20. http://www.ic.gc.ca/eic/site/crp-prda.nsf/eng/h_rp01151.html.

21. http://www.cla.ca/AM/Template.cfm?Section=News1&CONTENTID=5346&TEMPLATE=/CM/ContentDisplay.cfm.

22. http://www.ccarts.ca/en/advocacy/bulletins/2008/2008.htm.

23. http://www.cbc.ca/technology/story/2008/06/12/tech-copyright.html?ref=rss.

24. http://www.caut.ca/news_details.asp?nid=1132&page=490.

25. http://www.carl-abrc.ca/new/pdf/copyright_bill_press_release-final-june2008-e.pdf.

26. http://www.musiccreators.ca/wp/?p=264.

27. http://www.cria.ca/news.php.

28. http://www.iht.com/articles/ap/2008/09/07/news/Canada-Election.php.

29. http://www.international.gc.ca/consultations/active/index.aspx?menu_id=2&menu=R#acta.

30. http://www.theglobeandmail.com/servlet/Page/document/v5/content/subscribe?user_URL=
    http://www.theglobeandmail.com%2Fservlet%2Fstory%2FLAC.20080526.COPYRIGHT26
    %2F%2FTPStory%2FNational&ord=40298178&brand=theglobeandmail&force_login=true.

31. http://www.cla.ca/AM/Template.cfm?Section=News1&TEMPLATE=/CM/
    ContentDisplay.cfm&CONTENTID=5012

32. http://www.accesscopyright.ca/docs/Friedland%20Report.pdf.

33. http://www.poets.ca/linktext/links/pressreleases.htm.

34. http://network.nationalpost.com/np/blogs/fpposted/archive/2008/01/10/proposed-ipod-levy-
    killed-in-court.aspx.

35. http://www.cb-cda.gc.ca/news/pr-commercialradio20032007-e.pdf.

36. http://www.cb-cda.gc.ca/decisions/iinr200810240062008-e.pdf.

37. http://www.cb-cda.gc.ca/decisions/cnr20082009-e.pdf.

38. http://erg.environics.net/media_room/default.asp?aID=673.

39. http://www.friendsofchn.ca/picard.htm.

40. http://www.cbc.ca/canada/story/2008/05/02/cairs.html.

41. http://cmte.parl.gc.ca/cmte/committeepublication.aspx?sourceid=238040&lang=1.

42. http://cisti-icist.nrc-cnrc.gc.ca/pdo/partnership_e.html.

43. http://www.createchangecanada.ca.

44. http://www.cla.ca/AM/Template.cfm?Section=Position_Statements&Template=/CM/
    ContentDisplay.cfm&ContentID=5306.

45. http://www.aupress.ca.

46. http://www.ucalgary.ca/news/june2008/authorsfund.

47. http://www.ic.gc.ca/eic/site/ic1.nsf/eng//00345.html.

48. http://www.cla.ca/news/CLA%20Election%20Kit%202008.pdf.

49. http://www.cbc.ca/technology/story/2008/11/26/internet-access.html.

50. http://www.cata.ca/Communities/caip/resources/HighSpeedAccess.

51. http://www.crtc.gc.ca/eng/archive/2008/dt2008-108.htm.

52. http://www.crtc.gc.ca/eng/archive/2008/dt2008-116.htm.

53. http://www.canadianheritage.gc.ca/progs/ac-ca/progs/padie-bpidp/reports/rapport-report_
    2007/tdm_e.cfm.

54. http://www.statcan.ca/Daily/English/080226/d080226a.htm.

55. http://www.statcan.gc.ca/daily-quotidien/080710/dq080710a-eng.htm.

56. http://www.statcan.gc.ca/pub/81-595-m/81-595-m2008064-eng.pdf.

57. http://www.statcan.gc.ca/pub/81-595-m/81-595-m2008064-eng.pdf.

58. http://www.conferenceboard.ca/documents.asp?rnext=2671.

59. http://www.cipic.ca/en/publications.htm.

60. http://www.quillandquire.com/blog/index.php/2008/01/24/golden-compass-back-on-the-
    shelves-in-calgary.

61. http://pelhamlibrary.blogspot.com/2008/06/extraordinary-evil.html.

62. http://www.cla.ca/AM/Template.cfm?Section=News1&CONTENTID=4862&TEMPLATE=/CM/ContentDisplay.cfm.

63. http://www.canada.com/components/print.aspx?id=69970f8a-8f9a-4200-b41d-062707d8ea7c&sponsor=.

64. http://www.cbc.ca/canada/ottawa/story/2008/05/20/ot-archives-080520.html.

65. http://www.theglobeandmail.com/servlet/story/RTGAM.20080719.warchieves0719/BNStory/National.

66. http://www.collectionscanada.gc.ca/013/013-330-e.html.

67. http://www.news.utoronto.ca/campus-news/alumni-donate-10-million-to-robarts-library.html.

68. http://www.yorku.ca/yfile/archive/index.asp?Article=10507.

69. http://www.cbc.ca/canada/calgary/story/2008/01/22/uofc-funding.html.

70. http://www.journalofcommerce.com/article/id28731.

71. http://researchknowledge.ca/en/news/documents/OpenHouse01Apr08EFinal.pdf.

72. http://researchknowledge.ca/en/news/documents/mediareleaseEfinal-withphotolink.pdf.

73. http://www.canada.com/components/print.aspx?id=ca649676-749e-41c8-afa7-7756c6b9357e&k=67437.

74. http://www.theglobeandmail.com/servlet/story/LAC.20080218.BCLIBRARY18/TPStory/TPNational/BritishColumbia.

75. http://www.cupe410.ca/wordpress.

76. http://www.chathamdailynews.ca/PrintArticle.aspx?e=859896.

77. http://www.canada.com/windsorstar/news/local/story.html?id=11891547-0c00-4f32-8f5b-9b68949dd825&k=98676.

78. http://www.windsorstar.com/Entertainment/Windsor+libraries+dire+need+books/1059405/story.html.

79. http://www.accessola3.com/index.php?automodule=blog&blogid=9&&cmd=printentry&eid=488.

80. http://www.ischool.utoronto.ca/content/view/1371.

81. http://www.cbc.ca/canada/toronto/story/2008/06/17/library-food.html.

82. http://www.thestar.com/printArticle/534447.

83. http://www.gnb.ca/cnb/news/pet/2008e0352pe.htm.

84. http://www.cla.ca/docs/Digest_10_17_2008.pdf.

85. http://www.cla.ca/AM/TextTemplate.cfm?Section=CLTA&CONTENTID=5913&TEMPLATE=/CM/ContentDisplay.cfm.

86. http://alouette.canadiana.org.

87. http://www.collectionscanada.gc.ca/iela/005002-6040-e.html.

88. http://www.librarytechnology.org/ltg-displayarticle.pl?RC=13516.

89. http://www.cnib.ca/en/about/publications/corporate-reports/annual_review_2007_final.doc.

90. http://www.daisy.org/about_us/multimedia.shtml?PHPSESSID=bdef3dc40d602fa50cfc022880705c3f.

91. http://www.chla-absc.ca/nnlh/activities.html.

92. http://cisti-icist.nrc-cnrc.gc.ca/media/press/rds_group_e.html.

93. http://www.librariesincommunities.ca.

94. http://www.nnsl.com/inuvik/inuvik.html.

95. http://www.nnsl.com/yir/yirInuvik.html.

96. http://www2.news.gov.bc.ca/news_releases_2005-2009/2008EDUC0142-001731.htm.

97. http://www.alberta.ca/home/NewsFrame.cfm?ReleaseID=/acn/200809/24309479C41F4-B5B6-E989-DA6F16F3FCCFDF14.html.

98. http://gov.sk.ca/news?newsId=aa52a913-3305-412b-8323-c83c63c5c8c4.

99. http://www.gov.mb.ca/chc/press/top/2008/10/2008-10-16-113200-4601.html.

100. http://www.canada.com/edmontonjournal/news/local/story.html?id=7dd84b45-f971-40e0-b4f6-2a45ca1423ab.

101. http://www.canada.com/story.html?id=938866.

102. http://www.banq.qc.ca/portal/dt/a_propos_banq/communiques/2008/com_2008_05_15.jsp.

103. http://www.banq.qc.ca/portal/dt/a_propos_banq/communiques/2008/com_2008_10_08.jsp.

104. http://library.upei.ca/book/export/html/279.

105. http://www.oclc.org/news/releases/200846.htm.

106. http://www.gov.pe.ca/news/getrelease.php3?number=5783.

# Library and Archives Canada

395 Wellington St., Ottawa, ON K1A 0N4
866-578-7777, fax 613-995-6274
World Wide Web http://www.collectionscanada.gc.ca

## Ian E. Wilson
### Librarian and Archivist of Canada

Each generation creates its own narrative from objects, ideas, and records laid down by living beings in an earlier time. When libraries or archives create links between the past and the present, they take a history that may seem distant and make it personal. Once we have made the human connection, the facts and the dates and the particulars make sense.

During 2008 Library and Archives Canada (LAC) celebrated the role of libraries and archives in making this human connection, through technology, through on-site and virtual exhibitions, and through reaching out to audiences in innovative ways. This article reviews some of the year's highlights.

## Exhibitions

Millions of readers around the world are familiar with the exuberant orphan from *Anne of Green Gables*. LAC celebrated Anne and her creator, Lucy Maud Montgomery, with a multimedia exhibition in June to mark the centennial of one of Canada's most popular, successful, and enduring books. By bringing together archival materials, books, posters, audiovisual materials, paintings, stamps, and artwork, the exhibition provided a glimpse not only into the world of Lucy Maud Montgomery but also into how Anne's story has been interpreted and adapted over time. The core of the exhibition was a display of more than 40 versions of the book, including a dozen different editions and many foreign translations, all part of LAC's collection.

LAC also celebrated the 100th anniversary of the birth of one of Canada's most iconic visual artists, Yousuf Karsh. Karsh is internationally recognized as one of the leading portrait photographers of the 20th century. In November LAC launched "My Karsh," a chance for Canadians to share their own Karsh photographs and stories by posting them to a My Karsh Flickr group or sending them to the Portrait Gallery of Canada. Images and stories will also be considered for a major exhibition, "Karsh the Storyteller," scheduled for summer 2009 in cooperation with LAC and the Canada Science and Technology Museum.

### 1783: Subject or Citizen?

In collaboration with the National Archives and Records Administration (NARA) in the United States, LAC launched a unique international exhibition at its headquarters in Ottawa on the 225th anniversary of the signing of the Treaty of Paris. The exhibition—"1783: Subject or Citizen?"—marked the first collaborative educational initiative between the two national institutions.

The Treaty of Paris not only marked the end of the American Revolution but also provided the foundation for what was to become the Canadian nation. It shaped the political development and social fabric of Canada and led to the creation of new international relationships. The treaty also greatly affected the lives of North Americans including Canada's aboriginal First Peoples, Native Americans, African Americans, Loyalists, Patriots, and French Canadians in ways that are still felt today.

The exhibition included approximately 60 important documents, half of which were drawn from the LAC collection. Among items included were 18th-century maps, books, paintings, letters, a copy of the Loyalist Oath, and the *Quebec Gazette* newspaper from August 1790. The highlight of the exhibition was the actual Treaty of Paris document, which had never before been seen in Canada and had seldom been on view even in Washington, D.C.

After premiering at LAC in May 2008, the exhibition traveled to Washington in October.

**Virtual Exhibitions**

LAC digitizes roughly 1.7 million images a year from its collection. In 2008 it continued to share some of these images with Canadians and the world through virtual exhibitions.

One of the most compelling of these described life and death on the island of Grosse Île on the Saint Lawrence River east of Quebec City where a quarantine station was established in 1832 to cope with the thousands of immigrants who were arriving annually. Major cholera and smallpox epidemics were sweeping through Europe at that time, and through lists of births and deaths at sea, hospital registers, journals, letters, photographs, and maps preserved by LAC, the exhibition tells the story not only of the quarantine station, but of the individuals—both migrants and medical personnel—who experienced it firsthand. The exhibition is at http://www.collectionscanada.gc.ca/grosse-ile/index-e.html.

For a generation raised on speed dating and Internet romance, LAC offered a glimpse into the challenges faced by people looking for a spouse in the 1800s with the virtual exhibition "I Do: Love and Marriage in 19th Century Canada." The Web site (http://www.collectionscanada.gc.ca/love-and-marriage/index-e.html) includes the digitized letters and journals of famous French Canadians including former Prime Minister Sir Wilfrid Laurier and the notorious criminal William Donnelly of Black Donnellys fame.

Virtual exhibitions also included "Sir John A. Macdonald: Canada's Patriot Statesman," which profiles the nation's first prime minister through photographs, documentary art, and other documents from the LAC collection as well as a vivid documentary portrait of the political, social, cultural, economic, technological, and architectural changes experienced in Canada during its first 50 years after Confederation, as seen through the eyes of photographer William James Topley. The exhibition is at http://www.collectionscanada.gc.ca/sir-john-a-macdonald/index-e.html.

In December 2008 LAC and the Canadian Museum for Human Rights (CMHR) marked the 60th Anniversary of the Universal Declaration of Human

Rights by jointly launching a Web site. LAC was instrumental in mounting CMHR's first-ever virtual exhibition, "Everyone Has the Right: A Canadian and the Words that Changed the World" (http://www.humanrightsmuseum.ca). LAC's contribution to the exhibition has been substantial, including the identification of archival records, the provision of interpretive captions for each document, the digitization of all exhibition documents, and advisory services and support for copyright permission requests. Some of LAC's documents relating to human rights include information and original documents about Chinese, Ukrainian, black and aboriginal experiences in Canada. For more information or to undertake research, visit http://www.collectionscanada.gc.ca/index-e.html.

## Major Acquisitions

LAC owns the world's largest collection of documentary art relating to Canadian history, including more than 425,000 paintings, drawings, prints, posters, cartoons, and medals. A large and important addition to this collection was acquired in two separate purchases, the first in 2002 and the second in 2008. The Peter Winkworth Collection reflects more than four centuries of Canadian history. The 2008 acquisition comprises more than 1,000 pieces, including watercolors by Maria Morris, one of Canada's first recognized female artists, whose style has evoked comparisons to American wildlife artist John James Audubon.

The acquisition includes 13 oil paintings, 26 watercolors, four watercolor albums, 150 prints, 19 print albums, several map publications, two 19th century photo albums, and a number of other works. The acquisition was made possible through a partnership between LAC, the National Museum of Civilization Corporation, and the National Gallery of Canada.

Working in partnership with the Canadian Museum of Civilization, LAC also reached an agreement in principle early in 2008 with the present Earl of Elgin to acquire an extraordinary private collection of archival documents and museum artifacts accumulated by his family, notably the 19th century leader Lord Elgin (James Bruce, eighth Earl of Elgin). The treasures document life in Canada from 1847 until 1854, during Lord Elgin's term as Governor-in-Chief of the Province of Canada. This period was marked by events that shaped the development of Canada as a nation, including the implementation of Responsible Government in March 1848 and negotiating the Reciprocity Treaty with the United States in 1854. One interesting aspect of the collection is that much of it brings early Canada to life through the eyes of Lord Elgin's wife and daughter.

## Partnership with Ancestry.ca

Unprecedented online access to Canadian historical records is the result of a collaborative partnership between LAC and the Canadian online family history Web site Ancestry.ca. As part of the agreement announced in November 2008, Ancestry.ca will digitize and index microfilm and original records held by LAC and make them available to Ancestry.ca members. Eventually, all of the digitized records will be available free of charge to users of LAC's Web site.

## The Shamrock and the Maple Leaf

A growing interest in the field of Irish-Canadian studies led to a second Irish Studies Symposium hosted by LAC in November with the support of the National Archives of Ireland. As many as one-fifth of Canadians claim Irish heritage, and the symposium brought together historians, students, genealogists, and researchers with an interest in learning more about the collective history of the two countries.

The symposium is only one of a series of activities designed to celebrate Irish-Canadian documentary heritage, including the exhibition "Dubliners: Photographs from the National Library of Ireland," which showcased candid photographs of daily life in the heart of Ireland's capital between 1897 and 1904. The photographs were on loan from the National Library of Ireland. The exhibition was linked with LAC's inaugural Flickr/YouTube project, which presents a unique selection of Irish-Canadian images and videos.

Visitors to the Library and Archives Canada album at Flickr.com are encouraged to explore the interactive image collection, which allows for comments and tagging of content. The images on Flickr.com are tagged with geographical information so that visitors can explore history in the context of their surroundings by navigating the album on a virtual map of the world. "The Shamrock and the Maple Leaf" is at http://www.flickr.com/photos/28853433@N02/sets/72157606336243875.

## New Publications, New Portals

More than 5,000 library and information professionals from 120 countries gathered in Quebec City as Canada hosted the 74th conference of the International Federation of Library Associations and Institutions (IFLA) in August. As part of the conference, LAC launched a new publication developed in partnership with Bibliothèque et Archives Nationales du Québec, *Reaching Out: Innovations in Canadian Libraries.* The publication contains examples of innovation and experimentation in libraries across Canada, showing that the nation's libraries are models of community outreach, collaboration, and partnership.

Profiled examples include an automated library system to accommodate Inuktitut syllabics; library services that can benefit the poor, the homeless, and other marginalized groups; and new Canadian technologies, such as open source software now used throughout the world.

Participants also got a sneak preview of the Internet portal developed by the Réseau Francophone des Bibliothèques Nationales Numériques (RFBNN) (Network of Francophone Digital National Libraries), in cooperation with the national libraries of Canada, Belgium, France, Luxembourg, and Switzerland, as well as the Bibliothèque et Archives Nationales du Québec.

Visitors to the network's Web site, http://www.rfbnn.org, can consult digitized newspapers, magazines, books, maps, drawings, and archival materials from the collections of nearly a dozen recordkeeping organizations in the Francophone world. Through its participation in the portal, LAC helps to support the long-term preservation and dissemination of the documentary heritage of French-speaking communities and countries, materials that are not widely available and are in danger of disappearing.

The IFLA conference was also the site of the launch of *Access,* LAC's latest corporate publication. Illustrated with full-color images from the library's collection, *Access* describes LAC's work and its impact on Canadian life.

## International Roles

The International Council of Archives (ICA) represents 1,400 members in 190 countries and is dedicated to the preservation, development, and use of the world's archival heritage. In 2008 Librarian and Archivist of Canada Ian E. Wilson was elected president of ICA for a two-year term that began in July. LAC participation in international roles also involves many others, among them Richard Green, president of the International Association of Sound and Audiovisual Archives, and Ingrid Parent, chair of the IFLA Section on National Libraries.

## Summer Reading Club

During summer 2008 half a million children across Canada participated in the TD Summer Reading Club, a joint initiative between TD Bank Financial Group, LAC, and the Toronto Public Library. They read almost 2 million books and took part in close to 30,000 programs and activities in libraries across the country.

Participation in the TD Summer Reading Club has more than doubled since 2005, making it the most successful summer reading club in Canada. The program is offered free of charge in participating Canadian public libraries to children age 12 and younger, encouraging children to read for pleasure and providing an innovative approach to raising literacy levels. In 2008 the TD Summer Reading Club Library Awards were introduced, recognizing excellence in programming and innovation in participating libraries.

## Information Access

LAC works with the library community to ensure that information is accessible to all Canadians, including the more than 3 million Canadians with print disabilities. In December LAC hosted a forum with representatives of the library community, the publishing sector, consumers, and consumer groups to discuss the progress of the Initiative for Equitable Library Access (IELA).

The initiative was announced by LAC in 2007 as a means of creating a blueprint for equitable public library service through a national strategy. By promoting equitable library service and access to information in multiple formats, LAC can pave the way for all Canadians to share in the free exchange of knowledge, information, and ideas. LAC is looking into a fully accessible Internet portal that will serve as a gateway for information and resources, a toolkit for libraries on services and training, and an electronic clearinghouse to facilitate the production of materials in multiple formats. LAC has also commissioned a report, "Audio and Digital Publishing in Canada," which will be the first and most comprehensive of its kind in Canada. For more information on the initiative, visit http://www.collectionscanada.gc.ca/iela.

## New RSS Feeds

During 2008 LAC joined the world of RSS (Really Simple Syndication) by offering RSS feeds that offer links to new content on its Web site, updates to existing pages, and new finding aids and database descriptions. Eventually the RSS feed will also cover new content on the Portrait Gallery of Canada Web site.

## Tribute to Film Reconstruction

*Nass River Indians* is a 17-minute film documenting the activities of Marius Barbeau and Ernest MacMillan among the Nisga'a of the Nass River region of British Columbia in 1928. Barbeau, an ethnologist at the former National Museum of Canada, and MacMillan, then principal of the Toronto Conservatory of Music, are depicted transcribing and making wax cylinder recordings of the songs, dances, and rites of the Nisga'a people. On the UNESCO World Day for Audiovisual Heritage, October 27, 2008, LAC paid tribute to the late Bill O'Farrell and his team of film conservators at LAC who meticulously reconstructed the film.

LAC collects and preserves Canada's documentary heritage and makes it accessible to all Canadians, including 71,000 hours of short and full-length films dating back to 1897, and 270,000 hours of video and sound recordings.

## Portrait Gallery of Canada

The Portrait Gallery of Canada (PGC) and the National Capital Commission mounted "Portraits on the Ice" in 2008, showing huge, framed reproductions from LAC's National Portrait Collection around Ottawa's historic Byward Market Square and on the Rideau Canal Skateway. The Marquis de Vaudreuil, R. B. Bennett, Guido Molinari, and Wayne Gretzky were among notables whose portraits spent the winter gazing down from bridges and brick walls at passersby. "Portraits on the Ice" was so successful it was mounted again in 2009 with ten new portraits.

PGC also presented "In Your Face: The People's Portrait Project" in 2008, in collaboration with the Art Gallery of Ontario (AGO). Originally developed as an invitation to the people of Ontario to submit a 4- by 6-inch original portrait to AGO, the project immediately attracted interest across Canada and around the world. More than 17,000 portraits arrived from as far away as Australia, Britain, France, Germany, Italy, Japan, and South Korea.

Also in 2008, the Canadian public was invited for the first time to have a say on whose portraits should be commissioned for LAC's permanent collection. PGC is inviting all Canadians to suggest living persons who have made a significant contribution either to their community or to the country.

# Special Libraries Association

331 South Patrick St., Alexandria, VA 22314
703-647-4900, fax 703-647-4901, e-mail sla@sla.org
World Wide Web http://www.sla.org

Janice R. Lachance
Chief Executive Officer

Founded in 1909 and headquartered in Alexandria, Virginia, the Special Libraries Association (SLA) is a global organization for information professionals and their strategic partners. As an international professional association, SLA represents thousands of information experts and knowledge managers in more than 80 countries who collect, analyze, evaluate, package, and disseminate information to facilitate strategic decision making.

SLA members work in various settings including Fortune 500 companies, not-for-profit organizations, consulting firms, government agencies, technical and academic institutions, museums, law firms, and medical facilities. SLA promotes and strengthens its members through learning, advocacy, and networking initiatives.

## SLA Centennial

SLA was founded in 1909 by John Cotton Dana and a group of librarians who believed that libraries serving business, government, social agencies, and the academic community were very different from other libraries. The founders of SLA believed that these libraries operated using a different philosophy and more diverse resources than the typical public or school library.

These "special"—or, more aptly, "specialized"—libraries at first were distinguished by being subject collections with a specialized clientele, but gradually it was recognized that their chief characteristic was that they existed to serve the organization of which they were a part. Their purpose was not education per se, but the delivery of practical, focused, and even filtered information to the executives and other clients within their organizations. Specialist librarians, who have come to be called "information professionals," are unique in their relationship with their users and customers and are proactive partners in information and knowledge management.

Over the past century SLA members have been working on the technological edge, moving into knowledge services, and adapting to new roles to keep up with the times. They are entrepreneurial, embracing change and using their knowledge and vision to further the goals of their organizations. Corporate information professionals synthesize strategic information to help executives make the decisions necessary for business to thrive. Government information professionals organize and deliver information for congressional, parliamentary, judicial, and executive leaders to make policy decisions. Academic special librarians organize, digitize, and deliver research information so that professors and students can advance knowledge.

SLA's 11,000 members come from 75 nations. The association's strengths in serving its membership are in three areas: learning, networking, and advocacy.

These are the underpinnings that prompted the information pioneers of 1909 to come together in a cooperative association, and they are still the fundamental benefits that SLA provides the information pioneers of the 21st century.

## SLA's Core Values

The association's core values are

- Leadership—Strengthening members' roles as information leaders in their organizations and communities, including shaping information policy and ethical gathering and use of information
- Service—Responding to clients' needs, adding qualitative and quantitative value to information services and products
- Innovation and continuous learning—Embracing innovative solutions for the enhancement of services and intellectual advancement within the profession
- Results and accountability—Delivering measurable results in the information economy and members' organizations; the association and its members are expected to operate with the highest level of ethics and honesty
- Collaboration and partnering—Providing opportunities to meet, communicate, collaborate, and partner within the information industry and the business community

## Chapters, Divisions, and Caucuses

SLA chapter membership provides a network of information professionals in members' local community or region; SLA division membership links members to information professionals within their topical area of expertise. SLA membership includes membership in one chapter and in one division. For a small fee, members may join additional chapters, divisions, and caucuses. A caucus is an informal network of individuals with an interest in a discipline or topic not covered in other divisions.

SLA has 58 regional chapters in the United States, Canada, Europe, Asia, and the Middle East; 26 divisions representing a variety of industries; and 11 special-interest caucuses.

SLA chapters elect officers, issue bulletins or meeting announcements, hold three to nine program meetings a year, and initiate special projects. Members in all classes may affiliate with the chapter nearest to their own preferred mailing address (either business or residence).

SLA divisions represent subject interests, fields, or types of information-handling techniques. Each division elects officers and publishes a bulletin or newsletter. Most conduct professional programs during the association's annual conferences. SLA added an Academic Division in 2008 that focuses on broad-based topics of special librarianship in academic settings.

## Governance

SLA is governed by a board of directors elected by the membership. The board and the association both operate on a calendar year, with newly elected officers, as well as chapter and division leaders, taking office in January.

The 2009 officers are: president, Gloria Zamora, Sandia National Laboratories; president-elect, Anne Caputo, Dow Jones; past president, Stephen Abram, SirsiDynix; treasurer (2006–2009), Sylvia R. James, Sylvia James Consultancy; chapter cabinet chair, Susan Fifer Canby, National Geographic Society; chapter cabinet chair-elect, Ruth Wolfish, IEEE; division cabinet chair, Tom Rink, Northeastern State University; division cabinet chair-elect, Ann Sweeney, European Union/European Commission Delegation, Washington, D.C.; directors, 2006–2009, Kate L. Arnold, Cancer Research UK; Tamika McCollough, Environmental Protection Agency; directors 2008–2010, Deb Hunt, Exploratorium; Ty Webb, InfoWebb; directors 2009–2011, Daniel Lee, Navigator Ltd.; Nettie Seaberry, National Minority Supplier Development Council. SLA Chief Executive Officer Janice R. Lachance is a non-voting member.

## Programs and Services

### Click University

SLA's Click University, launched in 2005, is an online learning community focusing on continuing professional education for librarians, information professionals, and knowledge workers. "Click U" is primarily designed to provide SLA members with state-of-the-art learning opportunities in partnership with today's information industry experts. Courses on software and technology, management, communications, and leadership are designed to enhance skills acquired through traditional library education. Click U and its programs are available only to SLA members. As of January 2009, the majority of offerings from Click U are included in membership dues. Offerings that carry an additional fee include the Click U @ Annual Conference and Click U Certificate programs. Click U is constantly adding programs and courses on topics ranging from public speaking to copyright law.

### Innovation Laboratory

The SLA Innovation Laboratory is designed as a resource for SLA members to discover new technologies. The laboratory offers a wide variety of Web 2.0 software learning tools to help information professionals become more business-savvy and technologically adept. The program is included in member dues.

### Click U Certificate Programs (Premium)

Click U provides certificate programs for information professionals looking to take the next step into a new career and utilize their traditional information skills in such fields as competitive intelligence, knowledge management, and copyright management.

Click U @ Annual Conference (Premium)

SLA offers in-person training and continuing education at the SLA Annual Conference and INFO-EXPO. SLA workshops (half day) or learning forums (full day) are designed to educate and inspire participants to make an impact in their organizations.

### Advocacy

SLA serves the profession by advocating publicly on the value of the profession. Its activities range from communicating with executives and hiring professionals on the important role information professionals play in the workplace to sharing the membership's views and opinions with government officials worldwide.

SLA's Public Policy Program

Government bodies and related international organizations play a critical role in establishing the legal and social framework within which SLA members conduct information services. Because of the importance of governments and international organizations to its membership, SLA maintains an active public policy program. SLA staff and the association's Public Policy Advisory Council monitor and proactively work to shape legislation and regulatory proposals that affect SLA's membership.

SLA supports government policies that

- Strike a fair and equitable balance among the rights and interests of all parties in the creation, distribution, and use of information and other intellectual property
- Strengthen the library and information management operations of government agencies
- Promote access to government public information through the application of modern technologies and sound information management practices
- Encourage the development and application of new information and communications technologies to improve library services, information services, and information management
- Protect individual intellectual freedom and the confidentiality of library records, safeguard freedom of expression, and oppose government censorship
- Foster international exchange of information

With regard to the actions of government bodies and related international organizations in the policy areas listed above, the association will

- Monitor executive, legislative, and judicial actions and initiatives at the national and international level, and to the extent practical at the sub-national level
- Educate key decision-makers on the concerns of SLA's membership
- Provide timely updates to the membership on critical issues and actions

- Encourage members to influence actions by expressing their opinions
- Develop cooperative relationships with like-minded organizations so as to expand SLA's visibility and impact

## Legislative Action Center

SLA offers a Legislative Action Center tool on its Web site so that members can monitor legislation and other activities at the U.S. federal level. The Legislative Action Center provides automated and electronic proactive outreach to elected officials in an effort to shape legislation and regulatory proposals that affect SLA's membership.

## Employment and Career Services

The online SLA Career Center offers a variety of services to meet the career needs of members, including career coaching, articles and resources, and career disruption assistance mentoring. It includes a job bank serving the needs of employers as well as SLA members.

SLA Career Connection combines the power of the Web with the power of the face-to-face meeting. Job seekers and employers are able to connect online and then meet face-to-face at the next SLA Annual Conference.

## Information Center

The SLA Information Center provides access to resources to assist members in their day-to-day tasks and management decisions and in their roles as SLA leaders. Among its resources are Information Portals (links to articles, Web sites, books, and other resources on more than 40 topics); News Connections (industry news items summarized by topic); recent reports on information industry issues; research and surveys to help with benchmarking and strategic planning; and the SLA Podcast Center, which contains audio files from SLA Career Center experts as well as advice from the pages of the SLA magazine *Information Outlook.* SLA's Leadership Center guides members through resources created on best practices, training, guidelines, and responsibilities, and offers links to resources relevant to the operation and management of special libraries, from information portals to research and surveys.

## Professional and Student Networks

SLA's student groups are located throughout the world and are affiliated with accredited graduate schools of library and information science. Through membership in SLA, students gain valuable professional experience and make important industry contacts.

## Publications, Newsletters, and Blogs

SLA's monthly magazine, *Information Outlook,* provides news, features, and evaluation of trends in information management. SLA also produces a weekly e-newsletter, *SLA Connections,* that covers breaking news in the information industry as well as association news and updates on Click University. SLA also offers a number of blogs that keep members informed about important SLA and professional news.

**SLA Honors and Awards**

The SLA Awards and Honors Program was created in 1948 to honor exceptional individuals, achievements, and contributions to the association and the information profession. The purpose of the program is to bring attention to the important work of special librarians and information professionals within the corporate and academic setting.

Scholarships

Each year SLA awards scholarships to at least five students who have demonstrated their ability and desire to contribute to the special librarian and information management field. The SLA Scholarship Program consists of awards for graduate study leading to a master's degree, graduate study leading to a Ph.D., and for post-MLS study.

Grants

SLA offers grants for research projects for the advancement of library sciences; the support of programs developed by SLA chapters, divisions, or committees; and the support of the association's expanding international agenda. In addition, grants, scholarships, and stipends are offered by many of SLA's chapters and divisions.

[For a list of the winners of SLA's awards and grants, see "Library Scholarship and Award Recipients, 2008" in Part 3—*Ed.*]

## Events and Conferences

SLA's Annual Conference and INFO-EXPO brings together thousands of information professionals and provides a forum for discussion of issues shaping the information industry. The conference offers more than 400 events, programs, panel discussions, and seminars, and includes an exhibit hall with more than 300 participating companies.

Exhibition and attendance figures for the 2008 conference, held in Seattle June 15–18, exceeded planners' expectations and included, for the second year, SLA members from every chapter around the world.

Attendance figures totaled 5,011 from six continents, including 845 first-time conference participants. INFO-EXPO featured 283 companies and organizations and 464 booths. SLA welcomed 50 new exhibitors in 2008.

# Part 2
# Legislation, Funding, and Grants

# Legislation

## Legislation and Regulations Affecting Libraries in 2008

Emily Sheketoff
Executive Director, Washington Office, American Library Association

The second session of the 110th Congress proved extremely busy for the library community, though ultimately few of the bills of concern to the American Library Association (ALA) were actually passed. There were also active policy concerns relating to executive branch agencies. The long and hectic presidential campaign offered ALA many opportunities to contribute numerous proposals, continuing into President Barack Obama's transition process.

## Appropriations

During the second session of the 110th Congress, both the House and Senate Appropriations Committees included $171,500,000 for the Library Services and Technology Act (LSTA) State Grant program in the fiscal year (FY) 2009 Labor, Health and Human Services, Education and Related Agencies' appropriations bill. However, neither the full House nor the Senate voted on the bill. The 111th Congress will complete work on all unfinished FY 2009 appropriations bills by rolling them into one omnibus spending bill.

### LSTA Reauthorization

On September 11, 2008, Pennsylvania State Librarian M. Clare Zales testified before the House Education and Labor Subcommittee on Healthy Families and Communities on how libraries are essential to the American public in the 21st century.

Subcommittee Chairwoman Carolyn McCarthy (D-N.Y.), Ranking Member Todd Russell Platts (R-Pa.), and fellow members of the subcommittee showed great interest in Zales's testimony. Subcommittee members noted their support for libraries, asked several important follow-up questions, and set an overall positive tone for LSTA reauthorization in the coming year.

Zales's full testimony can be found at http://www.wo.ala.org/districtdispatch/wp-content/uploads/2008/09/zales_testimony910081.pdf.

## Higher Education

The Washington Office worked with key members of Congress to find ways to increase loan forgiveness opportunities for librarians during the 110th Congress.

In 2007 Congress passed and President Bush signed the College Cost Reduction Act of 2007, which included a program designed to encourage students to enter vital public service jobs by creating a new student loan forgiveness plan through the Direct Loan program for public service employees. Qualifying areas of employment include librarians.

The Higher Education Act was up for reauthorization in 2008 and was signed into law by President Bush on August 14, 2008. The bill extends Perkins loan forgiveness (which is subject to appropriations and available for borrowers who work in specific public service jobs) to additional categories of borrowers who meet eligibility criteria and work as librarians, pre-kindergarten or child care workers, full-time faculty at tribal colleges or universities, and speech and language therapists. Specifically, the language includes service as a librarian with a master's degree working in an elementary or secondary school eligible for assistance under Title I of the Elementary and Secondary Education Act, or in a public library serving an area containing an elementary or secondary school eligible for assistance under Title I of the Elementary and Secondary Education Act.

The bill authorized a discretionary loan forgiveness (excluding consolidation and PLUS loans) of $2,000 a year (up to $10,000) for service in "areas of national need." Under this program, librarians are specifically listed as an "area of national need" provided the individual is employed full-time in a high-poverty area for five consecutive years. Specifically, the individual must work in

- A public library that serves a geographic area within which the public schools have a combined average of 30 percent or more of their total student enrollments composed of children eligible for assistance under Title I of the Elementary and Secondary Education Act, or
- An elementary or secondary school with greater than 30 percent of its students eligible for assistance under Title I of the Elementary and Secondary Education Act

## Copyright

### Orphan Works Legislation

The ALA Office of Government Relations (OGR) actively advocated for a reasonable legislative solution in response to orphan works legislation that was introduced in both the House (H.R. 5889) and the Senate (S. 2913) during the 110th Congress. Activities included participating in strategy meetings, sending letters to key members of congress and their staff, and working with a consultant to help inform revisions being made to the bills. OGR advocated for the Senate version of the bill over the House version, and worked to amend the House version's additional provisions including eliminating the "dark archive" requirement (mandating that users file a notice with the U.S. Copyright Office before using an orphan work). In addition, OGR advocated for reasonable language on what constitutes best practices when conducting a qualifying/reasonable search for the copyright holder. S. 2913 passed the Senate on September 26, 2008, but the House did not take up the legislation.

### Section 108 Study Group

The final report of the Library of Congress Working Group on Section 108 was released in March 2008. The library community as a whole, and ALA in particular, continues to analyze the Working Group's report. The final results generated a mixed response from the library community, and further work on these issues will have to be done. The report can be viewed at http://www.section108.gov.

### Google Book Search Settlement Agreement

In late October Google, the Authors Guild, and the Association of American Publishers proposed a major settlement agreement resolving the class action lawsuit brought by book authors and publishers in response to Google's Book Search digitization project.

As of early February 2009, the ALA Washington Office continued to review the extensive agreement to determine possible implications—for all types of libraries—and to better understand the terms and conditions of the settlement agreement, with special emphasis on the provisions that apply directly to public and academic libraries. ALA was examining the possibility of filing comments with the judge who will decide whether the settlement will take effect.

### PRO-IP Act of 2008

At the end of 2008 President Bush signed into law the Prioritizing Resources and Organization for Intellectual Property (PRO-IP) Act of 2008 (S. 3325). Along with "gifting" President-elect Obama with an Intellectual Property Enforcement Coordinator ("I.P. Czar"), the new law allows the forfeiture of devices (such as computers) used in piracy, a provision of concern to libraries.

### International Copyright

ALA signed on to a number of letters urging the U.S. Trade Representative to share drafts of the Anti-Counterfeiting Trade Agreement (ACTA) and to warn Congress that trade law is being drafted without congressional participation. This multinational trade agreement—which was drafted outside of the review of international bodies including the United Nations Educational, Scientific, and Cultural Organization (UNESCO) and the World Intellectual Property Organization (WIPO) —could impose increased liabilities for infringement, involve the confiscation of personal electronic devices at international borders without a court order, and define incidental copies that are automatically created as a function of computer and digital technology as "copies" under the law even though they have no economic value and are temporary.

Additional emphasis was on secondary liability of Internet service providers (ISPs) that could greatly restrict the new application and use of Web 2.0 technologies and innovation. ALA was concerned because the negotiations have been conducted in secret, with no public interest representation. Leaks to the media from other involved countries suggested that ACTA's purpose is to meet the protectionist demands of the content industry.

### NIH Public Access Policy

Joining eight other library, publishing, and advocacy organizations, ALA signed a joint letter to the House Judiciary Subcommittee on Courts, the Internet, and Intellectual Property to express strong support for the recently instituted National Institutes of Health (NIH) Public Access Policy. Within days of the letter being sent, the Fair Copyright in Research Works Act (H.R. 6845) was introduced. This bill would have repealed the NIH Public Access Policy. ALA lobbied, and engaged targeted grassroots advocacy efforts, to express its strong opposition to the bill. ALA also worked to support the Scholarly Publishing and Academic Resources Coalition (SPARC) by helping to communicate that, in fact, the current NIH Public Access Policy does not affect copyright law. While the title of the bill implies that a copyright provision is at issue, in reality the issue is access to government (funded) information. H.R. 6845 was not released from committee before the end of the 110th Congress.

## Telecommunications and the Internet

The deployment of broadband services remains a high priority for ALA and the library community. Much of the effort during 2008 related to developing a long-term "fiber to the library" proposal and promoting it in Congress, with the Federal Communications Commission (FCC), and elsewhere. Other issues continued as well; network neutrality and reform of the Universal Service Fund were widely discussed but not acted upon either in Congress or by FCC.

Despite much debate in Washington about these telecommunications issues, the main bill passed in the 110th Congress was S. 1492—the Broadband Census of America Act of 2007. It requires FCC to conduct an annual assessment and report to the public on the nature and deployment of, and subscription to, broadband service capability throughout the states, including information comparing the extent of broadband service capability in other countries. The act also requires the National Telecommunications and Information Administration (NTIA) in the Department of Commerce to maintain a broadband inventory map. Although NTIA is now authorized to provide grants to local communities for technology planning, needs assessments, and related activities (but not for actual service or fiber build-out), no funding was appropriated for the activities.

### Internet Safety Education Legislation

ALA has long supported education as the best tool to promote safe Internet usage for young people. During the 110th Congress, there were various bills calling for different aspects of Internet safety education for libraries and schools receiving E-rate (lower "electronic" telecommunications rates) discounts and certain other federal funds. However, additional burdens placed on E-rate participants are not supported. ALA believes mandated blocking of all interactive Web applications denies access to materials and activities appropriate for children as well as limiting their abilities to learn the skills to utilize these new technologies and applications for education and career development, and that decisions about Internet safety education and/or blocking technologies are best made at the local level by library and school boards based upon community needs and standards.

H.R. 1120—the Deleting the Online Predators Act (DOPA) that originated in the 109th Congress—was reintroduced but died in committee. S. 49, the Protecting Children in the 21st Century Act sponsored by Sen. Ted Stevens (R-Alaska), was introduced in January 2007 and included DOPA, but also died in committee. Later, S. 1965, the Protecting Children in the 21st Century Act, also introduced by Sen. Stevens and proposed in August 2007 without DOPA, passed the Senate in May 2008 and was added to S. 1492, the Broadband Data Improvement Act, which became Public Law 110-385 in October 2008.

This new act requires a K–12 public or private school getting lower "electronic" telecommunications rates via the Universal Service Support (E-rate) system to certify "as part of its Internet safety policy" that it "is educating minors about appropriate online behavior . . ." As part of S. 1492, the act requires the Federal Trade Commission (FTC) to carry out a nationwide public awareness program on Internet safety and requires NTIA to establish an Online Safety and Technology Working Group to review and evaluate industry efforts to promote online safety and the development of Internet safety technologies.

In the 110th Congress, many bills calling for Internet safety education for libraries and schools receiving E-rate discounts were introduced. ALA has long supported education as the best tool to promote safe Internet usage for young people. However, additional burdens placed on E-rate participants are not supported.

Rep. Brad Ellsworth (D-Ind.) introduced the e-KIDS Act of 2007 (H.R. 3871) and Rep. Judy Biggert (R-Ill.) introduced the Protecting Our Children Online Act of 2008 (H.R. 6145). These bills were welcomed as alternatives to DOPA, H.R. 1120, reintroduced by Rep. Mark Kirk (R-Ill.). The "education" bills were clearly better bills than DOPA, which would block access to all interactive Web applications, such as MySpace, except under certain limited conditions. However, both bills remained in committee and were not voted on before the end of the 110th Congress.

**Fiber to the Library**

During 2008 ALA visited congressional offices to promote "fiber to the library" and share the results of two ALA telecommunications and connectivity studies. The two research projects, coordinated by ALA's Office of Information Technology Policy (OITP) and Office for Research and Statistics (ORS), were the basis both for congressional proposals and later transition proposals to President-elect Obama's staff in November and December 2008.

On September 16, 2008, Missouri State Librarian Margaret Conroy testified before the Senate Commerce, Energy, and Transportation Committee at a hearing on how communities use and benefit from broadband connectivity. She was one of six witnesses who emphasized that, even without wide broadband access in so many parts of the country, people are using connectivity where they can find it—in public libraries, for instance. Conroy focused on the varied needs of people, especially those without Internet service at home, school, or work, and how these individuals are using public libraries for job searching, online education, support for K–12 students, business information, and so forth.

Although this was an oversight hearing, not on any particular legislation, the discussions suggested the key issues that the Senate Commerce Committee, and all of Congress, must face in the 111th Congress: reform of the Universal Service Fund (which includes the E-rate discounts for libraries), network neutrality, and policies and mechanisms to push broadband build-out across the country.

### Farm Bill

In May 2008 libraries were added to the Farm Bill to assure that libraries are eligible entities to apply for the Rural Utilities Service (RUS) Distance Learning and Telemedicine program (DLT).

The insertion of the word "libraries" was the only statutory revision in the DLT program. The addition made it clear that Congress expects RUS to fund library-based DLT projects. The past law (which remained intact) provided for "financial assistance for the purpose of financing the construction of facilities and systems to provide telemedicine services and distance learning services in rural areas." ALA will have to make another legislative attempt to get its proposed language seeking additional resources and official recognition of the specialized broadband needs of libraries serving rural communities to address the specialized needs of libraries. The reauthorization of the farm bill, H.R. 2419, became law on May 22, 2008.

It was a modest victory to secure the small amendment in the bill "to encourage and improve telemedicine services and distance learning services in rural areas through the use of telecommunications, computer networks, and related advanced technologies by students, teachers, medical professionals, and rural residents." However, the definition of "distance learning" is narrow, focusing only on formal distance education courses. This may be of limited benefit to libraries until a broader definition is realized to include job training as "distance learning."

## Privacy

### FISA Reform Legislation

In August 2007 Congress enacted the Protect America Act very quickly as summer recess began. This bill expired on February 16, 2008. In March 2008 the House passed a new bill incorporating parts of the Senate's FISA (Foreign Intelligence Surveillance Act) Amendments Act of 2007 (S. 2248), and the House's original RESTORE Act (H.R. 3773). ALA signed on to numerous letters with organizations such as the Center for National Security Studies (CNSS) and the Center for Democracy and Technology (CDT), as the various iterations of these bills proceeded through Congress.

H.R. 6304, the "H.R. 3773 substitute bill," was felt by ALA to be substantially better than the Protect America Act or the bill passed by the Senate. The "substitute" included reporting requirements to ensure that Congress obtain access to the information needed for public and congressional consideration of what permanent amendments should ultimately be made to FISA. While the bill authorized the surveillance of Americans' international communications without a warrant (in some circumstances where the Fourth Amendment requires a warrant), it also contained some protections against such unconstitutional surveillance. These protections included

- Accountability for illegal surveillance by the administration that also guarantees future oversight
- A December 2009 "sunset" so that these powers will be reviewed in the new administration
- Creation of a commission to investigate and report about warrantless surveillance
- Stronger judicial oversight
- Requiring probable cause to target Americans who are overseas

H.R. 6304 became law on July 10, 2008.

### National Security Letter Reform Legislation

ALA—in conjunction with allies in the Campaign for Reader Privacy, which represents booksellers, librarians, publishers, and writers—released an open letter calling on Congress to pass legislation to restore the safeguards for reader privacy eliminated by the USAPatriot Act. In a letter published in the newspaper *Roll Call,* the American Booksellers Association, ALA, the Association of American Publishers, and PEN American Center urged approval of the National Security Letters Reform Act (S. 2088 and H.R. 3189). The letter cited two recent reports by the Inspector General of the Justice Department, which showed that the FBI had violated the law thousands of times since Congress expanded its authority to issue National Security Letters (NSLs), which it can use to seize records from bookstores and libraries without court approval. The letter stated that "the NSL Reform Act gives the FBI the tools it needs to conduct urgent investigations without sacrificing our most basic constitutional principles."

S. 2088 and H.R. 3189 would have restricted FBI searches to the records of those either suspected of or directly connected to terrorism or espionage. They also would have limited the time that booksellers and librarians are barred by a gag provision from revealing the receipt of an NSL, which is used to obtain Internet records, or a Section 215 order, which can be used to demand all other records.

S. 2088 included such reforms as limiting the reach of NSLs by allowing only less-sensitive personal information to be made available under this authority. Other existing authorities could still have been used to obtain the more-sensitive information that would no longer be available with an NSL. The bill would have required the government to determine that records sought with an NSL relate to someone who was connected to terrorism or espionage and would have required the attorney general to issue minimization procedures for information obtained through NSLs.

It would also have enhanced oversight by requiring additional reporting to Congress and making reasonable changes to the gag rules, requiring a gag to be narrowly tailored and limiting it to 30 days, extendable by a court. The bill would also have tightened standards for court-issued orders under Section 215 of the USAPatriot Act (the "library records" provision) by requiring the government to show that the records sought relate to a suspected terrorist or spy, or to someone directly linked to such a person.

Hearings were held in April and June, but neither bill moved out of committee.

### REAL ID Act and Related Issues

ALA opposed the REAL ID Act (P.L. 109-13) in 2005 and has continued to support efforts for its repeal. The act created a de facto national identification card by mandating standardized machine-readable driver's licenses in all states. The library community is concerned because such state driver's licenses are often used to apply for library cards. This would increase the opportunity to access and link multiple databases, including library-use records, threatening privacy rights and confidentiality with respect to information sought.

The REAL ID Act would create a national ID system lacking adequate privacy safeguards, and would put the burden of funding and managing this system on states' driver's license agencies (cost estimates exceed 100 times what Congress initially projected). Enactment of REAL ID would violate many states' privacy laws; 17 states have passed (and 20 have partially passed or introduced) legislation rejecting REAL ID. ALA adopted a resolution stating its concerns about the move to standardized machine-readable driver's licenses.

ALA supported the REAL ID Repeal and Identification Security Enhancement Act (H.R. 1117), introduced by Rep. Thomas Allen (D-Maine), and the Identification and Security Enhancement Act (S. 717), introduced by Sen. Daniel Akaka (D-Hawaii). Both bills remained in committee at the end of the 110th Congress.

### Data Mining and Personal Information

There was renewed debate in the 110th Congress on several employment-related bills that would require verification of an individual's residence status. The New Employee Verification Act (H.R. 5515) is an example. ALA monitored these proposals closely because of the implications for privacy, the problems inherent to such databases that currently exist, and the implications for libraries and their employees as well as for patrons.

The House passed a bill to reauthorize a pilot program for employment verification (H.R. 6633), but the Senate did not pass the bill.

## Government Information

### E-Government

The ALA Washington Office began a new initiative in November 2008, Veterans' Information @ your library. This project came from research illustrating the need for veterans' information to be more readily available. During the week of Veteran's Day in November, libraries around the country participated in a pilot program by displaying information about the Post-9-11 Veterans Educational Assistance Act of 2008 or "New GI Bill" and posting it to the libraries' Web sites.

ALA met with staff in the Senate's Homeland Security and Governmental Affairs Committee to generate awareness of and support for its E-Government efforts and to develop legislation that reflects the reality that public libraries are the primary providers of E-Government services. In June 2008 ALA also held a briefing session for Senate staffers on these issues.

A hearing on the reauthorization of the E-Government Act (S. 2321) was held on December 11, 2008. Although a vote was scheduled for the final days of the 110th Congress, it did not take place.

## Federal Libraries

Activities in the area of federal libraries focused mainly on addressing specific library threats or closings as well as on developing larger strategies to advocate for federal libraries.

- ALA gathered information on the Army's moving the Reimer Digital Library behind the password-protected Army Knowledge Online firewall; the Army decided to make the Reimer Digital Library once more available to the public.
- Discussions were held with key military librarians as well as with the chair of ALA's Federal and Armed Forces Libraries Round Table (FAFLRT) to discuss the most realistic options for preventing the closure of further base libraries.
- ALA monitored the efforts of the federal Environmental Protection Agency (EPA) to reopen its libraries.

ALA Washington Office staff had a conference call with EPA to learn about the Government Accountability Office (GAO) report "Environmental Protection: EPA Needs to Follow Best Practices and Procedures When Reorganizing Its Library Network," which prompted the House hearing mentioned below.

ALA's 2008–2009 president, James Rettig, testified at the House Science and Technology Subcommittee on Investigations and Oversight hearing on March 13, 2008. At the hearing, GAO released its report (mentioned above), which agreed with ALA's analysis of the EPA library situation. The chairman of the subcommittee, Rep. Brad Miller (D-N.C.), suggested that EPA consult with the groups represented there before submitting its report to Congress.

Throughout 2008 ALA was actively involved in the EPA libraries issue. Before the end of the year the EPA headquarters library officially reopened. EPA also reopened closed libraries in its National Library Network, with walk-in access for the public.

Other library locations will expand staffing, operating hours, or services. A Federal Register Notice of Access to EPA Library Services for Chicago, Dallas, Kansas City, and Washington, D.C. (both the Headquarters and Chemical Libraries) was published and went into effect September 30, 2008.

## Military Libraries

ALA, in conjunction with FAFLRT, worked actively on the concerns of military libraries. ALA staff made site visits to military libraries and the public libraries that serve those areas to learn the specific needs and challenges of military families and what role would be appropriate for ALA to take.

Additionally, ALA attended the Military OneSource online library launch. Librarians from all branches of the military came together on September 18, 2008, to announce new additions to Military OneSource, an effort to increase the online library offerings to all service members and their families. The new resources are a custom collection that has been compiled by the vendors with the help of the military librarians to best suit their patrons' needs. It is a combination of recreation and self-help material that comes in different formats including audio, interactive, and text. The vendors each spoke briefly about their contribution to the new capabilities on Military OneSource. The lead librarians of each service have worked to ensure that high-quality materials will be made available online around the clock to people of all ages. Not only will this new offering on Military OneSource be a more convenient way for service members and their families to access materials, it will also save the different branches from purchasing the same materials separately. These new resources will be especially helpful to National Guard and Reserve service members and families, in addition to men and women serving overseas who do not have regular access to a general military library. Now all service members can access the same materials in one place.

# Legislation and Regulations Affecting Publishing in 2008

Allan R. Adler

Vice President, Legal and Governmental Affairs

Emilia Varga-West

Assistant Director, Government and International Relations

Association of American Publishers
50 F St. N.W., Fourth Floor, Washington, DC 20001
202-347-3375, fax 202-347-3690
E-mail adler@publishers.org, evargawest@publishers.org

The Second Session of the 110th Congress was marked by partisan politics as Democratic control of Congress generated continuing disputes with the Republican administration of President George W. Bush. Given the brevity of the legislative period because of the presidential election campaign, many congressional initiatives were put on the legislative back burner. Nevertheless, a variety of activities of interest to Association of American Publishers (AAP) members continued to percolate in both the House and Senate.

This report focuses on legislative actions that affect book and journal publishing interests primarily concerning intellectual property protection, freedom of expression, and educational issues.

A summary, text, and status report for each piece of referenced legislation, whether enacted or not, can be found online in the Congressional Legislative Reference Service of the Library of Congress at http://thomas.loc.gov/home/multicongress/multicongress.html.

## Intellectual Property Issues

### NIH Enhanced Public Access

Despite the brevity of the Second Session of the 110th Congress due to elections, several pieces of copyright and copyright-related legislation required close monitoring by AAP staff.

Although AAP vigorously opposed efforts by the National Institutes of Health (NIH) in 2007 to make mandatory the voluntary manuscript submission aspect of its Enhanced Public Access Policy, NIH successfully convinced both the House and Senate Appropriations Committees to include obligatory statutory language in their respective versions of the Labor HHS (Health and Human Services) appropriations bills (H.R. 3043; S. 1710). Thus, NIH-funded researchers who wrote articles for publication in scientific journals were "requested" to submit an electronic version of their final, peer-reviewed manuscripts to NIH immediately upon acceptance by a journal for publication, so that the agency could make it freely available to the international online world through its PubMed Central Web site no more than 12 months after the date of journal publication.

Publishers argued that such a change would be inconsistent with policies embodied in U.S. copyright law, insofar as it would eliminate the concept of permission for NIH's use of the copyrighted work, and would effectively allow the agency to take important publisher property interests without compensation, including the value added to the article by the publishers' investments in the peer review process and other quality-assurance aspects of journal publication.

Journal publishers also argued that a mandatory policy would undermine publishers' ability to exercise their copyrights in the published articles, which is the means by which they support their investments in such value-adding operations. Journals published in the United States have strong markets abroad, and a government policy requiring these works to be made freely available for international distribution is inherently incompatible with the maintenance of global markets for these highly successful U.S. exports. Smaller and nonprofit scientific societies and their scholarly missions would be particularly at risk as their journal subscribers around the world turn to NIH for free access to the same content for which they would otherwise pay.

Nevertheless, the Second Session of the 110th Congress started with disappointing developments for the publishing industry. Following President Bush's veto of the Labor HHS appropriations bill that contained the controversial "mandatory NIH public access policy" provision, the same language was subsequently passed by Congress, as part of the omnibus Consolidated Appropriations Act of 2008 (H.R. 2764; P.L. 110-161), and signed into law by the president in December 2007. The mandatory NIH policy was enacted as Section 218 of Division G, Title II of that act.

AAP immediately expressed its objections to the newly enacted policy, and then submitted a joint petition with the DC Principles Coalition to the Department of Health and Human Services, calling for NIH implementation to occur through a public notice-and-comment rulemaking pursuant to the Administrative Procedure Act (APA). As the issue of the petition was forwarded to the White House for resolution, publishers were concerned that, instead of granting the rulemaking petition, the White House might compromise with NIH on a less-formal process for obtaining public input on implementation of the new mandatory policy. Thus, AAP continued to press for the formal rulemaking because the less-formal mechanisms would not require NIH to justify its probable refusal to change its announced implementation in response to publisher comments and would not provide the APA standards for judicial review of subsequent NIH implementation decisions.

On March 19, 2008, several journal-publisher representatives met with NIH Director Elias Zerhouni and his staff to discuss industry concerns and urge implementation of the new mandatory submission policy through an APA public notice-and-comment rulemaking. In general, the meeting was unproductive as it was confirmed that a Request for Information (RFI), rather than an APA notice, would be published in the *Federal Register* to solicit public comments about implementation of the new policy sometime after an NIH public meeting scheduled for March 20. It became evident that NIH was not willing to listen to publishers' requests when a senior NIH official announced during the public meeting that the RFI period would start on March 31 and end May 31.

Several AAP members submitted comments to NIH, which were evaluated by the agency in its report issued in September with the expected unsatisfactory responses to publishers' concerns. In the meantime, HHS passed responsibility for the rulemaking petition to Zerhouni, who, not surprisingly, rejected it in June. Refusing to give up, publishers turned to the staff and leadership of the House Judiciary Committee and its Intellectual Property subcommittee, lobbying for a hearing on the mandatory policy as well as for the introduction of legislation that would address issues arising from the NIH policy.

As a result, Judiciary Committee Chairman John Conyers (D-Mich.) introduced the Fair Copyright in Research Works Act (H.R. 6845) on September 9. His introductory remarks stated that the bill "would restore intellectual property protections for scientists, researchers, and publishers until a more thorough analysis of the access issues and a determination of an appropriate policy can be performed by the Register of Copyrights in consultation with economic experts." The proposal was intended to prevent harm to the peer review system that has been in place in journal publishing for more than 100 years.

Consequently, the House Judiciary Committee and its Intellectual Property Subcommittee held a hearing on September 11 discussing the legislation, which would roll back the mandatory NIH Public Access Policy and prevent the imposition of similar policies in the future by prohibiting federal agencies from conditioning grants of financial assistance for research on the agencies' ability to claim rights to exercise public distribution or display rights with respect to any "extrinsic work." H.R. 6845 focused on work that is (1) produced by a non-government person (2) who has created the work in connection with the receipt of financial assistance for research under a funding agreement with a federal agency, and is also (3) funded in substantial part by, or results from meaningful added value contributed by, one or more nonfederal entities that are not a party to the funding agreement. Although the hearing, which featured testimony from NIH Director Zerhouni, a former Register of Copyrights, and representatives of the opposing SPARC and DC Principles coalitions, concluded with mixed results, it provided a basis for determining what must be done to move the legislation forward in the new Congress.

As of early 2009, AAP expected that Conyers would reintroduce the Fair Copyright in Research Works Act early in the 111th Congress, and is hopeful of obtaining introduction of this legislation in the Senate as well.

**Prioritizing Resources and Organization for Intellectual Property**

**(PRO-IP) Act**
**(S. 3325; Public Law 110-403; October 13, 2008)**
During the past four years, AAP, along with other representatives of copyright-based industries, periodically engaged in ongoing discussions with the Department of Justice and key staff from the House and Senate Judiciary Committees regarding the development of a package of legislative proposals that would enhance civil and criminal enforcement capabilities for copyright owners and provide restructuring and additional resources for interagency efforts within the executive branch to address piracy and counterfeiting of copyrighted works in the international arena. Although AAP did not pursue any specific requests in this process, it was supported by other industry representatives in voicing its concerns about opening the Digital Millennium Copyright Act (DMCA) to possible amendment, as well as the possibility that certain controversial proposed amendments

(including, for example, one that would make it a felony to "attempt to infringe") might be viewed as overreaching by copyright interests.

Thus, AAP continued monitoring two bills concerning copyright enforcement that were introduced in 2007. The Senate advanced the Enforcement of Intellectual Property Rights Act (S. 3325) as a counterpart to the Prioritizing Resources and Organization for Intellectual Property (PRO-IP) Act of 2007 (H.R. 4279), which was passed by the House in May 2008. S. 3325 was signed into law in October under the House name of the PRO-IP Act (P.L. 110-403). It closely tracked the House-passed version of H.R. 4279, while incorporating certain provisions from S. 2317, the proposed Intellectual Property Enforcement Act, which had been introduced during the first session of the 110th Congress.

The new law contains a variety of measures to enhance civil and criminal copyright enforcement in specific ways, while also revamping the organizational structure and resources available within the executive branch for interagency coordination of intellectual property enforcement efforts in the international arena.

Like the House-passed bill, S. 3325 created an Intellectual Property Enforcement Coordinator (IPEC) position within the Executive Office of the President, subject to Senate confirmation, to devise and coordinate a joint strategic plan against counterfeiting and piracy.

Further, S. 3325 amended Section 411 of the Copyright Act to clarify that failure to register a copyrighted work affects only the ability to bring civil actions for infringement, not criminal actions. Like the House bill, it also contains amendments intended to harmonize civil and criminal asset forfeiture provisions as they apply across a variety of intellectual property laws. However, the civil forfeiture provisions of S. 3325 were originally more extensive than those proposed in the House version as they listed digital rights management (DRM) circumvention as an offense and mandated forfeiture of equipment used in the course of economic espionage. These provisions (derived from S. 2317) were criticized as creating penalties disproportionate to the offenses involved, and apply not only to infringing goods but to computers, cars, houses, and arguably any other real or personal property under the language embracing "any property used, or intended to be used, to commit or substantially facilitate the commission of an offense," but they were ultimately enacted with softening modifications.

Despite public controversy, based on earlier legislative proposals, S. 3325 also provided the Department of Justice with the ability to bring civil actions against any offender in lieu of criminal actions in circumstances where the infringing conduct would also qualify as a criminal offense. Critics derided this provision as an unnecessary and unjustifiable effort to effectively turn the Department of Justice into a private law firm for copyright owners; however, supporters of the provision claim it provides the department with an additional tool to use against criminal infringers even when criminal sanctions outweigh the offense.

Controversy also continued in 2008 regarding the House proposal in H.R. 4279 to change the existing rule on statutory damages that treats all parts of a compilation or derivative work as one work for purposes of such awards. The House bill would have given federal courts discretion to make multiple awards of statutory damages in such cases where the constituent parts of a compilation, or a derivative work and any previous existing work on which it is based, can be considered "distinct works having independent economic value." Critics claimed that the change in law would have resulted in awards of statutory damages that were greatly disproportionate to the harm suffered by the copyright owner. Although AAP members routinely publish derivative works, as well as anthologies and other types of compilations, they did not call for a change and were concerned regarding how such a change might impact them as users of third-party works who might be sued for infringement in such cases. The issue, however, was resolved for publishers during the markup of the PRO-IP (H.R. 4279) bill in March, when the House Judiciary Subcommittee deleted the controversial provision that would have allowed a court to grant multiple awards of statutory damages where a compilation or derivative work was infringed. The civil action authority for the Department of Justice was also dropped from the legislation before enactment.

## Orphan Works

Orphan works—copyrighted works whose owners are difficult or impossible to find—continued to be a priority on book publishers' agendas in 2008. The issue was reintroduced after the recess in 2007. It picked up the development of the legislation where the 109th Congress left it after H.R. 5439 was approved by the House Intellectual Property Subcommittee in May 2006 but expired upon adjournment later that year without further advancement.

Congress and the affected industries spent the first half of 2008 discussing and negotiating the controversial particulars of orphan works legislation. In March AAP's Allan Adler presented testimony at a hearing before the House Judiciary Intellectual Property Subcommittee, then continued to meet with subcommittee and Copyright Office staff on drafting an orphan works bill. In April the leaders of the House and Senate Judiciary Committees simultaneously introduced identical proposals largely based on the legislation from the previous Congress. Nevertheless, some of the provisions of House Committee Chairman Howard L. Berman's (D-Calif.) Orphan Works Act of 2008 (H.R. 5889) and Senate Committee Chairman Patrick Leahy's (D-Vt.) Shawn Bentley Orphan Works Act of 2008 (S. 2913) were different from the proposal in 2006, including: (1) moving from a "reasonably diligent search" to a "qualifying search" based on certain minimum search requirements for any user to qualify for the legislation's "limitations on remedies"; (2) a "notice of use" filing requirement, together with a requirement for the Copyright Office to establish and maintain a "dark archive" for such filings; (3) a "consent to federal court jurisdiction" provision for those who would assert the "orphan works" defense; (4) an exclusion for works "fixed on or in useful articles" (necessary to address concerns of textile and home furnishing producers); (5) a Government Accountability Office (GAO) study to examine the Copyright Office's deposit system; and (6) a "delayed effective date" provision for the legislation's application to pictorial, graphical, and sculptural (PGS) works that would have depended on when the Copyright Office "certified" the availability of databases with image search capabilities.

H.R. 5889 was marked up and approved by the House Judiciary Intellectual Property Subcommittee in May, with some improvements. Nevertheless, the

House bill still contained three provisions that publishers and other mainstream copyright organizations did not support:

- The photography, home furnishing, and textile industries were seeking a "notice of use" database, where the infringing user would have needed to deposit a notice of use that included a copy of the infringed work prior to making an infringing use of such work. It was contemplated that such a database would have been a "dark archive" rather than a publicly searchable resource. AAP has objected to such a requirement as unworkable and unnecessary, regardless of whether the database was publicly searchable or "dark." AAP has also pointed out that the expense of maintaining the database would have required funding from congressional appropriations or user fees, or both, which would contribute to bringing down the whole orphan works legislation.
- H.R. 5889 would have authorized the court to grant additional reasonable compensation ("value added") to the copyright owner who emerged subsequent to a diligent search and infringing use if the infringed work was registered with the Copyright Office. AAP noted the problems of defining what "value added" derived from registration, and how such "value" translated into additional compensation.
- AAP also opposed a provision that made the effective date of the legislation contingent upon whether the Copyright Office was able to certify the availability of at least two databases capable of both image and textual searches.

After the two bills were reported out of the House Judiciary Intellectual Property Subcommittee (H.R. 5889) and the full Senate Judiciary Committee (S. 2913), respectively, in May, the legislative efforts reached a serious impasse on the House side. The possible addition of "notice of use" provisions and efforts to rewrite the "qualifying search" and injunctive relief provisions further delayed the process to advance H.R. 5889. The House Judiciary Subcommittee urged AAP to compromise on several provisions that publishers opposed as unnecessary and unworkable, including "notice of use" requirements. The possibility of accepting compromises on such issues was further complicated by the fact that AAP had prevailed on those issues in S. 2913 as approved by the Senate Judiciary Committee. Furthermore, controversy also surrounded the House bill's "safe harbor" provisions that would have allowed certain nonprofit users to qualify for protection from monetary damages under the bill if there were no "direct or indirect commercial advantage" from use of the infringed work. Museums and libraries viewed this standard as too restrictive and also opposed the criterion where the subsequently emerging copyright owner would have had the right to obtain from the infringer any proceeds that were "directly attributable" to the use of the infringing work.

Following the August recess, however, prospects for movement of S. 2913 in the Senate appeared brighter. On September 29 the publishing industry applauded the Senate's swift passage of the Shawn Bentley Orphan Works Act of 2008 (S. 2913). Unfortunately, the bill expired in the House Judiciary Committee, as further advancement in the House was not possible because of conflicting views within the copyright community.

Although neither proposal was signed into law, Senate passage of S. 2913 was a significant step, establishing a benchmark for continuing efforts to enact meaningful orphan works legislation. It was expected that the legislation would be reintroduced in the 111th Congress.

### Other Intellectual Property Bills

Another bill of interest to book publishers was the International Intellectual Property Protection and Enforcement Act (S. 3464), which was introduced late in the Second Session on September 10 by the chairman of the Senate Finance Committee, Max Baucus (D-Mont.), and Sen. Orrin Hatch (R-Utah). The bill intended to strengthen the Special 301 sanction provisions of the Trade Policy Act, which provide the basis for an extensive annual report that AAP and its sister copyright industry associations (collectively as members of the International Intellectual Property Alliance) issue to rank countries for purposes of trade policy recommendations based on the degree to which the countries are meeting their intellectual property obligations under international treaties. The proposal, however, did not receive further consideration before the end of the Second Session.

With the exception of Rep. Rick Boucher's (D-Va.) proposed FAIR USE Act (H.R. 1201), which AAP had opposed in earlier versions in previous congresses and continued to oppose in the 110th Congress, S. 3464 was the only other copyright bill of interest to AAP, which expects to support its enactment if it is reintroduced in the new Congress.

## Freedom of Expression Issues

### Bills to Enhance National Security and to Protect Civil Liberties

### Libel Tourism

During the past decade, a new form of defamation litigation practice, popularly called "libel tourism," has emerged. The term is most frequently used in reference to the phenomenon of foreign plaintiffs bringing libel actions against U.S. authors or news organizations in British courts in connection with publications that have little connection with the United Kingdom. Essentially, these publications are considered "guilty until proven innocent" under the British common law approach to defamation, which differs significantly from the more defendant-friendly U.S. law of defamation as it has developed under the protections of the First Amendment. In perhaps the most notorious case of this kind, Khalid Salim bin Mahfouz, a billionaire Saudi businessman, brought suit in Britain against Rachel Ehrenfeld, an American author living and working in the United States, based on his claim that her 2003 book *Funding Evil* wrongfully asserted his involvement in the financing of Islamic terrorism. Although the book was not published in Britain, the public could obtain copies online, which bin Mahfouz claimed was the basis for alleging damage to his reputation there. When Ehrenfeld refused to appear before the British court, based on her view that it lacked jurisdiction over the case, the court issued a default ruling in favor of bin

Mahfouz, awarding damages against Ehrenfeld, ordering the destruction of extant copies of her book, and demanding that she make a formal apology to bin Mahfouz together with a retraction of her printed allegations against him. The highly publicized decision has not only served to restrict Ehrenfeld's further writing and travel activities, but has also been cited for its broader effect in intimidating and silencing other American authors and depriving the public of vital information on issues of public concern.

The persistent threat that victorious "libel tourist" plaintiffs like bin Mahfouz might attempt to enforce such foreign judgments against American defendants in the U.S. court system resulted, in the case of Ehrenfeld, in action by the New York State Legislature to revise the state's jurisdictional statute to bar its courts from enforcing libel judgments rendered in foreign jurisdictions whose laws do not provide the free speech protections embodied in the First Amendment to the Constitution. This action then prompted several members of Congress to seek changes in federal law to address the problem of libel tourism.

Hence, the Free Speech Protection Act of 2008 (H.R. 5814; S. 2977) was introduced in the House and Senate by Rep. Peter King (R-N.Y.) and Sens. Arlen Specter (R-Pa.) and Joe Lieberman (ID-Conn.) in April and May of last year, respectively. The identical bills would have allowed a U.S. person against whom a defamation lawsuit has been brought in a foreign jurisdiction, based on speech disseminated in the United States that does not constitute defamation under U.S. law, to sue the plaintiff in a U.S. federal district court to obtain a court order barring enforcement here of any foreign judgment obtained in the foreign lawsuit, and to seek an award of damages and legal expenses against the defamation plaintiff, including an award of treble damages if the jury in the U.S. action determines that the defamation plaintiff, in bringing the foreign lawsuit, "intentionally engaged in a scheme to suppress rights under the First Amendment" by discouraging media from publishing or supporting the speech of any individual.

Although no action was taken in either the House or Senate on the identical bills, another measure to address the "libel tourism" issue (H.R. 6146), which was introduced by Rep. Steve Cohen (D-Tenn.) in May 2008 and cosponsored by a number of House Judiciary Committee members including Chairman Conyers, was passed by the House on the suspension calendar, without hearings or other committee action, just before the end of the 110th Congress. Substantially similar to the state legislation enacted in New York, H.R. 6146 would have barred U.S. courts from recognizing a foreign defamation judgment "based upon a publication concerning a public figure or a matter of public concern" unless the U.S. court determined that the foreign judgment satisfied the free speech and free press protections guaranteed by the First Amendment. The bill, however, would not have established a "cause of action" for the U.S. defendant, as the other pending legislation proposed. Due to the press of end-of-Congress business, as well as the lack of hearings to consider the provisions of the bill as they differed from the other pending related legislation, H.R. 6146 received no action in the Senate and expired with the end of the Congress.

AAP expected to see these "libel tourism" bills, or some variations of them, introduced early in the new Congress, when hearings will likely be held to explore the related issues and build momentum for legislative action.

## National Security Letters Reform

Since the enactment of the USAPatriot Act little more than a month after the terrorist attacks of September 11, 2001, AAP has supported legislative proposals to cut back on the broadened "national security letter" (NSL) authority that was given to the FBI under that legislation. Despite denials of abusive use by the FBI, congressional hearings and reports from the Justice Department have revealed highly dubious uses of the FBI's sweeping administrative power to demand from any entity or organization records relating to identified individuals, without probable cause or judicial review but subject to a "gag order" prohibiting the recipient from disclosing the existence of the letter. For example, in August 2005, it was disclosed that the FBI used an NSL to demand records from the Library Connection, a consortium of 26 Connecticut libraries, including records concerning borrowed reading materials and Internet usage. Although the ensuing controversy eventually resulted in the FBI's abandonment of its demand, it took action by two federal courts to lift the "gag order" that prevented the libraries from publicly discussing receipt of the NSL.

The federal courts have held the NSL provisions of the USAPatriot Act to violate both the First Amendment and the constitutional doctrine of separation of powers among the three branches of the federal government, both before and after Congress amended the provisions as part of its reauthorization of the act in March 2006. Nevertheless, opponents of this authority continue to focus on legislation to curb offensive use of NSLs in light of those aspects of the 2006 amendments that added specific penalties for noncompliance or disclosure.

AAP continued in 2008 to support the proposed NSL Reform Act (S. 2088), which was introduced by Sen. Russell Feingold (D-Minn.), along with 11 cosponsors, in September 2007, as well as its similar House counterpart, the National Security Letters Reform Act (H.R. 3189), which was introduced by Rep. Jerry Nadler (D-N.Y.) two months earlier and eventually attracted 30 cosponsors. The House bill would have barred the use of NSLs by the FBI in connection with criminal investigations, except where the issuing official certified specific facts providing a reason to believe that information or records sought pertain to a foreign power or an agent of a foreign power. It also would have limited the uses of information acquired through the use of NSLs and provided a civil cause of action for the misuse of NSLs. The Senate bill would have more broadly allowed use of NSLs in "ongoing, authorized and specifically identified national security investigations," but would have specifically addressed their use to obtain third party records from wire or electronic communications service providers, financial institutions, and consumer credit reporting agencies, and would have revised criteria for judicial review of nondisclosure orders applicable to NSL recipients, required the attorney general to establish minimization and destruction procedures regarding records obtained pursuant to NSLs, and would have terminated certain authorities for use of NSLs. Neither bill advanced beyond committee.

With a new Democratic administration and strengthened Democratic majorities in the House and Senate, some version of these NSL reform bills was likely to be introduced early in the new Congress.

## Bills to Provide Confidential Source Protection for Journalists

Based on several highly publicized investigations and court actions in which journalists were subject to demands to reveal the identities of confidential news sources, debates over federal "shield law" legislation were prominent in the 110th Congress. Although unprecedented progress was made in 2007, when the House passed the Free Flow of Information Act (H.R. 2101) and the Senate Judiciary Committee approved a different version of identically titled legislation (S. 2035), the continued inability of advocates to reach consensus on a single version ultimately prevented enactment before the end of the 110th Congress.

After introduction of the House and Senate bills by Reps. Rick Boucher (D-Va.) and Mike Pence (R-Ind.) and Sen. Arlen Specter (R-Pa.), respectively, the legislation slowly continued to gather bipartisan cosponsorship (20 cosponsors in the Senate, 71 in the House). However, the progress of the legislation toward enactment stalled in disputes concerning the scope of the confidentiality privilege, the nature of permitted exceptions, and the question of who would be entitled to claim protection under the privilege.

Starting from the premise that journalists should have some protection from being compelled by a federal entity to produce documents, provide testimony, and identify confidential sources in connection with any "matter arising under federal law," the House-passed bill would have exempted a "covered person" from having to comply with a subpoena requiring documents or testimony, unless a court determined that (1) all reasonable alternative sources for the information sought had been exhausted; (2) there was a reasonable belief that a crime occurred and the information sought was critical to the resulting investigation, prosecution or defense; or (3) the information sought was critical to the successful completion of a non-criminal proceeding that was based on information provided by a third party.

Where the testimony or documents sought "could reveal the identity of a source of information or include any information that could reasonably be expected to lead to the discovery of the identity of such a source," the privilege would have attached unless disclosure of the identity of such source was "necessary" to (1) prevent or identify the perpetrator of an act of terrorism or significant and specified harm to national security; (2) prevent imminent death or significant bodily harm; or (3) identify someone who has disclosed a trade secret, individually identifiable health information, or nonpublic personal information about any consumer, in violation of federal law; or (4) was "essential" to identify, as part of a criminal investigation or prosecution, a person with authorized access to classified national security information who disclosed such information without authorization. The court also determined that "the public interest in compelling disclosure of the information or document involved outweighed the public interest in gathering or disseminating news or information."

The House-passed bill further provided an exception for "criminal or tortuous conduct," generally excluding an otherwise "covered person" from asserting the privilege if the information sought was obtained by that person through "eyewitness observation" of alleged criminal conduct or as a result of the commission of alleged criminal or tortuous conduct by such person.

With the exclusion of certain persons designated as a foreign power or agent of a foreign power, or persons affiliated with organizations or entities designated as terrorists or terrorist organizations, the House-passed bill defined a "covered person" as one who "regularly gathers, prepares, collects, photographs, records, writes, edits, reports, or publishes news or information that concerns local, national, or international events or other matters of public interest for dissemination to the public for a substantial portion of the person's livelihood or for substantial financial gain and included a supervisor, employer, parent, subsidiary, or affiliate of" such a person. It defined "journalism" as "the gathering, preparing, collecting, photographing, recording, writing, editing, reporting, or publishing of news or information that concerns local, national, or international events or other matters of public interest for dissemination to the public."

In determining who should have been eligible to claim the protection of the privilege provided by the bill, legislators argued over whether the coverage of Internet bloggers would unreasonably extend the privilege to any person with Internet access. The requirement that a "covered person" must engage in the described activities "for a substantial portion of the person's livelihood or for substantial financial gain" reflected the majority desire to restrict, if not entirely eliminate, the ability of bloggers to claim the bill's protections. Unfortunately, this qualification also excluded freelancers and many other types of writers and authors who couldn't meet its terms. The Senate bill (S. 2035), tracking the House-passed bill in most respects, contained the same definition of "covered person" but without this qualifying language.

Prior to the introduction of H.R. 2102, AAP expressed concerns that explicit reference to authors and publishers of books should have been included in the bill to ensure that they were able to assert the privilege against compelled disclosure. Similar expressions of concern that use of the term "journalist" to define parties eligible to claim the privilege had resulted in the addition of specific references to "book" authors and publishers in proposed "shield law" legislation in the previous Congress; however, with respect to H.R. 2102, the news media advocates, viewed as the primary constituency for this legislation, resisted such specificity, preferring the broader reference to "journalism" as a way of blurring the controversy over "blogger" coverage. AAP was successful in insisting that the definition of "journalism" should include "news or information that concerns local, national, or international events or other matters of public interest for dissemination to the public," and should not be limited to "current" or "contemporary" events, so that books—which may concern matters of historical interest and take more time to produce than "hot news" coverage—would not be excluded from a broad reading of the definition.

AAP expected to see federal "shield law" legislation introduced early in the new Congress, likely along the lines of the bill that passed the House last year.

### Improving Public Access to Presidential Records

As the Bush administration continued to polish its reputation as among the most secretive in the nation's history, congressional efforts to improve public access to federal records and promote accountability and openness in the executive branch continued during the first session of the 110th Congress. During 2008, however, the efforts subsided in the shadow of presidential politics and no further legislation was proposed or advanced.

The Presidential Records Act Amendments of 2007 (H.R. 1255), introduced by Rep. Henry Waxman (D-Calif.), chairman of the House Oversight and Government Reform Committee, in March 2007 was a response to a restrictive executive order issued by President Bush in 2001 that created new obstacles to public access to presidential records and was widely viewed as inconsistent with the letter and spirit of the Presidential Records Act of 1974.

The Presidential Records Act, enacted by Congress after the Watergate scandal raised questions about the wisdom of letting a former president have custodial authority over presidential records, established that such records belong to the American people, not to the president. It gave the Archivist of the United States custody of the records of a former president, with the "affirmative duty to make such records available to the public as rapidly and completely as possible . . . " Under its provisions, a president may restrict access to records for up to 12 years, after which records are to be released in accordance with the Freedom of Information Act (FOIA), excluding application of FOIA's "deliberative process" exemption. The Presidential Records Act recognizes presidential authority to assert executive privilege, maintaining the status quo with respect to whatever constitutionally based privilege may be available to an incumbent or former president.

The 1974 act was first applied to the records of former President Ronald Reagan, pursuant to the terms of an executive order he had issued to establish a process for dealing with potential executive privilege claims over records covered by the act. The executive order required the Archivist of the United States to give incumbent and former presidents 30 calendar days' advance notice before releasing presidential records. It authorized the archivist to release the records at the end of that period unless the incumbent or former president claimed executive privilege, or unless the incumbent president instructed the archivist to extend the period indefinitely. If the incumbent president decided to invoke executive privilege, the archivist would withhold the records unless directed to release them by a final court order. If the incumbent president decided not to support a former president's claim of privilege, the archivist would decide whether or not to honor the claim.

In November 2001 President Bush issued another executive order that overturned the Reagan executive order and gave current and former presidents and vice presidents broad authority to withhold presidential records or to delay their release indefinitely. In addition, it required the archivist to honor executive privilege claims made by either incumbent or former presidents; even if the incumbent disagrees with the former president's claim, the archivist must honor the claim and withhold the records.

Unlike the Reagan executive order, which stated that records were to be released on a schedule unless some other action occurred, the Bush executive order stated that records would be released only after actions by former and current presidents had occurred. Therefore, if either the current or former president does not respond to the archivist, the records would not be released. Moreover, under the Bush executive order, designees of a former president may assert privilege claims after the death of the president, in effect making the right to assert executive privilege an asset of the former president's estate. The Bush executive order also authorizes former vice presidents to assert executive privilege claims over their records.

H.R. 1255 proposed a set of guidelines regarding the process of publicly disclosing any presidential records for the first time. The bill required that both the incumbent and the former president during whose term the documents were created were notified of such action, and granted them the right to file privilege claims to hold the records for a specified time if necessary to review the files. However, without any time extension request, the records would have become publicly available within 20 days of providing initial notice to the incumbent and former presidents.

Despite unsurprising opposition from the Bush administration, H.R. 1255 passed the House in March during the First Session of the 110th Congress, and was approved by the Senate Committee on Homeland Security and Governmental Affairs without amendment just three months later. Unfortunately, since that time, with the bill subject to successive "holds" in the Senate, first by Sen. Jim Bunning (R-Ky.) and then by Sen. Tom Coburn (R-Okla.), it was not considered further before congressional adjournment.

AAP expected that legislation similar to the House-passed version of H.R. 1255 would be introduced early in the new Congress. In the wake of the perceived overreaching secrecy of the Bush administration, a new Democratic administration and strengthened Democratic majorities in both houses of Congress augur well for enactment of legislation securing public access to presidential records.

## Education Issues

### Higher Education Opportunity Act

**(H.R. 4137; Public Law 110-315; August 14, 2008)**
During the past six years, at the beginning of each academic semester, there has been a steady drumbeat of complaint about the prices students must pay for college textbooks and the perceived reasons for the claim that prices are unjustifiably high. These complaints have continued despite a 2005 study by the Government Accountability Office, which concluded that textbook prices had been largely driven by publishers' investments in additional instructional materials and new technologies in response to faculty needs and to enhance student success. Similarly, efforts to enact federal legislation addressing the cost of college textbooks continued last year, despite a subsequent study published in May 2007 by the Advisory Committee on Student Financial Assistance, a congressionally chartered federal advisory committee, which recommended against enactment of federal legislation that would compel stakeholders to take specific actions, impose price controls, or condition federal funding eligibility on particular actions by colleges with respect to textbook pricing.

Although the College Textbook Affordability Act (S. 945), sponsored by Sen. Richard Durbin (D-Ill.), and the College Textbook Affordability and Transparency Act (H.R. 3512), sponsored by Rep. Julia Carson (D-Ind.), received no further consideration after their introduction in 2007, they nevertheless served as stepping stones for provisions that were eventually added to the leading bill to reauthorize the Higher Education Act (HEA) of 1965, as amended, and the College Opportunity and Affordability Act (H.R. 4137) introduced by Rep. George Miller (D-Calif.), chairman of the House Education and Labor Committee, in November 2007. The identical bills (S. 945 and H.R. 3512) would have established federal policy with respect to the issue of college textbook affordability. Among other requirements, they would have required publishers informing teachers about available textbooks or supplements to include written information concerning (1) the price the publisher would charge the bookstore associated with such institution for such items; (2) the full history of revisions for such items; and (3) whether such items are available in other formats, including paperback and unbound, and the price the publisher would charge the bookstore for items in those formats. The bills also would have required any publisher that sells a textbook and any accompanying supplement as a single bundled item to also sell them as separately priced and unbundled items.

However, working with the sponsors of the legislation, as well as with the leadership and staff of the House Education and Labor Committee, AAP was able to negotiate a number of changes in these proposed requirements before they were included in H.R. 4137, the primary House vehicle for reauthorizing the substantive programs and policies of HEA. The revised language allowed publishers to provide faculty with a list of substantial content revisions, rather than a full list of all changes, as originally proposed; provided an exemption from the requirement to "unbundle" packages that include third-party materials that cannot be sold separately; and added flexibility for publishers providing information on custom textbooks.

When the House Education and Labor Committee took up H.R. 4137 in November 2007, AAP continued its fight for improvements in the two sets of proposed provisions affecting college textbook publishers, which sought to (1) expand transparency in textbook marketing and (2) make alternative formats of print course materials more readily available to students with print disabilities.

On textbook transparency, AAP obtained new language to enable the use of alternative means of communication between publishers and faculty, such as through e-mail or Web sites, to avoid unnecessary additional burdens and cost increases as a result of forcing publishers to provide price and product information "in writing" on paper.

On the accessibility issues, however, AAP first had to convince Rep. Raul Grijalva (D-Ariz.) not to offer an amendment proposed by the National Federation of the Blind (NFB) that basically would have extended the requirements of the IDEA Amendments of 2004 to higher education. The alternative provisions that resulted from these negotiations were added to H.R. 4137 and consequently approved by the House committee in mid-November, providing for establishment of a two-year federal commission to study the accessibility issue and a three-year grant program for model demonstration projects. Hopefully, this compromise will provide breathing room for AAP to continue developing an industry-based proposal for addressing the needs of college students with print disabilities, while also giving AAP the ability to argue that enactment of legislation in this area by individual states is neither necessary nor appropriate in light of the federal legislation.

In February 2008 the College Opportunity and Affordability Act (H.R. 4137) was placed on the legislative agenda again. After extensive discussions, the House and Senate reached an agreement in July, which was signed into law (P.L. 110-315) in August under the title of the Higher Education Opportunity Act. As enacted, the bill included a significant provision concerning integrated textbooks, which was finalized last year. AAP actively lobbied during the Second Session to differentiate an "integrated textbook" from a "bundle" of educational materials, since they were treated as the same in many pieces of related state legislation. Publishers' efforts resulted in clarification of those terms to provide clearer guidance for state legislation. Under the bill, an "integrated textbook" is "combined with materials developed by a third party and that, by third party contractual agreement, may not be offered by publishers separately from the college textbook with which the materials are combined; or combined with other materials that are so interrelated with the content of the college textbook that the separation of the college textbook from the other materials would render the college textbook unusable for its intended purpose." This clearly distinguishes the nature of such textbooks from the practice of "bundling" materials, where a "bundle" is more broadly defined as "one or more college textbooks or other supplemental materials that may be packaged together to be sold as course materials for one price."

It is worth noting a set of provisions in H.R. 4137 that were advocated by the motion picture and music industries in an effort to address the problem of illegal peer-to-peer "file-sharing" by college students of unauthorized copies of motion pictures and recorded music through campus Internet networks. Typically, efforts to address these problems have focused on proposed amendments to the federal Copyright Act, which means legislation within the jurisdiction of the judiciary committees. However, in an effort that bears watching by AAP regarding its own members' issues with "electronic reserves" and other unauthorized uses of copyrighted works in the form of electronic course content, these copyright-based industries have taken their efforts to the committees with jurisdiction over key legislation.

The copyright protection-related provisions of H.R. 4137 direct institutions that receive funds under Title IV of HEA to annually inform students about copyright law and campus policies on peer-to-peer copyright infringement; report on institutional policies and actions to prevent, detect, and punish peer-to-peer infringements by students; and, "to the extent practicable," develop plans to offer alternatives and explore technology-based deterrents to illegal downloading and peer-to-peer distribution of intellectual property.

Not surprisingly, the higher education community vigorously opposed these provisions as draconian threats against continued funding eligibility; however, despite their efforts, the provisions were enacted as part of the College Opportunity and Affordability Act.

## No Child Left Behind
In addition to HEA reauthorization, the other major task that remained on the education agenda of the Second Session of the 110th Congress was the reauthorization of the No Child Left Behind (NCLB) Act, which was enacted in 2002 as a successor to the Elementary and Secondary Education Act and has been considered the major domestic legislative achievement of the Bush administration.

Although enacted with strong bipartisan support, this federal law has increasingly become the subject of controversy regarding its effectiveness and the repeated refusal of the Bush administration to fully fund requirements that NCLB imposes on state and local educational agencies. Consequently, the debate over the act's merits prevented the reauthorization of act in March 2007, which prompted an automatic one-year extension of the programs.

AAP's School Division developed a position paper on the extension of NCLB, which was distributed to members of Congress in March 2007. The instructional programs, services, and assessments developed by AAP members play a critical role in NCLB programs, and AAP therefore expressed its strong support for the reauthorization of the act. Specifically, in order to help all students attain academic proficiency and to close achievement gaps, publishers recommended (1) access to up-to-date instructional materials in the classroom and at home; (2) authorization and expansion of reading programs for adolescents, such as the Striving Readers Program; (3) access to a selection of instructional materials, and assurance that programs implemented under the Reading First program should continue to meet rigorous and scientifically based criteria; (4) continuation of funding to expand math and science programs; (5) strengthened and expanded annual assessment systems for improved teaching and learning; (6) leveraging technology; and (7) improving teacher quality through training to effectively use and integrate instructional materials, assessments, and data.

Despite much activity surrounding NCLB reauthorization in 2007, the process ground to a halt and no further action took place before the end of First Session. Although a number of bills were introduced in 2008 regarding certain sections of NCLB, the House and Senate committees were unable to formally introduce reauthorization legislation. Thus, the programs were extended for the second time until March 2009.

AAP expected to see action toward reauthorization to begin early in the new Congress.

# Funding Programs and Grant-Making Agencies

## National Endowment for the Humanities

1100 Pennsylvania Ave. N.W., Washington, DC 20506
800-634-1121 or 202-606-8400
TDD (hearing impaired) 202-606-8282 or 866-372-2930 (toll free)
E-mail Info@neh.gov, World Wide Web http://www.neh.gov

The National Endowment for the Humanities (NEH) is an independent federal agency created in 1965. It is the largest funder of humanities programs in the United States.

Because democracy demands wisdom, NEH promotes excellence in the humanities and conveys the lessons of history to all Americans, seeking to develop educated and thoughtful citizens. It accomplishes this mission by providing grants for high-quality humanities projects in six funding areas: education, preservation and access, public programs, research, challenge grants, and digital humanities.

NEH grants enrich classroom learning, create and preserve knowledge, and bring ideas to life through television, radio, new technologies, museum exhibitions, and programs in libraries and other community places. Recipients typically are cultural institutions, such as museums, archives, libraries, colleges, universities, public television and radio stations, and individual scholars. The grants

- Strengthen teaching and learning in the humanities in schools and colleges
- Preserve and provide access to cultural and educational resources
- Provide opportunities for lifelong learning
- Facilitate research and original scholarship
- Strengthen the institutional base of the humanities

Over the past 40 years NEH has reached millions of Americans with projects and programs that preserve and study the nation's culture and history while providing a foundation for the future.

The endowment's mission is to enrich American cultural life by promoting the study of the humanities. According to the National Foundation on the Arts and the Humanities Act,

> The term "humanities" includes, but is not limited to, the study of the following: language, both modern and classical; linguistics; literature; history; jurisprudence; philosophy; archaeology; comparative religion; ethics; the history, criticism, and theory of the arts; those aspects of social sciences which have humanistic content and employ humanistic methods; and the study and application of the humanities to the human environment with particular attention to reflecting our diverse heritage, traditions, and history, and to the relevance of the humanities to the current conditions of national life.

The act, adopted by Congress 44 years ago, provided for the establishment of the National Foundation on the Arts and the Humanities in order to promote progress and scholarship in the humanities and the arts in the United States. The act included the following findings:

- The arts and the humanities belong to all the people of the United States.
- The encouragement and support of national progress and scholarship in the humanities and the arts, while primarily matters for private and local initiative, are also appropriate matters of concern to the federal government.
- An advanced civilization must not limit its efforts to science and technology alone, but must give full value and support to the other great branches of scholarly and cultural activity in order to achieve a better understanding of the past, a better analysis of the present, and a better view of the future.
- Democracy demands wisdom and vision in its citizens. It must therefore foster and support a form of education, and access to the arts and the humanities, designed to make people of all backgrounds and locations masters of technology and not its unthinking servants.
- It is necessary and appropriate for the federal government to complement, assist, and add to programs for the advancement of the humanities and the arts by local, state, regional, and private agencies and their organizations. In doing so, the government must be sensitive to the nature of public sponsorship. Public funding of the arts and humanities is subject to the conditions that traditionally govern the use of public money. Such funding should contribute to public support and confidence in the use of taxpayer funds. Public funds provided by the federal government ultimately must serve public purposes the Congress defines.
- The arts and the humanities reflect the high place accorded by the American people to the nation's rich culture and history and to the fostering of mutual respect for the diverse beliefs and values of all persons and groups.

## What NEH Grants Accomplish

Since its founding, NEH has awarded more than 65,875 competitive grants.

## Interpretive Exhibitions

Interpretive exhibitions provide opportunities for lifelong learning in the humanities for millions of Americans. Since 1967 the endowment has awarded nearly $250 million in grants for interpretive exhibitions, catalogs, and public programs, which are among the most highly visible activities supported by the agency. During 2009, more than 20 reading, viewing, and discussion programs, exhibitions, Web-based programs, and other public education programs will employ various delivery mechanisms at venues across the nation.

## Renewing Teaching

Over the years more than 70,000 high school and college teachers have deepened their knowledge of the humanities through intensive summer study supported by NEH; tens of thousands of students benefit from these better-educated teachers every year.

## Reading and Discussion Programs

Since 1982 the endowment has supported reading and discussion programs in the nation's libraries, bringing people together to discuss works of literature and history. Scholars in the humanities provide thematic direction for the discussion programs. Using selected texts and themes such as "Work," "Family," "Diversity," and "Not for Children Only," these programs have attracted more than 2 million Americans to read and talk about what they've read.

## Preserving the Nation's Heritage

NEH has launched an innovative program, the National Digital Newspaper Program, which is supporting projects to convert microfilm of historically important U.S. newspapers into fully searchable digital files and to mount these files on the Internet. Developed in partnership with the Library of Congress, this complex, long-term project ultimately will make more than 30 million pages of newspapers accessible online.

## Stimulating Private Support

More than $1.6 billion in humanities support has been generated by the NEH Challenge Grants program, which requires most grant recipients to raise $3 in nonfederal funds for every dollar they receive.

## Presidential Papers

Ten presidential papers projects have received support from the endowment, from Washington to Eisenhower. Matching grants for the ten projects have leveraged $7.6 million in nonfederal contributions.

## New Scholarship

NEH grants enable scholars to do in-depth study: Jack Rakove explored the making of the Constitution in his *Original Meanings* and James McPherson chronicled the Civil War in his *Battle Cry of Freedom.* Both won the Pulitzer Prize, as have 13 other recipients of NEH grants.

## History on Screen

Since 1967 the endowment has awarded nearly $274 million to support the production of films for broad public distribution, including the Emmy Award-winning series *The Civil War,* the Oscar-nominated films *Brooklyn Bridge, The Restless Conscience,* and *Freedom on My Mind,* and film biographies of John and Abigail Adams, Eugene O'Neill, and Ernest Hemingway. These films help Americans learn about the events and people that shaped the nation. Recently, two NEH-funded documentary films on World War II, *The Rape of Europa* and the Ken Burns series *The War,* received critical acclaim. *The Rape of Europa* tells the epic story of the systematic theft, deliberate destruction, and, in some cases, miraculous survival of Europe's art treasures during the war, and the seven-episode series *The War* details the experiences of American soldiers and their families through eyewitness testimony.

## Library of America

Millions of books have been sold as part of the Library of America series, a collection of the riches of the nation's literature. Begun with NEH seed money, the more than 170 published volumes include works by Henry Adams, Edith Wharton, William James, Eudora Welty, W. E. B. DuBois, and many others.

The Library of America also received a $150,000 grant for the publication of *American Poetry: The Seventeenth and Eighteenth Centuries* (two volumes) and an expanded volume of selected works by Captain John Smith—a key figure in the establishment of the first permanent English settlement in North America, at Jamestown, Virginia—and other early American narratives.

## Science and the Humanities

The scientific past is being preserved with NEH-supported editions of the letters of Charles Darwin, the works of Albert Einstein, and the 14-volume papers of Thomas A. Edison. Additionally, NEH and the National Science Foundation (NSF) have joined forces on Documenting Endangered Languages (DEL), a multiyear effort to preserve records of key languages before they become extinct.

## Learning Under the Tent

Across the country, state humanities councils bring a 21st-century version of Chautauqua to the public, embracing populations of entire towns, cities, even regions. Scholars portray significant figures such as Meriwether Lewis, Sojourner Truth, Willa Cather, Teddy Roosevelt, and Sacagawea, first speaking as the historic character and then giving audiences the opportunity to ask questions. The give-and-take between the scholar/performer and the audiences provides an entertaining, energetic, and thought-provoking exchange about experiences and attitudes in the present and the past.

## Special Initiatives

### We the People

We the People is a program launched by NEH to encourage the teaching, study, and understanding of American history and culture. Under this program, the endowment invites scholars, teachers, filmmakers, curators, librarians, and others to submit grant applications that explore significant events and themes in the nation's history and culture and that advance knowledge of the principles that define the United States. Since its inception in 2002, We the People has provided support to more than 1,700 projects.

Proposals responding to the initiative can take the form of

- New scholarship
- Projects to preserve and provide access to documents and artifacts significant to the national heritage
- Professional development programs for teachers and educators at every level, from kindergarten through college
- Public programs in libraries, museums, and historical societies, including exhibitions, film, radio, and Internet-based programs

NEH will accept We the People proposals in all programs and at all deadlines. Proposals are expected to meet the guidelines of the program that best fits the character of the project. A list of programs and deadlines is available on the NEH Web site, http://www.neh.gov.

Proposals will be evaluated through the endowment's established review process and will not receive special consideration. The chairman of NEH reserves the right to determine which grants will be designated as We the People projects.

The main components of We the People are

- A call for applications to the NEH for projects designed to explore significant events and themes in the nation's history
- Landmarks of American History and Culture workshops for K–12 teachers and community college faculty at important historical sites
- Interpreting America's Historic Places grants to enhance opportunities for local residents and the traveling public to learn more about American history and culture
- The National Digital Newspaper Program, which supports projects to digitize historically important U.S. newspapers and to make these files available on the Internet
- Picturing America, a program to provide schools and teachers with high-quality poster reproductions of some of the nation's greatest art, along with materials that help educators incorporate these art works into their teaching of history, literature, art history, and architecture
- The We the People Bookshelf, a set of classic books for young readers on significant American themes to be awarded to schools and libraries for use in local programs

## Picturing America

In February 2008 NEH launched Picturing America, an initiative designed to promote the teaching, study, and understanding of American history and its culture in K–12 schools and public libraries. Part of the We the People program, Picturing America is a free resource that provides an innovative way for people of all ages to explore the history and character of the United States through some of the nation's greatest works of art, including Emanuel Leutze's *Washington Crossing the Delaware* and Norman Rockwell's *Freedom of Speech.*

Picturing America features 40 high-quality reproductions (24 by 36 inches) of American art, an illustrated teachers resource book, and a comprehensive Web site, http://picturingamerica.neh.gov, with additional information about the artwork and the artists.

As of early 2009, more than 76,000 schools, public libraries, and Head Start centers nationwide had taken advantage of this educational resource.

## EDSITEment

NEH's EDSITEment Web site, http://www.edsitement.neh.gov, offers a selection of quality humanities resources on the Web, and draws more than 400,000 visitors every month. Incorporating these Internet resources, particularly primary documents, from more than 200 peer-reviewed Web sites, EDSITEment features 400-plus online lesson plans in all areas of the humanities. Educators use EDSITEment's digital resources to enhance their teaching and to engage students through interactive technology tools that hone critical-thinking skills.

# Federal-State Partnership

The NEH Office of Federal-State Partnership links the endowment with the nationwide network of 56 humanities councils, which are located in each state, the District of Columbia, Puerto Rico, the U.S. Virgin Islands, the Northern Mariana Islands, American Samoa, and Guam. Each humanities council funds humanities programs in its own jurisdiction.

### Directory of State Humanities Councils

#### Alabama

Alabama Humanities Foundation
1100 Ireland Way, Suite 101
Birmingham, AL 35205-7001
205-558-3980, fax 205-558-3981
http://www.ahf.net

#### Alaska

Alaska Humanities Forum
421 W. First Ave., Suite 300
Anchorage, AK 99501
907-272-5341, fax 907-272-3979
http://www.akhf.org

#### Arizona

Arizona Humanities Council
Ellis-Shackelford House
1242 N. Central Ave.
Phoenix, AZ 85004-1887
602-257-0335, fax 602-257-0392
http://www.azhumanities.org

#### Arkansas

Arkansas Humanities Council
10800 Financial Centre Pkwy., Suite 465
Little Rock, AR 72211

501-221-0091, fax 501-221-9860
http://www.arkhums.org

## California

California Council for the Humanities
312 Sutter St., Suite 601
San Francisco, CA 94108
415-391-1474, fax 415-391-1312
http://www.calhum.org

## Colorado

Colorado Humanities
1490 Lafayette St., Suite 101
Denver, CO 80218
303-894-7951, fax 303-864-9361
http://www.coloradohumanities.org

## Connecticut

Connecticut Humanities Council
37 Broad St.
Middletown, CT 06457
860-685-2260, fax 860-704-0429
http://www.ctculture.org

## Delaware

Delaware Humanities Forum
100 W. Tenth St., Suite 1009
Wilmington, DE 19801
302-657-0650, fax 302-657-0655
http://www.dhf.org

## District of Columbia

Humanities Council of Washington, D.C.
925 U St. N.W.
Washington, DC 20001
202-387-8393, fax 202-387-8149
http://wdchumanities.org

## Florida

Florida Humanities Council
599 Second St. S.
St. Petersburg, FL 33701-5005
727-873-2000, fax 727-873-2014
http://www.flahum.org

## Georgia

Georgia Humanities Council

50 Hurt Plaza S.E., Suite 595
Atlanta, GA 30303-2915
404-523-6220, fax 404-523-5702
http://www.georgiahumanities.org

## Hawaii

Hawaii Council for the Humanities
First Hawaiian Bank Bldg.
3599 Waialae Ave., Room 25
Honolulu, HI 96816
808-732-5402, fax 808-732-5432
http://www.hihumanities.org

## Idaho

Idaho Humanities Council
217 W. State St.
Boise, ID 83702
208-345-5346, fax 208-345-5347
http://www.idahohumanities.org

## Illinois

Illinois Humanities Council
17 N. State St., No. 1400
Chicago, IL 60602-3296
312-422-5580, fax 312-422-5588
http://www.prairie.org

## Indiana

Indiana Humanities Council
1500 N. Delaware St.
Indianapolis, IN 46202
317-638-1500, fax 317-634-9503
http://www.indianahumanities.org

## Iowa

Humanities Iowa
100 Oakdale Campus N310 OH
University of Iowa
Iowa City, IA 52242-5000
319-335-4153, fax 319-335-4154
http://www.humanitiesiowa.org

## Kansas

Kansas Humanities Council
112 S.W. Sixth Ave., Suite 210
Topeka, KS 66603
785-357-0359, fax 785-357-1723
http://www.kansashumanities.org

## Kentucky

Kentucky Humanities Council
206 E. Maxwell St.
Lexington, KY 40508
859-257-5932, fax 859-257-5933
http://www.kyhumanities.org

## Louisiana

Louisiana Endowment for the Humanities
938 Lafayette St., Suite 300
New Orleans, LA 70113-1027
504-523-4352, fax 504-529-2358
http://www.leh.org

## Maine

Maine Humanities Council
674 Brighton Ave.
Portland, ME 04102-1012
207-773-5051, fax 207-773-2416
http://www.mainehumanities.org

## Maryland

Maryland Humanities Council
108 W. Centre St.
Baltimore, MD 21201-4565
410-685-0095, fax 410-685-0795
http://www.mdhc.org

## Massachusetts

Mass Humanities
66 Bridge St.
Northampton, MA 01060
413-584-8440, fax 413-584-8454
http://www.masshumanities.org

## Michigan

Michigan Humanities Council
119 Pere Marquette Drive, Suite 3B
Lansing, MI 48912-1270
517-372-7770, fax 517-372-0027
http://michiganhumanities.org

## Minnesota

Minnesota Humanities Center
987 E. Ivy Ave.
St. Paul, MN 55106-2046
651-774-0105, fax 651-774-0205
http://www.minnesotahumanities.org

## Mississippi

Mississippi Humanities Council
3825 Ridgewood Rd., Room 311
Jackson, MS 39211
601-432-6752, fax 601-432-6750
http://www.mshumanities.org

## Missouri

Missouri Humanities Council
543 Hanley Industrial Court, Suite 201
St. Louis, MO 63144-1905
314-781-9660, fax 314-781-9681
http://www.mohumanities.org

## Montana

Humanities Montana
311 Brantly
Missoula, MT 59812-7848
406-243-6022, fax 406-243-4836
http://www.humanitiesmontana.org

## Nebraska

Nebraska Humanities Council
Lincoln Center Bldg., Suite 500
215 Centennial Mall South
Lincoln, NE 68508
402-474-2131, fax 402-474-4852
http://www.nebraskahumanties.org

## Nevada

Nevada Humanities
1034 N. Sierra St.
Reno, NV 89507
775-784-6587, fax 775-784-6527
http://www.nevadahumanities.org

## New Hampshire

New Hampshire Humanities Council
19 Pillsbury St.
Concord, NH 03302-2228
603-224-4071, fax 603-224-4072
http://www.nhhc.org

## New Jersey

New Jersey Council for the Humanities
28 W. State St.
Trenton, NJ 08608

609-695-4838, fax 609-695-4929
http://www.njch.org

## New Mexico

New Mexico Humanities Council
MSC06 3570
1 University of New Mexico
Albuquerque, NM 87131-0001
505-277-3705, fax 505-277-6056
http://www.nmhum.org

## New York

New York Council for the Humanities
150 Broadway, Suite 1700
New York, NY 10038
212-233-1131, fax 212-233-4607
http://www.nyhumanities.org

## North Carolina

North Carolina Humanities Council
200 S. Elm St., Suite 403
Greensboro, NC 27401
336-334-5325, fax 336-334-5052
http://www.nchumanities.org

## North Dakota

North Dakota Humanities Council
418 E. Broadway, Suite 8
P.O. Box 2191
Bismarck, ND 58502
701-255-3360, fax 701-223-8724
http://www.nd-humanities.org

## Ohio

Ohio Humanities Council
471 E. Broad St., Suite 1620
Columbus, OH 43215-3857
614-461-7802, fax 614-461-4651
http://www.ohiohumanities.org

## Oklahoma

Oklahoma Humanities Council
Festival Plaza
428 W. California, Suite 270
Oklahoma City, OK 73102
405-235-0280, fax 405-235-0289
http://www.okhumanitiescouncil.org

## Oregon

Oregon Council for the Humanities
813 S.W. Alder St., Suite 702
Portland, OR 97205
503-241-0543, fax 503-241-0024
http://www.oregonhum.org

## Pennsylvania

Pennsylvania Humanities Council
325 Chestnut St., Suite 715
Philadelphia, PA 19106-2607
215-925-1005, fax 215-925-3054
http://www.pahumanities.org

## Rhode Island

Rhode Island Council for the Humanities
385 Westminster St., Suite 2
Providence, RI 02903
401-273-2250, fax 401-454-4872
http://www.rihumanities.org

## South Carolina

Humanities Council of South Carolina
2711 Middleburg Drive, Suite 308
P.O. Box 5287
Columbia, SC 29254
803-771-2477, fax 803-771-2487
http://www.schumanities.org

## South Dakota

South Dakota Humanities Council
1215 Trail Ridge Rd., Suite A
Brookings, SD 57006
605-688-6113, fax 605-688-4531
http://web.sdstate.edu/humanities

## Tennessee

Humanities Tennessee
306 Gay St., Suite 306
Nashville, TN 37201
615-770-0006, fax 615-770-0007
http://www.humanitiestennessee.org

## Texas

Humanities Texas
1410 Rio Grande St.
Austin, TX 78701

512-440-1991, fax 512-440-0115
http://www.humanitiestexas.org

## Utah

Utah Humanities Council
202 W. 300 North
Salt Lake City, UT 84103
801-359-9670, fax 801-531-7869
http://www.utahhumanities.org

## Vermont

Vermont Humanities Council
11 Loomis St.
Montpelier, VT 05602
802-262-2626, fax 802-262-2620
http://www.vermonthumanities.org

## Virginia

Virginia Foundation for the Humanities and
   Public Policy
145 Ednam Dr.
Charlottesville, VA 22903-4629
434-924-3296, fax 434-296-4714
http://www.virginiafoundation.org

## Washington

Humanities Washington
1204 Minor Ave.
Seattle, WA 98101
206-682-1770, fax 206-682-4158
http://www.humanities.org

## West Virginia

West Virginia Humanities Council
1310 Kanawha Blvd. E.
Charleston, WV 25301
304-346-8500, fax 304-346-8504
http://www.wvhumanities.org

## Wisconsin

Wisconsin Humanities Council
222 S. Bedford St., Suite F
Madison, WI 53703-3688
608-262-0706, fax 608-263-7970
http://www.wisconsinhumanities.org

## Wyoming

Wyoming Humanities Council
1315 E. Lewis St.
Laramie, WY 82072-3459
307-721-9243, fax 307-742-4914
http://uwadmnweb.uwyo.edu/humanities

## American Samoa

Amerika Samoa Humanities Council
P.O. Box 5800
Pago Pago, AS 96799
684-633-4870, fax 684-633-4873

## Guam

Guam Humanities Council
222 Chalan Santo Papa
Reflection Center, Suite 106
Hagatna, Guam 96910
671-472-4460, fax 671-472-4465
http://www.guamhumanitiescouncil.org

## Northern Mariana Islands

Northern Mariana Islands Council for the
   Humanities
P.O. Box 506437
Saipan, MP 96950
670-235-4785, fax 670-235-4786
http://www.nmihumanities.org

## Puerto Rico

Fundación Puertorriqueña de las
   Humanidades
109 San Jose St.
Box 9023920
San Juan, PR 00902-3920
787-721-2087, fax 787-721-2684
http://www.fprh.org

## Virgin Islands

Virgin Islands Humanities Council
1826 Kongens Gade 5-6, Suite 2
St. Thomas, VI 00802-6746
340-776-4044, fax 340-774-3972
http://www.vihumanities.org

# NEH Overview

### Division of Education Programs

Through grants to educational institutions and professional development programs for scholars and teachers, this division is designed to support study of the humanities at all levels of education.

Grants support the development of curriculum and materials, faculty study programs among educational institutions, and conferences and networks of institutions.

| | |
|---|---|
| *Eligible applicants:* | Public and private elementary and secondary schools, school systems, colleges and universities, nonprofit academic associations, and cultural institutions, such as libraries and museums |
| *Application deadlines:* | Humanities Initiatives at Historically Black Colleges and Universities, Humanities Initiatives at Institutions with High Hispanic Enrollment, and Humanities Initiatives at Tribal Colleges and Universities, January 15, 2009; Picturing America School Collaboration Projects, October 1, 2009; Enduring Questions Course Grants, November 15, 2009 |
| *Contact:* | 202-606-8500, e-mail education@neh.gov |

## Seminars and Institutes

Grants support summer seminars and institutes in the humanities for college and school teachers. These faculty development activities are conducted at colleges and universities across the country, as well as at appropriate locations abroad. Those wishing to participate in seminars should submit their seminar applications to the seminar director.

| | |
|---|---|
| *Eligible applicants:* | Individuals and institutions of higher learning, as well as cultural institutions |
| *Application deadlines:* | Participants, March 2, 2009, for summer seminars and institutes in 2009; directors, March 2, 2009, for summer seminars and institutes in 2010 |

## Landmarks of American History and Culture

Grants for Landmarks workshops provide support to school teachers and to community college faculty. These professional development workshops are conducted at or near sites important to American history and culture (such as presidential residences or libraries, colonial-era settlements, major battlefields, historic districts, and sites associated with major writers or artists) to address central themes and issues in American history, government, literature, art history, and other related subjects in the humanities.

*Eligible applicants:* Individuals, institutions of higher learning, cultural institutions

*Application deadlines:* School teacher and community college faculty participants, March 16, 2009, for summer workshops in 2009; directors, March 16, 2009, for summer workshops in 2010

*Contact:* 202-606-8463, e-mail sem-inst@neh.gov

## Division of Preservation and Access

Grants are made for projects that will create, preserve, and increase the availability of resources important for research, education, and public programming in the humanities.

Projects may encompass books, journals, newspapers, manuscript and archival materials, maps, still and moving images, sound recordings, and objects of material culture held by libraries, archives, museums, historical organizations, and other repositories.

### Preservation and Access Projects

Support may be sought to preserve the intellectual content and aid bibliographic control of collections; to compile bibliographies, descriptive catalogs, and guides to cultural holdings; and to create dictionaries, encyclopedias, databases, and electronic archives. Applications may also be submitted for education and training projects dealing with issues of preservation or access; for research and development leading to improved preservation and access standards, practices, and tools; and for projects to digitize historic American newspapers and to document endangered languages. Grants are also made to help smaller cultural repositories preserve and care for their humanities collections.

Proposals may combine preservation and access activities within a single project.

*Eligible applicants:* Nonprofit institutions, cultural organizations, state agencies, and institutional consortia

*Application deadlines:* May 14, July 1, July 15, September 15, and November 4, 2009

*Contact:* 202-606-8570, e-mail preservation@neh.gov

## Division of Public Programs

Public humanities programs promote lifelong learning in American and world history, literature, comparative religion, philosophy, and other fields of the humanities. They offer new insights into familiar subjects and invite conversation about important humanities ideas and questions.

The Division of Public Programs supports a wide range of public humanities programs that reach large and diverse public audiences through a variety of program formats, including interpretive exhibitions, radio and television broadcasts, lectures, symposia, interpretive multimedia projects, printed materials, and reading and discussion programs.

Grants support the development and production of television, radio and digital media programs; the planning and implementation of museum exhibitions, the interpretation of historic sites, the production of related publications, multimedia components, and educational programs; and the planning and implementation of reading and discussion programs, lectures, symposia, and interpretive exhibitions of books, manuscripts, and other library resources.

*Eligible applicants:* Nonprofit institutions and organizations including public television and radio stations and state humanities councils

*Application deadlines:* Planning, implementation, development, production: August 26, 2009, and January 27, 2010

*Contact:* 202-606-8269, e-mail publicpgms@neh.gov

## Division of Research Programs

Through fellowships to individual scholars and grants to support complex and frequently collaborative research, the Division of Research Programs contributes to the creation of knowledge in the humanities.

### Fellowships and Stipends

Grants provide support for scholars to undertake full-time independent research and writing in the humanities. Grants are available for a maximum of one year and a minimum of two months of summer study.

*Eligible applicants:* Individuals

*Application deadlines:* Fellowships, May 5, 2009; Fellowships at Digital Humanities Centers, September 16, 2009; Teaching Development Fellowships, October 1, 2009; Summer Stipends, October 1, 2009

*Contact:* 202-606-8200, e-mail (fellowships) fellowships@neh.gov, (summer stipends) stipends@neh.gov

### Research

Grants provide up to three years of support for collaborative research in the preparation for publication of editions, translations, and other important works in the humanities, and in the conduct of large or complex interpretive studies including archaeology projects and humanities studies of science and technology. Grants also support research opportunities offered through independent research centers and international research organizations.

*Eligible applicants:* Individuals, institutions of higher education, nonprofit professional associations, scholarly societies, and other nonprofit organizations

*Application deadlines:* Collaborative Research and Scholarly Editions, October 28, 2009; fellowship programs at independent research institutions, August 19, 2009

*Contact:* 202-606-8200, e-mail research@neh.gov

## Office of Challenge Grants

Nonprofit institutions interested in developing new sources of long-term support for educational, scholarly, preservation, and public programs in the humanities can be assisted in these efforts by an NEH Challenge Grant. Grantees are required to raise $3 in nonfederal donations for every federal dollar offered. Both federal and nonfederal funds may be used to establish or increase institutional endowments and therefore guarantee long-term support for a variety of humanities needs. Funds also may be used for limited direct capital expenditures where such needs are compelling and clearly related to improvements in the humanities.

> *Eligible applicants:*        Nonprofit postsecondary, educational, research, or cultural institutions and organizations working within the humanities.
>
> *Application deadlines:*      Challenge Grants, May 5, 2009; We the People Challenge Grants, February 3, 2009
>
> *Contact:*                   202-606-8309, e-mail challenge@neh.gov

## Office of Digital Humanities

The NEH Office of Digital Humanities (ODH) encourages and supports projects that utilize or study the impact of digital technology on research, education, preservation, and public programming in the humanities. Launched as an initiative in 2006, Digital Humanities was made a permanent NEH office in 2008.

The endowment is interested in fostering the growth of digital humanities and lending support to a wide variety of projects, including those that deploy digital technologies and methods to enhance understanding of a topic or issue; those that study the impact of digital technology on the humanities; and those that digitize important materials, thereby increasing the public's ability to search and access humanities information.

ODH coordinates the endowment's efforts in the area of digital scholarship. Currently NEH has numerous programs throughout the agency that are actively funding digital scholarship, including Humanities Collections and Resources, Institutes for Advanced Topics in the Digital Humanities, Digital Humanities Challenge Grants, Digital Humanities Start-Up Grants, and many others. The endowment is also actively working with other funding partners, both within the United States and abroad, to better coordinate spending on digital infrastructure for the humanities.

> *Eligible applicants:*        Nonprofit postsecondary, educational, research, or cultural institutions and organizations working within the humanities
>
> *Application deadlines:*      Digital Humanities Start-Up Grants, April 8, 2009; Institutes for Advanced Topics in the Digital Humanities, February 18, 2009
>
> *Contact:*                   202-606-8401, e-mail odh@neh.gov

# Institute of Museum and Library Services Library Programs

1800 M St. N.W., Ninth Floor, Washington, DC 20036-5802
202-653-4657, fax 202-653-4625
World Wide Web http://www.imls.gov

Anne-Imelda M. Radice
Director, IMLS

Mary L. Chute
Deputy Director for Libraries

## Mission

The Institute of Museum and Library Services (IMLS) is the primary source of federal support for the nation's 122,000 libraries and 17,500 museums. The institute's mission is to create strong libraries and museums that connect people to information and ideas. The institute works at the national level and in coordination with state and local organizations to sustain heritage, culture, and knowledge; enhance learning and innovation; and support professional development.

## Overview

Libraries and museums help create vibrant, energized learning communities. Our achievement as individuals and our success as a democratic society depend on learning continually, adapting to change readily, and evaluating information critically.

As stewards of cultural heritage, information, and ideas, museums and libraries traditionally have played a vital role in helping us experience, explore, discover, and make sense of the world. That role is now more essential than ever. Through building technological infrastructure and strengthening community relationships, libraries and museums can offer the public unprecedented access and expertise in transforming information overload into knowledge.

The institute's role is to provide leadership and funding for the nation's museums and libraries, resources these institutions need to fulfill their mission of becoming centers of learning for life crucial to achieving personal fulfillment, a productive work force, and an engaged citizenry.

Specifically, the Museum and Library Services Act authorizes IMLS to support the following activities:

### Library Services and Technology Act (LSTA)

- To promote improvements in library services in all types of libraries to better serve the people of the United States

- To facilitate access to resources and in all types of libraries for the purpose of cultivating an educated and informed citizenry
- To encourage resource sharing among all types of libraries for the purpose of achieving economical and efficient delivery of library services to the public

## Museum Services Act

- To encourage and support museums in carrying out their public service role of connecting the whole society to cultural, artistic, historic, natural, and scientific understandings that constitute our heritage
- To encourage and support museums in carrying out their educational role as core providers of learning and in conjunction with schools, families, and communities
- To encourage leadership, innovation, and applications of the most current technologies and practices to enhance museum services
- To assist, encourage, and support museums in carrying out their stewardship responsibilities to achieve the highest standards in conservation and care of the cultural, historic, natural, and scientific heritage of the United States to benefit future generations
- To assist, encourage, and support museums in achieving the highest standards of management and service to the public, and to ease the financial burden borne by museums as a result of their increasing use by the public
- To support resource sharing and partnerships among museums, libraries, schools, and other community organizations

In fiscal year (FY) 2008, Congress appropriated $212,058,400 for the programs and administrative support authorized by LSTA. The Office of Library Services within IMLS, under the policy direction of the IMLS director and deputy director, administers LSTA programs. The office comprises the Division of State Programs, which administers the Grants to States program, and the Division of Discretionary Programs, which administers the National Leadership Grants for Libraries program, the Laura Bush 21st Century Librarian program, the Native American Library Services program, and the Native Hawaiian Library Services program. IMLS also presents annual awards to libraries through the National Medal for Museum and Library Service program. Additionally, IMLS is one of the sponsoring organizations supporting the Coming Up Taller awards (in conjunction with the President's Committee on the Arts and the Humanities, the National Endowment for the Arts [NEA], and the National Endowment for the Humanities); the Big Read program (in partnership with NEA); and Save America's Treasures (in partnership with the National Park Service, the National Trust for Historic Preservation, Heritage Preservation, NEA, and the National Park Foundation).

## Impact of Museum and Library Services

A general provision of the Museum and Library Services Act states that "the Director shall carry out and publish analyses of the impact of museum and library services. Such analyses

- Shall be conducted in ongoing consultation with state library administrative agencies; state, regional, and national library and museum organizations; and other relevant agencies and organizations
- Shall identify national needs for, and trends of, museum and library services provided with funds made available under subchapters II and III of this chapter
- Shall report on the impact and effectiveness of programs conducted with funds made available by the Institute in addressing such needs
- Shall identify, and disseminate information on, the best practices of such programs to the agencies and entities described."

## Library Statistics

The president's budget request for FY 2008 included funds for IMLS to continue administering the Public Libraries Survey and the State Library Agencies Survey, effective October 1, 2007. From their inception in 1989 through 2007, these two surveys were administered by the National Center for Education Statistics (NCES). NCES and IMLS have been working cooperatively to implement this policy. Current, accurate, and ongoing collection of library data is an essential foundation for quality library services, and IMLS is committed to the continued excellence of this program. [NCES continues to conduct the Academic Libraries Survey and the School Library Media Center Survey. For details, see "National Center for Education Statistics" in Part 1—*Ed.*]

In the Library Statistics section of the IMLS Web site (http://www.imls.gov/statistics), visitors can link to data search tools, the latest available data for each survey, other publications, data files, and survey definitions.

### Public Libraries Survey

Descriptive statistics for more than 9,000 public libraries are collected and disseminated annually through a voluntary census, the Public Libraries Survey (PLS). The survey is conducted through the Public Library Statistics Cooperative (PLSC, formerly FSCS). In FY 2009 IMLS will complete the 20th collection of this data.

PLS collects identifying information about public libraries and each of their service outlets, including address, telephone number, and Internet address. The survey collects data about public libraries, including data on staffing; type of legal basis; type of geographic boundary; type of administrative structure; type of interlibrary relationship; type and number of public service outlets; operating revenue and expenditures; capital revenue and expenditures; size of collection (including number of electronic books and databases); current serial subscriptions (including electronic); and such service measures as number of reference transactions, interlibrary loans, circulation, public service hours, library visits, circulation of children's materials, number of children's programs, children's program attendance, total number of library programs, total attendance at library programs, number of Internet terminals used by the general public, and number of users of electronic resources per year.

This survey also collects several data items about outlets, including the location of an outlet relative to a metropolitan area, number of books-by-mail-only outlets, number of bookmobiles by bookmobile outlet, and square footage of the outlet.

The 50 states and the District of Columbia participate in data collection. Beginning in 1993 the outlying areas of Guam, the Commonwealth of the Northern Mariana Islands, Puerto Rico, and the U.S. Virgin Islands joined in the survey. The first release of Public Libraries Survey data occurs with the release of the updated Compare Public Libraries Tool on the Library Statistics section of the IMLS Web site (http://www.imls.gov/statistics). The data used in this Web tool are final, but do not include imputations for missing data (imputation is a statistical means for providing an estimate for each missing data item).

Final imputed data files that contain FY 2006 data on more than 9,000 responding libraries and identifying information about their outlets were made available in November 2008 on the Library Statistics section of the IMLS Web site. The FY 2006 data were aggregated to state and national levels in a report, *Public Libraries Survey: Fiscal Year 2006,* and released in December 2008 on the Web site.

The Compare Public Libraries Tool and the Find Public Libraries Tool have been updated with FY 2006 data. FY 2007 data were expected to be available on these tools in spring 2009.

Continuing in FY 2009 with the FY 2007 data collection cycle, descriptive data on public libraries are collected via a Web-based data collection application called WebPLUS; this began in FY 2005. The resulting universe file has been a resource for use in drawing samples for special surveys on such topics as literacy, access for the disabled, and library construction. At the state level and in the outlying areas, data coordinators appointed by each state or outlying area's chief officer of the state library agency administer the PLSC, which is a working network. State data coordinators collect the requested data from public libraries and submit these data to IMLS, which aggregates the data to provide state and national totals. An annual training conference is provided for the state data coordinators, and the new IMLS Library Statistics Working Group (LSWG) that represents them is active in the development of the Public Libraries Survey and its Web-based data collection. Technical assistance to states is provided by state data coordinator mentors, by the Bureau of the Census, and by IMLS. The institute also works cooperatively with the Bureau of the Census, the Chief Officers of State Library Agencies (COSLA), and the American Library Association (ALA).

**State Library Agencies Survey**

The State Library Agencies Survey collects and disseminates information about the state library agencies in the 50 states and the District of Columbia. A state library agency (StLA) is the official unit of state government charged with statewide library development and the administration of federal funds under LSTA. StLAs' administrative and developmental responsibilities affect the operation of thousands of public, academic, school, and special libraries. StLAs provide important reference and information services to state government and sometimes also provide service to the general public. StLAs often administer state library and special operations such as state archives and libraries for the blind and physically handicapped and the state Center for the Book.

The State Library Agencies Survey began in 1994 and was administered by NCES until 2007. The FY 2007 StLA Survey collected data on the following areas: direct library services; adult literacy and family literacy; library development services; resources assigned to allied operations such as archive and records management; organizational and governance structure within which the agency operates; electronic networking; staffing; collections; and expenditures. The FY 2007 survey was the 14th in the StLA series. These data are edited electronically, and before FY 1999 missing data were not imputed. Beginning with FY 1999 data, however, national totals included imputations for missing data. Another change is that beginning with FY 1999 data, the StLA became a Web-based data collection system. The most recent data available are for FY 2007. The survey database and report were released in November 2008. [For sample findings of the Public Libraries Survey and the State Library Agencies Survey, see "Highlights of NCES and IMLS Surveys" in Part 4—*Ed.*]

# National Medal for Museum and Library Service

The National Medal for Museum and Library Service honors outstanding institutions that make significant and exceptional contributions to their communities. Selected institutions demonstrate extraordinary and innovative approaches to public service, exceeding the expected levels of community outreach and core programs generally associated with their services. The medal includes a prize of $10,000 for each recipient and an awards ceremony held in Washington, D.C.

The winners of the 2008 National Medal for Museum and Library Service were:

- Buffalo Bill Historical Center, Cody, Wyoming
- The Franklin Institute, Philadelphia
- General Lew Wallace Study and Museum, Crawfordsville, Indiana
- Jane Stern Dorado Community Library, Dorado, Puerto Rico
- Kansas City (Missouri) Public Library
- Lower East Side Tenement Museum, New York City
- Miami-Dade Public Library System, Florida
- Norton Museum of Art, West Palm Beach, Florida
- Skidompha Public Library, Damariscotta, Maine
- Skokie (Illinois) Public Library

## State-Administered Programs

In FY 2008 approximately 80 percent of the annual federal appropriation under LSTA was distributed through the Grants to States program to the State Library Administrative Agencies (SLAAs) according to a population-based formula. The formula consists of a minimum amount set by law plus a supplemental amount based on population. Population data were based on the information available from the Bureau of Census Web site on October 1, 2007. The 2003 reauthorization requires that base allotments of $340,000 to the states and $40,000 to the Pacific Territories be increased to $680,000 for the states and $60,000 for the Pacific Territories if IMLS is fully funded. The new base allotments will be phased in gradually as the total appropriation increases. For FY 2008 the adjusted base allotment to the states was $540,968; that for the Pacific Territories remained at $40,000.

For FY 2008 the Grants to States program total appropriation was $160,885,357 (see Table 1). State agencies may use the appropriation for statewide initiatives and services. They may also distribute the funds through competitive subgrants or cooperative agreements to public, academic, research, school, or special libraries. For-profit and federal libraries are not eligible applicants. LSTA state grant funds have been used to meet the special needs of children, parents, teenagers, the unemployed, senior citizens, the business community, and adult learners. Many libraries have partnered with community organizations to provide a variety of services and programs, including access to electronic databases, computer instruction, homework centers, summer reading programs, digitization of special collections, access to e-books and adaptive technology, bookmobile service, and development of outreach programs to the underserved. The act limits the amount of funds available for administration at the state level to 4 percent and requires a 34 percent match from nonfederal state or local funds.

Grants to the Pacific Territories and the Freely Associated States (FAS) are funded under a Special Rule, 20 USCA 9131(b)(3), which authorizes a small competitive grants program in the Pacific and the U.S. Virgin Islands. There are seven eligible entities: Guam (GU), American Samoa (AS), the Commonwealth of Northern Mariana Islands (CNMI), the Federated States of Micronesia (FSM), the Republic of the Marshall Islands (RMI), the Republic of Palau (PU), and the U.S. Virgin Islands (VI). The funds for this grant program are taken from the allotment amounts for the FAS (FSM, RMI, and PU). The territories (GU, AS, CNMI, VI) receive their allotments through the Grants to States program and, in addition, may apply for funds under the competitive program. In FY 2008 a total of $203,040 was available for the seven entities. This amount included a set-aside of 5 percent for Pacific Resources for Education and Learning (PREL), based in Hawaii, to facilitate the grants review process. Therefore, the total amount awarded in FY 2008 was $192,888.

The LSTA-funded programs and services delivered by each SLAA support the purposes and priorities set forth in legislation. The individual SLAAs set goals and objectives for the expenditure of Grants to States funds within the statutorily

*(text continues on page 324)*

Table 1 / Library Services and Technology Act, State Allotment Table, FY 2008
Total Distributed to States: $160,885,357[1]

| State | Federal Funds from IMLS (66%)[2] | State Matching Funds (34%) | Total Federal and State Funds |
|---|---|---|---|
| Alabama | $2,545,491 | $1,311,314 | $3,856,805 |
| Alaska | 833,016 | 429,129 | 1,262,145 |
| Arizona | 3,228,606 | 1,663,221 | 4,891,827 |
| Arkansas | 1,766,109 | 909,814 | 2,675,923 |
| California | 16,431,277 | 8,464,597 | 24,895,874 |
| Colorado | 2,612,765 | 1,345,970 | 3,958,735 |
| Connecticut | 2,068,566 | 1,065,625 | 3,134,191 |
| Delaware | 912,962 | 470,314 | 1,383,276 |
| Florida | 8,425,588 | 4,340,454 | 12,766,042 |
| Georgia | 4,622,315 | 2,381,193 | 7,003,508 |
| Hawaii | 1,101,262 | 567,317 | 1,668,579 |
| Idaho | 1,180,138 | 607,950 | 1,788,088 |
| Illinois | 6,133,883 | 3,159,879 | 9,293,762 |
| Indiana | 3,292,765 | 1,696,273 | 4,989,038 |
| Iowa | 1,840,733 | 948,256 | 2,788,989 |
| Kansas | 1,745,712 | 899,306 | 2,645,018 |
| Kentucky | 2,374,218 | 1,223,082 | 3,597,300 |
| Louisiana | 2,409,825 | 1,241,425 | 3,651,250 |
| Maine | 1,116,986 | 575,417 | 1,692,403 |
| Maryland | 2,988,627 | 1,539,596 | 4,528,223 |
| Massachusetts | 3,346,669 | 1,724,042 | 5,070,711 |
| Michigan | 4,941,233 | 2,545,484 | 7,486,717 |
| Minnesota | 2,793,089 | 1,438,864 | 4,231,953 |
| Mississippi | 1,809,550 | 932,192 | 2,741,742 |
| Missouri | 3,087,560 | 1,590,561 | 4,678,121 |
| Montana | 952,693 | 490,781 | 1,443,474 |
| Nebraska | 1,311,709 | 675,729 | 1,987,438 |
| Nevada | 1,628,664 | 839,009 | 2,467,673 |
| New Hampshire | 1,114,075 | 573,917 | 1,687,992 |
| New Jersey | 4,343,636 | 2,237,631 | 6,581,267 |
| New Mexico | 1,392,895 | 717,552 | 2,110,447 |
| New York | 8,955,719 | 4,613,552 | 13,569,271 |
| North Carolina | 4,401,145 | 2,267,257 | 6,668,402 |
| North Dakota | 818,116 | 421,454 | 1,239,570 |
| Ohio | 5,543,747 | 2,855,870 | 8,399,617 |
| Oklahoma | 2,100,996 | 1,082,331 | 3,183,327 |
| Oregon | 2,153,972 | 1,109,622 | 3,263,594 |
| Pennsylvania | 5,963,310 | 3,072,008 | 9,035,318 |
| Rhode Island | 1,006,294 | 518,394 | 1,524,688 |
| South Carolina | 2,424,418 | 1,248,943 | 3,673,361 |
| South Dakota | 881,774 | 454,247 | 1,336,021 |
| Tennessee | 3,173,028 | 1,634,590 | 4,807,618 |
| Texas | 10,787,020 | 5,556,950 | 16,343,970 |
| Utah | 1,652,433 | 851,253 | 2,503,686 |
| Vermont | 812,903 | 418,768 | 1,231,671 |
| Virginia | 3,872,179 | 1,994,759 | 5,866,938 |
| Washington | 3,328,627 | 1,714,747 | 5,043,374 |

**Table 1 / Library Services and Technology Act, State Allotment Table, FY 2008** *(cont.)*

| West Virginia | 1,333,562 | 686,986 | 2,020,548 |
|---|---|---|---|
| Wisconsin | 2,962,815 | 1,526,299 | 4,489,114 |
| Wyoming | 765,437 | 394,316 | 1,159,753 |
| District of Columbia | 794,432 | 409,253 | 1,203,685 |
| Puerto Rico | 2,252,920 | 1,160,595 | 3,413,515 |
| American Samoa | 65,133 | 33,553 | 98,686 |
| Northern Marianas | 76,850 | 39,589 | 116,439 |
| Guam | 115,602 | 59,553 | 175,155 |
| Virgin Islands | 87,268 | 44,956 | 132,224 |
| Pacific Territories[3] | 203,040 | 104,596 | 307,636 |
| Total | $160,885,357 | $82,880,335 | $243,765,692 |

1 The amount available to states is based on the balance remaining after enacted allocations have been subtracted from the total appropriation as follows:

| LIBRARY ALLOCATION, FY 2008 | $209,961,000 |
|---|---|
| Laura Bush 21st Century Librarian | $23,345,000 |
| National Leadership Grants | $12,159,000 |
| Native American/Native Hawaiian | $3,574,000 |
| Administration | $9,998,000 |
| Total Distributed to States | $160,885,000 |

2 Calculation is based on minimum set in the law (P.L. 108-81) and reflects appropriations enacted by P.L. 109-149.

Population data is from the Bureau of Census (BOC) estimates. Data used in the state allotment table are the most current published population estimates available the first day of the fiscal year. Therefore, the population data used in the 2007 table is what was available on the BOC Web site http://www.census.gov/popest/states/tables/ on October 1, 2007.

Population data for American Samoa, Northern Marianas, Guam, Virgin Islands, Marshall Islands, Federated States of Micronesia, and Palau can be accessed at http://www.census.gov/cgi-bin/ipc/idbrank.pl. This table reflects what was available on October 1, 2007.

3 Aggregate allotments (including administrative costs) for Palau, Marshall Islands, and Federated States of Micronesia are awarded on a competitive basis to eligible applicants, and are administered by Pacific Resources for Education and Learning (PREL).

*(continued from page 322)*

required five-year plan on file with IMLS. These goals and objectives are determined through a planning process that includes statewide needs assessment.

On a rotating basis, states program staff members conduct site visits to SLAAs to provide technical support and to monitor the states' success in administering the LSTA program. This year, program officers visited the eight SLAAs, in Oregon, North Dakota, Georgia, New York, Rhode Island, Missouri, Ohio, and the Virgin Islands. Each site visit includes critical review of the administration of the LSTA program at the SLAA as well as trips out into the field to visit libraries that are recipients of subgrants or beneficiaries of statewide LSTA projects.

## Discretionary Programs

IMLS began administering the discretionary programs of LSTA in 1998. In FY 2008 a total of $39,078,000 was allocated for discretionary programs, including National Leadership Grants, the Laura Bush 21st Century Librarian program, Native American Library Services, and Native Hawaiian Library Services.

The FY 2008 congressional appropriation for discretionary programs was

- National Leadership Grants
  (including Collaborative Planning Grants)        $12,159,000
- Laura Bush 21st Century Librarian program        $23,345,000
- Native American Library Services                  $3,063,500
- Native Hawaiian Library Services                    $510,500

**National Leadership Grants Program**

The National Leadership Grants program provides funding for innovative model programs to enhance the quality of library services nationwide. National Leadership Grants are competitive and intended to produce results useful for the broader library community.

During 2008 IMLS awarded 33 National Leadership Grants totaling $12,228,527. A total of 104 applications were received, requesting more than $37,000,000. Projects were funded in four categories: Advancing Digital Resources, Research, Demonstration, and Library and Museum Community Collaboration (see Table 2). In addition, IMLS offered Collaborative Planning Grants of up to $40,000 in all categories of the National Leadership Grants program. Collaborative Planning Grants enable project teams from libraries, museums, or other partner organizations to work together on a collaborative project in any of the National Leadership Grant categories. Partnerships with museums are not required for any projects except those in the Library and Museum Community Collaboration category.

Advancing Digital Resources (maximum award $1 million)

This category supports the creation, use, preservation, and presentation of significant digital resources as well as the development of tools to manage digital assets, incorporating new technologies or new technology practice. IMLS supported projects that

- Developed and disseminated new tools to facilitate management, preservation, sharing, and use of digital resources
- Increased community access to institutional resources through innovative use of existing technology-based tools
- Increased community access to institutional resources by improving practice in use, dissemination, and support of existing technology-based tools
- Developed or advanced participation in museum and/or library communities using social technologies in new ways
- Developed new approaches or tools for digital curation

Demonstration (maximum award $1 million)

Demonstration projects use available knowledge to address key needs and challenges facing libraries and museums, and transform that knowledge into formal practice. Funded projects

- Demonstrated and/or tested new practices in museum and/or library operations
- Demonstrated how museums and/or libraries serve their communities by fostering public value and implementing systemic changes in the field
- Established and/or tested standards and tools for innovative learning
- Demonstrated and/or tested an expansion of preservation or conservation practices

Research (maximum award $1 million)

Research grants support projects that have the potential to improve library and museum practice, resource use, programs, and services. Both basic and applied research projects are encouraged. Funded projects

- Evaluated the impact of library or museum services
- Investigated how learning takes place in museums and libraries and how use of library and/or museum resources enhances learning
- Investigated how to improve the quality, effectiveness, or efficiency of library or museum management programs or services
- Investigated ways to enhance the archiving, preservation, management, discovery, and use of digital assets and resources
- Investigated or conducted research to add new knowledge or make improvements in the conservation and preservation of collections

Library and Museum Community Collaboration (maximum award $1 million)

This category helps to create new opportunities for libraries and museums to engage with each other, and with other organizations as appropriate, to support the educational, economic, and social needs of their communities. In addition to libraries, archives, and museums, partners can include community organizations, public media, and other institutions and agencies that help libraries and museums to better serve their communities. A partnership of at least one eligible library entity and one eligible museum entity is required. Additional partners are encouraged where appropriate. Grant funds supported innovative collaborative projects, whether they were new partnerships or were building on an existing collaboration. Funded projects

- Addressed community civic and educational needs
- Increased the organizations' capacity to serve as effective venues and resources for learning
- Used technology in innovative ways to serve audiences more effectively

Collaborative Planning (maximum award $40,000)

This category enables project teams from libraries, museums, and other partnering organizations to work collaboratively in any of the National Leadership Grant categories. At least one of the partners must be an eligible library entity or an eli-

(text continues on page 332)

## Table 2 / National Leadership Grants, FY 2008

### Advancing Digital Resources

*Minnesota Historical Society* $243,363

The society will digitize and make available oral histories of recent Tibetan, Hmong, Somali, Indian, and Khmer immigrants. This rich collection will represent a unique source of contemporary history through the experiences of the newest Americans in their own words. The society will work with the communities, local school systems, and the Immigration History Research Center at the University of Minnesota to develop complementary resources and curriculum packets that will enhance the value of the collections to researchers, K–12 teachers, and the immigrant communities themselves.

*New York Public Library Astor, Lenox, and Tilden Foundation* $378,525

The New York Public Library, the Brooklyn Public Library, and the Queens Borough Public Library will create a set of digital tools for homework help that will be responsive to young people's information-gathering tendencies, research needs, and expectations. These activities will implement the findings of a successful 2007 IMLS Collaborative Planning Grant study awarded to the three library systems. The suite of tools, called Homework NYC Widgets, will provide students with a convenient and useful method of getting authoritative online homework assistance.

*Southern New Hampshire University* $500,000

Southern New Hampshire University will establish an institutional repository that will provide open, worldwide access to the university's research output. The project will initially focus on the works of the School of Community Economic Development and the International Business Program's faculty and students. These collections include important field-recorded research data sets, master's theses, doctoral dissertations, and working papers concerning low-income and marginalized communities around the world. The systems and workflows developed for preservation, digitization, and access to these collections will be extended to include all university departments.

*University Library, University of Michigan* $578,955

The library will create a Copyright Review Management System to increase the reliability of copyright status determinations for books published in the United States from 1923 to 1963, and to help create a point of collaboration for other institutions. The system will aid in the process of making vast numbers of these books available online to the general public. Nearly half a million books were published in the United States between 1923 and 1963, and although many of these are likely to be in the public domain, this can be difficult to check; the system will allow users to verify if a work's copyright status has been determined.

*Virginia Tech University Libraries* $250,000

Virginia Polytechnic Institute and State University will pursue further development of its highly successful LibX tool, which was created with funding from IMLS in 2006 and has been adopted by more than 275 libraries. This project will extend LibX by building a community platform for developing and delivering library services. The project will benefit a large community of librarians as well as library users.

### Demonstration

*Carnegie Library of Pittsburgh* $600,000

The Carnegie Library will combine preservation and digitization activities in an innovative process to bring its Iron and Steel Heritage Collection online and make it accessible to the world. Through the use of social networking software, the library will create an opportunity to grow a dynamic scholarly community around this significant collection. Using Web 2.0 functionality, users will be able to add personalized meaning and contribute important contextual information to items in the digitized collection. The project will demonstrate how public libraries can utilize digitization projects to promote their unique resources to communities far beyond their geographical location. More than 500,000 items will be made available online.

## Table 2 / National Leadership Grants, FY 2008 *(cont.)*

Carnegie Library will be working collaboratively with the library network PALINET (now merged with SOLINET to form Lyrasis) and Carnegie Mellon University on this project.

### *Hennepin County (Minnesota) Library* $271,391

Hennepin County Library, in partnership with the Science Museum of Minnesota, the Wilmette (Illinois) Public Library, the Public Library of Charlotte and Mecklenburg County (North Carolina), the Free Library of Philadelphia, the Seattle Public Library, and the Memphis Public Library, will develop a best practices framework for innovative technology program implementation. The project will evaluate literacy skills developed by youth participating in the creative technology workshops called Media MashUp. Participants' projects and their reflective responses to their work will be evaluated for evidence of such 21st century literacy practices as higher-order problem solving, collaboration, and risk taking.

### *Indiana University Digital Library Program* $481,987

Indiana University proposes to use the Variations digital music library system as a test bed for the Functional Requirements for Bibliographic Records (FRBR) conceptual model. The Library of Congress Working Group on the Future of Bibliographic Control report, released in January 2008, challenged the library community to create a model for testing the transformative promise of FRBR. In response to the challenge, the university will "FRBR-ize" records in the Cook Music Library's entire sound recording and score collections and make them available for evaluation and testing, both in a search interface designed to make the most of the FRBR model and as raw data for testing in other environments.

### *Orange County (Florida) Library System* $120,603

The library system will create a multifaceted learning experience called Citizenship Inspired, which will assist those seeking U.S. citizenship to take the required courses, making use of learning and communication methods that best suit their own situations and needs. Participants will have the opportunity to engage in one-on-one learning, learning in groups, live online learning, or self-paced online tutorial learning. The library will use social networking tools to support the continued collaboration of these communities outside of formal learning.

### *Syracuse University* $200,020

Syracuse will further develop the nationally recognized Web-based resource S.O.S. for Information Literacy. S.O.S is an innovative standards-based approach to improving K–16 information literacy teaching and learning through a freely accessible teaching support system. The project will expand S.O.S.'s structure and contents to include new national and state-level content standards, and provide examples of these standards in action with lesson plans, teaching ideas, videos, and other materials.

### *University of Florida, Center for Library Automation* $392,649

The Florida Center for Library Automation and its partners, the Cornell University Library and the New York University Libraries, will develop a proof-of-concept for the exchange of information between digital preservation repositories. Building on earlier work, the project will define a transfer format, modify three open source repository applications to import and export information packages in this format, and test a carefully developed set of use cases to verify the usability and flexibility of the format.

### *University of North Carolina at Chapel Hill, School of Information and Library Science* $334,699

The Metadata Research Center at the school and the National Evolutionary Synthesis Center (NESCent) in Durham, North Carolina, will use the Helping Interdisciplinary Vocabulary Engineering (HIVE) model to dynamically integrate multiple discipline-specific controlled vocabularies encoded with Simple Knowledge Organization Systems (SKOS). HIVE is an innovative approach and model designed to cater to the controlled-vocabulary needs of curatorial and cataloging information professionals in the library, museum, and archival communities.

## Table 2 / National Leadership Grants, FY 2008 *(cont.)*

### Research

*College of Information, Florida State University*                    $415,673

The research partnership of the College of Information at Florida State University, Chipola College, and Tallahassee Community College will investigate student perceptions of information literacy education and identify ways to ensure that all students develop essential learning skills. Research findings will provide important input for the design, development, and implementation of information services and resources, especially those aimed at reaching students who do not have proficient information literacy skills.

*New York University, Steinhardt School, Department of Music and*
*Music Professions*                    $615,405

New York University's Music Technology Program and Library Services will research and develop content-based approaches to automatic organization of, access to, and interaction with digital music archives. This research concentrates on encoding musical attributes, such as harmony and rhythm, to represent and characterize similarities that exist between songs and phrases, and showing how these methodologies can provide users with innovative modes of access to music.

*School of Information Resources and Library Science, University of Arizona*   $539,686

The school proposes to collaborate with the University of Arizona Library, the Harvard University Herbaria, the Missouri Botanical Gardens, and the University of Arizona University Information and Technology Services group to study project-based, hands-on learning using online laboratory environments as a way to enhance the teaching of advanced digital library technologies. The results will be applicable both to the library and information science curricula and to postgraduate on-the-job training and professional development.

*School of Information, University of Michigan*                    $649,941

In collaboration with the Center for History and New Media at George Mason University, the school will design, develop, test, and evaluate a computer game, Bibliobouts, to teach incoming undergraduate students essential information literacy skills. Five institutions— Chicago State University, Troy University Montgomery, Saginaw Valley State University, the University of Baltimore, and the University of Dubuque—will field test and evaluate Bibliobouts. Project evaluation will determine if gaming is effective for teaching incoming students information literacy skills, and whether students retain and apply these skills appropriately.

*School of Library and Information Sciences, University of North Texas*        $738,075

The Botanical Research Institute of Texas and the Texas Center for Digital Knowledge will study how computers and humans can work together to create meaningful, high-quality specimen label data for use in digitized biological collections. Digitizing these collections in a well-planned and standardized way increases their use by a wider audience, reduces the physical handling of the original object, and produces a permanent digital archive.

*Yale University*                    $749,990

Yale will investigate how topic modeling can be used to improve search and discovery for users of digital collections. Digital collections may contain hundreds of thousands of images associated with limited descriptions; Yale is seeking automated ways to connect users to the information they need. The project team will apply topic modeling to three important classes of digital library resources: full-text books, images, and tagged objects.

### Library and Museum Community Collaboration

*City of Salinas (California) Public Library*                    $713,899

Cultivating Knowledge: Life and Literature in Salinas is a two-year project of the Salinas Public Library, the National Steinbeck Center, and a partner council of other Salinas organizations. The project will explore the area's cultural past, present, and future through a series of

Table 2 / National Leadership Grants, FY 2008 (cont.)

integrated activities and events focused on reviving the city's civic life, promoting lifelong learning, and supporting community development efforts.

*ECHO Lake Aquarium and Science Center, Burlington, Vermont* $352,173

Voices for the Lake will create an online community network of and for the rural populations surrounding Lake Champlain dedicated to improving the health of the significantly polluted lake. The Lake Champlain Basin Science Center, in partnership with the Vermont and upstate New York public library systems and the Vermont Folklife Center, will tackle this problem with a program of public education and engagement designed to change personal behavior and reduce human impact on the deteriorating water quality of the basin.

*Lawrence Hall of Science, University of California, Berkeley* $499,455

Lawrence Hall of Science, the Berkeley Public Library, and the Oakland Public Library will partner in a three-year project to promote interest in and positive attitudes toward science in children ages 7 to 10 and their families. The science team will develop, promote, circulate, and evaluate "Check Out Science!" kits featuring a book with authentic science content and a hands-on activity for families to do together.

*Oregon Museum of Science and Industry* $249,876

Beyond Fact, a project partnership between the Oregon Museum of Science and Industry and the Multnomah County Library, will create a set of three public programs designed to engage adults in discussion-based learning and advance the science and information literacy skills that form the basis for future decision making. The programs will include science book discussion groups meeting in the library system's branches, forum events combining informal presentations and discussion, and a community-wide reading program highlighting an accessible science book.

*Poets House* $997,766

Poets House, a preeminent poetry library and literary center in Manhattan, will collaborate with public libraries and zoos across the United States to support library–zoo partnerships in five cities. The project teams will install exhibitions that use poetry as an interpretive tool to deepen visitor thinking about wildlife and conservation in each zoo. This project follows a year-long planning grant funded by IMLS and extends the success of an IMLS-funded partnership in New York City between Poets House and the Wildlife Conservation Society's Central Park Zoo, which pioneered the installation of poetry in the zoo.

*University of Maryland* $996,750

The university's Institute for Advanced Computer Studies and College of Information Studies will partner with the Indianapolis Museum of Art and 12 other museums to conduct research on new methods to improve user access to online museum images. This project will design and test a multi-institution image database containing search terms derived from several sources, including texts associated with exhibition catalogs, and terms contributed by online viewers, a technique known as "social tagging." The project will build on two previous projects, including the IMLS-funded "Steve" project, which created a database of user-contributed tags and investigated methods of labeling and categorizing these terms to make objects easier for the public to find.

## Collaborative Planning

*Eastern Washington University* $39,614

The Inland Northwest Network of Culture and History (INNCH), a collaboration led by the university, will develop organizational and action plans for this network and will outline the specific projects that will define the core collections and services of INNCH. The partners share a commitment to preserving regional cultural history and artifacts and to making information accessible and understandable to the public, historians, educators, rural communities, and other constituents.

## Table 2 / National Leadership Grants, FY 2008 *(cont.)*

*Ernst Mayr Library of the Museum of Comparative Zoology, Harvard University*                    $40,000

The Harvard University Botany Libraries and the Ernst Mayr Library of the Museum of Comparative Zoology—along with the partner institution libraries of the American Museum of Natural History, the Field Museum, the Missouri Botanical Garden, the New York Botanical Garden, the Academy of Natural Sciences, and the Internet Archive—will plan a cost-effective and efficient large-scale digitization workflow with enhanced metadata for biodiversity library materials designated as "special collections."

*Pacific Resources for Education and Learning, Honolulu*                    $40,000

Pacific Resources for Education and Learning (PREL) and the Republic of Palau Ministry of Health will work together to develop a plan for the creation of a regional, health-focused digital library. This project will undertake a systematic planning process for a digital project that will address specific health planning and policy information access challenges in the Republic of Palau.

*School of Library and Information Studies, San Jose State University*                    $39,826

San Jose State will systematically collect and analyze data regarding young adult spaces in libraries. The university will initiate planning for a full research project, which will include a broad dissemination of findings, helping library professionals design effective YA spaces that are developmentally appropriate and responsive to how today's youth prefer to use public spaces.

*Southeastern New York Library Resources Council*                    $39,600

The council, partnering with the Lower Hudson Conference of Historical Agencies and Museums and the Sound and Story Project of the Hudson Valley, will develop a plan for the identification, digital reformatting, and increased accessibility of sound recordings that document the history of the Hudson River Valley region. Many oral history collections exist throughout the region, but very few, if any, have been reformatted for digital access. This collaboration will lay the foundation for preserving endangered recordings throughout the region.

*University of Maryland, College Park*                    $39,955

The College of Information Studies at the University of Maryland and the School of Library and Information Studies at the University of Alabama will work collaboratively with libraries in Maryland and Alabama to create a model to strengthen public libraries' capacity to work effectively with government agencies, particularly in times of disaster or crisis. During the planning process, the team will conduct preliminary research regarding the libraries' existing resources, identify communities' assets and needs, and create an initial model to strengthen the libraries' potential for expanding and enhancing the public's access to vital information resources.

*University of Oregon Libraries*                    $38,844

The Orbis Cascade Alliance is a combination of 35 academic libraries in Washington and Oregon. One of the alliance's programs is the Northwest Digital Archives (NWDA), a 31-institution consortium of archives in Oregon, Washington, Alaska, Idaho, and Montana that currently maintains a database of finding aids for its members' archival collections. The grant, part of a long-range planning process, will support the second stage of planning, in which the group will determine solutions to specific problems that are currently impeding the development of sustainable digital programs. The project will be a collaborative effort of the alliance, Washington State University, Lewis and Clark College, Whitman College, and Whitworth University.

*University of Pittsburgh, Center for American Music*                    $39,826

The University of Pittsburgh and the Society for American Music will bring together librarians, archivists, and scholars to develop a sustainable digital reference tool for locating source materials in American music history; this will be an updated and online edition of the authoritative publication *Resources of American Music History: A Directory of Source Materials from*

**Table 2 / National Leadership Grants, FY 2008** *(cont.)*

*Colonial Times to World War II.* The planning project will focus on identifying the scope and types of materials to be included in the new edition, to be known as RAMH2; researching existing standards for, descriptions of, and access to these resources; determining tools needed to collect, store, and refresh collection data continuously; and establishing the online searching interface users will need.

*Vanderbilt University, Eskind Biomedical Library*                          $39,981

Vanderbilt University Medical Center will develop strategies for assessing children's interactions with health information. A team of librarians, psychologists, child development experts, pediatricians, informaticians, evaluators, and educators will employ a six-month planning period to develop techniques to assess health information needs and perceptions in children. Project partners include Meharry Medical College and Cumberland Pediatric Foundation, organizations that offer expertise in areas key to long-range work.

*(continued from page 326)*

gible museum entity. Funded projects were designed to result in deliverable products such as plans, prototypes, or proofs of concept for dissemination to and evaluation by appropriate audiences.

## Laura Bush 21st Century Librarian Program

The Laura Bush 21st Century Librarian program, which carries a maximum award of $1 million, was established in 2003 as the Librarians for the 21st Century program; the name was changed in 2006 in accordance with the provisions of IMLS's congressional appropriation. The program provides competitive funding to support projects to recruit and educate the next generation of librarians and library leaders, build institutional capacity in graduate schools of library and information science and develop faculty who will help in this endeavor, conduct needed research on the demographics and needs of the profession, and support programs of continuing education and training in library and information science for librarians and library staff.

In FY 2008 IMLS awarded 36 grants totaling $21,644,870 for the program (see Table 3). Ninety-three applications requesting $49,358,978 were received.

The 2008 priorities for program funding were:

Doctoral Programs

- To develop faculty to educate the next generation of library professionals; in particular, to increase the number of students enrolled in doctoral programs that will prepare faculty to teach master's students who will work in school, public, and academic libraries.

- To develop the next generation of library leaders; in particular, to increase the number of students enrolled in doctoral programs that will prepare them to assume positions as library managers and administrators.

Master's Programs

- To educate the next generation of librarians; in particular, to increase the number of students enrolled in nationally accredited graduate library programs preparing for careers of service in libraries.

Research

- *Early Career Development Program*—To support the early career development of new faculty members who are likely to become leaders in library and information science by supporting innovative research by untenured, tenure-track faculty.

- *Research*—To provide the library community with information needed to support successful recruitment and education of the next generation of librarians; in particular, through funded research, to establish baseline data on professional demographics and job availability, to evaluate current programs in library education for their capacity to meet the identified needs, and to conduct research and establish ongoing research capacity in the field of library and information science—particularly the evaluation of library and information services, assessment of the value and use of public libraries and their services by the public, and assessment of the public value and use of the Internet.

- *Preprofessional Programs*—To recruit future librarians; in particular, to attract promising junior high, high school, or college students to consider careers in librarianship through statewide or regional pilot projects employing recruitment strategies that are cost effective and measurable, and to introduce high school or college students to potential careers in library and information science by employing them to assist with library disaster recovery or service operation in areas that have suffered major disasters. Participation of at least one library, as the applicant or as an official partner, in a location certified by the Federal Emergency Management Agency as a major disaster area in 2005 or 2006 is required.

- *Programs to Build Institutional Capacity*—To develop or enhance curricula within graduate schools of library and information science; in particular, to develop or enhance courses or programs of study for library, museum, and archives professionals in the creation, management, preservation, presentation, and use of digital assets; to develop or enhance courses or programs of study relating to the development of critical thinking skills, such as organization leadership and research methods; to broaden the library and information science curriculum by incorporating perspectives from other disciplines and fields of scholarship, such as public policy, ethics, American studies, urban planning, mass communication, and instructional design; and to develop projects or programs in data curation as training programs for graduate students in library and information science.

- *Continuing Education*—To develop or enhance programs of continuing education and training in library and information science for librarians and library staff; to develop or enhance programs of continuing education and training for librarians and library staff to improve library services to specialized audiences such as at-risk youth, seniors, and those with ethnic, language, or other barriers to service; to develop or enhance programs to promote collaboration between educators and librarians employed in edu-

(text continues on page 339)

## Table 3 / Laura Bush 21st Century Librarian Program, FY 2008

### Doctoral Programs

*Regents of the University of California, Los Angeles*                $950,555

In "Building the Future of Archival Education and Research," the University of California, Los Angeles—along with the University of Maryland, University of Michigan, University of North Carolina at Chapel Hill, University of Pittsburgh, University of Texas, Simmons College, and the University of Wisconsin–Madison—will address the shortage of professors in archival science by providing at least four doctoral fellowships in archive-related topics. To strengthen the growing network of archival educators in library and information science programs, this project will also develop three annual week-long workshops for students, faculty, and working archivists to address pedagogical techniques, research methodology, and curriculum development, and technical and social issues relevant to the field.

*Simmons College*                $955,694

Building on a previously funded project, the Simmons College Graduate School of Library and Information Science will expand its Ph.D. concentration in managerial leadership in the information professions to include 18 rising leaders in the public and state library arenas. Until recently, students in this program have largely been drawn from the academic library community. Designed to provide mid- to upper-level library managers with the opportunities to prepare for senior-level leadership, this project will use face-to-face and online courses, research projects, and intensive interaction with library leaders acting as "professors of practice," along with a variety of supplementary activities, to develop the leadership and management potential of its students.

*Office of Sponsored Projects, University of Texas at Austin*                $978,617

The university will train four full-time doctoral students to become leaders in digital librarianship. Incorporating innovative coursework, in-depth research, teaching experiences, and wider engagement with the scholarly community, this project will develop library and information science faculty who will have both the theoretical understanding and practical skills required to develop the next generation of librarians.

### Master's Programs

*Association of Research Libraries*                $728,821

Partnering with the National Library of Medicine and libraries at the universities of Arizona, Kentucky, North Carolina State, and SUNY Albany, the association will provide 45 MLS students from under-represented racial and ethnic groups with internships in an academic or research library. It will also provide these ARL minority fellows with librarian mentors, opportunities for leadership development, and career placement.

*City of Dallas*                $545,909

With nearly half of its librarians projected to retire in the next five years and a paucity of Spanish-speaking librarians on its staff to serve its increasingly diverse population, Dallas Public Library will recruit 30 individuals from among its staff, especially targeting those who are Spanish-speaking, and provide them with scholarships to study for an MLS at Texas schools of library and information science.

*Queens College, City University of New York*                $99,999

The Graduate School of Library and Information Studies at Queens College will redevelop the coursework and internship requirements of its Archives, Records Management and Preservation Program to better prepare students to work in special collections and archives in the digital age.

*Indiana State Library*                $999,991

The library will increase the level of ethnic diversity in all types of libraries across the state by recruiting and providing scholarships for 30 MLS students from racially and ethnically diverse backgrounds who will commit to work in an Indiana library for at least two years.

## Table 3 / Laura Bush 21st Century Librarian Program, FY 2008 *(cont.)*

Scholarship recipients will also benefit from participation in state and regional library associations, as well as other supplementary activities, including special orientation meetings in various types of library settings, meetings with library directors, diversity and ethics workshops, transition to work programs, online and face-to-face support networks, and other special projects.

*North Carolina Central University* $839,073

Building on a previously funded project, the university's School of Library and Information Science—along with a wide range of North Carolina academic, public, and school library partners—will recruit and provide scholarships for MLS degrees to 20 minority students from 12 North Carolina counties. This extended, research-oriented master's program will focus on studying the "face-to-face" roles of the library, often abbreviated as "library as place," as well as issues relating to diversity in librarianship.

*Office of Commonwealth Libraries, Pennsylvania Department of Education* $537,600

MLS-educated librarians are needed in Pennsylvania, especially in the state's rural areas. To address this need, Pennsylvania's Office of Commonwealth Libraries, partnering with Clarion University, will provide scholarships for graduate school to 20 individuals working in the state's rural libraries. Special effort will be made to attract applicants who are bilingual.

*Pratt Institute* $756,324

The Pratt School of Information and Library Science and the Brooklyn Museum will recruit and provide scholarships to a highly diverse group of 30 students, educating them for careers in museum librarianship in the digital age. Students will take classes at Pratt and intern at the Brooklyn Museum, and upon completion will receive a master's degree and a certificate in museum librarianship. The partners will also produce and disseminate a study on the current state of museum library education.

*Regents of the University of Michigan* $631,816

The university's School of Information, along with nine partners—the Center for Research Libraries, the Florida Center for Library Automation, the LOCKSS program at Stanford University, the Northeast Document Conservation Center, OCLC, Smithsonian Institution Archives, Safe Sound Archive, the Inter-University Consortium for Political and Social Research (ICPSR), and the University of Michigan Libraries—will provide 30 digital curation/preservation administration summer internships to MLS students over three years.

*San Antonio Public Library Foundation* $963,420

The San Antonio Library Foundation and the San Antonio Public Library will recruit and provide MLS scholarships to 45 individuals to address the shortage of professional librarians in the San Antonio region while meeting the needs of their increasingly diverse community. At least half of the scholarship students will be bilingual.

*St. John's University* $990,892

St. John's University in Queens, New York, and two partners, the Metropolitan New York Library Council and the Law Librarians of Greater New York, will recruit and educate 40 MLS students interested in careers in special libraries such as those found in the corporate, legal, and media worlds. Special librarians provide expert, in-depth information support in dynamic, deadline-dominated, competitive environments.

*University of Denver* $999,370

The university will develop and integrate into its curriculum significant course offerings in law librarianship and will recruit and educate ten new law librarians through a comprehensive law librarianship program specifically designed to give students the general competencies, specialized subject training, and extensive practical experience necessary to be successful in this field.

**Table 3 / Laura Bush 21st Century Librarian Program, FY 2008** *(cont.)*

*University of Houston–Clear Lake*        $906,104

Seeking to increase the number of qualified professional librarians in the Houston area—where there is a demonstrable need for school librarians, especially those trained in collaboration and working with diverse and disadvantaged populations—the university will recruit and educate 30 school librarians with a special emphasis on collaborating with school administrators.

*University of North Carolina at Greensboro*        $862,014

The university's Department of Library and Information Studies and the university libraries, along with partners from ten North Carolina academic libraries, will recruit and provide scholarships to 12 minority students seeking MLS degrees and interested in working in academic libraries. Scholarship recipients will participate in professional conferences at the state and national level, and partner libraries will provide internships and mentors.

## Research

*Florida State University*        $754,755

Florida State, along with the New York University Research Center for Leadership in Action and local school districts, will follow 30 recipients from two previously funded IMLS school library media scholarship programs through their first year working in schools in order to gain a better understanding of the school library media specialist's role in integrating technology into the classroom. This project seeks to determine how library and information science education can better prepare school library media specialists to be leaders in technology integration in their schools.

## Early Career Development

*Drexel University*        $224,386

This early career development research grant will provide support for Assistant Professor Jung-ran Park to analyze interpersonal communication between librarians and the public in digital information service, using transcripts from the Internet Public Library's Question Answering Service.

*University of Colorado Denver*        $99,981

In this early career development project, Assistant Professor Laura Summers will investigate how professional development in culturally responsive school librarianship changes school library practices.

*University of Kentucky Research Foundation*        $339,420

This early career development grant will provide support for Assistant Professor Sujin Kim to study four existing methods of describing and representing medical pathology images, leading to one standardized descriptive framework so that clinicians and medical researchers can more readily share information about these images.

*University of South Carolina Research Foundation*        $155,885

Assistant Professor Jennifer Arns of the University of South Carolina School of Library and Information Science will gather, summarize, and integrate recent studies on the economic impact of public libraries in their communities, building a more comprehensive understanding of the capabilities and limitations of these studies.

*Office of Sponsored Projects, University of Texas at Austin*        $255,040

This early career development grant will provide support for Assistant Professor Megan Winget to study the collection and preservation of massively multiplayer online (MMO) games.

**Table 3 / Laura Bush 21st Century Librarian Program, FY 2008** *(cont.)*

## Preprofessional Programs

*Fairfax County (Virginia) Public Library*                                    $265,258

The library and a partner, Liberty's Promise, will collaborate to develop "An American Future: Library Service Opportunities for Immigrant Youth." The three-year project will recruit 90 low-income immigrant youth for paid internships in the library. The internships will provide support for these youth while introducing them to the vital role of the public library in American civic life.

## Programs to Build Institutional Capacity

*Arizona Board of Regents, University of Arizona*                              $999,860

Addressing a need for librarians from diverse backgrounds, especially those from the Hispanic and Native American communities, the university's School of Information Resources and Library Science—along with the University of Arizona Library; the University of Arizona Health Sciences Library; Pima County Public Library; Sunnyside Unified School District; and the Arizona State Library, Archives, and Public Records—will provide 48 scholarships to MLS students.

*Board of Trustees, University of Illinois at Urbana-Champaign*               $892,028

The university will extend its work in data curation in the sciences to include the humanities by developing a model humanities curation graduate curriculum and a related continuing-education institute. The project will recruit, provide scholarships, and fund internships for master's degree students interested in careers in humanities data curation.

*University of Maryland*                                                       $591,554

Addressing key recommendations in the American Council of Learned Societies' Commission on Cyberinfrastructure for the Humanities and Social Sciences report "Our Cultural Commonwealth," the university's College of Information Studies and the schools of information at the University of Michigan and the University of Texas at Austin will partner with three digital humanities centers—the Maryland Institute for Technology in the Humanities at the University of Maryland, the Center for Digital Research in the Humanities at the University of Nebraska, and MATRIX, the center for Humane Arts, Letters, and Social Sciences at Michigan State University—to create 18 internships for MLS students interested in careers in digital humanities centers and/or digital libraries.

*Office of Sponsored Research, University of North Carolina at Chapel Hill*    $878,634

Building on an earlier funded project, the university—partnering with the National Archives and Records Administration and the University of Glasgow, Scotland—will develop an international doctoral-level curriculum and educational network in digital curation (the management and preservation of digital materials across their life cycle).

## Continuing Education

*Carnegie Library of Pittsburgh*                                              $391,400

The library will conduct a staff development program that identifies and nurtures future leaders within its ranks in a year-long professional development program. Graduates of this program then enter a second tier of training that develops executive leadership skills and teaches nonprofit management skills.

*Florida State University*                                                    $81,206

Florida State will bring together approximately 40 attendees for a two-day workshop to identify the educational goals that LIS, museum studies, and archival studies programs have in common; identify the information needs and challenges facing cultural heritage organizations in the 21st century; and identify areas of convergence for educators and professionals working to meet the needs of the nation's cultural heritage organizations and the public they serve.

## Table 3 / Laura Bush 21st Century Librarian Program, FY 2008 *(cont.)*

*Louisiana State University, A&M College*   $279,672

In the continuing effort to address post-Hurricane Katrina issues in Gulf Coast cultural heritage institutions, Louisiana State University A&M's Graduate School of Library and Information Science will work to create the Mid-Gulf Coast Collaborative for Education, which will target the staffs of small, resource-challenged repositories in the states of Louisiana, Mississippi, and Alabama. The grant will provide them with various affordable workshops and other continuing education opportunities, based on a needs survey.

*Mississippi Library Commission*   $97,434

The commission will conduct an intensive, in-residence workshop to serve the continuing education needs of mid-level staff employed in public libraries in Mississippi. Thirty candidates will be selected each year to attend the Librarianship 201 Institute, which will cover topics in public library advocacy, management, ethics, and technology.

*New York University*   $788,747

The New York University Moving Image Archiving and Preservation Program (MIAP) will provide intensive work experience in libraries for MIAP interns and graduates. The funding will support 36 semester/summer internships and six postgraduate fellowships over the three years.

*State Library of Louisiana*   $155,946

The state library will provide executive leadership training for Louisiana public librarians. This grant will be the first in Louisiana to provide a statewide training program specifically tailored to public library leaders and potential leaders.

*Texas State Library and Archives Commission*   $535,556

The commission, with the University of North Texas Libraries, Amigos Library Services, and other partners, will develop Train to Share, a workshop program under the Texas Heritage Digitization Initiative for Texas librarians and other cultural heritage professionals. The three-year project will develop statewide workshops, adapted from the Library of Congress's "Cataloging for the 21st Century" series, to provide training on interoperability measures of digitization projects, and principles of sharable metadata developed in a project previously funded by IMLS.

*University of Illinois at Urbana-Champaign*   $499,895

The university libraries—in partnership with the university's Mortenson Center for International Library Programs, the Library Society of China, and the Chinese American Library Association—will develop a two-year partnership between librarians in the United States and China. The project will provide workshops for Chinese librarians and library educators, both in the United States and in China, on American practices in library public services. In return, U.S. librarians will learn about publicly available Chinese information resources that are or could be made available online to meet a growing demand for Chinese-language information about China.

*University of North Texas*   $544,514

The university, through its online continuing education arm, Lifelong Education @ Desktop, will develop, produce, and market 30 online courses to meet the need for training of both library professional and library support staff in core competencies for certification by state and regional agencies. These inexpensive online courses will meet the certification requirements for broad national certifying programs such as the American Library Association's Library Support Staff Certificate and the Western Council of Libraries' certificate programs.

(continued from page 333)
cation institutions; and to provide internships in conservation practice in libraries that have suffered disaster-related collections damage.

## Native American Library Services

The Native American Library Services program provides opportunities for improved library services to an important part of the nation's community of library users. The program offers three types of support to serve the range of needs of Indian tribes and Alaska Native villages, the latter coming under the definition of eligible Indian tribes as recognized by the secretary of the interior.

In 2008 IMLS distributed $3,114,281 in grants for American Indian tribes and Alaska Native villages. The program offers three types of support:

- Basic library services grants, in the amount of $5,000, that support core library operations on a noncompetitive basis for all eligible Indian tribes and Alaska Native villages that apply for such support. IMLS awarded basic grants to 34 tribes in 10 states in 2008.
- Basic library services grants with a supplemental education/assessment option of $1,000, totaling $6,000. IMLS awarded basic grants with the education/assessment option to 175 tribes in 25 states. The purpose of the education/assessment option is to provide funding for library staff to attend continuing education courses and/or training workshops on- or off-site, for library staff to attend or give presentations at conferences relating to library services, and/or to hire a consultant for an onsite professional library assessment.
- Enhancement grants, which support new levels of library service for activities specifically identified under LSTA. Of the 38 applications received, IMLS awarded 15 enhancement grants for a total of $1,894,281 (see Table 4).

## Native Hawaiian Library Services

The Native Hawaiian Library Services program provides opportunities for improved library services through grants to nonprofit organizations that primarily serve and represent Native Hawaiians, as the term "Native Hawaiian" is defined in section 7207 of the Native Hawaiian Education Act (20 U.S.C. 7517). In 2008 one Native Hawaiian Library Services grant was awarded to Alu Like, Inc. of Honolulu in the amount of $510,500.

# Partnerships

## National Endowment for the Arts—The Big Read

IMLS continued its partnership with the National Endowment for the Arts (NEA) to promote reading through the distribution of books to support community read-

(text continues on page 341)

### Table 4 / Native American Library Services Enhancement Grants, FY 2008

*Bear River Band of the Rohnerville Rancheria* $135,571

The Bear River Band of the Rohnerville Rancheria in Loleta, California, in response to a recent community survey and assessment, will meet the information needs of the tribe by hiring a library consultant to catalog and automate the existing collection and train current and new local staff in the ongoing operation of the library.

*Ely Shoshone Tribe of Nevada* $71,587

The grant will be used to expand the tribal library's collections and to purchase library automation software to catalog and organize materials, providing easy access for the public. With a recent donation of computer equipment, the library will be able to hire a trainer under this grant to offer community members in-depth instruction on word processing, spreadsheet, and graphics software programs that will help improve school and work performance.

*Fort Belknap Indian Community* $149,603

On behalf of the community, the Fort Belknap College Library, also serving the general Fort Belknap community in Harlem, Montana, will purchase furnishings and shelving for a new library building funded through the U.S. Department of Housing and Urban Development and the U.S. Department of Education. Ten computers with the latest technology will be added for public use, and library staff will provide training in computer and information literacy.

*Keweenaw Bay Indian Community* $120,374

The Ojibwa Community Library at Michigan's Keweenaw Bay Indian Community will focus on expanding and enhancing existing library services to senior and disabled tribal members. Project staff will implement in-home outreach services to homebound and limited-mobility community members, provide portable visual and audio assistance equipment, establish a collection of large-print books and periodicals, expand library services and assistive technology into the senior center, and improve accessibility through expanded evening and weekend hours.

*Makah Indian Tribe* $75,000

On behalf of the Makah Indian Tribe in Neah Bay, Washington, the Makah Cultural and Research Center will focus its grant activities on Makah Head Start students from 3 to 5 years old and the elders of the community. Project staff will teach the children how to create their own culturally based books to take home, instilling a sense of pride in reading, writing, and storytelling. Elders, parents, and teachers will read and tell culturally relevant stories to the Head Start students throughout the year, and 75 elders will be taught how to document their own life stories in scrapbook-style "Makah Memories" books.

*Miami Tribe of Oklahoma* $149,962

The tribe will use its grant to continue two successful projects and add new initiatives in response to community needs. Project staff will continue an oral history project that is documenting the ways in which local tribal leadership has worked together over the years. They will also enhance the multi-tribe library consortium known as the CHARLIE Network by adding library automation software and providing a circuit-rider librarian.

*Pueblo of Jemez* $143,262

The Jemez Community Library in New Mexico's Pueblo of Jemez will provide a wide variety of activities geared to school success and lifelong learning, including after-school tutoring for every grade level, computer literacy classes for all ages, family literacy nights for parents and children to read together, traditional arts classes, and story sessions conducted in the Towa language.

*Pueblo of Santa Clara* $75,000

The Pueblo of Santa Clara Community Library in Espanola, New Mexico, will implement an initiative focused on early childhood reading readiness. Library staff will teach parents and other caregivers how to help their children become successful readers and learners. They will also build on the intergenerational elder/child activities of the Tewa Language Program

Table 4 / Native American Library Services Enhancement Grants, FY 2008 *(cont.)*

by integrating it with the Relatives as Parents Program, which works with grandparents serving as surrogate parents.

*Sealaska Corporation*                                                                                      $148,375

On behalf of the Sealaska Corporation in Juneau, Alaska, the Sealaska Heritage Institute will pursue Project Ka-li-gaas'. The Tlingit phrase ka-li-gaas' captures the idea of moving upward. The project Ka-li-gaas' seeks to raise the effectiveness of the Sealaska library by implementing an online archival catalog that will provide online finding aids of all the library's archival and ethnographic collections. It will also begin the process of creating an online catalog of Sealaska's book collection by joining the Capital Cities Library Information Center, a catalog shared by the Juneau Public Library, the Alaska State Library, the University of Alaska/Southeast, and other libraries in the Juneau city and borough area.

*Sitka Tribe of Alaska*                                                                                      $139,136

The Sitka Tribe of Alaska will undertake the Treasures in the Attic project to digitize, translate, and transcribe Tlingit recordings and develop curriculum materials.

*Standing Rock Sioux Tribe*                                                                                 $132,604

On behalf of the Standing Rock Sioux Tribe of Fort Yates, North Dakota, Sitting Bull College Library—which serves as the community's public library—will purchase furnishings for its new library building, extend hours and service by adding a full-time staff person, pull together a vast number of Standing Rock historical documents, and gather and display 45 unique photographs of the legendary leader Sitting Bull.

*Torres Martinez Band of Cahuilla Mission Indians*                                                          $130,130

The California band's Spreading the Word project will develop a native literature reading skills program that will integrate Indian literature into the accelerated reader program for after-school enrichment.

*Tuolumne Band of Me-Wuk Indians*                                                                           $149,992

After its successful efforts to improve high school graduation rates, the Tuolumne Band of Me-Wuk Indians of Tuolumne, California, will expand its library from a K–12 focus to a facility serving all community members with a broad range of materials.

*Yerington (Nevada) Paiute Tribe*                                                                           $145,762

The Yerington Paiute Tribe will use its grant to strengthen the tribal library's outreach programs and services in response to community needs. A learning center coordinator will be hired to implement programming in which tribal elders and community experts will give hands-on presentations centered on cultural aspects of the tribe.

*Ysleta del Sur Pueblo of Texas*                                                                            $127,923

Ysleta del Sur Pueblo will implement its T-Life (Technology Library Innovations for Education) program by integrating the Tigua/IBM Achievement Center into the Tribal Empowerment Program. The project will integrate technology at all levels to increase youth enrichment, college/vocational preparation, and adult personal development services.

*(continued from page 339)*

ing and discussion programs based on selected works of fiction. The IMLS contribution was made through the Laura Bush 21st Century Librarian program.

**IMLS/NEH Digital Partnership**

IMLS continued a partnership with the National Endowment for the Humanities (NEH) to promote development of the digital humanities through two grant programs administered by NEH: Digital Humanities Start-up Grants at two levels (level I grants of up to $25,000, and level II grants of up to $50,000), and IMLS/ NEH Advancing Knowledge project grants of up to $350,000. IMLS funds were provided through the National Leadership Grants program. Four Advancing Knowledge grants totaling $884,491 were awarded in 2008:

- The Alexandria Archive Institute received $250,609 for its program "Enhancing Humanities Research Productivity in a Collaborative Data Sharing Environment." The Alexandria Archive Institute, in collaboration with the University of California, Berkeley, School of Information, will create best-practice guidelines for the development of humanities data-sharing software to meet user needs, as well as continue to develop Open Context, a collaborative, free, open-access resource to facilitate online sharing of archaeological field research among excavators, scholars, and cultural heritage institutions.
- The American Indian Higher Education Consortium (AIHEC) received $175,000 for its "AIHEC American Indian Collections Portal." AIHEC, using resources from the Autry National Center/Southwest Museum of the American Indian, the National Museum of the American Indian, the National Anthropological Archives, and the National Museum of Natural History, will federate databases focused on Native American collections and share the data in new ways with tribal colleges and community members.
- The City of Philadelphia Department of Records was granted $108,882 for "A Partnership to Increase Access to Our Nation's Historical Records." The department, in collaboration with the Free Library of Philadelphia, will develop an enhanced Web site (http://www.PhillyHistory.org) featuring historically significant collections at the department of records and the library, and will create tools to increase the level of access to and usefulness of these collections for researchers, students, and members of the general public.
- Ithaka Harbors, Inc./Portico was granted $350,000 for "Protecting Future Access Now: Developing a Prototype Preservation Model for Digital Books." Portico, in collaboration with Cornell University Library, will develop a prototype preservation service that will provide a practical model for the preservation of digitized books. The program will analyze electronic book data, identify a technological infrastructure to preserve electronic books, assess preservation costs and recovery options, create sample service-level agreements, and share the full preservation model with the cultural heritage community.

## Evaluation of IMLS Programs

IMLS encourages grant projects with strong evaluation components. In 2007 it awarded a grant of $362,490 through the Laura Bush 21st Century Librarian program to the Indiana University School of Library and Information Science to offer, enhance, and revise the online instructor-mediated courseware "Shaping

Outcomes" (http://www.shapingoutcomes.org/course). The course was developed and tested through a three-year collaborative agreement between IMLS and Indiana University-Purdue University Indianapolis's Museum Studies program and School of Library and Information Science. IMLS grantees and prospective applicants may enroll in the mediated course for a nominal fee or may use the unmediated online tutorial at no charge to improve their approaches to project planning, grant preparation, and measurement of results to successfully address the needs of audiences and users.

## IMLS Conferences and Activities

### Grants to States Conference

The eighth Grants to States Conference was held in Washington, D.C., October 31–November 2, 2007. There were 120 participants representing the SLAAs in the 50 states, the District of Columbia, Puerto Rico, and the Virgin Islands. The basic components of LSTA Grants to States program administration were covered, including statutory and regulatory overview, the life cycle of a grant, the building blocks of the program (determination and implementation of services and programs, matching allotment and activities to the grant calendar, and issues in the use of funds), management of the program at both the state and federal level (training, monitoring and tracking, attribution and copyright; dissemination of projects to the media and the library field; evaluation; record keeping and records retention; and audits), and IMLS resources for management of the LSTA Grants to States program.

### Pacific Region Grants Workshop

The second Pacific Region Grants Workshop was held in Honolulu February 19–20, 2008, with representation from American Samoa, the Commonwealth of Northern Mariana Islands, the Federated States of Micronesia, Guam, and the Republic of the Marshall Islands. The primary focus of the workshop was project planning, with an emphasis on the grant application for the FY 2008 competitive cycle. Individual meetings were held for each territory or freely associated state to review their grant projects and to provide technical assistance. Jane Barnwell, director of the Pacific Resource Center for PREL, was a guest speaker.

### WebWise

The Ninth Annual WebWise conference was held March 5–7, 2008, at the Miami Beach Convention Center. The 2008 conference was cosponsored by Wolfsonian–Florida International University, with additional support from the Florida Center for Library Automation and NEH. The theme was "WebWise 2.0: The Power of Community." More than 400 participants representing all types of museums and libraries nationwide attended. The conference focused on innovative ways that cultural heritage institutions can use technology to engage online audiences, create communities of interest, and build strong, sustainable programs to support research, education, and lifelong learning.

## IMLS Web Site and Publications

The IMLS Web site (http://www.imls.gov) provides information about the various grant programs, the National Medal for Museum and Library Service, and funded projects, plus application forms and staff contacts. The Web site also highlights model projects developed by libraries and museums throughout the country and provides materials on IMLS-sponsored conferences, publications, and studies. Through an electronic newsletter, *Primary Source,* IMLS provides information on grant deadlines and opportunities. Details on subscribing to the IMLS newsletter can be found on the Web site.

The following recent publications are available at the IMLS Web site: the 2009 "Grant and Award Opportunities" brochure; "Museums and Libraries Engaging America's Youth: Youth Practitioner's Guide"; the 2008 National Medal for Museum and Library Service brochure; and guidelines for each of the grant programs.

# Part 3
# Library/Information Science Education, Placement, and Salaries

# Employment Sources on the Internet

Catherine Barr
Contributing Editor

For the third year in a row, *US News & World Report* (http://www.usnews.com/
articles/business/best-careers/2008/12/11/best-careers-2009-librarian.html)
selected "librarian" as one of the best careers, based on criteria including job outlook, job satisfaction, prestige, and pay. Median national pay was given as
$51,400 and the job satisfaction and prestige received a higher rating than job
outlook. Special librarianship was again selected as the "smart specialty" and the
fastest-growing sector in an "underrated" field.

*Library Journal*'s "Placements and Salaries" report for 2008 was subtitled
"Library Jobs and Pay Both Up" and covered data received through 2007. The
"Where the Library Jobs Are" section shows public libraries accounting for 30
percent of placements; academic libraries, 26 percent; school libraries, 16 percent; other organizations, 15 percent; and special libraries, 8 percent. Government libraries, library cooperatives/networks, and vendors made up the
remaining 5 percent. The Midwest and Northeast offered the most positions. [See
the following article, "Placements and Salaries," for more details and discussion
of related topics—*Ed.*]

In *School Library Journal*'s Job Satisfaction survey, conducted in 2008, 74
percent of school and public librarians serving youth reported that they were
either very satisfied or satisfied with their jobs. Reports on the survey's results
(http://www.schoollibraryjournal.com/article/CA6624723.html?q=jobs) include
"The Money Gap," "Big Satisfactions," and "Librarians of Tomorrow."

The ALA-APA (American Library Association-Allied Professional Association) also reported 2008 findings (http://www.ala-apa.org/news/news.html#
survey08), including a 2 percent mean salary increase for librarians with ALA-
accredited master's degrees. Another survey was the Special Library Association's 2008 Salary Survey and Workplace Study (http://www.sla.org/content/
resources/research/salarysurveys/salsur2008/index.cfm), which shows a 5.3 percent mean increase for respondents in the United States in 2008.

*Library Journal*'s wide-ranging Job Satisfaction series, based on 2007 data,
includes articles that remain of interest ("Great Work, Genuine Problems,"
October 1, 2007, http://www.libraryjournal.com/article/CA6483878.html?q=
great+work) with reports on academic libraries ("Take This Job and Love It,"
February 1, 2008, http://www.libraryjournal.com/article/CA6523442.html?
q=take+this+job+and+love) and public libraries ("I ♥ Librarianship," March 1,
2008, http://www.libraryjournal.com/article/CA6533042.html?q=I+%3F+
Librarianship).

All these surveys, however, do not reflect the severe economic downturn of late 2008 and early 2009, and news of library layoffs and closures around the country.

The following is not a comprehensive list of the hundreds of job-related sites on the Internet of interest to librarians and information professionals. These are, however, the best starting places for a general job search in this area. Many offer additional information that will be helpful to those considering a career in librarianship, including advice on conducting a successful search, writing résumés, preparing for interviews, and negotiating salaries.

Before spending a lot of time on any Web site, users should check that the site has been updated recently and that out-of-date job listings no longer appear. The Directory of Organizations in Part 6 of this volume may also prove useful.

## Background Information

One particularly useful print resource, *The Information Professional's Guide to Career Development Online* (Information Today, Inc., 2002), has a companion Web site at http://www.lisjobs.com/careerdev. Both the print and the updated online versions present information on job hunting, networking, and online and continuing education. An article by the same authors—Rachel Singer Gordon and Sarah L. Nesbeitt—titled "Market Yourself Online!" appeared in the October/November 2001 issue of *Marketing Library Services*. The article presents practical advice on promoting yourself and your abilities on the Web; it is available at http://www.infotoday.com/mls/oct01/gordon&nesbeitt.htm.

The Bureau of Labor Statistics of the U.S. Department of Labor provides a thorough overview of the work of a librarian, necessary qualifications, and the job and salary outlook at http://stats.bls.gov/oco/ocos068.htm. Similar pages are available for archivists, curators, and museum technicians (http://stats.bls.gov/oco/ocos065.htm) and for library technicians (http://stats.bls.gov/oco/ocos113.htm). More-detailed employment and wage estimates can be found at http://stats.bls.gov/oes/current/oes254021.htm for librarians, at http://stats.bls.gov/oes/current/oes254011.htm for archivists, and at http://stats.bls.gov/oes/current/oes254031.htm for library technicians.

An excellent 2002 *American Libraries* feature article by Linda K. Wallace on the breadth of opportunities available to librarians and information professionals—"Places an MLS Can Take You"—is archived at http://www.ala.org/ala/educationcareers/careers/paths/al_mls.pdf.

The American Library Association (ALA) provides a user-friendly overview of librarianship at LibraryCareer.org (http://www.ala.org/ala/educationcareers/careers/librarycareerssite/home.cfm), and Info*Nation: Choose a Career in Libraries (http://www.cla.ca/infonation/welcome.htm) is an excellent Canadian site that describes the work of librarians, combining brief information on a variety of career options with statements by individual librarians about why they love their jobs. These two sites will be particularly useful for young people considering a possible career in librarianship.

Finally, How to Apply for a Library Job (http://www.liswiki.com/wiki/HOWTO:Apply_for_a_library_job) offers thoughtful advice and practical interview tips.

## General Sites/Portals

**American Library Association: Education and Careers**   http://www.ala.org/ala/educationcareers/index.cfm

Maintained by ALA. A useful source of information on library careers, education and professional development, scholarships, and salaries.

**ALA JobLIST**   http://joblist.ala.org

Sponsored by ALA and the Association of College and Research Libraries. This site incorporates the former job sites of *American Libraries* magazine and *C&RL News*. Registration is free for jobseekers, who can post their résumés and search jobs by library type, date, state, institution name, salary range, and other parameters. Employers can choose from a menu of print and electronic posting combinations.

**Canadian Library Association: Library Careers**   http://www.cla.ca/AM/Template.cfm?Section=Library_Careers

The Canadian Library Association lists Canadian job openings here and provides guidance on recognition of foreign credentials.

**Employment Resources: Organizations and Associations**   http://slisweb.sjsu.edu/resources/employment.htm

Maintained by San José State University's School of Library and Information Science. Gives links to organizations that will be of interest to students at the university, including a number of California sites. A related page, Professional Associations in the Information Sciences (http://slisweb.sjsu.edu/resources/orgs.htm), is a comprehensive listing of associations in the United States and abroad. And excellent information on conducting job searches and professional development in general can be found at http://slisgroups.sjsu.edu/alumni/jobseekers/index.html.

**LibGig**   http://www.libgig.com

This professional networking site offers jobs, "who's hiring" job alerts, résumé consultation, employer profiles, news, blogs, and so forth.

**Library Job Postings on the Internet**   http://www.libraryjobpostings.org

Compiled by Sarah (Nesbeitt) Johnson of Booth Library, Eastern Illinois University, coauthor of *The Information Professional's Guide to Career Development Online* (Information Today, Inc., 2002); there is a link to the book's companion Web site on this site. Provides links to library employment sites in the United States and abroad, with easy access by location and by category of job.

**LIScareer.com**   http://www.liscareer.com

Maintained by Priscilla Shontz and Richard Murray, coeditors of *A Day in the Life: Career Options in Library and Information Science* (Libraries Unlimited, 2007). Subtitled The Library & Information Science Professional's Career Development Center, this helpful and up-to-date site provides no job listings, but offers bibliographies of resources of interest in the areas of career planning, education, job hunting, experience, work/life balance, networking, mentoring, interpersonal skills, leadership, and publishing. This is an excellent place to begin research on library jobs.

**Lisjobs.com—Jobs for Librarians and**          http://www.lisjobs.com
**Information Professionals**
Maintained by Rachel Singer Gordon, author of books including *What's the Alternative? Career Options for Librarians and Info Pros* (Information Today, Inc., 2008), *Information Tomorrow: Reflections on Technology and the Future of Public and Academic Libraries* (Information Today, Inc., 2007), *The NextGen Librarian's Survival Guide* (Information Today, 2006), and *The Accidental Library Manager* (Information Today, Inc., 2005), and coauthor of *The Information Professional's Guide to Career Development Online* (Information Today, Inc., 2001).

This newly updated site includes a searchable database of job listings (RSS feed available), links to job banks, and useful job hunting and career development resources. Job seekers can post résumés for a small fee. The site also features an interesting professional development newsletter, *Info Career Trends* (http://lisjobs.com/career_trends), information on scholarships and funding for continuing education, and a section called "Career Q&A with the Library Career People," which provides detailed answers to users' questions.

**The Riley Guide: Employment Opportunities**          http://www.rileyguide.com
**and Job Resources on the Internet**
Compiled by Margaret F. Dikel, a private consultant and coauthor with Frances Roehm of *The Guide to Internet Job Searching* (McGraw-Hill, 2006). A general site rich in advice for the job seeker, from résumé writing and how to target a new employer to tips on networking and interviewing. Links to job sites are organized by type of opportunity; Information Delivery, Design, and Management is found under The Humanities, Social Sciences, and Personal Services.


## Sites by Sector

### Public Libraries

Public library openings can be found at all the general sites/portals listed above.

**Careers in Public Librarianship**          http://www.ala.org/
                                              ala/mgrps/divs/pla/placareers/index.cfm
The Public Library Association offers information on public librarianship, with a section on the experiences of PLA members.


### School Libraries

School library openings can be found at many of the sites listed above. Sites with interesting material for aspiring school librarians include those listed below.

**AASL: Recruitment to School Librarianship**          http://www.ala.org/ala/mgrps/
                                                        divs/aasl/aasleducation/recruitmentlib/aaslrecruitment.cfm

The American Association of School Librarians hosts this site, which describes the role of school librarians, salary and job outlooks, and mentoring programs; provides testimonials from working library media specialists; and offers state-by-state information on licensure, scholarships, library education, job hunting, mentoring, and recruitment efforts.

General education sites usually include school library openings. Among sites with nationwide coverage is:

**Education America**                    http://www.educationamerica.net
Library openings can be searched by geographic location.

### Special and Academic Libraries

**AALL Job Placement Hotline**          http://www.aallnet.org/hotline/hotline.asp
Maintained by the American Association of Law Librarians.

**Association of College and Research Libraries**
See ALA JobLIST above.

**ALISE: Job Placement**                       http://www.alise.org/
The Association for Library and Information Science Education posts jobs for deans, directors, and faculty.

**ASIS&T: Careers**                        http://www.asist.org/careers.html
A jobline maintained by the American Society for Information Science and Technology.

**Association of Research Libraries: Career Resources**     http://careers.arl.org/
In addition to listings of openings at ARL member institutions and at other organizations, there is information on ARL's Career Enhancement Program and Initiative to Recruit a Diverse Workforce plus a database of research library residency and internship programs.

**Chronicle of Higher Education**               http://chronicle.com/jobs
Listings can be browsed, with geographical options, under the category "Library/ information sciences" (found under "Professional fields") or searched by simple keyword such as "library." Articles and advice on job searching are also available.

**EDUCAUSE Job Posting Service**          http://www.educause.edu/jobpost
EDUCAUSE member organizations post positions "in the broad field of information technology in higher education."

**HigherEdJobs.com**                      http://www.higheredjobs.com
Published by Internet Employment Linkage, Inc. The category "Libraries" is found under Administrative Positions.

**Major Orchestra Librarians' Association**         http://www.mola-inc.org/
A nice site for a field that might be overlooked. The Resources section includes an introduction to the work of an orchestra librarian.

**Medical Library Association: Career Development**     http://www.mlanet.org/
career/index.html
The Medical Library Association offers much more than job listings here, with brochures on medical librarianship, a video, career tips, and a mentor program.

**Music Library Association Job Openings**   http://www.musiclibraryassoc.org/
employmentanded/joblist/openings.shtml
Along with job postings, this site features an article titled "Music Librarianship
—Is It for You?" and a listing of resources for the mid-career music librarian.

**SLA: Career Center**   http://www.sla.org/content/jobs/index.cfm
In addition to salary information and searchable job listings that are available to
all users, the Special Libraries Association provides many services for association members.

### Government

**Library of Congress**   http://www.loc.gov/hr/employment
Current job openings, internships, fellowships, and volunteering.

**National Archives and Records Administration**   http://www.archives.gov/
careers/
Employment opportunities, internships, and volunteering.

### Library Support Staff

**Library Support Staff**   http://www.ala.org/ala/aboutala/offices/hrdr/
**Resource Center**  librarysupportstaff/library_support_staff_resource_center.cfm
Maintained by ALA, this page includes information on the kinds of jobs available and the work environments, relevant events, certification requirements,
financial assistance, advancement opportunities, and so forth.

### Serials

**NASIG Jobs**   http://jobs.nasig.org/
Managed by the North American Serials Interest Group. Accepts serials-related
job postings.

## Library Periodicals

**American Libraries**
See ALA JobList above.

**Library Journal**   http://jobs.libraryjournal.com
Easy access to online job listings.

**School Library Journal**   http://www.schoollibraryjournal.com/
Click on the Jobs tab for access to a general list of job openings (jointly maintained with *Library Journal*; you must filter by Children's/Young Adult to access
school positions.

## Employment Agencies/Commercial Services

A number of employment agencies and commercial services in the United States
and abroad specialize in library-related jobs. Among those that keep up-to-date
listings on their Web sites are:

**Advanced Information Management**     http://www.aimusa.com
Specializes in librarians and support staff in a variety of types of libraries across the country.

**ASLIB**     http://www.aslib.co.uk/recruitment/index.htm
Lists jobs available in Britain.

**Library Associates**     http://www.libraryassociates.com/index.php4?page=jobs
An easy-to-use list of openings that can be sorted by state.

**TPFL: The Information People:**     http://www.tfpl.com/permanent_
**Recruitment and Executive Search**     recruitment/candidates/pjobs.cfm
Specializes in jobs in the fields of knowledge management, library and information management, records management, and Web and content management. Jobs around the world are listed, with the majority in the United Kingdom.

## Listservs

Many listservs allow members to post job openings on a casual basis.

**jESSE**     http://web.utk.edu/~gwhitney/jesse.html
This worldwide discussion group focuses on library and information science education; LIS faculty position announcements frequently appear here.

**LIBJOBS**     http://www.ifla.org/II/lists/libjobs.htm
Managed by the International Federation of Library Associations and Institutions (IFLA). Subscribers to this list receive posted job opportunities by e-mail.

**PUBLIB**     http://sunsite.berkeley.edu/PubLib
Public library job openings often appear on this list.

## Blogs

**The Blogging Libraries Wiki**     http://www.blogwithoutalibrary.net/
links/index.php?title=Welcome_to_the_Blogging_Libraries_Wiki
Provides lists of library blogs in the following fields: Academic Libraries, Public Libraries, School Libraries, Special Libraries, Internal Library Communication, Library Associations, and Library Director.

**Beyond the Job**     http://www.beyondthejob.org/
Maintained by Sarah Johnson and Rachel Singer Gordon, this blog focuses on job-hunting advice and professional development.

**Career Q&A with the Library Career People**     http://www.lisjobs.com/
careerqa_blog/
Formerly an advice column in the *Info Career Trends Newsletter*, this attractive and user-friendly blog is maintained by librarians Tiffany Allen and Susanne Markgren and is intended to "create an enlightening discussion forum of professional guidance and advice for librarians, library staff, and those thinking of entering the profession." Categories include job satisfaction, job seeking, and professional development.

# Placements and Salaries: Jobs and Pay Both Up

Stephanie Maatta

Assistant Professor, University of South Florida, Tampa

Despite a difficult economy and tightening budgets, both jobs and salaries rose for 2007 library and information science (LIS) graduates. Echoing the previous year's growth, reported annual salaries increased approximately 3.1 percent, from $41,014 in 2006 to $42,361. The picture was most positive for graduates in the Southeast, whose average annual starting salary surged past the $40,000 barrier that graduates there have been struggling to reach, increasing to $41,579, a significant gain of 8.2 percent. Minority graduates who found jobs in the Southeast also reported a reversal of fortunes, with average annual starting salaries up by 16.2 percent to $46,093, after falling to $39,674 in 2006.

In other highlights, academic libraries in the Northeast contributed to the improved job scene, with 11.8 percent more graduates hired and salaries up approximately 5.5 percent to $41,340. School library media specialists experienced higher placement rates in almost all regions of the United States and at worst held steady from the previous year, with commensurate salaries approximately 5.6 percent higher than in 2006.

There are many more positive aspects to note, with minorities and men faring even better than the 3.1 percent average overall rise in salaries, at 5.5 percent and 4.4 percent growth, respectively. The tremendous jump in salaries for new hires in the Southeast helped propel the overall average upward, with an additional boost from the extraordinarily high salaries garnered by the graduates of the University of Michigan (averaging $55,869, almost 32 percent above the rest). With the exception of the combined Canadian and international reporting, regional salaries across the board topped the $40,000 level, compared to 2006, when salaries in the Southeast, Midwest, and Southwest remained in the high $30,000s. Regionally, salary growth in the Northeast and in the Southwest was slightly lower than the average but nonetheless up from previous years. One real surprise was substantial growth in the number of graduates accepting professional positions as archivists. Compared with other types of jobs, archival placements comprise about 4.3 percent of the reported staffing. However, this was a 22 percent increase from the previous year. Archivists also experienced a 14.4 percent bump up in salary, to $40,286.

Nonetheless, 2007 was not without challenges. For a second year in a row, nonprofessional and temporary positions increased, hinting at the struggles many library systems face in maintaining high levels of service with fewer resources and personnel. The job search was a little longer and a little harder for many graduates, and reports indicate a continued rise in part-time positions.

Fewer responses from LIS graduates were received for 2007, though the response rate continues to fluctuate around 33 percent; over the last several survey periods it ranged from 30 percent to 40 percent. Of the approximate 5,300 reported graduates, 1,768 responded. This has implications for measuring some placements, but overall percentages were consistent with previous years.

Adapted from *Library Journal,* October 15, 2008.    *(text continues on page 360)*

## Table 1 / Status of 2007 Graduates*

| | Number of Schools Reporting | Number of Graduates Responding | Permanent Professional | Temporary Professional | Non-professional | Total | Graduates Outside of Profession | Unemployed or Status Unreported |
|---|---|---|---|---|---|---|---|---|
| Northeast | 12 | 476 | 289 | 38 | 65 | 392 | 14 | 70 |
| Southeast | 9 | 223 | 157 | 12 | 16 | 185 | 11 | 27 |
| Midwest | 11 | 577 | 419 | 36 | 49 | 504 | 26 | 47 |
| Southwest | 6 | 236 | 175 | 14 | 17 | 206 | 10 | 20 |
| West | 4 | 168 | 100 | 23 | 14 | 137 | 7 | 24 |
| Canada | 1 | 48 | 20 | 14 | 9 | 43 | — | 5 |
| Total | 43 | 1,768 | 1,189 | 140 | 170 | 1,499 | 70 | 199 |

* Table based on survey responses from schools and individual graduates. Figures will not necessarily be fully consistent with some of the other data reported. Tables do not always add up, individually or collectively, since both schools and individuals omitted data in some cases.

## Table 2 / Placements and Full-Time Salaries of 2007 Graduates/Summary by Region*

| Region | Number of Placements | Salaries | | | Low Salary | | High Salary | | Average Salary | | | Median Salary | | |
|---|---|---|---|---|---|---|---|---|---|---|---|---|---|---|
| | | Women | Men | Total | Women | Men | Women | Men | Women | Men | All | Women | Men | All |
| Northeast | 295 | 201 | 57 | 260 | $15,000 | $18,720 | $80,000 | $100,000 | $41,702 | $45,163 | $42,478 | $40,040 | $43,000 | $40,900 |
| Southeast | 221 | 150 | 45 | 199 | 14,400 | 17,000 | 121,000 | 87,500 | 41,145 | 43,158 | 41,579 | 40,000 | 42,000 | 40,000 |
| Midwest | 361 | 263 | 62 | 329 | 15,000 | 20,000 | 115,000 | 75,000 | 39,844 | 42,605 | 40,290 | 38,100 | 41,000 | 38,500 |
| Southwest | 176 | 133 | 23 | 157 | 20,300 | 28,000 | 93,000 | 88,000 | 40,795 | 42,841 | 41,047 | 40,000 | 40,000 | 40,000 |
| West | 141 | 98 | 28 | 127 | 20,000 | 30,000 | 93,000 | 150,000 | 49,639 | 55,068 | 50,736 | 47,000 | 50,000 | 48,000 |
| Canada/Int'l.* | 53 | 13 | 6 | 46 | 25,000 | 18,000 | 60,000 | 66,000 | 39,700 | 44,988 | 39,757 | 35,000 | 48,000 | 43,000 |
| Combined | 1,292 | 875 | 224 | 1,112 | $14,400 | $17,000 | $121,000 | $150,000 | $41,731 | $45,192 | $42,361 | $40,000 | $42,500 | $40,000 |

* All international salaries converted to American dollars based on conversion rates for August 18, 2008. This table represents only salaries and placements reported as full-time. Some data were reported as aggregate without breakdown by gender or region. Comparison with other tables will show different numbers of placements.

## Table 3 / Status of 2007 Graduates in Library Professions**

| Schools | Graduates | | | Employed | | | Unemployed | | | Students | | |
|---|---|---|---|---|---|---|---|---|---|---|---|---|
| | Women | Men | Total | Women | Men | Total | Women | Men | Total | Women | Men | Total |
| Alabama | 84 | 26 | 110 | 17 | 6 | 23 | 2 | 1 | 3 | — | 1 | 1 |
| Albany | 65 | 17 | 82 | 26 | 9 | 35 | 2 | — | 2 | — | — | — |
| Arizona** | 120 | 25 | 145 | — | — | — | — | — | — | — | — | — |
| Buffalo* | 31 | 12 | 43 | 29 | 10 | 39 | 2 | 1 | 3 | — | 1 | 1 |
| Denver | 75 | 15 | 90 | 18 | 5 | 24 | 1 | 1 | 1 | — | — | — |
| Dominican | 233 | 63 | 296 | 42 | 7 | 50 | 1 | 1 | 2 | — | — | — |
| Drexel | 141 | 40 | 181 | 38 | 16 | 56 | 5 | 1 | 6 | — | — | — |
| Emporia** | 74 | 18 | 92 | — | — | — | — | — | — | — | — | — |
| Florida State* | 53 | 19 | 73 | 47 | 17 | 65 | 6 | 1 | 7 | — | 1 | 1 |
| Hawaii | 37 | 11 | 48 | 18 | 4 | 22 | 1 | — | 1 | — | — | — |
| Illinois | 189 | 58 | 247 | 67 | 16 | 83 | 1 | — | 1 | 2 | — | 2 |
| Indiana | 175 | 46 | 221 | 40 | 12 | 52 | 4 | — | 4 | — | — | — |
| Iowa* | — | — | 5 | — | — | 5 | — | — | — | — | — | — |
| Kent State | 236 | 54 | 290 | 71 | 10 | 81 | 3 | 1 | 4 | — | 1 | 1 |
| Kentucky* | 25 | 9 | 35 | 21 | 7 | 29 | 4 | 1 | 5 | — | — | — |
| Long Island** | 166 | 41 | 207 | — | — | — | — | — | — | — | 1 | 1 |
| Louisiana State | 43 | 15 | 58 | 5 | — | 5 | — | — | — | — | — | — |
| Maryland* | 1 | — | 1 | 1 | — | 1 | — | — | — | — | — | — |
| Michigan* | — | — | — | 56 | 37 | 93 | — | — | — | 2 | 2 | 4 |
| Missouri–Columbia | 66 | 13 | 79 | 17 | 3 | 20 | 1 | — | 1 | — | — | — |
| N.C. Chapel Hill** | 82 | 31 | 113 | — | — | — | — | — | — | — | — | — |
| N.C. Greensboro | 64 | 10 | 74 | 12 | 4 | 16 | 1 | — | 1 | — | — | — |
| North Texas* | 108 | 19 | 127 | 101 | 17 | 118 | 4 | 2 | 6 | 3 | — | 3 |

| | | | | | | | | | | | | |
|---|---|---|---|---|---|---|---|---|---|---|---|---|
| Oklahoma | 41 | 10 | 51 | 8 | 1 | 9 | — | — | — | — | — | — |
| Pittsburgh* | 26 | 9 | 34 | 23 | 6 | 29 | 2 | 3 | 5 | 1 | — | 1 |
| Pratt | 119 | 29 | 148 | 24 | 3 | 27 | 1 | 1 | 2 | — | — | — |
| Rhode Island | 47 | 5 | 52 | 27 | 2 | 29 | 3 | 1 | 4 | 1 | — | 1 |
| Rutgers | 85 | 22 | 107 | 15 | 1 | 16 | 1 | — | 1 | — | — | — |
| San Jose | 420 | 157 | 577 | 85 | 15 | 100 | 5 | 1 | 6 | — | 3 | 3 |
| Simmons | 176 | 37 | 213 | 101 | 30 | 131 | 28 | 4 | 32 | 2 | — | 2 |
| So. Connecticut | 76 | 21 | 97 | 17 | 4 | 21 | 1 | — | 1 | — | — | — |
| South Florida | 142 | 30 | 172 | 30 | 2 | 32 | — | — | — | — | — | — |
| St. John's* | 9 | 1 | 10 | 9 | 1 | 10 | — | — | — | — | — | — |
| Syracuse | 79 | 18 | 97 | 7 | 5 | 12 | 2 | — | 2 | — | — | — |
| Tennessee* | 23 | 5 | 28 | 21 | 5 | 26 | 2 | — | 2 | 2 | — | 2 |
| Texas–Austin | 92 | 25 | 117 | 24 | 6 | 30 | 1 | — | 1 | 2 | — | 2 |
| Texas Women's | 164 | 8 | 172 | 35 | 2 | 37 | 4 | — | 4 | — | 3 | 3 |
| UCLA | 73 | 14 | 87 | 9 | — | 9 | 2 | — | 2 | 3 | — | 3 |
| Washington | 106 | 27 | 133 | 9 | 5 | 14 | 1 | — | 1 | — | — | — |
| Wayne State* | 83 | 16 | 99 | 71 | 14 | 85 | 7 | 2 | 9 | 5 | — | 5 |
| Western Ontario** | 116 | 31 | 147 | — | — | 43 | — | — | 4 | — | — | 1 |
| Wisconsin–Madison | 74 | 21 | 95 | 32 | 3 | 35 | 1 | — | 1 | — | — | — |
| Wisconsin–Milwaukee | 121 | 24 | 145 | 30 | 4 | 34 | 3 | — | 3 | — | 3 | 3 |
| Total | 4,140 | 1,052 | 5,317 | 1,203 | 289 | 1,546 | 102 | 20 | 125 | 21 | 9 | 31 |

Tables do not always add up, individually or collectively, since both schools and individuals omitted data in some cases.

* For schools that did not fill out the institutional survey, data were taken from graduate surveys, thus there is not full representation of their graduating classes.

** Some schools completed the institutional survey, but responses were not received from graduates; or schools conducted their own survey and provided reports. This table represents placements of any kind. Comparison with other tables will show different numbers of placements.

## Table 4 / Placements by Full-Time Salary of Reporting 2007 Graduates*

| | Average Salary | | | Median Salary | | Low Salary | | High Salary | | Salaries | | Total Placements |
|---|---|---|---|---|---|---|---|---|---|---|---|---|
| | Women | Men | All | Women | Men | Women | Men | Women | Men | Women | Men | |
| Michigan | $54,959 | $57,000 | $55,869 | $50,000 | $51,000 | $32,500 | $30,000 | $115,000 | $90,000 | 41 | 33 | 92 |
| Maryland | 52,500 | — | 52,500 | 52,500 | — | 52,500 | — | 52,500 | — | 1 | — | 1 |
| San Jose | 48,672 | 52,947 | 49,293 | 45,000 | 50,000 | 23,000 | 30,000 | 90,000 | 91,000 | 53 | 9 | 100 |
| Washington | 46,375 | 51,779 | 48,176 | 44,000 | 52,000 | 35,000 | 47,115 | 57,000 | 55,000 | 8 | 4 | 14 |
| UCLA | 47,550 | — | 47,689 | 47,500 | — | 41,200 | — | 55,000 | — | 8 | — | 9 |
| Western Ontario | — | — | 47,266 | — | — | — | — | — | — | — | — | 44 |
| Southern Connecticut | 47,909 | 43,550 | 46,975 | 47,000 | 44,000 | 20,000 | 39,650 | 82,000 | 47,000 | 11 | 3 | 21 |
| Rutgers | 46,870 | 42,000 | 46,428 | 46,695 | 42,000 | 33,613 | 42,000 | 59,000 | 42,000 | 10 | 1 | 16 |
| Pratt | 42,133 | 72,333 | 45,908 | 39,295 | 65,000 | 31,000 | 52,000 | 63,000 | 100,000 | 21 | 3 | 27 |
| Tennessee | 44,384 | 39,495 | 43,355 | 38,000 | 39,750 | 30,000 | 38,480 | 121,000 | 40,000 | 15 | 4 | 26 |
| Drexel | 40,359 | 53,419 | 43,280 | 39,000 | 51,000 | 24,000 | 34,000 | 60,000 | 90,000 | 27 | 11 | 56 |
| North Texas | 41,886 | 51,503 | 43,149 | 41,500 | 40,000 | 15,000 | 24,000 | 76,440 | 150,000 | 86 | 13 | 118 |
| Illinois | 41,875 | 47,115 | 43,011 | 40,000 | 51,000 | 15,000 | 24,000 | 80,000 | 58,000 | 54 | 14 | 83 |
| Texas Women's | 42,747 | 48,000 | 42,941 | 42,000 | 48,000 | 20,300 | 48,000 | 69,000 | 48,000 | 26 | 1 | 37 |
| Florida State | 42,534 | 40,689 | 42,283 | 42,000 | 40,000 | 26,000 | 32,500 | 63,000 | 53,000 | 30 | 11 | 65 |
| Syracuse | 42,100 | 41,900 | 42,000 | 46,000 | 45,000 | 33,500 | 25,500 | 48,000 | 52,000 | 5 | 5 | 12 |
| Hawaii | 42,818 | 37,667 | 41,714 | 45,000 | 40,000 | 20,000 | 32,000 | 60,000 | 41,000 | 11 | 3 | 22 |
| St. John's | 42,508 | 36,000 | 41,579 | 40,525 | 36,000 | 18,000 | 36,000 | 65,000 | 36,000 | 6 | 1 | 10 |
| Wayne State | 41,175 | 43,160 | 41,557 | 41,000 | 40,098 | 21,000 | 32,900 | 78,000 | 60,000 | 42 | 10 | 85 |

| School | | | | | | | | | | | | |
|---|---|---|---|---|---|---|---|---|---|---|---|---|
| Rhode Island | 40,956 | 49,000 | 41,379 | 40,500 | 49,000 | 30,000 | 49,000 | 58,000 | 49,000 | 18 | 1 | 29 |
| Texas (Austin) | 41,023 | 41,417 | 41,108 | 39,002 | 41,250 | 30,000 | 28,000 | 93,000 | 59,000 | 22 | 6 | 30 |
| Simmons | 39,575 | 44,235 | 40,818 | 39,000 | 40,800 | 12,000 | 25,778 | 62,500 | 80,000 | 55 | 20 | 131 |
| Dominican | 40,467 | 41,957 | 40,674 | 37,000 | 42,500 | 15,000 | 34,500 | 71,700 | 52,000 | 33 | 7 | 50 |
| Buffalo | 39,008 | 44,675 | 40,519 | 38,750 | 44,000 | 29,000 | 32,000 | 55,000 | 62,400 | 22 | 8 | 39 |
| South Florida | 40,027 | 44,968 | 40,407 | 39,795 | 44,968 | 31,512 | 44,936 | 56,000 | 62,400 | 24 | 2 | 32 |
| Denver | 41,153 | 39,075 | 40,345 | 40,000 | 36,250 | 30,000 | 34,000 | 62,454 | 45,000 | 15 | 4 | 24 |
| N.C. Greensboro | 40,147 | 39,333 | 39,925 | 41,000 | 37,000 | 32,575 | 34,000 | 46,600 | 49,800 | 8 | 3 | 16 |
| Albany | 39,018 | 40,701 | 39,424 | 40,023 | 39,250 | 26,500 | 24,000 | 50,000 | 47,000 | 22 | 7 | 35 |
| Oklahoma | 38,510 | 40,000 | 38,676 | 38,540 | 40,000 | 25,000 | 40,000 | 60,000 | 65,000 | 8 | 1 | 9 |
| Wisconsin–Milwaukee | 38,907 | 36,980 | 38,656 | 37,000 | 39,000 | 28,000 | 28,000 | 55,538 | 40,000 | 20 | 3 | 34 |
| Wisconsin–Madison | 38,959 | 34,500 | 38,651 | 38,000 | 34,500 | 19,000 | 33,000 | 70,000 | 43,939 | 27 | 2 | 35 |
| Kent State University | 37,226 | 37,039 | 37,204 | 38,000 | 38,000 | 23,000 | 20,000 | 56,000 | 36,000 | 51 | 7 | 81 |
| Pittsburgh | 37,497 | 35,537 | 37,045 | 37,750 | 39,250 | 19,440 | 18,720 | 54,500 | 59,000 | 20 | 6 | 29 |
| Missouri–Columbia | 35,888 | 41,933 | 36,896 | 36,700 | 37,800 | 25,000 | 35,000 | 50,000 | 52,000 | 15 | 3 | 20 |
| Iowa | — | — | 36,086 | — | — | — | — | — | 53,000 | — | — | 5 |
| Indiana | 34,970 | 38,296 | 35,726 | 33,825 | 39,000 | 20,500 | 18,000 | 55,000 | 50,000 | 34 | 10 | 52 |
| Alabama | 35,894 | 30,667 | 34,972 | 37,500 | 33,000 | 20,800 | 19,000 | 45,000 | 40,000 | 14 | 3 | 23 |
| Louisiana State | 34,330 | — | 34,330 | 36,960 | — | 24,400 | — | 39,000 | — | 4 | — | 5 |
| Kentucky | 34,044 | 27,857 | 32,150 | 34,000 | 32,000 | 22,000 | 17,000 | 47,700 | 40,000 | 17 | 7 | 29 |

* This table represents only placements and salaries reported as full-time. Some individuals or schools omitted some information, rendering information unusable. Comparisons with other tables will show different numbers of placement and salary. Table is sorted in descending order by average salary for all reported. Average overall salary = $42,361.

*(continued from page 354)*

## Public Libraries Drive Job Growth

Public libraries continue to be a popular choice for employment, averaging 28 percent of the overall reported placements. This figure has held steady over the last several years, consistently hovering around 27 percent to 29 percent. Increased hires were reported in the Midwest (up approximately 12 percent); in the Southwest, graduates reported 12.2 percent more public library hires. Unfortunately, public library salaries in the Midwest and Southwest did not follow suit, dipping an average of 3.0 percent below 2006 averages. An area of concern is children's services. Placements decreased, and salaries were flat for 2007. One possible explanation may be a redefining of the title to encompass both children's and youth services (teen and/or YA librarians), as there was a 3.6 percent increase in the number of graduates reporting their job as youth services rather than children's. However, average starting salaries for youth services librarians decreased 3.53 percent, to $35,929. The other possibility for decreased numbers is the overall economic impact on library funding and the number of public libraries, which employ the majority of children's and youth services librarians, suffering layoffs and reductions in services.

## School Library Snapshot

School library media centers showed some of the best growth among all types of library and information science agencies in 2007. Placements in the Midwest, Southwest, and West increased substantially, averaging 26.8 percent growth across the three regions. At the same time, the overall average starting salary for new school library media specialists took a giant step up to $44,935 (an impressive 5.6 percent increase from $42,420 in 2006). This improvement was spurred by a 9.9 percent growth in salaries in the Southwest and 20 percent in the West. Some caution needs to be applied to the salary growth for school library media specialists, however, as many graduates explain that their salaries are based on a standard teacher's pay scale for their states. As teachers move from the classroom to the media center, salary and compensation levels follow them; this means that the level they earned in the classroom will be their base for the media center positions and doesn't always indicate a pay increase with the achievement of a master's degree.

## A Changing Academic Environment

In light of recent professional discussions about tenure status for academic librarians, it seemed timely to explore graduate experiences in academic settings. Of the 416 graduates who accepted positions in academic libraries, 336 responded to inquiries regarding their faculty status and appointment. Surprisingly, 81.2 percent were hired for nontenured positions, and only 3.2 percent of the new hires had nine-month (or academic year) appointments. (A question that was not explored but may address the tenure/nontenure conundrum is the number of academic librarians in community or junior colleges compared with those at tiered research institutions.)

The more interesting responses were from the academic librarians who described their appointments as "other." This group comprised 21.9 percent of the responses to questions about the length of their service term (nine-month vs. 12-month). The appointments were described in a variety of ways, including grant-funded short-term, adjunct, semester by semester, and library fellows programs. One perhaps not unexpected finding was that the new academic librarians with tenure-earning status (18.8 percent of respondents) garnered starting salaries that were 8.8 percent higher than those of the nontenure-earning professionals and 6.7 percent higher than those of all new academic librarians ($43,634 compared to $40,090 and $40,911, respectively).

## I-school vs. L-school

This year's survey provided real opportunities to examine the debate between library science and information science in more detail. In 2006 and again in 2007, graduates were asked to define whether their jobs were information science (IS), library science (LS), or "other." Of the 1,347 graduates who responded to the question, 75.8 percent stated that their jobs were definitely LS, 9.2 percent claimed IS (down slightly from 2006), and the remaining 15 percent described their positions as falling into other professional areas, most frequently as grant-supported positions, corporate affiliation, or education (classroom teachers and higher education). The "other" category was also used for many of the reported archival positions.

The LS vs. IS question represents more than philosophical underpinnings and types of jobs (user experience interface designer vs. reference/information specialist, for example). For some it shows a significant difference in salary. A straight dollar-to-dollar comparison suggests that graduates describing their jobs as IS earned almost 20 percent more on average for their starting salaries than other graduates ($48,354 compared to $40,308). Five of the iSchools Caucus members reported average starting salaries significantly above the overall averages (ranging from 9.6 percent higher to a whopping 31.9 percent higher). Interestingly, though higher overall, the IS salaries remained flat between 2006 and 2007 while the salaries for LS jobs improved by 1.8 percent.

On the other hand, designation as an I-school and membership in the iSchools Caucus seem to have less impact on how the graduates defined themselves. The IS graduates who clearly identified themselves with information science made up only 28 percent of the IS pool.

The combination of regionality and IS designation also played a role in salary achievements. Graduates who accepted jobs on the West Coast historically attained higher salaries than others. In 2007 the pay difference was 19.7 percent (or $8,375) for all graduates. Salary differences were even more apparent when regional placement was compared among the IS graduates. Graduates identifying IS positions on the West Coast earned 36.3 percent higher salaries than the entire pool of IS graduates. The graduates who defined their jobs as IS-related in the

Midwest, where overall salaries were among the lowest in 2007, negotiated the lowest salaries for positions.

## Where the Jobs Are

In light of the LS vs. IS debate, a few unexpected trends among the individual schools' placements emerged along with several predictable ones. Graduates of University of Washington, an I-school, for example, reported 42.9 percent of their placements in public libraries when one might anticipate there would be higher placements in other types of agencies among I-school graduates. Despite high placements in libraries with traditionally lower salary ranges, Washington graduates maintained one the highest average salaries among all of the programs. Southern Connecticut State University, an L-school, followed the same trend of 42.9 percent placements in public libraries with better than average starting salaries. Comparatively, University of Kentucky, an I-school, saw graduates reporting 53.6 percent placement in public libraries but garnering the lowest average salary levels among the programs. In these instances, location played a more a significant role in determining salary than did the type of library, while being from an I-school or an L-school had little impact.

In a much more predictable pattern, the University of Michigan (UM), an I-school, dominated the "other" category, placing 56.3 percent of its graduates in agencies such as consulting, e-commerce, financial services, and interactive mar-

### Table 5 / Average Salary Index Starting Library Positions, 1990–2007

| Year | Library Schools | Average Beginning Salary | Dollar Increase in Average Salary | Salary Index | BLS-CPI* |
|------|------|------|------|------|------|
| 1990 | 38 | $25,306 | $725 | 143.03 | 130.7 |
| 1991 | 46 | 25,583 | 277 | 144.59 | 136.2 |
| 1992 | 41 | 26,666 | 1,083 | 150.71 | 140.5 |
| 1993 | 50 | 27,116 | 450 | 153.26 | 144.4 |
| 1994 | 43 | 28,086 | 970 | 158.74 | 148.4 |
| 1995 | 41 | 28,997 | 911 | 163.89 | 152.5 |
| 1996 | 44 | 29,480 | 483 | 166.62 | 159.1 |
| 1997 | 43 | 30,270 | 790 | 171.05 | 161.6 |
| 1998 | 47 | 31,915 | 1,645 | 180.38 | 164.3 |
| 1999 | 37 | 33,976 | 2,061 | 192.03 | 168.7 |
| 2000 | 37 | 34,871 | 895 | 197.26 | 175.1 |
| 2001 | 40 | 36,818 | 1,947 | 208.09 | 177.1 |
| 2002 | 30 | 37,456 | 638 | 211.70 | 179.9 |
| 2003 | 43 | 37,975 | 519 | 214.63 | 184.0 |
| 2004 | 46 | 39,079 | 1,104 | 220.87 | 188.9 |
| 2005 | 37 | 40,115 | 1,036 | 226.73 | 195.3 |
| 2006 | 45 | 41,014 | 899 | 231.81 | 201.6 |
| 2007 | 43 | 42,361 | 1,347 | 239.42 | 210.0 |

* U.S. Department of Labor, Bureau of Labor Statistics, Consumer Price index, All Urban Consumers (CPI-U), U.S. city average, all items, 1982–1984=100. The average beginning professional salary for that period was $17,693.

Table 6 / Salaries of Reporting Professionals* by Area of Job Assignment

| Assignment | No. | Percent of Total | Low Salary | High Salary | Average Salary | Median Salary |
|---|---|---|---|---|---|---|
| Acquisitions | 18 | 1.33 | $26,270 | $70,000 | $42,198 | $39,000 |
| Administration | 62 | 4.58 | 18,000 | 121,000 | 43,849 | 39,000 |
| Adult Services | 44 | 3.25 | 18,720 | 48,000 | 35,993 | 35,933 |
| Archives | 59 | 4.36 | 14,400 | 65,000 | 40,286 | 39,750 |
| Automation/Systems | 21 | 1.55 | 30,000 | 93,000 | 51,658 | 48,000 |
| Cataloging and Classification | 76 | 5.61 | 18,000 | 70,000 | 39,670 | 40,000 |
| Children's Services | 75 | 5.54 | 20,000 | 55,000 | 38,029 | 38,000 |
| Circulation | 51 | 3.77 | 19,000 | 55,000 | 32,089 | 33,000 |
| Collection Development | 18 | 1.33 | 30,000 | 53,000 | 40,746 | 41,000 |
| Database Management | 10 | 0.74 | 24,000 | 75,000 | 41,300 | 36,000 |
| Electronic or Digital Services | 51 | 3.77 | 24,000 | 70,000 | 44,657 | 42,500 |
| Government Documents | 8 | 0.59 | 32,000 | 50,000 | 38,571 | 38,000 |
| Indexing/Abstracting | 6 | 0.44 | 25,778 | 25,778 | 25,778 | 25,778 |
| Info Technology | 44 | 3.25 | 31,512 | 150,000 | 53,177 | 47,115 |
| Instruction | 41 | 3.03 | 17,000 | 70,000 | 42,485 | 41,250 |
| Interlibrary Loans/ Document Delivery | 19 | 1.40 | 20,500 | 44,600 | 33,779 | 32,000 |
| Knowledge Mgt. | 7 | 0.52 | 28,000 | 51,000 | 40,375 | 41,250 |
| Other | 110 | 8.12 | 15,000 | 115,000 | 45,895 | 42,500 |
| Reference/Info Services | 293 | 21.64 | 19,000 | 70,000 | 41,172 | 40,000 |
| School Library Media Specialist | 191 | 14.11 | 24,960 | 91,000 | 44,348 | 43,000 |
| Solo Librarian | 51 | 3.77 | 25,000 | 57,000 | 38,960 | 38,500 |
| Usability/ Usability Testing | 15 | 1.11 | 50,000 | 90,000 | 75,417 | 77,500 |
| Web Design | 1 | 0.07 | 45,000 | 45,000 | 45,000 | 45,000 |
| Youth Services | 83 | 6.13 | 20,000 | 52,332 | 35,929 | 36,000 |
| Total | 1,354 | 100.00 | $14,400 | $150,000 | $42,172 | $40,000 |

* This table represents placements of any type reported by job assignment, but only salaries reported as full-time.

Some individuals omitted placement information, rendering some information unusable. Comparison with other tables will show different numbers of placements.

keting. Many of these employers are private entities unaffected by public funding, thus allowing salaries to be highly competitive. Pratt, an L-school, and the University of Texas at Austin, an I-school, had the next highest percentages of placements in "other" agencies (28.6 percent and 26.7 percent, respectively). On average, the LIS graduates comprised 16.7 percent of the overall reported placements in "other" institutions, with UM making up 19.5 percent of the reported total.

Graduates of UCLA, Syracuse, and Oklahoma reported the highest percentage of positions in academic libraries, ranging from 50 percent to 75 percent of the reported placements. Alabama, Denver, and Illinois also had above-average placements in academic libraries. SUNY–Buffalo, University of North Texas,

*(text continues on page 366)*

Table 7 / Comparison of Salaries by Type of Organization*

| | Total Placements | Salaries | | Low Salary | | High Salary | | Average Salary | | | Median Salary | | |
|---|---|---|---|---|---|---|---|---|---|---|---|---|---|
| | | Women | Men | Women | Men | Women | Men | Women | Men | All | Women | Men | All |
| **Public Libraries** | | | | | | | | | | | | | |
| Northeast | 98 | 55 | 12 | $19,440 | $18,720 | $50,000 | $68,808 | $38,023 | $41,276 | $38,625 | $39,000 | $39,450 | $39,048 |
| Southeast | 57 | 38 | 9 | 22,000 | 30,000 | 52,571 | 44,936 | 34,989 | 37,004 | 35,727 | 34,695 | 37,000 | 35,500 |
| Midwest | 162 | 96 | 19 | 15,000 | 20,000 | 71,700 | 60,000 | 35,229 | 36,250 | 35,328 | 36,000 | 36,000 | 36,000 |
| Southwest | 55 | 37 | 6 | 23,000 | 29,000 | 65,000 | 41,000 | 36,425 | 42,704 | 36,261 | 36,000 | 36,000 | 36,000 |
| West | 62 | 34 | 11 | 20,000 | 30,000 | 76,440 | 53,000 | 42,994 | 45,338 | 43,997 | 41,250 | 48,000 | 42,000 |
| Canada/International | 15 | 1 | 1 | 47,900 | 43,939 | 47,900 | 43,939 | 47,900 | 43,939 | 45,920 | 47,900 | 43,939 | 45,920 |
| All Public | 470 | 267 | 58 | 15,000 | 18,720 | 76,440 | 68,808 | 37,023 | 39,160 | 37,414 | 37,000 | 39,000 | 37,000 |
| **School Libraries** | | | | | | | | | | | | | |
| Northeast | 62 | 42 | 5 | 29,000 | 40,000 | 62,000 | 57,500 | 43,448 | 47,200 | 43,847 | 42,600 | 47,000 | 44,000 |
| Southeast | 33 | 27 | 1 | 30,000 | 39,500 | 69,000 | 39,500 | 41,416 | 39,500 | 41,348 | 40,000 | 39,500 | 39,750 |
| Midwest | 58 | 54 | 1 | 24,960 | 59,000 | 78,000 | 59,000 | 42,921 | 59,000 | 43,213 | 40,000 | 59,000 | 40,000 |
| Southwest | 59 | 48 | 4 | 33,000 | 39,000 | 63,000 | 52,000 | 45,866 | 44,000 | 45,723 | 45,000 | 42,500 | 45,000 |
| West | 23 | 15 | 2 | 36,000 | 49,000 | 80,000 | 91,000 | 58,772 | 70,000 | 60,093 | 60,000 | 70,000 | 60,000 |
| Canada/International | 5 | 2 | — | 32,000 | — | 35,000 | — | 33,500 | — | 33,500 | 33,500 | — | 33,500 |
| All School | 255 | 199 | 13 | 24,960 | 39,000 | 80,000 | 91,000 | 44,602 | 50,038 | 44,935 | 43,000 | 47,000 | 43,220 |
| **College/University Libraries** | | | | | | | | | | | | | |
| Northeast | 119 | 60 | 23 | 15,000 | 24,000 | 65,000 | 70,000 | 40,116 | 44,244 | 41,340 | 40,000 | 44,000 | 41,125 |
| Southeast | 83 | 50 | 22 | 20,800 | 17,000 | 61,000 | 58,000 | 42,208 | 42,649 | 42,172 | 42,000 | 43,650 | 42,000 |
| Midwest | 103 | 62 | 23 | 19,000 | 24,000 | 70,000 | 55,500 | 39,506 | 42,055 | 40,159 | 40,000 | 41,000 | 40,000 |
| Southwest | 46 | 31 | 6 | 15,000 | 37,000 | 45,000 | 52,000 | 36,056 | 43,667 | 37,185 | 38,004 | 42,500 | 38,502 |
| West | 46 | 22 | 7 | 32,500 | 33,576 | 55,000 | 66,000 | 43,745 | 48,797 | 44,354 | 42,600 | 52,000 | 42,200 |
| Canada/International | 19 | 2 | 2 | 25,000 | 18,000 | 43,000 | 48,000 | 34,000 | 33,000 | 33,500 | 34,000 | 33,000 | 34,000 |
| All Academic | 416 | 227 | 84 | 15,000 | 17,000 | 70,000 | 70,000 | 40,153 | 43,175 | 40,911 | 40,000 | 43,500 | 40,000 |
| **Special Libraries** | | | | | | | | | | | | | |
| Northeast | 40 | 25 | 5 | 29,000 | 20,000 | 62,500 | 62,400 | 41,704 | 40,200 | 41,545 | 40,000 | 41,600 | 40,500 |
| Southeast | 32 | 14 | 1 | 14,400 | 40,000 | 63,000 | 40,000 | 41,833 | 40,000 | 41,710 | 43,500 | 40,000 | 42,000 |
| Midwest | 29 | 21 | 5 | 18,000 | 31,500 | 60,000 | 70,000 | 38,524 | 44,200 | 39,615 | 39,000 | 42,500 | 39,500 |
| Southwest | 9 | 7 | — | 25,000 | — | 52,000 | — | 48,010 | — | 38,371 | 41,600 | — | 41,600 |

| | | | | | | | | | | | | | |
|---|---|---|---|---|---|---|---|---|---|---|---|---|---|
| West | 17 | 11 | 1 | 38,000 | 50,000 | 90,000 | 50,000 | 52,591 | 50,000 | 52,375 | 48,000 | 50,000 | 49,000 |
| Canada/International | 3 | 1 | — | — | — | 90,000 | 70,000 | — | — | — | — | — | — |
| All Special | 121 | 81 | 13 | 14,400 | 20,000 | 90,000 | 70,000 | 42,066 | 41,231 | 41,951 | 41,000 | 41,600 | 41,300 |
| **Government Libraries** | | | | | | | | | | | | | |
| Northeast | 2 | — | 1 | — | 46,660 | — | 46,660 | — | 46,660 | 46,660 | 48,500 | 46,660 | 46,660 |
| Southeast | 12 | 9 | 2 | 29,000 | 25,778 | 121,000 | 32,000 | 56,278 | 28,889 | 42,010 | 38,160 | 28,889 | 46,000 |
| Midwest | 10 | 7 | 2 | 31,000 | 20,000 | 46,000 | 50,000 | 38,160 | 35,000 | 37,458 | 31,787 | 35,000 | 37,500 |
| Southwest | 4 | 1 | 2 | 31,787 | 28,000 | 31,787 | 49,800 | 31,787 | 38,900 | 36,529 | 39,427 | 38,900 | 31,787 |
| West | 4 | 2 | 2 | 38,854 | 41,000 | 40,000 | 50,000 | 39,427 | 45,500 | 42,464 | — | 45,500 | 40,500 |
| Canada/International | 1 | 1 | — | — | — | — | 50,000 | — | — | — | — | — | — |
| All Government | 39 | 20 | 9 | 29,000 | 20,000 | 121,000 | 50,000 | 46,540 | 38,138 | 43,839 | 41,000 | 41,000 | 41,000 |
| **Library Cooperatives/Networks** | | | | | | | | | | | | | |
| Northeast | 2 | 2 | — | 42,000 | — | 42,500 | — | 42,250 | — | 42,250 | 42,250 | — | 42,250 |
| Southeast | 3 | 2 | 1 | 32,000 | 70,000 | 36,000 | 70,000 | 34,000 | 70,000 | 46,000 | 34,000 | 70,000 | 36,000 |
| Midwest | 1 | 1 | 1 | — | 34,000 | — | 34,000 | — | 34,000 | 34,000 | — | 34,000 | 34,000 |
| Southwest | 3 | — | — | 25,000 | — | 45,000 | — | 35,667 | — | 35,667 | 37,000 | — | 37,000 |
| All Co-Op./Nets. | 9 | 7 | 2 | 25,000 | 34,000 | 45,000 | 70,000 | 37,071 | 52,000 | 40,389 | 37,000 | 52,000 | 37,000 |
| **Vendors** | | | | | | | | | | | | | |
| Northeast | 5 | 3 | 2 | 37,000 | 30,720 | 60,000 | 36,000 | 46,333 | 33,360 | 41,144 | 42,000 | 33,360 | 37,000 |
| Southeast | — | — | — | — | — | — | — | — | — | — | — | — | — |
| Midwest | 1 | 1 | — | 47,700 | — | 47,700 | — | 47,700 | — | 47,700 | 47,700 | — | 47,700 |
| West | 2 | — | 1 | — | 150,000 | — | 150,000 | — | 150,000 | 150,000 | — | 150,000 | 150,000 |
| All Vendors | 11 | 4 | 3 | 37,000 | 30,720 | 60,000 | 150,000 | 46,675 | 72,240 | 57,631 | 44,850 | 36,000 | 42,000 |
| **Other Organizations** | | | | | | | | | | | | | |
| Northeast | 45 | 22 | 10 | 20,000 | 36,000 | 80,000 | 100,000 | 48,059 | 54,700 | 50,134 | 45,500 | 47,500 | 45,500 |
| Southeast | 32 | 13 | 8 | 34,000 | 32,500 | 60,000 | 87,500 | 44,276 | 52,938 | 47,049 | 45,000 | 50,000 | 45,000 |
| Midwest | 51 | 26 | 12 | 20,500 | 27,000 | 115,000 | 75,000 | 51,192 | 51,792 | 51,382 | 44,500 | 50,500 | 45,000 |
| Southwest | 20 | 10 | 5 | 34,000 | 29,000 | 93,000 | 88,000 | 46,828 | 51,600 | 48,419 | 39,500 | 50,000 | 40,000 |
| West | 34 | 18 | 7 | 32,500 | 36,612 | 93,000 | 90,000 | 57,450 | 64,516 | 59,428 | 56,000 | 55,000 | 55,000 |
| Canada/International | 17 | 17 | 2 | 35,000 | 49,000 | 60,000 | 66,000 | 47,500 | 57,500 | 44,800 | 47,500 | 57,500 | 49,000 |
| All Other | 257 | 95 | 46 | 20,000 | 27,000 | 115,000 | 100,000 | 49,698 | 55,905 | 51,349 | 45,000 | 50,000 | 46,000 |

This table represents only full-time salaries and placements reported by type. Some individuals omitted placement information, rendering some information unusable.

* Comparison with other tables will show different numbers of total placements due to completeness of the data reported by individuals and schools.

*(continued from page 363)*
and Texas Woman's University had the strongest showing among the LIS programs in school library media centers, averaging 33.5 percent of the media specialist positions. The graduating class reported the fewest placements in special libraries, at 8.1 percent of the jobs; however, St. John's University, Louisiana State, and Simmons graduates were well above this average, with Simmons snagging 17.5 percent of the total positions in special libraries.

## Inside the Gender Gap

Recent issues of the annual placements and salaries survey have given cursory exploration of salary parity between the genders as well as minority comparisons. There is no doubt that the gaps continue to exist and even widen. Women experienced another year of salary growth in 2007, but for another year's running they lagged approximately 7.7 percent behind men. The question that begs to be answered is: "What factors are driving the differences?"

Proportionately, women continue to comprise 80 percent of the new members of the LIS work force. However, smaller proportions of women found positions in academic libraries (72.9 percent), government libraries (68.9 percent), and other agencies and organizations (67.4 percent) while dominating the school library media positions (93.9 percent). Average starting salaries for women in public libraries and special libraries fell while men experienced significant gains (as much as 9.1 percent compared to a loss of 8.4 percent for women) in the same types of agencies. Regionally, women who accepted school library media positions in the Southeast and the Southwest fared better than their male counterparts (slightly more than 4 percent and higher). The same situation occurred in special libraries in the Northeast and the Southeast, with women earning 3.7 percent and 4.6 percent more, respectively. Government libraries were the one agency where women dominated the salary game, with average starting pay 22 percent higher than men—$46,540 compared to $38,138.

Historically, school library media centers and "other" organizations generate higher average starting salaries. In both of these types of agencies, women experienced a comfortable salary growth, averaging just over 5 percent in each. School library media specialists are members of the teaching faculty and in most states are required to obtain formal teaching credentials. Much like the overall education profession, school library media positions are dominated by women (94 percent of the placements), and they have been subject to the same "glass ceiling" that many other female-dominated professions experience. Starting salaries for women in school media centers continue to fall below the levels men obtain. The rate of growth in salaries also reveals a gap, with a 12.2 percent differential between women and men ($44,602 compared to an average starting salary of $50,038).

## Women Up in 'Other' Agencies

Even though they continue to lag behind men with regard to starting salaries for "other" agencies, women gained 5.1 percent in their starting salaries (from

$47,163 in 2006). The best salary growth for women in "other "organizations was in the Midwest, with better than 17 percent upward movement. The percentage of women finding jobs in other agencies grew from 64 percent of the placements in 2006 to 66 percent of the placements in 2007. These positions included jobs in nonprofits, museums, Fortune 500 companies, and medical facilities.

Region seems to play a role in salary equity for women. In 2007 more women (approximately 30 percent) accepted positions in the Midwest than across the rest of the U.S. regions and Canada. In 2006 and again in 2007 average starting salaries were among the lowest in the Midwest, and women there followed the same pattern, taking among the lowest-paid spots accepted ($38,638 in 2006; $39,844 in 2007), although there was a trend toward modest growth from year to year. On a positive note, following the general rise in salaries in the Southeast, women gained just over 8 percent in average starting salary, narrowing the gender gap in the Southeast to 4.9 percent.

## First Careers Resonate

Background and experience are yet another piece in the gender puzzle. Interesting trends emerge from those who reported LIS as a second career (and in some cases "too many careers to name"). Women responding to the survey typically reported first careers in education, human services, nonprofit agencies, and the arts, while men reported jobs in law, medicine, science, and engineering. Starting salaries for women with prior professional experience were approximately 3.4 percent higher than the average starting salary for all women ($43,154 compared to $41,731); for men, the difference was more substantial, with $47,877 for those reporting previous careers to $45,192 for all men. This suggests that the "glass ceiling" migrates to the LIS professions along with career changers, although prior professional experience can help in general.

## Minorities Fare Well

The other gap that exists is one of diversity. That said, graduates claiming ethnic and racial minority status fared better in the marketplace than did women in general. In 2007 approximately 11.8 percent of the graduating class claimed minority status. This has been consistent across the last several reporting periods, ranging from 12 percent in 2005 to 10.7 percent in 2006. Along with the ALA Spectrum Scholarship program, several of the LIS schools have received grants from the Institute of Museum and Library Services (IMLS) and other funding to recruit actively and retain minority students, and the profession is seeing the fruits of these efforts.

From 2006 to 2007 average starting salaries for minority graduates increased by 5.1 percent, growing from $40,750 to $42,831 and exceeding the 2005 high of $42,233. Contributing to the surge was an unprecedented 10.9 percent rise in salaries for minorities in the Southeast. This echoes the other signs of health in that region. Unfortunately, a gender gap exists for minority graduates as well, with men earning 3.8 percent higher starting salaries than women ($44,828 compared to $43,656 in 2007). Much like the other positive trends for school library media centers, minority salaries sizzled for media specialists, with a 12.9 percent increase to $47,248.

While the proportion of minority placements remained steady in most library and information agency types between 2006 and 2007, an increasing number of graduates accepted positions in "other" agencies, and received higher salaries accordingly. In 2006 just over 11 percent of the minority graduates found jobs in such organizations, including nonprofits, private industry, and other nontraditional positions; in 2007 the placement rate grew to 16.8 percent. Average starting compensation in nonlibrary jobs for minority graduates grew from $45,203 to $47,963, although it still stumbled behind the overall salary ($51,349) for all new graduates in "other" organizations.

## Public vs. Private Sector Jobs

Over the past several years a greater and more diverse representation of job assignments and types of organizations has lured LIS graduates, especially in the area of information science. Schools and graduates are reporting many intriguing job titles and responsibilities, such as user experience design and interface, information preservation, social computing and networking, and e-commerce. The opportunities are boundless—though not always easy to find. Graduates also note employment in museums, archives, and public broadcasting (NPR, PBS, and so forth). Many of these jobs can be broken into three designations: nonprofits, private industry, and the ubiquitous "other."

In order to understand the distribution of the new job types better, we asked graduates to identify and describe "other" designations. Of the 297 graduates who responded, approximately 13.1 percent accepted positions in nonprofit agencies, 57.9 percent were in "other" agencies or outside of the LIS professions, and 29 percent described their employers as private industry. The salary implications were far reaching, both for the graduates claiming "other" status and compared to the rest of their graduating class. On average, graduates choosing "other" organizations reached salary levels approximately 21.2 percent higher than their counterparts ($51,349 compared to $42,361). But within the other category, salaries swung wildly, with the salaries of those describing positions in the nonprofit sector significantly lower than those in private industry ($43,519 vs. $60,677—a 39.4 percent difference).

Salary differentials also highlighted the gender gap, though, interestingly, salaries were basically equal in private industry, with women earning an average of $61,100 and men an average of $61,068. The salary disparity was greatest for women in the nonprofit sector, with a 34 percent gap between them and their male counterparts (an average of $39,975 compared to $53,643). Some of this may be owing to the small pool of men, thus a much smaller range of salaries. It also appears that many of the women accepted clerical-type positions while the men focused on information technology (IT) jobs in the nonprofits. However, the "other" organizations—including university units outside of the library or IT departments, hospitals, and other educational institutions—experienced a similar, though lesser, gap of almost 16 percent between salaries for women and men.

Two factors stood out in private industry in particular and the "other" category as a whole. First, the regional distribution of jobs in private industry had the highest placements in the West (approximately 26.7 percent of the placements), especially in California, which historically has shown the highest salaries. Graduates accepting positions in other organizations in the West reported an average starting salary of $59,428 (15.7 percent higher than other graduates reporting similar jobs). Secondly, the information school/library school dichotomy played out again, with the University of Michigan placing 41 percent of the graduates in private industry, and the combined I-schools placing 37.7 percent of the graduates in "other" organizations overall. As noted, Michigan graduates are at the pinnacle of the LIS salary scale, with an average annual starting salary of $55,869. Six of the other iSchool Caucus members top the list of above-average salaries as well.

## The Job Search

For some, the transition from graduate student to employed professional was seamless. Of the 1,546 graduates reporting employment, a full 41 percent remained with their current employer (compared to 36.9 percent in 2006 and 37 percent in 2005) while completing the master's degree; of these graduates, 77.3 percent were placed in professional positions. For some, this meant a promotion from support staff and library technical assistant to professional staff. For others, there was no change in professional status but simply the addition of an "official" credential for the job they were already doing.

Encouragingly, nearly 42 percent of all graduates found employment prior to graduation, which is slightly less than the previous year (46 percent) but well above the historical trends, ranging from 30 percent in 2003 to 25.2 percent in 2005. As in the past, graduates began the job search well in advance of graduation day to ensure a smooth transition and no loss of income. A number of recent graduates pointed to volunteer activities in libraries and other information agencies, previous experience, and fieldwork or internships as real boosts to landing positions.

The job search was an exercise in frustration for many graduates. It meant taking temporary work while seeking "better, more appropriate professional positions." In a disturbing pattern, temporary placements increased again in 2007, with approximately 12.5 percent graduates placed in temporary jobs (up from just over 10 percent in 2006 and 8.5 percent in 2005). While temporary status frequently implies that the job will cease at the end of a contractual period and without guarantees for the future, many graduates were quick to suggest that "temporary" is not always a bad thing. Temporary positions help them gain valuable work experience while continuing to search for permanent placements in areas and job types more suited to their needs.

The number of graduates with part-time positions held steady for a second year at approximately 16.2 percent. The majority of part-time positions were located in the Northeast (42.1 percent), followed by the Midwest (24 percent). The Southeast had the fewest reported part-time positions (7.3 percent). Public libraries and academic libraries continued to employ the highest levels of part-timers, with 40 percent and 23 percent of the part-time pool, respectively, comparable to 2006 levels. Part-time positions in both of these types of agencies may be another indication of the impact of a soft economy and lower operating budgets. An intriguing side note: numerous graduates said they had two or more part-time jobs, most frequently holding one in a public library along with one in an academic library. While one might assume the nonprofessional positions would be more likely to be part-time, positions in reference and information services saw the highest level of part-time staffing at 30 percent of the reported positions.

More than a few graduates shared their stories of many, many interviews but very few real job offers. The overall length of time from graduation to landing a professional position increased from four-and-a-half months in 2006 to just shy of five months in 2007, and some were still looking over a year after graduation. The most frequent advice graduates offered to their future colleagues included "Network, network, network, early in your program," "Find good mentors," and "Get as much experience as you can during your program to prepare yourself for the realities of the workplace."

## School Efforts

The LIS programs had a slightly different perspective, with more than 60 percent of the participating schools saying that they felt it was no harder placing graduates in 2007 than it had been the year before. In general, the LIS programs provided a broad range of access to job announcements and placement services, through electronic mail lists, bulletin boards, professional organizations and student chapters, and the schools' own Web sites. However, only approximately 30 percent of the reporting institutions offer a formal placement and/or career service for their graduates.

Several of the LIS programs created a variety of mentoring programs for incoming and current students as well as recent graduates. Drexel University launched a new Alumni Mentoring Program in which alumni of the iSchool programs serve as mentors for prospective students, current students, and other alumni. In a similar effort, Drexel also launched a Graduate Peer Mentoring Program to connect successful graduate students with new and continuing students. The University of Alabama features a Mentoring Day to assist its students with job placement. The University of Texas at Austin, University of Washington, University of Rhode Island, and Simmons each have either career mentoring, faculty mentoring, and/or peer-to-peer mentoring programs to help ensure the success of their graduates.

## Future Prospects

The LIS Class of 2007 experienced both tremendous opportunities and disappointments as they sought jobs in a slowing economic environment. Nationwide, library and information organizations suffered from loss of revenue, corporate slowdowns, and reduced spending. For some, this meant lower salaries, longer job searches, and temporary posts while waiting for permanent employment. On the flip side, salaries in the Southeast surged upward, and placements in many types of agencies around the nation increased. The gender gap widened, but women experienced solid growth in salaries in the Southeast and the Southwest and made significant progress in government libraries. All indications from the graduates and the programs responding were that the LIS profession continues to be viable, even healthy, and forward-looking.

# Accredited Master's Programs in Library and Information Studies

This list of graduate programs accredited by the American Library Association is issued by the ALA Office for Accreditation. Regular updates and additional details appear on the Office for Accreditation's Web site at http://www.ala.org/Template.cfm?Section=lisdirb&Template=/cfapps/lisdir/index.cfm. More than 200 institutions offering both accredited and nonaccredited programs in librarianship are included in the 62nd edition (2009–2010) of *American Library Directory* (Information Today, Inc.)

## Northeast: Conn., D.C., Md., Mass., N.J., N.Y., Pa., R.I.

Catholic University of America, School of Lib. and Info. Science, 620 Michigan Ave. N.E., Washington, DC 20064. Kimberly Kelley, dean. Tel. 202-319-5085, fax 202-219-5574, e-mail cua-slis@cua.edu, World Wide Web http://slis.cua.edu. Admissions contact: Jeannine Marino. Tel. 202-319-5085, e-mail marino@cua.edu.

Clarion University of Pennsylvania, College of Education and Human Services, Dept. of Lib. Science, 210 Carlson Lib. Bldg., 840 Wood St., Clarion, PA 16214. Andrea Miller, chair. Tel. 866-272-5612, fax 814-393-2150, World Wide Web http://www.clarion.edu/libsci. Admissions contact: Lois Dulavitch. Tel. 866-272-5612, e-mail ldulavitch@clarion.edu.

Drexel University, College of Info. Science and Technology, 3141 Chestnut St., Philadelphia, PA 19104-2875. David E. Fenske, dean. Tel. 215-895-2474, fax 215-895-2494, e-mail info@ischool.drexel.edu, World Wide Web http://www.ischool.drexel.edu. Admissions contact: Matthew Lechtenburg. Tel. 215-895-1951.

Long Island University, Palmer School of Lib. and Info. Science, C. W. Post Campus, 720 Northern Blvd., Brookville, NY 11548-1300. Mary L. Westermann-Cicio, dean pro tem. Tel. 516-299-2866, fax 516-299-4168, e-mail palmer@cwpost.liu.edu, World Wide Web http://www.cwpost.liu.edu/cwis/cwp/cics/palmer. Admissions contact: Rosemary Chu. Tel. 516-299-2487, e-mail rchu@liu.edu.

Pratt Institute, School of Info. and Lib. Science, 144 W. 14 St., New York, NY 10011. Tula Giannini, dean. Tel. 212-647-7682, fax 202-367-2492, e-mail infosils@pratt.edu, World Wide Web http://www.pratt.edu/sils. Admissions contact: Claire Moore.

Queens College, City Univ. of New York, Grad. School of Lib. and Info. Studies, Rm. 254, Rosenthal Lib., 65-30 Kissena Blvd., Flushing, NY 11367-1597. Virgil L. P. Blake, dir. Tel. 718-997-3790, fax 718-997-3797, e-mail gc_gslis@qc.cuny.edu, World Wide Web http://www.qc.edu/gslis. Admissions contact: Roberta Brody. E-mail roberta_brody@qc.edu.

Rutgers University, Dept. of Lib. and Info. Science, School of Communication, Info., and Lib. Studies, 4 Huntington St., New Brunswick, NJ 08901-1071. Michael Lesk, chair. Tel. 732-932-7500 ext. 8955, fax 732-932-2644, e-mail scilsmls@scils.rutgers.edu, World Wide Web http://www.scils.rutgers.edu. Admissions contact: Ross Todd.

Saint John's University, College of Liberal Arts and Sciences, Div. of Lib. and Info. Science, 8000 Utopia Pkwy., Queens, NY 11439. Jeffery E. Olson, dir. Tel. 718-990-6200, fax 718-990-2071, e-mail dlis@stjohns.edu, World Wide Web http://www.stjohns.edu/libraryscience. Admissions contact: Deborah Martinez. Tel. 618-990-6209.

Simmons College, Grad. School of Lib. and Info. Science, 300 The Fenway, Boston, MA 02115. Michèle Cloonan, dean. Tel. 617-521-2800, fax 617-521-3192, e-mail gslis@simmons.edu, World Wide Web http://www.simmons.edu/gslis.

Southern Connecticut State University, School of Communication, Info., and Lib. Science, 501 Crescent St., New Haven, CT 06515. Josephine Sche, chair. Tel. 203-392-5781, fax 203-392-5780, e-mail ils@southernct.edu, World Wide Web http://www.southernct.edu/ils. Admissions contact: Kathy Muldowney.

Syracuse University, School of Info. Studies, 343 Hinds Hall, Syracuse, NY 13244. Elizabeth D. Liddy, dean. Tel. 315-443-2911, fax 315-443-6886, e-mail ischool@syr.edu, World Wide Web http://www.ischool.syr.edu. Admissions contact: Scott Nicholson. Tel. 315-443-2911, e-mail mslis@syr.edu.

University at Albany, State Univ. of New York, College of Computing and Info., Dept. of Info. Studies, Draper 113, 135 Western Ave., Albany, NY 12222. Terrence A. Maxwell, chair. Tel. 518-442-5110, fax 518-442-5367, e-mail infostudies@albany.edu, World Wide Web http://www.albany.edu/cci/informationstudies/index.shtml. Admissions contact: Frances Reynolds. E-mail reynolds@albany.edu.

University at Buffalo, State Univ. of New York, Graduate School of Educ., Lib. and Info. Studies, 534 Baldy Hall, Box 1020, Buffalo, NY 14260. Judith Robinson, chair. Tel. 716-645-2412, fax 716-645-3775, e-mail ub-lis@buffalo.edu, World Wide Web http://www.gse.buffalo.edu/programs/lis. Admissions contact: Radhika Suresh. Tel. 716-645-2110, e-mail gse-info@buffalo.edu.

University of Maryland, College of Info. Studies, 4105 Hornbake Lib. Bldg., College Park, MD 20742. Jennifer Preece, dean. Tel. 301-405-2033, fax 301-314-9145, World Wide Web http://www.clis.umd.edu. Admissions tel. 301-405-2033, e-mail lbscgrad@deans.umd.edu.

University of Pittsburgh, School of Info. Sciences, 135 N. Bellefield Ave., Pittsburgh, PA 15260. Richard C. Cox, chair. Tel. 800-672-9435, fax 412-624-5231, e-mail lisinq@mail.sis.pitt.edu, World Wide Web http://www.sis.pitt.edu. Admissions contact: Shabana Reza. Tel. 412-624-3988.

University of Rhode Island, Grad. School of Lib. and Info. Studies, Rodman Hall, 94 W. Alumni Ave., Kingston, RI 02881. Gale Eaton, dir. Tel. 401-874-2878, fax 401-874-4964, e-mail gslis@etal.uri.edu, World Wide Web http://www.uri.edu/artsci/lsc.

## Southeast: Ala., Fla., Ga., Ky., La., Miss., N.C., S.C., Tenn., P.R.

Florida State University, College of Info., 142 Collegiate Loop, P.O. Box 3062100, Tallahassee, FL 32306-2100. Larry Dennis, dean. Tel. 850-644-5775, fax 850-644-9763, e-mail gradservices@ci.fus.edu, World Wide Web http://www.ci.fsu.edu. Admissions contact: Delores Bryant. Tel. 850-645-3280.

Louisiana State University, School of Lib. and Info. Science, 267 Coates Hall, Baton Rouge, LA 70803. Beth Paskoff, dean. Tel. 225-578-3158, fax 225-578-4581, e-mail slis@lsu.edu, World Wide Web http://slis.lsu.edu. Admissions contact: LaToya Coleman Joseph. E-mail lcjoseph@lsu.edu.

North Carolina Central University, School of Lib. and Info. Sciences, P.O. Box 19586, Durham, NC 27707. Irene Owens, dean. Tel. 919-530-6485, fax 919-530-6402, World Wide Web http://www.nccuslis.org. Admissions contact: Tysha Jacobs. Tel. 919-530-7320, e-mail tjacobs@nccu.edu.

University of Alabama, School of Lib. and Info. Studies, Box 870252, Tuscaloosa, AL 35487-0252. Elizabeth Aversa, dean. Tel. 205-348-4610, fax 205-348-3746, e-mail info@slis.ua.edu, World Wide Web http://www.slis.ua.edu. Admissions contact: Beth Riggs.

University of Kentucky, School of Lib. and Info. Science, 300 Little Lib., Lexington, KY 40506-0224. Jeffrey T. Huber, dir. Tel. 859-257-8876, fax 859-257-4205, e-mail ukslis@uky.edu, World Wide Web http://www.uky.edu/CIS/SLIS. Admissions contact: Will Buntin. Tel. 859-257-3317, e-mail wjbunt0@uky.edu.

University of North Carolina at Chapel Hill, School of Info. and Lib. Science, CB

3360, 100 Manning Hall, Chapel Hill, NC 27599-3360. José-Marie Griffiths, dean. Tel. 919-962-8366, fax 919-962-8071, e-mail info@ils.unc.edu, World Wide Web http://www.sils.unc.edu. Admissions contact: Lara Bailey.

University of North Carolina at Greensboro, Dept. of Lib. and Info. Studies, School of Educ., 349 Curry Bldg., Greensboro, NC 27402-6170. Lee Shiflett, chair. Tel. 336-334-3477, fax 336-334-5060, World Wide Web http://lis.uncg.edu. Admissions contact: Cindy Felts. E-mail cpfelts@uncg.edu.

University of Puerto Rico, Graduate School of Info. Sciences and Technologies, Box 21906, San Juan, PR 00931-1906. Luisa Vigo-Cepeda, acting dir. Tel. 787-763-6199, fax 787-764-2311, e-mail egcti@uprrp.edu, World Wide Web http://egcti.upr.edu. Admissions contact: Migdalia Dávila-Perez. Tel. 787-764-0000 ext. 3530, e-mail migdalia.davila@upr.edu.

University of South Carolina, College of Mass Communications and Info. Studies, School of Lib. and Info. Science, 1501 Greene St., Columbia, SC 29208. Samantha K. Hastings, dir. Tel. 803-777-3858, fax 803-777-7938, e-mail hastings@sc.edu, World Wide Web http://www.libsci.sc.edu. Admissions contact: Tilda Reeder. Tel. 800-304-3153, e-mail tildareeder@gwm.sc.edu.

University of South Florida, College of Arts and Sciences, School of Lib. and Info. Science, 4202 E. Fowler Ave., CIS 1040, Tampa, FL 33620. John N. Gathegi, dir. Tel. 813-974-3520, fax 813-974-6840, e-mail lis@cas.usf.edu, World Wide Web http://www.cas.usf.edu/lis. Admissions contact: Andrea LaRochelle. E-mail alaroche@cas.usf.edu.

University of Southern Mississippi, College of Educ. and Psychology, School of Lib. and Info. Science, 118 College Drive, No. 5146, Hattiesburg, MS 39406-0001. M. J. Norton, dir. Tel. 601-266-4228, fax 601-266-5774, e-mail slis@usm.edu, World Wide Web http://www.usm.edu/slis. Admissions tel. 601-266-5137, e-mail graduatestudies@usm.edu.

University of Tennessee, School of Info. Sciences, 451 Communication Bldg., Knox-ville, TN 37996-0341. Edwin M. Cortez, dir. Tel. 865-974-2148, fax 865-974-4967, World Wide Web http://www.sis.utk.edu. Admissions contact: Tanya Arnold. E-mail tnarnold@utk.edu.

Valdosta State Univ., Dept. of Info. Studies, 1500 N. Patterson St., Valdosta, GA 31698-0133. Wallace Koehler, dir. Tel. 229-333-5966, fax 229-259-5055, e-mail mlis@valdosta.edu, World Wide Web http://www.valdosta.edu/mlis. Admissions contact: Sheila Peacock.

## Midwest: Ill., Ind., Iowa, Kan., Mich., Mo., Ohio, Wis.

Dominican University, Grad. School of Lib. and Info. Science, 7900 W. Division St., River Forest, IL 60305. Susan Roman, dean. Tel. 708-524-6845, fax 708-524-6657, e-mail gslis@dom.edu, World Wide Web http://www.gslis.dom.edu. Admissions contact: Dianna K. Wiggins. Tel. 708-524-6848, e-mail dwiggins@dom.edu.

Emporia State University, School of Lib. and Info. Management, 1200 Commercial, Campus Box 4025, Emporia, KS 66801. Gwen Alexander, dean. Tel. 620-341-5203, fax 620-341-5233, e-mail slim info@emporia.edu, World Wide Web http://slim.emporia.edu. Admissions contact: Candace Boardman. Tel. 620-341-6159, e-mail sliminfo@emporia.edu.

Indiana University, School of Lib. and Info. Science, LI 011, 1320 E. 10 St., LI011, Bloomington, IN 47405-3907. Blaise Cronin, dean. Tel. 812-855-2018, fax 812-855-6166, e-mail slis@indiana.edu, World Wide Web http://www.slis.iu.edu. Admissions contact: Rhonda Spencer.

Kent State University, School of Lib. and Info. Science, Box 5190, Kent, OH 44242-0001. Richard E. Rubin, dir. Tel. 330-672-2782, fax 330-672-7965, e-mail inform@slis.kent.edu, World Wide Web http://www.slis.kent.edu. Admissions contact: Cheryl Tennant.

University of Illinois at Urbana-Champaign, Grad. School of Lib. and Info. Science, 501 E. Daniel St., Champaign, IL 61820-6211. John Unsworth, dean. Tel. 217-333-

3280, fax 217-244-3302, e-mail gslis@ Illinois.edu, World Wide Web http://www. lis.uiuc.edu. Admissions contact: Penny Ames. Tel. 217-333-7197, e-mail pames@ illinois.edu.

University of Iowa, School of Lib. and Info. Science, 3087 Main Lib., Iowa City, IA 52242-1420. James K. Elmborg, dir. Tel. 319-335-5707, fax 319-335-5374, e-mail slis@uiowa.edu, World Wide Web http:// slis.uiowa.edu/~slisweb. Admissions contact: Kit Austin. E-mail caroline-austin@ uiowa.edu.

University of Michigan, School of Info., 304 West Hall Bldg., 1085 S. University Ave., Ann Arbor, MI 48109-1092. Martha Pollack, dean. Tel. 734-763-2285, fax 734-764-2475, e-mail si.admissions@umich. edu, World Wide Web http://www.si. umich.edu. Admissions contact: Laura Elgas. E-mail si.admissions@umich.edu.

University of Missouri, College of Educ., School of Info. Science and Learning Technologies, 303 Townsend Hall, Columbia, MO 65211. John Wedman, dir. Tel. 877-747-5868, fax 573-884-0122, e-mail sislt@missouri.edu, World Wide Web http://sislt.missouri.edu.

University of Wisconsin–Madison, College of Letters and Sciences, School of Lib. and Info. Studies, Rm. 4217, H. C. White Hall, 600 N. Park St., Madison, WI 53706. Louise S. Robbins, dir. Tel. 608-263-2900, fax 608-263-4849, e-mail uw-slis@slis. wisc.edu, World Wide Web http://www. slis.wisc.edu. Admissions contact: Andrea Poehling. Tel. 608-263-2909, e-mail student-services@slis.wisc.edu.

University of Wisconsin–Milwaukee, School of Info. Studies, P.O. Box 413, Milwaukee, WI 53211. Johannes Britz, dean. Tel. 414-229-4707, fax 414-229-6699, e-mail info@sois.uwm.edu, World Wide Web http://www.uwm.edu/dept/sois.

Wayne State University, Lib. and Info. Science Program, 106 Kresge Lib., Detroit, MI 48202. Stephen T. Bajjaly, dir. Tel. 313-577-1825, fax 313-577-7563, e-mail asklis@wayne.edu, World Wide Web http://www.lisp.wayne.edu. Admissions contact: Matthew Fredericks. Tel. 313-577-2446, e-mail aj8416@wayne.edu.

## Southwest: Ariz., Okla., Texas

Texas Woman's University, School of Lib. and Info. Studies, P.O. Box 425438, Denton, TX 76204-5438. Ling Hwey Jeng, dir. Tel. 940-898-2602, fax 940-898-2611, e-mail slis@twu.edu, World Wide Web http://www.twu.edu/cope/slis. Admissions contact: Brenda Mallory. E-mail bmallory @mail.wu.edu.

University of Arizona, School of Info. Resources and Lib. Science, 1515 E. 1 St., Tucson, AZ 85719. Jana Bradley, dir. Tel. 520-621-3565, fax 520-621-3279, e-mail sirls@email.arizona.edu, World Wide Web http://www.sir.arizona.edu. Admissions contact: Geraldine Fragoso.

University of North Texas, School of Lib. and Info. Sciences, Box 311068, Denton, TX 76203-1068. Herman L. Totten, dean. Tel. 940-565-2445, fax 940-565-3101, e-mail slis@unt.edu, World Wide Web http://www.unt.edu/slis. Admissions contact: John Pipes. Tel. 940-565-3562, e-mail john.pipes@unt.edu.

University of Oklahoma, School of Lib. and Info. Studies, College of Arts and Sciences, Rm. 120, 401 W. Brooks, Norman, OK 73019-6032. Kathy Latrobe, dir. Tel. 405-325-3921, fax 405-325-7648, e-mail slisinfo@ou.edu, World Wide Web http:// www.ou.edu/cas/slis. Admissions contact: Maggie Ryan.

University of Texas at Austin, School of Info., Sanchez Bldg., Suite 564, 1 University Sta., D7000, Austin, TX 78712-0390. Andrew Dillon, dean. Tel. 512-471-3821, fax 512-471-3971, e-mail info@ischool. utexas.edu, World Wide Web http://www. ischool.utexas.edu. Admissions contact: Carla Criner. Tel. 512-471-5654, e-mail criner@ischool.utexas.edu.

## West: Calif., Colo., Hawaii, Wash.

San José State University, School of Lib. and Info. Science, 1 Washington Sq., San José, CA 95192-0029. Ken Haycock, dir. Tel. 408-924-2490, fax 408-924-2476, e-mail office@slis.sjsu.edu, World Wide Web http://slisweb.sjsu.edu. Admissions contact: Scharlee Phillips. Tel. 408-924-2417, e-mail sphillip@slis.sjsu.edu.

University of California, Los Angeles, Graduate School of Educ. and Info. Studies, Dept. of Info. Studies, Box 951520, Los Angeles, CA 90095-1520. Anne Gilliland, chair. Tel. 310-825-8799, fax 310-206-3076, e-mail info@gseis.ucla.edu, World Wide Web http://is.gseis.ucla.edu. Admissions contact: Susan Abler. Tel. 310-825-5269, e-mail abler@gseis.ucla.edu.

University of Denver, Morgridge College of Educ., Lib. and Info. Science Program, JMAC Bldg., 2450 S. Vine St., Denver, CO 80208. Mary Stansbury, chair. Tel. 303-871-2747, fax 303-871-2709, World Wide Web http://www.du.edu/lis. Admissions contact: Nick Heckart. E-mail nheckart@du.edu.

University of Hawaii, College of Natural Sciences, Lib. and Info. Science Program, 2550 McCarthy Mall, Honolulu, HI 96822. Andrew Wertheimer, chair. Tel. 808-956-7321, fax 808-956-3548, e-mail slis@hawaii.edu, World Wide Web http://www.hawaii.edu/slis. Admissions contact: Gail Morimoto.

University of Washington, The Info. School, 370 Mary Gates Hall, Box 352840, Seattle, WA 98195-2840. Harry Bruce, dean. Tel. 206-685-9937, fax 206-616-3152, e-mail info@ischool.washington.edu, World Wide Web http://www.ischool.washington.edu. Admissions contact: Admissions coordinator. Tel. 206-543-1794, e-mail mlis@ischool.washington.edu.

# Canada

Dalhousie University, School of Info. Management, Kenneth C. Rowe Management Bldg., Halifax, NS B3H 3J5. Fiona Black, dir. Tel. 902-494-3656, fax 902-494-2451, e-mail sim@dal.ca, World Wide Web http://www.sim.management.dal.ca. Admissions contact: JoAnn Watson. Tel. 902-494-3656, e-mail mlis@dal.ca.

McGill University, School of Info. Studies, 3459 McTavish St., Montreal, PQ H3A

1Y1. France Bouthillier, dir. Tel. 514-398-4204, fax 514-398-7193, e-mail sis@mcgill.ca, World Wide Web http://www.mcgill.ca/sis. Admissions contact: Kathryn Hubbard.

Université de Montréal, École de Bibliothéconomie et des Sciences de l'Information, C.P. 6128, Succursale Centre-Ville, Montreal, QC H3C 3J7. Jean-Michel Salaun, dir. Tel. 514-343-6400, fax 514-343-5753, e-mail ebsiinfo@ebsi.umontreal.ca, World Wide Web http://www.ebsi.umontreal.ca. Admissions contact: Céline Lapierre. E-mail celine.lapierre@umontreal.ca.

University of Alberta, School of Lib. and Info. Studies, 3-20 Rutherford S., Edmonton, AB T6G 2J4. Ann Curry, dir. Tel. 780-492-4578, fax 780-492-2430, e-mail slis@ualberta.ca, World Wide Web http://www.slis.ualberta.ca. Admissions contact: Joanne Hilger. Tel. 780-492-4140, e-mail joanne.hilger@ualberta.ca.

University of British Columbia, School of Lib., Archival, and Info. Studies, Irving K. Barber Learning Center, Suite 470, 1961 East Mall, Vancouver, BC V6T 1Z1. Edie Rasmussen, dir. Tel. 604-822-2404, fax 604-822-6006, e-mail slais@interchange.ubc.ca, World Wide Web http://www.slais.ubc.ca. Admissions contact: Michelle Mallette. E-mail slaisad@interchange.ubc.ca.

University of Toronto, Faculty of Info. Studies, Rm. 211, 140 George St., Toronto, ON M5S 3G6. Seamus Ross, dean. Tel. 416-978-3202, fax 416-978-5762, e-mail inquire@ischool.utoronto.ca, World Wide Web http://www.ischool.utoronto.ca. Admissions contact: Judy Dunn. Tel. 416-978-3934, e-mail judy.dunn@utoronto.ca.

University of Western Ontario, Grad. Programs in Lib. and Info. Science, Faculty of Info. and Media Studies, Rm. 240, North Campus Bldg., 1151 Richmond St., London, ON N6A 5B7. Thomas Carmichael, dean. Tel. 519-661-4017, fax 519-661-3506, e-mail mlisinfo@uwo.ca, World Wide Web http://fims.uwo.ca. Admissions contact: Shelley Long.

# Library Scholarship Sources

For a more complete list of scholarships, fellowships, and assistantships offered for library study, see *Financial Assistance for Library and Information Studies,* published annually by the American Library Association (ALA). The document is also available on the ALA Web site at http://www.ala.org/ala/educationcareers/education/financialassistance/index.cfm.

**American Association of Law Libraries.** (1) A varying number of scholarships of a minimum of $1,000 for graduates of an accredited law school who are degree candidates in an ALA-accredited library school; (2) a varying number of scholarships of varying amounts for library school graduates working on a law degree and nonlaw graduates enrolled in an ALA-accredited library school; (3) the George A. Strait Minority Stipend of $3,500 for varying numbers of minority librarians working toward a library or law degree; and (4) a varying number of $500 scholarships for law librarians taking courses relating to law librarianship. For information, write to: Scholarship Committee, AALL, 53 W. Jackson Blvd., Suite 940, Chicago, IL 60604.

**American Library Association.** (1) The Marshall Cavendish Scholarship of $3,000 for a varying number of students who have been admitted to an ALA-accredited library school; (2) the David H. Clift Scholarship of $3,000 for a varying number of students who have been admitted to an ALA-accredited library school; (3) the Tom and Roberta Drewes Scholarship of $3,000 for a varying number of library support staff; (4) the Mary V. Gaver Scholarship of $3,000 for a varying number of individuals specializing in youth services; (5) the Miriam L. Hornback Scholarship of $3,000 for a varying number of ALA or library support staff; (6) the Christopher J. Hoy/ERT Scholarship of $5,000 for a varying number of students who have been admitted to an ALA-accredited library school; (7) the Tony B. Leisner Scholarship of $3,000 for a varying number of library support staff; (8) the Peter Lyman Memorial/SAGE Scholarship in New Media of $2,500 for a student admitted to an ALA accredited library school and specializing in new media; (9) the Cicely Phippen Marks Scholarship of $3,000 for a varying number of students admitted to an ALA-accredited program and specializing in federal librarianship; (10) Spectrum Initiative Scholarships of $6,500 for a varying number of minority students admitted to an ALA-accredited library school. For information on all ALA scholarships, write to: ALA Scholarship Clearinghouse, 50 E. Huron St., Chicago, IL 60611. For information, write to: ALA Scholarship Clearinghouse, 50 E. Huron St., Chicago, IL 60611, or see http://www.ala.org/ala/educationcareers/education/scholarships/index.cfm.

**ALA/Association for Library Service to Children.** (1) The Bound to Stay Bound Books Scholarship of $6,500 each for four students who are U.S. or Canadian citizens, who have been admitted to an ALA-accredited program, and who will work with children in a library for one year after graduation; (2) the Frederic G. Melcher Scholarship of $6,000 each for two U.S. or Canadian citizens admitted to an ALA-accredited library school who will work with children in school or public libraries for one year after graduation. For information, write to: ALA Scholarship Clearinghouse, 50 E. Huron St., Chicago, IL 60611, or see http://www.ala.org/ala/educationcareers/education/scholarships/index.cfm.

**ALA/Association of College and Research Libraries and Thompson Reuters.** (1) The ACRL Doctoral Dissertation Fellowship of $1,500 for a student who has completed all coursework, and submitted a dissertation proposal that has been accepted, in the area of academic librarianship; (2) the Samuel Lazerow Fellowship of $1,000 for a research, travel, or writing project in acquisitions or technical services in an academic or research library; (3) the ACRL and Coutts Nijhoff International West European Specialist Study Grant of up to 4,500 euros to pay travel expenses, room, and board for a ten-day trip to Europe for an ALA member (selection is based on proposal outlining purpose of trip). For information, write to: Megan Griffin, ALA/ACRL, 50 E. Huron St., Chicago, IL 60611.

ALA/Association of Specialized and Cooperative Library Agencies. Century Scholarship of up to $2,500 for a varying number of disabled U.S. or Canadian citizens admitted to an ALA-accredited library school. For information, write to: ALA Scholarship Clearinghouse, 50 E. Huron St., Chicago, IL 60611, or see http://www.ala.org/ala/educationcareers/education/scholarships/index.cfm.

ALA/International Relations Committee. The Bogle Pratt International Library Travel Fund grant of $1,000 for a varying number of ALA members to attend a first international conference. For information, write to: Michael Dowling, ALA/IRC, 50 E. Huron St., Chicago, IL 60611.

ALA/Library and Information Technology Association. (1) The LITA/Christian Larew Memorial Scholarship of $3,000 for a disabled U.S. or Canadian citizen admitted to an ALA-accredited library school; (2) the LITA/OCLC Minority Scholarship in Library and Information Technology of $3,000 and (3) the LITA/LSSI Minority Scholarship of $2,500, each for a minority student admitted to an ALA-accredited program. For information, write to: ALA Scholarship Clearinghouse, 50 E. Huron St., Chicago, IL 60611, or see http://www.ala.org/ala/educationcareers/education/scholarships/index.cfm.

ALA/Public Library Association. The Demco New Leaders Travel Grant Study Award of up to $1,500 for a varying number of PLA members with MLS degrees and five years or less experience. For information, write to: PLA Awards Program, ALA/PLA, 50 E. Huron St., Chicago, IL 60611.

American-Scandinavian Foundation. Fellowships and grants for 25 to 30 students, in amounts from $3,000 to $18,000, for advanced study in Denmark, Finland, Iceland, Norway, or Sweden. For information, write to: Exchange Division, American-Scandinavian Foundation, 58 Park Ave., New York, NY 10026, or see http://www.amscan.org/fellowships_grants.html.

Association for Library and Information Science Education (ALISE). A varying number of research grants of up to $2,500 each for members of ALISE. For information, write to: Association for Library and Information Science Education, Box 7640, Arlington, VA 22207.

Association of Jewish Libraries. The AJL Scholarship Fund offers up to two scholarships of $500 each for MLS students who plan to work as Judaica librarians. For information, write to: Lynn Feinman, 92nd St. Y Library, 1395 Lexington Ave., New York, NY 10128, e-mail lfeinman@92Y.org.

Association of Seventh-Day Adventist Librarians. The D. Glenn Hilts Scholarship of $1,200 for a member of the Seventh-Day Adventist Church in a graduate library program. For information, write to: Lee Marie Wisel, Association of Seventh-Day Adventist Librarians, Columbia Union College, 7600 Flower Ave., Takoma Park, MD 20912.

Beta Phi Mu. (1) The Sarah Rebecca Reed Scholarship of $2,000 for a person accepted in an ALA-accredited library program; (2) the Frank B. Sessa Scholarship of $1,250 for a Beta Phi Mu member for continuing education; (3) the Harold Lancour Scholarship of $1,500 for study in a foreign country relating to the applicant's work or schooling; (4) the Blanche E. Woolls Scholarship for School Library Media Service of $1,500 for a person accepted in an ALA-accredited library program; (5) the Doctoral Dissertation Scholarship of $2,000 for a person who has completed course work toward a doctorate; (6) the Eugene Garfield Doctoral Dissertation Scholarship of $3,000 for a person who has approval of a dissertation topic. For information, write to: Executive Director, Beta Phi Mu, College of Information, Florida State University, Tallahassee, FL 32306-2100.

Canadian Association of Law Libraries. The Diana M. Priestly Scholarship of $2,500 for a student with previous law library experience or for entry to an approved Canadian law school or accredited Canadian library school. For information, write to: Janet Mass, Chair, CALL/ACBD Scholarship and Awards Committee, Gerard J. LaForest Law Library, University of New Brunswick, Bag Service 44999, Fredericton, NB E38 6C9.

Canadian Federation of University Women. (1) The Alice E. Wilson Award of $6,000 for five mature students returning to graduate studies in any field, with special consideration given to those returning to study after at least three years; (2) the Margaret McWilliams Pre-Doctoral Fellowship of $13,000 for a student who has completed at least one full year as a full-time student in doctoral level studies; (3) the Marion Elder Grand Fellowship of $11,000 for a full-time student at any level of a doctoral program (4) the Beverly Jackson Fellowship of $2,000 for a student over the age of 35 at the time of application who is enrolled in graduate studies at an Ontario university; (5) the 1989 Ecole Polytechnique Commemorative Award of $7,000 for graduate studies in any field; (6) the Bourse Georgette LeMoyne award of $7,000 for graduate study in any field at a Canadian university (the candidate must be studying in French); (7) the Margaret Dale Philp Biennial Award of $3,000 for studies in the humanities or social sciences; (8) the Canadian Home Economics Association Fellowship of $6,000 for a student enrolled in a postgraduate program in Canada. For information, write to: Fellowships Program Manager, Canadian Federation of University Women, 251 Bank St., Suite 305, Ottawa, ON K2P 1X3, Canada, or see http://www.cfuw.org.

Canadian Library Association. (1) The World Book Graduate Scholarship in Library and Information Science of $2,500; (2) the CLA Dafoe Scholarship of $5,000; and (3) the H. W. Wilson Scholarship of $2,000—each scholarship is given to a Canadian citizen or landed immigrant to attend an accredited Canadian library school; (4) the Library Research and Development Grant of $1,000 for a member of the Canadian Library Association, in support of theoretical and applied research in library and information science. For information, write to: CLA Membership Services Department, Scholarships and Awards Committee, 328 Frank St., Ottawa, ON K2P 0X8, Canada.

Catholic Library Association. (1) The World Book, Inc., Grant of $1,500 divided among no more than three CLA members for continuing education in children's or school librarianship; (2) the Rev. Andrew L. Bouwhuis Memorial Scholarship of $1,500 for a student accepted into a graduate program in library science. For information, write to: Jean R. Bostley, SSJ, Scholarship Chair, Catholic Library Association, 100 North St., Suite 224, Pittsfield, MA 01201-5109.

Chinese American Librarians Association. (1) The Sheila Suen Lai Scholarship and (2) the C. C. Seetoo/CALA Conference Travel Scholarship each offer $500 to a Chinese descendant who has been accepted in an ALA-accredited program. For information, write to: MengXiong Liu, Clark Library, San Jose State University, 1 Washington Sq., San Jose, CA 95192-0028.

Church and Synagogue Library Association. The Muriel Fuller Memorial Scholarship of $200 (including texts) for a correspondence course offered by the association. For information, write to: CSLA, 2920 S.W. Dolph Court, Suite 3A, Portland, OR 97280-0357.

Council on Library and Information Resources. (1) The Rovelstad Scholarship in International Librarianship, to enable a student enrolled in an accredited LIS program to attend the IFLA Annual Conference; (2) the A. R. Zipf Fellowship in Information Management of $10,000, awarded annually to a U.S. citizen enrolled in graduate school who shows exceptional promise for leadership and technical achievement. For more information, write to: A. R. Zipf Fellowship, Council on

Library and Information Resources, 1755 Massachusetts Ave. N.W., Suite 500, Washington, DC 20036.

Massachusetts Black Librarians' Network. Two scholarships of at least $500 and $1,000 for minority students entering an ALA-accredited master's program in library science with no more 12 semester hours completed toward a degree. For information, write to: Pearl Mosley, Chair, Massachusetts Black Librarians' Network, 17 Beech Glen St., Roxbury, MA 02119.

Medical Library Association. (1) The Cunningham Memorial International Fellowship of $3,500 for each of two health sciences librarians from countries other than the United States and Canada; (2) a scholarship of $5,000 for a person entering an ALA-accredited library program, with no more than one-half of the program yet to be completed; (3) a scholarship of $5,000 for a minority student for graduate study; (4) a varying number of Research, Development and Demonstration Project Grants of $100 to $1,000 for U.S. or Canadian citizens who are MLA members; (5) the MLA Doctoral Fellowship of $2,000 for doctoral work in medical librarianship or information science; (6) the Rittenhouse Award of $500 for a student enrolled in an ALA-accredited library program or a recent graduate working as a trainee in a library internship program; (7) Continuing Education Grants of $100 to $500 for U.S. or Canadian citizens who are MLA members. For information, write to: Professional Development Department, Medical Library Association, 65 E. Wacker Place, Suite 1900, Chicago, IL 60601-7298.

Mountain Plains Library Association. A varying number of grants of up to $600 each for MPLA members with at least two years of membership, for continuing education. For information, write to: Judy Zelenski, MPLA Executive Secretary, 14293 W. Center Drive, Lakewood, SD 80228.

Society of American Archivists. The Colonial Dames Awards, two grants of $1,200 each for specific types of repositories and collections. For information, write to: Debra Noland, Society of American Archivists, 521 S. Wells St., 5th fl., Chicago, IL 60607.

Southern Regional Education Board. A varying number of grants of varying amounts to cover in-state tuition for graduate or postgraduate study in an ALA-accredited library school for residents of various southern U.S. states (qualifying states vary year by year). For information, write to: Academic Common Market, c/o Southern Regional Education Board, 592 Tenth St. N.W., Atlanta, GA 30318-5790.

Special Libraries Association. (1) Three $6,000 scholarships for students interested in special-library work; (2) the Plenum Scholarship of $1,000 and (3) the ISI Scholarship of $1,000, each also for students interested in special-library work; (4) the Affirmative Action Scholarship of $6,000 for a minority student interested in special-library work; and (5) the Pharmaceutical Division Stipend Award of $1,200 for a student with an undergraduate degree in chemistry, life sciences, or pharmacy entering or enrolled in an ALA-accredited program. For information on the first four scholarships, write to: Scholarship Committee, Special Libraries Association, 331 South Patrick Street Alexandria, VA 22314-3501. For information on the Pharmaceutical Stipend, write to: Susan E. Katz, Awards Chair, Knoll Pharmaceuticals Science Information Center, 30 N. Jefferson St., Whippany, NJ 07981.

# Library Scholarship and Award Recipients, 2008

Scholarships and awards are listed by organization.

## American Association of Law Libraries (AALL)

AALL Scholarships. *Winners:* (Library Degree for Law School Graduates) Julia Michelle Byrd, Lisa Junghahn, Sean Kaneshiro, Jeff Woodmansee; (Library Degree for Non-Law School Graduates) Luz Evelyn Hernandez Carrion, Holly Gale, Lindsay Given.

AALL and Thomson West George A. Strait Minority Scholarship. *Winners:* Stephen Chan, Hsi-yen Chen, Pablo Sandoval.

Joseph L. Andrews Bibliographic Award. *Winner:* Edward Grosek for *The Secret Treaties of History,* second edition (Hein).

James F. Connolly LexisNexis Scholarship. To a law librarian interested in pursuing a law degree and who has demonstrated an interest in government publications. *Winner:* Not awarded in 2008.

Marian Gould Gallagher Distinguished Service Award. To recognize extended and sustained service to law librarianship. *Winner:* Robert L. Oakley (posthumously).

LexisNexis/John R. Johnson Memorial Scholarships. *Winners:* Jennifer Duperon, Stacy Hinkel, Robert Hudson, Mindy Rush.

## American Institute for the Conservation of Historic and Artistic Works (AIC)

Forbes Medal for Distinguished Contribution to the Field of Conservation. *Winner:* Anne-Imelda M. Radice.

## American Library Association (ALA)

ALA/Information Today Library of the Future Award ($1,500). For a library, consortium, group of librarians, or support organization for innovative planning for, applications of, or development of patron training programs about information technology in a library setting. *Donor:* Information Today, Inc. *Winner:* San Diego (California) County Library for a program to provide Internet and computer instruction to the region's immigrant Middle Eastern population.

Leo Albert Spectrum Scholarship. To a designated Spectrum Scholarship recipient. *Donor:* Leo Albert. *Winner:* Lisa Lavon Kidd.

Hugh C. Atkinson Memorial Award. For outstanding achievement (including risk taking) by academic librarians that has contributed significantly to improvements in library automation, management, and/or development or research. *Offered by:* ACRL, ALCTS, LLAMA, and LITA divisions. *Winner:* Not awarded in 2008.

Carroll Preston Baber Research Grant (up to $3,000). For innovative research that could lead to an improvement in library services to any specified group(s) of people. *Donor:* Eric R. Baber. *Winner:* Not awarded in 2008.

Beta Phi Mu Award ($1,000). For distinguished service in library education. *Donor:* Beta Phi Mu International Library Science Honorary Society. *Winner:* Ching-chih Chen.

Bogle Pratt International Library Travel Fund Award ($1,000). To ALA member(s) to attend their first international conference. *Donors:* Bogle Memorial Fund and Pratt Institute School of Information and Library Science. *Winner:* Rose Dotten.

W. Y. Boyd Literary Novel Award. *Winner:* See "Literary Prizes, 2008" in Part 5.

David H. Clift Scholarship ($3,000). To worthy U.S. or Canadian citizens enrolled in an ALA-accredited program toward an MLS degree. *Winner:* Linda Ann Christian.

Eileen Cooke State and Local James Madison Award. To recognize individuals or groups who have championed public access to government information. *Winner:* Not awarded in 2008.

Melvil Dewey Medal ($2,000). To an individual or group for recent creative professional achievement in library management, training, cataloging and classification, and the tools and techniques of librarianship. *Donor:* OCLC/Forest Press. *Winner:* Sandra Nelson.

Tom and Roberta Drewes Scholarship ($3,000). To a library support staff member pursuing a master's degree. *Donor:* Quality Books. *Winner:* Rebecca Marie Iserman.

EBSCO/ALA Conference Sponsorship Award (up to $1,000). To enable ten librarians to attend the ALA Annual Conference. *Donor:* EBSCO. *Winners:* A. Jade Alburo, Anne C. Behler, Sally Daniels, Ciara Healy, Laura Kortz, Sarah Elizabeth Miller, John J. Meier, Margaux DelGuidice, Kevin W. Merriman, Alice Wasielewski.

Equality Award ($1,000). To an individual or group for an outstanding contribution that promotes equality in the library profession. *Donor:* Scarecrow Press. *Winner:* Liana Zhou.

Elizabeth Futas Catalyst for Change Award ($1,000). To recognize and honor a librarian who invests time and talent to make positive change in the profession of librarianship. *Donor:* Elizabeth Futas Memorial Fund. *Winner:* Patricia Tarin.

Loleta D. Fyan Public Library Research Grant (up to $10,000). For projects in public library development. *Donor:* Fyan Estate. *Winner:* Not awarded in 2008.

Gale Cengage Learning Financial Development Award ($2,500). To a library organization for a financial development project to secure new funding resources for a public or academic library. *Donor:* Gale Cengage Learning. *Winner:* Elmont (New York) Memorial Library.

Mary V. Gaver Scholarship ($3,000). To a student pursuing an MLS degree and specializing in youth services. *Winner:* Kathleen Marvel.

Louise Giles Spectrum Scholarship. To a designated Spectrum Scholarship recipient. *Donor:* Louise Giles. *Winner:* Omar Jerome Poler.

William R. Gordon Spectrum Scholarship. To a designated Spectrum Scholarship recipient. *Donor:* William R. Gordon and friends. *Winner:* Harriett Elizabeth Green.

Greenwood Publishing Group Award for Best Book in Library Literature ($5,000). To recognize authors of U.S. or Canadian works whose books improve library management principles and practice. *Donor:* Greenwood Publishing Group. *Winner:* To be awarded first in 2009.

Ken Haycock Award ($1,000). For significant contribution to public recognition and appreciation of librarianship through professional performance, teaching, or writing. *Winner:* Larry Moore, former director of the Ontario Library Association.

Honorary ALA Membership. *Honorees:* Pat Mora, Effie Lee Morris, Peggy Sullivan.

Miriam L. Hornback Scholarship ($3,000). To an ALA or library support staff person pursuing a master's degree in library science. *Winner:* Oscar Rene Lanza-Galindo.

Paul Howard Award for Courage ($1,000). Awarded biennially to a librarian, library board, library group, or an individual for exhibiting unusual courage for the benefit of library programs or services. *Donor:* Paul Howard Memorial Fund. *Winner:* Not awarded in 2008.

John Ames Humphry/OCLC/Forest Press Award ($1,000). To an individual for significant contributions to international librarianship. *Donor:* OCLC/Forest Press. *Winner:* Barbara J. Ford.

Tony B. Leisner Scholarship ($3,000). To a library support staff member pursuing a master's degree program. *Donor:* Tony B. Leisner. *Winner:* Denelle Elaine Eads.

Joseph W. Lippincott Award ($1,000). To a librarian for distinguished service to the profession. *Donor:* Joseph W. Lippincott III. *Winner:* Duane Webster.

James Madison Award. To recognize efforts to promote government openness. *Winner:* U.S. Sen. Russ Feingold (D-Wis.).

Marshall Cavendish Excellence in Library Programming Award ($2,000). To recognize either a school library or public library that demonstrates excellence in library programming by providing programs that have community impact and respond to community need. *Winner:* Johnson County (Kansas) Library for "Literature in the Justice System: The Surprising Antidote."

Marshall Cavendish Scholarship ($3,000). To a worthy U.S. or Canadian citizen to begin an MLS degree in an ALA-accredited program. *Winner:* Maile Claire McGrew-Frede.

Grolier Foundation Award. See Scholastic Library Publishing Award.

Medical Library Association/National Library of Medicine Spectrum Scholarship. To a designated Spectrum Scholarship recipient or recipients. *Donor:* Medical Library Association. *Winner:* Rhonda J. Allard.

Schneider Family Book Awards (three awards of $5,000). To authors or illustrators of books that embody artistic expressions of the disability experience for child and adolescent audiences. *Donor:* Katherine Schneider. *Winners:* See "Literary Prizes, 2008" in Part 5.

Scholastic Library Publishing Award (formerly the Grolier Foundation Award) ($1,000). For stimulation and guidance of reading by children and young people. *Donor:* Scholastic Library Publishing. *Winner:* Carolyn S. Brodie.

Spectrum Doctoral Fellowships. To provide full tuition support and stipends to minority U.S. and Canadian LIS doctoral students. *Donor:* Institute of Museum and Library Services. *Winners:* Eric Chuk, Mónica Colón-Aguirre, Nicole Cooke, Stefani Gomez, Asher Isaac Jackson, Brenda Mitchell-Powell.

Spectrum Initiative Scholarships ($5,000). Presented to minority students admitted to ALA-accredited library schools. *Donors:* ALA and Institute of Museum and Library Services. *Winners:* Rhonda J. Allard, Kristen Armstrong, Steven De'Juan Booth, Letitia Jeremia Bulic, Orisanmi Burton, Charisse Nicole Byers, Leslie Elizabeth Campbell, Andrew Cano, Melissa Nicol Chance, Jeannie Chen, Haley Jessamyn Collazo, Linda Sue Collins, Deidra Catherine Garcia, Michelle Gorospe, George Edward Gottschalk, Harriett Elizabeth Green, K'Lani Green, Deana L. Greenfield, Nefertiti Guzman, Nicole Elaine Head, Katy Seon Hepner, Elizabeth Marie Hernandez, Elizabeth Hernandez, Adriana Alvarez Huertas, Rebecca D. Hunt, Harrison W. Inefuku, Marissa Jacobo, Boutsaba Janetvilay, Evone Jeffries, Suchitra Kamath, Melissa Nnasimbwa Kayongo, Aiza Rianna Keesey, Mojgan Khosravi, Lisa Lavon Kidd, Alice Kim, Kimberly Evette Ladson, Samantha Le Blanc, Hsin-I Desiree Leary, Hannah Kyung Lee, Letoria Gales Lewis, Melinda Maria Livas, Richard N. Ma, Lauren Elizabeth Mabry, Onaona Miller, Angela Patricia Murillo, Sonoe Tsulan Nakasone, Omar Jerome Poler, Margaret B. Puentes, Laksamee Anne Putnam, Refugio Ramirez, Michelle Anne Ruiz, Roy Saldaña, Jr., Pablo A. Sandoval, Ashley Lynn Shifflett, Juan de Jesus Soria, Amanda Michelle Stinso, Kimmy Szeto, Deborah Kazumi Takahashi, Laura Arizmendi Tamanaha, Manju Tanwar, Kimberly Rose Trinh-Sy, Serena Jennifer Vaquilar, Angela Lynette Watts, Jovanni M. Williams, Krystle R. Williams, Yani L. Yancey, Israel Yanez, Christine Jennifer Yontz-Orlando, Jamie L. Young.

Sullivan Award for Public Library Administrators Supporting Services to Children. To a library supervisor/administrator who has shown exceptional understanding and support of public library services to children. *Donor:* Peggy Sullivan. *Winner:* Harriet Henderson.

Howard M. and Gladys B. Teeple Spectrum Scholarship. To a designated Spectrum Scholarship recipient. *Donor:* Religion and Ethics Institute. *Winner:* Kimberly Evette Ladson.

H. W. Wilson Library Staff Development Grant ($3,500). To a library organization for a program to further its staff development goals and objectives. *Donor:* H. W. Wilson Company. *Winner:* Orange County (Florida) Library System.

Women's National Book Association Award. To a living American woman who derives part or all of her income from books and allied arts and who has done meritorious work in the world of books. *Winner:* Kathi Kamen Goldmark.

Women's National Book Association/Ann Heidbreder Eastman Grant ($750). To a librarian to take a course or participate in an institute devoted to aspects of publishing as a profession or to provide reimbursement for such study completed within the past year. *Winner:* Hanah Kim.

World Book/ALA Goal Grant (up to $10,000). To ALA units for the advancement of public, academic, or school library service and librarianship through support of programs that implement the goals and priorities of ALA. *Donor:* World Book. *Winner:* Not awarded in 2008.

## ALA/Allied Professional Association

SirsiDynix Award for Outstanding Achievement in Promoting Salaries and Status for Library Workers. *Donor:* SirsiDynix. *Winners:* Brian Keith ($3,000), Camilla B. Reid ($2,000).

## American Association of School Librarians (AASL)

AASL/ABC-CLIO Leadership Grant (up to $1,750). For planning and implementing leadership programs at state, regional, or local levels to be given to school library associations that are affiliates of AASL. *Donor:* ABC-CLIO. *Winner:* Colorado Association of School Libraries.

AASL/Baker & Taylor Distinguished Service Award ($3,000). For outstanding contributions to librarianship and school library development. *Donor:* Baker & Taylor Books. *Winner:* Nancy P. Zimmerman.

AASL Collaborative School Library Media Award ($2,500). For expanding the role of the library in elementary and/or secondary school education. *Donor:* Highsmith, Inc. *Winners:* Ronda Hassig and Kathy Hill, Harmony Middle School, Overland Park, Kansas.

AASL Crystal Apple Award. To an individual, individuals, or group for a significant impact on school libraries and students. *Winners:* "The Spokane Moms," Denette Hill, Lisa Layera-Brunkan, and Susan McBurney.

AASL Distinguished School Administrators Award ($2,000). For expanding the role of the library in elementary and/or secondary school education. *Donor:* ProQuest. *Winner:* Not Awarded in 2008.

AASL/Frances Henne Award ($1,250). To a school library media specialist with five or fewer years in the profession to attend an AASL regional conference or ALA Annual Conference for the first time. *Donor:* Greenwood Publishing Group. *Winner:* Sarah Prielipp.

AASL Innovative Reading Grant ($2,500). To support the planning and implementation of an innovative program for children that motivates and encourages reading, especially with struggling readers. *Sponsor:* Capstone Publishers. *Winner:* Barbara Powell-Schager, Big Shanty Intermediate School, Kennesaw, Georgia.

AASL School Librarian's Workshop Scholarship ($3,000). To a full-time student preparing to become a school library media specialist at the preschool, elementary, or secondary level. *Donor:* Jay W. Toor, president, Library Learning Resources. *Winner:* Charisse Nicole Byers.

Information Technology Pathfinder Award ($1,000 to the specialist and $500 to the library). To library media specialists for innovative approaches to microcomputer applications in the school library media center. *Donor:* Follett Software Company. *Winners:* Not awarded in 2008.

Intellectual Freedom Award ($2,000 plus $1,000 to the media center of the recipient's choice). To a school library media specialist and AASL member who has upheld the principles of intellectual freedom. *Donor:* ProQuest. *Winner:* Kristie Michalowski.

National School Library Media Program of the Year Award ($10,000). To school districts and two single schools for excellence and innovation in outstanding library media programs. *Donor:* Follett Library Resources. *Winners:* (district) Not awarded in 2008; (single schools) Luella Elementary School, Locust Grove, Georgia; Simsbury (Connecticut) High School.

## Association for Library Collections and Technical Services (ALCTS)

ALCTS George Cunha and Susan Swartzburg Preservation Award ($1,250). To recognize cooperative preservation projects and/or individuals or groups that foster collaboration for preservation goals. *Donor:* LBI. *Winner:* Becky Ryder.

ALCTS Presidential Citations for Outstanding Service. *Winners:* Janet Belanger Morrow, David Miller, Cathy Martyniak, Betsy Simpson.

Hugh C. Atkinson Memorial Award. *See under* American Library Association.

Ross Atkinson Lifetime Achievement Award. To recognize the contribution of an ALCTS member and library leader who has demonstrated exceptional service to ALCTS and its areas of interest. *Donor:* EBSCO. *Winner:* Carol Pitts Diedrichs.

Paul Banks and Carolyn Harris Preservation Award ($1,500). To recognize the contribution of a professional preservation specialist who has been active in the field of preservation and/or conservation for library and/or archival materials. *Donor:* Preservation Technologies. *Winner:* Janet Gertz.

Best of *LRTS* Award ($250). To the author(s) of the best paper published each year in the division's official journal. *Winner:* William H. Walters for "A Regression-based Approach to Library Fund Allocation."

Blackwell's Scholarship Award ($2,000 scholarship to the U.S. or Canadian library school of the recipient's choice). To honor the author(s) of the year's outstanding monograph, article, or original paper in the field of acquisitions, collection development, and related areas of resource development in libraries. *Donor:* Blackwell's. *Winner:* Lucy Eleonore Lyons for "The Dilemma for Academic Librarians with Collection Development Responsibilities: A Comparison of the Value of Attending Library Conferences versus Academic Conferences," published in *Journal of Academic Librarianship,* March 2007.

Coutts Award for Innovation in Electronic Resources Management ($2,000). To recognize significant and innovative contributions to electronic collections management and development practice. *Donor:* Coutts Information Services. *Winner:* Timothy Jewell.

CSA/Ulrich's Serials Librarianship Award ($1,500). For leadership in serials-related activities. *Donor:* CSA. *Winner:* Victoria Reich.

First Step Award (Wiley Professional Development Grant) ($1,500). For librarians new to the serials field to attend the ALA Annual Conference. *Donor:* John Wiley & Sons. *Winner:* Erin Leach.

Leadership in Library Acquisitions Award ($1,500). For significant contributions by an outstanding leader in the field of library acquisitions. *Donor:* Harrassowitz. *Winner:* Karen Darling.

Margaret Mann Citation (includes $2,000 award to the U.S. or Canadian library school of the winning author's choice). To a cataloger or classifier for achievement in the areas of cataloging or classification. *Donor:* Online Computer Library Center. *Winner:* Martha Yee.

Outstanding Collaboration Citation. For outstanding collaborative problem solving efforts in the areas of acquisition, access, management, preservation, or archiving of library materials. *Winners:* Adam Chandler and Oliver Pesch.

Esther J. Piercy Award ($1,500). To a librarian with no more than ten years' experience for contributions and leadership in the field of library collections and technical services. *Donor:* YBP Library Services. *Winner:* Daisy Waters.

SAGE Support Staff Travel Grants (up to $1,000). To enable support staff to attend an ALA Annual Conference. *Donor:* SAGE Publications. *Winners:* Behzad Allahyar, Gary Beer, Angela Hand, Michelle Schrade, Angela Slaughter, Israel Yanez.

Ulrich Serials Librarianship Award ($1,500). For distinguished contributions to serials librarianship. *Sponsor:* Ulrich's. *Winner:* Vicky Reich.

## Association for Library Service to Children (ALSC)

ALSC/Book Wholesalers, Inc. BWI Summer Reading Program Grant ($3,000). To an ALSC member for implementation of an outstanding public library summer reading program for children. *Donor:* Book Wholesalers, Inc. *Winner:* Wayne County Public Library, Goldsboro, North Carolina.

May Hill Arbuthnot Honor Lectureship. To an author, critic, librarian, historian, or teacher of children's literature who prepares a paper considered to be a significant contribution to the field of children's literature. *Winner:* Walter Dean Myers.

Mildred L. Batchelder Award. *Winner:* See "Literary Prizes, 2008" in Part 5.

Louise Seaman Bechtel Fellowship ($4,000). For librarians with 12 or more years of professional-level work in children's library collections, to read and study at the Baldwin Library, University of Florida. *Donor:* Bechtel Fund. *Winner:* Mary Elizabeth Land.

Pura Belpré Award. *Winners:* See "Literary Prizes, 2008" in Part 5.

Bookapalooza Program Awards. To provide three libraries with a collection of materials that will help transform their collection. *Winners:* Enid M. Baa Public Library, St. Thomas, Virgin Islands; Lena (Wisconsin) Public Library, Naturita Branch Library, Montrose (Colorado) Regional Library District.

ALSC/Booklist/YALSA Odyssey Award. To the producer of the best audiobook for children and/or young adults available in English in the United States. *Sponsor: Booklist. Winner:* Live Oak Media for *Jazz.*

Bound to Stay Bound Books Scholarships ($6,000 each). For men and women who intend to pursue an MLS or advanced degree and who plan to work in the area of library service to children. *Donor:* Bound to Stay Bound Books. *Winners:* Evan Bush, Emily Hersh, Christina Larrechea, Wendy Lee.

Randolph Caldecott Medal. *Winner:* See "Literary Prizes, 2008" in Part 5.

ALSC/Candlewick Press "Light the Way: Library Outreach to the Underserved" Grant ($5,000). To a library conducting exemplary outreach to underserved populations, presented in honor of author Kate DiCamillo. *Donor:* Candlewick Press. *Winner:* Rogers (Arkansas) Public Library.

Andrew Carnegie Medal. To the U.S. producer of the most distinguished video for children in the previous year. *Sponsor:* Carnegie Corporation of New York. *Winners:* Kevin Lafferty, John Davis, Amy Palmer Robertson, and Danielle Sterling for *Jump In! Freestyle Edition.*

Carnegie-Whitney Awards (up to $5,000). For the preparation of print or electronic reading lists, indexes, or other guides to library resources that promote reading or the use of library resources at any type of library. *Donors:* James Lyman Whitney and Andrew Carnegie Funds. *Winners:* Vivian Chan for *Facts and Fiction: Books about Asian Pacific Americans for K–12*; Virginia Dietrich, National Weather Center Library, for *All Weather Is Good*; Lois Gordon for *Environment, Health and Technology in the 21st Century: A Guide to Selected Popular Materials*; Carol Sibley for *Best Read-Aloud Picture Books*; Beth Thomsett-Scott for *STEM Girls: Resources to Interest Girls in STEM (Science, Technology, Engineering and Math) Careers*; Miriam Tuliao for *Contemporary Immigrant Voices in Poetry: A Selected Bibliography*; Karen Vargas for *Linking Older Adults to Quality Health Information*; Yunshan Ye for *Three Steps Toward Becoming a Proficient Researcher in East Asia.*

Distinguished Service to ALSC Award ($1,000). To recognize significant contributions to, and an impact on, library services to children and/or ALSC. *Winner:* Henrietta Smith.

Theodor Seuss Geisel Award. *Winner:* See "Literary Prizes, 2008" in Part 5.

Maureen Hayes Author/Illustrator Visit Award (up to $4,000). For an honorarium and travel expenses to enable a library talk to children by a nationally known author/illustrator. *Sponsor:* Simon & Schuster Children's Publishing. *Winners:* Robert Louis Stevenson Elementary School, San Francisco.

I Love My Librarian Awards. To recognize librarians for service to their communities, schools, and campuses. Winners are nominated by library patrons. *Sponsors:* Carnegie Corporation of New York and the *New York Times. Winners:* Linda Allen, Jean Amaral, Amy J. Cheney, Jennifer Lankford Dempsey, Carol W. Levers, Margaret "Gigi" Lincoln, Elaine McIlroy,

Paul McIntosh, Iona R. Malanchuk, Arezoo Moseni.

**Frederic G. Melcher Scholarship ($6,000).** To two students entering the field of library service to children for graduate work in an ALA-accredited program. *Winners:* Shauna Masella, Aileen Sanchez.

**John Newbery Medal.** *Winner:* See "Literary Prizes, 2008" in Part 5.

**Penguin Young Readers Group Awards ($600).** To children's librarians in school or public libraries with ten or fewer years of experience to attend the ALA Annual Conference. *Donor:* Penguin Young Readers Group. *Winners:* Barbara J. Head, Cheryl Fishman, Sara Jeffress, Madeline Walton-Hadlock.

**Robert F. Sibert Medal.** To the author of the most distinguished informational book for children published during the preceding year. *Donor:* Bound to Stay Bound Books. *Winner:* See "Literary Prizes, 2008" in Part 5.

**Tandem Library Books Literature Program Award ($1,000 toward ALA Annual Conference attendance for the development of an outstanding reading or literature program for children. *Donor:* Tandem Library Books. *Winner:* Lisa M. Shaia.

**Laura Ingalls Wilder Medal.** To an author or illustrator whose works have made a lasting contribution to children's literature. *Winner:* See "Literary Prizes, 2008" in Part 5.

## Association for Library Trustees and Advocates (ALTA)

**ALTA/Gale Outstanding Trustee Conference Grant Award ($750).** *Donor:* Gale Research. *Winner:* Not awarded in 2008.

**ALTA Literacy Award (citation).** To a library trustee or an individual who, in a volunteer capacity, has made a significant contribution to addressing the illiteracy problem in the United States. *Winner:* Not awarded in 2008.

**ALTA Major Benefactors Honor Award (citation).** To individuals, families, or corporate bodies that have made major benefactions to public libraries. *Winner:* Not awarded in 2008.

**Trustee Citations.** To recognize public library trustees for individual service to library development on the local, state, regional, or national level. *Winners:* Donald W. Green, Barbara Prentice.

## Association of College and Research Libraries (ACRL)

**ACRL Academic or Research Librarian of the Year Award ($5,000).** For outstanding contribution to academic and research librarianship and library development. *Donor:* YBP Library Services. *Winner:* Peter Hernon.

**ACRL Distinguished Education and Behavioral Sciences Librarian Award ($1,500).** To an academic librarian who has made an outstanding contribution as an education and/or behavioral sciences librarian through accomplishments and service to the profession. *Donor:* John Wiley & Sons. *Winner:* John William Collins III.

**ACRL/DLS Haworth Press Distance Learning Librarian Conference Sponsorship Award ($1,200).** To an ACRL member working in distance-learning librarianship in higher education. *Winner:* Harvey Gover.

**ACRL Doctoral Dissertation Fellowship ($1,500).** To a doctoral student in the field of academic librarianship whose research has potential significance in the field. *Donor:* Thomson Reuters. *Winner:* Donghua Tao for "Using Theory of Reasoned Action (TRA) in Understanding Selection and Use of Information Resources: An Information Resource Selection and Use Model."

**ACRL Special Presidential Recognition Award (plaque).** To recognize an individual's special career contributions to ACRL and the library profession. *Winner:* Not awarded in 2008.

**ACRL/WSS Award for Career Achievement in Women's Studies Librarianship ($1,000).** *Donors:* Greenwood Publishing Group and Routledge. *Winner:* Dolores Fidishun.

**ACRL/WSS Award for Significant Achievement in Women's Studies Librarianship ($1,000).** *Winner:* Jane Sloan.

**Hugh C. Atkinson Memorial Award.** *See under* American Library Association.

Community College Learning Resources Leadership/Library Achievement Awards ($500). To recognize outstanding achievement in library programs or leadership. *Sponsor:* EBSCO Information Services. *Winners:* (leadership) Not awarded in 2008; (programs) Hazard Community and Technical College, Hazard, Kentucky.

Coutts Nijhoff International West European Specialist Study Grant (up to 4,500 euros). Supports research pertaining to West European studies, librarianship, or the book trade. *Sponsor:* Coutts Information Services. *Winner:* Michelle Emanuel for her proposal to survey major film libraries in the Paris region in order to analyze and evaluate the collections and services provided to visiting scholars.

Miriam Dudley Instruction Librarian Award ($1,000). For a contribution to the advancement of bibliographic instruction in a college or research institution. *Donor:* Elsevier Science. *Winner:* Craig Gibson.

Excellence in Academic Libraries Awards ($3,000). To recognize outstanding community college, college, and university libraries. *Donor:* Blackwell's Book Services. *Winners:* (community college) Shatford Library, Pasadena (California) City College; (college) Lawrence McKinley Gould Library, Carleton College, Northfield, Minnesota; (university) McMaster University Libraries, Hamilton, Ontario.

Instruction Section Innovation Award ($3,000). To librarians or project teams in recognition of a project that demonstrates creative, innovative, or unique approaches to information literacy instruction or programming. *Donor:* LexisNexis. *Winner:* Susan Sharpless Smith, Wake Forest University, for the Embedded Librarian Project.

Marta Lange/CQ Press Award ($1,000). To recognize an academic or law librarian for contributions to bibliography and information service in law or political science. *Donor:* CQ Press. *Winner:* Lisa Norberg.

Samuel Lazerow Fellowship for Research in Acquisitions or Technical Services ($1,000). To foster advances in acquisitions or technical services by providing librarians a fellowship for travel or writing in those fields. *Sponsor:* Thomson Reuters. *Winners:* Ping Situ and Shuyong Jiang for their research project on vendor-provided records and the experience of a research library in outsourcing cataloging service for its Chinese-language materials.

Katharine Kyes Leab and Daniel J. Leab Exhibition Catalog Awards (citations). For the best catalogs published by American or Canadian institutions in conjunction with exhibitions of books and/or manuscripts. *Winners:* (division I–expensive) *Illustrating the Good Life: The Pissarros' Eragny Press, 1894–1914: A Catalogue of an Exhibition of Books, Prints and Drawings Related to the Work of the Press,* Groller Club; (division II–moderately expensive), *One Book, Many Interpretations,* Special Collections and Preservation Division, Chicago Public Library; division III–inexpensive) *Mapping America: 500 Years of Cartographic Depictions,* Vassar College; (division IV–brochures) *Collecting an Empire: The East India Company (1600–1900),* Beinecke Rare Book and Manuscript Library, Yale University; (division V–electronic exhibition) *B. W. Wells, Pioneer Ecologist,* Special Collections Research Center, North Carolina State University Libraries.

Oberly Award for Bibliography in the Agricultural or Natural Sciences. Biennially, for the best English-language bibliography in the field of agriculture or a related science in the preceding two-year period. *Donor:* Eunice Rockwood Oberly Memorial Fund. *Winner:* Not awarded in 2008.

Ilene F. Rockman Instruction Publication of the Year Award ($3,000). To recognize an outstanding publication relating to instruction in a library environment in the past two years. *Sponsor:* Emerald Group. *Winners:* Patrick Ragains, University of Nevada–Reno, for *Information Literacy Instruction That Works: A Guide to Teaching by Discipline and Student Population* (Neal-Schuman).

## Association of Specialized and Cooperative Library Agencies (ASCLA)

ASCLA Cathleen Bourdon Service Award. To recognize an ASCLA personal member for outstanding service and leadership to the division. *Winner:* Barbara H. Will.

ASCLA Century Scholarship ($2,500). For a library school student or students with disabilities admitted to an ALA-accredited library school. *Winner:* Lela Ellison.

ASCLA Exceptional Service Award. To recognize exceptional service to patients, the homebound, inmates, and to medical, nursing, and other professional staff in hospitals. *Winner:* Not awarded in 2008.

ASCLA Leadership and Professional Achievement Award. To recognize leadership and achievement in the areas of consulting, multitype library cooperation, statewide service and programs, and state library development. *Winners:* Public Library Interface Kit (PLINKIT) Collaborative.

Francis Joseph Campbell Award. For a contribution of recognized importance to library service for the blind and physically handicapped. *Winner:* Michael M. Moodie.

KLAS/National Organization on Disability Award for Library Service to People with Disabilities ($1,000). To a library organization to recognize an innovative project to benefit people with disabilities. *Donor:* Keystone Systems. *Winner:* Antioch (California) Public Library.

## Black Caucus of the American Library Association (BCALA)

BCALA Trailblazer's Award. Presented once every five years in recognition of outstanding and unique contributions to librarianship. *Winner:* To be awarded next in 2010.

DEMCO/BCALA Excellence in Librarianship Award ($500). To a librarian who has made significant contributions to promoting the status of African Americans in the library profession. *Winner:* John S. Page.

E. J. Josey Scholarship Awards ($2,000). To two African American students enrolled in or accepted by ALA accredited MLIS programs. *Winners:* Sandra Eddie, Teneka Taylor.

## Ethnic and Multicultural Information and Exchange Round Table (EMIERT)

David Cohen/EMIERT Multicultural Award ($300). To recognize articles of significant research and publication that increase understanding and promote multiculturalism in North American libraries. *Donor:* Routledge. *Winner:* Not awarded in 2008.

Gale/EMIERT Multicultural Award ($1,000). For outstanding achievement and leadership in serving the multicultural/multiethnic community. *Donor:* Gale Research. *Winner:* Not awarded in 2008.

## Exhibits Round Table (ERT)

Christopher J. Hoy/ERT Scholarship ($5,000). To an individual or individuals who will work toward an MLS degree in an ALA-accredited program. *Donor:* Family of Christopher Hoy. *Winner:* Kathryn Ruth Pettegrew.

## Federal and Armed Forces Librarians Round Table (FAFLRT)

FAFLRT Achievement Award. For achievement in the promotion of library and information service and the information profession in the federal government community. *Winner:* Robert E. Schnare, Jr., Naval War College Library.

Adelaide del Frate Conference Sponsorship Award ($1,000). To encourage library school students to become familiar with federal librarianship and ultimately seek work in federal libraries; for attendance at ALA Annual Conference and activities of the Federal and Armed Forces Librarians Round Table. *Winner:* Cynthia Blaschke.

Distinguished Service Award (citation). To honor a FAFLRT member for outstanding and sustained contributions to the association and to federal librarianship. *Winner:* Not awarded in 2008.

Ciccly Phippen Marks Scholarship ($1,500). To a library school student with an interest in working in a federal library. *Winner:* Alina J. Johnson.

## Gay, Lesbian, Bisexual, and Transgendered Round Table (GLBT)

Stonewall Book Awards. *Winners:* See "Literary Prizes, 2008" in Part 5.

## Government Documents Round Table (GODORT)

James Bennett Childs Award. To a librarian or other individual for distinguished lifetime contributions to documents librarianship. *Winner:* Larry Romans.

Bernadine Abbott Hoduski Founders Award. To recognize documents librarians who may not be known at the national level but who have made significant contributions to the field of local, state, federal, or international documents. *Winner:* Lily Wai.

LexisNexis Documents to the People Award. To an individual, library, organization, or noncommercial group that most effectively encourages or enhances the use of government documents in library services. *Winner:* Mary Webb Prophet.

NewsBank/Readex Catharine J. Reynolds Award. Grants to documents librarians for travel and/or study in the field of documents librarianship or area of study benefiting performance as documents librarians. *Donor:* NewsBank and Readex Corporation. *Winner:* Judith Downie.

W. David Rozkuszka Scholarship ($3,000). To provide financial assistance to an individual who is currently working with government documents in a library while completing a master's program in library science. *Winner:* Ray Walling.

## Intellectual Freedom Round Table (IFRT)

John Phillip Immroth Memorial Award for Intellectual Freedom ($500). For notable contribution to intellectual freedom fueled by personal courage. *Winners:* Jane Smith and Lisa Scherff.

Eli M. Oboler Memorial Award. See "Literary Prizes, 2008" in Part 5.

ProQuest/SIRS State and Regional Achievement Award ($1,000). To an innovative and effective intellectual freedom project covering a state or region during the calendar year. *Donor:* ProQuest Social Issues Resource Series (SIRS). *Winners:* Illinois Library Association Intellectual Freedom Committee

## Library Leadership and Management Association (LLAMA)

Hugh C. Atkinson Memorial Award. *See under* American Library Association.

Diana V. Braddom Fundraising and Financial Development Section Scholarship ($1,000). To enable attendance at the ALA Annual Conference. *Donor:* Diana V. Braddom. *Winner:* Susan E. Thomas.

John Cotton Dana Library Public Relations Awards ($5,000). To libraries or library organizations of all types for public relations programs or special projects ended during the preceding year. *Donors:* H. W. Wilson Company and H. W. Wilson Foundation. *Winners:* Gail Borden Public Library, Elgin, Illinois; Hamilton (Ontario) Public Library; Metropolitan Library Service Agency, St. Paul, Minnesota; Richmond (British Columbia) Public Library; University of California at Santa Barbara.

LLAMA/IIDA Library Interior Design Awards. To recognize excellence in library interior design. *Sponsors:* LLAMA Business and Equipment Section and the International Interior Design Association. *Winners:* (academic libraries, 30,000 square feet and smaller) Architecture Research Office (ARO) for Susan P. and Richard A. Friedman Study Center, Brown University; (academic libraries, over 30,000 square feet) SmithGroup for Hastings College of Law Library, University of California, San Francisco; (public libraries 30,000 square feet and smaller) richard + bauer for Arabian Public Library, Scottsdale, Arizona; (public libraries over 30,000 square feet) HGA Architects and Engineers for Ramsey County Library, Maplewood, Minnesota; (single space) Nagle Hartray Danker Kagan McKay Penney Architects and architectureisfun, Inc. for "The Loft" teen room, Evanston (Illinois) Public Library; (innovation in sustainable design) Shore Tilbe Irwin & Partners for

Hazel McCallion Academic Learning Center, University of Toronto, Mississauga; (historic restoration) Davis Brody Bond Aedas for Lionel Pincus and Princess Firyal Map Division, New York Public Library; (historic renovation-adaptive reuse) Office dA, Inc. for Fleet Library, Rhode Island School of Design; ("On the Boards" award) richard + bauer for Prescott Valley (Arizona) Public Library.

LLAMA Leadership Award. *Winner:* Janice Flug.

LLAMA President's Award. *Winner:* Not awarded in 2008.

## Library and Information Technology Association (LITA)

Hugh C. Atkinson Memorial Award. *See under* American Library Association.

Ex Libris Student Writing Award ($1,000 and publication in *Information Technology and Libraries*). For the best unpublished manuscript on a topic in the area of libraries and information technology written by a student or students enrolled in an ALA-accredited library and information studies graduate program. *Donor:* Ex Libris. *Winner:* Robin Sease for "Metaphor's Role in the Information Behavior of Humans Interacting with Computers."

LITA/Brett Butler Entrepreneurship Award ($5,000). To recognize a librarian or library for demonstrating exemplary entrepreneurship by providing innovative products or services through the application of information technology. *Donor:* Thomson Gale Group. *Winner:* Glenn Peterson for development of the library Web site service EngagedPatrons.org.

LITA/Christian Larew Memorial Scholarship ($3,000). To encourage the entry of qualified persons into the library and information technology field. *Sponsor:* Informata.com. *Winner:* Joanna DiPasquale.

LITA/Library Hi Tech Award ($1,000). To an individual or institution for a work that shows outstanding communication for continuing education in library and information technology. *Donor:* Emerald Press. *Winner:* Helene Blowers.

LITA/LSSI Minority Scholarship in Library and Information Science ($2,500). To encourage a qualified member of a principal minority group to work toward an MLS degree in an ALA-accredited program with emphasis on library automation. *Donor:* Library Systems and Services. *Winner:* Tiffany Chao.

LITA/OCLC Frederick G. Kilgour Award for Research in Library and Information Technology ($2,000 and expense-paid attendance at the ALA Annual Conference). To bring attention to research relevant to the development of information technologies. *Donor:* OCLC. *Winner:* Jane Greenberg.

LITA/OCLC Minority Scholarship in Library and Information Technology ($3,000). To encourage a qualified member of a principal minority group to work toward an MLS degree in an ALA-accredited program with emphasis on library automation. *Donor:* OCLC. *Winner:* Israel Yanez.

## Library History Round Table (LHRT)

Phyllis Dain Library History Dissertation Award ($500). To the author of a dissertation treating the history of books, libraries, librarianship, or information science. *Winner:* Not awarded in 2008.

Donald G. Davis Article Award (certificate). For the best article written in English in the field of U.S. and Canadian library history. *Winner:* Not awarded in 2008.

Eliza Atkins Gleason Book Award. Presented every third year to the author of the best book in English in the field of library history. *Winner:* Not awarded in 2008.

Justin Winsor Prize Essay ($500). To an author of an outstanding essay embodying original historical research on a significant subject of library history. *Winner:* Jeremy Dibbell for " 'A Library of the Most Celebrated and Approved Authors': The First Purchase Collection of Union College."

## Library Research Round Table (LRRT)

Ingenta Research Award (up to $6,000). To sponsor research projects about acquisition, use, and preservation of digital information; the award includes $1,000 to support travel to a conference to present the results of that research. *Sponsor:* Ingenta. *Winners:* Grace A. Ajuwon and

Prince B. Olorunsaye of the E. Latunde Odeku Medical Library, College of Medicine, University of Ibadan, Nigeria.

Jesse H. Shera Award for Distinguished Published Research ($500). For a research article on library and information studies published in English during the calendar year. *Winners:* Eric M. Meyers, Karen E. Fisher, and Elizabeth Marcoux for "Studying the Everyday Information Behaviors of 'Tweens: Notes from the Field."

Jesse H. Shera Award for Support of Dissertation Research ($500). To recognize and support dissertation research employing exemplary research design and methods. *Winner:* Sharon McQueen, University of Wisconsin–Madison, for "The Story of 'Ferdinand': The Creation of a Cultural Icon."

## Map and Geography Round Table (MAGERT)

MAGERT Honors Award. To recognize lifetime achievement and contributions to map and geography librarianship. *Winner:* Nancy A. Kandoian.

## New Members Round Table (NMRT)

NMRT/Marshall Cavendish Award (free tickets to the Newbery/Caldecott/Wilder Banquet at the ALA Annual Conference). *Winners:* Kris Baker, Judy Allen Dodson, Barbara M. Moon.

Shirley Olofson Memorial Award ($1,000). To an individual to help defray costs of attending the ALA Annual Conference. *Winner:* Annie Paprocki.

Student Chapter of the Year Award. To an ALA student chapter for outstanding contributions to ALA. *Winner:* Library and Information Science Student Association, University of South Carolina.

3M Professional Development Grant. To new NMRT members to encourage professional development and participation in national ALA and NMRT activities. *Donor:* 3M. *Winners:* Katie Dunneback, Deana Groves, Kate Zoellner.

## Office for Diversity

Achievement in Diversity Research Honor. To an ALA member who has made significant contributions to diversity research in the profession. *Winner:* Clara Chu.

Diversity Research Grants ($2,500). To the authors of research proposals that address critical gaps in the knowledge of diversity issues within library and information science. *Winners:* John Pruitt for "LGBT Book Discussion Groups in Public Libraries: Seeking Compatibility"; Jamie Campbell Naidoo for "Focus on MY Family: An Analysis of Gay-Themed Picturebooks and Public Library Services for LGBTQ Children and Children with Same-Sex Parents"; Eun-Young Yoo and Pauletta Bracy for "Cultural Authenticity Portrayed in Picture Books: A Systematic Approach Toward Diversity Education for Children."

## Office for Information Technology Policy

L. Ray Patterson Copyright Award. To recognize an individual who supports the constitutional purpose of U.S. copyright law, fair use, and the public domain. *Sponsor:* Freedom to Read Foundation. *Winner:* Peggy Hoon.

## Office for Intellectual Freedom

Freedom to Read Foundation Roll of Honor (citation): To recognize individuals who have contributed substantially to the foundation. *Winner:* Burton Joseph.

## Office for Literacy and Outreach Services

Jean E. Coleman Library Outreach Lecture. *Sponsor:* 15th of March, Inc. *Winner:* Clara M. Chu.

Diversity Fair Awards (total of $700). To outreach librarians for their institutions' diversity-in-action initiatives. *Winners:* (first place) Teaching Resources Center, University of North Carolina at Greensboro; (second place) Schaumburg Township District Library, Schaumburg, Illinois; (third place) Public Library of Charlotte and Mecklenburg County, North Carolina.

Estela and Raúl Mora Award ($1,000 and plaque). For the most exemplary program celebrating Día de Los Niños/Día de Los Libros. *Winners:* Public Library of Charlotte and Mecklenburg County, North Carolina, and Riverside County (California) Library System.

## Public Awareness Committee

Scholastic Library/Grolier National Library Week Grant ($5,000). To libraries or library associations of all types for a public awareness campaign in connection with National Library Week in the year the grant is awarded. *Sponsor:* Scholastic Library Publishing. *Winner:* Public Library of Charlotte and Mecklenburg County, North Carolina.

## Public Library Association (PLA)

Advancement of Literacy Award (plaque). To a publisher, bookseller, hardware and/or software dealer, foundation, or similar group that has made a significant contribution to the advancement of adult literacy. *Donor: Library Journal. Winner:* Mid South Reads, Memphis.

Baker & Taylor Entertainment Audio Music/ Video Product Grant ($2,500 worth of audio music or video products). To help a public library to build or expand a collection of either or both formats. *Donor:* Baker & Taylor. *Winner:* Kansas City (Missouri) Public Library.

Gordon M. Conable Award ($1,500). To a public library staff member, library trustee, or public library for demonstrating a commitment to intellectual freedom and the Library Bill of Rights. *Sponsor:* LSSI. *Winner:* Not awarded in 2008.

Demco New Leaders Travel Grants (up to $1,500). To PLA members who have not attended a major PLA continuing-education event in the past five years. *Winners:* Daisy Porter, Tracy Hokaj, Jennifer Tchida, Libby Feil.

EBSCO Excellence in Small and/or Rural Public Service Award ($1,000). Honors a library serving a population of 10,000 or less that demonstrates excellence of service to its community as exemplified by an overall service program or a special program of significant accomplishment. *Donor:* EBSCO Information Services. *Winner:* Thomas Memorial Library, Cape Elizabeth, Maine.

Highsmith Library Innovation Award ($2,000). To recognize a public library's innovative achievement in planning and implementing a creative community service program. *Donor:* Highsmith. *Winner:* Lake Agassiz Regional Library, Moorhead, Minnesota.

Allie Beth Martin Award ($3,000). To honor a public librarian who has demonstrated extraordinary range and depth of knowledge about books or other library materials and has distinguished ability to share that knowledge. *Donor:* Baker & Taylor. *Winner:* Janice Benedict.

Polaris Innovation in Technology John Iliff Award ($1,000). To a library worker, librarian, or library for the use of technology and innovative thinking as a tool to improve services to public library users. *Sponsor:* Polaris. *Winner:* Durham County (North Carolina) Library.

Charlie Robinson Award. Honors a public library director who, over a period of seven years, has been a risk taker, an innovator, and/or a change agent in a public library. *Donor:* Baker & Taylor. *Winner:* Sharon R. Quay.

## Public Programs Office

Sara Jaffarian School Library Program Award ($4,000). To honor a K–8 school library that has conducted an exemplary program or program series in the humanities. *Donors:* Sara Jaffarian and ALA Cultural Communities Fund. *Winner:* Woodsdale Elementary School, Wheeling, West Virginia.

## Reference and User Services Association (RUSA)

ABC-CLIO Online History Award ($3,000). A biennial award to recognize professional achievement in historical reference and librarianship. *Donor:* ABC-CLIO. *Winner:* Not awarded in 2008.

ALA/RUSA Zora Neale Hurston Award. To recognize the efforts of RUSA members in promoting African American literature. *Sponsored by:* Harper Perennial Publishing. *Winner:* Miriam Rodriguez, Dallas Public Library.

Virginia Boucher-OCLC Distinguished ILL Librarian Award ($2,000). To a librarian for outstanding professional achievement, leadership, and contributions to interlibrary loan and document delivery. *Winner:* Suzanne M. Ward.

BRASS Emerald Research Grant Awards ($5,000). To ALA members seeking support to conduct research in business librarianship. *Donor:* Emerald Group Publishing. *Winners:* Hyun-Duck Chung and Amy Van Scoy, Eleonora Dubicki.

BRASS Gale Cengage Learning Student Travel Award ($1,000). To enable a student enrolled in an ALA-accredited master's program to attend an ALA Annual Conference. *Donor:* Gale Cengage Learning. *Winner:* Daniel Hickey.

Sophie Brody Medal. *Winner:* See "Literary Prizes, 2008" in Part 5.

Dartmouth Medal. For creating current reference works of outstanding quality and significance. *Donor:* Dartmouth College. *Winners:* Oxford University Press for *Oxford Encyclopedia of Maritime History.*

Dun & Bradstreet Award for Outstanding Service to Minority Business Communities ($2,000). *Donor:* Dun & Bradstreet. *Winner:* Ka-Neng Au.

Dun & Bradstreet Public Librarian Support Award ($1,000). To support the attendance at the ALA Annual Conference of a public librarian who has performed outstanding business reference service. *Donor:* Dun & Bradstreet. *Winner:* Elizabeth Malafi.

Gale Cengage Award for Excellence in Business Librarianship ($3,000). For distinguished activities in the field of business librarianship *Donor:* Gale Cengage Learning. *Winner:* Gary White.

Gale Cengage Award for Excellence in Reference and Adult Library Services ($3,000). To recognize a library or library system for developing an imaginative and unique library resource to meet patrons' reference needs. *Donor:* Gale Cengage Learning. *Winner:* James Madison University Library and Educational Technologies.

Genealogical Publishing Company/History Section Award ($1,500). To encourage and commend professional achievement in historical reference and research librarianship. *Donor:* Genealogical Publishing Company. *Winner:* Carla Rickerson.

MARS Achievement Recognition Certificate. For excellence in service to the Machine-Assisted Reference Section. *Winner:* Mary Pagliero Popp.

Margaret E. Monroe Library Adult Services Award (citation). To a librarian for impact on library service to adults. *Winner:* Eileen Williams.

Isadore Gilbert Mudge–Gale Cengage Award ($5,000). For distinguished contributions to reference librarianship. *Donor:* Gale Cengage Learning. *Winner:* Margaret Stieg Dalton.

Reference Service Press Award ($2,500). To the author or authors of the most outstanding article published in *RUSQ* during the preceding two volume years. *Donor:* Reference Service Press. *Winner:* James Elmborg for "Libraries in the Contact Zone: On the Creation of Educational Space."

John Sessions Memorial Award (plaque). To a library or library system in recognition of work with the labor community. *Donor:* Department of Professional Employees, AFL/CIO. *Winner:* Walter P. Reuther Library of Labor and Urban Affairs, Wayne State University, Detroit.

Louis Shores–Greenwood Publishing Group Award ($3,000). To an individual, team, or organization to recognize excellence in reviewing of books and other materials for libraries. *Donor:* Greenwood Publishing Group. *Winner:* Ann Chambers Theis.

STARS-Atlas Systems Mentoring Award ($1,000). To a library practitioner new to the field of interlibrary loan, resource sharing, or electronic reserves, to attend an ALA Annual Conference. *Donor:* Atlas Systems. *Winner:* Pamela Flinton.

## Social Responsibilities Round Table (SRRT)

Coretta Scott King Awards. *Winners:* See "Literary Prizes, 2008" in Part 5.

Jackie Eubanks Memorial Award ($500). To honor outstanding achievement in promoting the acquisition and use of alternative media in libraries. *Donor:* SRRT Alternatives in Publication Task Force. *Winner:* Not awarded in 2008.

## Young Adult Library Services Association (YALSA)

Alex Awards. *Winners:* See "Literary Prizes, 2008" in Part 5.

Baker & Taylor/YALSA Scholarship Grants ($1,000). To young adult librarians in public or school libraries to attend an ALA Annual Conference for the first time. *Donor:* Baker & Taylor. *Winners:* Sudi Q. Napalan, Charlene Helsel-Kather.

BWI/YALSA Collection Development Grants ($1,000). To YALSA members who represent a public library and work directly with young adults, for collection development materials for young adults. *Donor:* Book Wholesalers, Inc. *Winners:* Sarah Daviau, Joan Light-Kraft.

Margaret A. Edwards Award ($2,000). *Winner:* See "Literary Prizes, 2008" in Part 5.

Great Book Giveaway (books, videos, CDs, and audiocassettes valued at a total of $25,000). *Winners:* Margaret Green Junior High School, Cleveland, Mississippi, Camden County (North Carolina) High School.

Frances Henne/VOYA Research Grant ($1,000). To provide seed money to an individual, institution, or group for a project to encourage research on library service to young adults. *Donor:* Scarecrow Press. *Winner:* Sarah Prielipp.

Michael L. Printz Award. *Winner:* See "Literary Prizes, 2008" in Part 5.

YALSA/Greenwood Publishing Group Service to Young Adults Achievement Award ($2,000). Awarded biennially to a YALSA member who has demonstrated unique and sustained devotion to young adult services. *Donor:* Greenwood. *Winner:* Michael Cart.

YALSA William C. Morris YA Debut Award. *Winner:* See "Literary Prizes, 2008" in Part 5.

YALSA/Sagebrush Award ($1,000). For an exemplary young adult reading or literature program. *Donor:* Sagebrush Corporation. *Winner:* Seth Cassel.

# American Society for Information Science and Technology (ASIS&T)

ASIS&T Award of Merit. For an outstanding contribution to the field of information science. *Winner:* Clifford Lynch.

ASIS&T Best Information Science Book. *Winner:* Christine Borgman for *Scholarship in the Digital Age: Information, Infrastructure, and the Internet* (MIT).

ASIS&T Proquest Doctoral Dissertation Award ($1,000 plus expense-paid attendance at ASIS&T Annual Meeting). *Winner:* Eric Meyer for "Socio-Technical Perspectives on Digital Photography."

ASIS&T Research in Information Science Award. For a systematic program of research in a single area at a level beyond the single study, recognizing contributions in the field of information science. *Winner:* Not awarded in 2008.

ASIS&T Special Award. To recognize long-term contributions to the advancement of information science and technology and enhancement of public access to information and discovery of mechanisms for improved transfer and utilization of knowledge. *Winner:* Not awarded in 2008.

James M. Cretsos Leadership Award. *Winners:* Elise Lewis and Phillip Edwards.

Watson Davis Award. For outstanding continuous contributions and dedicated service to the society. *Winner:* Samantha Hastings.

Pratt-Severn Best Student Research Paper Award. To recognize the outstanding work of a current student in a degree-granting program in the information field. *Sponsor:* Pratt Institute. *Winner:* Ann K. Irvine.

Thomson ISI Citation Analysis Research Grant. *Winners:* Isola Ajiferuke and Dietmar Wolfram for their proposal "Citer Analysis as a Measure of Research Impact."

Thomson ISI Doctoral Dissertation Proposal Scholarship. *Winner:* Christina M. Finneran for "Factors that Influence Users to Keep and/or Leave Information Items: A Case Study of College Students' Personal Information Management Behavior."

Thomson ISI Outstanding Information Science Teacher Award ($500). *Winner:* Eileen Abels.

John Wiley Best *JASIST* Paper Award. *Winners:* Teresa M. Harrison, Theresa Pardo, José Ramón Gil-García, Fiona Thompson, and Dubravka Juraga for "Geographic Information Technologies, Structuration Theory, and the World Trade Center Crisis."

## Art Libraries Society of North America (ARLIS/NA)

ARLIS/NA Conference Attendance Award. *Winner:* Ellie Ward.

ARLIS/NA Internship Award. To provide financial support for students preparing for a career in art librarianship or visual resource librarianship. *Winner:* Shilpa Rele.

AskART Conference Attendance Award ($1,000). *Winner:* Gabriela Zoller.

Andrew Cahan Photography Award ($1,000). To encourage conference participation of art information professionals in the field of photography. *Winner:* Tom Caswell.

Distinguished Service Award. To honor an individual whose exemplary service in art librarianship, visual resources curatorship, or a related field has made an outstanding national or international contribution to art information and/or art librarianship. *Winner:* Susan Craig.

Melva J. Dwyer Award. To the creators of exceptional reference or research tools relating to Canadian art and architecture. *Winner:* Philip Dombowsky for *Index to National Gallery of Canada Exhibition Catalogues and Checklists 1880–1930* (National Gallery of Canada).

Judith A. Hoffberg Student Award for Conference Attendance ($750). *Winner:* Yolanda Koscielski.

Howard and Beverly Joy Karno Award ($1,000). To provide financial assistance to a professional art librarian in Latin America through interaction with ARLIS/NA members and conference participation. *Winner:* Sandra Wiles.

Gerd Muehsam Award. To one or more graduate students in library science programs to recognize excellence in a graduate paper or project. *Winner:* Rachel Masilamani, University of Pittsburgh, for "Documenting Illegal Art: Collaborative Software, Online Environments and New York City's 1970s and 1980s Graffiti Art Movement."

Puvill Libros Award ($1,000). To encourage professional development of European art librarians through interaction with ARLIS/NA colleagues and conference participation. *Winners:* Not awarded in 2008.

Smithsonian American Art Museum Student Diversity Award for Conference Attendance ($750). *Winner:* Tiffany Chao.

Student Conference Attendance Award. *Winner:* Rebecca Cooper.

George Wittenborn Memorial Book Awards. See "Literary Prizes, 2008" in Part 5.

## Asian/Pacific Americans Libraries Association (APALA)

APALA Scholarship ($1,000). For a student of Asian or Pacific background who is enrolled, or has been accepted into, a master's or doctoral degree program in library and/or information science at an ALA-accredited school. *Winner:* Michael Habata.

APALA Travel Award ($500). To a library professional possessing a master's-level degree in library and/or information science to attend the ALA Annual Conference. *Winner:* Sally Ma.

## Association for Library and Information Science Education (ALISE)

ALISE Award for Teaching Excellence in the Field of Library and Information Science Education. *Winner:* Christine Jenkins.

ALISE/Eugene Garfield Doctoral Dissertation Award ($500). *Winner:* Kara Anne Reuter.

ALISE/Linworth Youth Services Paper Award. *Winner:* Kara Anne Reuter.

ALISE Pratt-Severn Faculty Innovation Award ($1,000). *Winner:* Faculty of the School of Library and Information Science at San José State University.

ALISE Professional Contribution to Library and Information Science Education Award. *Winners:* Catherine Ross, Linda Smith.

ALISE Research Grant Awards (one or more grants totaling $5,000): *Winners:* Joan Cherry, Luanne Freund, and Wendy Duff for "Learning From Our Students: Assessing Student Perceptions of Information Studies Programs and The Information Professions."

ALISE/Jean Tague-Sutcliffe Doctoral Student Research Poster Competition. *Winner:* Rachel A. Fleming.

ALISE/Bohdan S. Wynar Research Paper Competition. For a research paper concerning any aspect of librarianship or information studies by a member or members of ALISE. *Winners:* Rong Tang and Martin A. Safer for "Author-Rated Importance of Cited References in Biology and Psychology Publications."

ALISE/University of Washington Information School Youth Services Graduate Student Travel Award ($750). To support the costs associated with travel to and participation in the ALISE Annual Conference. *Winner:* To be awarded for the first time in 2009.

Doctoral Students to ALISE Grant. To enable one or more promising LIS doctoral students to attend the ALISE Annual Conference. *Winner:* Miriam Matteson.

OCLC/ALISE Research Grant Program. *Winners:* Rong Tang and Sheila Denn for "User-based Question Answering: An Exploratory Study of Community-generated Information Exchange in Yahoo! Answers"; Diane Kelly for "Developing and Evaluating a Query Recommendation Feature to Assist Users with Online Information Seeking and Retrieval"; Youngok Choi for "Analyzing Image Searching on the Web: How Do Undergraduates Search and Use Visual Information?"

Service to ALISE Award. *Winner:* Ken Haycock.

## Association of Jewish Libraries (AJL)

AJL Scholarships ($500). For students enrolled in accredited library schools who plan to work as Judaica librarians. *Winners:* Amanda (Miryem-Khaye) Seigel, Nachum Zitter.

## Association of Research Libraries

ARL Diversity Scholarships ($10,000 stipend). To a varying number of MLS students from under-represented groups who are interested in careers in research libraries. *Sponsors:* ARL member libraries and the Institute of Museum and Library Services. *Winners:* Nicole Branch, LaBae Daniels, Camille Chesley, Yesenia Figueroa, Andrea Gagliardi, Sorrel Goodwin, Harriett Green, Michelle Guitar, Jameka Lewis, Jennifer McDaniel, Shaneka Morris, Yujung Park, Elliot Polak, Mukhtar Raqib, Ayman Shabana, Jennifer Thompson, Linh Uong.

## Association of Seventh-Day Adventist Librarians

D. Glenn Hilts Scholarship ($1,200) for a member of the Seventh-Day Adventist Church in a graduate library program. *Winner:* Rebecca Macomber.

## Beta Phi Mu

Beta Phi Mu Award. *See under* American Library Association.

Eugene Garfield Doctoral Dissertation Fellowship. *Winners:* Serhiy Polyakov, Xiaoli Huang, Yong-Mi Kim, Maria Souden, Mary Jo Venetis. Pengyi Zhang.

Harold Lancour Scholarship for Foreign Study. For graduate study in a foreign country related to the applicant's work or schooling. *Winner:* Cristina Dominguez Ramirez.

Mary Jo Lynch Distinguished Lecture Award ($2,000). *Sponsors:* Florida State University Information Use Management and Policy Institute and Beta Phi Mu. *Winner:* Beta Lambda Chapter, Beta Phi Mu (University of North Texas/Texas Woman's University).

Sarah Rebecca Reed Scholarship. For study at an ALA-accredited library school. *Winner:* Emma Carbone.

Frank B. Sessa Scholarship for Continuing Professional Education. For continuing education for a Beta Phi Mu member. *Winner:* Sarah E. Wessel.

Blanche E. Woolls Scholarship ($1,000). For a beginning student in school library media services. *Winner:* Jennifer Lynn Ventura.

## Bibliographical Society of America (BSA)

BSA Fellowships ($1,500–$6,000). For scholars involved in bibliographical inquiry and research in the history of the book trades and in publishing history. *Winners:* Dee Andrews, Olga Duhl, Vincent Golden, Joseph J. Gwara, Grace Ioppolo, Jeffrey Knight, Miriam Mandel, Nikos Pappas, Catherine Parisian, Linda Quirk, Sydney Shep, Mei-Ying Sung, Deborah Wright.

William L. Mitchell Prize for Research on Early British Serials ($1,000). Awarded triennially for the best single work published in the previous three years. *Winner:* To be awarded next in 2009.

Justin G. Schiller Prize for Bibliographical Work on Pre-20th-Century Children's Books ($2,000). A triennial award to encourage scholarship in the bibliography of historical children's books. *Winner:* To be awarded next in 2010.

## Canadian Library Association (CLA)

Olga B. Bishop Award ($200). To a library school student for the best paper on government information or publications. *Winner:* Lori McCay-Peet.

CLA Award for the Advancement of Intellectual Freedom in Canada. *Winners:* Nancy Branscombe and Gina Barbar.

CLA Elizabeth Dafoe Scholarship ($5,000). *Winner:* Geoffrey Allen.

CLA/Information Today Award for Innovative Technology. *Donor:* Information Today, Inc. *Winner:* Richmond (British Columbia) Public Library.

CLA Outstanding Service to Librarianship Award. *Donor:* R. R. Bowker. *Winner:* Vivienne Monty.

CLA Research and Development Grant ($1,000). *Winner:* Kevin Manuel for "Working Together: Brock University Library's New Learning Commons."

CLA Student Article Award. *Winner:* Elizabeth Fulton-Lyne for "Casting Fresh Eyes on the CLA Statement on Intellectual Freedom."

CLA/3M Award for Achievement in Technical Services ($1,000). *Winner:* Not awarded in 2008.

CLA/YBP Award for Outstanding Contribution to Collection Development and Management ($1,000). To recognize a CLA/ACB member who has made an outstanding local, national, or international contribution in the field of library collection development or management. *Sponsor:* YBP Library Services. *Winner:* Merrill Distad.

Ken Haycock Award for Promoting Librarianship ($1,000). *See under* American Library Association.

W. Kaye Lamb Award for Service to Seniors. *Winner:* Oshawa (Ontario) Public Library.

H. W. Wilson Scholarship ($2,000). *Winner:* Allen Chase.

World Book Graduate Scholarship in Library Science ($2,500). *Winner:* Lorie Kloda.

### Canadian Association for School Libraries (CASL)

CASL Follett International Teacher Librarian of the Year Award. *Winner:* Diana Maliszewski.

CASL Margaret B. Scott Award of Merit. For the development of school libraries in Canada. *Winners:* Margaret Stimson and Donna DesRoches.

CASL Angela Thacker Memorial Award. For outstanding contribution to teacher-librarianship. *Winner:* Carlene Walter.

### Canadian Association of College and University Libraries (CACUL)

CACUL/Robert H. Blackburn Distinguished Paper Award ($200). To acknowledge notable research published by CACUL members. *Winner:* Donald Taylor.

CACUL/Miles Blackwell Award for Outstanding Academic Librarian. *Sponsor:* Blackwell's. *Winner:* Margaret Law.

CACUL Innovation Achievement Award ($1,000). *Sponsor:* SirsiDynix. *Winner:* Lois Hole Campus Alberta Digital Library.

CTCL Award for Outstanding College Librarian. *Winner:* Joanne Kemp, Grant MacEwan College.

CTCL Innovation Achievement Award. *Sponsor:* Micromedia ProQuest. *Winner:* SIAST Libraries.

### Canadian Association of Public Libraries (CAPL)

CAPL/Brodart Outstanding Public Library Service Award. *Winner:* Patricia Jobb.

### Canadian Association of Special Libraries and Information Services (CASLIS)

CASLIS Award for Special Librarianship in Canada. *Winner:* Not awarded in 2008.

### Canadian Library Trustees Association (CLTA)

CLTA/Stan Heath Achievement in Literacy Award. For an innovative literacy program by a public library board. *Donor:* ABC Canada. *Winner:* Ottawa Public Library.

CLTA Merit Award for Distinguished Service as a Public Library Trustee. *Winner:* Doug Dean.

## Chinese-American Librarians Association (CALA)

CALA Distinguished Service Award. To a librarian who has been a mentor, role model, and leader in the fields of library and information science. *Winner:* Hai Peng Li.

CALA President's Recognition Award. *Winner:* Not awarded in 2008.

Sheila Suen Lai Scholarship ($500). *Winner:* Stephen Chan.

C. C. Seetoo/CALA Conference Travel Scholarship ($500). For a student to attend the ALA Annual Conference and CALA program. *Winner:* Not awarded in 2008.

Sally T. Tseng Professional Development Grant ($1,000). *Winners:* Hwa-Wei Lee, Haipeng Li.

Huang Tso-ping and Wu Yao-yu Scholarship Memorial Research Grant ($200): *Winner:* Tiffany Chao.

## Church and Synagogue Library Association (CSLA)

CSLA Award for Outstanding Congregational Librarian. For distinguished service to the congregation and/or community through devotion to the congregational library. *Winner:* Marlene Moody.

CSLA Award for Outstanding Congregational Library. For responding in creative and innovative ways to the library's mission of reaching and serving the congregation and/or the wider community. *Winner:* Not awarded in 2008.

CSLA Award for Outstanding Contribution to Congregational Libraries. For providing inspiration, guidance, leadership, or resources to enrich the field of church or synagogue librarianship. *Winner:* Martha Huntley.

Helen Keating Ott Award for Outstanding Contribution to Children's Literature. *Winner:* Not awarded in 2008.

Pat Tabler Memorial Scholarship Award. *Winner:* Not awarded in 2008.

## Coalition for Networked Information

Paul Evan Peters Award. Awarded biennially to recognize notable and lasting international achievements relating to high-performance networks and the creation and use of information resources and services that advance scholarship and intellectual productivity. *Sponsors:* Association of Research Libraries, EDUCAUSE. *Winner:* Daniel E. Atkins.

Paul Evan Peters Fellowship ($5,000 a year for two years). Awarded biennially to a student pursuing a graduate degree in librarianship or the information sciences. *Sponsors:* Association of Research Libraries, EDUCAUSE. *Winner:* Elisabeth Jones.

## Council on Library and Information Resources (CLIR)

CLIR Postdoctoral Fellowships in Scholarly Information Resources. *Winners:* Gloria E. Chacon, Gabrielle N. O. Dean, Ernestina Osorio, Heather Waldroup, Susan Wiesner.

Mellon Fellowship Program for Dissertation Research in the Humanities in Original Sources (stipends of up to $20,000 to support dissertation research). *Winners:* Alex Borucki, Simonetta Marin, Noah Millstone, Tracy Neumann, Lata Parwani, Martin Renner, Kellie Warren, Alice Wolfram, Winnie Wong.

Rovelstad Scholarship in International Librarianship. To enable a student enrolled in an accredited LIS program to attend the IFLA World Library and Information Congress. *Winner:* Khue Duong.

A. R. Zipf Fellowship in Information Management ($10,000). To a student enrolled in graduate school who shows exceptional promise for leadership and technical achievement. *Winner:* Meredith Weiss.

## Friends of Libraries USA (FOLUSA)

FOLUSA/Baker & Taylor Awards ($2,000). To friends groups that have distinguished themselves in support of their libraries. *Winners:* (library without paid staff) Friends of the Blake Library in Stuart (Florida), Friends of the Morgan Hill (California) Library, Friends of the Westhampton (Massachusetts) Memorial Library; (library with paid staff) Friends of the Abilene (Texas) Public Library, Friends of the Ottawa (Ontario) Public Library Association.

FOLUSA Public Service Award. *Winner:* U.S. Rep. Vernon J. Ehlers (R-Mich.).

## Bill and Melinda Gates Foundation

Access to Learning Award ($1 million). To public libraries or similar organizations outside the United States for innovative programs that provide the public free access to information technology. *Administered by:* Gates Foundation Global Libraries initiative. *Winner:* The Vasconcelos Program, a mobile technology program that provides computer access and training for underserved communities in the state of Veracruz, Mexico.

## International Federation of Library Associations and Institutions (IFLA)

Harry Campbell Conference Attendance Grant. To support travel to the IFLA Conference from a developing country that has not had conference participants in recent years. *Winner:* Volatiana Ranaivozafy, Madagascar.

Dr. Shawky Salem Conference Grant (up to $1,900). To enable an expert in library and information science who is a national of an Arab country to attend the IFLA Conference for the first time. *Winner:* Mahmoud Khalifa, Library of Congress Overseas Office, Cairo.

Frederick Thorpe Individual Awards (up to £5,000 total). To librarians working in libraries for the blind. *Donor:* Ulverscroft Foundation. *Winners:* Hélène Kudzia of the Médiathèque de l'Association Valentin Haüy, Paris, £1,500 to spend 20 days at the Library of the Deutsche Blindenstudienanstalt, Marburg, Germany; Hosein Rohani Sadr of the National Library and Archives of Iran, £2,000 to study DAISY technology at the Swedish Library of Talking Books and Braille.

Frederick Thorpe Organizational Award (up to £15,000). To a library organization for development of service delivery to the visually impaired. *Winners:* Integrated Documentation System of the Cuyo National University, Mendoza, Argentina, £6,250; Centro para la Integración y el Desarrollo del Invidente, Lima, Peru, £10,000; Adaptive Technology Center for the Blind, Addis Ababa, Ethiopia, £5,000.

## Medical Library Association (MLA)

Virginia L. and William K. Beatty MLA Volunteer Service Award. To recognize a medical librarian who has demonstrated outstanding, sustained service to the Medical Library Association and the health sciences library profession. *Winner:* Logan Ludwig.

Estelle Brodman Award for the Academic Medical Librarian of the Year. To honor significant achievement, potential for leadership, and continuing excellence at mid-career in the area of academic health sciences librarianship. *Winner:* Not awarded in 2008.

Lois Ann Colaianni Award for Excellence and Achievement in Hospital Librarianship. To a member of MLA who has made significant contributions to the profession in the area of overall distinction or leadership in hospital librarianship. *Winner:* Jan Orick.

Cunningham Memorial International Fellowships ($3,500). Six-month grant and travel expenses in the United States and Canada for one or more foreign librarians. *Winners:* Lisa Kruesi, Vijay Padwal.

Louise Darling Medal. For distinguished achievement in collection development in the health sciences. *Winner:* The bimonthly *Grey Literature Report* produced by librarians at New York Academy of Medicine.

Janet Doe Lectureship. *Winner:* Thomas Basler. *Topic:* "There are No More Giants: Changing Leadership for Changing Times."

EBSCO/MLA Annual Meeting Grants (up to $1,000). *Winners:* Mary Lou Glazer, Laura Haines, Meredith Orlowski, Jason Young.

Ida and George Eliot Prize. For an essay published in any journal in the preceding calendar year that has been judged most effective in furthering medical librarianship. *Donor:* Login Brothers Books. *Winner:* Keith W. Cogdill for "Progress in Health Sciences Librarianship: 1970–2005" in *Advances in Librarianship*.

Murray Gottlieb Prize. For the best unpublished essay submitted by a medical librarian on the history of some aspect of health sciences or a detailed description of a library exhibit. *Donors:* Ralph and Jo Grimes. *Winner:* Heidi Heilemann for "Envisioning the Unborn: Art, Anatomy and the Printing Press in the Early Modern Era."

T. Mark Hodges International Service Award. To honor outstanding achievement in promoting, enabling, or delivering improved health information internationally. *Winner:* Carol Lefebvre.

Hospital Libraries Section/MLA Professional Development Grants. *Winners:* Amy Frey, Michelle Goodwin.

David A. Kronick Traveling Fellowship ($2,000). *Sponsor:* Bowden-Massey Foundation. *Winner:* Kathryn Kerdolff.

Joseph Leiter NLM/MLA Lectureship. *Winner:* Debra R. Lappin.

Donald A. B. Lindberg Research Fellowship ($9,945). *Winner:* Mark Puterbaugh.

Lucretia W. McClure Excellence in Education Award. To an outstanding educator in the field of health sciences librarianship and informatics. *Winner:* Sarah K. McCord.

Majors/MLA Chapter Project of the Year Award. *Sponsor:* J. A. Majors Co. *Winner:* New York-New Jersey Chapter of MLA for the digitization of chapter photographic archives.

Medical Informatics Section Career Development Grant (up to $1,500). To support a career development activity that will contribute to advancement in the field of medical informatics. *Winners:* Karen Albert, Maureen Knapp.

MLA Award for Distinguished Public Service. *Winner:* U.S. Rep. David Obey (D-Wis.).

MLA Continuing Education Awards. *Winners:* Patricia Hammond, Susan Schleper.

MLA Scholarship (up to $5,000). For graduate study at an ALA-accredited library school. *Winner:* Lisa O'Keefe.

MLA Scholarship for Minority Students (up to $5,000). For graduate study at an ALA-accredited library school. *Winner:* Manju Tanwar.

MLA Scholarship for Minority Students/Annual Meeting. A one-time award. *Winner:* Elana Churchill.

Marcia C. Noyes Award. For an outstanding contribution to medical librarianship. *Winner:* Rick B. Forsman.

Rittenhouse Award. For the best unpublished paper on medical librarianship submitted by a student enrolled in, or having been enrolled in, a course for credit in an ALA-accredited library school or a trainee in an internship program in medical librarianship. *Donor:* Rittenhouse Medical Bookstore. *Winner:* Bob Gerth for "Varicose Veins Pathfinder."

Thomson Reuters/MLA Doctoral Fellowship. To encourage superior students to conduct doctoral work in an area of health sciences librarianship or information. *Winner:* Lorie Kloda.

Thomson Scientific/Frank Bradway Rogers Information Advancement Award ($500). For an outstanding contribution to knowledge of health science information delivery. *Winner:* Linda Morgan Davis, Earlene Groseclose, and Louis J. Lafrado, creators of Digital Divide, a medical information service for rural American Indian communities.

## Music Library Association

Carol June Bradley Award. To support studies that involve the history of music libraries or special collections. *Winner:* Jocelyn Arem.

Vincent H. Duckles Award. For the best book-length bibliography or other research tool in music. *Winner:* Emilio Casares Rodicio for *Diccionario de la Zarzuela: España e Hispanoamérica* (Instituto Complutense de Ciencias Musicales, 2006).

Dena Epstein Award for Archival and Library Research in American Music. To support research in archives or libraries internationally on any aspect of American music. *Winners:* Steven Robert Swayne and Nikos Pappas.

Walter Gerboth Award. To members of MLA who are in the first five years of their professional library careers, to assist research-in-progress in music or music librarianship. *Winner:* Kristine Nelsen.

Richard S. Hill Award, For the best article on music librarianship or article of a music-bibliographic nature. *Winner:* James Deaville for "Publishing Paraphrases and Creating Collectors: Friedrich Hofmeister, Franz Liszt, and the Technology of Popularity," in *Franz Liszt and His World,* edited by Christopher H. Gibbs and Dana Gooley (Princeton).

MLA Citation. Awarded in recognition of contributions to the profession over a career. *Winner:* A. Ralph Papakhian.

Eva Judd O'Meara Award. For the best review published in *Notes. Winner:* John Wagstaff for his review of *Katharine Ellis's Interpreting the Musical Past: Early Music in Nineteenth-Century France* (Oxford).

Special Achievement Award. To recognize extraordinary service to the profession of music librarianship over a relatively short period of time. *Winner:* Nancy Bren Nuzzo.

# REFORMA (National Association to Promote Library and Information Services to Latinos and the Spanish-Speaking)

REFORMA scholarships ($1,500). To students who qualify for graduate study in library science and who are citizens or permanent residents of the United States. *Winners:* Tandra Frazier, Marissa Jacobo, Cristina E. Mitra, Rita A. Puig, Pablo A. Sandoval.

# K. G. Saur (Munich, Germany)

K. G. Saur Award for Best *LIBRI* Student Paper ($500). To author(s) to recognize the most outstanding article published in *LIBRI* during the preceding year. *Donor:* K. G. Saur Publishing. *Winner:* Michelle Caswell for "Irreparable damage: Violence, Ownership and Voice in an Indian Archive."

# Society of American Archivists (SAA)

C. F. W. Coker Award for Description. *Winner:* The Archivists' Toolkit (AT), an open-source archival data management system developed through a collaboration of several university libraries.

Colonial Dames of America and Donna Cutts Scholarships (up to $1,200). To enable new archivists to attend the Modern Archives Institute of the National Archives and Records Administration. *Winner:* Amy Moorman.

Distinguished Service Award. To recognize an archival institution, education program, nonprofit organization, or governmental organization that has given outstanding service to its public and has made an exemplary contribution to the archives profession. *Winner:* Thomas J. Dodd Research Center, University of Connecticut.

Fellows' Ernst Posner Award. For an outstanding essay dealing with a facet of archival administration, history, theory, or methodology, published in *American Archivist. Winners:* Magia Ghetu Krause and Elizabeth Yakel for "Interaction in Virtual Archives: The Polar Bear Expedition Digital Collections Next Generation Finding Aid."

Philip M. Hamer and Elizabeth Hamer Kegan Award. For individuals and/or institutions that have increased public awareness of a specific body of documents. *Winners:* Canadian Broadcasting Corporation (CBC) and the CBC Digital Archives for efforts to promote the use of CBC's radio and television collections.

Oliver Wendell Holmes Award. To enable overseas archivists already in the United States or Canada for training to attend the SAA annual meeting. *Winner:* Not awarded in 2008.

J. Franklin Jameson Award. For individuals and/or organizations that promote greater public awareness of archival activities and programs. *Winner:* The DICE (Data-Intensive Cyber Environments) group at the School of Library and Information Science at the University of North Carolina at Chapel Hill and the University of California, San Diego.

Sister M. Claude Lane, O.P., Memorial Award. For a significant contribution to the field of religious archives. *Winner:* Mark Thiel for his work on the five-volume "Guide to Catholic-Related Records About Native Americans."

Waldo Gifford Leland Prize. For writing of superior excellence and usefulness in the field of archival history, theory, or practice. *Winner:* Deidre Simmons *Keepers of the Record: The History of the Hudson's Bay Company Archives* (McGill-Queen's).

Theodore Calvin Pease Award. For the best student paper. *Winner:* Mary Samouelian for her research paper "Embracing Web 2.0: Archives and the Newest Generation of Web Applications."

Donald Peterson Student Scholarship Award (up to $1,000). To enable a student or recent graduate to attend the SAA Annual Meeting. *Winner:* Katherine Blank.

Harold T. Pinkett Minority Student Award. To encourage minority students to consider careers in the archival profession and promote minority participation in SAA. *Winners:* Monique Lloyd, Tiffany-Kay Sangwand.

Preservation Publication Award. To recognize an outstanding work published in North America that advances the theory or the practice of preservation in archival institutions. *Winner:* "The Digital Dilemma," produced by the Science and Technology Council of the Academy of Motion Picture Arts and Sciences.

SAA Fellows. Awarded to a limited number of members for their outstanding contribution to the archival profession. *Honored*: Danna Bell-Russel, Bill Landis, Dennis Meissner, Joan Schwartz, Robert Spindler, Sharon Thibodeau, Thomas Wilsted, Helena Zinkham.

SAA Spotlight Award. To recognize the contributions of individuals who work for the good of the profession and of archival collections, and whose work would not typically receive public recognition. *Winners:* staff of Afghan Film for their efforts to save films chronicling Afghanistan's culture and history.

# Special Libraries Association (SLA)

Diversity Leadership Development Award ($1,000 stipend). *Sponsor:* EBSCO. *Winners:* Prakriti R. Goswami, Jasmine Griffiths, Daniel P. Lee, Winter S. Shanck, Bing Wang.

Dow Jones Leadership Award ($2,000). For excellence in special librarianship. *Winner:* Richard Huffine.

SLA Affirmative Action Scholarship. *Winner:* Ximena Valdivia.

SLA John Cotton Dana Award. For exceptional support and encouragement of special librarianship. *Winner:* Bill Fisher.

SLA Fellows. *Honored:* Holly Chong Williams, Anne Caputo, Christina de Castell, David Stern, Betty Edwards.

SLA Hall of Fame Award. To a member or members of the association at or near the end of an active professional career for an extended and sustained period of distinguished service to the association. *Winners:* Sue O'Neil Johnson (posthumously), Toby Pearlstein, Dana Lincoln Roth.

SLA/LexisNexis Innovations in Technology Award ($1,000). *Winner:* Sabrina I. Pacifici.

SLA Presidential Citations. For notable or important contributions that enhance the association or further its goals and objectives. *Winners:* Linda Broussard, Susan Fifer-Canby, Judith J. Field, Sue Henczel, Deb Hunt, Jill Hurst-Wahl, Praveen Kumar "P. K." Jain, Debal C. Kar, Daniel Lee, Quan Logan, Douglas Newcomb, Gary Price, Cindy Romaine, Cara Schatz.

SLA Student Scholarships ($1,000). For graduate study in librarianship leading to a master's degree in library or information science. *Winners:* Sara Burns, Jennifer Cook, Holly Fisher.

Thomson Scientific Member Achievement Award. To an SLA member for raising visibility, awareness, and appreciation of profession, SLA unit, or the association at large. *Sponsors:* Thomson Scientific and Dialog. *Winner:* Rachel Kolsky.

Rose L. Vormelker Award. *Winner:* Shirley Loo.

H. W. Wilson Company Award ($500). For the most outstanding article in the past year's *Information Outlook*. *Donor:* H. W. Wilson Company. *Winners:* Belinda DeLisser, Julie Schien.

# Other Awards of Distinction

Presidential Citizens Medal. Awarded by the President of the United States to U.S. citizens who have performed exemplary deeds of service to the nation. *Among 2008 honorees:* James H. Billington, Librarian of Congress; Anne-Imelda M. Radice, director of the Institute of Museum and Library Services.

# Part 4
# Research and Statistics

# Library Research and Statistics

## Research and Statistics on Libraries and Librarianship in 2008

### Denise M. Davis

Director, Office for Research and Statistics, American Library Association

This report on library research and statistics will focus again this year on four key topics: library usage, the library work force, digital repositories and their impact on libraries, and general research methods used by the profession.

## Library Usage

### Serving Non-English-Speakers

About 21 million people in the United States speak little or no English—50 percent more than a decade ago. This principally affects public agencies in health care and education, but affects other public agencies as well. Staff at these agencies are faced daily with someone who needs services and doesn't speak English.

"Serving Non-English Speakers in U.S. Public Libraries: 2007 Analysis of Library Demographics, Services and Programs,"[1] published in 2008 by the American Library Association (ALA), is the first national study to consider the impact of providing specialized library services to non-English-speakers as reported through anecdotal information by library staff, both in terms of barriers to developing language-based services and regarding the perceived success of these services.

The study identified three principal findings:

- Spanish is far and away the most-supported non-English language in public libraries.
- Smaller communities are serving a larger proportion of non-English speakers.
- Low-level literacy is a barrier both for non-English-speakers using library services and for libraries in providing services and programs.

The study was made possible with the support of the ALA Offices for Literacy and Outreach Services, Public Programs, and Diversity, and by the 2006

World Book/ALA Goal Grant. It was conducted for ALA by Christie M. Koontz and Dean Jue of Florida State University.

A related report, "Immigration and Diversity," in the September 2008 *American School Board Journal,* is important for those interested in the impact of immigration and demographic relocation in the United States and the impact on public education (see http://www.asbj.com).

### Harris Poll on Public Library Usage

As America deals with a worsening economy, U.S. libraries are experiencing a dramatic increase in library card registration. According to a Harris Poll released in September, 68 percent of Americans had a library card, up 5 percent since 2006.[2] Survey results indicate that this was the greatest number of Americans with library cards since ALA started to measure library card usage in 1990.

In-person library visits were are up 10 percent compared with a 2006 ALA household survey. Seventy-six percent of Americans had visited their local public library in the past year, compared with 65.7 percent two years ago. Online visits to libraries were up even more substantially, with 41 percent of library card holders visiting their library Web sites in the past year, compared with 23.6 percent in 2006. This finding complements ALA's 2008 Public Library Funding and Technology Access study, detailed below, which found that public libraries had significantly increased the Internet services available to their communities, including online homework help, downloadable audio and video, and e-books. Detailed findings, including regional distributions, are available at http://www.harrisinteractive.com/harris_poll/printerfriend/index.asp?PID=949.

Other articles discussing population segmentation and libraries include Marc Futterman's October 15 *Library Journal* article "Finding the Underserved: Close Examination Using Market Segmentation Can Reveal Useful Surprises About the People Your Library Is Leaving Behind" (http://www.libraryjournal.com/article/CA6602835.html), and the OCLC study "From Awareness to Funding: A Study of Library Support in America" (available at http://www.oclc.org/reports/funding). A study using regression analysis of the government studies "Current Population Survey 2002" and the "Public Libraries Survey 2002" is presented in an article by Sei-Ching Joanna Sin and Kyung-Sun Kim (University of Wisconsin–Madison) titled "Use and Non-Use of Public Libraries in the Information Age: A Logistic Regression Analysis of Household Characteristics and Library Services Variables" (*Library and Information Science Research* (*LISR*) 30(3) (2008): 207–215, DOI 10.1016/j.lisr.2007.11.008).

### Funding and Technology Access Study

ALA released "Libraries Connect Communities: Public Library Funding and Technology Access Study 2007–2008" in September 2008. Among its key findings:

- Funding data indicate libraries are relying more on non-tax funding sources.
- Free wireless access is offered by 66 percent of public libraries, up about 12 percent from the previous year.

- Nearly two-thirds of all public libraries provide 1.5 Mbps or faster Internet access speeds, with a continuing disparity between urban (90 percent) and rural libraries (51.5 percent).
- Staff at 74 percent of libraries help patrons understand and use e-government services, including enrolling in Medicare and applying for unemployment compensation.
- Nearly three-quarters (73.4 percent) of libraries provide technology training to library patrons.
- While the number of Internet computers available to the public climbed for the first time in several years, one in five libraries reports there are consistently fewer computers than patrons who wish to use them throughout the day.

This is the most current national data available on technology access and funding in U.S. public libraries. The study collected data through surveys involving more than 5,400 public libraries, a questionnaire to the chief officers of state library agencies, and focus groups and site visits in New York, North Carolina, Pennsylvania, and Virginia. To view the final report, visit http://www.ala.org/plinternetfunding.

### Funding Models and Ranking Models

Articles tackling difficult library issues—funding models and public library ranking models—were "An Argument on Why the City Should Contribute to the Library Budget in a Means Similar to Corporate Funding of R&D" by Beatrice Priestly (*Library Administration and Management* 22(3): 125–128 [Summer 2008] and "The New *LJ* Index" by Keith Curry Lance and Ray Lyons (*Library Journal*, June 15, 2008, pp. 38–41).

## Library Work Force

### IMLS Study

The long-awaited national work force study funded by the Institute for Museum and Library Services (IMLS) was completed in 2008. The study results were released at a meeting of the project advisory committee during the ALA Midwinter Meeting in Denver. Highlighted were MLS librarian demographics (age, race, ethnicity, and so forth), evidence of career path, and attitudes toward librarianship. In addition to the data analysis, the study provides verbatim responses by librarians about their career experiences.

Among key findings were that remote Internet access has little, if any, effect on in-person visits to public libraries—people visit libraries online regardless of their level, in-person use—and that the demand for librarians is going to be significant over the next ten years. Another interesting finding was the increase in in-person library visits compared with five years ago; even libraries reporting library visits of fewer than 10,000 a year indicated increases of more than 5 percent (about 38 percent of libraries reported increases of 5 percent plus). A higher percentage of libraries (about 53 percent) with 250,000 or more in-person visits reported increases of more than 5 percent. There is much more of interest in the study. To review specific findings, see http://libraryworkforce.org/tiki-index.php.

### ALA-APA Salary Study

The ALA Allied Professional Association (ALA-APA) coordinates an annual salary study and additional research on library workers (see http://www.ala-apa.org/salaries/salaries.html).

According to the 2008 salary survey, the mean salary for librarians rose to $58,960, an increase of $1,151 from 2007 (about 2 percent). The modest increase was half that of the Consumer Price Index (CPI) for the same time period, 4.0 percent (CPI, February 2008). The average salary increase of public librarians was 2.7 percent and academic librarian salaries declined in all but two positions—academic library dean/director and manager/supervisor of support staff. More information about librarian salaries is available from the report summary (http://www.ala-apa.org/salaries/SalarySummary2008.pdf) or from the complete study, "ALA-APA Salary Survey: Librarian-Public and Academic (Librarian Salary Survey)."

The study included supplemental questions about employee benefits. Comparison of benefits data reported in 2003 and 2008 are available in "Library Employee Benefits 2003 and 2008: A Report from the 2008 Librarian Salary Survey" by ALA-APA Director Jenifer Grady (http://www.ala-apa.org/salaries/SalarySummary2008Benefits.pdf). Findings in the comparison study included these:

- In the insurance group of benefits for part-time library workers, academic libraries offered more options than did public libraries.
- Both academic and public libraries offered fewer financial benefits (retirement savings, professional memberships, pension plans) than in 2003.

Job satisfaction of library information technology (IT) workers based on regression analysis of three hypotheses—background variables, work-related variables, and a combination of both—was explored by Sook Lim in "Job Satisfaction of Information Technology Workers in Academic Libraries" (*LISR* 30 [2008]: 115–121, DOI 10.1016/j.lisr.2007.10.002). Gender and salary affected job satisfaction of academic library IT staff more than any other variables. Women IT workers were more satisfied than men, and those earning more (regardless of gender) were more satisfied than those earning less.

## Digital Books and Repositories

Digital books, repositories, and their impact on libraries continued to be a focus of scholarly communication in 2008. The following grouping of EDUCAUSE, Association for College and Research Libraries (ACRL), and Association for Research Libraries (ARL) articles provides context and overview of the changing landscape in academic libraries. In addition, the summer 2008 issue of *Library Trends* was devoted to the topic of digital books.

- "Digital Books and the Impact on Libraries" (Peter Brantley, editor), *Library Trends* 57(1), Summer 2008
- "Advancing Scholarship and Intellectual Productivity: An Interview with Clifford A. Lynch by Brian L. Hawkins," *EDUCAUSE Review,* May/June 2006 (http://www.educause.edu/er/erm06/erm0622.asp)
- "Tec(h)tonics: Reimagining Preservation" by Paul Conway, *C&RL News* 69(10), November 2008 (http://www.ala.org/ala/mgrps/divs/acrl/publications/crlnews/2008/nov/techtonics.cfm)
- "A Steady Vision for Libraries" by James G. Neal, *EDUCAUSEreview* May/June 2008, pp. 12–13, and "Publishing Services: An Emerging Role for Research Libraries" by Karla Hahn, *EDUCAUSE Review,* November/December 2008, pp. 16–17.
- "The Need to Formalize Trust Relationships in Digital Repositories" by Fran Berman, Ardys Kozbial, Robert H. McDonald, and Brian E. C. Schottlaender, *EDUCAUSE Review* May/June 2008, pp. 10–11

The ARL resources on digital repositories, including a SPEC Kit (SPEC Kit 292, ARL, July 2006) are online at http://www.arl.org/sc/models/repositories/index.shtml.

## General Research Methods

Some interesting general methodology articles and books should be mentioned. The fourth edition of *Designing Qualitative Research* by Catherine Marshall (University of North Carolina at Chapel Hill) and Gretchen B. Rossman (University of Massachusetts–Amherst) (SAGE, 2006) is a useful primer and presents information in sequence from hypothesis/purpose through resource allocation.

Issue 30 of *LISR* provides a number of useful "general research methodology" articles.

An editorial by Peter Hernon and Candy Schwartz (Simmons College), "A Research Study's Reflective Inquiry" (*LISR* 30 [2008]:163–164), provides brief yet detailed guidance on the parts of a research proposal. For those just learning about research, this editorial offers a useful synopsis.

For a review of the types of research being published, consult Phil Hider and Bob Pymm's (Charles Sturt University, Australia) article "Empirical Research Methods Reported in High-Profile LIS Journal Literature" (*LISR* 30 [2008]: 108–114). The authors propose that, because LIS is multi-disciplinary, no single research protocol is preferred. Through citation analysis for research published in 1975, 1985, and 2005, the authors discovered that data collection techniques in high-profile journal literature ranged from questionnaires and interviews to secondary use of data previously collected. The majority of analysis techniques were, however, quantitative rather than qualitative, and this held true for librarianship and non-librarianship journals. The reporting of empirical data has increased since 1985. This may be explained by such articles being published elsewhere rather than there being less qualitative research. Data collection technique "facets" recommended by the authors for future analysis vary significantly from the list they began with. Among the additions were bibliometric analysis and transaction log analysis—perhaps an indicator of the significance of library technology.

For those doing research and using census data, an article by Edward Herman (University of Buffalo), "The American Community Survey: An Introduction to the Basics" (*Government Information Quarterly* 25 [2008]: 504–519), provides helpful information about the integrity of the super-sampling, using multi-year averages, and the purpose of the American Community Survey interim data collection in addition to the comprehensive decennial census.

## Awards and Grants That Honor and Support Excellent Research

The professional library associations offer many awards and grants to recognize and encourage research. The 2008 awards and grants here are listed under the name of the sponsoring association, and in the case of ALA by the awarding division, in alphabetical order. More-detailed information about the prizes and prizewinners can be found at the association Web sites.

### American Library Association

**Jesse H. Shera Award for Excellence in Published Research**
*Winners:* Eric M. Meyers, Karen E. Fisher, and Elizabeth Marcoux, for "Studying the Everyday Information Behavior of Tweens: Notes from the Field," LISR 29, pp. 310–331.

**Jesse H. Shera Award for Support of Dissertation Research**
*Winner:* Sharon McQueen, University of Wisconsin–Madison, for "'The Story of Ferdinand': The Creation of a Cultural Icon."

### American Society for Information Science and Technology

**ASIS&T Best Information Science Book Award**
*Winner:* Christine Borgman for *Scholarship in the Digital Age: Information, Infrastructure, and the Internet* (MIT) (http://mitpress.mit.edu/catalog/item/default.asp?ttype=2&tid=11333).

**ProQuest Doctoral Dissertation Award**
*Winner:* Eric Meyer for "Socio-Technical Perspectives on Digital Photography."

**Thomson ISI Citation Analysis Research Grant** (formerly the ISI/ASIS&T Citation Analysis Research Grant)
*Winners:* Isola Ajiferuke and Dietmar Wolfram, University of Wisconsin–Milwaukee, for "Citer Analysis as a Measure of Research Impact."

**Thomson ISI Doctoral Dissertation Proposal Scholarship** (formerly the ASIS&T/ISI Doctoral Dissertation Proposal Scholarship)
*Winner:* Christina M. Finneran for "Factors That Influence Users to Keep and/or Leave Information Items: A Case Study of College Students' Personal Information Management Behavior."

## John Wiley Best *JASIST* Paper Award
*Winners:* Teresa M. Harrison, Theresa A. Pardo, José Ramón Gil-García, Fiona Thompson, and Dubravka Juraga, for "Geographic Information Technologies, Structuration Theory, and the World Trade Center Crisis" *JASIST* 58(14): 2240–2253.

### Association for Library and Information Science Education

## ALISE/Eugene Garfield Doctoral Dissertation Award
*Winner:* Kara Anne Reuter, University of Maryland, for "Children Selecting Books in a Library: Extending Models of Information Behavior to a Recreational Setting."

## ALISE Research Grant Award
*Winners:* Joan Cherry, Luanne Freund, and Wendy Duff, University of Toronto, for "Learning From Our Students: Assessing Student Perceptions of Information Studies Programs and the Information Professions."

### Association of College and Research Libraries (ACRL)

## Coutts Nijhoff International West European Specialist Study Grant
*Winner:* Michelle Emanuel, University of Mississippi, for her proposal to survey major film libraries in the Paris region in order to analyze and evaluate the collections and services provided to visiting scholars, with some focus on the films of Francis Veber.

## Doctoral Dissertation Fellowship
*Winner:* Donghua Tao for "Using Theory of Reasoned Action (TRA) in Understanding Selection and Use of Information Resources: An Information Resource Selection and Use Model."

## Samuel Lazerow Fellowship for Research in Collections and Technical Services in Academic and Research Libraries
*Winners:* Ping Situ and Shuyong Jiang for their research project on vendor-provided records and the experience of a research library in outsourcing cataloging service for its Chinese-language materials.

## Ilene F. Rockman Instruction Publication of the Year Award (formerly the IS Publication Award)
*Winner:* Patrick Ragains, University of Nevada–Reno, for his book *Information Literacy Instruction That Works: A Guide to Teaching by Discipline and Student Population* (Neal-Schuman).

### Beta Phi Mu

## Mary Jo Lynch Distinguished Lecture Award
*Winner:* Beta Lambda Chapter (University of North Texas/Texas Woman's University); the lecturer was Danny P. Wallace, University of Oklahoma at Norman, who presented "Using Technology to Effectively Serve Older Adults and Baby Boomers in Your Local Library."

**Library and Information Technology Association/OCLC**

## Frederick G. Kilgour Award for Research in Library and Information Technology

*Winner:* Jane Greenberg, University of North Carolina–Chapel Hill School of Information and Library Science (see http://www.ala.org/ala/mgrps/divs/lita/newandnoteworthy/kilgourwinner08.cfm).

**Medical Library Association**

### Ida and George Eliot Prize

*Winner:* Keith W. Cogdill, National Library of Medicine, for "Progress in Health Sciences Librarianship: 1970–2005."

### Janet Doe Lectureship for 2009

*Winner:* J. Michael Homan, Mayo Clinic Libraries.

### Donald A. B. Lindberg Research Fellowship

*Winner:* Mark Puterbaugh, Warner Memorial Library, Eastern University.

## Notes

1. American Library Association, Office for Research and Statistics. *Serving Non-English Speakers in U.S. Public Libraries: 2007 Analysis of Library Demographics, Services and Programs* (2008), http://www.ala.org/nonenglishspeakers.

2. The Harris Poll is a non-commissioned survey that was conducted online within the United States Aug. 11–17, 2008, among 2,710 adults (ages 18 and over). Figures for age, sex, race, education, region, and household income were weighted to bring them into line with their actual proportions in the population. Propensity score weighting was also used to adjust for respondents' propensity to answer online. A full methodology is available at http://www.harrisinteractive.com.

# Library Budget Dollars Shrinking in Real Terms— Are We Eating Our Seed Corn?

Robert E. Molyneux

The current economic news is discouraging for the library community. Anecdotes abound about individual libraries, but what are the trends? What is going on nationally?

Presented here are results of an analysis of the most current national-level data about public libraries in the United States—for fiscal year (FY) 2006. Alas, they don't tell us about today, but they do give us strong evidence that what we sensed some time ago is true: the fortunes of U.S. public libraries have been strained for a number of years.

The analysis of these data, combined with current glum anecdotal evidence, produce a dark picture of the fortunes of the nation's more than 9,000 public library systems.

The conclusion drawn here is that the downturn in the fortunes of U.S. public libraries began in the late 1990s, with FY 2002 marking a peak in funding in real terms, followed by a noticeable year-by-year drop since then. Meanwhile, of course, circulations continue to rise. Not all libraries were affected, but the impact is visible across libraries of all sizes and states. In other words, it is systemic.

This analysis continues that done for *Public Library Quarterly* (*PLQ*) by this author: "Squeeze Play: Public Library Circulation and Budget Trends, FY1992–FY2004,"[1] which attempted to interweave a dynamic interpretation of forces at work on public libraries and responses by public libraries to those forces. It was a view in aggregate. One clear conclusion was that in the late 1990s and early years of this century, library budgets seen in aggregate were under stress. We pick up the story there.

Two data series are used here, and they are discussed at more length at the end of the article. One is a longitudinal (that is, usable for trend analysis) file of the NCES-IMLS (National Center for Education Statistics-Institute of Museum and Library Services) state summary/state characteristics data files (that is, state summary data), and the other is a longitudinal file of data reported in the NCES-IMLS public library data file. The state summary data give us the best look at trends in national-level aggregates. This second file reports on individual libraries and is used here for aggregates of individual libraries seen over time.

Table 1 presents state summary data about U.S. public libraries from FY 1992 through FY 2006. The first three columns (Total Circulations, Population Served, and Total Circulations per Capita) make it clear that during this period the total items circulated by U.S. public libraries increased steadily, as did the population served by those libraries. Moreover, the total circulations per capita (figured by both appropriate methods) bounced around a bit during the 1990s before we begin to see steady increases they have shown since then. Those fig-

Robert E. Molyneux has worked on compiling, documenting, and analyzing library data for more than 25 years and has taught a variety of library school classes dealing with the integration of computers and networking technology in libraries. He is vice president for business development at Equinox Software, Inc.

ures are impressive and bespeak the national system of public libraries serving more people who are checking out more items. Public libraries must be doing something right.

This article uses total operating expenditures as a means to assess the state of U.S. public libraries. It is the best variable we have to measure their financial health. As the *PLQ* article indicated, libraries as a whole modified their behavior and what they purchased through the years. However, an abiding fact was the constraint in the total amount that was available to spend on operations.

"Current dollars" are the dollars as reported each year. But, as we are all aware, the dollar has been losing value steadily, and analysts have wrestled with the problem of comparing what a dollar could buy in one year with what a dollar could buy in another. This is a difficult problem, and a simple expedient is used here to get a rough idea: these dollar figures are discounted by using the consumer price index to give us another column: Total Library Expenditures (in 1992 dollars). Sometimes these are referred to as "constant dollars." In any case, this is an approximation of what we know is true: library budget dollars, whatever the numbers, are shrinking in real terms. Inflation is a decline in the value of a currency that manifests itself in prices rising. We have more dollars, but everything seems to have gone up in price. The hurrier we go, the behinder we get.

What do we see in this "1992 dollars" column? The figures rise steadily until FY 2002, when they peak. In aggregate, U.S. public libraries were getting more dollars each year but could do less with them. In FY 2006, the total expenditures in constant 1992 dollars were at about the level they were in 1999 when total annual circulations were about 400 million or 25 percent lower than they were in 2006. The numbers speak for themselves.

Of course, circulations are only one thing libraries do, but they are often taken as a good proxy for all library activities. Another item that is important is total expenditures on collections. These peaked in current dollars in FY 2002 and in constant dollars in FY 2001. In the latest 2006 data the expenditures for collections in constant dollars were a bit above the 1994 figures—when total circulations were much lower. We are eating our seed corn, and the circulation trends reviewed here are unsustainable given these collection expenditure figures.

After a steady rise from FY 1992, the *PLQ* article mentioned showed that total full-time-equivalent (FTE) staff fell from 2002 through 2004. Table 1 shows that total FTE employees have risen since FY 2004. It is a reasonable speculation that increases in demand for library services compelled a reallocation of budgets to increase staff. However, given that the purchasing power of the public library dollar has been falling, this reallocation just moved the pain to another place. Circulations are up; staffs are up; budgets are down.

## Does Size Matter?

The distribution of public libraries by size is skewed. That term means that there are very few big libraries and many small ones. For instance, if we take the U.S. public libraries in the FY 2006 data that reported their total expenditures, and took the top 25 percent of those libraries that spent the most, these 2,200 libraries spent 89 percent of every dollar spent by public libraries while the other 75 per-

## Table 1 / Summary Data on US Public Libraries, FY1992–FY2006

| Fiscal Year | Total Circulations | Population Served | Total Circulations per capita 1 | Total Circulations per capita 2 | Total Library expenditures (current dollars) | Total Library expenditures (in 1992 dollars) | Total expenditures on collections (current dollars) | Total expenditures on collections (in 1992 dollars) | Total Staff |
|---|---|---|---|---|---|---|---|---|---|
| 1992 | 1,564,380,576 | 243,252,828 | 6.4 | 6.7 | $4,546,748,000 | $4,546,748,000 | $690,392,523 | $690,392,523 | 110,319 |
| 1993 | 1,595,167,482 | 246,691,014 | 6.5 | 6.7 | 4,720,699,198 | 4,579,078,222 | 707,236,576 | 686,019,479 | 112,397 |
| 1994 | 1,578,458,404 | 248,615,499 | 6.3 | 6.6 | 4,949,622,071 | 4,652,644,747 | 736,127,946 | 691,960,269 | 113,350 |
| 1995 | 1,609,871,741 | 250,273,781 | 6.4 | 6.7 | 5,226,215,759 | 4,755,856,341 | 788,715,213 | 717,730,844 | 115,968 |
| 1996 | 1,642,625,448 | 252,723,153 | 6.5 | 6.7 | 5,555,415,682 | 4,888,765,800 | 841,526,051 | 740,542,925 | 117,812 |
| 1997 | 1,690,203,336 | 256,026,905 | 6.6 | 6.9 | 5,857,721,522 | 5,037,640,509 | 890,898,746 | 766,172,922 | 120,750 |
| 1998 | 1,701,183,676 | 258,982,791 | 6.6 | 6.8 | 6,193,640,435 | 5,202,657,965 | 953,144,846 | 800,641,671 | 123,443 |
| 1999 | 1,693,415,906 | 262,603,622 | 6.4 | 6.7 | 6,631,995,976 | 5,371,916,741 | 1,014,120,972 | 821,437,987 | 127,890 |
| 2000 | 1,713,966,658 | 265,985,006 | 6.4 | 6.7 | 7,027,907,527 | 5,411,488,796 | 1,069,974,873 | 823,880,652 | 130,102 |
| 2001 | 1,789,927,072 | 273,921,496 | 6.5 | 6.8 | 7,571,645,315 | 5,603,017,533 | 1,148,349,376 | 849,778,538 | 133,456 |
| 2002 | 1,897,874,169 | 277,252,717 | 6.8 | 7.1 | 8,024,132,936 | 5,777,375,714 | 1,158,577,244 | 834,175,616 | 136,219 |
| 2003 | 1,964,999,696 | 280,368,429 | 7.0 | 7.2 | 8,297,707,518 | 5,725,418,187 | 1,153,831,960 | 796,144,052 | 136,172 |
| 2004 | 2,010,777,017 | 283,434,546 | 7.1 | 7.3 | 8,643,027,806 | 5,617,968,074 | 1,143,743,151 | 743,433,048 | 136,014 |
| 2005 | 2,062,960,991 | 286,472,011 | 7.2 | 7.5 | 9,066,039,651 | 5,530,284,187 | 1,197,062,468 | 730,208,105 | 137,855 |
| 2006 | 2,101,533,003 | 288,693,216 | 7.3 | 7.6 | 9,595,567,855 | 5,373,517,999 | 1,262,231,935 | 706,849,884 | 140,442 |

Total Circulations per capita have been figured two ways: 1 By dividing the total circulations by total population served, by year; 2 The mean of the annual value for all states, by year.

cent (that is, about 6,600) spent the remaining 11 percent. Or, of the $9.4 billion spent by all public libraries reporting, the top 25 percent spent $8.3 billion and the smaller libraries spent $1.1 billion.

This skewed characteristic of library data is well known, of course, but it might suggest that the expenditure figures presented in Table 1 may actually be biased by these large libraries and their data. Suppose the large libraries are having budget problems but the small libraries are healthy. Is this so? Is there good news in the smaller libraries?

Apparently not. Table 2 presents summary data from four groups of libraries. GT100K are the 521 U.S. public libraries serving a population greater than 100,000 in FY 2006. This group of libraries was then analyzed 1992–2006, as were the three other groups of libraries in this table. This procedure is awkward but informative. The 144 U.S. members of the Urban Libraries Council (ULC) in FY 2006 are in the second group. Both of these groups have a substantial portion (58 percent and 36 percent, respectively) of the total expenditures of all public libraries in FY 2006. Their totals in 1992 dollars also peaked in 2002. In both cases, their collection expenditures in 1992 dollars peaked in 2001.

The more than 4,400 that were in the lower half of total expenditures also showed a peak in FY 2002, as did the 2,200 library in the lowest quarter of expenditures.

It would appear that, in aggregate, the size of the library did not save it from this downturn in spending power.

**Table 2 / Dates of the Downturn in Constant Dollar Expenditures, by Group**

| | Number of libraries | Total Expenditures | % of total expenditures | Year of the downturn in 1992 dollars |
|---|---|---|---|---|
| GT100K | 521 | $5.5 billion | 58.0 | 2003 |
| ULC | 145 | 3.3 billion | 36.0 | 2003 |
| 1st & 2nd quartiles | 4,432 | 280 million | 3.0 | 2003 |
| 1st quartile | 2,216 | 58 million | 0.6 | 2003 |

| | |
|---|---|
| GT100K | US public libraries with greater than 100,000 population served in FY 2006 |
| ULC | US members of the Urban Libraries Council in FY 2006 |
| 1st & 2nd quartiles | US Public Libraries in the first or second quartiles of total expenditures in FY 2006 |
| 1st quartile | US Public Libraries in the first quartile of total expenditures in FY 2006 |

## What About the States?

All states but Delaware showed a decline in the purchasing power of their libraries from FY 2002 through FY 2006. Massachusetts, Ohio, West Virginia, and Pennsylvania showed declines of greater than 20 percent, using the consumer price index as a guide.

It should be noted that public libraries in three states—Alaska, Hawaii, and West Virginia—have lost purchasing power since FY 1992. The devastation, then, is broad-based and we know, anecdotally, that the situation is worse now.

## The Data Used

IMLS is now managing the collection and reporting of two major library data series formerly under the aegis of NCES—the State Library Agencies Survey (StLA), which surveys and reports data on the various state libraries, and the Public Libraries survey. IMLS makes the data, documentation, and a report on these two series available as NCES did in the past; NCES continues to collect and report on data in two other series, on academic library statistics and school library media centers. The StLA data have been published for FY 1994–2007 (FY 2006 was the first year that IMLS managed these data).

The Public Libraries Survey has three parts: the Public Library Data File (PLDF in NCES/IMLS parlance), which reports on data on each public library system in the country; the Public Library State Summary/State Characteristics (PUSUM), which provides summary data that present state library statistics in aggregate (for instance, it would report total annual circulations from all public libraries in a state for a given year); and the Public Library Outlet File, which reports basic data on each branch library in the United States.

A limitation of all NCES and IMLS series—indeed all regularly published annual library data series—is that they are issued without creating a longitudinal series for trend analysis. The reasons for this fact appear to be related to why the data are collected, which do not have to do with analyzing trends. To analyze trends you need the data with an infrastructure that supports trend analysis.

When I was at the now-defunct National Commission on Libraries and Information Services (NCLIS), I created two longitudinal series that I have continued to update since NCLIS closed in 2007. One is PLDF3, created from the annual compilations of institutional data from FY 1987–FY 2006 and PUSUM for the state summary data from FY 1992–FY 2006. These data were used here.

## Note

1. Molyneux, Robert E. "Squeeze Play: Public Library Circulation and Budget Trends, FY 1992–FY 2004," *Public Library Quarterly,* 26, 3/4, 2007, pp. 101–107.

# Number of Libraries in the United States and Canada

Statistics are from *American Library Directory (ALD) 2008–2009* (Information Today, Inc., 2008). Data are exclusive of elementary and secondary school libraries.

## Libraries in the United States

| | |
|---|---|
| Public Libraries | 17,022* |
| Public libraries, excluding branches | 9,763† |
| Main public libraries that have branches | 1,410 |
| Public library branches | 7,259 |
| Academic Libraries | 3,772* |
| Community college | 1,171 |
| Departmental | 179 |
| Medical | 11 |
| Religious | 9 |
| University and college | 2,601 |
| Departmental | 1,397 |
| Law | 181 |
| Medical | 247 |
| Religious | 234 |
| Armed Forces Libraries | 296* |
| Air Force | 86 |
| Medical | 7 |
| Army | 138 |
| Medical | 26 |
| Marine Corps | 11 |
| Navy | 61 |
| Law | 1 |
| Medical | 13 |
| Government Libraries | 1,159* |
| Law | 402 |
| Medical | 162 |
| Special Libraries (excluding public, academic, armed forces, and government) | 7,773* |
| Law | 928 |
| Medical | 1,529 |
| Religious | 545 |
| Total Special Libraries (including public, academic, armed forces, and government) | 9,066 |
| Total law | 1,512 |
| Total medical | 1,995 |
| Total religious | 1,055 |
| Total Libraries Counted(*) | 30,022 |

# Libraries in Regions Administered by the United States

| | |
|---|---:|
| Public Libraries | 28 * |
|   Public libraries, excluding branches | 10 † |
|     Main public libraries that have branches | 3 |
|   Public library branches | 18 |
| Academic Libraries | 37 * |
|   Community college | 6 |
|     Departmental | 3 |
|     Medical | 0 |
|   University and college | 31 |
|     Departmental | 22 |
|     Law | 3 |
|     Medical | 2 |
|     Religious | 1 |
| Armed Forces Libraries | 2 * |
|   Air Force | 1 |
|   Army | 1 |
|   Navy | 0 |
| Government Libraries | 6 * |
|   Law | 1 |
|   Medical | 2 |
| Special Libraries (excluding public, academic, armed forces, and government) | 7 * |
|   Law | 3 |
|   Medical | 1 |
|   Religious | 1 |
| Total Special Libraries (including public, academic, armed forces, and government) | 16 |
|   Total law | 7 |
|   Total medical | 5 |
|   Total religious | 2 |
| Total Libraries Counted(*) | 80 |

*Note:* Numbers followed by an asterisk are added to find "Total libraries counted" for each of the three geographic areas (United States, U.S.-administered regions, and Canada). The sum of the three totals is the "Grand total of libraries listed" in *ALD*. For details on the count of libraries, see the preface to the 61st edition of *ALD—Ed.*

† Federal, state, and other statistical sources use this figure (libraries *excluding* branches) as the total for public libraries.

## Libraries in Canada

| | |
|---|---|
| Public Libraries | 2,063* |
|   Public libraries, excluding branches | 827† |
|     Main public libraries that have branches | 133 |
|   Public library branches | 1,236 |
| Academic Libraries | 350* |
|   Community college | 85 |
|     Departmental | 15 |
|     Medical | 0 |
|     Religious | 3 |
|   University and college | 265 |
|     Departmental | 176 |
|     Law | 17 |
|     Medical | 21 |
|     Religious | 36 |
| Government Libraries | 303* |
|   Law | 34 |
|   Medical | 5 |
| Special Libraries (excluding public, academic, armed forces, and government) | 969* |
|   Law | 108 |
|   Medical | 182 |
|   Religious | 27 |
| Total Special Libraries (including public, academic, armed forces, and government) | 1,085 |
|   Total law | 159 |
|   Total medical | 208 |
|   Total religious | 97 |
| Total Libraries Counted(*) | 3,685 |

## Summary

| | |
|---|---|
| Total U.S. Libraries | 30,022 |
| Total Libraries Administered by the United States | 80 |
| Total Canadian Libraries | 3,685 |
| Grand Total of Libraries Listed | 33,787 |

# Highlights of NCES and IMLS Surveys

The National Center for Education Statistics (NCES) and the Institute of Museum and Library Services (IMLS) collect and disseminate statistical information about libraries in the United States and its outlying areas. Two major surveys are conducted by NCES, the Academic Libraries Survey and the School Library Media Centers Survey; two others, the Public Libraries Survey and the State Library Agencies Survey, were formerly conducted by NCES, but are now handled by IMLS.

This article presents highlights from three of the most recently conducted surveys. For more information, see "National Center for Education Statistics Library Statistics Program" in Part 1 and "Institute of Museum and Library Services Library Programs" in Part 2.

## Academic Libraries

The following are highlights from the First Look publication *Academic Libraries, 2006,* released in July 2008 by NCES.

The report summarizes services, staff, collections, and expenditures of academic libraries in two- and four-year, degree-granting postsecondary institutions in the 50 states and the District of Columbia.

### Services

- During fiscal year (FY) 2006, there were 144.1 million circulation transactions from academic libraries' general collections.
- Academic libraries loaned 10.8 million documents to other libraries and borrowed 10.3 million documents from other libraries. In addition to the interlibrary loans, academic libraries received 1.2 million documents from commercial services.
- During a typical week in fall 2006, of the 3,600 academic libraries in the United States, 31 were open 24 hours a day, 7 days a week.
- During a typical week, approximately 1.1 million academic library reference transactions were conducted, including computer searches.

### Collections

- At the end of FY 2006, there were 221 academic libraries that held 1 million or more books, serial backfiles, and other paper materials, including government documents.
- The nation's 3,600 academic libraries held 1 billion books, serial backfiles, and other paper materials, including government documents.
- During the fiscal year, academic libraries added 22.2 million books, serial backfiles, and other paper materials, including government documents.

**Staff**

- Academic libraries reported 93,600 full-time-equivalent (FTE) staff working in academic libraries.
- Librarians accounted for 28 percent of the total number of FTE staff working in academic libraries.

**Expenditures**

- Academic libraries' expenditures totaled $6.2 billion during the fiscal year. They spent $3.1 billion on salaries and wages, representing 50 percent of total library expenditures.
- Academic libraries spent $2.4 billion on information resources during the year, of which $94 million was for electronic books, serials backfiles, and other materials. Expenditures for electronic current serial subscriptions were $692 million.
- During FY 2006 academic libraries spent $106.3 million for bibliographic utilities, networks, and consortia.

**Electronic Services**

- In fall 2006 about 72 percent of academic libraries provided library reference service by e-mail or the Internet.
- Fifty percent of academic libraries reported providing technology to assist patrons with disabilities.

**Information Literacy**

- About 48 percent of academic libraries reported that their postsecondary institution defined information literacy or the information-literate student.
- Thirty-four percent of academic libraries reported that their postsecondary institution had incorporated information literacy into its mission.

## Public Libraries

The following are highlights from the publication *Public Libraries Survey, Fiscal Year 2006,* released in December 2008 by IMLS. The survey is the result of a collaborative effort between IMLS and NCES.

### Number of Public Libraries and Population of Legal Service Area

- There were 9,208 public libraries (administrative entities) in the 50 states and the District of Columbia in FY 2006.
- Public libraries served 97 percent of the total population of the states and the District of Columbia, either in legally established geographic service areas or in areas under contract.

- Twelve percent of the public libraries served 73 percent of the population of legally served areas in the United States. Each of these public libraries had a legal service area population of 50,000 or more.

## Service Outlets

- During FY 2006, 81 percent of public libraries had one direct-service outlet (an outlet that provides service directly to the public), and 19 percent had more than one direct-service outlet. Types of direct-service outlets include central library outlets, branch library outlets, and bookmobiles.
- A total of 1,543 public libraries (17 percent) had one or more branch library outlets, with a total of 7,542 branch outlets. The total number of central library outlets was 9,050. The total number of stationary outlets (central library outlets and branch library outlets) was 16,592. Eight percent of public libraries had one or more bookmobile outlets, with a total of 819 bookmobiles.
- Eleven percent of public libraries had an average number of weekly public service hours per outlet of less than 20 hours, 39 percent had weekly public service hours per outlet of 20–39 hours, and 51 percent had weekly public service hours per outlet of 40 hours or more.

## Legal Basis and Interlibrary Relationships

- In FY 2006, 53 percent of public libraries were part of a municipal government, 15 percent were nonprofit association libraries or agency libraries, 14 percent were separate government units known as library districts, 10 percent were part of a county or parish, 3 percent had multijurisdictional legal basis under an intergovernmental agreement, 2 percent were part of a school district, 1 percent were part of a city or county, and 2 percent reported their legal basis as "other."
- Seventy-six percent of public libraries were members of a federation or cooperative service, while 23 percent were not. One percent served as the headquarters of a federation or cooperative service.

## Library Services

- In FY 2006 total nationwide circulation of public library materials was 2.1 billion, or 7.3 materials circulated per capita. Among the 50 states and the District of Columbia, Ohio had the highest per capita circulation at 15.5, while the District of Columbia had the lowest, at 2.1.
- During the year 43.7 million library materials were loaned by public libraries to other libraries.
- Reference transactions in public libraries totaled 295 million, or 1.0 reference transactions per capita.
- Visits to public libraries totaled 1.4 billion, or 4.8 per capita.
- Circulation of children's materials was 728.1 million, or 35 percent of total circulation. Attendance at children's programs was 57.6 million.

- Nationwide, uses of public-use Internet-connected computers totaled 334 million, or 1.2 uses per capita.
- The number of Internet-connected computers available for public use in public libraries totaled 196,000, or 3.4 per 5,000 people. The average number of Internet-connected computers available for public use per stationary outlet was 11.8.

## Collections

- Nationwide, public libraries had 807.2 million print materials in their collections, or 2.8 volumes per capita. By state, the number of print materials per capita ranged from 1.5 in Arizona to 5.4 in Maine.
- Public libraries nationwide had 42.6 million audio materials and 43.9 million video materials in their collections.

## Staff

- Public libraries had a total of 140,000 paid FTE staff in FY 2006, or 12 paid FTE staff per 25,000 population. Librarians accounted for 33 percent of total FTE staff; 67 percent were in other positions. More than two-thirds of the librarians—68 percent—had master's degrees from programs of library and information studies accredited by the American Library Association (ALA-MLS degrees).
- A total of 4,348 public libraries (47 percent) had librarians with ALA-MLS degrees.

## Operating Revenue and Expenditures

- In FY 2006 about 82 percent of public libraries' total operating revenue of about $10.3 billion came from local sources, 9 percent from state sources, 1 percent from federal sources, and 9 percent from other sources, such as monetary gifts and donations, interest, library fines, fees, or grants.
- Nationwide, the average total per capita operating revenue for public libraries was $35.64. Of that amount, $29.11 was from local sources, $3.27 was from state sources, $0.17 from federal sources, and $3.09 from other sources.
- Per capita operating revenue from local sources was under $3 for 7 percent of public libraries, $3 to $14.99 for 27 percent of libraries, $15 to $29.99 for 32 percent of libraries, and $30 or more for 34 percent of libraries.
- Total operating expenditures for public libraries were $9.6 billion in FY 2006. Of this, 66 percent was spent for paid staff and 13 percent for the library collection. The remaining 21 percent was used on a variety of "other" expenditures.
- Twenty-six percent of public libraries had operating expenditures of less than $50,000, 42 percent spent $50,000 to $399,999, and 33 percent spent $400,000 or more.

- Nationwide, the average per capita operating expenditure for public libraries was $33.24. The highest average per capita operating expenditure was $58.20 (Ohio), and the lowest was $13.57 (Mississippi).
- Expenditures for library collection materials in electronic format were 10 percent of total operating expenditures for public libraries.

## State Library Agencies

The following are highlights from the publication *State Library Agencies: Fiscal Year 2007,* released in November 2008 by the Institute of Museum and Library Services.

### Collections

- In FY 2007 the number of book and serial volumes held by state library agencies totaled 24.1 million. Two state library agencies each had book and serial volumes exceeding 2 million: New York had 2.7 million and Michigan had 2.4 million. The number of books and serial volumes in the Connecticut, New Jersey, Texas, and Virginia state libraries exceeded 1 million. The state library agencies for Hawaii, Idaho, Maryland, Minnesota, and the District of Columbia did not maintain collections.
- Thirty-five state library agencies held a total of 23.2 million uncataloged government documents in FY 2007. The five states with the largest collections of uncataloged government documents were California (4.6 million), Illinois (3.4 million), Arkansas (2.8 million), Oklahoma (2.7 million), and Connecticut (1.7 million).
- Thirty-six state library agencies housed nearly 284,000 audio materials. Nearly 60 percent of these materials were held by two states: Tennessee (106,000) and Florida (60,000).
- Forty-six state library agencies held a total of 144,000 video materials. Four states held more than 10,000 video materials: Tennessee (23,000), Florida (16,000), Louisiana (13,000), and Wisconsin (11,000).
- Forty-six states held a total of 51,000 serial subscriptions. New York had the largest serials collection by far (14,000), followed by Connecticut (5,600), Michigan (5,000), California (3,000), and South Carolina (2,100).

### Service Transactions

- In FY 2007 there were 1.6 million visits to state library agencies. The states with the largest number of visits were Washington (269,000), Virginia (193,000), and Michigan (152,000).
- State library agencies reported 2.4 million circulations during the fiscal year. Washington reported the most circulation transactions (776,000). Other states with circulations of 100,000 or more were Maine (259,000), Virginia (235,000), Tennessee (233,000), Michigan (233,000), and New Mexico (144,000).

- State library agencies conducted 917,000 reference transactions during the year. Washington reported the most reference transactions (104,000), followed by Florida (101,000), Indiana (71,000), and New York (70,000).

- State library agencies provided 397,000 interlibrary loans in FY 2007. The four state libraries that provided the most interlibrary loans were Vermont (56,000), Maine (41,000), South Dakota (32,000), and New York (31,000).

- State library agencies received 181,000 interlibrary loans. The five state library agencies receiving the most interlibrary loans were Maine (43,000), South Dakota (23,000), Ohio (21,000), North Dakota (18,000), and Louisiana (11,000).

- Nationwide, nearly 9,000 Library Services and Technology Act (LSTA) and state grants were awarded. The most grants (2,000) were awarded by the Illinois state library agency, followed by New York's state library agency (1,000). These states accounted for more than one-third of the LSTA and state grants that were disbursed in FY 2007.

- State library agencies hosted 7,200 events during the year. These events were attended by 134,000 individuals.

- The four state library agencies that hosted the largest number of events were New York (939), California (532), Texas (421), and Ohio (375). The states with event attendance of more than 5,000 individuals were California (12,600), New York (8,800), Colorado (6,300), Ohio (5,700), and Alabama (5,500).

### Internet Access and Electronic Services

- All state library agencies facilitated library access to the Internet in one or more of the following ways: providing Internet training or consultation to state or local library staff or state library end users; providing direct funding to libraries for Internet access; providing equipment to libraries for Internet access; providing access to directories, databases, or online catalogs via the Internet; managing a Web site, file server, bulletin boards, or electronic mailing lists.

- Most state library agencies (46 states and the District of Columbia) planned or monitored the development of electronic networks. State library agencies in 43 states and the District of Columbia operated electronic networks.

- State library agencies in 47 states and the District of Columbia supported the development of bibliographic databases via electronic networks, and state library agencies in 46 states and the District of Columbia supported the development of full-text or data files via electronic networks.

- Thirty-four state library agencies provided funds or facilitated their own digitization or digital programs or services. Other libraries or library cooperatives received financial support or the facilitation of digitization or digital programs or services in 32 states.

- All of the state library agencies except Nevada, Washington, and the District of Columbia facilitated or subsidized electronic access to a union catalog—a list of titles of works (usually periodicals) in physically separate library collections. Nine state libraries offered union catalog access via a Telnet gateway, and three (Montana, New York, and Pennsylvania) provided union catalog access on CD-ROM.

## Staffing and Hours

- The total number of budgeted FTE positions in state library agencies was 3,500 as of October 1, 2007, although there was a high degree of variability across the states. The range of budgeted FTE positions ran from 6 in Hawaii to 226 in Virginia.
- Most of the budgeted FTE positions (52 percent) were in library services; 19 percent were in library development, 13 percent were in administration, and 16 percent were in other services such as allied operations.
- Every state library agency except Hawaii's offered public service hours in FY 2007. The number of hours at the main outlet that served the general public or state employees ranged from 60 hours a week in Tennessee to 32 hours a week in California. Forty-three state library agencies had main general public/state employee outlets that were open for 40 or more hours a week.
- Two state library agencies (Colorado and Idaho) did not offer public service hours at their main outlets.

## Expenditures

- State library agencies reported total expenditures of $1.2 billion in FY 2007. Total expenditures of state library agencies were received from state funds (83 percent), federal funds (14 percent), and funds from other sources (3 percent).
- State library agencies' total expenditures averaged $3.93 per capita. The three agencies with the highest total per capita expenditures (excluding the District of Columbia and Hawaii) were Delaware ($15.70), Rhode Island ($12.83), and Maryland ($10.53).
- The three agencies with the lowest per capita expenditures were Washington ($1.62), Texas ($1.32), and Colorado ($1.10). The median per capita expenditure across all states (again excluding the District of Columbia and Hawaii) was $3.22.
- Operating expenditures, financial assistance for library expenditures, and other expenditures (all expenditures except capital outlay) were supported by revenue from federal, state, and other sources. In FY 2007 state library agencies reported $164.3 million in expenditures from federal revenue sources, $981.2 million from state sources, and an additional $37.4 million from other sources.
- Revenue for operating expenditures was received from various public and private sources; 69 percent ($234.4 million) of FY 2007 operating expen-

ditures came from state revenue, 26 percent ($89.7 million) of operating expenditures were funded by the federal government, and the remaining 5 percent ($15.8 million) of operating expenditures was funded by other sources.

- Expenditures for financial assistance to libraries totaled $817.7 million. The largest expenditures for financial assistance to libraries in FY 2007 were reported by New York ($115.2 million), Pennsylvania ($94.1 million), and Maryland ($56.8 million). State library agencies' financial assistance to libraries is funded by federal, state, and other revenue sources. In FY 2007, 90 percent ($732.8 million) of financial assistance to libraries by state library agencies came from state sources.

- In five state library agencies (Louisiana, Maine, Michigan, New Mexico, and Virginia), 100 percent of the support for financial assistance to libraries was from state revenue.

- State library agencies reported capital outlay expenditures of $2.4 million in FY 2007.

- State revenue was the source of 76 percent of capital outlay expenditures.

- Federal revenue represented 12 percent of state library agencies' capital outlay expenditures. Eight state library agencies had capital outlay expenditures from federal revenue: Arkansas, Colorado, Florida, Idaho, Kansas, Kentucky, Mississippi, and North Carolina.

- In FY 2007 state library agencies had $25.3 million in "other" expenditures (expenditures not included in operating expenditures, financial assistance to libraries, or capital outlay; these other expenditures may include expenditures for allied operations, if the expenditures are from the state library agency budget).

- Most (56 percent) of state library agencies' other expenditures ($14.1 million) were supported by state revenue. Federal revenue supported 30 percent ($7.6 million) of state library agencies' other expenditures. "Other" sources of funding accounted for 14 percent ($3.6 million) of expenditures in the "other" category.

- Expenditures are categorized as total, operating expenditures, financial assistance to libraries, capital outlay, and "other." Financial assistance to libraries represented the largest percentage of expenditures (69 percent) in FY 2007, accounting for $817.7 million of expenditures by state library agencies, followed by operating expenditures (29 percent), which accounted for $339.9 million. Operating expenditures include staff (salaries, wages, and employee benefits), collection expenditures, and other related spending. Staff expenditures accounted for the largest share of state library operating expenses (56 percent), followed by "other" (36 percent) and collection expenditures (8 percent).

- State library agencies' total expenditures reported in FY 2007 for financial assistance to individual public libraries were $477.5 million, representing 58 percent of all expenditures for financial assistance to libraries.

- Library cooperatives serving only public libraries received $123.8 million in financial support from state library agencies in FY 2007. Fifteen percent of all financial assistance to libraries was targeted to library cooperatives serving public libraries only.

- Per capita expenditures of state library agencies for financial assistance to libraries in FY 2007 were $1.58 for individual public libraries and $0.41 for library cooperatives serving only public libraries.
- State library agencies' financial assistance to libraries from state sources totaled $732.8 million. Individual public libraries received $438.8 million of those state funds, representing 60 percent of state revenue for financial assistance for libraries. Library cooperatives serving only public libraries received $113.5 million in financial support from state library agencies, from state sources, in FY 2007; this accounted for 16 percent of state-funded spending on financial assistance to libraries.
- Per capita expenditures of state library agencies for financial assistance to libraries, from state sources, were $1.45 for individual public libraries and $0.38 for library cooperatives serving only public libraries.
- In FY 2007 state library agencies had expenditures of $160.7 million in LSTA funds for statewide services, grants, or LSTA administration. The vast majority of the LSTA funds were targeted to statewide services (56 percent) or grants (41 percent).
- Library technology, connectivity, and services accounted for 54 percent of LSTA expenditures by state library agencies. Other activities that were targeted were services to persons having difficulty using libraries (19 percent) and services for lifelong learning (24 percent). LSTA administration costs accounted for 3 percent of all LSTA expenditures by state library agencies during the fiscal year.

**Revenue**

- Sources of state library agency revenue were the federal government, state government, and other sources, such as local, regional, or multijurisdictional sources, or through fines or fees for services.
- State library agencies may receive income from private sources, such as foundations, corporations, friends of libraries groups, and individuals. In FY 2007 state library agencies reported total revenue of $1.2 billion. Most revenue was from state sources (84 percent), followed by federal sources (14 percent) and other sources (3 percent).
- In FY 2007 federal revenue to state library agencies totaled $161.3 million and state revenue was $989.7 million. California ($16.5 million), Texas ($10.6 million), New York ($9.3 million), and Florida ($8.3 million) received the most federal revenue in 2007; North Dakota ($705,000), Wyoming ($738,000) and Vermont ($783,000) received the least.
- Of the federal revenue to state library agencies in FY 2007, 98 percent ($158 million) was LSTA funds.
- Most of the $989.7 million in state revenue available in FY 2007 funded state aid to libraries (64 percent). Thirty percent of state revenue supported state library agency operations. The remaining 6 percent of state rev-

enue supported other activities, such as interagency transfers. Hawaii, New Hampshire, South Dakota, and the District of Columbia applied 100 percent of their state revenue to state library agency operations.

**Services to Libraries and Cooperatives**

- In FY 2007 nearly all state library agencies (46 to 50 agencies) provided consulting services, continuing education, interlibrary loan referral services, library legislation preparation or review, and summer reading program support.
- Services to public libraries provided by 39 to 41 state library agencies included administration of state aid, literacy program support, reference referral services, state standards or guidelines, or statewide public relations or library promotion campaigns.
- Thirteen state library agencies reported accreditation of public libraries, 15 reported preservation/conservation services, and 21 reported certification of public librarians.
- More than two-thirds of state library agencies (35 to 40 agencies) provided the following services to academic libraries: administration of LSTA grants, continuing education, interlibrary loan referral services, or reference referral services.
- Three state library agencies (Illinois, Montana, and New York) administered state aid to academic libraries.
- Thirty-three state library agencies provided consulting services, 26 provided union list development, and 20 provided statewide public relations/ library promotion campaigns to academic libraries.
- No state library agency reported accreditation of academic libraries. The state library agencies in Indiana, Massachusetts, New Mexico, and Washington reported certification of academic librarians.
- More than two-thirds of state library agencies (37 to 39) provided administration of LSTA grants, continuing education programs, or interlibrary loan referral services to school library media centers (LMCs) in FY 2007.
- Thirty-one agencies provided reference referral services, an additional 31 provided consulting services, 22 provided union list development, and 21 provided statewide public relations/library promotion campaigns to LMCs.
- State library agencies in Illinois and Montana administered state aid to LMCs.
- No state library agencies reported accreditation of LMCs, but three state library agencies (Indiana, Massachusetts, and Pennsylvania) reported certification of library media specialists.
- In FY 2007 more than two-thirds of state library agencies (34 to 40 agencies) served special libraries through administration of LSTA grants, consulting services, continuing education, interlibrary loan referral, and reference referral services.

# Library Acquisition Expenditures, 2007–2008: U.S. Public, Academic, Special, and Government Libraries

The information in these tables is taken from *American Library Directory* (*ALD*) *2008–2009* (Information Today, Inc., 2008). The tables report acquisition expenditures by public, academic, special, and government libraries.

The total number of libraries in the United States and in regions administered by the United States listed in this 61st edition of *ALD* is 29,804, including 17,050 public libraries, 3,809 academic libraries, 7,780 special libraries, and 1,165 government libraries.

## Understanding the Tables

*Number of libraries* includes only those U.S. libraries in *ALD* that reported annual acquisition expenditures (2,223 public libraries, 870 academic libraries, 169 special libraries, and 55 government libraries). Libraries that reported annual income but not expenditures are not included in the count. Academic libraries include university, college, and junior college libraries. Special academic libraries, such as law and medical libraries, that reported acquisition expenditures separately from the institution's main library are counted as independent libraries.

The amount in the *total acquisition expenditures* column for a given state is generally greater than the sum of the categories of expenditures. This is because the total acquisition expenditures amount also includes the expenditures of libraries that did not itemize by category.

Figures in *categories of expenditure* columns represent only those libraries that itemized expenditures. Libraries that reported a total acquisition expenditure amount but did not itemize are only represented in the total acquisition expenditures column.

**Table 1 / Public Library Acquisition Expenditures**

| State | Number of Libraries | Total Acquisition Expenditures | Books | Other Print Materials | Periodicals/ Serials | Manuscripts & Archives | AV Equipment | AV Materials | Microforms | Electronic Reference | Preservation |
|---|---|---|---|---|---|---|---|---|---|---|---|
| Alabama | 32 | 18,839,145 | 1,788,544 | 22,105 | 65,271 | 0 | 18,297 | 255,459 | 16,963 | 35,414 | 1,800 |
| Alaska | 12 | 871,804 | 162,396 | 7,500 | 22,522 | 0 | 0 | 15,079 | 500 | 19,389 | 0 |
| Arizona | 26 | 15,727,605 | 6,123,617 | 4,600,648 | 251,770 | 0 | 0 | 2,197,963 | 47,269 | 1,619,370 | 29,968 |
| Arkansas | 17 | 3,953,826 | 2,226,610 | 1,750 | 148,727 | 0 | 1,500 | 310,726 | 1,640 | 251,821 | 8,270 |
| California | 80 | 80,679,451 | 34,737,979 | 2,176,744 | 4,551,881 | 37,000 | 0 | 9,185,893 | 318,263 | 7,107,064 | 112,002 |
| Colorado | 33 | 15,608,314 | 5,517,074 | 1,000 | 554,783 | 0 | 17,200 | 3,065,685 | 1,081 | 1,079,515 | 586 |
| Connecticut | 74 | 10,223,967 | 5,050,041 | 570,742 | 803,079 | 0 | 7,984 | 821,629 | 131,175 | 1,257,202 | 15,795 |
| Delaware | 5 | 497,229 | 142,294 | 0 | 2,300 | 0 | 1,000 | 26,263 | 0 | 1,500 | 0 |
| District of Columbia | 0 | 0 | 0 | 0 | 0 | 0 | 0 | 0 | 0 | 0 | 0 |
| Florida | 41 | 34,972,173 | 13,514,945 | 585,250 | 3,160,465 | 1,500 | 41,000 | 6,267,650 | 106,301 | 2,620,108 | 2,000 |
| Georgia | 19 | 14,394,448 | 2,281,089 | 19,678 | 139,940 | 0 | 3,876 | 622,452 | 28,286 | 431,228 | 3,777 |
| Hawaii | 1 | 5,030,113 | 0 | 0 | 275,320 | 0 | 0 | 0 | 54,902 | 1,580,296 | 0 |
| Idaho | 17 | 762,907 | 172,486 | 515 | 19,570 | 0 | 3,800 | 25,014 | 900 | 3,589 | 1,500 |
| Illinois | 159 | 45,249,012 | 14,896,999 | 229,992 | 1,206,918 | 13,000 | 127,393 | 3,851,389 | 111,301 | 4,090,530 | 16,235 |
| Indiana | 152 | 30,484,342 | 11,908,414 | 622 | 1,612,410 | 0 | 148,188 | 3,979,635 | 186,990 | 1,316,223 | 67,944 |
| Iowa | 81 | 7,058,004 | 2,145,974 | 28,601 | 262,700 | 1,300 | 18,313 | 480,928 | 2,044 | 142,300 | 1,369 |
| Kansas | 42 | 11,680,902 | 2,608,747 | 37,712 | 852,540 | 15 | 26,379 | 851,625 | 3,050 | 638,931 | 300 |
| Kentucky | 26 | 5,362,521 | 2,439,179 | 10,486 | 119,808 | 0 | 15,329 | 851,311 | 13,685 | 323,038 | 1,200 |
| Louisiana | 13 | 5,718,397 | 2,926,937 | 4,000 | 387,001 | 3,000 | 151,405 | 761,239 | 50,500 | 330,453 | 0 |
| Maine | 55 | 2,048,113 | 1,054,068 | 1,623 | 216,694 | 2,100 | 11,350 | 133,213 | 1,200 | 202,034 | 1,000 |
| Maryland | 7 | 16,486,268 | 2,837,419 | 47,425 | 175,577 | 0 | 0 | 1,076,131 | 0 | 678,370 | 0 |
| Massachusetts | 101 | 10,846,968 | 3,991,064 | 87,414 | 500,012 | 0 | 6,036 | 1,103,414 | 56,233 | 499,910 | 3,200 |
| Michigan | 82 | 23,574,041 | 7,692,044 | 5,760 | 574,935 | 0 | 34,000 | 1,738,960 | 26,440 | 1,059,559 | 13,589 |
| Minnesota | 36 | 14,520,440 | 3,572,798 | 9,283 | 202,788 | 0 | 6,500 | 1,039,551 | 5,749 | 397,069 | 1,750 |
| Mississippi | 9 | 3,734,685 | 457,249 | 0 | 29,950 | 0 | 1,795 | 147,152 | 5,973 | 1,273,709 | 2,162 |

| | | | | | | | | | | |
|---|---|---|---|---|---|---|---|---|---|---|
| Missouri | 66 | 24,174,943 | 8,708,917 | 45,656 | 678,972 | 160 | 33,507 | 1,978,424 | 234,293 | 3,333,899 | 40,765 |
| Montana | 16 | 1,050,488 | 449,443 | 2,253 | 82,998 | 6,700 | 5,316 | 114,379 | 5,016 | 31,612 | 3,231 |
| Nebraska | 35 | 1,671,903 | 499,725 | 550 | 46,166 | 278 | 540 | 60,523 | 540 | 50,797 | 2,346 |
| Nevada | 5 | 1,420,591 | 125,504 | 1,193 | 10,558 | 0 | 0 | 19,634 | 200 | 20,000 | 0 |
| New Hampshire | 78 | 3,321,969 | 1,279,586 | 3,000 | 170,094 | 0 | 2,500 | 295,221 | 18,675 | 118,912 | 12,150 |
| New Jersey | 98 | 25,350,159 | 13,793,945 | 83,917 | 1,492,065 | 0 | 38,800 | 3,302,420 | 152,487 | 1,894,588 | 18,850 |
| New Mexico | 11 | 2,546,123 | 1,343,130 | 427 | 57,430 | 0 | 9,225 | 215,439 | 10,518 | 85,985 | 0 |
| New York | 164 | 47,451,166 | 22,347,206 | 367,124 | 5,018,720 | 5,500 | 233,818 | 3,915,256 | 258,170 | 2,510,390 | 70,590 |
| North Carolina | 25 | 10,750,453 | 6,318,255 | 78,806 | 197,181 | 0 | 26,040 | 626,969 | 20,745 | 445,548 | 413 |
| North Dakota | 15 | 1,620,389 | 724,835 | 59,000 | 80,726 | 0 | 37,000 | 124,172 | 4,500 | 101,637 | 1,000 |
| Ohio | 54 | 50,867,816 | 23,193,445 | 484,913 | 3,925,792 | 1,153 | 159,924 | 10,365,352 | 590,199 | 6,939,593 | 394,853 |
| Oklahoma | 11 | 10,828,357 | 5,007,047 | 4,647 | 859,003 | 0 | 0 | 1,195,925 | 4,800 | 782,110 | 0 |
| Oregon | 45 | 5,976,517 | 2,401,559 | 22,400 | 319,248 | 0 | 0 | 423,676 | 18,191 | 168,702 | 0 |
| Pennsylvania | 90 | 11,868,037 | 5,334,948 | 255,211 | 1,189,123 | 0 | 41,343 | 1,246,940 | 527,385 | 1,022,381 | 222,880 |
| Rhode Island | 13 | 10,695,088 | 1,287,199 | 54,994 | 142,433 | 0 | 1,846 | 252,257 | 0 | 141,700 | 7,974 |
| South Carolina | 21 | 13,339,567 | 6,736,304 | 22,222 | 206,523 | 5,000 | 90,907 | 1,508,259 | 1,592 | 1,124,865 | 10,832 |
| South Dakota | 18 | 1,786,591 | 849,613 | 1,000 | 94,601 | 530 | 395 | 279,916 | 2,164 | 118,201 | 0 |
| Tennessee | 22 | 7,324,222 | 3,162,496 | 27,413 | 202,708 | 0 | 10,100 | 290,374 | 1,200 | 219,724 | 1,518 |
| Texas | 105 | 39,930,506 | 11,675,961 | 281,732 | 1,095,349 | 0 | 38,835 | 2,287,913 | 70,887 | 1,503,698 | 8,660 |
| Utah | 14 | 5,047,200 | 1,773,072 | 1,400 | 117,363 | 245,000 | 19,900 | 479,869 | 10,650 | 114,385 | 72,000 |
| Vermont | 46 | 1,301,985 | 608,282 | 0 | 34,639 | 120 | 2,500 | 100,494 | 276 | 51,191 | 500 |
| Virginia | 29 | 11,318,576 | 4,209,286 | 13,307 | 690,438 | 106,278 | 0 | 1,299,171 | 117,429 | 784,248 | 1,472,810 |
| Washington | 24 | 30,852,948 | 3,033,501 | 123,263 | 204,988 | 0 | 55,765 | 1,094,151 | 4,100 | 364,000 | 900 |
| West Virginia | 15 | 4,598,452 | 1,680,728 | 86 | 104,088 | 0 | 15,000 | 249,329 | 10,310 | 750,207 | 6,000 |
| Wisconsin | 64 | 7,541,027 | 4,231,918 | 24,862 | 246,516 | 0 | 8,857 | 1,115,630 | 10,419 | 629,916 | 2,700 |
| Wyoming | 18 | 2,005,767 | 434,571 | 4,694 | 45,806 | 0 | 6,000 | 69,384 | 55 | 33,908 | 0 |
| U.S. Virgin Islands | 1 | 8,000 | 7,000 | 1,000 | 1,000 | 0 | 0 | 0 | 0 | 0 | 0 |
| Total | 2,223 | 712,973,515 | 259,465,443 | 10,412,920 | 33,451,489 | 428,634 | 1,479,463 | 71,719,438 | 3,245,246 | 50,300,819 | 2,635,419 |
| Estimated % of Acquisition Expenditures | | | 36.39 | 1.46 | 4.69 | 0.06 | 0.21 | 10.06 | 0.46 | 7.06 | 0.37 |

Table 2 / Academic Library Acquisition Expenditures

| State | Number of Libraries | Total Acquisition Expenditures | Books | Other Print Materials | Periodicals/ Serials | Manuscripts & Archives | AV Equipment | AV Materials | Microforms | Electronic Reference | Preservation |
|---|---|---|---|---|---|---|---|---|---|---|---|
| Alabama | 18 | 21,088,305 | 3,664,164 | 46,908 | 8,888,251 | 3,000 | 38,056 | 138,693 | 149,235 | 2,416,681 | 146,340 |
| Alaska | 5 | 4,987,013 | 360,433 | 0 | 846,408 | 0 | 19,000 | 59,087 | 15,307 | 886,392 | 18,827 |
| Arizona | 11 | 4,193,372 | 927,114 | 75,816 | 780,236 | 17,979 | 3,465 | 157,643 | 50,205 | 1,386,418 | 18,403 |
| Arkansas | 7 | 11,408,029 | 1,517,471 | 77,560 | 6,423,385 | 0 | 87,429 | 103,268 | 182,409 | 2,921,216 | 95,294 |
| California | 75 | 100,653,611 | 13,520,108 | 391,362 | 21,892,848 | 30,149 | 97,059 | 541,223 | 1,068,224 | 14,624,062 | 780,248 |
| Colorado | 14 | 25,924,256 | 3,123,631 | 469,768 | 10,042,527 | 0 | 0 | 83,767 | 11,630 | 7,300,517 | 86,147 |
| Connecticut | 13 | 40,306,360 | 1,360,581 | 38,025 | 4,045,230 | 0 | 8,202 | 106,317 | 111,755 | 1,473,117 | 103,740 |
| Delaware | 3 | 8,346,310 | 40,000 | 0 | 8,419 | 0 | 0 | 0 | 0 | 0 | 0 |
| District of Columbia | 7 | 19,639,228 | 2,382,273 | 53,241 | 5,937,180 | 5,000 | 26,300 | 9,718 | 74,773 | 1,142,522 | 115,267 |
| Florida | 34 | 27,057,345 | 4,746,563 | 867,143 | 8,007,023 | 0 | 26,000 | 471,528 | 325,499 | 10,271,607 | 289,557 |
| Georgia | 23 | 19,476,106 | 1,803,495 | 2,000 | 5,178,981 | 0 | 10,872 | 107,266 | 1,771,479 | 999,345 | 105,895 |
| Hawaii | 2 | 659,932 | 128,000 | 0 | 176,200 | 0 | 3,000 | 16,047 | 14,000 | 77,438 | 18,700 |
| Idaho | 4 | 9,055,479 | 788,510 | 0 | 3,712,670 | 0 | 0 | 19,968 | 0 | 882,478 | 69,641 |
| Illinois | 39 | 48,056,793 | 7,418,810 | 260,634 | 15,352,084 | 1,000 | 205,695 | 273,017 | 110,137 | 2,702,156 | 130,198 |
| Indiana | 25 | 26,568,274 | 4,386,074 | 24,211 | 14,003,645 | 7,460 | 74,002 | 189,074 | 133,752 | 2,118,989 | 149,493 |
| Iowa | 22 | 29,087,312 | 3,677,673 | 177,205 | 11,068,004 | 0 | 31,139 | 111,949 | 84,870 | 2,391,178 | 137,633 |
| Kansas | 21 | 9,542,289 | 2,046,144 | 2,000 | 5,052,125 | 2,000 | 16,766 | 60,357 | 18,753 | 2,241,578 | 24,811 |
| Kentucky | 15 | 44,232,968 | 2,070,147 | 0 | 9,600,619 | 59,037 | 2,825 | 99,814 | 189,516 | 27,439,802 | 148,634 |
| Louisiana | 10 | 4,902,499 | 953,196 | 35,173 | 2,358,675 | 4,781 | 3,720 | 1,228 | 38,521 | 766,795 | 49,192 |
| Maine | 5 | 8,257,711 | 1,651,579 | 0 | 5,884,041 | 0 | 0 | 37,664 | 62,500 | 227,000 | 104,427 |
| Maryland | 13 | 11,210,582 | 1,638,962 | 15,065 | 3,289,154 | 500 | 15,000 | 134,026 | 175,574 | 1,301,805 | 69,718 |
| Massachusetts | 26 | 180,036,359 | 4,093,953 | 49,578 | 10,022,579 | 0 | 186,288 | 171,357 | 115,015 | 8,447,610 | 179,039 |
| Michigan | 27 | 19,498,027 | 3,265,189 | 162,070 | 7,662,429 | 26,000 | 48,426 | 145,217 | 224,184 | 5,819,305 | 146,105 |
| Minnesota | 18 | 13,247,217 | 2,498,345 | 0 | 4,823,541 | 0 | 33,954 | 248,549 | 118,602 | 2,300,583 | 102,401 |
| Mississippi | 7 | 3,799,429 | 415,867 | 0 | 1,446,001 | 0 | 19,000 | 38,853 | 116,000 | 1,334,212 | 45,818 |

|  | | | | | | | | | | | |
|---|---|---|---|---|---|---|---|---|---|---|---|
| Missouri | 20 | 27,517,733 | 1,135,364 | 95,477 | 2,530,806 | 3,863 | 15,221 | 129,118 | 136,251 | 1,361,955 | 202,660 |
| Montana | 5 | 357,358 | 164,342 | 0 | 154,828 | 0 | 10,000 | 5,018 | 3,000 | 20,000 | 170 |
| Nebraska | 7 | 10,460,874 | 485,858 | 101,451 | 1,214,073 | 0 | 34,909 | 83,047 | 82,297 | 302,552 | 42,695 |
| Nevada | 2 | 415,295 | 136,754 | 0 | 11,877 | 0 | 0 | 15,908 | 217 | 49,926 | 613 |
| New Hampshire | 6 | 8,714,685 | 1,195,883 | 0 | 4,118,752 | 0 | 740 | 1,584 | 20,416 | 1,241,302 | 74,271 |
| New Jersey | 17 | 11,912,185 | 1,537,110 | 114,617 | 3,796,833 | 7,000 | 22,576 | 117,105 | 58,514 | 1,647,049 | 23,635 |
| New Mexico | 8 | 6,524,063 | 77,280 | 0 | 1,700 | 0 | 20,000 | 24,000 | 0 | 5,000 | 0 |
| New York | 57 | 111,801,498 | 11,120,827 | 349,772 | 20,501,718 | 39,883 | 246,161 | 452,078 | 351,899 | 15,355,319 | 408,879 |
| North Carolina | 29 | 41,157,685 | 9,706,110 | 219,478 | 20,113,415 | 2,000 | 35,886 | 398,809 | 462,238 | 2,606,256 | 274,833 |
| North Dakota | 4 | 2,766,611 | 446,664 | 10,000 | 1,546,634 | 0 | 1,080 | 15,129 | 0 | 493,296 | 31,976 |
| Ohio | 30 | 27,281,785 | 6,035,879 | 102,617 | 8,281,145 | 2,461 | 44,415 | 243,383 | 208,877 | 5,786,541 | 275,209 |
| Oklahoma | 9 | 4,479,174 | 692,456 | 56,186 | 2,440,267 | 2,000 | 54,951 | 150,125 | 13,818 | 162,865 | 10,000 |
| Oregon | 17 | 29,729,582 | 1,562,654 | 831 | 3,826,416 | 0 | 900 | 91,745 | | 1,143,615 | 99,939 |
| Pennsylvania | 29 | 18,303,220 | 3,918,684 | 102,780 | 8,039,436 | 36,303 | 80,641 | 184,531 | 299,894 | 4,523,694 | 236,048 |
| Rhode Island | 6 | 3,883,220 | 1,070,585 | 2,100 | 1,520,596 | 9,500 | 112,500 | 60,433 | 31,000 | 968,600 | 21,804 |
| South Carolina | 17 | 9,307,263 | 2,069,592 | 108,196 | 3,002,711 | 20,000 | 5,000 | 123,059 | 144,809 | 1,533,692 | 102,020 |
| South Dakota | 6 | 3,893,861 | 300,380 | 0 | 1,091,925 | 0 | 1,170 | 13,652 | 12,362 | 725,849 | 26,473 |
| Tennessee | 14 | 8,137,310 | 1,095,135 | 300 | 1,875,761 | 0 | 0 | 85,663 | 95,537 | 2,628,761 | 39,323 |
| Texas | 44 | 60,476,362 | 11,302,389 | 22,340 | 24,119,871 | 8,050 | 198,871 | 530,436 | 390,653 | 4,502,377 | 453,918 |
| Utah | 5 | 5,201,669 | 1,261,480 | 0 | 3,040,758 | 0 | 1,000 | 90,332 | 4,247 | 735,327 | 2,414 |
| Vermont | 7 | 1,867,911 | 459,122 | 0 | 650,029 | 3,000 | 5,000 | 37,710 | 10,190 | 378,809 | 13,441 |
| Virginia | 27 | 30,331,678 | 6,986,620 | 459,942 | 13,168,053 | 2,000 | 41,688 | 316,853 | 152,305 | 6,041,309 | 112,402 |
| Washington | 18 | 12,946,702 | 2,575,518 | 11,644 | 7,433,920 | 14,360 | 37,400 | 169,592 | 37,013 | 1,134,675 | 63,014 |
| West Virginia | 14 | 3,235,809 | 388,351 | 123,755 | 906,903 | 14,336 | 47,692 | 40,240 | 79,289 | 1,061,522 | 3,071 |
| Wisconsin | 17 | 21,586,248 | 2,665,332 | 6,056 | 6,024,088 | 0 | 26,239 | 142,093 | 116,239 | 885,690 | 69,414 |
| Wyoming | 3 | 3,629,698 | 346,806 | 0 | 2,178,087 | 0 | 0 | 0 | 0 | 326,744 | 0 |
| Mariana Islands | 1 | 102,000 | 74,000 | 0 | 15,000 | 0 | 5,000 | 5,000 | 0 | 8,000 | 0 |
| Puerto Rico | 7 | 6,439,522 | 356,421 | 1,000 | 2,177,466 | 5,000 | 34,527 | 29,638 | 0 | 318,075 | 10,000 |
| Total | 870 | 1,163,695,836 | 137,645,878 | 4,636,301 | 310,285,323 | 326,662 | 2,033,865 | 6,881,911 | 7,873,905 | 157,421,606 | 5,733,750 |
| Estimated % of Acquisition Expenditures | | | 11.83 | 0.40 | 26.66 | 0.03 | 0.17 | 0.59 | 0.68 | 13.53 | 0.49 |

Table 3 / Special Library Acquisition Expenditures

| State | Number of Libraries | Total Acquisition Expenditures | Books | Other Print Materials | Periodicals/ Serials | Manuscripts & Archives | AV Equipment | AV Materials | Microforms | Electronic Reference | Preservation |
|---|---|---|---|---|---|---|---|---|---|---|---|
| | | | | | | | | | | Categories of Expenditure (in U.S. dollars) | |
| Alabama | 1 | 1,375 | 250 | 0 | 525 | 0 | 0 | 0 | 0 | 500 | 100 |
| Alaska | 0 | 0 | 0 | 0 | 0 | 0 | 0 | 0 | 0 | 0 | 0 |
| Arizona | 5 | 21,824 | 0 | 0 | 0 | 0 | 0 | 0 | 0 | 0 | 0 |
| Arkansas | 0 | 0 | 0 | 0 | 0 | 0 | 0 | 0 | 0 | 0 | 0 |
| California | 13 | 445,098 | 102,198 | 2,000 | 205,059 | 0 | 2,500 | 1,100 | 0 | 74,741 | 7,500 |
| Colorado | 1 | 10,000 | 7,000 | 0 | 1,000 | 0 | 0 | 2,000 | 0 | 0 | 0 |
| Connecticut | 0 | 0 | 0 | 0 | 0 | 0 | 0 | 0 | 0 | 0 | 0 |
| Delaware | 0 | 0 | 0 | 0 | 0 | 0 | 0 | 0 | 0 | 0 | 0 |
| District of Columbia | 3 | 878,578 | 124,130 | 0 | 57,871 | 0 | 0 | 261 | 25,000 | 13,000 | 504,877 |
| Florida | 6 | 102,900 | 50,350 | 1,000 | 36,800 | 0 | 0 | 0 | 0 | 7,500 | 3,300 |
| Georgia | 0 | 0 | 0 | 0 | 0 | 0 | 0 | 0 | 0 | 0 | 0 |
| Hawaii | 0 | 0 | 0 | 0 | 0 | 0 | 0 | 0 | 0 | 0 | 0 |
| Idaho | 0 | 0 | 0 | 0 | 0 | 0 | 0 | 0 | 0 | 0 | 0 |
| Illinois | 20 | 3,070,508 | 201,990 | 20,862 | 225,566 | 2,400 | 5,900 | 9,000 | 1,900 | 135,250 | 19,400 |
| Indiana | 3 | 49,225 | 37,725 | 0 | 120 | 500 | 0 | 0 | 3,780 | 0 | 1,500 |
| Iowa | 3 | 204,558 | 35,862 | 0 | 12,408 | 0 | 0 | 0 | 155,288 | 0 | 1,000 |
| Kansas | 3 | 44,849 | 4,037 | 4,000 | 3,029 | 0 | 0 | 0 | 0 | 683 | 100 |
| Kentucky | 1 | 17,500 | 11,000 | 0 | 6,500 | 0 | 0 | 0 | 0 | 0 | 0 |
| Louisiana | 0 | 0 | 0 | 0 | 0 | 0 | 0 | 0 | 0 | 0 | 0 |
| Maine | 1 | 200 | 0 | 0 | 0 | 0 | 0 | 0 | 0 | 0 | 0 |
| Maryland | 5 | 181,550 | 34,000 | 1,000 | 130,900 | 50 | 1,000 | 0 | 0 | 13,000 | 100 |
| Massachusetts | 7 | 1,035,894 | 379,592 | 50 | 100,800 | 0 | 0 | 7,000 | 0 | 348,000 | 27,100 |
| Michigan | 0 | 0 | 0 | 0 | 0 | 0 | 0 | 0 | 0 | 0 | 0 |
| Minnesota | 3 | 57,850 | 21,350 | 5,000 | 11,500 | 0 | 0 | 1,000 | 0 | 16,000 | 0 |
| Mississippi | 0 | 0 | 0 | 0 | 0 | 0 | 0 | 0 | 0 | 0 | 0 |

| | | | | | | | | | | | |
|---|---|---:|---:|---:|---:|---:|---:|---:|---:|---:|---:|
| Missouri | 1 | 67,500 | 24,000 | 0 | 29,500 | 0 | 0 | 0 | 0 | 14,000 | 0 |
| Montana | 2 | 57,592 | 15,123 | 0 | 3,500 | 0 | 9,546 | 0 | 26,423 | 1,500 | 0 |
| Nebraska | 1 | 1,800 | 650 | 0 | 1,000 | 0 | 0 | 0 | 0 | 0 | 0 |
| Nevada | 1 | 1,000 | 0 | 0 | 0 | 0 | 0 | 0 | 0 | 0 | 0 |
| New Hampshire | 2 | 83,000 | 16,000 | 2,000 | 4,000 | 15,000 | 0 | 0 | 0 | 37,000 | 9,000 |
| New Jersey | 5 | 65,600 | 35,500 | 0 | 13,400 | 0 | 0 | 6,000 | 0 | 2,500 | 7,200 |
| New Mexico | 0 | 0 | 0 | 0 | 0 | 0 | 0 | 0 | 0 | 0 | 0 |
| New York | 29 | 860,540 | 198,952 | 3,050 | 278,870 | 23,000 | 5,827 | 11,662 | 1,000 | 70,375 | 21,020 |
| North Carolina | 0 | 0 | 0 | 0 | 0 | 0 | 0 | 0 | 0 | 0 | 0 |
| North Dakota | 2 | 11,598 | 2,660 | 0 | 5,475 | 2,000 | 0 | 0 | 0 | 0 | 1,463 |
| Ohio | 13 | 1,635,557 | 148,842 | 550 | 677,564 | 1,200 | 150 | 1,008 | 1,500 | 776,321 | 11,222 |
| Oklahoma | 4 | 66,000 | 8,950 | 800 | 33,100 | 2,500 | 20,000 | 0 | 0 | 0 | 0 |
| Oregon | 2 | 2,300 | 200 | 100 | 1,050 | 0 | 0 | 0 | 50 | 0 | 0 |
| Pennsylvania | 8 | 384,625 | 47,969 | 66,089 | 76,953 | 30,721 | 0 | 10,859 | 10,000 | 110,391 | 23,143 |
| Rhode Island | 1 | 50,895 | 32,695 | 0 | 8,000 | 0 | 0 | 0 | 0 | 0 | 10,200 |
| South Carolina | 1 | 29,600 | 14,000 | 0 | 5,000 | 0 | 0 | 6,000 | 3,000 | 0 | 0 |
| South Dakota | 0 | 0 | 0 | 0 | 0 | 0 | 0 | 0 | 0 | 0 | 0 |
| Tennessee | 2 | 26,000 | 12,500 | 0 | 6,000 | 0 | 500 | 3,000 | 0 | 4,000 | 0 |
| Texas | 10 | 1,191,489 | 45,324 | 45,992 | 27,674 | 500 | 167 | 622 | 0 | 115,000 | 500 |
| Utah | 1 | 75,000 | 5,000 | 5,000 | 10,000 | 0 | 5,000 | 0 | 0 | 50,000 | 0 |
| Vermont | 0 | 0 | 0 | 0 | 0 | 0 | 0 | 0 | 0 | 0 | 0 |
| Virginia | 5 | 593,450 | 114,753 | 12,600 | 46,030 | 40,197 | 49,849 | 5,276 | 4,200 | 27,675 | 90,962 |
| Washington | 1 | 1,500 | 0 | 0 | 0 | 0 | 0 | 0 | 0 | 0 | 0 |
| West Virginia | 2 | 236,000 | 9,000 | 0 | 125,000 | 0 | 0 | 500 | 0 | 101,500 | 0 |
| Wisconsin | 1 | 1,400 | 1,200 | 0 | 0 | 0 | 0 | 0 | 0 | 0 | 0 |
| Wyoming | 0 | 0 | 0 | 0 | 0 | 0 | 0 | 0 | 0 | 0 | 0 |
| Total | 169 | 11,564,355 | 1,742,802 | 170,093 | 2,144,194 | 118,068 | 100,439 | 65,288 | 232,141 | 1,918,936 | 739,687 |
| Estimated % of Acquisition Expenditures | | | 15.07 | 1.47 | 18.54 | 1.02 | 0.87 | 0.56 | 2.01 | 16.59 | 6.40 |

Table 4 / Government Library Acquisition Expenditures

| State | Number of Libraries | Total Acquisition Expenditures | Books | Other Print Materials | Periodicals/ Serials | Manuscripts & Archives | AV Equipment | AV Materials | Microforms | Electronic Reference | Preservation |
|---|---|---|---|---|---|---|---|---|---|---|---|
| | | | | | Categories of Expenditure (in U.S. dollars) | | | | | | |
| Alabama | 2 | 715,875 | 234,829 | 0 | 575 | 0 | 0 | 0 | 0 | 480,000 | 471 |
| Alaska | 0 | 0 | 0 | 0 | 0 | 0 | 0 | 0 | 0 | 0 | 0 |
| Arizona | 1 | 228,291 | 0 | 0 | 0 | 0 | 0 | 0 | 0 | 14,049 | 0 |
| Arkansas | 0 | 0 | 0 | 0 | 0 | 0 | 0 | 0 | 0 | 0 | 0 |
| California | 11 | 2,656,285 | 828,500 | 187,758 | 537,590 | 0 | 7,472 | 6,245 | 17,804 | 348,008 | 4,432 |
| Colorado | 0 | 0 | 0 | 0 | 0 | 0 | 0 | 0 | 0 | 0 | 0 |
| Connecticut | 0 | 0 | 0 | 0 | 0 | 0 | 0 | 0 | 0 | 0 | 0 |
| Delaware | 0 | 0 | 0 | 0 | 0 | 0 | 0 | 0 | 0 | 0 | 0 |
| District of Columbia | 2 | 1,755,881 | 7,200 | 0 | 17,779 | 0 | 0 | 0 | 0 | 44,118 | 0 |
| Florida | 2 | 154,545 | 45,750 | 0 | 89,170 | 0 | 0 | 1,625 | 0 | 18,000 | 0 |
| Georgia | 0 | 0 | 0 | 0 | 0 | 0 | 0 | 0 | 0 | 0 | 0 |
| Hawaii | 0 | 0 | 0 | 0 | 0 | 0 | 0 | 0 | 0 | 0 | 0 |
| Idaho | 0 | 0 | 0 | 0 | 0 | 0 | 0 | 0 | 0 | 0 | 0 |
| Illinois | 0 | 0 | 0 | 0 | 0 | 0 | 0 | 0 | 0 | 0 | 0 |
| Indiana | 0 | 0 | 0 | 0 | 0 | 0 | 0 | 0 | 0 | 0 | 0 |
| Iowa | 0 | 0 | 0 | 0 | 0 | 0 | 0 | 0 | 0 | 0 | 0 |
| Kansas | 2 | 835,175 | 286,783 | 0 | 330,566 | 0 | 0 | 0 | 0 | 212,543 | 5,283 |
| Kentucky | 0 | 0 | 0 | 0 | 0 | 0 | 0 | 0 | 0 | 0 | 0 |
| Louisiana | 3 | 4,452,018 | 14,313 | 0 | 105,100 | 0 | 0 | 500 | 0 | 0 | 0 |
| Maine | 1 | 257,079 | 0 | 0 | 0 | 0 | 0 | 0 | 0 | 0 | 0 |
| Maryland | 5 | 10,678,130 | 538,000 | 21,800 | 6,196,000 | 0 | 0 | 7,700 | 0 | 2,500,000 | 3,500 |
| Massachusetts | 4 | 435,768 | 195,036 | 0 | 0 | 0 | 0 | 0 | 0 | 68,332 | 7,500 |
| Michigan | 1 | 40,000 | 8,000 | 10,000 | 10,000 | 0 | 1,000 | 1,000 | 0 | 10,000 | 0 |
| Minnesota | 2 | 137,500 | 21,000 | 0 | 61,500 | 0 | 0 | 0 | 0 | 55,000 | 0 |
| Mississippi | 1 | 2,500 | 0 | 0 | 0 | 0 | 0 | 0 | 0 | 0 | 0 |

|  | | | | | | | | | | | |
|---|---|---|---|---|---|---|---|---|---|---|---|
| Missouri | 0 | 0 | 0 | 0 | 0 | 0 | 0 | 0 | 0 | 0 | 0 |
| Montana | 1 | 260,000 | 0 | 0 | 0 | 0 | 0 | 0 | 0 | 0 | 0 |
| Nebraska | 0 | 0 | 0 | 0 | 0 | 0 | 0 | 0 | 0 | 0 | 0 |
| Nevada | 0 | 0 | 0 | 0 | 0 | 0 | 0 | 0 | 0 | 0 | 0 |
| New Hampshire | 1 | 70,000 | 0 | 0 | 0 | 0 | 0 | 0 | 0 | 0 | 0 |
| New Jersey | 0 | 0 | 0 | 0 | 0 | 0 | 0 | 0 | 0 | 0 | 0 |
| New Mexico | 0 | 0 | 0 | 0 | 0 | 0 | 0 | 0 | 0 | 0 | 0 |
| New York | 3 | 1,367,180 | 0 | 0 | 0 | 0 | 0 | 0 | 0 | 0 | 5,300 |
| North Carolina | 1 | 40,000 | 5,000 | 0 | 30,000 | 0 | 0 | 0 | 0 | 5,000 | 0 |
| North Dakota | 1 | 0 | 0 | 0 | 0 | 0 | 0 | 0 | 0 | 2,500 | 0 |
| Ohio | 1 | 69,800 | 24,000 | 0 | 17,600 | 0 | 7,500 | 1,000 | 0 | 0 | 0 |
| Oklahoma | 0 | 0 | 0 | 0 | 0 | 0 | 0 | 0 | 0 | 0 | 0 |
| Oregon | 0 | 0 | 0 | 0 | 0 | 0 | 0 | 0 | 0 | 0 | 0 |
| Pennsylvania | 6 | 649,151 | 229,500 | 0 | 500 | 0 | 0 | 0 | 0 | 10,000 | 0 |
| Rhode Island | 1 | 43,425 | 9,961 | 0 | 31,764 | 0 | 0 | 814 | 0 | 886 | 0 |
| South Carolina | 0 | 0 | 0 | 0 | 0 | 0 | 0 | 0 | 0 | 0 | 0 |
| South Dakota | 0 | 0 | 0 | 0 | 0 | 0 | 0 | 0 | 0 | 0 | 0 |
| Tennessee | 1 | 125,000 | 0 | 0 | 0 | 0 | 0 | 0 | 0 | 0 | 0 |
| Texas | 2 | 207,616 | 156,313 | 0 | 33,434 | 0 | 0 | 14,692 | 0 | 3,177 | 0 |
| Utah | 0 | 0 | 0 | 0 | 0 | 0 | 0 | 0 | 0 | 0 | 0 |
| Vermont | 0 | 0 | 0 | 0 | 0 | 0 | 0 | 0 | 0 | 0 | 0 |
| Virginia | 1 | 63,090 | 13,355 | 0 | 42,453 | 0 | 0 | 6,271 | 0 | 1,011 | 0 |
| Washington | 0 | 0 | 0 | 0 | 0 | 0 | 0 | 0 | 0 | 0 | 0 |
| West Virginia | 0 | 0 | 0 | 0 | 0 | 0 | 0 | 0 | 0 | 0 | 0 |
| Wisconsin | 0 | 0 | 0 | 0 | 0 | 0 | 0 | 0 | 0 | 0 | 0 |
| Wyoming | 0 | 0 | 0 | 0 | 0 | 0 | 0 | 0 | 0 | 0 | 0 |
| Total | 55 | 25,244,309 | 2,617,540 | 219,558 | 7,504,031 | 0 | 15,972 | 39,847 | 17,804 | 3,772,624 | 26,486 |
| Estimated % of Acquisition Expenditures | | | 10.37 | 0.87 | 29.73 | 0.00 | 0.06 | 0.16 | 0.07 | 14.94 | 0.10 |

# Public Library State Rankings, 2006

| State | Library Visits per Capita* | Reference Transactions per Capita | Circulation Transactions per Capita | Interlibrary Loans per 1,000 Population | Internet Terminals per Outlet |
|---|---|---|---|---|---|
| Alabama | 46 | 34 | 46 | 33 | 15 |
| Alaska | 24 | 48 | 34 | 24 | 47 |
| Arizona | 41 | 27 | 30 | 44 | 3 |
| Arkansas | 44 | 45 | 45 | 43 | 37 |
| California | 36 | 25 | 40 | 25 | 11 |
| Colorado | 11 | 10 | 6 | 22 | 13 |
| Connecticut | 5 | 9 | 15 | 14 | 23 |
| Delaware | 22 | 42 | 11 | 12 | 26 |
| District of Columbia | 49 | 1 | 51 | 50 | 12 |
| Florida | 34 | 8 | 37 | 38 | 1 |
| Georgia | 42 | 16 | 44 | 31 | 5 |
| Hawaii | 35 | 38 | 41 | 51 | 32 |
| Idaho | 15 | 43 | 19 | 28 | 40 |
| Illinois | 17 | 4 | 17 | 6 | 10 |
| Indiana | 3 | 17 | 4 | 35 | 9 |
| Iowa | 14 | 40 | 10 | 18 | 45 |
| Kansas | 4 | 11 | 7 | 10 | 39 |
| Kentucky | 37 | 37 | 33 | 39 | 14 |
| Louisiana | 50 | 19 | 49 | 34 | 27 |
| Maine | 19 | 44 | 23 | 11 | 49 |
| Maryland | 25 | 6 | 12 | 30 | 2 |
| Massachusetts | 12 | 32 | 21 | 4 | 36 |
| Michigan | 27 | 26 | 28 | 8 | 18 |
| Minnesota | 23 | 29 | 9 | 13 | 21 |
| Mississippi | 51 | 50 | 50 | 47 | 38 |
| Missouri | 28 | 12 | 14 | 27 | 29 |
| Montana | 33 | 51 | 35 | 16 | 42 |
| Nebraska | 6 | 21 | 13 | 32 | 43 |
| Nevada | 39 | 46 | 36 | 36 | 30 |
| New Hampshire | 26 | 47 | 22 | 17 | 51 |
| New Jersey | 20 | 18 | 31 | 15 | 20 |
| New Mexico | 31 | 24 | 32 | 42 | 31 |
| New York | 18 | 5 | 24 | 7 | 24 |
| North Carolina | 38 | 7 | 39 | 49 | 8 |
| North Dakota | 29 | 41 | 26 | 21 | 48 |
| Ohio | 1 | 2 | 1 | 5 | 7 |
| Oklahoma | 32 | 36 | 27 | 40 | 33 |
| Oregon | 10 | 33 | 2 | 2 | 34 |
| Pennsylvania | 40 | 39 | 38 | 9 | 28 |
| Rhode Island | 16 | 22 | 29 | 3 | 19 |
| South Carolina | 43 | 13 | 42 | 45 | 6 |
| South Dakota | 21 | 30 | 20 | 23 | 46 |
| Tennessee | 48 | 28 | 48 | 48 | 25 |
| Texas | 47 | 31 | 43 | 41 | 4 |
| Utah | 2 | 3 | 3 | 46 | 22 |
| Vermont | 9 | 35 | 25 | 19 | 50 |

| State | Library Visits per Capita* | Reference Transactions per Capita | Circulation Transactions per Capita | Interlibrary Loans per 1,000 Population | Internet Terminals per Outlet |
|---|---|---|---|---|---|
| Virginia | 30 | 20 | 18 | 37 | 16 |
| Washington | 8 | 15 | 5 | 29 | 17 |
| West Virginia | 45 | 49 | 47 | 26 | 44 |
| Wisconsin | 13 | 23 | 8 | 1 | 35 |
| Wyoming | 7 | 14 | 16 | 20 | 41 |

| State | Internet Terminals per 5,000 Population** | Book and Serial Volumes per Capita | Audio Materials per 1,000 Population | Video Materials per 1,000 Population | Current Serials (Print) Subscriptions per 1,000 Population |
|---|---|---|---|---|---|
| Alabama | 15 | 40 | 40 | 32 | 49 |
| Alaska | 12 | 19 | 21 | 5 | 11 |
| Arizona | 47 | 51 | 44 | 45 | 41 |
| Arkansas | 42 | 39 | 47 | 47 | 43 |
| California | 49 | 43 | 45 | 43 | 47 |
| Colorado | 26 | 34 | 19 | 15 | 28 |
| Connecticut | 18 | 9 | 12 | 6 | 16 |
| Delaware | 48 | 36 | 32 | 30 | 22 |
| District of Columbia | 46 | 17 | 34 | 34 | 18 |
| Florida | 40 | 48 | 35 | 29 | 38 |
| Georgia | 31 | 49 | 50 | 50 | 51 |
| Hawaii | 50 | 32 | 41 | 46 | 44 |
| Idaho | 24 | 23 | 27 | 28 | 34 |
| Illinois | 9 | 16 | 6 | 7 | 10 |
| Indiana | 6 | 10 | 3 | 3 | 8 |
| Iowa | 7 | 11 | 9 | 8 | 2 |
| Kansas | 4 | 3 | 13 | 2 | 9 |
| Kentucky | 36 | 42 | 39 | 40 | 37 |
| Louisiana | 14 | 33 | 49 | 35 | 20 |
| Maine | 5 | 1 | 20 | 10 | 13 |
| Maryland | 38 | 30 | 23 | 33 | 25 |
| Massachusetts | 25 | 2 | 16 | 12 | 15 |
| Michigan | 17 | 22 | 18 | 24 | 27 |
| Minnesota | 16 | 25 | 24 | 27 | 30 |
| Mississippi | 44 | 45 | 51 | 48 | 48 |
| Missouri | 20 | 21 | 25 | 21 | 7 |
| Montana | 19 | 24 | 36 | 31 | 32 |
| Nebraska | 2 | 4 | 11 | 18 | 5 |
| Nevada | 51 | 50 | 29 | 25 | 45 |
| New Hampshire | 23 | 7 | 17 | 11 | 1 |
| New Jersey | 29 | 18 | 28 | 23 | 21 |
| New Mexico | 21 | 26 | 33 | 39 | 26 |
| New York | 30 | 15 | 5 | 14 | 4 |
| North Carolina | 33 | 47 | 48 | 51 | 42 |
| North Dakota | 11 | 12 | 26 | 26 | 19 |
| Ohio | 10 | 14 | 1 | 1 | 6 |
| Oklahoma | 27 | 38 | 38 | 44 | 39 |

| State | Internet Terminals per 5,000 Population** | Book and Serial Volumes per Capita | Audio Materials per 1,000 Population | Video Materials per 1,000 Population | Current Serials (Print) Subscriptions per 1,000 Population |
|---|---|---|---|---|---|
| Oregon | 34 | 27 | 10 | 20 | 29 |
| Pennsylvania | 41 | 35 | 15 | 36 | 33 |
| Rhode Island | 13 | 13 | 30 | 19 | 23 |
| South Carolina | 32 | 41 | 43 | 42 | 36 |
| South Dakota | 3 | 6 | 22 | 16 | 17 |
| Tennessee | 43 | 46 | 46 | 49 | 50 |
| Texas | 35 | 44 | 42 | 41 | 46 |
| Utah | 45 | 31 | 4 | 17 | 31 |
| Vermont | 1 | 5 | 8 | 13 | 3 |
| Virginia | 37 | 37 | 31 | 38 | 35 |
| Washington | 28 | 28 | 14 | 99 | 24 |
| West Virginia | 39 | 29 | 37 | 37 | 40 |
| Wisconsin | 22 | 20 | 7 | 4 | 14 |
| Wyoming | 8 | 8 | 2 | 9 | 12 |

| State | Paid FTE Staff per 25,000 Population | Paid FTE Librarians per 25,000 Population | ALA-MLS Librarians per 25,000 Population | Other Paid FTE Staff per 25,000 Population | Total Operating Income per Capita |
|---|---|---|---|---|---|
| Alabama | 41 | 31 | 43 | 43 | 47 |
| Alaska | 32 | 30 | 27 | 29 | 15 |
| Arizona | 46 | 47 | 29 | 37 | 39 |
| Arkansas | 44 | 44 | 50 | 39 | 46 |
| California | 49 | 48 | 26 | 41 | 29 |
| Colorado | 15 | 13 | 15 | 9 | 9 |
| Connecticut | 5 | 28 | 2 | 10 | 7 |
| Delaware | 40 | 7 | 41 | 40 | 24 |
| District of Columbia | 8 | 36 | 1 | 11 | 40 |
| Florida | 38 | 8 | 21 | 35 | 26 |
| Georgia | 47 | 43 | 34 | 36 | 44 |
| Hawaii | 33 | 51 | 11 | 26 | 2 |
| Idaho | 27 | 37 | 48 | 17 | 36 |
| Illinois | 6 | 35 | 9 | 5 | 4 |
| Indiana | 3 | 11 | 8 | 2 | 6 |
| Iowa | 17 | 3 | 28 | 38 | 27 |
| Kansas | 4 | 2 | 17 | 12 | 13 |
| Kentucky | 28 | 14 | 42 | 42 | 32 |
| Louisiana | 26 | 27 | 37 | 21 | 25 |
| Maine | 16 | 6 | 14 | 27 | 31 |
| Maryland | 14 | 16 | 16 | 15 | 11 |
| Massachusetts | 12 | 9 | 6 | 20 | 18 |
| Michigan | 23 | 24 | 12 | 22 | 16 |
| Minnesota | 29 | 32 | 22 | 23 | 21 |
| Mississippi | 35 | 22 | 51 | 45 | 51 |
| Missouri | 13 | 33 | 32 | 6 | 17 |
| Montana | 42 | 19 | 45 | 50 | 43 |

| State | Paid FTE Staff per 25,000 Population | Paid FTE Librarians per 25,000 Population | ALA-MLS Librarians per 25,000 Population | Other Paid FTE Staff per 25,000 Population | Total Operating Income per Capita |
|---|---|---|---|---|---|
| Nebraska | 18 | 10 | 35 | 25 | 30 |
| Nevada | 43 | 49 | 40 | 32 | 23 |
| New Hampshire | 9 | 1 | 10 | 28 | 19 |
| New Jersey | 11 | 29 | 7 | 7 | 5 |
| New Mexico | 31 | 25 | 30 | 34 | 35 |
| New York | 7 | 17 | 4 | 4 | 3 |
| North Carolina | 45 | 50 | 31 | 31 | 42 |
| North Dakota | 39 | 21 | 46 | 49 | 45 |
| Ohio | 1 | 12 | 5 | 1 | 1 |
| Oklahoma | 34 | 23 | 38 | 44 | 38 |
| Oregon | 25 | 34 | 18 | 16 | 12 |
| Pennsylvania | 36 | 41 | 25 | 30 | 37 |
| Rhode Island | 10 | 15 | 3 | 13 | 14 |
| South Carolina | 37 | 42 | 23 | 33 | 41 |
| South Dakota | 22 | 18 | 44 | 24 | 33 |
| Tennessee | 51 | 45 | 49 | 48 | 49 |
| Texas | 50 | 46 | 36 | 46 | 48 |
| Utah | 30 | 40 | 39 | 19 | 28 |
| Vermont | 21 | 4 | 24 | 47 | 34 |
| Virginia | 24 | 39 | 19 | 14 | 22 |
| Washington | 19 | 38 | 13 | 8 | 8 |
| West Virginia | 48 | 26 | 47 | 51 | 50 |
| Wisconsin | 20 | 20 | 20 | 18 | 20 |
| Wyoming | 2 | 5 | 33 | 3 | 10 |

| State | State Operating Income per Capita | Local Operating Income per Capita | Other Operating Income per Capita | Operating Expenditures per Capita | Collection Expenditures per Capita |
|---|---|---|---|---|---|
| Alabama | 28 | 45 | 32 | 46 | 47 |
| Alaska | 25 | 13 | 28 | 15 | 25 |
| Arizona | 44 | 31 | 51 | 41 | 33 |
| Arkansas | 19 | 43 | 43 | 48 | 45 |
| California | 30 | 24 | 30 | 30 | 41 |
| Colorado | 47 | 6 | 15 | 10 | 8 |
| Connecticut | 37 | 10 | 3 | 7 | 12 |
| Delaware | 7 | 33 | 12 | 28 | 29 |
| District of Columbia | 2 | 1 | 26 | 2 | 9 |
| Florida | 17 | 22 | 41 | 32 | 30 |
| Georgia | 9 | 47 | 49 | 45 | 48 |
| Hawaii | 51 | 51 | 35 | 38 | 19 |
| Idaho | 34 | 34 | 18 | 39 | 43 |
| Illinois | 11 | 3 | 10 | 4 | 3 |
| Indiana | 8 | 8 | 14 | 6 | 2 |
| Iowa | 29 | 25 | 20 | 23 | 17 |
| Kansas | 35 | 11 | 11 | 14 | 11 |
| Kentucky | 21 | 29 | 25 | 37 | 35 |

| State | State Operating Income per Capita | Local Operating Income per Capita | Other Operating Income per Capita | Operating Expenditures per Capita | Collection Expenditures per Capita |
|---|---|---|---|---|---|
| Louisiana | 18 | 27 | 16 | 25 | 40 |
| Maine | 42 | 36 | 4 | 26 | 38 |
| Maryland | 5 | 15 | 6 | 13 | 5 |
| Massachusetts | 22 | 18 | 17 | 16 | 13 |
| Michigan | 24 | 12 | 23 | 17 | 22 |
| Minnesota | 23 | 19 | 19 | 20 | 26 |
| Mississippi | 10 | 49 | 36 | 51 | 51 |
| Missouri | 32 | 16 | 13 | 21 | 6 |
| Montana | 36 | 39 | 31 | 44 | 42 |
| Nebraska | 39 | 23 | 45 | 29 | 23 |
| Nevada | 20 | 35 | 1 | 31 | 15 |
| New Hampshire | 49 | 14 | 21 | 18 | 21 |
| New Jersey | 27 | 2 | 27 | 5 | 7 |
| New Mexico | 13 | 32 | 44 | 33 | 16 |
| New York | 12 | 5 | 2 | 3 | 10 |
| North Carolina | 15 | 40 | 42 | 42 | 44 |
| North Dakota | 26 | 44 | 24 | 43 | 39 |
| Ohio | 1 | 41 | 8 | 1 | 1 |
| Oklahoma | 33 | 30 | 46 | 36 | 34 |
| Oregon | 41 | 9 | 22 | 11 | 20 |
| Pennsylvania | 4 | 46 | 9 | 35 | 36 |
| Rhode Island | 3 | 28 | 7 | 12 | 18 |
| South Carolina | 16 | 38 | 48 | 40 | 31 |
| South Dakota | 48 | 26 | 34 | 34 | 32 |
| Tennessee | 46 | 48 | 39 | 49 | 50 |
| Texas | 43 | 42 | 50 | 47 | 46 |
| Utah | 38 | 21 | 38 | 24 | 14 |
| Vermont | 45 | 37 | 5 | 27 | 37 |
| Virginia | 14 | 20 | 37 | 22 | 24 |
| Washington | 40 | 4 | 40 | 8 | 4 |
| West Virginia | 6 | 50 | 47 | 50 | 49 |
| Wisconsin | 31 | 17 | 33 | 19 | 27 |
| Wyoming | 50 | 7 | 29 | 9 | 28 |

| State | Staff Expenditures per Capita | Salary and Wages Expenditures per Capita | Average Rank | Rank of Ranks |
|---|---|---|---|---|
| Alabama | 45 | 45 | 38.32 | 44 |
| Alaska | 15 | 17 | 23.45 | 25 |
| Arizona | 39 | 39 | 38.59 | 45 |
| Arkansas | 48 | 49 | 43.18 | 49 |
| California | 25 | 30 | 34.86 | 38 |
| Colorado | 12 | 12 | 16.14 | 10 |
| Connecticut | 5 | 4 | 11.68 | 5 |
| Delaware | 31 | 32 | 27.50 | 29 |
| District of Columbia | 1 | 1 | 20.45 | 18 |
| Florida | 34 | 34 | 29.36 | 30 |

| State | Staff Expenditures per Capita | Salary and Wages Expenditures per Capita | Average Rank | Rank of Ranks |
|---|---|---|---|---|
| Georgia | 43 | 43 | 38.95 | 46 |
| Hawaii | 38 | 25 | 35.91 | 41 |
| Idaho | 35 | 35 | 31.09 | 33 |
| Illinois | 6 | 5 | 9.23 | 3 |
| Indiana | 10 | 11 | 8.50 | 2 |
| Iowa | 22 | 23 | 19.82 | 14 |
| Kansas | 16 | 15 | 11.95 | 6 |
| Kentucky | 41 | 41 | 33.68 | 37 |
| Louisiana | 32 | 33 | 29.86 | 31 |
| Maine | 23 | 22 | 21.82 | 21 |
| Maryland | 13 | 13 | 16.64 | 12 |
| Massachusetts | 14 | 7 | 15.77 | 9 |
| Michigan | 20 | 21 | 20.50 | 19 |
| Minnesota | 19 | 19 | 22.23 | 23 |
| Mississippi | 51 | 51 | 44.32 | 50 |
| Missouri | 24 | 24 | 20.05 | 16 |
| Montana | 44 | 44 | 36.27 | 42 |
| Nebraska | 28 | 27 | 22.14 | 22 |
| Nevada | 30 | 29 | 33.41 | 36 |
| New Hampshire | 17 | 14 | 20.14 | 17 |
| New Jersey | 4 | 6 | 16.36 | 11 |
| New Mexico | 33 | 38 | 30.41 | 32 |
| New York | 3 | 3 | 9.95 | 4 |
| North Carolina | 42 | 42 | 37.64 | 43 |
| North Dakota | 47 | 46 | 33.09 | 35 |
| Ohio | 2 | 2 | 5.64 | 1 |
| Oklahoma | 36 | 36 | 35.55 | 40 |
| Oregon | 11 | 16 | 19.82 | 15 |
| Pennsylvania | 37 | 37 | 31.23 | 34 |
| Rhode Island | 9 | 9 | 14.91 | 7 |
| South Carolina | 40 | 40 | 35.09 | 39 |
| South Dakota | 29 | 28 | 26.18 | 28 |
| Tennessee | 49 | 48 | 45.55 | 51 |
| Texas | 46 | 47 | 41.86 | 48 |
| Utah | 27 | 31 | 25.14 | 26 |
| Vermont | 26 | 26 | 22.77 | 24 |
| Virginia | 21 | 20 | 26.14 | 27 |
| Washington | 8 | 8 | 21.14 | 20 |
| West Virginia | 50 | 50 | 41.68 | 47 |
| Wisconsin | 18 | 18 | 18.55 | 13 |
| Wyoming | 7 | 10 | 15.00 | 8 |

FTE = full-time equivalent

\* Per capita is based on the unduplicated population of legal service areas.

\*\* Average number of public-use terminals per 5,000 population.

\*\*\* The District of Columbia, while not a state, is included in the state rankings. Special care should be taken in comparing the data to state data.

Source: Compiled by Julia C. Miller from *Public Libraries in the United States: Fiscal Year 2006,* Institute of Museum and Library Services (2008).

# Library Buildings 2008:
# Keeping The 'Eco' in Economy

Bette-Lee Fox

Managing Editor, *Library Journal*

The latest calamities to befall the economy aren't reflected in the 2008 compilation of library building projects. These 183 public libraries and 30 academic facilities, completed between July 1, 2007, and June 30, 2008, squeaked through before the repercussions from the current financial debacles began. Yet we certainly can't ignore the money side of things. Funding is at the heart of libraries and their future. The root of economy means "to manage." The root of eco means "environment." Managing our library environment this past year showed distinct signs of going green and saving green as design ramped up sustainability elements.

## Public in a Big Way

Though cost-consciousness is always a focus in libraries, some projects still went big, like the new Lewis Library and Technology Center in Fontana, California ($64 million), the Champaign Public Library in Illinois ($28.3 million), and *Library Journal*'s (*LJ*'s) 2007 Library of the Year, Laramie County Library in Wyoming ($25.4 million). Among the larger addition/renovation projects were the Hartford (Connecticut) Public Library ($42 million) and the Medina Library in Ohio ($20 million). Managing costs also provides opportunities for some creative mixed use space, as a branch of the Omaha Public Library combines with a community college, for example, and the East Anaheim (California) Branch joins forces with a police station and a community center.

## Recycling on a Large Scale

*LJ* asked respondents to this year's architecture survey to include "sustainable" features that made an impact on their designs. And what could be a better green project than to repurpose and reuse an existing structure? The largest project in our 2008 list of academic libraries is the Harrington Learning Commons, Sobrato Technology Center, and Orradre Library at Santa Clara University in California, which totaled a mind-blowing $92 million and 194,000 square feet. This sustainable project includes reused clay roof tiles, double-height clerestory windows, dimmable lighting zones, reclaimed water, and reflective white "cool-roofs." The remodeling of the Gentry Public Library in Arkansas converted a century-old hardware store, while the Bond Hill Branch of the Public Library of Cincinnati and Hamilton County, Ohio, took over a department store, and the Cutchogue-New Suffolk Free Library in New York transformed an 1862 church.

Remodels of historic libraries were able to resurrect and restore original woodwork and classic building features. For example, the Stephenson Public

Adapted from *Library Journal,* December 2008.

Library in Marinette, Wisconsin, renovated a 1902 facility, reclaimed its rotunda and stained glass skylights, and uncovered several fireplaces. Also, a number of early 20th-century Carnegie libraries have been revived for the 21st century. Salvaged windows and furniture, high-performance lighting, proximity to public transportation, high R-value insulation, formaldehyde-free composite wood, xeriscaping (landscaping designed to cope with dry conditions), cork and bamboo flooring, and solar panels have contributed to the environmentally friendly and economically sound projects we are highlighting this year. The Looscan Neighborhood Library, Houston, Texas, was one of several libraries that combined these features to achieve Leadership in Energy and Environmental Design (LEED) certification.

## Table 1 / New Academic Library Buildings, 2008

| Institution | Project Cost | Gross Area (Sq. Ft.) | Square Foot Cost | Construction Cost | Equipment Cost | Book Capacity | Architect |
|---|---|---|---|---|---|---|---|
| Harrington Learning Commons, Sobrato Technology Center and Orradre Library, Santa Clara University, CA | $92,000,000 | 194,000 | $357.53 | $69,400,000 | $7,000,000 | 1,150,000 | Pfeiffer Partners Architects |
| Utah Valley University Library, Orem | 48,000,000 | 190,000 | 210.53 | 40,000,000 | 4,500,000 | 600,000 | Alspector Architecture |
| Richard J. Klarchek Information Commons, Loyola University, Chicago | 32,000,000 | 67,000 | n.a. | n.a. | n.a. | 0 | Solomon Cordwell Buenz |
| East Campus Library, James Madison University, Harrisonburg, VA | 31,122,747 | 108,200 | 210.66 | 22,793,442 | 5,040,000 | 168,000 | Design Collective |
| Canizaro Library, Ave Maria University, FL | 30,522,855 | 91,799 | 192.33 | 17,655,910 | 1,227,855 | 400,000 | Cannon Design |
| Anschutz Medical Center Library, University of Colorado at Denver Health Sciences Center | 25,000,000 | 118,875 | n.a. | n.a. | n.a. | n.a. | Davis Partnership; Design Architect: Centerbrook |
| William Atkinson Hall Information and Technology Center, Jackson Community College, MI | 16,500,000 | 53,000 | 221.48 | 11,738,300 | 866,743 | 42,000 | SHW Group |
| B. Thomas Golisano Library, Roberts Wesleyan College, Rochester, NY | 11,500,000 | 45,500 | 195.48 | 8,894,320 | 925,400 | 222,500 | Leo A. Daly; SWBR Architects |
| Christine and Steven F. Udvar-Hazy Library, Embry-Riddle Aeronautical University–Prescott Campus, AZ | 10,200,000 | 35,711 | 246.42 | 8,800,000 | 800,000 | 50,000 | DLR Group |
| Tunxis Community College Library, Farmington, CT | n.a. | 40,300 | 203.42 | 8,197,799 | 626,070 | 89,380 | Du Bose Associates |
| Ford Library, Fuqua School of Business, Duke University, Durham, NC | 8,400,000 | 17,300 | 364.16 | 6,300,000 | 1,600,000 | 50,000 | Perkins + Will |
| Clayton Glass Library, Motlow State Community College, Lynchburg, TN | 7,435,000 | 32,000 | 184.37 | 5,900,000 | 415,000 | 62,000 | Kline Swinney Associates |
| South Omaha Library, Metropolitan Community College* | 6,567,652 | 23,300 | 189.51 | 4,415,669 | 366,641 | 65,000 | Engberg Anderson; DLR Group |
| Associated Mennonite Biblical Seminary Library, Elkhart, IN | 6,190,300 | 29,970 | 170.76 | 5,117,721 | 194,193 | 190,000 | The Troyer Group |
| University of Puerto Rico Library, Utuado Campus | n.a. | 27,000 | 203.70 | 5,500,000 | 572,000 | 30,290 | Marvel & Marchand |

* A joint project with the Omaha Public Library.

n.a. = not available

# Table 2 / Academic Library Buildings, Additions and Renovations, 2008

| Institution | Status | Project Cost | Gross Area (Sq. Ft.) | Square Foot Cost | Construction Cost | Equipment Cost | Book Capacity | Architect |
|---|---|---|---|---|---|---|---|---|
| Case Library and Geyer Center for Information Technology, Colgate University, Hamilton, NY | Total | $57,500,000 | 152,000 | $242.76 | $36,900,000 | n.a. | 1,000,000 | Shepley Bulfinch Richardson... |
| | New | n.a. | 51,000 | n.a. | n.a. | n.a. | n.a. | |
| | Renovated | n.a. | 101,000 | n.a. | n.a. | n.a. | n.a. | |
| John Spoor Broome Library, California State University Channel Islands, Camarillo | Total | 56,000,000 | 137,750 | 351.22 | 48,380,186 | $3,100,000 | 300,000 | Foster + Partners |
| | New | n.a. | n.a. | n.a. | n.a. | n.a. | n.a. | |
| | Renovated | n.a. | n.a. | n.a. | n.a. | n.a. | n.a. | |
| Georgia State University Library, Atlanta | Total | 23,000,000 | n.a. | n.a. | 16,769,666 | n.a. | 1,300,000 | Leo A. Daly |
| | New | n.a. | 25,000 | n.a. | n.a. | n.a. | n.a. | |
| | Renovated | n.a. | n.a. | n.a. | n.a. | n.a. | n.a. | |
| Rothrock Library, Lehigh Carbon Community College, Schnecksville, PA | Total | 4,533,760 | 28,760 | 119.14 | 3,426,602 | 1,107,158 | 55,000 | MKSD Architects |
| | New | 740,410 | 2,638 | 249.81 | 659,000 | 81,410 | 200 | |
| | Renovated | 3,793,350 | 26,122 | 105.95 | 2,767,602 | 1,025,748 | 54,800 | |
| Lewis Walpole Library, Yale University, Farmington, CT | Total | n.a. | 16,266 | n.a. | n.a. | n.a. | * | Centerbrook Architects |
| | New | n.a. | 13,238 | n.a. | n.a. | n.a. | * | |
| | Renovated | n.a. | 3,028 | n.a. | n.a. | n.a. | * | |

* The Walpole Library collection now includes 35,000 volumes, 30,000 prints and manuscripts, and 3,000-plus letters.

# Table 3 / Academic Library Buildings, Renovations Only, 2008

| Institution | Project Cost | Gross Area (Sq. Ft.) | Square Foot Cost | Construction Cost | Equipment Cost | Book Capacity | Architect |
|---|---|---|---|---|---|---|---|
| Gleason Library, University of Rochester, NY | $5,000,000 | 22,000 | $131.00 | $2,882,000 | $704,000 | n.a. | Ayers/Saint/Gross DesignGroup |
| Pelletier Library, Allegheny College, Meadville, PA | 4,600,000 | 80,000 | 36.04 | 2,882,813 | 1,018,283 | 772,000 | DesignGroup |
| Richard Bland College Library, College of William and Mary, Petersburg, VA | 2,651,738 | 23,085 | 101.87 | 2,351,738 | 300,000 | 69,000 | The Lukmire Partnership |
| Frank Lee Martin Journalism Library, University of Missouri/Missouri School of Journalism, Columbia | 2,079,100 | 7,150 | 274.00 | 1,959,100 | 185,000 | 30,000 | SFS Architecture |
| Mary Norton Clapp Library, Occidental College, Los Angeles | 1,500,000 | 7,025 | 156.58 | 1,100,000 | 15,000 | n.a. | Harley Ellis Devereaux DesignGroup |
| Vernon Alden Library, Ohio University, Athens | 1,062,000 | 11,878 | 72.57 | 862,000 | 200,000 | n.a. | College at Brockport |
| Drake Memorial Library, College at Brockport, State University of New York | 730,749 | 8,636 | 69.47 | 600,000 | 130,749 | n.a. | |
| F. Franklin Moon Library, State University of New York College of Environmental Science and Forestry | 378,341 | 11,830 | n.a. | n.a. | n.a. | n.a. | Campus physical plant staff |
| Franklin D. Schurz Library, Indiana University South Bend | 301,719 | 4,252 | 48.44 | 205,948 | 95,771 | 10,000 | Maregatti Interiors |
| Library-Student-Faculty Building, Purdue University North Central, Westville, IN | 265,000 | 32,000 | 6.31 | 202,000 | n.a. | 85,000 | Woollen, Molzan & Partners |

n.a. = not available

## Table 4 / New Public Library Buildings, 2008

| Community | Pop ('000) | Code | Project Cost | Const. Cost | Gross Sq. Ft. | Sq. Ft. Cost | Equip. Cost | Site Cost | Other Costs | Volumes | Federal Funds | State Funds | Local Funds | Gift Funds | Architect |
|---|---|---|---|---|---|---|---|---|---|---|---|---|---|---|---|
| *Alaska* | | | | | | | | | | | | | | | |
| Girdwood | 5 | B | $5,189,000 | $4,000,000 | 9,394 | $425.80 | $614,000 | Owned | $575,000 | 2,025 | $1,000,000 | $2,500,000 | $1,000,000 | $689,000 | RIM Architects |
| *Arizona* | | | | | | | | | | | | | | | |
| Scottsdale | 50 | B | 9,874,683 | 7,771,987 | 20,000 | 388.60 | 832,581 | Owned | 1,270,115 | 80,000 | 0 | 0 | 9,824,683 | 50,000 | Richárd+Bauer |
| Tucson (Marana) | 19 | B | 6,247,800 | 5,251,000 | 20,000 | 262.55 | 293,500 | Owned | 703,300 | 80,000 | 0 | 0 | 6,247,800 | 0 | Richárd+Bauer |
| Tucson | 17 | B | 1,878,500 | 1,300,000 | 5,000 | 260.00 | 293,500 | Owned | 285,000 | 12,000 | 0 | 0 | 1,878,500 | 0 | Burns Wald-Hopkins… |
| Wellton | 7 | B | 2,553,835 | 2,200,000 | 8,675 | 253.60 | 95,000 | $120,000 | 138,835 | 2,952 | 0 | 0 | 2,433,835 | 120,000 | Barry Patterson Archs. |
| *California* | | | | | | | | | | | | | | | |
| Calabasas | 22 | M | 13,930,000 | 12,530,000 | 31,033 | 403.76 | n.a. | Owned | n.a. | 60,000 | 0 | 2,733,000 | 11,197,000 | 0 | R.A.M. Stern; Harley |
| Encinitas | 54 | B | 19,180,000 | 14,700,000 | 26,798 | 548.55 | 491,000 | 1,139,000 | 2,850,000 | 90,000 | 0 | 0 | 18,900,000 | 280,000 | Manuel Oncina |
| Fontana | 220 | O | 64,000,000 | 44,000,000 | 93,000 | 473.12 | 20,000,000 | Owned | n.a. | 150,000 | 0 | 14,900,000 | 33,500,000 | 15,600,000 | RNL |
| Irvine | 35 | O | 6,530,000 | 5,830,647 | 11,250 | 518.28 | 250,000 | Leased | 449,353 | 786 | 0 | 0 | 5,530,000 | 1,000,000 | Thirtieth Street Archs. |
| La Mesa | 59 | O | 4,748,428 | 3,918,000 | 10,000 | 391.80 | 280,000 | Owned | 550,428 | 7,462 | 0 | 0 | 4,748,428 | 0 | Leach Mounce |
| Lincoln | 40 | M | 17,045,000 | 11,135,751 | 39,343 | 283.04 | 615,383 | 1,250,000 | 4,043,866 | 173,171 | 0 | 10,422,338 | 6,894,772 | 0 | NTD Architecture |
| Mecca | 10 | O | 4,394,000 | 4,044,000 | 10,086 | 400.95 | 175,000 | 175,000 | 0 | 15,000 | 4,044,000 | 0 | 350,000 | 0 | Hill Partnership |
| Mendota | 10 | O | 5,398,725 | 4,126,039 | 12,600 | 327.46 | 360,180 | 129,173 | 783,333 | 46,000 | 0 | 3,525,962 | 1,898,572 | 39,527 | Taylor Teter; Fresno |
| Riverside | 15 | B | 5,885,000 | 5,635,000 | 10,086 | 558.70 | 250,000 | Owned | 250,000 | 30,000 | 30,000 | 0 | 5,855,000 | 0 | HMC Architects |
| Roseville | 44 | B | 8,918,069 | 7,512,759 | 14,000 | 536.63 | 502,802 | Owned | 902,508 | 4,209 | 0 | 102,240 | 8,815,829 | 0 | Williams + Paddon |
| San Diego | 42 | M | 11,000,000 | 7,900,000 | 16,020 | 493.13 | 270,000 | Owned | 2,830,000 | 7,384 | 0 | 0 | 11,000,000 | 0 | Harley Ellis; Platt/… |
| San Francisco | 15 | B | 5,988,200 | 1,591,737 | 7,185 | 221.54 | 500,000 | 3,455,160 | 441,303 | 35,000 | 0 | 0 | 5,488,200 | 500,000 | Tom Eliot; Sf Bureau |
| San Jose | 48 | B | 10,370,293 | 7,799,314 | 22,222 | 350.97 | 463,649 | Owned | 2,107,330 | 119,600 | 0 | 0 | 10,370,293 | 0 | CWA AIA |
| San Jose | 26 | B | 9,928,276 | 7,307,397 | 14,500 | 503.96 | 335,964 | Owned | 2,284,915 | 72,300 | 0 | 0 | 9,928,276 | 0 | Tetra Design |
| San Jose | 27 | B | 8,480,159 | 6,212,483 | 13,885 | 447.42 | 340,510 | Owned | 1,927,166 | 78,600 | 0 | 0 | 8,480,159 | 0 | Anderson Brulé |
| San Jose | 31 | B | 9,124,119 | 7,091,919 | 13,380 | 530.04 | 422,137 | Owned | 1,610,063 | 67,900 | 0 | 0 | 9,124,119 | 0 | Krong Design |
| San Marino | 13 | MS | 15,110,607 | 11,387,364 | 29,467 | 386.44 | 416,433 | Owned | 3,306,810 | 100,000 | 0 | 0 | 5,397,607 | 9,713,000 | Harley Ellis Devereaux |
| Suisun City | 27 | O | 5,731,521 | 4,719,348 | 10,000 | 471.93 | 326,403 | Owned | 685,770 | 50,000 | 0 | 0 | 5,731,521 | 0 | Paul Roberts |
| Watsonville | 58 | M | 10,944,593 | 8,788,270 | 43,000 | 204.38 | 1,298,913 | Owned | 857,410 | 175,634 | 0 | 315,000 | 10,629,593 | 0 | Hidell & Associates |
| *Colorado* | | | | | | | | | | | | | | | |
| Erie | 17 | B | 6,907,500 | 4,800,000 | 20,000 | 240.00 | 725,000 | 550,000 | 832,500 | 80,000 | 0 | 200,000 | 6,057,500 | 650,000 | Klipp |
| Firestone | 25 | B | 9,175,000 | 6,500,000 | 34,500 | 188.41 | 1,075,000 | 400,000 | 1,200,000 | 116,000 | 0 | 200,000 | 8,475,000 | 500,000 | Klipp |

Symbol Code: B=Branch Library; BS=Branch and System Headquarters; M=Main Library; MS=Main and System Headquarters; S=System Headquarters; O=combined use space; n.a.=not available

| Location | | | | | | | | | | | | | | | |
|---|---|---|---|---|---|---|---|---|---|---|---|---|---|---|---|
| **Florida** | | | | | | | | | | | | | | | |
| Boca Raton | 86 | BS | 17,742,845 | 12,249,845 | 40,970 | 298.97 | 1,543,845 | 350,000 | 3,600,000 | 100,000 | 0 | 500,000 | 16,242,845 | 1,000,000 | Harvard Jolly |
| Clermont | 25 | B | 8,396,699 | 6,934,706 | 30,125 | 230.20 | 619,551 | 100,000 | 742,442 | 43,007 | 198,000 | 500,000 | 7,396,361 | 302,000 | Harvard Jolly |
| Miami | 53 | M | 5,576,361 | 4,555,664 | 7,500 | 607.42 | 1,020,697 | Owned | 0 | 25,000 | 0 | 500,000 | 5,076,361 | 0 | Miami-Dade Cty. |
| Oldsmar | 14 | M | 5,794,474 | 4,971,196 | 19,800 | 251.07 | 179,267 | 225,000 | 419,011 | 72,000 | 0 | 700,000 | 5,024,474 | 70,000 | Harvard Jolly |
| Plantation | 330 | B | 18,495,860 | 14,711,000 | 72,000 | 204.30 | 2,047,500 | Owned | 1,787,360 | 200,000 | 0 | 500,000 | 18,045,860 | 0 | Pierce Architectural |
| **Georgia** | | | | | | | | | | | | | | | |
| Ellijay | 28 | B | 4,054,419 | 3,310,615 | 20,000 | 165.53 | 400,491 | Owned | 343,313 | 4,731 | 0 | 2,000,000 | 2,000,000 | 54,419 | Pope/Partners |
| Flowery Branch | 61 | B | 5,341,718 | 3,131,592 | 22,460 | 139.43 | 1,085,762 | 500,000 | 624,364 | 129,000 | 0 | 2,000,000 | 3,276,718 | 65,000 | Pope/Partners |
| Newnan | 190 | MS | 8,000,000 | 5,821,108 | 29,000 | 200.73 | 465,682 | Owned | 1,713,210 | 8,460 | 0 | 2,000,000 | 6,000,000 | 0 | Gardner Spencer… |
| **Idaho** | | | | | | | | | | | | | | | |
| Coeur D'alene | 45 | M | 7,600,000 | 5,840,000 | 38,000 | 153.68 | 385,000 | 1,000,000 | 375,000 | 5,000 | 0 | 0 | 4,600,000 | 3,000,000 | Architects West |
| **Illinois** | | | | | | | | | | | | | | | |
| Addison | 37 | M | 15,000,000 | 12,162,633 | 54,600 | 222.76 | 792,755 | Owned | 2,044,612 | 16,692 | 0 | 0 | 15,000,000 | 0 | Burnidge Cassell |
| Champaign | 75 | M | 28,300,000 | 20,772,500 | 122,600 | 169.43 | 4,043,300 | Owned | 3,484,200 | 29,907 | 0 | 150,000 | 25,300,000 | 2,850,000 | Ross Barney |
| Harwood Heights | 23 | M | 15,763,920 | 11,254,586 | 44,575 | 252.49 | 788,843 | 1,900,000 | 1,820,491 | 168,791 | 0 | 42,800 | 15,721,120 | 0 | WCT Architects |
| La Grange | 16 | M | 10,396,096 | 7,682,782 | 34,417 | 223.23 | 788,202 | 200,000 | 1,925,112 | 3,348 | 0 | 0 | 10,364,465 | 31,631 | Burnidge Cassell |
| Washington | 21 | M | 2,666,572 | 2,331,572 | 19,300 | 120.81 | 130,000 | 200,000 | 5,000 | 55,000 | 0 | 0 | 2,536,572 | 130,000 | P.J. Hoerr Inc. |
| **Indiana** | | | | | | | | | | | | | | | |
| Lake Station | 18 | B | 3,940,000 | 3,280,000 | 16,000 | 205.00 | 260,450 | 150,000 | 249,550 | 60,000 | 0 | 0 | 3,940,000 | 0 | Carras-Szany-Kuhn |
| Trafalgar | 95 | B | 6,021,140 | 4,744,957 | 20,800 | 228.12 | 628,233 | 350,000 | 297,950 | 72,000 | 0 | 0 | 5,753,177 | 0 | VPS Architecture |
| Williamsport* | 2 | M | 1,500,000 | 800,000 | 10,500 | 76.19 | 400,000 | Owned | 300,000 | 80,000 | 267,963 | 0 | 1,500,000 | 0 | H.L. Mohler & Assocs. |
| **Iowa** | | | | | | | | | | | | | | | |
| Humeston | 1 | M | 480,000 | 440,000 | 3,850 | 114.29 | 15,000 | 5,000 | 20,000 | 11,500 | 0 | 19,000 | 461,000 | 0 | Ron Lehman |
| **Kansas** | | | | | | | | | | | | | | | |
| Basehor | 7 | M | 3,549,268 | 2,343,324 | 17,800 | 131.65 | 507,458 | 300,000 | 398,486 | 75,000 | 0 | 0 | 3,249,268 | 300,000 | Treanor Architects |
| **Kentucky** | | | | | | | | | | | | | | | |
| Berea | 81 | B | 4,099,696 | 3,152,853 | 12,483 | 252.57 | 207,343 | 550,000 | 189,500 | 4,862 | 0 | 0 | 4,099,696 | 0 | 5253 Design Group |
| Burlington | 112 | M | 17,437,854 | 10,879,772 | 75,000 | 145.06 | 1,886,036 | 3,240,618 | 1,431,428 | 200,000 | 0 | 0 | 17,437,854 | 0 | Robert Ehmet Hayes |
| Flemingsburg | 15 | M | 2,637,086 | 1,945,647 | 12,000 | 162.14 | 236,797 | 255,229 | 199,413 | 50,000 | 0 | 1,600,000 | 1,037,086 | 0 | Sherman Carter… |
| Owensboro | 97 | M | 9,315,000 | 7,200,000 | 52,000 | 138.46 | 1,140,000 | Owned | 975,000 | 264,054 | 0 | 40,000 | 9,249,000 | 26,000 | Tuck-Hinton Archs. |
| Somerset | 60 | M | 12,231,000 | 9,055,000 | 45,750 | 197.92 | 1,005,000 | 1,176,000 | 995,000 | 154,864 | 0 | 0 | 12,079,000 | 152,000 | McClorey & Savage |
| **Louisiana** | | | | | | | | | | | | | | | |
| Carencro | 35 | B | 3,096,209 | 2,297,723 | 12,564 | 182.88 | 489,571 | Owned | 308,915 | 35,000 | 0 | 41,125 | 3,039,334 | 15,750 | Angelle Architects |
| Glenmora | 4 | B | 620,743 | 510,515 | 4,000 | 127.64 | 27,818 | 35,000 | 47,410 | 350 | 0 | 0 | 585,743 | 35,000 | Alliance Design |

* The Williamsport-Washington Township Public Library building was funded through insurance money

Symbol Code: B=Branch Library; BS=Branch and System Headquarters; M=Main Library; MS=Main and System Headquarters; O=combined use space; S=System Headquarters; n.a.=not available

Table 4 / New Public Library Buildings, 2008 *(cont.)*

| Community | Pop ('000) | Code | Project Cost | Const. Cost | Gross Sq. Ft. | Sq. Ft. Cost | Equip. Cost | Site Cost | Other Costs | Volumes | Federal Funds | State Funds | Local Funds | Gift Funds | Architect |
|---|---|---|---|---|---|---|---|---|---|---|---|---|---|---|---|
| Hineston | 4 | B | $616,117 | $507,717 | 4,000 | $126.93 | $27,741 | $35,000 | $45,659 | 350 | 0 | 0 | $581,117 | $35,000 | Alliance Design |
| Lake Charles | 21 | B | 1,262,547 | 1,096,255 | 7,020 | 156.16 | 133,795 | 13,285 | 19,212 | 20,000 | 0 | 0 | 1,262,547 | 0 | Randy M. Goodloe |
| *Maryland* | | | | | | | | | | | | | | | |
| Boonsboro | 12 | B | 2,375,642 | 2,057,000 | 9,983 | 206.05 | 135,286 | 85,000 | 98,356 | 22,000 | $196,000 | 400,000 | 933,404 | 846,238 | Murphy & Dittenhafer |
| Frederick | 18 | B | 8,193,905 | 6,199,294 | 25,088 | 247.10 | 1,545,000 | Owned | 449,611 | 75,000 | 0 | 0 | 8,193,905 | 0 | PSA-Dewberry |
| Ocean City | 7 | B | 6,181,787 | 5,271,994 | 12,691 | 415.41 | 398,208 | Owned | 511,585 | 33,000 | 0 | 67,500 | 6,092,816 | 21,471 | Buck Simpers |
| Perryville | 12 | B | 6,905,020 | 4,747,290 | 15,190 | 312.53 | 618,000 | 382,000 | 1,157,730 | 70,000 | 0 | 90,000 | 6,800,020 | 15,000 | Grimm + Parker |
| *Michigan* | | | | | | | | | | | | | | | |
| Ann Arbor | 36 | B | 9,756,886 | 7,000,000 | 16,600 | 421.67 | 600,000 | 1,400,000 | 756,000 | 2,938 | 0 | 0 | 9,746,000 | 10,000 | inFORM studio |
| Lansing | 30 | M | 7,535,500 | 6,220,000 | 31,294 | 198.76 | 609,000 | Owned | 706,500 | 65,000 | 0 | 0 | 7,535,500 | 0 | Fishbeck, Thompson |
| Presque Isle | 3 | B | 569,000 | 475,000 | 4,000 | 118.75 | 40,000 | 50,000 | 4,000 | 11,000 | 0 | 0 | 569,000 | 0 | Charles Winters |
| Warren | 138 | M | 8,213,280 | 6,565,259 | 33,936 | 193.46 | 1,039,630 | Owned | 608,391 | 151,835 | 0 | 0 | 8,213,280 | 0 | Hidell & Associates |
| *Minnesota* | | | | | | | | | | | | | | | |
| Forest Lake | 23 | B | 7,089,886 | 4,344,477 | 24,600 | 176.61 | 648,931 | 571,522 | 1,524,956 | 120,000 | 0 | 250,000 | 6,839,886 | 0 | Ankeny Kell Archs. |
| *Mississippi* | | | | | | | | | | | | | | | |
| Southaven | 41 | B | 5,285,000 | 4,500,000 | 43,000 | 104.65 | 285,000 | Owned | 500,000 | 200,000 | 0 | 401,000 | 4,884,000 | 0 | Marvin Johnson |
| *Missouri* | | | | | | | | | | | | | | | |
| Independence | 700 | B | 9,555,032 | 7,498,055 | 50,330 | 148.97 | 386,661 | 800,000 | 870,316 | 10,431 | 0 | 0 | 9,305,032 | 250,000 | Sapp Design |
| Springfield | 16 | B | 256,926 | 110,979 | 3,100 | 35.80 | 130,572 | Leased | 15,375 | 3,700 | 0 | 0 | 6,926 | 250,000 | Buxton-Kubik-Dodd |
| *Nebraska* | | | | | | | | | | | | | | | |
| Omaha* | 27 | O | 6,567,472 | 4,415,669 | 23,300 | 189.51 | 366,641 | 344,602 | 1,440,560 | 65,000 | 0 | 0 | 6,017,472 | 550,000 | DLR; Engberg... |
| *New Mexico* | | | | | | | | | | | | | | | |
| Rio Rancho | 67 | M | 6,697,150 | 5,575,402 | 32,000 | 174.23 | 596,873 | Owned | 524,875 | 125,000 | 0 | 0 | 6,347,150 | 350,000 | Hidell & Associates |
| *New York* | | | | | | | | | | | | | | | |
| W. Hempstead | 17 | M | 12,521,074 | 7,228,573 | 27,300 | 265.00 | 340,187 | 1,691,892 | 3,260,422 | 75,001 | 0 | 18,435 | 12,502,639 | 0 | Gibbons Heidtmann... |
| *North Dakota* | | | | | | | | | | | | | | | |
| Fargo | 40 | B | 3,679,899 | 2,899,374 | 14,474 | 200.32 | 333,087 | 155,000 | 292,438 | 50,078 | 0 | 0 | 2,554,899 | 1,125,000 | Meyer, Scherer... |
| *Ohio* | | | | | | | | | | | | | | | |
| Carroll | 5 | B | 1,547,609 | 1,200,000 | 8,000 | 150.00 | 170,549 | 77,000 | 100,060 | 55,000 | 0 | 0 | 170,549 | 1,377,060 | Lupton Rausch |

* A joint project with the Metropolitan Community College of Omaha.

Symbol Code: B=Branch Library; BS=Branch and System Headquarters; M=Main Library; MS=Main and System Headquarters; S=System Headquarters; O=combined use space; n.a.=not available

| Location | | | | | | | | | | | | | | | Architect |
|---|---|---|---|---|---|---|---|---|---|---|---|---|---|---|---|
| Cleveland | 3 | B | 350,138 | 230,765 | 3,517 | 65.61 | 119,373 | Leased | 0 | 10,000 | 0 | 0 | 350,138 | 0 | none |
| Medina | 17 | B | 4,630,199 | 3,092,749 | 12,325 | 250.93 | 556,000 | Owned | 981,450 | 2,980 | 0 | 0 | 4,628,454 | 1,745 | David Milling Archs. |
| Toledo | 26 | B | 2,266,302 | 1,828,320 | 9,849 | 185.64 | 160,000 | 147,000 | 130,982 | 107,000 | 0 | 0 | 2,266,302 | 0 | Spring Valley Archs. |
| *Oklahoma* | | | | | | | | | | | | | | | |
| Tulsa | 585 | B | 2,331,927 | 1,891,991 | 11,280 | 167.73 | 176,454 | Leased | 263,482 | 50,000 | 0 | 0 | 0 | 2,331,927 | Larry Edmondson |
| *Oregon* | | | | | | | | | | | | | | | |
| Gold Beach | 5 | M | 2,239,726 | 1,224,859 | 8,200 | 149.37 | 113,000 | 225,000 | 676,867 | 42,000 | 0 | 0 | 1,070,000 | 1,169,726 | Richard P. Turi |
| Mount Angel | 4 | O | 1,070,299 | 895,511 | 4,100 | 218.41 | 78,600 | Owned | 96,188 | 2,902 | 609,411 | 0 | 228,947 | 231,941 | LDN Architecture |
| *Pennsylvania* | | | | | | | | | | | | | | | |
| Berwick Group | 19 | M | 2,841,115 | 2,434,115 | 20,560 | 118.39 | 186,000 | Owned | 221,000 | 75,000 | 0 | 40,000 | 0 | 2,801,115 | Larson Design |
| Biglerville | 13 | B | 2,651,203 | 2,217,771 | 13,428 | 165.16 | 198,320 | 33,000 | 202,112 | 28,000 | 0 | 0 | 0 | 2,651,203 | Murphy & Dittenhafer |
| Cresco | 7 | M | 2,699,184 | 2,244,834 | 7,800 | 287.80 | 216,719 | 90,000 | 147,631 | 2,329 | 0 | 60,000 | 717,940 | 1,921,244 | Robert Strunk |
| Intercourse | 20 | M | 1,350,000 | 989,000 | 8,600 | 115.00 | 11,000 | 285,000 | 65,000 | 40,000 | 0 | 0 | 350,000 | 1,000,000 | S. E. Smoker |
| *Rhode Island* | | | | | | | | | | | | | | | |
| Harrisville | 16 | M | 9,343,079 | 5,544,467 | 24,900 | 222.67 | 431,183 | 2,337,498 | 1,029,931 | 87,060 | 372,000 | 335,000 | 7,686,079 | 950,000 | Newport Collaborative |
| *Tennessee* | | | | | | | | | | | | | | | |
| Sparta | 25 | M | 1,862,831 | 1,260,000 | 15,000 | 84.00 | 462,163 | 75,000 | 65,668 | 4,440 | 80,483 | 100,000 | 1,003,416 | 678,932 | Stamps Design Group |
| *Texas* | | | | | | | | | | | | | | | |
| Arlington | 61 | B | 3,420,000 | 1,880,000 | 11,200 | 167.86 | 1,125,800 | Owned | 414,200 | 5,418 | 0 | 0 | 3,280,000 | 140,000 | PETRELLI assocs. |
| Haskell | 6 | M | 995,000 | 568,849 | 5,960 | 95.44 | 294,163 | Owned | 131,988 | 10,000 | 0 | 0 | 25,000 | 970,000 | Cadco Architects |
| Houston | 39 | B | 8,172,000 | 5,050,000 | 20,400 | 247.55 | 1,151,000 | 1,000,000 | 971,000 | 4,959 | 0 | 0 | 6,972,000 | 1,200,000 | Jackson & Ryan |
| Irving | 34 | B | 4,242,685 | 3,497,125 | 26,000 | 134.50 | 295,560 | Owned | 450,000 | 85,000 | 0 | 0 | 4,242,685 | 0 | PSA-Dewberry |
| Rockwall | 72 | M | 12,339,225 | 9,600,000 | 52,000 | 184.62 | 600,000 | 900,000 | 1,239,225 | 150,000 | 0 | 0 | 11,939,225 | 400,000 | PSA-Dewberry |
| San Antonio | 58 | B | 5,495,100 | 3,678,083 | 16,000 | 229.88 | 407,609 | Owned | 1,409,408 | 58,000 | 0 | 0 | 5,095,100 | 400,000 | Rehler Vaughn Koone |
| Waco | 31 | B | 1,967,666 | 1,639,285 | 11,200 | 146.36 | 127,879 | 159,430 | 41,072 | 68,000 | 0 | 0 | 459,669 | 1,507,997 | Rogers Company |
| *Virginia* | | | | | | | | | | | | | | | |
| Burke | 58 | B | 10,750,000 | 5,651,389 | 16,720 | 338.00 | 595,000 | 3,302,000 | 1,201,611 | 75,000 | 0 | 0 | 10,750,000 | 0 | Grimm + Parker |
| Fairfax | 68 | B | 20,002,092 | 13,053,833 | 43,886 | 297.45 | 1,605,714 | Owned | 5,342,545 | 220,000 | 0 | 0 | 20,002,092 | 0 | Lukmire Partnership |
| Oakton | 29 | B | 7,845,000 | 5,247,700 | 17,304 | 303.27 | 535,800 | 1,340,000 | 721,500 | 75,000 | 0 | 0 | 6,665,000 | 1,180,000 | PSA-Dewberry |
| *Washington* | | | | | | | | | | | | | | | |
| St. John | 1 | B | 627,775 | 557,913 | 3,200 | 174.35 | 4,862 | Owned | 65,000 | 360 | 0 | 0 | 500,000 | 127,775 | zimmerraystudios |
| *Wyoming* | | | | | | | | | | | | | | | |
| Cheyenne | 86 | MS | 25,466,154 | 16,487,286 | 103,000 | 160.07 | 2,879,520 | 3,276,620 | 2,822,728 | 27,258 | 0 | 230,615 | 24,066,434 | 1,169,105 | Anderson Mason… |

Symbol Code: B=Branch Library; BS=Branch and System Headquarters; M=Main Library; MS=Main and System Headquarters; S=System Headquarters; O=combined use space; n.a.=not available

## Table 5 / Public Library Buildings, Additions and Renovations, 2008

| Community | Pop ('000) | Code | Project Cost | Constr. Cost | Gross Sq. Ft. | Sq. Ft. Cost | Equip. Cost | Site Cost | Other Costs | Volumes | Federal Funds | State Funds | Local Funds | Gift Funds | Architect |
|---|---|---|---|---|---|---|---|---|---|---|---|---|---|---|---|
| *Arizona* | | | | | | | | | | | | | | | |
| Cave Creek | 5 | M | $3,426,348 | $2,958,848 | 19,300 | $153.31 | $216,000 | Owned | $251,500 | 80,000 | 0 | 0 | $40,000 | $3,386,348 | Hidell & Assocs. |
| Phoenix | 82 | B | 2,820,000 | 1,510,000 | 10,500 | 143.81 | 978,000 | Owned | 332,000 | 71,805 | 0 | 0 | 2,820,000 | 0 | Durkin+Durkin |
| *Arkansas* | | | | | | | | | | | | | | | |
| Gentry | 7 | M | 1,583,081 | 1,218,081 | 11,970 | 101.76 | 50,000 | $120,000 | 195,000 | 34,080 | 0 | 10,000 | 1,083,081 | 493,718 | Marlon Blackwell |
| *California* | | | | | | | | | | | | | | | |
| Anaheim | 25 | O | 3,404,790 | 2,768,925 | 10,546 | 262.56 | 295,081 | Owned | 340,784 | 50,000 | 0 | 0 | 3,369,790 | 35,000 | Robert Borders |
| Beaumont | 52 | M | 845,000 | 740,000 | 3,800 | 194.74 | 20,000 | Owned | 85,000 | 480 | 50,000 | 0 | 780,000 | 15,000 | JLP Archs./ James Pirdy |
| Calipatria | 8 | B | 197,293 | 178,010 | 854 | 208.45 | 9,500 | Leased | 9,783 | 41 | 0 | 0 | 0 | 197,293 | Sanders, Inc. |
| Mountain House | 7 | B | 580,265 | 43,200 | 5,400 | 8.00 | 296,427 | Leased | 240,638 | 20,000 | 0 | 0 | 580,265 | 0 | Huff Construction |
| Orangevale | 25 | B | 281,000 | 180,000 | 1,200 | 150.00 | 66,192 | Leased | 34,808 | 34,000 | 0 | 0 | 281,000 | 0 | Sacramento Cty. Svcs. |
| Palo Alto | 62 | B | 4,147,381 | 3,172,776 | 6,043 | 525.03 | 402,080 | Owned | 572,525 | 37,000 | 357,217 | 0 | 2,205,075 | 1,585,089 | Architectural Resources |
| San Francisco | 22 | B | 6,207,318 | 4,197,799 | 6,069 | 688.62 | 500,000 | Owned | 1,509,519 | 2,026 | 0 | 0 | 5,707,318 | 500,000 | Carey & Co. |
| San Francisco | 43 | B | 4,893,500 | 2,963,240 | 8,000 | 370.41 | 500,000 | Owned | 1,430,260 | 4,338 | 0 | 0 | 4,348,500 | 545,000 | SF Bureau of Arch. |
| San Francisco | 20 | B | 4,424,500 | 2,822,923 | 7,633 | 369.83 | 500,000 | Owned | 1,101,577 | 35,000 | 0 | 0 | 3,924,500 | 500,000 | TomEliotFisch; Field Paoli |
| *Colorado* | | | | | | | | | | | | | | | |
| Colorado Springs | 20 | B | 1,209,276 | 973,881 | 4,909 | 198.39 | 117,208 | Owned | 118,187 | 23,000 | 0 | 399,583 | 592,549 | 403,102 | Gifford Spurck |
| *Connecticut* | | | | | | | | | | | | | | | |
| Hartford | 1,000 | MS | 42,000,000 | 33,000,000 | 37,750 | 874.17 | 4,500,000 | Owned | 4,500,000 | 409,900 | 321,000 | 500,000 | 37,000,000 | 4,179,000 | FHCM•S; Sevigny Archs. |
| Wallingford | 45 | M | 12,565,000 | 9,898,000 | 67,000 | 147.73 | 913,400 | 300,000 | 1,453,600 | 265,000 | 0 | 500,000 | 11,065,000 | 1,000,000 | Tuthill & Wells |
| West Hartford | 61 | M | 10,007,500 | 7,993,970 | 59,961 | 133.32 | 907,500 | Owned | 1,106,030 | 205,000 | 325,000 | 500,000 | 8,000,500 | 1,182,000 | Tuthill & Wells |
| *Delaware* | | | | | | | | | | | | | | | |
| Hockessin | 32 | B | 8,500,000 | 5,284,897 | 25,000 | 211.40 | 594,530 | Owned | 2,620,573 | 82,000 | 0 | 3,521,000 | 4,413,286 | 813,791 | ikon.5 Architects |
| *Florida* | | | | | | | | | | | | | | | |
| Lakeland | 35 | B | 472,888 | 231,010 | 4,525 | 51.05 | 153,297 | Leased | 88,581 | 8,000 | 0 | 0 | 472,888 | 0 | Furr & Wegman |
| Lighthouse Point | 11 | M | 1,180,227 | 739,926 | 8,200 | 90.23 | 217,562 | 137,739 | 85,000 | 49,263 | 0 | 285,000 | 190,400 | 704,827 | Cubellis |
| Wellington | 57 | B | 7,506,504 | 6,250,000 | 29,981 | 208.46 | 902,304 | Owned | 354,200 | 174,000 | 0 | 500,000 | 7,006,504 | 0 | Slattery & Assocs. |

Symbol Code: B=Branch Library; BS=Branch and System Headquarters; M=Main Library; MS=Main and System Headquarters; O=combined use space; n.a.=not available

| Location | | Code | | | | | | | Owned/Leased | | | | | | | Architect |
|---|---|---|---|---|---|---|---|---|---|---|---|---|---|---|---|---|
| **Illinois** | | | | | | | | | | | | | | | | |
| Evanston | 74 | M | 2,397,809 | 1,723,213 | 21,140 | 81.51 | 246,520 | Owned | 428,076 | 4,073 | 0 | 200,000 | 1,347,809 | 850,000 | | Nagle Hartray Danker… |
| Evergreen Park | 21 | M | 3,830,255 | 3,303,000 | 23,350 | 141.45 | 192,222 | Owned | 335,033 | 70,000 | 0 | 317,633 | 3,437,622 | 75,000 | | PSA-Dewberry |
| Hinsdale | 18 | M | 3,537,000 | 2,715,000 | 32,360 | 83.90 | 245,000 | Owned | 577,000 | 124,370 | 0 | 0 | 3,292,000 | 245,000 | | PSA-Dewberry |
| Lisle | 30 | M | 1,620,000 | 1,300,000 | 20,000 | 65.00 | 200,000 | Owned | 120,000 | 160,000 | 0 | 0 | 1,618,000 | 2,000 | | LZT/Fillung Archs. |
| Palos Hills | 32 | M | 6,425,546 | 5,425,366 | 30,696 | 176.75 | 507,445 | Owned | 492,735 | 66,555 | 0 | 39,144 | 6,346,402 | 40,000 | | Gilfillan Callahan Nelson |
| **Indiana** | | | | | | | | | | | | | | | | |
| Auburn | n/a | S | 571,000 | 390,000 | 4,936 | 79.01 | 50,000 | 75,000 | 56,000 | n/a | 0 | 0 | 285,500 | 285,500 | | WKM & Assocs. |
| Muncie | 74 | B | 2,237,146 | 2,020,146 | 17,000 | 118.83 | 65,000 | Owned | 152,000 | 100,000 | 0 | 1,900,000 | 350,000 | 0 | | Woollen Molzan… |
| **Maryland** | | | | | | | | | | | | | | | | |
| Baltimore | 33 | B | 5,300,000 | 3,000,000 | 9,500 | 315.79 | 500,000 | Owned | 1,800,000 | 25,000 | 0 | 250,000 | 3,300,000 | 2,000,000 | | Alexander Design |
| Rosedale/Baltimore | 47 | B | 1,026,713 | 768,687 | 2,588 | 297.02 | 167,938 | Owned | 90,088 | 1,607 | 112,500 | | 401,596 | 262,617 | | James Bradberry |
| **Massachusetts** | | | | | | | | | | | | | | | | |
| Chariton | 15 | M | 7,202,174 | 6,084,523 | 27,000 | 225.35 | 418,374 | Owned | 699,277 | 6,740 | 0 | 2,413,314 | 3,625,000 | 1,163,860 | | J. Stewart Roberts |
| Falmouth | 32 | M | 11,122,175 | 7,715,000 | 37,000 | 208.51 | 1,000,000 | Owned | 2,407,175 | 10,845 | 0 | 3,071,749 | 7,050,426 | 1,000,000 | | Beacon Architectural |
| Georgetown | 8 | M | 4,157,460 | 3,518,223 | 18,000 | 195.46 | 88,543 | Owned | 550,694 | 6,015 | 1,644,694 | 0 | 2,400,000 | 144,500 | | Beacon Architectural |
| North Brookfield | 5 | M | 4,236,890 | 3,472,734 | 12,662 | 274.26 | 181,519 | Owned | 582,637 | 32,895 | 0 | 1,257,173 | 2,754,337 | 225,380 | | J. Stewart Roberts |
| Wendell | 1 | M | 1,818,933 | 1,248,497 | 4,200 | 297.26 | 50,000 | 270,685 | 249,751 | 1,822 | 0 | 1,015,092 | 773,841 | 30,000 | | Margo Jones Archs. |
| **Michigan** | | | | | | | | | | | | | | | | |
| Petersburg | 4 | O | 625,000 | 445,000 | 4,000 | 111.25 | 130,000 | Owned | 50,000 | 30,000 | 0 | 0 | 625,000 | 5,000 | | David Arthur |
| Saline | 25 | M | 5,539,488 | 4,278,679 | 33,000 | 129.66 | 593,988 | Owned | 666,821 | 200,000 | 0 | 0 | 5,615,142 | 122,517 | | Michael F. Pogliano |
| **Minnesota** | | | | | | | | | | | | | | | | |
| West St. Paul | 37 | B | 1,059,727 | 598,304 | 8,000 | 74.79 | 370,102 | Owned | 91,321 | 119,306 | 0 | 277,793 | 781,934 | 0 | | Perkins & Will |
| **Mississippi** | | | | | | | | | | | | | | | | |
| Eupora | 10 | O | 167,216 | 102,187 | 3,850 | 26.54 | 36,361 | Owned | 28,668 | 9,500 | 0 | 125,412 | 41,804 | 0 | | BelindaStewart |
| **Missouri** | | | | | | | | | | | | | | | | |
| Carthage | 14 | M | 4,500,000 | 3,854,652 | 22,464 | 171.59 | 250,000 | Owned | 395,348 | 7,908 | 0 | 0 | 2,500,000 | 2,000,000 | | Gould Evans |
| Kansas City | 428 | MS | 3,800,000 | 3,018,000 | 17,000 | 177.53 | 195,000 | Owned | 587,000 | n.a. | 0 | 0 | 0 | 3,800,000 | | ASAI Architecture |
| Kansas City | 605 | MS | 700,000 | 463,830 | 9,868 | 47.00 | 126,000 | Owned | 110,170 | 2,032 | 0 | 0 | 0 | 700,000 | | Helix Architecture |
| **Nebraska** | | | | | | | | | | | | | | | | |
| Grand Island | 44 | M | 8,636,518 | 4,955,687 | 48,852 | 101.44 | 709,432 | 1,789,896 Leased | 1,181,503 | 160,000 | 0 | 0 | 7,000,000 | 1,636,518 | | Cannon Moss/Durrant |
| **Nevada** | | | | | | | | | | | | | | | | |
| Las Vegas | 21 | B | 1,254,491 | 641,836 | 5,740 | 111.82 | 512,335 | Leased | 100,320 | 137,278 | 0 | 200,000 | 1,054,491 | 0 | | Winston Henderson |

Symbol Code: B=Branch Library; BS=Branch and System Headquarters; M=Main Library; MS=Main and System Headquarters; S=System Headquarters; O=combined use space; n.a.=not available

Table 5 / Public Library Buildings, Additions and Renovations, 2008 (cont.)

| Community | Pop ('000) | Code | Project Cost | Constr. Cost | Gross Sq. Ft. | Sq. Ft. Cost | Equip. Cost | Site Cost | Other Costs | Volumes | Federal Funds | State Funds | Local Funds | Gift Funds | Architect |
|---|---|---|---|---|---|---|---|---|---|---|---|---|---|---|---|
| *New Jersey* | | | | | | | | | | | | | | | |
| Old Tappan | 6 | M | $1,757,000 | $1,450,000 | 11,875 | $122.11 | $42,000 | Owned | $265,000 | 60,000 | 0 | 0 | $1,427,000 | $330,000 | Arcari + Iovino |
| Shrewsbury | 170 | B | 10,915,000 | 8,765,000 | 45,000 | 194.78 | 1,100,000 | Owned | 1,050,000 | 295,000 | 0 | $1,365,000 | 9,550,000 | 0 | Thomas Assocs. |
| *New Mexico* | | | | | | | | | | | | | | | |
| Belen | 21 | M | 2,467,516 | 2,052,516 | 17,800 | 115.31 | 256,000 | Owned | 159,000 | 40,000 | 0 | 1,405,250 | 1,062,266 | 0 | Molzen-Corbin |
| *New York* | | | | | | | | | | | | | | | |
| Cutchogue | 3 | M | 3,126,264 | 2,423,861 | 12,261 | 197.68 | 277,733 | Owned | 424,670 | 4,345 | 0 | 121,825 | 2,741,939 | 262,500 | Nemschick Silverman |
| East Meadow | 52 | M | 313,028 | 232,281 | 1,400 | 165.92 | 57,519 | Owned | 23,228 | 600 | 0 | 80,963 | 202,773 | 29,292 | LAS Associates |
| Lyons | 7 | M | 2,290,902 | 1,950,703 | 12,994 | 150.12 | 40,877 | Owned | 299,322 | 2,970 | 0 | 348,484 | 1,783,898 | 158,520 | Holmes, King, Kallquist |
| Merrick* | 23 | B | 507,214 | 468,714 | 2,500 | 187.49 | 0 | Owned | 38,500 | n/a | 0 | 0 | 507,214 | 0 | Holzmacher McLendon... |
| Scarsdale | 18 | M | 345,870 | 266,250 | 3,360 | 79.24 | 44,670 | Owned | 34,950 | 846 | 0 | 0 | 0 | 345,870 | Arcari + Iovino |
| *North Dakota* | | | | | | | | | | | | | | | |
| Dickinson | 24 | M | 3,756,600 | 3,043,552 | 24,200 | 125.76 | 500,000 | Owned | 213,048 | 130,000 | 0 | 0 | 500,000 | 3,256,600 | Hulsing & Assocs. |
| *Ohio* | | | | | | | | | | | | | | | |
| Brunswick | 45 | B | 7,385,743 | 4,451,439 | 39,000 | 114.14 | 1,240,408 | Leased | 1,693,896 | 12,700 | 0 | 0 | 7,371,958 | 13,785 | David Milling Archs. |
| Cincinnati | 18 | B | 778,244 | 497,070 | 12,000 | 41.42 | 217,038 | Leased | 64,136 | 70,000 | 0 | 0 | 0 | 778,244 | K4 Architecture |
| Cincinnati | 860 | M | 1,799,694 | 1,068,332 | 225,000 | 4.75 | 331,610 | Owned | 399,752 | 487,872 | 0 | 1,799,694 | 0 | 0 | GBBN Architects |
| Lakewood | 57 | MS | 17,500,000 | 13,421,000 | 44,019 | 304.89 | 1,200,000 | Owned | n/a | 320,800 | 0 | 2,733,000 | 14,767,000 | 0 | R.A.M. Stern; CBLH |
| Medina | 47 | MS | 20,802,417 | 13,359,378 | 75,000 | 178.13 | 2,705,896 | Owned | 4,737,143 | 38,700 | 0 | 0 | 20,673,683 | 128,734 | David Milling Archs. |
| Perry | 9 | M | 1,915,821 | 1,629,914 | 18,410 | 88.53 | 104,918 | Owned | 180,989 | 5,151 | 0 | 0 | 1,915,821 | 0 | Ziska Architecture |
| South Charleston | 2 | B | 1,175,000 | 895,000 | 5,000 | 179.00 | 87,000 | $94,000 | 99,000 | 27,000 | 0 | 0 | 1,159,000 | 16,000 | MKC Associates |
| Upper Sandusky | 11 | M | 54,582 | 49,620 | 14,700 | 3.38 | 0 | Owned | 4,962 | n/a | 0 | 0 | 54,582 | 0 | Joseph Bolish |
| *Oregon* | | | | | | | | | | | | | | | |
| Sumpter | 170 | B | 40,153 | 24,438 | 707 | 34.57 | 15,715 | Leased | 0 | 3,120 | 0 | 0 | 24,203 | 15,950 | none reported |
| Waldport | 5 | M | 230,076 | 208,000 | 3,156 | 65.91 | 16,840 | Owned | 5,236 | 2,046 | 0 | 0 | 85,940 | 144,136 | Mark A. Seder |
| *Pennsylvania* | | | | | | | | | | | | | | | |
| Mcmurray | 18 | M | 1,035,308 | 818,030 | 4,814 | 169.93 | 90,975 | Owned | 126,303 | 50,000 | 0 | 500,000 | 0 | 535,308 | Ross Schonder... |

* The Historic Merrick Library underwent renovations following significant fire damage, but efforts were made to restore the building's original 1880s features in an ecofriendly way.

Symbol Code: B=Branch Library; BS=Branch and System Headquarters; M=Main Library; MS=Main and System Headquarters; S=System Headquarters; O=combined use space; n.a.=not available

| Location | # | Code | | | | | | | | | | | | | | Architect |
|---|---|---|---|---|---|---|---|---|---|---|---|---|---|---|---|---|
| *South Carolina* | | | | | | | | | | | | | | | | |
| Greenville | 36 | B | 760,837 | 479,266 | 12,050 | 39.77 | 169,001 | Owned | 112,570 | 6,608 | 0 | 0 | 0 | 760,837 | 0 | Craig Gaulden Davis |
| Irmo | 48 | B | 165,100 | 40,034 | 2,300 | 17.41 | 109,933 | Leased | 15,133 | 7,500 | 0 | 0 | 23,825 | 11,427 | 129,848 | CDA Architects |
| *South Dakota* | | | | | | | | | | | | | | | | |
| Hudson | 1 | O | 24,485 | 493 | 114 | 4.32 | 992 | 23,000 | | 483 | 0 | 0 | 0 | 23,823 | 662 | none |
| *Texas* | | | | | | | | | | | | | | | | |
| Austin | 42 | B | 1,012,673 | 536,366 | 11,056 | 48.51 | 48,210 | Owned | 386,588 | 90,000 | 0 | 0 | 0 | 1,012,673 | 0 | O'Connell Robertson... |
| Austin | 45 | B | 680,575 | 545,776 | 14,500 | 37.64 | 21,579 | Owned | 113,220 | 7,100 | 0 | 0 | 0 | 680,575 | 0 | The Lawrence Group |
| Bastrop | 25 | M | 2,848,434 | 2,260,834 | 19,800 | 114.18 | 372,600 | Owned | 215,000 | 50,000 | 0 | 0 | 0 | 2,463,434 | 385,000 | Hidell & Assocs. |
| Fort Worth | 20 | B | 4,350,000 | 3,500,000 | 12,590 | 278.00 | 377,150 | Owned | 445,750 | 26,000 | 4,350,000 | 0 | 0 | 0 | 0 | Dennehy Architects |
| Hidalgo | 14 | M | 600,921 | 522,321 | 4,934 | 105.86 | 40,200 | Owned | 38,400 | 20,000 | 367,556 | 0 | 0 | 178,365 | 55,000 | EGV Architects |
| Highland Park | 14 | MS | 2,500,000 | 2,070,000 | 5,800 | 356.90 | 150,000 | Owned | 280,000 | 766 | 0 | 0 | 0 | 0 | 2,500,000 | Komatsu Architecture |
| Houston | 2,229 | O | 155,000 | 80,000 | 450 | 177.78 | 50,000 | Leased | 25,000 | 366 | 0 | 0 | 0 | 155,000 | 0 | mArchitects |
| Houston | 65 | O | 1,582,000 | 750,000 | 3,636 | 206.27 | 716,000 | Owned | 116,000 | 72 | 0 | 0 | 0 | 1,582,000 | 0 | mArchitects |
| Houston | 2,229 | B | 19,286,000 | 13,825,000 | 268,663 | 51.46 | 2,619,000 | Owned | 2,842,000 | 53,844 | 0 | 0 | 0 | 19,286,000 | 0 | Prozign Architects |
| Plano | 35 | B | 437,938 | 284,181 | 10,000 | 28.42 | 84,757 | Owned | 69,000 | 9,484 | 0 | 0 | 0 | 437,938 | 0 | PSA-Dewberry |
| Plano | 44 | MS | 405,273 | 233,716 | 10,000 | 23.37 | 102,557 | Owned | 69,000 | 21,645 | 0 | 0 | 0 | 405,273 | 0 | PSA-Dewberry |
| San Antonio | 140 | B | 1,625,000 | n/a | 5,252 | n/a | 0 | Owned | n/a | 25,000 | 0 | 0 | 0 | 40,000 | 1,585,000 | Arizpe Group; Shows |
| *Virginia* | | | | | | | | | | | | | | | | |
| Danville | 18 | B | 111,148 | 2,927 | 2,250 | 1.32 | 59,362 | Leased | 48,859 | 10,000 | 0 | 0 | 52,874 | 52,408 | 5,866 | none |
| Fishersville | 71 | M | 1,166,165 | 950,446 | 6,105 | 155.68 | 120,700 | Owned | 95,019 | 65,000 | 0 | 0 | 0 | 1,161,028 | 5,137 | Frazier Associates |
| Floyd | 15 | B | 1,573,675 | 1,170,465 | 11,883 | 98.50 | 246,799 | Owned | 156,411 | 60,000 | 0 | 0 | 0 | 1,035,000 | 600,000 | Thompson & Litton |
| Haysi | 8 | O | 279,979 | 96,425 | 3,200 | 30.13 | 20,406 | Owned | 1,148 | 1,497 | 0 | 0 | 11,208 | 66,177 | 202,594 | Thompson & Litton |
| *Washington* | | | | | | | | | | | | | | | | |
| Seattle | 72 | B | 7,049,907 | 5,148,067 | 15,000 | 343.20 | 465,910 | Owned | 834,375 | 66,700 | 0 | 0 | 0 | 7,032,250 | 18,000 | Miller Hayashi Archs. |
| Seattle | 27 | B | 1,067,534 | 787,480 | 7,931 | 99.99 | 86,127 | Owned | 193,927 | 37,000 | 0 | 0 | 0 | 992,534 | 75,000 | Hoshide Williams |
| Seattle | 23 | B | 1,273,910 | 954,191 | 8,140 | 117.22 | 93,977 | Owned | 225,742 | 40,000 | 0 | 0 | 0 | 1,150,361 | 123,549 | Hoshide Williams |
| Seattle | 10 | B | 1,145,110 | 926,082 | 1,707 | 542.52 | 92,949 | Owned | 126,079 | 15,000 | 0 | 0 | 0 | 1,120,110 | 25,000 | Heliotrope Architects |
| Seattle | 19 | B | 4,512,000 | 3,250,000 | 7,800 | 416.67 | 112,000 | Owned | 1,150,000 | 21,000 | 0 | 0 | 0 | 4,497,000 | 15,000 | SHKS Architects |
| *Wisconsin* | | | | | | | | | | | | | | | | |
| Marinette | 45 | MS | 4,044,339 | 3,044,116 | 22,000 | 138.37 | 612,711 | Owned | 387,512 | 200,000 | 206,000 | 0 | 0 | 2,000,000 | 1,850,000 | Frye Gillan Molinaro |

Symbol Code: B=Branch Library; BS=Branch and System Headquarters; M=Main Library; MS=Main and System Headquarters; S=System Headquarters; O=combined use space; n.a.=not available

Table 6 / Public Library Buildings, Six-Year Cost Summary

| | Fiscal 2003 | Fiscal 2004 | Fiscal 2005 | Fiscal 2006 | Fiscal 2007 | Fiscal 2008 |
|---|---|---|---|---|---|---|
| Number of new buildings | 103 | 99 | 91 | 81 | 82 | 95 |
| Number of ARRs* | 92 | 102 | 94 | 79 | 86 | 88 |
| Sq. ft. new buildings | 2,340,374 | 3,178,027 | 2,349,670 | 2,050,087 | 2,245,929 | 2,235,854 |
| Sq. ft. ARRs | 1,725,902 | 2,096,243 | 1,530,382 | 1,505,326 | 2,300,619 | 1,782,204 |
| *New Buildings* | | | | | | |
| Construction cost | $420,486,065 | $655,261,309 | $420,241,028 | $421,856,723 | $491,240,609 | $539,109,943 |
| Equipment cost | 51,738,413 | 72,422,017 | 57,152,920 | 51,541,695 | 60,666,368 | 73,468,236 |
| Site cost | 30,095,454 | 30,873,801 | 43,892,631 | 43,897,019 | 37,089,067 | 36,331,029 |
| Other cost | 69,981,113 | 157,419,044 | 75,384,007 | 90,240,356 | 105,271,399 | 86,508,406 |
| Total—Project cost | 573,531,535 | 916,026,171 | 596,670,586 | 611,502,793 | 705,543,661 | 736,767,614 |
| ARRs—Project cost | 263,624,575 | 326,410,267 | 235,915,173 | 293,982,768 | 426,681,990 | 334,871,847 |
| New and ARR Project cost | $837,156,110 | $1,242,436,438 | $832,585,759 | $905,485,561 | $1,132,225,651 | $1,071,639,461 |
| *Fund Sources* | | | | | | |
| Federal, new buildings | $9,106,615 | $3,765,492 | $3,657,196 | $9,733,136 | $9,701,152 | $6,797,857 |
| Federal, ARRs | 6,482,225 | 6,202,088 | 3,692,293 | 4,150,883 | 2,971,210 | 7,733,967 |
| Federal, total | $15,588,840 | $9,967,580 | $7,349,489 | $13,884,019 | $12,672,362 | $14,531,824 |
| State, new buildings | $18,465,123 | $115,846,277 | $28,458,752 | $26,218,139 | $65,941,808 | $47,484,015 |
| State, ARRs | 16,090,024 | 24,889,690 | 12,816,996 | 28,803,122 | 23,951,016 | 25,725,016 |
| State, total | $34,555,147 | $140,735,967 | $41,275,748 | $55,021,261 | $89,892,824 | $73,209,031 |
| Local, new buildings | $507,445,956 | $703,245,493 | $537,391,416 | $534,202,531 | $560,754,782 | $619,928,229 |
| Local, ARRS | 207,977,217 | 237,027,037 | 193,115,934 | 236,808,805 | 369,691,281 | 258,453,050 |
| Local, total | 715,423,173 | 940,272,530 | 730,507,350 | 771,011,336 | 930,446,063 | 878,381,279 |
| Gift, new buildings | $39,094,374 | $93,284,817 | $27,464,751 | $43,422,990 | $71,784,153 | $62,835,806 |
| Gift, ARRs | 31,972,475 | 58,402,733 | 26,579,726 | 24,780,729 | 31,906,464 | 43,718,655 |
| Gift, total | $71,066,849 | $151,687,550 | $54,044,477 | $68,203,719 | $103,690,617 | $106,554,461 |
| Total funds used | $836,634,009 | $1,242,663,627 | $833,177,064 | $908,120,335 | $1,136,701,866 | $1,072,785,748 |

* ARR: Additions, Renovations, And Remodels

# Expenditures for Resources in
# School Library Media Centers, 2007–2008

Lesley Farmer

Professor of Library Media Technology, California State University, Long Beach

Marilyn Shontz

Associate Professor, School Library Media Program, Rowan University

It was a Dickens of a year for school librarians—the best of times and the worst of times. Although the nation's economy has gone down in flames, we're hoping that the Obama administration will turn things around. *School Library Journal*'s (*SLJ*'s) survey of school expenditures and collections arrives at a time when many media specialists are thinking about ways to improve their programs. To use a cliché, they're busy turning lemons into lemonade. Although our data reflects last year's funding realities (before the recession officially began), it offers insight into what we might expect in the near future. We know the road ahead won't be easy. As one respondent put it, "Next year's survey should be a true test of how schools support their library programs because of the drastic budget cuts that will occur due to depressed local economies."

## Staffing

Despite the recession, the vast majority of media centers around the country have retained their credentialed media specialists. For example, almost 85 percent of elementary schools and more than 95 percent of middle and high schools have a full-time certified librarian (Table 1). While there are still several states that don't require media specialists to earn post-baccalaureate degrees, almost all of them have advanced degrees, most often in library/information science. About a quarter of these library media specialists (LMSs) have earned a master's degree in education, and high school librarians are most likely to have an advanced degree that focuses on librarianship. Almost always, if a full-time media specialist is not present, a half-time professional (either certificated or with a master's degree in librarianship) oversees the library.

In addition, salaries have not declined. While elementary school librarians' salaries remained the same as in 2004–2005 ($48,000, which does not take inflation into account), both middle/junior and high school librarians experienced a median $2,000 raise (to $54,500 and $52,000, respectively), with average salaries gaining $4,000 for middle/junior high librarians (to $56,219) and even more for senior high librarians (to $56,960). The salary range for LMSs is surprisingly wide, probably because some K–8 librarians are supervised by a district media specialist. For those LMSs who work at least 30 hours per week, elementary

Adapted from *School Library Journal*, April 2009.

Table 1 / School Library Media Specialists' Experience, Salary, and Supporting Staff, 2007–2008 by Grade Levels

| | Elementary n=250 | | Middle/Jr. High n=168 | | Senior High n=259 | | K–8, K–12, and Other n=103 | | Total All n=780 | |
|---|---|---|---|---|---|---|---|---|---|---|
| | Median | Mean | Median | Mean | Median | Mean | Median | Mean | Median | Mean |
| Number of media specialists in school | 1.00 | 1.00 | 1.00 | 1.03 | 1.00 | 1.19 | 1.00 | 1.07 | 1.00 | 1.08 |
| Support staff/paid clerks | 0.50 | 0.73 | 1.00 | 0.76 | 1.00 | 0.88 | 0.50 | 0.64 | 0.50 | 0.77 |
| Years experience in K–12 schools | 16 | 18 | 16 | 18 | 18 | 19 | 15 | 17 | 17 | 18 |
| Years experience in library/media | 9 | 11 | 10 | 12 | 12 | 14 | 10 | 11 | 10 | 12 |
| Salary of head media specialist | $48,000 | $47,864 | $54,500 | $56,219 | $52,000 | $56,960 | $42,000 | $44,165 | $50,000 | $52,209 |
| Student assistants | 1.00 | 5.57 | 1.00 | 5.29 | 3.00 | 6.60 | 1.00 | 4.89 | 2.00 | 5.76 |
| Adult volunteers | 1.00 | 3.66 | 0.00 | 2.86 | 0.00 | 2.87 | 1.00 | 3.83 | 0.00 | 3.24 |

school salaries ranged from $15,680 to $113,000, middle/junior high salaries from $13,000 to $120,000, and senior high salaries from $28,000 to $95,000.

Generally, the higher the grade level taught, the greater the number of years of LMS experience. Nevertheless, the mean number of years of school experience has declined from 15 years in 2004–2005 to 12 years in 2007–2008. Furthermore, elementary school and middle/junior high LMSs are now averaging a year less experience (both averaged 19 years in 2004–2005 and 18 years in 2007–2008), with high school librarians averaging three years less experience— from 20 years' experience in 2004–2005 to 17 in our most recent survey. Interestingly, the spread in years of experience is very "flat." Although many observers had predicted there would be a shortage of media specialists—given the high number of those retiring or soon-to-be retiring—the survey's figures seem to belie the expected crisis.

On the other hand, the percentage of library media centers (LMCs) with paraprofessional staff has declined since the 2004–2005 data, from an average of one in 2004–2005 to 0.77 in 2007–2008 (Table 1). Adding the number of full-time and part-time staff, the average number of paid library staff held steady across all grade levels. In elementary schools, such staff are likely to be part-time, and by high school about three-fourths have a full-time paraprofessional. The median number of parent volunteers has also decreased, to practically zero. On a happy note, the number of student volunteers has increased about 20 percent across all grades since 2004–2005, which might correspond to the rise in community service requirements for some schools.

## Budget Constraints

Comparisons between 2007–2008 expenditures and the 2004–2005 figures show consistent decline or stasis except for purchases of CDs and other software,

Table 2 / Comparison of Mean and Median
Expenditures for All Resources, All Funding Sources

|  | Number Responding | | Mean | | Median | |
|---|---|---|---|---|---|---|
|  | 2004–2005 | 2007–2008 | 2004–2005 | 2007–2008 | 2004–2005 | 2007–2008 |
| *Local* | | | | | | |
| Total all local funds | 476 | 742 | $16,599 | $13,715 | $11,000 | $8,600 |
| *Federal* | | | | | | |
| Total all federal funds | 123 | 146 | $6,232 | $5,663 | $3,620 | $2,437 |
| *Gift funds* | | | | | | |
| Total all gift/fundraising | 270 | 403 | $3,599 | $2,800 | $1,308 | $1,200 |
| *Total all funds* | | | | | | |
| Books | 480 | 772 | $10,832 | $9,731 | $7,997 | $6,500 |
| Periodicals | 460 | 668 | $1,366 | $1,032 | $1,000 | $650 |
| AV resources/equipment | 411 | 598 | $2,987 | $2,193 | $1,600 | $1,000 |
| Computer resources/equipment | 372 | 506 | $6,568 | $5,666 | $2,386 | $2,200 |
| Total expenditures | 493 | 777 | $20,029 | $15,614 | $13,591 | $10,283 |

Table 3 / Median Expenditures per School for LMC Resources:
A 10-Year Comparison, 1998–2008

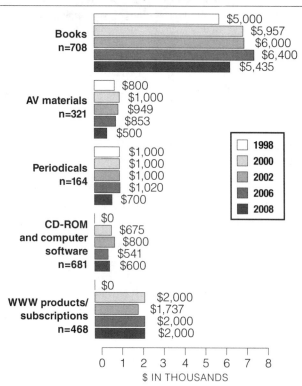

which were 11 percent higher than in 2004–2005 (Tables 2 and 3). While Internet subscriptions held constant at $2,000, the median expenditures for books declined 15 percent to $5,435, AV purchases dropped 41 percent to $500, and periodicals declined 31 percent to $700. Several media specialists in rural areas and in older and smaller schools felt they were negatively affected by budget constraints. Respondents mentioned how districts "took back" library budgets or considered media centers a second priority. Budget cuts did affect technology support.

What are some ways media specialists are trying to cope? They're buying paperbacks instead of hardbacks, writing grants, holding book fairs, increasing interlibrary loan services, depending on public library databases, collaborating with other school districts to leverage purchases, spending more time weeding— and sometimes dipping into their own pockets. "We haven't had a formal library budget since 2001," wrote one middle school media specialist. "We are always thinking 'outside the box' to find ways to fund new technology and new books."

Table 4 / LMC Collection Size and Expenditures by Grade Level, 2007–2008 Local Funds Only

| | Elementary n=250 | | Middle/Jr. High n=168 | | High School n=259 | | Other, K–12, K–8 n=103 | |
|---|---|---|---|---|---|---|---|---|
| | Median | Mean | Median | Mean | Median | Mean | Median | Mean |
| *Collections* | | | | | | | | |
| Size of book collection | 11,000 | 11,852 | 12,267 | 12,913 | 12,868 | 14,985 | 13,000 | 14,899 |
| Number of books per pupil | 24 | 27 | 18 | 19 | 14 | 16 | 14 | 16 |
| Volumes added, 2007–2008 | 400 | 739 | 500 | 650 | 400 | 692 | 500 | 830 |
| Volumes discarded, 2007–2008 | 200 | 471 | 250 | 490 | 300 | 673 | 300 | 482 |
| Combined video/DVD collections | 210 | 254 | 225 | 364 | 348 | 516 | 225 | 383 |
| Number of videos/DVDs per pupil | 0.42 | 0.56 | 0.37 | 0.54 | 0.42 | 0.56 | 0.39 | 0.78 |
| Size of audiotapes/CD collection | 28 | 58 | 28 | 52 | 25 | 60 | 20 | 51 |
| Size of software/CD-ROM collections | 5 | 26 | 1 | 18 | 5 | 12 | 3.00 | 12 |
| *Expenditures* | | | | | | | | |
| Books | $5,500.00 | $7,420.75 | $5,419.00 | $8,213.87 | $5,505.00 | $7,748.87 | $5,005.00 | $11,690.50 |
| Books per pupil | 11.11 | 18.84 | 8.26 | 13.20 | 6.07 | 10.12 | 9.35 | 26.67 |
| Periodicals | 700.00 | 971.87 | 700.00 | 1,052.40 | 670.00 | 1,024.55 | 663.00 | 1,433.46 |
| Periodicals per pupil | 1.54 | 2.35 | 0.87 | 1.81 | 0.71 | 1.31 | 1.33 | 4.28 |
| Audiovisual resources | 500.00 | 1,123.45 | 500.00 | 1,136.65 | 500.00 | 931.61 | 500.00 | 1,302.94 |
| Audiovisual resources per pupil | 1.10 | 2.37 | 0.71 | 1.69 | 0.59 | 1.16 | 0.86 | 4.05 |
| Software and CD-ROM resources | 600.00 | 1,425.00 | 300.00 | 1,190.28 | 949.00 | 1,288.36 | 900.00 | 1,613.07 |
| Software and CD-ROM resources per pupil | 1.33 | 3.58 | 0.44 | 1.80 | 0.60 | 1.42 | 1.01 | 2.81 |
| Online products | 2,550.00 | 4,455.65 | 2,000.00 | 4,724.00 | 1,725.00 | 3,671.53 | 1,500.00 | 5,296.57 |
| Online products per pupil | 5.31 | 11.31 | 2.62 | 6.80 | 1.61 | 4.50 | 3.85 | 30.19 |
| Total materials expenditures (TME) | $8,000.00 | $11,689.20 | $8,550.00 | $12,795.65 | $8,450.00 | $12,314.62 | $8,500.00 | $18,592.16 |
| TME per pupil | $13.96 | $31.03 | $11.58 | $20.15 | $9.04 | $15.42 | $16.2 | $52.86 |

## Collections Remain Static

School library collections have been getting smaller since 2004–2005 (Table 4). The average net gain of books for the 2007–2008 academic year varied from 268 in elementary school libraries to 30 in high school libraries, largely because media specialists weeded out more volumes than in 2004–2005. Interestingly, even though more LMSs got rid of additional items, about 42 percent of respondents stated that 11 percent to 30 percent of their collection was outdated.

On average, elementary and middle schools added fewer than 10 videos and CDs in 2007–2008; even DVD additions only topped at a mean of 23 for high schools. Software collections range from zero to 1,320 (at an elementary school library), but the average collection has fewer than 30 volumes at any site, although that figure reflects a 44 percent increase over 2004–2005 in elementary school libraries and increases of 12 percent in middle/junior schools and 71 percent in high schools.

School libraries continue to purchase electronic subscription databases, but the representative titles have changed since the 2004–2005 report (Table 5). It is likely that budget constraints have prompted librarians to cautiously choose a couple of stable, reputable vendors and leverage funding through joint subscriptions to regional and state databases (the case for half of the respondents).

## Technology Access

Almost all of the respondents have Internet-accessible computers in their media centers. That said, more than 95 percent have some type of filtering or blocking software, such as NetNanny, CyberPatrol, or BSafe. The average number of computers in school libraries rose by grade level—from 10 computers in elementary school media centers to 18 in middle/junior school to 27 in high schools. Similarly, the likelihood that media specialists would manage a computer lab also increased with grade level, and slightly more than half had such responsibilities. It should be noted that the average number of computers in a lab peaked at 34 in middle school, which might reflect more project-based learning or larger class sizes. Oddly, about 10 percent of elementary school libraries still don't have a telephone.

Most schools—a whopping 97.4 percent—have 24/7 online access to their media center's resources. In two-thirds of the cases, the system was installed on a school or district server—and almost 30 percent use a vendor Web-based system, such as Destiny or Athena. In more than 90 percent of these school libraries, students can access an online computer catalog (OPAC). While the median number of OPAC stations in a library is 13, the most likely number of OPAC stations is four. Almost all schools with OPACs permit classroom access and two-thirds enable every classroom to access the databases (Table 6).

It's much more common for a library to have a Web page now than a few years ago. In 2004–2005, 60 percent of all media centers had a home page. Now two-thirds of elementary school libraries and four-fifths of high school libraries have one. About 60 percent of all media specialists manage their library's Web page, regardless of level, while at another 8 percent of elementary schools and 12

Table 5 / Comparison of Electronic Resources Available in LMCs, 2004–2005 and 2007–2008

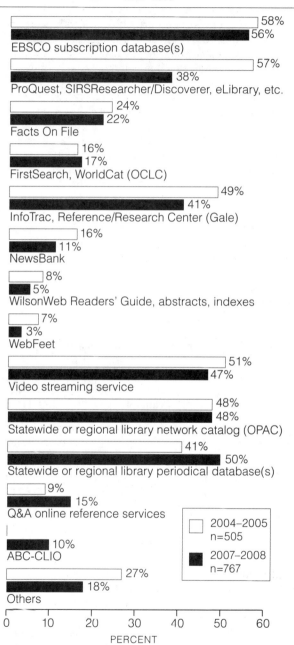

Table 6 / Comparison of Available LMC Technologies,
2004–2005 and 2007–2008

|  | 2004–2005 Percentage responding YES | 2007–2008 Percentage responding YES |
|---|---|---|
| LMC has online library catalog (OPAC) | 92 | 94 |
| LMC has computerized circulation system | 99 | 98 |
| *LMC uses:* | | |
| Cable or satellite TV | 50 | 39 |
| Broadcast TV | 24 | 30 |
| Closed-circuit TV | 31 | 23 |
| Distance education, 1-2 way audio-video | 4 | 6 |
| Distance education, video conferencing | 8 | 7 |
| *LMC has:* | | |
| Telephone | 97 | 96 |
| Local area network | 64 | 59 |
| Wide area network | 67 | 59 |
| Computers with modem | 8 | 3 |
| Wireless network | 38 | 57 |
| Laptop computers on mobile carts | 32 | 31 |
| LMC is member of resource sharing network | 68 | 60 |
| Network is linked electronically | 60 | 55 |
| LMC has online home page | 60 | 75 |
| School or LMC uses filtering software | 98 | 97 |

percent of high schools, the library Web page is managed by technical support personnel.

Surprisingly, technology has not grown substantially since 2005, but the formats have sometimes changed. For instance, broadcast TV has outdistanced cable and closed-circuit TV, but overall availability is down slightly or down by as much as 25 percent. Both LAN and WAN network availability has decreased (from 64 percent to 59 percent for LANs, and from 67 percent to 59 percent for WANs), while WiFi availability has risen to about 50 percent. The evidence overall seems to indicate that media center technology is at a mature stage: used when effective. Not that its priority has been reduced: "Our library/media center is in the process of transitioning to a library/media center of the 21st century and that has been the major push for activities/budget expenses," wrote a middle school media specialist.

## Technology Use

The use of technology for administrative tasks is now the norm, with specific functions such as acquisitions, cataloging, and circulation incorporating technology to about the same degree in 2007–2008 as in 2004–2005 (Table 7). Interlibrary loans at all levels have increased slightly (from 54 percent to 58 percent), possibly owing to fewer acquisitions. Formal library reports are produced by almost 90 percent of respondents, probably reflecting the emphasis on school—and media center—accountability.

**Table 7 / Comparison of Computers Used for Library Administration Tasks, 2004–2005 and 2007–2008**

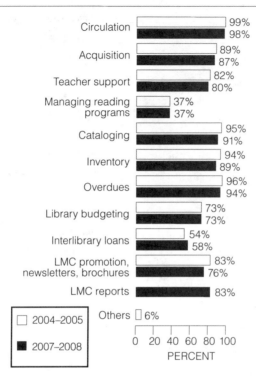

Use of technology by LMSs for teaching and learning has also changed since 2004–2005, reflecting shifts in production emphases, reading strategies, instruction, and communication. Certainly the use of the Internet is dominant—especially e-mail (Table 8). As it becomes increasingly difficult for librarians to find time to interact with their colleagues, e-mail has provided a reliable way for 86 percent of the respondents to keep in touch. Second in popularity, at 85 percent, is Web searching and reference. Most schools take online information in their media centers as a given, and librarians can leverage that by helping students and staff select the most appropriate resources and navigate the Web. Indeed, these services now outrank general information/computer skills instruction, which has fallen by 11 percent to 76 percent. The use of WebQuests and similar Web pages has declined precipitately as well. Interestingly, the use of library reading rooms has dropped almost 50 percent, which may be because that function has been farmed out to other school personnel or is now considered a schoolwide function rather than just the librarian's. On the other hand, the use of technology for book reviews and reading guidance was reported by a majority of librarians, suggesting an increased realization of the positive impact of value-added services.

Some people had great things to say about programs that promote reading at all ages. "We have a very active book club with 90-plus student members and a

**Table 8 / Comparison of Computers Used in LMC Teaching and Learning, 2004–2005 and 2007–2008**

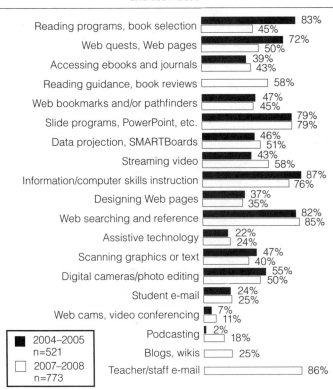

successful coffee shop in the library," reported one media specialist. Tragically, the use of assistive technologies, such as modified keyboards, activation switches, and screen readers, has inched up insignificantly.

## Web 2.0

Current trends may indicate that "traditional" computer instruction is needed less now and that the more interactive, dynamic, skills—such as creating blogs—are more useful. For example, almost one-fifth of the respondents now use podcasts and a quarter use blogs and wikis. In 2004–2005 only a couple of respondents mentioned these Web 2.0 applications. Computer-based photo-editing services have declined, replaced by online photo- and video-sharing, which increased by a quarter of the respondents.

Table 8 also shows that these Web 2.0 resources are incorporated by and large into the teaching and learning aspects of library programs. While use of virtual realities, such as Second Life, remains insignificant, and much controversy still surrounds the educational use of social networks such as Facebook, partici-

Table 9 / LMC Uses of Web 2.0 Resources

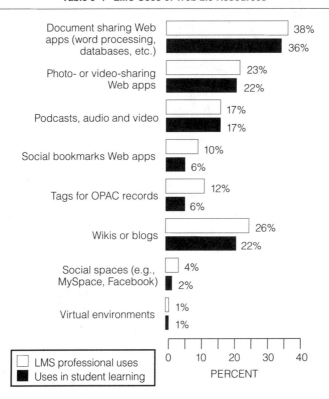

| Resource | LMS professional uses | Uses in student learning |
|---|---|---|
| Document sharing Web apps (word processing, databases, etc.) | 38% | 36% |
| Photo- or video-sharing Web apps | 23% | 22% |
| Podcasts, audio and video | 17% | 17% |
| Social bookmarks Web apps | 10% | 6% |
| Tags for OPAC records | 12% | 6% |
| Wikis or blogs | 26% | 22% |
| Social spaces (e.g., MySpace, Facebook) | 4% | 2% |
| Virtual environments | 1% | 1% |

☐ LMS professional uses
■ Uses in student learning

PERCENT

pation in library-related services such as bookmarking and tagging (which have made library catalogs more responsive) could help make many library programs more relevant.

The main reason for *not* using Web 2.0 resources was the need to train staff and students (58.1 percent), closely followed by software filtering issues (56.5 percent). Running a distant third at 37.8 percent was the fact that many librarians didn't know enough about interactive technologies (for instance, one respondent wrote, "What is 2.0?"). The status of technology and tech support (such as troubleshooting and maintenance) also impacts Web 2.0 incorporation. Only 4 percent of respondents mentioned time or money as a barrier, but several people noted those issues anecdotally. "While we want to use new technologies, no one is yet willing to support former services to allow extensive time to develop and use Web 2.0," explained one librarian. Other respondents asserted that the school district or teachers weren't ready for social networking. In addition, Web 2.0 tends to be more developmentally appropriate for students in higher grades. Nevertheless, Web 2.0 applications constitute a worthy area for LMS self-development and an opportunity to share that new expertise with the rest of the school community.

## Collaboration and Planning

School libraries are open more hours as grade levels increase and scheduling becomes more flexible. About two-thirds of elementary school librarians have fixed schedules, and nearly another third use a combination of fixed and flexible schedules. Middle school librarians flip-flop these percentages: about one-third use a flexible schedule, and two-thirds employ a mixed fixed/flexible schedule. In high schools, 85 percent of media specialists have a flexible schedule, and 11 percent use a combination fixed/flexible schedule.

About half of elementary school librarians, two-thirds of middle school librarians, and almost three-quarters of high school librarians plan regularly with their classroom counterparts. While a smaller percentage of classroom teachers plan with librarians as grade levels increase, the amount of time in formal and informal planning steadily increases with grade level. The message is that the higher the grade level, the more teachers and librarians collaborate, probably because their lessons are more complex and nuanced.

## Conclusions

This new survey data shows that regional differences have largely disappeared. Additionally, the actions of beginning and veteran librarians show little difference in practices, although newer media specialists tend to use more Web 2.0 technologies, and more experienced media specialists subscribe to more databases. Nevertheless, three trends emerged from the current 2007–2008 survey responses:

- School librarians have opted for "lean and clean" collections. Fewer items have been added, and more weeding means less outdated material. Media specialists are subscribing to fewer databases, or at least are being more selective about them.
- "Traditional" library technology has hit a plateau. There are no great plans to add more equipment. Overall, it appears that librarians have reached a mature level of technology use: transcending the novelty and potential of technology to choose effective resources that provide a unique niche for library services built on their specialized knowledge and experience.
- Participatory technology—and participation in general—seems to be the next wave that media specialists need to ride. Web 2.0 offers a wonderful chance for the school community to contribute to the library and the school's knowledge base in general, and the library can emphasize its support of authentic student knowledge production.

The bottom line? Librarians are hunkering down during these lean times, presenting their best face and prioritizing expenditures carefully.

# Book Trade Research and Statistics

## Cutbacks, Consolidations, Takeovers, Layoffs Hit Publishing in 2008

Jim Milliot
Business and News Director, *Publishers Weekly*

It was a wild year for the publishing industry in 2008, and in early 2009 it appeared the disruptions might continue indefinitely.

Two of the industry's most prominent executives, Peter Olson, chairman of Random House, and Jane Friedman, president of HarperCollins, stepped down in the first part of the year.

Olson, who resurfaced as a senior lecturer at Harvard Business School, was succeeded at Random by Markus Dohle who had run Arvato, the printing group of Bertelsmann, which is also the parent company of Random House. Within three months of Dohle's appointment, Random Deputy Chairman Ed Volini resigned.

Meanwhile, Harper's owner, News Corp., promoted Brian Murray to succeed Friedman. Murray then named Michael Morrison and Amanda Barnsley as his top aides. Harper COO Glenn D'Agnes was replaced by Rick Schwartz; D'Agnes would later join Workman.

The departures of Olson and Friedman would turn out to be precursors to major changes at a significant number of publishers during the year. The severe economic downturn in the fall prompted publishers to initiate a wide range of cost-saving measures, ranging from salary freezes to layoffs.

Among the publishers cutting jobs in fall 2008 was Simon & Schuster, which eliminated 34 jobs, 2 percent of its work force. Macmillan cut 64 jobs (including 10 at *Scientific American* magazine), while the religious publisher Thomas Nelson cut 54 people, 10 percent of its staff. Earlier in the year, Nelson had eliminated 60 positions as part of its plan to cut its title output by 50 percent. Nelson's major competitor, Zondervan, reorganized in May, cutting 17 positions, including that of longtime publisher Scott Bolinder, as it worked to streamline its organization.

Independent publishers were not immune to the downturn. Chronicle Books eliminated 10 positions late in 2008, while earlier in the year Bloomsbury cut 7 positions. Rodale eliminated 111 positions across its organization, including about eight jobs in the book group. The company also closed its Modern Times imprint and Editorial Director Leigh Haber left the firm. Macadam/Cage cut several positions and suspended releasing new titles for a period. In Canada, Raincoast Books ended its publishing operation to focus on its distribution business.

In December, six months after his appointment at Random, Dohle announced the framework for a restructuring of the nation's largest trade publisher. The reorganization included the consolidation of the company's five publishing groups into three with the elimination of the Doubleday Broadway Publishing Group and the Bantam Dell Publishing Group. The reorganization resulted in the departure of Irwyn Applebaum, head of Bantam Dell, while Doubleday President Stephen Rubin was in discussions with Dohle for a new position within Random. Although the major reorganization of Random was not expected to take place until early 2009, a total of 16 positions at Doubleday Broadway were eliminated as that group was divided into the Random House and Crown Publishing groups. Earlier in the year, Doubleday closed its Harlem Moon imprint and founder Janet Hill left the company.

Meredith all but exited the book business in 2008. The company pulled back from its plans to expand beyond its traditional cooking and do-it-yourself/home improvement segments early in the year, and just before the close of 2008 signed a licensing agreement with John Wiley giving Wiley the right to publish books based on Meredith's magazines. Overall, Meredith's departure from the book business resulted in the loss of about 100 jobs. The slowdown in the housing market hurt all publishers who target that area. Creative Homeowner cut back its title output and reduced its payroll by approximately $1 million in 2008. Sales at Creative were down by more than 20 percent.

The downsizing at Macmillan was accompanied by the creation of a new children's publishing group at the company, the Macmillan Publishing Children's Group. The new group brought together all of Macmillan's children's publishing lines under the direction of Dan Farley, who also maintained his role as president of Macmillan's Henry Holt imprint. Farley joined Macmillan earlier in the year when John Sterling stepped down as the head of Holt to assume a corporate position with Macmillan. Farley became available as the integration of Houghton Mifflin into Harcourt was completed. Farley, the former head of the Harcourt Trade Group, lost out to Gary Gentel, the president of Houghton Mifflin Trade and Reference, as new head of the combined Houghton Mifflin Harcourt (HMH) Trade Group. The consolidation of those companies involved the closure of Harcourt's San Diego office and the elimination of about 70 jobs. Later in the year, the Houghton Mifflin Harcourt Trade Group cut about another dozen positions and instituted a freeze on acquiring new titles due to slowing sales. Among those leaving the company late in the year was Becky Saletan, who served briefly as senior vice president and publisher of the HMH trade and reference group.

Downsizing wasn't limited to trade and religious publishers. McGraw-Hill Education had two rounds of cuts, eliminating a total of 455 jobs spread across its school group and higher education/professional/international group. The combination of Harcourt and Houghton Mifflin's elementary operations also resulted in widespread layoffs, and although a figure was never announced it was reported that the total reduction was about 700 positions. Scholastic cut its work force by about 300 during the year; an early retirement offer was accepted by 110 employees.

In bookselling circles, over the summer Borders eliminated 274 jobs in its headquarters and distribution centers as part of its effort to turn around the struggling bookstore chain. Earlier, the chain had eliminated eight positions at the vice president and director level.

Some of the country's best-known independent booksellers closed their doors during the year. In California two landmark stores—Cody's and Dutton's—closed, while Olsson's Books closed all five of its stores in the Washington, D.C., area. Among wholesalers, Baker & Taylor eliminated 80 jobs last year. The comics/graphic novel publisher TokyoPop eliminated 19 jobs, while Virgin Comics closed after two years, eliminating eight positions.

The bad news was not limited to downsizing. The giant Canadian publisher Quebecor filed for Chapter 11 bankruptcy in January 2008, but the company continued to operate throughout the year and hoped to emerge from Chapter 11 protection in early 2009. The specialty printer Stinehour Press closed after being unable to find a buyer in the spring. Children's publisher Playmore filed for Chapter 11 in the summer and was struggling to reorganize late in the year. Sports Publishing filed for Chapter 11 and hoped to sell some assets to reduce debt, but no deal had been completed by the end of the year.

On the publishing front, books about Barack Obama proliferated in 2008 as the Illinois senator continued his march to the White House. The surprise selection of Sarah Palin as the Republican vice presidential nominee turned into a boon for the indie house Epicenter; that small Washington State publisher was the only company to have a book about the Alaska governor in print at the time of her selection and was overwhelmed with orders. Eventually Epicenter signed a deal with Tyndale House for that company to take over publication and distribution of the book.

In a similar agreement, Hachette assumed publication of the Christian fiction megaseller *The Shack* and additional titles developed by Windblown Media, a small company formed only about a year earlier.

## Mergers, Acquisitions, Start-Ups

The largest deal in a relatively quiet year for acquisitions was the sale of Bertelsmann's North America Direct Group (parent company of the Bookspan book clubs and Columbia music clubs) to the private investment firm Najafi Companies. The company was renamed Direct Brands.

Amazon made three book-related purchases during the year, acquiring the leading audiobook distributor Audible, Inc. as well as Shelfari and Abebooks. Random House made a couple of acquisitions in 2008, buying the illustrated book publisher Monacelli Press as well as Watson-Guptill. Random's Ballantine division partnered with ESPN for a new imprint.

Among the deals made by independent presses, Chronicle Books purchased the children's publisher Handprint Books, and Sourcebooks acquired Cumberland Press. Publisher of books for infants Softplay, Inc. bought Kidsbooks. Educational Development Corp., distributor of the Usborne book line in the United States, bought the children's publisher Kane-Miller. Keen Communications, parent company of Menasha Ridge Press and Clerisy Press, bought Wilderness Press. The children's publisher Albert Whitman & Company was acquired by two of its executives, John Quattrochi and Patrick McPartland, who took on the roles of president and vice president, respectively.

Macmillan bought the college custom textbook publisher Hayden-McNeil. Rowman & Littlefield Publishing Group acquired Bernan Associates, publisher and distributor of U.S. government publications, and followed that up with the acquisition of the assets of the supplementary publisher Sundance/Newbridge from Haights Cross. Professional and educational publisher SAGE bought CQ Press from Congressional Quarterly. Globe Pequot Press bought the British travel publisher Compass Maps. Audio Holdings acquired fellow audiobook publisher Durkin Hayes. School and library publisher Capstone Publishers acquired Heinemann-Raintree library reference from Pearson. In the fall, ABC-CLIO took over the operation of Greenwood Publishing from Houghton Mifflin Harcourt. Reader's Digest sold its Books Are Fun (BAF) division to BAF founder Earl Kaplan for $17.5 million. Reader's Digest had acquired the display sales company for $380 million.

On the technology front, Firebrand Technologies took over the operations of netGalley, a startup aimed at delivering electronic galleys to reviewers and critics. In wholesaling, Follett acquired the Varsity Group, which uses the Web as an online bookstore for private high schools and small colleges. In need of cash, Borders sold its Australian and New Zealand store group to A&R Whitcoulls.

The tight credit market contributed to the cancellation of a few deals in 2008. The acquisition of Publication International's children's group by toy manufacturer RC2 Corp. was derailed by a lack of funding, while Reed Elsevier canceled the sale of Reed Business Information (parent company of *Publishers Weekly, Library Journal,* and *School Library Journal*) when bids were below expectations.

The worsening economy did not stop some companies from starting new ventures. Bob Miller, longtime president of Hyperion, stepped down to join HarperCollins, where he established HarperStudio, a new imprint that focused on offering authors smaller advances for higher royalties and hoped to sell books on a nonreturnable basis. Reagan Arthur established her own imprint at Little, Brown with plans to publish 15 to 20 books annually. Little, Brown parent Hachette also combined its Orbit and Yen Press imprints into a single imprint, known as Orbit, headed by Tim Holman. BookMasters, the privately held company owned by Dave Wurster, hired distribution veteran Rich Freese to launch a new distribution unit, BookMasters Distribution Services (BDS). The unit's first client was Imagine Publishing, a new publisher started by Charles Nurnberg, former CEO of Sterling Publishing. Imagine will focus on nonfiction adult titles while also having a small children's list. Earlier in the year BookMasters's Atlas Books division acquired Biblio Distribution from National Book Network. Biblio specializes in the distribution of small and micro presses. Kensington Publishing expanded in the African American market, launching the Souls of My Sisters imprint and buying Holloway House Publishing, whose list features classic black crime writers. Blue Mountain Arts, publisher of cards and gift items, started a book division. National Geographic started a photographer imprint, Focal Point. The British firm Octopus Books formed Octopus Books USA and Jonathan Stolper was named associate publisher.

In children's publishing, Christy Ottaviano launched her own eponymous imprint at Henry Holt Books for Young Readers. Donna Bray and Alessandra Balzer went from Hyperion Books for Children to HarperCollins, where they formed the Balzer & Bray imprint. Lisa Holton, former president of Scholastic Trade Publishing, launched Fourth Story Media, a studio that integrates books and the Internet to develop children's properties.

## Issues and Trends

Newspapers and magazines continued to cut back space given to book reviews in 2008. As part of that trend, the two top editors at the *San Francisco Chronicle* accepted buyouts and John McMurtie was appointed to oversee book coverage.

Confronted by a bad economy and dwindling book buyer attendance, North America's two book trade shows faced some tough questions in 2008. BookExpo Canada (BEC) began offering prefabricated booths to attendees in an attempt to lower booth costs and announced plans to launch a consumer-oriented show in the fall. Still, Random House Canada said it would not attend the BEC scheduled for June. In the United States, executives at BookExpo America (BEA) were in discussions with publishers on ways to make the show more effective after the 2008 show in Los Angeles proved a disappointment to many houses. One suggestion under consideration is holding the convention in New York most years. Late in 2008 Macmillan said it would not have a display on the BEA exhibit floor, but would instead take a conference room in a move to control costs.

Two major events in the book search field took place in 2008. Just prior to BEA, Microsoft abruptly announced that it was immediately closing its Book Search program, which it had started several years earlier in a bid to catch up to Google in the search field. (The search programs for both companies scan books into their search engines.) In the fall Google reached an out-of-court settlement with the Authors Guild and the Association of American Publishers, ending three years of litigation. The organizations had filed separate lawsuits against Google in October of 2005 charging that Google's Library Project—which scans copyrighted books held by various libraries without the permission of the rights-holder—involved copyright infringement. The $125 million agreement established a framework allowing Google to continue to scan copyrighted materials with the permission of publishers and authors and also created a new agency, the Book Rights Registry, which will collect and disburse payments made for use of the scanned material by the public.

Another lawsuit that had drawn the attention of the industry came to a conclusion in 2008—J. K. Rowling's copyright infringement suit against RDR Books charging that a lexicon based on Rowling's Harry Potter books being developed by Steve Vander Ark violated Rowling's copyright. After a three-day trial, the judge found in favor of Rowling. RDR dropped its appeal in the fall when RDR reached an agreement with Rowling's representatives to publish a new lexicon that met with the approval of the author.

While the Google and Rowling cases were wrapped up in 2008, a new case began that is likely to last for several years. In May Amazon filed a lawsuit against New York State charging that New York's decision to collect sales tax on items sold in the state was unconstitutional. The question of whether Amazon is required to collect taxes in states where it has no physical presence had been debated almost since the company opened its doors. The issue came to a head in April when New York decided that by buying Amazon products over the Internet, state residents effectively gave Amazon a presence in the state, and therefore Amazon needed to collect sales tax. New York's action was cheered by independent booksellers (as well as Barnes & Noble), who have argued that Amazon's exclusion from charging sales tax gave it an unfair advantage against bricks-and-mortar stores.

New York was also the site of the nation's first "libel tourism" bill, which was enacted following a growing number of libel lawsuits filed against American authors by people in other countries. The Libel Terrorism Protection Act prohibits the enforcement of a foreign libel judgment unless a New York court determines that it satisfies the free speech and free press protections guaranteed by the First Amendment and the New York Constitution.

The American Booksellers Association introduced a new comprehensive marketing program to replace BookSense. IndieBound is designed to take advantage of the growing buy-local movements springing up in communities across the country. In addition to providing materials to promote the concept of buying locally, IndieBound includes information on how booksellers can form buy-local chapters involving all types of independent retailers.

The buy-local movement tapped into another growing trend affecting both the publishing industry and consumers—the green movement. The Book Industry Study Group released the first major study of the industry's impact on the environment. The report found that the use of paper had the most significant negative environmental impact. The report urged publishers and printers to use more recycled paper in the production of books in a bid to reduce the number of new trees needed to meet the production needs of the industry. Finding ways to reduce returns was another recommendation, as transportation of books from publishers to stores and back again was reported to be another major detriment to the environment. Many publishers and printers embraced the report, and some of the largest publishers, including Random House and Scholastic, established goals for increasing the use of recycled paper over the next few years.

At the chain level, Borders opened ten new concept stores that combine books with a host of media and digital products.

Thanks in part to Amazon's November 2007 introduction of its wireless reading device, the Kindle, sales of e-books began to gain traction in 2008. Amazon said demand for the Kindle was stronger than expected in both the 2007 and 2008 holiday season and more than 150,000 titles were available for sale on the Kindle. Sony began offering its e-book Reader through a growing number of retailers, including Target. In November, Sony introduced an upgraded version of the Reader that includes a touch screen and note-taking capabilities.

## People

A couple of Americans moved to Europe in new roles during 2008. Madeline McIntosh left Random House, where she was senior vice president and publisher of the audio publishing and large-print groups, to work for Amazon in Luxembourg. She was succeeded at Random House by Amanda D'Acierno. Chuck Lang, vice president of publishing and marketing at Langenscheidt Publishing, moved to England to become managing director of Harry N. Abrams's British office.

Juan Garcia de Oteyza was named executive director of Aperture. John Owen—cofounder of the international publisher Weldon Owen, which was acquired by the Bonnier Publishing group in 2006—was named group publisher of Bonnier. Karen Rinaldi left Bloomsbury USA to join Rodale, where she was appointed publishing director of its book group. Rinaldi soon hired Colin Dickerman and Pam Krauss as senior vice presidents and publishing directors of the book group. Liz Perl, who had directed the Rodale book operation, resigned and joined Simon & Schuster in a senior marketing post. With Dickerman's departure from Bloomsbury, George Gibson was named to head that house. Former Random House executive David Naggar joined the online media company iAmplify as president. Marcus Leaver was promoted to the top spot at Sterling Publishing early in the year, replacing Charlie Nurnberg. Simon & Schuster named Elinor Hirschhorn to the newly created position of chief digital officer. Will Schwalbe left Hyperion where he was editor-in-chief. Later in the year, following the departure of Bob Miller, Karen Archer was promoted to president of Hyperion. Janet Silver, who left Houghton Mifflin in the integration with Harcourt, was named editor-at-large at Random's Nan Talese imprint. Susan Kamil was named editor-in-chief of Little Random. Marjorie Braman was named editor-in-chief of Henry Holt; she had been an executive editor with HarperCollins. Ken Siman resigned as publisher of Virgin Books USA. Former *Publishers Weekly* publisher David Nudo signed on with Shelfari. After two years with Weinstein Books, Rob Weisbach stepped down.

Changes came at the top at Baker & Taylor in 2008 where Thomas Morgan was named chairman and CEO in July, succeeding Jack Eugster who had taken over those roles from Richard Willis at the beginning of the year. David Cully, who held executive spots at Simon & Schuster and Barnes & Noble, joined Baker & Taylor in the newly created position of executive vice president of merchandising. At Ingram, the company consolidated its Lightning Source and book group into one unit under the direction of Skip Prichard, who was named president of the Ingram Book Group in January. Kirby Best, head of Lightning, stepped down and was replaced by David Taylor. Longtime Barnes & Noble.com CEO Marie Toulantis stepped down at the end of the summer and was not directly replaced. Peter Davis was named president of McGraw-Hill Education, succeeding Henry Hirschberg.

The biggest change in children's publishing was the appointment of Don Weisberg as president of Penguin Young Readers. The former head of Random House sales and an executive vice president there, Weisberg took over from Doug Whiteman, who was promoted to executive vice president of business operations for all of Penguin. Barbara Marcus, longtime head of Scholastic's children's publishing group, was named a strategic advisor to the group. Another of the country's largest children's publishers, Simon & Schuster, saw a change in leadership when President Rick Richter resigned. Regina Griffin, editor-in-chief of Holiday House, was named executive editor of Egmont USA, the new U.S.

children's division of the Swedish-based house. Joanna Cotler, publisher of her own imprint at HarperCollins children's group, stepped down from that role and became editor-at-large. Laura Geringer, who operated her own children's imprint at HarperCollins for 17 years, left the company in the summer. Stephen Roxburgh resigned as publisher of Boyds Mills Press.

Dana Gioia stepped down at the end of the year as chairman of the National Endowment for the Arts (NEA). Under Gioia, NEA released several studies on the decline of reading in America and launched the Big Read initiative to encourage more interest in reading.

## Bestsellers

Stephenie Meyer was the hot author of the year in 2008. The three titles in Meyer's Twilight series all hit the bestsellers list in the year and the books—*Twilight, The Host,* and the newest, *Eclipse,* were the most sought-after books during the holiday shopping season. *The Host* had the longest run of all titles on *Publishers Weekly*'s hardcover fiction list during the year, sitting on the list for 30 weeks. Barack Obama also posted more than one book on the bestsellers list with *The Audacity of Hope* and *Dreams from My Father* remaining on the trade paperback list for 41 and 28 weeks, respectively. Eckhart Tolle, whose *A New Earth* was one of the most popular Oprah selections ever, hit the list for 36 weeks with that title, while his *The Power of Now* made the list for 27 weeks.

By virtue of its size, Random House, as usual, had the most hardcover titles reach the bestsellers list with 88 titles appearing as bestsellers for at least one week. Random's titles, however, stayed on the list for a shorter period of time than in 2007, and as a result the company's share of the hardcover bestsellers list fell from 23.5 percent in 2007 to 21.7 percent last year. Simon & Schuster's titles accounted for 18.5 percent of the hardcover bestsellers list in 2008, a decline of 1.9 percent, but good enough for second place. Hachette Book Group increased its market share of the hardcover list by 2.3 percent, giving it a 14.1 percent share of bestsellers, tying with Penguin USA for third place. HarperCollins's share fell by just under 1 percent in 2008 to 10.8 percent. Moderate-sized Hyperion placed 9 books on the bestsellers list, increasing its market share by 2.7 percent, giving it 5.0 percent of hardcover bestseller slots.

In paperback, the clear winner was Penguin USA, which placed 81 books on the trade paperback and mass market paperback lists, giving it a commanding 32.5 percent share of paperback bestsellers, up 8.3 percent from 2008. Random House had a difficult year in the paperback segment with its share of paperback bestsellers falling by 6.2 percent, which gave it a 17.3 percent market share. The number of Random paperbacks hitting the bestsellers list fell to 50 from 77 in 2007. Simon & Schuster was a distant third among publishers, occupying 8.7 percent of the paperback spots in 2008, just ahead of Hachette and HarperCollins, which had shares of 8.5 percent and 8.4 percent, respectively. Harlequin, which has expanded its presence into different areas of the romance market, increased its share of the paperback market by 2.3 percent, to 5.2 percent in 2008.

# Prices of U.S. and Foreign Published Materials

Narda Tafuri

Editor, ALA ALCTS Library Materials Price Index Editorial Board

The Library Materials Price Index (LMPI) Editorial Board of the American Library Association's Association for Library Collections and Technical Services' Publications Committee continues to monitor prices for a range of library materials from sources within North America and from other key publishing centers around the world.

During 2008 price increases for library materials generally outperformed the U.S. Consumer Price Index (CPI)—some by a significant margin—but trade paperbacks showed a dramatic decline. As usual, periodicals significantly outperformed the CPI, as did hardcover, mass market paperback, and audiobook prices. The cost of books has continued to exhibit inflationary activity. Over the past few years, prices for U.S. hardcover, paperback, and audiobooks continued to be mixed, according to data from book wholesaler Baker & Taylor; the figures for all years are revised and reflect enhancements to the Baker & Taylor database. Data for college books show a substantial increase in 2008 compared with 2007. CPI data are obtained from the Bureau of Labor Statistics Web site at http://www.bls.gov/cpi.

Two indexes that were unavailable last year have been reestablished and updated. Several factors continue to hamper data collection and index preparation. These include, but are not limited to, mergers and acquisitions in the publishing and distribution world that make it more difficult to determine what is published in a foreign country by "multinational" firms; the conversion of several key countries to the euro; and migrations by vendors to new internal systems. Due to these difficulties, we have not been able to update one index (Table 9), and it is being repeated from last year. We plan to retire the newspaper indexes (Tables 8A and 8B) this year.

|  | Percent Change | | | | |
| Index | 2004 | 2005 | 2006 | 2007 | 2008 |
| --- | --- | --- | --- | --- | --- |
| CPI | 3.3 | 3.4 | 2.5 | 4.1 | 0.1 |
| Periodicals | 6.5 | 7.8 | 7.3 | 7.2 | 8.0 |
| Serials services | 7.1 | n.a. | n.a. | n.a. | n.a. |
| *Hardcover books | n.a. | -2.9 | 5.44 | -3.12 | 3.13 |
| Academic books | 1.9 | 6.4 | 2.9 | 1.1 | n.a. |
| College books | 4.4 | 1.7 | 3.0 | 0.47 | 3.3 |
| *Mass market paperbacks | n.a. | 1.12 | 0.95 | 0.47 | 1.4 |
| *Trade paperbacks | n.a. | 6.66 | 1.57 | 12.83 | -9.18 |
| *Audiobooks | n.a. | 15.33 | -9.73 | 8.99 | 10.21 |
| Newspapers | 2.1 | -0.9 | 1.8 | -2.0 | 4.1 |

n.a. = not available * = figures revised

## U.S. Published Materials

Tables 1 through 8B indicate average prices and price indexes for library materials published primarily in the United States. These indexes are U.S. Periodicals (Table 1), U.S. Serials Services (Table 2), U.S. Hardcover Books (Table 3), North American Academic Books (Table 4), U.S. College Books (Table 5), U.S. Mass Market Paperback Books (Table 6), U.S. Paperback Books (Excluding Mass Market) (Table 7), U.S. Audiobooks (Table 7A), and U.S. Daily Newspapers and International Newspapers (Tables 8A and 8B).

### Periodical and Serials Prices

The LMPI Editorial Board and Swets Information Services jointly produce the U.S. Periodicals Price Index (USPPI) (Table 1). The subscription prices shown are publishers' list prices, excluding publisher discount or vendor service charges. This report includes 2007, 2008 and 2009 data indexed to the base year of 1984.

Compiled by Brenda Dingley, this table shows that U.S. periodical prices, excluding Russian translations, increased by 8 percent from 2007 to 2008, and by 7.1 percent from 2008 to 2009. This compares with the overall rate of inflation from the last (2007) report at 7.3 percent. Including the Russian translation category, the single-year increase was exactly the same percentage for 2008 at 8 percent, but was 7.8 percent from 2008 to 2009. These figures compare with the 7.1 percent increase for the entire sample in 2007. In 2008, as in most previous years, the overall greatest price increases were in the sciences, which averaged an 8.8 percent overall increase in 2008, with Zoology posting the greatest increase of any single category at 12.7 percent. In 2009 the sciences posted the lowest average increase, at 6.5 percent, with the social sciences showing the greatest increases, averaging 7.5 percent. Unlike 2007, when no subject category showed the double-digit increases of previous years, in 2008 both Zoology and Industrial Arts increased more than 10 percent. Medicine posted the third-highest increase at 9.9 percent. In 2009 Children's Literature, which in most years is the category posting the lowest increase, saw the highest inflationary increase, at 11.5 percent. This was followed by Russian translations, which increased 10 percent, and by Labor and Industrial Relations, which increased by 9.9 percent. The lowest increases in 2008 were, in order, General Interest Periodicals at 1.8 percent, Library and Information Sciences at 4.2 percent, and Children's Periodicals at 4.4 percent. In 2009 the lowest rates of increase were posted in Industrial Arts at 1 percent, Fine and Applied Arts at 5.3 percent, and by both the Law category and the Journalism and Communications category, which each saw a 5.7 percent inflationary increase.

More extensive reports on the periodicals price index were published annually in the April 15 issue of *Library Journal* through 1992, in the May issue of *American Libraries* from 1993 to 2002, and in the October 2003 issue of *Library Resources and Technical Services*. The full reports for the 1999–2006 studies are available on the Web site of the Association for Collections and Library Technical Services (ALCTS) at the URL http://www.ala.org/ala/mgrps/divs/alcts/resources/collect/serials/periodicalsindex/index.cfm. Future editions of the USPPI will also be posted on the ALCTS Web site as they are completed.

**Table 1 / U.S. Periodicals: Average Prices and Price Indexes, 2007–2009**

Index Base: 1984 = 100

| Subject Area | 1984 Average Price | 2007 Average Price | 2007 Index | 2008 Average Price | 2008 Index | 2009 Average Price | 2009 Index |
|---|---|---|---|---|---|---|---|
| U.S. periodicals excluding Russian translations | $54.97 | $404.40 | 735.7 | $436.90 | 794.8 | $467.82 | 851.1 |
| U.S. periodicals including Russian translations | 72.47 | 518.55 | 715.6 | 559.96 | 772.7 | 603.85 | 833.3 |
| Agriculture | 24.06 | 159.51 | 663.0 | 169.99 | 706.5 | 181.40 | 754.0 |
| Business and economics | 38.87 | 231.66 | 596.0 | 245.27 | 631.0 | 263.64 | 678.3 |
| Chemistry and physics | 228.90 | 2,189.67 | 956.6 | 2,333.37 | 1,019.4 | 2,482.16 | 1,084.4 |
| Children's periodicals | 12.21 | 28.71 | 235.2 | 29.98 | 245.5 | 33.43 | 273.8 |
| Education | 34.01 | 222.05 | 652.9 | 240.80 | 708.0 | 258.73 | 760.8 |
| Engineering | 78.70 | 634.85 | 806.7 | 688.98 | 875.5 | 734.14 | 932.8 |
| Fine and applied arts | 26.90 | 77.63 | 288.6 | 84.94 | 315.8 | 89.40 | 332.4 |
| General interest periodicals | 27.90 | 59.03 | 211.6 | 60.11 | 215.5 | 63.91 | 229.1 |
| History | 23.68 | 101.40 | 428.2 | 106.55 | 450.0 | 113.94 | 481.2 |
| Home economics | 37.15 | 210.05 | 511.8 | 225.51 | 549.5 | 246.26 | 600.1 |
| Industrial arts | 30.40 | 154.84 | 509.4 | 170.51 | 560.9 | 172.22 | 566.5 |
| Journalism and communications | 39.25 | 174.51 | 444.6 | 182.41 | 464.8 | 192.89 | 491.4 |
| Labor and industrial relations | 29.87 | 186.87 | 625.6 | 201.12 | 673.3 | 220.96 | 739.8 |
| Law | 31.31 | 133.46 | 426.2 | 141.02 | 450.4 | 149.04 | 476.0 |
| Library and information sciences | 38.85 | 154.73 | 398.3 | 161.15 | 414.8 | 172.63 | 444.4 |
| Literature and language | 23.02 | 91.80 | 398.8 | 96.35 | 418.5 | 102.92 | 447.1 |
| Mathematics, botany, geology, general science | 106.56 | 853.36 | 800.8 | 925.61 | 868.6 | 991.88 | 930.8 |
| Medicine | 125.57 | 1,113.97 | 887.1 | 1,224.41 | 975.1 | 1,317.81 | 1,049.5 |
| Philosophy and religion | 21.94 | 93.00 | 423.9 | 99.33 | 452.8 | 107.44 | 489.7 |
| Physical education and recreation | 20.54 | 76.28 | 371.4 | 81.79 | 398.2 | 87.73 | 427.1 |
| Political science | 32.43 | 222.77 | 686.9 | 241.37 | 744.3 | 261.05 | 805.0 |
| Psychology | 69.74 | 579.93 | 831.6 | 631.79 | 905.9 | 686.52 | 984.4 |
| Russian translations | 381.86 | 2,856.72 | 748.1 | 3,080.51 | 806.7 | 3,390.04 | 887.8 |
| Sociology and anthropology | 43.87 | 335.16 | 764.0 | 367.59 | 837.9 | 400.08 | 912.0 |
| Zoology | 78.35 | 809.07 | 1,032.6 | 911.89 | 1,163.9 | 980.66 | 1,251.6 |
| Total number of periodicals | | | | | | | |
| Excluding Russian translations | 3,731 | 3,728 | | 3,728 | | 3,728 | |
| Including Russian translations | 3,942 | 3,910 | | 3,910 | | 3,910 | |

Compiled by Brenda Dingley, University of Missouri, Kansas City, based on subscription information supplied by Swets Information Services.

The U.S. Serials Services Index (Table 2) has been jointly prepared by the LMPI Editorial Board and Swets Information Services. It is compiled by Ajaye Bloomstone. Pricing for legal serial titles is obtained directly from vendors of those services. Stephanie Braunstein collected the data for the other titles, including the government documents subscription titles. Braunstein used the U.S. Government Online Bookstore for the government titles and used listings provided by the Swets Subscription Services Company for the other categories.

This report marks the beginning of a new base year for reporting and comparing prices for domestic serial publications. Therefore, the index and table only show pricing information for 2009; next year's table will provide cost inflation data.

It is important to note, however, that finding serial publications that are available in print is challenging now and will undoubtedly become more challenging in the future as more and more of these publications migrate to electronic-only status. This index tracks serial publications most commonly found in library collections—not in private collections—and print versions are therefore more likely to be discontinued in favor of electronic versions. There is concern that meaningful comparisons will be difficult to make as the pool of available print titles becomes smaller. Already this new base year shows smaller dollar amounts for the average costs in part because the more expensive materials are now online. This smaller dollar amount also reflects the smaller sample available. The notable exception to this change is in the law materials area; the supposition is that most legal materials, whether in print or online, are notably more expensive than materials from other disciplines.

For this year—the new base year—titles were selected on the basis of their format (print) and their representation of the topic under which they fall. For certain topic areas, finding print titles was especially challenging—for the reason noted above.

Please refer to earlier editions of the *Bowker Annual Library and Book Trade Almanac* for historical information.

### Table 2 / U.S. Serials Services: Average Prices, 2009

| Subject Area | Average Price |
| --- | --- |
| Business | $680.99 |
| General and humanities | 156.22 |
| Law | 1,646.45 |
| Science and technology | 241.68 |
| Social sciences | 168.59 |
| U.S. documents | 341.52 |
| Total number of services | 359 |

**Book Prices**

Tables 3 (U.S. Hardcover Books), 6 (U.S. Mass Market Paperback Books), 7 (U.S. Paperback Books [Excluding Mass Market]), and 7A (Audiobooks), prepared by Catherine Barr, are once again derived from data provided by Baker &

*(text continues on page 495)*

**Table 3 / U.S. Hardcover Books: Average Prices and Price Indexes, 2005–2008**

Index Base: 2004 = 100

| Category | 2004 Average Price | 2005 Final Volumes | 2005 Final Average Price | 2005 Final Index | 2006 Final Volumes | 2006 Final Average Price | 2006 Final Index | 2007 Final Volumes | 2007 Final Average Price | 2007 Final Index | 2008 Preliminary Volumes | 2008 Preliminary Average Price | 2008 Preliminary Index |
|---|---|---|---|---|---|---|---|---|---|---|---|---|---|
| Agriculture | $72.87 | 670 | $61.63 | 84.6 | 591 | $68.57 | 94.1 | 680 | $70.90 | 97.3 | 555 | $73.50 | 100.9 |
| Arts | 72.43 | 3,472 | 62.51 | 86.3 | 3,962 | 77.37 | 106.8 | 4,241 | 77.03 | 106.4 | 4,284 | 80.55 | 111.2 |
| Biography | 50.47 | 1,601 | 48.12 | 95.3 | 1,587 | 52.95 | 104.9 | 1,669 | 53.60 | 106.2 | 1,509 | 57.70 | 114.3 |
| Business | 122.65 | 2,031 | 123.70 | 100.9 | 2,010 | 130.44 | 106.4 | 2,154 | 139.48 | 113.7 | 2,244 | 152.00 | 123.9 |
| Careers | 82.71 | 679 | 86.39 | 104.5 | 726 | 85.91 | 103.9 | 758 | 78.89 | 95.4 | 772 | 91.76 | 110.9 |
| Children | 22.42 | 12,567 | 22.79 | 101.7 | 12,373 | 22.73 | 101.4 | 14,689 | 23.53 | 105.0 | 12,811 | 26.39 | 117.7 |
| Computers | 106.15 | 772 | 110.58 | 104.2 | 906 | 109.57 | 103.2 | 765 | 113.25 | 106.7 | 724 | 146.46 | 138.0 |
| Cooking | 28.81 | 861 | 28.46 | 98.8 | 881 | 29.98 | 104.1 | 865 | 27.42 | 95.2 | 965 | 29.52 | 102.5 |
| Education | 101.26 | 1,151 | 93.08 | 91.9 | 1,306 | 103.86 | 102.6 | 1,264 | 109.01 | 107.7 | 1,315 | 110.25 | 108.9 |
| Fiction | 28.13 | 4,732 | 28.39 | 100.9 | 4,489 | 28.75 | 102.2 | 4,591 | 33.59 | 119.4 | 4,740 | 29.37 | 104.4 |
| General works | 123.39 | 1,711 | 114.42 | 92.7 | 1,679 | 119.24 | 96.6 | 1,616 | 143.02 | 115.9 | 1,560 | 155.93 | 126.4 |
| Graphic novels | 31.73 | 237 | 33.43 | 105.4 | 294 | 32.29 | 101.8 | 337 | 33.29 | 104.9 | 479 | 32.83 | 103.5 |
| History | 84.55 | 4,574 | 84.66 | 100.1 | 4,794 | 91.77 | 108.5 | 4,952 | 84.86 | 100.4 | 4,856 | 85.43 | 101.0 |
| How-to, home arts | 33.32 | 478 | 31.44 | 94.4 | 465 | 31.47 | 94.4 | 499 | 32.81 | 98.5 | 394 | 36.46 | 109.4 |
| Language | 105.87 | 1,279 | 111.02 | 104.9 | 1,233 | 111.02 | 104.9 | 1,482 | 113.85 | 107.5 | 1,249 | 110.82 | 104.7 |
| Law | 151.58 | 1,280 | 153.03 | 101.0 | 1,400 | 172.55 | 113.8 | 1,430 | 163.84 | 108.1 | 1,466 | 158.97 | 104.9 |
| Literature | 97.80 | 1,847 | 115.71 | 118.3 | 1,875 | 100.62 | 102.9 | 2,289 | 109.33 | 111.8 | 2,059 | 101.74 | 104.0 |
| Medicine | 159.09 | 2,746 | 155.08 | 97.5 | 2,959 | 158.37 | 99.5 | 2,965 | 150.67 | 94.7 | 2,936 | 155.01 | 97.4 |
| Music | 77.11 | 411 | 78.17 | 101.4 | 395 | 77.79 | 100.9 | 484 | 75.94 | 98.5 | 479 | 68.87 | 89.3 |
| Philosophy | 152.76 | 861 | 124.17 | 81.3 | 962 | 103.55 | 67.8 | 1,022 | 89.63 | 58.7 | 985 | 96.84 | 63.4 |
| Poetry, drama | 36.58 | 468 | 40.76 | 111.4 | 377 | 45.56 | 124.5 | 431 | 46.39 | 126.8 | 517 | 46.28 | 126.5 |
| Religion | 68.13 | 2,704 | 62.81 | 92.2 | 2,630 | 70.98 | 104.2 | 2,662 | 68.17 | 100.1 | 2,587 | 69.71 | 102.3 |
| Science | 172.53 | 4,632 | 172.81 | 100.2 | 4,845 | 168.87 | 97.9 | 4,650 | 174.11 | 100.9 | 4,451 | 170.96 | 99.1 |
| Self-help, psychology | 61.47 | 1,894 | 65.02 | 105.8 | 2,075 | 67.62 | 110.0 | 2,026 | 73.05 | 118.8 | 2,028 | 72.50 | 117.9 |
| Sociology, economics | 101.43 | 4,856 | 101.01 | 99.6 | 5,411 | 116.32 | 114.7 | 5,527 | 104.98 | 103.5 | 5,761 | 96.51 | 95.1 |
| Sports, recreation | 47.05 | 922 | 36.47 | 77.5 | 1,000 | 36.28 | 77.1 | 911 | 36.89 | 78.4 | 957 | 40.59 | 86.3 |
| Technology | 154.91 | 1,965 | 167.17 | 107.9 | 2,183 | 149.01 | 96.2 | 2,128 | 140.41 | 90.6 | 2,361 | 144.24 | 93.1 |
| Travel | 47.97 | 421 | 37.13 | 77.4 | 400 | 43.43 | 90.5 | 754 | 54.29 | 113.2 | 402 | 34.08 | 71.0 |
| Young adult | 41.44 | 2,450 | 49.45 | 119.3 | 2,298 | 47.97 | 115.8 | 2,739 | 49.71 | 120.0 | 2,248 | 49.36 | 119.1 |
| Totals | $81.83 | 64,272 | $79.46 | 97.1 | 66,106 | $83.78 | 102.4 | 70,580 | $81.17 | 99.2 | 67,694 | $83.71 | 102.3 |

Compiled by Catherine Barr from data supplied by Baker & Taylor.

Table 4 / North American Academic Books: Average Prices and Price Indexes 2005–2007
Index Base: 1989 = 100

| Subject Area | LC Class | 1989 | | 2005 | | 2006 | | 2007 | | | |
|---|---|---|---|---|---|---|---|---|---|---|---|
| | | No. of Titles | Average Price | No. of Titles | Average Price | No. of Titles | Average Price | No. of Titles | Average Price | % Change 2006–2007 | Index |
| Agriculture | S | 897 | $45.13 | 971 | $68.95 | 963 | $65.14 | 995 | $76.22 | 17.0 | 168.9 |
| Anthropology | GN | 406 | 32.81 | 377 | 62.04 | 368 | 67.94 | 416 | 67.88 | -0.1 | 206.9 |
| Botany | QK | 251 | 69.02 | 198 | 94.29 | 239 | 115.31 | 178 | 107.34 | -6.9 | 155.5 |
| Business and economics | H | 5,979 | 41.67 | 7,377 | 68.74 | 7,485 | 71.64 | 6,534 | 72.44 | 1.1 | 173.9 |
| Chemistry | QD | 577 | 110.61 | 533 | 187.38 | 484 | 176.72 | 485 | 175.33 | -0.8 | 158.5 |
| Education | L | 1,685 | 29.61 | 2,787 | 51.30 | 3,011 | 56.86 | 2,822 | 58.83 | 3.5 | 198.7 |
| Engineering and technology | T | 4,569 | 64.94 | 5,832 | 105.58 | 5,666 | 98.67 | 5,156 | 100.13 | 1.5 | 154.2 |
| Fine and applied arts | M-N | 3,040 | 40.72 | 4,215 | 48.16 | 4,652 | 52.77 | 4,761 | 53.28 | 1.0 | 130.9 |
| General works | A | 333 | 134.65 | 85 | 52.06 | 97 | 72.40 | 109 | 74.80 | 3.3 | 55.6 |
| Geography | G | 396 | 47.34 | 803 | 76.54 | 788 | 80.11 | 706 | 80.60 | 0.6 | 170.3 |
| Geology | QE | 303 | 63.49 | 191 | 104.50 | 203 | 100.12 | 191 | 118.23 | 18.1 | 186.2 |
| History | C-D-E-F | 5,549 | 31.34 | 7,174 | 49.47 | 7,296 | 52.54 | 6,838 | 55.45 | 5.5 | 176.9 |
| Home economics | TX | 535 | 27.10 | 700 | 37.74 | 683 | 41.23 | 686 | 43.62 | 5.8 | 161.0 |
| Industrial arts | TT | 175 | 23.89 | 179 | 35.48 | 237 | 32.54 | 248 | 36.01 | 10.7 | 150.7 |
| Law | K | 1,252 | 51.10 | 2,568 | 86.69 | 2,701 | 87.26 | 2,788 | 98.78 | 13.2 | 193.3 |
| Library and information science | Z | 857 | 44.51 | 489 | 69.93 | 479 | 62.89 | 480 | 66.85 | 6.3 | 150.2 |
| Literature and language | P | 10,812 | 24.99 | 12,391 | 41.53 | 12,551 | 45.69 | 12,595 | 44.91 | -1.7 | 179.7 |

| Subject | LC class | | | | | | | | | | |
|---|---|---|---|---|---|---|---|---|---|---|---|
| Mathematics and computer science | QA | 2,707 | 44.68 | 3,552 | 82.41 | 3,365 | 76.47 | 2,939 | 79.16 | 3.5 | 177.2 |
| Medicine | R | 5,028 | 58.38 | 6,226 | 83.45 | 6,550 | 85.21 | 5,757 | 86.01 | 0.9 | 147.3 |
| Military and naval science | U-V | 715 | 33.57 | 548 | 56.67 | 643 | 58.96 | 603 | 56.40 | -4.3 | 168.0 |
| Philosophy and religion | B | 3,518 | 29.06 | 5,636 | 53.31 | 5,745 | 59.32 | 5,448 | 56.25 | -5.2 | 193.6 |
| Physical education and recreation | GV | 814 | 20.38 | 1,179 | 38.26 | 1,226 | 41.23 | 1,134 | 42.58 | 3.3 | 208.9 |
| Physics and astronomy | QB | 1,219 | 64.59 | 1,273 | 105.76 | 1,285 | 104.67 | 1,100 | 101.91 | -2.6 | 157.8 |
| Political science | J | 1,650 | 36.76 | 2,094 | 63.95 | 2,300 | 65.94 | 2,195 | 66.69 | 1.1 | 181.4 |
| Psychology | BF | 890 | 31.97 | 980 | 56.85 | 1,010 | 55.27 | 1,027 | 59.04 | 6.8 | 184.7 |
| Science (general) | Q | 433 | 56.10 | 384 | 86.82 | 416 | 84.02 | 328 | 92.59 | 10.2 | 165.1 |
| Sociology | HM | 2,742 | 29.36 | 4,513 | 53.47 | 4,856 | 60.55 | 4,440 | 62.64 | 3.5 | 213.4 |
| Zoology | QH,L,P,R | 1,967 | 71.28 | 2,129 | 104.04 | 2,235 | 107.34 | 2,006 | 110.43 | 2.9 | 154.9 |
| Average for all subjects | | 59,299 | $41.69 | 75,384 | $65.42 | 77,534 | $67.29 | 72,965 | $68.01 | 1.1 | 163.1 |

Compiled by Stephen Bosch, University of Arizona, from electronic data provided by Blackwells and YBP Library Services. The data represent all titles (hardcover, trade, and paperback books, as well as annuals and electronic books) treated for all approval plan customers serviced by the vendors. This table covers titles published or distributed in the United States and Canada during the calendar years listed.

This index does not include paperback editions. The inclusion of these items does impact pricing in the index.

## Table 5 / U.S. College Books: Average Prices and Price Indexes, 1989, 2006–2008

Index Base: 1989 = 100

| Subject | 1989 | | 2006 | | | | 2007 | | | | 2008 | | | | |
|---|---|---|---|---|---|---|---|---|---|---|---|---|---|---|---|
| | No. of Titles | Avg. Price per Title | No. of Titles | Avg. Price per Title | Indexed to 1989 | Indexed to 2005 | No. of Titles | Avg. Price per Title | Indexed to 1989 | Indexed to 2006 | No. of Titles | Avg. Price per Title | Indexed to 1989 | Indexed to 2007 | Percent Change 2007–2008 |
| General[1] | 19 | $40.19 | n.a. | n.a. | n.a. | n.a. | n.a. | n.a. | n.a. | n.a. | n.a. | n.a. | n.a. | n.a. | n.a. |
| Humanities | 21 | 32.33 | 63 | $55.45 | 171.51 | 113.07 | 61 | $55.00 | 170.12 | 99.19 | 73 | $56.95 | 176.15 | 103.55 | 3.55 |
| Art and architecture | 276 | 55.56 | 155 | 53.26 | 95.86 | 101.91 | 152 | 57.55 | 103.58 | 108.05 | 150 | 57.84 | 104.10 | 100.50 | 0.50 |
| Fine arts[2] | n.a. | n.a. | 182 | 58.48 | n.a. | 99.37 | 226 | 61.02 | n.a. | 104.34 | 116 | 68.77 | n.a. | 112.70 | 12.70 |
| Architecture[2] | n.a. | n.a. | 81 | 54.07 | n.a. | 96.99 | 75 | 57.00 | n.a. | 105.42 | 50 | 77.12 | n.a. | 135.30 | 35.30 |
| Photography | 24 | 44.11 | 50 | 50.34 | 114.12 | 87.95 | 48 | 51.76 | 117.34 | 102.82 | 18 | 46.64 | 105.74 | 90.11 | -9.89 |
| Communication | 42 | 32.70 | 77 | 51.01 | 155.99 | 100.53 | 93 | 58.83 | 179.91 | 115.33 | 98 | 54.17 | 165.66 | 92.08 | -7.92 |
| Language and literature | 110 | 35.17 | 71 | 62.81 | 178.59 | 110.48 | 95 | 54.88 | 156.04 | 87.37 | 70 | 64.77 | 184.16 | 118.02 | 18.02 |
| African and Middle Eastern[3] | n.a. | n.a. | 15 | 56.18 | n.a. | 97.38 | 24 | 49.58 | n.a. | 88.25 | 26 | 49.03 | n.a. | 98.89 | -1.11 |
| Asian and Oceanian[3] | n.a. | n.a. | 26 | 56.21 | n.a. | 127.26 | 40 | 54.07 | n.a. | 96.19 | 25 | 62.27 | n.a. | 115.17 | 15.17 |
| Classical | 75 | 43.07 | 29 | 68.94 | 160.07 | 120.40 | 27 | 77.23 | 179.31 | 112.02 | 29 | 81.64 | 189.55 | 105.71 | 5.71 |
| English and American | 547 | 30.27 | 424 | 57.36 | 189.49 | 106.38 | 401 | 57.70 | 190.62 | 100.59 | 420 | 58.83 | 194.35 | 101.96 | 1.96 |
| Germanic | 38 | 32.18 | 23 | 64.99 | 201.96 | 102.44 | 29 | 61.66 | 191.61 | 94.88 | 29 | 66.89 | 207.86 | 108.48 | 8.48 |
| Romance | 97 | 30.30 | 70 | 56.89 | 187.76 | 94.66 | 89 | 51.28 | 169.24 | 90.14 | 70 | 53.94 | 178.02 | 105.19 | 5.19 |
| Slavic | 41 | 27.92 | 15 | 42.98 | 153.94 | 95.83 | 15 | 67.01 | 240.01 | 155.91 | 20 | 44.41 | 159.06 | 66.27 | -33.73 |
| Other | 63 | 25.09 | n.a. | n.a. | n.a. | n.a. | n.a. | n.a. | n.a. | n.a. | n.a. | n.a. | n.a. | n.a. | n.a. |
| Performing arts | 20 | 29.41 | 18 | 71.31 | 242.47 | 203.16 | 25 | 50.55 | 171.88 | 70.89 | 29 | 54.42 | 185.04 | 107.66 | 7.66 |
| Film | 82 | 33.00 | 118 | 52.00 | 157.58 | 118.32 | 133 | 52.44 | 158.91 | 100.85 | 159 | 58.12 | 176.12 | 110.83 | 10.83 |
| Music | 156 | 35.34 | 156 | 49.02 | 138.71 | 94.00 | 145 | 53.60 | 151.67 | 109.34 | 157 | 56.97 | 161.21 | 106.29 | 6.29 |
| Theater and dance[4] | 58 | 34.18 | 38 | 57.62 | 168.58 | 102.13 | 43 | 51.20 | 149.80 | 88.86 | 41 | 64.11 | 187.57 | 125.21 | 25.21 |
| Philosophy | 185 | 37.25 | 164 | 60.13 | 161.42 | 122.69 | 187 | 58.64 | 157.42 | 97.52 | 183 | 58.00 | 155.70 | 98.91 | -1.09 |
| Religion | 174 | 33.49 | 200 | 46.47 | 138.76 | 98.98 | 232 | 50.73 | 151.48 | 109.17 | 250 | 48.32 | 144.28 | 95.25 | -4.75 |
| Total Humanities[5] | 2,009 | $36.09 | 1,975 | $55.11 | 152.70 | 105.23 | 2,140 | $56.09 | 155.42 | 101.78 | 2,013 | $58.37 | 161.73 | 104.06 | 4.06 |

| | | | | | | | | | | | | | | | |
|---|---|---|---|---|---|---|---|---|---|---|---|---|---|---|---|
| Science/technology | 99 | $46.90 | 57 | $44.15 | 94.14 | 94.64 | 65 | $46.46 | 99.06 | 105.23 | 109 | $53.68 | 114.46 | 115.54 | 15.54 |
| History of science and technology | 74 | 40.56 | 112 | 41.06 | 101.23 | 90.18 | 95 | 47.73 | 117.68 | 116.24 | 96 | 46.72 | 115.19 | 97.88 | -2.12 |
| Astronautics and astronomy | 22 | 50.56 | 50 | 54.56 | 107.91 | 107.13 | 71 | 50.37 | 99.62 | 92.32 | 68 | 50.64 | 100.16 | 100.54 | 0.54 |
| Biology | 97 | 51.01 | 116 | 69.65 | 136.54 | 106.16 | 138 | 58.18 | 114.06 | 83.53 | 145 | 71.31 | 139.80 | 122.57 | 22.57 |
| *Botany* | 29 | 63.91 | 54 | 73.06 | 114.32 | 127.13 | 48 | 55.62 | 87.03 | 76.13 | 85 | 77.65 | 121.50 | 139.61 | 39.61 |
| *Zoology* | 53 | 49.21 | 71 | 66.16 | 134.44 | 100.93 | 76 | 76.36 | 155.17 | 115.42 | 94 | 67.63 | 137.43 | 88.57 | -11.43 |
| Chemistry | 21 | 70.76 | 60 | 110.55 | 156.23 | 90.73 | 76 | 116.67 | 164.88 | 105.54 | 70 | 109.05 | 154.11 | 93.47 | -6.53 |
| Earth science | 34 | 79.44 | 46 | 61.15 | 76.98 | 73.92 | 54 | 79.63 | 100.24 | 130.22 | 95 | 73.74 | 92.82 | 92.60 | -7.40 |
| Engineering | 87 | 66.74 | 96 | 108.70 | 162.87 | 99.83 | 90 | 90.31 | 135.32 | 83.08 | 90 | 95.23 | 142.69 | 105.45 | 5.45 |
| Health sciences | 94 | 34.91 | 122 | 57.19 | 163.82 | 124.57 | 151 | 52.75 | 151.10 | 92.24 | 156 | 56.29 | 161.24 | 106.71 | 6.71 |
| Information and computer science | 70 | 40.35 | 43 | 71.10 | 176.21 | 112.57 | 55 | 63.55 | 157.50 | 89.38 | 90 | 75.86 | 188.00 | 119.37 | 19.37 |
| Mathematics | 60 | 48.53 | 93 | 70.90 | 146.10 | 96.61 | 90 | 65.38 | 134.72 | 92.21 | 98 | 68.98 | 142.14 | 105.51 | 5.51 |
| Physics | 22 | 43.94 | 72 | 67.93 | 154.60 | 91.96 | 81 | 79.13 | 180.09 | 116.49 | 65 | 63.43 | 144.36 | 80.16 | -19.84 |
| Sports and physical education | 18 | 27.46 | 54 | 40.39 | 147.09 | 112.07 | 20 | 37.52 | 136.64 | 92.89 | 65 | 38.72 | 141.01 | 103.20 | 3.20 |
| Total Science/ Technology | 780 | $49.54 | 1,046 | $67.06 | 135.37 | 100.93 | 1,110 | $66.15 | 133.53 | 98.64 | 1,326 | $67.34 | 135.93 | 101.80 | 1.80 |

## Table 5 / U.S. College Books: Average Prices and Price Indexes, 1989, 2006–2008 (cont.)

Index Base: 1989 = 100

| Subject | 1989 No. of Titles | 1989 Avg. Price per Title | 2006 No. of Titles | 2006 Avg. Price per Title | 2006 Indexed to 1989 | 2006 Indexed to 2005 | 2007 No. of Titles | 2007 Avg. Price per Title | 2007 Indexed to 1989 | 2007 Indexed to 2006 | 2008 No. of Titles | 2008 Avg. Price per Title | 2008 Indexed to 1989 | 2008 Indexed to 2007 | 2008 Indexed Percent Change 2007–2008 |
|---|---|---|---|---|---|---|---|---|---|---|---|---|---|---|---|
| Social/behavioral sciences | 92 | $37.09 | 103 | $49.98 | 134.75 | 99.58 | 102 | $60.65 | 163.52 | 121.35 | 108 | $60.31 | 162.60 | 99.44 | -0.56 |
| Anthropology | 96 | 39.94 | 130 | 57.11 | 142.99 | 101.75 | 96 | 67.55 | 169.13 | 118.28 | 142 | 56.41 | 141.24 | 83.51 | -16.49 |
| Business, management, and labor | 145 | 35.72 | 139 | 48.49 | 135.75 | 93.70 | 132 | 50.78 | 142.16 | 104.72 | 151 | 53.01 | 148.40 | 104.39 | 4.39 |
| Economics | 332 | 40.75 | 239 | 58.16 | 142.72 | 102.30 | 261 | 63.37 | 155.51 | 108.96 | 263 | 62.36 | 153.03 | 98.41 | -1.59 |
| Education | 71 | 34.50 | 169 | 53.52 | 155.13 | 109.18 | 159 | 51.75 | 150.00 | 96.69 | 163 | 52.71 | 152.78 | 101.86 | 1.86 |
| History, geography, and area studies | 59 | 42.10 | 137 | 54.99 | 130.62 | 119.26 | 105 | 49.33 | 117.17 | 89.71 | 111 | 51.33 | 121.92 | 104.05 | 4.05 |
| Africa | 44 | 34.85 | 36 | 57.29 | 164.39 | 112.91 | 29 | 54.94 | 157.65 | 95.90 | 29 | 62.02 | 177.96 | 112.89 | 12.89 |
| Ancient history | n.a. | n.a. | 47 | 70.66 | n.a. | 116.83 | 57 | 71.50 | n.a. | 101.19 | 48 | 80.66 | n.a. | 112.81 | 12.81 |
| Asia and Oceania | 76 | 34.75 | 81 | 53.67 | 154.45 | 94.31 | 83 | 56.04 | 161.27 | 104.42 | 86 | 54.73 | 157.50 | 97.66 | -2.34 |
| Central and Eastern Europe | n.a. | n.a. | 53 | 51.67 | n.a. | 99.58 | 60 | 55.80 | n.a. | 107.99 | 60 | 57.24 | n.a. | 102.58 | 2.58 |
| Latin America and Caribbean | 42 | 37.23 | 61 | 56.17 | 150.87 | 107.61 | 56 | 52.06 | 139.83 | 92.68 | 71 | 53.15 | 142.76 | 102.09 | 2.09 |
| Middle East and North Africa | 30 | 36.32 | 37 | 51.83 | 142.70 | 103.21 | 45 | 64.82 | 178.47 | 125.06 | 45 | 50.17 | 138.13 | 77.40 | -22.60 |
| North America | 349 | 30.56 | 396 | 40.51 | 132.56 | 99.31 | 406 | 42.53 | 139.17 | 104.99 | 382 | 45.07 | 147.48 | 105.97 | 5.97 |
| United Kingdom[6] | n.a. | n.a. | 73 | 58.14 | n.a. | 111.57 | 73 | 56.88 | n.a. | 97.83 | 91 | 58.62 | n.a. | 103.06 | 3.06 |
| Western Europe[6] | 287 | 42.08 | 141 | 57.51 | 136.67 | 99.00 | 168 | 48.88 | 116.16 | 84.99 | 134 | 65.03 | 154.54 | 133.04 | 33.04 |
| Political science | 28 | 33.56 | 22 | 48.11 | 143.36 | 91.97 | 37 | 60.88 | 181.41 | 126.54 | 6 | 54.30 | 161.80 | 89.19 | -10.81 |
| Comparative politics[7] | 236 | 37.82 | 219 | 58.80 | 155.47 | 102.98 | 228 | 58.17 | 153.81 | 98.93 | 207 | 60.16 | 159.07 | 103.42 | 3.42 |
| International relations[7] | 207 | 35.74 | 157 | 56.49 | 158.06 | 112.80 | 156 | 53.02 | 148.35 | 93.86 | 166 | 59.46 | 166.37 | 112.15 | 12.15 |
| Political theory[7] | 59 | 37.76 | 57 | 55.68 | 147.48 | 114.31 | 60 | 60.41 | 159.98 | 108.49 | 81 | 62.43 | 165.33 | 103.34 | 3.34 |

| | | | | | | | | | | | | | | |
|---|---|---|---|---|---|---|---|---|---|---|---|---|---|---|
| U.S. politics[7] | 212 | 29.37 | 158 | 48.94 | 166.63 | 109.24 | 160 | 46.88 | 159.62 | 95.79 | 218 | 49.15 | 167.35 | 104.84 | 4.84 |
| Psychology | 179 | 36.36 | 122 | 59.00 | 162.27 | 108.32 | 130 | 59.19 | 162.79 | 100.32 | 125 | 61.59 | 169.39 | 104.05 | 4.05 |
| Sociology | 178 | 36.36 | 198 | 52.05 | 143.15 | 98.65 | 257 | 57.14 | 157.15 | 109.78 | 237 | 61.09 | 168.01 | 106.91 | 6.91 |
| Total Social/Behavioral Sciences | 2,722 | $36.43 | 2,775 | $52.98 | 145.43 | 104.00 | 2,860 | $54.46 | 149.49 | 102.79 | 2,924 | $56.40 | 154.82 | 103.56 | 3.56 |
| Total General, Humanities, Science/Technology, Social/Behavioral Sciences | 5,530 | $38.16 | 5796 | $56.24 | 147.38 | 103.33 | 6,110 | $57.15 | 149.76 | 101.62 | 6,263 | $59.35 | 155.53 | 103.85 | 3.85 |
| Reference | 636 | $61.02 | n.a. | n.a. | n.a. | n.a. | n.a. | n.a. | n.a. | n.a. | n.a. | n.a. | n.a. | n.a. | n.a. |
| General[8] | n.a. | n.a. | 35 | $92.25 | n.a. | 106.38 | 33 | $136.26 | n.a. | 147.71 | 20 | $72.36 | n.a. | 53.10 | -46.90 |
| Humanities[8] | n.a. | n.a. | 152 | 131.80 | n.a. | 105.18 | 139 | 114.51 | n.a. | 86.88 | 144 | 102.95 | n.a. | 89.90 | -10.10 |
| Science and technology[8] | n.a. | n.a. | 73 | 147.50 | n.a. | 115.50 | 64 | 96.76 | n.a. | 65.60 | 89 | 145.94 | n.a. | 150.83 | 50.83 |
| Social and behavioral sciences[8] | n.a. | n.a. | 198 | 144.69 | n.a. | 112.47 | 253 | 143.28 | n.a. | 99.03 | 198 | 162.60 | n.a. | 113.48 | 13.48 |
| Total Reference | 636 | $61.02 | 458 | $136.85 | 224.27 | 110.61 | 489 | $128.54 | 210.65 | 93.93 | 451 | $136.26 | 223.30 | 106.01 | 6.01 |
| Grand Total (incl. Reference) | 6,166 | $40.52 | 6,254 | $62.15 | 153.38 | 103.02 | 6,599 | $62.44 | 154.10 | 100.47 | 6,714 | $64.52 | 159.23 | 103.33 | 3.33 |

Compiled by Frederick C. Lynden

n.a. = not available

1 General category no longer appears after 1999.

2 Began appearing after 1999.

3 Began appearing as separate sections in September 1995.

4 Separate sections for Theater and Drama combined in September 1995.

5 1983 totals include Linguistics (incorporated into Language and literature in 1985, non-European/Other (replaced by Africa and Middle Eastern and Asian and Oceanian in September 1995), and Europe (replaced by Central and Eastern Europe, United Kingdom, and Western Europe in July 1997).

6 Began appearing as separate sections, replacing Europe in July 1997.

7 Began appearing as separate sections in March 1998.

8 Began appearing as separate sections in July 1997.

## Table 6 / U.S. Mass Market Paperback Books: Average Per-Volume Prices, 2005–2008

Index Base: 2004 = 100

| | 2004 | | 2005 Final | | | 2006 Final | | | 2007 Final | | | 2008 Preliminary | | |
|---|---|---|---|---|---|---|---|---|---|---|---|---|---|---|
| | Average Prices | Volumes | Average Prices | Volumes | Index | Average Prices | Volumes | Index | Average Prices | Volumes | Index | Average Prices | Volumes | Index |
| Agriculture | n.a. | n.a. | n.a. | n.a. | n.a. | n.a. | n.a. | n.a. | n.a. | n.a. | n.a. | $7.99 | 1 | n.a. |
| Arts | $8.32 | 4 | $8.23 | 4 | 98.9 | $7.99 | 3 | 96.0 | $8.64 | 3 | 103.8 | 9.99 | 1 | 120.1 |
| Biography | 7.85 | 21 | 7.77 | 21 | 99.0 | 7.83 | 13 | 99.7 | 7.87 | 9 | 100.3 | 7.99 | 8 | 101.8 |
| Business | n.a. | 1 | 16.95 | 1 | n.a. | n.a. | n.a. | n.a. | n.a. | n.a. | n.a. | n.a. | n.a. | n.a. |
| Education | n.a. | n.a. | n.a. | n.a. | n.a. | n.a. | n.a. | n.a. | n.a. | n.a. | n.a. | n.a. | n.a. | n.a. |
| Careers | 7.99 | 1 | 7.99 | 1 | 100.0 | n.a. | n.a. | n.a. | n.a. | n.a. | n.a. | 7.99 | 1 | 100.0 |
| Children | 5.71 | 281 | 5.26 | 281 | 92.1 | 5.63 | 270 | 98.6 | 5.72 | 272 | 100.2 | 6.11 | 239 | 107.0 |
| Computers | n.a. | n.a. | n.a. | n.a. | n.a. | n.a. | n.a. | n.a. | n.a. | n.a. | n.a. | n.a. | n.a. | n.a. |
| Cooking | 6.99 | 1 | 7.50 | 1 | 107.3 | 6.99 | 1 | 100.0 | n.a. | n.a. | n.a. | n.a. | n.a. | n.a. |
| Fiction | 6.22 | 4,259 | 6.30 | 4,259 | 101.3 | 6.33 | 4,329 | 101.8 | 6.39 | 4,216 | 102.7 | 6.47 | 4,160 | 104.0 |
| General works | 7.14 | 62 | 7.39 | 62 | 103.5 | 8.2 | 69 | 114.8 | 7.48 | 67 | 104.8 | 7.24 | 69 | 101.4 |
| Graphic novels | n.a. | 2 | 8.47 | 2 | n.a. | n.a. | n.a. | n.a. | n.a. | n.a. | n.a. | 3.99 | 1 | n.a. |
| History | 7.44 | 25 | 7.81 | 25 | 105.0 | 7.62 | 16 | 102.4 | 7.76 | 13 | 104.3 | 5.49 | 3 | 73.8 |
| How-to, home arts | n.a. | 1 | 5.99 | 1 | n.a. | n.a. | n.a. | n.a. | n.a. | n.a. | n.a. | n.a. | n.a. | n.a. |
| Language | n.a. | n.a. | 6.99 | 1 | n.a. | 5.99 | 1 | n.a. | 6.24 | 4 | n.a. | 5.99 | 4 | n.a. |
| Law | 7.99 | n.a. | n.a. | n.a. | n.a. | n.a. | n.a. | n.a. | n.a. | n.a. | n.a. | n.a. | n.a. | n.a. |
| Literature | n.a. | 1 | 7.95 | 1 | n.a. | 7.95 | 1 | n.a. | n.a. | n.a. | n.a. | 5.98 | 3 | n.a. |
| Medicine | 6.99 | 3 | 7.83 | 3 | 112.0 | 6.62 | 4 | 94.7 | 6.87 | 4 | 98.3 | 7.5 | 1 | 107.3 |
| Music | 7.95 | 2 | 7.95 | 2 | 100.0 | n.a. | n.a. | n.a. | n.a. | n.a. | n.a. | n.a. | n.a. | n.a. |
| Philosophy | 5.45 | 2 | 6.99 | 2 | 128.3 | 7.38 | 5 | 135.4 | 7.78 | 5 | 142.8 | 5.45 | 2 | 100.0 |
| Poetry, drama | 6.13 | 24 | 6.39 | 24 | 104.2 | 7.52 | 9 | 122.7 | 6.37 | 5 | 103.9 | 5.47 | 4 | 89.2 |
| Religion | 7.61 | 4 | 11.21 | 4 | 147.3 | 7.32 | 6 | 96.2 | 6.99 | 2 | 91.9 | 7.74 | 4 | 101.7 |
| Science | 6.99 | n.a. | n.a. | n.a. | n.a. | 7.99 | 1 | 114.3 | n.a. | n.a. | n.a. | 6.95 | 1 | 99.4 |
| Self-help, psychology | 7.22 | 49 | 7.93 | 49 | 109.8 | 7.25 | 78 | 100.4 | 7.57 | 46 | 104.8 | 7.62 | 35 | 105.5 |
| Sociology, economics | 7.35 | 6 | 7.08 | 6 | 96.3 | 7.47 | 4 | 101.6 | 7.49 | 2 | 101.9 | 7.99 | 2 | 108.7 |
| Sports, recreation | 7.36 | 19 | 7.46 | 19 | 101.4 | 7.13 | 14 | 96.9 | 5.99 | 24 | 81.4 | 6.44 | 20 | 87.5 |
| Technology | n.a. | 1 | 12.95 | 1 | n.a. | n.a. | n.a. | n.a. | n.a. | n.a. | n.a. | n.a. | n.a. | n.a. |
| Travel | n.a. | n.a. | n.a. | n.a. | n.a. | 7.99 | 1 | n.a. | n.a. | n.a. | n.a. | 6.95 | 1 | n.a. |
| Young adult | 6.33 | 237 | 6.57 | 237 | 103.8 | 7.18 | 197 | 113.4 | 6.97 | 156 | 110.1 | 7.06 | 139 | 111.5 |
| Totals | $6.25 | 5,007 | $6.32 | 5,007 | 101.1 | $6.38 | 5,022 | 102.1 | $6.41 | 4,828 | 102.6 | $6.50 | 4,699 | 104.0 |

Compiled by Catherine Barr from data supplied by Baker & Taylor. n.a. = not available

**Table 7 / U.S. Paperback Books (Excluding Mass Market): Average Prices and Price Indexes, 2005–2008**

Index Base: 2004 = 100

| | 2004 | | 2005 Final | | | 2006 Final | | | 2007 Final | | | 2008 Preliminary | | |
|---|---|---|---|---|---|---|---|---|---|---|---|---|---|---|
| | Average Prices | Volumes | Average Prices | Volumes | Index | Average Prices | Volumes | Index | Average Prices | Volumes | Index | Volumes | Average Prices | Index |
| Agriculture | $27.82 | 934 | $28.21 | 934 | 101.4 | $30.92 | 875 | 111.1 | $32.97 | 833 | 118.5 | 872 | $28.01 | 100.7 |
| Arts | 31.94 | 3,922 | 30.78 | 3,922 | 96.4 | 32.46 | 3,929 | 101.6 | 33.95 | 4,351 | 106.3 | 4,028 | 38.20 | 119.6 |
| Biography | 19.59 | 1,800 | 19.40 | 1,800 | 99.0 | 19.86 | 1,803 | 101.4 | 20.87 | 2,007 | 106.5 | 1,921 | 20.14 | 102.8 |
| Business | 55.64 | 4,960 | 70.37 | 4,960 | 126.5 | 76.12 | 3,990 | 136.8 | 89.61 | 8,626 | 161.1 | 3,674 | 78.49 | 141.1 |
| Careers | 37.81 | 1,434 | 40.30 | 1,434 | 106.6 | 42.03 | 1,415 | 111.2 | 43.31 | 1,514 | 114.5 | 1,445 | 43.26 | 114.4 |
| Children | 11.24 | 8,826 | 10.89 | 8,826 | 96.9 | 10.22 | 9,027 | 90.9 | 10.32 | 8,665 | 91.8 | 8,439 | 10.58 | 94.1 |
| Computers | 55.28 | 3,636 | 54.83 | 3,636 | 99.2 | 60.19 | 3,112 | 108.9 | 60.11 | 3,430 | 108.7 | 2,649 | 58.77 | 106.3 |
| Cooking | 17.34 | 1,186 | 18.17 | 1,186 | 104.8 | 18.95 | 987 | 109.3 | 17.59 | 1,063 | 101.4 | 1,230 | 18.74 | 108.1 |
| Education | 33.29 | 4,913 | 34.90 | 4,913 | 104.8 | 36.46 | 4,996 | 109.5 | 36.12 | 4,505 | 108.5 | 4,193 | 35.04 | 105.3 |
| Fiction | 15.37 | 8,098 | 15.43 | 8,098 | 100.4 | 16.00 | 7,999 | 104.1 | 17.50 | 9,492 | 113.9 | 8,984 | 17.47 | 113.7 |
| General works | 31.78 | 3,453 | 33.31 | 3,453 | 104.8 | 40.12 | 3,494 | 126.2 | 38.73 | 3,291 | 121.9 | 3,205 | 42.30 | 133.1 |
| Graphic novels | 12.68 | 2,106 | 12.88 | 2,106 | 101.6 | 13.66 | 2,078 | 107.7 | 15.15 | 2,216 | 119.5 | 2,439 | 14.42 | 113.7 |
| History | 29.48 | 5,767 | 33.40 | 5,767 | 113.3 | 32.90 | 5,996 | 111.6 | 34.51 | 6,831 | 117.1 | 5,743 | 31.88 | 108.1 |
| How-to, home arts | 21.09 | 1,390 | 19.52 | 1,390 | 92.6 | 20.47 | 1,365 | 97.1 | 21.64 | 1,252 | 102.6 | 1,266 | 21.69 | 102.8 |
| Language | 41.42 | 3,388 | 47.53 | 3,388 | 114.8 | 44.97 | 3,125 | 108.6 | 43.68 | 3,001 | 105.5 | 2,582 | 47.09 | 113.7 |
| Law | 54.73 | 1,944 | 61.77 | 1,944 | 112.9 | 54.25 | 3,344 | 99.1 | 74.14 | 3,135 | 135.5 | 3,823 | 82.13 | 150.1 |
| Literature | 33.69 | 2,312 | 30.86 | 2,312 | 91.6 | 34.31 | 1,744 | 101.8 | 38.01 | 2,064 | 112.8 | 1,783 | 39.24 | 116.5 |
| Medicine | 57.36 | 3,597 | 63.65 | 3,597 | 111.0 | 62.66 | 3,840 | 109.2 | 68.26 | 3,932 | 119.0 | 3,698 | 74.16 | 129.3 |
| Music | 22.77 | 2,695 | 23.11 | 2,695 | 101.5 | 25.73 | 2,657 | 113.0 | 27.84 | 2,474 | 122.3 | 2,793 | 21.81 | 95.8 |
| Philosophy | 31.89 | 1,202 | 31.09 | 1,202 | 97.5 | 32.97 | 1,100 | 103.4 | 31.87 | 1,589 | 99.9 | 1,165 | 30.20 | 94.7 |
| Poetry, drama | 15.72 | 2,234 | 16.10 | 2,234 | 102.4 | 16.10 | 2,101 | 102.4 | 17.38 | 2,406 | 110.6 | 2,177 | 16.80 | 106.9 |
| Religion | 20.96 | 5,599 | 20.54 | 5,599 | 98.0 | 20.75 | 5,788 | 99.0 | 20.59 | 5,696 | 98.2 | 5,949 | 19.93 | 95.1 |
| Science | 58.31 | 3,901 | 64.55 | 3,901 | 110.7 | 62.26 | 3,810 | 106.8 | 63.89 | 3,905 | 109.6 | 3,422 | 55.76 | 95.6 |
| Self-help, psychology | 26.53 | 4,906 | 26.54 | 4,906 | 100.0 | 27.29 | 4,872 | 102.9 | 26.61 | 5,190 | 100.3 | 4,525 | 25.68 | 96.8 |
| Sociology, economics | 35.34 | 7,107 | 39.61 | 7,107 | 112.1 | 39.88 | 6,873 | 112.8 | 43.90 | 7,802 | 124.2 | 6,931 | 39.49 | 111.7 |
| Sports, recreation | 20.05 | 2,465 | 19.10 | 2,465 | 95.3 | 19.66 | 2,516 | 98.1 | 20.00 | 2,298 | 99.8 | 2,104 | 20.24 | 100.9 |
| Technology | 74.85 | 1,941 | 76.41 | 1,941 | 102.1 | 72.49 | 2,207 | 96.8 | 87.64 | 2,076 | 117.1 | 1,542 | 73.01 | 97.5 |
| Travel | 17.40 | 2,171 | 19.01 | 2,171 | 109.3 | 19.71 | 2,885 | 113.3 | 21.07 | 3,383 | 121.1 | 2,861 | 19.61 | 112.7 |
| Young adult† | 14.40 | 2,609 | 13.79 | 2,609 | 95.8 | 14.25 | 2,547 | 99.0 | 13.71 | 3,029 | 95.2 | 2,454 | 13.90 | 96.5 |
| Totals | $31.09 | 100,496 | $33.16 | 100,496 | 106.7 | $33.68 | 100,475 | 108.3 | $38.00 | 110,056 | 122.2 | 97,897 | $34.51 | 111.0 |

Compiled by Catherine Barr from data supplied by Baker & Taylor.

## Table 7A / U.S. Audiobooks: Average Prices and Price Indexes, 2005–2008
Index Base: 2004 = 100

| | 2004 | 2005 Final | | | 2006 Final | | | 2007 Final | | | 2008 Preliminary | | |
|---|---|---|---|---|---|---|---|---|---|---|---|---|---|
| | Average Prices | Volumes | Average Prices | Index | Volumes | Average Prices | Index | Volumes | Average Prices | Index | Volumes | Average Prices | Index |
| Agriculture | $17.63 | 4 | $29.78 | 168.9 | 12 | $30.13 | 170.9 | 19 | $32.50 | 184.3 | 22 | $36.05 | 204.5 |
| Arts | 27.28 | 28 | 44.92 | 164.7 | 38 | 32.87 | 120.5 | 23 | 28.59 | 104.8 | 47 | 38.49 | 141.1 |
| Biography | 36.35 | 295 | 38.53 | 106.0 | 341 | 38.23 | 105.2 | 419 | 45.14 | 124.2 | 600 | 47.61 | 131.0 |
| Business | 32.47 | 79 | 46.84 | 144.3 | 139 | 42.41 | 130.6 | 161 | 36.01 | 110.9 | 229 | 39.51 | 121.7 |
| Careers | 28.16 | 60 | 39.31 | 139.6 | 92 | 37.75 | 134.1 | 103 | 29.72 | 105.5 | 167 | 40.43 | 143.6 |
| Children | 23.38 | 561 | 26.58 | 113.7 | 533 | 27.08 | 115.8 | 857 | 29.12 | 124.6 | 705 | 31.37 | 134.2 |
| Computers | n.a. | 5 | 41.39 | n.a. | 2 | 27.45 | n.a. | n.a. | n.a. | n.a. | 4 | 31.23 | n.a. |
| Cooking | 22.95 | 24 | 14.45 | 63.0 | 14 | 16.60 | 72.3 | 7 | 35.40 | 154.2 | 4 | 14.71 | 64.1 |
| Education | 31.53 | 36 | 27.60 | 87.5 | 49 | 30.84 | 97.8 | 36 | 41.11 | 130.4 | 20 | 32.09 | 101.8 |
| Fiction | 38.62 | 2,914 | 41.58 | 107.7 | 3,126 | 39.97 | 103.5 | 3,636 | 44.16 | 114.3 | 4,225 | 47.73 | 123.6 |
| General works | 28.94 | 80 | 27.77 | 96.0 | 133 | 30.86 | 106.6 | 147 | 33.07 | 114.3 | 208 | 39.92 | 137.9 |
| History | 33.07 | 194 | 41.56 | 125.7 | 311 | 39.92 | 120.7 | 487 | 48.01 | 145.2 | 571 | 53.74 | 162.5 |
| How-to, home arts | n.a. | 1 | 25.00 | n.a. | 4 | 22.25 | n.a. | 11 | 27.23 | n.a. | 9 | 42.20 | n.a. |
| Language | 49.70 | 663 | 69.42 | 139.7 | 436 | 40.74 | 82.0 | 335 | 41.56 | 83.6 | 363 | 38.72 | 77.9 |
| Law | 57.66 | 44 | 55.51 | 96.3 | 48 | 75.82 | 131.5 | 24 | 59.46 | 103.1 | 19 | 51.25 | 88.9 |
| Literature | 24.96 | 15 | 25.10 | 100.6 | 30 | 23.13 | 92.7 | 34 | 32.38 | 129.7 | 49 | 47.02 | 188.4 |
| Medicine | 77.48 | 7 | 147.25 | 190.0 | 22 | 42.28 | 54.6 | 20 | 68.55 | 88.5 | 23 | 101.06 | 130.4 |
| Music | 28.68 | 104 | 29.54 | 103.0 | 163 | 24.50 | 85.4 | 111 | 26.95 | 94.0 | 141 | 29.11 | 101.5 |
| Philosophy | 18.81 | 17 | 33.50 | 178.1 | 72 | 26.14 | 139.0 | 24 | 40.01 | 212.7 | 33 | 39.70 | 211.1 |
| Poetry, drama | 20.91 | 80 | 23.47 | 112.2 | 118 | 23.41 | 112.0 | 80 | 27.14 | 129.8 | 93 | 31.97 | 152.9 |
| Religion | 30.60 | 367 | 26.78 | 87.5 | 369 | 26.67 | 87.2 | 386 | 28.12 | 91.9 | 346 | 30.69 | 100.3 |
| Science | 32.52 | 34 | 36.96 | 113.7 | 49 | 34.37 | 105.7 | 46 | 39.32 | 120.9 | 85 | 46.20 | 142.1 |
| Self-help, psychology | 27.05 | 363 | 26.35 | 97.4 | 304 | 27.42 | 101.4 | 461 | 29.70 | 109.8 | 379 | 32.47 | 120.0 |
| Sociology, economics | 30.64 | 91 | 39.03 | 127.4 | 168 | 31.69 | 103.4 | 229 | 39.87 | 130.1 | 259 | 43.72 | 142.7 |
| Sports, recreation | 31.76 | 39 | 30.33 | 95.5 | 45 | 34.91 | 109.9 | 64 | 36.59 | 115.2 | 73 | 38.91 | 122.5 |
| Technology | 39.98 | 5 | 54.78 | 137.0 | 6 | 36.33 | 90.9 | 11 | 34.60 | 86.5 | 9 | 45.21 | 113.1 |
| Travel | 21.62 | 13 | 41.91 | 193.8 | 13 | 22.35 | 103.4 | 45 | 46.66 | 215.8 | 38 | 44.28 | 204.8 |
| Young adult | 33.29 | 196 | 35.84 | 107.7 | 239 | 42.26 | 126.9 | 273 | 39.91 | 119.9 | 259 | 44.18 | 132.7 |
| Totals | $35.04 | 6,319 | $40.41 | 115.3 | 6,876 | $36.48 | 104.1 | 8,049 | $39.76 | 113.5 | 8,980 | $43.82 | 125.1 |

Compiled by Catherine Barr from data supplied by Baker & Taylor. n.a. = not available

(continued from page 484)

Taylor and are not directly comparable with earlier data that came from R. R. Bowker's Books in Print. Differences in the two databases have inevitably resulted in variations in totals and across categories. For this reason, the index base for these tables has been changed to 2004.

Enhancements to the Baker & Taylor database have resulted in slightly different results for earlier years, and therefore these tables provide all-new data for 2004 forward.

Last year we added a new category—graphic novels, which can include both fiction and nonfiction—and a new table on audiobooks (Table 7A). The graphic novels category is not included in Table 7A.

This year we have added a number of additional categories that we believe will be of interest: Careers, Computers, Cooking, How-to and Home Arts, and Self-help and Psychology (Psychology was previously included in a category with Philosophy). We have also broken down the former Juveniles category into two categories: Children (PreK–6) and Young Adults (7–12).

Book prices were mixed in 2007 and preliminary figures indicated a similar situation in 2008. List prices for hardcovers (Table 3) fell by 3.12 percent in 2007 but returned in 2008 to almost exactly the same position as in 2006. Mass market paperback prices (Table 6) continued to show slow but steady increases, up 0.47 percent and a further 1.4 percent in 2008, while trade paperback prices (Table 7) rose a strong 12.83 percent in 2007 but declined in 2008. Audiobook prices (Table 7A), which had dipped in 2006, recovered by 8.99 percent in 2007 and were showing a strong 10.21 percent increase in preliminary data for 2008.

The North American Academic Books Price Index (Table 4) is prepared by Stephen Bosch. The average price of North American Academic Books in 2007 (Table 4) increased by 1.1 percent as compared with the 2006 average price. The growth of electronic books is now influencing book prices. Starting in 2006 and continuing into the foreseeable future, the major vendors have been very aggressive in adding electronic books to their offerings. In most academic settings e-books are not cheaper than the print counterparts and a portion of the price increase is due to the addition of the more expensive e-book versions. To be sure that this is truly the case, Bosch reports, "I redid the 2006 data using a file from one vendor that included no electronic books, and the number of titles in the combined index dropped by 8,334 and the average price declined 5.5 percent. Due to customer demands, vendors offer multiple platforms and pricing models for e-books; consequently there can be multiple prices for the same title. Since this is where the market is going, it is appropriate to have e-books in the index, but it is also good to know that this is a driver for price increases, not a price decrease at this time. Publishers are still very concerned that selling e-books to libraries will hurt overall sales, so pricing to libraries is higher than print pricing."

For the past two years the average prices had been trending higher (up 6.4 percent in 2005–2006), but this year the increase has leveled off. In addition to the growth of e-books being a driver in earlier years, there are some other factors that may help explain this. The number of titles treated this year declined from 2006 (77,534 to 72,965). One vendor reported a decrease of a little more than 3,000 titles in what they treated while the other vendor stayed relatively the same. The additional drop was due to increased overlap in the title lists. When an

Figure 1 / Comparison of Titles in Sample Grouped by Price

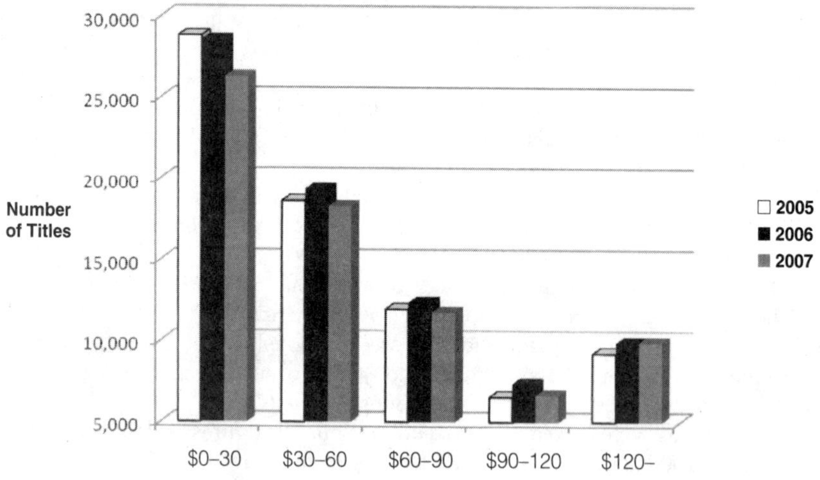

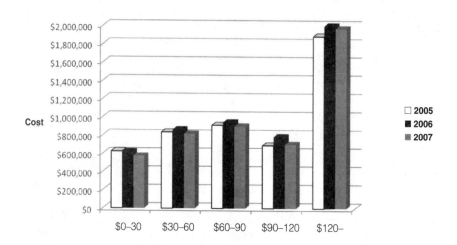

Figure 2 / Comparison of Costs in Sample Grouped by Price

analysis is done on the data by looking at price grouped into "bands," the largest drop in number of titles in the index was in the group priced less than $30. See Figure 1.

However, if you look at the actual dollar values in groups, this drop in the number of titles was not what held down the price index for 2007. Although the $0–30 price area has the largest number of titles, dollar wise it is the smallest portion as far as cost (sum of all prices) goes in the index. The decline in the prices in the upper end of the index was what caused the drop in the level of increase. Since STM (scientific, technical, and medical) publishers were early adopters of e-books and STM titles still tend to be more expensive, it may be that growth in the top end has slowed. Also, as budgets tighten it may be that publishers are bringing fewer expensive titles to market. See Figure 2.

The data used for this index are derived from all titles treated by Blackwell Book Services and YBP in their approval plans during the calendar years listed. The index does include paperback editions as supplied by these vendors and this inclusion has clearly influenced the prices reflected in the index figures. In addition, e-books are now being treated in approval plans and these are consequently part of the data reports and of the index. The inclusion of both paperbacks and e-books has resulted in the numbers of titles increasing, since each has a unique ISBN and is treated as a separate edition. So drivers for this price increase include general price inflation as well as increases from the inclusion of e-books, which generally are more expensive than print counterparts. Many e-book pricing models add extra charges of as much as 50 percent to the retail price. Paperbacks and e-books will continue to be a part of this index, as they are included in the approval plan data and represent a viable part of the North American book market. The direct impact on inflation caused by hardback/paperback/e-book pricing continues to be unquantifiable, but it is clear that the increases in overall price inflation for academic books during the past few years seems to correlate to increases in paperback numbers and now the impact of e-books. This may change, as publishers have started to "up" the size and price of paperbacks or as e-books find pricing levels closer to normal retail.

Analysis of the data as it is processed shows that the overlap titles that are excluded from the index tend to be more expensive than the unique titles processed by each vendor. This fact will tend to hold down the average prices in the index. This year a drop in titles from one vendor tended to occur in the lower part of the price range. In all cases, the average price of a book for each vendor is 4 percent to 6 percent higher than the aggregate average price. This shows that when the titles are combined in the aggregate index, the unique titles each vendor handles tend to be cheaper than the titles that overlap. This makes sense because publications from small publishers tend to be cheaper than those from mainstream publishers and the small publishers will tend to make up more of the unique titles handled by each vendor. All vendors will carry the full title list from Macmillan or Oxford University Press, but a small regional press may not be supplied by all vendors. Current trends reported by vendors indicate that increases are going to grow in 2008, and there should also be increases in the titles and formats available.

Price changes vary, as always, among subject areas. This year there were several double-digit increases in subject areas and several areas saw prices decrease. If you look at the top areas for price increases, 2007 shows that STM areas are back as those with the largest price increases. The areas showing double-digit increases were: Science (general), Industrial arts, Law, Agriculture, and Geology. It is interesting to note that some areas that showed high increases last year (Botany and Literature) are now at the other end of the spectrum of price increases. It is also interesting to note that some STM areas that have seen large price increases in the past, Physics and Chemistry, showed price decreases this year.

It is good to bear in mind that price indexes become less accurate at describing price changes the smaller the sample becomes. Geology is a small sampling and showed an 18.1 percent increase, but to then conclude that all books in the area increased 18.1 percent is not correct. This area has a small sample size of only 191 books and the inclusion of just a few expensive items can have a major impact on prices for the category.

This compilation of the U.S. College Books Price Index (Table 5), prepared by Frederick C. Lynden, contains price and indexing information for the years 2006 through 2008 (index base year of 1989), and also the percentage change between 2007 and 2008. The index is based on titles reviewed in *Choice* magazine, a publication of the Association for College and Research Libraries, a division of the American Library Association. Data for this index were compiled from 6,766 reviews of books published in *Choice* during 2008; expensive titles ($500 or more) were omitted from the analysis, thus the total number of titles reported is smaller. As with Table 4 (North American Academic Books), this index includes some paperback prices; as a result, the average price of books is less than if only hardcover books were included.

For 2008 the overall average price for books in the Humanities, Sciences, and Social and Behavioral Sciences (including reference books) was $64.52, a moderate price increase of 3.3 percent over the average 2007 price of $62.44. Reference books had the highest average price at $136.26 and also the highest increase—6 percent over the previous year. Excluding reference books, the 2008 book price was $59.35, or a 3.85 percent increase over the average 2007 price of $57.15.

The average 2008 price for Humanities titles increased by 4 percent over the previous year. The average price for Science and Technology titles increased by 1.8 percent, whereas the price for Social and Behavioral Sciences titles increased by 3.6 percent. Since 1989 there has been an overall average book price increase of 59 percent when reference books are included (and 55 percent when reference books are excluded). Calculated separately, reference books showed a 6 percent increase over the previous year (2007). Last year's decrease in the average price for a reference book will probably soon be forgotten. Since 1989 there has been a 233 percent increase in the average price of reference books.

This year there are no appendixes listing data for non-book and higher-priced titles, which are excluded from the index. The author will supply this information upon request.

**Newspaper Prices**

The indexes for U.S. (Table 8A) and international (Table 8B) newspapers are compiled by Genevieve S. Owens. Both indexes reversed their trends this year. For U.S. titles, the average price for mail delivery of a daily newspaper went up by 4.1 percent. For international titles, the average price for the most expedient mail delivery of a newspaper went down by 10.2 percent. The effects of postage costs and papers' attempts to retain print subscribers factor into both indexes.

The number of titles being tracked by both instruments declined again this year. In the case of international titles, papers continue to convert to "Order Direct" status. This trend affects U.S. titles, too. Domestic papers continue to cease publication. This year, a few titles also became available through electronic mail or online access only. These changes are challenging for libraries to manage. As acquisitions budgets tighten, moreover, libraries are increasingly can-

### Table 8A / U.S. Daily Newspapers:
### Average Prices and Price Indexes, 1990–2009
Index Base: 1990 = 100

| Year | Number of Titles | Average Price | Percent Change | Index |
|------|------|------|------|------|
| 1990 | 165 | $189.58 | 0.0 | 100.0 |
| 1991 | 166 | 198.13 | 4.5 | 104.5 |
| 1992 | 167 | 222.68 | 12.4 | 117.5 |
| 1993 | 171 | 229.92 | 3.3 | 121.3 |
| 1994 | 171 | 261.91 | 13.9 | 138.2 |
| 1995 | 172 | 270.22 | 3.2 | 142.5 |
| 1996 | 166 | 300.21 | 11.1 | 158.4 |
| 1997 | 165 | 311.77 | 3.9 | 164.5 |
| 1998 | 163 | 316.60 | 1.5 | 167.0 |
| 1999 | 162 | 318.44 | 0.6 | 168.0 |
| 2000 | 162 | 324.26 | 1.8 | 171.0 |
| 2001 | 160 | 330.78 | 2.0 | 174.5 |
| 2002 | 158 | 340.38 | 2.9 | 179.5 |
| 2003 | 156 | 352.65 | 3.6 | 186.0 |
| 2004 | 154 | 364.97 | 3.5 | 192.5 |
| 2005 | 154 | 372.64 | 2.1 | 196.6 |
| 2006 | 154 | 369.24 | -0.9 | 194.8 |
| 2007 | 152 | 375.76 | 1.8 | 198.2 |
| 2008 | 149 | 368.30 | -2.0 | 194.3 |
| 2009 | 144 | 383.33 | 4.1 | 202.2 |

Compiled by Genevieve S. Owens, Williamsburg (Virginia) Regional Library, from data supplied by EBSCO Information Services. Thanks to Kathleen Born of EBSCO for her assistance with this project.

### Table 8B / International Newspapers:
### Average Prices and Price Indexes, 1993–2009
Index Base: 1993 = 100

| Year | Number of Titles | Average Price | Percent Change | Index |
|------|------|------|------|------|
| 1993 | 46 | $806.91 | 0.0 | 100.0 |
| 1994 | 46 | 842.01 | 4.3 | 104.3 |
| 1995 | 49 | 942.13 | 11.9 | 116.3 |
| 1996 | 50 | 992.78 | 5.4 | 123.0 |
| 1997 | 53 | 1,029.49 | 3.7 | 127.6 |
| 1998 | 52 | 1,046.72 | 1.7 | 129.7 |
| 1999 | 50 | 1,049.13 | 0.2 | 130.0 |
| 2000 | 50 | 1,050.88 | 0.2 | 130.2 |
| 2001 | 50 | 1,038.26 | -1.2 | 128.7 |
| 2002 | 49 | 1,052.69 | 1.4 | 130.5 |
| 2003 | 46 | 1,223.31 | 16.2 | 151.6 |
| 2004 | 43 | 1,301.71 | 6.4 | 161.3 |
| 2005 | 47 | 1,352.23 | 3.9 | 167.6 |
| 2006 | 45 | 1,306.79 | -3.4 | 161.9 |
| 2007 | 44 | 1,354.60 | 3.7 | 167.9 |
| 2008 | 40 | 1,568.71 | 15.8 | 194.4 |
| 2009 | 38 | 1,409.39 | -10.2 | 174.7 |

Compiled by Genevieve S. Owens, Williamsburg (Virginia) Regional Library, from data supplied by EBSCO Information Services. Thanks to Kathleen Born of EBSCO for her assistance with this project.

celling print newspaper subscriptions (especially for expensive international titles) and referring users to newspapers' Web sites for current events coverage.

Given these circumstances, the LMPI Editorial Board expects to discontinue both newspaper indexes. Please contact compiler Genevieve Owens (gowens@ wrl.org) with concerns about this decision or ideas about ways to develop new, more useful newspaper indexes.

### Prices of Other Media

The U.S. nonprint media index (former Table 9) does not appear this year. Those wishing historical information can find data for 1997 and 1998, indexed to a base of 1980, in the 2001 edition of the *Bowker Annual*. The database, compiled in previous years by Dana Alessi, collected information from titles reviewed in *Booklist, Library Journal, School Library Journal,* and *Video Librarian.*

The CD-ROM price inventory that formerly appeared as Table 10 also has been discontinued. As with U.S. Serials Services, many of the titles that were published in CD-ROM format have migrated to Web editions. Additionally, the changes from single workstation pricing to network pricing or site licenses made tracking of the prices for this category of material difficult.

The LMPI Editorial Board has been working on developing a price index for electronic journals. Factors hindering progress in this area include, but are not limited to, the continued volatility of pricing models, consortial pricing, and institution-specific package deals. The Association of Research Libraries is also considering ways to gather this important economic data for libraries.

## Foreign Prices

Exchange rates were closely watched during 2008. The dollar proved much stronger against the euro, the pound, and the Canadian dollar compared with 2007. However, the dollar lost ground against the Japanese yen. Continued inflation of book and serials prices may offset this slight advantage in currency exchange.

| Dates | 112/31/03* | 12/31/04** | 12/31/05** | 12/31/06** | 12/30/07** | 12/31/08** |
|---|---|---|---|---|---|---|
| Canada | 1.2958 | 1.1880 | 1.1680 | 1.1720 | .9990 | 1.1910 |
| Euro | 0.7913 | 0.7530 | 0.8470 | 0.7590 | .6800 | .7310 |
| U.K. | 0.5478 | 0.5240 | 0.5820 | 0.5120 | .4860 | .6570 |
| Japan | 106.2700 | 103.1100 | 117.9400 | 119.5300 | 110.8800 | 92.6500 |

* Data from the regional Federal Reserve Bank of St. Louis (http://www.stls.frb.org/fred/data/exchange.html).

**Data from Financial Management Services. U.S. Treasury Department (http://fms.treas.gov/intn.html). The change is due to the Federal Reserve Bank of St. Louis no longer reporting Euro to U.S. and U.K. to U.S. rates.

The foreign price index that follows is British Academic Books (Table 9). Tables showing prices for Latin American Periodicals, German academic books, German academic periodicals, and Dutch English-language periodicals have not been updated and are not included in this volume. Please refer to earlier editions of the *Bowker Annual* for historical information.

**British Prices**

The price index for British academic books (Table 9) is compiled by Curt Holleman from information supplied by Blackwell's Book Services. This index is being repeated from last year because current pricing was not available at the time this publication was being produced. Information concerning this index is available in the 2008 edition of the *Bowker Annual.*

## Using the Price Indexes

Librarians are encouraged to monitor trends in the publishing industry and changes in economic conditions when preparing budget forecasts and projections. The ALA ALCTS Library Materials Price Index Editorial Board endeavors to make information on publishing trends readily available by sponsoring the annual compilation and publication of price data contained in Tables 1 to 9. The indexes cover newly published library materials and document prices and rates of percent changes at the national and international level. They are useful benchmarks against which local costs can be compared, but because they reflect retail prices in the aggregate, they are not a substitute for cost data that reflect the collecting patterns of individual libraries, and they are not a substitute for specific cost studies.

Differences between local prices and those found in national indexes arise partially because these indexes exclude discounts, service charges, shipping and handling fees, and other costs that the library might incur. Discrepancies may also relate to a library's subject coverage; mix of titles purchased, including both current and backfiles; and the proportion of the library's budget expended on domestic or foreign materials. These variables can affect the average price paid by an individual library, although the individual library's rate of increase may not differ greatly from the national indexes.

LMPI is interested in pursuing studies that would correlate a particular library's costs with the national prices. The group welcomes interested parties to its meetings at ALA Annual and Midwinter conferences.

The LMPI Editorial Board consists of compilers Catherine Barr, Ajaye Bloomstone, Stephen Bosch, Stephanie Braunstein, Brenda Dingley, Virginia Gilbert, Curt Holleman, Frederick Lynden, Janet Belanger Morrow, Genevieve S. Owens, and editor Narda Tafuri.

**Table 9 / British Academic Books: Average Prices and Price Indexes, 2005–2007**

Index Base: 1985 = 100; prices listed are pounds sterling

| Subject Area | 1985 | | 2005 | | | 2006 | | | 2007 | | |
|---|---|---|---|---|---|---|---|---|---|---|---|
| | No. of Titles | Average Price | No. of Titles | Average Price | Index | No. of Titles | Average Price | Index | No. of Titles | Average Price | Index |
| General works | 29 | £30.54 | 26 | £33.59 | 110.0 | 33 | £43.04 | 140.9 | 34 | 39.86 | 130.5 |
| Fine arts | 329 | 21.70 | 603 | 29.94 | 138.0 | 456 | 32.68 | 150.6 | 457 | 32.12 | 148.0 |
| Architecture | 97 | 20.68 | 199 | 36.38 | 175.9 | 152 | 44.31 | 214.3 | 179 | 41.68 | 201.5 |
| Music | 136 | 17.01 | 134 | 38.44 | 226.0 | 141 | 37.73 | 221.8 | 181 | 42.49 | 249.8 |
| Performing arts except music | 110 | 13.30 | 290 | 31.42 | 236.2 | 277 | 36.60 | 275.2 | 271 | 40.05 | 301.1 |
| Archaeology | 146 | 18.80 | 129 | 40.87 | 217.4 | 104 | 39.61 | 210.7 | 107 | 48.71 | 259.1 |
| Geography | 60 | 22.74 | 55 | 50.01 | 219.9 | 29 | 50.50 | 222.1 | 35 | 56.10 | 246.7 |
| History | 1,123 | 16.92 | 1,198 | 36.02 | 212.9 | 1,031 | 40.54 | 239.6 | 1,077 | 40.91 | 241.8 |
| Philosophy | 127 | 18.41 | 359 | 43.54 | 236.5 | 388 | 45.45 | 246.9 | 385 | 46.90 | 254.8 |
| Religion | 328 | 10.40 | 601 | 40.00 | 384.6 | 667 | 40.85 | 392.8 | 684 | 40.93 | 393.6 |
| Language | 135 | 19.37 | 292 | 45.68 | 235.8 | 268 | 49.25 | 254.3 | 257 | 49.28 | 254.4 |
| Miscellaneous humanities | 59 | 21.71 | 37 | 37.92 | 174.7 | 42 | 34.84 | 160.5 | 20 | 25.91 | 119.3 |
| Literary texts | 570 | 9.31 | 1,138 | 14.68 | 157.7 | 1,046 | 16.14 | 173.4 | 1,000 | 15.22 | 163.5 |
| Literary criticism | 438 | 14.82 | 619 | 43.62 | 294.3 | 545 | 44.46 | 300.0 | 680 | 46.58 | 314.3 |
| Law | 188 | 24.64 | 674 | 63.17 | 256.4 | 614 | 62.42 | 253.3 | 683 | 67.41 | 273.6 |
| Library science and book trade | 78 | 18.69 | 65 | 40.65 | 217.5 | 79 | 45.47 | 243.3 | 73 | 45.27 | 242.2 |
| Mass communications | 38 | 14.20 | 170 | 41.68 | 293.5 | 180 | 42.42 | 298.7 | 151 | 44.67 | 314.6 |
| Anthropology and ethnology | 42 | 20.71 | 72 | 50.57 | 244.2 | 51 | 49.73 | 240.1 | 80 | 47.51 | 229.4 |
| Sociology | 136 | 15.24 | 276 | 47.74 | 313.3 | 238 | 50.55 | 331.7 | 239 | 49.86 | 327.2 |
| Psychology | 107 | 19.25 | 156 | 42.56 | 221.1 | 191 | 47.02 | 244.3 | 161 | 48.25 | 250.6 |
| Economics | 334 | 20.48 | 603 | 56.20 | 274.4 | 542 | 58.44 | 285.4 | 491 | 62.03 | 302.9 |
| Political science and intl. relations | 314 | 15.54 | 879 | 46.23 | 297.5 | 813 | 48.23 | 310.4 | 839 | 50.23 | 323.2 |
| Miscellaneous social sciences | 20 | 26.84 | 33 | 65.90 | 245.5 | 33 | 54.06 | 201.4 | 43 | 60.37 | 224.9 |
| Military science | 83 | 17.69 | 58 | 40.48 | 228.8 | 85 | 49.24 | 278.3 | 85 | 46.20 | 261.2 |
| Sports and recreation | 44 | 11.23 | 131 | 37.23 | 331.5 | 143 | 38.48 | 342.7 | 103 | 39.86 | 354.9 |
| Social service | 56 | 12.17 | 99 | 40.41 | 332.0 | 101 | 36.79 | 302.3 | 94 | 42.90 | 352.5 |
| Education | 295 | 12.22 | 429 | 38.92 | 318.5 | 449 | 44.54 | 364.5 | 425 | 45.59 | 373.1 |
| Management and business administration | 427 | 19.55 | 890 | 47.74 | 244.2 | 870 | 49.19 | 251.6 | 812 | 49.33 | 252.3 |
| Miscellaneous applied social studies | 13 | 9.58 | 28 | 39.90 | 416.5 | 28 | 45.14 | 471.2 | 33 | 47.09 | 491.5 |

|  | | | | | | | | | | | |
|---|---|---|---|---|---|---|---|---|---|---|---|
| Criminology | 45 | 11.45 | 150 | 43.17 | 377.0 | 134 | 44.37 | 387.5 | 141 | 44.22 | 386.2 |
| Applied inter-discip. soc. studies | 254 | 14.17 | 595 | 47.20 | 333.1 | 581 | 50.61 | 357.2 | 563 | 52.30 | 369.1 |
| General science | 43 | 13.73 | 59 | 38.57 | 280.9 | 39 | 39.98 | 291.2 | 39 | 47.84 | 348.4 |
| Botany | 55 | 30.54 | 38 | 53.26 | 174.4 | 27 | 63.40 | 207.6 | 19 | 68.37 | 223.9 |
| Zoology | 85 | 25.67 | 51 | 59.64 | 232.3 | 42 | 51.95 | 202.4 | 35 | 52.38 | 204.1 |
| Human biology | 35 | 28.91 | 45 | 50.65 | 175.2 | 35 | 52.25 | 180.7 | 27 | 49.59 | 171.5 |
| Biochemistry | 26 | 33.57 | 19 | 69.10 | 205.8 | 21 | 63.67 | 189.7 | 14 | 67.43 | 200.9 |
| Miscellaneous biological sciences | 152 | 26.64 | 138 | 54.08 | 203.0 | 130 | 57.76 | 216.8 | 117 | 54.79 | 205.7 |
| Chemistry | 109 | 48.84 | 70 | 69.91 | 143.1 | 60 | 64.10 | 131.2 | 54 | 87.53 | 179.2 |
| Earth sciences | 87 | 28.94 | 87 | 63.34 | 218.9 | 92 | 60.86 | 210.3 | 71 | 64.09 | 221.5 |
| Astronomy | 43 | 20.36 | 74 | 42.92 | 210.8 | 73 | 47.59 | 233.7 | 68 | 41.73 | 205.0 |
| Physics | 76 | 26.58 | 185 | 56.22 | 211.5 | 165 | 53.87 | 202.7 | 96 | 54.92 | 206.6 |
| Mathematics | 123 | 20.20 | 225 | 49.39 | 244.5 | 203 | 44.41 | 219.9 | 154 | 49.55 | 245.3 |
| Computer sciences | 150 | 20.14 | 142 | 41.49 | 206.0 | 123 | 37.49 | 186.1 | 133 | 38.73 | 192.3 |
| Inter-disciplinary technical fields | 38 | 26.14 | 36 | 51.61 | 197.4 | 42 | 55.02 | 210.5 | 51 | 57.39 | 219.5 |
| Civil engineering | 134 | 28.68 | 128 | 80.38 | 280.3 | 126 | 80.40 | 280.3 | 115 | 75.02 | 261.6 |
| Mechanical engineering | 27 | 31.73 | 24 | 54.62 | 172.1 | 30 | 78.76 | 248.2 | 18 | 66.38 | 209.2 |
| Electrical and electronic engineering | 100 | 33.12 | 126 | 65.63 | 198.2 | 113 | 59.21 | 178.8 | 123 | 61.66 | 186.2 |
| Materials science | 54 | 37.93 | 48 | 90.58 | 238.8 | 38 | 97.71 | 257.6 | 47 | 93.64 | 246.9 |
| Chemical engineering | 24 | 40.48 | 30 | 77.60 | 191.7 | 21 | 79.59 | 196.6 | 15 | 72.93 | 180.2 |
| Miscellaneous technology | 217 | 36.33 | 286 | 54.89 | 151.1 | 279 | 55.48 | 152.7 | 251 | 55.64 | 153.2 |
| Food and domestic science | 38 | 23.75 | 90 | 30.98 | 130.4 | 78 | 34.13 | 143.7 | 88 | 28.05 | 118.1 |
| Non-clinical medicine | 97 | 18.19 | 181 | 43.80 | 240.8 | 234 | 38.64 | 212.4 | 178 | 47.78 | 262.7 |
| General medicine | 73 | 21.03 | 87 | 50.53 | 240.2 | 65 | 54.02 | 256.9 | 53 | 55.00 | 261.5 |
| Internal medicine | 163 | 27.30 | 185 | 60.74 | 222.5 | 185 | 57.74 | 211.5 | 149 | 60.01 | 219.8 |
| Psychiatry and mental disorders | 71 | 17.97 | 238 | 34.42 | 191.5 | 225 | 38.23 | 212.7 | 170 | 39.88 | 221.9 |
| Surgery | 50 | 29.37 | 57 | 67.95 | 231.4 | 58 | 62.31 | 212.2 | 37 | 69.51 | 236.7 |
| Miscellaneous medicine | 292 | 22.08 | 318 | 49.31 | 223.3 | 274 | 51.28 | 232.2 | 289 | 51.50 | 233.2 |
| Dentistry | 20 | 19.39 | 17 | 34.86 | 179.8 | 19 | 51.41 | 265.1 | 15 | 49.23 | 253.9 |
| Pharmacy* | n.a. | n.a. | 5 | 29.79 | n.a. | 9 | 41.05 | n.a. | 9 | 73.21 | na |
| Nursing | 71 | 8 | 105 | 29.42 | 367.8 | 106 | 25.11 | 313.9 | 86 | 28.00 | 350.0 |
| Agriculture and forestry | 78 | 23.69 | 63 | 48.47 | 204.6 | 56 | 47.95 | 202.4 | 52 | 57.94 | 244.6 |
| Animal husbandry and vet. medicine | 34 | 20.92 | 59 | 43.88 | 209.8 | 53 | 48.59 | 232.3 | 46 | 55.67 | 266.1 |
| Natural resources and conservation | 58 | 22.88 | 50 | 60.39 | 263.9 | 62 | 57.10 | 249.6 | 60 | 52.74 | 230.5 |
| Total, All Books (NT) | 9,049 | £19.07 | 14,260 | £43.37 | 227.4 | 13,400 | £45.09 | 236.4 | 13,065 | £46.39 | 243.3 |

* New category introduced in 2001.
Last year's average price was £45.09 and the overall inflation rate is 2.9%.
n.a. = not available

# Book Title Output and Average Prices: 2004–2008

Catherine Barr
Contributing Editor

Constance Harbison
Baker & Taylor

American book title output continued to climb over the four-year period from 2004 to 2007, rising by 3.7 percent in 2005, just over 1 percent in 2006, and 8.07 percent in 2007. Preliminary figures for 2008—publishers were still submitting late 2008 titles in early 2009—suggest that output for the year will be considerably lower than the 2007 total, probably a result of the economic downturn and slumping book industry.

As was the case last year, the figures in this edition of the *Library and Book Trade Almanac* were provided by book wholesaler Baker & Taylor. They are not directly comparable with earlier data that came from R. R. Bowker's Books in Print, and for this reason the index base for these tables has been changed to 2004.

The final figures in this year's tables for 2004, 2005, 2006, and 2007 have been revised to reflect improvements that have been made in the Baker & Taylor database.

Last year we added a new table on Audiobooks (Table 6) and a new category—Graphic Novels—that appears in all tables except Table 6. The Graphic Novel category includes both fiction and nonfiction. This year we have added a number of additional categories that we believe will be of interest: Careers, Computers, Cooking, How-to and Home Arts, and Self-help and Psychology (Psychology was previously included in a category with Philosophy). We have also broken down the former Juveniles category into two categories: Children (PreK–6) and Young Adults (7–12).

## Output by Format and by Category

Output of hardcovers and paperbacks generally held steady or grew in 2007, with overall hardcover titles and editions increasing by 4,474 (6.77 percent) following a gain of 1,834 (2.85 percent) in 2006. Hardcovers priced at less than $81—nearly 70 percent of the hardcover market—increased by 3,913 titles (8.81 percent) in 2007 after falling by 306 (0.68 percent) in 2006. Mass market paperback output fell by 194 titles (3.86 percent) in 2007, but trade paperbacks registered an increase of 9,581 titles (9.54 percent). In 2006 mass market and trade paperback output was virtually unchanged. Output of audiobooks continued to rise in 2007, with a jump of 1,173 titles or 17.1 percent following the increase of 557 titles (8.81 percent) registered in 2006. This trend seemed set to continue, with preliminary 2008 data showing an increase of 11.6 percent. Preliminary 2008 figures for other formats indicate that most will see declines for the year.

Fiction, a key category, showed mixed results across formats. Trade paperback fiction grew by 1,493 titles in 2007 (18.66 percent), while mass market fiction fell by 113 titles (2.6 percent) and hardcover fiction (less than $81) fell by 14 titles (0.32 percent). Only the hardcover and audio formats seemed poised to increase in 2008.

The important juveniles category is now broken into children's and young adult (YA) titles. Children's hardcover titles priced at less than $81 jumped by 2,260 units or 18.7 percent in 2007, but trade paperback titles fell 4.01 percent in the same period. YA hardcover titles under $81 also showed strong growth (21.55 percent) as did trade paperbacks (rising 18.92 percent). Audiobooks for children increased a dramatic 60.79 percent in 2007, with the YA category trailing at 14.23 percent growth.

Graphic novels—a category that can include both fiction and nonfiction—continued to show impressive increases. In hardcovers under $81, graphic novels registered a rise of 13.3 percent in 2007 following an increase of 23.9 percent in 2006 and with estimated growth of 39.3 percent in 2008. Trade paperback increases were less dramatic, with a 6.6 percent increase in 2007 and a projected increase of 10.1 in 2008.

A review of performance in nonfiction categories shows considerable variations. Output in the overall arts category rose 6.7 percent in 2006, 8.9 percent in 2007, and appeared set to do well in 2008. The careers category has been showing slow but steady growth. Travel output had been strong in 2006 and 2007 (up 26.8 and 25.9 percent, respectively), but was headed downward in 2008. History was up 4.2 percent in 2006 and 9.2 percent in 2007, but estimates for 2008 projected a fall in the range of 10 percent. Categories showing large one-year spikes in 2007 were literature (up 20.2 percent), philosophy (up 26.6 percent), poetry/drama (up 14.3 percent), and YA (up 17.3 percent). Business titles shot up 79.1 percent in 2007 after falling 14.1 percent in 2006, but output in 2008 was down an estimated 45.1 percent. Most other categories show mixed results, up one year and down the next, or vice versa.

## Average Book Prices

Average book prices were mixed in 2007 and preliminary figures indicated a similar situation in 2008. List prices for hardcovers (Table 2) fell in 2007, by $2.62 or 3.1 percent, but returned in 2008 to almost exactly the same position as in 2006. Prices for hardcovers under $81 (Table 3), on the other hand, rose by 0.8 percent in 2007 and by 3.1 percent in 2008. Mass market paperback prices (Table 4) continued to show slow but steady increases, up 0.4 percent in 2007 to $6.41 and a further 1.4 percent in 2008, while trade paperback prices (Table 5) rose a strong 12.9 percent in 2007, to $38.00, but declined in 2008. Audiobook prices (Table 6), which had dipped in 2006, recovered to $39.76 in 2007 (an increase of $3.28 or 9.0 percent) and were showing a strong 10.2 percent increase in preliminary data for 2008.

Average book prices for fiction rose for all formats in 2007. Hardcover fiction titles priced at less than $81 increased 31 cents (1.2 percent) to $27.28. Mass market fiction increased 6 cents (1.0 percent), and trade fiction increased $1.50 (9.4 percent). Audiobook fiction rose a strong $4.20 (10.5 percent). Preliminary data for 2008 indicated that these trends would continue, with only trade paperbacks showing weaker growth or a potential decline.

Prices for children's titles increased in 2007 and in 2008. Hardcover prices under $81 increased 18 cents (0.1 percent) and 51 cents (2.7 percent), respectively. Children's mass market paperbacks rose 9 cents (1.6 percent) and 39 cents (6.8 percent), trade paperbacks increased 10 cents (0.9 percent) and 26 cents (2.5 percent), and audiobooks were up by $2.04 (7.5 percent) and $2.26 (7.8 percent). Young adult prices showed more volatility. After falling 2.6 percent in 2006 in the hardcovers under $81 sector, prices rebounded by 54 cents or 2.1 percent in 2007; preliminary figures for 2008, however, showed another drop. Mass market paperback prices fell by 21 cents or 2.9 percent in 2007 but rose by 9 cents or 1.3 percent in 2008, a pattern mirrored by trade paperbacks, which fell 54 cents or 3.8 percent in 2007 but rose 19 cents or 1.4 percent in 2008, and by audiobooks,

Table 1 / American Book Production, 2004–2008

| Category | 2004 Final | 2005 Final | 2006 Final | 2007 Final | 2008 Preliminary |
|---|---|---|---|---|---|
| Agriculture | 1,473 | 1,606 | 1,467 | 1,516 | 1,429 |
| Arts | 7,176 | 7,403 | 7,896 | 8,599 | 8,315 |
| Biography | 3,418 | 3,422 | 3,403 | 3,685 | 3,437 |
| Business | 6,139 | 7,030 | 6,042 | 10,820 | 5,946 |
| Careers | 1,847 | 2,153 | 2,172 | 2,306 | 2,247 |
| Children | 20,244 | 21,692 | 21,728 | 23,683 | 21,524 |
| Computers | 3,964 | 4,410 | 4,020 | 4,201 | 3,376 |
| Cooking | 1,891 | 2,060 | 1,883 | 1,938 | 2,203 |
| Education | 5,465 | 6,089 | 6,318 | 5,782 | 5,521 |
| Fiction | 15,873 | 17,094 | 16,913 | 18,391 | 17,894 |
| General works | 5,360 | 5,236 | 5,261 | 4,994 | 4,843 |
| Graphic novels | 1,708 | 2,345 | 2,372 | 2,553 | 2,919 |
| History | 10,978 | 10,368 | 10,806 | 11,800 | 10,605 |
| How-to, home arts | 1,830 | 1,870 | 1,831 | 1,756 | 1,664 |
| Language | 4,143 | 4,685 | 4,367 | 4,496 | 3,848 |
| Law | 3,337 | 3,265 | 4,786 | 4,615 | 5,353 |
| Literature | 3,862 | 4,166 | 3,621 | 4,353 | 3,845 |
| Medicine | 6,114 | 6,362 | 6,839 | 6,949 | 6,642 |
| Music | 3,423 | 3,110 | 3,052 | 2,961 | 3,272 |
| Philosophy | 2,027 | 2,065 | 2,067 | 2,616 | 2,154 |
| Poetry, drama | 2,626 | 2,726 | 2,487 | 2,843 | 2,698 |
| Religion | 8,549 | 8,316 | 8,453 | 8,367 | 8,571 |
| Science | 8,222 | 8,552 | 8,672 | 8,605 | 7,930 |
| Self-help, psychology | 7,088 | 6,858 | 7,040 | 7,272 | 6,607 |
| Sociology, economics | 12,152 | 11,981 | 12,307 | 13,351 | 12,716 |
| Sports, recreation | 3,515 | 3,409 | 3,536 | 3,234 | 3,082 |
| Technology | 4,589 | 3,912 | 4,402 | 4,210 | 3,915 |
| Travel | 2,223 | 2,593 | 3,289 | 4,140 | 3,266 |
| Young adult | 4,784 | 5,300 | 5,059 | 5,933 | 4,841 |
| Total | 164,020 | 170,078 | 172,089 | 185,969 | 170,663 |

which fell by $2.35 or 5.6 percent in 2007 but more than made up for that decline with an estimated increase of $4.28 or 10.7 percent.

Hardcover categories showing double-digit increases in 2007 include general works (up 20 percent and showing further growth in 2008) and travel (up 25 percent, although this increase appeared to be erased by a sharp decline in 2008).

In trade paperbacks, double-digit increases registered in the following categories in 2007: business, up 17.8 percent but with a preliminary dip of 12.4 percent in 2008; graphic novels, up 10.9 percent with a 4.9 percent decline foreseen for 2008; law, up a whopping 36.7 percent with further growth of 10.8 percent forecast for 2008; literature, up 10.8 percent with further growth of 3.2 percent in 2008; sociology and economics, up 10.1 percent (an increase that appears to be have been wiped out in 2008); and technology, up 20.9 percent but with a decline of 16.7 percent in 2008. Other categories showing price increases over the two years are arts, how-to and home arts, medicine, and sports and recreation.

The generally strong audiobook format registered sharp price increases in some categories in 2007, led by cooking (up 113.3 percent) and travel (up 108.8 percent). Double-digit increases were registered by biography (up 18.1 percent), education (33.3 percent), history (20.3 percent), how-to and home arts (22.4 percent), literature (40.0 percent), medicine (62.1 percent), philosophy (53.1 percent), poetry and drama (15.9 percent), science (14.4 percent), and sociology and economics (25.8 percent). Most of these categories posted further increases for 2008.

Note: Restated total average prices for 2004 were as follows: Table 2, $81.83; Table 3, $33.22; Table 4, $6.25; Table 5, $31.09; Table 6, $35.04.

## Table 2 / Hardcover Average Per-Volume Prices, 2005–2008

| Category | 2005 Final | | | 2006 Final | | | 2007 Final | | | 2008 Preliminary | | |
|---|---|---|---|---|---|---|---|---|---|---|---|---|
| | Vols. | $ Total | Prices | Vols. | $ Total | Prices | Vols. | $ Total | Prices | Vols. | $ Total | Prices |
| Agriculture | 670 | $41,289.97 | $61.63 | 591 | $40,527.41 | $68.57 | 680 | $48,214.26 | $70.90 | 555 | $40,790.85 | $73.50 |
| Arts | 3,472 | 217,028.47 | 62.51 | 3,962 | 306,536.09 | 77.37 | 4,241 | 326,674.20 | 77.03 | 4,284 | 345,090.73 | 80.55 |
| Biography | 1,601 | 77,034.98 | 48.12 | 1,587 | 84,029.32 | 52.95 | 1,669 | 89,461.04 | 53.60 | 1,509 | 87,066.31 | 57.70 |
| Business | 2,031 | 251,227.39 | 123.70 | 2,010 | 262,175.51 | 130.44 | 2,154 | 300,443.17 | 139.48 | 2,244 | 341,078.44 | 152.00 |
| Careers | 679 | 58,656.40 | 86.39 | 726 | 62,367.71 | 85.91 | 758 | 59,801.12 | 78.89 | 772 | 70,839.19 | 91.76 |
| Children | 12,567 | 286,434.30 | 22.79 | 12,373 | 281,228.72 | 22.73 | 14,689 | 345,684.34 | 23.53 | 12,811 | 338,108.81 | 26.39 |
| Computers | 772 | 85,365.61 | 110.58 | 906 | 99,272.77 | 109.57 | 765 | 86,637.65 | 113.25 | 724 | 106,038.94 | 146.46 |
| Cooking | 861 | 24,507.51 | 28.46 | 881 | 26,411.82 | 29.98 | 865 | 23,719.75 | 27.42 | 965 | 28,485.30 | 29.52 |
| Education | 1,151 | 107,129.47 | 93.08 | 1,306 | 135,636.36 | 103.86 | 1,264 | 137,790.60 | 109.01 | 1,315 | 144,974.72 | 110.25 |
| Fiction | 4,732 | 134,334.84 | 28.39 | 4,489 | 129,038.01 | 28.75 | 4,591 | 154,214.54 | 33.59 | 4,740 | 139,198.29 | 29.37 |
| General works | 1,711 | 195,778.93 | 114.42 | 1,679 | 200,208.53 | 119.24 | 1,616 | 231,122.61 | 143.02 | 1,560 | 243,248.66 | 155.93 |
| Graphic novels | 237 | 7,921.87 | 33.43 | 294 | 9,492.74 | 32.29 | 337 | 11,219.64 | 33.29 | 479 | 15,727.95 | 32.83 |
| History | 4,574 | 387,232.75 | 84.66 | 4,794 | 439,966.89 | 91.77 | 4,952 | 420,250.26 | 84.86 | 4,856 | 414,835.38 | 85.43 |
| How-to, home arts | 478 | 15,029.82 | 31.44 | 465 | 14,633.68 | 31.47 | 499 | 16,372.44 | 32.81 | 394 | 14,367.05 | 36.46 |
| Language | 1,279 | 141,999.52 | 111.02 | 1,233 | 136,892.14 | 111.02 | 1,482 | 168,723.05 | 113.85 | 1,249 | 138,418.59 | 110.82 |
| Law | 1,280 | 195,875.35 | 153.03 | 1,400 | 241,573.95 | 172.55 | 1,430 | 234,284.82 | 163.84 | 1,466 | 233,047.33 | 158.97 |
| Literature | 1,847 | 213,714.09 | 115.71 | 1,875 | 188,656.13 | 100.62 | 2,289 | 250,266.53 | 109.33 | 2,059 | 209,476.92 | 101.74 |
| Medicine | 2,746 | 425,838.23 | 155.08 | 2,959 | 468,619.58 | 158.37 | 2,965 | 446,722.59 | 150.67 | 2,936 | 455,116.18 | 155.01 |
| Music | 411 | 32,125.84 | 78.17 | 395 | 30,727.19 | 77.79 | 484 | 36,753.43 | 75.94 | 479 | 32,987.70 | 68.87 |
| Philosophy | 861 | 106,906.62 | 124.17 | 962 | 99,611.86 | 103.55 | 1,022 | 91,599.67 | 89.63 | 985 | 95,383.72 | 96.84 |
| Poetry, drama | 468 | 19,076.30 | 40.76 | 377 | 17,175.35 | 45.56 | 431 | 19,994.64 | 46.39 | 517 | 23,924.76 | 46.28 |
| Religion | 2,704 | 169,836.51 | 62.81 | 2,630 | 186,686.54 | 70.98 | 2,662 | 181,472.34 | 68.17 | 2,587 | 180,336.73 | 69.71 |
| Science | 4,632 | 800,435.57 | 172.81 | 4,845 | 818,180.93 | 168.87 | 4,650 | 809,591.36 | 174.11 | 4,451 | 760,950.73 | 170.96 |
| Self-help, psychology | 1,894 | 123,142.16 | 65.02 | 2,075 | 140,305.31 | 67.62 | 2,026 | 148,003.71 | 73.05 | 2,028 | 147,020.69 | 72.50 |
| Sociology, economics | 4,856 | 490,490.96 | 101.01 | 5,411 | 629,419.76 | 116.32 | 5,527 | 580,250.33 | 104.98 | 5,761 | 555,998.73 | 96.51 |
| Sports, recreation | 922 | 33,627.62 | 36.47 | 1,000 | 36,276.33 | 36.28 | 911 | 33,605.28 | 36.89 | 957 | 38,842.70 | 40.59 |
| Technology | 1,965 | 328,486.49 | 167.17 | 2,183 | 325,289.63 | 149.01 | 2,128 | 298,794.97 | 140.41 | 2,361 | 340,555.11 | 144.24 |
| Travel | 421 | 15,632.44 | 37.13 | 400 | 17,370.41 | 43.43 | 754 | 40,935.77 | 54.29 | 402 | 13,700.32 | 34.08 |
| Young adult | 2,450 | 121,161.32 | 49.45 | 2,298 | 110,225.24 | 47.97 | 2,739 | 136,149.89 | 49.71 | 2,248 | 110,961.40 | 49.36 |
| Totals | 64,272 | $5,107,321.33 | $79.46 | 66,106 | $5,538,535.91 | $83.78 | 70,580 | $5,728,754.00 | $81.17 | 67,694 | $5,666,572.23 | $83.71 |

**Table 3 / Hardcover Average Per-Volume Prices, Less Than $81, 2005–2008**

| Category | 2005 Final | | | 2006 Final | | | 2007 Final | | | 2008 Preliminary | | |
|---|---|---|---|---|---|---|---|---|---|---|---|---|
| | Vols. | $ Total | Prices | Vols. | $ Total | Prices | Vols. | $ Total | Prices | Vols. | $ Total | Prices |
| Agriculture | 506 | $15,136.65 | $29.91 | 423 | $13,090.91 | $30.95 | 470 | $14,389.26 | $30.62 | 382 | $12,667.77 | $33.16 |
| Arts | 2,863 | 127,321.80 | 44.47 | 3,219 | 145,407.08 | 45.17 | 3,386 | 157,996.49 | 46.66 | 3,346 | 159,135.18 | 47.56 |
| Biography | 1,443 | 44,746.28 | 31.01 | 1,422 | 44,170.77 | 31.06 | 1,481 | 46,911.55 | 31.68 | 1,327 | 41,987.76 | 31.64 |
| Business | 879 | 38,204.94 | 43.46 | 851 | 36,989.02 | 43.47 | 912 | 38,608.07 | 42.33 | 1,024 | 44,916.87 | 43.86 |
| Careers | 406 | 14,522.12 | 35.77 | 435 | 14,685.43 | 33.76 | 498 | 17,392.91 | 34.93 | 471 | 17,131.95 | 36.37 |
| Children | 12,287 | 228,226.72 | 18.57 | 12,106 | 226,703.66 | 18.73 | 14,366 | 271,656.13 | 18.91 | 12,431 | 241,381.71 | 19.42 |
| Computers | 282 | 17,455.03 | 61.90 | 283 | 17,495.49 | 61.82 | 273 | 16,427.84 | 60.18 | 251 | 15,641.02 | 62.31 |
| Cooking | 839 | 21,672.42 | 25.83 | 854 | 22,063.00 | 25.83 | 852 | 22,053.68 | 25.88 | 938 | 24,819.37 | 26.46 |
| Education | 640 | 30,408.41 | 47.51 | 729 | 37,791.15 | 51.84 | 678 | 37,133.72 | 54.77 | 651 | 37,266.80 | 57.25 |
| Fiction | 4,688 | 125,349.54 | 26.74 | 4,444 | 119,844.66 | 26.97 | 4,430 | 120,854.89 | 27.28 | 4,698 | 131,394.05 | 27.97 |
| General works | 1,253 | 36,107.63 | 28.82 | 1,229 | 36,219.67 | 29.47 | 1,129 | 33,426.12 | 29.61 | 1,067 | 30,223.05 | 28.33 |
| Graphic novels | 230 | 7,091.20 | 30.83 | 285 | 8,494.78 | 29.81 | 323 | 9,708.30 | 30.06 | 450 | 12,752.24 | 28.34 |
| History | 3,182 | 136,888.07 | 43.02 | 3,161 | 139,318.88 | 44.07 | 3,209 | 144,434.15 | 45.01 | 3,286 | 144,044.00 | 43.84 |
| How-to, home arts | 462 | 13,296.62 | 28.78 | 453 | 12,844.98 | 28.36 | 479 | 13,705.34 | 28.61 | 379 | 11,426.06 | 30.15 |
| Language | 567 | 28,936.31 | 51.03 | 534 | 27,643.96 | 51.77 | 625 | 34,133.49 | 54.61 | 554 | 30,819.93 | 55.63 |
| Law | 329 | 17,063.03 | 51.86 | 295 | 15,949.96 | 54.07 | 321 | 17,256.12 | 53.76 | 330 | 17,431.98 | 52.82 |
| Literature | 984 | 48,409.66 | 49.20 | 1,019 | 52,572.67 | 51.59 | 1,175 | 62,917.23 | 53.55 | 1,125 | 61,472.29 | 54.64 |
| Medicine | 696 | 37,971.90 | 54.56 | 646 | 36,020.75 | 55.76 | 613 | 34,370.49 | 56.07 | 549 | 31,525.11 | 57.42 |
| Music | 283 | 10,686.50 | 37.76 | 253 | 10,435.44 | 41.25 | 317 | 13,198.02 | 41.63 | 348 | 14,966.75 | 43.01 |
| Philosophy | 432 | 22,541.50 | 52.18 | 437 | 23,125.54 | 52.92 | 474 | 25,558.95 | 53.92 | 507 | 27,344.92 | 53.93 |
| Poetry, drama | 433 | 13,106.16 | 30.27 | 342 | 10,860.61 | 31.76 | 369 | 11,629.09 | 31.52 | 459 | 16,078.39 | 35.03 |
| Religion | 2,086 | 60,742.04 | 29.12 | 1,889 | 58,320.75 | 30.87 | 1,902 | 59,278.74 | 31.17 | 1,915 | 62,050.66 | 32.40 |
| Science | 1,213 | 56,645.36 | 46.70 | 1,152 | 56,353.57 | 48.92 | 1,275 | 63,134.12 | 49.52 | 1,248 | 62,454.83 | 50.04 |
| Self-help, psychology | 1,328 | 45,255.16 | 34.08 | 1,402 | 46,689.05 | 33.30 | 1,349 | 47,680.88 | 35.35 | 1,309 | 45,991.45 | 35.13 |
| Sociology, economics | 2,469 | 124,846.85 | 50.57 | 2,619 | 131,737.52 | 50.30 | 2,791 | 143,974.27 | 51.59 | 3,084 | 159,491.20 | 51.72 |
| Sports, recreation | 875 | 26,669.38 | 30.48 | 946 | 27,829.40 | 29.42 | 868 | 26,378.54 | 30.39 | 894 | 28,843.20 | 32.26 |
| Technology | 511 | 23,397.78 | 45.79 | 517 | 24,441.66 | 47.28 | 490 | 23,841.30 | 48.66 | 542 | 27,119.62 | 50.04 |
| Travel | 394 | 11,187.19 | 28.39 | 378 | 11,853.01 | 31.36 | 733 | 29,318.27 | 40.00 | 385 | 10,907.92 | 28.33 |
| Young adult | 2,148 | 58,587.63 | 27.28 | 2,079 | 55,213.70 | 26.56 | 2,527 | 68,488.58 | 27.10 | 2,100 | 56,659.49 | 26.98 |
| Totals | 44,708 | $1,442,473.88 | $32.26 | 44,402 | $1,464,167.07 | $32.98 | 48,315 | $1,605,856.54 | $33.24 | 46,050 | $1,577,945.57 | $34.27 |

## Table 4 / Mass Market Paperbacks Average Per-Volume Prices, 2005–2008

| Category | 2005 Final | | | 2006 Final | | | 2007 Final | | | 2008 Preliminary | | |
|---|---|---|---|---|---|---|---|---|---|---|---|---|
| | Vols. | $ Total | Prices | Vols. | $ Total | Prices | Vols. | $ Total | Prices | Vols. | $ Total | Prices |
| Agriculture | n.a. | n.a. | n.a. | n.a. | n.a. | n.a. | n.a. | n.a. | n.a. | 1 | $7.99 | $7.99 |
| Arts | 4 | $32.92 | $8.23 | 3 | $23.97 | $7.99 | 3 | $25.93 | $8.64 | 1 | 9.99 | 9.99 |
| Biography | 21 | 163.18 | 7.77 | 13 | 101.83 | 7.83 | 9 | 70.87 | 7.87 | 8 | 63.92 | 7.99 |
| Business | 1 | 16.95 | 16.95 | n.a. | n.a. | n.a. | n.a. | n.a. | n.a. | n.a. | n.a. | n.a. |
| Education | n.a. | n.a. | n.a. | n.a. | n.a. | n.a. | n.a. | n.a. | n.a. | n.a. | n.a. | n.a. |
| Careers | 1 | 7.99 | 7.99 | n.a. | n.a. | n.a. | n.a. | n.a. | n.a. | 1 | 7.99 | 7.99 |
| Children | 281 | 1,476.84 | 5.26 | 270 | 1,520.37 | 5.63 | 272 | 1,555.40 | 5.72 | 239 | 1,460.21 | 6.11 |
| Computers | n.a. | n.a. | n.a. | n.a. | n.a. | n.a. | n.a. | n.a. | n.a. | n.a. | n.a. | n.a. |
| Cooking | 1 | 7.50 | 7.50 | 1 | 6.99 | 6.99 | n.a. | n.a. | n.a. | n.a. | n.a. | n.a. |
| Fiction | 4,259 | 26,830.97 | 6.30 | 4,329 | 27,403.60 | 6.33 | 4,216 | 26,959.26 | 6.39 | 4,160 | 26,933.75 | 6.47 |
| General works | 62 | 458.38 | 7.39 | 69 | 565.81 | 8.20 | 67 | 500.84 | 7.48 | 69 | 499.33 | 7.24 |
| Graphic novels | 2 | 16.94 | 8.47 | n.a. | n.a. | n.a. | n.a. | n.a. | n.a. | 1 | 3.99 | 3.99 |
| History | 25 | 195.20 | 7.81 | 16 | 121.84 | 7.62 | 13 | 100.87 | 7.76 | 3 | 16.48 | 5.49 |
| How-to, home arts | 1 | 5.99 | 5.99 | n.a. | n.a. | n.a. | n.a. | n.a. | n.a. | n.a. | n.a. | n.a. |
| Language | 1 | 6.99 | 6.99 | 1 | 5.99 | 5.99 | 4 | 24.96 | 6.24 | 4 | 23.96 | 5.99 |
| Law | n.a. | n.a. | n.a. | n.a. | n.a. | n.a. | n.a. | n.a. | n.a. | n.a. | n.a. | n.a. |
| Literature | 1 | 7.95 | 7.95 | 1 | 7.95 | 7.95 | n.a. | n.a. | n.a. | 3 | 17.93 | 5.98 |
| Medicine | 3 | 23.48 | 7.83 | 4 | 26.47 | 6.62 | 4 | 27.47 | 6.87 | 1 | 7.50 | 7.50 |
| Music | 2 | 15.90 | 7.95 | n.a. | n.a. | n.a. | n.a. | n.a. | n.a. | n.a. | n.a. | n.a. |
| Philosophy | 2 | 13.98 | 6.99 | 5 | 36.91 | 7.38 | 5 | 38.91 | 7.78 | 2 | 10.90 | 5.45 |
| Poetry, drama | 24 | 153.24 | 6.39 | 9 | 67.64 | 7.52 | 5 | 31.83 | 6.37 | 4 | 21.88 | 5.47 |
| Religion | 4 | 44.84 | 11.21 | 6 | 43.90 | 7.32 | 2 | 13.98 | 6.99 | 4 | 30.96 | 7.74 |
| Science | n.a. | n.a. | n.a. | 1 | 7.99 | 7.99 | n.a. | n.a. | n.a. | 1 | 6.95 | 6.95 |
| Self-help, psychology | 49 | 388.74 | 7.93 | 78 | 565.84 | 7.25 | 46 | 348.36 | 7.57 | 35 | 266.61 | 7.62 |
| Sociology, economics | 6 | 42.45 | 7.08 | 4 | 29.88 | 7.47 | 2 | 14.98 | 7.49 | 2 | 15.98 | 7.99 |
| Sports, recreation | 19 | 141.81 | 7.46 | 14 | 99.80 | 7.13 | 24 | 143.72 | 5.99 | 20 | 128.80 | 6.44 |
| Technology | 1 | 12.95 | 12.95 | n.a. | n.a. | n.a. | n.a. | n.a. | n.a. | n.a. | n.a. | n.a. |
| Travel | n.a. | n.a. | n.a. | 1 | 7.99 | 7.99 | n.a. | n.a. | n.a. | 1 | 6.95 | 6.95 |
| Young adult | 237 | 1,557.70 | 6.57 | 197 | 1,413.59 | 7.18 | 156 | 1,087.04 | 6.97 | 139 | 981.23 | 7.06 |
| Totals | 5,007 | $31,622.89 | $6.32 | 5,022 | $32,058.36 | $6.38 | 4,828 | $30,944.42 | $6.41 | 4,699 | $30,523.30 | $6.50 |

n.a. = not available

**Table 5 / Trade Paperbacks Average Per-Volume Prices, 2005–2008**

| Category | 2005 Final | | | 2006 Final | | | 2007 Final | | | 2008 Preliminary | | |
|---|---|---|---|---|---|---|---|---|---|---|---|---|
| | Vols. | $ Total | Prices | Vols. | $ Total | Prices | Vols. | $ Total | Prices | Vols. | $ Total | Prices |
| Agriculture | 934 | $26,347.77 | $28.21 | 875 | $27,052.34 | $30.92 | 833 | $27,466.61 | $32.97 | 872 | $24,424.22 | $28.01 |
| Arts | 3,922 | 120,723.64 | 30.78 | 3,929 | 127,554.72 | 32.46 | 4,351 | 147,710.87 | 33.95 | 4,028 | 153,880.20 | 38.20 |
| Biography | 1,800 | 34,913.34 | 19.40 | 1,803 | 35,810.63 | 19.86 | 2,007 | 41,887.65 | 20.87 | 1,921 | 38,692.84 | 20.14 |
| Business | 4,960 | 349,030.84 | 70.37 | 3,990 | 303,710.76 | 76.12 | 8,626 | 773,007.56 | 89.61 | 3,674 | 288,379.49 | 78.49 |
| Careers | 1,434 | 57,788.23 | 40.30 | 1,415 | 59,479.03 | 42.03 | 1,514 | 65,564.17 | 43.31 | 1,445 | 62,515.94 | 43.26 |
| Children | 8,826 | 96,148.26 | 10.89 | 9,027 | 92,293.21 | 10.22 | 8,665 | 89,425.92 | 10.32 | 8,439 | 89,250.59 | 10.58 |
| Computers | 3,636 | 199,367.33 | 54.83 | 3,112 | 187,298.82 | 60.19 | 3,430 | 206,189.12 | 60.11 | 2,649 | 155,669.28 | 58.77 |
| Cooking | 1,186 | 21,554.28 | 18.17 | 987 | 18,706.05 | 18.95 | 1,063 | 18,695.42 | 17.59 | 1,230 | 23,046.99 | 18.74 |
| Education | 4,913 | 171,479.08 | 34.90 | 4,996 | 182,165.13 | 36.46 | 4,505 | 162,710.50 | 36.12 | 4,193 | 146,906.99 | 35.04 |
| Fiction | 8,098 | 124,982.99 | 15.43 | 7,999 | 127,977.69 | 16.00 | 9,492 | 166,074.12 | 17.50 | 8,984 | 156,918.58 | 17.47 |
| General works | 3,453 | 115,022.27 | 33.31 | 3,494 | 140,188.18 | 40.12 | 3,291 | 127,467.92 | 38.73 | 3,205 | 135,576.66 | 42.30 |
| Graphic novels | 2,106 | 27,131.50 | 12.88 | 2,078 | 28,393.78 | 13.66 | 2,216 | 33,583.01 | 15.15 | 2,439 | 35,162.87 | 14.42 |
| History | 5,767 | 192,605.57 | 33.40 | 5,996 | 197,279.33 | 32.90 | 6,831 | 235,750.38 | 34.51 | 5,743 | 183,073.59 | 31.88 |
| How-to, home arts | 1,390 | 27,128.23 | 19.52 | 1,365 | 27,936.64 | 20.47 | 1,252 | 27,099.51 | 21.64 | 1,266 | 27,461.51 | 21.69 |
| Language | 3,388 | 161,022.05 | 47.53 | 3,125 | 140,526.95 | 44.97 | 3,001 | 131,079.92 | 43.68 | 2,582 | 121,574.21 | 47.09 |
| Law | 1,944 | 120,075.51 | 61.77 | 3,344 | 181,425.75 | 54.25 | 3,135 | 232,424.94 | 74.14 | 3,823 | 313,988.10 | 82.13 |
| Literature | 2,312 | 71,356.10 | 30.86 | 1,744 | 59,843.24 | 34.31 | 2,064 | 78,452.47 | 38.01 | 1,783 | 69,958.55 | 39.24 |
| Medicine | 3,597 | 228,958.12 | 63.65 | 3,840 | 240,596.89 | 62.66 | 3,932 | 268,406.81 | 68.26 | 3,698 | 274,229.67 | 74.16 |
| Music | 2,695 | 62,291.41 | 23.11 | 2,657 | 68,362.24 | 25.73 | 2,474 | 68,876.40 | 27.84 | 2,793 | 60,922.08 | 21.81 |
| Philosophy | 1,202 | 37,368.55 | 31.09 | 1,100 | 36,263.41 | 32.97 | 1,589 | 50,635.54 | 31.87 | 1,165 | 35,178.76 | 30.20 |
| Poetry, drama | 2,234 | 35,962.66 | 16.10 | 2,101 | 33,825.67 | 16.10 | 2,406 | 41,827.30 | 17.38 | 2,177 | 36,579.41 | 16.80 |
| Religion | 5,599 | 115,021.14 | 20.54 | 5,788 | 120,077.65 | 20.75 | 5,696 | 117,290.31 | 20.59 | 5,949 | 118,563.96 | 19.93 |
| Science | 3,901 | 251,820.56 | 64.55 | 3,810 | 237,199.09 | 62.26 | 3,905 | 249,476.41 | 63.89 | 3,422 | 190,826.19 | 55.76 |
| Self-help, psychology | 4,906 | 130,211.90 | 26.54 | 4,872 | 132,947.28 | 27.29 | 5,190 | 138,125.34 | 26.61 | 4,525 | 116,205.77 | 25.68 |
| Sociology, economics | 7,107 | 281,491.71 | 39.61 | 6,873 | 274,099.23 | 39.88 | 7,802 | 342,483.36 | 43.90 | 6,931 | 273,671.35 | 39.49 |
| Sports, recreation | 2,465 | 47,078.20 | 19.10 | 2,516 | 49,458.25 | 19.66 | 2,298 | 45,969.57 | 20.00 | 2,104 | 42,585.19 | 20.24 |
| Technology | 1,941 | 148,321.19 | 76.41 | 2,207 | 159,980.47 | 72.49 | 2,076 | 181,938.31 | 87.64 | 1,542 | 112,580.60 | 73.01 |
| Travel | 2,171 | 41,262.71 | 19.01 | 2,885 | 56,859.49 | 19.71 | 3,383 | 71,288.87 | 21.07 | 2,861 | 56,117.42 | 19.61 |
| Young adult | 2,609 | 35,968.93 | 13.79 | 2,547 | 36,304.51 | 14.25 | 3,029 | 41,534.17 | 13.71 | 2,454 | 34,116.15 | 13.90 |
| Totals | 100,496 | $3,332,434.07 | $33.16 | 100,475 | $3,383,616.43 | $33.68 | 110,056 | $4,182,442.48 | $38.00 | 97,897 | $3,378,057.16 | $34.51 |

## Table 6 / Audiobook Average Per-Volume Prices, 2005–2008

| Category | 2005 Final | | | 2006 Final | | | 2007 Final | | | 2008 Preliminary | | |
|---|---|---|---|---|---|---|---|---|---|---|---|---|
| | Vols. | $ Total | Prices | Vols. | $ Total | Prices | Vols. | $ Total | Prices | Vols. | $ Total | Prices |
| Agriculture | 4 | $119.13 | $29.78 | 12 | $361.60 | $30.13 | 19 | $617.50 | $32.50 | 22 | $792.99 | $36.05 |
| Arts | 28 | 1,257.78 | 44.92 | 38 | 1,248.94 | 32.87 | 23 | 657.64 | 28.59 | 47 | 1,809.21 | 38.49 |
| Biography | 295 | 11,365.30 | 38.53 | 341 | 13,037.80 | 38.23 | 419 | 18,915.34 | 45.14 | 600 | 28,563.01 | 47.61 |
| Business | 79 | 3,700.45 | 46.84 | 139 | 5,894.37 | 42.41 | 161 | 5,797.99 | 36.01 | 229 | 9,046.87 | 39.51 |
| Careers | 60 | 2,358.58 | 39.31 | 92 | 3,472.74 | 37.75 | 103 | 3,061.40 | 29.72 | 167 | 6,751.83 | 40.43 |
| Children | 561 | 14,912.93 | 26.58 | 533 | 14,432.92 | 27.08 | 857 | 24,953.19 | 29.12 | 705 | 22,119.30 | 31.37 |
| Computers | 5 | 206.96 | 41.39 | 2 | 54.90 | 27.45 | n.a. | n.a. | n.a. | 4 | 124.91 | 31.23 |
| Cooking | 24 | 346.80 | 14.45 | 14 | 232.33 | 16.60 | 7 | 247.78 | 35.40 | 4 | 58.83 | 14.71 |
| Education | 36 | 993.61 | 27.60 | 49 | 1,511.02 | 30.84 | 36 | 1,479.95 | 41.11 | 20 | 641.78 | 32.09 |
| Fiction | 2,914 | 121,150.61 | 41.58 | 3,126 | 124,939.08 | 39.97 | 3,636 | 160,581.21 | 44.16 | 4,225 | 201,647.00 | 47.73 |
| General works | 80 | 2,221.25 | 27.77 | 133 | 4,104.34 | 30.86 | 147 | 4,860.72 | 33.07 | 208 | 8,303.68 | 39.92 |
| History | 194 | 8,062.95 | 41.56 | 311 | 12,415.78 | 39.92 | 487 | 23,381.04 | 48.01 | 571 | 30,684.64 | 53.74 |
| How-to, home arts | 1 | 25.00 | 25.00 | 4 | 88.98 | 22.25 | 11 | 299.53 | 27.23 | 9 | 379.79 | 42.20 |
| Language | 663 | 46,025.55 | 69.42 | 436 | 17,761.36 | 40.74 | 335 | 13,922.53 | 41.56 | 363 | 14,056.21 | 38.72 |
| Law | 44 | 2,442.45 | 55.51 | 48 | 3,639.22 | 75.82 | 24 | 1,426.92 | 59.46 | 19 | 973.75 | 51.25 |
| Literature | 15 | 376.54 | 25.10 | 30 | 693.89 | 23.13 | 34 | 1,100.95 | 32.38 | 49 | 2,303.96 | 47.02 |
| Medicine | 7 | 1,030.74 | 147.25 | 22 | 930.26 | 42.28 | 20 | 1,371.08 | 68.55 | 23 | 2,324.38 | 101.06 |
| Music | 104 | 3,072.49 | 29.54 | 163 | 3,993.56 | 24.50 | 111 | 2,991.30 | 26.95 | 141 | 4,103.91 | 29.11 |
| Philosophy | 17 | 569.47 | 33.50 | 72 | 1,882.06 | 26.14 | 24 | 960.23 | 40.01 | 33 | 1,310.20 | 39.70 |
| Poetry, drama | 80 | 1,877.45 | 23.47 | 118 | 2,762.69 | 23.41 | 80 | 2,171.10 | 27.14 | 93 | 2,972.77 | 31.97 |
| Religion | 367 | 9,826.83 | 26.78 | 369 | 9,840.19 | 26.67 | 386 | 10,853.69 | 28.12 | 346 | 10,619.89 | 30.69 |
| Science | 34 | 1,256.77 | 36.96 | 49 | 1,684.09 | 34.37 | 46 | 1,808.64 | 39.32 | 85 | 3,926.73 | 46.20 |
| Self-help, psychology | 363 | 9,565.65 | 26.35 | 304 | 8,335.80 | 27.42 | 461 | 13,691.22 | 29.70 | 379 | 12,304.66 | 32.47 |
| Sociology, economics | 91 | 3,551.89 | 39.03 | 168 | 5,323.20 | 31.69 | 229 | 9,129.35 | 39.87 | 259 | 11,323.06 | 43.72 |
| Sports, recreation | 39 | 1,182.87 | 30.33 | 45 | 1,570.80 | 34.91 | 64 | 2,341.54 | 36.59 | 73 | 2,840.66 | 38.91 |
| Technology | 5 | 273.88 | 54.78 | 6 | 217.97 | 36.33 | 11 | 380.63 | 34.60 | 9 | 406.92 | 45.21 |
| Travel | 13 | 544.79 | 41.91 | 13 | 290.57 | 22.35 | 45 | 2,099.75 | 46.66 | 38 | 1,682.45 | 44.28 |
| Young adult | 196 | 7,024.72 | 35.84 | 239 | 10,099.66 | 42.26 | 273 | 10,895.11 | 39.91 | 259 | 11,443.80 | 44.18 |
| Totals | 6,319 | $255,343.44 | $40.41 | 6,876 | $250,820.12 | $36.48 | 8,049 | $319,997.33 | $39.76 | 8,980 | $393,517.19 | $43.82 |

# Book Sales Statistics, 2008: AAP Estimates

Association of American Publishers

Net sales by the U.S. publishing industry are estimated to have decreased by 2.8 percent from 2007 to 2008. The 2008 grand total was $24.26 billion, according to figures released by the Association of American Publishers (AAP).

The AAP report, which uses data from the U.S. Bureau of the Census as well as sales data from 81 publishers, indicates a compound growth rate of 1.6 percent a year since 2002.

Trade sales of adult and juvenile books fell 5.2 percent from 2007 to $8.08 billion, and the compound annual growth rate (CAGR) for that category fell to 2.1 percent. Growth in 2008 was found in paperbound books for adults and children, with rates of 3.6 percent and 6.4 percent, respectively. Sales in the hardcover category fell 13 percent for adult books and 12.4 percent for children's books.

The CAGR for hardbound books was 0.4 percent for adult books and 1.5 percent for juvenile. Paperbound book sales in those categories grew 3.9 percent and 2.8 percent over the six years.

Educational titles had a mixed year in 2008. Sales in the el–hi category—books produced for K–12 education—fell 4.4 percent to just under $6.08 billion in 2008, and the CAGR for this category was 0.8 percent. The Higher Education category, which includes sales of college textbooks, fared better. Total sales reached nearly $3.78 billion, up 2.7 percent in 2008. This brought the CAGR for college textbooks to 3.8 percent.

Mass market paperbacks decreased 3.0 percent and brought the category CAGR to minus 1.9 percent. Total sales were $1.09 billion in 2008. Book clubs and mail order fell for the sixth year to $600 million, a fall of 3.4 percent for the year and a CAGR of minus 5.7 percent.

Audiobook sales for 2008 totaled $172 million, down 21 percent from 2007, but the CAGR for this category was still healthy at 3.1 percent. E-books continued to grow significantly; sales topped $113 million in 2008, up 68.4 percent.

Religious book sales dropped 7.6 percent to just under $724 million in 2008. Over the six years of the estimate the category has performed well, however, with a CAGR of 4.5 percent.

Figures for the six years in all categories are shown on the following page. For more data on 2008 sales estimates, prepared by Management Practice, Inc., visit the AAP Web site at http://www.publishers.org. For additional information, contact Tina Jordan at AAP's New York office (212-255-0200 ext. 263, tjordan@publishers.org).

**Table 1 / Estimated Book Publishing Industry Net Sales, 2002–2008**
(figures in thousands of dollars)

| | 2002 Census $ | 2003 $ | % Change from 2002 | 2004 $ | % Change from 2003 | 2005 $ | % Change from 2004 | 2006 $ | % Change from 2005 | 2007 $ | % Change from 2006 | 2008 $ | % Change from 2006 | Compound Growth Rate 2002–2008 |
|---|---|---|---|---|---|---|---|---|---|---|---|---|---|---|
| Trade (total) | 7,144,188 | 6,872,190 | -3.8 | 7,504,458 | 9.2 | 8,043,471 | 7.2 | 8,274,103 | 2.9 | 8,525,932 | 3.0 | 8,079,423 | -5.2 | 2.1 |
| Adult hardbound | 2,371,553 | 2,314,636 | -2.4 | 2,460,458 | 6.3 | 2,495,175 | 1.4 | 2,597,477 | 4.1 | 2,800,080 | 7.8 | 2,436,070 | -13.0 | 0.4 |
| Adult paperbound | 1,876,620 | 1,865,360 | -0.6 | 1,917,590 | 2.8 | 2,099,187 | 9.5 | 2,277,618 | 8.5 | 2,282,173 | 0.2 | 2,364,331 | 3.6 | 3.9 |
| Juvenile hardbound | 1,636,248 | 1,484,077 | -9.3 | 1,902,587 | 28.2 | 2,100,456 | 10.4 | 2,058,447 | -2.0 | 2,048,155 | -0.5 | 1,794,184 | -12.4 | 1.5 |
| Juvenile paperbound | 1,259,767 | 1,208,117 | -4.1 | 1,223,823 | 1.3 | 1,348,653 | 10.2 | 1,340,561 | -0.6 | 1,395,524 | 4.1 | 1,484,838 | 6.4 | 2.8 |
| Book clubs and mail order | 852,384 | 775,669 | -9.0 | 706,634 | -8.9 | 659,290 | -6.7 | 639,511 | -3.0 | 621,605 | -2.8 | 600,470 | -3.4 | -5.7 |
| Mass market paperback | 1,216,710 | 1,196,026 | -1.7 | 1,089,580 | -8.9 | 1,091,759 | 0.2 | 1,141,980 | 4.6 | 1,119,140 | -2.0 | 1,085,566 | -3.0 | -1.9 |
| Audiobooks | 143,410 | 161,049 | 12.3 | 159,922 | -0.7 | 206,299 | 29.0 | 182,162 | -11.7 | 218,230 | 19.8 | 172,402 | -21.0 | 3.1 |
| Religious | 556,799 | 836,312 | 50.2 | 883,145 | 5.6 | 829,273 | -6.1 | 744,687 | -10.2 | 783,411 | 5.2 | 723,872 | -7.6 | 4.5 |
| E-books | 7,337 | 19,772 | 169.5 | 30,271 | 53.1 | 43,832 | 44.8 | 54,396 | 24.1 | 67,233 | 23.6 | 113,220 | 68.4 | 57.8 |
| Professional | 3,155,191 | 3,268,778 | 3.6 | 3,334,154 | 2.0 | 3,300,812 | -1.0 | 3,376,731 | 2.3 | 3,474,656 | 2.9 | 3,457,283 | -0.5 | 1.5 |
| El-hi (K–12 education) | 5,795,044 | 5,939,920 | 2.5 | 5,945,860 | 0.1 | 6,570,175 | 10.5 | 6,189,105 | -5.8 | 6,356,211 | 2.7 | 6,076,538 | -4.4 | 0.8 |
| Higher education | 3,025,029 | 3,133,930 | 3.6 | 3,190,341 | 1.8 | 3,359,429 | 5.3 | 3,453,493 | 2.8 | 3,677,970 | 6.5 | 3,777,275 | 2.7 | 3.8 |
| All other | 136,488 | 153,932 | 12.8 | 161,629 | 5.0 | 158,558 | -1.9 | 140,641 | -11.3 | 115,185 | -18.1 | 168,976 | 46.7 | 3.6 |
| Total | 22,032,580 | 22,357,578 | 1.5 | 23,005,994 | 2.9 | 24,262,898 | 5.5 | 24,196,809 | -0.3 | 24,959,573 | 3.2 | 24,255,025 | -2.8 | 1.6 |

# U.S. Book Exports and Imports in 2008: A Year of Economic Uncertainty

Albert N. Greco

Senior Researcher
The Institute for Publishing Research
201-439-1839, e-mail angreco@aol.com

In 2008 U.S. exports of books to other nations (the shipment of physical books, excluding foreign rights payments) topped $2,187,049,000, up 2.4 percent over 2007 ($2,135,195,000). Imports dipped nearly 3 percent to $2,213,812,000 from 2007's total of $2,281,275,000.

At first glance, these results confirm classical macroeconomic theories (Moss, 2007). When the value of the dollar declines relative to foreign currencies, then the cost of U.S. books on overseas markets declines, effectively making exports cheaper and increasing sales. When it comes to imports, a weaker dollar poses a problem. The cost to purchase books from abroad and to import them into the United States increases.

This is precisely what happened in 2008; exports were up and imports were down. So it appears that the "invisible hand" of the marketplace was at work, stimulating exports and dampening imports.

In reality, international macroeconomics began to unravel in June 2007 when Bear Stearns & Co. (Cohan, 2009) was forced to close two of its high-profile hedge funds. During the rest of 2007, concerns emerged in the United States and abroad about sub-prime mortgages, structured investment vehicles, mortgage-backed securities, and other complex investment instruments (Emanuel Derman describes these and other instruments in his book about "quants" working in the financial service sector in Wall Street and elsewhere [Derman, 2004].) To many observers in Washington, London, and New York, problems with risk and uncertainty had been addressed and corrected after the debilitating 1987 "Asian currency contagion" and the fall of Long-Term Capital Management (Lowenstein, 2000). Obviously, they were not corrected. By March 2008 Bear Stearns & Co. was absorbed into JPMorgan Chase, and the complete unraveling of a number of major international financial service firms became a reality in the following months, among them Lehman Bros., Merrill Lynch, Washington Mutual, A.I.G., Fannie Mae, and Freddie Mac. These events have been analyzed by a number of authors, including Carroll and Mui (2008), Muolo and Padilla (2008), and Phillips (2008).

Regrettably, financial uncertainty quickly filtered into the global marketplace (Cinquetti, 2008). Financial service organizations in Europe, Asia, the Pacific Rim, and elsewhere sustained drops in revenues, spilling over to consumers in those regions who saw declines in income and savings. These developments cast doubt on many of the highly publicized studies stressing the decoupling of Asia from the U.S. market (Gabor and Peltonen, 2009) and the emergence of a strengthened Chinese manufacturing sector (Chung, Chinn, and Fujii, 2009). The end results in the United States and in many foreign markets included higher unemployment rates and lower increases—and some decreases—in gross domestic product (GDP).

The U.S. book industry was not spared. During 2008 monthly book sales sagged, and most of the major trade publishers sustained declines in domestic sales in certain book categories.

Even though exports grew in 2008, the outlook for continued growth in this sector was questionable, especially for most of 2009, because of the global economic turmoil. The bottom line was unsettling. Classic macroeconomic theory, which appeared to work according to standard rules and theories during periods of economic expansion, did not perform so well during an international fiscal crisis.

However, while economic theory is rather exciting (if not daunting at times) —revealing the close, intense business connections between countries (Greco, 2005; Greco, Rodriguez, and Wharton, 2007)—the goal of this article is to review and explain the intricate 2008 data on exports and imports.

## Overview of U.S. Exports and Imports

The ratio of exports as a percentage of U.S. shipments sagged from 1997 to 2006, with a modest uptick in 2005, but slim increases were evident in both 2007 (0.94 percent) and 2008 (0.95 percent). Table 1 outlines these developments.

### Table 1 / U.S. Trade in Books: 1970–2008
($ million)

| Year | U.S. Book Exports | U.S. Book Imports | Ratio: U.S. Book Exports/Imports |
|------|------------------|-------------------|----------------------------------|
| 1970 | $174.9 | $92.0 | 1.90 |
| 1975 | 269.3 | 147.6 | 1.82 |
| 1980 | 518.9 | 306.5 | 1.69 |
| 1985 | 591.2 | 564.2 | 1.05 |
| 1990 | 1,415.1 | 855.1 | 1.65 |
| 1995 | 1,779.5 | 1,184.5 | 1.50 |
| 1996 | 1,775.6 | 1,240.1 | 1.43 |
| 1997 | 1,896.6 | 1,297.5 | 1.46 |
| 1998 | 1,841.8 | 1,383.7 | 1.33 |
| 1999 | 1,871.1 | 1,441.4 | 1.30 |
| 2000 | 1,877.0 | 1,590.5 | 1.18 |
| 2001 | 1,712.3 | 1,627.8 | 1.05 |
| 2002 | 1,681.2 | 1,661.2 | 1.01 |
| 2003 | 1,693.6 | 1,755.9 | 0.96 |
| 2004 | 1,740.5 | 1,934.4 | 0.90 |
| 2005 | 1,894.3 | 2,026.3 | 0.93 |
| 2006 | 1,948.1 | 2,124.3 | 0.92 |
| 2007 | 2,135.2 | 2,281.3 | 0.94 |
| 2008 | 2,187.0 | 2,213.8 | 0.99 |

Source: U.S. Department of Commerce, International Trade Administration. All totals are rounded off to one decimal point. Data for individual categories may not add to totals due to statistical rounding. Due to changes in the classification of "U.S. traded products" and what constitutes products classified as "books," data prior to 1990 are not strictly comparable with data beginning in 1990.

The equally important ratio of exports as a percentage of total U.S. shipments (that is, total net publishers' revenues) declined from 7.3 percent in 2007 to 6.9 percent in 2008, basically matching the results of 2005–2006, hardly a positive sign for 2009. Table 2 provides data from 1970 through 2008.

**Table 2 / U.S. Book Industry Shipments Compared with U.S. Book Exports: 1970–2008**
($ million)

| Year | Total Shipments | U.S. Book Exports | Exports as a Percent of Total Shipments |
|------|-----------------|-------------------|------------------------------------------|
| 1970 | $2,434.2 | $174.9 | 7.2 |
| 1975 | 3,536.5 | 269.3 | 7.6 |
| 1980 | 6,114.4 | 518.9 | 8.5 |
| 1985 | 10,165.7 | 591.2 | 5.8 |
| 1990 | 14,982.6 | 1,415.1 | 9.4 |
| 1995 | 19,471.0 | 1,779.5 | 9.1 |
| 1996 | 20,285.7 | 1,775.6 | 8.8 |
| 1997 | 21,131.9 | 1,896.6 | 9.0 |
| 1998 | 22,480.0 | 1,841.8 | 8.2 |
| 1999 | 24,129.9 | 1,871.1 | 7.8 |
| 2000 | 25,235.0 | 1,877.0 | 7.4 |
| 2001 | 26,096.0 | 1,712.3 | 6.6 |
| 2002 | 27,203.0 | 1,681.2 | 6.2 |
| 2003 | 26,326.0 | 1,693.6 | 6.4 |
| 2004 | 27,903.0 | 1,740.5 | 6.2 |
| 2005 | 27,905.0 | 1,894.3 | 6.8 |
| 2006 | 28,236.0 | 1,948.1 | 6.9 |
| 2007 | 29,296.0 | 2,135.2 | 7.3 |
| 2008 | 31,812.4 | 2,187.0 | 6.9 |

Source: U.S. Department of Commerce, International Trade Administration; and calculations by the author. Due to changes in the classification of U.S. traded products and what constitutes products classified as "books," data prior to 1990 are not strictly comparable with data beginning in 1990. All totals are rounded off to one decimal point. Data for individual categories may not add to totals due to statistical rounding.

## Book Exports in 2008

What happened in 2008? What book categories increased in 2008? What can the book publishing industry do to strengthen its world trade position?

Canada remained the best customer for U.S. exported books, easily surpassing the United Kingdom. However, seven of the next eight export markets posted declines in their purchase of U.S. books, with Germany sliding 41.1 percent between 2007 and 2008 and China in tenth place with just $28 million (down 5.6 percent from 2007); among those nations, only Singapore saw an increase, an impressive 11.1 percent. Table 3 outlines these unsettling developments.

An analysis of the top 25 nations revealed additional troubles. In 2007 these countries purchased 93.17 percent of all exports; in 2008 their total declined to 92.64 percent. While not a major shift, this decline should be investigated by the U.S. Department of Commerce to ascertain what can be done to stimulate more

Table 3 / Top Ten Export Destinations for U.S. Books, 1999–2008
($'000)

| Country | 1999 | 2000 | 2001 | 2002 | 2003 | 2004 | 2005 | 2006 | 2007 | 2008 | Percent Change 2007–2008 |
|---|---|---|---|---|---|---|---|---|---|---|---|
| Canada | 807,541 | 756,667 | 727,698 | 742,619 | 776,441 | 812,833 | 866,173 | 918,250 | 962,509 | 999,309 | 3.8 |
| United Kingdom | 253,646 | 264,230 | 250,031 | 270,622 | 274,596 | 289,196 | 284,993 | 291,376 | 300,150 | 340,864 | 13.6 |
| Australia | 139,588 | 116,302 | 66,010 | 70,806 | 76,067 | 78,549 | 100,769 | 107,754 | 110,922 | 110,922 | -4.6 |
| Mexico | 65,599 | 73,886 | 63,804 | 64,938 | 68,132 | 66,087 | 102,658 | 71,316 | 79,685 | 78,578 | -1.4 |
| Japan | 101,146 | 123,100 | 129,316 | 100,804 | 95,835 | 98,436 | 93,394 | 78,219 | 78,301 | 76,594 | -2.2 |
| Singapore | 41,135 | 60,669 | 48,985 | 49,570 | 48,358 | 57,974 | 53,395 | 49,734 | 52,689 | 58,541 | 11.1 |
| Germany | 43,134 | 34,341 | 34,007 | 29,081 | 34,128 | 27,174 | 35,789 | 38,298 | 76,176 | 44,837 | -41.1 |
| South Korea | 24,627 | 36,793 | 35,499 | 29,131 | 24,698 | 26,670 | 38,557 | 33,432 | 44,400 | 42,922 | -3.3 |
| India | 11,954 | 14,430 | 15,992 | 19,513 | 16,807 | 18,967 | 22,497 | 21,757 | 40,022 | 32,537 | -18.7 |
| China | 12,414 | 12,019 | 10,711 | 11,739 | 15,491 | 18,110 | 16,532 | 25,777 | 29,715 | 28,058 | -5.6 |

Source: U.S. Department of Commerce, International Trade Administration.
Note: Individual shipments are excluded from the foreign trade data if valued under $2,500. All totals are rounded off to one decimal point. Data for individual categories may not add to totals due to statistical rounding.

exports. Table 4 lists the results for the top 25 nations, for the remaining cluster, and the grand total.

Table 4 / U.S. Book Exports to 25 Principal Countries: 2006–2008

| Country | Value ($'000) | | | Percent Change 2006–2007 | Percent Change 2007–2008 |
|---|---|---|---|---|---|
| | 2006 | 2007 | 2008 | | |
| Canada | $918,250 | $962,509 | $999,309 | 4.8 | 3.8 |
| United Kingdom | 291,376 | 300,150 | 340,864 | 3.0 | 13.6 |
| Australia | 107,754 | 110,922 | 105,822 | 2.9 | -4.6 |
| Mexico | 71,316 | 79,685 | 78,578 | 11.7 | -1.4 |
| Japan | 78,219 | 78,301 | 76,594 | 0.1 | -2.2 |
| Singapore | 49,734 | 52,689 | 58,541 | 5.9 | 11.1 |
| Germany | 38,298 | 76,176 | 44,837 | 98.9 | -41.1 |
| South Korea | 33,432 | 44,400 | 42,922 | 32.8 | -3.3 |
| India | 21,757 | 40,022 | 32537 | 84.0 | -18.7 |
| China | 25,777 | 29,715 | 28,058 | 15.3 | -5.6 |
| South Africa | 21,172 | 18,627 | 22,772 | -12.0 | 22.2 |
| Philippines | 19,131 | 18,883 | 19,997 | -1.3 | 0.7 |
| Brazil | 13,758 | 21,676 | 21829 | 57.6 | 5.9 |
| Hong Kong | 17,844 | 19,722 | 18,879 | 10.5 | -4.3 |
| United Arab Emirates | 5,483 | 9,999 | 17349 | 82.47 | 3.5 |
| Taiwan | 16,144 | 18,663 | 15,065 | 15.6 | -19.3 |
| Belgium | 11,113 | 13,852 | 14,600 | 24.6 | 5.4 |
| Nigeria | 7,970 | 11,635 | 14,044 | 46.0 | 20.7 |
| Saudi Arabia | 9,804 | 10,109 | 12,770 | 3.1 | 26.3 |
| New Zealand | 11,731 | 14,385 | 12,000 | 22.6 | -16.6 |
| Netherlands | 11,879 | 12,260 | 11,759 | 3.2 | -4.1 |
| Thailand | 6,799 | 7,922 | 10,102 | 16.5 | 27.5 |
| Malaysia | 9,801 | 9,913 | 9,946 | 1.1 | 0.3 |
| Colombia | 7,711 | 8,333 | 8,739 | 8.1 | 4.9 |
| France | 7,487 | 7,803 | 8,089 | 4.2 | 3.7 |
| Total, Top 25 countries | $1,817,023 | $1,989,336 | $2,025,999 | 9.9 | 2.4 |
| All Others | $131,080 | $145,858 | $161,051 | 5.6 | 2.7 |
| Grand Total | $1,948,103 | $2,135,195 | $2,187,049 | 9.6 | 2.4 |

Source: U.S. Department of Commerce, International Trade Administration. Note: Individual shipments are excluded from the foreign trade data if valued under $2,500. All totals are rounded off to one decimal point. Data for individual categories may not add to totals due to statistical rounding.

An additional assessment of specific book export categories indicates a number of unusual occurrences. Clearly, Commerce's aggregation of numerous book categories into something called "hardcover books" or "textbooks" poses a serious problem for researchers because of the use of the "harmonious trade system" (HTS). Ideally, Commerce should be encouraged to "translate" the HTS categories and results into the book categories utilized for decades by the U.S. book industry.

A second problem centers on the fact that there were declines in the export of book categories long dominated by U.S. publishers, including religious books (down 7.1 percent in revenues); and technical, scientific, and professional books, off a surprising 10.2 percent in revenues and 14.8 percent in units. Declines in dictionaries and thesauruses were expected; increases in art book units (17.2 percent) and encyclopedias (6.67 percent) were a pleasant surprise. Table 5 outlines these developments.

**Table 5 / U.S. Exports of Books: 2008**

| Category | Value ($'000) | Percent Change 2007–2008 | Units ('000) | Percent Change 2007–2008 |
|---|---|---|---|---|
| Dictionaries and thesauruses | $3,338 | -12.0 | 478 | -1.8 |
| Encyclopedias | 7,017 | 9.0 | 800 | 6.67 |
| Art books | 32,477 | 23.4 | 4,869 | 17.2 |
| Textbooks | 513,022 | 19.3 | 35,987 | 18.6 |
| Religious books | 106,001 | -7.1 | 38,147 | 1.2 |
| Technical, scientific, and professional | 504,002 | -10.2 | 31,847 | -14.8 |
| Hardcover books, n.e.s. | 193,006 | 20.5 | 22,763 | 18.5 |
| Mass market paperbacks | 271,768 | 13.5 | 83,556 | 8.6 |

Source: U.S. Department of Commerce, International Trade Administration.
Note: Individual shipments are excluded from the foreign trade data if valued under $2,500. All totals are rounded off to one decimal point. Data for individual categories may not add to totals due to statistical rounding.
n.e.s. = not elsewhere specified

Mass market paperbacks (sometimes called rack-sized paperbacks) traditionally have been a robust export category. Very large increases were recorded by the United Kingdom (up 23.7 percent in revenues and 11.3 percent in units), Australia (up 39.1 percent in revenues, 35.5 percent in units), South Africa (up 29.6 percent in revenues, 19.2 percent in units), the Philippines (up 17.1 percent in revenues, 28.5 percent in units), and Thailand (up 139.8 percent in revenues, 105.9 percent in units). Declines were evident in Japan (down 3 percent in revenues, 4.8 percent in units), Singapore (down 6.4 percent in units), and Brazil (down in revenues by 23.3 percent and units by 21.7 percent). Table 6 lists the results for 2008.

**Table 6 / U.S. Exports of Mass Market Paperbacks (Rack Sized): Top Ten Markets 2008**

| Country | Value ($'000) | Percent Change 2007–2008 | Units ('000) | Percent Change 2007–2008 |
|---|---|---|---|---|
| Canada | $14,158 | 17.7 | 50,000 | 7.1 |
| United Kingdom | 23,226 | 23.7 | 6,037 | 11.3 |
| Australia | 15,572 | 39.1 | 5,623 | 35.5 |
| South Africa | 13,445 | 29.6 | 2,764 | 19.2 |
| Japan | 12,884 | -3.0 | 4,244 | -4.8 |
| Philippines | 10,866 | 17.1 | 3,811 | 28.5 |
| China | 5,181 | -1.7 | 1,501 | 1.4 |
| Singapore | 4,991 | 0.8 | 1,100 | -6.4 |
| Brazil | 3,577 | -23.3 | 736 | -21.7 |
| Thailand | 3,541 | 139.8 | 650 | 105.9 |

Source: U.S. Department of Commerce, International Trade Administration. All totals are rounded off to one decimal point. Data for individual categories may not add to totals due to statistical rounding.

Technical, scientific, and professional books posted distressing results, especially in light of the extensive research facilities and the impressive amount of original research conducted in the United States. Six of the top ten nations recorded sharp declines in units, including Canada (down 16 percent), Germany (down 55.2 percent), and Australia (down 14.3 percent). Only Japan (up 15.8 percent in units) and Mexico (up 31.7 percent in units) had solid double-digit unit increases in 2008. See Table 7.

### Table 7 / U.S. Exports of Technical, Scientific, and Professional Books: Top Ten Markets

| Country | Value ($'000) | Percent Change 2007–2008 | Units ('000) | Percent Change 2007–2008 |
|---|---|---|---|---|
| Canada | $167,992 | -7.5 | 12,583 | -16.0 |
| United Kingdom | 94,808 | -5.7 | 4,328 | 4.6 |
| Japan | 32,018 | -0.3 | 1,626 | 15.8 |
| Germany | 25,790 | -52.4 | 1,377 | -55.2 |
| Australia | 23,381 | -14.4 | 1,948 | -14.3 |
| Singapore | 16,339 | 6.1 | 3,204 | 8.8 |
| Mexico | 14,140 | -10.1 | 1,341 | 31.7 |
| India | 13,698 | -22.9 | 671 | -14.5 |
| Belgium | 12,397 | 2.4 | 441 | -27.4 |
| Hong Kong | 12,380 | 38.5 | 424 | -5.1 |

Source: U.S. Department of Commerce, International Trade Administration. All totals are rounded off to one decimal point. Data for individual categories may not add to totals due to statistical rounding.

### Table 8 / U.S. Exports of Textbooks 2008: Top Ten Markets

| Country | Value ($'000) | Percent Change 2007–2008 | Units ('000) | Percent Change 2007–2008 |
|---|---|---|---|---|
| United Kingdom | $143,045 | 61.8 | 12,951 | 49.9 |
| Canada | 109,393 | 7.4 | 6,816 | 8.7 |
| Australia | 39,677 | 3.9 | 3,198 | 0.7 |
| South Korea | 31,890 | 14.1 | 2,295 | 15.3 |
| Singapore | 31,101 | 17.8 | 3,221 | 8.9 |
| Japan | 22,674 | 5.6 | 1,160 | -4.8 |
| Mexico | 10,821 | -9.0 | 883 | -15.3 |
| United Arab Emirates | 9,053 | 116.1 | 543 | 88.3 |
| India | 7,373 | -12.7 | 528 | -16.3 |
| China | 7,073 | 2.4 | 435 | -1.8 |

Source: U.S. Department of Commerce, International Trade Administration. All totals are rounded off to one decimal point. Data for individual categories may not add to totals due to statistical rounding.

Another odd development was observed in the textbook sector, another strong book category because of the important titles published in the United States in many of the key international sectors, including business administration-economics-accounting, mathematics, computer science, and so forth. Unit declines were evident in four nations (Japan down 4.8 percent, Mexico down 15.3 percent, India down 16.3 percent, and China down 1.8 percent), with a fifth

(Australia) barely posting any growth; only 0.7 percent. Fortunately, only two countries saw drops in revenues (Mexico, down 9 percent, and India, down 12.7 percent).

Clearly, currency conversion issues plagued publishers in 2008, and it was likely this predicament would continue throughout 2009. However, since many of the same firms publish titles in the technical, scientific, and professional area as well as textbooks, executives at these firms should discuss these declines with their sales representatives as well as with the Commerce Department and the Treasury Department. If these two sectors cannot grow, even during periods of economic recession, then the future of exports in most sectors will be in jeopardy. Table 8 lists the uneven results for 2008.

A similar unit-downturn pattern was evident in the religious book category. Australia (down 7.4 percent), Canada, Argentina, and Colombia all posted declines (Canada by 16.4 percent, Argentina by 56.0 percent, and Colombia by 3.9 percent); the only significant changes were generated in Kenya (up 114.6 percent) and Guatemala (up 67.5 percent). The United Kingdom, long the primary market for U.S. religious books, was barely up (0.8 percent). Revenues, on the other hand, showed somewhat better results, with growth rates reported for Venezuela (up 43.7 percent), Kenya (up 68.1 percent), and Guatemala (up 31.3 percent). See Table 9 for details.

### Table 9 / U.S. Exports of Religious Books 2008: Top Ten Markets

| Country | Value ($'000) | Percent Change 2007–2008 | Units ('000) | Percent Change 2007–2008 |
|---|---|---|---|---|
| United Kingdom | $15,780 | -5.3 | 6,533 | 0.8 |
| Australia | 11,912 | -22.6 | 3,154 | -7.4 |
| Canada | 13,204 | -7.0 | 3,517 | -16.4 |
| Nigeria | 12,932 | 25.2 | 3,931 | 25.0 |
| Mexico | 8,045 | -11.8 | 4,778 | 14.5 |
| Argentina | 3,146 | -50.9 | 2,027 | -56.0 |
| Venezuela | 2,646 | 43.7 | 943 | 7.3 |
| Kenya | 2,441 | 68.1 | 1,725 | 114.6 |
| Guatemala | 2,355 | 31.3 | 1,051 | 67.5 |
| Colombia | 2,291 | 3.9 | 610 | -3.9 |

Source: U.S. Department of Commerce, International Trade Administration. All totals are rounded off to one decimal point. Data for individual categories may not add to totals due to statistical rounding.

The critically important hardbound book category, an eclectic collection of adult trade and other categories, sustained the deepest, most unsettling unit decline in 2008 with seven nations showing negative numbers. Traditionally strong trading partners purchased fewer hardbound books last year, paced by the United Kingdom (down 4.9 percent), India (down 1.8 percent), Australia (down 41.8 percent), and China (down 53.4 percent). This pattern was not an anomaly; it was, clearly, the result of the global economic crisis and an erosion in the value of the U.S. dollar.

On the revenue side, fortunately, seven nations were up (Canada, India, Singapore, the United Arab Emirates, Japan, Mexico, and the Philippines).

Table 10 outlines this situation.

### Table 10 / U.S. Exports of Hardbound Books 2008: Top Ten Markets

| Country | Value ($'000) | Percent Change 2007–2008 | Units ('000) | Percent Change 2007–2008 |
|---|---|---|---|---|
| Canada | $144,075 | 35.5 | 1,7273 | 29.3 |
| United Kingdom | 10,677 | -18.7 | 1,892 | -4.9 |
| India | 4,982 | 17.1 | 709 | -1.8 |
| Singapore | 3,502 | 27.0 | 516 | 23.7 |
| Australia | 2,805 | -50.2 | 417 | -41.8 |
| United Arab Emirates | 2,329 | 7.4 | 134 | -7.7 |
| Japan | 2,307 | 32.1 | 255 | 30.7 |
| China | 1,517 | -26.0 | 83 | -53.4 |
| Mexico | 1,484 | 3.5 | 195 | -4.3 |
| Philippines | 1,483 | 24.1 | 166 | -2.0 |

Source: U.S. Department of Commerce, International Trade Administration. All totals are rounded off to one decimal point. Data for individual categories may not add to totals due to statistical rounding.

As in past years, exports of encyclopedias and serial installments, as well as dictionaries, were undermined by the global movement toward digital products. This is the last year these books will be tracked as separate categories. See Tables 11 and 12 for the 2008 results.

Fortunately, art and pictorial books remain a viable—albeit small—export category, with the United Kingdom (up 96 percent), Canada (down 0.3 percent), and Japan (up 81.7 percent) as the largest export designations in terms of units for 2008. This sector also showed impressive annual increases in terms of revenue, topped by the United Kingdom's strong 102.6 percent. Table 13 lists the ten largest markets for U.S. books in this sector.

### Table 11 / U.S. Exports of Encyclopedias and Serial Installments 2008: Top Ten Markets

| Country | Value ($'000) | Percent Change 2007–2008 | Units ('000) | Percent Change 2007–2008 |
|---|---|---|---|---|
| Japan | $1,274 | -26.2 | 135 | -22.1 |
| Canada | 1,812 | -10.1 | 206 | -21.1 |
| Australia | 539 | 72.6 | 51 | 86.2 |
| Pakistan | 536 | 1,393.4 | 70 | 1,396.8 |
| Ghana | 520 | n.a. | 62 | n.a. |
| Mexico | 414 | 72.8 | 92 | 144.0 |
| United Kingdom | 373 | 165.3 | 38 | 230.4 |
| South Africa | 314 | -0.8 | 28 | -14.6 |
| Philippines | 281 | 108.2 | 34 | 100.7 |
| India | 150 | -15.8 | 17 | -13.2 |

Source: U.S. Department of Commerce, International Trade Administration. All totals are rounded off to one decimal point. Data for individual categories may not add to totals due to statistical rounding.
n.a. = no data available.

**Table 12 / U.S. Exports of Dictionaries (Including Thesauruses) 2008: Top Ten Markets**

| Country | Value ($'000) | Percent Change 2007–2008 | Units ('000) | Percent Change 2007–2008 |
|---|---|---|---|---|
| Canada | $1,225 | -10.7 | 165 | -8.1 |
| South Korea | 662 | 178.4 | 94 | 356.3 |
| United Kingdom | 347 | 1,055.8 | 48 | 1,396.6 |
| Mexico | 231 | -45.8 | 58 | -18.4 |
| Germany | 120 | 70.6 | 17 | 70.6 |
| Brazil | 82 | -90.5 | 12 | -90.5 |
| Costa Rica | 53 | 1.5 | 10 | -10.1 |
| Saudi Arabia | 51 | 131.9 | 6 | 56.3 |
| Dominican Republic | 44 | n.a. | 3 | n.a. |
| Poland | 44 | n.a. | 6 | n.a. |

Source: U.S. Department of Commerce, International Trade Administration. All totals are rounded off to one decimal point. Data for individual categories may not add to totals due to statistical rounding.
n.a. = no data available.

**Table 13 / U.S. Exports of Art and Pictorial Books 2008: Top Ten Markets**

| Country | Value ($'000) | Percent Change 2007–2008 | Units ('000) | Percent Change 2007–2008 |
|---|---|---|---|---|
| United Kingdom | $22,070 | 102.6 | 3,501 | 96.0 |
| Canada | 3,135 | 28.2 | 312 | -0.3 |
| Japan | 1,036 | 64.5 | 169 | 81.7 |
| Germany | 869 | -57.1 | 129 | -60.4 |
| Switzerland | 565 | 313.7 | 96 | 312.5 |
| Australia | 548 | 9.2 | 93 | 22.2 |
| Mexico | 505 | -2.5 | 69 | 3.2 |
| Israel | 420 | 38.0 | 64 | 37.7 |
| Spain | 343 | 20.7 | 52 | 1.2 |
| France | 323 | -10.0 | 48 | -12.1 |

Source: U.S. Department of Commerce, International Trade Administration. All totals are rounded off to one decimal point. Data for individual categories may not add to totals due to statistical rounding.
n.a. = no data available.

## U.S. Book Imports, 2008

The nation's total book imports declined 1.42 percent in 2008. This decline is troubling since a significant portion of imported books in certain categories (including juvenile, mass market, professional, textbooks, and religious books) are printed abroad for U.S. publishers, not books printed and published abroad. The reason is economics. For example, printing, paper, and binding (PPB) in the United States for a higher education textbook might cost $16.50 a unit, while the PPB cost for that same book abroad (in China, for instance) might be 50 percent lower.

What undermined the importation of books printed abroad in 2008 (five of the top ten nations posted declines) was the surge in petroleum prices in 2008,

Table 14 / Top Ten Import Sources of Books: 1999–2008
($'000)

| Country | 1999 | 2000 | 2001 | 2002 | 2003 | 2004 | 2005 | 2006 | 2007 | 2008 | Percent Change 2007–2008 |
|---|---|---|---|---|---|---|---|---|---|---|---|
| China | 142,459 | 220,895 | 267,582 | 338,489 | 413,065 | 533,524 | 605,229 | 724,742 | 815,677 | 806,695 | -1.1 % |
| Canada | 221,462 | 229,045 | 243,689 | 251,085 | 275,053 | 289,423 | 281,120 | 292,273 | 298,633 | 308,340 | 3.3 |
| United Kingdom | 278,252 | 317,660 | 303,897 | 267,853 | 287,972 | 304,619 | 307,517 | 286,624 | 332,579 | 289,280 | -13.0 |
| Singapore | 89,000 | 86,630 | 96,325 | 100,610 | 103,383 | 113,900 | 115,314 | 115,609 | 120,867 | 115,740 | -4.2 |
| Hong Kong | 229,293 | 224,834 | 229,719 | 223,452 | 189,783 | 185,963 | 176,079 | 136,617 | 125,138 | 107,406 | -14.2 |
| Japan | 55,087 | 59,268 | 49,956 | 47,198 | 45,277 | 48,726 | 50,765 | 63,822 | 88,062 | 96,681 | 9.8 |
| Germany | 57,082 | 57,345 | 53,092 | 55,993 | 52,055 | 57,353 | 68,211 | 76,657 | 82,088 | 88,075 | 7.3 |
| Italy | 100,475 | 94,983 | 87,779 | 83,360 | 84,167 | 78,567 | 69,463 | 69,571 | 69,393 | 62,430 | -10.0 |
| South Korea | 29,728 | 29,430 | 35,559 | 40,459 | 39,083 | 46,265 | 54,303 | 54,398 | 54,252 | 55,545 | 2.4 |
| Spain | 46,590 | 55,506 | 50,474 | 50,994 | 48,407 | 49,330 | 38,725 | 36,901 | 32,646 | 32,679 | 0.1 |

Source: U.S. Department of Commerce, International Trade Administration. All totals are rounded off to one decimal point. Data for individual categories may not add to totals due to statistical rounding.

which reached about $150 a barrel in summer 2008. Oil prices declined in the fall, but then climbed back into the $40-a-barrel range in early 2009. If oil again reaches the $70-plus range, the cost to print and ship books from Asia to the United States could pose a problem for U.S. publishers, triggering additional declines in imports in 2009.

Another factor is typesetting and fulfillment done abroad for U.S. publishers. Type is often set in India and fulfillment work is performed in Singapore to reduce the total cost of goods sold (COGS). Since these tasks involve relatively inexpensive data transfers from the United States to India and Singapore via the Internet, these processes are not adversely affected by surges in energy costs.

### Table 15 / U.S. Book Imports from 25 Principal Countries 2006–2008

| Country | Value ($'000) | | | Percent Change 2006–2007 | Percent Change 2007–2008 |
|---|---|---|---|---|---|
| | 2006 | 2007 | 2008 | | |
| China | $724,742 | $815,677 | $806,695 | 12.5% | -1.1% |
| United Kingdom | 286,624 | 332,579 | 289,280 | 16.0 | -13.0 |
| Canada | 292,273 | 298,633 | 308,340 | 2.2 | 3.3 |
| Hong Kong | 136,617 | 125,138 | 107,406 | -8.4 | -14.2 |
| Singapore | 115,609 | 120,867 | 115,740 | 4.5 | -4.2 |
| Germany | 76,657 | 82,088 | 88,075 | 7.1 | 7.3 |
| Italy | 69,571 | 69,393 | 62,430 | -0.3 | -10.0 |
| Japan | 63,822 | 88,062 | 96,681 | 38.0 | 9.8 |
| South Korea | 54,398 | 54,252 | 55,545 | -0.3 | 2.4 |
| Mexico | 47,089 | 32,380 | 30,667 | -31.2 | -5.3 |
| Spain | 36,901 | 32,646 | 32,679 | -11.5 | 0.1 |
| France | 31,006 | 25,562 | 22,503 | -17.6 | -12.0 |
| Colombia | 22,102 | 36,274 | 31,159 | 64.1 | -14.1 |
| Thailand | 19,476 | 18,747 | 15,454 | -3.7 | -17.6 |
| Belgium | 15,113 | 12,860 | 8,087 | -14.9 | -37.1 |
| India | 14,222 | 16,439 | 16,161 | 15.6 | -1.7 |
| Malaysia | 14,011 | 13,816 | 15,063 | -1.4 | 9.0 |
| Israel | 12,874 | 14,309 | 13,686 | 11.1 | -4.4 |
| Taiwan | 8,860 | 9,866 | 10,303 | 11.4 | 4.4 |
| Netherlands | 8,570 | 8,084 | 21,557 | -5.7 | 166.9 |
| Australia | 6,828 | 6,811 | 6,564 | -0.2 | -3.6 |
| United Arab Emirates | 6,748 | 6,075 | 6,578 | -10.0 | 8.3 |
| Indonesia | 3,431 | 3,254 | 6,145 | -5.2 | 88.8 |
| Switzerland | 9,541 | 5,441 | 5,410 | -43.0 | -0.6 |
| Sweden | 5,527 | 5,526 | 3,974 | -0.02 | -28.1 |
| Total: Top 25 Countries | $2,081,643 | $2,238,936 | $2,176,202 | 7.6 | -19.1 |
| All Others | $42,663 | $42,338 | $37,610 | -0.8 | -19.1 |
| Grand Total | $2,124,306 | $2,281,275 | $2,113,812 | 7.4 | -3.0 |

Source: U.S. Department of Commerce, International Trade Administration. All totals are rounded off to one decimal point. Data for individual categories may not add to totals due to statistical rounding. Individual shipments are excluded from the foreign trade data if valued under $2,500.

China has been the largest source of imported books since 2000 even though it posted a 1.1 percent decline in 2008. Five additional countries also had declines in 2008, including the United Kingdom (13 percent), Hong Kong (14.2 percent), Singapore (4.2 percent), and Italy (10.0 percent). Table 14 lists the top 10 import sources.

Table 15 lists the top 25 nations that exported books to the United State in 2008. Fifteen countries—among them France, Thailand, Belgium, and India— also reported declines, some of which were significant. The well-publicized slowdown in the U.S. economy affected these results, which are likely to be replicated in 2009.

In 2008, as in previous years, hardcover books remained the largest, most important import book category. However, the value of this category dropped 0.9 percent in 2008 to $718.6 million (in 2007 it was $725 million). Textbooks remained the second largest category, but also saw a drop (6.0 percent). The third category in size is the technical, scientific, and professional cluster (down 4.9 percent to $262 million in 2008). Table 16 lists these declines as well as the results for the other categories.

#### Table 16 / U.S. Imports of Books: 2006–2008

| Category | Value ($'000) | | | Percent Change 2006–2007 | Percent Change 2007–2008 |
|---|---|---|---|---|---|
| | 2006 | 2007 | 2008 | | |
| Encyclopedias | $5,912 | $3,110 | $5,662 | -47.4 | 82.0 |
| Textbooks | 243,489 | 310,491 | 291,914 | 27.5 | -6.0 |
| Religious books | 114,254 | 132,687 | 131,858 | 16.1 | -0.6 |
| Technical, scientific and professional | 249,248 | 275,844 | 262,352 | 10.7 | -4.9 |
| Hardcover books, n.e.s. | 657,237 | 725,052 | 718,631 | 10.3 | -0.9 |
| Mass market paperbacks | 108,524 | 108,883 | 112,537 | 0.3 | 3.4 |
| Art and pictorial books | 49,961 | 48,974 | 31,803 | -2.8 | 6.3 |
| Dictionaries and thesauruses | 11,775 | 9,907 | 7,534 | -15.9 | -24.0 |

Source: U.S. Department of Commerce, International Trade Administration. All totals are rounded off to one decimal point. Data for individual categories may not add to totals due to statistical rounding. Individual shipments are excluded from the foreign trade data if valued under $2,500.

## Book Import Categories in 2008

Imports of textbooks also saw some declines in 2008. Canada was the largest source of printed textbooks (almost all of them printed, but not printed and published, in Canada), growing 21.5 percent in revenues and 18.3 percent in units. China posted a modest increase (3.1 percent) in revenues, but sustained a 14.6 percent decline in units.

Five countries were down in terms of revenue (the United Kingdom, Hong Kong, Singapore, Colombia, and Spain), with upticks reported by Mexico, Germany, and France. Table 17 contains data on these trends.

### Table 17 / U.S. Imports of Textbooks 2008: Top Ten Markets

| Country | Value ($'000) | Percent Change 2007–2008 | Units ('000) | Percent Change 2007–2008 |
|---|---|---|---|---|
| Canada | $78,583 | 21.5 | 12,668 | 18.3 |
| China | 67,181 | 3.1 | 18,458 | -14.6 |
| United Kingdom | 67,143 | -14.7 | 3,865 | 18.1 |
| Hong Kong | 17,050 | -48.2 | 5,305 | -23.7 |
| Singapore | 10,968 | -23.8 | 4,688 | -3.4 |
| Mexico | 6,816 | 12.0 | 2,638 | -3.1 |
| Germany | 5,428 | 2.6 | 284 | 3.9 |
| Colombia | 4,998 | -23.2 | 1,158 | -8.0 |
| Spain | 4,200 | -14.0 | 422 | 7.6 |
| France | 3,691 | 25.5 | 393 | -10.1 |

Source: U.S. Department of Commerce, International Trade Administration. All totals are rounded off to one decimal point. Data for individual categories may not add to totals due to statistical rounding.

For a number of years, the religious book category was unquestionably the fastest-growing import book category for the United States, generating annual increases in the 5 percent to 7 percent range. This trend abated in 2006, although there was a 16.1 percent increase in 2007.

In 2008 four nations posted declines in revenues and units for religious books, including South Korea (revenues down 5.1 percent, units 1.5 percent), Colombia (revenues down 17.8 percent, units 20.1 percent), Belgium (revenues down 48.2 percent, units 65.4 percent), and Hong Kong (revenues down 1.8 percent, units 10.3 percent). China remained the largest source of religious books in terms of revenues (up 15.2 percent) and units (up 21.4 percent). Italy posted a staggering 150.8 percent increase in revenues, outpacing both Canada (up 73.4 percent) and the United Kingdom (up 33.8 percent). Table 18 contains data on this sector.

### Table 18 / U.S. Imports of Bibles, Testaments, Prayer Books, and Other Religious Books: Top Ten Markets 2008

| Country | Value ($'000) | Percent Change 2007–2008 | Units ('000) | Percent Change 2007–2008 |
|---|---|---|---|---|
| China | $34,917 | 15.2 | 15,757 | 21.4 |
| South Korea | 18,978 | -5.1 | 11,730 | -1.5 |
| Colombia | 17,021 | -17.8 | 10,052 | -20.1 |
| Israel | 11,280 | -4.9 | 3,525 | 2.6 |
| United Kingdom | 5,880 | 33.8 | 701 | -32.4 |
| Canada | 5,687 | 73.4 | 1,620 | -74.3 |
| Italy | 4,492 | 150.8 | 1,090 | 2.4 |
| Belgium | 3,922 | -48.2 | 1,027 | -65.4 |
| Spain | 3,756 | 0.6 | 586 | -28.3 |
| Hong Kong | 3,371 | -1.8 | 6,391 | -10.3 |

Source: U.S. Department of Commerce, International Trade Administration. All totals are rounded off to one decimal point. Data for individual categories may not add to totals due to statistical rounding.

For a number of years, the United Kingdom and Canada dominated the technical, scientific, and professional book import sector. Recently China overtook these two nations as the largest source of such books, but in 2008 China was overtaken by both Japan (up 10.8 percent in revenues) and Germany (up 0.7 percent).

Overall, five nations saw declines in both revenues and units, including China (revenues down 34.6 percent, units 9.1 percent), Hong Kong (revenues down 13.1 percent, units 48.7 percent), Mexico (revenues down 3.2 percent, units 15.6 percent), Italy (revenues down 29.4 percent, units 15.7 percent), and Singapore (revenues down 3.1 percent, units 10.7 percent).

As of 2008, reliable data about digital books in this category became available, although the Department of Commerce does not release any e-book data. It is likely that by 2010 or 2011 the concept of a "technical, scientific, and professional book unit" will become an anachronism since the publishers active in this field record only dollars (and not units) in their quarterly and annual financial reports. This trend will be monitored, and, in the near future, only revenues will be analyzed. See Table 19 for additional information.

**Table 19  /  U.S. Imports of Technical, Scientific, and Professional Books: Top Ten Markets 2008**

| Country | Value ($'000) | Percent Change 2007–2008 | Units ('000) | Percent Change 2007–2008 |
|---|---|---|---|---|
| Japan | $60,913 | 10.8 | 876 | -7.4 |
| Germany | 44,570 | 0.7 | 1,406 | -26.9 |
| China | 38,990 | -34.6 | 9,552 | -9.1 |
| Canada | 36,017 | 2.9 | 4,880 | -20.9 |
| United Kingdom | 30,208 | 8.7 | 3,430 | 26.1 |
| France | 7,150 | 14.7 | 273 | -6.4 |
| Hong Kong | 6,911 | -13.1 | 1,284 | -48.7 |
| Mexico | 5,619 | -3.2 | 3,176 | -15.6 |
| Italy | 4,669 | -29.4 | 270 | -15.7 |
| Singapore | 4,468 | -3.1 | 1,186 | -10.7 |

Source: U.S. Department of Commerce, International Trade Administration. All totals are rounded off to one decimal point. Data for individual categories may not add to totals due to statistical rounding.

Despite declines in both revenues (3.2 percent) and units (12.7 percent), China's hegemony in the hardcover book category remained intact, easily outpacing the United Kingdom. See Table 20 for details.

However, structural volatility was also evident in this category, and three other nations reported declines in revenues and units, including the United Kingdom (revenues down 21.4 percent, units 45.8 percent), Singapore (revenues down 5.0 percent, units 3.5 percent), and Italy (revenues down 10.6 percent, units 27.0 percent). Remarkable revenue growth patterns were reported for Germany (up 59.7 percent) and Spain (up 35.6 percent).

As it did in many other categories, China maintained the top position in the mass market paperback sector even with a rather modest increase in revenues (4.5 percent) and a sharp 8.7 percent decline in units.

Table 20 / U.S. Imports of Hardbound Books: Top Ten Markets 2008

| Country | Value ($'000) | Percent Change 2007–2008 | Units ('000) | Percent Change 2007–2008 |
|---|---|---|---|---|
| China | $358,421 | -3.2 | 151,162 | -12.7 |
| United Kingdom | 88,544 | -21.4 | 4,958 | -45.8 |
| Singapore | 56,969 | -5.0 | 24,765 | -3.5 |
| Hong Kong | 39,298 | 15.1 | 12,662 | -11.1 |
| Canada | 35,014 | 1.6 | 7,016 | -1.7 |
| Italy | 30,213 | -10.6 | 4,217 | -27.0 |
| Netherlands | 14,820 | n.a. | 1,132.8 | n.a. |
| Germany | 14,062 | 59.7 | 2,122 | 104.0 |
| Japan | 12,862 | 19.3 | 3,411 | 5.4 |
| Spain | 12,386 | 35.6 | 1,866 | 15.3 |

Source: U.S. Department of Commerce, International Trade Administration. All totals are rounded off to one decimal point. Data for individual categories may not add to totals due to statistical rounding.

n.a. = no data available for previous year.

The United Kingdom also had an uneven year, solidifying its position as the second-largest source of mass market paperbacks. Canada's results were bumpy, up a razor-thin 0.7 percent in revenues despite a staggering increase in units (66.2 percent). The United Kingdom and Canada remain the largest sources of these books after China. The other seven "top ten" nations generated mixed results in this sector. See Table 21 for details on revenues and units.

Table 21 / U.S. Imports of Mass Market Paperbacks (Rack Size): Top Ten Markets 2008

| Country | Value ($'000) | Percent Change 2007–2008 | Units ('000) | Percent Change 2007–2008 |
|---|---|---|---|---|
| China | $35,086 | 4.5 | 20,468 | -8.7 |
| United Kingdom | 25,668 | 3.5 | 6,423 | -10.3 |
| Canada | 22,408 | 0.7 | 13,243 | 66.2 |
| Hong Kong | 6,817 | 70.7 | 3,555 | 78.7 |
| Singapore | 5,738 | -1.5 | 5,022 | -4.2 |
| Italy | 4,591 | 16.9 | 1,879 | 77.0 |
| Spain | 2,836 | -1.8 | 1,584 | 67.1 |
| Japan | 1,321 | -9.8 | 296 | 27.0 |
| Mexico | 1,306 | -44.4 | 432 | -52.3 |
| South Korea | 967 | -28.2 | 743 | -39.9 |

Source: U.S. Department of Commerce, International Trade Administration. All totals are rounded off to one decimal point. Data for individual categories may not add to totals due to statistical rounding.

This is the last year that data for encyclopedias and serial installments, as well as dictionaries and thesauruses, will be included in this analysis, but Tables 21 and 22 list detailed information about these small categories.

Table 22 / U.S. Imports of Encyclopedias and Serial Installments:
Top Ten Markets 2008

| Country | Value ($'000) | Percent Change 2007–2008 | Units ('000) | Percent Change 2007–2008 |
|---|---|---|---|---|
| China | $3,114 | 228.5 | 1,398 | 384.1 |
| Mexico | 834 | 33.9 | 84 | -35.5 |
| Canada | 431 | 93.2 | 71 | 506.4 |
| Singapore | 408 | 110.7 | 72 | 65.4 |
| Hong Kong | 257 | -21.9 | 40 | -57.6 |
| Italy | 147 | 122.3 | 16 | -15.1 |
| Taiwan | 78 | 241.2 | 35 | 246.9 |
| United Kingdom | 72 | 105.9 | 6 | 1,875.0 |
| Germany | 69 | 92.1 | 59 | 7,236.1 |
| United Arab Emirates | 65 | -11.6 | 50 | 12.0 |

Source: U.S. Department of Commerce, International Trade Administration. All totals are rounded off to one decimal point. Data for individual categories may not add to totals due to statistical rounding. Calculations used two decimal points because of the size of the totals.

Table 23 / U.S. Imports of Dictionaries and Thesauruses: Top Ten Markets 2008

| Country | Value ($'000) | Percent Change 2007–2008 | Units ('000) | Percent Change 2007–2008 |
|---|---|---|---|---|
| China | $2,443 | 72.4 | 655 | -3.0 |
| United Kingdom | 1,072 | -51.2 | 255 | -51.5 |
| Germany | 490 | -71.1 | 137 | -68.8 |
| Italy | 485 | -42.1 | 84 | -66.3 |
| Canada | 454 | -31.7 | 294 | -62.7 |
| Spain | 307 | -62.0 | 97 | -42.7 |
| Japan | 227 | 391.4 | 7 | 425.5 |
| Hong Kong | 196 | -52.6 | 45 | -50.4 |
| Colombia | 173 | -32.8 | 38 | -34.0 |
| Singapore | 904 | 265.0 | 254 | 260.3 |

Source: U.S. Department of Commerce, International Trade Administration. All totals are rounded off to one decimal point. Data for individual categories may not add to totals due to statistical rounding. Calculations used two decimal points because of the size of the totals.

Art books remain a popular import category because of the impressive printing and binding done in several other parts of the world, notably China, Western Europe, and the Pacific Rim nations.

However, Canada emerged as a significant source of these books in 2008, and it is likely that it will continue to burnish its reputation in this highly competitive category. See Table 24 for details.

### Table 24 / U.S. Imports of Art and Pictorial Books (Minimum Values $5): Top Ten Markets 2008

| Country | Value ($'000) | Percent Change 2007–2008 | Units ('000) | Percent Change 2007–2008 |
|---|---|---|---|---|
| China | $6,179 | -0.2 | 675 | -12.0 |
| Italy | 5,274 | 6.2 | 307 | -4.2 |
| Germany | 4,231 | -31.7 | 350 | -31.2 |
| United Kingdom | 3,012 | 67.6 | 194 | 54.3 |
| France | 2,225 | 106.9 | 34 | -25.0 |
| Hong Kong | 1,910 | -14.2 | 213 | -12.2 |
| Singapore | 1,866 | 34.2 | 198 | 49.9 |
| Netherlands | 1,493 | 88.3 | 67 | 52.1 |
| Canada | 1,386 | 298.1 | 52 | 46.9 |
| Spain | 621 | -21.2 | 35 | -18.3 |

Source: U.S. Department of Commerce, International Trade Administration. All totals are rounded off to one decimal point. Data for individual categories may not add to totals due to statistical rounding. Calculations used two decimal points because of the size of the totals.

## Conclusions

Book exports remain an important distribution channel for many U.S. book publishers. Yet, for the first time in decades, publishers and editors became acutely aware of the impact of global economics on this revenue source.

Second, in spite of a significant amount of publicity and an inordinate amount of "buzz" about the inevitability of digital books replacing printed books, the amount of net publishers' revenues generated in the trade sector by this new format remained exceptionally small, unlike digital books in the professional category.

However, certain book categories (such as technical books and educational textbooks) are currently in the process of transforming content from "print only" to a "print and electronic" format and an "electronic and print" business model; and they will report increased revenues from digital books.

The remaining major book categories (adult, juvenile, mass market paperbacks, and religious books) will move more slowly into digital books because of well-documented consumer preferences, technological issues, and, in the current recession, financial concerns about the cost of electronic hand-held digital book readers.

Ultimately, this digital metamorphosis will have far-reaching consequences, impacting readers, book publishers, book retailers, and book distributors—in effect the entire industry supply chain.

Third, if regional economic "decoupling" from the United States has occurred (for instance, on the part of the so-called BRIC countries—Brazil, Russia, India, and China), it was not very evident in 2008.

Fourth, the credit liquidity and mortgage crises in the United States will not end in 2009.

Fifth, book piracy remains a significant problem, as indicated in the latest statistical data from the International Intellectual Property Alliance (2009), which reported that U.S. publishers lost more than half a billion dollars to book piracy in 2008; the actual sum, in fact, is $1.5 billion to $2 billion.

Last, the entire book industry needs to pay more attention to collecting and analyzing basic, critical macroeconomic data that will assist U.S. publishers in understanding their current domestic markets and help them to increase the export channel of distribution. Recent work undertaken by the Institute for Publishing Research and *Publishers Weekly* shows great promise in this area.

## References

Carroll, P. B., and C. Mui. *Billion Dollar Lessons: What You Can Learn from the Most Inexcusable Business Failures of the Last 25 Years* (Portfolio, 2008).

Chung, Y., M. Chinn, and E. Fujii. "China's Current Account and Exchange Rate," National Bureau of Economic Research, NBER Working Papers 2009: No. 14673.

Cinquetti, C. "Multinationals and Exports in a Large and Protected Developing Country," *Review of International Economics* 16:5 (November 2008), 904–918.

Cohan, William D. *House of Cards: A Tale of Hubris and Wretched Excess on Wall Street* (Doubleday, 2009).

Derman, Emanuel. *My Life As a Quant: Reflections on Physics and Finance* (John Wiley, 2004).

Gabor, P., and T. A. Peltonen. "Has Emerging Asia Decoupled? An Analysis of Production and Trade Linkages Using the Asian International Input-Output Table," European Central Bank, Working Paper Series 2009: No. 993.

Greco, A. N. *The Book Publishing Industry* (Lawrence Erlbaum Associates, 2005).

Greco, A. N., Clara E. Rodriguez, and Robert M. Wharton. *The Culture and Commerce of Publishing in the 21st Century* (Stanford University Press, 2007).

International Intellectual Property Alliance (2009). "Appendix A: IIPA 'Special 301' Recommendations; International Intellectual Property Alliance 2008 'Special 301 Report'; Appendix B: Methodology" (http://www.iipa.com/special301.html).

Kehoe, T., and K. Ruhl. "Are Shocks to the Terms of Trade Shocks to Productivity?" *Review of Economic Dynamics* 11:4 (October 2008), 804–819.

Lowenstein, R. *When Genius Failed: The Rise and Fall of Long-Term Capital Management* (Random, 2000).

Moss, D. A. *A Concise Guide to Macroeconomics* (Harvard Business School Press, 2007).

Muolo, P., and M. Padilla. *Chain of Blame: How Wall Street Caused the Mortgage and Credit Crisis* (Wiley, 2008).

Phillips, K. *Bad Money: Reckless Finance, Failed Politics, and the Global Crisis of American Capitalism* (Viking, 2008).

# Number of Book Outlets
# in the United States and Canada

The *American Book Trade Directory* (Information Today, Inc.) has been published since 1915. Revised annually, it features lists of booksellers, wholesalers, periodicals, reference tools, and other information about the U.S. and Canadian book markets. The data shown in Table 1, the most current available, are from the 2009–2010 edition of the directory.

The 19,920 stores of various types shown are located throughout the United States, Canada, and regions administered by the United States. "General" bookstores stock trade books and children's books in a general variety of subjects. "College" stores carry college-level textbooks. "Educational" outlets handle school textbooks up to and including the high school level. "Mail order" outlets sell general trade books by mail and are not book clubs; all others operating by mail are classified according to the kinds of books carried. "Antiquarian" dealers sell old and rare books. Stores handling secondhand books are classified as "Used." "Paperback" stores have more than 80 percent of their stock in paperbound books. Stores with paperback departments are listed under the appropriate major classification ("General," "Department Store," "Stationer," and so forth.). Bookstores with at least 50 percent of their stock on a particular subject are classified by subject.

### Table 1 / Bookstores in the United States and Canada, 2008

| Category | United States | Canada |
|---|---|---|
| Antiquarian General | 837 | 74 |
| Antiquarian Mail Order | 315 | 12 |
| Antiquarian Specialized | 161 | 4 |
| Art Supply Store | 67 | 2 |
| College General | 3,235 | 174 |
| College Specialized | 123 | 6 |
| Comics | 218 | 26 |
| Computer Software | 2 | 0 |
| Cooking | 264 | 8 |
| Department Store | 1,618 | 4 |
| Educational* | 188 | 37 |
| Federal Sites† | 221 | 1 |
| Foreign Language* | 22 | 3 |
| General | 4,113 | 628 |
| Gift Shop | 158 | 7 |
| Juvenile* | 125 | 21 |
| Mail Order General | 129 | 12 |
| Mail Order Specialized | 398 | 21 |
| Metaphysics, New Age, and Occult | 167 | 22 |
| Museum Store and Art Gallery | 498 | 32 |
| Nature and Natural History | 41 | 7 |
| Newsdealer | 30 | 2 |
| Office Supply | 17 | 2 |
| Other‡ | 2,326 | 443 |

**Table 1 / Bookstores in the United States and Canada, 2008** *(cont.)*

| Category | United States | Canada |
|---|---|---|
| Paperback§ | 114 | 5 |
| Religious* | 2,160 | 187 |
| Self Help/Development | 24 | 6 |
| Stationer | 5 | 4 |
| Toy Store | 53 | 20 |
| Used* | 435 | 86 |
| Totals | 18,064 | 1,856 |

\* Includes Mail Order Shops for this topic, which are not counted elsewhere in this survey.
† National Historic Sites, National Monuments, and National Parks.
‡ Stores specializing in subjects or services other than those covered in this survey.
§ Includes Mail Order. Excludes used paperback bookstores, stationers, drugstores, or wholesalers handling paperbacks.

# Review Media Statistics

Compiled by the staff of the *Library and Book Trade Almanac*

## Number of Books and Other Media Reviewed by Major Reviewing Publications

| 2007EN]2008 | Adult | | Juvenile | | Young Adult | | Total | |
|---|---|---|---|---|---|---|---|---|
| | 2007 | 2008 | 2007 | 2008 | 2007 | 2008 | 2007 | 2008 |
| *Booklist*[1] | 4,939 | 4,673 | 2,849 | 3,138 | — | — | 7,788 | 7,811 |
| *Bookmarks* | n.a. | 716 | — | — | n.a. | 20 | n.a. | 736 |
| *BookPage*[2] | n.a. | 533 | n.a. | 77 | n.a. | 20 | n.a. | 630 |
| *Bulletin of the Center for Children's Books*[3] | — | — | 855 | 849 | — | — | 855 | 849 |
| *Chicago Sun Times* | 525 | n.a. | 95 | n.a. | — | — | 610 | n.a. |
| *Chicago Tribune Sunday Book Section* | 500 | 400 | 250 | 225 | 100 | 50 | 850 | 675 |
| *Choice*[4] | 6,672 | 6,766 | — | — | — | — | 6,672 | 6,766 |
| *Horn Book Guide* | — | — | 3,421 | 3,3240 | 751 | 1,154 | 4,172 | 4,478 |
| *Horn Book Magazine*[5] | 3 | 2 | 297 | 320 | 79 | 106 | 379 | 428 |
| *Kirkus Reviews*[6] | 2,725 | 2,532 | 1,998 | 2,096 | — | — | 4,723 | 4,628 |
| *Library Journal*[7] | 6,166 | 5,814 | — | — | — | — | 6,166 | 5,814 |
| *Los Angeles Times* | n.a. | n.a. | — | — | — | — | n.a. | n.a. |
| *New York Review of Books* | n.a. | 332 | — | — | — | — | n.a. | 332 |
| *New York Times Sunday Book Review*[6] | 1,075 | 1,050 | 125 | 115 | — | — | 1,200 | 1,165 |
| *Publishers Weekly*[8] | 6,004 | 6,284 | 878 | 1,030 | — | — | 6,882 | 7,912 |
| *School Library Journal*[6] | 250 | 280 | 4,283 | 4,853 | — | — | 4,533 | ,5,133 |
| *Washington Post Book World* | 1,200 | n.a. | 100 | n.a. | 50 | n.a. | 1,350 | n.a. |

n.a. = not available

1 All figures are for a 12-month period from September 1, 2007, to August 31, 2008 (vol. 104). YA books are included in the juvenile total. *Booklist* also reviewed 563 other media.

2 BookPage also reviewed 51 audiobooks.

3 All figures are for a 12-month period beginning September and ending July/August. YA books are included in the juvenile total. The *Bulletin* also reviewed 21 professional books.

4 All materials reviewed in *Choice* are scholarly publications intended for undergraduate libraries. *Choice* also reviewed 418 Internet sites, 4 CD-ROMs, and 2 e-books.

5 *Horn Book Magazine* also reviewed 2 audiobooks.

6 YA books are included in the juvenile total.

7 In addition, *Library Journal* reviewed 314 audiobooks, 438 DVDs/videos, 106 magazines, 268 books in Collection Development, and 85 online databases, and previewed 1,119 books in "Prepub Alert," "Prepub Mystery," and "Prepub Audio."

8 Of the total of 7,912 reviews, 1,009 were online only. *Publishers Weekly* also reviewed 462 audiobooks.

# Part 5
# Reference Information

# Bibliographies

## The Librarian's Bookshelf

Mary Ellen Quinn

Editor, *Booklist/Reference Books Bulletin,* American Library Association

Most of the books on this selective bibliography have been published since 2006; a few earlier titles are retained because of their continuing importance.

## General Works

*American Library Directory, 2009–2010.* 2 vols. Information Today, Inc., 2009. $309. Also available online.

*Annual Review of Information Science and Technology (ARIST).* Ed. by Blaise Cronin. Information Today, Inc., 2009. $99.95.

*The Bowker Annual Library and Book Trade Almanac, 2009.* See *Library and Book Trade Almanac.*

*Encyclopedia of Library and Information Science.* 2nd ed. Ed. by Miriam A. Drake. Taylor & Francis, 2003. $1,500. Also available online.

*Library and Book Trade Almanac, 2009* (Bowker Annual). Information Today, Inc., 2009. $199.95.

*Library Literature and Information Science Full Text.* H. W. Wilson (http://vnweb.hwwilsonweb.com/hww/Journals).

*Library Literature and Information Science Index.* H. W. Wilson, 1921–. Also available online, 1984–.

*Library Literature and Information Science Retrospective: 1905–1983.* H. W. Wilson (http://vnweb.hwwilsonweb.com/hww/Journals).

*The Oxford Guide to Library Research.* 3rd ed. By Thomas Mann. Oxford University, 2005. Paper $18.95.

*The Whole Library Handbook 4.* Ed. by George Eberhart. American Library Association, 2006. Paper $46.

## Academic Libraries

*The Academic Library and the Net Gen Student: Making the Connection.* By Susan Gibbons. American Library Association, 2007. Paper $50.

*The Academic Library Manager's Forms, Policies, and Procedures Handbook with CD-ROM.* By Rebecca Brumley. Neal-Schuman, 2007. Paper and CD-ROM $149.95.

*Academic Library Trends and Statistics, 2006.* Association of College and Research Libraries/American Library Association, 2006. 3 vols. $440. Also available online (http://secure200.telusys.net/trendstat/2006).

*ARL Statistics.* Association of Research Libraries. Annual. 1962– (http://www.arl.org/stats/annualsurveys/arlstats).

*Beyond Survival: Managing Academic Libraries in Transition.* By Elizabeth J. Wood and Rush Miller. Libraries Unlimited, 2006. Paper $45.

*CLIP* (College Library Information Packet) *Notes.* Association of College and Research Libraries/American Library Association,

1980–. Most recent volume is No. 39, 2008. Paper $45.

*Convergence and Collaboration of Campus Information Services.* Ed. by Peter Hernon and Ronald R. Powell. Libraries Unlimited, 2008. Paper $50.

*Creating the Customer-Driven Academic Library.* By Jeannette Woodward. American Library Association, 2008. Paper $58.

*Making a Difference: Leadership and Academic Libraries.* By Peter Hernon and Nancy Rossiter. Libraries Unlimited, 2007. Paper $45.

*Real-Life Marketing and Promotion Strategies in College Libraries: Connecting with Campus and Community.* Ed. by Barbara Whitney Petruzzelli. Haworth, 2006. Paper $22.95.

*Revisiting Outcomes Assessment in Higher Education.* Ed. by Peter Hermon, Robert E. Dugan, and Candy Schwartz. Libraries Unlimited, 2006. Paper $50.

*SPEC Kits.* Association of Research Libraries. 1973–. 10/yr. $285.

*Transforming Library Service Through Information Commons: Case Studies for the Digital Age.* By D. Russell Bailey and Barbara Gunter Tierney. American Library Association, 2008. Paper $60.

## Administration and Personnel

*Achieving Diversity: A How-To-Do-It Manual for Libraries.* Ed. by Barbara I. Dewey and Loretta Parham. Neal-Schuman, 2006. Paper $75.

*Advances in Library Administration and Organization.* Most recent volume is No. 25. Ed. by Edward D. Garten and Delmus E. Williams. Elsevier Science, 2007. $94.95.

*Crash Course in Library Supervision.* By Dennis C. Tucker and Shelley Elizabeth Mosley. Libraries Unlimited, 2007. Paper $30.

*Dealing with Natural Disasters in Libraries.* Ed. by William Miller and Rita M. Pellen. Haworth, 2008. Paper $65.

*Field Guide to Emergency Response.* Heritage Preservation Trust, 2006. Paper $29.95.

*Human Resources for Results: The Right Person for the Right Job.* By Jeanne Goodrich and Paula M. Singer. American Library Association, 2007. Paper $60.

*Library and Information Center Management.* 7th ed. By Robert D. Stueart and Barbara B. Moran. Libraries Unlimited, 2007. Paper $50.

*Library Board Strategic Guide: Going to the Next Level.* By Ellen G. Moore and Patricia H. Fisher. Scarecrow, 2007. Paper $35.

*The Library Security and Safety Guide to Prevention, Planning, and Response.* By Miriam B. Kahn. American Library Association, 2008. Paper $45.

*Management Basics for Information Professionals.* 2nd ed. By G. Edward Evans and Patricia Layzell Ward. Neal-Schuman, 2007. Paper $65.

*The New OPL Sourcebook: A Guide for Solo and Small Libraries.* By Judith A. Siess. Information Today, Inc., 2006. Paper $39.50.

*Our New Public, A Changing Clientele: Bewildering Issues or New Challenges for Managing Libraries?* Ed. by James R. Kennedy, Lisa Vardaman, and Gerard B. McCabe. Libraries Unlimited, 2008. $45.

*Putting Customers First.* 40-minute video. Library Information Network, 2007. DVD or VHS $99.

*The Quality Library: Guide to Staff-Driven Improvement, Better Efficiency, and Happier Customers.* By Sara Laughlin and Ray W. Wilson. American Library Association, 2008. Paper $55.

*Running a Small Library: A How-To-Do-It Manual.* Ed. by John Moorman. Neal-Schuman, 2006. Paper $59.95.

*Small Change, Big Problems: Detecting and Preventing Financial Misconduct in Your Library.* By Herbert Snyder. American Library Association, 2006. Paper $45.

*Strategic Planning for Results.* By Sandra Nelson. American Library Association, 2008. Paper $58.50.

*Streamlining Library Services: What We Do, How Much Time It Takes, What It Costs, and How We Can Do It Better.* By Richard M. Dougherty. Scarecrow, 2008. Paper $45.

*Supervising Staff: A How-To-Do-It Manual.* By Marcia Trotta. Neal-Schuman, 2006. Paper $59.95.

*Training Library Staff and Volunteers to Provide Extraordinary Customer Service.* By Julie Todaro and Mark L. Smith. Neal-Schuman, 2006. Paper $65.

## Buildings and Space Planning

*Designing a School Library Media Center for the Future.* By Rolf Erikson and Carolyn Markuson. American Library Association, 2007. Paper $50.

*Libraries Designed for Kids.* By Nolan Lushington. Neal-Schuman, 2008. Paper $85.

*Library Furnishings: A Planning Guide.* By Tish Murphy. McFarland, 2007. Paper $55.

*Managing Your Library Construction Project.* By Richard C. McCarthy. American Library Association, 2007. Paper $64.

*The New Downtown Library.* By Shannon Mattern. University of Minnesota, 2006. Paper $39.95.

*Planning New and Remodeled Archival Facilities.* By Thomas P. Wilsted. Society of American Archivists, 2007. Paper $49.

## Cataloging and Bibliographic Control

*Catalog It: A Guide to Cataloging School Library Materials.* 2nd ed. By Allison Kaplan and Ann Riedling. Linworth, 2006. Paper $46.95.

*Cataloging Cultural Objects: A Guide to Describing Cultural Works and Their Images.* By Murtha Baca, Patricia Harpring, Elisa Lanzi, Linda McRae, and Ann Whiteside. American Library Association, 2006. Paper $94.

*Education for Library Cataloging: International Perspectives.* Ed. by Dajin D. Sun and Ruth C. Carter. Haworth, 2006. Paper $49.95.

*FRBR: A Guide for the Perplexed.* By Robert L. Maxwell. American Library Association, 2008. Paper $55.

*From Catalog to Gateway: Charting a Course for Future Access.* Ed. by Bill Sleeman and Pamela Blum. Association for Library Collections and Technical Services/American Library Association, 2006. Paper $54.

*Introduction to Cataloging and Classification.* 10th ed. By Arlene G. Taylor. Libraries Unlimited, 2006. Paper $50.

*Knowledge Without Boundaries: Organizing Information for the Future.* Ed. by Michael A. Chopey. Association for Library Collections and Technical Services/American Library Association, 2006. Paper $49.

*Metadata.* By Marcia Lei Zeng and Jian Qin. Neal-Schuman, 2008. Paper $65.

*Moving Image Cataloging: How to Create and How to Use a Moving Image Catalog.* By Martha M. Yee. Libraries Unlimited, 2007. Paper $45.

*Organizing Audiovisual and Electronic Resources for Access.* 2nd ed. By Ingrid Hsieh-Yee. Libraries Unlimited, 2006. Paper $45.

*Radical Cataloging: Essays at the Front.* Ed. by K. R. Roberto. McFarland, 2008. Paper $45.

*Standard Cataloging for School and Public Libraries.* 4th ed. By Sheila S. Intner and Jean Weihs. Libraries Unlimited, 2007. Paper $50.

*Understanding FRBR: What It Is and How It Will Affect Our Retrieval Tools.* By Arlene G. Taylor. Libraries Unlimited, 2008. Paper $45.

## Children's and Young Adult Services and Materials

*Children's Books: A Practical Guide to Selection.* By Phyllis J. Van Orden and Sunny Strong. Neal-Schuman, 2007. Paper $59.95.

*Children's Literature in Action: A Librarian's Guide.* By Sylvia Vardell. Libraries Unlimited, 2008. Paper $50.

*Connecting with Reluctant Teen Readers: Tips, Titles, and Tools.* By Patrick Jones. Neal-Schuman, 2006. Paper. $59.95.

*Core Collection for Children and Young Adults.* By Rachel E. Schwedt and Janice DeLong. Scarecrow, 2008. $50.

*Dynamic Youth Services Through Outcome-Based Planning and Evaluation.* By Eliza T. Dresang, Melissa Gross, and Leslie Edmonds Holt. American Library Association, 2006. Paper $42.

*Extreme Teens: Library Services to Nontraditional Young Adults.* By Sheila B. Anderson. Libraries Unlimited, 2006. Paper $46.

*The Guy-Friendly YA Library.* By James Rollie Welch. Libraries Unlimited, 2007. Paper $40.

*Managing Children's Services in the Public Library.* 3rd ed. By Adele M. Fasick and Leslie E. Holt. Libraries Unlimited, 2007. Paper $45.

*The Newbery and Caldecott Awards 2008: A Guide to the Medal and Honor Books.* Association for Library Service to Children/American Library Association, 2007. Paper $20.

*The Newbery/Printz Companion: Booktalk and Related Materials for Award Winners and Honor Books.* By John T. Gillespie and Corinne J. Naden. 3rd ed. Libraries Unlimited, 2006. $75.

*Outstanding Library Service to Children: Putting the Core Competencies to Work.* By Rosanne Cerny, Penny Markey, and Amanda Williams. Association for Library Services to Children/American Library Association, 2006. Paper $30.

*Serving Urban Teens.* By Paula Brehm-Heeger. Libraries Unlimited. Paper $40.

*Serving Young Teens and 'Tweens.* Ed. by Sheila B. Anderson. Libraries Unlimited, 2006. $40.

*Sex, Brains, and Video Games: A Librarian's Guide to Teens in the 21st Century.* By Jennifer Burek Pierce. American Library Association. Paper $40.

*Sizzling Summer Reading Programs for Young Adults.* 2nd ed. By Katharine L. Kan. American Library Association, 2006. Paper $32.

*Youth Information-Seeking Behavior II: Context, Theories, Models, and Issues.* Ed. by Mary K. Chelton and Colleen Cool. Scarecrow, 2006. Paper $45.

# Collection Development

*Collection Development Issues in the Online Environment.* Ed. by Di Su. Haworth, 2006. Paper $19.95.

*The Collection Program in Schools: Concepts, Practices, and Information Sources.* 4th ed. By Kay Bishop. Libraries Unlimited, 2007. Paper $50.

*Community, Collaboration, and Collections: The Writings of Ross Atkinson.* Ed. by Robert Alan and Bonnie MacEwan. Association for Library Collections and Technical Services/American Library Association, 2006. Paper $75.

*Crash Course in Collection Development.* By Wayne Disher. Libraries Unlimited, 2007. Paper $30.

*E-Metrics for Library and Information Professionals: How to Use Data for Managing and Evaluating Electronic Resource Collections.* By Andrew White and Eric Djiva Kamal. Neal-Schuman, 2006. $75.

*Fundamentals of Collection Development and Management.* 2nd ed. By Peggy Johnson. American Library Association, 2009. Paper $70.

# Copyright

*The Complete Copyright Liability Handbook for Librarians and Educators.* By Thomas A. Lipinski. Neal-Schuman, 2006. Paper $125.

*Copyright Issues Relevant to Digital Preservation and Dissemination of Pre-1972 Commercial Sound Recordings by Libraries and Archives.* By June M. Besek. Council on Library and Information Resources, 2006. Paper $20.

*Intellectual Property: Everything the Digital-Age Librarian Needs to Know.* By Timothy Lee Wherry. American Library Association, 2007. Paper $55.

*Intellectual Property Rights: A Critical History.* By Christopher May and Susan K. Sell. Lynne Rienner, 2006. $55.

## Distance Education

*Going the Distance: Library Instruction for Remote Users.* Ed. by Susan J. Clayton. Neal-Schuman, 2007. Paper $65.

*Libraries Without Walls 6: Evaluating the Distributed Delivery of Library Services.* Ed. by Peter Brophy, Jenny Craven, and Margaret Markland. Neal-Schuman, 2006. $125.

## The Electronic Library

*Building Digital Libraries.* By Terry Reese, Jr. and Kyle Banerjee. Neal-Schuman, 2008. Paper $75.

*Digital Library Development: The View from Kanazawa.* Ed. by Deanna B. Marcum and Gerald George. Libraries Unlimited, 2006. Paper $70.

*The Information Commons Handbook.* By Donald Robert Beagle. Neal-Schuman, 2006. $125.

*What Every Librarian Should Know about Electronic Privacy.* By Jeanette Woodward. Libraries Unlimited, 2008. Paper $40.

*The Whole Digital Library Handbook.* Ed. by Diane Kresh. American Library Association, 2007. Paper $60.

## Evaluation of Library Services

*Demonstrating Results: Using Outcome Measurement in Your Library.* By Rhea Joyce Rubin. American Library Association, 2006. Paper $60.

*Evaluating the Impact of Your Library.* By Sharon Markless and David Streatfield. Facet, 2006. $99.95.

*The Evaluation and Measurement of Library Services.* By Joseph R. Matthews. Libraries Unlimited, 2007. Paper $50.

*Library Assessment in Higher Education.* By Joseph R. Matthews. Libraries Unlimited, 2007. Paper $45.

*Measuring Your Library's Value: How to Do a Cost-Benefit Analysis for Your Public Library.* By Donald S. Elliot, Glen E. Holt, Sterling W. Hayden, and Leslie Edmonds Holt. American Library Association, 2007. Paper $60.

## History

*African American Librarians in the Far West: Pioneers and Trailblazers.* Ed. by Binnie Tate Wilkin. Scarecrow, 2006. Paper $55.

*Libraries and Librarianship: Sixty Years of Challenge and Change, 1945–2005.* By George Bobinski. Scarecrow, 2007. $40.

## Information Literacy

*The Blue Book on Information Age Inquiry, Instruction, and Literacy.* By Daniel Callison and Leslie Preddy. Libraries Unlimited, 2006. Paper $45.

*Information Literacy Assessment: Standards-Based Tools and Assignments.* By Teresa Y. Neely. Association of College and Research Libraries/American Library Association, 2006. Paper $46.

*Proven Strategies for Building an Information Literacy Program.* Ed. by Susan Carol Curzon and Lynn D. Lampert. Neal-Schuman, 2007. Paper $65.

*Student Engagement and Information Literacy.* Ed. by Craig Gibson. Association of College and Research Libraries/American Library Association, 2006. Paper $27.

## Information Science

*Fundamentals of Information Studies: Understanding Information and Its Environment.* 2nd ed. By June Lester and Wallace C. Koehler, Jr. Neal-Schuman, 2007. Paper $65.

## Intellectual Freedom

*Banned Books Resource Guide.* Office for Intellectual Freedom/American Library Association, 2007. Paper $39.

*Burning Books.* By Haig Bosmajian. McFarland, 2006. $55.

*Burning Books and Leveling Libraries: Extremist Violence and Cultural Destruction.* By Rebecca Knuth. Praeger, 2006. $39.95.

*IFLA/FAIFE Theme Report.* International Association of Library Associations and Institutions, biannual. 27 euros.

*IFLA/FAIFE World Report.* International Association of Library Associations and Institutions, biannual. 27 euros.

*The New Inquisition: Understanding and Managing Intellectual Freedom Challenges.* By James LaRue. Libraries Unlimited, 2007. Paper $40.

## The Internet/Web

*Archiving Websites: A Practical Guide for Information Management Professionals.* By Adrian Brown. Facet, 2006. $99.95.

*Creating Database-Backed Library Web Pages Using Open Source Tools.* By Stephen R. Westman. American Library Association, 2006. Paper $53.

*Making Library Web Sites Usable: A LITA Guide.* Ed. by Tom Lehman and Terry Nikkel. Neal-Schuman, 2008. Paper $65.

*XHTML and CSS Essentials for Library Web Design.* By Michael Sauers. Neal-Schuman, 2006. Paper $75.

## Knowledge Management

*The Knowledge Entrepreneur.* By Stan Skrzeszewski. Scarecrow, 2006. Paper $27.

*Perspectives on Knowledge Management.* Ed. by I. V. Malhan and Shivirama Rao K. Scarecrow, 2008. Paper $65.

*What They Didn't Tell You About Knowledge Management.* By Jay Liebowitz. Scarecrow, 2006. Paper $35.

## Librarians and Librarianship

*The ALA-APA Salary Survey 2007: Librarian—Public and Academic.* ALA-Allied Professional Association and ALA Office for Research and Statistics. American Library Association, 2006. Paper $70.

*The ALA-APA Salary Survey 2008: Librarian—Public and Academic.* ALA-Allied Professional Association and ALA Office for Research and Statistics. American Library Association, 2008. Paper $90.

*The ALA-APA Salary Survey 2007: Non-MLS—Public and Academic.* ALA-Allied Professional Association and ALA Office for Research and Statistics. American Library Association, 2007. Paper $100.

*ARL Annual Salary Survey, 2007–2008.* Association of Research Libraries, 2008. Download from http://www.arl.org/bm~doc/ss07.pdf.

*A Day in the Life: Career Options in Library and Information Science.* Ed. by Priscilla K. Schontz and Richard A. Murray. Libraries Unlimited, 2007. $45.

*Information Technology in Librarianship: New Critical Approaches.* Ed. by Gloria J. Leckie and John E. Buschman. Libraries Unlimited, 2009. Paper $50.

*Introduction to the Library and Information Professions.* By Roger C. Greer, Robert J. Grover, and Susan G. Fowler. Libraries Unlimited, 2007. Paper $60.

*Leadership Basics for Librarians and Information Professionals.* By G. Edward Evans and Patricia Layzell Ward. Scarecrow, 2007. $40.

*Library as Place: History, Community, and Culture.* Ed. by John E. Buschman and Gloria J. Leckie. Libraries Unlimited, 2006. Paper $50.

*Library Ethics.* By Jean Preer. Libraries Unlimited, 2008. Paper $45.

*The Portable MLIS: Insights from the Experts.* Ed. by Ken Haycock and Brooke E. Sheldon. Libraries Unlimited, 2008. Paper $50.

*Résumé Writing and Interviewing Techniques That Work: A How-To-Do-It Manual for Librarians.* By Robert R. Newlen. Neal-Schumann, 2006. Paper $55.

*The Romance of Libraries.* By Madeleine Lefebvre. Scarecrow, 2006. Paper $27.

*Sacred Stacks: The Higher Purpose of Libraries and Librarianship.* By Nancy Kalikow Maxwell. American Library Association, 2006. Paper $37.

*Self-Examination: The Present and Future of Librarianship.* By John M. Budd. Libraries Unlimited, 2008. Paper $60.

# Library 2.0

*Blogging and RSS: A Librarian's Guide.* By Michael Sauers. Information Today, Inc., 2006. Paper $29.95.

*Gamers . . . In the Library?!* By Eli Neiburger. American Library Association, 2007. Paper $46.

*Library 2.0 and Beyond: Innovative Technologies and Tomorrow's Users.* Ed. by Nancy Courtney. Libraries Unlimited, 2007. Paper $45.

*Social Software in Libraries: Building Collaboration, Communication, and Community Online.* By Meredith G. Farkas. Information Today, Inc., 2007. Paper $39.50.

*Web 2.0 for Librarians and Information Professionals.* By Ellyssa Kroski. Neal-Schuman, 2008. Paper $65.

# Preservation

*Leading and Managing Archives and Records Programs: Strategies for Success.* Ed. by Bruce W. Dearstyne. Neal-Schuman, 2008. Paper $75.

*Photographs: Archival Care and Management.* Rev. ed. By Mary Lynn Ritzenthaler and Diane Vogt-O'Connor. Society of American Archivists, 2006. $84.95.

*Preparing for the Worst, Planning for the Best: Protecting our Cultural Heritage from Disaster.* Ed. by Johanna G. Wellheiser and Nancy E. Gwinn. K. G. Saur, 2005. 78 euros.

*Preservation in the Age of Large-Scale Digitization: A White Paper.* By Oya Y. Rieger. Council on Library and Information Resources, 2008. Download from http://www.clir.org/pubs/abstract/pub141abst.html.

# Public Libraries

*Breaking the Mold: Innovative Libraries and Programs.* 25-minute video, Library Video Network, 2007. DVD or VHS $99.

*Defining Relevancy: Managing the New Public Library.* Ed. by Janet McNeil Hurlbert. Libraries Unlimited, 2008. Paper $45.

*Pop Goes the Library: Using Pop Culture to Connect with Your Whole Community.* By Sophie Brookover and Elizabeth Burns. Information Today, Inc., 2008. Paper, $39.50.

*Public Libraries and Internet Service Roles: Measuring and Maximizing Internet Services.* By Charles R. McClure and Paul T. Jaeger. American Library Association, 2008. Paper $65.

*Public Library Data Service Statistical Report.* Public Library Association/American Library Association, 2008. Paper $120.

*The Public Library Policy Writer: A Guidebook with Model Policies on CD-ROM.* By Jeanette C. Larson and Herman L. Totten. Neal-Schuman, 2008. Paper and CD-ROM $75.

*The Small Public Library Survival Guide: Thriving on Less.* By Herbert B. Landau. American Library Association, 2008. Paper $38.

*The Thriving Library: Successful Strategies for Challenging Times.* By Marylaine Block. Information Today, Inc., 2007. Paper $39.50.

# Public Relations/Marketing

*Crash Course in Marketing for Libraries.* By Susan Webreck Alman. Libraries Unlimited, 2007. Paper $30.

*Creating Your Library Brand: Communicating Your Relevance and Value to Your Patrons.* By Elizabeth Doucett. American Library Association, 2008. Paper $45.

*Look, It's Books! Marketing Your Library with Displays and Promotions.* By Gayle Skaggs. McFarland, 2008. Paper $45.

*Merchandising Made Simple: Using Standards and Dynamite Displays to Boost Circulation.* By Jenny LaPierre and Trish Christiansen. Libraries Unlimited, 2008. Paper $36.

# Readers' Advisory

*I Need a Book: Reader's Advisory for Adults.* 19-minute video. Library Services Network, 2006. DVD or VHS $99.

*Nonfiction Readers' Advisory.* By Neal Wyatt. American Library Association, 2007. Paper $53.

*The Real Story: A Guide to Nonfiction Reading Interests.* By Sarah Statz Cord. Libraries Unlimited, 2006. $55.

*Research-Based Readers' Advisory.* By Jessica E. Moyer. American Library Association, 2008. Paper $55.

*Serving Teens Through Readers' Advisory.* By Heather Booth. American Library Association, 2007. Paper $40.

## Reference Services

*Crash Course in Reference.* By Charlotte Ford. Libraries Unlimited, 2008. Paper $30.

*Reference and Information Services in the 21st Century: An Introduction.* By Kay Ann Cassell and Uma Hiremath. Neal-Schuman, 2006. Paper. $65.

*The Reference Librarian's Policies, Forms, Guidelines, and Procedures Handbook with CD-ROM.* By Rebecca Brumley. Neal-Schuman, 2006. Paper and CD-ROM $125.

*Virtual Reference Best Practices: Tailoring Services to Your Library.* By M. Kathleen Kern. American Library Association, 2008. Paper $50.

*The Virtual Reference Desk: Creating a Reference Future.* Ed. by R. David Lankes, Eileen G. Abels, Marilyn Domas White, and Saira N. Haque. Neal-Schuman, 2006. Paper $75.

*Virtual Reference on a Budget: Case Studies.* Ed. by Teresa Dalston and Michael Pullin. Linworth, 2008. Paper $39.95.

*Virtual Reference Service: From Competencies to Assessment.* Ed. by R. David Lankes, Scott Nicholson, Marie L. Radford, Joanne Silverstein, Lynn Westbrook, and Philip Nast. Neal-Schumann, 2008. Paper $75.

## School Libraries/Media Centers

*Collaborating with Administrators and Educational Support Staff.* By Lesley S. J. Farmer. Neal-Schuman, 2007. Paper $65.

*Enhancing Teaching and Learning: A Leadership Guide for School Library Media Specialists.* 2nd ed. By Jean Donham. Neal-Schuman, 2008. Paper $65.

*Ensuring Intellectual Freedom and Access to Information in the School Library Media Program.* By Helen R. Adams. Libraries Unlimited, 2008. Paper $40.

*Facilities Planning for School Library Media and Technology Centers.* By Steven M. Baule. Linworth, 2007. Paper $39.95.

*Leadership and the School Librarian: Essays from Leaders in the Field.* Ed. by Mary Lankford. Linworth, 2006. Paper $44.95.

*Leadership for Excellence: Insights of National School Library Media Programs of the Year Award Winners.* Ed. by Joanne Carr. American Library Association, 2008. Paper $39.

*Less Is More: A Practical Guide to Weeding School Library Collections.* By Donna J. Baumbach and Linda L. Miller. American Library Association, 2006. Paper $37.

*Library 101: A Handbook for the School Library Media Specialist.* By Claire Gatrell Stephens and Patricia Franklin. Libraries Unlimited, 2007. Paper $35.

*New on the Job: A School Library Media Specialist's Guide to Success.* By Ruth Toor and Hilda K. Weisburg. American Library Association, 2006. Paper $42.

*Reviving Reading: School Library Programming, Author Visits, and Books that Rock!* By Alison M. G. Follos. Libraries Unlimited, 2006. Paper $32.

*The School Library Media Manager.* 4th ed. By Blanche Woolls. Libraries Unlimited, 2008. Paper $45.

*School Reform and the School Library Media Specialist.* By Sandra Hughes-Hassell and Violet H. Harada. Libraries Unlimited, 2007. Paper $40.

*Technology and the School Library: A Comprehensive Guide for Media Specialists and Other Educators.* By Odin L. Jurowski. Scarecrow, 2006. Paper $45.

*Toward a 21st-Century School Media Program.* Ed. by Esther Rosenfeld and David V. Loertscher. Scarecrow, 2007. Paper $40.

# Serials

*Serials in Libraries: Issues and Practices.* By Steve Black. Libraries Unlimited, 2006. Paper $45.

# Services for Special Groups

*Adult Learners Welcome Here.* By Margaret Crowley Weibel. Neal-Schuman, 2007. Paper $75.

*Crash Course in Serving Spanish-Speakers.* By Salvador Avila. Libraries Unlimited, 2008. $30.

*Improving the Quality of Library Services for Students with Disabilities.* Ed. by Peter Hernon. Libraries Unlimited, 2006. Paper $48.

*Library Services to the Incarcerated: Applying the Public Library Model in Correctional Facility Libraries.* By Sheila Clark and Erica MacCreaigh. Libraries Unlimited, 2006. Paper $40.

*Libros Esenciales: Building, Marketing, and Programming a Core Collection of Spanish-Language Children's Materials.* By Tim Wadham. Neal-Schuman, 2006. Paper $65.

*Serving Latino Communities: A How-To-Do-It Manual.* 2nd ed. By Camila Alire and Jacqueline Ayala. Neal-Schuman, 2007. Paper $59.95.

*Serving New Immigrant Communities in the Library.* By Sondra Cuban. Libraries Unlimited, 2007. Paper $40.

# Technical Services

*Fundamentals of Technical Services Management.* By Sheila S. Intner, with Peggy Johnson. American Library Association, 2008. Paper $46.

*Teams in Library Technical Services.* Ed. by Rosann Bazirjian and Rebecca Mugridge. Scarecrow, 2006. Paper $40.

# Technology

*The Accidental Technology Trainer: A Guide for Libraries.* By Stephanie Gerding. Information Today, Inc., 2007. Paper $29.50.

*Audio and Video Equipment Basics for Libraries.* By Jim Farrington. Scarecrow, 2006. Paper $45.

*Automation Primer for School Library Media Centers and Small Libraries.* By Barbara Schultz-Jones. Linworth, 2006. Paper $39.95.

*Core Technology Competencies for Librarians and Library Staff: A LITA Guide.* Ed. by Susan M. Thompson. Neal-Schuman, 2009. Paper $65.

*Information Tomorrow: Reflections on Technology and the Future of Public and Academic Libraries.* Ed. by Rachel Singer Gordon. Information Today, 2007. Paper $35.

*Listen Up! Podcasting for Schools and Libraries.* By Linda W. Braun. Information Today, 2007. Paper $29.50.

*The Neal-Schuman Library Technology Companion: A Basic Guide for Library Staff.* 2nd ed. By John Burke. Neal-Schuman, 2006. Paper $59.95.

*Technologies for Education: A Practical Guide.* 5th ed. By Ann E. Barron, Karen S. Ivers, Nick Lilavois, and Julie A. Wells. Libraries Unlimited, 2006. Paper $48.

*Technology Made Simple: An Improvement Guide for Small and Medium Libraries.* By Kimberly Bolan and Robert Cullin. American Library Association, 2006. Paper $40.

*Wireless Networking: A How-To-Do-It Manual for Libraries.* By Louise E. Alcorn and Maryellen Mott Allen. Neal Schuman, 2006. Paper $65.

# Periodicals

*ARL*
*Acquisitions Librarian*
*Advanced Technology Libraries*
*Against the Grain*
*American Archivist*
*American Libraries*
*Behavioral and Social Sciences Librarian*
*Book Links*
*Booklist*
*Booklist Online*
*Bookmobile and Outreach Services*
*The Bottom Line: Managing Library Finances*
*Cataloging and Classification Quarterly*

Catholic Library World

Children and Libraries: The Journal of the Association for Library Services to Children

CHOICE

CHOICE Reviews Online

Church and Synagogue Libraries

Collection Management

College and Research Libraries

College and Undergraduate Libraries

Communicator (Librarian's Guild)

Community and Junior College Libraries

Computers in Libraries

FYI: The Journal for the School Information Professional

IFLA Journal

Information Outlook (formerly Special Libraries)

Information Technology and Libraries

Journal of Academic Librarianship

Journal of Education for Library and Information Science

Journal of Information Ethics

Journal of Interlibrary Loan, Document Delivery and Information Supply

Journal of Library Administration

Journal of the American Society for Information Science and Technology

Journal of the Medical Library Association

Knowledge Quest

Law Library Journal

Legal Reference Services Quarterly

Libraries & Culture

Library Administration and Management

Library Administrator's Digest

Library and Archival Security

Library and Information Science Research (LIBRES)

Library Hi-Tech News

Library Issues: Briefings for Faculty and Academic Administrators

Library Journal

Library Media Connection (formerly Book Report and Library Talk)

Library Quarterly

Library Resources and Technical Services

Library Technology Reports

Library Trends

Librarysparks

Medical Reference Services Quarterly

MultiMedia and Internet @ Schools

Music Library Association Notes

Music Reference Services Quarterly

NetConnect

New Review of Children's Literature and Librarianship

The One-Person Library

portal: Libraries and the Academy

Progressive Librarian

Public Libraries

Public Library Quarterly

Reference and User Services Quarterly (formerly RQ)

Reference Librarian

Resource Sharing & Information Networks

RSR: Reference Services Review

Rural Libraries Journal

School Library Journal

School Library Media Research

Science & Technology Libraries

Searcher: The Magazine for Database Professionals

Serials Librarian

Serials Review

Technical Services Quarterly

Technicalities

Video Librarian

Voice of Youth Advocates (VOYA)

World Libraries

Young Adult Library Services

## Blogs

AASL Blog (http://www.aasl.ala.org/aaslblog)

ACRLog (http://acrlog.org)

ALA TechSource (http://www.alatechsource.org/blog)

ASCL Blog (http://www.alsc.ala.org/blog)

Audiobooker. By Mary Burkey (http://audiobooker.booklistonline.com)

Blue Skunk. By Doug Johnson (http://doug-johnson.squarespace.com)

Book Group Buzz (http://bookgroupbuzz.booklistonline.com)

Catalogblog. By David Bigwood (http://catalogablog.blogspot.com)

David Lee King. By David Lee King (http://www.davidleeking.com)

Early Word. By Nora Rawlinson (http://www.earlyword.com)

Free Range Librarian. By Karen G. Schneider (http://freerangelibrarian.com)

Hey Jude. By Judy O'Connell (http://heyjude.wordpress.com)

Information Wants to Be Free. By Meredith Farkas (http://meredith.wolfwater.com/wordpress)

Librarian.net. By Jessamyn West (http://www.librarian.net)

LibrarianInBlack. By Sarah Houghton-Jan (http://librarianinblack.typepad.com/librarianinblack)

Library Juice. By Rory Litwin (http://libraryjuicepress.com/blog)

LibraryBytes. By Helene Blowers (http://www.librarybytes.com)

LibraryLaw Blog. By Mary Minow (http://blog.librarylaw.com)

Likely Stories. By Keir Graff (http://blog.booklistonline.com)

LIS News. By Blake Carver (http://lisnews.org)

LITA Blog (http://litablog.org)

Lorcan Dempsey's Weblog. By Lorcan Dempsey (http://orweblog.oclc.org)

No Shelf Required. By Sue Polanka (http://www.libraries.wright.edu/noshelfrequired)

Phil Bradley's weblog. By Phil Bradley (http://www.philbradley.typepad.com)

PLA Blog (http://plablog.org)

Pop Goes the Library. By Sophie Brookover, Liz Burns, Melissa Rabey, Susan Quinn, John Klima, Carlie Webber, Karen Corday, and Eli Neiburger (http://www.popgoesthelibrary.com)

ResourceShelf. By Gary Price (http://www.resourceshelf.com)

RUSA Blog (http://rusa.ala.org/blog)

The Shifted Librarian. By Jenny Levine (http://www.theshiftedlibrarian.com)

Stephen's Lighthouse. By Stephen Abram (http://stephenslighthouse.sirsidynix.com)

Swiss Army Librarian. By Brian Herzog (http://www.swissarmylibrarian.net)

Tame the Web: Libraries and Technology. By Michael Stephens (http://tametheweb.com)

Walking Paper. By Aaron Schmidt (http://www.walkingpaper.org)

Walt at Random. By Walt Crawford (http://walt.lishost.org)

What I Learned Today. By Nicole C. Engard (http://www.web2learning.net)

YALSA Blog (http://yalsa.ala.org/blog)

# Ready Reference

## How to Obtain an ISBN

Andy Weissberg and Louise Timko
United States ISBN/SAN Agency

The International Standard Book Numbering (ISBN) system was introduced into the United Kingdom by J. Whitaker & Sons Ltd. in 1967 and into the United States in 1968 by R. R. Bowker. The Technical Committee on Documentation of the International Organization for Standardization (ISO TC 46) is responsible for the international standard.

The purpose of this standard is to "establish the specifications for the International Standard Book Number (ISBN) as a unique international identification system for each product form or edition of a monographic publication published or produced by a specific publisher." The standard specifies the construction of an ISBN, the rules for assignment and use of an ISBN, and all metadata associated with the allocation of an ISBN.

Types of monographic publications to which an ISBN may be assigned include printed books and pamphlets (in various product formats); electronic publications (either on the Internet or on physical carriers such as CD-ROMs or diskettes); educational/instructional films, videos, and transparencies; educational/instructional software; audiobooks on cassette or CD or DVD; braille publications; and microform publications.

Serial publications, printed music, and musical sound recordings are excluded from the ISBN standard as they are covered by other identification systems.

The ISBN is used by publishers, distributors, wholesalers, bookstores, and libraries, among others, in 217 countries and territories as an ordering and inventory system. It expedites the collection of data on new and forthcoming editions of monographic publications for print and electronic directories used by the book trade. Its use also facilitates rights management and the monitoring of sales data for the publishing industry.

The "new" ISBN consists of 13 digits. As of January 1, 2007, a revision to the ISBN standard was implemented in an effort to substantially increase the numbering capacity. The 10-digit ISBN identifier (ISBN-10) is now replaced by the ISBN 13-digit identifier (ISBN-13). All facets of book publishing are now expected to use the ISBN-13, and the ISBN agencies throughout the world are now issuing only ISBN-13s to publishers. Publishers with existing ISBN-10s need to convert their ISBNs to ISBN-13s by the addition of the EAN prefix 978 and recalculation of the new check digit:

ISBN-10: 0-8352-8235-X
ISBN-13: 978-0-8352-8235-2

When the inventory of the ISBN-10s has been exhausted, the ISBN agencies will start assigning ISBN-13s with the "979" prefix instead of the "978." There is no 10-digit equivalent for 979 ISBNs.

## Construction of an ISBN

An ISBN currently consists of 13 digits separated into the following parts:

1 A prefix of "978" for an ISBN-10 converted to an ISBN-13
2 Group or country identifier, which identifies a national or geographic grouping of publishers
3 Publisher identifier, which identifies a particular publisher within a group
4 Title identifier, which identifies a particular title or edition of a title
5 Check digit, the single digit at the end of the ISBN that validates the ISBN-13

For more information regarding ISBN-13 conversion services provided by the U.S. ISBN Agency at R. R. Bowker, LLC, visit the ISBN Agency Web site at http://www.isbn.org, or contact the U.S. ISBN Agency at isbn-san@bowker.com.
Publishers requiring their ISBNs to be converted from the ISBN-10 to ISBN-13 format can use the U.S. ISBN Agency's free ISBN-13 online converter at http://isbn.org/converterpub.asp. Large list conversions can be requested by e-mailing isbnconversion@bowker.com. Publishers can also subscribe to view their ISBN online log book by accessing their personal account at http://www.bowkerlink.com.

## Displaying the ISBN on a Product or Publication

When an ISBN is written or printed, it should be preceded by the letters ISBN, and each part should be separated by a space or hyphen. In the United States, the hyphen is used for separation, as in the following example: ISBN 978-0-8352-8235-2. In this example, 978 is the prefix that precedes the ISBN-13, 0 is the group identifier, 8352 is the publisher identifier, 8235 is the title identifier, and 2 is the check digit. The group of English-speaking countries, which includes the United States, Australia, Canada, New Zealand, and the United Kingdom, uses the group identifiers 0 and 1.

## The ISBN Organization

The administration of the ISBN system is carried out at three levels—through the International ISBN Agency in the United Kingdom, through the national agencies, and through the publishing houses themselves. The International ISBN Agency, which is responsible for assigning country prefixes and for coordinating the worldwide implementation of the system, has an advisory panel that represents the International Organization for Standardization (ISO), publishers, and libraries. The International ISBN Agency publishes the *Publishers International ISBN Directory,* which is a listing of all national agencies' publishers with their assigned ISBN publisher prefixes. R. R. Bowker, as the publisher of *Books In Print* with its extensive and varied database of publishers' addresses, was the obvious place to initiate the ISBN system and to provide the service to the U.S. publishing industry. To date, the U.S. ISBN Agency has entered more than 180,000 publishers into the system.

## ISBN Assignment Procedure

Assignment of ISBNs is a shared endeavor between the U.S. ISBN Agency and the publisher. Publishers can make online application through the ISBN Agency's Web site, or by phone or fax. After an application is received and processed by the agency, an ISBN Publisher Prefix is assigned, along with a computer-generated block of ISBNs that is mailed or e-mailed to the publisher. The publisher then has the responsibility to assign an ISBN to each title, keep an accurate record of each number assigned, and register each title in the Books In Print database at http://www.bowkerlink.com. It is the responsibility of the ISBN Agency to validate assigned ISBNs and keep a record of all ISBN publisher prefixes in circulation.

ISBN implementation is very much market-driven. Major distributors, wholesalers, retailers, and so forth recognize the necessity of the ISBN system and request that publishers register with the ISBN Agency. Also, the ISBN is a mandatory bibliographic element in the International Standard Bibliographical Description (ISBD). The Library of Congress Cataloging in Publication (CIP) Division directs publishers to the agency to obtain their ISBN prefixes.

## Location and Display of the ISBN

On books, pamphlets, and other printed material, the ISBN shall be printed on the verso of the title leaf or, if this is not possible, at the foot of the title leaf itself. It should also appear on the outside back cover or on the back of the jacket if the book has one (the lower right-hand corner is recommended). The ISBN shall also appear on any accompanying promotional materials following the provisions for location according to the format of the material.

On other monographic publications, the ISBN shall appear on the title or credit frames and any labels permanently affixed to the publication. If the publication is issued in a container that is an integral part of the publication, the ISBN shall be displayed on the label. If it is not possible to place the ISBN on the item or its label, then the number should be displayed on the bottom or the back of the container, box, sleeve, or frame. It should also appear on any accompanying material, including each component of a multi-type publication.

## Printing of ISBN in Machine-Readable Coding

All books should carry ISBNs in the EAN-13 bar code machine-readable format. All ISBN EAN-13 bar codes start with the EAN prefix 978 for books. As of January 1, 2007, all EAN bar codes should have the ISBN-13 appearing immediately above the bar code in eye-readable format, preceded by the acronym "ISBN." The recommended location of the EAN-13 bar code for books is in the lower right-hand corner of the back cover (see Figure 1).

**Figure 1 / Printing the ISBN in Bookland/EAN Symbology**

## Five-Digit Add-On Code

In the United States, a five-digit add-on code is used for additional information. In the publishing industry, this code is used for price information. The lead digit of the five-digit add-on has been designated a currency identifier, when the add-on is used for price. Number 5 is the code for the U.S. dollar, 6 denotes the Canadian dollar, 1 the British pound, 3 the Australian dollar, and 4 the New Zealand dollar. Publishers that do not want to indicate price in the add-on should print the code 90000 (see Figure 2).

**Figure 2 / Printing the ISBN Bookland/EAN Number in Bar Code with the Five-Digit Add-On Code**

978 = ISBN Bookland/EAN prefix
5 = Code for U.S. $
2499 = $24.99

90000 means no information
in the add-on code

## Reporting the Title and the ISBN

After the publisher reports a title to the ISBN Agency, the number is validated and the title is listed in the many R. R. Bowker hard-copy and electronic publications, including *Books in Print; Forthcoming Books; Paperbound Books in Print; Books in Print Supplement; Books Out of Print; Books in Print Online; Books in Print Plus-CD ROM; Children's Books in Print; Subject Guide to Children's Books in Print; Books Out Loud: Bowker's Guide to AudioBooks; Bowker's Complete Video Directory; Software Encyclopedia; Software for Schools;* and other specialized publications.

For an ISBN application and information, visit the ISBN Agency Web site at http://www.isbn.org, call the toll-free number 877-310-7333, fax 908-219-0188, or write to the United States ISBN Agency, 630 Central Ave., New Providence, NJ 07974.

# How to Obtain an ISSN

U.S. ISSN Center
Library of Congress

In the early 1970s the rapid increase in the production and dissemination of information and an intensified desire to exchange information about serials in computerized form among different systems and organizations made it increasingly clear that a means to identify serial publications at an international level was needed. The International Standard Serial Number (ISSN) was developed and became the internationally accepted code for identifying serial publications.

The ISSN is an international standard, ISO 3297: 2007, as well as a U.S. standard, ANSI/NISO Z39.9. The 2007 edition of ISO 3297 expands the scope of the ISSN to cover continuing resources (serials, as well as updating databases, looseleafs, and some Web sites).

The number itself has no significance other than as a brief, unique, and unambiguous identifier. The ISSN consists of eight digits in Arabic numerals 0 to 9, except for the last—or check—digit, which can be an X. The numbers appear as two groups of four digits separated by a hyphen and preceded by the letters ISSN—for example, ISSN 1234-5679.

The ISSN is not self-assigned by publishers. Administration of the ISSN is coordinated through the ISSN Network, an intergovernmental organization within the UNESCO/UNISIST program. The ISSN Network consists of national ISSN centers, coordinated by the ISSN International Centre, located in Paris. National ISSN Centers are responsible for registering serials published in their respective countries. The ISSN International Centre handles ISSN assignments for international organizations and for countries that do not have a national center. It also maintains and distributes the ISSN Register and makes it available online as the ISSN Portal. The ISSN Register contains bibliographic records corresponding to each ISSN assignment as reported by national ISSN centers. The database contains records for about 1.5 million ISSNs.

The ISSN is used all over the world by serial publishers to identify their serials and to distinguish their titles from others that are the same or similar. It is used by subscription services and libraries to manage files for orders, claims, and back issues. It is used in automated check-in systems by libraries that wish to process receipts more quickly. Copyright centers use the ISSN as a means to collect and disseminate royalties. It is also used as an identification code by postal services and legal deposit services. The ISSN is included as a verification element in interlibrary lending activities and for union catalogs as a collocating device. In recent years, the ISSN has been incorporated into bar codes for optical recognition of serial publications and into the standards for the identification of issues and articles in serial publications. Another growing use for the ISSN is in online systems where it can serve to connect catalog records or citations in abstracting and indexing databases with full-text journal content via OpenURL resolvers or reference linking services.

Because serials are generally known and cited by title, assignment of the ISSN is inseparably linked to the key title, a standardized form of the title derived from information in the serial issue. Only one ISSN can be assigned to a title in a particular medium. For titles issued in multiple media—e.g., print, online, CD-ROM—a separate ISSN is assigned to each medium version. If a title change occurs or the medium changes, a new ISSN must be assigned. Centers responsible for assigning ISSNs also construct the key title and create an associated bibliographic record.

A significant new feature of the 2007 ISSN standard is the Linking ISSN (ISSN-L), a mechanism that enables collocation or linking among different media versions of a continuing resource. The Linking ISSN allows a unique designation (one of the existing ISSNs) to be applied to all media versions of a continuing resource while retaining the separate ISSN that pertains to each version. When an ISSN is functioning as a Linking ISSN, the eight digits of the base ISSN are prefixed with the designation "ISSN-L." The Linking ISSN facilitates search, retrieval, and delivery across all medium versions of a serial or other continuing resource for improved ISSN functionality in OpenURL linking, search engines, library catalogs, and knowledge bases. The 2007 standard also supports interoperability by specifying the use of ISSN and ISSN-L with other systems such as DOI, OpenURL, URN, and EAN bar codes. ISSN-L was implemented in the ISSN Register in 2008. To help ISSN users implement the ISSN-L in their databases, two free tables are available from the ISSN International Centre's home page: one lists each ISSN and its corresponding ISSN-L; the other lists each ISSN-L and its corresponding ISSNs.

In the United States, the U.S. ISSN Center at the Library of Congress is responsible for assigning and maintaining the ISSNs for all U.S. serial titles. Publishers wishing to have an ISSN assigned should request an application form, or download one from the Center's Web site, and mail, e-mail, or fax the form to the U.S. ISSN Center. Assignment of the ISSN is free, and there is no charge for use of the ISSN.

For further information about the ISSN or the ISSN Network, U.S. libraries, publishers, and other ISSN users should contact the U.S. ISSN Center, Library of Congress, Washington, DC 20540-4284 (telephone 202-707-6452, fax 202-707-6333, e-mail issn@loc.gov). ISSN application forms and instructions for obtaining an ISSN are also available via the Library of Congress World Wide Web site, http://www.loc.gov/issn.

Non-U.S. parties should contact the ISSN International Centre, 20 rue Bachaumont, 75002 Paris, France (telephone 33-1-44-88-22-20, fax 33-1-40-26-32-43, e-mail issnic@issn.org, World Wide Web http://www.ISSN.org).

# How to Obtain an SAN

Andy Weissberg and Louise Timko

United States ISBN/SAN Agency

SAN stands for Standard Address Number. The SAN system, an American National Standards Institute (ANSI) standard, assigns a unique identification number that is used to positively identify specific addresses of organizations in order to facilitate buying and selling transactions within the industry. It is recognized as the identification code for electronic communication within the industry.

For purposes of this standard, the book industry includes book publishers, book wholesalers, book distributors, book retailers, college bookstores, libraries, library binders, and serial vendors. Schools, school systems, technical institutes, and colleges and universities are not members of this industry, but are served by it and therefore included in the SAN system.

The purpose of the SAN is to ease communications among these organizations, of which there are several hundreds of thousands that engage in a large volume of separate transactions with one another. These transactions include purchases of books by book dealers, wholesalers, schools, colleges, and libraries from publishers and wholesalers; payments for all such purchases; and other communications between participants. The objective of this standard is to establish an identification code system by assigning each address within the industry a unique code to be used for positive identification for all book and serial buying and selling transactions.

Many organizations have similar names and multiple addresses, making identification of the correct contact point difficult and subject to error. In many cases, the physical movement of materials takes place between addresses that differ from the addresses to be used for the financial transactions. In such instances, there is ample opportunity for confusion and errors. Without identification by SAN, a complex record-keeping system would have to be instituted to avoid introducing errors. In addition, problems with the current numbering system—such as errors in billing, shipping, payments, and returns—are significantly reduced by using the SAN system. The SAN also eliminates one step in the order fulfillment process: the "look-up procedure" used to assign account numbers. Previously a store or library dealing with 50 different publishers was assigned a different account number by each of the suppliers. The SAN solved this problem. If a publisher prints its SAN on its stationery and ordering documents, vendors to whom it sends transactions do not have to look up the account number, but can proceed immediately to process orders by SAN.

Libraries are involved in many of the same transactions as book dealers, such as ordering and paying for books and charging and paying for various services to other libraries. Keeping records of transactions—whether these involve buying, selling, lending, or donations—entails operations suited to SAN use. SAN stationery speeds up order fulfillment and eliminate errors in shipping, billing, and crediting; this, in turn, means savings in both time and money.

# History

Development of the Standard Address Number began in 1968 when Russell Reynolds, general manager of the National Association of College Stores (NACS), approached R. R. Bowker and suggested that a "Standard Account Number" system be implemented in the book industry. The first draft of a standard was prepared by an American National Standards Institute (ANSI) Committee Z39 subcommittee, which was co-chaired by Russell Reynolds and Emery Koltay of Bowker. After Z39 members proposed changes, the current version of the standard was approved by NACS on December 17, 1979.

# Format

The SAN consists of six digits plus a seventh *Modulus 11* check digit; a hyphen follows the third digit (XXX-XXXX) to facilitate transcription. The hyphen is to be used in print form, but need not be entered or retained in computer systems. Printed on documents, the Standard Address Number should be preceded by the identifier "SAN" to avoid confusion with other numerical codes (SAN XXXXXXX).

# Check Digit Calculation

The check digit is based on *Modulus 11,* and can be derived as follows:

1. Write the digits of the basic number.               2 3 4 5 6 7
2. Write the constant weighting factors associated with each position by the basic number.             7 6 5 4 3 2
3. Multiply each digit by its associated weighting factor.     14 18 20 20 18 14
4. Add the products of the multiplications.    $14 + 18 + 20 + 20 + 18 + 14 = 104$
5. Divide the sum by *Modulus 11* to find the remainder.      $104 \div 11 = 9$
                                                  plus a remainder of 5
6. Subtract the remainder from the *Modulus 11* to generate the required check digit. If there is no remainder, generate a check digit of zero. If the check digit is 10, generate a check digit of X to represent 10, since the use of 10 would require an extra digit.    $11 - 5 = 6$
7. Append the check digit to create the standard seven-digit Standard Address Number.                SAN 234-5676

# SAN Assignment

R. R. Bowker accepted responsibility for being the central administrative agency for SAN, and in that capacity assigns SANs to identify uniquely the addresses of organizations. No SANs can be reassigned; in the event that an organization should cease to exist, for example, its SAN would cease to be in circulation entirely. If an organization using an SAN should move or change its name with no change in ownership, its SAN would remain the same, and only the name or address would be updated to reflect the change.

The SAN should be used in all transactions; it is recommended that the SAN be imprinted on stationery, letterheads, order and invoice forms, checks, and all other documents used in executing various book transactions. The SAN should always be printed on a separate line above the name and address of the organization, preferably in the upper left-hand corner of the stationery to avoid confusion with other numerical codes pertaining to the organization, such as telephone number, zip code, and the like.

## SAN Functions

The SAN is strictly a Standard Address Number, becoming functional only in applications determined by the user; these may include activities such as purchasing, billing, shipping, receiving, paying, crediting, and refunding. It is the method used by Pubnet and PubEasy systems and is required in all electronic data interchange communications using the Book Industry Systems Advisory Committee (BISAC) EDI formats. Every department that has an independent function within an organization could have a SAN for its own identification.

For additional information or to make suggestions, write to ISBN/SAN Agency, R. R. Bowker, LLC, 630 Central Ave., New Providence, NJ 07974, call 908-219-0276, or fax 908-219-0188. The e-mail address is san@bowker.com. The SAN Web site for online applications is at http://www.isbn.org.

# Distinguished Books

## Notable Books of 2008

The Notable Books Council of the Reference and User Services Association, a division of the American Library Association, selected these titles for their significant contribution to the expansion of knowledge or for the pleasure they can provide to adult readers.

### Fiction

Alameddine, Rabih. *The Hakawati* (Knopf).

Aslam, Nadeem. *The Wasted Vigil* (Knopf).

Bausch, Richard. *Peace* (Knopf).

Benioff, David. *City of Thieves* (Viking).

Erdrich, Louise. *The Plague of Doves* (HarperCollins).

Galchen, Rivka. *Atmospheric Disturbances* (Farrar, Straus & Giroux).

Lahiri, Jhumpa. *Unaccustomed Earth* (Knopf).

Millhauser, Steven. *Dangerous Laughter: Thirteen Stories* (Knopf).

Sheers, Owen. *Resistance* (Doubleday).

Strout, Elizabeth. *Olive Kitteridge* (Random).

Talarigo, Jeff. *The Ginseng Hunter* (Doubleday).

### Nonfiction

Coll, Steve. *The Bin Ladens: An Arabian Family in the American Century* (Penguin).

Faust, Drew Gilpin. *This Republic of Suffering: Death and the American Civil War* (Knopf).

Filkins, Dexter. *The Forever War* (Knopf).

Gilmore, Glenda Elizabeth. *Defying Dixie: The Radical Roots of Civil Rights, 1919–1950* (Norton).

Gordon-Reed, Annette. *The Hemingses of Monticello: An American Family* (Norton).

Harris, Mark. *Pictures at a Revolution: Five Movies and the Birth of the New Hollywood* (Penguin).

Horwitz, Tony. *A Voyage Long and Strange: Rediscovering the New World* (Holt).

Mayer, Jane *The Dark Side: The Inside Story of How The War on Terror Turned into a War on American Ideals* (Doubleday).

Pollan, Michael. *In Defense of Food: An Eater's Manifesto* (Penguin).

Taylor, Nick. *American-Made: The Enduring Legacy of the WPA* (Bantam).

Vanderbilt, Tom. *Traffic: Why We Drive the Way We Do (and What It Says About Us)* (Knopf).

Wickersham, Joan. *The Suicide Index: Putting My Father's Death in Order* (Harcourt).

### Poetry

Hirsch, Edward. *Special Orders: Poems* (Knopf).

Tate, James. *Ghost Soldiers: Poems* (Ecco).

# Best Books for Young Adults

Each year a committee of the Young Adult Library Services Association (YALSA), a division of the American Library Association, compiles a list of the best fiction and nonfiction appropriate for young adults ages 12 to 18. Selected on the basis of each book's proven or potential appeal and value to young adults, the titles span a variety of subjects as well as a broad range of reading levels.

## Fiction

Almond, David. *The Savage.* Candlewick (978-0-7636-3932-7).

Anderson, Laurie Halse. *Chains.* Simon & Schuster (978-1-4169-0585-1).

Anderson, M. T. *The Astonishing Life of Octavian Nothing, Traitor to the Nation: Vol. II: The Kingdom on the Waves.* Candlewick (978-0-7636-2950-2).

Bartoletti, Susan Campbell. *The Boy Who Dared.* Scholastic (978-0-439-68013-4).

Bell, Hilari. *The Last Knight.* HarperCollins (978-0-06-082503-4).

Benway, Robin. *Audrey, Wait!* Penguin (978-1-59514-191-0).

Blundell, Judy. *What I Saw and How I Lied.* Scholastic (978-0-439-90346-2).

Booth, Coe. *Kendra.* Scholastic (978-0-439-92536-5).

Bradbury, Jennifer. *Shift.* Simon & Schuster (978-1-4169-4732-5).

Brothers, Meagan. *Debbie Harry Sings in French.* Henry Holt (978-0-8050-8080-3).

Bunce, Elizabeth. *A Curse Dark as Gold.* Scholastic (978-0-439-89576-7).

Caletti, Deb. *The Fortunes of Indigo Skye.* Simon & Schuster (978-1-1469-1007-7).

Cashore, Kristin. *Graceling.* Harcourt (978-0-15-206396-2).

Colfer, Eoin. *Airman.* Hyperion (978-1-4231-0750-7).

Collins, Suzanne. *The Hunger Games.* Scholastic (978-0-439-02348-1).

Conner, Leslie. *Waiting for Normal.* HarperCollins (978-0-06-089088-9).

De la Peña, Matt. *Mexican WhiteBoy.* Delacorte (978-0-385-73310-6).

Doctorow, Cory. *Little Brother.* Tor (978-0-7653-1985-2).

Dowd, Siobhan. *Bog Child.* Random (978-0-385-75169-8).

Dowd, Siobhan. *The London Eye Mystery.* Random (978-0-375-84976-3).

Fleischman, Sid. *The Entertainer and the Dybbuk.* HarperCollins (978-0-06-134445-9).

Gaiman, Neil. *The Graveyard Book.* Harper-Collins (978-0-06-053092-1).

Gardner, Sally. *The Red Necklace: A Story of the French Revolution.* Penguin/Dial (978-0-8037-3100-4).

Geerling, Marjetta. *Fancy White Trash.* Penguin/Viking (978-0-670-01082-0).

George, Jessica Day. *Sun and Moon, Ice and Snow.* Bloomsbury (978-1-59990-109-1).

George, Madeleine. *Looks.* Viking (978-0-670-06167-9).

Green, John. *Paper Towns.* Penguin (978-0-25-47818-8).

Harmon, Michael. *The Last Exit to Normal.* Knopf (978-0-375-94098-9).

Hernandez, David. *Suckerpunch.* Harper-Collins (978-0-06-117330-1).

Hijuelos, Oscar. *Dark Dude.* Simon & Schuster (978-1-4169-4804-9).

Jenkins, A. M. *Night Road.* HarperCollins (978-0-06-054604-5).

Johnson, Maureen. *Suite Scarlett.* Scholastic (978-0-439-89927-7).

Juby, Susan. *Another Kind of Cowboy.* HarperCollins (978-0-06-076518-7).

Katcher, Brian. *Playing With Matches.* Random (978-0-385-73544-5).

Kibuishi, Kazu. *Amulet: Book 1, The Stone Keeper.* Scholastic (978-0-439-84680-6).

Lanagan, Margo. *Tender Morsels.* Knopf (978-0-375-84811-7).

Lester, Julius. *Guardian.* HarperCollins (978-0-06-155890-0).

Link, Kelly. *Pretty Monsters.* Viking (978-0-670-01090-5).

Lockhart, E. *The Disreputable History of Frankie Landau-Banks.* Hyperion (978-0-7868-3818-9).

McMullan, Margaret. *When I Crossed No-Bob.* Houghton Mifflin (978-0-618-71715-6).

McNamee, Graham. *Bonechiller.* Random (978-0-385-74658-8).

Marchetta, Melina. *Jellicoe Road.* Harper-Collins (978-0-06-143183-8).

Marillier, Juliet. *Cybele's Secret.* Knopf (978-0-375-83365-6).

Mazer, Norma Fox. *The Missing Girl.* HarperCollins (978-0-06-623777-0).

Meldrum, Christina. *Madapple.* Knopf (978-0-375-95176-3).

Meyer, Stephenie. *The Host.* Little, Brown (978-0-316-06804-8).

Monninger, Joseph. *Baby.* Front Street (978-1-59078-502-7).

Murphy, Pat. *The Wild Girls.* Viking/Penguin (978-0-670-06226-3).

Napoli, Donna Jo. *Hush: An Irish Princess' Tale.* Atheneum (978-0-689-86176-5).

Ness, Patrick. *The Knife of Never Letting Go: Chaos Walking, Book One.* Candlewick (978-0-7636-3931-0).

Padian, Maria. *Brett McCarthy: Work in Progress.* Knopf (978-0-375-94675-2).

Pearson, Mary E. *The Adoration of Jenna Fox.* Henry Holt (978-0-8050-7668-4).

Pratchett, Terry. *Nation.* HarperCollins (978-0-06-143302-3).

Reeve, Philip. *Here Lies Arthur.* Scholastic (978-0-545-09334-1).

Reinhardt, Dana. *How to Build a House.* Random (978-0-375-84453-9).

Schmidt, Gary D. *Trouble.* Clarion (978-0-618-92766-1).

Schumacher, Julie *Black Box.* Random (978-0-385-73542-1).

Scott, Elizabeth. *Living Dead Girl.* Simon & Schuster (978-1-4169-6059-1).

Scott, Elizabeth. *Stealing Heaven.* Harper-Collins (978-0-06-112280-4).

Sheth, Kashmira. *Keeping Corner.* Hyperion (978-0-7868-3859-2).

Shusterman, Neal. *Antsy Does Time.* Penguin (978-0-525-47825-6).

Smith, Andrew. *Ghost Medicine.* Feiwel & Friends (978-0-312-37557-7).

Smith, Roland. *Elephant Run.* Hyperion (978-1-4231-0402-5).

Tamaki, Mariko, and Jillian Tamaki. *Skim.* House of Anansi (978-0-88899-753-1).

Tharp, Tim. *The Spectacular Now.* Random House (978-0-375-95179-4).

Valentine, Jenny. *Me, the Missing, and the Dead.* HarperCollins (978-0-06-085068-5).

Venkatraman, Padma. *Climbing the Stairs.* Penguin (978-0-399-24746-0).

Voorhees, Coert. *The Brothers Torres.* Hyperion (978-1-4231-0304-2).

Werlin, Nancy. *Impossible.* Penguin (978-0-8037-3002-1).

Wood, Don. *Into the Volcano.* Scholastic (978-0-439-72671-9).

Woodson, Jacqueline. *After Tupac and D Foster.* Putnam (978-0-399-24654-8).

Zarr, Sara. *Sweethearts.* Little, Brown (978-0-316-01455-7).

## Nonfiction

Aronson, Marc, and Patty Campbell. *War Is . . . : Soldiers, Survivors, and Storytellers Talk About War.* Candlewick (978-0-7636-3625-8).

Barry, Lynda. *What It Is.* Drawn and Quarterly (978-1-897299-35-7).

Bowman, Robin. *It's Complicated: The American Teenager.* Umbrage (978-1-884167-69-0).

Engle, Margarita. *The Surrender Tree: Poems of Cuba's Struggle for Freedom.* Henry Holt (978-0-8050-8674-4).

Fleischman, Sid. *The Trouble Begins at 8: A Life of Mark Twain in the Wild, Wild West.* HarperCollins (978-0-06-134431-2).

Kuklin, Susan. *No Choirboy: Murder, Violence, and Teenagers on Death Row.* Henry Holt (978-0-8050-7950-0).

Menzel, Peter, and Faith D'Aluisio. *What the World Eats.* Ten Speed (978-1-58246-246-2).

Nelson, Scott Reynolds. *Ain't Nothing But a Man: My Quest to Find the Real John Henry.* National Geographic (978-1-4263-0000-4).

Parker, David L. *Before Their Time: The World of Child Labor.* Quantuck Lane (978-0-618-23378-6).

Porcellino, John. *Thoreau at Walden.* Hyperion (978-1-4231-0038-6).

Shields, Charles J. *I Am Scout: The Biography of Harper Lee.* Henry Holt (978-0-8050-8334-7).

Weatherford, Carole Boston. *Becoming Billie Holiday.* Wordsong (978-1-59078-507-2).

Wendel, Tim, and Jose Luis Villegas. *Far From Home: Latino Baseball Players in America.* National Geographic (978-1-4262-0216-2).

# Quick Picks for Reluctant Young Adult Readers

The Young Adult Library Services Association, a division of the American Library Association, annually chooses a list of outstanding titles that will stimulate the interest of reluctant teen readers. This list is intended to attract teens who, for whatever reason, choose not to read.

The list, compiled by a 12-member committee, includes fiction and nonfiction titles published from late 2007 through 2008.

## Fiction

Bodeen, S. A. *The Compound*. Feiwel & Friends.

Booth, Coe. *Kendra*. Scholastic.

Collins, Suzanne. *Hunger Games*. Scholastic.

Divine, L. *Drama High* (series). Dafina.

Fahy, Thomas. *The Unspoken*. Simon & Schuster.

Fields, Terri. *My Father's Son*. Roaring Brook.

Giles, Gail. *Right Behind You*. Little, Brown.

Golden, Christopher. *Poison Ink*. Random.

Hernandez, David. *Suckerpunch*. HarperCollins.

High, Linda Oatman. *Planet Pregnancy*. Boyds Mills.

Hopkins, Ellen. *Identical*. McElderry.

James, Brian. *Thief*. Push.

Jordan, Dream. *Hot Girl*. St. Martin's.

Kern, Peggy. *No Way Out*. Townsend.

Kropp, Paul. *Behind the Door*. HIP Edge.

Krovatin, Christopher, and Kelly Yates (illustrator). *Venomous*. Ginee Seo.

Langan, Paul. *Schooled*. Townsend.

Mac, Carrie. *Pain and Wastings*. Orca Soundings.

McDaniel, Lurlene. *Prey*. Random.

McDonnell, Margot. *Torn to Pieces*. Random.

McMann, Lisa. *Wake*. Simon & Schuster.

Mancusi, Mari. *Gamer Girl*. Dutton.

Mead, Richelle. *Frostbite: A Vampire Academy Novel*. Penguin.

Millner, Denene, and Mitzi Miller. *Hotlanta* (series). Point.

Neri, G., and Jesse Joshua Watson, illustrator. *Chess Rumble*. Lee & Low.

Olsen, Sylvia. *Middle Row*. Orca.

Pauley, Kimberly. *Sucks to Be Me: The All-True Confessions of Mina Hamilton, Teen Vampire (Maybe)*. Mirrorstone.

Perez, Marlene. *Dead Is the New Black*. Harcourt.

Reisz, Kristopher. *Unleashed*. Simon Pulse.

Schroeder, Lisa. *I Heart You, You Haunt Me*. Simon & Schuster.

Schumacher, Julie. *Black Box*. Delacorte.

Scott, Elizabeth. *Living Dead Girl*. Simon Pulse.

Shiraz, Yasmin. *Retaliation*. Rolling Hills.

Sitomer, Alan Lawrence. *The Secret Story of Sonia Rodriguez*. Hyperion.

Snow, Carol. *Switch*. Harper Teen.

Stolarz, Laurie Faria. *Project 17*. Hyperion.

Taylor, Brooke. *Undone*. Walker.

Trondheim, Lewis. *Kaput and Zosky*. Roaring Brook.

Varrato, Tony. *Fakie*. Lobster.

Varrato, Tony. *Outrage*. HIP Edge.

Weaver, Will. *Saturday Night Dirt*. Farrar, Straus & Giroux.

## Nonfiction

Abel, Jessica, and Gabriel Soria. *Life Sucks*. First Second.

Badillo, Steve, and Doug Werner. *Skateboarding: Legendary Tricks*. Tracks.

Black, Holly, and Ted Naifeh, illustrator. *Good Neighbors: Kin*. Scholastic.

Boos, Ben. *Swords: An Artist's Devotion*. Candlewick.

Bower, Crai S., and Travis Millard, illustrator. *Farts: A Spotter's Guide*. Chronicle.

Bowman, Robin. *It's Complicated: The American Teenager*. Umbrage.

Carey, Percy, and Ronald Wimberly, illustrator. *Sentences: The Life of M. F. Grimm.* Vertigo.

Comickers Magazine. *Comickers Art 2: Create Amazing Manga Characters.* HarperCollins.

Conley, Erin Elisabeth. *Uncool: A Girl's Guide to Misfitting In.* Orange Avenue.

D'Arcy, Sean. *Freestyle Soccer Tricks.* Firefly.

Ecclesine, Patrick. *Faces of Sunset Boulevard.* Santa Monica.

Editors of Cosmogirl. *All the Questions About Hair, Makeup, Skin and More.* Hearst.

Eminem. *The Way I Am.* Dutton.

Fardon, John. *Do Not Open: An Encyclopedia of the World's Best-Kept Secrets.* DK.

Franco, Betsy, editor. *Falling Hard: 100 Love Poems by Teenagers.* Candlewick.

Franzini, Michael. *One Hundred Young Americans.* HarperCollins.

Fulbeck, Kip. *Permanence.* Chronicle.

Garza, Mario. *More Stuff on My Cat: 2x the Stuff +2x the Cats = 4x the Awesome.* Chronicle.

Greenberg, Steve. *Gadget Nation: A Journey Through the Eccentric World of Invention.* Sterling.

Haden, Christen. *Creepy Cute Crochet: Zombies, Ninjas, Robots, and More!* Quirk.

Hague, Michael. *In the Small.* Little, Brown.

Harrison, Ian. *Take Me to Your Leader: Weird, Strange, and Totally Useless Information.* DK.

Horowitz, Anthony, and Antony Johnston. *Point Blank: The Graphic Novel.* Philomel.

Hudson, Noel. *The Band Name Book.* Boston Mills.

Khidekel, Marina. *The Quiz Life.* Delacorte.

Kibuishi, Kazu. *Flight: Vol. 4.* Villard.

King, Dennis. *Art of Modern Rock: Mini No. 1: A–Z.* Chronicle.

Kuklin, Susan. *No Choirboy: Murder, Violence and Teenagers on Death Row.* Henry Holt.

Li, Yishan. *500 Manga Creatures.* HarperCollins.

The Manga University Culinary Institute and Chihiro Hattori. *The Manga Cookbook.* Japanime.

Ngo, Karen. *Indognito.* Little, Brown.

O'Meara, Donna. *Volcano: A Visual Guide.* Firefly.

Paglen, Trevor. *I Could Tell You But Then You Would Have to Be Destroyed by Me.* Melville House.

Peckham, Aaron. *Mo'Urban Dictionary: Ridonkulous Street Slang Defined.* Andrews McMeel.

Powell, Ben. *Skateboarding Skills: The Reader's Guide.* Firefly.

Reber, Deborah. *Chill: Stress-Reducing Techniques for a More Balanced, Peaceful You.* Simon & Schuster.

Redd, Nancy Amanda. *Body Drama.* Penguin.

Saffel, Steve. *Spider-Man, the Icon.* Titan.

Sanchez, Reymundo, and Sonia Rodriguez. *Lady Q: The Rise and Fall of a Latin Queen.* Chicago Review.

Scalin, Noah. *Skulls.* Lark.

Shapiro, Bill. *Other People's Love Letters: 150 Letters You Were Never Meant to See.* Crown.

Smith, Larry, and Rachel Fershleiser. *Not Quite What I Was Planning: Six Word Memoirs by Writers Famous and Obscure.* Harper Perennial.

Smits, Kim, and Matthijs Maat. *Custom Kicks.* Laurence King.

Spears, Rick, and Chuck BB, illustrator. *Black Metal, Vol. 1.* Oni.

Steinberger, Major Aimee. *Japan Ai: A Tall Girl's Adventures in Japan.* Go! Media.

Tanen, Sloan, and Stefan Hagen. *Appetite for Detention.* Bloomsbury.

Willin, Melvyn. *Ghosts: Caught on Film.* David & Charles.

Wilson, Daniel H. *How to Build a Robot Army: Tips on Defending the Earth Against Alien Invaders.* Bloomsbury.

Zinczeko, David. *Eat This, Not That!* Rodale.

# Audiobooks for Young Adults

Each year a committee of the Young Adult Library Services Association, a division of the American Library Association, compiles a list of the best audiobooks for young adults ages 12 to 18. The titles are selected for their teen appeal and recording quality, and because they enhance the audience's appreciation of any written work on which the recordings may be based. While the list as a whole addresses the interests and needs of young adults, individual titles need not appeal to this entire age range but rather to parts of it.

## Nonfiction

*The Burn Journals,* by Brent Runyon, read by Christopher Evan Welch. Recorded Books, 8 hours, 7 discs (978-1-4361-3876-5) or 7 cassettes (978-1-4361-3871-0).

## Fiction

*The Absolutely True Diary of a Part-time Indian,* by Sherman Alexie, read by the author. Recorded Books, 5 hours, 5 discs (978-1-4281-8297-4) or 5 cassettes (978-1-4281-8292-9).

*The Adoration of Jenna Fox,* by Mary E. Pearson, read by Jenna Lamia. Macmillan Audio, 7 hours and 30 minutes, 6 discs (978-1-4272-0443-1).

*A Bloody Jack Adventure, Book 2. Curse of the Blue Tattoo: Being an Account of the Misadventures of Jacky Faber, Midshipman and Fine Lady,* by L. A. Meyer, read by Katherine Kellgren. Listen & Live Audio, 14 hours, 11 discs (978-1-5931-6134-7).

*A Bloody Jack Adventure, Book 3. Under the Jolly Roger: Being an Account of the Further Nautical Adventures of Jacky Faber,* by L. A. Meyer, read by Katherine Kellgren. Listen & Live Audio, 15 hours, 12 discs (978-1-59316-141-5).

*A Clockwork Orange,* by Anthony Burgess, read by Tom Hollander. HarperAudio, 8 hours, 7 discs (978-0-06-117062-1).

*The Compound,* by S. A. Bodeen, read by Christopher Lane. Brilliance Audio, 6 hours, 6 discs (978-1-4233-6558-7) or 5 cassettes (978-1-4233-6556-3).

*The Declaration,* by Gemma Malley, read by Charlotte Parry. Recorded Books, 7 hours and 45 minutes, 7 discs (978-1-4281-7281-4) or 7 cassettes (978-1-4281-7276-0).

*Elijah of Buxton,* by Christopher Paul Curtis, read by Mirron Willis. Listening Library, 7 discs, 8 hours and 30 minutes (978-0-7393-6719-3).

*Fairest,* by Gail Carson Levine, read by Sarah Naughton. Full Cast Audio, 8 hours and 15 minutes, 8 discs, library edition (978-1-934180-13-6) or retail edition (978-1-934180-08-2).

*The Graveyard Book,* by Neil Gaiman, read by the author. Recorded Books, 7 hours and 45 minutes, 7 discs (978-1-4361-5884-8) or 7 cassettes (978-1-4361-5879-4).

*How to Build a House,* by Dana Reinhardt, read by Caitlin Greer. Listening Library, 5 hours and 24 minutes, 5 discs (978-0-7393-6412-3).

*The Last Apprentice, Book 3: Night of the Soul Stealer,* by Joseph Delaney, read by Christopher Evan Welch. Recorded Books, 7 hours and 30 minutes, 6 discs (978-1-4281-7251-7) or 6 cassettes (978-1-4281-7246-3).

*Lock and Key,* by Sarah Dessen, read by Rebecca Soler. Penguin Audio, 11 hours, 10 discs (978-0-14-314305-5).

*Nation,* by Terry Pratchett, read by Stephen Briggs. Harper Children's Audio, 8 discs, 9 hours and 30 minutes (978-0-06-143301-6).

*Sebastian Darke: Prince of Fools,* by Philip Caveney, read by Maxwell Caulfield. Listening Library, 8 hours and 25 minutes (978-0-7393-6318-8).

*Skybreaker* by Kenneth Oppel, read by David Kelly. Full Cast Audio, 11 hours and 30 minutes, 10 discs (978-1-934180-33-4).

*Slam,* by Nick Hornby, read by Nicholas Hoult. Penguin Audio, 7 hours, 6 discs (978-0-14-314283-6).

*Story of a Girl,* by Sara Zarr, read by the author. Listening Library, 4 hours and 48 minutes, 4 discs (978-0-7393-7133-6).

*Tallgrass,* by Sandra Dallas, read by Lorelei King. Macmillan Audio, 8 hours and 30 minutes, 7 discs (978-1-4272-0045-7).

*A Thousand Never Evers,* by Shana Burg, read by Kenya Brome. Listening Library, 8 hours and 8 minutes, 7 discs (978-0-7393-6742-1).

# The Reading List

Established in 2007 by the Reference and User Services Association (RUSA), a division of the American Library Association, this list highlights outstanding genre fiction that merits special attention by general adult readers and the librarians who work with them.

RUSA's Reading List Council, which consists of ten librarians who are experts in readers' advisory and collection development, selects books in eight categories: Adrenaline (suspense, thrillers, and action adventure), Fantasy, Historical Fiction, Horror, Mystery, Romance, Science Fiction, and Women's Fiction.

## Adrenaline

*Blue Heaven* by C. J. Box (St. Martin's).

## Fantasy

*Veil of Gold* by Kim Wilkins (Tor).

## Historical Fiction

*The Steel Wave* by Jeff Shaara (Ballantine).

## Horror

*Sharp Teeth* by Toby Barlow (Harper).

## Mystery

*The Garden of Evil* by David Hewson (Bantam Dell).

## Romance

*The Spymaster's Lady* by Joanna Bourne (Berkley).

## Science Fiction

*Hunter's Run* by George R. R. Martin, Gardner Dozois, and Daniel Abraham (Eos).

## Women's Fiction

*Every Last Cuckoo* by Kate Maloy (Algonquin)

# Notable Recordings for Children

This list of notable CD recordings for children was selected by the Association for Library Service to Children, a division of the American Library Association. Recommended titles are chosen by children's librarians and educators on the basis of their originality, creativity, and suitability.

*The 39 Clues: The Maze of Bones.* Scholastic AudioBooks, 5 hours and 11 minutes. Grades 4–8. Amy and Dan Cahill are given the choice of receiving a fortune or uncovering the 39 clues that will lead to the source of their family's power. Narrated by David Pittu.

*The Absolutely True Diary of a Part-Time Indian.* Recorded Books, 5 hours. Ages 14–up. Author Sherman Alexie narrates his award-winning story of a 14-year-old's fight to overcome physical and other obstacles.

*Alice's Adventures in Wonderland.* Listening Library, 3 hours. Grades 4–up. Jim Dale tells the classic tale of Alice's strange experiences down the rabbit hole.

*Beethoven's Wig 4: Dance Along Symphonies.* Rounder Records, 44 minutes. Grades 4–up. Listeners are invited to sing and dance along with 26 symphonic songs, 12 of which feature amusing lyrics.

*A Bloody Jack Adventure, Book 2. Curse of the Blue Tattoo: Being an Account of the Misadventures of Jacky Faber, Midshipman and Fine Lady.* Listen & Live Audio, 14 hours. Middle School/YA. Narrator Katherine Kellgren tells the story of young Jacky Faber's enrolling at fancy finishing school in this sequel to *Bloody Jack.*

*Brooklyn Bridge.* Macmillan Audio, 4 hours and 45 minutes. Grades 4–9. Fred Berman narrates Karen Hesse's story of Joseph Michtom, 14-year-old son of the couple who created the teddy bear in 1903, and his world in downtown Manhattan.

*Celia Cruz: Queen of Salsa.* Live Oak, 16 minutes. Grades K–5. With narration and singing by Michelle Manzo, this read-along offers a glimpse into the Cuban-born singer's life.

*Clementine's Letter.* Recorded Books, 2 hours and 30 minutes. Grades 2–5. Young Clementine concocts a plan to keep her favorite teacher, Mr. D'Matz, from leaving for a new job. Jessica Almasy is the narrator.

*The Dead and the Gone.* Listening Library, 8 hours and 51 minutes. Grades 6–12. Robertson Dean reads Susan Beth Pfeffer's story of a boy's struggle for survival after an asteroid hits New York City.

*Elijah of Buxton.* Listening Library, 8 hours 30 minutes. Grades 5–8. Mirron Willis narrates Christopher Paul Curtis's award-winning tale of 11-year-old Elijah, whose life changes when he embarks on a dangerous journey and encounters the horrors of slavery.

*Good Masters! Sweet Ladies! Voices from a Medieval Village.* Recorded Books, 1 hour and 30 minutes. Grades 4–9. Christina Moore and a full cast present author Laura Amy Schlitz's slice of life in medieval England.

*Grandfather's Journey.* Weston Woods Studios, 8 minutes. Grades K–5. B. D. Wong narrates Allen Say's memoir of his grandfather's yearning for two countries. An interview with the author is included.

*The Graveyard Book.* Recorded Books, 7 hours and 45 minutes. Grades 5–8. Neil Gaiman tells his story of little Nobody Owens, who flees his family's killer and finds refuge among ghosts in a graveyard.

*Gregor and the Code of Claw.* Listening Library, 9 hours and 4 minutes. Grades 4–8. Narrator Paul Boehmer presents the final segment of the Underland Chronicles, featuring the battle of the warrior Gregor with the Bane and the breaking of the Code of Claw.

*Hawaiian Playground.* Putumayo Kids, 26 minutes. All Ages. Ukuleles, native Hawaiian language, and the sliding sounds of slack-key guitars enliven this collection of island songs by various performers.

*I'm Dirty!* Weston Woods Studios, 6 minutes. Preschool–2. Steve Buscemi is the voice of a busy backhoe in this adventure featuring music by David Mansfield.

*Martina the Beautiful Cockroach: A Cuban Folktale.* Peachtree Publishers, 10 minutes. Elementary. Carmen Agra Deedy brings spirited wit and cultural touches to a telling of the traditional Cuban tale of Martina's quest for a husband. A Spanish-language version is included.

*Miss Spitfire.* Recorded Books, 6 hours and 45 minutes. Grades 6–up. Terry Donnelly voices the joys and frustrations of blind and deaf Helen Keller's early tutor, Anne Sullivan.

*The Possibilities of Sainthood.* Brilliance Audio, 7 hours. Grades 7–10. Fifteen-year-old Antonia harbors an ambition to become a saint while at the same time hankering for romance. Emily Bauer tells the story by Donna Freitas.

*Red Moon at Sharpsburg.* Recorded Books, 7 hours. Grades 5–8. Coming of age during the Civil War, 13-year-old India faces danger and heartbreak. Julia Gibson narrates Rosemary Wells's novel.

*Shooting the Moon.* Recorded Books, 3 hours and 15 minutes. Grades 4–7. Jessica Almasy voices the story of Jamie, whose adventure begins when she receives a roll of film to process from her brother who is serving in Vietnam.

*Skybreaker.* Full Cast Audio. 11 hours and 30 minutes. Grades 5–up. Continuing the adventures of Matt and Kate as they try to salvage a long-lost treasure ship.

*The True Story of the Three Little Pigs.* Weston Woods Studios, 8 minutes. Grades K–4. Paul Giamatti tells Jon Scieszka's story of the classic tale as seen from the wolf's point of view.

# Notable Children's Books

A list of notable children's books is selected each year by the Notable Children's Books Committee of the Association for Library Service to Children, a division of the American Library Association. Recommended titles are selected by children's librarians and educators based on originality, creativity, and suitability for children. [See "Literary Prizes, 2008" later in Part 5 for Caldecott, Newbery, and other award winners—*Ed.*]

## Books for Younger Readers

Becker, Bonny. *A Visitor for Bear.* Illus. by Kady MacDonald Denton. Candlewick.

Bee, William. *Beware of the Frog.* Illus. by the author. Candlewick.

Campbell, Sarah C. *Wolfsnail: A Backyard Predator.* Photographs by Sarah C. and Richard P. Campbell. Boyds Mills.

Davis, Eleanor. *Stinky.* Illus. by the author. RAW Junior/TOON.

Dorros, Arthur. *Papá and Me.* Illus. by Rudy Gutierrez. HarperCollins.

Fleming, Denise. *Buster Goes to Cowboy Camp.* Illus. by the author. Henry Holt.

Frazee, Marla. *A Couple of Boys Have the Best Week Ever.* Illus. by the author. Harcourt.

George, Jean Craighead. *Goose and Duck.* Illus. by Priscilla Lamont. HarperCollins.

Graham, Bob. *How to Heal a Broken Wing.* Illus. by the author. Candlewick.

Grant, Judyann Ackerman. *Chicken Said, "Cluck!"* Illus. by Sue Truesdell. HarperCollins.

Harris, Robie H. *Maybe a Bear Ate It!* Illus. by Michael Emberley. Scholastic.

Henkes, Kevin. *Old Bear.* Illus. by the author. HarperCollins.

Hills, Tad. *What's Up, Duck? A Book of Opposites.* Illus. by the author. Random.

Hole, Stian. *Garmann's Summer.* Illus. by the author, tr. by Don Bartlett. Eerdmans.

Kohara, Kazuno. *Ghosts in the House!* Illus. by the author. Roaring Brook.

McDonald, Megan. *The Hinky Pink.* Illus. by Brian Floca. Atheneum.

Morales, Yuyi. *Just in Case: A Trickster Tale and Spanish Alphabet Book.* Illus. by the author. Roaring Brook.

Seeger, Laura Vaccaro. *One Boy.* Illus. by the author. Roaring Brook.

Swanson, Susan Marie. *The House in the Night.* Illus. by Beth Krommes. Houghton Mifflin.

Tafolla, Carmen. *What Can You Do with a Rebozo?* Illus. by Amy Cordova. Ten Speed.

Weatherford, Carole Boston. *Before John Was a Jazz Giant: A Song of John Coltrane.* Illus. by Sean Qualls. Henry Holt.

Willems, Mo. *Are You Ready to Play Outside?* Illus. by the author. Disney.

## Middle Readers

Appelt, Kathi. *The Underneath.* Illus. by David Small. Atheneum.

Bishop, Nic. *Frogs.* Photographs by the author. Scholastic.

Broach, Elise. *Masterpiece.* Illus. by Kelly Murphy. Henry Holt.

Brown, Don. *All Stations! Distress! April 15, 1912, the Day the Titanic Sank.* Illus. by the author. Roaring Brook.

Bryant, Jen. *A River of Words: The Story of William Carlos Williams.* Illus. by Melissa Sweet. Eerdmans.

Dowd, Siobhan. *The London Eye Mystery.* Random.

Elliott, Zetta. *Bird.* Illus. by Shadra Strickland. Lee & Low.

Erdrich, Louise. *The Porcupine Year.* HarperCollins.

Fern, Tracey E. *Buffalo Music.* Illus. by Lauren Castillo. Clarion.

Gaiman, Neil. *The Graveyard Book.* Illus. by Dave McKean. HarperCollins.

González, Lucía. *The Storyteller's Candle/La Velita de los Cuentos.* Illus. by Lulu Delacre. Children's Book Press.

Greenberg, Jan, and Sandra Jordan. *Christo and Jeanne-Claude: Through the Gates and Beyond.* Illus. with photographs. Roaring Brook.

Hale, Shannon, and Dean Hale. *Rapunzel's Revenge.* Illus. by Nathan Hale. Bloomsbury.

Hopkinson, Deborah. *Abe Lincoln Crosses a Creek: A Tall, Thin Tale (Introducing His Forgotten Frontier Friend).* Illus. by John Hendrix. Random.

Kerley, Barbara. *What to Do About Alice? How Alice Roosevelt Broke the Rules, Charmed the World, and Drove Her Father Teddy Crazy!* Illus. by Edwin Fotheringham. Scholastic.

Law, Ingrid. *Savvy.* Dial.

Lewin, Ted, and Betsy Lewin. *Horse Song: The Naadam of Mongolia.* Illus. by the authors. Lee & Low.

McGill, Alice. *Way Up and Over Everything.* Illus. by Jude Daly. Houghton Mifflin.

Nicholls, Sally. *Ways to Live Forever.* Scholastic.

Nivola, Claire A. *Planting the Trees of Kenya: The Story of Wangari Maathai.* Illus. by the author. Farrar, Straus & Giroux.

Nobleman, Marc Tyler. *Boys of Steel: The Creators of Superman.* Illus. by Ross MacDonald. Knopf.

Parker, Robert Andrew. *Piano Starts Here: The Young Art Tatum.* Illus. by the author. Random.

Patent, Dorothy Hinshaw. *When the Wolves Returned: Restoring Nature's Balance in Yellowstone.* Photographs by Dan Hartman and Cassie Hartman. Walker.

Preller, James. *Six Innings.* Feiwel & Friends.

Ray, Deborah Kogan. *Wanda Gág: The Girl Who Lived to Draw.* Illus. by the author. Viking/Penguin.

Rumford, James. *Silent Music: A Story of Baghdad.* Illus. by the author. Roaring Brook.

Scieszka, Jon. *Knucklehead: Tall Tales and Mostly True Stories About Growing Up Scieszka.* Illus. by the author. Viking/Penguin.

Schulman, Janet. *Pale Male: Citizen Hawk of New York City.* Illus. by Meilo So. Knopf.

Shulevitz, Uri. *How I Learned Geography.* Illus. by the author. Farrar, Straus & Giroux.

Stone, Tanya Lee. *Elizabeth Leads the Way: Elizabeth Cady Stanton and the Right to Vote.* Illus. by Rebecca Gibbon. Henry Holt.

Thomas, Joyce Carol. *The Blacker the Berry.* Illus. by Floyd Cooper. HarperCollins.

Uehashi, Nahoko. *Moribito: Guardian of the Spirit.* Illus. by Yuko Shimizu, tr. by Cathy Hirano. Scholastic.

## Older Readers

Anderson, Laurie Halse. *Chains.* Simon & Schuster.

Collins, Suzanne. *The Hunger Games.* Scholastic.

Connor, Leslie. *Waiting for Normal.* HarperCollins.

Deem, James M. *Bodies from the Ice: Melting Glaciers and the Recovery of the Past.* Illus. Houghton Mifflin.

Engle, Margarita. *The Surrender Tree: Poems of Cuba's Struggle for Freedom.* Henry Holt.

Fleischman, Sid. *The Trouble Begins at 8: A Life of Mark Twain in the Wild, Wild West.* Illus. HarperCollins.

Fleming, Candace. *The Lincolns: A Scrapbook Look at Abraham and Mary.* Illus. Random House.

Freedman, Russell. *Washington at Valley Forge.* Illus. Holiday House.

Jiménez, Francisco. *Reaching Out.* Houghton Mifflin.

Macaulay, David, with Richard Walker. *The Way We Work: Getting to Know the Amazing Human Body.* Illus. by the author. Houghton Mifflin.

Michaelis, Antonia. *Tiger Moon.* Tr. by Anthea Bell. Amulet.

Nelson, Kadir. *We Are the Ship: The Story of Negro League Baseball.* Illus. by the author. Disney.

Nelson, Scott Reynolds, with Marc Aronson. *Ain't Nothing But a Man: My Quest to*

*Find the Real John Henry.* Illus. National Geographic.

O'Brien, Tony, and Mike Sullivan. *Afghan Dreams: Young Voices of Afghanistan.* Photographs by Tony O'Brien. Bloomsbury.

Pratchett, Terry. *Nation.* HarperCollins.

Reeve, Philip. *Here Lies Arthur.* Scholastic.

Smith, Hope Anita. *Keeping the Night Watch.* Illus. by E. B. Lewis. Henry Holt.

Woodson, Jacqueline. *After Tupac and D Foster.* Putnam.

## All Ages

Arnosky, Jim. *Wild Tracks! A Guide to Nature's Footprints.* Illus. by the author. Sterling.

Johnson, Stephen T. *A Is for Art: An Abstract Alphabet.* Illus. by the author. Simon & Schuster.

National Children's Book and Literacy Alliance. *Our White House: Looking In, Looking Out.* Candlewick.

# Notable Children's Videos

These DVD titles are selected by a committee of the Association for Library Service to Children, a division of the American Library Association. Recommendations are based on originality, creativity, and suitability for children.

*Art.* Weston Woods Studios, 6 minutes. Ages 3–7.

*Bats at the Beach.* Nutmeg Media, 10 minutes. Ages 4–8.

*A Box Full of Kittens.* Nutmeg Media, 17 minutes. Ages 3–7.

*The Boy Who Cried Wolf.* Weston Woods Studios, 7 minutes. Ages 4–9.

*Bugs! Bugs! Bugs!* Weston Woods Studios, 8 minutes. Ages 2–6.

*Come Again in Spring.* National Film Board of Canada, 12 minutes. Ages 12–up.

*Diary of a Fly.* Weston Woods Studios, 9 minutes. Ages 3–8.

*Do Unto Otters: A Book About Manners.* Weston Woods Studios, 10 minutes. Ages 4–8.

*Getting to Know the World's Greatest Artists: Mary Cassatt.* Getting to Know, Inc., 24 minutes. Ages 8–14.

*Grandfather's Journey.* Weston Woods Studios, 10 minutes. Ages 5–10.

*Hannah's Story.* National Film Board of Canada, 29 minutes. Ages 8–up.

*I'm Dirty.* Weston Woods Studios, 8 minutes. Ages 5–10.

*Mack Made Movies.* Live Oak Media, 14 minutes. Ages 4–8.

*Madam President.* Weston Woods Studios, 9 minutes. Ages 6–10.

*A Mama for Owen.* Nutmeg Media, 9 minutes. Ages 4–8.

*March On! The Day My Brother Martin Changed the World.* Weston Woods Studios, 20 minutes. Ages 8–up.

*Pharm Parties: A Lethal Mix.* Human Relations Media, 24 minutes. Ages 13–up.

*The True Story of the Three Little Pigs.* Weston Woods Studios, 8 minutes. Ages 3–8.

*Understanding Fetal Alcohol Syndrome.* Human Relations Media, 13 minutes. Ages 12–up.

*What Do You Do with a Tail like This?* Weston Woods Studios, 8 minutes. Ages 4–8.

*You're All My Favorites.* Candlewick, 10 minutes. Ages 2–6.

# Great Interactive Software for Kids

This list is chosen by a committee of the Association for Library Service to Children, a division of the American Library Association. Titles are selected on the basis of their originality, creativity, and suitability for children.

*Beep.* Tool Factory (http://www.toolfactory. com). Grades K–2. Children can choose among six activities, combining art, music, reading, and problem solving. Windows and Mac.

*GollyGee Blocks: 3-D Modeling for Kids.* Grades 1–5. GollyGee Software (http:// www.gollygee.com). Players can build anything, and decorate it, in a 3-D environment that encourages creativity and exploration. An intuitive interface features easy-to-understand icons and instructions. Once built, the work can be rotated to be seen from different angles, viewed in close-up, saved, or printed. Windows and Mac.

*LEGO Indiana Jones: The Original Adventures.* Lucasarts Entertainment (http:// www.lucasarts.com). Ages 10–14. The fictional archaeologist comes alive in this LEGO-style video game. Players must switch between the various characters—each of whom has specific skills—in order to solve some of the puzzles, illustrating the need for social interaction and the rewards of helping one another. Nintendo Wii, Multiplayer.

*Mastering Elementary School.* Weekly Reader Corp. (http://weeklyreader.com). This 2-disc DVD-ROM set provides lessons covering the topics of math, English, literature, history, and science at the elementary school level. Users watch videos and take lessons and quizzes. Progress reports show children's advancement. Windows and Mac.

*Mastering Elementary and Middle School Math.* Weekly Reader Corp. (http://www. weeklyreader.com). Grades 1–8. Audio- and video-powered lessons make learning math fun, fostering children's understanding of both core and complex mathematics concepts. A progress-report function tracks the user's advancement. Windows and Mac.

*Nancy Drew and the Phantom of Venice.* Her Interactive (http://www.herinteractive. com). Ages 10–adult. Nancy finds herself in Venice, where a phantom thief has the authorities baffled. Working with local police, she manages to infiltrate a crime syndicate. Players help Nancy interview suspects, interpret clues, solve puzzles, and disguise herself in order to successfully penetrate the secret organization. Windows.

# Bestsellers of 2008

## Hardcover Bestsellers: Old and New

### Dermot McEvoy and Michael Coffey
*Publishers Weekly*

John Grisham's aptly titled *Appeal* had the most of it, as far as the novel-buying reading public went, earning the No. 1 slot on *Publishers Weekly*'s hardcover fiction list in 2008—just enough to beat out *The Story of Edgar Sawtelle* by David Wroblewski, which sold 1.3 million. The top 15 fiction titles look much like 2007's, with the notable absence of Khaled Hosseini, who was top dog that year. The prolific James Patterson racked up three in the top echelon, and Nicholas Sparks, Patricia Cornwell, Dean Koontz, and David Baldacci made returns. The new kids on the block, in addition to Wroblewski, were Stephenie Meyer, seamlessly crossing over from the young adult genre with *The Host,* and Glenn Beck, whose *Christmas Sweater* apparently warmed the hearts of his faithful.

In nonfiction, as usual, the top spots went to heart-string tuggers (Randy Pausch, Rick Warren), humor (David Sedaris) and self-empowerment (Roizen and Oz—doctors Michael F. Roizen and Mehmet C. Oz), but Pausch's *The Last Lecture* outsold the next bestselling book by 4 to 1. Of course, the power of television and celebrity was obvious; of the top 15 authors, seven had prominent regular media exposure: Warren, Bill O'Reilly, Barbara Walters, Ina Garten, Jon and Kate Gosselin, Chelsea Handler, and Maria Shriver. Together the "media seven" sold a remarkable 4,800,000 books.

Going deeper into the nonfiction list, it appears that Americans are fixated on Barack Obama, cooking, and money. Obama be the world's most charismatic figure. Books by, for, and against the 44th president—it hardly mattered—did very well in 2008. First were Obama's own memoirs, *Dreams from My Father* and *The Audacity of Hope,* which together sold just over 239,000 copies. The anti-Obama forces did well with *Obama Nation* by Jerome R. Corsi and *The Case Against Barack Obama* by David Freddoso, which together sold just over 470,000 copies. There were also a couple of Obama photography books: *The American Journey of Barack Obama* by the editors of *Life* and *The Rise of Barack Obama* by Pete Souza (now the official White House photographer). Together they sold more than 325,000 copies.

Food had a place at the table, too. The Food Network is well represented with Rachael Ray, Giada De Laurentiis, Paula Deen, and Ina Garten. Also prominent were Martha Stewart, Jessica Seinfeld, Phyllis Pellman Good, and Trisha Yearwood.

And with the United States facing the worst financial crisis since the Depression, it's not surprising that people turned to two trusted financial advisers— Dave Ramsey and Suze Orman. Ramsey's *Total Money Makeover* sold 252,000 copies and Orman's *Women & Money* weighed in at 179,396.

Adapted from *Publishers Weekly,* March 23, 2009

# Publishers Weekly 2008 Bestsellers

## FICTION

1. **The Appeal** by John Grisham. Doubleday (11/08) #
2. **The Story of Edgar Sawtelle** by David Wroblewski. Ecco (9/08) 1,320,000
3. **The Host** by Stephenie Meyer. Little, Brown (5/08) 1,240,005
4. **Cross Country** by James Patterson. Little, Brown (11/08) 1,181,458
5. **The Lucky One** by Nicholas Sparks. Grand Central (9/08) 1,150,023
6. **Fearless Fourteen** by Janet Evanovich. St. Martin's (6/08)1,058,427
7. **Christmas Sweater** by Glenn Beck. Threshold (11/08) 900,800
8. **Scarpetta** by Patricia Cornwell. Putnam (12/08) 800,000
9. **Your Heart Belongs to Me** by Dean Koontz. Bantam (11/08) 784,645
10. **Plum Lucky** by Janet Evanovich. St. Martin's (1/08) 748,414
11. **7th Heaven** by James Patterson. Little, Brown (08) 700,313
12. **Sail** by James Patterson. Little, Brown (1/08) 665,358
13. **A Good Woman** by Danielle Steel. Delacorte (10/08) 636,375
14. **Divine Justice** by David Baldacci. Grand Central (11/08) 633,607
15. **The Gate House** by Nelson DeMille. Grand Central (10/08) 606,845

## NONFICTION

1. **The Last Lecture** by Randy Pausch. Hyperion (4/08) 4,388,137
2. **The Purpose of Christmas** by Rick Warren. Howard (11/08) #1,290,000
3. **You: Being Beautiful** by Michael F. Roizen and Mehmet C. Oz. Free Press (11/08) #910,000
4. **Outliers** by Malcolm Gladwell. Little, Brown (11/08) 821,721
5. **A Bold, Fresh Piece of Humanity** by Bill O'Reilly. Broadway (9/08) 776,608
6. **Dewey** by Vicki Myron with Brett Witter. Grand Central (9/08) 758,931
7. **Audition** by Barbara Waters. Knopf (1/08) 702,000
8. **Barefoot Contessa Back to Basics** by Ina Garten. Clarkson Potter (10/08) 641,741
9. **The Snowball** by Alice Schroeder. Bantam (9/08) 634,546
10. **Hot, Flat and Crowded** by Thomas L. Friedman. Farrar, Straus & Giroux (9/08) 625,363
11. **When You Are Engulfed in Flames** by David Sedaris. Little, Brown (6/08) 621,873
12. **Multiple Blessings** by Jon and Kate Gosselin and Beth Carson. Zondervan (10/08) 523,000
13. **American Lion** by Jon Meacham. Random (11/08) 463,678
14. **Are You There, Vodka? It's Me, Chelsea** by Chelsea Handler. Simon Spotlight (4/08) #460,000
15. **Just Who Will You Be?** by Maria Shriver. Hyperion (4/08) 418,721

---

All sales figures reflect books sold in calendar year 2008.

# Sales figures were submitted to *Publishers Weekly* in confidence, for use in placing titles on the lists. Numbers shown are rounded down to indicate relationship to sales figures for other titles.

Note: Rankings are determined by sales figures provided by publishers; the numbers generally reflect reports of copies "shipped and billed" in calendar year 2008. Publishers were instructed to adjust sales figures to include returns through January 31, 2009. Publishers did not at that time know what total returns would be—indeed, the majority of returns occur after that cutoff date—so none of these figures should be regarded as final net sales. (Dates in parentheses indicate month and year of publication.)

## The Fiction Runners-Up

16. *Tribute* by Nora Roberts. Putnam (600,005)
17. *Duma Key* by Stephen King. Scribner (#595,000)
18. *Arctic Drift* by Clive Cussler with Dirk Cussler. Putnam (588,247)
19. *Sundays at Tiffany's* by James Patterson. Little, Brown (581,250)
20. *Just After Sunset* by Stephen King. Scribner (#565,000)
21. *The Front* by Patricia Cornwell. Putnam (529,200)
22. *Extreme Measures* by Vince Flynn. Atria (454,543)
23. *Dashing Through the Snow* by Mary Higgins Clark and Carol Higgins Clark. S&S (#450,000)
24. *Love the One You're With* by Emily Giffin. St. Martin's (442,046)
25. *The Brass Verdict* by Michael Connelly. Little, Brown (439,007)
26. *Phantom Prey* by John Sandford. Putnam (423,687)
27. *The Whole Truth* by David Baldacci. Grand Central (420,724)
28. *The Hour I First Believed* by Wally Lamb. Harper (411,460)
29. *Where Are You Now* by Mary Higgins Clark. S&S (#410,000)
30. *Tailspin* by Catherine Coulter. Putnam (408,904)

### 400,000+

*Strangers in Death* by J. D. Robb. Putnam (403,000)

*Odd Hours* by Dean Koontz. Bantam (401,522)

### 300,000+

*Plague Ship* by Clive Cussler. Putnam (387,480)

*Change of Heart* by Jodi Picoult. Atria (378,857)

*Salvation in Death* by J. D. Robb. Putnam (378,500)

*A Lion Among Men* by Gregory Maguire. Morrow (377,458)

*Honor Thyself* by Danielle Steel. Delacorte (375,509)

*The Guernsey Literary and Potato Peel Pie Society* by Mary Ann Shaffer and Annie Barrows. Dial (368,288)

*Rogue* by Danielle Steel. Delacorte (362,237)

*Remember Me?* by Sophie Kinsella. Dial (336,870)

*Heat Lightning* by John Sandford. Putnam (324,935)

### 200,000+

*One Fifth Avenue* by Candace Bushnell. Voice/ Hyperion (290,004)

*A Mercy* by Toni Morrison. Knopf (284,000)

*Moscow Rules* by Daniel Silva. Putnam (282,047)

*Grace* by Richard Paul Evans. S&S (#280,000)

*Dark Summer* by Iris Johansen. St. Martin's (274,586)

*Unaccustomed Earth* by Jhumpa Lahiri. Knopf (274,000)

*Bones* by Jonathan Kellerman. Ballantine (269,856)

*Chasing Harry Winston* by Lauren Weisberger. S&S (#265,000)

*Smoke Screen* by Sandra Brown. S&S (#255,000)

*The Given Day* by Dennis Lehane. Morrow (250,716)

*The Art of Racing in the Rain* by Garth Stein. Harper (250,412)

*A Cedar Cove Christmas* by Debbie Macomber. Mira (250,000)

*Robert Ludlum's The Bourne Sanction* by Eric Van Lustbader. Grand Central (244,229)

*Twenty Wishes* by Debbie Macomber. Mira (242,000)

*Quicksand* by Iris Johansen. St. Martin's (238,554)

*Nothing to Lose* by Lee Child. Delacorte (237,120)

*Hot Mahogany* by Stuart Woods. Putnam (236,704)

*The Private Patient* by P. D. James. Knopf (235,000)

*Acheron* by Sherrilyn Kenyon. St. Martin's (232,027)

*Devil Bones* by Kathy Reichs. Scribner (#230,000)

*The Charlemagne Pursuit* by Steve Berry. Ballantine (229,074)

*Married Lovers* by Jackie Collins. St. Martin's (228,395)

*The Other Queen* by Philippa Gregory. Touchstone (#225,000)

*Blood Noir* by Laurell K. Hamilton. Berkley (216,121)

*Hold Tight* by Harlan Coben. Dutton (214,159)

*People of the Book* by Geraldine Brooks. Viking (212,498)

*The Last Oracle* by James Rollins. Morrow (210,231)

*A Wolfe at the Table* by Augusten Burroughs. St. Martin's (208,869)

*A Prisoner of Birth* by Jeffrey Archer. St. Martin's (207,441)

*Fire and Ice* by Julie Garwood. Ballantine (203,984)

*Santa Fe Dead* by Stuart Woods. Putnam (200,716)

## 125,000+

*Compulsion* by Jonathan Kellerman. Ballantine (199,774)

*Silent Thunder* by Iris Johansen and Roy Johansen. St. Martin's (198,755)

*Black Ops* by W. E. B. Griffin. Putnam (198,586)

*Book of Lies* by Brad Meltzer. Grand Central (198,036)

*The Last Patriot* by Brad Thor. Atria (197,462)

*Stranger in Paradise* by Robert B. Parker. Putnam (194,847)

*Knit Two* by Kate Jacobs. Putnam (194,057)

*The Girl with the Dragon Tattoo* by Stieg Larsson. Knopf (192,000)

*Belong to Me* by Marisa de los Santos. Morrow (185,751)

*A Most Wanted Man* by John le Carré. Scribner (#185,000)

*Certain Girls* by Jennifer Weiner. Atria (184,792)

*Shadow of Power* by Steve Martini. Morrow (181,993)

*The Treasure* by Iris Johansen. Bantam (180,839)

*The Beach House* by Jane Green. Viking (179,738)

*Testimony* by Anita Shreve. Little, Brown (178,093)

*Foreign Body* by Robin Cook. Putnam (175,460)

*Rough Weather* by Robert B. Parker. Putnam (172,978)

*Dark Curse* by Christine Feehan. Berkley (172,258)

*Swine Not?* by Jimmy Buffett. Little, Brown (168,730)

*Swallowing Darkness* by Laurell K. Hamilton. Ballantine (167,958)

*The Bodies Left Behind* by Jeffery Deaver. S&S (#165,000)

*The Killing Ground* by Jack Higgins. Putnam (161,898)

*What's Your Poo Telling You?* by Anish Sheth, M.D., and Josh Richman. Chronicle (161,000)

*Careless in Red* by Elizabeth George. Harper (160,697)

*The Lace Reader* by Brunonia Barry. Morrow (160,285)

*Death and Honor* by W. E. B. Griffin. Putnam (158,713)

*Anathem* by Neal Stephenson. Morrow (157,215)

*The Mercedes Coffin* by Faye Kellerman. Morrow (155,397)

*Sizzle and Burn* by Jayne Ann Krentz. Putnam (152,600)

*The Miracle at Speedy Motors* by Alexander McCall Smith. Pantheon (150,000)

*The Broken Window* by Jeffery Deaver. S&S (#150,000)

*Silks* by Dick Francis. Putnam (147,005)

*Midnight* by Sister Souljah. Atria (145,762)

*From Dead to Worse* by Charlaine Harris. Ace (145,000)

*Dead Heat* by Joel. C. Rosenberg. Tyndale (144,347)

*Top Chef* by The creators of *Top Chef*. Chronicle (144,000)

*A Wallflower Christmas* by Lisa Kleypas. St. Martin's (143,023)

*Rough Justice* by Jack Higgins. Putnam (135,795)

*American Wife* by Curtis Sittenfeld. Random (134,013)

*Being Elizabeth* by Barbara Taylor Bradford. St. Martin's (131,038)

*Holidays on Ice* by David Sedaris. Little, Brown (130,506)

*The Fire* by Katherine Neville. Ballantine (128,939)

*Snuff* by Chuck Palahniuk. Doubleday (126,842)

*Bright Shiny Morning* by James Frey. Harper (125,380)

*First Patient* by Michael Palmer. St. Martin's (125,016)

## 100,000+

*Small Favor* by Jim Butcher. Roc (124,188)

*Say Goodbye* by Lisa Gardner. Bantam (123,222)

*The Keepsake* by Tess Gerritsen. Ballantine (122,393)

*The Senator's Wife* by Sue Miller. Knopf (122,000)

*Damage Control* by J. A. Jance. Morrow (121,853)

*Blood Sins* by Kay Hooper. Bantam (121,510)

*The Dark Tide* by Andrew Gross. Morrow (121,162)

*Bulls Island* by Dorothea Benton Frank. Morrow (118,533)

*World Without End* by Ken Follett. Dutton (116,660)

*Swan Peak* by James Lee Burke. S&S (#115,000)

*Death Angel* by Linda Howard. Ballantine (114,947)

*Off Season* by Anne Rivers Siddons. Grand Central (113,372)

*Christ the Lord: The Road to Cana* by Anne Rice. Knopf (112,000)

*The Steel Wave* by Jeff Shaara. Ballantine (111,187)

*Sin No More* by Kimberla Lawson Roby. Morrow (109,447)

*Firefly Lane* by Kristen Hannah. St. Martin's (109,156)

*The Outlaw Demon Wails* by Kim Harrison. Morrow (108,528)

*Charm!* by Kendall Hart. Hyperion (108,000)

*Ender in Exile* by Orson Scott Card. Tor (107,792)

*Blue Smoke and Murder* by Elizabeth Lowell. Morrow (106,219)

*Assassin* by Stephen Coonts. St. Martin's (105,855)

*The Gypsy Morph* by Terry Brooks. Del Rey (105,838)

*Just Too Good to Be True* by E. Lynn Harris. Doubleday (104,046)

*Lady Killer* by Lisa Scottoline. Harper (103,933)

*Star Wars: The Force Unleashed* by Sean Williams. Del Rey (103,232)

*The Enchantress of Florence* by Salman Rushdie. Random (102,512)

*Blasphemy* by Douglas Preston. Forge (101,621)

*Days of Infamy* by Newt Gingrich and William R. Forstchen. St. Martin's/Dunne (101,288)

*Star Wars: The Clone Wars* by Karen Traviss. Del Rey (101,146)

*Sweetheart* by Chelsea Cain. St. Martin's (101,042)

*Star Wars: Legacy of the Force: Invincible* by Troy Denning. Del Rey (101,034)

*Liberty* by Garrison Keillor. Viking (101,000)

*The Widows of Eastwick* by John Updike. Knopf (101,000)

*Blue-Eyed Devil* by Lisa Kleypas. St. Martin's (100,826)

*Pleasure* by Eric Jerome Dickey. Dutton (100,210)

*Zapped* by Carol Higgins Clark. Scribner (#100,000)

*Lost Souls* by Lisa Jackson. Kensington (100,000)

*Something on the Side* by Carl Weber. Kensington (100,000)

*The Garden of Last Days* by Andre Dubus III. Norton (#100,000)

## The Nonfiction Runners-Up

16. *StrengthsFinder 2.0* by Tom Rath. Gallup (399,473)
17. *Stori Telling* by Tori Spelling. Simon Spotlight (#375,000)
18. *Against Medical Advice* by James Patterson with Hal Friedman. Little, Brown (371,513)
19. *The War Within* by Bob Woodward. S&S (#345,000)
20. *Love Your Life* by Victoria Osteen. Free Press (#325,000)
21. *Call Me Ted* by Ted Turner with Bill Burke. Grand Central (322,117)
22. *Too Fat to Fish* by Artie Lange with Anthony Bozza. Spiegel & Grau (318,600)
23. *Martha Stewart's Cooking School* by Martha Stewart. Clarkson Potter (317,992)
24. *Breakthrough* by Suzanne Somers. Crown (311,274)
25. *Obama Nation* by Jerome R. Corsi. Threshold (310,575)
26. *You* by Michael F. Roizen, M.D., and Mehmet C. Oz, M.D. Collins (306,000)
27. *Giada's Kitchen* by Giada De Laurentiis. Clarkson Potter (301,663)
28. *What's Age Got to Do with It?* by Robin McGraw. Nelson (289,000)
29. *Fleeced* by Dick Morris. Harper (280,246)
30. *The Taste of Home Cookbook* (New Rev.) by the editors of Taste of Home Magazine. Reader's Digest (264,343)

### 200,000+

*Stolen Innocence* by Elissa Wall. Morrow (259,186)

*The Longest Trip Home* by John Grogan. Morrow (258,025)

*Secret Daily Teachings* by Rhonda Byrne. Atria (253,812)

*Total Money Makeover* by Dave Ramsey. Nelson (252,000)

*Become a Better You* by Joel Osteen. Free Press (#250,000)

*Letter to My Daughter* by Maya Angelou. Random (247,584)

*What Happened* by Scott McClellan. PublicAffairs (247,183)

*The Post-American World* by Fareed Zakaria. Norton (#245,000)

*The Best Life Cookbook* by Bob Greene. S&S (#245,000)

*Here's the Story* by Maureen McCormick. Morrow (244,416)

*Yum-O!* by Rachael Ray. Clarkson Potter (243,470)

*Life with My Sister Madonna* by Christopher Ciccone. Simon Spotlight (#235,000)

*Losing It* by Valerie Bertinelli. Free Press (#235,000)

*Mistaken Identity* by Don and Susie Van Ryn, et al. Howard (#235,000)

*Do the Right Thing* by Mike Huckabee. Sentinel (232,357)

*What in the World Is Going On?* by David Jeremiah. Nelson (223,000)

*My Stroke of Insight* by Jill Bolte Taylor. Viking (219,458)

*The American Journey of Barack Obama* by the Editors of Life Magazine. Little, Brown (214,825)

*Before You Do* by T. D. Jakes. Atria (212,984)

*Home* by Julie Andrews. Hyperion (208,004)

*Why We Suck* by Denis Leary. Viking (207,437)

*The Secret* by Rhonda Byrne. Atria (201,141)

*No Limits* by Michael Phelps with Alan Abrahamson. Free Press (#200,000)

**125,000+**

*The 4-Hour Workweek* by Timothy Ferriss. Crown (193,368)

*The Secret to True Happiness* by Joyce Meyer. Faithwords (190,851)

*A Member of the Family* by Cesar Millan and Melissa Jo Peltier. Harmony (184,921)

*Women & Money* by Suze Orman. Spiegel & Grau (179,396)

*Paula Deen's Kitchen Wisdom and Recipe Journal* by Paula Deen. S&S (#170,000)

*You: Staying Young* by Michael F. Roizen, M.D., and Mehmet C. Oz, M.D. Free Press (#170,000)

*John Lennon* by Philip Norman. Ecco (166,795)

*Ladies of Liberty* by Cokie Roberts. Morrow (166,657)

*Liberal Fascism* by Jonah Goldberg. Doubleday (163,010)

*Freakonomics* (Rev. Ed.) by Steven Levitt and Stephen Dubner. Morrow (160,653)

*The Case Against Barack Obama* by David Freddoso. Regnery (159,485)

*Start Your New Life Today* by Joyce Meyer. Faithwords (158,676)

*Deceptively Delicious* by Jessica Seinfeld. Collins (156,000)

*The Reason for God* by Timothy Keller. Dutton (155,104)

*Vindicated* by Jose Canseco. Simon Spotlight (#155,000)

*You: On a Diet* by Michael F. Roizen, M.D., and Mehmet C. Oz, M.D. Free Press (#155,000)

*The Revolution* by Ron Paul. Grand Central (152,935)

*Pocket Dangerous Book for Boys* by Conn Iggulden. Collins (146,000)

*Predictably Irrational* by Dan Ariely. Harper (145,243)

*Real Life* by Dr. Phil McGraw. Free Press (#140,000)

*The Way of the World* by Ron Suskind. Harper (138,547)

*Our Iceberg Is Melting* by John Kotter. St. Martin's (137,708)

*How Not to Look Old* by Charla Krupp. Springboard (137,275)

*Pieces of My Heart* by Robert Wagner. Morrow (137,076)

*Pocket Daring Book for Girls* by Andrea J. Buchanan. Collins (137,000)

*Go Put Your Strengths to Work* by Marcus Buckingham. Free Press (#135,000)

*The Road to Wealth* (Rev.) by Suze Orman. Riverhead (136,136)

*Dreams from My Father* by Barack Obama. Crown (134,877)

*Real Change* by Newt Gingrich. Regnery (134,129)

*Jeff Foxworthy's Complete Redneck* by Jeff Foxworthy. Villard (133,099)

*Mother Warriors* by Jenny McCarthy. Dutton (130,042)

*Michelle* by Lisa Mundy. S&S (#130,000)

*Gorgeously Green* by Sophie Uliano. Collins (129,000)

*Joy's Life Diet* by Joy Bauer. Collins (128,000)

*Quantum Wellness* by Kathy Freston. Weinstein (125,000)

**100,000+**

*The Black Swan* by Nassim Nicholas Taleb. Random (123,083)

*The Monster of Florence* by Douglas Preston with Mario Speci. Grand Central (121,779)

*Fix-It and Forget-It Big Cookbook* by Phyllis Pellman Good. Good Books (121,433)

*The Winners Manual* by Jim Tressel with Chris Fabry. Tyndale (120,504)

*Now, Discover Your Strengths* by Marcus Buckingham and Donald O. Clifton. Free Press (#120,000)

*Anticancer* by David Servan-Schreiber. Viking (118,989)

*Goodnight Bush* by Eric Origen and Gan Golan. Little, Brown (118,564)

*Walking with God* by John Eldredge. Nelson (118,000)

*The Downhill Lie* by Carl Hiaasen. Knopf (117,000)

*Stop Whining, Start Living* by Dr. Laura Schlessinger. Harper (110,860)

*The Rise of Barack Obama* by Pete Souza. Triumph (110,826)

*Cast of Characters* by Max Lucado. Nelson (110,000)

*The House at Sugar Beach* by Helene Cooper. S&S (#110,000)

*The Greatest Stories Never Told* by Rick Beyer. Collins (110,000)

*The Third Jesus* by Deepak Chopra. Harmony (109,153)

*Armageddon in Retrospect* by Kurt Vonnegut. Putnam (107,636)

*Annie Leibovitz at Work* by Annie Leibovitz. Random (107,531)

*Escape* by Carolyn Jessop. Broadway (106,769)

*The Audacity of Hope* by Barack Obama. Crown (104,205)

*Looking for Lincoln* by Philip B. Kunhardt III and Peter W. Kunhardt. Knopf (103,000)

*Georgia Cooking in an Oklahoma Kitchen* by Trisha Yearwood. Clarkson Potter (102,856)

*Made to Stick* by Chip Heath and Dan Heath. Random (102,794)

*Alex & Me* by Irene Pepperberg. Collins (102,000)

*The Forever War* by Dexter Filkins. Knopf (102,000)

*Me of Little Faith* by Lewis Black. Riverhead (101,981)

*Bad Money* by Kevin Philips. Viking (100,543)

*The Dark Side* by Jane Mayer. Doubleday (101,520)

*The Intelligent Investor* (Rev.) by Benjamin Graham. Collins (101,000)

*Things I've Been Silent About* by Azar Nafisi. Random (100,305)

*Up Till Now* by William Shatner. St. Martin's (100,232)

*Ghosts Among Us* by James Van Praagh. HarperOne (100,000)

## Paperback Bestsellers: The Usual Suspects

### Dermot McEvoy

"Round up the usual suspects," Captain Renault famously said in *Casablanca,* and if ever there was a movie line that could apply year after year to the fiction side of paperback publishing, that would be it, for the more things change in publishing on a daily basis the more they stay the same in paperback fiction bestsellerdom.

The following listings show a lopsided fiction-to-nonfiction ratio (fiction wins) and a repeat of the big-money names: Nora Roberts (12 titles), James Patterson (9), Janet Evanovich (4) and John Grisham (3, including the top mass market seller of the year, *The Appeal*). And, of course, there are the big names with more than one title: Fern Michaels (with 5), Dean Koontz (2), Clive Cussler (3), and Danielle Steel (3).

Novels far outdistance nonfiction titles, but the nonfiction titles tell us something about where the country is going. As usual, there are a fair number of cookbooks with the same bestselling authors—Rachael Ray, Martha Stewart, and Paula Deen—but the domestic titles that grab attention are books on pregnancy and child care. The leader of this trend is Heidi Murkoff, who had three titles from Workman (*What to Expect When You're Expecting, What to Expect the First Year,* and *What to Expect: The Toddler Years*) that sold more than 1,313,300 books in 2008 alone.

As usual, a presidential election year generated a lot of books, with the bestselling author eventually ending up as the electoral champ, too. Barack Obama's two memoirs (*The Audacity of Hope* and *Dreams from My Father*) sold just under 3 million copies in trade paperback and mass market. He also sold another 280,428 copies of a campaign policy book, *Change We Can Believe In,* putting him over the 3 million mark for the year.

Interestingly, although Republican presidential nominee John McCain has had several bestsellers over the years, the campaign did not give him any kind of a backlist bump in sales. However, a book on his running mate (*Sarah Palin: A New Kind of Leader* by Joe Hilley) sold 140,000 copies for Zondervan. Michael Moore also did well (268,592) with *Mike's Election Guide* for Grand Central.

The one thing on the mind of almost every American in 2008 was the ongoing financial crisis. CNBC has been getting its share of criticism recently from the likes of Jon Stewart and White House press secretary Robert Gibbs, with on-air CNBC personalities Rick Santelli and Jim Cramer coming in for the heaviest bombardment. Well, guess which CNBC personality topped the bestseller charts for 2008—none other than Suze Orman, with *Suze Orman's 2009 Action Plan,* which sold 886,529 copies for Spiegel & Grau. It should be noted that Orman, unlike the rest of CNBC's cheerleaders, was out front in warning about the housing and credit card bubbles and the shenanigans of the financial industry in general. Also showing up with financial advice was Robert T. Kiyosaki—*Rich Dad, Poor Dad* and *Rich Dad's Increase Your Financial IQ* sold close to 390,000 copies for Grand Central.

So as the big names in fiction continue to dominate year after year, paperback bestsellers tell us something about the American mind set: they are becoming more family-oriented (cooking and childcare books), are concerned about the leadership of the country (political tomes), and are keeping a sharp eye on the economy (Orman and Kiyosaki). The publishing industry continues to reflect what's on the minds of Americans.

Listed on the following pages are trade paperbacks and mass market titles published in 2007 and 2008; the rankings are based only on 2008 sales. To qualify, trade paperbacks had to have sold more than 100,000 copies in 2008; for mass markets, sales of more than 500,000 were required. A single asterisk (*) indicates the book was published in 2007; a double asterisk (**) means the book was published earlier but either remained or reappeared on *Publishers Weekly*'s bestseller charts in 2008. These reappearances are most often movie tie-ins. A pound sign (#) indicates that the shipped-and-billed figure was rounded down to the nearest 5,000 to indicate the books' sales relationship to other titles. The actual figures were given to *Publishers Weekly* in confidence for use only in placing titles on these lists.

## Mass Market

### Two Million+

*The Appeal* by John Grisham. Rep. Dell (2,185,722)

### One Million+

*The Hollow* by Nora Roberts. Orig. Jove (1,912,349)

*The Pagan Stone* by Nora Roberts. Orig. Jove (1,838,137)

*Double Cross* by James Patterson. Rep. Grand Central (1,609,619)

*Playing for Pizza* by John Grisham. Rep. Dell (1,532,428)

*The 5th Horseman* by James Patterson. Rep. Grand Central (1,447,295)

*High Noon* by Nora Roberts. Rep. Jove (1,447,282)

*Simple Genius* by James Patterson. Rep. Grand Central (1,435,672)

*Step on a Crack* by James Patterson. Rep. Grand Central (1,430,472)

*You've Been Warned* by James Patterson. Rep. Grand Central (1,310,188)

*Plum Lovin'* by Janet Evanovich. Rep. St. Martin's (1,250,000)

*Book of the Dead* by Patricia Cornwell. Rep. Berkley (1,239,465)

*Lean Mean Thirteen* by Janet Evanovich. Rep. St. Martin's (1,200,000)

*Stone Cold* by David Baldacci. Rep. Grand Central (1,199,109)

*The 6th Target* by James Patterson. Rep. Grand Central (1,144,299)

*Pandora's Daughter* by Iris Johansen. Rep. St. Martin's (1,100,000)

*I Heard That Song Before* by Mary Higgins Clark. Rep. Pocket (1,065,000)

*The Darkest Evening of the Year* by Dean Koontz. Rep. Bantam (1,060,474)

*Quicksand* by Iris Johansen. Rep. St. Martin's (1,000,000)

### 750,000+

*Double Take* by Catherine Coulter. Rep. Jove (997,115)

*Dear John* by Nicholas Sparks. Rep. Grand Central (977,102)

*Sisters* by Danielle Steel. Rep. Dell (971,600)

*The Overlook* by Michael Connelly. Rep. Grand Central (958,838)

*The Good Guy* by Dean Koontz. Rep. Bantam (940,235)

*Amazing Grace* by Danielle Steel. Rep. Dell (908,614)

*Shadow Music* by Julie Garwood. Rep. Ballantine (899,055)

*Suze Orman's 2009 Action Plan* by Suze Orman. Orig. Spiegel & Grau (886,529)

*Robert Ludlum's The Bourne Betrayal* by Eric Van Lustbader. Rep. Grand Central (851,321)

*Someday Soon* by Debbie Macomber. Reissue. Avon (850,000)

*Invisible Prey* by John Sandford. Rep. Berkley (847,150)

*T Is for Trespass* by Sue Grafton. Rep. Berkley (838,431)

*Creation in Death* by J. D. Robb. Rep. Berkley (828,045)

*Naughty Neighbor* by Janet Evanovich. Reissue. Harper (825,000)

*The Judas Strain* by James Rollins. Rep. Harper (800,000)

*Marley & Me* by John Grogan. Rep. Harper (800,000)

*Nineteen Minutes* by Jodi Picoult. Rep. Washington Square (790,447)

*Dark of the Moon* by John Sandford. Rep. Berkley (780,147)

*Whitethorn Woods* by Maeve Binchy. Rep. Anchor (776,635)

*Nights in Rodanthe* by Nicholas Sparks. Movie tie-in. Grand Central (771,828)

*The Woods* by Harlan Coben. Rep. Signet (755,210)

*Foul Play* by Janet Evanovich. Reissue. Harper (750,000)

*Dream Chaser* by Sherrilyn Kenyon. Orig. St. Martin's (750,000)

### 500,000+

*Strangers in Death* by J. D. Robb. Rep. Berkley (735,321)

*The Manning Sisters* by Debbie Macomber. Reissue. Mira (721,000)

*8 Sandpiper Way* by Debbie Macomber. Orig. Mira (718,000)

*The Lost Duke of Wyndham* by Julia Quinn. Orig. Avon (700,000)

*Mr. Cavendish, I Presume* by Julia Quinn. Orig. Avon (700,000)

*Left to Die* by Lisa Jackson. Orig. Zebra (700,000)

*Collateral Damage* by Fern Michaels. Orig. Zebra (700,000)

*\*Hide and Seek* by Fern Michaels. Orig. Zebra (700,000)

*The 6th Target* by James Patterson. Rep. Grand Central (681,200)

*The Edge of Desire* by Stephanie Laurens. Orig. Avon (675,000)

*The Quickie* by James Patterson. Rep. Grand Central (662,216)

*The Chase* by Clive Cussler. Rep. Berkley (661,184)

*Compulsion* by Jonathan Kellerman. Rep. Ballantine (656,935)

*Hokus Pokus* by Fern Michaels. Orig. Zebra (650,000)

*Fast Track* by Fern Michaels. Orig. Zebra (650,000)

*Three in Death* by J. D. Robb. Reissue. Berkley (636,422)

*The Navigator* by Clive Cussler. Rep. Berkley (617,109)

*Hide* by Lisa Gardner. Rep. Bantam (614,804)

*Sacred Stone* by Clive Cussler. Rep. Berkley (607,000)

*Daddy's Girl* by Lisa Scottoline. Rep. Harper (600,000)

*Innocent as Sin* by Elizabeth Lowell. Rep. Avon (600,000)

*Absolute Fear* by Lisa Jackson. Rep. Zebra (600,000)

*The Choice* by Nicholas Sparks. Rep. Grand Central (594,539)

*First Impressions* by Nora Roberts. Reissue. Silhouette (592,000)

*Bungalow 2* by Danielle Steel. Rep. Dell (591,644)

*Back on Blossom Street* by Debbie Macomber. Reissue. Mira (585,000)

*Seduce Me at Sunrise* by Lisa Kleypas. Orig. St. Martin's (575,000)

*Lady Killer* by Lisa Scottoline. Rep. Harper (575,000)

*Tom Clancy's EndWar* by David Michaels. Orig. Berkley (571,177)

*The Alibi Man* by Tami Hoag. Rep. Bantam (570,885)

*The Audacity of Hope* by Barack Obama. Rep. Vintage (562,149)

*Small Town Christmas* by Debbie Macomber. Reissue. Mira (558,000)

*Sugar Daddy* by Lisa Kleypas. Rep. St. Martin's (550,000)

*The Sanctuary* by Raymond Khoury. Rep. Signet (547,364)

*The Manning Bridges* by Debbie Macomber. Reissue. Mira (542,000)

*Blood Drams* by Kay Hooper. Rep. Bantam (540,388)

*Prisoner of Birth* by Jeffrey Archer. Rep. St. Martin's (535,000)

*Natural Born Charmer* by Susan Elizabeth Phillips. Rep. Avon (525,000)

*Justice Denied* by J. A. Jance. Rep. Harper (525,000)

*The Burnt House* by Faye Kellerman. Rep. Harper (525,000)

*The River Knows* by Amanda Quick. Rep. Jove (524,243)

*Light of the Moon* by Luanne Rice. Rep. Bantam (524,053)

*Devil May Cry* by Sherrilyn Kenyon. Rep. St. Martin's (520,000)

*One Silent Night* by Sherrilyn Kenyon. Orig. St. Martin's (510,000)

*Shoot Him if He Runs* by Stuart Woods. Rep. Signet (508,214)

*\*Stars* by Nora Roberts. Reissue. Silhouette (507,000)

*Mysterious* by Nora Roberts. Reissue. Silhouette (506,000)

*White Lies* by Jayne Ann Krents. Rep. Jove (505,200)

*The Venetian Betrayal* by Steve Berry. Rep. Ballantine (503,439)

*Dead Until Dark* by Charlaine Harris. TV Tie-In. Ace (502,456)

*Obsession* by Jonathan Kellerman. Rep. Ballantine (501,119)

*The Ruins* by Scott Smith. Movie tie-in. Vintage (500,887)

*Family Tree* by Barbara Delinsky. Rep. Anchor (500,501)

*Deep Storm* by Lincoln Child. Rep. Anchor (500,095)

*Turbulent Sea* by Christine Feehan. Orig. Jove (500,059)

*Bad Luck and Trouble* by Lee Child. Rep. Dell (500,038)

*Silver Bells* by Fern Michaels, JoAnn Ross, et al. Orig. Zebra (500,000)

*The Blue Zone* by Andrew Gross. Rep. Harper (500,000)

*The Heart-Shaped Box* by Joe Hill. Rep. Harper (500,000)

*Keeping Faith* by Jodi Picoult. Reissue. Avon (500,000)

*Everlasting* by Kathleen E. Woodiwiss. Rep. Avon (500,000)

*First Patient* by Michael Palmer. Rep. St. Martin's (500,000)

*The Alchemist* by Paulo Coelho. Rep. HarperOne (500,000)

## Trade Paperbacks

### 1 Million+

*A New Earth* by Eckhart Tolle. Oprah Edition. Plume (5,298,355)

*The Shack* by William P. Young. Orig. Windblown Media (4,432,439)

*\*Three Cups of Tea* by Greg Mortenson. Rep. Penguin (1,346,204)

*The Audacity of Hope* by Barack Obama. Rep. Three Rivers (1,214,728)

*Dreams from My Father* by Barack Obama. Rep. Three Rivers (1,206,867)

*Eat This, Not That!* by David Zinczenko and Matt Goulding. Orig. Rodale (1,200,000)

*Eat, Pray, Love* by Elizabeth Gilbert. Rep. Penguin (1,177,953)

**The Secret Life of Bees* by Sue Monk Kidd. Rep. Penguin (1,037,531)

## 750,000+

*The Friday Night Knitting Club* by Kate Jacobs. Rep. Berkley (963,147)

**The Power of Now* by Eckhart Tolle. Rep./ Oprah pick. New World Library (934,378)

*Key* by Stephen King. Rep. Pocket (871,000)

*Marley & Me* by John Grogan. Movie tie-in. Harper (860,000)

*Play Dirty* by Sandra Brown. Rep. Pocket (803,500)

*90 Minutes in Heaven* by Don Piper. Orig. Revell (801,801)

*What to Expect When You're Expecting* by Heidi Murkoff. Revised. Workman (782,653)

*A Thousand Splendid Suns* by Khaled Hosseini. Rep. Riverhead (758,281)

**The Road* by Cormac McCarthy. Rep. Vintage (750,467)

## 500,000+

*The Appeal* by John Grisham. Rep. Delta (719,375)

**Water for Elephants* by Sarah Gruen. Rep. Algonquin (707,000)

***The Kite Runner* by Khaled Hosseinui. Rep. Riverhead (700,094)

***Skinny Bitch* by Rory Freedman and Kim Barnouin. Rep. Running Press (622,229)

**Into the Wild* by Jon Krakauer. Movie tie-in. Anchor (608,982)

***The Five Love Languages* by Dr. Gary Chapman. Rep. Moody (567,696)

*Hungry Girl* by Lisa Lillien. Orig. St. Martin's/ Griffin (550,000)

***The Memory Keeper's Daughter* by Kim Edwards. Rep. Penguin (548,028)

*Third Degree* by Greg Iles. Rep. Pocket (542,000)

*Protect and Defend* by Vince Flynn. Rep. Pocket (535,200)

*World Without End* by Ken Follett. Rep. NAL (521,158)

*Hello, Cupcake!* by Karen Tack and Alan Richardson. Orig. Houghton Mifflin (520,101)

*Eat This, Not That for Kids* by David Zinczenko and Matt Goulding. Orig. Rodale (500,000)

## 250,000+

*Rachael Ray's Big Orange Book* by Rachael Ray. Orig. Clarkson Potter (496,168)

*The MacGregor Grooms* by Nora Roberts. Reissue. Silhouette (495,000)

***Big Russ and Me* by Tim Russert. Rep. Hyperion (492,773)

*Change of Heart* by Jodi Picoult. Rep. Washington Square (455,647)

*Nights in Rodanthe* by Nicholas Sparks. Movie tie-in. Grand Central (442,966)

*For One More Day* by Mitch Albom. Hyperion (428,720)

**Atonement* by Ian McEwan. Movie tie-in. Anchor (414,678)

*Loving Frank* by Nancy Horan. Rep. Ballantine (406,450)

*Marked* by P. C. Cast. Orig. St. Martin's/ Griffin (400,000)

*What to Expect the First Year* by Heidi Murkoff. Revised. Workman (374,934)

*Body Surfing* by Anita Shreve. Rep. Little, Brown (358,281)

*Confessions of a Shopaholic* by Sophia Kinsella. Movie tie-in. Dial (354,513)

**The Pillars of Earth* by Ken Follett. Rep. NAL (340,123)

***In the Woods* by Tana French. Rep. Penguin (338,758)

*Untamed* by P. C. Cast. Orig. St. Martin's/ Griffin (330,000)

#*John Adams* by David McCullough. Movie tie-in. S&S (325,000)

#*The Other Boleyn Girl* by Philippa Gregory. Movie tie-in. Touchstone (325,000)

*Barefoot* by Elin Hilderbrand. Rep. Little, Brown (317,265)

**Chosen* by P. C. Cast. Orig. St. Martin's/ Griffin (315,000)

**The Omnivore's Dilemma* by Michael Pollan. Rep. Penguin (310,150)

*The Longing* by Beverly Lewis. Rep. Bethany (302,489)

**Betrayed* by P. C. Cast. Orig. St. Martin's/Griffin (300,000)

*Eat This, Not That Supermarket Survival Guide* by David Zinczenko and Matt Goulding. Orig. Rodale (300,000)

**Tipping Point* by Malcolm Gladwell. Rep. Little, Brown (299,481)

*Martha Stewart's Cookies* by Martha Stewart Living Magazine. Orig. Clarkson Potter (299,283)

*Sunset* by Karen Kingsbury. Orig. Tyndale (291,363)

**Purpose Driven Life* by Rick Warren. Rep. Zondervan (290,000)

**No Country for Old Men* by Cormac McCarthy. Movie tie-in. Vintage (286,992)

**Blink* by Malcolm Gladwell. Rep. Little, Brown (286,866)

*Revolutionary Road* by Richard Yates. Movie tie-in. Vintage (282,216)

#**The 7 Habits of Highly Effective People* by Stephen R. Covey. Rep. Free Press (280,000)

*Change We Can Believe In* by Barack Obama. Orig. Three Rivers (280,428)

***Change Your Brain, Change Your Life* by Daniel G. Amen, M.D. Rep. Three Rivers (279,450)

*The Last Summer (of You and Me)* by Ann Brashares. Rep. Riverhead (273,314)

*The Brief Wondrous Life of Oscar Wao* by Junot Díaz. Rep. Riverhead (272,388)

*Mike's Election Guide* by Michael Moore. Orig. Grand Central (268,592)

*Second Chance* by Jane Green. Rep. Plume (265,615)

*The Wednesday Letters* by Jason F. Wright. Rep. Berkley (259,212)

*Someday* by Karen Kingsbury. Orig. Tyndale (257,749)

*The Forbidden* by Beverly Lewis. Rep. Bethany (257,530)

***Battlefield of the Mind* by Joyce Meyer. Orig. Faith Words (256,909)

*The Reader* by Bernhard Schlink. Movie tie-in. Vintage (254,701)

*A Long Way Gone* by Ishmael Beah. Rep. Sarah Crichton/FSG (250,000)

## 100,000+

**Wisdom of Our Fathers* by Tim Russert. Rep. Random (249,737)

*Same Kind of Different As Me* by Ron Hall and Denver Moore. Rep. Nelson (237,940)

***Choke* by Chuck Palahaniuk. Rep. Anchor (236,810)

***Rich Dad, Poor Dad* by Robert T. Kiyosaki with Sharon L. Lechter, C.P.A. Orig. Grand Central (233,826)

*Quiet Strength* by Tony Dungy with Nathan Whitaker. Rep. Tyndale (233,115)

*Lone Survivor* by Marcus Luttrell. Rep. Little, Brown (230,731)

*Home in Holly Springs* by Jan Karon. Rep. Penguin (229,315)

*Taming Natasha & Luring a Lady* by Nora Roberts. Reissue. Silhouette (229,000)

*I Feel Bad About My Neck* by Nora Ephron. Rep. Vintage (226,141)

*Peony in Love* by Lisa See. Rep. Random (223,924)

***Caring for Your Baby and Young Child* by Steven P. Shelov, et al. Rep. Bantam (223,040)

*Every Now and Then* by Karen Kingsbury. Orig. Zondervan (222,000)

*People of the Book* by Geraldine Brooks. Rep. Penguin (220,082)

*Falling for Rachel & Convincing Alex* by Nora Roberts. Reissue. Silhouette (220,000)

*Sarah's Key* by Tatiana de Rosnay. Rep. St. Martin's/Griffin (220,000)

*The Almost Moon* by Alice Sebold. Rep. Little, Brown (217,707)

*A Year of Fog* by Micelle Richmond. Rep. Bantam (217,069)

**A Raisin in the Sun* by Lorraine Hansberry. Movie tie-in. Vintage (210,574)

**The World Is Flat* by Thomas L. Friedman. Rep. Picador (210,000)

***Miracle Ball Method* by Elaine Petrone. Orig. Workman (205,878)

*The Double Bind* by Chris Bohjalian. Rep. Vintage (204,808)

*Animal, Vegetable, Miracle* by Barbara Kingsolver. Rep. Harper Perennial (200,000)

*Gatecrasher* by Madeleine Wickham. Rep. St. Martin's/Griffin (200,000)

*Second Glance* by Jodi Picoult. Rep. Washington Square (197,557)

*Making the Cut* by Jillian Michaels. Rep. Three Rivers (196,402)

*Out Stealing Horses* by Per Petterson. Rep. Picador (195,000)

**Broken Open* by Elizabeth Lesser. Rep. Villard (194,622)

*Homeport* by Nora Roberts. Reissue. Berkley (194,354)

*The Soloist* by Steve Lopez. Movie tie-in. Berkley (194,015)

*The Children of Hurin* by J. R. R. Tolkien. Rep. Houghton Mifflin (191,435)

#*Best Life Diet* by Bob Green. Revised. S&S (190,000)

**Fix-It and Forget-It Cookbook* by Dawn J. Ranck and Phyllis Pellman Good. Orig. Good Books (190,500)

**1000 Places to See Before You Die* by Patricia Schultz. Orig. Workman (187,173)

**The Lovely Bones* by Alice Sebold. Rep. Little, Brown (184,923)

*The Age of Turbulence* by Alan Greenspan. Rep. Penguin (179,855)

**Harvesting the Heart* by Jodi Picoult. Movie tie-in. Penguin (176,815)

*Halo* by Tobias S. Buckell. Orig. Tor (176,453)

**Your Best Life Now* by Joel Osteen. Rep. Faith Words (173,499)

**1000 Places to See Before You Die USA & Canada* by Patricia Schultz. Orig. Workman (172,150)

*The Duchess* by Amanda Foreman. Movie tie-in. Random (170,619)

**Cesar's Way* by Cesar Millan and Melissa Jo Peltier. Rep. Three Rivers (169,289)

**Love Walked In* by Marisa de los Santos. Rep. Plume (168,738)

*Godo Husband of Zebra Drive* by Alexander McCall Smith. Rep. Anchor (166,786)

*On Chesil Beach* by Ian McEwan. Rep. Anchor (166,775)

*Bridge of Sighs* by Richard Russo. Rep. Vintage (166,184)

**A Whole New Mind* by Daniel H. Pink. Rep. Riverhead (166,157)

*Shoe Addicts Anonymous* by Beth Harbison. Rep. St. Martin's/Griffin (165,000)

#*The Speed of Trust* by Stephen R. Covey. Rep. Free Press (165,000)

*Sarah* by Kaylene Johnson. Orig. Tyndale (159,919)

*#*The Boleyn Inheritance* by Philippa Gregory. Rep. Touchstone (160,000)

**Getting Things Done* by David Allen. Rep. Penguin (158,345)

*Heart Of Texas Vol. 3* by Debbie Macomber. Reissue. Mira (158,000)

**The Zombie Survival Guide* by Max Brooks. Orig. Three Rivers (157,748)

*What to Expect: The Toddler Years* by Heidi Murkoff. Revised. Workman (155,727)

*Rich Dad's Increase Your Financial IQ* by Robert T. Kiyosaki. Orig. Grand Central (155,634)

*Rant* by Chuck Palahaniuk. Rep. Anchor (154,584)

*Reflections & Dreams* by Nora Roberts. Reissue. Silhouette (154,000)

#*Einstein* by Walter Isaacson. Rep. S&S (155,000)

*Stuff White People Like* by Christian Lander. Orig. Random (151,598)

#*The White Tiger* by Aravind Adiga. Rep. Free Press (150,000)

*The Yiddish Policeman's Union* by Michael Chabon. Rep. Harper Perennial (150,000)

**Baby Proof* by Emily Giffin. Rep. St. Martin's/Griffin (150,000)

*Boom!* by Tom Brokaw. Rep. Random (148,668)

*Plain Truth* by Jodi Picoult. Rep. Washington Square (148,603)

**What Is the What* by Dave Eggers. Rep. Vintage (147,826)

*Barbecue Bible* by Steven Raichlen. Revised. Workman (145,549)

*A Sister's Hope* by Wanda Brunstetter. Orig. Barbour (145,500)

**Darkly Dreaming Dexter* by Jeff Lindsay. TV tie-in. Vintage (145,273)

*The Assault on Reason* by Al Gore. Rep. Penguin (144,543)

*Such a Pretty Fat* by Jen Lancaster. Orig. NAL (143,025)

*I Can Has Cheezburger?* by Professor Happycat, et al. Orig. Gotham (141,133)

**Suite Française* by Irene Nemirovsky. Rep. Vintage (140,810)

*Bakugan Battle Brawlers* by Cartoon Network. Movie tie-in. Del Rey (140,124)

*Better* by Atul Gawande. Rep. Picador (140,000)

*Sarah Palin: A New Kind of Leader* by Joe Hilley. Orig. Zondervan (140,000)

*Age of Miracles* by Marianne Williamson. Hay House (138,000)

*Away* by Amy Bloom. Rep. Random (136,316)

*Fireproof* by Eric Wilson. Orig./movie tie-in. Nelson (132,959)

*The Nine* by Jeffrey Toobin. Rep. Anchor (131,137)

*White Christmas Pie* by Wanda Brunstetter. Orig. Barbour (130,700)

*1000 Recordings to Hear Before You Die* by Tom Moon. Orig. Workman (130,328)

*Be the Pack Leader* by Cesar Millan and Melissa Jo Peltier. Rep. Three Rivers (129,621)

*Grace (Eventually)* by Anne Lamott. Rep. Riverhead (128,146)

*True to the Game III* by Teri Woods. Orig. Grand Central (127,803)

**Snow Flower and the Secret Fan* by Lisa See. Rep. Random (127,353)

*4th of July* by James Patterson. Rep. Grand Central (127,156)

#*Infidel* by Ayaan Hirsi Ali. Rep. Free Press (125,000)

*Then We Came to the End* by Joshua Ferris. Rep. Little, Brown (126,163)

*Quantum Wellness* by Kathy Freston. Orig. Weinstein (125,000)

*The World Without Us* by Alan Weisman. Rep. Picador (125,000)

*The Shock Doctrine* by Naomi Klein. Rep. Picador (125,000)

**Skinny Bitch in the Kitch* by Rory Freedman and Kim Barnouin. Rep. Running Press (123,589)

*Captivating* by John and Stasi Eldredge. Rep. Nelson (120,858)

*The Taste of Home Simple & Delicious Cookbook* by the editors of Taste of Home. Orig. Reader's Digest (120,000)

*Let's Play Doctor* by Mark Leyner and Billy Goldberg, M.D. Orig. Three Rivers (119,373)

**The Truth About Chuck Norris* by Ian Spector. Orig. Gotham (119,311)

*A Sister's Test* by Wanda Brunstetter. Orig. Barbour (118,850)

*Dear to Me* by Wanda Brunstetter. Repackage. Barbour (118,500)

**The Lady & Sons Savannah Country Cookbook* by Paula H. Deen. Rep. Random (118,108)

*An Irish Country Doctor* by Patrick Taylor. Rep. Tor (118,107)

#*21* by Ben Mazrich. Movie tie-in. Free Press (115,000)

*Plato and a Platypus Walk into a Bar* by Thomas Cathcart and Daniel Klein. Rep. Penguin (115,676)

**The American Academy of Pediatrics New Mother's Guide to Breastfeeding* by American Academy of Pediatrics, et al. Rep. Bantam (115,629)

#*The Zookeeper's Wife* by Diane Ackerman. Rep. Norton (115,000)

**Everyday Food* by Martha Stewart Living Magazine. Orig. Clarkson Potter (114,664)

*I Was Told There'd Be Cake* by Sloane Crosley. Orig. Riverhead (114,219)

**Emperor's Children* by Claire Messud. Rep. Vintage (113,595)

**Porn for Women* by Cambridge Women's Pornography Cooperative and Susan Anderson. Orig. Chronicle (113,000)

*The God Delusion* by Richard Dawkins. Rep. Mariner (110,946)

*Twilight Companion* by Lois Gresh. Orig. St. Martin's/Griffin (110,000)

*A New Way of Living* by Joyce Meyer. Orig. Faith Words (110,000)

**Wreck This Journal* by Keri Smith. Orig. Perigee (109,142)

*The Secret Between Us* by Barbara Delinsky. Rep. Anchor (108,792)

**Mountains Beyond Mountains* by Tracy Kidder. Rep. Random (108,459)

*Musicophilia* by Oliver Sacks. Rep. Vintage (108,308)

*Blessings* by Kim Vogel Sawyer. Orig. Barbour (108,250)

*Generation Kill* by Evan Wright. TV tie-in. Berkley (108,212)

*Last Child in the Woods* by Richard Louv. Revised. Algonquin (107,345)

**World War Z* by Max Brooks. Rep. Three Rivers (106,305)

**The Brain That Changed Itself* by Norman Doidge. Rep. Penguin (104,908)

#*Body of Lies* by David Ignatius. Movie tie-in. Norton (105,000)

*Allison's Journey* by Wanda Brunstetter. Repackage. (102,800)

*Look Me in the Eye* by John Elder Robinson. Rep. Three Rivers (102,791)

*Reposition Yourself* by T. D. Jakes. Rep. Atria (102,615)

*Captivated & Entranced* by Nora Roberts. Reissue. Silhouette (101,000)

*Dexter in the Dark* by Jeff Lindsay. TV tie-in. Vintage (100,630)

**Dearly Devoted Dexter* by Jeff Lindsay. TV tie-in. Vintage (100,420)

*The Best American Short Stories 2008* edited by Salman Rushdie. Orig. Houghton Mifflin (100,146)

*Divisadero* by Michael Ondaatje. Rep. Vintage (100,090)

*Legacy of Ashes* by Tim Weiner. Rep. Anchor (100,070)

*Last Child in the Woods* by Richard Louv. Updated. Algonquin (100,000)

*Middlesex* by Jeffrey Eugenides. Rep. Picador (100,000)

**Running with Scissors* by Augusten Burroughs. Rep. Picador (100,000)

*A Little History of the World* by E. H. Gombrich. Rep. Yale (100,000)

*Biggest Loser Family Cookbook* by Devin Alexander, et al. Orig. Rodale (100,000)

*Abs Diet for Women* by David Zinczenko and Ted Spiker. Rep. Rodale (100,000)

## Almanacs, Atlases and Annuals

*The World Almanac and Book of Facts 2009* by the editors of the World Almanac, C. Alan Joyce and Sarah Janssen. Annual. Reader's Digest (300,000)

*The Old Farmer's Almanac 2008.* Annual. Yankee (167,553)

*Europe TravelBook, 9th edition.* Annual. AAA (166,233)

*What Color Is Your Parachute? 2009* by Richard Nelson Bolles. Revised. Ten Speed (160,000)

*2008 AAA Road Atlas.* Annual. AAA (158,650)

# Children's Bestsellers: Meyer's Deep Run

### Diane Roback

Early last year booksellers were bemoaning the end of Harry Potter. That series, which ended in 2007, sold 19 million copies in its final year, and it didn't seem as though anything would be replacing it anytime soon. But how quickly things change!

In 2008, as the final volume in Stephenie Meyer's Twilight series was published (6 million copies sold) and *Twilight* the movie was released (domestic box office: $191 million), Little, Brown sold 27.5 million copies of Meyer's four vampire novels; with her adult novel *The Host* added in, that's 28.7 million Stephenie Meyer novels sold last year. A new queen has been crowned.

Sales for other blockbuster series also proved strong. The third volume in Christopher Paolini's Inheritance Cycle, *Brisingr,* sold 2.6 million copies (the series sold 3.2 million in total last year); two frontlist Wimpy Kid books sold a combined 1.8 million (3 million total for the series in 2008); and Rick Riordan's latest Percy Jackson installment sold a million copies (2.2 million for the series). Other series still doing well are Fancy Nancy, Warriors, Artemis Fowl, and Maximum Ride. And though it wasn't a new Potter title per se, J. K. Rowling's *The Tales of Beedle the Bard* sold 3.5 million copies.

One perennial kid favorite that shows no sign of slowing down is the Magic Tree House series (635,000 hardcovers sold, plus 4.2 million—mostly backlist—

paperbacks). And in more good news for Random House, parents can't get enough of Dr. Seuss; just over 5 million copies of his books sold in 2008, all (obviously) backlist.

Last summer belonged to The Clique, with the publication of five Summer Collection titles that sold a total of 1.4 million copies (along with another 1.4 million regular Clique titles).

Such media stars as the Jonas Brothers, Paula Deen, and Hannah Montana all had books by or about them turn into bestsellers. Movie versions of *The Tale of Despereaux, Prince Caspian, Inkheart, City of Ember,* and *Marley & Me* sent books for those properties soaring up the charts. And some newcomers made a splash too, including the 39 Clues series and Rufus Butler Seder's two Scanimation books, *Gallop!* and *Swing!*

## Children's Hardcover Frontlist

**300,000+**

1.  *Breaking Dawn* by Stephenie Meyer. Little, Brown/Tingley (6,051,981)
2.  *The Tales of Beedle the Bard* by J. K. Rowling, illus. by Mary GrandPré. Scholastic/Levine (3,577,183)
3.  *Brisingr* (The Inheritance Cycle) by Christopher Paolini. Knopf (2,604,642)
4.  *Diary of a Wimpy Kid No. 2: Rodrick Rules* by Jeff Kinney. Abrams/Amulet (1,222,091)
5.  *Burning Up: On Tour with the Jonas Brothers* by Kevin, Joe, and Nick Jonas. Disney-Hyperion (1,000,000)
6.  *Percy Jackson and the Olympians, Book Four: The Battle of the Labyrinth* by Rick Riordan. Disney-Hyperion (1,000,000)
7.  *Diary of a Wimpy Kid: Do-It-Yourself Book* by Jeff Kinney. Abrams/Amulet (635,240)
8.  *If You Give a Cat a Cupcake* by Laura Numeroff, illus. by Felicia Bond. HarperCollins (556,859)
9.  *Fancy Nancy's Favorite Fancy Words* by Jane O'Connor, illus. by Robin Preiss Glasser. HarperCollins (554,154)
10. *Swing!* by Rufus Butler Seder. Workman (528,212)
11. *The Final Warning* (Maximum Ride) by James Patterson. Little, Brown (519,444)
12. *The Dangerous Days of Daniel X* by James Patterson. Little, Brown (517,918)
13. *Fancy Nancy: Bonjour, Butterfly* by Jane O'Connor, illus. by Robin Preiss Glasser. HarperCollins (464,387)
14. *Artemis Fowl: The Time Paradox* by Eoin Colfer. Disney-Hyperion (406,687)
15. *Eclipse* (Special Edition) by Stephenie Meyer. Little, Brown/Tingley (345,669)
16. *The 39 Clues Book 1: The Maze of Bones* by Rick Riordan. Scholastic (321,054)

**200,000+**

17. *Paula Deen's My First Cookbook* by Paula Deen, illus. by Susan Mitchell. S&S (292,390)

18. *Hannah Montana: Backstage Pass* by M. C. King. Disney (275,069)

19. *Big Words for Little People* by Jamie Lee Curtis, illus. by Laura Cornell. HarperCollins (270,272)

20. *The 39 Clues Book 2: One False Note* by Gordon Korman. Scholastic (255,832)

21. *Dark Day in the Deep Sea* (Magic Tree House No. 39) by Mary Pope Osborne, illus. by Sal Murdocca. Random (254,699)

22. *Inkdeath* by Cornelia Funke. Scholastic/Chicken House (254,176)

23. *A Very Marley Christmas* by John Grogan, illus. by Richard Cowdrey. HarperCollins (231,061)

24. *Eve of the Emperor Penguin* (MTH No. 40) by Mary Pope Osborne, illus. by Sal Murdocca. Random (225,765)

25. *Old Bear* by Kevin Henkes. Greenwillow (212,717)

26. *Dirt on My Shirt* by Jeff Foxworthy, illus. by Steve Björkman. Harper-Collins (201,812)

**150,000+**

27. *Time for School, Mouse!* (board book) by Laura Numeroff, illus. by Felicia Bond. HarperFestival (187,772)

28. *Vote for SpongeBob* by Erica Pass, illus. by Harry Moore. Simon Spotlight (187,093)

29. *Don't Bump the Glump!* by Shel Silverstein. HarperCollins (186,592)

30. *Wall-E.* Random/Disney (184,813)

31. *Barack Obama* by Nikki Grimes, illus. by Bryan Collier. S&S (174,474)

32. *Read All About It!* by Laura Bush and Jenna Bush, illus. by Denise Brunkus. HarperCollins (170,427)

33. *Warriors: Powers of Three No. 3: Outcast* by Erin Hunter. HarperCollins (161,986)

34. *Seekers No. 1: The Quest Begins* by Erin Hunter, illus. by Gary Chalk. HarperCollins (159,893)

35. *The Pigeon Wants a Puppy!* by Mo Willems. Hyperion Books for Children (158,421)

36. *Lock and Key* by Sarah Dessen. Viking (155,604)

37. *Septimus Heap, Book Four: Queste* by Angie Sage, illus. by Mark Zug. HarperCollins (155,002)

38. *Gingerbread Friends* by Jan Brett. Putnam (152,742)

39. *The Hunger Games* by Suzanne Collins. Scholastic Press (150,873)

40. *Fancy Nancy: Let's Get Fancy Together!* by Jane O'Connor, illus. by Robin Preiss Glasser. HarperCollins (150,352)

41. *Rock the Waves* by Suzanne Harper. Disney (150,033)

**100,000+**

42. *Bolt.* Random/Disney (144,926)
43. *Alphabet* by Matthew Van Fleet. S&S/Wiseman (144,677)
44. *Tweak* by Nic Sheff. S&S/Atheneum (142,294)
45. *Warriors: Power of Three No. 4: Eclipse* by Erin Hunter. HarperCollins (136,949)
46. *Dog* by Matthew Van Fleet. S&S/Atheneum (134,857)
47. *The Battle for Skandia* (Ranger's Apprentice) by John Flanagan. Philomel (132,941)
48. *Warriors: Power of Three No. 5: Long Shadows* by Erin Hunter. Harper-Collins (132,938)
49. *Baby Einstein: Touch and Feel Farm Animals* by Julie Aigner-Clark, illus. by Nadeem Zaidi. Disney (132,850)
50. *Peek-a-Baby* by Karen Katz. S&S/Little Simon (132,552)
51. *No No Yes Yes* by Leslie Patricelli. Candlewick (132,267)
52. *It's Sharing Day!* by Kirsten Larsen, illus. by Ron Zalme. Simon Spotlight (129,039)
53. *A Giant Problem* by Holly Black, illus. by Tony DiTerlizzi. S&S (128,872)
54. *Revelations* (Blue Bloods) by Melissa de la Cruz. Disney-Hyperion (126,270)
55. *Handy Manny: Manny's Book of Tools* by Marcy Kelman. Disney (124,941)
56. *Christmas Cookies* by Amy Krouse Rosenthal, illus. by Jane Dyer. Harper-Collins (124,425)
57. *Raven Rise* by D. J. MacHale. S&S/Aladdin (124,018)
58. *How to Talk to Girls* by Alec Greven, illus. by Kei Acedera. Collins (122,720)
59. *The Graveyard Book* by Neil Gaiman, illus. by Dave McKean. Harper-Collins (122,559)
60. *The Sorcerer of the North* (Ranger's Apprentice) by John Flanagan. Philomel (120,449)
61. *Twilight* (Collector's Edition) by Stephenie Meyer. Little, Brown/Tingley (120,435)
62. *The Nixie's Song* by Holly Black, illus. by Tony DiTerlizzi. S&S (115,953)
63. *Baby Einstein: Touch and Feel Baby Animals* by Julie Aigner-Clark, illus. by Nadeem Zaidi. Disney (115,952)
64. *In Grandma's Arms* by Jayne Shelton, illus. by Karen Katz. Scholas-tic/Cartwheel (115,193)
65. *It's Time to Sleep, My Love* by Nancy Tillman, illus. by Eric Metaxas. Fei-wel and Friends (113,290)
66. *Warriors: Cats of the Clans* by Erin Hunter, illus. by Wayne McLoughlin. HarperCollins (109,918)

67.  *Big Blue Book of Beginner Books* by P. D. Eastman. Random (109,120)
68.  *The Magician* (The Secrets of the Immortal Nicholas Flamel) by Michael Scott. Delacorte (107,522)
69.  *Baby Signs* by Joy Allen. Dial (107,406)
70.  *Barack* by Jonah Winter, illus. by A. G. Ford. Collins (107,147)
71.  *Barbie and the Diamond Castle* by Mary Man-Kong. Random/Golden (105,546)
72.  *The Diamond of Darkhold* by Jeanne DuPrau. Random (105,142)
73.  *Spyology* by Spencer Blake, ed. by Dugald A. Steer. Candlewick (103,911)
74.  *Harry Potter and the Sorcerer's Stone* (anniversary edition) by J. K. Rowling, illus. by Mary GrandPré. Scholastic/Levine (103,450)
75.  *Let's Dance, Little Pookie* by Sandra Boynton. Random/Corey (102,757)
76.  *Allie Finkle's Rules for Girls Book No. 1: Moving Day* by Meg Cabot. Scholastic Press (101,543)
77.  *Old MacDonald Had a Farm* by Salina Yoon. Price Stern Sloan (100,723)

**75,000+**

78.  *Change Has Come.* Illus. by Kadir Nelson. S&S (98,793)
79.  *Fisher Price: Spring Is Here.* Reader's Digest (97,224)
80.  *The Lump of Coal* by Lemony Snicket, illus. by Brett Helquist. HarperCollins (95,990)
81.  *On a Scary Scary Night (Can You See What I See?)* by Walter Wick. Scholastic/Cartwheel (95,398)
82.  *Fisher Price: Christmas Time Is Here.* Reader's Digest (94,701)
83.  *Unbelievable* (Pretty Little Liars No. 4) by Sara Shepard. HarperTeen (93,140)
84.  *Identical* by Ellen Hopkins. S&S/McElderry (93,015)
85.  *Monsterology* by Dr. Ernest Drake, ed. by Dugald A. Steer. Candlewick (92,696)
86.  *The Big Field* by Mike Lupica. Philomel (92,208)
87.  *Disney Nursery Rhymes & Fairy Tales.* Disney (91,761)
88.  *Tinker Bell: Two Magical Tales* (Disney Fairies) by Kiki Thorpe. Random/Disney (90,900)
89.  *Narnia Chronology* by C. S. Lewis, illus. by Mark Edwards. HarperCollins (90,383)
90.  *Someday* by Alison McGhee, illus. by Peter Reynolds. S&S/Atheneum (90,211)
91.  *The Hidden World of Fairies* by Tennant Redbank. Disney (89,508)
92.  *Ladybug Girl* by Jacky Davis and David Soman. Dial (88,878)
93.  *Smash! Crash!* by Jon Scieszka, illus. by David Shannon. S&S (87,530)

94. *7 Habits of Happy Kids* by Sean Covey, illus. by Stacy Curtis. S&S (86,967)

95. *Tea for Ruby* by Sarah Ferguson, illus. by Robin Preiss Glasser. S&S/Wiseman (86,653)

96. *My Little Girl* by Tim McGraw and Tom Douglas, illus. by Julia Denos. Nelson (85,925)

97. *Snow Fairies' Skating Party* by Irene Kilpatrick, illus. by Dave Aikins. Simon Spotlight (85,456)

98. *If You Were a Penguin* by Florence Minor, illus. by Wendell Minor. HarperCollins (84,929)

99. *Grace for President* by Kelly DiPucchio, illus. by LeUyen Pham. Disney-Hyperion (84,106)

100. *Bats at the Library* by Brian Lies. Houghton (83,859)

101. *The Way We Work* by David Macaulay. Houghton/Lorraine (83,137)

102. *Barbie Magnetic Fashions: Book and Playset* by Cappi Novell. Reader's Digest (82,691)

103. *Thump, Quack, Moo* by Doreen Cronin, illus. by Betsy Lewin. S&S/Atheneum (82,223)

104. *Baby Einstein: First Words* by Julie Aigner-Clark. Disney (81,767)

105. *The Dream Collection* by Random/Disney (80,852)

106. *Glass* by Ellen Hopkins. S&S/McElderry (80,268)

107. *Save the Reindeer!* by Tone Thyne. Simon Spotlight (80,199)

108. *The House That Jack Built.* Illus. by J. P. Miller. Random/Golden Books (79,753)

109. *The Tale of Despereaux: The Deluxe Movie Storybook.* Candlewick (79,135)

110. *Where Is Baby's Birthday Cake?* by Karen Katz. S&S/Little Simon (78,316)

111. *Wicked* (Pretty Little Liars No. 5) by Sara Shepard. HarperTeen (78,155)

112. *The Battle Begins* by Rob Valois. Grosset & Dunlap (78,137)

113. *ABC3D* by Marion Bataille. Roaring Brook/Porter (78,000)

114. *Behold, No Cavities!* by Sarah Willson, illus. by Harry Moore. Simon Spotlight (77,948)

115. *We the People* by Lynne Cheney, illus. by Greg Harlin. S&S/Wiseman (77,308)

116. *Ink Exchange* by Melissa Marr. HarperCollins (77,141)

117. *Airhead* by Meg Cabot. Scholastic Point (75,747)

118. *Rumors: A Luxe Novel* by Anna Godbersen. HarperCollins (75,636)

119. *Too Many Toys* by David Shannon. Scholastic/Blue Sky (75,590)

120. *Influence* by Mary Kate and Ashley Olsen. Razorbill (75,562)

121. *Charlie Bone and the Shadow* by Jenny Nimmo. Scholastic/Orchard (75,074)

## Children's Hardcover Backlist

**300,000+**

1. *Eclipse* by Stephenie Meyer. Little, Brown/Tingley, 2007 (4,525,238)
2. *New Moon* by Stephenie Meyer. Little, Brown/Tingley, 2006 (1,430,167)
3. *Diary of a Wimpy Kid* by Jeff Kinney. Abrams/Amulet, 2007 (1,171,687)
4. *Twilight* by Stephenie Meyer. Little, Brown/Tingley, 2005 (1,138,588)
5. *Gallop!* by Rufus Butler Seder. Workman, 2007 (1,083,767)
6. *Goodnight Moon* (board book) by Margaret Wise Brown, illus. by Clement Hurd. HarperFestival, 1991 (697,763)
7. *Horton Hears a Who!* by Dr. Seuss. Random, 1954 (690,024)
8. *Green Eggs and Ham* by Dr. Seuss. Random, 1960 (554,477)
9. *The Cat in the Hat* by Dr. Seuss. Random, 1957 (430,753)
10. *Dr. Seuss's ABC: An Amazing Alphabet Book!* (board book) by Dr. Seuss. Random, 1996 (411,506)
11. *One Fish Two Fish Red Fish Blue Fish* by Dr. Seuss. Random, 1960 (395,535)
12. *Oh, the Places You'll Go!* by Dr. Seuss. Random, 1990 (383,122)
13. *The Poky Little Puppy* by Janette Lowery Sebring, illus. by Gustaf Tenggren. Golden, 2001 (382,293)
14. *Guess How Much I Love You* (all editions) by Sam McBratney, illus. by Anita Jeram. Candlewick, 1995 (356,346)
15. *Brown Bear, Brown Bear, What Do You See?* (board book) by Bill Martin, Jr., illus. by Eric Carle. Holt, 1996 (350,000)
16. *The Very Hungry Caterpillar* (board book) by Eric Carle. Philomel, 1994 (318,770)

**200,000+**

17. *Mr. Brown Can Moo! Can You?* (board book) by Dr. Seuss. Random, 1996 (299,390)
18. *I Love You Through and Through* (board book) by Bernadette Rossetti Shustak, illus. by Caroline Jay Church. Scholastic/Cartwheel, 2005 (296,188)
19. *Where Is Baby's Belly Button?* by Karen Katz. S&S/Little Simon, 2000 (277,757)
20. *Are You My Mother?* (board book) by P. D. Eastman. Random, 1998 (274,679)
21. *The Polar Express* by Chris Van Allsburg. Houghton, 1985 (273,320)
22. *The Giving Tree* by Shel Silverstein. HarperCollins, 1964 (263,523)
23. *Baby Farm Animals* by Garth Williams. Golden, 1993 (254,421)
24. *Cars.* Illus. by Ben Smiley. Golden/Disney, 2006 (252,565)
25. *Where Do Kisses Come From?* by Maria Fleming, illus. by Janice Kinnealy. Golden, 1999 (244,661)
26. *Fancy Nancy* by Jane O'Connor, illus. by Robin Preiss Glasser. HarperCollins, 2005 (238,819)
27. *Disney Bedtime Favorites.* Disney, 2007 (236,545)

28. *The Jolly Barnyard* by Annie North Bedford, illus. by Tibor Gergely. Golden, 2004 (230,495)

29. *The Story of Jesus* by Jane Werner Watson, illus. by Jerry Smath. Golden Christian, 2007 (226,865)

30. *Going-to-Bed-Book* by Sandra Boynton. S&S/Little Simon, 1982 (225,388)

31. *Mater and the Ghost Light.* Golden/Disney, 2006 (224,340)

32. *Disney High School Musical: All Access.* Disney, 2007 (217,512)

33. *Baby Einstein: Mirror Me!* by Julie Aigner-Clark. Disney, 2002 (217,189)

34. *The Monster at the End of This Book* by Jon Stone, illus. by Michael Smollin. Golden, 1999 (212,379)

35. *The Little Red Hen* by J. P. Miller. Golden, 2001 (210,721)

36. *My First Counting Book* by Lillian Moore. Golden, 2001 (208,831)

37. *Are You My Mother?* by P. D. Eastman. Random, 1960 (208,590)

38. *How the Grinch Stole Christmas* by Dr. Seuss. Random, 1957 (207,907)

**150,000+**

39. *Hop on Pop* by Dr. Seuss. Random, 1963 (196,891)

40. *On the Night You Were Born* by Nancy Tillman. Feiwel and Friends, 2006 (195,000)

41. *Moo, Baa, La La La!* by Sandra Boynton. S&S/Little Simon, 1982 (194,105)

42. *Pinkalicious* by Elizabeth Kann and Victoria Kann, illus. by Victoria Kann. HarperCollins, 2006 (192,241)

43. *Barnyard Dance!* by Sandra Boynton. Workman, 1993 (188,539)

44. *Thomas and the Big, Big Bridge* by Rev. W. Awdry. Golden, 2003 (188,048)

45. *My Little Golden Book About God* by Eloise Wilkin. Golden Christian, 2000 (187,139)

46. *Fancy Nancy and the Posh Puppy* by Jane O'Connor, illus. by Robin Preiss Glasser. HarperCollins, 2007 (184,326)

47. *Go, Dog, Go!* by P. D. Eastman. Random, 1961 (183,287)

48. *The Invention of Hugo Cabret* by Brian Selznick. Scholastic Press, 2007 (181,425)

49. *Toes, Ears, & Nose* by Marion Dane Bauer, illus. by Karen Katz. S&S/Little Simon, 2003 (171,912)

50. *The Little Mermaid.* Golden/Disney, 2003 (170,307)

51. *Belly Button Book* by Sandra Boynton. Workman, 2005 (164,187)

52. *Dress-Up.* Disney, 2004 (163,286)

53. *Good Night, Gorilla* (board book) by Peggy Rathmann. Putnam, 1996 (161,135)

54. *Fox in Socks* by Dr. Seuss. Random, 1965 (158,880)

55. *Dr. Seuss's ABC* by Dr. Seuss. Random, 1960 (157,340)

56. *Go, Dog, Go!* (board book) by P. D. Eastman. Random, 1997 (157,272)

57. *Disney Pixar Storybook Collection.* Disney, 2006 (156,894)

58. *Snuggle Puppy* by Sandra Boynton. Workman, 2003 (150,276)

**100,000+**

59. *The Absolutely True Diary of a Part-Time Indian* by Sherman Alexie. Little, Brown, 2007 (146,766)

60. *Tails* by Matthew Van Fleet. Harcourt, 2003 (144,214)

61. *Big Red Barn* (board book) by Margaret Wise Brown, illus. by Felicia Bond. HarperFestival, 1995 (140,908)

62. *Hop on Pop* (board book) by Dr. Seuss. Random, 2004 (139,718)

63. *Thomas Breaks a Promise.* Illus. by Richard Courtney. Golden, 2006 (137,234)

64. *Thirteen Reasons Why* by Jay Asher. Razorbill, 2007 (136,452)

65. *Colors* by Justine Smith, illus. by Fiona Land. Little Scholastic, 2007 (135,459)

66. *Fisher Price: Let's Go to the Zoo* (Lift the Flap). Reader's Digest (134,449)

67. *Five Little Pumpkins* (board book). Illus. by Dan Yaccarino. HarperFestival, 2003 (130,452)

68. *The Lorax* by Dr. Seuss. Random, 1971 (130,070)

69. *The Fire Engine Book* by Tibor Gergely. Golden, 2001 (125,095)

70. *If You Give a Mouse a Cookie* by Laura Numeroff, illus. by Felicia Bond. HarperCollins, 1985 (124,812)

71. *The Girls' Book: How to Be the Best at Everything* by Juliana Foster, illus. by Amanda Enright. Scholastic Nonfiction, 2007 (122,385)

72. *Hand, Hand, Fingers, Thumb* (board book) by Al Perkins. Random, 1998 (121,825)

73. *Happily Ever After Stories.* Disney, 2007 (121,780)

74. *The Boys' Book: How to Be the Best at Everything* by Dominique Enright and Guy Macdonald, illus. by Nikalas Catlow. Scholastic Nonfiction, 2007 (121,639)

75. *I Can Read with My Eyes Shut!* by Dr. Seuss. Random, 1978 (118,606)

76. *Disney Princess Collection.* Disney, 2006 (118,411)

77. *Sleeping Beauty* by Michael Teitelbaum. Random/Disney, 2004 (116,914)

78. *The Foot Book* (board book) by Dr. Seuss. Random, 1996 (114,275)

79. *Harry Potter and the Deathly Hallows* by J. K. Rowling, illus. by Mary GrandPré. Scholastic/Levine, 2007 (113,376)

80. *Noah's Ark* by Barbara Shook Hazen, illus. by Mircea Catusanu. Golden, 2003 (111,504)

81. *Where the Wild Things Are* by Maurice Sendak. HarperCollins, 1963 (111,005)

82. *Ten Apples Up On Top!* by Dr. Seuss as Theo. LeSieg. Random, 1961 (110,658)

83. *Bad Dog, Marley!* by John Grogan, illus. by Richard Cowdrey. Harper-Collins, 2007 (110,568)

84. *Put Me in the Zoo* (board book) by Robert Lopshire. Random, 2001 (110,412)

85. *The Nose Book* (board book) by Al Perkins, illus. by Joe Mathieu. Random, 2003 (110,254)

86. *Polar Bear, Polar Bear, What Do You Hear?* (board book) by Bill Martin, Jr., illus. by Eric Carle. Holt, 2006 (110,000)

87. *Put Me in the Zoo* by Robert Lopshire. Random, 1960 (109,470)

88. *Clap Your Hands.* Illus. by Joseph Ewers. Random, 2002 (108,484)

89. *The Saggy Baggy Elephant Book* by K. and B. Jackson, illus. by Gustaf Tenggren. Golden, 1999 (108,051)

90. *Disney Storybook Collection.* Disney, 2006 (106,058)

91. *Purplicious* by Elizabeth Kann and Victoria Kann, illus. by Victoria Kann. HarperCollins, 2007 (105,631)

92. *Where's Spot?* (board book) by Eric Hill. Putnam, 2003 (104,582)

93. *Sesame Street: Guess Who, Elmo!* Reader's Digest (103,404)

94. *Eldest* (The Inheritance Cycle) by Christopher Paolini. Knopf, 2005 (102,882)

95. *Baby's First Book* by Garth Williams. Golden, 2007 (102,183)

96. *Eragon* (The Inheritance Cycle) by Christopher Paolini. Knopf, 2003 (100,744)

97. *Scholastic Children's Dictionary.* Scholastic Reference, 2007 (100,326)

98. *Panda Bear, Panda Bear, What Do You See?* (board book) by Bill Martin, Jr., illus. by Eric Carle. Holt, 1997 (100,000)

**75,000+**

99. *So Big!* by Anna Jane Hays, illus. by Christopher Moroney. Random, 2003 (99,658)

100. *Baby Einstein: Alphabooks* by Julie Aigner-Clark, illus. by Nadeem Zaidi. Disney, 2005 (99,574)

101. *Where Is Baby's Pumpkin?* by Karen Katz. S&S/Little Simon, 2006 (98,974)

102. *There's a Wocket in My Pocket!* (board book) by Dr. Seuss. Random, 1996 (98,620)

103. *100 Bible Stories, 100 Bible Songs* by Stephen Elkins, illus. by Tim O'Connor. Nelson (98,418)

104. *I Love You Because You're You* (board book) by Lisa Baker, illus. by David McPhail. Scholastic/Cartwheel, 2007 (97,430)

105. *Fisher Price: My Little People Farm.* Reader's Digest (96,767)

106. *Dora's Backpack* by Sarah Willson, illus. by Robert Roper. Simon Spotlight, 2002 (96,314)

107. *The Alphabet Book* (board book) by P. D. Eastman. Random, 2000 (95,562)

108. *Ten Apples Up on Top!* (board book) by Dr. Seuss. Random, 1998 (95,480)

109. *The Runaway Bunny* (board book) by Margaret Wise Brown, illus. by Clement Hurd. HarperFestival, 1991 (95,382)

110. *Good Masters! Sweet Ladies!* by Laura Amy Schlitz, illus. by Robert Byrd. Candlewick, 2007 (95,378)

111. *Rudolph the Red-Nosed Reindeer.* Illus. by Arkadia. Golden, 2000 (94,277)

112. *I Spy Christmas* by Jean Marzollo and Carol D. Carson, illus. by Walter Wick. Scholastic/Cartwheel, 1992 (93,032)

113. *Field Guide* (The Spiderwick Chronicles) by Holly Black, illus. by Tony DiTerlizzi. S&S, 2003 (92,325)

114. *Fisher-Price: Who Lives in the Rainforest?* by Nora Pelizzari. HarperFestival, 2007 (91,840)

115. *What's Wrong, Little Pookie?* by Sandra Boynton. Random/Corey, 2007 (90,105)

116. *Cross My Heart and Hope to Spy* by Ally Carter. Disney-Hyperion, 2007 (89,899)

117. *The Christmas Story* by Jane Werner Watson. Golden, 2000 (89,443)

118. *The Sweet Far Thing* (Gemma Doyle Trilogy) by Libba Bray. Delacorte, 2007 (88,127)

119. *101 Dalmatians* by Justine Korman, illus. by Bill Langley and Ron Dias. Golden/Disney, 2007 (87,491)

120. *Yertle the Turtle and Other Stories Party Edition* by Dr. Seuss. Random, 1958 (87,290)

121. *Junie B., First Grader: Jingle Bells, Batman Smells! (P.S. So Does May.)* (Junie B. Jones) by Barbara Park, illus. by Denise Brunkus. Random, 2005 (87,176)

122. *Warriors: Power of Three No. 2: Dark River* by Erin Hunter. HarperCollins, 2007 (85,295)

123. *Knuffle Bunny Too: A Case of Mistaken Identity* by Mo Willems. Hyperion Books for Children, 2007 (85,282)

124. *I'm a Big Sister* by Joanna Cole, illus. by Maxie Chambliss. HarperCollins, 1997 (84,513)

125. *The Night Before Christmas* by Clement C. Moore, illus. by Mircea Catusanu. Golden, 2001 (84,324)

126. *The Shy Little Kitten* by Cathleen Schurr, illus. by Gustaf Tenggren. Golden, 1999 (83,843)

127. *Scuffy the Tugboat* by Gertrude Crampton, illus. by Tibor Gergely. Golden, 2001 (83,108)

128. *Counting Kisses* by Karen Katz. S&S/Little Simon, 2003 (83,040)

129. *Don't Let the Pigeon Drive the Bus!* by Mo Willems. Hyperion Books for Children, 2003 (82,724)

130. *I'm a Big Brother* by Joanna Cole, illus. by Maxie Chambliss. HarperCollins, 1997 (82,107)

131. *Blue Hat, Green Hat* by Sandra Boynton. S&S/Little Simon, 1984 (81,604)

132. *My First Read and Learn Book of Prayers.* American Bible Society. Scholastic/Little Shepherd, 2007 (80,050)

133. *Where the Sidewalk Ends 30th Anniversary Edition* by Shel Silverstein. HarperCollins, 2003 (79,971)

134. *Oh, the Thinks You Can Think!* by Dr. Seuss. Random, 1975 (79,734)

135. *Haunted Castle on Hallows Eve* (Magic Tree House No. 30) by Mary Pope Osborne, illus. by Sal Murdocca. Random, 2003 (79,713)

136. *The Night Before Christmas* by Clement C. Moore, illus. by Mary Engelbreit. HarperCollins, 2002 (79,379)

137. *Knuffle Bunny: A Cautionary Tale* by Mo Willems. Hyperion Books for Children, 2004 (77,670)

138. *Fisher-Price: All About My Day* by Laura Marchesani. HarperFestival, 2007 (76,893)

139. *There's No Place Like Space* by Tish Rabe, illus. by Aristides Ruiz. Random, 1999 (76,803)

140. *The Little Red Caboose* by Marian Potter. Golden, 2000 (76,722)

141. *I Am Not Going to Get Up Today!* by Dr. Seuss, illus. by James Stevenson. Random, 1987 (76,500)

142. *I Love You, Stinky Face* (board book) by Lisa McCourt, illus. by Cyd Moore. Scholastic/Cartwheel, 2004 (76,037)

143. *From Head to Toe* (board book) by Eric Carle. HarperFestival, 1999 (75,743)

144. *Star Wars: A Pop-Up Guide to the Galaxy* by Matthew Reinhart. Scholastic/Orchard, 2007 (75,711)

145. *Sesame Street: Music Player and Storybook.* Reader's Digest (75,631)

146. *Wacky Wednesday* by Dr. Seuss as Theo. LeSieg. Random, 1974 (75,577)

147. *Olivia* by Ian Falconer. S&S/Atheneum, 2004 (75,567)

148. *First the Egg* by Laura Vaccaro Seeger. Roaring Brook/Porter, 2007 (75,500)

149. *Summer of the Sea Serpent* (MTH No. 31) by Mary Pope Osborne, illus. by Sal Murdocca. Random, 2004 (75,402)

150. *My Best Friend Is a Princess: A Princess Friendship Treasury.* Random/Disney, 2007 (75,333)

151. *Horton Hatches the Egg* by Dr. Seuss. Random, 1940 (75,025)

## Children's Paperback Frontlist

**300,000+**

1. *New Moon* by Stephenie Meyer. Little, Brown/Tingley (5,309,229)

2. *Twilight* (mass market edition) by Stephenie Meyer. Little, Brown/Tingley (1,872,408)

3. *Twilight* (media tie-in edition) by Stephenie Meyer. Little, Brown/Tingley (982,034)

4. *Saving the World and Other Extreme Sports* (Maximum Ride) (mass market edition) by James Patterson. Little, Brown (799,631)

5. *Fancy Nancy and the Boy from Paris* by Jane O'Connor, illus. by Robin Preiss Glasser. HarperCollins (730,499)

6. *Fancy Nancy at the Museum* by Jane O'Connor, illus. by Robin Preiss Glasser. HarperCollins (657,311)

7. *Bratfest at Tiffany's* (Clique No. 9) by Lisi Harrison. Little, Brown/Poppy (463,502)

8. *Twilight: The Complete Illustrated Movie Companion* by Mark Cotta Vaz. Little, Brown (442,361)

9. *Marley* by John Grogan. Collins (394,681)

10. *Disney High School Musical 3 Junior Novel* by N. B. Grace. Disney (367,518)

11. *Fancy Nancy Sees Stars* by Jane O'Connor, illus. by Robin Preiss Glasser. HarperCollins (366,037)

12. *Prince Caspian* (movie tie-in edition) by C. S. Lewis, illus. by Pauline Baynes. HarperFestival (364,864)

13. *Percy Jackson and the Olympians, Book Three: The Titan's Curse* by Rick Riordan. Disney-Hyperion (341,192)

14. *Massie* (Clique Summer Collection No. 1) by Lisi Harrison. Little, Brown/Poppy (340,343)

15. *Hannah Montana: Don't Bet on It* by Ann Lloyd. Disney (336,815)

16. *Dora Saves the Snow Princess* by Phoebe Beinstein, illus. by Dave Aikins. Simon Spotlight (321,933)

**200,000+**

17. *A Fairy Tale* (Step into Reading). Random/Disney (299,969)

18. *Dylan* (Clique Summer Collection No. 2) by Lisi Harrison. Little, Brown/Poppy (297,941)

19. *Alicia* (Clique Summer Collection No. 3) by Lisi Harrison. Little, Brown/Poppy (285,793)

20. *Forever in Blue: The Fourth Summer of the Sisterhood* by Ann Brashares. Delacorte (279,779)

21. *Camp Rock: The Junior Novel* by Lucy Ruggles. Disney (278,546)

22. *Smash Trash!* (Step into Reading). Random/Disney (252,394)

23. *Kristen* (Clique Summer Collection No. 4) by Lisi Harrison. Little, Brown/Poppy (237,426)

24. *Thomas and the Treasure* by Schuyler Hooke, illus. by Richard Courtney. Random (232,579)

25. *A Guide to Pixie Hollow.* Random/Disney (228,122)

26. *Claire* (Clique Summer Collection No. 5) by Lisi Harrison. Little, Brown/Poppy (224,924)

27. *Roadwork.* Illus. by Art Mawhinney. Random/Disney (223,768)

28. *The Sweetest Spring* (Step into Reading) by Apple Jordan, illus. by Gabriella Matta and Francesco Legramandi. Random/Disney (223,285)
29. *Just Listen* by Sarah Dessen. Puffin (209,631)
30. *Barbie and the Diamond Castle: A Storybook* by Mary Man-Kong. Golden (207,225)
31. *Love at First Beep* (Step into Reading). Random/Disney (201,592)
32. *Barbie: Mariposa* by Mary Man-Kong, illus. by Golden Books. Golden (200,328)

## 150,000+

33. *Hannah Montana: Sweet Revenge* by M. C. King. Disney (197,428)
34. *The Great Fairy Race* (Step into Reading). Random/Disney (194,488)
35. *Star Wars: The Clone Wars* by Tracey West. Grosset & Dunlap (190,700)
36. *Inheritance Cycle Omnibus: Eragon and Eldest* by Christopher Paolini. Knopf (188,613)
37. *Battle at Teth* (Star Wars: The Clone Wars) by Kirsten Mayer. Grosset & Dunlap (186,282)
38. *Marley & Me: Meet Marley* by Natalie Engel. HarperCollins (185,318)
39. *Revenge of the Living Dummy* (Goosebumps HorrorLand No. 1) by R. L. Stine. Scholastic (184,669)
40. *The Sisterhood of the Traveling Pants 2* by Ann Brashares. Delacorte (182,804)
41. *Jammin' with the Jonas Brothers: An Unauthorized Biography* by Lexi Ryals. Price Stern Sloan (177,561)
42. *The Mysterious Benedict Society* by Trenton Lee Stewart. Little, Brown/Tingley (175,066)
43. *Madagascar: Escape 2 Africa: Father and Son Save the Day* by Gail Herman, illus. by Lydia Halverson. HarperCollins (170,184)
44. *Mickey Mouse Clubhouse: Minnie's Rainbow* by Sheila Sweeny Higginson. Disney (169,825)
45. *Gossip Girl: The Carlyles No. 1.* Cecily von Ziegesar. Little, Brown/Poppy (169,753)
46. *Who Bob What Pants?* by Emily Sollinger, illus. by Stephen Reed. Simon Spotlight (166,528)
47. *Creep from the Deep* (Goosebumps HorrorLand No. 2) by R. L. Stine. Scholastic (165,933)
48. *Disney High School Musical: Stories from East High: Friends 4Ever?* by Catherine Hapka. Disney (164,205)
49. *Thomas and Friends: Steam Engine Stories* by Rev. W. Awdry, illus. by Richard Courtney. Random (158,400)
50. *Dragon of the Red Dawn* (Magic Tree House No. 37) by Mary Pope Osborne, illus. by Sal Murdocca. Random (157,695)
51. *The Little Mermaid: Ariel's Beginning.* Random/Disney (157,459)

52. *Clementine* by Sara Pennypacker. Disney-Hyperion (156,832)
53. *Hannah Montana: True Blue* by Laurie McElroy. Disney (155,074)
54. *Hannah Montana: Win or Lose* by Heather Alexander. Disney (154,252)
55. *The New Padawan* (Star Wars: The Clone Wars) by Eric Stevens. Grosset & Dunlap (152,661)
56. *Silvermist and the Ladybug Curse* (Disney Fairies) by Gail Herman. Random/Disney (150,457)
57. *Disney High School Musical: Stories from East High: Get Your Vote On!* by N. B. Grace and Beth Beechwood. Disney (150,220)
58. *My Hero* (Step into Reading). Random/Disney (150,181)

**100,000+**

59. *Iron Man: I Am Iron Man!* by Lisa Rao, illus. by Guido Guidi. Harper-Collins (149,832)
60. *Camp Rock Poster Book.* Disney (146,804)
61. *Dulcie's Taste of Magic* (Disney Fairies) by Gail Herman. Random/Disney (144,301)
62. *Fancy Nancy's Fashion Parade!* by Jane O'Connor, illus. by Robin Preiss Glasser. HarperFestival (140,916)
63. *Kung Fu Panda: Meet the Masters* by Catherine Hapka, illus. by Lydia Halverson. HarperCollins (139,156)
64. *Rogue Robots!* Random/Disney (138,841)
65. *Tinker Bell Junior Novel.* Random/Disney (138,315)
66. *Disney High School Musical 3: A Prom to Remember* by Sarah Nathan. Disney (137,274)
67. *The Scream of the Haunted Mask* (Goosebumps HorrorLand No. 4) by R. L. Stine. Scholastic (135,016)
68. *Camp Rock: Say What? A Jammin' Fill-in Story* by Avery Scott. Disney (134,163)
69. *Kung Fu Panda: The Junior Novel* by Susan Korman. HarperFestival (133,952)
70. *Disney High School Musical 3: Making Memories* by Sarah Nathan. Disney (133,536)
71. *Barbie Mariposa* (Step into Reading) by Christy Webster. Random (133,485)
72. *The Tale of Despereaux Movie Tie-In Junior Novelization* by Jamie Michalak. Candlewick (131,430)
73. *Mia* by Laurence Yep, illus. by Robert Papp. American Girl (131,368)
74. *Barbies and the Diamond Castle* (Step into Reading) by Kristen Depken. Random (128,769)
75. *Super Friends: Flying High* (Step into Reading). Illus. by DC Comics. Random (126,633)
76. *Monster Blood for Breakfast* (Goosebumps HorrorLand No. 3) by R. L. Stine. Scholastic (125,113)

77. *The Lost Colony* by Eoin Colfer. Disney-Hyperion (123,943)

78. *Tempted* (The It Girl No. 6) by Cecily von Ziegesar. Poppy (123,302)

79. *Emily Windsnap and the Castle in the Mist* by Liz Kessler, illus. by Sarah Gibb. Candlewick (122,600)

80. *Warriors: Power of Three No. 1: The Sight* by Erin Hunter. HarperCollins (121,389)

81. *Just Jonas! The Jonas Brothers Up Close and Personal.* Scholastic (120,484)

82. *Marley & Me: Marley to the Rescue!* by M. K. Gaudet. HarperCollins (120,406)

83. *Intergalactic Adventure: Activity Book* (Star Wars: The Clone Wars). Grosset & Dunlap (119,621)

84. *Madagascar: Escape 2 Africa: The Gang's All Here!* by Annie Auerbach. HarperFestival (117,078)

85. *Night World No. 1* by L. J. Smith. Simon Pulse (116,488)

86. *Hannah Montana: The Official Trivia & Quiz Book* by Emma Harrison. Disney (116,241)

87. *Shadow Kiss* (Vampire Academy 3) by Richelle Mead. Razorbill (116,125)

88. *The Alchemyst* (The Secrets of the Immortal Nicholas Flamel) by Michael Scott. Delacorte (115,422)

89. *Indiana Jones and the Kingdom of the Crystal Skull.* Scholastic (115,161)

90. *Prince Caspian: This Is Narnia* by Jennifer Frantz. HarperCollins (114,045)

91. *The Fairy Berry Bake-Off* (Step into Reading). Random/Disney (113,590)

92. *Camp Rock: Second Session: Play It Again* by Phoebe Appleton. Disney (113,297)

93. *SpongeBob's Slap Shot* by David Lewman, illus. by Harry Moore. Simon Spotlight (113,054)

94. *Warriors Super Edition: Firestar's Quest* by Erin Hunter, illus. by Gary Chalk. HarperCollins (112,775)

95. *Rapunzel* (Littlest Pet Shop). Scholastic (112,646)

96. *Lights, Camera, Action!* Random/Disney (112,350)

97. *Wall-E Junior Novel.* Random/Disney (112,002)

98. *Hannah Montana: Season's Greetings: A Book of Rockin' Holiday Cards.* Disney (111,098)

99. *Katie the Kitten Fairy* (Pet Fairies No. 1). Scholastic (110,551)

100. *Small Steps* by Louis Sachar. Delacorte (109,384)

101. *Lauren the Puppy Fairy* (Pet Fairies No. 4). Scholastic (109,302)

102. *Marley* (movie tie-in edition) by John Grogan. HarperFestival (108,950)

103. *The Dark Knight: I Am Batman* by Catherine Hapka, illus. by Adrian Barrios. HarperCollins (108,631)

104. *Masquerade* (Blue Bloods) by Melissa de la Cruz. Disney-Hyperion (108,611)

105. *Warriors: Tigerstar and Sasha No. 1: Into the Woods* by Erin Hunter, illus. by Don Hudson. HarperCollins (108,186)

106. *Fancy Nancy: Poison Ivy Expert* by Jane O'Connor, illus. by Robin Preiss Glassser. HarperCollins (107,762)

107. *Prince Caspian: Lucy's Journey* by Jennifer Frantz. HarperCollins (107,279)

108. *Teacher's Pet* (Littlest Pet Shop). Scholastic (107,266)

109. *Wicked Lovely* by Melissa Marr. HarperTeen (107,031)

110. *The Icebound Land* (Ranger's Apprentice) by John Flanagan. Puffin (106,787)

111. *The Cricket in Times Square* by George Selden, illus. by Garth Williams. Macmillan/Square Fish (106,680)

112. *Disney High School Musical: Stories from East High Super Special: Under the Stars* by Helen Perelman-Bernstein. Disney (106,615)

113. *Little Critter: It's Earth Day!* by Mercer Mayer. HarperFestival (105,698)

114. *Disney High School Musical 3 Poster Book.* Disney (105,684)

115. *You Just Can't Get Enough* (Gossip Girl: The Carlyles No. 2) by Cecily von Ziegesar. Little, Brown/Poppy (103,599)

116. *Hannah Montana: On the Road* by Kitty Richards. Disney (103,214)

117. *Star Wars Fandex* by Christopher Cerasi. Workman (103,191)

118. *Tranformers Animated: Robot Roll Call* by Jennifer Frantz. HarperCollins (102,886)

119. *Fawn and the Mysterious Trickster* (Disney Fairies) by Laura Driscoll. Random (102,666)

120. *Septimus Heap, Book Three: Physik* by Angie Sage, illus. by Mark Zug. HarperCollins (101,837)

121. *Stink and the World's Worst Super-Stinky Sneakers* by Megan McDonald, illus. by Peter H. Reynolds. Candlewick (101,639)

122. *Never Underestimate Your Dumbness* (Dear Dumb Diary No. 7) by Jim Benton. Scholastic (101,272)

123. *Wow! Wow! Wubsy! Special Delivery.* Scholastic (101,192)

124. *Never Glue Your Friends to Chairs* (Roscoe Riley Rules No. 1) by Katherine Applegate, illus. by Brian Biggs. HarperCollins (101,008)

125. *The Tale of Despereaux: No Ordinary Mouse.* Candlewick (100,528)

126. *Frostbite (*Vampire Academy 2) by Richelle Mead. Razorbill (100,476)

## Children's Paperback Backlist

**300,000+**

1. *Twilight* by Stephenie Meyer. Little, Brown/Tingley, 2006 (5,698,941)

2. *The Tale of Despereaux* by Kate DiCamillo, illus. by Timothy Basil Ering. Candlewick, 2006 (507,054)

3. *Percy Jackson and the Olympians: Book One: The Lightning Thief* by Rick Riordan. Disney-Hyperion, 2006 (502,372)

4. *The Giver* by Lois Lowry. Delacorte/Laurel Leaf, 1994 (470,315)

5. *Dinosaurs Before Dark* (Magic Tree House No. 1) by Mary Pope Osborne, illus. by Sal Murdocca. Random, 1992 (396,008)

6. *Prince Caspian* by C. S. Lewis, illus. by Pauline Baynes. HarperCollins, 2002 (393,405)

7. *Eldest* (The Inheritance Cycle) by Christopher Paolini. Knopf, 2007 (369,546)

8. *The Outsiders* by S. E. Hinton. Puffin, 1997 (357,855)

9. *The City of Ember* (The Books of Ember) by Jeanne DuPrau. Random/Yearling, 2004 (349,038)

10. *Hannah Montana: Keeping Secrets* by Beth Beechwood. Disney, 2006 (341,361)

11. *Percy Jackson and the Olympians: Book Two: The Sea of Monsters* by Rick Riordan. Disney-Hyperion, 2007 (336,895)

12. *Hannah Montana: Super Sneak* by Laurie McElroy. Disney, 2006 (328,324)

13. *Old, New, Red, Blue!* (Step into Reading). Random/Disney, 2006 (315,167)

14. *The Care & Keeping of You: The Body Book for Girls* by Valorie Schaefer, illus. by Norm Bendel. American Girl, 1998 (312,783)

15. *The Lion, the Witch and the Wardrobe* by C. S. Lewis, illus. by Pauline Baynes. HarperCollins, 2002 (311,413)

16. *What Is a Princess?* (Step into Reading). Random/Disney, 2004 (310,066)

17. *Hannah Montana: Face-Off* by Alice Alfonsi. Disney, 2006 (305,030)

18. *Hannah Montana: Truth or Dare* by M. C. King. Disney, 2007 (302,654)

**200,000+**

19. *Hannah Montana: Face the Music* by Beth Beechwood. Disney, 2007 (296,064)

20. *The Second Summer of the Sisterhood* by Ann Brashares. Delacorte, 2004 (295,246)

21. *The Book Thief* by Markus Zusak. Knopf, 2007 (291,661)

22. *Eragon* (The Inheritance Cycle) by Christopher Paolini. Knopf, 2005 (289,521)

23. *Mummies in the Morning* (MTH No. 3) by Mary Pope Osborne, illus. by Sal Murdocca. Random, 1993 (265,730)

24. *Amelia Bedelia* by Peggy Parish, illus. by Fritz Siebel. HarperCollins, 1992 (262,865)

25. *The Knight at Dawn* (MTH No. 2) by Mary Pope Osborne, illus. by Sal Murdocca. Random, 1993 (261,812)

26. *Pirates Past Noon* (MTH No. 4) by Mary Pope Osborne, illus. by Sal Murdocca. Random, 1994 (256,431)

27. *The Sisterhood of the Traveling Pants* by Ann Brashares. Delacorte/Dell, 2003 (255,173)

28. *Holes* by Louis Sachar. Yearling/Laurel Leaf, 2000 (249,251)

29. *The Magician's Nephew* by C. S. Lewis, illus. by Pauline Baynes. Harper-Collins, 2002 (247,034)

30. *Where the Wild Things Are* by Maurice Sendak. HarperCollins, 1988 (242,186)

31. *Hannah Montana: Seeing Green* by M. C. King. Disney, 2007 (238,329)

32. *Biscuit's Day at the Farm* by Alyssa Satin Capucilli, illus. by Pat Schories. HarperCollins, 2007 (236,719)

33. *Biscuit* by Alyssa Satin Capucilli, illus. by Pat Schories. HarperCollins, 1997 (232,280)

34. *A Horse to Love* (Enchanted Stables). Random/Disney, 2007 (229,844)

35. *Hannah Montana: Nightmare on Hannah Street* by Laurie McElroy. Disney, 2007 (225,028)

36. *Danny and the Dinosaur* by Syd Hoff. HarperCollins, 1992 (224,184)

37. *A Wrinkle in Time* by Madeleine L'Engle. Macmillan/Square Fish, 2007 (223,625)

38. *Number the Stars* by Lois Lowry. Yearling/Laurel Leaf, 1990 (223,495)

39. *Speak* by Laurie Halse Anderson. Puffin, 2006 (214,018)

40. *Love You Forever* by Robert Munsch, illus. by Sheila McGraw. Firefly, 1986 (208,830)

41. *The Horse and His Boy* by C. S. Lewis, illus. by Pauline Baynes. HarperCollins, 2002 (206,672)

42. *Transformers: Meet the Autobots* by Jennifer Frantz, illus. by Guido Guidi. HarperCollins, 2007 (206,435)

43. *Junie B. Jones and the Stupid Smelly Bus* (Junie B. Jones No. 1) by Barbara Park, illus. by Denise Brunkus. Random, 1992 (202,416)

44. *Night of the Ninjas* (MTH No. 5) by Mary Pope Osborne, illus. by Sal Murdocca. Random, 1995 (201,150)

## 150,000+

45. *The Voyage of the Dawn Treader* by C. S. Lewis, illus. by Pauline Baynes. HarperCollins, 2002 (197,407)

46. *Fancy Nancy Loves! Loves!! Loves!!!* by Jane O'Connor, illus. by Robin Preiss Glasser. HarperFestival, 2007 (192,332)

47. *The Boy in the Striped Pajamas* by John Boyne. Random/Fickling, 2007 (191,596)

48. *The Silver Chair* by C. S. Lewis, illus. by Pauline Baynes. HarperCollins, 2002 (190,467)

49. *Barbie Loves Pets.* Illus. by Jiyoung An. Golden, 2007 (189,235)

50. *The Last Battle* by C. S. Lewis, illus. by Pauline Baynes. HarperCollins, 2002 (189,101)

51. *Pat the Bunny* by Dorothy Kunhardt. Golden, 2001 (188,341)

52. *Hannah Montana: Hold on Tight* by Laurie McElroy. Disney, 2007 (184,527)

53. *Hannah Montana: Crush-Tastic!* by Beth Beechwood. Disney, 2007 (182,372)

54. *Junie B., First Grader: Toothless Wonder* (JBJ No. 20) by Barbara Park, illus. by Denise Brunkus. Random, 2003 (181,699)

55. *Biscuit Goes to School* by Alyssa Satin Capucilli, illus. by Pat Schories. HarperCollins, 2003 (177,898)

56. *Afternoon on the Amazon* (MTH No. 6) by Mary Pope Osborne, illus. by Sal Murdocca. Random, 1995 (177,542)

57. *Harry Potter and the Sorcerer's Stone* by J. K. Rowling, illus. by Mary GrandPré. Scholastic/Levine, 1999 (177,133)

58. *The Cat in the Hat: Cooking with the Cat* by Bonnie Worth, illus. by Christopher Moroney. Random, 2003 (177,053)

59. *Driving Buddies* (Step into Reading). Random/Disney, 2006 (177,019)

60. *Midnight on the Moon* (MTH No. 8) by Mary Pope Osborne, illus. by Sal Murdocca. Random, 1996 (176,363)

61. *Dolphins at Daybreak* (MTH No. 9) by Mary Pope Osborne, illus. by Sal Murdocca. Random, 1997 (175,492)

62. *Maniac Magee* by Jerry Spinelli. Little, Brown, 1999 (175,378)

63. *Ramona Quimby, Age 8* by Beverly Cleary, illus. by Tracy Dockray. HarperCollins, 1992 (175,077)

64. *Frog and Toad Are Friends* by Arnold Lobel. HarperCollins, 1979 (172,449)

65. *Junie B. Jones and Her Big Fat Mouth* (JBJ No. 3) by Barbara Park, illus. by Denise Brunkus. Random, 1993 (172,017)

66. *Polar Bears Past Bedtime* (MTH No. 12) by Mary Pope Osborne, illus. by Sal Murdocca. Random, 1998 (171,942)

67. *Meet Kit* by Valerie Tripp, illus. by Walter Rane. American Girl, 2000 (171,908)

68. *Harry Potter and the Half-Blood Prince* by J. K. Rowling, illus. by Mary GrandPré. Scholastic/Levine, 2006 (171,680)

69. *Island of the Blue Dolphins* by Scott O'Dell. Yearling/Laurel Leaf, 1987 (167,710)

70. *Frindle* by Andrew Clements, illus. by Brian Selznick. S&S/Aladdin, 1998 (167,432)

71. *Junie B. Jones and Some Sneaky Peeky Spying* (JBJ No. 4) by Barbara Park, illus. by Denise Brunkus. Random, 1994 (166,793)

72. *Junie B. Jones and a Little Monkey Business* (JBJ No. 2) by Barbara Park, illus. by Denise Brunkus. Random, 1993 (161,953)

73. *I'd Tell You I Love You, but Then I'd Have to Kill You* by Ally Carter. Disney-Hyperion, 2007 (159,730)

74. *Blizzard of the Blue Moon* (MTH No. 36) by Mary Pope Osborne, illus. by Sal Murdocca. Random, 2007 (159,662)

75. *Blue Bloods* by Melissa de la Cruz. Disney-Hyperion, 2007 (159,587)

76. *Hatchet* by Gary Paulsen. S&S/Aladdin, 2006 (159,459)

77. *Sunset of the Sabertooth* (MTH No. 7) by Mary Pope Osborne, illus. by Sal Murdocca. Random, 1996 (158,020)

78. *Tales of a Fourth Grade Nothing* by Judy Blume. Puffin (155,360)

79. *Ghost Town at Sundown* (MTH No. 10) by Mary Pope Osborne, illus. by Sal Murdocca. Random, 1997 (155,113)

80. *The Clique* by Lisi Harrison. Little, Brown/Poppy, 2004 (154,102)

81. *The Lost Dinosaur Bone* (Little Critter) by Mercer Mayer. HarperFestival, 2007 (152,756)

82. *Vacation Under the Volcano* (MTH No. 13) by Mary Pope Osborne, illus. by Sal Murdocca. Random, 1998 (151,813)

83. *Warriors No. 1: Into the Wild* by Erin Hunter. HarperCollins, 2003 (150,637)

**100,000+**

84. *Warriors: The New Prophecy No. 1: Midnight* by Erin Hunter. Harper-Collins, 2006 (149,146)

85. *Where the Red Fern Grows* by Wilson Rawls. Yearling/Laurel Leaf, 1997 (149,118)

86. *Uglies* by Scott Westerfeld. Simon Pulse, 2005 (147,998)

87. *Hour of the Olympics* (MTH No. 16) by Mary Pope Osborne, illus. by Sal Murdocca. Random, 1998 (147,293)

88. *Captain Underpants and the Perilous Plot of Professor Poopypants* by Dav Pilkey. Scholastic, 2000 (147,085)

89. *B Is for Books!* (Step into Reading) by Annie Cobb. Random, 1996 (146,761)

90. *Monster* by Walter Dean Myers. HarperCollins/Amistad, 2001 (146,075)

91. *The Vampire Diaries: The Awakening and The Struggle.* L. J. Smith. Harper-Teen, 2007 (144,990)

92. *Patch* (Stablemates). Scholastic, 2007 (144,784)

93. *The Mouse and the Motorcycle* by Beverly Cleary, illus. by Tracy Dockray. HarperCollins, 1990 (144,504)

94. *Day of the Dragon-King* (MTH No. 14) by Mary Pope Osborne, illus. by Sal Murdocca. Random, 1998 (143,587)

95. *Lions at Lunchtime* (MTH No. 11) by Mary Pope Osborne, illus. by Sal Murdocca. Random, 1998 (142,541)

96. *Bud, Not Buddy* by Christopher Paul Curtis. Yearling/Laurel Leaf, 2002 (142,514)

97. *Disney High School Musical: Stories from East High: Wildcat Spirit* by Catherine Hapka. Disney, 2007 (142,128)

98. *Bathtime for Biscuit* by Alyssa Satin Capucilli, illus. by Pat Schories. HarperCollins, 1999 (140,768)

99. *Flat Stanley: His Original Adventure!* by Jeff Brown, illus. by Macky Pamintuan. HarperCollins, 2003 (140,287)

100. *The Adventures of Captain Underpants* by Dav Pilkey. Scholastic, 1997 (140,071)

101. *Crank* by Ellen Hopkins. S&S/Aladdin, 2004 (139,962)

102. *Junie B. Jones Has a Monster Under Her Bed* (JBJ No. 8) by Barbara Park, illus. by Denise Brunkus. Random, 1997 (138,739)

103. *The Berenstain Bears Forget Their Manners* by Stan and Jan Berenstain. Random, 1985 (138,701)

104. *Frog and Toad Together* by Arnold Lobel. HarperCollins, 1979 (137,971)

105. *Junie B. Jones Is a Party Animal* (JBJ No. 7) by Barbara Park, illus. by Denise Brunkus. Random, 1997 (136,366)

106. *Inkheart* by Cornelia Funke. Scholastic/Chicken House, 2005 (135,425)

107. *Grandma, Grandpa, and Me* (Little Critter) by Mercer Mayer. HarperFestival, 2007 (135,252)

108. *Best Friends for Never* (The Clique No. 2) by Lisi Harrison. Little, Brown/Poppy, 2004 (135,050)

109. *Biscuit and the Little Pup* by Alyssa Satin Capucilli, illus. by Pat Schories. HarperCollins, 2007 (133,499)

110. *The Tail of Emily Windsnap* by Liz Kessler, illus. by Sarah Gibb. Candlewick, 2006 (133,465)

111. *Girls in Pants: The Third Summer of the Sisterhood* by Ann Brashares. Delacorte, 2006 (133,185)

112. *Junie B., First Grader: Aloha-ha-ha!* (JBJ No. 26) by Barbara Park, illus. by Denise Brunkus. Random, 2007 (132,829)

113. *The Watsons Go to Birmingham—1963.* Christopher Paul Curtis. Yearling/Laurel Leaf, 1997 (132,686)

114. *Tonight on the Titanic* (MTH No. 17) by Mary Pope Osborne, illus. by Sal Murdocca. Random, 1999 (131,979)

115. *Charlotte's Web* by E. B. White, illus. by Garth Williams. HarperCollins, 1974 (130,462)

116. *Hoot* by Carl Hiaasen. Knopf/Yearling, 2004 (129,450)

117. *Thomas Goes Fishing* (Step into Reading) by Rev. W. Awdry, illus. by Richard Courtney. Random, 2005 (129,321)

118. *Frog and Toad All Year* by Arnold Lobel. HarperCollins, 1984 (128,502)

119. *Disney High School Musical: Stories from East High: Crunch Time* by N. B. Grace. Disney, 2007 (128,491)

120. *Junie B., First Grader: BOO . . . and I MEAN It!* (JBJ No. 24) by Barbara Park, illus. by Denise Brunkus. Random, 2005 (128,251)

121. *Judy Moody* by Megan McDonald, illus. by Peter H. Reynolds. Candlewick, 2002 (128,149)

122. *Junie B. Jones Is a Beauty Shop Guy* (JBJ No. 11) by Barbara Park, illus. by Denise Brunkus. Random, 1998 (127,796)

123. *The Revenge of the Wannabes* (The Clique No. 3) by Lisi Harrison. Little, Brown/Poppy, 2005 (127,757)

124. *Captain Underpants and the Wrath of the Wicked Wedgie Woman* by Dav Pilkey. Scholastic, 2001 (127,239)

125. *Disney High School Musical: Stories from East High: Battle of the Bands* by N. B. Grace. Disney, 2007 (126,475)

126. *The Vampire Diaries: The Fury and Dark Reunion* by L. J. Smith. Harper-Teen, 2007 (126,279)

127. *Harry Potter and the Goblet of Fire* by J. K. Rowling, illus. by Mary Grand-Pré. Scholastic/Levine, 2002 (125,195)

128. *Disney High School Musical: Stories from East High: Heart to Heart* by Helen Perelman. Disney, 2007 (124,768)

129. *The People of Sparks* (The Books of Ember) by Jeanne DuPrau. Yearling, 2005 (124,672)

130. *Go Ask Alice* by Anonymous. Simon Pulse, 2006 (124,432)

131. *This Lullaby* by Sarah Dessen. Puffin, 2004 (124,272)

132. *Vampire Academy* by Richelle Mead. Razorbill, 2007 (122,961)

133. *The Berenstain Bears and Too Much Junk Food* by Stan and Jan Berenstain. Random, 1985 (122,703)

134. *Captain Underpants and the Big, Bad Battle of the Bionic Booger Boy, Part 2.* Dav Pilkey. Scholastic, 2003 (122,402)

135. *Junie B. Jones and That Meanie Jim's Birthday* (JBJ No. 6) by Barbara Park, illus. by Denise Brunkus. Random, 1996 (121,621)

136. *Junie B. Jones Loves Handsome Warren* (JBJ No. 7) by Barbara Park, illus. by Denise Brunkus. Random, 1996 (121,459)

137. *Junie B., First Grader (at last!)* (JBJ No. 18) by Barbara Park, illus. by Denise Brunkus. Random, 2002 (121,101)

138. *Harry Potter and the Chamber of Secrets* by J. K. Rowling, illus. by Mary GrandPré. Scholastic/Levine, 2000 (120,480)

139. *Tuck Everlasting* by Natalie Babbitt. Macmillan/Square Fish, 2007 (120,230)

140. *Miss Daisy Is Crazy!* (My Weird School No. 1) by Dan Gutman, illus. by Jim Paillot. HarperCollins, 2004 (119,623)

141. *Biscuit and the Baby* by Alyssa Satin Capucilli, illus. by pat Schories. HarperCollins, 2005 (119,061)

142. *Harry Potter and the Order of the Phoenix* by J. K. Rowling, illus. by Mary GrandPré. Scholastic/Levine, 2004 (118,543)

143. *Stargirl* by Jerry Spinelli. Knopf/Laurel Leaf, 2002 (118,372)

144. *Junie B. Jones Is (Almost) a Flower Girl* (JBJ No. 13) by Barbara Park, illus. by Denise Brunkus. Random, 1999 (118,293)

145. *Viking Ships at Sunrise* (MTH No. 15) by Mary Pope Osborne, illus. by Sal Murdocca. Random, 1998 (117,423)

146. *The Berenstain Bears Get the Gimmies* by Stan and Jan Berenstain. Random, 1988 (117,307)

147. *Thomas-saurus Rex* by Rev. W. Awdry, illus. by Richard Courtney. Random, 2006 (117,074)

148. *Bridge to Terabithia* by Katherine Paterson. HarperCollins, 1987 (116,157)

149. *Among the Hidden* by Margaret Peterson Haddix. S&S/Aladdin, 2000 (115,456)

150. *High Tide in Hawaii* (MTH No. 28) by Mary Pope Osborne, illus. by Sal Murdocca. Random, 2003 (115,314)

151. *Because of Winn-Dixie* by Kate DiCamillo. Candlewick, 2001 (114,778)

152. *Captain Underpants and the Big, Bad Battle of the Bionic Booger Boy, Part 1.* Dav Pilkey. Scholastic, 2003 (114,716)

153. *Warriors No. 2: Fire and Ice* by Erin Hunter. HarperCollins, 2004 (113,957)

154. *Captain Underpants and the Attack of the Talking Toilets* by Dav Pilkey. Scholastic, 1999 (113,852)

155. *Mad Libs on the Road* by Roger Price. Price Stern Sloan, 1999 (113,252)

156. *Dial L for Loser* (The Clique No. 6) by Lisi Harrison. Little, Brown/Poppy, 2006 (112,941)

157. *The Berenstain Bears and the Truth* by Stan and Jan Berenstain. Random, 1983 (112,748)

158. *Just Me and My Mom* by Mercer Mayer. Random, 2001 (112,032)

159. *Roll of Thunder, Hear My Cry* by Mildred Taylor. Puffin, 1997 (112,002)

160. *The Boxcar Children* by Gertrude Chandler Warner, illus. by L. Kate Deal. Albert Whitman, 1942 (111,810)

161. *The Best Christmas Pageant Ever* by Barbara Robinson. HarperCollins, 2005 (111,352)

162. *Harry Potter and the Prisoner of Azkaban* by J. K. Rowling, illus. by Mary GrandPré. Scholastic/Levine, 2001 (111,022)

163. *Bye-Bye, Mom and Dad* (Little Critter) by Mercer Mayer. HarperFestival, 2004 (110,406)

164. *The Ruins of Gorlan* (Ranger's Apprentice) by John Flanagan. Puffin, 2006 (110,204)

165. *The Little Old Lady Who Was Not Afraid of Anything* by Linda Williams, illus. by Megan Lloyd. HarperCollins, 1988 (110,063)

166. *The Berenstain Bears Learn About Strangers* by Stan and Jan Berenstain. Random, 1985 (110,015)

167. *Freak the Mighty* by Rodman Philbrick. Scholastic, 2001 (110,003)

168. *The Pretty Committee Strikes Back* (The Clique No. 5) by Lisi Harrison. Little, Brown/Poppy, 2006 (109,693)

169. *Junie B. Jones and the Yucky Blucky Fruitcake* (JBJ No. 5) by Barbara Park, illus. by Denise Brunkus. Random, 1995 (109,027)

170. *Touching Spirit Bear* by Ben Mikaelson. HarperCollins, 2002 (108,941)

171. *Junie B. Jones Is Not a Crook* (JBJ No. 9) by Barbara Park, illus. by Denise Brunkus. Random, 1997 (108,704)

172. *The Truth About Forever* by Sarah Dessen. Puffin, 2006 (108,480)

173. *Junie B., First Grader: Cheater Pants* (JBJ No. 21) by Barbara Park, illus. by Denise Brunkus. Random, 2004 (108,462)

174. *Junie B. Jones Is a Graduation Girl* (JBJ No. 7) by Barbara Park, illus. by Denise Brunkus. Random, 2001 (108,456)

175. *It's Not Easy Being Mean* (The Clique No. 7) by Lisi Harrison. Little, Brown/Poppy, 2007 (108,172)

176. *The Berenstain Bears and Too Much TV* by Stan and Jan Berenstain. Random, 1984 (108,026)

177. *The Night Before Kindergarten* by Natasha Wing. Grosset & Dunlap, 2001 (107,685)

178. *Little Bear* by Else Holmelund Minarik, illus. by Maurice Sendak. HarperCollins, 1978 (107,080)

179. *Captain Underpants and the Invasion of the Incredibly Naughty Cafeteria Ladies of Outer Space* by Dav Pilkey. Scholastic, 1999 (106,799)

180. *Little Engines Can Do Big Things.* Illus. by Ted Gadecki. Random, 2000 (106,533)

181. *Junie B. Jones Smells Something Fishy* (JBJ No. 12) by Barbara Park, illus. by Denise Brunkus. Random, 1998 (106,214)

182. *Disney High School Musical: Stories from East High: Poetry in Motion* by Alice Alfonsi. Disney, 2007 (106,170)

183. *Seedfolks* by Paul Fleischman. HarperTeen, 1999 (105,752)

184. *Invasion of the Boy Snatchers* (The Clique No. 4) by Lisi Harrison. Little, Brown/Poppy, 2005 (105,640)

185. *Pretties* by Scott Westerfeld. Simon Pulse, 2005 (105,621)

186. *Sealed with a Diss* (The Clique No. 8) by Lisi Harrison. Little, Brown/Poppy, 2007 (105,563)

187. *Goodnight Moon* by Margaret Wise Brown, illus. by Clement Hurd. HarperCollins, 1977 (104,521)

188. *Junie B. Jones and the Mushy Gushy Valentine* (JBJ No. 14) by Barbara Park, illus. by Denise Brunkus. Random, 1999 (104,457)

189. *Are You There God? It's Me, Margaret* by Judy Blume. Yearling/Laurel Leaf, 1986 (104,367)

190. *Junie B., First Grader: Boss of Lunch* (JBJ No. 19) by Barbara Park, illus. by Denise Brunkus. Random, 2003 (104,190)

191. *Maximum Ride: The Angel Experiment* (mass market edition) by James Patterson. Little, Brown, 2006 (103,326)

192. *A Smart Girl's Guide to Starting Middle School* by Julie Williams, illus. by Angela Martini. American Girl, 2003 (103,268)

193. *Esperanza Rising* by Pam Muñoz Ryan. Scholastic, 2002 (103,078)

194. *Stink* by Megan McDonald, illus. by Peter H. Reynolds. Candlewick, 2006 (103,077)

195. *Johnny Tremain* by Esther Forbes. Yearling/Laurel Leaf, 1987 (102,978)

196. *Cloudy with a Chance of Meatballs* by Judi Barrett, illus. by Ron Barrett. S&S/Aladdin, 1982 (102,833)

197. *The Phantom Tollbooth* by Norton Juster. Yearling, 1988 (102,685)

198. *Someone Like You* by Sarah Dessen. Puffin, 2004 (102,494)

199. *Nick & Norah's Infinite Playlist* by Rachel Cohn and David Levithan. Knopf, 2007 (101,902)

200. *Hot Dog* (Step into Reading) by Molly Coxe. Random, 1998 (101,703)

201. *The Cay* by Theodore Taylor. Yearling/Laurel Leaf, 2002 (101,537)

202. *Warriors No. 3: Forest of Secrets* by Erin Hunter. HarperCollins, 2004 (101,099)

203. *Freckle Juice* by Judy Blume. Yearling, 1978 (100,889)

204. *Dingoes at Dinnertime* (MTH No. 20) by Mary Pope Osborne, illus. by Sal Murdocca. Random, 2000 (100,712)

205. *Night of the New Magicians* (MTH No. 35) by Mary Pope Osborne, illus. by Sal Murdocca. Random, 2007 (100,654)

206. *A Great and Terrible Beauty* (Gemma Doyle Trilogy) by Libba Bray. Delacorte, 2005 (100,500)

207. *Good Morning, Gorillas* (MTH No. 26) by Mary Pope Osborne, illus. by Sal Murdocca. Random, 2002 (100,448)

208. *The Sign of the Beaver* by Elizabeth George Speare. Yearling, 1984 (100,424)

209. *Dinosaur Days* (Step into Reading) by Joyce Milton. Random, 1985 (100,350)

210. *Junie B. Jones Has a Peep in Her Pocket* (JBJ No. 15) by Barbara Park, illus. by Denise Brunkus. Random, 2000 (100,332)

211. *The Prophet of Yonwood* (The Books of Ember) by Jeanne DuPrau. Yearling, 2007 (100,234)

212. *The Trouble with Tink* (Disney Fairies) by Kiki Thorpe. Random/Disney, 2006 (100,215)

213. *The Penderwicks* by Jeanne Birdsall. Yearling, 2007 (100,211)

214. *Tigers at Twilight* (MTH No. 19) by Mary Pope Osborne, illus. by Sal Murdocca. Random, 1999 (100,104)

215. *Revolutionary War on Wednesday* (MTH No. 22) by Mary Pope Osborne, illus. by Sal Murdocca. Random, 2000 (100,101)

# Literary Prizes, 2008

Compiled by the Staff of the *Library and Book Trade Almanac*

**Agatha Awards.** For mystery novels written in the method exemplified by author Agatha Christie. *Offered by:* Malice Domestic Ltd. *Winners:* (best novel) Louise Penny for *A Fatal Grace* (St. Martin's); (best first novel) Hank Phillippi Ryan for *Prime Time* (Harlequin); (nonfiction) Jon Lellenberg, Daniel Stashower, and Charles Foley for *Arthur Conan Doyle: A Life In Letters* (Penguin); (short story) Donna Andrews for "A Rat's Tale" in *Ellery Queen Mystery Magazine,* September/October 2007; (children's/young adult novel) Sarah Masters Buckey for *A Light in the Cellar* (American Girl).

**Alex Awards.** To the authors of ten books published for adults that have high potential appeal to teenagers. *Sponsor:* Margaret Alexander Edwards Trust and *Booklist. Winners:* Matthew Polly for *American Shaolin: Flying Kicks, Buddhist Monks, and the Legend of Iron Crotch: An Odyssey in the New China* (Penguin); Matt Ruff for *Bad Monkeys* (HarperCollins); Jeff Lemire for *Essex County Volume 1: Tales from the Farm* (Top Shelf); Conn Iggulden for *Genghis: Birth of an Empire* (Delacorte); Aryn Kyle for *The God of Animals* (Scribner); Ishmael Beah for *A Long Way Gone: Memoirs of a Boy Soldier* (Farrar, Straus & Giroux); Lloyd Jones for *Mister Pip* (Random); Patrick Rothfuss for *The Name of the Wind* (DAW); Thomas Maltman for *The Night Birds* (Soho); Lisa Lutz for *The Spellman Files* (Simon & Schuster).

**Ambassador Book Awards:** To honor an exceptional contribution to the interpretation of life and culture in the United States. *Offered by:* English-Speaking Union of the United States. *Winners:* (American Studies) Rebecca Solnit for *Storming the Gates of Paradise: Landscapes for Politics* (University of California); (autobiography) Robert Stone for *Prime Green: Remembering the Sixties* (HarperCollins); (biography) Hermione Lee for *Edith Wharton* (Knopf); (fiction) Mohsin Hamid for *The Reluctant Fundamentalist* (Harcourt); (poetry) Henri Cole for *Blackbird and Wolf* (Farrar, Straus & Giroux); (lifetime achievement) John Ashbery.

**American Academy of Arts and Letters Awards in Literature ($7,500).** To honor writers of exceptional accomplishment in any genre. *Offered by:* American Academy of Arts and Letters. *Winners:* Dan Chiasson, Brian Doyle, Rikki Ducornet, Will Eno, Edith Grossman, Fanny Howe, Richard Nelson, Mona Simpson.

**American Academy of Arts and Letters Rome Fellowships.** For a one-year residency at the American Academy in Rome for young writers of promise. *Offered by:* American Academy of Arts and Letters. *Winners:* Brad Kessler, Dana Spiotta.

**American Book Awards.** For literary achievement by people of various ethnic backgrounds. *Offered by:* Before Columbus Foundation. *Winners:* Moustafa Bayoumi for *How Does It Feel to Be a Problem? Being Young and Arab in America* (Penguin); Douglas A. Blackmon for *Slavery by Another Name: The Re-Enslavement of Black Americans from the Civil War to World War II* (Doubleday); Nora Marks Dauenhauer, Richard Dauenhauer, Lydia T. Black, and Anóoshi Lingít Aaní Ká for *Russians in Tlingit America: The Battles of Sitka, 1802 and 1804* (University of Washington); Maria Mazziotti Gillan for *All That Lies Between Us* (Guernica); Nikki Giovanni for *The Collected Poetry of Nikki Giovanni: 1968–1998* (HarperCollins) C. S. Giscombe for *Prairie Style* (Dalkey Archive); Angela Jackson for *Where I Must Go* (TriQuarterly); L. Luis Lopez for *Each Month I Sing* (Farolito); Tom Lutz for *Doing Nothing: A History of Loafers, Loungers, Slackers, and Bums in America* (Farrar, Straus & Giroux); Fae Myenne Ng for *Steer Toward Rock* (Hyperion); Yuko Taniguchi for *The Ocean in the Closet* (Coffee House); Lorenzo Thomas and Aldon Lynn Nielsen (editor) for *Don't Deny My Name: Words and Music and the*

*Black Intellectual Tradition* (University of Michigan); Frank B. Wilderson III for *Incognegro: A Memoir of Exile and Apartheid* (South End); Jonathan Curiel for *Al' America: Travels Through America's Arab and Islamic Roots* (New Press); (lifetime achievement) J. J. Phillips.

Rudolfo and Patricia Anaya Premio Aztlan Literary Prize. To honor a Chicano or Chicana fiction writer who has published no more than two books. *Offered by:* University of New Mexico. *Winner:* Veronica Gonzalez for *Twin Time: Or, How Death Befell Me* (Semiotext(e)).

Hans Christian Andersen Awards. To an author and an illustrator whose body of work has made an important and lasting contribution to children's literature. *Offered by:* International Board of Books for Young People (IBBY). *Winners:* (author) Jürg Schubiger; (illustrator) Roberto Innocenti.

Anthony Awards. For superior mystery writing. *Offered by:* Boucheron World Mystery Convention. *Winners:* (best novel) Laura Lippman for *What the Dead Know* (William Morrow); (best first novel) Tana French for *In the Woods* (Viking); (best paperback original) P. J. Parrish for *A Thousand Bones* (Pocket); (best short story) Laura Lippman for "Hardly Knew Her" in *Dead Man's Hand* (Harcourt); (critical work) Jon Lellenberg, Daniel Stashower, and Charles Foley for *Arthur Conan Doyle: A Life in Letters* (Penguin).

Asian/Pacific American Awards for Literature. For books that promote Asian/Pacific American culture and heritage. *Sponsor:* Asian/Pacific American Librarians Association (APALA). *Winners:* (adult nonfiction) Jean Pfaelzer for *Driven Out: The Forgotten War Against Chinese Americans* (Random); (illustration in children's literature) Richard Waldrep for *Surfer of the Century* by Ellie Crowe (Lee and Low); (young adult literature) Kelly Easton for *Hiroshima Dreams* (Dutton).

Bad Sex in Fiction Award (United Kingdom). *Sponsor: Literary Review. Winner:* (annual prize) Rachel Johnson for *Shire Hell* (Penguin); (lifetime achievement) John Updike.

Bakeless Literary Publication Prizes. For promising new writers. *Offered by:* Bread Loaf Writers' Conference of Middlebury College. *Winners:* (fiction) Skip Horack for *The Southern Cross* (Houghton Mifflin); (creative nonfiction) Vicki Forman for *This Lovely Life* (Houghton Mifflin); (poetry) Leslie Harrison for *Displacement* (Houghton Mifflin).

Bancroft Prizes ($10,000). For books of exceptional merit and distinction in American history, American diplomacy, and the international relations of the United States. *Offered by:* Columbia University. *Winners:* Allan M. Brandt for *The Cigarette Century: The Rise, Fall, and Deadly Persistence of the Product that Defined America* (Basic); Charles Postel for *The Populist Vision* (Oxford); Peter Silver for *Our Savage Neighbors: How Indian War Transformed Early America* (Norton).

Barnes & Noble Discover Great New Writers Awards. To honor a first novel and a first work of nonfiction by American authors. *Offered by:* Barnes & Noble, Inc. *Winners:* (fiction) Gin Phillips for *The Well and the Mine* (Hawthorne); (nonfiction) David Sheff for *Beautiful Boy: A Father's Journey Through His Son's Addiction* (Houghton Mifflin).

Margaret L. Batchelder Award. For an American publisher of a children's book originally published in a foreign country and subsequently published in English in the United States. *Offered by:* American Library Association, Association for Library Service to Children. *Winner:* VIZ Media for *Brave Story* by Miyuki Miyabe, translated from Japanese by Alexander O. Smith.

Pura Belpré Awards. To a Latino/Latina writer and illustrator whose work portrays, affirms, and celebrates the Latino cultural experience in an outstanding work of literature for children and youth. *Offered by:* American Library Association, Association for Library Service to Children. *Winners:* (author) Margarita Engle for *The Poet Slave of Cuba: A Biography of Juan Francisco Manzano,* illustrated by Sean Qualls (Holt); (illustrator) Yuyi Morales for *Los Gatos Black on Halloween,* written by Marisa Montes (Holt).

Curtis Benjamin Award. To an outstanding individual within the U.S. publishing industry who has shown exceptional innovation and creativity in the field of publishing. *Offered by:* Association of American Publishers. *Winner:* Not awarded in 2008.

Helen B. Bernstein Award. To a journalist who has written at book length about an issue of contemporary concern. *Offered by:* New York Public Library. *Winner:* Charlie Savage for *Takeover: The Return of the Imperial Presidency and the Subversion of American Democracy* (Little, Brown).

Black Caucus of the American Library Association (BCALA) Literary Awards. *Winners:* (fiction) Stephen L. Carter for *New England White* (Knopf); (nonfiction) Arnold Rampersad for *Ralph Ellison: A Biography* (Knopf); (first novelist award) Chantal Ellen for *The Rise: Where Neighbors Are Sometimes More* (Lion's Den); (outstanding contribution to publishing) Deborah Willis for *Let Your Motto Be Resistance: African American Portraits* (USMTH).

James Tait Black Memorial Prize (United Kingdom) (£10,000). To recognize literary excellence in biography and fiction. *Offered by:* University of Edinburgh. *Winners:* (fiction) Rosalind Belben for *Our Horses in Egypt* (Chatto & Windus); (biography) Rosemary Hill for *God's Architect: Pugin and the Building of Romantic Britain* (Allen Lane).

Rebekah Johnson Bobbitt National Prize for Poetry. *Offered by:* Library of Congress. *Winners:* Bob Hicok for *This Clumsy Living* (University of Pittsburgh); (lifetime achievement) Charles Wright.

Booksellers Association/Nielsen Author of the Year (United Kingdom) (£1,000). *Sponsor:* Nielsen Book Data. *Winner:* Clarissa Dickson Wright.

BookSense Book of the Year Awards. To honor titles that member stores most enjoyed handselling during the past year. *Offered by:* American Booksellers Association. *Winners:* (fiction) Khaled Hosseini

for *A Thousand Splendid Suns* (Riverhead/Penguin); (nonfiction) Barbara Kingsolver, with Steven L. Hopp and Camille Kingsolver, for *Animal, Vegetable, Miracle: A Year of Food Life* (HarperCollins); (children's literature) Brian Selznick for *The Invention of Hugo Cabret* (Scholastic); (children's illustrated) Mo Willems for *Knuffle Bunny Too: A Case of Mistaken Identity* (Hyperion).

Booktrust Teenage Prize (United Kingdom) (£2,500). *Offered by:* Booktrust. *Winner:* Patrick Ness for *The Knife of Never Letting Go* (Walker).

Boston Globe/Horn Book Awards. For excellence in children's literature. *Winners:* (fiction and poetry) Sherman Alexie and Ellen Forney (illustrator) for *The Absolutely True Diary of a Part-Time Indian* (Little, Brown); (nonfiction) Peter Sís for *The Wall* (Farrar, Straus & Giroux); (picture book) Jonathan Bean for *At Night* (Farrar, Straus & Giroux); (special citation) Shaun Tan for *The Arrival* (Scholastic).

W. Y. Boyd Literary Novel Award ($5,000). For a military novel that honors the service of American veterans during a time of war. *Offered by:* American Library Association. *Winner:* Robert N. Macomber for *A Different Kind of Honor* (Pineapple).

Michael Braude Award for Light Verse ($5,000). *Offered by:* American Academy of Arts and Letters. *Winner:* Christopher Reid.

Bridport International Creative Writing Prizes (United Kingdom). For poetry and short stories. *Offered by:* Bridport Arts Centre. *Winners:* (poetry) (first prize, £5,000) Anne Stewart for "Still Water, Orange, Apple, Tea"; (second prize, £1,000) Elizabeth Speller for "Finistère"; (third prize, £500) Ama Bolton for "Time-Travel"; (short story) (first prize, £5,000) Elaine Chiew for "Face"; (second prize, £1,000) Joanna Quinn for "A Pocket Guide to Infidelity for Girls"; (third prize, £500) Sara Levine for "Little Bad."

Sophie Brody Medal. For the U.S. author of the most distinguished contribution to Jewish literature for adults published in the preceding year. *Offered by:* Reference and User Services Association, American

Library Association, Brodart Foundation. *Winner:* Nathan Englander for *The Ministry of Special Classes* (Knopf).

Randolph Caldecott Medal. For the artist of the most distinguished picture book. *Offered by:* American Library Association, Association for Library Service to Children. *Winner:* Brian Selznick for *The Invention of Hugo Cabret* (Scholastic).

California Book Awards. To California residents to honor books of fiction, nonfiction, and poetry published in the previous year. *Offered by:* Commonwealth Club of California. *Winners:* (fiction) Michael Chabon for *The Yiddish Policeman's Union* (HarperCollins); (nonfiction) Arnold Rampersad for *Ralph Ellison: A Biography* (Knopf); (poetry) W. S. Di Piero for *Chinese Apples* (Knopf).

John W. Campbell Memorial Award. For science fiction writing. *Offered by:* Center for the Study of Science Fiction. *Winner:* Kathleen Ann Goonan for *In War Times* (Tor).

Canadian Library Association Amelia Frances Howard-Gibbon Illustrator's Award. *Winner:* Mélanie Watt (illustrator and author) for *Chester* (Kids Can).

Canadian Library Association Book of the Year for Children *Winner:* Christopher Paul Curtis for *Elijah of Buxton* (Scholastic).

Canadian Library Association Young Adult Canadian Book Award. *Winner:* Martha Brooks for *Mistik Lake* (Groundwood).

Children's Book Council of Australia Children's Book of the Year Awards. *Winners:* (picture book) Matt Ottley for *Requiem for a Beast* (Lothian); (early childhood) Aaron Blabey for *Pearl Bailey and Charlie Parsley* (Viking); (younger readers) Carole Wilkinson for *Dragon Moon* (Black Dog); (older readers) Sonya Hartnett for *The Ghost's Child* (Viking).

Children's Poet Laureate ($25,000). For lifetime achievement in poetry for children. Honoree holds the title for two years. *Offered by:* The Poetry Foundation. *Winner:* Mary Ann Hoberman.

Chinese American Librarians Association Book Awards. *Winners:* (adult nonfiction) Guangqiu Xu for *Congress and the U.S.-China Relationship: 1949–1979* (University of Akron); (adult fiction) Ruthanne Lum McCunn for *God of Luck* (Soho); (juvenile) Ying Chang Compestine for *Revolution Is Not a Dinner Party* (Henry Holt); (juvenile) Belle Yang for *Always Come Home to Me* (Candlewick).

Cholmondeley Awards for Poets (United Kingdom) (£1,500). For a poet's body of work and contribution to poetry. *Winners:* John Burnside, John Greening, David Harsent, Sarah Maguire.

CILIP Carnegie Medal (United Kingdom). For the outstanding children's book of the year. *Offered by:* CILIP: The Chartered Institute of Library and Information Professionals (formerly the Library Association). *Winner:* Philip Reeve for *Here Lies Arthur* (Scholastic).

CILIP Kate Greenaway Medal (United Kingdom). For children's book Illustration. *Offered by:* CILIP: The Chartered Institute of Library and Information Professionals. *Winner:* Emily Gravett for *Little Mouse's Big Book of Fears* (Macmillan).

Chicago Tribune Heartland Prize for Fiction ($7,500). *Offered by: Chicago Tribune. Winner:* Aleksandar Hemon for *The Lazarus Project* (Riverhead).

Chicago Tribune Heartland Prize for Nonfiction ($7,500). *Offered by: Chicago Tribune. Winner:* Garry Wills for *Head and Heart: American Christianities* (Penguin) and *What the Gospels Meant* (Penguin).

Chicago Tribune Literary Prize. For a lifetime of literary achievement by an author whose body of work has had great impact on American society. *Offered by: Chicago Tribune. Winner:* David McCullough.

Chicago Tribune Nelson Algren Award ($5,000). For short fiction. *Offered by: Chicago Tribune. Winner:* John K. Wilson, Kari Lydersen.

Chicago Tribune Young Adult Literary Prize. To recognize a distinguished literary career. *Winner:* S. E. Hinton.

Arthur C. Clarke Award (United Kingdom). For the best science fiction novel published in the United Kingdom. *Offered by:* British Science Fiction Association. *Winner:* Richard Morgan for *Black Man* (Gollancz).

David Cohen Prize (United Kingdom). Awarded biennially to a living British writer, novelist, poet, essayist, or dramatist in recognition of an entire body of work written in the English language. *Offered by:* David Cohen Family Charitable Trust. *Winner:* To be awarded next in 2009.

Matt Cohen Award (Canada). To a Canadian author whose life has been dedicated to writing as a primary pursuit, for a body of work. *Offered by:* Writers' Trust of Canada. *Winner:* Sylvia Fraser.

Commonwealth Writers' Prize (United Kingdom). To reward and encourage new Commonwealth fiction and ensure that works of merit reach a wider audience outside their country of origin. *Offered by:* Commonwealth Institute. *Winners:* (best book) (£10,000) Lawrence Hill for *The Book of Negroes* (U.S. title *Someone Knows My Name*) (HarperCollins); (best first book) (£5,000) Tahmima Anam for *A Golden Age* (John Murray).

Olive Cook Award (United Kingdom) (£1,000). Awarded biennially for a short story of a traditional rather than experimental character. *Winner:* Alison MacLeod for "Dirty Weekend" from *Fifteen Tales of Attraction* (Hamish Hamilton).

Costa Book Awards (United Kingdom) (formerly the Whitbread Book Awards). For literature of merit that is readable on a wide scale. *Offered by:* Booksellers Association of Great Britain and Costa Coffee. *Winners:* (novel and book of the year, £5,000 plus £25,000) Sebastian Barry for *The Secret Scripture* (Viking); (first novel, £5,000) Sadie Jones for *The Outcast* (Vintage); (biography, £5,000) Diana Athill for *Somewhere Towards the End* (Granta); (poetry, £5,000) Adam Foulds for *The Broken Word* (Jonathan Cape); (children's, £5,000) Michelle Magorian for *Just Henry* (Egmont).

Roald Dahl Funny Prize (United Kingdom) (£2,500). *Offered by:* Booktrust. *Winners:* (ages 6 and under) Ursula Jones and Russell Ayto for *The Witch's Children Go to School* (Orchard); (ages 7 to 14) Andy Stanton and David Tazzyman, illustrator, for *Mr. Gum and the Dancing Bear* (Egmont).

Benjamin H. Danks Award ($20,000). To a promising young playwright. *Offered by:* American Academy of Arts and Letters. *Winner:* A. E. Stallings.

Philip K. Dick Award. For a distinguished science fiction paperback published in the United States. *Offered by:* Norwescon. *Winner:* M. John Harrison for *Nova Swing* (Bantam).

Glen Dimplex New Writers Awards (Ireland). *Sponsors:* Glen Dimplex Group and Irish Writers Centre. *Winners:* (new writer of the year) Sally Nicholls for *Ways to Live Forever* (Scholastic); (fiction) Allan Bush for *Last Bird Singing* (Seren); (biography/nonfiction) Nia Wyn for *Blue Sky July* (Seren); (poetry) Will Stone for *Glaciation* (Salt); (best Irish-language book) Simon Ó Faoláin for *Anam Mhadra* (Coiscéim).

Margaret A. Edwards Award ($2,000). To an author whose book or books have provided young adults with a window through which they can view their world and which will help them to grow and to understand themselves and their role in society. *Donor: School Library Journal. Winner:* Orson Scott Card for *Ender's Game* and *Ender's Shadow* (Tor).

Will Eisner Comic Industry Awards. *Winners:* (best anthology) Gabriel Bá, Becky Cloonan, Fabio Moon, Vasilis Lolos, and Rafael Grampa for *5* (self-published); (best reality-based work) James Sturm and Rich Tomasso for *Satchel Paige: Striking Out Jim Crow* (Hyperion); (best children's publication) *Mouse Guard: Fall 1152* and *Mouse Guard: Winter 1152* (Archaia); (best publication for teens) Nick Abadzis for *Laika* (First Second); (best humor publication) Nicholas Gurewitch for *Perry Bible Fellowship: The Trial of Colonel Sweeto and Other Stories* (Dark Horse); (best archival collection—comic strips) *Complete Terry and the Pirates, Vol. 1* by Milton Caniff (IDW); (best archival collection—comic books) *I Shall Destroy All the Civilized Planets!* by Fletcher Hanks (Fantagraphics).

Marian Engel Award (Canada). To a female writer in mid-career for a body of work.

*Offered by:* Writers' Trust of Canada. *Winner:* Diane Schoemperlen.

Timothy Findley Award (Canada). To a male Canadian author in mid-career for a body of work. *Offered by:* Writers' Trust of Canada. *Winner:* Michael Crummey.

E. M. Forster Award ($20,000). To a young writer from England, Ireland, Scotland, or Wales, for a stay in the United States. *Offered by:* American Academy of Arts and Letters. *Winner:* John Lanchester.

Forward Prizes (United Kingdom). For poetry. *Offered by: The Forward. Winners:* (best collection, £10,000) Mick Imlah for *The Lost Leader* (Faber & Faber); (best first collection, £5,000) Kathryn Simmons for *Sunday at the Skin Launderette* (Seren); (best single poem, £1,000) Don Paterson for "Love Poem for Natalie 'Tusja' Beridze."

Josette Frank Award (formerly the Children's Book Award). For a work of fiction in which children or young people deal in a positive and realistic way with difficulties in their world and grow emotionally and morally. *Offered by:* Bank Street College of Education and the Florence M. Miller Memorial Fund. *Winner:* Katherine Applegate for *Home of the Brave* (Feiwel and Friends).

George Freedley Memorial Award. For the best English-language work about live theater published in the United States. *Offered by:* Theatre Library Association. *Winner:* Felicia Hardison Londrè for *The Enchanted Years of the Stage: Kansas City at the Crossroads of American Theater, 1870–1930* (University of Missouri).

French-American Foundation Translation Prize ($10,000). For a translation or translations from French into English of a work of fiction and nonfiction. *Offered by:* French-American Foundation. *Winners:* (fiction) Linda Coverdale for *Ravel* by Jean Echenoz (New Press); (nonfiction) Linda Asher for *The Curtain* by Milan Kundera (HarperCollins).

Frost Medal. To recognize achievement in poetry over a lifetime. *Offered by:* Poetry Society of America. *Winner:* Michael S. Harper.

Lewis Galantière Award. A biennial award for a literary translation into English from any language other than German. *Offered by:* American Translators Association. *Winner:* Norman R. Shapiro for *The Complete Fables of Jean de La Fontaine* (University of Illinois).

Galaxy British Book Awards. *Offered by: Publishing News. Winners:* (Galaxy Book of the Year) Ian McEwan for *On Chesil Beach* (Jonathan Cape); (Bookpeople Outstanding Achievement Award) J. K. Rowling; (Richard & Judy Best Read of the Year) Khaled Hosseini for *A Thousand Splendid Suns* (Bloomsbury); (Reader's Digest Author of the Year) Ian McEwan for *On Chesil Beach* (Jonathan Cape); (Tesco Biography of the Year) Russell Brand for *My Booky Wook* (Hodder & Stoughton); (WHSmith Children's Book of the Year) Francesca Simon for *Horrid Henry and the Abominable Snowman* (Orion); (BooksDirect Crime Thriller of the Year) Patricia Cornwell for *Book of the Dead* (Little, Brown); (Waterstone's Newcomer of the Year) Catherine O'Flynn for *What Was Lost* (Tindal Street); (Sainsbury's Popular Fiction Award) Kim Edwards for *The Memory Keeper's Daughter* (Penguin); (Play.com Popular Nonfiction Award) Ewan McGregor and Charlie Boorman for *Long Way Down* (Sphere).

Theodor Seuss Geisel Medal. For the best book for beginning readers. *Offered by:* American Library Association, Association for Library Service to Children. *Winner:* Mo Willems for *There Is a Bird on Your Head!* (Hyperion).

Giller Prize (Canada) (C$40,000). For the best novel or short story collection written in English. *Offered by:* Giller Prize Foundation and Scotiabank. *Winner:* Joseph Boyden for *Through Black Spruce* (Viking).

Goldberg Prize for Fiction by Emerging Writers ($2,500). To highlight new works by contemporary writers exploring Jewish themes. *Offered by:* Foundation for Jewish Culture and *Moment* magazine. *Winner:* Anya Ulinich for *Petropolis* (Penguin).

Golden Kite Awards ($2,500). For children's books. *Offered by:* Society of Children's Book Writers and Illustrators. *Winners:*

(fiction) Katherine Applegate for *Home of the Brave* (Feiwel and Friends); (nonfiction) Ann Bausum for *Muckrakers* (National Geographic); (picture book text) Sara Pennypacker for *Pierre in Love,* illustrated by Petra Mathers (Orchard); (picture book illustration) Yuyi Morales for *Little Night,* written by the illustrator (Roaring Brook).

Governor General's Literary Awards (Canada) (C$25,000). For works, in English and in French, of fiction, nonfiction, poetry, drama, and children's literature, and for translation. *Offered by:* Canada Council for the Arts. *Winners:* (fiction, English) Nino Ricci for *The Origin of Species* (Doubleday); (fiction, French) Marie-Claire Blais for *Naissance de Rebecca à l'Ère des Tourments* (Éditions du Boréal); (poetry, English) Jacob Scheier for *More to Keep Us Warm* (ECW); (poetry, French) Michel Pleau for *La Lenteur du Monde* (Éditions David); (drama, English) Catherine Banks for *Bone Cage* (Playwrights Canada); (drama, French) Jennifer Tremblay for *La Liste* (Éditions de la Bagnole); (nonfiction, English) Christie Blatchford for *Fifteen Days: Stories of Bravery, Friendship, Life and Death from Inside the New Canadian Army* (Doubleday); (nonfiction, French) Pierre Ouellet for *Hors-Temps: Poétique de la Posthistoire* (VLB Éditeur); (children's literature text, English) John Ibbitson for *The Landing* (Kids Can); (children's literature text, French) Sylvie Desrosiers for *Les Trois Lieues* (Éditions de la Courte Échelle); (children's literature illustration, English) Stéphane Jorisch for *The Owl and the Pussycat* by Edward Lear (Kids Can); (children's illustration, French) Janice Nadeau for *Ma Meilleure Amie* by Gilles Tibo (Québec Amérique); (translation into English) Lazer Lederhendler for *Nikolski* by Nicolas Dickner (Knopf); (translation into French) Claire Chabalier and Louise Chabalier for *Tracey en Mille Morceaux* (Éditions Les Allusifs), translation of *The Tracey Fragments* by Maureen Medved (House of Anansi).

Eric Gregory Awards (United Kingdom) (£4,000). For a collection by poets under the age of 30. *Winners:* Emily Berry, Rhiannon Hooson, James Midgley, Adam O'Riordan, Heather Phillipson.

Griffin Poetry Prizes (Canada) (C$100,000 total). To a living Canadian poet or translator and a living poet or translator from any country, which may include Canada. *Offered by:* Griffin Trust. *Winners:* (Canadian) Robin Blaser for *The Holy Forest: Collected Poems of Robin Blaser* (University of California); (international) John Ashbery for *Notes From the Air: Selected Later Poems* (HarperCollins).

Gryphon Award ($1,000). To recognize a noteworthy work of fiction or nonfiction for younger children. *Offered by:* The Center for Children's Books. *Winner:* Michael Townsend for *Billy Tartle in Say Cheese!* (Knopf).

Guardian Children's Fiction Prize (United Kingdom) (£1,500). For an outstanding children's or young adult novel. *Offered by:* The Guardian. *Winner:* Patrick Ness for *The Knife of Never Letting Go* (Walker).

Guardian First Book Award (United Kingdom) (£10,000). For recognition of a first book. *Offered by:* The Guardian. *Winner:* Alex Ross for *The Rest Is Noise* (Farrar, Straus & Giroux).

Handelsman Prize for Jewish Nonfiction. *Offered by:* Foundation for Jewish Culture and *Moment* magazine. *Winner:* Harry Bernstein for *The Invisible Wall* (Ballantine).

O. B. Hardison, Jr. Poetry Prize ($10,000). To a U.S. poet who has published at least one book in the past five years, and has made important contributions as a teacher, and is committed to furthering the understanding of poetry. *Offered by:* Folger Shakespeare Library. *Winner:* Mary Kinzie.

Harvey Awards. To recognize outstanding work in comics and sequential art. *Winners:* (best anthology) *Popgun Volume 1,* edited by Joe Keatinge and Mark Andrew Smith (Image); (best original graphic album) *Scott Pilgrim Gets It Together* (Oni); (best biographical, historical, or journalistic presentation) Douglas Wolk for *Reading Comics: How Graphic Albums Work and What They Mean* (Da Capo); (best writer) Brian K. Vaughan; (best artist) Frank Quietly; (best cartoonist) Darwyn Cooke.

R. R. Hawkins Award. For the outstanding professional/scholarly work of the year. *Offered by:* Association of American Publishers. *Winner:* Princeton University Press for *The Dream of the Poem* by Peter Cole.

Heartland Prizes ($7,500). To recognize an outstanding work of fiction and an outstanding work of nonfiction, each about people and places in America's heartland. *Offered by: Chicago Tribune. Winners:* (fiction) Aleksandar Hemon for *The Lazarus Project* (Riverhead); (nonfiction) Garry Wills for *Head and Heart: American Christianities* (Penguin) and *What the Gospels Meant* (Penguin).

Ernest Hemingway Foundation Award. For a distinguished work of first fiction by an American. *Offered by:* PEN New England. *Winner:* Joshua Ferris for *Then We Came to the End* (Back Bay).

O. Henry Awards. To honor the year's best short stories published in American and Canadian magazines and written by American or Canadian authors. *Winners:* Ha Jin for "A Composer and His Parakeets" in *Zoetrope*; Lore Segal for "Other People's Deaths" in the *New Yorker*; Anthony Doerr for "Village 113" in *Tin House*; Steven Millhauser for "A Change in Fashion" in *Harper's Magazine*; Sheila Kohler for "The Transitional Object" in *Boulevard*; Olaf Olafsson for "On the Lake" in *Zoetrope*; Brittani Sonnenberg for "Taiping" in *xconnect*; Alice Munro for "What Do You Want to Know For?" in *The American Scholar*; Shannon Cain for "The Necessity of Certain Behaviors" in *New England Review*; Rose Tremain for "A Game of Cards" in *Paris Review*; Alexi Zentner for "Touch" in *Tin House*; Edward P. Jones for "Bad Neighbors" in the *New Yorker*; David Malouf for "Every Move You Make" in *Granta*; Tony Tulathimutte for "Scenes from the Life of the Only Girl in Water Shield, Alaska" in *Threepenny Review*; Roger McDonald for "The Bullock Run" in *MĀNOA*; Yiyun Li for "Prison" in *Tin House*; Michel Faber for "Bye-bye Natalia" in *Granta*; William

Trevor for "Folie à Deux" in the *New Yorker*; Mary Gaitskill for "The Little Boy" in *Harper's Magazine*; William H. Gass for "A Little History of Modern Music" in *Conjunctions.*

William Dean Howells Medal. In recognition of the most distinguished novel published in the preceding five years. *Offered by:* American Academy of Arts and Letters. *Winner:* To be awarded next in 2010.

Hugo Awards. For outstanding science fiction writing. *Offered by:* World Science Fiction Convention. *Winners:* (novel) Michael Chabon for *The Yiddish Policemen's Union* (HarperCollins); (novella) Connie Willis for "All Seated on the Ground" in *Asimov's*; (novelette) Ted Chiang for "The Merchant and the Alchemist's Gate" in *Fantasy & Science Fiction*; (short story) Elizabeth Bear for "Tideline" in *Asimov's*; (nonfiction book) Jeff Prucher for *Brave New Words: The Oxford Dictionary of Science Fiction* (Oxford).

Hurston/Wright Legacy Awards. To writers of African American descent for a book of fiction, a book of nonfiction, a book of first fiction, and a book of poetry. *Offered by:* Hurston/Wright Foundation and Borders Books. *Winners:* (fiction) Junot Díaz for *The Brief Wondrous Life of Oscar Wao* (Riverhead); (nonfiction) Edwidge Danticat for *Brother, I'm Dying* (Vintage); (first fiction) Kwame Dawes for *She's Gone* (Akashic); (poetry) Kyle Dargan for *Bouquet of Hungers: Poems* (University of Georgia).

Ignatz Awards. To recognize outstanding achievement in comics and cartooning. *Offered by:* SPX Cartoons and Comic Arts festival. *Winners:* (outstanding artist) Laura Park for *Do Not Disturb My Waking Dream* (self-published); (outstanding anthology or collection) Greg Means (editor) for *Papercutter No. 7* (Tugboat); (outstanding graphic novel) Mariko Tamaki and Jillian Tamaki for *Skim* (Groundwood); (outstanding series) Chuck Forsman for *Snake Oil* (self-published); (outstanding comic) Chuck Forsman for *Snake Oil No. 1* (self-published).

IMPAC Dublin Literary Award (Ireland) (€100,000). For a book of high literary merit, written in English or translated into English. *Offered by:* IMPAC Corp. and the City of Dublin. *Winner:* Rawi Hage for *De Niro's Game* (House of Anansi).

IRA Children's and Young Adult Book Awards. For first or second books in any language published for children or young adults. *Offered by:* International Reading Association. *Winners:* (primary fiction) Lita Judge for *One Thousand Tracings: Healing the Wounds of World War II* (Hyperion); (intermediate fiction) Constance Leeds for *The Silver Cup* (Viking); (young adult fiction) Laura Resau for *Red Glass* (Delacorte); (primary nonfiction) Bill Wise and Bill Farnsworth (illustrator) for *Louis Sockalexis: Native American Baseball Pioneer* (Lee & Low); (intermediate nonfiction) Loree Griffin Burns for *Tracking Trash: Flotsam, Jetsam, and the Science of Ocean Motion* (Houghton Mifflin); (young adult nonfiction) Ibtisam Barakat for *Tasting the Sky: A Palestinian Childhood* (Farrar, Straus & Giroux).

Rona Jaffe Foundation Writers' Awards ($25,000). To identify and support women writers of exceptional talent in the early stages of their careers. *Offered by:* Rona Jaffe Foundation. *Winners:* Jennifer Culkin, Joanne Dominique Dwyer, Amy Leach, Jolie Lewis, Hasanthika Sirisena, Therese Stanton.

Jerusalem Prize (Israel). Awarded biennially to a writer whose works best express the theme of freedom of the individual in society. *Offered by:* Jerusalem International Book Fair. *Winner:* To be awarded next in 2009.

Samuel Johnson Prize for Nonfiction (United Kingdom) (£30,000). For an outstanding work of nonfiction. *Offered by:* British Broadcasting Corporation. *Winner:* Orlando Figes for *The Whisperers* (Allen Lane).

Sue Kaufman Prize for First Fiction ($5,000). For a first novel or collection of short stories. *Offered by:* American Academy of Arts and Letters. *Winner:* Frances Hwang for *Transparency* (Back Bay).

Ezra Jack Keats Awards. For children's picture books. *Offered by:* New York Public Library and the Ezra Jack Keats Foundation. *Winners:* (new writer award) David Ezra Stein for *Leaves,* illustrated by the author (Putnam); (new illustrator award) Jonathan Bean for *The Apple Pie that Papa Baked,* written by Lauren Thompson (Simon & Schuster).

Kerlan Award. To recognize singular attainments in the creation of children's literature and in appreciation for generous donation of unique resources to the Kerlan Collection for the study of children's literature. *Offered by:* Kerlan Children's Literature Research Collections, University of Minnesota. *Winners:* Robert Kraus, Walter Dean Myers.

Coretta Scott King Awards. For works that promote the cause of peace and brotherhood. *Offered by:* American Library Association, Social Responsibilities Roundtable. *Winners:* (author) Christopher Paul Curtis for *Elijah of Buxton* (Scholastic); (illustrator) Ashley Bryan for *Let It Shine* (Atheneum).

Coretta Scott King/John Steptoe Award for New Talent. To offer visibility to a writer or illustrator at the beginning of a career. *Sponsor:* Coretta Scott King Book Award Committee. *Winner:* Sundee T. Frazier for *Brendan Buckley's Universe and Everything in It"* (Delacorte).

Kiriyama Pacific Rim Book Prizes. For a book of fiction or a book of nonfiction that best contributes to a fuller understanding among the nations and peoples of the Pacific Rim. *Offered by:* Kiriyama Pacific Rim Institute. *Winner:* (fiction) Lloyd Jones for *Mister Pip* (Dial); (nonfiction) Julia Whitty for *The Fragile Edge: Diving and Other Adventures in the South Pacific* (Houghton Mifflin).

Robert Kirsch Award for Lifetime Achievement. To a living author whose residence or focus is the American West, and whose contributions to American letters clearly merit body-of-work recognition. *Offered by: Los Angeles Times. Winner:* Maxine Hong Kingston.

Lambda Literary Awards. To honor outstanding lesbian, gay, bisexual, and transgendered (LGBT) literature. *Offered by:* Lambda Literary Foundation. *Winners:* (anthology) Richard Labonte and Lawrence Schimel for *First Person Queer*

(Arsenal Pulp); (arts and culture) Matthew Hays for *The View From Here* (Arsenal Pulp); (bisexual) Brent Hartinger for *Split Screen* (HarperCollins); (children's/young adult) Perry Moore for *Hero* (Hyperion); (drama/theater) Steve Susoyev and George Birimisa, editors, for *Return to the Caffe Cino* (Moving Finger); (erotica) Simon Sheppard for *Homosex: 60 Years of Gay Erotica* (Running Press); (gay debut fiction) Christopher Kelly for *A Push and a Shove* (Alyson); (lesbian debut fiction) Aoibheann Sweeney for *Among Other Things, I've Taken Up Smoking* (Penguin); (LGBT studies) Sharon Marcus for *Between Women* (Princeton University); (men's fiction) Andre Aciman for *Call Me By Your Name* (Farrar, Straus & Giroux); (men's memoir/biography) Kevin Sessums for *Mississippi Sissy* (St. Martin's); (men's mystery) Greg Herren for *Murder in the Rue Chartres* (Alyson); (men's romance) Michael Thomas Ford for *Changing Tides* (Kensington); (nonfiction) Michael S. Sherry for *Gay Artists in Modern American Culture* (University of North Carolina); (poetry) Henri Cole for *Blackbird and Wolf* (Farrar, Straus & Giroux); (science fiction/fantasy/horror) Lee Thomas for *The Dust of Wonderland* (Alyson); (transgender) Cris Beam for *Transparent* (Harcourt); (women's fiction) Ali Liebegott for *The IHOP Papers* (Carroll & Graf); (women's memoir/biography) Nicola Griffith for *And Now We Are Going to Have a Party* (Payseur & Schmidt); (women's romance) K. G. MacGregor for *Out-of-Love* (Bella); (women's mystery) Gabrielle Goldsby for *Wall of Silence* (Bold Strokes).

Harold Morton Landon Translation Award ($1,000). For a book of verse translated into English by a single translator. *Offered by:* Academy of American Poets. *Winner:* Clayton Eshleman for *The Complete Poetry of Cesar Vallejo* (University of California).

Lannan Foundation Literary Awards. To honor both established and emerging writers whose work is of exceptional quality. *Offered by:* Lannan Foundation. *Winners:* (notable books) Philip Kitcher for *Living with Darwin: Evolution, Design, and the Future of Faith* (Oxford University); John Gray for *Black Mass: Apocalyptic Religion and the Death of Utopia* (Farrar, Straus & Giroux); Sheldon S. Wolin for *Democracy Incorporated: Managed Democracy and the Specter of Inverted Totalitarianism* (Princeton University); (poetry award) August Kleinzahler.

Lannan Foundation Literary Fellowships. To recognize young and mid-career writers of distinctive literary merit who demonstrate potential for continued outstanding work. *Offered by:* Lannan Foundation. *Winners:* Charles D'Ambrosio, Katie Ford, Ilya Kaminsky, Glenn Patterson.

James Laughlin Award. To commend and support a second book of poetry. *Offered by:* Academy of American Poets. *Winner:* Rusty Morrison for *the true keeps calm biding its story* (Small Press Distribution).

Claudia Lewis Award. For the year's best poetry book or books for young readers. *Offered by:* Bank Street College of Education and the Florence M. Miller Memorial Fund. *Winners:* Jane Yolen, Andrew Fusek Peters, and Polly Dunbar (illustrator) for *Here's a Little Poem: A Very First Book of Poetry* (Candlewick); Joyce Sidman and Pamela Zagarenski (illustrator) for *This Is Just to Say: Poems of Apology and Forgiveness* (Houghton Mifflin).

Library of Congress Lifetime Achievement Award for the Writing of Fiction. For a distinguished body of work. *Offered by:* Library of Congress. *Winner:* Herman Wouk.

Ruth Lilly Poetry Prize ($100,000). To a U.S. poet in recognition of lifetime achievement. *Offered by:* The Poetry Foundation. *Winner:* Gary Snyder.

Astrid Lindgren Award (Sweden) (approximately $830,000). In memory of children's author Astrid Lindgren to honor outstanding children's literature and efforts to promote it. *Offered by:* Government of Sweden. *Winner:* Sonya Hartnett.

Locus Awards. For science fiction writing. *Offered by:* Locus Publications. *Winners:* (science fiction novel) Michael Chabon for *The Yiddish Policemen's Union* (HarperCollins); (fantasy novel) Terry Pratchett for *Making Money* (HarperCollins); (young adult book) China Miéville for *Un Lun Dun* (Ballantine); (first novel) Joe Hill for *Heart-Shaped Box* (Morrow); (novella) Cory Doctorow for "After the Siege" in *The Infinite Matrix* January 2007; (novelette) Neil Gaiman for "The Witch's Headstone" in *Wizards*; (short story) Michael Swanwick for "A Small Room in Koboldtown" in *Asimov's* April/May 2007; (collection) Connie Willis for *The Winds of Marble Arch and Other Stories* (Subterranean); (anthology) Gardner Dozois and Jonathan Strahan, editors, for *The New Space Opera* (Eos); (nonfiction) Barry N. Malzberg for *Breakfast in the Ruins* (Baen); (art book) Shaun Tan for *The Arrival* (Scholastic).

Elizabeth Longford Prize for Historical Biography (United Kingdom) (£5,000). *Sponsors:* Flora Fraser and Peter Soros. *Winner:* Rosemary Hill for *God's Architect—Pugin and the Building of Romantic Britain* (Allen Lane).

Los Angeles Times Book Prizes. To honor literary excellence. *Offered by: Los Angeles Times. Winners:* (biography) Simon Sebag Montefiore for *Young Stalin* (Knopf); (current interest) Elizabeth D. Samet for *Soldier's Heart: Reading Literature Through Peace and War at West Point* (Farrar, Straus & Giroux); (fiction) Andrew O'Hagan for *Be Near Me* (Harcourt); (Art Seidenbaum Award for First Fiction) Dinaw Mengestu for *The Beautiful Things That Heaven Bears* (Riverhead); (history) Tim Weiner for *Legacy of Ashes: The History of the CIA* (Doubleday); (mystery/thriller) Karin Fossum for *The Indian Bride* translated by Charlotte Barslund (Harcourt); (poetry) Stanley Plumly for *Old Heart: Poems* (Norton); (science and technology) Douglas Hofstadter for *I Am a Strange Loop* (Basic); (young adult fiction) Philip Reeve for *A Darkling Plain* (The Hungry City Chronicles) (HarperCollins).

Amy Lowell Poetry Travelling Scholarship. For a U.S. poet to spend one year outside North America in a country the recipient feels will most advance his or her work. *Offered by:* Amy Lowell Poetry Travelling Scholarship. *Winner:* Kathleen Graber.

J. Anthony Lukas Awards. For nonfiction writing that demonstrates literary grace, serious research, and concern for an important aspect of American social or political life. *Offered by:* Columbia University Graduate School of Journalism and the Nieman Foundation for Journalism at Harvard. *Winners:* (book prize) ($10,000) Jeffrey Toobin for *The Nine: Inside the Secret World of the Supreme Court* (Doubleday); (history prize) ($10,000) Peter Silver for *Our Savage Neighbors: How Indian War Transformed Early America* (Norton); (work-in-progress) ($30,000) Michelle Goldberg for *The Means of Reproduction* (to be published by Penguin).

McKitterick Prize (United Kingdom) (£4,000). To an author over the age of 40 for a first novel, published or unpublished. *Winner:* Jennie Walker for *24 for 3* (Bloomsbury).

James Madison Book Award ($10,000). To honor books representing excellence in bringing knowledge and understanding of American history to children ages 5 to 14. *Offered by:* James Madison Book Award Fund. *Winner:* James Cross Giblin for *The Many Rides of Paul Revere* (Scholastic).

Man Asian Literary Prize ($10,000 plus $3,000 for translator, if applicable). For an Asian novel as yet unpublished in English. *Sponsored by:* Man Group. *Winner:* Miguel Syjuco for *Ilustrado.*

Man Booker International Prize (United Kingdom) (£60,000). Awarded biennially to a living author for a significant contribution to world literature. *Offered by:* Man Group. *Winner:* To be awarded next in 2009.

Man Booker Prize for Fiction (United Kingdom) (£50,000). For the best novel written in English by a Commonwealth author. *Offered by:* Booktrust and the Man Group. *Winner:* Aravind Adiga for *The White Tiger* (Atlantic).

Lenore Marshall Poetry Prize. For an outstanding book of poems published in the United States. *Offered by:* Academy of American Poets. *Winner:* Henri Cole for *Blackbird and Wolf* (Farrar, Straus & Giroux).

Somerset Maugham Awards (United Kingdom). For works in any genre except drama by a writer under the age of 35, to enable young writers to enrich their work by gaining experience of foreign countries. *Winners:* Gwendoline Riley for *Joshua Spassky* (Cape); Steven Hall for *The Raw Shark Texts* (Canongate); Nick Laird for *On Purpose* (Faber); Adam Thirlwell for *Miss Herbert* (Cape).

Addison M. Metcalf Award. To a young writer of great promise. *Offered by:* American Academy of Arts and Letters. *Winner:* To be awarded next in 2009.

Vicky Metcalf Award for Children's Literature (Canada) ($20,000). To a Canadian writer of children's literature for a body of work. *Offered by:* Metcalf Foundation. *Winner:* Michael Kusugak

Midwest Booksellers Choice Awards. *Offered by:* Midwest Booksellers Association. *Winners:* (fiction) Nancy Horan for *Loving Frank* (Ballantine); (nonfiction) Mildred Armstrong Kalish for *Little Heathens: Hard Times and High Spirits on an Iowa Farm During the Great Depression* (Bantam); (poetry) Ted Kooser and Robert Hanna (illustrator) for *Valentines: Poems* (University of Nebraska); (children's picture book) Joy Morgan Dey and Nikki Johnson for *Agate: What Good Is a Moose?* (Lake Superior Port Cities); (children's literature) Anne Ylvisaker for *Little Klein* (Candlewick).

Moonbeam Children's Book Awards. To honor the year's best independently published children's books. *Offered by:* Jenkins Group and Independent Publisher Online. *Winners:* (board book/cloth book) Catherine Maria Woolf for *My First Hike* (Dawn); (alphabet/counting book) Dianna Bonder for *Dogabet* (Walrus); (pop-up/cut-out) Pascale Hedelin and Robert Barborini, illustrator, for *The Human Body* (Owlkids); (activity book—games, arts and crafts) Karen Thalacker and Mindy Dwyer, illustrator, for *Gigi Knits . . . and Purls* (Martingale); (activity book—educational, science, history) Joan Marie Galat and Lorna Bennett, illustrator, for *Dot to Dot in the Sky: Stories of the Zodiac* (Walrus); (book with music/theatrical) CeCe

Winans, Keith Thomas, Alvin Love III, and Melodee Strong, illustrator, for *Colorful World* (Maren Green); (audiobook) Eugenia Miller, Talmadge Ragan, narrator, and Worth Keeter, producer, for *The Sign of the Salamander* (Blue Kiss); (picture book—preschool) Margie Blumberg and June Goulding, illustrator, for *Sunny Bunnies* (MB); (picture book—ages 4–8) (tie) Janet Marie Sinke and Craig Pennington, illustrator, for *Priscilla McDoodleNut DoodleMcMae Asks, "Why?"* (My Grandma and Me), Jennifer Fosberry and Mike Litwin for *My Name Is Not Isabella* (Monkey Barrel); (picture book—all ages) (tie) Vivian French and Jackie Morris, illustrator, for *Singing to the Sun: A Fairy Tale* (Kane/Miller), John Matthews and Pavel Tatarnikov, illustrator, for *Arthur of Albion* (Barefoot); (juvenile fiction—early reader) Zoe Weil for *Claude and Medea: The Hellburn Dogs* (Lantern); (pre-teen fiction) Shane Peacock for *Eye of the Crow* (Tundra); (young adult fiction) Maureen Ulrich for *Power Plays* (Coteau); (young adult fiction—mature issues) Christine Hart for *Watching July* (Sumach); (children's poetry) Mozz for *In Search of the Holey Whale* (Goofy Guru); (nonfiction—picture book) Selene Castrovilla and Bill Farnsworth, illustrator, for *By the Sword* (Boyds Mills); (nonfiction—young adult) (tie) Michael Smith for *What in the World!* (East West Discovery ), Ken Beller and Heather Chase for *Great Peacemakers* (LTS); (multicultural—picture book) (tie) David Bouchard and Andy Everson for *I Am Raven* (More Than Words), Karen Cogan and Blanche Davidson, illustrator, for *Pancho Finds a Home* (Azro); (multicultural fiction—chapter book) Guo Yue and Clare Farrow for *Little Leap Forward* (Barefoot); (multicultural nonfiction) Maya Ajmera, Yvonne Wakim Dennis, Arlene Hirschfelder, and Cynthia Pon for *Children of the USA* (Charlesbridge); (comic/graphic novel) J. Gunderson and Brent Schoonover, illustrator, for *Ropes of Revolution* (Stone Arch); (religion/spirituality) (tie) Sally Lloyd-Jones and Igor Oleynikov, illustrator, for *Tiny Bear's Bible* (Zonderkidz), Christopher Nye and

Henri Sørensen, illustrator, for *The Old Shepherd's Tale* (Housatonic); (holiday) Alastair MacDonald and Adel Nassief, illustrator, for *First Christmas* (Welcome); (book with merchandise—e.g., toy) Wendy Lokken, Gwendy Mangiamele, Edna Cucksey Stephens, and Heather Drescher, illustrator, for *You and Me Make Three* (EDCO); (Spanish-language book) (tie) Jorge Betancourt Polanco for *Ensonacion y el Jardin de Suenos/Dreamygirl's Field of Wishes* (Stephens), Michelle Markel and Bo Young Kim, illustrator, for *El Tiburón Que Me Enseñó Ingles/The Shark That Taught Me English* (Lectura); (environmental issues) Michael Driscoll, Dennis Driscoll, and Meredith Hamilton, illustrator, for *A Child's Introduction to the Environment* (Black Dog & Leventhal); (health issues) Yopi Havlik and April Willy, illustrator, for *Why Is Mommy Sleeping?* (Yopi's Pledge); (mind, body, spirit) Chuck Stump and Jim Strawn for *The Sad Mad Glad Book: The Anatomy of Your Attitude* (Four Dolphins); (best first book) (tie) Jessica Solberg and Robert Rath, illustrator, for *First Dog: Unleashed in the Montana Capitol* (Farcountry); Deanna Neil, David Erickson, Tom Newsom, David Lowe, and David Neil for *The Land of Curiosities: Adventures in Yellowstone, 1871–1872* (EcoSeekers); (best illustration) (tie) Jeri Landers for *The Journey of Bushky Bushybottom* (Ochre Moon), Barry Moser for *Jack London's Dog* by Dirk Wales (Great Plains); (reading skills/literacy) (tie) Sheila Moore and Carol Holsinger, illustrator, for *Abadaba Alphabet: Learning Letter Sounds* (Abadaba Reading); Barbara Mariconda and Sherry Rogers, illustrator, for *Sort It Out!* (Sylvan Dell).

Moonbeam Peacemaker Award. To honor the best book promoting world peace and human tolerance. *Offered by:* Jenkins Group and Independent Publisher Online. *Winner:* Natalie Maydell, Sep Riahi, and Heba Amin, illustrator, for *Extraordinary Women from the Muslim World* (Global Content).

Moonbeam Spirit Awards. For books that show dedication and compassion about children, humanity, and literacy. *Offered by:* Jenkins Group and Independent Publisher Online. *Winners:* Terri Saville-Sewell for *Can You See?* (self-published/BookSurge); Denise Vanderlugt for *Where Rainbows Live* (self-published/Bookbuilders); Donna Lee and Ann Gates Fiser, illustrator, for *Beatrice and the Magic Garden Hat* (Chi Whiz Creations); S. K. Carnes for *My Champion* (self-published/Illumina).

William C. Morris YA Debut Award. To honor a debut book published by a first-time author writing for teens and celebrating impressive new voices in young adult literature. *Offered by:* Young Adult Library Services Association, American Library Association. *Donor:* William C. Morris Endowment. *Winner:* To be awarded first in 2009.

Gustavus Myers Awards. For outstanding books that extend understanding of the root causes of bigotry. *Offered by:* Gustavus Myers Center for the Study of Bigotry and Human Rights in North America. *Winners:* Douglas A. Blackmon for *Slavery by Another Name: The Re-Enslavement of Black Americans from the Civil War to World War II* (Doubleday); Paula J. Giddings for *Ida—A Sword Among Lions: Ida B. Wells and the Campaign Against Lynching* (HarperCollins); Lawrence Hill for *Someone Knows My Name* (Norton); David Ngaruri Kenney and Philip G. Schrag for *Asylum Denied: A Refugee's Struggle for Safety in America* (University of California); Mahvish Rukhsana Khan for *My Guantanamo Diary: The Detainees and the Stories They Told Me* (Public Affairs); Suzanne Braun Levine and Mary Thom for *Bella Abzug: How One Tough Broad from the Bronx Fought Jim Crow and Joe McCarthy, Pissed Off Jimmy Carter, Battled for the Rights of Women and Workers . . .* (Farrar, Straus & Giroux); Mica Pollock, editor, for *Everyday Antiracism: Getting Real About Race in School* (New Press); Cynthia Soohoo, Catherine Albisa, and Martha Davis, editors, for *Bringing Human Rights Home, Vols. 1–3* (Greenwood); Kai Wright for *Drifting Toward Love: Black, Brown, Gay and Coming of Age on the Streets of New*

*York* (Beacon); Kao Kalia Yang for *The Latehomecomer: A Hmong Family Memoir* (Coffee House).

National Book Awards. For the best books of the year published in the United States. *Offered by:* National Book Foundation. *Winners:* (fiction) Peter Matthiessen for *Shadow Country* (Modern Library); (nonfiction) Annette Gordon-Reed for *The Hemingses of Monticello: An American Family* (Norton); (poetry) Mark Doty for *Fire to Fire: New and Collected Poems* (HarperCollins); (young people's literature) Judy Blundell for *What I Saw and How I Lied* (Scholastic).

National Book Critics Circle Awards. For literary excellence. *Offered by:* National Book Critics Circle. *Winners:* (fiction) Junot Diaz for *The Brief Wondrous Life of Oscar Wao* (Riverhead); (general nonfiction) Harriet Washington for *Medical Apartheid: The Dark History of Medical Experiments on Black Americans from Colonial Times to the Present* (Doubleday); (biography) Tim Jeal for *Stanley: The Impossible Life of Africa's Greatest Explorer* (Yale University); (autobiography) Edwidge Danticat for *Brother, I'm Dying* (Knopf); (poetry) Mary Jo Bang for *Elegy* (Graywolf); (criticism) Alex Ross for *The Rest Is Noise: Listening to the Twentieth Century* (Farrar, Straus & Giroux); (Ivan Sandrof Lifetime Achievement Award) Emilie Buchwald; (Nona Balakian Citation for Excellence in Reviewing) Sam Anderson, *New York* magazine.

National Book Foundation Literarian Award for Outstanding Service to the American Literary Community. *Offered by:* National Book Foundation. *Winner:* Barney Rosset.

National Book Foundation Medal for Distinguished Contribution to American Letters. To a person who has enriched the nation's literary heritage over a life of service or corpus of work. *Offered by:* National Book Foundation. *Winner:* Maxine Hong Kingston.

National Translation Award ($2,500). To honor a translator whose work has made the most valuable contribution to literary translation into English. *Offered by:* American Literary Translators Association.

*Winner:* Richard Wilbur for his translation from French of Pierre Corneille's *The Theatre of Illusion* (Harvest).

Nebula Awards. For science fiction writing. *Offered by:* Science Fiction and Fantasy Writers of America. *Winners:* (best novel) Michael Chabon for *The Yiddish Policemen's Union* (HarperCollins); (best novella) Nancy Kress for "Fountain of Age" in *Asimov's*; (best novelette) Ted Chiang for "The Merchant and the Alchemist's Gate" (Subterranean); (best short story) Karen Joy Fowler for "Always" in *Asimov's*; (best script) Guillermo del Toro for "Pan's Labyrinth"; (Andre Norton Award for Young Adult Science Fiction and Fantasy) J. K. Rowling for *Harry Potter and the Deathly Hallows*; (Damon Knight Grand Master for 2008) Michael Moorcock.

Nestlé Children's Book Prizes (formerly Smarties Book Prizes) (United Kingdom). To encourage high standards and to stimulate interest in books for children. *Offered by:* Nestlé UK Ltd. *Winners:* Discontinued in 2008.

John Newbery Medal. For the most distinguished contribution to literature for children. *Offered by:* American Library Association, Association for Library Service to Children. *Winner:* Laura Amy Schlitz for *Good Masters! Sweet Ladies! Voices from a Medieval Village* (Candlewick).

Nobel Prize in Literature (Sweden). For the total literary output of a distinguished career. *Offered by:* Swedish Academy. *Winner:* Jean-Marie Gustave Le Clézio.

Eli M. Oboler Memorial Award. Biennially, to an author of a published work in English or in English translation dealing with issues, events, questions, or controversies in the area of intellectual freedom. *Offered by:* Intellectual Freedom Round Table, American Library Association. *Winner:* Christopher M. Finan for *From the Palmer Raids to the Patriot Act* (Beacon).

Flannery O'Connor Awards for Short Fiction. For collections of short fiction. *Offered by:* University of Georgia Press. *Winners:* Andrew Porter for *The Theory of Light and Matter* (University of Georgia); Peter Selgin for *Drowning Lessons* (University of Georgia).

Scott O'Dell Award. For historical fiction. *Offered by: Bulletin of the Center for Children's Books,* University of Chicago. *Winner:* Christopher Paul Curtis for *Elijah of Buxton* (Scholastic).

Orange Broadband Award for New Writers (United Kingdom). For a first novel or short story collection written by a woman and published in the United Kingdom. *Offered by:* Orange plc. *Winner:* Joanna Kavenna for *Inglorious* (Picador).

Orange Broadband Prize for Fiction (United Kingdom). For the best novel written by a woman and published in the United Kingdom. *Offered by:* Orange plc. *Winner:* Rose Tremain for *The Road Home* (Little, Brown).

Orbis Pictus Award. For outstanding nonfiction for children. *Offered by:* National Council of Teachers of English. *Winner:* Tonya Bolden for *M.L.K.: Journey of a King* (Abrams).

Pegasus Awards. For outstanding works of poetry. *Offered by:* The Poetry Foundation. *Winners:* (Neglected Master Award, $50,000). For the life's work of a significant but under-recognized American poet. Not awarded in 2008; (Emily Dickinson First Book Award, $10,000). To a writer over the age of 50 who has never published a book. Not awarded in 2008; (Randall Jarrell Award in Poetry Criticism, $10,000). Not awarded in 2008; (Verse Drama Prize, $10,000) to honor a living poet who has written a previously unpublished, outstanding original verse drama in English. Not awarded in 2008.

PEN Award for Poetry in Translation. For a book-length translation of poetry from any language into English and published in the United States. *Offered by:* PEN American Center. *Winner:* Rosmarie Waldrop for her translation from German of *Lingos I-IX* by Ulf Stolterfoht (Burning Deck).

PEN/Saul Bellow Award for Achievement in American Fiction. Awarded biennially to a distinguished living American author of fiction. *Offered by:* PEN American Center. *Winner:* To be awarded next in 2009.

PEN Beyond Margins Awards. For book-length writings by authors of color, published in the United States during the current calendar year. *Offered by:* PEN American Center. *Winners:* Chris Abani for *Song for Night* (Akashic); Amiri Baraka (LeRoi Jones) for *Tales of the Out and the Gone* (Akashic); Frances Hwang for *Transparency: Stories* (Back Bay); Naeem Murr for *The Perfect Man* (Random); Joseph M. Marshall III for *The Day the World Ended at Little Big Horn* (Viking).

PEN/Robert Bingham Fellowship ($35,000). To a writer whose first novel or short story collection represents distinguished literary achievement and suggests great promise. *Offered by:* PEN American Center. *Winner:* Dalia Sofer for *The Septembers of Shiraz* (Ecco).

PEN/Jacqueline Bograd Weld Award for Biography ($10,000). To the author of a distinguished biography published in the United States during the previous calendar year. *Offered by:* PEN American Center. *Winner:* Janet Malcolm for *Two Lives: Gertrude and Alice* (Yale University).

PEN Book-of-the-Month Club Translation Prize. For a book-length literary translation from any language into English. *Offered by:* PEN American Center. *Winner:* Margaret Jull Costa for her translation from Portuguese of *The Maias* by Eça de Queirós (New Directions).

PEN/Faulkner Award for Fiction ($15,000). To honor the best work of fiction published by an American. *Winner:* Kate Christensen for *The Great Man* (Doubleday).

PEN/John Kenneth Galbraith Award ($10,000). For a distinguished book of general nonfiction. *Offered by:* PEN American Center. *Winner:* Not awarded in 2008.

PEN/Nora Magid Award ($2,500). To honor a magazine editor whose high literary standards and taste have contributed significantly to the excellence of the publication he or she edits. *Offered by:* PEN American Center. *Winner:* Not awarded in 2008.

PEN/Malamud Award ($5,000). To an author or authors who have demonstrated long-term excellence in short fiction. *Offered by:* PEN American Center. *Winners:* Cynthia Ozick, Peter Ho Davies.

PEN/Ralph Manheim Medal for Translation. Given every three years to a translator whose career has demonstrated a commitment to excellence. *Winner:* To be awarded next in 2009.

PEN/Nabokov Award ($20,000). To celebrate the accomplishments of a living author whose body of work, either written in or translated into English, represents achievement in a variety of literary genres. *Offered by:* PEN American Center. *Winner:* Cynthia Ozick.

PEN/Phyllis Naylor Working Writer Fellowship ($5,000). *Offered by:* PEN American Center. *Winner:* Theresa Nelson.

PEN/Joyce Osterweil Award for Poetry. Given in odd-numbered years to recognize a new and emerging American poet. *Offered by:* PEN American Center. *Winner:* Not awarded in 2008.

PEN/Laura Pels Foundation Awards for Drama. To recognize a master American dramatist and an American playwright in mid-career. *Offered by:* PEN American Center. *Winners:* (playwright) Richard Nelson; (mid-career prize) Sarah Ruhl.

PEN Prison Writing Awards. To provide support and encouragement to prison inmates whose writing shows merit or promise. *Offered by:* PEN American Center. *Winners:* (fiction) Chris Everly for "Hook Island Traveler"; (poetry) Yvette Louisell for "Prison Eulogies"; (essay) Michael Rothwell for "Check Out Day"; (drama) Jodi L. Serino for "Metamorphosis"; (memoir) Charles P. Norman for "Fighting the Ninja."

PEN Translation Fund grants. To promote the publication and reception of translated world literature in English. *Winners:* Bernard Adams for his translation from Hungarian of *Kornél Esti* by Dezső Kosztolányi; Jeffrey Angles for his translation from Japanese of *Twelve Perspectives* by Mutsuo Takahashi; Andrea Lingenfelter for her translation from Chinese of *Padma* by Annie Baobei; Jessica Moore for her translation from French of *Turkana Boy* by Jean-François Beauchemin; Sean Redmond for his translation from medieval Latin of Felix Fabri's 1483 travel memoir *Another Holy Land: Felix Fabri's Voyage to Medieval Egypt*; Mira Rosenthal for her translation from Polish of *Colonies,* son-

nets by Tomasz Różycki; Damion Searls for his translation from Dutch of *The Freeloader and Other Stories* by Nescio (J. H. F. Grönloh); Simon Wickham-Smith for his translation from Mongolian of *The Battle for Our Land Has Begun,* poems and political writings by Ochirbatyn Dashbalbar.

PEN/Voelcker Award for Poetry. Given in even-numbered years to an American poet at the height of his or her powers. *Offered by:* PEN American Center. *Winner:* Kimiko Hahn.

Maxwell E. Perkins Award. To honor an editor, publisher, or agent who has discovered, nurtured, and championed writers of fiction in the United States. *Offered by:* Mercantile Library of New York. *Winner:* Jonathan Galassi.

Phoenix Award. To the author of an English-language children's book that failed to win a major award at the time of its publication 20 years earlier. *Winner:* Peter Dickinson for *Eva* (Delacorte).

Edgar Allan Poe Awards. For outstanding mystery, suspense, and crime writing. *Offered by:* Mystery Writers of America. *Winners:* (novel) John Hart for *Down River* (St. Martin's); (first novel by an American author) Tana French for *In the Woods* (Penguin); (paperback original) Megan Abbott for *Queenpin* (Simon & Schuster); (critical/biographical) Jon Lellenberg, Daniel Stashower, and Charles Foley for *Arthur Conan Doyle: A Life in Letters* (Penguin); (fact crime) Vincent Bugliosi for *Reclaiming History: The Assassination of President John F. Kennedy* (Norton); (short story) Susan Straight for "The Golden Gopher" in *Los Angeles Noir* (Akashic); (best young adult) Tedd Arnold for *Rat Life* (Penguin); (best juvenile) Katherine Marsh for *The Night Tourist* (Hyperion); (play) Joseph Goodrich for *Panic* (International Mystery Writers' Festival); (Robert L. Fish Memorial Award) Mark Ammons for "The Catch" in *Still Waters* (Level Best); (Simon & Schuster–Mary Higgins Clark Award) Sandi Ault for *Wild Indigo* (Penguin); (grand master) Bill Pronzini.

Katherine Anne Porter Award ($20,000). Awarded biennially to a prose writer of demonstrated achievement. *Offered by:* American Academy of Arts and Letters. *Winner:* John Edgar Wideman.

Michael L. Printz Award. For excellence in literature for young adults. *Offered by:* American Library Association, Young Adult Library Services Association. *Winner:* Geraldine McCaughrean for *The White Darkness* (HarperCollins).

V. S. Pritchett Memorial Prize (United Kingdom) (£1,000). For a previously unpublished short story. *Offered by:* Royal Society of Literature. *Winner:* Cynthia Rogerson for "A Dangerous Place."

Prix Goncourt (France). For "the best imaginary prose work of the year." *Offered by:* Société des Gens des Lettres. *Winner:* Atiq Rahimi for *Syngué Sabour—La Pierre de Patience* (French and European Publications).

Pulitzer Prizes in Letters. To honor distinguished work dealing preferably with American themes. *Offered by:* Columbia University Graduate School of Journalism. *Winners:* (fiction) Junot Diaz for *The Brief Wondrous Life of Oscar Wao* (Riverhead); (history) Daniel Walker Howe for *What Hath God Wrought: The Transformation of America, 1815–1848* (Oxford University); (biography) John Matteson for *Eden's Outcasts: The Story of Louisa May Alcott and Her Father* (Norton); (general nonfiction) Saul Friedländer for *The Years of Extermination: Nazi Germany and the Jews, 1939–1945* (Harper); (drama) Tracy Letts for "August: Osage County" (Theatre Communications Group); (poetry) Robert Hass for *Time and Materials* (HarperCollins) and Philip Schultz for "Failure" (Harcourt).

Quill Awards. To honor excellence in book publishing. *Offered by:* Reed Business Information and the NBC Universal Television Stations. *Winners:* Program suspended in 2008.

Raiziss/De Palchi Translation Award. For a translation into English of a significant work of modern Italian poetry by a living translator. *Offered by:* Academy of American Poets. *Winner:* Patrick Barron for *The Selected Poetry and Prose of Andrea Zanzotto* (University of Chicago).

Raven Awards. For outstanding achievement in the mystery field outside the realm of creative writing. *Offered by:* Mystery Writers of America. *Winners:* Center for the Book, Library of Congress; Kate Mattes of Kate's Mystery Books, North Cambridge, Massachusetts.

Rea Award for the Short Story. To honor a living writer who has made a significant contribution to the short story as an art form. *Offered by:* Dungannon Foundation. *Winner:* Amy Hempel.

Arthur Rense Poetry Prize ($20,000). To an exceptional poet. *Offered by:* American Academy of Arts and Letters. *Winner:* Hayden Carruth.

John Llewellyn Rhys Prize (United Kingdom) (£5,000). For a work of literature by a British or Commonwealth author 35 or younger and published in the United Kingdom. *Offered by:* Booktrust. *Winner:* Henry Hitchings for *The Secret Life of Words* (John Murray).

Harold U. Ribalow Prize. For Jewish fiction published in English. *Sponsor: Hadassah Magazine. Winner:* Nathan Englander for *The Ministry of Special Cases* (Vintage).

Rita Awards. *Offered by:* Romance Writers of America. *Winners:* (best first book) Terri Garey for *Dead Girls Are Easy* (HarperCollins); (best contemporary series romance) Janice Johnson for *Snowbound* (Harlequin); (best contemporary series romance—suspense/adventure) Helen Brenna for *Treasure* (Harlequin); (best contemporary single title romance) Kristan Higgins for *Catch of the Day* (Harlequin); (best historical romance) Madeline Hunter for *Lessons of Desire* (Bantam Dell); (best inspirational romance) Linda Goodnight for *A Touch of Grace* (Harlequin); (best novel with strong romantic elements) Deanna Raybourn for *Silent in the Grave* (Harlequin); (best paranormal romance) J. R. Ward for *Lover Revealed* (Penguin); (best Regency historical romance) Julia Quinn for *The Secret Diaries of Miss Miranda Cheever* (HarperCollins); (best romance novella) Jennifer Greene for "Born in My Heart" in *Like Mother, Like*

*Daughter* (Harlequin); (best romantic suspense) Anne Stuart for *Ice Blue* (Harlequin); (best young adult romance) Melissa Marr for *Wicked Lovely* (HarperCollins); (Nora Roberts Lifetime Achievement Award) Vicki Lewis Thompson.

Rodda Book Award. To recognize a book that exhibits excellence in writing and has contributed significantly to congregational libraries through promotion of spiritual growth. The award is given to books for adults, young adults, and children on a three-year-rotational basis. *Offered by:* Church and Synagogue Library Association. *Winner:* (children's) Ingrid Hess for *Sleep in Peace* (Herald).

Rogers Writers' Trust Fiction Prize (Canada) (C$25,000). To a Canadian author of a novel or short story collection. *Offered by:* Rogers Communications. *Winner:* Miriam Toews for *The Flying Troutmans* (Knopf Canada).

Sami Rohr Prize for Jewish Literature ($100,000). *Offered by:* Family of Sami Rohr. *Winner:* Lucette Lagnado for *The Man in the White Sharkskin Suit: My Family's Exodus from Old Cairo to the New World* (Harper Perennial).

Rosenthal Family Foundation Award ($5,000). To a young novelist of considerable literary talent for a work. *Offered by:* American Academy of Arts and Letters. *Winner:* Richard Lange for *Dead Boys* (Back Bay).

Royal Society of Literature/Jerwood Awards for Nonfiction (United Kingdom). For authors engaged on their first major commissioned works of nonfiction. *Offered by:* Royal Society of Literature. *Winners:* (£10,000) Rachel Hewitt for the historical biography *Map of a Nation,* to be published by Granta; (£5,000) Matthew Hollis for his study of the poet Edward Thomas, *Edward Thomas—The Final Years,* to be published by Faber; (£5,000) poets Michael Symmons Roberts and Paul Farley for *Edgelands—Journeys into England's Last Wilderness,* to be published by Cape.

Royal Society of Literature Ondaatje Prize. For a distinguished work of fiction, nonfiction or poetry evoking the spirit of a place. *Offered by:* Royal Society of Litera-

ture. *Winner:* Graham Robb for *The Discovery of France* (Picador).

Juan Rulfo International Latin American and Caribbean Prize (FIL Literature Prize) (Mexico) ($100,000). For lifetime achievement in any literary genre. *Offered by:* Juan Rulfo International Latin American and Caribbean Prize Committee. *Winner:* António Lobo Antunes.

Carl Sandburg Literary Award. To honor a significant body of work that has enhanced public awareness of the written word. *Sponsor:* Chicago Public Library Foundation. *Winner:* Tom Wolfe.

Ivan Sandrof Life Achievement Award. To honor long-standing and outstanding dedication to book culture. *Sponsor:* National Book Critics Circle. *Winner:* PEN American Center.

John Sargent, Sr. First Novel Prize. *Offered by:* Mercantile Library Center for Fiction. *Winner:* Hannah Tinti for *The Good Thief* (Dial).

Schneider Family Book Awards. To honor authors and illustrators for books that embody artistic expressions of the disability experience of children and adolescents. *Offered by:* American Library Association. *Winners:* (ages 0–10) Andrea Stenn Stryer and Bert Dodson (illustrator) for *Kami and the Yaks* (Bay Otter); (ages 11–13) Tracie Vaughn Zimmer for *Reaching for Sun* (Bloomsbury); (ages 13–18) Ginny Rorby for *Hurt Go Happy* (Starscape).

Shelley Memorial Award. To a poet living in the United States who is chosen on the basis of genius and need. *Offered by:* Poetry Society of America. *Winner:* Ed Roberson.

Robert F. Sibert Medal. For the most distinguished informational book for children. *Offered by:* American Library Association, Association for Library Service to Children. *Winner:* Peter Sís for *The Wall: Growing Up Behind the Iron Curtain* (Farrar, Straus & Giroux).

Spur Awards. *Offered by:* Western Writers of America. *Winners:* (long novel) Aryn Kyle for *The God of Animals* (Scribner); (short novel) Sandra Dallas for *Tallgrass* (St. Martin's); (original mass market paperback) Max McCoy for *Hellfire Canyon*

(Pinnacle); (first novel) Thomas Maltman for *The Night Birds* (Soho); (nonfiction biography) Robert W. Larson for *Gall: Lakota War Chief* (University of Oklahoma); (nonfiction historical) Annette Atkins for *Creating Minnesota* (Minnesota Historical Society); (nonfiction contemporary) Robert M. Utley for *Lone Star Lawmen: The Second Century of the Texas Rangers* (Oxford University); (short fiction story) Marcia Muller and Bill Pronzini for "Crucifixion River" (Five Star); (short nonfiction) Joseph B. Herring for "Selling the 'Noble Savage' Myth: George Catlin and the Iowa Indians in Europe, 1843–1845" in *Kansas History* (Winter 2007); (juvenile fiction) Johnny D. Boggs for *Doubtful Cañon* (Five Star); (juvenile nonfiction) Nancy Plain for *Sagebrush and Paintbrush: The Story of Charlie Russell, the Cowboy Artist* (Mondo); (drama) Andrew Dominik for *The Assassination of Jesse James by the Coward Robert Ford* (Warner Bros. Pictures); (documentary) Jayne McKay and Daniel Dixon for *Maynard Dixon: Art and Spirit* (Cloud World); (poem) John Duncklee for "El Corrido de Antonio Beltran" from *Open Range: Poetry of the Reimagined West* (Ghost Road).

Wallace Stevens Award. To recognize outstanding and proven mastery in the art of poetry. *Offered by:* Academy of American Poets. *Winner:* Louise Glück.

Bram Stoker Awards. For superior horror writing. *Offered by:* Horror Writers Association. *Winners:* (novel) Sarah Langan for *The Missing* (Harper); (first novel) Joe Hill for *Heart-Shaped Box* (Morrow); (long fiction) Gary Braunbeck for *Afterward, There Will Be a Hallway*; (short fiction) David Niall Wilson for "The Gentle Brush of Wings; (fiction collection) (tie) Michael A. Arnzen for *Proverbs for Monsters* (Dark Regions); Peter Straub for *Five Stories*; (anthology) Gary Braunbeck and Hank Schwaeble, editors, for *Five Strokes to Midnight* (Haunted Pelican); (nonfiction) Jonathan Maberry and David F. Kramer for *The Cryptopedia: A Dictionary of the Weird, Strange and Downright Bizarre* (Citadel); (poetry collection) (tie) Linda Addison for *Being Full of Light,*

*Insubstantial* (Space and Time); Charlee Jacob and Marge Simon for *Vectors: A Week in the Death of a Planet* (Dark Regions); (lifetime achievement) John Carpenter, Robert Weinberg; (Richard Laymon President's Award) Mark Worthen, Stephen Dorato, Christopher Fulbright.

Stonewall Book Awards. *Offered by:* Gay, Lesbian, Bisexual, and Transgendered Round Table, American Library Association. *Winners:* (Barbara Gittings Literature Award) Ellis Avery for *The Teahouse Fire* (Riverhead); (Israel Fishman Nonfiction Award) Mark Doty for *Dog Years: A Memoir* (HarperCollins).

The Story Prize. For a collection of short fiction. *Offered by: Story* magazine. *Winner:* Jim Shepard for *Like You'd Understand, Anyway* (Knopf).

Flora Stieglitz Straus Award. For nonfiction books that serve as an inspiration to young readers. *Offered by:* Bank Street College of Education and the Florence M. Miller Memorial Fund. *Winners:* Lauren Thompson and James Estrin, photographer, for *Ballerina Dreams* (Feiwel and Friends); Russell Freedman for *Who Was First? Discovering the Americas* (Clarion).

Tanizaki Prize (Japan). *Winner:* Serai Yuici for *Bakushin.*

Charles Taylor Prize for Literary Nonfiction (Canada). To honor a book of creative nonfiction widely available in Canada and written by a Canadian citizen or landed immigrant. *Offered by:* Charles Taylor Foundation. *Winner:* John Gwyn for *John A.—The Man Who Made Us: The Life and Times of John A. McDonald, Vol. 1, 1815–1867* (Random).

Sydney Taylor Children's Book Awards. For a distinguished contribution to Jewish children's literature. *Offered by:* Association of Jewish Libraries. *Winners:* (younger readers) Richard Michelson for *As Good as Anybody: Martin Luther King, Jr. and Abraham Joshua Heschel's Amazing March Toward Freedom,* illustrated by Raul Colon (Knopf); (older readers) Karen Hesse for *Brooklyn Bridge* (Macmillan); (teen readers) Valerie Zenatti for *A Bottle in the Gaza Sea* (Bloomsbury).

Theatre Library Association Award. For the best English-language book about recorded performance, including motion pictures, television, and radio. *Offered by:* Theatre Library Association. *Winner:* Jeanine Basinger for *The Star Machine* (Knopf).

Dylan Thomas Prize (United Kingdom) (£60,000). Awarded biennially for the year's best eligible commercially published work of literature. *Offered by:* David Cohen Family Charitable Trust and the Arts Council of England. *Winner:* Nam Le for *The Boat* (Knopf).

Thriller Awards. *Offered by:* International Thriller Writers. *Winners:* (novel) Robert Harris for *The Ghost* (Simon & Schuster); (first novel) Joe Hill for *Heart-Shaped Box* (Morrow); (paperback original) Tom Piccirilli for *The Midnight Road* (Bantam).

Thurber Prize for American Humor. For a humorous book of fiction or nonfiction. *Offered by:* Thurber House. *Winner:* Larry Doyle for *I Love You, Beth Cooper* (HarperCollins).

Betty Trask Prize and Awards (United Kingdom). To Commonwealth writers under the age of 35 for "romantic or traditional" first novels. *Offered by:* Society of Authors. *Winner:* (Betty Trask Prize, £10,000) David Szalay for *London and the South-East* (Cape); (£2,000–£6,000) Ross Raisin for *God's Own Country* (Viking), Thomas Leveritt for *The Exchange Rate Between Love and Money* (Harvill Secker), Anna Ralph for *The Floating Island* (Hutchinson).

Kate Tufts Discovery Award ($10,000). For a first or very early book of poetry by an emerging poet. *Offered by:* Claremont Graduate School. *Winner:* Janice Harrington for *Even the Hollow My Body Made Is Gone* (BOA Editions).

Kingsley Tufts Poetry Award ($100,000). For a book of poetry by a mid-career poet. *Offered by:* Claremont Graduate School. *Winner:* Tom Sleigh for *Space Walk* (Mariner).

Mark Twain Poetry Award ($25,000). To recognize a poet's contribution to humor in American poetry. *Offered by:* The Poetry Foundation. *Winner:* Albert Goldbarth.

21st Century Award. To honor recent achievement in writing by an author with ties to Chicago. *Sponsor:* Chicago Public Library Foundation. *Winner:* Theresa Schwegel.

Harold D. Vursell Memorial Award ($10,000). To a writer whose work merits recognition for the quality of its prose style. *Offered by* American Academy of Arts and Letters. *Winner:* Maxine Swann.

Kim Scott Walwyn Prize (United Kingdom). To recognise the professional achievements of women in publishing. *Offered by:* Booktrust. *Winner:* Clare Alexander.

George Washington Book Prize ($50,000). To recognize an important new book about America's founding era. *Offered by:* Washington College and the Gilder Lehrman Institute of American History. *Winner:* Marcus Rediker for *The Slave Ship: A Human History* (Viking).

Whitbread Book Awards. See Costa Book Awards.

Whiting Writers' Awards ($50,000). For emerging writers of exceptional talent and promise. *Offered by:* Mrs. Giles Whiting Foundation. *Winners:* (fiction) Mischa Berlinski, Laleh Khadivi, Manuel Muñoz, Benjamin Percy, Lysley Tenorio; (poetry) Rick Hilles, Douglas Kearney, Julie Sheehan; (nonfiction) Donovan Hohn; (plays) Dael Orlandersmith.

Walt Whitman Award ($5,000). To a U.S. poet who has not published a book of poems in a standard edition. *Offered by:* Academy of American Poets. *Winner:* Jonathan Thirkield for *The Waker's Corridor* (LSU Press).

Laura Ingalls Wilder Award. Awarded biennially to an author or illustrator whose books have made a substantial and lasting contribution to children's literature. *Offered by:* American Library Association, Association for Library Service to Children. *Winner:* Not awarded in 2008.

Robert H. Winner Memorial Award. To a mid-career poet over 40 who has published no more than one book of poetry. *Offered by:* Poetry Society of America. *Winner:* Jocelyn Emerson.

L. L. Winship Award. For a book of fiction, poetry, or creative nonfiction with a New

England subject or written by a New England author. *Offered by:* PEN New England. *Winners:* (fiction) Rishi Reddi for *Karma and Other Stories* (Harper Perennial); (nonfiction) Kristen Laine for *American Band: Music, Dreams, and Coming of Age in the Heartland* (Gotham); (poetry) Ann Killough for *Beloved Idea* (Alice James).

George Wittenborn Memorial Book Awards. To North American art publications that represent the highest standards of content, documentation, layout, and format. *Offered by:* Art Libraries Society of North America (ARLIS/NA). *Winner:* Cindi Strauss for *Ornament as Art: Avant-Garde Jewelry from the Helen Williams Drutt Collection* (Arnoldsche Verlagsanstalt in association with the Museum of Fine Arts, Houston); Ani Boyajian and Mark Rutkoski, editors, for *Stuart Davis: A Catalogue Raisonné* (Yale University).

Thomas Wolfe Award and Lecture. To honor writers with distinguished bodies of work. *Offered by:* Thomas Wolfe Society and University of North Carolina at Chapel Hill. *Winner:* Robert Morgan.

Helen and Kurt Wolff Translator's Prize. For an outstanding translation from German into English, published in the United States. *Offered by:* Goethe Institut Inter Nationes, Chicago. *Winner:* David Dollenmayer for his translation of Moses Rosenkranz's *Childhood: An Autobiographical Fragment* (*Kindheit. Fragment einer Autobiographie*) (Syracuse University).

World Fantasy Convention Awards. For outstanding fantasy writing. *Offered by:* World Fantasy Convention. *Winners:* (novel) Guy Gavriel Kay for *Ysabel* (Viking/Penguin); (novella) Elizabeth Hand for *Illyria* (PS Publishing); (short story) Theodora Goss for "Singing of Mount Abora" in *Logorrhea* (Bantam); (anthology) Ellen Datlow, editor, for *Inferno: New Tales of Terror and the Supernatural* (Tor); (collection) Robert Shearman for *Tiny Deaths* (Comma); (lifetime achievement) Leo and Diane Dillon, Patricia McKillip.

Writers' Trust Nonfiction Prize (Canada) (C\$25,000). *Offered by:* Writers' Trust. *Winner:* Taras Grescoe for *Bottomfeeder: How to Eat Ethically in a World of Vanishing Seafood* (HarperCollins).

Writers' Trust/McClelland & Stewart Journey Prize (Canada) (C\$10,000). To a new, developing Canadian author for a short story or an excerpt from a novel in progress. *Offered by:* McClelland & Stewart and James A. Michener. *Winner:* Saleema Nawaz for "My Three Girls," published in *Prairie Fire*.

Writers' Trust Notable Author (Canada) (C\$25,000). To a writer in mid-career for a body of work. *Winner:* Michael Winter.

Young Lions Fiction Award. For a novel or collection of short stories by an American under the age of 35. *Offered by:* Young Lions of the New York Public Library. *Winner:* Ron Currie, Jr. for *God Is Dead* (Viking).

Morton Dauwen Zabel Award (\$10,000). To a progressive and experimental writer. *Offered by:* American Academy of Arts and Letters. *Winner:* Ben Marcus.

Zoetrope Short Fiction Prizes. *Offered by:* Zoetrope: All-Story. *Winners:* (first, \$1,000) Bernie McGill for "Sleepwalkers"; (second, \$500) Doug Ramspeck for "The Owl That Carries Us Away"; (third, \$250) Akenji Ndumu for "The Fireside Kitchen."

Charlotte Zolotow Award. To the author of the best children's picture book published in the United States in the previous year. *Offered by:* Cooperative Children's Book Center, University of Wisconsin–Madison. *Winner:* Greg Foley for *Thank You, Bear* (Viking).

# Part 6
# Directory of Organizations

# Directory of Library and Related Organizations

## Networks, Consortia, and Other Cooperative Library Organizations

### United States

#### Alabama

Alabama Health Libraries Assn., Inc. (ALHeLa), Univ. of Alabama, Lister Hill Lib., Birmingham 35294-0013. SAN 372-8218. Tel. 205-975-8313, fax 205-934-2230. *Pres.* Lee Vacovich.

Library Management Network, Inc. (LMN), 2132 6th Ave. S.E., Suite 106, Decatur 35601. SAN 322-3906. Tel. 256-308-2529, fax 256-308-2533. *Systems Coord.* Charlotte Moncrief.

Marine Environmental Sciences Consortium, Dauphin Island Sea Lab, Dauphin Island 36528. SAN 322-0001. Tel. 251-861-2141, fax 251-861-4646, e-mail disl@disl.org. *Coord.* John Dindo.

Network of Alabama Academic Libraries, c/o Alabama Commission on Higher Education, Montgomery 36104. SAN 322-4570. Tel. 334-242-2211, fax 334-242-0270. *Dir.* Sue O. Medina.

#### Alaska

Alaska Library Network (ALN), P.O. Box 100585, Anchorage 99501-0585. SAN 371-0688. Tel. 907-269-6587. *Cataloger* Keri Canepa.

#### Arizona

Maricopa County Community College District/Library Technology Services, 2411 W. 14 St., Tempe 85281-6942. SAN 322-0060. Tel. 480-731-8774, fax 480-731-8787. *Dir. Technical Services* Thomas Saudargas.

#### Arkansas

Arkansas Area Health Education Center Consortium (AHEC), Sparks Regional Medical Center, Fort Smith 72901-4992. SAN 329-3734. Tel. 479-441-5337, fax 479-441-5339. *Dir.* Grace Anderson.

Arkansas Independent Colleges and Universities, Firstar Bldg., 1 Riverfront Place, Suite 610, North Little Rock 72114. SAN 322-0079. Tel. 501-378-0843, fax 501-374-1523. *Pres.* Kearney E. Dietz.

Northeast Arkansas Hospital Library Consortium, 223 E. Jackson, Jonesboro 72401. SAN 329-529X. Tel. 870-972-1290, fax 870-931-0839. *Dir.* Karen Crosser.

South Arkansas Film Cooperative, c/o Malvern-Hot Spring County Lib., Malvern 72104. SAN 321-5938. Tel. 501-332-5441, fax 501-332-6679, e-mail hotspringcountylibrary@yahoo.com. *Dir.* Tammy Carter.

#### California

Bay Area Library and Information Network (BayNet), c/o San Francisco Public Lib., San Francisco 94702. SAN 371-0610. Tel. 415-355-2826, e-mail infobay@baynetlibs.org. *Pres.* Linda Suzukie.

Berkeley Information Network (BIN), Berkeley Public Lib., Berkeley 94704. Tel. 510-981-6166, 510-981-6150, fax 510-981-6246. *Mgr.* Jane Scantlebury.

Califa, 32 W. 25 Ave., Suite 201, San Mateo 94403. Tel. 650-572-2746, fax 650-349-5089, e-mail califa@califa.org. *Exec. Dir.* Linda Crowe.

Central Assn. of Libraries (CAL), 605 N. El Dorado St., Stockton 95202-1999. SAN 322-0125. Tel. 209-937-8649, fax 209-937-8292, e-mail 4999@ci.stockton.ca.us. *Dir.* Darla Gunning.

Claremont University Consortium (CUC), 150 E. 8 St., Claremont 91711. Tel. 909-621-8026, 909-621-8150, fax 909-621-8681. *CEO* Robert Walton.

Consortium for Open Learning, 333 Sunrise Ave., No. 229, Roseville 95661-3480. SAN 329-4412. Tel. 916-788-0660, fax 916-788-0696. *Operations Mgr.* Sandra Scott-Smith.

Consumer Health Information Program and Services (CHIPS), 12350 Imperial Hwy., Norwalk 90650. SAN 372-8110. Tel. 562-868-4003, fax 562-868-4065, e-mail referenceservices@gw.colapl.org, chips@librarylacounty.gov. *Libn.* Amy Beteilho.

Gold Coast Library Network, 3437 Empresa Drive, Suite C, San Luis Obispo 93401-7355. Tel. 805-543-6082, fax 805-543-9487. *Admin.* Maureen Theobald.

Kaiser Permanente Library System–Southern California Region (KPLS), Health Sciences Lib., Riverside 92505. SAN 372-8153. Tel. 951-353-3659, fax 951-353-3262, e-mail scal.rsvd-medical-library@kp.org. *Dir.* William Paringer.

Metropolitan Cooperative Library System (MCLS), 248 E. Foothill Blvd., Suite 101, Monrovia 91016-5522. SAN 371-3865. Tel. 626-359-6111, fax 626-359-2999, e-mail mclshq@mcls.org. *Dir.* Rosario Garza.

Mountain Valley Library System (MVLS), 55 E St., Santa Rosa 95404. Tel. 707-544-0142, fax 707-544-8411 ext. 101. *Exec. Dir.* Annette Milliron.

National Network of Libraries of Medicine–Pacific Southwest Region (NN/LM PSR), Louise M. Darling Biomedical Lib., Los Angeles 90095-1798. SAN 372-8234. Tel. 310-825-1200, fax 310-825-5389, e-mail psr-nnlm@Lib.ucla.edu. *Dir.* Judy Consales.

Nevada Medical Library Group (NMLG), Barton Memorial Hospital Lib., South Lake Tahoe 96150. SAN 370-0445. Tel. 530-543-5844, fax 530-541-4697. *Senior Exec. Coord.* Laurie Anton.

Northern California Assn. of Law Libraries (NOCALL), 268 Bush St., No. 4006, San Francisco 94104. SAN 323-5777. E-mail admin@nocall.org. *Pres.* Coral Henning.

Northern California Consortium of Psychology Libraries (NCCPL), San Francisco Bay Area Campus, Argosy Univ., Alameda 94133. SAN 371-9006. Tel. 510-837-3715. *Pres.* Julie Griffith.

OCLC Western Service Center, 3281 E. Guasti Rd., Suite 560, Ontario 91761. SAN 370-0747. Tel. 909-937-3300, fax 909-937-3384, e-mail western@oclc.org. *Dir.* Pamela Bailey.

Peninsula Libraries Automated Network (PLAN), 2471 Flores St., San Mateo 94403-4000. SAN 371-5035. Tel. 650-349-5538, fax 650-349-5089. *Dir., Info. Technology* Monica Schultz.

San Bernardino, Inyo, Riverside Counties United Library Services (SIRCULS), 3581 Mission Inn Ave., Riverside 92501-3377. SAN 322-0222. Tel. 951-369-7995, fax 951-784-1158, e-mail sirculs@inlandlib.org. *Exec. Dir.* Kathleen F. Aaron.

San Francisco Biomedical Library Network (SFBLN), San Franscisco General Hospital UCSF/Barnett-Briggs Medical Lib., San Francisco 94110. SAN 371-2125. Tel. 415-206-6639, e-mail fishbon@itsa.ucfs.edu.

Santa Clarita Interlibrary Network (SCIL-NET), Powell Lib., Santa Clarita 91321. SAN 371-8964. Tel. 661-259-3540 ext. 3420, fax 661-222-9159. *Libn.* John Stone.

Serra Cooperative Library System, 820 E St., San Diego 92101. SAN 372-8129. Tel. 619-232-1225, fax 619-696-8649, e-mail serral@serralib.org. *Contact* Ralph DeLauro.

Substance Abuse Librarians and Information Specialists (SALIS), P.O. Box 9513, Berkeley 94709-0513. SAN 372-4042. Fax 510-985-6459, e-mail salis@salis.org. *Exec. Dir.* Andrea L. Mitchell.

## Colorado

Automation System Colorado Consortium (ASCC), c/o Delta Public Lib., Delta 81416. Tel. 970-872-4317. *Technology Consultant* Connie Wolfrom.

Bibliographical Center for Research, Inc. (BCR), Rocky Mountain Region, 14394 E. Evans Ave., Aurora 80014-1478. SAN 322-0338. Tel. 303-751-6277, fax 303-751-9787, e-mail admin@bcr.org. *Exec. Dir.* Brenda Bailey-Hayner.

Colorado Alliance of Research Libraries, 3801 E. Florida Ave., Suite 515, Denver 80210. SAN 322-3760. Tel. 303-759-3399, fax 303-759-3363. *Exec. Dir.* Alan Charnes.

Colorado Assn. of Law Libraries, P.O. Box 13363, Denver 80201. SAN 322-4325. Tel. 303-492-7535, fax 303-492-2707. *Pres.* Karen Selden.

Colorado Council of Medical Librarians (CCML), P.O. Box 101058, Denver 80210-1058. SAN 370-0755. Tel. 303-724-2124, fax 303-724-2154. *Pres.* Gene Gardner.

Colorado Library Consortium (CLiC), 770 W. Hampden Ave., Suite 105, Centennial 80112. SAN 371-3970. Tel. 303-422-1150, fax 303-431-9752. *Dir.* Valerie Horton.

## Connecticut

Bibliomation, 32 Crest Rd., Middlebury 06762. Tel. 203-577-4070, fax 203-577-4077. *CEO* Mike Simonds.

Capital Area Health Consortium, 270 Farmington Ave., Suite 352, Farmington 06032-1994. SAN 322-0370. Tel. 860-676-1110, fax 860-676-1303, e-mail info@cahc.org. *Pres.* Karen Goodman.

Connecticut Library Consortium, 234 Court St., Middletown 06457-3304. SAN 322-0389. Tel. 860-344-8777, fax 860-344-9199, e-mail clc@ctlibrarians.org. *Exec. Dir.* Christine Bradley.

Council of State Library Agencies in the Northeast (COSLINE), Connecticut State Lib., Hartford 06106. SAN 322-0451. Tel. 860-757-6510, fax 860-757-6503.

CTW Library Consortium, Olin Memorial Lib., Middletown 06459-6065. SAN 329-4587. Tel. 860-685-3889, fax 860-685-2661. *System Libn.* Steve Bischof.

Hartford Consortium for Higher Education, 950 Main St., Suite 314, Hartford 06103. SAN 322-0443. Tel. 860-906-5016, fax 860-906-5118. *Exec. Dir.* Rosanne Druckman.

LEAP, 110 Washington Ave., North Haven 06473. SAN 322-4082. Tel. 203-239-1411, fax 203-239-9458. *Exec. Dir.* Diana Sellers.

Libraries Online, Inc. (LION), 100 Riverview Center, Suite 252, Middletown 06457. SAN 322-3922. Tel. 860-347-1704, fax 860-346-3707. *Exec. Dir.* Alan Hagyard.

Library Connection, Inc., 599 Matianuck Ave., Windsor 06095-3567. Tel. 860-298-5322, fax 860-298-5328. *Exec. Dir.* George Christian.

North Atlantic Health Sciences Libraries, Inc. (NAHSL), Dana Medical Lib., Univ. of Vermont Medical School, Burlington 05405. SAN 371-0599. Tel. 508-656-3483, fax 508-656-0762. *Chair* Marianne Burke.

## Delaware

Central Delaware Library Consortium, Dover Public Lib., Dover 19901. SAN 329-3696. Tel. 302-736-7030, fax 302-736-5087. *Dir.* Margery Kirby Cyr.

Delaware Library Consortium (DLC), Delaware Academy of Medicine, Newark 19713. SAN 329-3718. Tel. 302-733-1122, fax 302-733-3885, e-mail library@delamed.org. *Dir.* P. J. Grier.

## District Of Columbia

Computer Sciences Corporation/ERIC Project, 655 15th St. N.W., Suite 500, Washington 20005. SAN 322-161X. Tel. 202-741-4200, fax 202-628-3205. *Dir.* Lawrence Henry.

Council for Christian Colleges and Universities, 321 8th St. N.E., Washington 20002. SAN 322-0524. Tel. 202-546-8713, fax 202-546-8913, e-mail council@cccu.org. *Pres.* Paul R. Corts.

District of Columbia Area Health Science Libraries (DCAHSL), American College of Obstetrics and Gynecology Resource Center, Washington 20024. SAN 323-9918. Tel. 202-863-2518, fax 202-484-

1595, e-mail resources@acog.org. *Pres.* Rudine Anderson.

EDUCAUSE, 1150 18th St. N.W., Suite 1010, Washington 20036. SAN 371-487X. Tel. 202-872-4200, fax 202-872-4318, e-mail info@educause.edu. *Pres.* Brian Hawkins.

FEDLINK/Federal Library and Information Network, c/o Federal Lib. and Info. Center Committee, Washington 20540-4935. SAN 322-0761. Tel. 202-707-4800, fax 202-707-4818, e-mail flicc@loc.gov. *Exec. Dir.* Roberta I. Shaffer.

Interlibrary Users Assn. (IUA), c/o Urban Institute Lib., Washington 20037. SAN 322-1628. Tel. 202-261-5534, fax 202-223-3043. *Pres.* Nancy L. Minter.

Library of Congress, National Library Service for the Blind and Physically Handicapped (NLS), 1291 Taylor St. N.W., Washington 20542. SAN 370-5870. Tel. 202-707-5100, fax 202-707-0712, e-mail nls@loc.gov. *Dir.* Frank Kurt Cylke.

OCLC Eastern, 11 Dupont Circle N.E., Suite 550, Washington 20036-3430. SAN 321-5954. Tel. 202-331-5771, 202-331-5771, fax 202-331-5788, e-mail eastern@oclc.org. *Exec. Dir.* Irene M. Hoffman.

Transportation Research Board, 500 5th St. N.W., Washington 20001. SAN 370-582X. Tel. 202-334-2990, fax 202-334-2527. *Mgr. Info. Services* Barbara Post.

Veterans Affairs Library Network (VAL-NET), Lib. Programs Office 19E, Washington 20420. SAN 322-0834. *Dir. of Lib. Programs* Ginny DuPont.

Washington Theological Consortium, 487 Michigan Ave. N.E., Washington 20017-1585. SAN 322-0842. Tel. 202-832-2675, fax 202-526-0818, e-mail wtc@washtheocon.org. *Exec. Dir.* John Crossin.

## Florida

Central Florida Library Cooperative (CFLC), 431 E. Horatio Ave., Suite 230, Maitland 32751. SAN 371-9014. Tel. 407-644-9050, fax 407-644-7023, e-mail contactus @cflc.net. *Exec. Dir.* Marta Westall.

College Center for Library Automation (CCLA), 1753 W. Paul Dirac Drive, Tallahassee 32310. Tel. 850-922-6044, fax 850-

922-4869, e-mail servicedesk@cclaflorida. org. *Exec. Dir.* Richard Madaus.

Consortium of Southeastern Law Libraries (COSELL), Lawton Chiles Legal Info. Center, Gainesville 32611. SAN 372-8277. Tel. 352-273-0710, fax 352-392-5093.

Florida Center for Library Automation (FCLA), 5830 N.W. 39 Ave., Gainesville 32606. Tel. 352-392-9020, fax 352-392-9188, e-mail fclmin@ufl.edu. *Dir.* James Corey.

Florida Library Information Network, R. A. Gray Bldg., Tallahassee 32399-0250. SAN 322-0869. Tel. 850-245-6600, fax 850-245-6744, e-mail library@dos.state.fl.us. *Lending Services Libn.* Linda Pulliam.

Miami Health Sciences Library Consortium (MHSLC), Miami VA Healthcare System, Miami 33125-1624. SAN 371-0734. Tel. 305-575-3187, fax 305-575-3118, e-mail vhamialibrary@va.gov. *Pres.* Devica Samsundar.

Northeast Florida Library Information Network (NEFLIN), 2233 Park Ave., Suite 402, Orange Park 32073. Tel. 904-278-5620, fax 904-278-5625, e-mail office@neflin.org. *Exec. Dir.* Brad Ward.

Panhandle Library Access Network (PLAN), Five Miracle Strip Loop, Suite 8, Panama City Beach 32407-3850. SAN 370-047X. Tel. 850-233-9051, fax 850-235-2286. *Exec. Dir.* William P. Conniff.

Southeast Florida Library Information Network, Inc. (SEFLIN), Wimberly Lib., Office 452, Boca Raton 33431. SAN 370-0666. Tel. 561-208-0984, fax 561-208-0995. *Exec. Dir.* Tom Sloan.

Southwest Florida Library Network (SWFLN), Bldg. III, Unit 7, Fort Myers 33913. Tel. 239-225-4225, fax 239-225-4229, e-mail swfln@fgcu.edu. *Exec. Dir.* Sondra Taylor-Furbee.

Tampa Bay Library Consortium, Inc., 1202 Tech Blvd., Suite 202, Tampa 33619. SAN 322-371X. Tel. 813-740-3963, 813-622-8252, fax 813-628-4425. *Exec. Dir.* Charlie Parker.

Tampa Bay Medical Library Network (TABAMLN), Florida Hospital College of Health Sciences, Orlando 32803-1226. SAN 322-0885. Tel. 407-303-9798, fax 407-303-9408. *Pres.* Deanna Stevens.

## Georgia

Assn. of Southeastern Research Libraries (ASERL), c/o Lyrasis, 1438 W. Peachtree St. N.W., Suite 200, Atlanta 30309-2955. SAN 322-1555. Tel. 404-892-0943, fax 404-892-7879. *Exec. Dir.* John Burger.

Atlanta Health Science Libraries Consortium, Fran Golding Medical Lib. at Scottish Rite, Atlanta 30342-1600. Tel. 404-785-2157, fax 404-785-2155. *Pres.* Kate Daniels.

Atlanta Regional Council for Higher Education (ARCHE), 50 Hurt Plaza, Suite 735, Atlanta 30303-2923. SAN 322-0990. Tel. 404-651-2668, fax 404-651-1797, e-mail arche@atlantahighered.org. *Pres.* Michael Gerber.

Georgia Interactive Network for Medical Information (GAIN), c/o Mercer Univ. School of Medicine, Macon 31207. SAN 370-0577. Tel. 478-301-2515, fax 478-301-2051, e-mail gain.info@gain.mercer. edu. *Dir.* Jan H. LaBeause.

Georgia Online Database (GOLD), c/o Public Lib. Services, Atlanta 30345-4304. SAN 322-094X. Tel. 404-235-7200, fax 404-235-7201. *Lib. Services Mgr.* Elaine Hardy.

Lyrasis, 1438 W. Peachtree St. N.W., Suite 200, Atlanta 30309-2955. SAN 322-0974. Tel. 404-892-0943, fax 404-892-7879; 3000 Market St., Suite 200, Philadelphia, PA 19104-2801. SAN 322-3000. Tel. 215-382-7031, fax 215-382-0022. *CEO* Kate Nevins. E-mail knevins@solinet.net; *Pres.* Catherine C. Wilt. E-mail wilt@palinet. org.

Metro Atlanta Library Assn. (MALA), P.O. Box 14948, Atlanta 30324. SAN 378-2549. Tel. 678-915-7207, fax 678-915-7471, e-mail mala-a@comcast.net. *Pres.* Steven Vincent.

Southeastern Library Network (SOLINET). See Lyrasis above.

## Hawaii

Hawaii Library Consortium (HLC), c/o Hawaii State Lib., Honolulu 96813-2994. Tel. 808-586-3494; 808-586-3614, e-mail hlcboard-1@hawaii.edu, hslser@libraries hawaii.org. *Pres.* Charles L. King.

Hawaii-Pacific Chapter of the Medical Library Assn. (HPC-MLA), Health Sciences Lib., Honolulu 96813. SAN 371-3946. Tel. 808-692-0810, fax 808-692-1244. *Chair* A. Lee Adams.

## Idaho

Canyon Owyhee Library Group, Ltd. (COLG), 203 E. Owyhee Ave., Homedale 83628. Tel. 208-454-2221, 337-4613, fax 208-337-4933. *Coord.* Glynda Pflieger.

Cooperative Information Network (CIN), 8385 N. Government Way, Hayden 83835-9280. SAN 323-7656. Tel. 208-772-5612, fax 208-772-2498, e-mail hay@cin.kcl. org. *Fiscal Agent* John W. Hartung.

Idaho Health Information Assn. (IHIA), c/o Eastern Idaho Regional Medical Center, Idaho Falls 83403. SAN 371-5078. Tel. 208-529-6077, fax 208-529-7014, e-mail library@dataway.net. *Dir.* Kathy Fatkin.

Library Consortium of Eastern Idaho (LCEI), 5210 Stuart Ave., Chubbuck 83202. SAN 323-7699. Tel. 208-237-2192. *Chair* Linda Rasmussen.

LYNX Consortium, c/o Boise Public Lib., Boise 83702-7195. SAN 375-0086. Tel. 208-384-4238, fax 208-384-4025, e-mail askalibrarian@cityofboise.org.

## Illinois

Alliance Library System, 600 High Point Lane, East Peoria 61611. SAN 371-0637. Tel. 309-694-9200, fax 309-694-9230. *Exec. Dir.* Kitty Pope.

American Theological Library Assn. (ATLA), 300 S. Wacker Drive, Suite 2100, Chicago 60606-5889. SAN 371-9022. Tel. 312-454-5100, fax 312-454-5505, e-mail atla@ atla.com. *Exec. Dir.* Dennis A. Norlin.

Areawide Hospital Library Consortium of Southwestern Illinois (AHLC), c/o St. Elizabeth Hospital Health Sciences Lib., Belleville 62222. SAN 322-1016. Tel. 618-234-2120 ext. 2011, fax 618-222-4614.

Assn. of Chicago Theological Schools (ACTS), Wiggin Lib. at Meadville/Lombard Theological School, Chicago 60637. SAN 370-0658. Tel. 773-256-3000 ext. 225. *Chair* Neil Gerdes.

Capital Area Consortium, 701 N. 1 St., Springfield 62781. *Coord.* Lynne Ferrell.

Center for Research Libraries, 6050 S. Kenwood, Chicago 60637-2804. SAN 322-1032. Tel. 773-955-4545, fax 773-955-4339. *Pres.* Bernard F. Reilly.

Chicago and South Consortium, Jackson Park Hospital and Medical Center, Chicago 60649-3993. SAN 322-1067. Tel. 773-947-7653. *Coord.* Andrew Paradise.

Chicago Area Museum Libraries (CAML), c/o Lib., Field Museum, Chicago 60605-2496. SAN 371-392X. Tel. 312-665-7887, fax 312-665-7893. *Assoc. Libn., Reference and Circulation Services* Christine Giannoni.

Committee on Institutional Cooperation, 1819 S. Neil St., Suite D, Champaign 61820-7271. Tel. 217-333-8475, fax 217-244-7127, e-mail cic@staff.cic.net. *Dir.* Barbara Mcfadden Allen.

Consortium of Academic and Research Libraries in Illinois (CARLI), 100 Trade Center Drive, Suite 303, Champaign 61820. SAN 322-3736. Tel. 217-244-7593, fax 217-244-7596, e-mail support@carli.illinois.edu. *Exec. Dir.* Susan Singleton.

Council of Directors of State University Libraries in Illinois (CODSULI), Southern Illinois Univ. School of Medicine Lib., Springfield 62702-4910. SAN 322-1083. Tel. 217-545-0994, fax 217-545-0988.

East Central Illinois Consortium, Booth Lib., Eastern Illinois Univ., Charleston 61920. SAN 322-1040. Tel. 217-581-7549, fax 217-581-7534. *Mgr.* Stacey Knight-Davis.

Fox Valley Health Science Library Consortium, c/o Delnor-Community Hospital, Geneva 60134. SAN 329-3831. Tel. 630-208-4299.

Heart of Illinois Library Consortium, 511 N.E. Greenleaf, Peoria 61603. SAN 322-1113. *Chair* Leslie Menz.

Illinois Library and Information Network (ILLINET), c/o Illinois State Lib., Springfield 62701-1796. SAN 322-1148. Tel. 217-782-2994, fax 217-785-4326. *Dir.* Anne Craig.

Illinois Office of Educational Services, 2450 Foundation Drive, Suite 100, Springfield 62703-5464. SAN 371-5108. Tel. 217-786-3010, fax 217-786-3020, e-mail info @ioes.org. *Dir.* Rebecca Woodhull.

LIBRAS, Inc., North Park Univ., Chicago 60625-4895. SAN 322-1172. Tel. 773-244-5584, fax 773-244-4891. *Pres.* Mark Vargas.

Metropolitan Consortium of Chicago, Chicago School of Professional Psychology, Chicago 60610. SAN 322-1180. Tel. 312-329-6633, fax 312-644-6075. *Coord.* Margaret White.

National Network of Libraries of Medicine–Greater Midwest Region (NNLM–GMR), c/o Lib. of Health Sciences, Univ. of Illinois, Chicago 60612-4330. SAN 322-1202. Tel. 312-996-2464, fax 312-996-2226, e-mail gmr4u@uic.edu. *Dir.* Kathryn Carpenter.

Network of Illinois Learning Resources in Community Colleges (NILRC), 719 William St., River Forest 60305-1925. Tel. 608-523-4094, fax 608-523-4072. *Exec. Dir.* John W. Berry.

Quad Cities Libraries in Cooperation (Quad-LINC), 220 W. 23 Ave., Coal Valley 61240. SAN 373-093X. Tel. 309-799-3155 ext. 3254, fax 309-799-7916.

System Wide Automated Network (SWAN), c/o Metropolitan Lib. System, Burr Ridge 60527-5783. Tel. 630-734-5000, fax 630-734-5050. *Dir.* Aaron Skog.

## Indiana

Central Indiana Health Science Libraries Consortium, Indiana Univ. School of Medicine Lib., Indianapolis 46202. SAN 322-1245. Tel. 317-274-8358, fax 317-274-4056. *Contact* Elaine Skopelja.

Collegiate Consortium of Western Indiana, c/o Cunningham Memorial Lib., Terre Haute 47809. SAN 329-4439. Tel. 812-237-3700, fax 812-237-3376. *Interim Dean* Alberta Comer.

Consortium of College and University Media Centers (CCUMC), Indiana Univ., Bloomington 47405-1223. SAN 322-1091. Tel. 812-855-6049, fax 812-855-2103, e-mail ccumc@ccumc.org. *Exec. Dir.* Aileen Scales.

Consortium of Foundation Libraries, IUPUI Univ. Lib., Indianapolis 46202. SAN 322-

2462. Tel. 317-278-2329. *Chair* Brenda Burk.

Evansville Area Library Consortium, 3700 Washington Ave., Evansville 47750. SAN 322-1261. Tel. 812-485-4151, fax 812-485-7564. *Coord.* Jane Saltzman.

Indiana Cooperative Library Services Authority (INCOLSA), 6202 Morenci Trail, Indianapolis 46268-2536. SAN 322-1296. Tel. 317-298-6570, fax 317-328-2380. *Exec. Dir.* Michael Piper.

Indiana State Data Center, Indiana State Lib., Indianapolis 46204-2296. SAN 322-1318. Tel. 317-232-3733, fax 317-232-3728. *Coord.* Katie Springer.

Northeast Indiana Health Science Libraries Consortium (NEIHSL), Vann Lib., Univ. of Saint Francis, Fort Wayne 46808. SAN 373-1383. Tel. 260-399-7700 ext. 6065, fax 260-399-8166. *Coord.* Lauralee Aven.

Northwest Indiana Health Science Library Consortium (NIHSLC), c/o NW Center for Medical Education, Gary 46408-1197. SAN 322-1350. Tel. 219-980-6852, 219-980-6709, fax 219-980-6524, 219-980-6566. *Coord. Lib. Services* Corona Wiley.

## Iowa

Consortium of User Libraries (CUL), Lib. for the Blind and Physically Handicapped, Des Moines 50309-2364. Tel. 515-281-1333, fax 515-281-1378; 515-281-1263. *Pres.* Karen Keninger.

Dubuque Area Library Information Consortium, c/o Burton Payne Lib., Northeast Iowa Community College, Peosta 52068. Tel. 563-556-5110 ext. 269, fax 563-557-0340. *Coord.* Deb Seiffert.

Iowa Private Academic Library Consortium (IPAL), c/o Buena Vista Univ. Lib., Storm Lake 50588. SAN 329-5311. Tel. 712-749-2127, 749-2203, fax 712-749-2059, e-mail library@bvu.edu. *Univ. Libn.* Jim Kennedy.

Linn County Library Consortium, Russell D. Cole Lib., Mount Vernon 52314-1012. SAN 322-4597. Tel. 319-895-4259. *Pres.* Aileen Chang-Matus.

Polk County Biomedical Consortium, c/o Broadlawns Medical Center Lib., Des Moines 50314. SAN 322-1431. Tel. 515-

282 2394, fax 515-282 5634. *Treas.* Elaine Hughes.

Quad City Area Biomedical Consortium, Great River Medical Center Lib., West Burlington 52655. SAN 322-435X. Tel. 319-768-4075, fax 319-768-4080. *Coord.* Judy Hawk.

Sioux City Library Cooperative (SCLC), c/o Sioux City Public Lib., Sioux City 51101-1203. SAN 329-4722. Tel. 712-255-2933 ext. 251, fax 712-279-6432. *Chair* Betsy Thompson.

State of Iowa Libraries Online (SILO), State Lib. of Iowa, Des Moines 50319. SAN 322-1415. Tel. 515-281-4105, fax 515-281-6191. *State Libn.* Mary Wegner.

## Kansas

Associated Colleges of Central Kansas (ACCK), 210 S. Main St., McPherson 67460. SAN 322-1474. Tel. 620-241-5150, fax 620-241-5153.

Dodge City Library Consortium, c/o Comanche Intermediate Center, Dodge City 67801. SAN 322-4368. Tel. 620-227-1609, fax 620-227-4862.

Kansas Regents Library Database Consortium (RLDC), c/o Emporia State Univ., Emporia 66801. Tel. 620-341-5480, e-mail rldc@ku.edu. *Chair* Cynthia Akers.

State Library of Kansas, Statewide Resource Sharing Division, 300 S.W. 10 Ave., Room 343N, Topeka 66612-1593. SAN 329-5621. Tel. 785-296-3875, fax 785-368-7291. *Dir.* Patti Butcher.

## Kentucky

Assn. of Independent Kentucky Colleges and Universities (AIKCU), 484 Chenault Rd., Frankfort 40601. SAN 322-1490. Tel. 502-695-5007, fax 502-695-5057. *Pres.* Gary S. Cox.

Eastern Kentucky Health Science Information Network (EKHSIN), c/o Camden-Carroll Lib., Morehead 40351. SAN 370-0631. Tel. 606-783-6860, fax 606-784-2178. *Lib. Dir.* Tammy Jenkins.

Kentuckiana Metroversity, Inc., 109 E. Broadway, Louisville 40202. SAN 322-1504. Tel. 502-897-3374, fax 502-895-1647.

Kentucky Medical Library Assn., Lib. Services 142D, VA Medical Center, Louisville 40206-1499. SAN 370-0623. Tel. 502-287-6240, fax 502-287-6134. *Head Libn.* Gene M. Haynes.

Kentucky Virtual Library (KVL), 1024 Capital Center Drive, Suite 320, Frankfort 40601. Tel. 502-573-1555, fax 502-573-0222, e-mail kyvl@ky.gov. *Dir.* Enid Wohlstein.

Southeastern Chapter of the American Assn. of Law Libraries (SEAALL), c/o Law Lib., Univ. of Kentucky, Lexington 40506-0048. Tel. 859-257-8347, fax 859-323-4906. *Pres.* Osborne Amy.

Theological Education Assn. of Mid America (TEAM-A), Southern Baptist Theological Seminary, Louisville 40280. SAN 377-5038. Tel. 502-897-4807, fax 502-897-4600. *Dir., Info. Resources* Ken Boyd.

### Louisiana

Central Louisiana Medical Center Library Consortium (CLMLC), P.O. Box 8784, Alexandria 71306-1784. Tel. 318-619-9102, fax 318-619-9144, e-mail clmlc8784 @yahoo.com. *Coord.* Miriam J. Brown.

Health Sciences Library Assn. of Louisiana (HSLAL), LSUHSC Lib., Shreveport 71103. SAN 375-0035. *Pres.* Donna Timm.

Loan SHARK, State Library of Louisiana, Baton Rouge 70802. SAN 371-6880. Tel. 225-342-4920, 342-4918, fax 225-219-4725. *Head, Access Services* Kytara A. Gaudin.

LOUIS/The Louisiana Library Network, Info. Technology Services, Baton Rouge 70803. *Exec. Dir.* Ralph Boe.

Louisiana Government Information Network (LaGIN), c/o State Lib. of Louisiana, Baton Rouge 70802. SAN 329-5036. Tel. 225-342-4920, e-mail lagin@pelican.state. lib.la.us. *Coord.* Virginia Smith.

New Orleans Educational Telecommunications Consortium, 2 Canal St., Suite 2038, New Orleans 70130. SAN 329-5214. Tel. 504-524-0350, fax 504-524-0327, e-mail noetc@noetc.org. *Exec. Dir.* Michael Adler.

### Maine

Health Science Library Information Consortium (HSLIC), 211 Marginal Way, No 245, Portland 04101. SAN 322-1601. Tel. 207-795-2561, fax 207-795-2569. *Chair* Kathy Brunjes.

### Maryland

Library Video Network (LVN), 320 York Rd., Towson 21204. SAN 375-5320. Tel. 410-887-2090, fax 410-887-2091, e-mail lvn@bcpl.net. *Mgr.* Carl Birkmeyer.

Maryland Assn. of Health Science Librarians (MAHSL), Medical Lib., VA Medical HealthCare System, Baltimore 21201. SAN 377-5070. Tel. 401-605-7093. *Contact* Brittany Rice.

Maryland Interlibrary Loan Organization (MILO), c/o Enoch Pratt Free Lib., Baltimore 21201-4484. SAN 343-8600. Tel. 410-396-5498, fax 410-396-5837, e-mail milo@prattLib.org. *Mgr.* Emma E. Beaven.

National Library of Medicine (NLM), 8600 Rockville Pike, Bethesda 20894. SAN 322-1652. Tel. 301-594-5983, fax 301-402-1384, e-mail custserv@nlm.nih.gov. *Coord.* Martha Fishel.

National Network of Libraries of Medicine (NNLM), National Lib. of Medicine, Bethesda 20894. SAN 373-0905. Tel. 301-496-4777, fax 301-480-1467. *Dir.* Angela Ruffin.

National Network of Libraries of Medicine–Southeastern Atlantic Region (NNLM–SEA), Univ. of Maryland Health Sciences and Human Services Lib., Baltimore 21201-1512. SAN 322-1644. Tel. 410-706-2855, fax 410-706-0099, e-mail hshsl-nimsea@ hshsl.umaryland.edu. *Dir.* Mary J. Tooey.

Regional Alcohol and Drug Abuse Resource Network (RADAR), National Clearinghouse on Alcohol and Drug Info., Rockville 20852. Tel. 301-468-2600, fax 301-468-6433, e-mail ncadi-info @samhsa.hhs.gov.

Washington Research Lib. Consortium (WRLC), 901 Commerce Drive, Upper Marlboro 20774. SAN 373-0883. Tel. 301-390-2031, fax 301-390-2020. *Exec. Dir.* Lizanne Payne.

## Massachusetts

Boston Biomedical Library Consortium (BBLC), c/o Dana Farber Cancer Trust, Boston 02115. SAN 322-1725. *Pres.* Christine Fleuried.

Boston Library Consortium, Inc., McKim Bldg., Boston 02117. SAN 322-1733. Tel. 617-262-0380, fax 617-262-0163, e-mail admin@blc.org. *Exec. Dir.* Barbara G. Preece.

Boston Regional Library System (BRLS), c/o Boston Public Lib., Boston 02117. Tel. 617-859-2380, fax 617-424-8617, e-mail brl@bpl.org. *Regional Admin.* Michael Colford.

Cape Libraries Automated Materials Sharing Network (CLAMS), 270 Communication Way, Unit 4E, Hyannis 02601. SAN 370-579X. Tel. 508-790-4399, fax 508-771-4533. *Exec. Dir.* Gayle Simundza.

Catholic Library Assn., 100 North St., Suite 224, Pittsfield 01201-5109. SAN 329-1030. Tel. 413-443-2252, fax 413-442-2252, e-mail cla@cathla.org. *Exec. Dir.* Jean R. Bostley, SSJ.

Central and Western Massachusetts Automated Resource Sharing (C/W MARS), 67 Millbrook St., Suite 201, Worcester 01606. SAN 322-3973. Tel. 508-755-3323 ext. 30, fax 508-755-3721. *Exec. Dir.* Joan Kuklinski.

Cooperating Libraries of Greater Springfield (CLGS), Springfield College, Springfield 01109. SAN 322-1768. Tel. 413-748-3609, fax 413-748-3631. *Coord.* Lynn Coakley.

Fenway Libraries Online, Inc. (FLO), c/o Wentworth Institute of Technology, Boston 02115. SAN 373-9112. Tel. 617-442-2384, fax 617-442-1519. *Exec. Dir.* Walter Stine.

Massachusetts Health Sciences Libraries Network (MAHSLIN), Brigham and Women's Hospital Medical Library, Boston 02115. SAN 372-8293. Tel. 617-632-2489. *Chair* Christine Fleuriel.

Merrimack Valley Library Consortium, 123 Tewksbury St., Andover 01810. SAN 322-4384. Tel. 978-475-7632, fax 978-475-7179, e-mail netmail@mailserv.mvlc.lib.ma.us. *Exec. Dir.* Lawrence Rungren.

Metrowest Massachusetts Regional Library System (METROWEST), 135 Beaver St., Waltham 02452. Tel. 781-398-1819, fax 781-398-1821. *Admin.* Sondra H. Vandermark.

Minuteman Library Network, 10 Strathmore Rd., Natick 01760-2419. SAN 322-4252. Tel. 508-655-8008, fax 508-655-1507. *Exec. Dir.* Susan McAlister.

National Network of Libraries of Medicine–New England Region (NNLM–NER), Univ. of Massachusetts Medical School, Shrewsbury 01545-2732. SAN 372-5448. Tel. 508-856-5979, fax 508-856-5977. *Dir.* Elaine Martin.

NELINET, Inc., 153 Cordaville Rd., Suite 200, Southborough 01772. SAN 322-1822. Tel. 508-460-7700 ext. 1934, fax 508-460-9455. *Exec. Dir.* Arnold Hirshon.

North of Boston Library Exchange, Inc. (NOBLE), 26 Cherry Hill Drive, Danvers 01923. SAN 322-4023. Tel. 978-777-8844, fax 978-750-8472. *Exec. Dir.* Ronald A. Gagnon.

Northeast Consortium of Colleges and Universities In Massachusetts (NECCUM), Merrimack College, North Andover 01845. SAN 371-0602. Tel. 978-556-3400, fax 978-556-3738. *Pres.* Richard Santagati.

Northeastern Consortium for Health Information (NECHI), Lowell General Hospital Health Science Lib., Lowell 01854. SAN 322-1857. Tel. 978-937-6247, fax 978-937-6855. *Libn.* Donna Beales.

SAILS, Inc., 547 W. Groves St., Suite 4, Middleboro 02346. SAN 378-0058. Tel. 508-946-8600, fax 508-946-8605. *Pres.* Robin Glasser.

Southeastern Massachusetts Consortium of Health Science Libraries (SEMCO), Caritius Norwood Youngdahl Lib., Norwood 02062. SAN 322-1873. Tel. 781-278-6243, fax 781-769-9622. *Chair* Denise Corless.

Southeastern Massachusetts Regional Library System (SEMLS), 10 Riverside Drive, Lakeville 02347. Tel. 508-923-3531, fax 508-923-3539, e-mail semls@semls.org. *Admin.* Cynthia A. Roach.

West of Boston Network (WEBNET), Horn Lib., Babson College, Babson Park 02457.

SAN 371-5019. Tel. 781-239-4308, fax 781-239-5226. *Pres.* Marilyn Bregoli.
Western Massachusetts Health Information Consortium, Baystate Medical Center Health Sciences Lib., Springfield 01199. SAN 329-4579. Tel. 413-794-1291, fax 413-794-1974. *Pres.* Susan La Forter.

## Michigan

Detroit Area Consortium of Catholic Colleges, c/o Sacred Heart Seminary, Detroit 48206. SAN 329-482X. Tel. 313-883-8500, fax 313-883-8594. *Acting Dir.* Chris Spilker.
Detroit Area Library Network (DALNET), 5048 Gullen Mall, Detroit 48202. Tel. 313-577-6789, fax 313-577-1231. *Dir.* Steven K. Bowers.
Kalamazoo Consortium for Higher Education (KCHE), Kalamazoo College, Kalamazoo 49006. SAN 329-4994. Tel. 269-337-7220, fax 269-337-7219. *Pres.* Eileen B. Wilson-Oyelaran.
Lakeland Library Cooperative, 4138 Three Mile Rd. N.W., Grand Rapids 49534-1134. SAN 308-132X. Tel. 616-559-5253, fax 616-559-4329. *Dir.* Sandra Wilson.
Michigan Health Sciences Libraries Assn. (MHSLA), 1407 Rensen St., Suite 4, Lansing 48910. SAN 323-987X. Tel. 517-394-2774, fax 517-394-2675. *Pres.* Janet Zimmerman.
Michigan Library Consortium (MLC), 1407 Rensen St., Suite 1, Lansing 48910-3657. SAN 322-192X. Tel. 517-394-2420, fax 517-394-2096, e-mail reception@mlcnet. org. *Assoc. Dir.* Ruth Dukelow.
PALnet, 1040 W. Bristol Rd., Flint 48507. Tel. 810-766-4070. *Dir.* Stephanie C. John.
Southeastern Michigan League of Libraries (SEMLOL), Lawrence Technological Univ., Southfield 48075. SAN 322-4481. Tel. 248-204-3000, fax 248-204-3005. *Treas.* Gary Cocozzoli.
Southwest Michigan Library Cooperative (SMLC), c/o Niles District Lib., Niles 49120-2620. SAN 371-5027. Tel. 269-683-8545, fax 269-657-4494. *Pres.* Jennifer Ray.
Suburban Library Cooperative (SLC), 44750 Delco Blvd., Sterling Heights 48313. SAN

373-9082. Tel. 586-685-5750, fax 586-685-3010. *Interim Dir.* Arthur M. Woodford.
The Library Network (TLN), 13331 Reeck Rd., Southgate 48195-3054. SAN 370-596X. Tel. 734-281-3830, fax 734-281-1817. *Interim Co-Dir.* Anne Neville.
Upper Peninsula of Michigan Health Science Library Consortium, c/o Marquette Health System Hospital, Marquette 49855. SAN 329-4803. Tel. 906-225-3429, fax 906-225-3524. *In Charge* Janis Lubenow.
Upper Peninsula Region of Library Cooperation, Inc., 1615 Presque Isle Ave., Marquette 49855. SAN 329-5540. Tel. 906-228-7697, fax 906-228-5627. *Treas.* Suzanne Dees.
Valley Library Consortium, 3210 Davenport Ave., Saginaw 48602-3495. Tel. 989-497-0925, fax 989-497-0918. *Exec. Dir.* Karl R. Steiner.

## Minnesota

Capital Area Library Consortium (CALCO), c/o Library MS155, Minnesota Dept. of Transportation, Saint Paul 55155. SAN 374-6127. Tel. 651-296-5272, fax 651-297-2354. *Libn.* Shirley Sherkow.
Central Minnesota Libraries Exchange (CMLE), Miller Center, Rm. 130-D, Saint Cloud 56301-4498. SAN 322-3779. Tel. 320-308-2950, fax 320-654-5131, e-mail cmle@stcloudstate.edu. *Dir.* Patricia A. Post.
Cooperating Libraries in Consortium (CLIC), 1619 Dayton Ave., Suite 204, Saint Paul 55104. SAN 322-1970. Tel. 651-644-3878, fax 651-644-6258. *System Admin.* Deb Bergeron.
Metronet, 1619 Dayton Ave., Suite 314, Saint Paul 55104. SAN 322-1989. Tel. 651-646-0475, fax 651-649-3169, e-mail information@metrolibraries.net. *Exec. Dir.* Ann Walker Smalley.
Metropolitan Library Service Agency (MELSA), 1619 Dayton Ave., No. 314, Saint Paul 55104-6206. SAN 371-5124. Tel. 651-645-5731, fax 651-649-3169, e-mail melsa@melsa.org. *Exec. Dir.* Chris D. Olson.
MINITEX Library Information Network, 15 Andersen Lib., Univ. of Minnesota–Twin

Cities, Minneapolis 55455-0439. SAN 322-1997. Tel. 612-624-4002, fax 612-624-4508. *Dir.* William DeJohn.

Minnesota Library Information Network (MnLINK), Univ. of Minnesota–Twin Cities, Minneapolis 55455-0439. Tel. 612-624-8096, fax 612-624-4508. *Info. Specialist* Nick Banitt.

Minnesota Theological Library Assn. (MTLA), Luther Seminary Lib., Saint Paul 55108. SAN 322-1962. Tel. 651-641-3447. *Chair* David Stewart.

North Country Library Cooperative, 5528 Emerald Ave., Mountain Iron 55768-2069. SAN 322-3795. Tel. 218-741-1907, fax 218-741-1908. *Dir.* Linda J. Wadman.

Northern Lights Library Network, 103 Graystone Plaza, Detroit Lakes 56501-3041. SAN 322-2004. Tel. 218-847-2825, fax 218-847-1461, e-mail nloffice@nlln.org. *Dir.* Ruth Solie.

SMILE (Southcentral Minnesota Inter-Library Exchange), 1400 Madison Ave., No. 622, Mankato 56001. SAN 321-3358. Tel. 507-625-7555, fax 507-625-4049, e-mail smile@tds.lib.mn.us. *Dir.* Nancy Katharine Steele.

Southeastern Libraries Cooperating (SELCO), 2600 19th St. N.W., Rochester 55901-0767. SAN 308-7417. Tel. 507-288-5513, fax 507-288-8697. *Exec. Dir.* Ann B. Hutton.

Southwest Area Multicounty Multitype Interlibrary Exchange (SAMMIE), 109 S. 5 St., Suite 30, Marshall 56258-1240. SAN 322-2039. Tel. 507-532-9013, fax 507-532-2039, e-mail info@sammie.org. *Dir.* Robin Chaney.

Twin Cities Biomedical Consortium (TCBC), c/o Fairview Univ. Medical Center, Minneapolis 55455. SAN 322-2055. Tel. 612-273-6595, fax 612-273-2675. *Mgr.* Colleen Olsen.

West—A Thomson Reuters Business, P.O. Box 64526, Saint Paul 55164-0526. SAN 322-4031. Tel. 651-687-7000, fax 651-687-5614, e-mail west.customer.service@thomson.com.

## Mississippi

Central Mississippi Library Council (CMLC), c/o Millsaps College Lib., Jackson 39210. SAN 372-8250. Tel. 601-974-1070, fax 601-974-1082. *Admin./Treas.* Tom Henderson.

Mississippi Electronic Libraries Online (MELO), Mississippi State Board for Community and Junior Colleges, Jackson 39211. Tel. 601-432-6518, fax 601-432-6363, e-mail melo@colin.edu. *Dir.* Audra Kimball.

## Missouri

Greater Western Library Alliance (GWLA), 5109 Cherry St., Kansas City 64110. Tel. 816-926-8765, fax 816-926-8790. *Exec. Dir.* Joni Blake.

Health Sciences Library Network of Kansas City, Inc. (HSLNKC), Univ. of Missouri–Kansas City Health Sciences Lib., Kansas City 64108-2792. SAN 322-2098. Tel. 816-235-1880, fax 816-235-6570. *Dir.* Peggy Mullaly-Quijas.

Kansas City Library Consortium (KCLC), Kansas City Public Lib., 14 W. 10 St., Kansas City 64105. Tel. 816-701-3400, fax 816-701-3464, e-mail kclcsupport@kclibrary.org. *Exec. Dir.* Debbie Siratusa.

Kansas City Metropolitan Library and Information Network, 15624 E. 24 Hwy., Independence 64050. SAN 322-2101. Tel. 816-521-7257, fax 816-461-0966. *Exec. Dir.* Susan Burton.

Missouri Library Network Corp. (MLNC), 8045 Big Bend Blvd., Suite 202, Saint Louis 63119-2714. SAN 322-466X. Tel. 314-918-7222, fax 314-918-7727, e-mail support@mlnc.org. *Exec. Dir.* Tracy Byerly.

Saint Louis Regional Library Network, 341 Sappington Rd., Saint Louis 63122. SAN 322-2209. Tel. 314-395-1305.

## Nebraska

ICON Library Consortium, McGoogan Lib. of Medicine, Univ. of Nebraska, Omaha 68198-6705. Tel. 402-559-7099, fax 402-559-5498.

NEBASE, c/o Nebraska Lib. Commission, Lincoln 68508-2023. SAN 322-2268. Tel. 402-471-2045, fax 402-471-2083, e-mail nedase@nlc.state.ne.us.

Southeast Nebraska Library System, 5730 R St., Suite C1, Lincoln 68505. SAN 322-

4732. Tel. 402-467-6188, fax 402-467-6196. *Pres.* Glenda Willnerd.

## Nevada

Desert States Law Library Consortium, Wiener-Rogers Law Lib., William S. Boyd School of Law, Las Vegas 89154-1080. Tel. 702-895-2400, fax 702-895-2416. *Collection Development Libn.* Matthew Wright.

Information Nevada, Interlibrary Loan Dept., Nevada State Lib. and Archives, Carson City 89701-4285. SAN 322-2276. Tel. 775-684-3328, fax 775-684-3330. *Coord., ILL* Hope Williams.

## New Hampshire

Carroll County Library Cooperative, c/o Freedom Lib., Freedom 03836. SAN 371-8999. Tel. 603-367-8545, fax 603-539-5176, e-mail librarian@madison.lib.nh.us. *Dir.* Elizabeth Rhymer.

GMILCS, Inc., 1701B Hooksett Rd., Hooksett 03106. Tel. 603-485-4286, fax 603-485-4246, e-mail helpdesk@gmilcs.org. *Chair* Janet Angus.

Health Sciences Libraries of New Hampshire and Vermont, Breene Memorial Lib., New Hampshire Hospital, Concord 03246. SAN 371-6864. Tel. 603-527-2837, fax 603-527-7197. *Admin. Coord.* Marion Allen.

Librarians of the Upper Valley Cooperative (LUV Coop), c/o Hanover Town Lib., Etna 03750. SAN 371-6856. Tel. 603-643-3116. *Coord.* Barbara Prince.

Merri-Hill-Rock Library Cooperative, c/o Kimball Lib., Atkinson 03811-2299. SAN 329-5338. Tel. 603-362-5234, fax 603-362-4791. *Interim Dir.* Caroline Birr.

New England Law Library Consortium, Inc. (NELLCO), 9 Drummer Rd., Keene 03431. SAN 322-4244. Tel. 603-357-3385, fax 603-357-2075. *Exec. Dir.* Tracy L. Thompson.

New Hampshire College and University Council, Three Barrell Court, Suite 100, Concord 03301-8543. SAN 322-2322. Tel. 603-225-4199, fax 603-225-8108. *Pres.* Thomas R. Horgan.

Nubanusit Library Cooperative, c/o Peterborough Town Lib., Peterborough 03458.

SAN 322-4600. Tel. 603-924-8040, fax 603-924-8041.

Scrooge and Marley Cooperative, 695 Main St., Laconia 03246. SAN 329-515X. Tel. 603-524-4775. *In Charge* Randy Brough.

## New Jersey

Basic Health Sciences Library Network (BHSL), Overlook Hospital Health Science Lib., Summit 07902. SAN 371-4888. Tel. 908-522-2886, fax 908-522-2274. *Coord.* Pat Regenberg.

Bergen Passaic Health Sciences Library Consortium, c/o Englewood Hospital and Medical Center, Health Sciences Lib., Englewood 07631. SAN 371-0904. Tel. 201-894-3069, fax 201-894-9049. *Coord.* Lia Sabbagh.

Burlington Libraries Information Consortium (BLINC), Five Pioneer Blvd., Westampton 08060. Tel. 609-267-9660, fax 609-267-4091, e-mail hq@bcls.lib.nj.us. *Coord.* Gale Sweet.

Central Jersey Regional Lib. Cooperative (CJRLC), 4400 Rte. 9 S., Suite 3400, Freehold 07728-4232. SAN 370-5102. Tel. 732-409-6484, fax 732-409-6492, e-mail carol@cjrlc.org. *Exec. Dir.* Connie S. Paul.

Central New Jersey Health Science Libraries Consortium (CNJHSLA), Saint Francis Medical Center Medical Lib., Trenton 08629. SAN 370-0712. Tel. 609-599-5068, fax 609-599-5773. *Libn.* Donna Barlow.

Cosmopolitan Biomedical Library Consortium (CBLC), Overlook Hospital Medical Lib., Summit 07902. SAN 322-4414. Tel. 908-522-2699, fax 908-522-2274. *Coord.* Pat Regenberg.

Health Sciences Library Assn. of New Jersey (HSLANJ), Saint Michaels Medical Center, Newark 07102. SAN 370-0488. Tel. 973-877-5471, fax 973-877-5378. *Dir.* Peter Cole.

Highlands Regional Library Cooperative, 400 Morris Ave., Suite 202, Denville 07834. SAN 329-4609. Tel. 973-664-1776, fax 973-664-1780. *Exec. Dir.* Joanne P. Roukens.

INFOLINK/Eastern New Jersey Regional Library Cooperative, Inc., 44 Stelton Rd., Suite 330, Piscataway 08854. SAN 371-

5116. Tel. 732-752-7720, fax 732-752-7785. *Exec. Dir.* Cheryl O'Connor.

Integrated Information Solutions, 600 Mountain Ave., Rm. 1B 202, Murray Hill 07974. SAN 329-5400. Tel. 908-582-4840, fax 908-582-3146, e-mail librarymh@alcatel-lucent. *Mgr.* M. E. Brennan.

Libraries of Middlesex Automation Consortium (LMxAC), 1030 Saint Georges Ave., Suite 203, Avenel 07001. SAN 329-448X. Tel. 732-750-2525, fax 732-750-9392. *Exec. Dir.* Eileen Palmer.

Monmouth-Ocean Biomedical Information Consortium (MOBIC), Community Medical Center, Toms River 08755. SAN 329-5389. Tel. 732-557-8117, fax 732-557-8354. *Libn.* Reina Reisler.

Morris Automated Information Network (MAIN), P.O. Box 900, Morristown 07963-0900. SAN 322-4058. Tel. 973-631-5353, fax 973-631-5366. *Dir.* Jeremy Jenynak.

Morris-Union Federation, 214 Main St., Chatham 07928. SAN 310-2629. Tel. 973-635-0603, fax 973-635-7827.

New Jersey Health Sciences Library Network (NJHSN), Overlook Hospital Lib., Summit 07902. SAN 371-4829. Tel. 908-522-2886, fax 908-522-2274. *Lib. Mgr.* Pat Regenberg.

New Jersey Library Network, Lib. Development Bureau, Trenton 08608. SAN 372-8161. Tel. 609-278-2640 ext. 152. *Assoc. State Libn. for Lib. Development* Kathleen Moeller-Peiffer.

South Jersey Regional Library Cooperative, Paint Works Corporate Center, Gibbsboro 08026. SAN 329-4625. Tel. 856-346-1222, fax 856-346-2839. *Exec. Dir.* Karen Hyman.

Virtual Academic Library Environment (VALE), William Paterson Univ. Lib., Wayne 07470-2103. Tel. 973-720-3179, fax 973-720-3171. *Coord.* Judy Avrin.

## New Mexico

Alliance for Innovation in Science and Technology Information (AISTI), 369 Montezuma Ave., No. 237, Santa Fe 87501. *Exec. Dir.* Corinne Lebrunn.

Estacado Library Information Network (ELIN), 509 N. Shipp, Hobby 88240. Tel.

505-397-9328, fax 505-397-1508. *System Admin.* Cristine Adams.

New Mexico Consortium of Academic Libraries, Dean's Office, Albuquerque 87131-0001. SAN 371-6872. *Pres.* Ruben Aragon.

New Mexico Consortium of Biomedical and Hospital Libraries, c/o St. Vincent Hospital, Santa Fe 87505. SAN 322-449X. Tel. 505-820-5218, fax 505-989-6478. *Chair* Albert Robinson.

## New York

Academic Libraries of Brooklyn, Long Island Univ. Lib. 517, Brooklyn 11201. SAN 322-2411. Tel. 718-488-1081, fax 718-780-4057.

Associated Colleges of the Saint Lawrence Valley, SUNY Potsdam, Potsdam 13676-2299. SAN 322-242X. Tel. 315-267-3331, fax 315-267-2389. *Exec. Dir.* Anneke J. Larrance.

Capital District Library Council for Reference and Research Resources, 28 Essex St., Albany 12206. SAN 322-2446. Tel. 518-438-2500, fax 518-438-2872. *Exec. Dir.* Jean K. Sheviak.

Central New York Library Resources Council (CLRC), 6493 Ridings Rd., Syracuse 13206-1195. SAN 322-2454. Tel. 315-446-5446, fax 315-446-5590. *Exec. Dir.* Penelope J. Klein.

Connect NY, Rochester Institute of Technology, Rochester 14623. Tel. 585-475-2050. *Dir. of Technology* Chris Lerch.

Council of Archives and Research Libraries in Jewish Studies (CARLJS), 330 7th Ave., 21st flr., New York 10001. SAN 371-053X. Tel. 212-629-0500, fax 212-629-0508, e-mail fjc@jewishculture.org. *Operations Dir.* Michelle Moskowitz Brown.

Library Association of Rockland County (LARC), P.O. Box 917, New City 10956-0917. Tel. 845-357-1237 ext. 11. *Pres.* Ruth A. Bolin.

Library Consortium of Health Institutions in Buffalo (LCHIB), Abbott Hall, SUNY at Buffalo, Buffalo 14214. SAN 329-367X. Tel. 716-829-3900 ext. 143, fax 716-829-2211, e-mail hubnet@buffalo.edu. *Exec. Dir.* Martin E. Mutka.

Long Island Library Resources Council (LILRC), Melville Lib. Bldg., Suite E5310, Stony Brook 11794-3399. SAN 322-2489. Tel. 631-632-6650, fax 631-632-6662. *Dir.* Herbert Biblo.

Medical and Scientific Libraries of Long Island (MEDLI), c/o Palmer School of Lib. and Info. Science, Brookville 11548. SAN 322-4309. Tel. 516-299-2866, fax 516-299-4168. *Pres.* Mahnaz Tehrani.

Metropolitan New York Library Council (METRO), 57 E. 11 St., 4th flr., New York 10003-4605. SAN 322-2500. Tel. 212-228-2320, fax 212-228-2598. *Exec. Dir.* Dottie Hiebing.

National Network of Libraries of Medicine–Middle Atlantic Region (NNLM–MAR), NYU Medical Center, New York 10010. E-mail rml@library.med.nyu.edu. *Assoc. Dir.* Kathel Dunn.

New York State Higher Education Initiative (NYSHEI), 22 Corporate Woods Blvd., Albany 12211-2350. Fax 518-432-4346, e-mail nyshei@nyshei.org. *Exec. Dir.* Jason Kramer.

Northeast Foreign Law Libraries Cooperative Group, Columbia Univ. Lib., New York 10027. SAN 375-0000. Tel. 212-854-1411, fax 212-854-3295. *Coord.* Silke Sahl.

Northern New York Library Network, 6721 U.S. Hwy. 11, Potsdam 13676. SAN 322-2527. Tel. 315-265-1119, fax 315-265-1881, e-mail info@nnyln.org. *Exec. Dir.* John J. Hammond.

Nylink, 22 Corporate Woods, 3rd flr., Albany 12211. SAN 322-256X. Tel. 518-443-5444, fax 518-432-4346, e-mail nylink@nylink.org. *Exec. Dir.* David Penniman.

Research Library Association of South Manhattan, Bobst Lib., New York Univ., New York 10012. SAN 372-8080. Tel. 212-998-2477, fax 212-995-4366. *Dean of Lib.* Carol Mandel.

Rochester Regional Library Council, 390 Packetts Landing, Fairport 14450. SAN 322-2535. Tel. 585-223-7570, fax 585-223-7712, e-mail rrlc@rrlc.org. *Exec. Dir.* Kathleen M. Miller.

South Central Regional Library Council, Clinton Hall, Ithaca 14850. SAN 322-2543. Tel. 607-273-9106, fax 607-272-0740, e-mail scrlc@lakenet.org. *Exec. Dir.* Mary-Carol Lindbloom.

Southeastern New York Library Resources Council (SENYLRC), 21 S. Elting Corners Rd., Highland 12528-2805. SAN 322-2551. Tel. 845-883-9065, fax 845-883-9483. *Exec. Dir.* John L. Shaloiko.

SUNYConnect, Office of Lib. and Info. Services, Albany 12246. Tel. 518-443-5577, fax 518-443-5358. *Assistant Provost for Lib. and Info. Services* Carey Hatch.

United Nations System Electronic Information Acquisitions Consortium (UNSEIAC), c/o Dag Hammarskjold Lib., Rm. L-166A, New York 10017. SAN 377-855X. Tel. 212-963-2026, fax 212-963-2608, e-mail unseiac@un.org. *Coord.* Noriko Gines.

Western New York Library Resources Council, 4455 Genesee St., Buffalo 14225. SAN 322-2578. Tel. 716-633-0705, fax 716-633-1736. *Exec. Dir.* Sheryl Knab.

## North Carolina

Cape Fear Health Sciences Information Consortium, 1601 Owen Drive, Fayetteville 28301. SAN 322-3930. Tel. 910-671-5046, fax 910-671-5337. *Pres.* Rita Johnson.

Dialog Corp., 11000 Regency Pkwy., Suite 10, Cary 27518. SAN 322-0176. Tel. 919-462-8600, fax 919-468-9890. *In Charge* Kevin Bonson.

North Carolina Area Health Education Centers, Univ. of North Carolina Health Sciences Lib., CB 7585, Chapel Hill 27599-7585. SAN 323-9950. Tel. 919-962-0700. *Dir.* Diana McDuffee.

North Carolina Community College System, 200 W. Jones St., Raleigh 27603-1379. SAN 322-2594. Tel. 919-807-7100, fax 919-807-7175; 919-807-7164. *Assoc. V.P. for Learning Technology Systems* Bill Randall.

North Carolina Library and Information Network, State Lib. of North Carolina, Raleigh 27601-2807. SAN 329-3092. Tel. 919-807-7400, fax 919-733-8748. *State Libn.* Mary L. Boone.

Northwest AHEC Library at Hickory, Catawba Medical Center, Hickory 28602. SAN 322-4708. Tel. 828-326-3662, fax 828-326-3484. *Dir.* Karen Lee Martinez.

Northwest AHEC Library at Salisbury, c/o Rowan Regional Medical Center, Salisbury 28144. SAN 322-4589. Tel. 704-210-5069, fax 704-636-5050.

Northwest AHEC Library and Information Network, Wake Forest Univ. School of Medicine, Winston-Salem 27157-1060. SAN 322-4716. Tel. 336-713-7700, fax 336-713-7701. *Dir.* Mike Lischke.

Triangle Research Libraries Network, Wilson Lib., Chapel Hill 27514-8890. SAN 329-5362. Tel. 919-962-8022, fax 919-962-4452. *Dir.* Mona C. Couts.

Western North Carolina Library Network (WNCLN), c/o Appalachian State Univ., Boone 28608. SAN 376-7205. Tel. 828-262-2774, fax 828-262-3001. *Libn.* Catherine Wilkinson.

## North Dakota

Central Dakota Library Network, Morton Mandan Public Lib., Mandan 58554-3149. SAN 373-1391. Tel. 701-667-5365. *Dir.* Kelly Steckler.

Mid-America Law School Library Consortium (MALSLC), Univ. of North Dakota School of Law, Grand Forks 58202. SAN 371-6813. Tel. 701-777-2204, fax 701-777-4956. *Interim Dir.* Rhonda Schwartz.

Tri-College University Libraries Consortium, NDSU Downtown Campus, Fargo 58102. SAN 322-2047. Tel. 701-231-8170, fax 701-231-7205. *In Charge* Sonia Hohnadel.

## Ohio

Assn. of Christian Librarians (ACL), P.O. Box 4, Cedarville 45314. Tel. 937-766-2255, fax 937-766-5499, e-mail info@acl.org. *Pres.* Linda Poston.

Central Ohio Hospital Library Consortium, 127 S. Davis Ave., Columbus 43222. SAN 371-084X. Tel. 614-234-5214, fax 614-234-1257, e-mail library@mchs.com. *Dir.* Stevo Roksandic.

Christian Library Consortium (CLC), c/o ACL, Cedarville 45314. Tel. 937-766-2255, fax 937-766-5499, e-mail info@acl.org. *Coord.* Beth Purtee.

Cleveland Area Metropolitan Library System (CAMLS), 20600 Chagrin Blvd., Suite 500, Shaker Heights 44122-5334. SAN 322-2632. Tel. 216-921-3900, fax 216-921-7220. *Exec. Dir.* Michael G. Snyder.

Columbus Area Library and Information Council of Ohio (CALICO), c/o Westerville Public Lib., Westerville 43081. SAN 371-683X. Tel. 614-882-7277, fax 614-882-5369.

Consortium of Popular Culture Collections in the Midwest (CPCCM), c/o Popular Culture Lib., Bowling Green 43403-0600. SAN 370-5811. Tel. 419-372-2450, fax 419-372-7996. *Head Libn.* Nancy Down.

Five Colleges of Ohio, 102 Allen House, Gambier 43022. Tel. 740-427-5377, fax 740-427-5390, e-mail ohiofive@gmail.com. *Exec. Dir.* Susan Palmer.

Northeast Ohio Regional Library System (NEO-RLS), 4445 Mahoning Ave. N.W., Warren 44483. SAN 322-2713. Tel. 330-847-7744, fax 330-847-7704, e-mail nola@nolanet.org. *Exec. Dir.* William Martino.

Northwest Regional Library System (NOR-WELD), 181½ S. Main St., Bowling Green 43402. SAN 322-273X. Tel. 419-352-2903, fax 419-353-8310. *Dir.* Allan Gray.

OCLC (Online Computer Library Center, Inc.), 6565 Kilgour Place, Dublin 43017-3395. SAN 322-2748. Tel. 614-764-6000, fax 614-718-1017, e-mail oclc@oclc.org. *Pres./CEO* Jay Jordan.

Ohio Health Sciences Library Assn. (OHSLA), South Pointe Hospital, Medical Lib., Warrensville Heights 44122. Tel. 216-491-7454, fax 216-491-7650. *Pres.* Michelle Kraft.

Ohio Library and Information Network (OhioLINK), 2455 N. Star Rd., Suite 300, Columbus 43221. SAN 374-8014. Tel. 614-728-3600, fax 614-728-3610, e-mail info@ohiolink.edu. *Exec. Dir.* Thomas J. Sanville.

Ohio Network of American History Research Centers, Ohio Historical Society Archives Lib., Columbus 43211-2497. SAN 323-9624. Tel. 614-297-2510, fax 614-297-2546, e-mail ohsref@ohiohistory.org, reference@ohiohistory.org. *Research* Louise Jones.

Ohio Public Library Information Network (OPLIN), 2323 W. 5th Ave., Suite 130, Columbus 43204. Tel. 614-728-5252, fax

614-728-5256, e-mail support@oplin.org. *Exec. Dir.* Stephen Hedges.

OHIONET, 1500 W. Lane Ave., Columbus 43221-3975. SAN 322-2764. Tel. 614-486-2966, fax 614-486-1527. *Exec. Dir./ CEO* Michael P. Butler.

Rural Ohio Valley Health Sciences Library Network (ROVHSLN), Southern State Community College South, Sardinia 45171. Tel. 937-695-0307 ext. 3681, fax 937-695-1440. *Mgr.* Mary Ayres.

Southeast Regional Library System (SERLS), 252 W. 13 St., Wellston 45692. SAN 322-2756. Tel. 740-384-2103, fax 740-384-2106, e-mail dirserls@oplin.org. *Exec. Dir.* Mary Leffler.

SouthWest Ohio and Neighboring Libraries (SWON), 10815 Indeco Drive, Suite 200, Cincinnati 45241-2926. SAN 322-2675. Tel. 513-751-4422, fax 513-751-0463, e-mail info@swonlibraries.org. *Exec. Dir.* Anne K. Abate.

Southwestern Ohio Council for Higher Education (SOCHE), Miami Valley Research Park, Dayton 45420-4015. SAN 322-2659. Tel. 937-258-8890, fax 937-258-8899, e-mail soche@soche.org.

State Assisted Academic Library Council of Kentucky (SAALCK), c/o SWON Libraries, Cincinnati 45241. SAN 371-2222. Tel. 513-751-4422, fax 513-751-0463, e-mail saalck@saalck.org. *Exec. Dir.* Anne Abate.

Theological Consortium of Greater Columbus (TCGC), Trinity Lutheran Seminary, Columbus 43209-2334. Tel. 614-384-4646, fax 614-238-0263. *Lib. Systems Mgr.* Ray Olson.

## Oklahoma

Greater Oklahoma Area Health Sciences Library Consortium (GOAL), Mercy Memorial Health Center/Resource Center, Ardmore 73401. SAN 329-3858. Tel. 580-220-6625, fax 580-220-6599. *Pres.* Catherine Ice.

Oklahoma Health Sciences Library Assn. (OHSLA), HSC Bird Health Science Lib., Univ. of Oklahoma, Oklahoma City 73190. SAN 375-0051. Tel. 405-271-2285 ext. 48755, fax 405-271-3297. *Dir.* Clinton M. Thompson.

## Oregon

Chemeketa Cooperative Regional Library Service, c/o Chemeketa Community College, Salem 97305-1453. SAN 322-2837. Tel. 503-399-5105, fax 503-399-7316, e-mail cocl@chemeketa.edu. *Coord.* Linda Cochrane.

Coastal Resource Sharing Network (CRSN), c/o Tillamook County Lib., Tillamook 97141. Tel. 503-842-4792, fax 503-815-8194, e-mail webmaster@beachbooks.org. *Pres.* Peter Rayment.

Coos County Library Service District, 1988 Newmark, Coos Bay 97420. SAN 322-4279. Tel. 541-888-1529, fax 541-888-1529. *Dir.* Mary Jane Fisher.

Gorge LINK Library Consortium, c/o Hood River County Lib., Hood River 97031. Tel. 541-387-4659, 541-386-2535, fax 541-386-3835, e-mail gorge.link@co.hood-river.or.us. *System Admin.* Jayne Guidinger.

Library Information Network of Clackamas County, 16239 S.E. McLoughlin Blvd., Suite 208, Oak Grove 97267-4654. SAN 322-2845. Tel. 503-723-4888, fax 503-794-8238, e-mail webmaster@lincc.org. *Mgr.* Joanna Rood.

Orbis Cascade Alliance, 1501 Kincaid, No. 4, Eugene 97401-4540. SAN 377-8096. Tel. 541-346-1832, fax 541-346-1968, e-mail orbcas@uoregon.edu. *Chair* Lee Lyttle.

Oregon Health Sciences Libraries Assn. (OHSLA), Oregon Health and Science Univ. Lib., Portland 97239-3098. SAN 371-2176. Tel. 503-494-3462, fax 503-494-3322, e-mail Lib.@ohsu.edu. *Dir.* James Morgan.

Portland Area Library System (PORTALS), Port Community College, SYLIB202, Portland 97219. Tel. 503-977-4571, fax 503-977-4977. *Coord.* Roberta Richards.

Southern Oregon Library Federation, c/o Klamath County Lib., Klamath Falls 97601. SAN 322-2861. Tel. 541-882-8894, fax 541-882-6166. *Dir.* Andy Swanson.

Southern Oregon Library Information System (SOLIS), 724 S. Central Ave., Suite 112, Medford 97501. Tel. 541-772-2141, fax 541-772-2144, e-mail solis_97501@yahoo.com. *System Admin.* Marian Stoner.

Washington County Cooperative Library Services, 111 N.E. Lincoln St., MS No. 58, Hillsboro 97124-3036. SAN 322-287X. Tel. 503-846-3222, fax 503-846-3220. *Mgr.* Eva Calcagno.

## Pennsylvania

Associated College Libraries of Central Pennsylvania, P.O. Box 39, Grantham 17027. E-mail aclcp@aclcp.org. *Pres.* Gregory Crawford.

Berks County Library Assn. (BCLA), Reading Public Lib., Reading 19602. SAN 371-0866. Tel. 610-655-6350, 610-478-9035. *Pres.* Jennifer Balas.

Central Pennsylvania Consortium (CPC), Dickinson College, Carlisle 17013. SAN 322-2896. Tel. 717-245-1984, fax 717-245-1807, e-mail cpc@dickinson.edu. *Pres.* Katherine Haley Will.

Central Pennsylvania Health Sciences Library Assn. (CPHSLA), Office for Research Protections, Pennsylvania State Univ., University Park 16802. SAN 375-5290. Fax 814-865-1775. *Pres.* Tracie Kahler.

Cooperating Hospital Libraries of the Lehigh Valley Area, Estes Lib., Saint Luke's Hospital, Bethlehem 18015. SAN 371-0858. Tel. 610-954-3407, fax 610-954-4651. *Chair* Sharon Hrabina.

Delaware Valley Information Consortium (DEVIC), St. Mary Medical Center Medical Lib., Langhorne 19047. Tel. 215-710-2012, fax 215-710-4638, e-mail info@devic-libraries.net. *Dir.* Rita Haydar.

Eastern Mennonite Associated Libraries and Archives (EMALA), 2215 Millstream Rd., Lancaster 17602. SAN 372-8226. Tel. 717-393-9745, fax 717-393-8751. *Chair* Edsel Burdge.

Erie Area Health Information Library Cooperative (EAHILC), Nash Lib., Gannon Univ., Erie 16541. SAN 371-0564. Tel. 814-871-7667, fax 814-871-5566. *Chair* Deborah West.

Greater Philadelphia Law Library Assn. (GPLLA), P.O. Box 335, Philadelphia 19105. SAN 373-1375. *Pres.* Monica Almendarez.

HSLC/Access PA (Health Sciences Libraries Consortium), 3600 Market St., Suite 550, Philadelphia 19104-2646. SAN 323-9780.

Tel. 215-222-1532, fax 215-222-0416, e-mail support@hslc.org. *Exec. Dir.* Joseph C. Scorza.

Interlibrary Delivery Service of Pennsylvania (IDS), c/o Bucks County IU, No. 22, Doylestown 18901. SAN 322-2942. Tel. 215-348-2940 ext. 1620, fax 215-348-8315, e-mail ids@bucksiu.org. *Admin. Dir.* Beverly J. Carey.

Keystone Library Network, Dixon Univ. Center, Harrisburg 17110-1201. Tel. 717-720-4088, fax 717-720-4453. *Coord.* Mary Lou Sowden.

Laurel Highlands Health Science Library Consortium, 361 Sunrise Rd., Dayton 16222. SAN 322-2950. Tel. 814-341-0242, fax 814-266-8230. *Dir.* Rhonda Yeager.

Lehigh Valley Assn. of Independent Colleges, 130 W. Greenwich St., Bethlehem 18018. SAN 322-2969. Tel. 610-625-7888, fax 610-625-7891. *Exec. Dir.* Tom A. Tenges.

Lyrasis. See under Georgia.

Montgomery County Library and Information Network Consortium (MCLINC), 301 Lafayette St., 2nd flr., Conshohocken 19428. Tel. 610-238-0580, fax 610-238-0581, e-mail webmaster@mclinc.org. *Pres.* Carrie L. Turner.

Northeastern Pennsylvania Library Network, c/o Marywood Univ. Lib., Scranton 18509-1598. SAN 322-2993. Tel. 570-348-6260, fax 570-961-4769. *Exec. Dir.* Catherine H. Schappert.

Northwest Interlibrary Cooperative of Pennsylvania (NICOP), Mercyhurst College Lib., Erie 16546. SAN 370-5862. Tel. 814-824-2190, fax 814-824-2219. *Archivist* Earleen Glaser.

PALINET, see Lyrasis under Georgia.

Pennsylvania Library Assn., 220 Cumberland Pkwy., Suite 10, Mechanicsburg 17055. Tel. 717-766-7663, fax 717-766-5440. *Exec. Dir.* Glenn R. Miller.

Philadelphia Area Consortium of Special Collections Libraries (PACSCL), c/o Historical Society of Pennsylvania, Philadelphia 19107. SAN 370-7504. Tel. 215-985-1445, fax 215-985-1446, e-mail pacsl@pacscl.org. *Exec. Dir.* Laura Blanchard.

Southeastern Pennsylvania Theological Library Assn. (SEPTLA), c/o Biblical Seminary, Hatfield 19440. SAN 371-0793. Tel. 215-368-5000 ext. 234. *Chair* Daniel LaValla.

State System of Higher Education Library Cooperative (SSHELCO), c/o Bailey Lib., Slippery Rock 16057. Tel. 724-738-2630, fax 724-738-2661. *Dir.* Philip Tramdack.

Susquehanna Library Cooperative (SLC), Stevenson Lib., Lock Haven Univ. of Pennsylvania, Lock Haven 17745. SAN 322-3051. Tel. 570-484-2310, fax 570-484-2506. *Dean of Lib. and Info. Services* Tara Lynn Fulton.

Tri-State College Library Cooperative (TCLC), c/o Rosemont College Lib., Rosemont 19010-1699. SAN 322-3078. Tel. 610-525-0796, fax 610-525-1939, e-mail office@tclclibs.org. *Coord.* Ellen Gasiewski.

## Rhode Island

Library of Rhode Island Network (LORI), c/o Office of Lib. and Info. Services, Providence 02908-5870. SAN 371-6821. Tel. 401-574-9300, fax 401-574-9320. *Lib. Services Dir.* Howard Boksenbaum.

Ocean State Libraries (OSL), 600 Sandy Lane, Warwick 02886. SAN 329-4560. Tel. 401-738-2200, fax 401-736-8949, e-mail support@oslri.net. *Exec. Dir.* Joan Gillespie.

## South Carolina

Charleston Academic Libraries Consortium (CALC), P.O. Box 118067, Charleston 29423-8067. SAN 371-0769. Tel. 843-574-6088, fax 843-574-6484. *Chair* Drucie Gullion.

Columbia Area Medical Librarians' Assn. (CAMLA), School of Medicine Lib., Univ. of South Carolina, Columbia 29209. SAN 372-9400. Tel. 803-733-3361, fax 803-733-1509. *Pres.* Roz Anderson.

Partnership Among South Carolina Academic Libraries (PASCAL), 1333 Main St., Suite 305, Columbia 29201. Tel. 803-734-0900, fax 803-734-0901. *Exec. Dir.* Rick Moul.

South Carolina AHEC, c/o Medical Univ. of South Carolina, Charleston 29425. SAN 329-3998. Tel. 843-792-4431, fax 843-792-4430. *Exec. Dir.* David Garr.

South Carolina State Library/South Carolina Library Network, 1430 and 1500 Senate St., Columbia 29201. SAN 322-4198. Tel. 803-734-8666, fax 803-734-8676, e-mail reference@stateLib.sc.gov. *Dir., Lib. and Info. Services* Mary Morgan.

## South Dakota

South Dakota Library Network (SDLN), 1200 University, Unit 9672, Spearfish 57799-9672. SAN 371-2117. Tel. 605-642-6835, fax 605-642-6472, e-mail help@sdln.net. *Dir.* Warren Wilson.

## Tennessee

Consortium of Southern Biomedical Libraries (CONBLS), Meharry Medical College, Nashville 37208. SAN 370-7717. Tel. 615-327-6728, fax 615-327-6448. *Chair* Barbara Shearer.

Knoxville Area Health Sciences Library Consortium (KAHSLC), Preston Medical Lib., Univ. of Tennessee, Knoxville 37920. SAN 371-0556. Tel. 865-305-9525, fax 865-305-9527. *Pres.* Cynthia Vaughn.

Mid-Tennessee Health Science Librarians Assn., VA Medical Center, Nashville 37212. SAN 329-5028. Tel. 615-327-4751 ext. 5523, fax 615-321-6336.

Tennessee Health Science Library Assn. (THeSLA), Holston Valley Medical Center Health Sciences Lib., Kingsport 37660. SAN 371-0726. Tel. 423-224-6870, fax 423-224-6014, e-mail sharon_m_brown@wellmont.org. *Coord., Lib. Services* Sharon M. Brown.

Tri-Cities Area Health Sciences Libraries Consortium (TCAHSLC), James H. Quillen College of Medicine, East Tennessee State Univ., Johnson City 37614. SAN 329-4099. Tel. 423-439-6252, fax 423-439-7025. *Dir.* Biddanda Ponnappa.

Wolf River Library Consortium, c/o Germantown Community Lib., Germantown 38138-2815. Tel. 901-757-7323, fax 901-756-9940. *Dir.* Melody Pittman.

## Texas

Abilene Library Consortium, 3305 N. 3rd St., Suite 301, Abilene 79603. SAN 322-4694. Tel. 325-672-7081, fax 325-672-7082. *Coord.* David Bavousett.

Amigos Library Services, Inc., 14400 Midway Rd., Dallas 75244-3509. SAN 322-3191. Tel. 972-851-8000, fax 972-991-6061, e-mail amigos@amigos.org. *Exec. Dir.* Bonnie Juergens.

Council of Research and Academic Libraries (CORAL), P.O. Box 290236, San Antonio 78280-1636. SAN 322-3213. Tel. 210-458-4885. *Coord.* Rosemary Vasquez.

Del Norte Biosciences Library Consortium, El Paso Community College, El Paso 79998. SAN 322-3302. Tel. 915-831-4149, fax 915-831-4639. *Coord.* Becky Perales.

Harrington Library Consortium, 413 E. 4 Ave., Amarillo 79101. SAN 329-546X. Tel. 806-378-6037, fax 806-378-6038. *Dir.* Donna Littlejohn.

Health Libraries Information Network (Health LINE), UT Southwestern Medical Center Lib., Dallas 75390-9049. SAN 322-3299. Tel. 214-648-2626, fax 214-648-2826.

Houston Area Library Automation Network (HALAN), Houston Public Lib., Houston 77002. Tel. 832-393-1411, fax 832-393-1427, e-mail website@hpl.lib.tx.us. *In Charge* Violet Johnson.

Houston Area Research Library Consortium (HARLiC), c/o Univ. of Houston Libraries, Houston 77204-2000. SAN 322-3329. Tel. 713-743-9807, fax 713-743-9811. *Pres.* Dana Rooks.

National Network of Libraries of Medicine–South Central Region (NNLM–SCR), c/o HAM-TMC Lib., Houston 77030-2809. SAN 322-3353. Tel. 713-799-7880, fax 713-790-7030, e-mail nnlm-scr@exch.library.tmc.edu. *Dir.* Elizabeth K. Eaton.

Northeast Texas Library System (NETLS), 625 Austin St., Garland 75040-6365. SAN 370-5943. Tel. 972-205-2566, fax 972-205-2767. *Major Resource Center Dir.* Claire Bausch.

South Central Academic Medical Libraries Consortium (SCAMeL), c/o Lewis Lib.–UNTHSC, Fort Worth 76107. SAN 372-8269. Tel. 817-735-2380, fax 817-735-

5158. *Assoc. V.P. for Info. Resources* Bobby Carter.

Texas Council of Academic Libraries (TCAL), VC/UHV Lib., Victoria 77901. SAN 322-337X. Tel. 361-570-4150, fax 361-570-4155. *Chair* Joe Dahlstrom.

Texnet, P.O. Box 12927, Austin 78711. SAN 322-3396. Tel. 512-463-5406, fax 512-936-2306, e-mail ill@tsl.state.tx.us.

## Utah

National Network of Libraries of Medicine–MidContinental Region (NNLM–MCR), Spencer S. Eccles Health Sciences Lib., Univ. of Utah, Salt Lake City 84112-5890. SAN 322-225X. Tel. 801-587-3412, fax 801-581-3632. *Dir.* Wayne J. Peay.

Utah Academic Library Consortium (UALC), Univ. of Utah, Salt Lake City 84112-0731. SAN 322-3418. Tel. 801-581-3386; 801-581-6594, fax 801-585-3033, e-mail UALCmail@library.utah.edu. *Dir.* Rita Reusch.

Utah Health Sciences Library Consortium, c/o Spencer S. Eccles Health Sciences Lib., Univ. of Utah, Salt Lake City 84112-5890. SAN 376-2246. Tel. 801-585-5743, fax 801-581-3632. *Chair* John Bramble.

## Vermont

Vermont Resource Sharing Network, c/o Vermont Dept. of Libs., Montpelier 05609-0601. SAN 322-3426. Tel. 802-828-3261, fax 802-828-1481. *Libn.* Gerrie Denison.

## Virginia

American Indian Higher Education Consortium (AIHEC), 121 Oronoco St., Alexandria 22314. SAN 329-4056. Tel. 703-838-0400, fax 703-838-0388, e-mail aihec@aihec.org.

Defense Technical Information Center, 8725 John J. Kingman Rd., Suite 0944, Fort Belvoir 22060-6218. SAN 322-3442. Tel. 703-767-8180, fax 703-767-8179. *Admin.* R. Paul Ryan.

Lynchburg Area Library Cooperative, c/o Sweet Briar College Lib., Sweet Briar 24595. SAN 322-3450. Tel. 434-381-6315, fax 434-381-6173.

Lynchburg Information Online Network (LION), 2315 Memorial Ave., Lynchburg 24503. SAN 374-6097. Tel. 434-381-6311, fax 434-381-6173. *Dir.* John G. Jaffee.

NASA Libraries Information System, NASA Galaxie, NASA Langley Research Center, MS 185–Technical Lib., Hampton 23681-2199. SAN 322-0788. Tel. 757-864-2356, fax 757-864-2375, e-mail tech-library@larc.nasa.gov. *Coord.* Manjula Ambur.

Richmond Academic Library Consortium (RALC), James Branch Cabell Lib., Virginia Commonwealth Univ., Richmond 23284. SAN 322-3469. Tel. 804-828-1110; 804-828-1107, fax 804-828-1105, 804-828-0151. *Univ. Libn.* John E. Ulmschneider.

Southside Virginia Library Network (SVLN), Longwood Univ., Farmville 23909-1897. SAN 372-8242. Tel. 434-395-2431; 434-395-2433, fax 434-395-2453. *Dir.* Wendell Barbour.

Southwestern Virginia Health Information Librarians (SWVAHILI), Carilion Health Sciences Lib., Roanoke 24033. SAN 323-9527. Tel. 540-433-4166, fax 540-433-3106. *Chair* George Curran.

United States Army Training and Doctrine Command (TRADOC)/Library Program Office, U.S. Army Hq. TRADOC, Fort Monroe 23651. SAN 322-418X. Tel. 757-788-2155, fax 757-788-5544. *Dir.* Amy Loughran.

Virginia Independent College and University Library Assn., c/o Mary Helen Cochran Lib., Sweet Briar 24595. SAN 374-6089. Tel. 434-381-6139, fax 434-381-6173. *Dir.* John Jaffee.

Virginia Tidewater Consortium for Higher Education (VTC), 4900 Powhhatan Ave., Norfolk 23529. SAN 329-5486. Tel. 757-683-3183, fax 757-683-4515, e-mail lgdotolo@aol.com. *Pres.* Lawrence G. Dotolo.

Virtual Library of Virginia (VIVA), George Mason Univ., Fairfax 22030. Tel. 703-993-4652, fax 703-993-4662. *Dir.* Katherine Perry.

## Washington

Cooperating Libraries in Olympia (CLIO), Evergreen State College Lib., L2300, Olympia 98505. SAN 329-4528. Tel. 360-867-6260, fax 360-867-6790. *Dean, Lib. Services* Lee Lyttle.

Inland NorthWest Health Sciences Libraries (INWHSL), P.O. Box 10283, Spokane 99209-0283. SAN 370-5099. Tel. 509-368-6973, fax 509-358-7928. *Treas.* Robert Pringle.

National Network of Libraries of Medicine–Pacific Northwest Region (NNLM–PNR), Univ. of Washington, Seattle 98195-7155. SAN 322-3485. Tel. 206-543-8262, fax 206-543-2469, e-mail nnlm@u.washington.edu. *Dir.* Sherrilynne S. Fuller.

Palouse Area Library Information Services (PALIS), c/o Neill Public Lib., Pullman 99163. SAN 375-0132. Tel. 509-334-3595, fax 509-334-6051. *Dir.* Andriette Pieron.

VALNet, Asotin County Lib., Clarkston 99403. SAN 323-7672. Tel. 509-758-5454, fax 509-751-1460, e-mail admin.acl@valnet.org. *Dir.* Jennifer Ashby.

Washington Idaho Network (WIN), Foley Center Lib., Gonzaga Univ., Spokane 99258. Tel. 509-323-6545, fax 509-324-5398, e-mail winsupport@gonzaga.edu. *Pres.* Eileen Bell-Garrison.

Western Council of State Libraries, Washington State Lib., Olympia 48504-2460. Tel. 360-704-5253, fax 360-586-7575. *Pres.* Jan Walsh.

## West Virginia

Mid-Atlantic Law Library Cooperative (MALLCO), College of Law Lib., Morgantown 26506-6135. SAN 371-0645. Tel. 304-293-7641, fax 304-293-6020. *Lib. Dir.* Camille M. Riley.

## Wisconsin

Arrowhead Health Sciences Library Network, Wisconsin Indianhead Technical College, Shell Lake 54817. SAN 322-1954. Tel. 715-468-2815 ext. 2298, fax 715-468-2819. *Coord.* Judy Lyons.

Fox River Valley Area Library Consortium (FRVALC), c/o Polk Lib., Univ. of Wisconsin–Oshkosh, Oshkosh 54901. SAN 322-3531. Tel. 920-424-3348; 920-424-4333, fax 920-424-2175. *Coord.* Erin Czech.

Fox Valley Library Council, c/o OWLS, Appleton 54911. SAN 323-9640. Tel. 920-832-6190, fax 920-832-6422. *Pres.* Joy Schwarz.

Library Council of Southeastern Wisconsin, Inc., 814 W. Wisconsin Ave., Milwaukee 53233-2309. SAN 322-354X. Tel. 414-271-8470, fax 414-286-2798. *Exec. Dir.* Susie M. Just.

North East Wisconsin Intertype Libraries, Inc. (NEWIL), 515 Pine St., Green Bay 54301. SAN 322-3574. Tel. 920-448-4412, fax 920-448-4420. *Dir.* Mark Merrifield.

Northwestern Wisconsin Health Science Library Consortium, c/o Gundersen Lutheran Medical Center, Lacrosse 54601. Tel. 608-775-5410, fax 608-775-6343. *Treas.* Eileen Severson.

South Central Wisconsin Health Science Library Consortium, c/o Fort Healthcare Medical Lib., Fort Atkinson 53538. SAN 322-4686. Tel. 920-568-5194, fax 920-568-5195. *Coord.* Carrie Garity.

Southeastern Wisconsin Health Science Library Consortium, VA Center Medical Lib., Milwaukee 53295. SAN 322-3582. Tel. 414-384-2000 ext. 42342, fax 414-382-5334. *Coord.* Janice Curnes.

Southeastern Wisconsin Information Technology Exchange, Inc. (SWITCH), 6801 N. Yates Rd., Milwaukee 53217-3985. SAN 371-3962. Tel. 414-351-2423, fax 414-228-4146. *Coord.* William A. Topritzhofer.

University of Wisconsin System School Library Education Consortium (UWSSLEC), Graduate and Continuing Education, Univ. of Wisconsin–Whitewater, Whitewater 53190. Tel. 262-472-1463, fax 262-472-5210, e-mail lenchoc@uww.edu. *Co-Dir.* E. Anne Zarinnia.

Wisconsin Library Services (WILS), 728 State St., Rm. 464, Madison 53706-1494. SAN 322-3612. Tel. 608-265-4167, 608-265-0580, 608-263-4981, fax 608-263-

3684, 608-262-6067. *Dir.* Kathryn Schneider Michaelis.

Wisconsin Public Library Consortium (WPLC), c/o South Central Lib. System, Madison 53718. *Dir.* Phyllis Davis.

Wisconsin Valley Library Service (WVLS), 300 N. 1 St., Wausau 54403. SAN 371-3911. Tel. 715-261-7250, fax 715-261-7259. *Dir.* Marla Rae Sepnafski.

WISPALS Library Consortium, c/o Gateway Technical College, Kenosha 53144-1690. Tel. 262-564-2602, fax 262-564-2787. *Coord.* Rebecca Dougherty.

## Wyoming

WYLD Network, c/o Wyoming State Lib., Cheyenne 82002-0060. SAN 371-0661. Tel. 307-777-6339, fax 307-777-6289, e-mail wyldstaff@will.state.wy.us. *State Libn.* Lesley Boughton.

## Virgin Islands

Vilinet/Virgin Islands Library and Information Network, c/o Division of Libs., Archives, and Museums, Saint Thomas 00802. SAN 322-3639. Tel. 340-773-5715, fax 340-773-3257, e-mail info@vilinet.net. *Territorial Dir. of Libs., Archives, and Museums.* Ingrid Bough.

# Canada

## Alberta

NEOS Library Consortium, 1-01H Rutherford Library South, University of Alberta, Edmonton T6G 2J8. Tel. 780-492-0075, fax 780-492-5083. *Mgr.* Anne Carr-Wiggin.

The Alberta Library (TAL), 6-14, 7 Sir Winston Churchill Sq., Edmonton T5J 2V5. Tel. 780-414-0805, fax 780-414-0806. *Acting CEO* Karla Palichuk.

## British Columbia

British Columbia Academic Health Council (BCAHC), 402-1770 W. 7 Ave., Vancouver V6J 4Y6. Tel. 604-739-3910 ext. 228, fax 604-739-3931, e-mail info@bcahc.ca. *CEO* George Eisler.

British Columbia College and Institute Library Services, Langara College Lib., Vancouver V5Y 2Z6. SAN 329-6970. Tel. 604-323-5639, fax 604-323-5544, e-mail cils@langara.bc.ca. *Dir.* Mary Anne Epp.

British Columbia Electronic Library Network (BC ELN), WAC Bennett Lib., 7th fl., Simon Fraser Univ., Burnaby V5A 1S6. Tel. 778-782-7003, fax 778-782-3023, e-mail office@eln.bc.ca. *Exec. Dir.* Anita Cocchia.

Council of Prairie and Pacific University Libraries (COPPUL), 2005 Sooke Rd., Victoria V9B 5Y2. Tel. 250-391-2554, fax 250-391-2556, e-mail coppul@royalroads. ca. *Exec. Dir.* Alexander Slade.

Electronic Health Library of British Columbia (e-HLbc), c/o Bennett Lib., Burnaby V5A 1S6. Tel. 778-782-5440, fax 778-782-3023, e-mail info@ehlbc.ca. *Coord.* Leigh Anne Palmer.

Public Library InterLINK, c/o Kingsway Branch, Burnaby Public Lib., Burnaby V5E 1G3. SAN 318-8272. Tel. 604-517-8441, fax 604-517-8410, e-mail plilink@moon.bcpl.gov.bc.ca. *Operations Mgr.* Rita Avigdor.

## Manitoba

Manitoba Government Libraries Council (MGLC), c/o Instructional Resources Unit, Winnipeg R3G 0T3. SAN 371-6848. Tel. 204-945-7833, fax 204-945-8756. *Chair* John Tooth.

Manitoba Library Consortium, Inc. (MLCI), c/o Lib. Administration, Univ. of Winnipeg, Winnipeg R3B 2E9. SAN 372-820X. Tel. 204-786-9801, fax 204-783-8910. *Chair* Rick Walker.

## Nova Scotia

Maritimes Health Libraries Association (MHLA-ABSM), W. K. Kellogg Health Sciences Lib., Tupper Medical Bldg., 5850 College St., Dalhousie Univ., Halifax B3H 1X5. Tel. 902-494-2483, email mckibbon @dal.ca. *Pres.* Shelley McKibbon.

NOVANET, 1550 Bedford Hwy., No. 501, Bedford B4A 1E6. SAN 372-4050. Tel. 902-453-2461, fax 902-453-2369, e-mail office@novanet.ns.ca. *Mgr.* Bill Slauenwhite.

## Ontario

Bibliocentre, 31 Scarsdale Rd., North York M3B 2R2. SAN 322-3663. Tel. 647-722-9300, fax 647-722-9301. *Exec. Dir.* Janice Hayes.

Canadian Association of Research Libraries (Association des Bibliothéques de Recherche du Canada), Morisset Hall, Rm. 238, Ottawa K1N 9A5. SAN 323-9721. Tel. 613-562-5385, fax 613-562-5195, e-mail carladm@uottawa.ca. *Exec. Dir.* Brent Roe.

Canadian Health Libraries Association (CHLA-ABSC), 39 River St., Toronto M5A 3P1. SAN 370-0720. Tel. 416-646-1600, fax 416-646-9460, e-mail info@chla-absc.ca. *Pres.* Dianne Kharouba.

Canadian Research Knowledge Network (CRKN), 200-343 Preston St., Preston Sq., Tower II, Ottawa K1S 1N4. Tel. 613-907-7040, fax 866-903-9094. *Exec. Dir.* Deb deBruijn.

Consortium of Ontario Academic Health Libraries (COAHL), Gerstein Science Information Centre, Univ. of Toronto, 9 King's College Circle, Toronto M5S 1A5. Tel. 416-978-6370, fax 416-971-2848. *Chair* Sandra Langlands.

Hamilton and District Health Library Network, c/o St. Joseph's Hospital, Hamilton L8N 4A6. SAN 370-5846. Tel. 905-522-1155 ext. 3410. *Coord.* Jean Maragno.

Health Science Information Consortium of Toronto, c/o Gerstein Science Info. Center, Univ. of Toronto, Toronto M5S 1A5. SAN 370-5080. Tel. 416-978-6359, fax 416-971-2637. *Exec. Dir.* Miriam Ticoll.

Ontario Council of University Libraries (OCUL), 130 Saint George St., Toronto M5S 1A5. Tel. 416-946-0578, fax 416-978-6755. *Exec. Dir.* Kathy Scardellato.

Ontario Health Libraries Association (OHLA), c/o Health Sciences Lib., Sault Area Hospital, Sault Ste. Marie P6A 2C4. SAN 370-0739. Tel. 705-759-3434 ext. 4368, fax 705-759-3640. *Pres.* Kimberley Aslett.

Ontario Library Consortium (OLC), c/o Middlesex County Lib., 399 Ridout St. N., London N6A 2P1. *Pres.* Marzio Apolloni.

Parry Sound and Area Access Network, c/o Parry Sound Public Lib., Parry Sound P2A 1E3. Tel. 705-746-9601, fax 705-746-9601, e-mail pslib@zeuter.com. *Chair* Laurine Tremaine.

Perth County Information Network (PCIN), c/o Stratford Public Lib., Stratford N5A 1A2. Tel. 519-271-0220, fax 519-271-3843, e-mail webmaster@pcin.on.ca. *CEO* Ted Boniface.

Shared Library Services (SLS), South Huron Hospital, Exeter N0M 1S2. SAN 323-9500. Tel. 519-235-4002 ext. 249, fax 519- 235-2742, e-mail linda.wilcox@shha. on.ca. *Dir.* Linda Wilcox.

Southwestern Ontario Health Libraries and Information Network (SOHLIN), South Huron Hospital, Exeter N0M 1S2. Tel. 519-235-5168, fax 519-235-4476. *Pres.* Linda Wilcox.

Toronto Health Libraries Association (THLA), 3409 Yonge St., Toronto M4N 2L0. SAN 323-9853. Tel. 416-485-0377, fax 416-485-6877, e-mail president@thla. ca. *Pres.* Weina Wang.

Toronto School of Theology, 47 Queen's Park Crescent E., Toronto M5S 2C3. SAN 322-452X. Tel. 416-978-4039, fax 416-978-7821.

## Quebec

Association des Bibliothèques de la Santé Affiliées a l'Université de Montréal (ABSAUM), c/o Health Library Univ., Montreal H3C 3J7. SAN 370-5838. Tel. 514-343-6826, fax 514-343-2350.

Canadian Heritage Information Network (CHIN), 15 Eddy St., 4th fl., Gatineau K1A 0M5. SAN 329-3076. Tel. 819-994-1200, fax 819-994-9555, e-mail service@ chin.gc.ca. *Dir.-Gen.* Gabrielle Blais.

# National Library and Information-Industry Associations, United States and Canada

## American Association of Law Libraries

Executive Director, Kate Hagan
53 W. Jackson Blvd., Ste. 940, Chicago, IL 60604
312-939-4764, fax 312-431-1097, e-mail khagan@aall.org
World Wide Web http://www.aallnet.org

### Object

The American Association of Law Libraries (AALL) is established for educational and scientific purposes. It shall be conducted as a nonprofit corporation to promote and enhance the value of law libraries to the public, the legal community, and the world; to foster the profession of law librarianship; to provide leadership in the field of legal information; and to foster a spirit of cooperation among the members of the profession. Established 1906.

### Membership

Memb. 5,000+. Persons officially connected with a law library or with a law section of a state or general library, separately maintained. Associate membership available for others. Dues (Indiv.) $208; (Retired) $52; (Student) $52. Year. July 1–June 30.

### Officers

*Pres.* James E. Duggan, Dir. Law Lib. and Professor of Law, Tulane Univ. Law Lib., 320C John Giffen Weinmann Hall, 6329 Freret St., New Orleans, LA 70118-6231. Tel. 504-865-5950, e-mail duggan@tulane. edu; *V.P.* Catherine Lemann; *Secy.* Ruth J. Hill; *Treas.* David S. Mao; *Past Pres.* Ann T. Fessenden.

### Executive Board

Carol Bredemeyer, Christine L. Graesser, Janice E. Henderson, Jean M. Wenger, Cornell H. Winston, Sally Wise.

## American Library Association

Executive Director, Keith Michael Fiels
50 E. Huron St., Chicago, IL 60611
800-545-2433, 312-280-1392, fax 312-440-9374
World Wide Web http://www.ala.org

### Object

The mission of the American Library Association (ALA) is to provide leadership for the development, promotion, and improvement of library and information services and the profession of librarianship in order to enhance learning and ensure access to information for all. Founded 1876.

### Membership

Memb. (Indiv.) 63,522; (Inst.) 3,396; (Corporate) 260; (Total) 67,178 (as of November 13, 2008). Any person, library, or other organization interested in library service and librarians. Dues (Indiv.) 1st year, $65; 2nd year, $98; 3rd year and later, $130; (Trustee and Assoc. Memb.) $59; (Lib. Support Staff)

$46; (Student) $33; (Foreign Indiv.) $78; (Other) $46; (Inst.) $110 and up, depending on operating expenses of institution.

## Officers (2008–2009)

*Pres.* Jim Rettig, University Libn., Boatwright Memorial Lib., Univ. of Richmond. Tel. 804-289-8456, fax 804-289-8757, e-mail jrettig@richmond.edu; *Pres.-Elect* Camila Alire, Dean Emerita, Univ. of New Mexico and Colorado State Univ. E-mail calire@att.net; *Past Pres.* Loriene Roy, Professor, School of Info., Univ. of Texas at Austin. E-mail loriene@ischool.utexas.edu; *Treas.* Rod Hersberger, Dean, Univ. Lib., California State University-Bakersfield. E-mail rhersberger@csub.edu.

## Executive Board

Diane R. Chen (2011), Joseph M. Eagan (2011), Mario M. Gonzalez (2009), Terri G. Kirk (2009), Em Claire Knowles (2011), Charles E. Kratz, Jr. (2010), Larry Romans (2010), Roberta A. Stevens (2009).

## Endowment Trustees

Daniel J. Bradbury (2009), John Vitali (2010), Robert A. Walton (2010); *Exec. Board Liaison* Rod Hersberger; *Staff Liaison* Gregory L. Calloway.

## Divisions

See the separate entries that follow: American Assn. of School Libns.; Assn. for Lib. Collections and Technical Services; Assn. for Lib. Service to Children; Assn. for Lib. Trustees, Advocates, Friends and Foundations; Assn. of College and Research Libs.; Assn. of Specialized and Cooperative Lib. Agencies; Lib. Leadership and Management Assn.; Lib. and Info. Technology Assn.; Public Lib. Assn.; Reference and User Services Assn.; Young Adult Lib. Services Assn.

## Publications

*ALA Handbook of Organization* (ann.).

*American Libraries* (10 a year; memb.; organizations $70; foreign $80; single copy $7.50).

*Book Links* (6 a year; U.S. $39.95; foreign $46; single copy $8).

*Booklist* (22 a year; U.S. and possessions $99.50; foreign $115; single copy $8).

## Round Table Chairpersons

(ALA staff liaison in parentheses)

Continuing Library Education Network and Exchange. Stacy Schrank (Darlena Davis).

Ethnic and Multicultural Information Exchange. Myra Appel (Elliot Mandel).

Exhibits. Kathy Young (Deidre I. Ross).

Federal and Armed Forces Libraries. Nancy Gomez Faget (Patricia May).

Gay, Lesbian, Bisexual, Transgendered. K. R. Roberto, Mary Callaghan Zunt (Elliot Mandel).

Government Documents. Cassandra Hartnett (Patricia May).

Intellectual Freedom. Robert Holley (Nanette Perez).

International Relations. Judith Lin Hunt (Michael Dowling).

Library History. Kenneth Potts (Denise M. Davis).

Library Instruction. Linda Colding (Darlena Davis).

Library Research. Denise Agosto (Denise M. Davis).

Library Support Staff Interests. Dorothy Morgan (Darlena Davis).

Map and Geography. Carolyn Kadri (Danielle M. Alderson).

New Members. Laurel Bliss (Kimberly Sanders).

Social Responsibilities. Alison Lewis (Elliot Mandel).

Staff Organizations. Leon S. Bey (Darlena Davis).

Video. Justin Michael Wadland (Danielle M. Alderson).

## Committee Chairpersons

(ALA staff liaison in parentheses)

Accreditation (Standing). Richard E. Rubin (Karen L. O'Brien).

*American Libraries* Advisory (Standing). Laurel Minott (Leonard Kniffel).

Appointments (Standing). Camila Alire (Eileen Hardy).

Awards (Standing). Susan Stroyan (Cheryl Malden).

Budget Analysis and Review (Standing). James Neal (Gregory L. Calloway).

Chapter Relations (Standing). Molly Fogarty (Michael P. Dowling).

Committee on Committees (Elected Council Committee). Camila Alire (Eileen Hardy).

Conference Committee (Standing). Janice Ison (Deidre I. Ross).

Conference Program Coordinating Team. Rhonda Putney (Deidre I. Ross).

Constitution and Bylaws (Standing). Thomas Wilding (JoAnne M. Kempf).

Council Orientation (Standing). Barbara Genco (Lois Ann Gregory-Wood).

Diversity (Standing). Ismail Abdullahi (Wendy Prellwitz).

Education (Standing). Michael Groman (Lorelle R. Swader).

Election (Standing). Peter Hepburn (Al Companio).

Human Resource Development and Recruitment (Standing). Vicki Varner Burger (Lorelle R. Swader).

Information Technology Policy Advisory (Standing). Maurice Freedman (Alan Inouye).

Intellectual Freedom (Standing). Douglas Archer (Judith F. Krug).

International Relations (Standing). Beverly Lynch (Michael P. Dowling).

Legislation (Standing). Kendall French Wiggin (Lynne E. Bradley).

Literacy (Standing). Sandra O. Newell (Dale P. Lipschultz).

Literacy and Outreach Services Advisory (Standing). Constance Lynn Purcell (Satia M. Orange).

Membership (Standing). Dora T. Ho (John F. Chrastka, Cathleen Bourdon).

Organization (Standing). Stephen Matthews (Eileen Hardy).

Orientation, Training, and Leadership Development. Teri Switzer (Lorelle Swader).

Policy Monitoring (Standing). Janet Swan Hill (Lois Ann Gregory-Wood).

Professional Ethics (Standing). Nancy Zimmerman (Judith F. Krug).

Public and Cultural Programs Advisory (Standing). Timothy Grimes (Deborah Anne Robertson).

Public Awareness (Standing). Leslie Burger (Mark R. Gould).

Publishing (Standing). Sara McLaughlin (Donald E. Chatham).

Research and Statistics (Standing). Stephen Wiberley (Denise M. Davis).

Resolutions. Michael Golrick (Lois Ann Gregory-Wood).

Rural, Native, and Tribal Libraries of All Kinds. David C. Ongley (Satia M. Orange).

Scholarships and Study Grants. Julie Brewer (Lorelle R. Swader).

Status of Women in Librarianship (Standing). Mary Callaghan Zunt (Lorelle R. Swader).

Web Site Advisory. Michael Stephens (Robert P. Carlson, Sherri L. Vanyek).

## Joint Committee Chairpersons

ALA/SAA/AAM: American Library Association–Society of American Archivists–American Association of Museums. Christian Yves Dupont (ALA); Holly Witchey (AAM); Mary W. Ghikas (ALA staff liaison).

Association of American Publishers–ALA. To be appointed (AAP); Loriene Roy (ALA); Keith Michael Fiels (ALA staff liaison).

Children's Book Council–ALA. David Mowery (ALA); Diane Foote (ALA staff liaison).

# American Library Association
# American Association of School Librarians

Executive Director, Julie A. Walker
50 E. Huron St., Chicago, IL 60611
312-280-4382, 800-545-2433, ext. 4382, fax 312-280-5276, e-mail aasl@ala.org
World Wide Web http://www.aasl.org.

## Object

The mission of the American Association of School Librarians (AASL) is to advocate excellence, facilitate change, and develop leaders in the school library media field. AASL works to ensure that all members of the field collaborate to provide leadership in the total education program; participate as active partners in the teaching/learning process; connect learners with ideas and information; and prepare students for lifelong learning, informed decision making, a love of reading, and the use of information technologies.

Established in 1951 as a separate division of the American Library Association.

## Membership

Memb. 7,200+. Open to all libraries, school library media specialists, interested individuals, and business firms, with requisite membership in ALA.

## Officers (2008–2009)

*Pres.* Ann M. Martin; *Pres.-Elect* Cassandra Barnett; *Treas.* Floyd Pentlin; *Past Pres.* Sara Kelly Johns.

## Board of Directors

Rosina Alaimo, Alice Bryant, Linda Collins, Nancy M. Dickinson, Gail M. Formanack, Louis Greco, Carl Harvey, Marilyn Z. Joyce, Allison G. Kaplan, Karen Lemmons, Cathie Marriott, Robbie L. Nickel, Sylvia K. Norton, Barbara J. Ray, Paul K. Whitsitt.

## Publications

*AASL Hotlinks* (mo.; electronic, memb.).
*Knowledge Quest* (5 a year; $50, $60 outside U.S.A.). *Ed.* Debbie Abilock (kq@abilock. net).
*School Library Media Research* (electronic, free, at http://www.ala.org/aasl.slmr). *Eds.* Jean Donham (jdonham@cornellcollege. edu), Carol L. Tilley (ctilley@uiuc.edu).

## Committee Chairpersons

AASL/ACRL Joint Information Literacy Committee. Judi Repman.
AASL/ALSC/YALSA Interdivisional Committee on School/Public Library Cooperation. Connie Champlin.
AASL/ELMSS Executive Committee. Gail Dickinson.
AASL/ISS Executive Committee. Elizabeth Burke.
AASL/SPVS Executive Committee. Donna Helvering.
Advocacy. Deb Logan.
Affiliate Assembly. Irene Kwidzinski.
Alliance for Association Excellence. Floyd Pentlin.
American University Press Book Selection. Terri Lent.
Annual Conference 2009. Karen Gavigan.
Appointments. Merlyn Miller.
Awards. Janice Ostram.
Blog Editorial Board. Laura Pearle.
Bylaws and Organization. Carol Doll.
Intellectual Freedom. Helen Adams.
*Knowledge Quest* Editorial Board. Debbie Abilock.
Legislation. Robert Roth.
National Conference 2009. Jay Bansbach, Ann Marie Pipkin.
National Institute 2010. Hilda K. Weisburg.

NCATE Coordinating Committee. Audrey Church.
Nominating. Dee Gwaltney.
Professional Development Coordinating Committee. Mary Lewis.
Promotion and Marketing Special Committee. Susan Kowalski.
Publications. Don Adcock.
Research/Statistics. Marcia Mardis.
*SLMR* Editorial Board. Jean Donham, Carol Tilley.
Web Site Resource Guides Editorial Board. Donna Nix.

## Task Force Chairpersons

AASL 2.0. Lisa E. Perez.
Best List for Teacher Resources. Pam Berger.
Diversity in the Organization. Pauletta Brown Bracy.
Guidelines Editing. Bonnie Grimble.
International Relations. Johan H. Koren.
Learning Standards Indicators and Assessment. Kathy Lowe.
Library Media Specialist's Role in Reading. Judi Moreillon.
No Child Left Behind. J. Linda Williams.

Parent Outreach. LaDawna Harrington.
Quantitative Measures. Nancy Dickinson.
School Library Media Month. Melissa Johnston.
Standards and Guidelines Implementation. Susan Ballard.
State Department Inquiry. Sandra Andrews.

## Awards Committees and Chairpersons

ABC/CLIO Leadership Grant. Mary Betz Lord.
Collaborative School Library Media Award. Val Edwards.
Distinguished School Administrator Award. Lynn Caruthers.
Distinguished Service Award. Melinda Yonger.
Frances Henne Award. Joanne Proctor.
Information Technology Pathfinder Award. Janice Krueger.
Innovative Reading Grant. Linda Underwood.
Intellectual Freedom Award. Emily Peterson.
National School Library Media Program of the Year Award. Cyndi Phillip.

# American Library Association
# Association for Library Collections and Technical Services

Executive Director, Charles Wilt
50 E. Huron St., Chicago, IL 60611
800-545-2433 ext. 5030, fax 312-280-5033, e-mail cwilt@ala.org
World Wide Web http://www.ala.org/alcts

## Object

The Association for Library Collections and Technical Services (ALCTS) envisions an environment in which traditional library roles are evolving. New technologies are making information more fluid and raising expectations. The public needs quality information anytime, anyplace. ALCTS provides frameworks to meet these information needs.

ALCTS provides leadership to the library and information communities in developing principles, standards, and best practices for creating, collecting, organizing, delivering, and preserving information resources in all forms. It provides this leadership through its members by fostering educational, research, and professional service opportunities. ALCTS is committed to quality information, universal access, collaboration, and lifelong learning.

*Standards*—Develop, evaluate, revise, and promote standards for creating, collecting, organizing, delivering, and preserving information resources in all forms.

*Best practices*—Research, develop, evaluate, and implement best practices for creating, collecting, organizing, delivering, and preserving information resources in all forms.

*Education*—Assess the need for, sponsor, develop, administer, and promote educational programs and resources for lifelong learning.

*Professional development*—Provide opportunities for professional development through research, scholarship, publication, and professional service.

*Interaction and information exchange*—Create opportunities to interact and exchange information with others in the library and information communities.

*Association operations*—Ensure efficient use of association resources and effective delivery of member services.

Established 1957; renamed 1988.

## Membership

Memb. 4,850. Any member of the American Library Association may elect membership in this division according to the provisions of the bylaws.

## Officers (2008–2009)

*Pres.* Dina Giambi, Univ. of Delaware Lib., 181 S. College Ave., Newark, DE 19717. Tel. 302-831-2829, fax 302-831-1046, e-mail dinag@udel.edu; *Pres.-Elect* Mary M. Case, Univ. of Illinois–Chicago Lib., 801 S. Morgan St., Chicago, IL 60661 Tel. 312-996-2716, fax 312-413-0424, e-mail marycase@uic.edu; *Past Pres.* Pamela M. Bluh, Thurgood Marshall Law Lib., Univ. of Maryland, 501 W. Fayette St., Baltimore, MD 2120 Tel. 410-706-2736, fax 410-706-2372, e-mail pbluh@umaryland.edu; *Councilor* Diane Dates Casey, Governors State Univ. Lib., 1 University Pkwy., University Park, IL 60466. Tel. 708-534-4110, fax 708-534-4564, e-mail d-casey@govst.edu.

Address correspondence to the executive director.

## Board of Directors

Robert Alan, Pamela Bluh, Beth Picknally Camden, Mary M. Case, Diane Dates Casey, Walter T. Cybulski, Felicity A. Dykas, Dina Giambi, Janet Lee-Smeltzer, Rebecca Mugridge, Carolynne Myall, Genevieve Owens, Dale Swensen, Mary Beth Thomson, Kay Walter, Mary Beth Weber, Charles Wilt, Mary Woodley.

## Publications

*ALCTS Newsletter Online* (bi-mo.; free; posted at http://www.ala.org/alcts). *Ed.* Mary Beth Weber, Cataloging Dept., Rutgers Univ. Libs., 47 Davidson Rd., Piscataway, NJ 08854. Tel. 732-445-0500, fax 732-445-5888, e-mail mbfecko@rci.rutgers.edu.

*Library Resources and Technical Services* (q.; memb. $75; nonmemb. $85; international $95). *Ed.* Peggy Johnson, Univ. of Minnesota Libs., 499 Wilson Lib., 309 19th Ave. S., Minneapolis, MN 55455. Tel. 612-624-2312, fax 612-626-9353, e-mail m-john@tc.umn.edu.

## Section Chairpersons

Acquisitions. Robert Alan.
Cataloging and Classification. Mary Woodley.
Collection Management and Development. Genevieve Owens.
Continuing Resources. Felicity A. Dykas.
Preservation and Reformatting. Walter T. Cybulski.

## Committee Chairpersons

Hugh C. Atkinson Memorial Award (ALCTS/ ACRL/LAMA/LITA). Sarah Michalak.
Ross Atkinson Lifetime Achievement Award Jury. Ann Swartzell.
Paul Banks and Carolyn Harris Preservation Award Jury. Nancy Kraft.
Best of *LRTS* Award Jury. Ellen Safley.
Blackwell's Scholarship Award Jury. Narda Tafuri.

Budget and Finance. Mary Beth Thomson.
Education. Julia Gammon.
Fund Raising. Susan Davis.
International Relations. Susan Matveyeva.
Leadership Development. Melinda Flannery.
*LRTS* Editorial Board. Peggy Johnson.
Membership. Becky Ryder.
Nominating. Bruce Chr. Johnson.
Organization and Bylaws. Dale Swensen.
Outstanding Collaboration Citation Jury.
    Karen Wilhoit.
Esther J. Piercy Award Jury. Keith Powell.
Planning. Carolynne Myall.
Program. Tim Strawn.
Publications. Norm Medeiros.

### Interest Groups

Authority Control (ALCTS/LITA). Mary
    Mastraccio.

Automated Acquisitions/In-Process Control
    Systems. Michael Zeoli.
Creative Ideas in Technical Services. Linda
    Lomker.
Electronic Resources. Jennifer Lang.
FRBR. Richard Greene.
MARC Formats (ALCTS/LITA). To be an-
    nounced.
Newspapers. Errol Somay.
Out of Print. William Kane.
Role of the Professional in Academic Re-
    search Technical Service Departments.
    Angela Laack, Michael Rice.
Scholarly Communications. Brian Quinn.
Technical Services Administrators of Medi-
    um-Sized Research Libraries. Roberta
    Winjum.
Technical Services Directors of Large Re-
    search Libraries. Mechael Charbonneau.
Technical Services Workflow Efficiency.
    Catherine Grove.

# American Library Association
## Association for Library Service to Children

Executive Director, Diane Foote
50 E. Huron St., Chicago, IL 60611
312-280-2162, 800-545-2433 ext. 2162, fax 312-280-5271, e-mail dfoote@ala.org
World Wide Web http://www.ala.org/alsc

### Object

The core purpose of the Association for
Library Service to Children (ALSC) is to create a better future for children through
libraries. Its primary goal is to lead the way
in forging excellent library services for all
children. ALSC offers creative programming,
information about best practices, continuing
education, a prestigious award and media
evaluation program, and professional connections. Founded 1901.

### Membership

Memb. 4,237. Open to anyone interested in
library services to children. For information
on dues, see ALA entry.

Address correspondence to the executive
director.

### Officers

*Pres.* Pat Scales; *V.P./Pres.-Elect* Thom
Barthelmess; *Past Pres.* Jane B. Marino; *Fis-
cal Officer* Sue Zeigler; *Division Councilor*
Linda Perkins.

### Directors

Mary Fellows, Marge Loch-Wouters, Penny
Markey, Leslie Molnar, Elizabeth Orsburn,
Tim Wadham, Judy Zuckerman.

## Publications

*Children and Libraries: The Journal of the Association for Library Service to Children* (q.; memb.; nonmemb. $40; foreign $50).
*ALSConnect* (q., electronic; memb. Not available by subscription.)

## Committee Chairpersons

AASL/ALSC/YALSA Interdivisional Committee on School/Public Library Cooperation. Connie Champlin.
ALSC/*Booklist*/YALSA Odyssey Award Selection 2008. Pam Spencer Holley.
ALSC BWI Summer Reading Grant. Marilyn Zielinski.
Arbuthnot Honor Lecture 2009. Amy Kellman.
Arbuthnot Honor Lecture 2010. Kristi Jemtegaard.
Mildred L. Batchelder Award 2009. Sandra Imdieke.
Bechtel Fellowship. Nancy J. Johnson.
Pura Belpré Award 2009. Claudette McLinn.
Budget. Andrew Medlar.
Randolph Caldecott Award 2009. Nell Colburn.
Andrew Carnegie Award 2009. Margaret Tice.
Children and Libraries Advisory Committee. Sharon Deeds.
Children and Technology. Christopher Borawski.
Distinguished Service Award 2009. Tish Wilson.
Early Childhood Programs and Services. Kevin Delecki.
Education. Emily Chandler.
Theodor Seuss Geisel Award 2009. Joan L. Atkinson.
Great Interactive Software for Kids. Angelique Kopa.

Great Web Sites. Karen Lemmons, Becki Bishop.
Maureen Hayes Award. Linda Ernst.
Intellectual Freedom. Lisa Dennis.
International Relations. Elizabeth Poe.
Legislation. Kathy Toon.
Liaison with National Organizations. Laurina Cashin, Marna Elliott.
Library Service to Special Population Children and Their Caregivers. Sarah English.
Local Arrangements (Chicago). Shilo Pearson.
Managing Children's Services. Susan Pannebaker.
Membership. Betsy Crone.
National Planning of Special Collections. Mary Beth Dunhouse.
John Newbery Award 2009. Rose Treviño.
Nominating 2009. Carol Edwards.
Notable Children's Books. Caroline Ward.
Notable Children's Recordings. Jane Claes.
Notable Children's Videos. Kathy Krasniwiecz.
Oral History. Carole Fiore.
Organization and Bylaws. Tali Balas, Julie Dietzel-Glair.
Penguin Young Readers Group Award. Beth Blankley.
Preconference Planning (Chicago). Megan Schliesman.
Program Coordinating. Kate Schiavi.
Public Awareness. Rhonda Puntney.
Quicklists Consulting. Barbara Brand, Victor Schill, Bettye L. Smith.
Research and Development. To be announced.
Charlemae Rollins President's Program 2009. Deborah Taylor, Laura Jenkins.
Scholarships. To be announced.
School Age Programs and Service. Deborah Wright.
Robert F. Sibert Award 2009. Carol K. Phillips.
Laura Ingalls Wilder Award 2009. Cathryn Mercier.

# American Library Association
## Association for Library Trustees, Advocates, Friends and Foundations

Executive Director Sally Gardner Reed
109 S. 13 St., Suite 3N, Philadelphia, PA 19107
Tel. 215-790-1674, fax 215-545-3821, e-mail sreed@ala.org
World Wide Web http://www.ala.org/ala/mgrps/divs/altaff/index.cfm

## Object

The Association for Library Trustees, Advocates, Friends and Foundations (ALTAFF) was founded in 1890 as the American Library Trustee Association (ALTA). It is the only division of the American Library Association dedicated to promoting and ensuring outstanding library service through educational programs that develop excellence in trusteeship and promote citizen involvement in the support of libraries. In 2008 the members of ALTA voted to expand the division to more aggressively address the needs of friends of libraries and library foundations, and through a merger with Friends of Libraries USA (FOLUSA) became ALTAFF. ALTA became an ALA division in 1961.

## Membership

Memb. 4,200. Open to all interested persons and organizations. For dues and membership year, see ALA entry.

## Officers (2008–2009)

*Pres.* Margaret J. Danhof; *1st V.P./Pres.-Elect* Rose Mosley; *V.P.* Claire Gritzer; *Councilor* Shirley Bruursema; *Past Pres.* Donald L. Roalkvam.

## Publications

*The Voice* (q.; memb.).
*News Update*

## Committees

### Advocacy Committees Cluster

Chair. Jane Rowland.
Advocacy. Joan Ress Reeves.
Awards. Denise Botto.
Intellectual Freedom. Sherman Banks.
Legislative. Debbie Miller.

### Business Committees Cluster

Chair. G. Vic Johnson.
Development. To be announced.
Leadership Development. Lenore Gall.
Membership Committee. Gwendolyn Welch.
Nominations Committee. Donald L. Roalkvam.

### Education Committees Cluster

Chair. Sharon Saulmon.
Annual Conference Program. Kim Denise Johnson.
PLA National Conference. Gail Griffin.
President's Event. Donna Sample.
Regional Programming. Claire Gritzer.

### Publications Committee Cluster

Chair. Christine Lind Hage.
Newsletter. To be announced.
Publication. Donna McDonald.
Web Site Development. David Hargett.

# American Library Association
# Association of College and Research Libraries

Executive Director, Mary Ellen K. Davis
50 E. Huron St., Chicago, IL 60611-2795
312-280-2523, 800-545-2433 ext. 2523, fax 312-280-2520, e-mail acrl@ala.org
World Wide Web http://www.ala.org/acrl

## Object

The Association of College and Research Libraries (ACRL) leads academic and research librarians and libraries in advancing learning and scholarship. Founded 1938.

## Membership

Memb. 13,083. For information on dues, see ALA entry.

## Officers

*Pres.* Erika C. Linke, Assoc. Dean, Univ. Libs., Carnegie Mellon Univ., 5000 Forbes Ave., Pittsburgh, PA 15213-3890. Tel. 412-268-7800, fax 412-268-2793, e-mail el08@andrew.cmu.edu; *Pres.-Elect* Lori Goetsch, Dean of Libs., 504 Hale Lib., Kansas State Univ., Manhattan, KS 66506. Tel. 785-532-7400, fax 785-532-7415, e-mail lgoetsch@ksu.edu; *Past Pres.* Julie B. Todaro, Dean, Lib. Services, Rio Grande Campus, Austin Community College, 1212 Rio Grande, Austin, TX 78701-1710. Tel. 512-223-3071, fax 512-223-3431, e-mail jtodaro@austincc.edu; *Budget and Finance Chair* Theresa S. Byrd, Dir. of Libs., Ohio Wesleyan Univ., 43 Rowland Ave., Delaware, OH 43015-2333. Tel. 740-368-3246, fax 740-368-3222, e-mail fsbyrd@owu.edu; *ACRL Councilor* Locke J. Morrisey, Head, Collections/Reference and Research Services, Gleeson Lib., Univ. of San Francisco, San Francisco, CA 94117-1080. Tel. 415-422-5399, e-mail morrisey@usfca.edu.

## Board of Directors

Officers; Janis M. Bandelin, Mary M. Carr, Elizabeth A. Dupuis, Linda Kopecky, Michael J. LaCroix, John Lehner, Debbie L. Malone, Karen A. Williams.

## Publications

*Choice* (12 a year; $325; Canada and Mexico $375; other international $445). *Ed.* Irving Rockwood.

*Choice Reviews-on-Cards* (available only to subscribers of *Choice* and/or *Choice Reviews Online*; $395; Canada and Mexico $445; other international $525).

*ChoiceReviews.Online 2.0* ($390 and $135).

*College & Research Libraries* (*C&RL*) (6 a year; memb.; nonmemb. $70; Canada and other PUAS countries $75; other international $80). *Ed.* Joseph J. Branin.

*College & Research Libraries News* (*C&RL News*) (11 a year; memb.; nonmemb. $46; Canada and other PUAS countries $52; other international $57 ). *Ed.* David Free.

*Publications in Librarianship* (formerly ACRL Monograph Series) (occasional). *Ed.* Charles A. Schwartz.

*RBM: A Journal of Rare Books, Manuscripts, and Cultural Heritage* (s. ann.; $42; Canada and other PUAS countries $47; other international $58). *Ed.* Beth M. Whittaker.

## Committee and Task Force Chairpersons

AASL/ACRL Information Literacy (interdivisional). Judi Repman.

Academic/Research Librarian of the Year Award. Robin Wagner.

ACRL/LLAMA Interdivisional Committee on Building Resources. Charles Forrest.

ACRLog Advisory Board. Lisa Janicke Hinchliffe.

Appointments. Steven Bell.

Assessment. Vicki Coleman.

Assessment Skills Task Force. Steven Hiller.

Hugh C. Atkinson Memorial Award. Barbara J. Ford.

Budget and Finance. Theresa S. Byrd.

Bylaws. Wilbur A. Stolt.

*Choice* Editorial Board. Edward Warro.

Colleagues. Frank A. D'Andraia, Julia M. Gelfand.

*College & Research Libraries* Editorial Board. Joseph Branin.

*College & Research Libraries News* Editorial Board. Lucia Snowhill.

Coordinating Committee for ACRL Advocacy Initiatives. Dawn Thistle.

Copyright. Becky S. Albitz.

Council of Liaisons. Susan Kroll.

Doctoral Dissertation Fellowship. Nancy H. Seamans.

Effective Practices Review Committee. Todd Digby.

Ethics. Lori J. Phillips.

Excellence in Academic Libraries Award (Nominations). Andrew Scrimgeour.

Excellence in Academic Libraries Award (Selection). Pam Snelson.

Friends Fund. Lisa M. Browar.

Friends Fund Disbursement. Jane Schillie.

Government Relations. Jonathan Miller.

Immersion Program. Stephanie Michel.

Information Literacy Advisory. Debra Gilchrist.

Information Literacy Standards. To be announced.

Information Literacy Web Site. To be announced.

Intellectual Freedom. Julianne P. Hinz, Paul Beavers.

International Relations. Ravindra N. Sharma.

E. J. Josey Spectrum Scholar Mentor. To be announced.

Samuel Lazerow Fellowship. Jacqueline Samples.

Leadership Recruitment and Nomination. Cynthia Steinhoff.

Marketing Academic and Research Libraries. Toni Tucker.

Membership Advisory. Susanna D. Boylston.

National Conference Executive Committee, Seattle, 2009. Lizabeth Wilson.

New Publications Advisory. Joan Lippincott.

President's Program Planning Committee, Chicago, 2009. Barbara Preece.

Professional Development Coordinating. Trevor A. Dawes.

Publications Coordinating. Daren Callahan.

*Publications in Librarianship* Editorial Board. Craig Gibson.

Racial and Ethnic Diversity. Michele L. Saunders.

*RBM* Editorial Board. Beth Whittaker.

REAL Advisory Board. Pam Snelson.

Research Coordinating. Scott Walter.

Research Planning and Review. Ryan Johnson.

Research Program. Ruth Vondraceck.

*Resources for College Libraries* Editorial Board. Brian E. Coutts.

Scholarly Communications. Kimberly Douglas, Richard Fyffe.

Standards and Accreditation. William N. Nelson.

Statistics. William Miller.

Status of Academic Librarians. Elizabeth Kocevar-Weidinger.

## Discussion Group Chairpersons

Australian-Canadian-New Zealand Studies. Margaret Brill.

Balancing Baby and Book. Cynthia Dudenhoffer.

Consumer and Family Studies. Lore Guilmartin.

Continuing Education/Professional Development. Beth Avery.

Copyright. Becky Albitz.

Electronic Reserves. Laureen Esser.

Information Commons. Scott B. Mandernack, Michael Whitchurch, Leslie Haas.

Librarianship in For-Profit Educational Institutions. David Bickford.

Libraries and Information Science Collections. Susan Searing.

Library Development. Charlene Baldwin.

Media Resources. Thomas Ipri, Amanda Hornby.

MLA International Bibliography. Gregory Heald.

New Members. Merinda Kaye Hensley.

Personnel Administrators and Staff Development Officers. Pat Hawthorne, Marilyn McClaskey.

Philosophical, Religious, and Theological Studies. Richard Terry Chaffin.

Popular Cultures. Sarah Sogigian, Inga Barnello.

Regional Campus Libraries. Alica C. White, Anna Salyer.

Scholarly Communications. Michael Furlough.

Senior Administrators. Faye C. Backie, Charles Gilreath.

Sports and Recreation. Mila C. Su.

Team-Based Organizations. Robert Patrick Mitchell.

Undergraduate Libraries. Leah G. McGinnis, Jill Morrison McKinstry.

## Section Chairpersons

African American Studies Librarians. Thomas Weissinger.

Anthropology and Sociology. Randal Hertzler.

Arts. Lucie Wall Stylianopoulos.

Asian, African, and Middle Eastern. Rajwant Singh Chilana.

College Libraries. Irene Herold.

Community and Junior College Libraries. Lora Mirza.

Distance Learning. Patrick Mahoney.

Education and Behavioral Sciences. Deborah Schaeffer.

Instruction. Sarah McDaniel.

Law and Political Science. Ann Marshall.

Literatures in English. Karen Munro.

Rare Books and Manuscripts. Mary Lacy.

Science and Technology. Virginia Ann Baldwin.

Slavic and East European. Terri Tickle Miller.

University Libraries. Barbara Baxter Jenkins.

Western European Studies. Laura Dale Bischof.

Women's Studies. Diana Leigh King.

# American Library Association
# Association of Specialized and Cooperative Library Agencies

Executive Director, Barbara A. Macikas
50 E. Huron St., Chicago, IL 60611-2795
312-280-4398, 800-545-2433 ext. 4398, fax 312-280-5273
World Wide Web http://www.ala.org/ascla

## Object

The Association of Specialized and Cooperative Library Agencies (ASCLA) enhances the effectiveness of library service by providing networking, enrichment, and educational opportunities for its diverse members, who represent state library agencies, libraries serving special populations, multitype library organizations, and independent librarians. Within the interests of these library organizations, ASCLA has specific responsibility for

1. Development and evaluation of goals and plans for state library agencies, specialized library agencies, and multitype library cooperatives to facilitate the implementation, improvement, and extension of library activities designed to foster improved user services, coordinating such activities with other appropriate units of the American Library Association (ALA)

2. Representation and interpretation of the role, functions, and services of state library agencies, specialized

library agencies, multitype library cooperatives, and independent librarians within and outside the profession, including contact with national organizations and government agencies

3. Development of policies, studies, and activities in matters affecting state library agencies, specialized library agencies, multitype library cooperatives, and independent librarians relating to (a) state and local library legislation, (b) state grants-in-aid and appropriations, and (c) relationships among state, federal, regional, and local governments, coordinating such activities with other appropriate ALA units

4. Establishment, evaluation, and promotion of standards and service guidelines relating to the concerns of this association

5. Identifying the interests and needs of all persons, encouraging the creation of services to meet these needs within the areas of concern of the association, and promoting the use of these services provided by state library agencies, specialized library agencies, multitype library cooperatives, and independent librarians

6. Stimulating the professional growth and promoting the specialized training and continuing education of library personnel at all levels in the areas of concern of this association and encouraging membership participation in appropriate type-of-activity divisions within ALA

7. Assisting in the coordination of activities of other units within ALA that have a bearing on the concerns of this association

8. Granting recognition for outstanding library service within the areas of concern of this association

9. Acting as a clearinghouse for the exchange of information and encouraging the development of materials, publications, and research within the areas of concern of this association

## Membership

Memb. 900.

## Board of Directors (2008–2009)

*Pres.* Carol Ann Desch; *Pres.-Elect* Brenda K. Bailey-Hainer; *Past Pres.* Barbara T. Mates; *Dirs.-at-Large* Yolanda J. Cuesta, Ann Joslin, Jerome W. Krois; *Div. Councilor* Kendall French Wiggin; *Ed.* Emily Inlow-Hood; *Ex Officio* Barbara A. Macikas.

## Section Chairpersons

Independent Librarian's Exchange Section (ILEX). Jean F. Porter.
Interlibrary Cooperation and Networking Section (ICAN). Deborah A. Littrell.
Libraries Serving Special Populations Section (LSSPS). Glennor Loy Shirley.
LSSPS Board Representative. Diana Reese.
State Library Agency Section (SLAS). Barbara A. Reading.

## Publication

*Interface* (q.; memb.; single copies $7). *Ed.* Emily Inlow-Hood; e-mail ascla@ala.org.

## Committee Chairpersons

Accessibility Assembly. Simon J. M. Healey.
Awards. Kathleen B. Hegarty.
Legislation. Barratt Wilkins.
Membership Promotion. Valerie J. Horton.
Nominating. Rahye L. Puckett.
Planning and Budget. Brenda K. Bailey-Hainer, Barbara T. Mates.
President's Program. Jerome W. Krois.
Publications. Sara G. Laughlin.
Standards Review. Jeannette P. Smithee.

# American Library Association
## Library Leadership and Management Association

Executive Director, Kerry Ward
50 E. Huron St., Chicago, IL 60611
312-280-5032, 800-545-2433 ext. 5032, fax 312-280-5033, e-mail kward@ala.org
World Wide Web http://www.ala.org/lama

## Object

The Library Leadership and Management Association (LLAMA) Strategic Plan (2006–2010) sets out the following:

Mission: The Library Leadership and Management Association encourages and nurtures current and future leaders, and develops and promotes outstanding leadership and management practices.

Vision: LLAMA will be the foremost organization developing present and future leaders in library and information services.

Image: LLAMA is a welcoming community where aspiring and experienced leaders from all types of libraries, as well as those who support libraries, come together to gain skills in a quest for excellence in library management, administration, and leadership.

In addition,

- LLAMA will be an organization in which value to its members drives decisions.
- LLAMA will expand and strengthen leadership and management expertise at all levels for all libraries.
- LLAMA will facilitate professional development opportunities to enhance leadership and management.
- LLAMA will be the preeminent professional organization that develops and supports library leaders and managers.

Established 1957.

## Membership

Memb. 4,800.

## Officers (July 2008–June 2009)

*Pres.* Molly Raphael; *V.P.* Gina Millsap; *Secy.* Emily A. Bergman; *Dirs.-at-Large* Robert Daugherty, Janice Simmons-Welburn *Div. Councilor* Charles Forrest; *Past Pres.* W. Bede Mitchell.

Address correspondence to the executive director.

## Publications

*Library Administration and Management* (q.; memb.; nonmemb. $65; foreign $75). *Ed.* Gregg Sapp.

*LEADS from LLAMA* (approx. biweekly; electronic; free). To subscribe, send to listproc@ala.org the message *subscribe lamaleads [first name last name]*.

## Committee Chairpersons

Budget and Finance. Teri R. Switzer.
Continuing Education. Roderick MacNeil.
Cultural Diversity Grants. Susan Marks.
Financial Advancement. Andrea Lapsley.
Leadership Development. Deborah Tenofsky.
Marketing Communications. Marilyn Wilt.
Membership. Catherine Friedman.
Mentoring. Neely Tang.
Nominating. Paul Anderson.
Organization. Mary Frances Burns.
President's Program. Karen Danczak-Lyons.
Program. Frank R. Allen.
Publications Editorial Advisory Board. Diane Bisom.
Recognition of Achievement. Thomas Wilding.
Strategic Planning Implementation. Anne Edwards.
Web Site Advisory Board. Marsha Iverson.

# American Library Association
# Library and Information Technology Association

Executive Director, Mary C. Taylor
50 E. Huron St., Chicago, IL 60611
312-280-4267, 800-545-2433, e-mail mtaylor@ala.org
World Wide Web http://www.lita.org

## Object

As a center of expertise about information technology, the Library and Information Technology Association (LITA) leads in exploring and enabling new technologies to empower libraries. LITA members use the promise of technology to deliver dynamic library collections and services.

LITA educates, serves, and reaches out to its members, other ALA members and divisions, and the entire library and information community through its publications, programs, and other activities designed to promote, develop, and aid in the implementation of library and information technology.

## Membership

Memb. 4,333.

## Officers (2008–2009)

*Pres.* Andrew K. Pace; *V.P./Pres.-Elect* Michelle L. Frisque; *Past Pres.* Mark A. Beatty.

## Directors

Officers; Mary Alice Ball, Mona C. Couts, Colleen Cuddy, Susan Logue, Jonathan Edward Rothman, Debra S. Shapiro, Lorre B. Smith; *Councilor* Colby Mariva Riggs; *Bylaws and Organization* Clara A. Ruttenberg; *Exec. Dir.* Mary C. Taylor.

## Publication

*Information Technology and Libraries (ITAL)* (q.; memb.; nonmemb. $65; single copy $30). *Ed.* Marc Truitt. For information or to send manuscripts, contact the editor.

## Committee Chairpersons

Assessment and Research. Diane Bisom, Bonnie Postlethwaite.

Budget Review. Mark Beatty.

Bylaws and Organization. Clara A. Ruttenberg.

Committee Chair Coordinator. Scott P. Muir.

Education. Mandy Havert, David Ward.

Executive. Andrew Pace.

International Relations. Teri Sierra.

*ITAL* Editorial Board. Marc Truitt.

Legislation and Regulation. Kristin A. Antelman.

LITA/Brett Butler Entrepreneurship Award. Martin Halbert.

LITA/Ex Libris Student Writing Award. Barbara L. Spivey.

LITA/Library Hi Tech Award. Cindi Trainor.

LITA/LSSI and LITA/OCLC Minority Scholarships. Sophia Guevara.

LITA National Forum 2009. Elizabeth A. Steward-Marshall.

LITA/OCLC Kilgour Award. Michael Gorman.

LITA/Christian Larew Scholarship. Maribeth Manoff.

Membership Development. Donald W. Lemke.

Nominating. Bonnie Postlethwaite.

Program Planning. Jason Griffey.

Publications. Walt Crawford.

Technology and Access. David J. Nutty.

TER Board. Martin R. Kalfatovic.

Top Technology Trends. Maurice York.

Web Coordinating. Jean Rainwater.

## Interest Group Coordinators

Authority Control in the Online Environment (LITA/ALCTS). Edward Swanson.
Blogs, Interactive Media, Groupware, and Wikis. Jason Griffey.
Digital Library Technologies. Tyra Grant.
Distance Learning. Lauren Marie Pressley.
Electronic Resources Management (LITA/ALCTS). Clara A. Ruttenberg.
Emerging Technologies. Joseph B. Ford.
Heads of Library Technology. Richard B. Wayne.

Imagineering. Cara V. W. Kinsey.
Interest Groups Coordinator. Holly Hong Yu.
Internet Resources and Services. Joseph Fisher.
JPEG 2000 in Archives and Libraries. Peter Murray.
Library Consortia Automated Systems. Jon Mark Bolthouse.
Next Generation Catalog. Sharon M. Shafer.
Open Source Systems. George J. Harmon.
Public Libraries Technology. Paul Keith.
RFID Technology. Vicki Terbovich.
Standards. Judy J. Jeng.

# American Library Association
# Public Library Association

Executive Director, Greta K. Southard
50 E. Huron St., Chicago, IL 60611
312-280-5752, 800-545-2433 ext. 5752, fax 312-280-5029, e-mail pla@ala.org
World Wide Web http://www.pla.org

The Public Library Association (PLA) has specific responsibility for

1. Conducting and sponsoring research about how the public library can respond to changing social needs and technical developments

2. Developing and disseminating materials useful to public libraries in interpreting public library services and needs

3. Conducting continuing education for public librarians by programming at national and regional conferences, by publications such as the newsletter, and by other delivery means

4. Establishing, evaluating, and promoting goals, guidelines, and standards for public libraries

5. Maintaining liaison with relevant national agencies and organizations engaged in public administration and human services, such as the National Association of Counties, the Municipal League, and the Commission on Postsecondary Education

6. Maintaining liaison with other divisions and units of ALA and other library organizations, such as the Association for Library and Information Science Education and the Urban Libraries Council

7. Defining the role of the public library in service to a wide range of user and potential user groups

8. Promoting and interpreting the public library to a changing society through legislative programs and other appropriate means

9. Identifying legislation to improve and to equalize support of public libraries

PLA enhances the development and effectiveness of public librarians and public library services. This mission positions PLA to

- Focus its efforts on serving the needs of its members

- Address issues that affect public libraries

- Commit to quality public library services that benefit the general public

The goals of PLA are

- Advocacy and recognition: public libraries will be recognized as the destination for a wide variety of valuable services and their funding will be a community priority.
- A literate nation: PLA will be a valued partner of public library initiatives to create a nation of readers.
- Staffing and recruitment: public libraries will be recognized as exciting places to work and will be staffed by skilled professionals who are recognized as the information experts, are competitively paid, and reflect the demographics of their communities.
- Training and knowledge transfer: PLA will be nationally recognized as the leading source for continuing education opportunities for public library staff and trustees.

## PLAspace

PLAspace (http://www.plaspace.org) is a tool that connects members of PLA with one another to exchange ideas, share knowledge, make professional connections, and collaborate virtually. Members create and join PLAspace communities of practice (CoPs) based on their interest in learning about, discussing, and sharing insights about a subject related to public libraries and public librarianship.

## Membership

Memb. 11,000+. Open to all ALA members interested in the improvement and expansion of public library services to all ages in various types of communities.

## Officers (2008–2009)

*Pres.* Carol Sheffer, Troy, New York. Tel. 518-233-1740, email csheffer@live.com;

*Pres.-Elect* Sari Feldman, Cuyahoga County Public Lib., 2111 Snow Rd., Parma, OH 44134. Tel 216-749-9490, e-mail sfeldman@cuyahogalibrary.org; *Past Pres.* Jan Sanders, Pasadena Public Lib., 285 E. Walnut St., Pasadena, CA 91101. Tel. 626-744-4066, e-mail jsanders@cityofpasadena.net.

## Publication

*Public Libraries* (bi-mo.; memb.; nonmemb. $50; foreign $60; single copy $10). *Managing Ed.* Kathleen Hughes, PLA, 50 E. Huron St., Chicago, IL 60611. E-mail khughes@ala.org.

## Committee Chairs

Advancement of Literacy Award Jury. Melissa E. Jones.

Allie Beth Martin Award Jury. Kim E. Becnel.

Annual Conference Program (2009). Kathleen S. Reif.

Annual Conference Program (2010). Carol E. Simmons.

Baker & Taylor Entertainment Audio Music/Video Product Award Jury. Sandy Wee.

Budget and Finance. Marilyn H. Boria.

Charlie Robinson Award Jury. Claudya Muller.

DEMCO New Leaders Travel Grant Jury. Cynthia A. DeLanty.

EBSCO Excellence in Small and/or Rural Public Library Service Award Jury. Patricia Linville.

Endowment Task Force. Marilyn H. Boria.

Every Child Ready to Read Evaluation Task Force. Clara Nalli Bohrer.

Gordon M. Conable Award Jury. Sara Dallas.

Highsmith Library Innovation Award Jury. Sylvia Y. Sprinkle-Hamlin.

Intellectual Freedom Advisory Group. Sara Dallas.

Leadership Development Task Force. Luis Herrera.

Legislative Advisory Group. Cathy Elizabeth Sanford.

Monographs Work Groups. To be announced.

National Conference Committee (2010). Elizabeth E. Bingham, Kay K. Runge.

National Conference Local Arrangements (2010). Vailey B. Oehlke.

National Conference Program (2010). Kathleen R. T. Imhoff.

Nominating Committee (2009). Susan Hildreth.

Nominating Committee (2010). Jan W. Sanders.

PLDS Statistical Report Advisory Committee. Susan G. Waxter.

Polaris Innovation in Technology John Iliff Award Jury. Alan Harkness.

Program Committee. Kathleen R. T. Imhoff.

Public Libraries Advisory Committee. Luren E. Dickinson.

Spring Symposium Program Subcommittee. To be announced.

# American Library Association
# Reference and User Services Association

President, Neal Wyatt
50 E. Huron St., Chicago, IL 60611-2795
312-280-4398, 800-545-2433 ext. 4398, fax 312-280-5273, e-mail rusa@ala.org
World Wide Web http://www.ala.org/rusa

## Object

The Reference and User Services Association (RUSA) is the foremost organization of reference and information professionals who make the connections between people and the information sources, services, and collection materials they need. Responsible for supporting the delivery of reference/information services to all groups, regardless of age, in all types of libraries, RUSA facilitates the development and conduct of direct service to library users, the development of programs and guidelines for service to meet the needs of these users, and assists libraries in reaching potential users.

The specific responsibilities of RUSA are

1. Conduct of activities and projects within the association's areas of responsibility

2. Encouragement of the development of librarians engaged in these activities and stimulation of participation by members of appropriate type-of-library divisions

3. Synthesis of the activities of all units within the American Library Association that have a bearing on the type of activities represented by the association

4. Representation and interpretation of the association's activities in contacts outside the profession

5. Planning and development of programs of study and research in these areas for the total profession

6. Continuous study and review of the association's activities

## Membership

Memb. 4,877.

## Officers (July 2008–June 2009)

*Pres.* Neal Wyatt; *Pres.-Elect* Susan J. Beck; *Secy.* Naomi Lederer; *Past Pres.* David A. Tyckoson.

## Directors-at-Large

Corinne M. Hill, Mary Alison Hollerich, Mary M. D. Parker, Joseph A. Thompson, Jr., Suzanne M. Ward, Gary W. White; *Councilor* Pamela C. Sieving; *Ed., RUSQ* Diane M. Zabel; *Ex Officio* Daniel C. Mack; *Exec. Dir.* Barbara A. Macikas.

## Publication

*RUSQ* (q.; memb. $25 (included in dues), U.S. $65, foreign memb. $75, single copies $25). *Ed.* Diane M. Zabel.

## Section Chairpersons

Business Reference and Services. Rita W. Moss.
Collection Development and Evaluation. Michael Levine-Clark.
History. David A. Lincove.
Machine-Assisted Reference. Rosemary Long Meszaros.
Reference Services. Judy L. Solberg.
Sharing and Transforming Access to Resources. Stephanie S. Atkins.

## Committee Chairpersons

Access to Information. Karen Jung.

AFL/CIO Joint Committee on Library Services to Labor Groups. Mary M. D. Parker.
Awards Coordinating. Cathleen Alice Towey.
Budget and Finance. David A. Tyckoson.
Conference Program Coordinating. Diane M. Zabel.
Membership. Lisa A. Romero.
Margaret E. Monroe Adult Services Award. Steve Alleman.
Isadore Gilbert Mudge Award. Teresa Portilla Omidsalar.
Nominating. Diane M. Zabel.
Organization and Planning. Corinne M. Hill.
President's Program Planning. Joyce G. Saricks.
Professional Development. Nancy Huling.
Publications and Communications. Gwen Arthur.
Reference Services Press Award. Judith A. Druse.
Services. Anne Charlotte Behler.
John Sessions Memorial Award. Laura L. Leavitt.
Standards and Guidelines. Charles B. Thurston.

# American Library Association
# Young Adult Library Services Association

Executive Director, Beth Yoke
50 E. Huron St., Chicago, IL 60611
312-280-4390, 800-545-2433 ext. 4390, fax 312-280-5276
E-mail yalsa@ala.org, World Wide Web http://www.ala.org/yalsa
Blog http://yalsa.ala.org/blog, MySpace page http://www.myspace.com/yalsa
Wiki http://wikis.ala.org/yalsa, Twitter http://www.ala.org/twitter, Facebook
http://www.facebook.com/pages/YALSA/35222707784

## Object

In every library in the nation, quality library service to young adults is provided by a staff that understands and respects the unique informational, educational, and recreational needs of teenagers. Equal access to information, services, and materials is recognized as a right, not a privilege. Young adults are actively involved in the library decision making process. The library staff collaborates and cooperates with other youth-serving agencies

to provide a holistic, community-wide network of activities and services that support healthy youth development. To ensure that this vision becomes a reality, the Young Adult Library Services Association (YALSA)

1. Advocates extensive and developmentally appropriate library and information services for young adults ages 12 to 18

2. Promotes reading and supports the literacy movement

3. Advocates the use of information and communications technologies to provide effective library service

4. Supports equality of access to the full range of library materials and services, including existing and emerging information and communications technologies, for young adults

5. Provides education and professional development to enable its members to serve as effective advocates for young people

6. Fosters collaboration and partnerships among its individual members with the library community and other groups involved in providing library and information services to young adults

7. Influences public policy by demonstrating the importance of providing library and information services that meet the unique needs and interests of young adults

8. Encourages research and is in the vanguard of new thinking concerning the provision of library and information services for youth

## Membership

Memb. 5,700. Open to anyone interested in library services, literature, and technology for young adults. For information on dues, see ALA entry.

## Officers

*Pres.* Sarah Debraski. E-mail slcornish@gmail.com; *V.P./Pres.-Elect* Linda Braun. E-mail lbraun@leonline.com; *Past Pres.* Paula Brehm-Heeger. E-mail paulabrehmheeger@fuse.net; *Division Councilor* Christine Allen. E-mail callen@rusd.k12.ca.us; *Fiscal Officer* Mary Hastler. E-mail mhastler@bcpl.net; *Secy.* Francisca Goldsmith. E-mail fgoldsmith@gmail.com.

## Directors

Ruth Cox Clark. E-mail clarkr@ecu.edu; Michele Gorman. E-mail comixlibrarian@aol.com; Erin V. Helmrich. E-mail helmriche@aadl.org; Kimberly Anne Patton. E-mail kpatton@lawrence.lib.ks.us; Sandra Payne. E-mail spayne@nypl.org; Melissa Rabey (ex-officio). E-mail melinwonderland@gmail.com; Dawn Rutherford. E-mail drutherford@sno-isle.org; Sheila Schofer (ex-officio). E-mail sschofer@brooklynpubliclibrary.org; Cindy Welch. E-mail cwelch2@gmail.com.

## Publications

*Young Adult Library Services* (q.) (memb.; nonmemb. $50; foreign $60). *Ed.* Rose-Mary Honnold.

*YAttitudes* (memb.) *Ed.* Erin Downey Howerton.

# AIIM—The Enterprise Content Management Association

President, John F. Mancini
1100 Wayne Ave., Suite 1100, Silver Spring, MD 20910
800-477-2446, 301-587-8202, fax 301-587-2711
E-mail aiim@aiim.org, World Wide Web http://www.aiim.org
European Office: The IT Centre, 8 Canalside, Lowesmoor Wharf, Worcester WR1 2RR,
England. Tel. 44-1905-727600, fax 44-1905-727609, e-mail info@aiim.org.uk

## Object

AIIM is an international authority on enterprise content management, the tools and technologies that capture, manage, store, preserve, and deliver content in support of business processes. Founded 1943 as the Association for Information and Image Management.

## Officers

*Chair* Robert W. Zagami, DataBank IMX; *V. Chair* Lynn Fraas, Crown Partners; *Treas.* Mike Alsup, Gimmal Group; *Past Chair* Jan Andersson, ReadSoft AB.

## Publication

*AIIM E-DOC Magazine* (bi-mo.; memb.).

# American Indian Library Association

President, Susan Hanks, California State Library
World Wide Web http://www.ailanet.org

## Objective

To improve library and information services for American Indians. Founded 1979; affiliated with American Library Association 1985.

## Membership

Any person, library, or other organization interested in working to improve library and information services for American Indians may become a member. Dues (Inst.) $30; (Indiv.) $15; (Student) $10.

## Officers (July 2008–June 2009)

*Pres.* Susan Hanks, Development Services, California State Lib., P.O. Box 942837, Sacramento, CA 94237-0001. Tel. 916-653-0661, e-mail shanks@library.ca.gov; *V.P./ Pres.-Elect* Liana Juliano. E-mail lj12116@yahoo.com; *Secy.* Holly Tomren. E-mail htomren@uci.edu; *Treas.* Joan Howland. E-mail howla001@umn.edu; *Past. Pres.* Janice Rice. E-mail jrice@library.wisc.edu.

## Publication

*AILA Newsletter* (q.).

## Committee Chairs

Children's Literature Award. Lisa Mitten.

Communications and Publications. Liana Juliano.

Development and Fund Raising. Richenda Wilkinson.

Nominating. Kelly Webster, Joan Howland.

Programming. Janice Rice.

Scholarship Review Board. Joan Howland, Jody Gray.

Subject Access and Classification. Mario Klimiades.

# American Merchant Marine Library Association

(An affiliate of United Seamen's Service)

Executive Director, Roger T. Korner
635 Fourth Ave., Brooklyn, NY 11232
Tel. 718-369-3818, e-mail ussammla@ix.netcom.com
World Wide Web http://uss-ammla.com

## Object

Provides ship and shore library service for American-flag merchant vessels, the Military Sealift Command, the U.S. Coast Guard, and other waterborne operations of the U.S. government. Established 1921.

## Officers (2008–2009)

*Pres.* Edward R. Morgan; *V.P.s* Thomas J. Bethel, John M. Bowers, Capt. Timothy A. Brown, James Capo, David Cockroft, Ron Davis, Capt. Remo Di Fiore, Yoji Fujisawa, John Halas, Rene Lioeanjie, George E. Murphy, Capt. Gregorio Oca, Michael Sacco, John J. Sweeney; *Secy.* Donald E. Kadlac; *Treas.* William D. Potts; *Gen. Counsel* John L. DeGurse, Jr.; *Exec. Dir.* Roger T. Korner.

# American Society for Information Science and Technology

Executive Director, Richard B. Hill
1320 Fenwick Lane, Suite 510, Silver Spring, MD 20910
301-495-0900, fax 301-495-0810, e-mail asis@asis.org
World Wide Web http://www.asis.org

## Object

The American Society for Information Science and Technology (ASIS&T) provides a forum for the discussion, publication, and critical analysis of work dealing with the design, management, and use of information, information systems, and information technology.

## Membership

Memb. (Indiv.) 3,500; (Student) 800; (Inst.) 250. Dues (Indiv.) $140; (Student) $40; (Inst.) $650 and $800.

## Officers

*Pres.* Donald O. Case, Univ. of Kentucky; *Pres.-Elect* Gary Marchionini, Univ. of North Carolina at Chapel Hill; *Treas.* Vicki Gregory, Univ. of South Florida; *Past Pres.* Nancy Roderer, Johns Hopkins Univ.

Address correspondence to the executive director.

## Board of Directors

*Dirs.-at-Large* Deborah Barreau, Efthimis Efthimiadis, Katherine McCain, Peter Morville, Julian Warner, Barbara Wildemuth.

## Publications

*ASIS&T Thesaurus of Information Science, Technology, and Librarianship,* 3rd edition, ed. by Alice Redmond-Neal and Marjorie M. K. Hlava.

*Computerization Movements and Technology Diffusion: From Mainframes to Ubiquitous Computing,* ed. by Margaret S. Elliott and Kenneth L. Kraemer.

*Covert and Overt: Recollecting and Connecting Intelligence Service and Information Science,* ed. by Robert V. Williams and Ben-Ami Lipetz.

*Editorial Peer Review: Its Strengths and Weaknesses,* by Ann C. Weller.

*Electronic Publishing: Applications and Implications,* ed. by Elisabeth Logan and Myke Gluck.

*Evaluating Networked Information Services: Techniques, Policy and Issues,* by Charles R. McClure and John Carlo Bertot.

*From Print to Electronic: The Transformation of Scientific Communication,* by Susan Y. Crawford, Julie M. Hurd, and Ann C. Weller.

*Historical Information Science: An Emerging Unidiscipline,* by Lawrence J. McCrank.

*Historical Studies in Information Science,* ed. by Trudi Bellardo Hahn and Michael Buckland.

*The History and Heritage of Scientific and Technological Information Systems,* ed. by W. Boyd Rayward and Mary Ellen Bowden.

*Information and Emotion: The Emergent Affective Paradigm in Information Behavior Research and Theory,* ed. by Diane Nahl and Dania Bilal.

*Information Management for the Intelligent Organization: The Art of Environmental Scanning,* 3rd edition, by Chun Wei Choo.

*Information Representation and Retrieval in the Digital Age,* by Heting Chu.

*Intelligent Technologies in Library and Information Service Applications,* by F. W. Lancaster and Amy Warner.

*Introductory Concepts in Information Science,* by Melanie J. Norton.

*Knowledge Management for the Information Professional,* ed. by T. Kanti Srikantaiah and Michael E. D. Koenig.

*Knowledge Management in Practice: Connections and Context,* ed. by T. Kanti Srikantaiah and Michael E. D. Koenig.

*Knowledge Management Lessons Learned: What Works and What Doesn't,* ed. by T. Kanti Srikantaiah and Michael E. D. Koenig.

*Knowledge Management: The Bibliography,* compiled by Paul Burden.

*Proceedings of ASIS&T Annual Meetings.*

*Statistical Methods for the Information Professional,* by Liwen Vaughan.

*Theories of Information Behavior,* ed. by Karen E. Fisher, Sanda Erdelez, and Lynne E. F. McKechnie.

*The Web of Knowledge: A Festschrift in Honor of Eugene Garfield,* ed. by Blaise Cronin and Helen Barsky Atkins.

The above publications are available from Information Today, Inc., 143 Old Marlton Pike, Medford, NJ 08055.

# American Theological Library Association

300 S. Wacker Drive, Suite 2100, Chicago, IL 60606-6701
Tel. 888-665-2852, 312-454-5100, fax 312-454-5505. e-mail atla@atla.com
World Wide Web http://www.atla.com/atlahome.html

## Mission

The mission of the American Theological Library Association (ATLA) is to foster the study of theology and religion by enhancing the development of theological and religious libraries and librarianship. In pursuit of this mission, the association undertakes

- To foster the professional growth of its members, and to enhance their ability to serve their constituencies as administrators and librarians
- To advance the profession of theological librarianship, and to assist theological librarians in defining and interpreting the proper role and function of libraries in theological education
- To promote quality library and information services in support of teaching, learning, and research in theology, religion, and related disciplines and to create such tools and aids (including publications) as may be helpful in accomplishing this
- To stimulate purposeful collaboration among librarians of theological libraries and religious studies collections, and to develop programmatic solutions to information-related problems common to those librarians and collections

## Membership

(Inst.) 265; (International Inst.) 13; (Indiv.) 492; (Student) 67; (Lifetime) 90; (Affiliates) 71.

## Officers

*Pres.* David R. Stewart, Dir. of Lib. Services, Luther Seminary, 2481 Como Ave., St. Paul, MN 55108. Tel. 651-641-3592, fax 651-641-3280, e-mail dstewart@luthersem.edu; *V.P.* Roberta A. Schaafsma, Dir., Bridwell Lib., Perkins School of Theology, Southern Methodist Univ., P.O. Box 750476, Dallas, TX 75275-0476. Tel. 214-768-1867, fax 214-768-4295, e-mail schaafsm@smu.edu; *Secy.* Eileen Crawford, Assoc. Dir., Vanderbilt Univ. Divinity Lib., 419 21st Ave. South, Nashville, TN 37240-0007. Tel. 615-343-9880, fax 615-343-2918, e-mail eileen.k.crawford@vanderbilt.edu; *Past Pres.* Martha Lund Smalley, Research Services Libn., Yale Univ. Divinity School Lib., 409 Prospect St., New Haven, CT 06511. Tel. 203-432-6374, fax 203-432-3906, e-mail martha.smalley@yale.edu.

## Directors

Cheryl L. Adams, Carrisse Mickey Berryhill, M. Patrick Graham, Duane Harbin, Cait Kokolus, Saundra Lipton, Allen W. Mueller, James C. Pakala, Laura Wood.

## Publications

ATLA Indexes in MARC Format (2 a year).
ATLA Religion Database on CD-ROM, 1949–.
ATLA Religion Database: Ten-Year Subset on CD-ROM, 1993–.
Biblical Studies on CD-ROM (ann.).
Catholic Periodical and Literature Index on CD-ROM (ann.).

*Index to Book Reviews in Religion* (ann.).
*Newsletter* (q.; memb.; nonmemb. $55). *Ed.*
Sara Corkery.
Old Testament Abstracts on CD-ROM (ann.).
*Proceedings* (ann.; memb.; nonmemb. $55).

*Ed.* Sara Corkery.
*Religion Index One: Periodicals* (2 a year).
*Research in Ministry: An Index to Doctor of Ministry Project Reports* (ann.), print and online.

## Archivists and Librarians in the History of the Health Sciences

President, Lisa A. Mix, Manager, Archives and Special Collections, UCSF Library and
Center for Knowledge Management, 530 Parnassus Ave., San Francisco, CA 94143-0840
415-514-3706, e-mail lisa.mix@library.ucsf.edu
World Wide Web http://www.alhhs.org/

### Object

The association was established exclusively
for educational purposes, to serve the professional interests of librarians, archivists, and
other specialists actively engaged in the
librarianship of the history of the health sciences by promoting the exchange of information and by improving the standards of
service.

### Membership

Memb. 170. Dues $15 (Americas), $21 (other
countries).

### Officers

*Pres.* Lisa A. Mix. E-mail lisa.mix@library.
ucsf.edu; *Secy./Treas.* Brooke Fox. E-mail
ebf2@musc.edu; *Membs.-at-Large* Judy M.
Chellnick, K. Garth Huston, Jr., Christopher
Lyons, Howard Rootenberg; *Past Pres.*
Micaela Sullivan-Fowler msullivan@library.
wisc.edu.

### Publication

*Watermark* (q.; memb.). *Ed.* Christopher
Lyons, Osler Lib. of the History of Medicine, McGill Univ. E-mail christopher.
lyons@mcgill.ca.

## ARMA International

Executive Director, Marilyn Bier
13725 W. 109 St., Suite 101, Lenexa, KS 66215
800-422-2762, 913-341-3808, fax 913-341-3742
World Wide Web http://www.arma.org

### Object

To advance the practice of records and information management as a discipline and a profession; to organize and promote programs of
research, education, training, and networking
within that profession; to support the enhancement of professionalism of the membership; and to promote cooperative endeavors with related professional groups.

### Membership

Memb. 11,000. Annual dues $150 for inter-
national affiliation (student/retired $25).
Chapter dues vary.

## Officers (July 2009–June 2010)

*Pres./Chair* John Frost, IBM Corp., 12408 John Simpson Court, Austin, TX 78732. Tel. 877-622-9929; *Pres.-Elect* Douglas Allen, Global 360, 3103 Sasparilla Cove, Austin, TX 78748. Tel. 512-791-8027; *Treas.* Fred Pulzello, 26 Holt Court, Glen Rock, NJ 07452. Tel. 201-723-5865; *Past Pres.* Carol E. B. Choksy, IRAD Consulting, 4103 Gold Grove Rd., Greenwood, IN 46143. Tel. 317-294-8329.

## Directors

Sharon Alexander-Gooding, Beth Chiaiese, Galina Datskovsky, Nicholas De Laurentis, Pamela Duane, Komal Gulich, Michael Langstone, Susan Lord, Juana Walker, Paula Uscian, Gita Werapitiya, Jesse Wilkins.

## Publication

*Information Management* (*IM*) (bi-mo.).

# Art Libraries Society of North America

Executive Director, Elizabeth Clarke
38 Steffler Drive, Guelph, ON N1G 3N5
519-827-1506, fax 519-827-1825, e-mail eclarke33@rogers.com
World Wide Web http://www.arlisna.org

## Object

To foster excellence in art librarianship and visual resources curatorship for the advancement of the visual arts. Established 1972.

## Membership

Memb. 1,100. Dues (Inst./Business Affiliate) $145; (Indiv.) $85; (Student) $45; (Retired/Unemployed) $45; (Sustaining) $250; (Sponsor) $500; (Overseas) $65. Year. Jan. 1–Dec. 31. Membership is open to all those interested in visual librarianship, whether they be professional librarians, students, library assistants, art book publishers, art book dealers, art historians, archivists, architects, slide and photograph curators, or retired associates in these fields.

## Officers

*Pres.* Ken Soehner, Thomas J. Watson Lib., Metropolitan Museum of Art, 1000 Fifth Ave., New York, NY 10028. Tel. 212-570-3934, fax 212-570-3847, e-mail ken.soehner @metmuseum.org; *V.P./Pres.-Elect* Amy Lucker, Institute of Fine Arts Lib., 1 E. 78 St., New York, NY 10075. Tel. 212-992-5826, e-mail amy.lucker@nyu.edu; *Secy.* Rebecca Price, 2396 Duderstadt Center, Ann Arbor, MI 48109-2094. Tel. 734-647-2094, e-mail rpw@umich.edu; *Treas.* Edward ("Ted") Goodman, Avery Lib., Columbia Univ., 1172 Amsterdam Ave., MC 0301, New York, NY 10027. Tel. 212-854-8407, fax 212-854-8904, e-mail goodman@ columbia.edu; *Past Pres.* Deborah K. Ultan Boudewyns, 170B Wilson Lib., Univ. of Minnesota, 309 19th Ave S., Minneapolis, MN 55455. Tel. 612-625-6438, e-mail ultan004 @umn.edu.

Address correspondence to the executive director.

## Publications

*ARLIS/NA Update* (bi-mo.; memb.).
*Art Documentation* (2 a year; memb., subscription).
*Handbook and List of Members* (ann.; memb.).
Occasional papers (price varies).
Miscellaneous others (request current list from headquarters).

## Committee Chairpersons

ARLIS/NA and VRA Summer Educational Institute for Visual Resources and Image Management. Amy Lucker, Karin Whalen, Eileen Fry, Jeanne Keefe.
Awards. Susan Moon.
Cataloging Advisory. Kay Teel.
Development. Jon Evans.
Distinguished Service Award. Betsy Peck-Learned.
Diversity. Vanessa Kam, Laurel Bliss.
Finance. Lynda White.

International Relations. Kristen Regina.
Membership. Rachel Resnik.
Gerd Muehsam Award. Tony White.
Nominating. Carole Ann Fabian.
Professional Development. Tom Caswell.
Public Policy. Tim Shipe.
Publications. Roger Lawson.
Research Awards. Alan Michelson, Hannah Bennett.
Standards. Aprille Nace.
Travel Awards. Jennifer Parker.
George Wittenborn Award. Margaret Culbertson.

# Asian/Pacific American Librarians Association

Executive Director, Gerardo ("Gary") Colmenar
E-mail colmenar@library.ucsb.edu
World Wide Web http://www.apalaweb.org

## Object

To provide a forum for discussing problems and concerns of Asian/Pacific American librarians; to provide a forum for the exchange of ideas by Asian/Pacific American librarians and other librarians; to support and encourage library services to Asian/Pacific American communities; to recruit and support Asian/Pacific American librarians in the library/information science professions; to seek funding for scholarships in library/information science programs for Asian/Pacific Americans; and to provide a vehicle whereby Asian/Pacific American librarians can cooperate with other associations and organizations having similar or allied interests. Founded 1980; incorporated 1981; affiliated with American Library Association 1982.

## Membership

Open to all librarians and information specialists of Asian/Pacific descent working in U.S. libraries and information centers and other related organizations, and to others who support the goals and purposes of APALA. Asian/Pacific Americans are defined as people residing in North America who self-identify as Asian/Pacific American. Dues (Inst.) $50; (Indiv.) $20; (Students/Unemployed Librarians) $10.

## Officers (July 2008–June 2009)

*Pres.* Michelle Baildon, MIT Humanities Lib. E-mail baildon@mit.edu; *V.P./Pres.-Elect* Sherise Kimura, Gleeson Lib., Univ. of San Francisco. E-mail kimura@usfca.edu; *Secy.* Saima Fazli, Collection Core Services Div., Univ. of California, Berkeley. E-mail sfazli@library.berkeley.edu; *Treas.* Angela Boyd, Davidson Lib., Univ. of California, Santa Barbara. E-mail aboyd@library.ucsb.edu; *Past Pres.* Buenaventura ("Ven") B. Basco, Univ. of Central Florida Libs. E-mail bbasco@mail.ucf.edu.

## Publication

*APALA Newsletter* (q.).

## Committee Chairs

Constitution and Bylaws. Thaddeus Bejnar.
Finance and Fund Raising. Sherise Kimura.
Literary Awards. Dora Ho.
Membership. Michelle Baildon.
Newsletter and Publications. Suhasini Kumar,
  Gary Colmenar.

Nomination. Ben Wakashige.
Program. Ven Basco.
Publicity. Angela Boyd, Maria Hudson Carpenter.
Research and Travel. Alanna Aiko Moore.
Scholarships. Sarah Jeong.
Web. Andrienne Z. Gaerlan, Holly Yu.

# Association for Library and Information Science Education

Executive Director, Kathleen Combs
ALISE Headquarters, 65 E. Wacker Place, Suite 1900, Chicago, IL 60601-7246
312-795-0996, fax 312-419-8950, e-mail contact@alise.org
World Wide Web http://www.alise.org

The Association for Library and Information Science Education (ALISE) is an independent, nonprofit professional association whose mission is to promote excellence in research, teaching, and service for library and information science (LIS) education through leadership, collaboration, advocacy, and dissemination of research. Its enduring purpose is to promote research that informs the scholarship of teaching and learning for library and information science, enabling members to integrate research into teaching and learning. The association provides a forum in which to share ideas, discuss issues, address challenges, and shape the future of education for library and information science. Founded in 1915 as the Association of American Library Schools, it has had its present name since 1983.

## Membership

600+ in four categories: Personal, Institutional, International Affiliate Institutional, and Associate Institutional. Personal membership is open to anyone with an interest in the association's objectives.

## Officers (2009–2010)

*Pres.* Linda Smith, Univ. of Illinois at Urbana-Champaign; *V.P./Pres.-Elect* Lorna Peterson, Univ. at Buffalo; *Past Pres.* Michèle Cloonan, Simmons College; *Secy.-Treas.* Jean Preer, Indiana Univ., Indianapolis.

## Publications

*Journal of Education for Library and Information Science (JELIS)* (q.). *Co-Eds.* Kathleen Burnett and Michelle Kazmer.
*ALISE News* (q.)

# Association of Academic Health Sciences Libraries

Executive Director, Louise S. Miller
2150 N. 107 St., Ste. 205, Seattle, WA 98133
206-367-8704, fax 206-367-8777, e-mail aahsl@sbims.com
World Wide Web http://www.aahsl.org

## Object

The Association of Academic Health Sciences Libraries (AAHSL) is composed of the directors of libraries of more than 140 accredited U.S. and Canadian medical schools belonging to the Association of American Medical Colleges. Its goals are to promote excellence in academic health science libraries and to ensure that the next generation of health practitioners is trained in information-seeking skills that enhance the quality of healthcare delivery, education, and research. Founded 1977.

## Membership

Memb. 140+. Regular membership is available to nonprofit educational institutions operating a school of health sciences that has full or provisional accreditation by the Association of American Medical Colleges. Regular members are represented by the chief administrative officer of the member institution's health sciences library. Associate membership (and nonvoting representation) is available to organizations having an interest in the purposes and activities of the association.

## Officers (2008–2009)

*Pres.* Julia Sollenberger, Univ. of Rochester Medical Center; *Pres.-Elect* Connie Poole, School of Medicine Lib., Southern Illinois Univ.; *Secy./Treas.* Paul Schoening, Bernard Becker Medical Lib., Washington Univ. School of Medicine; *Past Pres.* Linda Watson, Health Sciences Libs., Univ. of Minnesota–Twin Cities.

## Directors

Jim Bothmer, Health Science Lib., Creighton Univ.; Mary Ryan, Univ. of Arkansas for Medical Sciences Lib.; M. J. Tooey, Health Sciences and Human Services Lib., Univ. of Maryland, Baltimore.

# Association of Independent Information Professionals

8550 United Plaza Blvd., Suite 1001, Baton Rouge, LA 70809
225-408-4400, fax 225-408-4422, e-mail office@aiip.org
World Wide Web http://www.aiip.org

## Object

AIIP's members are owners of firms providing such information-related services as online and manual research, document delivery, database design, library support, consulting, writing, and publishing. The objectives of the association are

- To advance the knowledge and understanding of the information profession
- To promote and maintain high professional and ethical standards among its members
- To encourage independent information professionals to assemble to discuss common issues
- To promote the interchange of information among independent information professionals and various organizations
- To keep the public informed of the profession and of the responsibilities of the information professional

## Membership

Memb. 650+.

## Officers (2008–2009)

*Pres.* Edward Vawter, QD Information Services. Tel. 503-999-7347; *Pres.-Elect* Marcy Phelps, Phelps Research. Tel. 303-239-0657; *Secy.* Mark Goldstein, International Research Center. Tel. 602-470-0389; *Treas.* Cliff Kalibjian, Mr. Health Search. Tel. 925-830-8439; *Past Pres.* Jane John, On Point Research. Tel. 207-373-1755.

## Publications

*Connections* (q.).
*Membership Directory* (ann.).
Professional paper series.

# Association of Jewish Libraries

P.O. Box 1118, Teaneck, NJ 07666
212-725-5359, e-mail ajlibs@osu.edu
World Wide Web http://www.jewishlibraries.org

## Object

The Association of Jewish Libraries (AJL) promotes Jewish literacy through enhancement of libraries and library resources and through leadership for the profession and practitioners of Judaica librarianship. The association fosters access to information, learning, teaching, and research relating to Jews, Judaism, the Jewish experience, and Israel.

## Goals

- Maintain high professional standards for Judaica librarians and recruit qualified individuals into the profession
- Facilitate communication and exchange of information on a global scale
- Encourage quality publication in the field in all formats and media

- Stimulate publication of high-quality children's literature
- Facilitate and encourage establishment of Judaica library collections
- Enhance information access for all through application of advanced technologies
- Publicize the organization and its activities in all relevant venues
- Stimulate awareness of Judaica library services among the public at large
- Promote recognition of Judaica librarianship within the wider library profession
- Encourage recognition of Judaica library services by other organizations and related professions
- Ensure continuity of the association through sound management, financial security, effective governance, and a dedicated and active membership

## Membership

Memb. 1,100. Dues $50; (Student/Retired) $30. Year. July 1–June 30.

## Officers (July 2009–June 2010)

*Pres.* Susan Dubin; *V.P./Pres.-Elect* David Hirsch; *V.P. Memb.* Laurie Haas; *V.P. Publications* Deborah Stern; *Treas.* Schlomit Schwarzer; *Recording Secy.* Elana Gensler; *Corresponding Secy.* Rachel Glasser; *Treas.* Sheryl Stahl; *Past Pres.* Laurel S. Wolfson.
   Address correspondence to the association.

## Publications

*AJL Newsletter* (q.). *Ed.* Libby K. White, Baltimore Hebrew Univ., 5800 Park Heights Ave., Baltimore, MD 21215.
*Judaica Librarianship* (irreg.). *Ed.* Zachary M. Baker, Green Lib. 321, ASRG, Stanford Univ. Libs., Stanford, CA 94305-6004.

## Division Presidents

Research Libraries, Archives, and Special Libraries. Elliot H. Gertel, Univ. of Michigan.
Synagogue, School, and Center Libraries. Etta D. Gold, Temple Beth Am, Miami.

# Association of Research Libraries

Executive Director, Charles B. Lowry
21 Dupont Circle N.W., Suite 800, Washington, DC 20036
202-296-2296, fax 202-872-0884, e-mail arlhq@arl.org
World Wide Web http://www.arl.org

## Object

The Association of Research Libraries (ARL) influences the changing environment of scholarly communication and the public policies that affect research libraries and the diverse communities they serve. ARL pursues this mission by advancing the goals of its member research libraries, providing leadership in public and information policy to the scholarly and higher education communities, fostering the exchange of ideas and expertise, and shaping a future environment that leverages its interests with those of allied organizations.

## Membership

Memb. 123. Membership is institutional. Dues: $23,704 for 2009.

## Officers

*Pres.* Thomas C. Leonard, Univ. of California, Berkeley; *V.P./Pres.-Elect*; Brinley Franklin, Univ. of Connecticut; *Past Pres.* Marianne Gaunt, Rutgers Univ.

## Board of Directors

Colleen Cook, Texas A&M Univ.; Barbara Dewey, Univ. of Tennessee; Brinley Franklin, Univ. of Connecticut; Tom Leonard, Univ. of California, Berkeley; Charles B. Lowry, ex officio, ARL; Carol A. Mandel, New York Univ.; Sarah Michalak, ex officio, Univ. of North Carolina at Chapel Hill; James Mullins, Purdue Univ.; James G. Neal, ex officio, Univ. of Columbia; Dana C. Rooks, Univ. of Houston; Winston Tabb, Johns Hopkins Univ.; Karin Trainer, Princeton Univ.; Paul Wiens, Queens Univ.; Sandra Yee, Wayne State Univ.

## Publications

*ARL: A Bimonthly Report on Research Library Issues and Actions from ARL, CNI, and SPARC* (bi-mo.).
*ARL Academic Health Sciences Library Statistics* (ann.).
*ARL Academic Law Library Statistics* (ann.).
*ARL Annual Salary Survey* (ann.).
*ARL Preservation Statistics* (ann.).
*ARL Statistics* (ann.).
*SPEC Kits* (6 a year).

## Committee and Working Group Chairpersons

Diversity Initiatives. Karin Trainer, Princeton Univ.
E-Science Working Group. Wendy Pradt Lougee, Univ. of Minnesota.
Fair Use and Related Exemptions. Mary Case, Univ. of Illinois, Chicago.
Membership. Marilyn Sharrow, Univ. of California, Davis.

Public Policies Affecting Research Libraries. Sarah Michalak, Univ. of North Carolina at Chapel Hill.
Regional Federal Depository Libraries Working Group. Joan Giesecke, Univ. of Nebraska.
Research, Teaching, and Learning. Barbara Dewey, Univ. of Tennessee.
Scholarly Communication. James G. Neal, Columbia Univ.
Special Collections Working Group, Alice Prochaska, Yale Univ.
Statistics and Assessment. Colleen Cook, Texas A&M Univ.

## ARL Membership

### Nonuniversity Libraries

Boston Public Lib., Canada Inst. for Scientific and Technical Info., Center for Research Libs., Lib. and Archives Canada, Lib. of Congress, National Agricultural Lib., National Lib. of Medicine, New York Public Lib., New York State Lib., Smithsonian Institution Libs.

### University Libraries

Alabama; Albany (SUNY); Alberta; Arizona; Arizona State; Auburn; Boston College; Boston Univ.; Brigham Young; British Columbia; Brown; Buffalo (SUNY); California, Berkeley; California, Davis; California, Irvine; California, Los Angeles; California, Riverside; California, San Diego; California, Santa Barbara; Case Western Reserve; Chicago; Cincinnati; Colorado; Colorado State; Columbia; Connecticut; Cornell; Dartmouth; Delaware; Duke; Emory; Florida; Florida State; George Washington; Georgetown; Georgia; Georgia Inst. of Technology; Guelph; Harvard; Hawaii; Houston; Howard; Illinois, Chicago; Illinois, Urbana-Champaign; Indiana; Iowa; Iowa State; Johns Hopkins; Kansas; Kent State; Kentucky; Laval; Louisiana State; Louisville; McGill; McMaster; Manitoba; Maryland; Massachusetts; Massachusetts Inst. of Technology; Miami (Florida); Michigan; Michigan State; Minnesota; Missouri; Montreal; Nebraska, Lincoln; New Mexico; New York; North Carolina; North Carolina State; Northwestern; Notre Dame; Ohio; Ohio State; Oklahoma; Oklahoma State; Oregon; Pennsylvania; Pennsylvania State; Pittsburgh; Princeton; Purdue; Queen's (Kingston, Ontario); Rice; Rochester; Rutgers; Saskatchewan; South Carolina; South-ern California; Southern Illinois; Stony Brook (SUNY); Syracuse; Temple; Tennessee; Texas; Texas A&M; Texas Tech; Toronto; Tulane; Utah; Vanderbilt; Virginia; Virginia Tech; Washington; Washington (Saint Louis): Washington State; Waterloo; Wayne State; Western Ontario; Wisconsin; Yale; York.

# Association of Vision Science Librarians

Chair 2009, Pamela C. Sieving, Informationist, NIH Lib., 10 Center Drive, Rm. 1L09G, MSC 1150, Bethesda, MD 20892-1150. Tel. 301-451-5862, fax 301-402-0254, e-mail pamsieving@nih.gov World Wide Web http://spectacle.berkeley.edu/~library/AVSL.htm

## Object

To foster collective and individual acquisition and dissemination of vision science information, to improve services for all persons seeking such information, and to develop standards for libraries to which members are attached. Founded 1968.

## Membership

Memb. (U.S.) 62; (International) 60.

## Publications

*Core List of Audio-Visual Related Serials.*
*Guidelines for Vision Science Libraries.*
*Opening Day Book, Journal and AV Collection—Visual Science.*
*Publication Considerations in the Age of Electronic Opportunities.*
*Standards for Vision Science Libraries.*
*Union List of Vision-Related Serials* (irreg.).

## Meetings

Annual meeting held in the fall, midyear mini-meeting with the Medical Library Association in the spring.

# Beta Phi Mu
## (International Library and Information Studies Honor Society)

Executive Director, Christie Koontz
College of Information, Florida State University, Tallahassee, FL 32306-2100
850-644-3907, fax 850-644-9763, e-mail ckoontz@ci.fsu.edu
World Wide Web http://www.beta-phi-mu.org

## Object

To recognize distinguished achievement in and scholarly contributions to librarianship, information studies, or library education, and to sponsor and support appropriate professional and scholarly projects related to these fields. Founded at the University of Illinois in 1948.

## Membership

Memb. 35,000. Open to graduates of library school programs accredited by the American Library Association who fulfill the following requirements: complete the course requirements leading to a fifth year or other advanced degree in librarianship with a scholastic average of 3.75 where A equals 4 points (this provision shall also apply to planned programs of advanced study beyond the fifth year that do not culminate in a degree but that require full-time study for one or more academic years) and rank in the top 25 percent of their class; and receive a letter of recommendation from the faculty of their respective library schools attesting to their professional promise.

## Officers

*Pres.* Nancy Zimmerman, School of Lib. and Info. Science, Univ. of South Carolina, 1501 Green St., Columbia, SC 29208; *V.P./Pres.-Elect* Sue Stroyan, Milner Lib., Illinois State Univ., Campus Box 8900, Normal, IL 61700-8900; *Treas.* David Whisenant, College Center for Lib. Automation, 1753 W. Paul Dirac Drive, Tallahassee, FL 32310; *Exec. Dir.* Christie Koontz, College of Info., Florida State Univ., Tallahassee, FL 32306-2100. Tel. 850-644-3907, fax 850-644-9763, e-mail betaphimuinfo@admin.fsu.edu.

## Directors

*Dirs.* Alice Calabrese-Berry, George Gaumond, Eloise May, Ron Miller, Beth Paskoff, Blanche Woolls; *Dirs.-at-Large* Marie L. Radford, Sue Searing.

## Publications

Beta Phi Mu Monograph Series. Book-length scholarly works based on original research in subjects of interest to library and information professionals. Available from Greenwood Press, 130 Cremona Dr., Santa Barbara, CA 93117.
Chapbook Series. Limited editions on topics of interest to information professionals.
*Newsletter* (electronic only). *Ed.* JP Walters.

## Chapters

*Alpha.* Univ. of Illinois, Grad. School of Lib. and Info. Science; *Gamma.* Florida State Univ., College of Info.; *Epsilon.* Univ. of North Carolina, School of Info. and Lib. Science; *Theta.* Pratt Inst., Grad. School of Lib. and Info. Science; *Iota.* Catholic Univ. of America, School of Lib. and Info. Science; Univ. of Maryland, College of Lib. and Info. Services; *Lambda.* Univ. of Oklahoma, School of Lib. and Info. Studies; *Mu.* Univ. of Michigan, School of Info; *Xi.* Univ. of Hawaii, Grad. School of Lib. Studies; *Omicron.* Rutgers Univ., Grad. School of Communication, Info. and Lib. Studies; *Pi.* Univ. of Pittsburgh, School of Info. Sciences; *Rho.* Kent State Univ., School of Lib. and Info. Science; *Sigma.* Drexel Univ., College of Info. Science and Technology; *Upsilon.* Univ. of Kentucky, School of Lib. and Info. Science; *Phi.* Univ. of Denver, Grad. School of Lib. and Info. Science; *Chi.* Indiana Univ.,

School of Lib. and Info. Science; *Psi.* Univ. of Missouri at Columbia, School of Lib. and Info. Science; *Omega.* San Jose State Univ., School of Lib. and Info. Science; *Beta Alpha.* Queens College, City College of New York, Grad. School of Lib. and Info. Studies; *Beta Beta.* Simmons College, Grad. School of Lib. and Info. Science; *Beta Delta.* State Univ. of New York at Buffalo, Dept. of Info. and Lib. Studies; *Beta Epsilon.* Emporia State Univ., School of Lib. and Info. Management; *Beta Zeta.* Louisiana State Univ., Grad. School of Lib. and Info. Science; *Beta Eta.* Univ. of Texas at Austin, Grad. School of Lib. and Info. Science; *Beta Iota.* Univ. of Rhode Island, Grad. School of Lib. and Info. Studies; *Beta Kappa.* Univ. of Alabama, Grad. School of Lib. and Info. Studies; *Beta Lambda.* North Texas State Univ., School of Lib. and Info. Science; Texas Woman's Univ., School of Lib. and Info. Sciences; *Beta Mu.* Long Island Univ., Palmer Grad. School of Lib. and Info. Science; *Beta Nu.* Saint John's Univ., Div. of Lib. and Info. Science; *Beta Xi.* North Carolina Central Univ., School of Lib. and Info. Sciences; *Beta Omicron.* Univ. of Tennessee at Knoxville, Grad. School of Info. Sciences; *Beta Pi.* Univ. of Arizona, Grad. School of Info. Resources and Lib. Science; *Beta Rho.* Univ. of Wisconsin at Milwaukee, School of Info.; *Beta Sigma.* Clarion Univ. of Pennsylvania, Dept. of Lib. Science; *Beta Tau.* Wayne State Univ., Lib. and Info. Science Program; *Beta Phi.* Univ. of South Florida, Grad. School of Lib. and Info. Science; *Beta Psi.* Univ. of Southern Mississippi, School of Lib. and Info. Science; *Beta Omega.* Univ. of South Carolina, College of Lib. and Info. Science; *Beta Beta Alpha.* Univ. of California at Los Angeles, Grad. School of Lib. and Info. Science; *Beta Beta Gamma.* Dominican Univ., Grad. School of Lib. and Info. Science; *Beta Beta Epsilon.* Univ. of Wisconsin at Madison, School of Lib. and Info. Studies; *Beta Beta Zeta.* Univ. of North Carolina at Greensboro, Dept. of Lib. and Info. Studies; *Beta Beta Theta.* Univ. of Iowa, School of Lib. and Info. Science; *Beta Beta Iota.* State Univ. of New York, Univ. at Albany, School of Info. Science and Policy; *Beta Beta Kappa.* Univ. of Puerto Rico, Grad. School of Info. Sciences and Technologies; *Pi Lambda Sigma.* Syracuse Univ., School of Info. Studies; *Beta Beta Mu.* Valdosta State Univ., School of Lib. and Info. Science.

# Bibliographical Society of America

Executive Secretary, Michèle E. Randall
P.O. Box 1537, Lenox Hill Station, New York, NY 10021
212-452-2710 (tel./fax), e-mail bsa@bibsocamer.org
World Wide Web http://www.bibsocamer.org

## Object

To promote bibliographical research and to issue bibliographical publications. Organized 1904.

## Membership

Memb. 1,200. Dues (Indiv.) $65; (Sustaining) $250; (Contributing) $100; (Student) $20; (Inst.) $75. Year. Jan.–Dec.

## Officers

*Pres.* John Neal Hoover. E-mail jhoover@ umsl.edu; *V.P.* Claudia Funke. E-mail ccf6@ columbia.edu; *Secy.* David R. Whitesell. E-mail whitesel@fas.harvard.edu; *Treas.* G. Scott Clemons. E-mail scott.clemons@bbh. com; *Past Pres.* John Bidwell. E-mail jbidwell@morganlibrary.org.

## Council

(2010) Eugene S. Flamm, James N. Green, Arthur L. Schwarz, Carolyn L. Smith; (2011) Douglas F. Bauer, John Crichton, Joan Friedman, Gregory A. Pass; (2012) David L. Gants, Barbara Shailor, Daniel Slive, David Supino.

## Publication

*Papers of the Bibliographical Society of America* (q.; memb.). *Ed.* Trevor Howard-Hill, Thomas Cooper Lib., Univ. of South Carolina, Columbia, SC 29208. Tel./fax 803-777-7046, e-mail ralphcrane@msn.com.

# Bibliographical Society of Canada
## (La Société Bibliographique du Canada)

President, David McKnight
P.O. Box 575, Postal Station P, Toronto, ON M5S 2T1
World Wide Web http://www.library.utoronto.ca/bsc/bschomeeng.html

## Object

The Bibliographical Society of Canada is a bilingual (English/French) organization that has as its goal the scholarly study of the history, description, and transmission of texts in all media and formats, with a primary emphasis on Canada, and the fulfillment of this goal through the following objectives:

- To promote the study and practice of bibliography: enumerative, historical, descriptive, analytical, and textual
- To further the study, research, and publication of book history and print culture
- To publish bibliographies and studies of book history and print culture
- To encourage the publication of bibliographies, critical editions, and studies of book history and print culture
- To promote the appropriate preservation and conservation of manuscript, archival, and published materials in various formats
- To encourage the utilization and analysis of relevant manuscript and archival sources as a foundation of bibliographical scholarship and book history
- To promote the interdisciplinary nature of bibliography, and to foster relationships with other relevant organizations nationally and internationally

- To conduct the society without purpose of financial gain for its members, and to ensure that any profits or other accretions to the society shall be used in promoting its goal and objectives

## Membership

The society welcomes as members all those who share its aims and wish to support and participate in bibliographical research and publication.

## Officers

*Pres.* David McKnight; *1st V.P.* Anne Dondertman; *2nd V.P.* Paul Aubin; *Secy.* Greta Golick. E-mail gretagolick@rogers.com; *Assoc. Secy.* Roger Meloche; *Treas.* Tom Vincent.

## Publications

*The Bulletin* (s.ann).
For a full list of the society's publications, see http://www.library.utoronto.ca/bsc/publicationseng.html.

## Committee Chairpersons

Awards. Randall Speller.
Fellowships. Nancy Vogan.
Publications. Patricia Fleming.

# Black Caucus of the American Library Association

President, Karolyn S. Thompson, Univ. Libs., Univ. of Southern Mississippi, 118 College Drive, No. 5053, Hattiesburg, MS 39406-0001
Tel. 601-266-5111, fax 601-266-4410, e-mail karolyn.thompson@usm.edu
World Wide Web http://www.bcala.org

## Mission

The Black Caucus of the American Library Association (BCALA) serves as an advocate for the development, promotion, and improvement of library services and resources to the nation's African American community and provides leadership for the recruitment and professional development of African American librarians. Founded in 1970.

## Membership

Membership is open to any person, institution, or business interested in promoting the development of library and information services for African Americans and other people of African descent and willing to maintain good financial standing with the organization. The membership is currently composed of librarians and other information professionals, library support staff, libraries, publishers, authors, vendors, and other library-related organizations in the United States and abroad. Dues (Corporate) $200; (Institutional) $60; (Regular) $45; (Student) $10.

## Officers

*Pres.* Karolyn S. Thompson. E-mail karolyn. thompson@usm.edu; *V.P./Pres.-Elect* Jos N. Holman. Tel. 765-429-0118, e-mail jholman @tcpl.lib.in.us; *Secy.* Eboni Curry. Tel. 202-727-1248, e-mail eboni.curry@dc.gov; *Treas.* Stanton F. Biddle. E-mail treasurer@ bcala.org; *Past Pres.* Wanda K. Brown. E-mail brownw@wfu.edu.

## Executive Board

Talia Abdullah, Gladys Smiley Bell, Vivian Bordeaux, Lisa Boyd, Jannie Cobb, Denyvetta Davis, Sharon Epps, LaVerne Gray, S. D. Harris, Gerald Holmes, Julius Jefferson, Jr., Alys Jordan, Carolyn Norman, Kelvin Watson, Joel White.

## Publication

*BCALA Newsletter* (bi-mo; memb.). *Interim Ed.* S. D. Harris. E-mail sdh.newsletter@ bcala.org.

## Committee Chairpersons

Affiliated Chapters. Sylvia Sprinkle-Hamlin, Lainey Westbrooks.
Affirmative Action. Howard F. McGinn, Darren Sweeper.
ALA Relations. Allene Hayes.
Awards. Richard Bradberry, ayo dayo.
Budget/Audit. Bobby Player.
Constitution and Bylaws. D. L. Grant, Gerald Holmes.
Fund Raising. Makiba J. Foster, Kelvin Watson.
History. Sibyl E. Moses.
International Relations. Vivian Bordeaux, Eboni M. Stokes.
E. J. Josey Scholarship. Billy Beal, Joyce E. Jelks.
Literary Awards. Virginia Toliver, Joel White.
Membership. Rudolph Clay, Allison M. Sutton.
Newsletter. George Grant, S. D. Harris.
Nominations/Elections. Wanda K. Brown.
Programs. Jos Holman.
Public Relations. Barbara E. Martin.
Recruitment and Professional Development. Jannie R. Cobb, Andrew P. Jackson (Sekou Molefi Baako).
Services to Children of Families of African Descent. Karen Lemmons.
Smiley Fund. Gladys Smiley Bell.

Technology Advisory. H. Jamane Yeager.

Dr. John C. Tyson Award. Alys Jordan, Esmeralda M. Kale.

## Awards

BCALA Literary Awards.

BCALA Trailblazer's Award.

DEMCO/ALA Black Caucus Award for Excellence in Librarianship.

Distinguished Service Award.

E. J. Josey Scholarship Award.

Smiley Student Fund.

John Tyson Award.

# Canadian Association for Information Science
## (L'Association Canadienne des Sciences de l'Information)

President, Joan Bartlett
School of Info. Studies, McGill Univ.
3459 McTavish, Montreal, QC H3A 1Y1
Tel. 514-398-6976, fax 514-398-7193, e-mail joan.bartlett@mcgill.ca
World Wide Web http://www.cais-acsi.ca

## Object

To promote the advancement of information science in Canada and encourage and facilitate the exchange of information relating to the use, access, retrieval, organization, management, and dissemination of information.

## Membership

Institutions and individuals interested in information science and involved in the gathering, organization, and dissemination of information (such as information scientists, archivists, librarians, computer scientists, documentalists, economists, educators, journalists, and psychologists) and who support CAIS's objectives can become association members. Dues (Inst.) $165; (Personal) $75; (Senior) $40; (Student) $40.

## Directors

*Pres.* Joan Bartlett, McGill Univ.; *V.P.* Catherine Johnson, Univ. of Western Ontario; *Treas.* Ali Shiri, Univ. of Alberta; *Dir., Communications* Luanne Freund, Univ. of British Columbia; *Dir., Membership* Clément Arsenault, Univ. de Montréal; *Secy.* Kimiz Dalkir, McGill Univ.; *Past Pres.* Gloria Leckie, Univ. of Western Ontario.

## Publication

*Canadian Journal of Information and Library Science. Ed.* Heidi Julien, Univ. of Alberta.

# Canadian Association of Research Libraries
## (Association des Bibliothèques de Recherche du Canada)

Brent Roe, Executive Director
Morisset Hall, 65 University St., Suite 239, University of Ottawa, Ottawa, ON K1N 9A5.
Tel. 613-562-5800, fax 613.562.5297, e-mail carl@uottawa.ca
World Wide Web http://www.carl-abrc.ca

## Membership

The Canadian Association of Research Libraries (CARL) was established in 1976 and consists of 27 university libraries plus Library and Archives Canada, Canada Institute for Scientific and Technical Information (CISTI), and the Library of Parliament. Membership is institutional, and is open primarily to libraries of Canadian universities that have doctoral graduates in both the arts and the sciences.

CARL has three basic goals:

• To provide organized leadership for the Canadian research library community in the development of policies and programs that maintain and improve the cycle of scholarly communication

• To work toward the realization of a national research library resource-sharing network in the areas of collection development, preservation, and access

• To increase the capacity of individual member libraries to provide effective support and encouragement to postgraduate study and research at national, regional, and local levels

Areas of interest to the association include automation, collections inventory projects, copyright, joint purchasing consortia, preservation, and resource sharing. CARL is an affiliate member of the Association of Universities and Colleges of Canada (AUCC), and is incorporated as a nonprofit organization under the Canada Corporations Act.

## Officers

*Pres.* Leslie Weir, Univ. of Ottawa Lib. Network, 65 University St., Ottawa, ON K1N 9A5. E-mail lweir@uottawa.ca; *V.P./Pres.-Elect* Ernie Ingles, 5-07 Cameron Lib., Univ. of Alberta, Edmonton, AB T6G 2J8. E-mail ernie.ingles@ualberta.ca; *Secy.* Margaret Haines, Maxwell MacOdrum Lib., Carleton Univ., 1125 Colonel By Drive, Ottawa, ON K1S 5B6. E-mail margaret_haines@carleton.ca; *Treas.* Lorraine Busby, Queen Elizabeth II Lib., Memorial Univ. of Newfoundland, St. John's, NF A1C 5S7. E-mail librarian@mun.ca; *Dir.* Lucie Gardner, Univ. of Quebec at Montreal, CP 8888 Succ. Centre-ville, Montreal, QC H3C 3P8. E-mail gardner.lucie@uqam.ca; Carol Hixson, Univ. of Regina, Room LY 416.1, 3737 Wascana Pkwy., Regina, SK S4S 0A2. E-mail carol.hixson@uregina.ca.

## Member Institutions

Univ. of Alberta; Univ. of British Columbia; Univ. of Calgary; Carleton Univ.; CISTI (Canada Institute for Scientific and Technical Information); Concordia Univ.; Dalhousie Univ.; Univ. of Guelph; Université Laval; Univ. of Manitoba; Lib. and Archives Canada; Lib. of Parliament; McGill Univ.; McMaster Univ.; Memorial Univ. of Newfoundland; Université de Montréal; Univ. of New Brunswick; Univ. of Ottawa; Université du Québec à Montréal; Queen's Univ.; Univ. of Regina; Univ. of Saskatchewan; Université de Sherbrooke; Simon Fraser Univ.; Univ. of Toronto; Univ. of Victoria; Univ. of Waterloo; Univ. of Western Ontario; Univ. of Windsor; York Univ.

## Publications

For a full list of publications, see http://www.carl-abrc.ca/publications/publications-e.html.

# Canadian Library Association
# (Association Canadienne des Bibliothèques)

Executive Director, Kelly Moore
328 Frank St., Ottawa, ON K2P 0X8
613-232-9625 ext. 306, fax 613-563-9895, e-mail kmoore@cla.ca
World Wide Web http://www.cla.ca

## Object

The Canadian Library Association (CLA) is its members' advocate and public voice, educator, and network. It builds the Canadian library and information community by promoting, developing, and supporting library and information services and advancing today's information professionals, through cooperation with all who share its values. The association represents Canadian librarianship to the federal government and media, carries on international liaison with other library associations and cultural agencies, offers professional development programs, and supports such core library values as intellectual freedom and access to information, particularly for disadvantaged populations. Founded in 1946, CLA is a nonprofit voluntary organization governed by an elected executive council.

## Membership

Memb. (Indiv.) 1,900; (Inst.) 500. Open to individuals, institutions, and groups interested in librarianship and in library and information services.

## Officers

*Pres.* Ken Roberts, Hamilton Public Lib.; *V.P./Pres.-Elect* John Teskey, University of New Brunswick; *Treas.* Theresa Tomchyshyn, Department of National Defense Communications Security Establishment.

## Publications

*Feliciter: Linking Canada's Information Professionals* (6 a year; magazine/journal).
*CLA Digest* (bi-weekly; electronic newsletter).

## Divisions

Canadian Association for School Libraries (CASL).
Canadian Association of College and University Libraries (CACUL).
Canadian Association of Public Libraries (CAPL).
Canadian Association of Special Libraries and Information Services (CASLIS).
Canadian Library Trustees Association (CLTA).

# Catholic Library Association

Executive Director, Jean R. Bostley, SSJ
100 North St., Suite 224, Pittsfield, MA 01201-5109
413-443-2252, fax 413-442-2252, e-mail cla@cathla.org
World Wide Web http://www.cathla.org

## Object

The promotion and encouragement of Catholic literature and library work through cooperation, publications, education, and information. Founded 1921.

## Membership

Memb. 1,000. Dues $45–$500. Year. July–June.

## Officers (2007–2009)

*Pres.* Nancy K. Schmidtmann, 174 Theodore Drive, Coram, NY 11727; *V.P./Pres.-Elect* Malachy R. McCarthy, Claretian Missionaries Archives, 205 W. Monroe St., Chicago, IL 60606; *Past Pres.* Catherine M. Fennell, Gertrude Kistler Memorial Lib., Rosemont College, 1400 Montgomery Ave., Rosemont, PA 19010.

Address correspondence to the executive director.

## Executive Board

Officers; Sara B. Baron, Regent Univ. Lib., 1000 Regent University Drive, Virginia Beach, VA 23464; Jean Elvekrog, 401 Doral Court, Waunakee, WI 53597; Cait C. Kokolus, St. Charles Borromeo Seminary, 100 E. Wynnewood Rd., Wynnewood, PA 19096; Frances O'Dell, OSF, Barry Univ. Lib., 11300 N.E. 2 Ave., Miami Shores, FL 33161; Annette B. Thibodeaux, Archbishop Chapelle H.S., 8800 Veterans Blvd., Metairie, LA 70003.

## Publications

*Catholic Library World* (q.; memb.; nonmemb. $60). *General Ed.* Mary E. Gallagher, SSJ.

*Catholic Periodical and Literature Index* (*CLPI*) (q.; $400 calendar year; abridged ed., $125 calendar year; *CPLI* online, inquire). *Ed.* Deborah A. Winarski.

# Center for the Study of Rural Librarianship

Dept. of Lib. Science, Clarion Univ. of Pennsylvania, 840 Wood St., Clarion, PA 16214.
Tel. 814-393-2014, fax 814-393-2150, e-mail vavrek@clarion.edu or csrl@clarion.edu
World Wide Web http://jupiter.clarion.edu/~csrl/csrlhom.htm

## Object

The Center for the Study of Rural Librarianship (CSRL) is a research, publishing, consultative, and continuing education facility established in the Department of Library Science at Clarion University of Pennsylvania in 1978. Its mission is to extend knowledge relative to the nature and role of rural and small libraries worldwide, whose defining characteristics are a limited budget and a diverse clientele. CSRL is concerned with the development and use of information technology in rural communities, and its recent endeavors include library outreach and, particularly, bookmobile services in the United States and overseas.

Its objectives are

- To stimulate imaginative thinking relative to rural library services
- To identify problems endemic with library services—for those currently being served and those who are not yet served
- To provide consultative services in designing new service patterns in rural libraries
- To conduct and/or coordinate research relative to identifiable library problems
- To stimulate continuing education
- To coordinate physical and human resources which could be lent to analyze library services
- To collect data relevant to the needs of rural libraries

Two professional associations are affiliated with CSRL: the Association for Rural and Small Libraries and the Association of Bookmobile and Outreach Services.

The Association for Rural and Small Libraries (ARSL) (http://www.webjunction.org/arsl) includes members among public, school, small urban branch, special, corporate, and small academic libraries. The association's mission is to provide a network of people and materials to support rural and small library staff, volunteers, and trustees to integrate the library thoroughly with the life and work of the community it serves.

The Association of Bookmobile and Outreach Services (ABOS) (http://www.abos-outreach.org) encompasses libraries of all types. The association's mission is to support and encourage government officials, library administrators, trustees, and staff in the provision of quality bookmobile and outreach services to meet diverse community information and programming needs.

Membership in ARSL and ABOS and attendance at their annual conferences are open to all individuals and institutions seeking to champion rural libraries and outreach services. Both associations are supported by CSRL in cooperation with the H. W. Wilson Foundation.

## Publications

CSRL has published the journal *Rural Libraries* since 1980 and the journal *Bookmobile and Outreach Services* since 1998. Both are printed twice a year, with annual subscription rates of $20 for domestic and $30 for international subscribers. Back copies are available at $10 each, and selected full-text articles are available at http://www.clarion.edu/rural. CSRL also publishes a variety of monographs, bibliographies, and other resources.

CSRL maintains listservs for ARSL and ABOS to provide forums for discussion, sharing of best practices and success stories, relevant library news, and professional networking.

# Chief Officers of State Library Agencies

Director, Tracy Tucker
201 E. Main St., Suite 1405, Lexington, KY 40507
859-514-9151, fax 859-514-1966, e-mail ttucker@amrms.com
World Wide Web http://www.cosla.org

## Object

The purpose of the Chief Officers of State Library Agencies (COSLA) is to identify and address issues of common concern and national interest, to further state library agency relationships with federal government and national organizations, and to initiate cooperative action for the improvement of library services to the people of the United States. It provides a continuing mechanism for dealing with the problems and challenges faced by the heads of the state agencies that are responsible for statewide library development.

## Membership

COSLA is an independent organization of the chief officers of state and territorial agencies designated as the state library administrative agency and responsible for statewide library development. Its membership consists solely of these top library officers of the states and territories, variously designated as state librarian, director, commissioner, or executive secretary.

## Officers (2008–2010)

*Pres.* Susan McVey, Dir., Dept. of Libs., 200 N.E. 18 St., Oklahoma City, OK 73105-3298. Tel. 405-521-2502, fax 405-525-7804, e-mail smcvey@oltn.odl.state.ok.us; *V.P./Pres.-Elect* Lamar Veatch, State Libn., Georgia Public Lib. Service, 1800 Century Place, Suite 150, Atlanta, GA 30345-4304. Tel. 404-235-7200, fax 404-235-7201, e-mail lveatch@georgialibraries.org; *Secy.* Donna Jones Morris, Dir./State Libn., Utah State Lib., 250 N. 1950 W., Suite A, Salt Lake City, UT 84116-7901. Tel. 801-715-6777, fax 801-715-6767, e-mail dmorris@utah.gov; *Treas.* Ann Joslin, State Libn., State Lib., 325 W. State St., Boise, ID 83702. Tel. 208-334-2150, ann.joslin@libraries.idaho.gov; *Dirs.* Jan Walsh, State Libn., Washington State Lib. Div., Office of the Secy. of State, 6880 Capitol Blvd., Tumwater, WA 98504-2460. Tel. 360-704-5253, fax 360-586-7575, e-mail jwalsh@secstate.wa.gov; Jeanne Sugg, State Libn. and Archivist, Tennessee State Lib. and Archives, 403 Seventh Ave. N., Nashville, TN 37243-0312. Tel. 615-741-7996, fax 615-532-9293, e-mail jeanne.sugg@state.tn.us.

# Chinese American Librarians Association

Executive Director, Haipeng Li
E-mail haipeng.li@oberlin.edu
World Wide Web http://www.cala-web.org

## Object

To enhance communications among Chinese American librarians as well as between Chinese American librarians and other librarians; to serve as a forum for discussion of mutual problems and professional concerns among Chinese American librarians; to promote Sino-American librarianship and library services; and to provide a vehicle whereby Chinese American librarians can cooperate with other associations and organizations having similar or allied interests.

## Membership

Memb. 1,100+. Open to anyone who is interested in the association's goals and activities. Dues (Regular) $30; (International/Student/Nonsalaried) $15; (Inst.) $100; (Affiliated) $100; (Life) $300.

## Officers

*Pres. (2008–2009)* Sha Li Zhang. E-mail slzhang@uncg.edu; *V.P./Pres.-Elect (2008–2009)* Xudong Jin. E-mail xdjin@owu.edu; *V.P./Pres.-Elect (2009–2010)* Zhijia Shen. E-mail zhijia@u.washington.edu; *Exec. Dir. (2008–2009)* Haipeng Li. E-mail haipeng.li@oberlin.edu; *Treas. (2008–2010)* Shuyong Jiang. E-mail shyjiang@uiuc.edu.

## Publications

*Journal of Library and Information Science* (2 a year; memb.; online).
*Membership Directory* (memb.).
*Newsletter* (2 a year; memb.; online). *Ed.* Shuyong Jiang.
Occasional Paper Series (OPS) (occasional, online). *Ed.* Judy Jeng.

## Committee Chairpersons

Annual Conference, Local Arrangements. Qi Chen, Lisa Zhao.
Annual Conference, Program Planning (2008–2009). Xudong Jin.
Annual Conference, Program Planning (2009–2010). Zhijia Shen.
Awards. Cathy Yang.
Best Book Award. Julia Tung, Miao Jin.
Constitution and Bylaws. Karen Wei.
Finance. Ai-Hua Chen.
International Relations. Lisa Zhao.
Membership. Elaine Dong, Songqian Lu.
Mentorship Program. Wenwen Zhang.
Nominating. Dora Ho.
Public Relations/Fund Raising. Esther Lee, Ai-hua Chen.
Publications. Hong Miao, Mia Bassham.
Sally C. Tseng's Professional Development Grant. Lian Ruan.
Scholarship. Ying Xu.
Web. Bin Zhang, Vincci Kwong.

# Church and Synagogue Library Association

2920 S.W. Dolph Court, Suite 3A, Portland, OR 97219
503-244-6919, 800-542-2752, fax 503-977-3734, e-mail CSLA@worldaccessnet.com
World Wide Web http://www.cslainfo.org

## Object

The Church and Synagogue Library Association (CSLA) provides educational guidance in the establishment and maintenance of congregational libraries.

Its purpose is to act as a unifying core for church and synagogue libraries; to provide the opportunity for a mutual sharing of practices and problems; to inspire and encourage a sense of purpose and mission among church and synagogue librarians; to study and guide the development of church and synagogue librarianship toward recognition as a formal branch of the library profession. Founded 1967.

## Membership

Memb. 1,800. Dues (Inst.) $200; (Affiliated) $100; (Congregational) $60 ($65 foreign); (Indiv.) $40 ($45 foreign).

## Officers (July 2008–July 2009)

*Pres.* J. Theodore Anderson; *Pres.-Elect* Rusty Tryon; *2nd V.P.* Judy Birch; *Treas.* Bill Anderson; *Admin.* Judith Janzen; *Past*

*Pres.* Craig Kubic; *Ed., Congregational Libraries Today* Mark Olson, 1225 Dandridge St., Fredricksburg, VA 22401; *Book Review Ed.* Monica Tenney, 399 Blenheim Rd., Columbus, OH 43214-3219. E-mail motenney@aol.com.

## Executive Board

Officers; committee chairpersons.

## Publications

Bibliographies (1–5; price varies).
*Congregational Libraries Today* (bi-mo.; memb.; nonmemb. $50; Canada $60).
*CSLA Guides* (1–20; price varies).

## Committee Chairpersons

Awards. Jeri Baker.
Conference. Beth French.
Library Services. Esther Beirbaum.
Nominations and Elections. Jane Hope.
Publications. Alice Hamilton, Rod McClendon.

# Coalition for Networked Information

Executive Director, Clifford A. Lynch
21 Dupont Circle, Suite 800, Washington, DC 20036
202-296-5098, fax 202-872-0884, e-mail info@cni.org
World Wide Web http://www.cni.org

## Mission

The Coalition for Networked Information (CNI) is an organization to advance the transformative promise of networked information technology for the advancement of scholarly communication and the enrichment of intellectual productivity.

## Membership

Memb. 224. Membership is institutional. Dues $6,600. Year. July–June.

## Steering Committee

Richard P. West, California State Univ. (*Chair*); Daniel Cohen, George Mason Univ.; Timothy Lance, NYSERNet; Charles B. Lowry, Assn. of Research Libs.; Richard E. Luce, Emory Univ.; Clifford A. Lynch, CNI; Deanna B. Marcum, Lib. of Congress; Diana G. Oblinger, EDUCAUSE; Brian E. C. Schottlaender, Univ. of California, San Diego; George O. Strawn, National Science Foundation; Donald J. Waters, Andrew W. Mellon Foundation.

## Publication

*CNI-Announce* (subscribe by e-mail to cni-announce-subscribe@cni.org).

# Council on Library and Information Resources

1752 N St. N.W., Suite 800, Washington, DC 20036
202-939-4750, fax 202-939-4765
World Wide Web http://www.clir.org

## Object

In 1997 the Council on Library Resources (CLR) and the Commission on Preservation and Access (CPA) merged and became the Council on Library and Information Resources (CLIR). CLIR's mission is to expand access to information, however recorded and preserved, as a public good. CLIR identifies and defines the key emerging issues related to the welfare of libraries and the constituencies they serve, convenes the leaders who can influence change, and promotes collaboration among the institutions and organizations that can achieve change. The council's interests embrace the entire range of information resources and services from traditional library and archival materials to emerging digital formats. It assumes a particular interest in helping institutions cope with the accelerating pace of change associated with the transition into the digital environment.

CLIR is an independent, nonprofit organization. While maintaining appropriate collaboration and liaison with other institutions and organizations, the council operates independently of any particular institutional or vested interests. Through the composition of its board, it brings the broadest possible perspective to bear upon defining and establishing the priority of the issues with which it is concerned.

## Board

CLIR's Board of Directors currently has 15 members.

## Officers

*Chair* Paula T. Kaufman; *Pres.* Charles Henry. E-mail chenry@clir.org; *Treas.* Herman Pabbruwe.

Address correspondence to headquarters.

## Publications

*Annual Report.*
*CLIR Issues* (bi-mo.).
Technical reports.

# Council on Library/Media Technicians

Executive Director, Margaret Barron
PMB 168, 28262 Chardon Rd., Willoughby Hills, OH 44092
216-261-0776, e-mail margaretrbarron@aol.com
World Wide Web http://colt.ucr.edu

The Council on Library/Media Technicians (COLT), an affiliate of the American Library Association, is an international organization that works to address the issues and concerns of library and media support staff personnel.

Since 1967 COLT has addressed issues covering such areas as technical education, continuing education, certification, job description uniformity, and the more elusive goals of gaining recognition and respect for the professional work that its members do.

## Objectives

COLT's objectives are

- To function as a clearinghouse for information relating to library support staff personnel
- To advance the status, employment, and certification of library staff
- To promote effective communication and cooperation with other organizations whose purposes and objectives are similar to those of COLT

COLT's Web site, http://colt.ucr.edu, provides information on library technician programs, a speaker exchange listing for help in organizing workshops and conferences, bibliographies on needed resources, and jobline resource links.

COLT holds an annual conference, generally immediately preceding the American Library Association Annual Conference.

## Membership

Membership is open to all library employees. Dues (Inst.) $70 ($95 foreign); (Indiv.) $45 ($70 foreign); (Student) $35. Year Jan.–Dec.

## Officers

*Pres.* Jackie Hite. E-mail jmhite0@dia.mil; *V.P./Pres.-Elect.* Chris Egan. E-mail egan@rand.org; *Secy.* Robin Martindill. E-mail rmartind@sdccd.edu; *Treas.* Stan Cieplinski. E-mail stan.cieplinski@domail.maricopa.edu; *Past Pres.* Jackie Lakatos. E-mail jlakatos@lemontlibrary.org; *Exec. Dir.* Margaret Barron, PMB 168, 28262 Chardon Rd., Willoughby Hills, OH 44092.

# Federal Library and Information Center Committee

Executive Director, Roberta I. Shaffer
Library of Congress, Washington, DC 20540-4935
202-707-4800
World Wide Web http://www.loc.gov/flicc

## Object

The Federal Library and Information Center Committee (FLICC) makes recommendations on federal library and information policies, programs, and procedures to federal agencies and to others concerned with libraries and information centers. The committee coordinates cooperative activities and services among federal libraries and information centers and serves as a forum to consider issues and policies that affect federal libraries and information centers, needs and priorities in providing information services to the government and to the nation at large, and efficient and cost-effective use of federal library and information resources and services. Furthermore, the committee promotes improved access to information, continued development and use of the Federal Library and Information Network (FEDLINK), research and development in the application of new technologies to federal libraries and information centers, improvements in the management of federal libraries and information centers, and relevant education opportunities. Founded 1965.

## Membership

Libn. of Congress, Dir. of the National Agricultural Lib., Dir. of the National Lib. of Medicine, Dir. of the National Lib. of Educ., representatives of each of the cabinet-level executive departments, and representatives of each of the following agencies: National Aeronautics and Space Admin., National Sci-ence Foundation, Smithsonian Institution, U.S. Supreme Court, National Archives and Records Admin., Admin. Offices of the U.S. Courts, Defense Technical Info. Center, Government Printing Office, National Technical Info. Service (Dept. of Commerce), Office of Scientific and Technical Info. (Dept. of Energy), Exec. Office of the President, Dept. of the Army, Dept. of the Navy, Dept. of the Air Force, and chair of the FEDLINK Advisory Council. Fifteen additional voting member agencies are selected on a rotating basis by the voting members of FEDLINK. These rotating members serve three-year terms. One representative of each of the following agencies is invited as an observer to committee meetings: Government Accountability Office, General Services Admin., Joint Committee on Printing, Office of Mgt. and Budget, Office of Personnel Mgt., and U.S. Copyright Office.

## Officers

*Chair* James H. Billington, Libn. of Congress; *Chair* Deanna Marcum, Assoc. Libn. for Lib. Services, Lib. of Congress; *Co-Chair* Kathryn Mendenhall; *V. Chair* Elaine Cline; *Exec. Dir.* Roberta I. Shaffer.

Address correspondence to the executive director.

## Publication

*FEDLINK Technical Notes* (every other month).

# Federal Publishers Committee

Chair, John Ward
International Trade Administration, Washington, DC 20230
202-482-5489, fax 202-482-5819, e-mail john.ward@mail.doc.gov

## Object

To foster and promote effective management of data development and dissemination in the federal government through exchange of information, and to act as a focal point for federal agency publishing.

agencies, and corporations, as well as independent organizations concerned with federal government publishing and dissemination. Some key federal government organizations represented are the Joint Committee on Printing, Government Printing Office, National Technical Info. Service, and the Lib. of Congress.

## Membership

Memb. 500. Membership is available to persons involved in publishing and dissemination in federal government departments,

## Publication

*Guide to Federal Publishing* (occasional).

# Medical Library Association

Executive Director, Carla Funk
65 E. Wacker Place, Suite 1900, Chicago, IL 60601-7298
312-419-9094, fax 312-419-8950, e-mail info@mlahq.org
World Wide Web http://www.mlanet.org

## Object

The Medical Library Association (MLA) is a nonprofit educational organization composed of health sciences information professionals and organized exclusively for scientific and educational purposes. It is dedicated to the support of health sciences research, education, and patient care. MLA fosters excellence in the professional achievement and leadership of health sciences library and information professionals to enhance the quality of health care, education, and research.

## Membership

Memb. (Inst.) 850+; (Indiv.) 3,600+, in 43 countries. Institutional members are medical

and allied scientific libraries. Individual members are people who are (or were at the time membership was established) engaged in professional library or bibliographic work in medical and allied scientific libraries or people who are interested in medical or allied scientific libraries. Members can be affiliated with one or more of MLA's more than 20 special-interest sections and its regional chapters.

## Officers

*Pres.* Mary L. Ryan. E-mail president@ mlahq.org; *Pres-Elect* Connie Schardt. E-mail schar005@mc.duke.edu; *Past Pres.* Mark E. Funk. E-mail mefunk@mail.med. cornell.edu.

## Directors

Jane Blumenthal (2011), Judy Burnham (2011), Gary A. Freiberger (2010), Julia Kochi (2011), Beverly Murphy (2011), T. Scott Plutchak (2009), Paula Raimondo (2010), Laurie L. Thompson (2010), Linda Walton (2009).

## Publications

*Journal of the Medical Library Association* (q.; $163).

*MLA News* (10 a year; $58).

Miscellaneous (request current list from association headquarters).

# Music Library Association

8551 Research Way, Suite 180, Middleton, WI 53562
608-836-5825, e-mail mla@areditions.com
World Wide Web http://www.musiclibraryassoc.org

## Object

To promote the establishment, growth, and use of music libraries; to encourage the collection of music and musical literature in libraries; to further studies in musical bibliography; to increase efficiency in music library service and administration; and to promote the profession of music librarianship. Founded 1931.

## Membership

Memb. 1,274. Dues (Inst.) $125; (Indiv.) $90; (Retired or Associate) $60; (Paraprofessional) $45; (Student) $35. Year. July 1–June 30.

## Officers

*Pres.* Ruthann B. McTyre, 2000 Voxman Music Bldg., Univ. of Iowa, Iowa City 52242-1795. Tel. 319-335-3088, fax 319-335-2637; ruthann-mctyre@uiowa.edu; *Rec.*

*Secy.* Karen Little. E-mail klittle@louisville.edu; *Treas./Exec. Secy.* Brad Short. E-mail short@wustl.edu; *Past Pres.* Philip R. Vandermeer, Music Lib., Wilson Lib. CB3906, Univ. of North Carolina at Chapel Hill, Chapel Hill 27514. Tel. 919-966-1113, fax 919-843-0418, e-mail vanderme@email.unc.edu.

## Members-at-Large

Members-at-Large (2008–2010) Paul Cary, Lois Kuyper-Rushing, Nancy Lorimer; (2009–2011) Linda Fairtile, Steve Mantz, Jenn Riley.

## Publications

MLA Index and Bibliography Series (irreg.; price varies).
*MLA Newsletter* (q.; memb.).
MLA Technical Reports (irreg.; price varies).
*Music Cataloging Bulletin* (mo.; $25).
*Notes* (q.; indiv. $85; inst. $100).

# National Association of Government Archives and Records Administrators

90 State St., Suite 1009, Albany, NY 12207
518-463-8644, fax 518-463-8656, e-mail nagara@caphill.com
World Wide Web http://www.nagara.org

## Object

Founded in 1984, NAGARA is a growing nationwide association of local, state, and federal archivists and records administrators, and others interested in improved care and management of government records. NAGARA promotes public awareness of government records and archives management programs, encourages interchange of information among government archives and records management agencies, develops and implements professional standards of government records and archival administration, and encourages study and research into records management problems and issues.

## Membership

Most NAGARA members are federal, state, and local archival and records management agencies.

## Officers

*Pres.* Tracey Berezansky, Alabama Dept. of Archives and History, P.O. Box 300100, Montgomery, AL 36130-0100. Tel. 334-353-4604, fax 334-353-4321, e-mail tracey. berezansky@archiveds.alabama.gov; *V.P.* Paul R. Bergeron, City Clerk, 229 Main St., Nashua, NH 03060. Tel. 603-589-3010, fax 603-589-3029, e-mail BergeronP@nashuanh. gov; *Secy.* Caryn Wojcik, Michigan Histori-cal Center, 3405 N. Martin Luther King, Jr. Blvd., Lansing, MI 48909. Tel. 517-335-8222, fax 517-335-9418, e-mail wojcikc@ michigan.gov; *Treas.* John Stewart, National Archives and Records Admin., Great Lakes Region, 7358 S. Pulaski Rd., Chicago, IL 60629-5898. Tel. 773-581-7816, fax 312-886-7883, e-mail john.stewart@nara.gov; *Past Pres.* Mary Beth Herkert, Archives Div., Offices of the Secy. of State, 800 Summer St. N.E., Salem, OR 97310. Tel. 503-373-0701, fax 503-373-0953, e-mail mary.e.herkert@ state.or.us.

## Directors

Jelain Chubb, Missouri State Archives; Bonnie Curtin, Federal Trade Commission; Ken Feith, Metro Archives; Nancy Fortna, National Archives and Records Admin., Washington, D.C.; Sandy Hart, McKinney, Texas; Sandra Jaramillo, New Mexico State Records Center and Archives; Kay Lanning Minchew, Troup County (Georgia) Archives.

## Publications

*Clearinghouse* (q.; memb.).
*Crossroads* (q.; memb.).
Government Records Issues (series).
*Preservation Needs in State Archives.*
*Program Reporting Guidelines for Government Records Programs.*

# National Church Library Association

Executive Director, Susan Benish
275 S. 3 St., Suite 101A, Stillwater, MN 55082
651-430-0770, e-mail info@churchlibraries.org
World Wide Web http://www.churchlibraries.org

## Object

The National Church Library Association (NCLA, formerly the Lutheran Church Library Association) is a nonprofit organization that serves the unique needs of congregational libraries and those who manage them. NCLA provides inspiration, solutions, and support to church librarians in the form of printed manuals and guidelines, booklists, the quarterly journal *Libraries ALIVE*, national conferences, a mentoring program, online support, and personal advice. Regional chapters operate throughout the United States.

## Membership

Memb. $55. Year. Jan.–Jan.

## Officers

*Pres.* Charles Mann; *V.P.* Phyllis Wendorf;
*Secy.* Chris Magnusson; *Treas.* to be announced; *Past Pres.* Karen Gieseke.

Address correspondence to the executive director.

## Directors

Kathleen Bowman, Deanna Gordon, Darlene Kalfahs, Carol Spaulding, Melissa Taylor, Diane Volzer.

## Publication

*Libraries ALIVE* (q.; memb.).

## Committee Chairpersons

Advisory. Marlys Johnson.
Librarian Resources. Deanna Gordon, Doreen Knudson.

# National Federation of Advanced Information Services

Executive Director, Bonnie Lawlor
1518 Walnut St., Suite 1004, Philadelphia, PA 19102
215-893-1561, fax 215-893-1564, e-mail nfais@nfais.org
World Wide Web http://www.nfais.org

## Object

The National Federation of Advanced Information Services (NFAIS) is an international nonprofit membership organization composed of leading information providers. Its membership includes government agencies, nonprofit scholarly societies, and private sector businesses. NFAIS is committed to promoting the value of authoritative content. It serves all groups that create, aggregate, organize, or facilitate access to such information. In order to improve members' capabilities and to contribute to their ongoing success, NFAIS provides opportunities for education, advocacy, and a forum in which to address common interests. Founded 1958.

## Membership

Memb. 60. Full members are organizations whose main focus is any of the following activities: information creation, organization, aggregation, dissemination, access, or retrieval. Organizations are eligible for associate member status if they do not meet the qualifications for full membership.

## Officers (2008–2009)

*Pres.* David Brown; *Pres.-Elect* Terry Ford; *Secy.* Judith Russell; *Treas.* Barbara Dobbs Mackenzie; *Past Pres.* Kevin Bouley.

## Directors

David Gillikin, Ellen Herbst, Keith MacGregor, Janice Mears, Lucian Parziale, Rafael Sidi, Marisa Westcott.

## Staff

*Exec. Dir.* Bonnie Lawlor. E-mail blawlor@nfais.org; *Dir., Planning and Communications* Jill O'Neill. E-mail jilloneill@nfais.org; *Customer Service* Margaret Manson. E-mail mmanson@nfais.org.

## Publications

For a detailed list of NFAIS publications, see the NFAIS Web site.

# National Information Standards Organization

Managing Director, Todd Carpenter
1 N. Charles Ave., Suite 1905, Baltimore, MD 21201
301-654-2512, fax 410-685-5278, e-mail nisohq@niso.org
World Wide Web http://www.niso.org

## Object

NISO, the National Information Standards Organization, a nonprofit association accredited by the American National Standards Institute (ANSI), identifies, develops, maintains, and publishes technical standards to manage information in our changing and ever-more-digital environment. NISO standards apply both traditional and new technologies to the full range of information-related needs, including discovery, retrieval, repurposing, storage, metadata, business information, and preservation.

Experts from the information industry, libraries, systems vendors, and publishing participate in the development of NISO standards. The standards are approved by the consensus body of NISO's voting membership, which consists of nearly 80 voting members representing libraries, publishers, vendors, government, associations, and private businesses and organizations. In addition, approximately 25 libraries are NISO Library Standards Alliance members. NISO is supported by its membership and corporate grants. NISO is a nonprofit educational organization. NISO is accredited by ANSI and serves as the U.S. Technical Advisory Group to ISO/TC 46 Information and Documentation.

## Membership

Memb. Approx. 80. Open to any organization, association, government agency, or company willing to participate in and having substantial concern for the development of NISO standards. Libraries support NISO as members of the Library Standards Alliance.

## Officers

*Chair* James Neal, 517 Butler Lib., Columbia Univ., 535 W. 114 St., New York, NY 10027. Tel. 212-854-2247, fax 212-854-4972, e-mail jneal@columbia.edu; *V. Chair/Chair-Elect* to be announced; *Immediate Past Chair* Carl Grant, CARE Affiliates, 4445 Pearman Rd., Blacksburg, VA 24060. Tel. 540-529-7885, fax 540-557-1210, e-mail carl@care-affiliates. com; *Treas.* Winston Tabb, Milton S. Eisenhower Lib., Johns Hopkins Univ., 3400 N. Charles St., Baltimore, MD 21218. Tel. 410-516-8328, fax 410-516-5080, e-mail wtabb@jhu.edu.

## Directors

Nancy Davenport, Lorcan Dempsey, John Erickson, John Harwood, Michael Jensen, Chuck Koscher, Oliver Pesch, Bruce Rosenblum.

## Publications

*Information Standards Quarterly* ($120/year, foreign $150, back issues $40/each).
*NISO Newsline* (free monthly e-letter released on the first Wednesday of each month. See the NISO Web site for details on subscribing and archived issues).

For other NISO publications, see the article "National Information Standards Organization (NISO) Standards" later in Part 6.

NISO published standards are available free of charge as downloadable pdf files from the NISO Web site (http://www.niso.org). Standards in hard copy are available for sale on the Web site. The *NISO Annual Report* is available on request.

# Patent and Trademark Depository Library Association

World Wide Web http://www.ptdla.org

## Object

The Patent and Trademark Depository Library Association (PTDLA) provides a support structure for the 84 patent and trademark depository libraries (PTDLs) affiliated with the U.S. Patent and Trademark Office (USPTO). The association's mission is to discover the interests, needs, opinions, and goals of the PTDLs and to advise USPTO in these matters for the benefit of PTDLs and their users, and to assist USPTO in planning and implementing appropriate services. Founded in 1983 as the Patent Depository Library Advisory Council; name changed to Patent and Trademark Depository Library Association in 1988; became an American Library Association affiliate in 1996.

## Membership

Open to any person employed in a patent and trademark depository library whose responsibilities include the patent collection. Affiliate membership is also available. Dues $25.

## Officers (2008–2009)

*Pres.* Karon King. E-mail karon.king@lib. state.ia.us; *V.P./Pres-Elect* Andrew Wohrley. E-mail wohrlaj@auburn.edu; *Secy.* Marian Armour Gemmen. E-mail marmour@wvu. edu; *Treas.* Jim Miller. E-mail jmiller2@umd.edu; *Past Pres.* Leena Lalwani. E-mail llalwani@umich.edu.

## Regional Representatives

Region 1, Martin Wallace. E-mail martin. wallace@umit.maine.edu; Region 2, Connie Wu. E-mail conniewu@rci.rutgers.edu; Region 3, Marian Armour Gemmen. E-mail marmour@wvu.edu; Region 4, Jan Comfort. E-mail comforj@clemson.edu; Region 5, Robert Klein. E-mail patents@mdpls.org; Region 6, Esther Crawford. E-mail crawford @rice.edu; Region 7, Ran Raider. E-mail ran.raider@wright.edu; Region 8, Nancy Spitzer; Region 9, Michael Strickland. E-mail mstrickland@asl.lib.ar.us; Region 10,

Walt Johnson. E-mail wjohnson@mplib.org; Region 11, Patrick Ragains. E-mail ragains@ unr.edu; Region 12, Marjory Cameron. E-mail mcameron@ci.sunnyvale.ca.us.

## Publications

*PTDLA Newsletter. Ed.* Suzanne Holcombe. E-mail suzanne.holcombe@okstate.edu.
*Intellectual Property (IP), Journal of the PTDLA.* Electronic at http://www.ptdla. org/ipjournal.html. *Co-Eds.* Michael White, Claudine Jenda, Andrew Wohrley.

# REFORMA (National Association to Promote Library and Information Services to Latinos and the Spanish-Speaking)

President, Luis Chaparro
National Office Manager, Sandra Rios Balderrama
P.O. Box 4386, Fresno, CA 93744
Tel. 480-734-4460, e-mail reformaoffice@riosbalderrama.com
World Wide Web http://www.reforma.org

## Object

Promoting library services to the Spanish-speaking for nearly 40 years, REFORMA, an affiliate of the American Library Association, works in a number of areas to promote the development of library collections to include Spanish-language and Latino-oriented materials; the recruitment of more bilingual and bicultural professionals and support staff; the development of library services and programs that meet the needs of the Latino community; the establishment of a national network among individuals who share its goals; the education of the U.S. Latino population in regard to the availability and types of library services; and lobbying efforts to preserve existing library resource centers serving the interest of Latinos.

## Membership

Memb. 800+. Any person who is supportive of the goals and objectives of REFORMA.

## Officers

*Pres.* Luis Chaparro. El Paso Community College, P.O. Box 20500, El Paso TX 79998. Tel. 915-831-2132, fax 915-831-2886, e-mail lchapa13@epcc.edu; *Pres.-Elect* Loida García Febo, Queens Lib., 89-11 Merrick Blvd., Jamaica, NY 11209. Tel. 718-990-0891, fax 718-297-3404, e-mail loidagarciafebo@ gmail.com; *Secy.* Siobhan Champ-Blackwell; *Treas.* Robin Imperial; *Memb.-at-Large* Toni Anaya; *Past Pres.* Mario A. Ascencio, Corcoran Lib., 500 17th St. N.W., Washington, DC 2006. Tel. 202-478-1543, fax 202-628-7908, e-mail masencio@corcoran.org.

## Committees

Pura Belpré Award. Lucía González.
Children's and Young Adult Services. Lucia González.
Education. Romelia Salinas.
Finance. Mario A. Ascencio.
International Relations. Miguel Garcia Colon.

Legislative. Miguel Garcia Colon.

Membership. Isabel Espinal.

Nominations. Oscar Baeza.

Organizational Development. Yolanda Valentín.

Public Relations. Selina Gómez-Beloz.

Recruitment and Mentoring. Toni Anaya.

Translations. Armando Trejo.

## Publication

*REFORMA Newsletter* (s. ann; memb.).

## Meetings

General membership and board meetings take place at the American Library Association Midwinter Meeting and Annual Conference.

# Society for Scholarly Publishing

Executive Director, Francine Butler
10200 W. 44 Ave., Suite 304, Wheat Ridge, CO 80033
303-422-3914, fax 303-422-8894, e-mail ssp@resourcenter.com
World Wide Web http://www.sspnet.org

## Object

To draw together individuals involved in the process of scholarly publishing. This process requires successful interaction of the many functions performed within the scholarly community. The Society for Scholarly Publishing (SSP) provides the leadership for such interaction by creating opportunities for the exchange of information and opinions among scholars, editors, publishers, librarians, printers, booksellers, and all others engaged in scholarly publishing.

## Membership

Memb. 900. Open to all with an interest in the scholarly publishing process and dissemination of information. Dues (Indiv.) $150; (Libn.) $75; (Early Career) $75; (New Stu-dent) $30; (Supporting) $1,300; (Sustaining) $2,900. Year. Jan. 1–Dec. 31.

## Executive Committee

*Pres.* October Ivins, Ivins eContent Solutions. E-mail october.ivins@mindspring.com; *Pres.-Elect* Ray Fastiggi, Rockefeller Univ. Press. E-mail fastigg@rockefeller.edu; *Past Pres.* Sue Kesner, Copyright Clearance Center. E-mail skesner@copyright.com; *Secy./Treas.* Mady Tissenbaum, Journal of Bone and Joint Surgery. E-mail madyt@jbjs.org.

## Meetings

An annual meeting is held in late May/early June. SSP also conducts several seminars throughout the year and a Top Management Roundtable each fall.

# Society of American Archivists

Executive Director, Nancy Perkin Beaumont
17 N. State St., Suite 1425, Chicago, IL 60602
888-722-7858, 312-606-0722, fax 312-606-0728, e-mail nbeaumont@archivists.org
World Wide Web http://www.archivists.org

## Object

Provides leadership to ensure the identification, preservation, and use of records of historical value. Founded 1936.

## Membership

Memb. 5,035. Dues (Indiv.) $77–$216, graduated according to salary; (Assoc.) $77, domestic; (Student) $44; (Inst.) $247; (Sustaining) $484.

## Officers (2008–2009)

*Pres.* Frank Boles, Clarke Historical Lib., Central Michigan Univ., Park 142, Mt. Pleasant, MI 48859. Tel. 989-774-3352, fax 989-774-2160, e-mail boles1Fj@cmich.edu; *V.P.* Peter Gottlieb, Wisconsin Historical Society, 816 State St., No. 422, Madison, WI 53706-1488. Tel. 608-264-6480, 608-264-6486, e-mail peter.gottlieb@wisconsinhistory.org; *Treas.* Ann Russell, 131 Rollingwood Lane, Concord, MA 01742, e-mail drannrussell@live.com.

## Staff

*Exec. Dir.* Nancy Perkin Beaumont; *Dir., Memb. and Technical Services* Brian P. Doyle; *Publishing Dir.* Teresa Brinati; *Educ. Dir.* Solveig DeSutter; *Dir., Finance and Admin.* Thomas Jurczak.

## Publications

*American Archivist* (q.; individual print edition, $120; print and online, $145; institutional $145 print, $145 online, $170 print and online). *Ed.* Mary Jo Pugh; *Reviews Ed.* Jeannette A. Bastian.

*Archival Outlook* (bi-mo.; memb.). *Ed.* Teresa Brinati.

# Software and Information Industry Association

1090 Vermont Ave. N.W., Washington, DC 20005
Tel. 202-289-7442, fax 202-289-7097
World Wide Web http://www.siia.net

## Membership

Memb. 520 companies. Formed January 1, 1999, through the merger of the Software Publishers Association (SPA) and the Information Industry Association (IIA). Open to companies involved in the creation, distribution, and use of software, information products, services, and technologies. For details on membership and dues, see the SIIA Web site.

## Staff

*Pres.* Kenneth Wasch. E-mail kwasch@siia.net.

## Officers

*Chair* Robert Merry, Congressional Quarterly; *V. Chair* Stuart Udell, Penn Foster; *Secy.*

Kathy Hurley, Pearson; *Treas.* Rom Rabon, Red Hat.

## Board of Directors

Cindy Braddon, McGraw-Hill; Daniel Burton, Salesforce.com; Paul Despins, Houghton Mifflin; Kenneth Glueck, Oracle; Jim Parkinson, Sun Microsystems; Alan Scott, Dow Jones; Joseph Fitzgerald, Symantec; Kathy Hurley, Pearson; Steven Manzo, Reed Elsevier; Bernard McKay, Intuit; Robert Merry, Congressional Quarterly; Randy Marcinko, MEI; Tim Sheehy, IBM; Fred Hawrysh, Thomson; Stuart Udell, Penn Foster; Tom Rabon, Red Hat; Ken Wasch, SIIA.

# SPARC

Executive Director, Heather Joseph
21 Dupont Circle, Suite 800, Washington, DC 20036
202-296-2296, fax 202-872-0884, e-mail sparc@arl.org
World Wide Web http://www.arl.org/sparc

SPARC, the Scholarly Publishing and Academic Resources Coalition, is an international alliance of academic and research libraries working to correct imbalances in the scholarly publishing system. Developed by the Association of Research Libraries, SPARC has become a catalyst for change. Its pragmatic focus is to stimulate the emergence of new scholarly communication models that expand the dissemination of scholarly research and reduce financial pressures on libraries. Action by SPARC in collaboration with stakeholders—including authors, publishers, and libraries—builds on the unprecedented opportunities created by the networked digital environment to advance the conduct of scholarship.

SPARC's role in stimulating change focuses on

- Advocating policy changes that advance the potential of technology to advance scholarly communication and that explicitly recognize that dissemination is an essential, inseparable component of the research process
- Educating stakeholders about the problems facing scholarly communication and the opportunities for change
- Incubating real-world demonstrations of business and publishing models

that advance changes benefiting scholarship and academe

SPARC is a visible advocate for changes in scholarly communication that benefit more than the academic community alone. Founded in 1997, SPARC has expanded to represent more than 800 academic and research libraries in North America, Britain, Europe, and Japan.

## Membership

SPARC membership is open to North American and international academic and research institutions, organizations, and consortia that share an interest in creating a more open and diverse marketplace for scholarly communication. Dues are scaled by membership type and budget. For more information, visit SPARC's Web site at http://www.arl.org/sparc, SPARC Europe at http://www.sparceurope.org, or SPARC Japan at http://www.nii.ac.jp/sparc.

## Publications

*The Right to Research: The Student Guide to Opening Access to Scholarship* (2008), part of a campaign to engage students on the issue of research access.

*Author Rights* (2006), an educational initiative and introduction to the SPARC Author Addendum, a legal form that enables authors of journal articles to modify publishers' copyright transfer agreements and allow authors to keep key rights to their articles.

*Open Access News Blog,* daily updates on the worldwide movement for open access to science and scholarship, written by Peter Suber and cosponsored by SPARC.

*SPARC Open Access Newsletter,* a monthly roundup of developments relating to open access publishing written by Peter Suber.

*SPARC e-news,* SPARC's monthly newsletter featuring SPARC activities, an industry roundup, upcoming workshops and events, and articles relating to developments in scholarly communication.

*Sponsorships for Nonprofit Scholarly and Scientific Journals: A Guide to Defining and Negotiating Successful Sponsorships* (2005), a resource for nonprofit publishers. A more complete list of SPARC publications, including brochures, articles, and guides, is available at http://www.arl.org/sparc.

# Special Libraries Association

Chief Executive Officer, Janice R. Lachance
331 S. Patrick St., Alexandria, VA 22314
703-647-4900, fax 703-647-4901, e-mail sla@sla.org, janice@sla.org
World Wide Web http://www.sla.org

## Mission

To advance the leadership role of the association's members in putting knowledge to work for the benefit of decision-makers in corporations, government, the professions, and society; to shape the destiny of today's information- and knowledge-based society.

## Membership

Memb. 11,000. Dues (Organizational) $650; (Indiv.) $99–$160; (Student/Retired/Salary Less Than $18,000 a year) $35.

## Officers (January 2009–December 2010)

*Pres.* Gloria Zamora. E-mail gzamora@sandia.gov; *Pres.-Elect* Anne Caputo. E-mail acaupto@dowjones.com; *Treas.* Sylvia R. James. E-mail dajames@11daymer.freeserve.co.uk; *Chapter Cabinet Chair* Susan Fifer Canby. E-mail sfiferca@ngs.org; *Chapter Cabinet Chair-Elect* Ruth Wolfish. E-mail r.wolfish@ieee.org; *Div. Cabinet Chair* Tom Rink. E-mail rink@suok.edu; *Div. Chapter*

*Chair-Elect* Ann Sweeney. E-mail ann.sweeney@ec.europa.eu; *Past Pres.* Stephen Abram. E-mail stephen.abram@sirsidynix.com.

## Directors

Officers; Kate L. Arnold, Deb Hunt, Daniel Lee, Tamika McCollough, Nettie Seaberry, Ty Webb.

## Publication

*Information Outlook* (mo.) (memb., nonmemb. $125/yr.)

## Committee Chairpersons

Awards and Honors. Rebecca Vargha.
Conference Planning James Manasco.
Bylaws. Julie Stich.
Cataloging. John Gallwey.
Diversity Leadership Development. Lyle Minter.
Information Ethics. Toni Carbo, Thomas Froelich.

Professional Development. Roberta Brody.
Public Policy. Ann Shea.
Public Relations. Jill Strand.

Research. Eileen Abels.
Scholarship. Doris Helfer.
Technical Standards. Michael Kim.

# Theatre Library Association

c/o New York Public Library for the Performing Arts
40 Lincoln Center Plaza, New York, NY 10023
World Wide Web http://tla.library.unt.edu

## Object

To further the interests of collecting, preserving, and using theater, cinema, and performing arts materials in libraries, museums, and private collections. Founded 1937.

## Membership

Memb. 337. Dues (Indiv.) $20–$40, (Inst.) $40–$50. Year. Jan. 1–Dec. 31.

## Officers

*Pres.* Kenneth Schlesinger, Lehman College, City Univ. of New York; *V.P.* Susan Brady, Yale Univ.; *Exec. Secy.* David Nochimson, New York Public Lib.; *Treas.* Angela Weaver, Univ. of Washington.

## Executive Board

William Boatman, Phyllis Dircks, John Frick, Nancy Friedland, Stephen Johnson, Beth Kerr, Stephen Kuehler, Francesca Marini, Tobin Nellhaus, Karen Nickeson, Ellen Truax, Angela Weaver; *Honorary* Marian Seldes; *Historian* Louis A. Rachow; *Legal Counsel* Georgia Harper; *Past Pres.* Martha S. LoMonaco.

## Publications

*Broadside* (3 a year; memb.). *Ed.* Angela Weaver.
*Performing Arts Resources* (occasional; memb.).
*Membership Directory* (annual; memb.). *Ed.* David Nochimson.

## Committee Chairpersons

Conference Planning. Susan Brady.
Membership. Angela Weaver.
Nominating. Martha S. LoMonaco.
Professional Award. Maryann Chach, Phyllis Dircks, Don B. Wilmeth.
Publications. Robert W. Melton.
Strategic Planning. Susan Brady.
TLA/Freedley Book Awards. Brook Stowe.

# Urban Libraries Council

125 S. Wacker Drive, Suite 1050, Chicago, IL 60606
312-676-0999, fax 312-676-0950, e-mail info@urbanlibraries.org
World Wide Web http://www.urbanlibraries.org

## Object

The object of the Urban Libraries Council (ULC) is to strengthen the public library as an essential part of urban life; to identify and make known the opportunities for urban libraries; to facilitate the exchange of ideas and programs of member libraries and other libraries; to develop programs that enable libraries to act as a focus of community development and to supply the informational needs of the new urban populations; to conduct research and educational programs that will benefit urban libraries and to solicit and accept grants, contributions, and donations essential to their implementation.

ULC's Foresight 2020 initiative, launched in 2008, is teaching libraries how to spot trends and adapt quickly, putting them in a proactive mode regardless of how their environment changes.

## Membership

Membership is open to public libraries serving populations of 100,000 or more located in a Standard Metropolitan Statistical Area and to corporations specializing in library-related materials and services. The organization also offers associate memberships.

## Officers (2008–2009)

*Chair* Patrick A. Losinski, Columbus Metropolitan Lib., 96 S. Grant, Columbus, OH 43215; *V. Chair/Chair-Elect* Raymond Santiago, Miami-Dade Public Lib. System, 101 W. Flagler St., Miami, FL 33130; *Secy./Treas.* Dorothy Ridings, 505 Altagate Rd.,

Louisville, KY 40206; *Past Chair* Charles Higueras, San Francisco Dept. of Public Works, Bureau of Project Mgt., 30 Van Ness, San Francisco, CA 94102.

Officers serve one-year terms, members of the executive board two-year terms. New officers are elected and take office at the summer annual meeting of the council.

## Executive Board

Susan W. Adams. E-mail bereasue@sbcglobal.net; Melinda Cervantes. E-mail melinda.cervantes@lib.sccgov.org; Ginnie Cooper. E-mail ginnie.cooper@dc.gov; Charles Higueras. E-mail chiggy515@gmail.com; John Kretzmann. E-mail j-kretzmann@northwestern.edu; Okeima Lawrence. E-mail olawrence@youthchallengefund.org; Patrick Losinski. E-mail plosinski@columbuslibrary.org; Robert Martin. E-mail rsmartin@tx.rr.com; Dennis B. Martinez. E-mail dmartinez@dennismartinez.com; Clement Alexander Price. E-mail caprice@andromeda.rutgers.edu; Joan Marie Prince. E-mail jrpince@uwm.edu; Dorothy Ridings. E-mail dridings@aol.com; Raymond Santiago. E-mail santiagor@mdpls.org; Rivkah Sass. E-mail rsass@omahapubliclibrary.org; Keith B. Simmons. E-mail ksimmons@bassberry.com; John Szabo. E-mail john.szabo@fultoncountyga.gov.

## Key Staff

*Chief Operating Officer* Rick J. Ashton; *V.P. Finance* Angela Goodrich; *V.P. Membership and Communications* Veronda J. Pitchford; *Office Mgr.* Jeanie Ramsey.

# State, Provincial, and Regional Library Associations

The associations in this section are organized under three headings: United States, Canada, and Regional. Both the United States and Canada are represented under Regional associations.

## United States

### Alabama

Memb. 1,200. Term of Office. Apr. 2008–Apr. 2009. Publication. *The Alabama Librarian* (q.).

*Pres.* Engle Kneeland, Auburn Public Lib., 479 E. Thach Ave., Auburn 36839. Tel. 334-501-3196, e-mail eengle@auburnalabama.org; *Pres.-Elect* Eve Dennis Nichols, Homewood Public Lib., 1721 Oxmoor Rd., Homewood 35209. Tel. 205-332-6620, e-mail dnichols@bham.lib.al.us; *Secy.* Tim Dodge, RBD Lib., Auburn Univ., 231 Mell St., Auburn 36849. Tel. 334-844-1729, e-mail dodgeti@auburn.edu; *Treas.* Paul O. Blackmon, Alabama Southern Community College, P.O. Box 2000, Thomasville 36784. Tel. 334-636-9642 ext. 646; *Past Pres.* Theresa C. Trawick, MacArthur Campus, Lurleen B. Wallace Community College, P.O. Drawer 910, Opp 36467. Tel. 334-493-5368, e-mail ttrawick@lbwcc.edu.

Address correspondence to the association, 9154 Eastchase Pkwy., Suite 418, Montgomery 36117. Tel. 334-414-0113, e-mail administrator@allanet.org.

World Wide Web http://allanet.org.

### Alaska

Memb. 450+. Publication. *Newspoke* (q.).

*Pres.* Mary Jo Joiner. E-mail mjoiner@ci.kenai.ak.us; *V.P.–Committees* Susan Mitchell. E-mail afsm1@uaa.alaska.edu; *V.P.–Conference* David Ongley. E-mail david.ongley@tuzzy.org; *Secy.* Joyce McCombs. E-mail deltalibrary@wildak.net; *Treas.* Catherine Powers; *Past Pres.* Jane Fuerstenau. E-mail ifjef@uaa.alaska.edu; *Exec. Officer* Mary Jennings. E-mail maryj@gci.net.

Address correspondence to the secretary, Alaska Lib. Assn., P.O. Box 81084, Fairbanks 99708. Fax 877-863-1401, e-mail akla@akla.org.

World Wide Web http://www.akla.org.

### Arizona

Memb. 1,000. Term of Office. Nov. 2008–Nov. 2009. Publication. *AzLA Newsletter* (mo.).

*Pres.* Denise C. Keller, Pinal County Lib. Dist., P.O. Box 2974, Florence 85232. Tel. 520-866-6457, fax 520-866-6533, e-mail denise.keller@pinalcountyaz.gov; *Pres.-Elect* Cynthia Landrum, Glendale Public Lib., 5959 W. Brown St., Glendale 85302. Tel. 623-930-3566, e-mail clandrum@glendaleaz.com; *Secy.* McKay Wellikson, Central Arizona College, 8470 N. Overfield Rd., Coolidge 85228. Tel. 520-494-5416, e-mail mckay.wellikson@centralaz.edu; *Treas.* Linda Renfro, Blue Ridge Unified School Dist. Tel. 928-368-6119, e-mail lrenfro@brusd.k12.az.us; *Past Pres.* Angela Creel-Erb, Arizona Western College, 2020 S. Ave. 8E, Yuma 85365. Tel. 928-344-7776, e-mail angie.creel-erb@azwestern.edu; *Exec. Dir.* Debbie J. Hanson. Tel. 480-609-3999, e-mail admin@azla.org.

Address correspondence to the executive director, AzLA, 1030 E. Baseline Rd., Suite 105-1025, Tempe 85283.

World Wide Web http://www.azla.org.

### Arkansas

Memb. 600. Term of Office. Jan.–Dec. 2009. Publication. *Arkansas Libraries* (bi-mo.).

*Pres.* Jerrie Townsend, Phillips Community College, 2807 Hwy. 165 S., Box A, Stuttgart 72160. Tel. 870-673-4201 ext. 1818, e-mail jtownsend@pccua.edu; *V.P./Pres.-Elect* Connie Zimmer, Arkansas Tech Univ., 305 W. Q St., Russellville 72801. Tel. 479-

968-0434, e-mail czimmer@atu.edu; *Secy./ Treas.* Jamie Melson, Main Lib., Central Arkansas Lib. System, 100 Rock St., Little Rock 72201. Tel. 501-918-3074, fax 501-376-1830, e-mail jamiem@cals.lib.ar.us; *Past Pres.* Deborah Hall, Arkansas State Lib., 1 Capitol Mall, Little Rock 72201. Tel. 501-682-2845, fax 501-682-1899, e-mail dhall@asl.lib.ar.us; *Exec. Admin.* Barbara Martin, P.O. Box 958, Benton 72018-0958. Tel. 501-860-7585, fax 501-776-9709, e-mail arlib2@sbcglobal.net.

Address correspondence to the executive administrator.

World Wide Web http://www.arlib.org.

## California

Memb. 2,500. Publication. *Clarion* (s. ann.).

*Pres.* Barbara Roberts, Palm Springs Public Lib. Tel. 760-322-8375, e-mail Barbara. Roberts@palmsprings-ca.gov; *V.P./Pres.-Elect* Ken Haycock, San Jose State Univ. Tel. 408-924-2491, e-mail ken.haycock@sjsu.edu; *Treas.* Annette Milliron DeBacker, North Bay Cooperative Lib. System. Tel. 707-544-0142, e-mail annetnbc@sonic.net; *Past Pres.* Monique le Conge, Richmond Public Lib. Tel. 510-620-6555, e-mail monique_leconge @ci.richmond.ca.us; *Interim Exec. Dir.* Claudia Foutz, California Lib. Assn., 717 20th St., Suite 200, Sacramento 95814. Tel. 916-447-8541. e-mail cfoutz@cla-net.org.

Address correspondence to the executive director.

World Wide Web http://www.cla-net.org.

## Colorado

Memb. 1,100. Publication. *Colorado Libraries* (q.). *Co-Eds.* (content) Nina McHale. E-mail nina.mchale@cudenver.edu; (advertising) Melissa Powell. E-mail thelibrarygirl@comcast.net; (peer review) Sandra Macke. E-mail sandra.macke@du.edu.

*Pres.* Jody Howard. Tel. 303-859-1242, e-mail jodyhoward@comcast.net; *V.P./Pres.-Elect* Rochelle Logan. Tel. 303-688-7603, e-mail rlogan@dclibraries.org; *Secy.* Sharon Morris. Tel. 303-866-6946, e-mail morris_s @cde.state.co.us; *Treas.* Shannon Cruthers. Tel. 303-556-6701, e-mail shannon.cruthers @cudenver.edu; *Past Pres.* Martin Garnar.

Tel. 303-964-5459, e-mail mgarnar@regis. edu; *Exec. Dir.* Kathleen Noland, Colorado Assn. of Libs., 12081 W. Alameda Pkwy., No. 427, Lakewood 80228. Tel. 303-463-6400, e-mail kathleen@cal-webs.org.

Address correspondence to the executive director.

World Wide Web http://www.cal-webs.org.

## Connecticut

Memb. 1,000+. Term of Office. July 2008–June 2009. Publication. *Connecticut Libraries* (11 a year). *Ed.* David Kapp, 4 Llynwood Drive, Bolton 06040. Tel. 203-647-0697, e-mail dkapp@aol.com.

*Pres.* Kathy Leeds, Wilton Lib. Assn. Tel. 203-762-7196, fax 203-834-1166, e-mail kathy_leeds@wiltonlibrary.org; *V.P./Pres.-Elect* Randi Ashton-Pritting, Univ. of Hartford, Bloomfield. Tel. 860-768-4268, e-mail pritting@hartford.edu; *Treas.* Alison Wang, Naugatuck Community College, Waterbury. Tel. 203-575-8250, e-mail awang@nvcc. commnet.edu; *Past Pres.* Carl Antonucci, Capital CC, Hartford. Tel. 860-906-5021, e-mail cantonucci@ccc.commnet.edu; *Coord.* Pam Najarian, Connecticut Lib. Assn., P.O. Box 75, Middletown 06457. Tel. 860-346-2444, fax 860-344-9199, e-mail cla@ ctlibrarians.org.

Address correspondence to the coordinator.

World Wide Web http://www.ctlibrary association.org.

## Delaware

Memb. 200+. Term of Office. Apr. 2008–Apr. 2009. Publication. *DLA Bulletin* (online only).

*Pres.* Rebecca C. Knight, Univ. of Delaware Lib., 181 S. College Ave., Newark 19717-5267. Tel. 302-831-1730, fax 302-831-1631, e-mail knight@udel.edu; *V.P.* Peggy Dillner, Educ. Resource Center, Univ. of Delaware, Newark 19716. Tel. 302-831-2335, fax 302-831-8404, e-mail mpd@udel. edu; *Secy.* Sonja Brown, Delaware Div. of Libs., 43 S. DuPont Hwy., Dover 19901. Tel. 302-739-4748 ext. 120, fax 302-739-6787, e-mail sonja.brown@state.de.us; *Treas.* Michael Gutiérrez, Univ. of Delaware Lib., 181 S.

College Ave., Newark 19717-5267. Tel. 302-831-6076, fax 302-831-1631, e-mail mgutierr @udel.edu; *Past Pres.* Lynne Haines, Sussex County Dept. of Libs., P.O. Box 589, Georgetown 19947. Tel. 302-855-7890, fax 302-855-7895, e-mail lynne.haines@lib.de.us.

Address correspondence to the association, Box 816, Dover 19903-0816. E-mail dla@ dla.lib.de.us.

World Wide Web http://www2.lib.udel. edu/dla/index.htm.

## District of Columbia

Memb. 300+. Term of Office. July 2008–June 2009. Publication. *Capital Librarian* (s. ann.).

*Pres.* M-J Oboroceanu. E-mail moboroceanu @crs.loc.gov; *V.P./Pres.-Elect* Angela Fisher Jaffee; *Secy.* Colleen Semitekol; *Treas.* Carol Bursik; *Past Pres.* Barbara Folensbee-Moore.

Address correspondence to the association, Box 14177, Benjamin Franklin Sta., Washington 20044. Tel. 202-872-1112.

World Wide Web http://www.dcla.org.

## Florida

Memb. (Indiv.) 1,400+. Term of Office. April 2008–March 2009. Publications. *Florida Libraries* (s. ann.). *Ed.* Gloria Colvin, 2505 Blarney Drive, Tallahassee 32309. Tel. 850-645-1680, e-mail gpcolvin@yahoo.com; *FLA News Digest* (online). *Ed.* Laura Kirkland, du Pont-Ball Lib., Stetson Univ., 421 N. Woodland Blvd., Unit 8418, DeLand 32720-3757. Tel. 386-822-4027, e-mail lkirklan@stetson.edu.

*Pres.* Mercedes Clement, Daytona Beach Community College, 1200 W. International Speedway Blvd., Daytona Beach 32120. Tel. 386-506-3440, e-mail clemenm@daytona state.edu; *V.P./Pres.-Elect* Wendy Breeden, Lake County Lib. System, 2401 Woodlea Rd., Tavares 32778. Tel. 352-253-6180, e-mail wbreeden@lakeline.lib.fl.us; *Secy.* Barbara Stites, Florida Gulf Coast Univ., 10501 FGCU Blvd. S., Fort Myers 33965-7602. Tel. 239-590-7602, e-mail bstites@fgcu.edu; *Treas.* Alan Kornblau, Delray Beach Public Lib., 100 W. Atlantic Ave., Delray Beach 33444-3662. Tel. 561-266-9488, e-mail alan.kornblau@delraylibrary.org; *Past Pres.*

Charles Parker, Tampa Bay Lib. Consortium, 1201 Tech Blvd., Suite 202, Tampa 33619. Tel. 813-622-8252, e-mail cparker@tblc.org; *Exec. Dir.* Faye Roberts, P.O. Box 1571, Lake City 32056-1571. Tel. 386-438-5795, e-mail faye.roberts@comcast.net.

Address correspondence to the executive director.

World Wide Web http://www.flalib.org.

## Georgia

Memb. 1,000+. Publication. *Georgia Library Quarterly. Ed.* Susan Cooley, Sara Hightower Regional Lib., 205 Riverside Pkwy., Rome 30161. Tel. 706-236-4609, fax 706-236-4631, e-mail scooley@romelibrary.org.

*Pres.* Jim Cooper, West Georgia Regional Lib., 710 Rome St., Carrollton 30117. Tel. 770-836-6711, e-mail cooperj@wgrl.net; *1st V.P./Pres.-Elect* Carol Stanley, Athens Technical College. Tel. 706-213-2116, e-mail cstanley@athenstech.edu; *2nd V.P.* Bill Richards, Georgia College and State Univ. Tel. 478-445-0977, e-mail bill.richards@ gcsu.edu; *Secy.* Jeff Heck, Reese Lib., Augusta State Univ. Tel. 706-737-1745, e-mail jheck@aug.edu; *Treas.* Ray Calvert, Coastal Georgia Community College Lib. Tel. 912-262-3293, e-mail calverr@cgcc.edu; *Past Pres.* Betty Paulk, Odum Lib., Valdosta State Univ. Tel. 229-333-5870, e-mail bpaulk@ valdosta.edu.

Address correspondence to the president, c/o Georgia Lib. Assn., P.O. Box 793, Rex 30273-0793.

World Wide Web http://gla.georgia libraries.org.

## Hawaii

Memb. 320. Publication. *HLA Newsletter* (3 a year).

*Pres.* Becky Rathgeber, Brigham Young Univ.–Hawaii. Tel. 808-675-3946, e-mail rathgebb@byuh.edu; *V.P.* Sheryl Lynch, Kapolei Public Lib. Tel. 808-693-7050; *Secy.* Loraine Oribio, Tokai Univ. E-mail loribio@ tokai.edu; *Treas.* To be announced; *Past Pres.* Douglas Bates, Brigham Young Univ.–Hawaii. Tel. 808-675-3851, e-mail batesd@ byuh.edu.

Address correspondence to the president.

## Idaho

Memb. 500. Term of Office. Oct. 2008–Oct. 2009.

*Pres.* Susan Tabor-Boesch, Wood River Middle School, 900 N. 2 Ave., Hailey 83333. Tel. 208-578-5030 ext. 2323, e-mail staborboesch@blaineschools.org; *V.P./Pres.-Elect* Bette Ammon, Coeur d'Alene Public Lib., 702 E. Front, Coeur d'Alene 83814. E-mail bammon@cdalibrary.org; *Secy.* Jody Vestal, Boise Public Lib., 715 S. Capitol Blvd., Boise 83702. Tel. 208-562-4034, e-mail jvestal@cityofboise.org; *Treas.* Steve Poppino, College of Southern Idaho, 315 Falls Ave., Twin Falls 83383-1238. Tel. 208-732-6504, fax 208-732-3087, e-mail spoppino@csi.edu; *Past Pres.* Sandra Shropshire, E. M. Oboler Lib., Idaho State Univ., P.O. Box 8089, Pocatello 83209-8089. Tel. 208-282-2671, e-mail shrosand@isu.edu.

Address correspondence to the association, P.O. Box 8533, Moscow 83844.

World Wide Web http://www.idaholibraries.org.

## Illinois

Memb. 3,000. Term of Office. July 2008–July 2009. Publication. *ILA Reporter* (bimo.).

*Pres.* Donna Dziedzic, Naperville Public Lib., 200 W. Jefferson, Naperville 60540. Tel. 630-961-4100 ext. 151, fax 630-637-6149, e-mail ddziedzic@naperville-lib.org; *V.P./Pres.-Elect* Carole A. Medal, Gail Borden Public Lib. Dist., 270 N. Grove Ave., Elgin 60120-5505. Tel. 847-429-4699, fax 847-742-0485, e-mail cmedal@gailborden. info; *Treas.* Jamie Bukovac, Indian Prairie Public Lib., 401 Plainfield Rd., Darien 60561. Tel. 630-887-8760, fax 630-887-1018, e-mail bukovacj@indianprairielibrary. org; *Past Pres.* Bradley F. Baker, Ronald Williams Lib., Northeastern Illinois Univ., 5500 N. St. Louis Ave., Chicago 60625-4625. Tel. 773-442-4470, fax 773-442-4531, e-mail b-baker@neiu.edu; *Exec. Dir.* Robert P. Doyle, 33 W. Grand Ave., Suite 301, Chicago 60654. Tel. 312-644-1896, fax 312-644-1899, e-mail doyle@ila.org.

Address correspondence to the executive director.

World Wide Web http://www.ila.org.

## Indiana

Memb. 3,000+. Term of Office. March 2008–April 2009. Publication. *Indiana Libraries* (s. ann.). *Ed.* Karen Evans, Cunningham Memorial Lib., Indiana State Univ., 650 Sycamore St., Terre Haute 47809. Tel. 812-237-8824, fax 812-237-2567, e-mail kevans4@isugw. indstate.edu.

*Pres.* Cheryl Truesdell, Helmke Lib., Indiana Univ. Purdue Univ.–Fort Wayne, 2101 E. Coliseum Blvd., Fort Wayne 46805. Tel. 260-481-6506, fax 260-481-6509, e-mail truesdel@ipfw.edu; *V.P.* Nancy Dowell, Vigo County Public Lib., 1 Library Sq., Terre Haute 47807. Tel. 812-232-1113, fax 812-235-1439, e-mail ndowell@vigo.lib.in. us; *Secy.* Janet Pfadt, Fox Hill Elementary, 802 Fox Hill Drive, Indianapolis 46228-1476. Tel. 317-259-5371, fax 317-259-5383, e-mail jpfadt@msdwt.k12.in.us; *Treas.* Jim Cline, Porter County Public Lib. System, 103 E. Jefferson St., Valparaiso 46383-4820. Tel. 219-462-0524, fax 219-477-4866, e-mail jcline@pcpls.lib.in.us; *Past Pres.* Carl A. Harvey II, North Elementary, 440 N. 10 St., Noblesville 46060-2099. Tel. 317-773-0482, fax 317-776-6274, e-mail carl_harvey@mail. nobl.k12.in.us; *Exec. Dir.* Linda Kolb. E-mail lkolb@ilfonline.org.

Address correspondence to Indiana Lib. Federation, 941 E. 86 St., Suite 260, Indianapolis 46240. Tel. 317-257-2040, fax 317-257-1389, e-mail ilf@indy.net.

World Wide Web http://www.ilfonline.org.

## Iowa

Memb. 1,700. Term of Office. Jan.–Dec. Publication. *The Catalyst* (bi-mo.). *Ed.* Laurie Hews.

*Pres.* Ellen Neuhaus, Rod Lib., Univ. of Northern Iowa, 1227 W. 27 St., Cedar Falls 50613. Tel. 319-273-3739, fax 319-273-2913, e-mail ellen.neuhaus@uni.edu; *V.P./ Pres.-Elect* Dale H. Ross, Ames Public Lib., 515 Douglas Ave., Ames 50010. Tel. 515-233-2998, e-mail dross24704@aol.com;

*Secy.* Marilyn Murphy, Busse Center Lib., Mount Mercy College, 1330 Elmhurst Drive N.E., Cedar Rapids 52402. Tel. 319-363-8213 ext. 1244, fax 319-363-9060, e-mail marilyn@mtmercy.edu; *Past Pres.* Barbara Peterson, Council Bluffs Public Lib., 400 Willow Ave., Council Bluffs 51503. Tel. 712-323-7553, fax 712-323-1269, e-mail bpeterson@cbpl.lib.ia.us; *Exec. Dir.* Laurie Hews. Tel. 515-273-5322, fax 515-309-4576, e-mail lhews@mcleodusa.net.

Address correspondence to the association, 3636 Westown Pkwy., Suite 202, West Des Moines 50266.

World Wide Web http://www.iowalibrary association.org.

### Kansas

Memb. 1,500. Term of Office. July 2008–June 2009. Publication. *KLA Connects* (q.). *Ed.* Royce Kitts. E-mail roycekitts@gmail.com.

*Pres.* Laura Loveless, West Wyandotte Branch, Kansas City Public Lib., 1737 N. 82, Kansas City 66112. Tel. 913-596-5800, fax 913-596-5809, e-mail llove@kckpl.lib.ks.us; *1st V.P.* Denise Smith, Stanton County Lib., 103 E. Sherman, P.O. Box 480, Johnson City 67855. Tel. 620-492-2302, fax 620-492-2203, e-mail dolliesmith@hotmail.com; *2nd V.P.* Emily Sitz, Southwest Kansas Lib. System, 100 Military Ave., Suite 210, Dodge City 67801. Tel. 620-225-1231, e-mail esitz@swkls.org; *Secy.* Joyce Armstrong, Hamilton County Lib., 102 W. Ave. C, P.O. Box 1307, Syracuse 67878. Tel. 620-384-5622, fax 620-384-5623, e-mail hamcolib@yahoo.com; *Treas.* Marie Pyko, Topeka and Shawnee County Public Lib., 1515 S.W. 10, Topeka 66604. Tel. 785-580-4481, fax 785-580-4496, e-mail mpyko@tscpl.org; *Past Pres.* Cynthia Akers, William Allen White Lib., Emporia State Univ., 1200 Commercial Campus, Box 4051, Emporia 66801. Tel. 620-341-5480, fax 620-341-5997, e-mail cakers@emporia.edu; *Exec. Dir.* Rosanne Siemens, Kansas Lib. Assn., 1020 S.W. Washburn, Topeka 66604. Tel. 785-580-4518, fax 785-580-4595, e-mail kansas libraryassociation@yahoo.com.

Address correspondence to the executive director.

World Wide Web http://www.kansas libraryassociation.org.

### Kentucky

Memb. 1,900. Term of Office. Oct. 2008–Oct. 2009. Publication. *Kentucky Libraries* (q.).

*Pres.* Debbe Oberhausen, Crescent Hill Branch, Louisville Free Public Lib., 2762 Frankfort Ave., Louisville 40206. Tel. 502-574-1793, e-mail debra.oberhausen@lfpl.org; *Pres.-Elect* Emmalee Hoover, Dixie Heights H.S., 3010 Dixie Hwy., Edgewood 41017. Tel. 859-341-7650, e-mail emmalee.hoover@ Kenton.kyschools.us; *Secy.* Leoma Dunn, Thomas More College Lib., 333 Thomas More Pkwy., Crestview Hills 41017. Tel. 859-344-3524, e-mail leoma.dunn@ thomasmore.edu; *Past Pres.* Fannie Cox, Ekstrom Lib., Univ. of Louisville, Louisville 40292. Tel. 502-852-2705, e-mail fmcox@ louisville.edu; *Exec. Secy.* Tom Underwood, 1501 Twilight Trail, Frankfort 40601. Tel. 502-223-5322, fax 502-223-4937, e-mail info@kylibasn.org.

Address correspondence to the executive secretary.

World Wide Web http://www.kylibasn.org.

### Louisiana

Memb. 1,100+. Term of Office. July 2008–June 2009. Publication. *Louisiana Libraries* (q.).

*Pres.* Melissa Hymel. Tel. 225-638-7593, fax 318-865-5041, e-mail melrod@cadddo. k12.la.us; *1st V.P./Pres.-Elect* Melanie Sims. Tel. 225-578-8815, fax 225-578-5773, e-mail melanie.sims@law.lsu.edu; *Secy.* Melinda Matthews. Tel. 318-342-1060, fax 318-342-1075, e-mail matthews@ulm.edu; *Past Pres.* Melissa Elrod. Tel. 318-865-7949, fax 318-868-2978, e-mail melrod@addo.k12.la.us.

Address correspondence to Louisiana Lib. Assn., 8550 United Plaza Blvd., Suite 1001, Baton Rouge 70809. Tel. 225.922.4642, fax 225-408-4422, e-mail office@llaonline.org.

World Wide Web http://www.llaonline.org.

## Maine

Memb. 950. Term of Office. (Pres., V.P.) July 2008–July 2009. Publication. *MLA-To-Z* (q., online).

*Pres.* Molly Larson, Rockport Public Lib., P.O. Box 8, Rockport 04856-0008. Tel. 207-236-3642, e-mail mlarson@rockport.lib.me.us; *V.P./Pres.-Elect* Sonja Plummer-Morgan, Mark and Emily Turner Memorial Lib., 39 Second St., Presque Isle 04769. Tel. 207-764-2571; *Secy.* Carrie Rossiter, Camden Public Lib., 55 Main St., Camden 04843. Tel. 207-236-3440; *Treas.* Alisia Wygant, Colby College, 5146 Mayflower Hill, Waterville 04901. Tel. 207-859-5146; *Past Pres.* Rich Boulet, Blue Hill Public Lib., P.O. Box 824, Parker Point Rd., Blue Hill 04614. Tel. 207-374-5515, fax 207-374-5254, e-mail rboulet @bluehill.lib.me.us.

Address correspondence to the association, P.O. Box 634, Augusta 04332-0634. Tel. 207-441-1410.

World Wide Web http://mainelibraries.org.

## Maryland

Memb. 1,100. Term of office. July 2008–July 2009. Publications. *Happenings* (mo.); *The Crab* (q).

*Pres.* Darrell Batson, Frederick County Public Lib. Tel. 301-600-1613, e-mail dbatson@fredco-md.net; *V.P./Pres.-Elect* James Fish, Baltimore County Public Lib. Tel. 410-887-6160, e-mail jfish@bcpl.net; *Past Pres.* Marion Francis, Anne Arundel County Public Lib. Tel. 410-222-7234, e-mail mfrancis@aacpl.net; *Exec. Dir.* Margaret Carty.

Address correspondence to the association, 1401 Hollins St., Baltimore 21223. Tel. 410-947-5090, fax 410-947-5089, e-mail mla@mdlib.org.

World Wide Web http://mdlib.org.

## Massachusetts

Memb. (Indiv.) 1,000; (Inst.) 100. Term of Office. July 2008–June 2009. Publication. *Bay State Libraries* (4 a year).

*Pres.* Richard Callaghan. Tel. 781-275-9440, fax 781-275-3590, e-mail rcallaghan@minlib.net; *Exec. Mgr.* Elizabeth Hacala, Massachusetts Lib. Assn., P.O. Box 535, Bedford 01730. Tel. 781-275-7729, fax 781-998-0393, e-mail mlaoffice@masslib.org.

Address correspondence to the executive manager.

World Wide Web http://www.masslib.org.

## Michigan

Memb. (Indiv.) 2,100+. Term of Office. July 2008–June 2009. Publications. *Michigan Librarian Newsletter* (6 a year), *Michigan Library Association Forum* (s. ann., online).

*Pres.* Kathy Irwin, Univ. of Michigan–Dearborn Lib.; *Pres.-Elect* Larry Neal, Clinton Macomb Public Lib.; *Secy.* Elizabeth Bolinger, Michigan State Univ.; *Treas.* Ed Repik, Howell Carnegie District Lib.; *Past Pres.* Josie Parker, Ann Arbor District Lib.

Address correspondence to Gretchen Couraud, Exec. Dir., Michigan Lib. Assn., 1407 Rensen St., Suite 2, Lansing 48910. Tel. 517-394-2774 ext. 224, e-mail couraudg @mlcnet.org.

World Wide Web http://www.mla.lib.mi.us.

## Minnesota

Memb. 1,100. Term of Office. (Pres., Pres.-Elect) Jan.–Dec. 2009.

*Pres.* Ken Behringer. E-mail ken.behringer @co.dakota.mn.us; *Pres.-Elect* Kathleen James. E-mail kathleen@melsa.org; *Secy.* Lynne Young. E-mail lynne.young@ci. northfield.mn.us; *Treas.* Robin Chaney. E-mail robin@sammie.org; *Past Pres.* Wendy Wendt, Marhall-Lyon County Lib., Marshall 56258. Tel. 507-537-7003, e-mail wendyw@marshalllyonlibrary.org.

Address correspondence to the association, 1619 Dayton Ave., Suite 314, Saint Paul 55104. Tel. 651-641-0982, fax 651-641-3169, e-mail mlaoffice@mnlibraryassociation.org.

World Wide Web http://www.mnlibrary association.org.

## Mississippi

Memb. 650. Term of Office. Jan.–Dec. 2009. Publication. *Mississippi Libraries* (q.).

*Pres.* Jan Willis, Lee-Itawama Lib. System. Tel. 662-841-9029, e-mail jwillis@li. lib.ms.us; *V.P.* Ann Branton, Univ. Libs., Univ. of Southern Mississippi. Tel. 601-266-4350, e-mail ann.branton@usm.edu; *Secy.* Marsha A. Case, Jackson-Hinds Lib. System. Tel. 601-968-5828, e-mail mcase@jhlibrary. com; *Treas.* Amanda Clay Powers, Mitchell Memorial Lib., Mississippi State Univ. Tel. 662-325-7677, e-mail apowers@library. msstate.edu; *Past Pres.* Jeff Slagell, Roberts-LaForge Lib., Delta State Univ. Tel. 662-846-4441, e-mail jslagell@deltastate.edu; *Exec. Secy.* Mary Julia Anderson, P.O. Box 13687, Jackson 39236-3687. Tel. 601-981-4586, fax 601-981-4501, e-mail info@ misslib.org.

Address correspondence to the executive secretary.

World Wide Web http://www.misslib.org.

## Missouri

Memb. 800+. Term of Office. Jan.–Dec. 2009. Publication. *MO INFO* (bi-mo.). *Ed.* Margaret Booker.

*Pres.* Kimberlee Ried, National Archives and Records Admin., 2312 E. Bannister Rd., Kansas City 64131. Tel. 816-268-8072, fax 816-268-8037, e-mail mlaprez09@gmail.com; *Pres.-Elect* Sharon McCaslin, Fontbonne Univ., 275 Union Blvd., Apt. 1409, St. Louis 63108. Tel. 314-889-4567, fax 314-719-8040, e-mail smccaslin@fontbonne.edu; *Secy.* Frances Piesbergen, Thomas Jefferson Lib.–UMSL, 1 University Blvd., St. Louis 63121. Tel. 314-516-5084, fax 314-516-5853, e-mail sfrpies@umsl.edu; *Treas.* Tony Garrett, Thomas Jefferson Lib.–UMSL, 1 University Blvd., St. Louis 63121. Tel. 314-516-7993, fax 314-516-5853, e-mail garrettwa@umsl.edu; *Past Pres.* Karen Hayden, Little Dixie Regional Libs., 111 N. 4 St., Moberly 65270. Tel. 660-263-4426, fax 660-263-4024, e-mail khayden@little-dixie.lib. mo.us; *Exec. Dir.* Margaret Booker, Missouri Lib. Assn., 3212-A LeMone Industrial Blvd.,

Columbia 65201. Tel. 573-449-4627, fax 573-449-4655, e-mail mla001@more.net.

Address correspondence to the executive director.

World Wide Web http://www.molib.org.

## Montana

Memb. 600. Term of Office. July 2008–June 2009. Publication. *Focus* (bi-mo.).

*Pres.* Della Dubbe, Glacier County Lib., 21 First Ave. S.E., Cut Bank 59427. Tel. 406-873-4572, fax 406-873-4845, e-mail glibrary@northerntel.net; *V.P.* Eva English, Fort Belknap College Lib., P.O. Box 159, Harlem 59526-0159. Tel. 406-353-2607 ext. 262, fax 406-353-2898, e-mail evaenglish@ yahoo.com; *Secy./Treas.* Dee Ann Redman, Parmly Billings Lib., 510 N. Broadway, Billings 59101-1196. Tel. 406-657-8258, e-mail redmand@ci.billings.mt.us; *Past Pres.* Honore Bray, Missoula Public Lib., P.O. Box 21, Hall 59837. Tel. 406-258-3860, fax 406-728-5900; *Exec. Dir.* Debra Kramer, Montana Lib. Assn., P.O. Box 1085, Manhattan 59741. Tel. 406-670-8449, e-mail debkmla@ hotmail.com.

Address correspondence to the executive director.

World Wide Web http://www.mtlib.org.

## Nebraska

Term of Office. Jan.–Dec. 2009. Publication. *Nebraska Library Association Quarterly (NLAQ)* (q.).

*Pres.* Pam Bohmfalk, Hastings Public Lib. E-mail pbohmfal@hastings.lib.ne.us; *V.P./ Pres.-Elect* Scott Childers, UNL. E-mail schilder1@unl.edu; *Secy.* Joanne Ferguson Cavanaugh, Omaha Public Lib.; *Treas.* Julie Hector, Lincoln City Libs. E-mail j.hector@ lincolnlibraries.org; *Past Pres.* Lisa Olivigni, Crete Public Lib. E-mail lolivigni@crete-ne.gov; *Exec. Dir.* Kathy Thomsen, 1402 N. Jackson, Lexington 68850. E-mail katet323@ msn.com.

Address correspondence to the executive director.

World Wide Web http://www.nebraska libraries.org.

## Nevada

Memb. 450. Term of Office. Jan.–Dec. 2009. Publication. *Nevada Libraries* (q.).

*Pres.* Jeanette Hammons, Elko County Lib. E-mail jmhammon@clan.lib.nv.us; *V.P./Pres.-Elect* Joan Vaughan, Paseo Verde Lib. E-mail jevaughan@hdpl.org; *Treas.* Linda Pizarro. E-mail pizarrol@lvccld.org; *Past Pres.* Denise Gerdes, Las Vegas–Clark County Lib. Dist. E-mail gerdesd@lvccld.org; *Exec. Secy.* Robbie DeBuff. E-mail rjdebuff @hotmail.com.

Address correspondence to the executive secretary.

World Wide Web http://www.nevada libraries.org.

## New Hampshire

Memb. 700. Publication. *NHLA News* (q.).

*Pres.* Steve Butzel, Portsmouth Public Lib., 175 Parrott Ave., Portsmouth 03801. Tel. 603-766-1711, e-mail skbutzel@lib. cityofportsmouth.com; *V.P./Pres.-Elect* Judith Haskell, Hampton Falls Free Lib., 7 Drinkwater Rd., Hampton Falls 03844-2116. Tel. 603-926-3682, e-mail judyhaskell@ comcast.net; *Secy.* Sue Hoadley, Pelham Public Lib., 24 Village Green, Pelham 03016. Tel. 603-508-3060, e-mail shoadley@ pelhamweb.com; *Treas.* Carl Heidenblad, Nesmith Lib., P.O. Box 60, Windham 03087. Tel. 603-432-7154, e-mail cheidenblad@ library.windham.nh.us; *Past Pres.* Amy Thurber, Canaan Town Lib., 1173 U.S. Rte. 4, P.O. Box 368, Canaan 03714. Tel. 603-523-9650, e-mail athurber@canaanlibrary. org.

Address correspondence to the association, c/o LGC, P.O. Box 617, Concord 03302-0617.

World Wide Web http://webster.state.nh. us/nhla.

## New Jersey

Memb. 1,700. Term of Office. July 2008–June 2009. Publication. *New Jersey Libraries Newsletter* (mo.).

*Pres.* Heidi Lynn Cramer, Newark Public Lib.–Washington St., P.O. Box 630, Newark 07101. Tel. 973-733-7837, fax 973-733-

8539, e-mail hcramer@npl.org; *V.P.* Susan Briant, Haddonfield Public Lib., 60 Haddon Ave., Haddonfield 08033. Tel. 856-429-1304, fax 856-429-3760, e-mail sbriant@ haddonfieldlibrary.org; *2nd V.P.* Jennifer Lang, Firestone Lib., Princeton Univ., 1 Washington Rd., Princeton 08544. Tel. 609-258-5476, fax 609-258-0441, e-mail lang@ princeton.edu; *Secy.* Nancy Weiner, Chang Lib., William Paterson Univ., 300 Pompton Rd., Wayne 07470. Tel. 973-720-2161, e-mail weinern@wpunj.edu; *Treas.* Keith McCoy, Roselle Public Lib., 104 W. 4 Ave., Roselle 07203. Tel. 908-245-5809, fax 908-298-8881, e-mail wkmccoy@lmxac.org; *Past Pres.* Michele Reutty, Oakland Public Lib., 2 Municipal Plaza, Oakland 07436. Tel. 201-337-3742, fax 201-337-0261, e-mail reutty@ bccls.org; *Exec. Dir.* Patricia Tumulty, NJLA, P.O. Box 1534, Trenton 08607. Tel. 609-394-8032, fax 609-394-8164, e-mail ptumulty@njla.org.

Address correspondence to the executive director.

World Wide Web http://www.njla.org.

## New Mexico

Memb. 550. Term of Office. Apr. 2008–Apr. 2009. Publication. *New Mexico Library Association Newsletter* (6 a year).

*Pres.* Cassandra Osterloh. E-mail cassandra. osterloh@gmail.com; *V.P.* Dan Kammer. E-mail dkammer@nmsu.edu; *Secy.* Kathleen Teaze. E-mail kteaze@las-cruces.org; *Treas.* Tracy Thompson. E-mail thomptd@nmsu. edu; *Past Pres.* Louise Hoffmann. E-mail hoffmannl@sanjuancollege.edu; *Admin.* Lorie Christian. E-mail admin@nmla.org.

Address correspondence to the association, Box 26074, Albuquerque 87125. Tel. 505-400-7309, fax 505-891-5171, e-mail admin@ nmla.org.

World Wide Web http://www.nmla.org.

## New York

Memb. 3,000. Term of Office. Oct. 2008–Oct. 2009. Publication. *NYLA Bulletin* (6 a year). *Ed.* Michael J. Borges.

*Pres.* Josh Cohen. Tel. 845-471-6060 ext. 17, e-mail jcohen@midhudson.org; *Pres.-Elect* Kathy Miller. Tel. 585-223-7570, e-mail kmiller@rrlc.org; *Treas.* Ed Falcone. Tel. 914-375-7951, e-mail efalcone@ypl.org; *Past Pres.* Rosina Alaimo. Tel. 716-626-8846, e-mail rosella@att.net; *Exec. Dir.* Michael J. Borges.

Address correspondence to the executive director, New York Lib. Assn., 6021 State Farm Rd., Guilderland 12084. Tel. 800-252-6952 (toll-free), 518-432-6952, fax 518-427-1697, e-mail director@nyla.org.

World Wide Web http://www.nyla.org.

## North Carolina

Memb. 1,100. Term of Office. Oct. 2007–Oct. 2009. Publications. *North Carolina Library Association E-news* (bi-mo.). *Ed.* Marilyn Schuster, Local Documents/Special Collections, Univ. of North Carolina–Charlotte. E-mail mbschust@email.uncc.edu; *North Carolina Libraries Online* (2 a year). *Ed.* Ralph Lee Scott, Joyner Lib., ECU, Greenville 27858. Tel. 252-328-0265, e-mail scottr@ecu.edu.

*Pres.* Phil Barton, Rowan Public Lib., 714 Brookmont Ave., Salisbury 28146-7293. Tel. 704-633-5462, e-mail pbarton2@carolina.rr. com; *V.P./Pres.-Elect* Sherwin Rice, Bladen Community College, P.O. Box 266, Dublin 28332. Tel. 910-879-5641, e-mail srice@bladen.cc.nc.us; *Secy.* Caroline Walters, 1110 W. Murray Ave., Durham 27704. Tel. 919-962-6402, e-mail carolinejwalters@verizon. net; *Treas.* Andrea Tullos, Orange County Lib., P.O. Box 8181, Hillsboro 27278. Tel. 919-245-2529, e-mail tullos.andrea@gmail. com; *Past Pres.* Robert Burgin, North Carolina Central Univ., 307 Swiss Lake Drive, Cary 27513. Tel. 919-462-0134, fax 919-380-8074, e-mail rburgin@mindspring.com; *Admin. Asst.* Kim Parrott, North Carolina Lib. Assn., 1811 Capital Blvd., Raleigh 27604. Tel. 919-839-6252, fax 919-839-6253, e-mail nclaonline@ibiblio.org.

Address correspondence to the administrative assistant.

World Wide Web http://www.nclaonline. org.

## North Dakota

Memb. (Indiv.) 400; (Inst.) 18. Term of Office. Sept. 2008–Sept. 2009. Publication.

*The Good Stuff* (q.). *Ed.* Marlene Anderson, Bismarck State College Lib., Box 5587, Bismarck 58506-5587. Tel. 701-224-5578.

*Pres.* Phyllis Ann K. Bratton, Raugust Lib., Jamestown College, 6070 College Lane, Jamestown 58405-0002. Tel. 701-252-3467 ext. 2433, fax 701-253-4318, e-mail pbratton@jc.edu; *Pres.-Elect* Laurie L. McHenry, Chester Fritz Lib., Univ. of North Dakota, P.O. Box 14626, Grand Forks 58208-4626. Tel. 701-777-2919, fax 701-777-3319, e-mail lauriemchenry@mail.und.nodak.edu; *Secy.* Zachary B. Packineau, Bismarck Public Lib., 515 N. 5 St., Bismarck 58501-4057. Tel. 701-355-1490, fax 701-221-3729, e-mail z.packineau@mail.infolynx.org; *Treas.* Michael Safratowich, Harley French Lib. of the Health Sciences, Univ. of North Dakota, Box 9002, Grand Forks 58202-9002. Tel. 701-777-2602, fax 701-777-4790, e-mail msafrat@medicine.nodak.edu; *Past Pres.* Donna James, Allen Memorial Lib., Valley City State Univ., 101 College St. S.W., Valley City 58072-4098. Tel. 701-845-7275, fax 701-845-7437, e-mail donna.james@vcsu. edu.

Address correspondence to the president.

World Wide Web http://www.ndla.info.

## Ohio

Memb. 3,400+. Term of Office. Jan.–Dec. 2009. Publication. *Access* (11 a year).

*Pres.* Scott Shafer, Lima Public Lib., 650 W. Market St., Lima 45801. Tel. 419-228-5113, e-mail shafers@limalibrary.com; *V.P./Pres.-Elect* Beverly Cain, Portsmouth Public Lib., 1220 Gallia St., Portsmouth 45662. Tel. 740-353-5990, e-mail bcain@yourppl.org; *Secy./Treas.* Molly Carver, Bellevue Public Lib., 224 E. Main St., Bellevue 44811-1409. Tel. 419-483-4769 ext. 14, e-mail mcarver@bellevue.lib.oh.us; *Past Pres.* Margaret Danziger, Toledo–Lucas County Public Lib., Toledo 43624-1614. Tel. 419-259-5260, e-mail mdanziger@toledo library.org; *Exec. Dir.* Douglas S. Evans.

Address correspondence to the executive director, OLC, 1105 Schrock Rd., Suite 440, Columbus 43229-1174. Tel. 614-410-8092, fax 614-410-8098, e-mail olc@olc.org.

World Wide Web http://www.olc.org.

## Oklahoma

Memb. (Indiv.) 1,000; (Inst.) 60. Term of Office. July 2008–June 2009. Publication. *Oklahoma Librarian* (bi-mo.).

*Pres.* Kathy Latrobe. E-mail klatrobe@ou. edu; *V.P./Pres.-Elect* Charles Brooks. E-mail charles-brooks@utulsa.edu; *Secy.* Tim Miller. E-mail tim.miller@wplibs.com; *Treas.* Sarah Robbins. E-mail srobbins@ou.edu; *Past Pres.* Jan Bryant. E-mail ljanbryant@eok.lib.ok.us; *Exec. Dir.* Kay Boies, 300 Hardy Drive, Edmond 73013. Tel. 405-525-5100, fax 405-525-5103, e-mail kboies@sbcglobal.net.

Address correspondence to the executive director.

World Wide Web http://www.oklibs.org.

## Oregon

Memb. (Indiv.) 1,000+. Publications. *OLA Hotline* (bi-w.), *OLA Quarterly*.

*Pres.* Mary Ginnane, Eugene Public Lib. E-mail mary.j.ginnane@ci.eugene.or.us; *V.P./Pres.-Elect* Connie Anderson-Cohoon, Southern Oregon Univ. E-mail anderson@sou.edu; *Secy.* Bill Baars, Lake Oswego Public Lib. E-mail bbaars@ci.Oswego.or.us; *Treas.* Shirley Roberts, Eastern Oregon Univ. E-mail sroberts@eou.edu; *Past Pres.* Sarah Beasley, Portland State Univ. Tel. 503-725-3688, e-mail beasleys@pdx.edu.

Address correspondence to Oregon Lib. Assn., P.O. Box 2042, Salem 97308. Tel. 503-370-7019, e-mail olaweb@olaweb.org, World Wide Web http://www.olaweb.org.

## Pennsylvania

Memb. 1,900+. Term of Office. Jan.–Dec. 2009. Publication. *PaLA Bulletin* (10 a year).

*Pres.* Joe Fennewald, Penn State–Hazleton. Tel. 570-450-3172, e-mail jaf23@psu. edu; *1st V.P.* Margie Stern, Delaware County Lib. System. Tel. 610-891-8622, e-mail mstern@delco.lib.pa.us; *2nd V.P.* Robin Lesher, Adams County Lib. System. Tel. 717-334-5716, e-mail robinl@adamslibrary. org; *Treas.* Jo Ellen Kenney, Carnegie Lib. of McKeesport. Tel. 412-678-7076, e-mail kenneyj@einetwork.net; *Past Pres.* Mary O. Garm, Lackawanna County Lib. System. E-mail garm@albright.org; *Exec. Dir.* Glenn R. Miller, Pennsylvania Lib. Assn., 220 Cumberland Pkwy., Suite 10, Mechanicsburg 17055. Tel. 717-766-7663, fax 717-766-5440, e-mail glenn@palibraries.org.

Address correspondence to the executive director.

World Wide Web http://www.palibraries. org.

## Rhode Island

Memb. (Indiv.) 350+; (Inst.) 50+. Term of Office. June 2007–June 2009. Publication. *Rhode Island Library Association Bulletin.*

*Pres.* Christopher La Roux, Greenville Public Lib., 573 Putnam Pike, Greenville 02828. Tel. 401-949-3630, e-mail president @rilibraryassoc.org; *V.P./Pres.-Elect* Laura Marlane, Central Falls Free Public Lib., 205 Central St., Central Falls 02863. Tel. 401-727-7440, e-mail vicepresident@rilibrary assoc.org; *Secy.* Jenifer Bond, Douglas and Judith Krupp Lib., Bryant Univ., Smithfield 02917. Tel. 401-232-6299, e-mail secretary@rilibraryassoc.org; *Treas./Past Pres.* Cindy Lunghofer, East Providence Public Lib., 41 Grove Ave., East Providence 02914. Tel. 401-434-2453, e-mail book_n@yahoo.com.

World Wide Web http://www.rilibrary assoc.org.

## South Carolina

Memb. 550+. Term of Office. Jan.–Dec. 2009. Publication. *News and Views.*

*Pres.* Libby Young, Furman Univ., 10 W. Earle St., Greenville 29609. Tel. 864-294-2260, fax 864-294-3004, e-mail libby.young @furman.edu; *1st V.P./Pres.-Elect* Rayburne Turner, Charleston County Public Lib., 2261 Otranto Rd., North Charleston 29406. Tel. 843-572-4094, fax 843-572-4190, e-mail greeklife@lowcountry.com; *Secy.* Karen Brown, Thomas Cooper Lib., Univ. of South Carolina, Columbia 29208. Tel. 803-777-4267, fax 803-777-4661, e-mail kwbrown@gwm.sc.edu; *Treas.* Jeronell "Nell" Bradley, Florence Darlington Technical College. Tel. 843-661-8032, e-mail jeronell.bradley@fdtc. edu; *Past Pres.* Curtis R. Rogers, South Carolina State Lib., 1430 Senate St., Columbia 29211. Tel. 803-734-8928, fax 803-734-

8676, e-mail crogers@statelibrary.sc.gov; *Exec. Secy.* Gabrielle Barnes, South Carolina Lib. Assn., P.O. Box 1763, Columbia 29202. Tel. 803-252-1087, e-mail scla@capconsc. com.

Address correspondence to the executive secretary.

World Wide Web http://www.scla.org.

## South Dakota

Memb. (Indiv.) 451; (Inst.) 74. Term of Office. Oct. 2008–Oct. 2009. Publication. *Book Marks* (bi-mo.).

*Pres.* Nancy Sabbe, Madison Public Lib., Madison. E-mail nsabbe@sdln.net; *V.P./ Pres.-Elect* Kay Christensen, Augustana College Lib., Sioux Falls. E-mail kchristie@ augie.edu; *Recording Secy.* Julie Erickson, South Dakota State Lib. E-mail julie.erickson @state.sd.us; *Past Pres.* Robin Schrupp, Grant County Public Lib. E-mail gclibrary21 @hotmail.com; *Exec. Secy./Treas.* Brenda Hemmelman. E-mail bkstand@rap.midco. net.

Address correspondence to the executive secretary, SDLA, Box 1212, Rapid City 57709-1212. Tel. 605-343-3750, e-mail bkstand@rap.midco.net.

World Wide Web http://www.sdlibrary association.org.

## Tennessee

Memb. 639. Term of Office. July 2008–June 2009. Publications. *Tennessee Librarian* (q.), *TLA Newsletter* (bi-mo.) Both online only at http://www.tnla.org.

*Pres.* Sue Szostak, Motlow State Community College, Lynchburg 37352. E-mail sszostak@mscc.edu; *V.P./Pres.-Elect* Kevin Reynolds. E-mail kreynold@sewanee.edu; *Recording Secy.* Bess Robinson. E-mail merobnsn@memphis.edu; *Past Pres.* Jane Pinkston. E-mail jane.pinkston@state.tn.us; *Exec. Dir.* Annelle R. Huggins, Tennessee Lib. Assn., Box 241074, Memphis 38124. Tel. 901-485-6952, e-mail arhuggins1@ comcast.net

Address correspondence to the executive director.

World Wide Web http://tnla.org.

## Texas

Memb. 7,433. Term of Office. Apr. 2008–Apr. 2009. Publications. *Texas Library Journal* (q.), *TLACast* (9 a year).

*Pres.* Melody Kelly, Univ. of North Texas. E-mail melody.kelly@unt.edu; *Pres.-Elect* Patrick Heath. E-mail patrickheath@ windstream.net; *Treas.* Jane Clausen, Lubbock Public Lib. E-mail jclausen@mail.ci. Lubbock.tx.us; *Past Pres.* Steve Brown, North Richland Hills Public Lib. E-mail sbrown@nrhtx.com; *Exec. Dir.* Patricia H. Smith, TXLA, 3355 Bee Cave Rd., Suite 401, Austin 78746-6763. Tel. 512-328-1518, fax 512-328-8852, e-mail pats@txla.org.

Address correspondence to the executive director.

World Wide Web http://www.txla.org.

## Utah

Memb. 650. Term of Office. May 2008–May 2009. Publication. *Utah Libraries News* (bi-mo.) (online at http://www.ula.org/newsletter).

*Pres.* Steven D. Decker, Cedar City Public Lib., Cedar City 84720. Tel. 435-586-6661 ext. 1001, fax 435-865-7280, e-mail dsteve@ cedarcity.org; *V.P./Pres.-Elect* Ruby Cheesman, Hunter Lib., Salt Lake County. Tel. 801) 944-7597, e-mail rcheesman@slco. lib.ut.us; *Past Pres.* Dorothy Horan, Family History Lib., 50 E. North Temple, COB 3, Salt Lake City 84602. Tel. 801-240-6125, e-mail horandm@ldschurch.org; *Exec. Secy.* Ranny Lacanienta, Harold B. Lee Lib., Brigham Young Univ., Provo 84602. Tel. 801-422-6278, fax 801-422-0466, e-mail ranny@byu.edu.

Address correspondence to the executive secretary, Utah Lib. Assn., P.O. Box 708155, Sandy 84070-8155.

World Wide Web http://www.ula.org.

## Vermont

Memb. 400. Publication. *VLA News* (6 a year).

*Pres.* Judah S. Hamer, 1571 Rte. 30, Cornwall 05753. Tel. 802-462-2096, e-mail jshamer@gmail.com; *V.P./Pres.-Elect* John K. Payne, Saint Michael's College, Box L 1 Winooski Park, Colchester 05439. Tel. 802-

654-2401, e-mail jpayne@smcvt.edu; *Secy.* Brenda Ellis, Middlebury College Lib., 110 Storrs Ave., Middlebury 05753. Tel. 802-443-5497, e-mail bellis@middlebury.edu; *Treas.* Wynne Browne, Downs Rachlin Martin, St. Johnsbury 05819-0099. Tel. 802-473-4216, e-mail wbrowne@drm.com; *Past Pres.* Barbara Doyle-Wilch, Middlebury College Lib., 110 Storrs Ave., Middlebury 05753. Tel. 802-443-5490, e-mail bdoylewi@middlebury.edu.

Address correspondence to VLA, Box 803, Burlington 05402.

World Wide Web http://www.vermont libraries.org.

## Virginia

Memb. 1,100+. Term of Office. Oct. 2008–Oct. 2009. Publications. *Virginia Libraries* (q.); *VLA Newsletter* (10 a year, online only).

*Pres.* Robin Benke, Univ. of Virginia–Wise, 116 Dotson Ave., Wise 24293. Tel. 276-328-0151, e-mail rbenke@virginia.edu; *V.P./Pres.-Elect* John Moorman, Williamsburg Public Lib., 7770 Croaker Rd., Williamsburg 23188. Tel. 757-259-7777, e-mail jmoorman@wrl.org; *2nd V.P.* Caryl Gray, Univ. Libs., Virginia Tech, 304 Fincastle Drive, Blacksburg 24060. Tel. 540-231-9229, e-mail cegray@vt.cdu; *Secy.* Connie Gilman, Chinn Park Regional Lib., 13065 Chinn Park Drive, Prince William 22192. Tel. 703-792-6199, e-mail cgilman@pwcgov.org; *Treas.* Matt Todd, Northern Virginia Community College, 3001 N. Beauregard St., Alexandria 22331. Tel. 703-845-6033, e-mail mtodd@nvcc.edu; *Exec. Dir.* Linda Hahne, P.O. Box 8277, Norfolk 23503-0277. Tel. 757-583-0041, fax 757-583-5041, e-mail lhahne@coastalnet.com.

Address correspondence to the executive director.

World Wide Web http://www.vla.org.

## Washington

Memb. 1,040+. Term of Office. Apr. 2007–Apr. 2009. Publication. *ALKI* (3 a year). *Ed.* Margaret Thomas, Box 43165, Olympia 98504. Tel. 360-481-1250, e-mail alkieditor @wla.org.

*Pres.* Martha Parsons, WSU Energy Program Lib., 925 Plum St. S.E., Olympia 98501. Tel. 360-956-2159, fax 360-236-2159, e-mail president@wla.org; *V.P./Pres.-Elect* Tim Mallory, Timberland Regional Lib., 415 Tumwater Blvd. S.W., Tumwater 98501. Tel. 360-704-4502, fax 360-586-6838, e-mail vicepresident@wla.org; *Secy.* Karen Highum, Allen Lib., Univ. of Washington, Box 35290, Seattle 98195-2900. Tel. 425 Harvard Ave. E., Seattle 98102. Tel. 206-685-3981, e-mail highum@u.washington. edu; *Treas.* Priscilla Ice, Spokane Valley Lib. Dist., 12004 E. Main, Spokane 99206. Tel. 509-893-8451, fax 509-893-8478, e-mail treasurer@wla.org; *Past Pres.* Carolynne Myall, John F. Kennedy Lib., Eastern Washington Univ., 816 F St., Cheney 99004. Tel. 509-359-6967, fax 509-359-2476, e-mail cmyall@ewu.edu; *Exec. Dir.* Kristin Crowe, Washington Lib. Assn., 23607 Hwy. 99, Suite 2-C, Edmonds 98026. Tel. 425-967-0739, fax 425-771-9588, e-mail kristin@wla. org.

Address correspondence to the executive director.

World Wide Web http://www.wla.org.

## West Virginia

Memb. 650+. Publication. *West Virginia Libraries* (6 a year). *Ed.* Pam Coyle, Martinsburg Public Lib., 101 W. King St., Martinsburg 25401. Tel. 304-267-8933, fax 304-267-9720, e-mail pcoyle@martin.lib.wv.us.

*Pres.* Barbara LaGodna, Evansdale Lib., WVU, P.O. Box 6105, Morgantown 26505-6105. Tel. 304-293-9748, e-mail blagodna @wvu.edu; *1st V.P./Pres.-Elect* Brian Raitz, Parkersburg and Wood County Public Lib., 3100 Emerson Ave., Parkersburg 26104-2414. Tel. 304-420-4587 ext. 11, e-mail raitzb@park.lib.wv.us; *2nd V.P.* Sarah Cranstoun, Summersville Public Lib., 6201 Webster Rd., Summersville 26651. Tel. 304-872-0844, e-mail sarahc@mail.mln.lib.wv.us; *Secy.* Martha Yancey, Evansdale Lib., WVU, P.O. Box 6105, Morgantown 26506-6105. Tel. 304-293-5039, e-mail myancey@wvu. edu; *Treas.* Beth Royall, Evansdale Lib., WVU, P.O. Box 6105, Morgantown 26506-6105. Tel. 304-293-9755, e-mail beth.royall

@mail.wvu.edu; *Past Pres.* Ann Farr, Greenbrier County Public Lib., 301 Courtney Drive, Lewisburg 24901. Tel. 304-647-7568, e-mail farrann@mail.mln.lib.wv.us.

Address correspondence to the president. World Wide Web http://www.wvla.org.

## Wisconsin

Memb. 1,800. Term of Office. Jan.–Dec. Publication. *WLA Newsletter* (q.).

*Pres.* Pat Chevis, Stoughton Public Lib., 304 S. 4 St., Stoughton 53589. E-mail pchevis@scls.lib.wi.us; *Pres.-Elect* Walter Burkhalter, Mid-Wisconsin Federated Lib. System, 112 Clinton St., Horicon 53032. E-mail wburkh@mwfls.org; *Secy.* Tasha Saecker, Elisha D. Smith Public Lib., 440 First St., Menasha 54952-3191. E-mail saecker@menashalibrary.org; *Treas.* Jan Berg, DeForest Public Lib., 203 Library St., DeForest 53532. E-mail bergjd@scls.lib.wi.us; *Past Pres.* Becca Berger, Door County Lib., 107 S. 4 Ave., Sturgeon Bay 54235. E-mail rberger@mail.nfls.lib.wi.us; *Exec. Dir.* Lisa K. Strand, Wisconsin Lib. Assn., 5250 E. Terrace Drive, Suite A1, Madison 53718-8345. Tel. 608-245-3640, fax 608-245-3646, e-mail strand@scls.lib.wi.us.

Address correspondence to the association. World Wide Web http://www.wla.lib.wi.us.

## Wyoming

Memb. 450+. Term of Office. Oct. 2008–Oct. 2009.

*Pres.* Cynthia Twing, Johnson County Public Lib. Tel. 307-684-5546, fax 307-684-7888, e-mail ctwing@will.state.wy.us; *V.P./Pres.-Elect* Jamie Markus, Wyoming State Lib. Tel. 307-777-5914, fax 307-777-6289, e-mail jmarku@state.wy.us; *Recording Secy.* Meg Martin, Wyoming State Law Lib. Tel. 307-777-8564, e-mail mmartin@courts.state.wy.us; *Past Pres.* Brian Greene, Wyoming State Lib. Tel. 307-777-6339, fax 307-777-6289, e-mail bgreen@state.wy.us; *Exec. Secy.* Laura Grott, Box 1387, Cheyenne 82003. Tel. 307-632-7622, fax 307-638-3469, e-mail grottski@aol.com.

Address correspondence to the executive secretary. World Wide Web http://www.wyla.org.

# Canada

## Alberta

Memb. 500. Term of Office. May 2008–Apr. 2009. Publication. *Letter of the LAA* (4 a year).

*Pres.* Karla Palichuk, Alberta Lib. E-mail kpalichuk@thealbertalibrary.ab.ca; *V.P.* Renee Reaume, Univ. of Calgary. E-mail renee.reaume@ucalgary.ca; *Past Pres.* Della Paradis, Northern Alberta Institute of Technology. E-mail dellap@nait.ca; *2nd V.P.* Diane Clark, Univ. of Alberta. E-mail diane.clark@ualberta.ca; *Treas.* Melanie Johnson, Edmonton Public Lib. E-mail siljohn@telusplanet.net; *Exec. Dir.* Christine Sheppard, 80 Baker Crescent N.W., Calgary T2L 1R4. Tel. 403-284-5818, fax 403-282-6646, e-mail info@laa.ca.

Address correspondence to the executive director.

World Wide Web http://www.laa.ca.

## British Columbia

Memb. 820. Term of Office. April 2008–April 2009. Publication. *BCLA Browser. Ed.* Sandra Wong.

*Pres.* Lynne Jordon, Greater Victoria Public Lib., 735 Broughton St., Victoria V8W 3H2. E-mail ljordon@gvpl.ca; *V.P./Pres.-Elect* Ken Cooley, McPherson Lib., Univ. of Victoria, P.O. Box 1800, STN CSC, Victoria V8W 3H5. E-mail kcooley@uvic.ca; *Treas.* Christina de Castell, Vancouver Public Lib., 350 W. Georgia St., Vancouver V6B 6B1. E-mail chrisdec@vpl.ca; *Past Pres.* Deborah Thomas, Burnaby Public Lib., 7252 Kingsway, Burnaby V5E 1G3. E-mail deborah.thomas@bpl.bc.ca; *Exec. Dir.* Alane Wilson. E-mail execdir@bcla.bc.ca.

Address correspondence to the association, 900 Howe St., Suite 150, Vancouver V6Z 2M4. Tel. 604-683-5354, fax 604-609-0707, e-mail office@bcla.bc.ca.

World Wide Web http://www.bcla.bc.ca.

## Manitoba

Memb. 500+. Term of Office. May 2008–May 2009. Publication. *Newsline* (mo.).

*Pres.* Carolyn Minor, Millennium Lib., 251 Donald St., Winnipeg R3C 3P5. Tel.

204-986-4206, e-mail northwest@hotmail. com; *V.P.* C. J. de Jong, Univ. of Winnipeg Lib., 515 Portage Ave., Winnipeg R3B 2E9. Tel. 204-786-9802, e-mail c.dejong@ uwinnipeg.ca; *Treas.* Bonita "Bunny" Cobb, Manitoba Lib. Assn., 606-100 Arthur St., Winnipeg R3B 1H3. Tel. 204-475-1724, e-mail gbcobb@shaw.ca; *Past Pres.* H. Rainer Schira, John E. Robbins Lib., Brandon Univ., 270 18th St., Brandon R7A 6A9. Tel. 204-727-7463, fax 204-726-1072, e-mail schirar @brandonu.ca.

Address correspondence to the association, 606-100 Arthur St., Winnipeg R3B 1H3. Tel. 204-943-4567, e-mail manitobalibrary@ gmail.com.

World Wide Web http://www.mla.mb.ca.

## Ontario

Memb. 5,200+. Publications. *Access* (q.); *Teaching Librarian* (3 a year).

*Pres.* Peggy Thomas. E-mail peggy. thomas@tel.tdsb.on.ca; *V.P./Pres.-Elect* Mary Ann Mavrinac. E-mail maryann. mavrinac@utoronto.ca; *Treas.* Paul Takala. E-mail ptakala@hpl.ca; *Past Pres.* Sam Coghlan. E-mail scoghlan@city.stratford. on.ca; *Exec. Dir.* Shelagh Paterson. E-mail spaterson@accessola.com.

Address correspondence to the association, 50 Wellington St. E., Suite 201, Toronto M5E 1C8. Tel. 416-363-3388, fax 416-941-9581, e-mail info@accessola.com.

World Wide Web http://www.accessola. com.

## Quebec

Memb. (Indiv.) 110+. Term of Office. May 2008–April 2009. Publication. *ABQLA Bulletin* (3 a year).

*Pres.* Lisa Milner; *V.P.* Maria Morales; *Secy.* Cathy Maxwell; *Exec. Secy./Treas.* Janet Ilavsky, Box 1095, Pointe-Claire H9S 4H9. Tel. 514-697-0146, e-mail abqla@ abqla.qc.ca; *Past Pres.* Janine West.

Address correspondence to the executive secretary.

World Wide Web http://www.abqla.qc.ca.

## Saskatchewan

Memb. 200+. Term of Office. May 2008–May 2009. Publication. *Forum* (4 a year).

*Pres.* Erin O. Romanyshyn, Saskatoon Public Lib., 311 23rd St. E., Saskatoon S7K 0J6. Tel. 306-975-7597, fax 306-975-7542, e-mail e.romanyshyn@saskatoonlibrary.ca; *V.P.* Barbara Kelly, Connaught Lib., 3435 13th Ave., P.O. Box 2311, Regina S4P 3Z5. Tel. 306-777-6079, fax 306-949-7266, e-mail bkelly@reginalibrary.ca; *Treas.* Brett Waytuck, Provincial Lib., Ministry of Educ., 1945 Hamilton St., Regina S4P 2C8. Tel. 306-787-8020, fax 306-787-2029, e-mail brett. waytuck@gov.sk.ca; *Past Pres.* Amy Rankin, RCMP Resource Centre, P.O. Box 6500, Regina S4P 3J7. Tel. 306-780-5824, fax 306-780-7599, e-mail arankin-library@hotmail. com; *Exec. Dir.* Caroline Selinger, Saskatchewan Lib. Assn., 2010 Seventh Ave., No. 15, Regina S4R 1C2. Tel. 306-780-9413, fax 306-780-9447, e-mail slaexdir@sasktel.net.

Address correspondence to the executive director.

World Wide Web http://www.lib.sk.ca/sla.

## Regional

### Atlantic Provinces: N.B., N.L., N.S., P.E.

Memb. (Indiv.) 200+; (Inst.) 26. Publications. *APLA Bulletin* (bi-mo.), *Membership Directory* (ann.).

*Pres.* Su Cleyle, Queen Elizabeth II Lib., Memorial Univ. of Newfoundland, St. John's, NL A1B 3Y1. Tel. 709-737-3188, fax 709-737-2153, e-mail scleyle@mun.ca; *V.P./ Pres.-Elect* Donald Moses, Lib. Services, Holland College, 140 Weymouth St., Charlottetown, PE C1A 4Z1. Tel. 902-566-9577, fax 902-566-9522, e-mail dmoses@hollandc. pe.ca; *V.P., Membership* Ruthmary Macpherson, Mount Allison Univ. Libs. and Archives, 49 York St., Sackville, NB E4L 1C6. Tel. 506-364-2691, fax 506-364-2617, e-mail macpherson@mta.ca; *Secy.* Lynn Somers, Keshen Goodman Public Lib., 330 Lacewood Drive, Halifax, NS B3S 0A3. Tel. 902-490-6441, e-mail somersl@halifax.ca; *Treas.* Penny Logan, Capital Health, 1796 Summer

St., Rm. 2212, Halifax, NS B3H 3A7. Tel. 902-473-4383, fax 902-473-8651, e-mail apla_executive@yahoo.ca; *Past Pres.* Donna Bourne-Tyson, Mount Saint Vincent Univ., 166 Bedford Hwy., Halifax, NS B3M 2J6. Tel. 902-457-6108, fax 902-457-6445, e-mail donna.bourne-tyson@msvu.ca.

Address correspondence to Atlantic Provinces Lib. Assn., c/o School of Info. Mgt., Faculty of Mgt., Kenneth C. Rowe Mgt. Bldg., 6100 University Ave., Halifax, NS B3H 3J5.

World Wide Web http://www.apla.ca.

**Mountain Plains: Ariz., Colo., Kan., Mont., Neb., Nev., N.Dak., N.M., Okla., S.Dak., Utah, Wyo.**

Memb. 820. Term of Office. May 2008–May 2009. Publications. *MPLA Newsletter* (bi-mo.). *Ed./Advertising Mgr.* Judy Zelenski, 14293 W. Center Drive, Lakewood, CO 80228. Tel. 303-985-7795, e-mail mpla_execsecretary@operamail.com.

*Pres.* Robert Banks, Topeka and Shawnee County Public Lib., 1515 S.W. 10 Ave., Topeka, KS 66604. Tel. 785-580-4481, fax 785-580-4496, e-mail rbanks@mail.tscpl.org; *V.P./Pres.-Elect* Eileen Wright, Billings Lib., Montana State Univ., 1500 University Drive, Billings, MT 59101. Tel. 406-657-1656, fax 406-657-2037, e-mail ewright@msubillings.edu; *Recording Secy.* Annie Epperson, Michener Lib., Univ. of Northern Colorado, Campus Box 48, Greeley, CO 80639-0091, Tel. 970-351-1535, fax 970-351-2963, e-mail annie.epperson@unco.edu; *Past Pres.* Wayne Hanway, Southeastern Public Lib. System, 401 N. 2 St., McAlester, OK 74501. Tel. 918-426-0456, fax 918-423-0550, e-mail whanway@sepl.lib.ok.us; *Exec. Secy.* Judy Zelenski, 14293 W. Center Drive, Lakewood, CO 80228. Tel. 303-985-7795, e-mail mpla_execsecretary@operamail.com.

Address correspondence to the executive secretary, Mountain Plains Lib. Assn.

World Wide Web http://www.mpla.us.

**New England: Conn., Maine, Mass., N.H., R.I., Vt.**

Memb. (Indiv.) 800. Term of Office. Nov. 2008–Oct. 2009. Publications. *New England Libraries* (annual), *NELA News* (electronic, mo.). *Ed.* David Bryan, 1 Salty Ridge Rd., Orleans, MA 02653. Tel. 508-240-2357, e-mail publicationsmanager@nelib.org.

*Pres.* Mary Ann Tricarico, New England Institute of Art, 10 Brookline Place West, Brookline, MA 02445. Tel. 800-903-4425, e-mail president@nelib.org; *V.P./Pres.-Elect* Rick Taplin, Minuteman Lib. Network, 10 Strathmore Rd., Natick, MA 01760. Tel. 508-655-8008, e-mail vicepresident@nelib.org; *Secy.* Marija Sanderling, Lane Memorial Lib., 2 Academy Ave., Hampton, NH 03842. Tel. 603-926-3368, fax 603-926-1348, e-mail secretary@nelib.org; *Treas.* Kerry Cronin, Rye Public Lib., 581 Washington Rd., Rye, NH 03870. Tel. 603-964-8401, fax 603-964-7065, e-mail treasurer@nelib.org; *Past Pres.* Kristin M. Jacobi, J. Eugene Smith Lib., Eastern Connecticut State Univ., 83 Windham St., Willimantic, CT 06226. Tel. 860-465-4508, fax 860-465-5523, e-mail pastpresident@nelib.org; *Exec. Mgr.* Mary Ann Rupert, New England Lib. Assn., 31 Connor Lane, Wilton, NH 03086. Tel. 603-654-3533, fax 603-654-3526, e-mail maryann@nelib.org.

Address correspondence to the executive manager.

World Wide Web http://www.nelib.org.

**Pacific Northwest: Alaska, Idaho, Mont., Ore., Wash., Alberta, B.C.**

Memb. (Active) 172. Term of Office. Aug. 2008–Aug. 2009. Publication. *PNLA Quarterly.* *Ed.* Mary Bolin, 322B Love Lib., Univ. of Nebraska, P.O. Box 881140, Lincoln, NE 68588-4100. Tel. 402-472-4281, e-mail mbolin2@unlnotes.unl.edu.

*Pres.* Kathy Waston, Marshall Public Lib., 113 S. Garfield, Pocatello, ID 83204. Tel. 208-232-1263 ext. 30, fax 208-232-9266, e-mail kwatson@marshallpl.org; *1st V.P./Pres.-Elect* Samantha Hines, Mansfield Lib., Univ. of Montana, Missoula, MT 59812-9936. Tel. 406-243-4558, fax 406-243-4067, e-mail samantha.hines@umontana.edu; *2nd V.P.* Jason Openo, Edmonton Public Lib., 145 Whitemud Crossing Shopping Centre, 4211 106th St., Edmonton, AB T6J 6L7. Tel. 780-496-8348, e-mail jopeno@epl.ca; *Secy.* Brent

Roberts, Montana State Univ.–Billings. E-mail broberts@msubillings.edu; *Treas.* Katie Cargill, Eastern Washington Univ. Libs., 816 F St., Cheney, WA 99004. Tel. 509-359-2385, fax 509-359-2476, e-mail kcargill@mail.ewu.edu; *Past Pres.* Susannah Price, Boise Public Lib., 715 Capitol Blvd., Boise, ID 83702-7195. Tel. 208-384-4026, e-mail sprice@cityofboise.org.

Address correspondence to the president, Pacific Northwest Lib. Assn.

World Wide Web http://www.pnla.org.

### Southeastern: Ala., Ark., Fla., Ga., Ky., La., Miss., N.C., S.C., Tenn., Va., W.Va.

Memb. 500. Publication. *The Southeastern Librarian* (q.). *Ed.* Perry Bratcher, 503A Steely Lib., Northern Kentucky Univ., Highland Heights, KY 41099. Tel. 859-572-6309, fax 859-572-6181, e-mail bratcher@nku.edu.

*Pres.* Faith A. Line, Anderson County Lib., P.O. Box 4047, 300 McDuffie St., Anderson, SC 29621. Tel. 864-260-4500, fax 864-260-4510, e-mail fline@andersonlibrary.org; *1st V.P./Pres.-Elect* Kathleen R. T. Imhoff, Lexington Public Lib., 140 E. Main St., Lexington, KY 40507. Tel. 859-231-5599, e-mail kimhoff@lexpublib.org; *Secy.* Gordon N. Baker, Clayton State Univ. Tel. 678-466-4325, e-mail gordonbaker@clayton.edu; *Treas.* William N. Nelson, Augusta State Univ. Lib. Tel. 706-737-1745, e-mail wnelson@aug.edu; *Past Pres.* Judith A. Gibbons, Kentucky Dept. for Libs. and Archives. Tel. 502-564-8300, fax 502-564-5773, e-mail judith.gibbons@ky.gov.

Address correspondence to Southeastern Lib. Assn., Administrative Services, P.O. Box 950, Rex, GA 30273-0950. Tel. 770-961-3520, fax 770-961-3712.

World Wide Web http://sela.jsu.edu.

# State and Provincial Library Agencies

The state library administrative agency in each of the U.S. states will have the latest information on its state plan for the use of federal funds under the Library Services and Technology Act (LSTA). The directors and addresses of these state agencies are listed below.

## Alabama

Rebecca Mitchell, Dir., Alabama Public Lib. Service, 6030 Monticello Dr., Montgomery 36130-6000. Tel. 334-213-3902, fax 334-213-3993, e-mail rmitchell@apls.state.al.us.

## Alaska

Kathryn H. Shelton, State Libn. and Dir., Alaska Dept. of Educ., Div. of Libs., Archives, and Museums, Box 110571, Juneau 99811-0571. Tel. 907-465-2911, fax 907-465-2151, e-mail kay.shelton@Alaska.gov. World Wide Web http://library.state.ak.us.

## Arizona

GladysAnn Wells, State Libn., Arizona State Lib., Archives and Public Records, Rm. 200, 1700 W. Washington, Phoenix 85007-2896. Tel. 602-926-4035, fax 602-256-7983, e-mail gawells@lib.az.us. World Wide Web http://www.lib.az.us.

## Arkansas

Carolyn Ashcraft, State Libn., Arkansas State Lib., 1 Capitol Mall, 5th fl., Little Rock 72201-1081. Tel. 501-682-1526, fax 501-682-1899, e-mail cashcraft@asl.lib.ar.us. World Wide Web http://www.asl.lib.ar.us.

## California

Susan Hildreth, State Libn., California State Lib., P.O. Box 942837, Sacramento 94237-0001. Tel. 916-654-0266, fax 916-653-7818, e-mail shildreth@library.ca.gov. World Wide Web http://www.library.ca.gov.

## Colorado

Eugene Hainer, Dir., Colorado State Lib., Rm. 309, 201 E. Colfax Ave., Denver 80203. Tel. 303-866-6733, fax 303-866-6940, e-mail hainer_g@cde.state.co.us. World Wide Web http://www.cde.state.co.us/index_library.htm.

## Connecticut

Kendall F. Wiggin, State Libn., Connecticut State Lib., 231 Capitol Ave., Hartford 06106-1537. Tel. 860-757-6510, fax 860-757-6503, e-mail kwiggin@cslib.org. World Wide Web http://www.cslib.org.

## Delaware

Anne Norman, State Libn., Delaware Div. of Libs., 43 S. DuPont Hwy., Dover 19901. Tel. 302-739-4748 ext. 126, fax 302-739-6787, e-mail norman@lib.de.us. World Wide Web http://www.state.lib.de.us.

## District of Columbia

Ginnie Cooper, Chief Libn., District of Columbia Public Lib., 901 G St. N.W., Washington 20001. Tel. 202-727-1101, fax 202-727-1129, e-mail ginnie.cooper@dc.gov. World Wide Web http://www.dclibrary.org.

## Florida

Judith A. Ring, State Libn., Div. of Lib. and Info. Services, R. A. Gray Bldg., 500 S. Bronough St., Tallahassee 32399-0250. Tel. 850-245-6604, fax 850-488-2746, e-mail jring@dos.state.fl.us. World Wide Web http://dlis.dos.state.fl.us/stlib.

## Georgia

Lamar Veatch, State Libn., Georgia Public Lib. Services, 1800 Century Place, Suite 150, Atlanta 30345-4304. Tel. 404-235-7200, fax 404-235-7201, e-mail lveatch@georgia libraries.org. World Wide Web http://www.georgialibraries.org.

## Hawaii

Richard Burns, State Libn., Hawaii State Public Lib. System, 44 Merchant St., Honolulu 96813. Tel. 808-586-3704, fax 808-586-3715, e-mail stlib@librarieshawaii.org. World Wide Web http://www.librarieshawaii.org.

## Idaho

Ann Joslin, State Libn., Idaho Commission for Libs., 325 W. State St., Boise 83713. Tel. 208-334-2150, fax 208-334-4016, e-mail ann.joslin@libraries.idaho.gov. World Wide Web http://libraries.idaho.gov.

## Illinois

Anne Craig, Dir., Illinois State Lib., 300 S. 2 St., Springfield 62701-1796. Tel. 217-782-2994, fax 217-782-6062, e-mail acraig@ilsos.net. World Wide Web http://www.cyberdriveillinois.com/departments/library/home.html.

## Indiana

Roberta L. Brooker, Dir. and State Libn., Indiana State Lib., 140 N. Senate Ave., Indianapolis 46204. Tel. 317-232-3693, fax 317-232-3713, e-mail rbrooker@library.in.gov. World Wide Web http://www.in.gov/library.

## Iowa

Mary Wegner, State Libn., State Lib. of Iowa, 1112 E. Grand Ave., Des Moines 50319. Tel. 515-281-4105, fax 515-281-6191, e-mail mary.wegner@lib.state.ia.us. World Wide Web http://www.statelibraryofiowa.org.

## Kansas

Christie Pearson Brandau, State Libn., Kansas State Lib., 300 S.W. 10 Ave., Topeka 66612-1593. Tel. 785-296-5466, fax 785-296-6650, e-mail christieb@kslib.org. World Wide Web http://skyways.lib.ks.us/KSL.

## Kentucky

Wayne Onkst, State Libn./Commissioner, Kentucky Dept. for Libs. and Archives, 300 Coffee Tree Rd., Frankfort 40602-0537. Tel. 502-564-8300 ext. 312, fax 502-564-5773, e-mail wayne.onkst@ky.gov. World Wide Web http://www.kdla.ky.gov.

## Louisiana

Rebecca Hamilton, State Libn., State Lib. of Louisiana, 701 N. 4 St., P.O. Box 131, Baton Rouge 70821-0131. Tel. 225-342-4923, fax 225-219-4804, e-mail rhamilton@crt.state.la.us. World Wide Web http://www.state.lib.la.us.

## Maine

J. Gary Nichols, State Libn., Maine State Lib., 64 State House Sta., Augusta 04333-0064. Tel. 207-287-5600, fax 207-287-5615, e-mail gary.nichols@maine.gov. World Wide Web http://www.maine.gov/msl.

## Maryland

Irene Padilla, Asst. State Superintendent for Lib. Development and Services, Maryland State Dept. of Educ., 200 W. Baltimore St., Baltimore 21201. Tel. 410-767-0435, fax 410-333-2507, e-mail ipadilla@msde.state.md.us. World Wide Web http://www.marylandpublicschools.org/MSDE/divisions/library.

## Massachusetts

Robert C. Maier, Dir., Massachusetts Board of Lib. Commissioners, 98 N. Washington St., Suite 401, Boston 02114. Tel. 617-725-1860 ext. 249, fax 617-421-0149, e-mail robert.maier@state.ma.us. World Wide Web http://mblc.state.ma.us.

## Michigan

Nancy R. Robertson, State Libn., Lib. of Michigan, 702 W. Kalamazoo St., P.O. Box 30007, Lansing 48909-7507. Tel. 517-373-5504, fax 517-373-4480, e-mail nrobertson@michigan.gov. World Wide Web http://www.michigan.gov/hal.

## Minnesota

Suzanne Miller, State Libn. and Dir., Div. of State Lib. Services, Minnesota Dept. of

Educ., 1500 Hwy. 36 W., Roseville 55113-4266. Tel. 651-582-8251, fax 651-582-8752, e-mail suzanne.miller@state.mn.us. World Wide Web http://education.state.mn.us/MDE/Learning_Support/Library_Services/index.html.

## Mississippi

Sharman Bridges Smith, Exec. Dir., Mississippi Lib. Commission, 3881 Eastwood Dr., Jackson 39211. Tel. 601-432-4039, fax 601-432-4480, e-mail sharman@mlc.lib.ms.us. World Wide Web http://www.mlc.lib.ms.us.

## Missouri

Margaret Conroy, Dir., Missouri State Lib., 600 W. Main, P.O. Box 387, Jefferson City 65102-0387. Tel. 573-751-2751, fax 573-751-3612, e-mail margaret.conroy@sos.mo.gov. World Wide Web http://www.sos.mo.gov/library.

## Montana

Darlene Staffeldt, State Libn., Montana State Lib., 1515 E. 6 Ave., P.O. Box 201800, Helena 59620-1800. Tel. 406-444-3115, fax 406-444-0266, e-mail dstaffeldt@mt.us. World Wide Web http://msl.state.mt.us.

## Nebraska

Rodney G. Wagner, Dir., Nebraska Lib. Commission, Suite 120, 1200 N St., Lincoln 68508-2023. Tel. 402-471-4001, fax 402-471-2083, e-mail rwagner@nlc.state.ne.us. World Wide Web http://www.nlc.state.ne.us.

## Nevada

Daphne Arnaiz-DeLeon, Admin., Nevada State Lib. and Archives, 100 N. Stewart St., Carson City 89710-4285. Tel. 775-684-3315, fax 775-684-3311, e-mail ddeleon@nevadaculture.org. World Wide Web http://www.nevadaculture.org/docs/nsla.

## New Hampshire

Michael York, State Libn., New Hampshire State Lib., 20 Park St., Concord 03301. Tel. 603-271-2397, fax 603-271-6826, e-mail michael.york@dcr.nh.gov. World Wide Web http://www.state.nh.us/nhsl.

## New Jersey

Norma E. Blake, State Libn., New Jersey State Lib., P.O. Box 520, Trenton 08625-0520. Tel. 609-278-2640 ext. 101, fax 609-292-2746, e-mail nblake@njstatelib.org. World Wide Web http://www.njstatelib.org.

## New Mexico

Susan Oberlander, State Libn., New Mexico State Lib., 1209 Camino Carlos Rey, Santa Fe 87505-6980. Tel. 505-476-9762, fax 505-476-9761, e-mail susan.oberlander@state.nm.us. World Wide Web http://www.nmstatelibrary.org.

## New York

Bernard A. Margolis, State Libn., New York State Lib., Rm. 10A33, Cultural Educ. Center, Albany 12230. Tel. 518-474-5930, fax 518-486-6880, e-mail jcannell@mail.nysed.gov. World Wide Web http://www.nysl.nysed.gov.

## North Carolina

Mary L. Boone, State Libn., State Lib. of North Carolina, 4640 Mail Service Center, 109 E. Jones St., Raleigh 27699-4640. Tel. 919-807-7410, fax 919-733-8748, e-mail mary.boone@ncmail.net. World Wide Web http://statelibrary.dcr.state.nc.us.

## North Dakota

Doris Ott, State Libn., North Dakota State Lib., Dept. 250, 604 E. Boulevard Ave., Bismarck 58505-0800. Tel. 701-328-2492, fax 701-328-2040, e-mail dott@nd.us. World Wide Web http://ndsl.lib.state.nd.us.

## Ohio

Jo Budler, State Libn., State Lib. of Ohio, 274 E. 1 Ave., Columbus 43201. Tel. 614-644-7061, fax 614-466-3584, e-mail jbudler@sloma.state.ohio.us. World Wide Web http://www.library.ohio.gov.

## Oklahoma

Susan McVey, Dir., Oklahoma Dept. of Libs., 200 N.E. 18 St., Oklahoma City 73105. Tel. 405-522-3173, fax 405-525-7804, e-mail smcvey@oltn.odl.state.ok.us. World Wide Web http://www.odl.state.ok.us.

## Oregon

James B. Scheppke, State Libn., Oregon State Lib., 250 Winter St. N.E., Salem 97310-0640. Tel. 503-378-4367, fax 503-585-8059, e-mail jim.b.scheppke@state.or.us. World Wide Web http://oregon.gov/OSL.

## Pennsylvania

M. Clare Zales, Deputy Secy. of Educ. for Commonwealth Libs. (State Libn.), Office of Commonwealth Libs., 333 Market St., Harrisburg 17105-1745. Tel. 717-787-2646, fax 717-772-3265, e-mail mzales@state.pa.us. World Wide Web http://www.statelibrary. state.pa.us/libraries/site/default.asp.

## Rhode Island

Howard Boksenbaum, Chief Lib. Officer, Rhode Island Office of Lib. and Info. Services, 1 Capitol Hill, Providence 02908-5803. Tel. 401-574-9301, fax 401-574-9320, e-mail howardbm@olis.ri.gov. World Wide Web http://www.olis.ri.gov.

## South Carolina

David S. Goble, Dir. and State Libn., South Carolina State Lib., P.O. Box 11469, Columbia 29211. Tel. 803-734-8656, fax 803-734-8676, e-mail dgoble@statelibrary.sc.gov. World Wide Web http://www.statelibrary.sc. gov.

## South Dakota

Dan Siebersma, State Libn., South Dakota State Lib., 800 Governors Dr., Pierre 57501-2294. Tel. 605-773-3131, fax 605-773-6962, e-mail dan.siebersma@state.sd.us. World Wide Web http://library.sd.gov.

## Tennessee

Jeanne D. Sugg, State Libn./Archivist, Tennessee State Lib. and Archives, 403 Seventh Ave. N., Nashville 37243-0312. Tel. 615-741-7996, fax 615-532-9293, e-mail jeanne. sugg@state.tn.us. World Wide Web http:// www.state.tn.us/tsla.

## Texas

Peggy Rudd, Dir./Libn., Texas State Lib. and Archives Commission, P.O. Box 12927, Austin 78711-2927. Tel. 512-463-5460, fax 512-463-5436, e-mail peggy.rudd@tsl.state. tx.us. World Wide Web http://www.tsl.state. tx.us.

## Utah

Donna Jones Morris, State Libn./Dir., Utah State Lib. Div., Suite A, 250 N. 1950 W., Salt Lake City 84115-7901. Tel. 801-715-6770, fax 801-715-6767, e-mail dmorris@ utah.gov. World Wide Web http://library. utah.gov.

## Vermont

Martha Reid, State Libn., Vermont Dept. of Libs., 109 State St., Montpelier 05609-0601. Tel. 802-828-3265, fax 802-828-2199, e-mail martha.reid@mail.dol.state.vt.us. World Wide Web http://dol.state.vt.us.

## Virginia

Sandra Gioia Treadway, Libn. of Virginia, Lib. of Virginia, 800 E. Broad St., Richmond 23219-8000. Tel. 804-692-3535, fax 804-692-3594, e-mail sandra.treadway@lva. virginia.gov. World Wide Web http://www. lva.virginia.gov.

## Washington

Jan Walsh, State Libn., Washington State Lib., P.O. Box 42460, Olympia 98504-2460. Tel. 360-704-5253, fax 360-586-7575, e-mail jwalsh@secstate.wa.gov. World Wide Web http://www.secstate.wa.gov/library.

## West Virginia

James D. Waggoner, Secy., West Virginia Lib. Commission, Cultural Center, 1900 Kanawha Blvd. E., Charleston 25305-0620. Tel. 304-558-2041, fax 304-558-2044, e-mail waggoner@wvlc.lib.wv.us. World Wide Web http://librarycommission.lib.wv.us.

## Wisconsin

Richard Grobschmidt, State Libn., Asst. Superintendent, Div. for Libs. and Community Learning, Dept. of Public Instruction, P.O. Box 7841, Madison 53707-7841. Tel. 608-266-2205, fax 608-267-1052, e-mail richard.grobschmidt@dpi.state.wi.us. World Wide Web http://dpi.wi.gov/dltcl/index.html.

## Wyoming

Lesley Boughton, State Libn., Wyoming State Lib., 516 S. Greeley Hwy., Cheyenne 82002. Tel. 307-777-5911, fax 307-777-6289, e-mail lbough@state.wy.us. World Wide Web http://will.state.wy.us.

## American Samoa

Cheryl Morales, Territorial Libn., Feleti Barstow Public Lib., P.O. Box 997687, Pago Pago, AS 96799. Tel. 684-633-5816, fax 684-633-5823, e-mail feletibarstow@yahoo.com. World Wide Web http://fbpl.org.

## Federated States of Micronesia

Rufino Mauricio, Secy., National Archives, Culture, and Historic Preservation, P.O. Box PS 175, Palikir, Pohnpei, FM 96941. Tel. 691-320-2643, fax 691-320-5634, e-mail npo@mail.fm. World Wide Web http://www.fsmgov.org.

## Guam

Teresita L. G. Kennimer, Acting Dir./Territorial Libn., Guam Public Lib. System, 254 Martyr St., Hagatna 96910. Tel. 671-475-4754, fax 671-477-9777, e-mail gpls@gpls. guam.gov. World Wide Web http://gpls. guam.gov.

## Northern Mariana Islands

Erlinda Naputi, Acting State Libn., Joeten-Kiyu Public Lib., Box 501092, Saipan, MP 96950. Tel. 670-235-7324, fax 670-235-7550, e-mail naputi@saipan.com. World Wide Web http://www.cnmilibrary.com.

## Palau

Mario Katosang, Minister of Educ., Republic of Palau, P.O. Box 189, Koror, PW 96940. Tel. 680-488-2973, fax 680-488-1465, e-mail mariok@palaumoe.net. World Wide Web http://www.palaugov.net/PalauGov/Executiv e/Ministries/MOE/MOE.htm.

## Puerto Rico

Aura M. Rodriguez Ramos, Dir., Lib. Services and Info. Program, P.O. Box 190759, San Juan, PR 00919-0759. Tel. 787-754-1120, fax 787-754-0843, e-mail rodriguez ram@de.gobierno.pr. World Wide Web http://de.gobierno.pr/dePortal/Escuelas/Bibli otecas/Bibliotecarios.aspx.

## Republic of the Marshall Islands

Wilbur Heine, Secy. of Internal Affairs, Alele Inc., P.O. Box 629, Majuro, MH 96960. Tel. 692-625-8240, fax 692-625-3226, e-mail alele@ntamar.net. World Wide Web http://rmigovernment.org/index.jsp.

## Virgin Islands

Ingrid A. Bough, Territorial Dir. of Libs., Archives, and Museums, V.I. Dept. of Planning and Natural Resources, 1122 Kings Street, Christiansted, St. Croix VI 00802. Tel. 340-773-5715, fax 340-773-5327, e-mail ingrid.bough@dpnr.gov.vi. World Wide Web http://www.virginislandspace.org/Division% 20of%20Libraries/dlamwhat'snew.htm.

# Canada

## Alberta

Bonnie Gray, Mgr., Public Lib. Services, Alberta Municipal Affairs, 803 Standard Life Centre, 10405 Jasper Ave., Edmonton T5J 4R7. Tel. 780-415-0295, fax 780-415-8594, e-mail bonnie.gray@gov.ab.ca.

## British Columbia

Jacqueline van Dyk, Dir., Public Lib. Services Branch, Ministry of Education, P.O. Box 9831 Stn, Provincial Government, Victoria BC V8W 9T1. Tel. 250-356-1791, fax 250-953-3225, e-mail Jacquenline.vanDyk@gov.bc.ca

## Manitoba

Trevor Surgenor, Dir., Public Lib. Services, Manitoba Dept. of Culture, Heritage, Tourism, and Sport, 301-1011 Rosser Ave., Brandon R7A OL5. E-mail pls@gov.mb.ca.

## New Brunswick

Sylvie Nadeau, Exec. Dir., New Brunswick Public Lib. Service, 250 King St., Place 2000, P.O. Box 6000, Fredericton E3B 5H1. Tel. 506-453-2354, fax 506-444-4064, e-mail Sylvie.NADEAU@gnb.ca. World Wide Web http://www.gnb.ca/0003/index-e.asp.

## Newfoundland and Labrador

Shawn Tetford, Exec. Dir., Provincial Info. and Lib. Resources Board, 48 St. George's Ave., Stephenville A2N 1K9. Tel. 709-643-0900, fax 709-643-0925, e-mail stetford@nlpl.ca, World Wide Web http://www.nlpl.ca.

## Northwest Territories

Alison Hopkins, Territorial Libn., NWT Lib. Services, 75 Woodland Dr., Hay River X0E 1G1. Tel. 867-874-6531, fax 867-874-3321, e-mail Alison_Hopkins@gov.nt.ca. World Wide Web http://www.nwtpls.gov.nt.ca.

## Nova Scotia

Jennifer Evans, Dir., Nova Scotia Provincial Lib., 2021 Brunswick St., P.O. Box 578, Halifax B3J 2S9. Tel. 902-424-2457, fax 902-424-0633, e-mail evansjl@gov.ns.ca.

## Nunavut

Ron Knowling, Mgr., Nunavut Public Lib. Services, Box 270, Baker Lake X0C 0A0. Tel. 867-793-3353, fax 867-793-3360, e-mail rknowling@gov.nu.ca.

## Ontario

Aileen Carroll, Minister, Ontario Government Ministry of Culture, 900 Bay St., 5th fl., Mowat, Toronto M7A 1L2. Tel. 416-212-0644. Ontario Lib. Service—North, 334 Regent St., Sudbury, ON P3C 4E2. Tel. 705-675-6467; Southern Ontario Lib. Service, 111 Peter St., Suite 902, Toronto M5V 2H1. Tel. 416-961-1669 ext. 5118.

## Prince Edward Island

Kathleen Eaton, Provincial Libn., Province of Prince Edward Island, 89 Red Head Rd., P.O. Box 7500, Morell COA 1S0. Tel. 902-961-7320, fax 902-961-7322, e-mail plshq@gov.pe.ca.

## Quebec

Lise Bissonnette, Chair and CEO; Hélène Roussel, Dir. Gen. of Distribution, Bibliothèque et Archives Nationales du Québec (BAnQ), 475 Bvld. de Maisonneuve Est, Montreal H2L 5C4. Tel. 514-873-1100, fax 514-873-9312, e-mail pdg@banq.qc.ca or info@banq.qc.ca.

## Saskatchewan

Joylene Campbell, Provincial Libn., Saskatchewan Learning, 1945 Hamilton St., Regina S4P 2C8. Tel. 306-787-2972, fax 306-787-2029, e-mail jcampbell@library.gov.sk.ca.

## Yukon Territory

Julie Ourom, Dir., Public Libs., Community Development Div., Dept. of Community Services, Box 2703, Whitehorse Y1A 2C6. Tel. 867-667-5447, fax 867-393-6333, e-mail julie.ourom@gov.yk.ca.

# State School Library Media Associations

## Alabama

Children's and School Libns. Div., Alabama Lib. Assn. Memb. 650. Publication. *The Alabama Librarian* (q.).

*Chair* Barbara Curry, Autauga-Prattville Public Lib., 254 Doster St., Prattville 36067. E-mail bcurry@appl.info; *V. Chair/Chair-Elect* Dorothy Hunt, MacMillan International Academy, 25 Covington St., Montgomery 36104. E-mail jahunt62@knology.net; *Past Chair* Deidra Brewer, Highland Park/Webster Elementary, Muscle Shoals. E-mail dbrewer@mscs.k12.al.us; *Assn. Admin.* Dena Luce, Nichols Lib., Faulkner Univ., 5345 Atlanta Hwy., Montgomery 36109. Tel. 334-386-7482, email dluce@faulkner.edu.

Address correspondence to the association administrator.

World Wide Web http://allanet.org.

## Alaska

Alaska Assn. of School Libns. Memb. 200+. Publication. *The Puffin* (3 a year). *Ed.* Laura Guest. E-mail lauraguest@mtaonline.net.

*Pres.* Suzanne Metcalfe, Diamond H.S., Anchorage. E-mail metcalfe_suzanne@asdk12.org; *Pres.-Elect* Ann Morgester, Lib. Curriculum Coord., Anchorage. E-mail annm@alaska.net; *Secy.* Kari Sagel, Blatchley Middle School, Sitka. E-mail sagelk@mail.ssd.k12.ak.us; *Treas.* Janet Madsen, West Valley H.S., Fairbanks. E-mail jmadsen@northstar.k12.ak.us; *Past Pres.* Lynn Ballam, North Pole Middle School. E-mail lballam@mac.com.

World Wide Web http://www.akla.org/akasl.

## Arizona

Teacher-Libn. Div., Arizona Lib. Assn. Memb. 1,000. Publication. *AZLA Newsletter.*

*Chair* Sally Roof, Madison Meadows Middle School, 225 W. Ocotillo Rd. Phoenix 85013. Tel. 602-664-7640, e-mail sroofhott@cox.net; *Co-Chairs-Elect* Jean Kilker, 160 E. Estero Lane, Litchfield Park 85340. Tel. 602-764-2134 or 623-935-1464, e-mail jkilker@phxhs.k12.az.us or jean.kilker@gmail.com; Kerrita Westrick, Verrado Middle School, 553 Plaza Circle, Litchfield Park 85340. Tel. 623-547-1324 or 623-935-1911, e-mail kerrlita@cox.net or westrick@lesd.k12.az.us; *Past Chair* Linda Renfro, Blue Ridge Unified School Dist. Tel. 928-368-6119, e-mail lrenfro@brusd.k12.az.us.

Address correspondence to the chairperson.

World Wide Web http://www.azla.affiniscape.com.

## Arkansas

Arkansas Assn. of Instructional Media. Term of Office. Apr. 2008–April 2009.

*Pres.* Lori Bush. E-mail lori.bush@lh.k12.ar.us; *Pres.-Elect* Diane Hughes. E-mail dianeallenhughes@gmail.com; *Secy.* Glenda Jenkins. E-mail gjenkins@indian.dsc.k12.ar.us; *Treas.* Devona Pendergrass. E-mail dpendergrass@mtnhome.k12.ar.us; *Past Pres.* Devona Pendergrass.

Address correspondence to the president.

World Wide Web http://aaim.k12.ar.us.

## California

California School Lib. Assn. Memb. 2,000. Publication. *CSLA Journal* (2 a year); *CSLA Bulletin* (9 a year).

*Pres.* Connie Hamner Williams, Petaluma H.S., 201 Fair St., Petaluma 94952. Tel. 707-778-4662, e-mail chwms@mac.com; *Pres.-Elect* Rosemarie Bernier, Alexander Hamilton Senior H.S., 2955 Robertson Blvd., Los Angeles 90034. Tel. 310-280-1430, e-mail rbernier@lausd.net; *Past Pres.* Sandra Yoon, Bakersfield City ESD, 1300 Baker St., Bakersfield 93305. Tel. 661-631-4808, e-mail yoons@bcsd.com; *Exec. Dir.* Deidre Bryant, California School Lib. Assn., 950 Glenn Drive, Suite 150, Folsom 95630. Tel. 916-447-2684, fax 916-447-2695, e-mail diedreb@csla.net.

Address correspondence to the executive director.

World Wide Web http://www.schoolibrary.org.

## Colorado

Colorado Assn. of School Libns. Memb. 300+. Term of Office. Nov. 2008–Oct. 2010. *Pres.* Susan Gilbert, Clear Lake Middle School. Tel. 720-542-4606, e-mail gilbert.susan@comcast.net; *V.P./Pres.-Elect* Jen Cotton, Colorado Academy. Tel. 303-986-1501, e-mail jen.cotton@coloradoacademy.org; *Secy.* Nancy White, Academy School Dist. 20, 1110 Chapel Hill Drive, Colorado Springs 80904. Tel. 719-234-1362, e-mail nwhite@asd20.org; *Past Pres.* Su Eckhardt, 10930 W. Powers Ave., Littleton 80127. Tel. 303-979-7799, fax 970-245-7854, e-mail sueckhardt@earthlink.net; *Exec. Dir.* Kathleen Sagee Noland, Colorado Assn. of School Libns., 12081 W. Alameda Pkwy., No. 427, Lakewood 80228. Tel. 303-463-6400, fax 303-798-2485, e-mail kathleen@cal-webs.org or executivedirector@cal-webs.org.

World Wide Web http://www.cal-webs.org/associations2.html.

## Connecticut

Connecticut Assn. of School Libns. (formerly Connecticut Educational Media Assn.). Memb. 1,000+. Term of Office. July 2008–June 2009. Publication. *CEMAGram* (9 a year).

*Pres.* David Bilmes. E-mail bilmesd@new-milfordps.org; *V.P.* Lucia Rafala. E-mail luciarafala@sbcglobal.net; *Recording Secy.* Christopher Barlow. E-mail christophbarlow@sbcglobal.net; *Treas.* Sewell Pruchnik. E-mail spruchnik@snet.net; *Admin. Secy.* Anne Weimann, 25 Elmwood Ave., Trumbull 06611. Tel. 203-372-2260, e-mail anneweimann@gmail.com.

Address correspondence to the administrative secretary.

World Wide Web http://www.ctcasl.com

## Delaware

Delaware School Lib. Media Assn., Div. of Delaware Lib. Assn. Memb. 100+. Term of Office. May 2008–May 2009. Publications.

*DSLMA Newsletter* (online; irreg.); column in *DLA Bulletin* (3 a year).

*Pres.* Barb Fitzpatrick, Lulu M. Ross Elementary, 310 Lovers Lane, Milford 19963. E-mail bfitzpat@mail.milford.k12.de.us; *V.P./Pres.-Elect* Sharon Lyons, Central Middle School, 211 Delaware Ave., Dover 19901. E-mail slyons@capital.k12.de.us; *Secy.* Pat Bartoshesky, Highlands Elementary, 2100 Gilpin St., Wilmington 19806. E-mail patricia.bartoshesky@redclay.k12.de.us; *Past Pres.* Jane Stewart, W. B. Simpson Elementary, 5 Old North Rd., Camden 19934. E-mail jane.stewart@cr.k12.de.us.

Address correspondence to the president.

World Wide Web http://www.udel.edu/erc/dslma.

## District of Columbia

District of Columbia Assn. of School Libns. Memb. 35. Publication. *Newsletter* (4 a year).

*Pres.* André Maria Taylor. E-mail diva librarian2@aol.com; *V.P.* Gloria Reaves. E-mail gjenkn@comcast.net.

Address correspondence to Virginia Moore, 330 10th St. N.E., Washington DC 20002. Tel. 301-502-4203.

## Florida

Florida Assn. for Media in Educ. Memb. 1,400+. Term of Office. Nov. 2008–Oct. 2009. Publication. *Florida Media Quarterly.* *Ed.* Pat Dedicos. E-mail dedicosp@duval schools.org.

*Pres.* Deb Svec. E-mail dsvec@bellsouth.net; *Pres.-Elect* Cecelia Solomon. E-mail buckysmom@tampabay.rr.com; *Secy.* Gail Przeclawski. E-mail przeclg@ocps.net; *Treas.* Joanne Seale. E-mail seale.joanne@brevardschools.org; *Past Pres.* Miriam Needham. E-mail miriam.needham@marion.k12.fl.us; *Exec. Dir.* Larry E. Bodkin, Jr. Tel. 850-531-8351, fax 850-531-8344, e-mail lbodkin@floridamedia.org.

Address correspondence to FAME, 2563 Capital Medical Blvd., Tallahassee 32308. E-mail info@floridamedia.org.

World Wide Web http://www.floridamedia.org.

## Georgia

Georgia Lib. Assn., School Lib. Media Div. *Chair* Tim Wojcik, Our Lady of Mercy Catholic H.S. Tel. 770-461-2202, e-mail wojcikt@bellsouth.net; *Chair-Elect* Judi Repman, Georgia Southern Univ. Tel. 912-681-5394, e-mail jrepman@georgiasouthern.edu; *Secy.* Brian W. Jones, Forest Park H.S. Tel. 404-362-3890; *Past Chair* Pam Nutt, Moore Elementary. Tel. 770-229-3756, e-mail pnutt@spalding.k12.ga.us.

World Wide Web http://gla.georgialibraries.org/div_media.htm.

Georgia Lib. Media Assn. Memb. 700+. Term of Office. Jan.–Dec. 2009. *Pres.* Sherry Grove. E-mail grove.sherry@gmail.com; *Pres.-Elect* Susan Grigsby. E-mail susan.grigsby@gmail.com; *Secy.* Esther Brenneman. E-mail esther.brenneman@cherokee.k12.ga.us; *Treas.* Rebecca Amerson. E-mail rebecca.amerson@cherokee.k12.ga.us; *Past Pres.* Rosalind L. Dennis. E-mail rosalind_l_dennis@fc.dekalb.k12.ga.us.

World Wide Web http://www.glma-inc.org.

## Hawaii

Hawaii Assn. of School Libns. Memb. 200+. Term of Office. June 2008–May 2009. Publication. *HASL Newsletter* (4 a year).

*Co-Pres.* Grace Fujiyoshi. E-mail gracef@hawaii.rr.com; Linda Kim, Mililaniwaena Elementary. E-mail tklinda@hawaii.rr.com; *V.P., Programming* Jamie Ahlman, Salt Lake Elementary. E-mail jeahlman@gmail.com; *V.P., Membership* Deb Peterson, Punahou School. E-mail dpeterson@punahou.edu; *Secy.* Karen Graham, Noelani Elementary. E-mail kgraham@hawaii.rr.com; *Treas.* Jo-An Goss. E-mail gossj002@hawaii.rr.com; *Past Pres.* Linda Marks, Kalihi Uka Elementary. E-mail flcadiz@aol.com.

Address correspondence to the association, Box 235019, Honolulu 96823.

World Wide Web http://hasl.ws.

## Idaho

Educational Media Div., Idaho Lib. Assn. Term of Office. Oct. 2007–Oct. 2009. Publication. Column in *Idaho Librarian* (q.).

*Chair* Glynda Pflieger, Melba School District. E-mail gpflieger@melbaschools.org; *V. Chair/Chair-Elect* Susan Nickel, Capital H.S. E-mail susan.nickel@boiseschools.org.

Address correspondence to the chairperson.

World Wide Web http://www.idaholibraries.org.

## Illinois

Illinois School Lib. Media Assn. Memb. 1,100. Term of Office. July 2008–June 2009. Publications. *ISLMA News* (4 a year); *Linking for Learning: The Illinois School Library Media Program Guidelines; Powerful Libraries Make Powerful Learners: The Illinois Study.*

*Pres.* Randee Hudson, Millburn School, 18550 W. Millburn Rd., Wadsworth 60083. Tel. 847-356-8331, fax 847-356-9722, e-mail rhudson@millburn24.net; *Pres.-Elect* Gail Janz, Morris Community H.S., 1000 Union St., Morris 60450-1297. Tel. 815-941-5328, fax 815-941-5409, e-mail gjanz@mchs.grundy.k12.il.us; *Past Pres.* Jane A. Sharka, 0N655 Winfield Scott Drive, Winfield 60190. Tel. 630-668-6554, e-mail jane@sharka.org; *Exec. Secy.* Kay Maynard, ISLMA, P.O. Box 598, Canton 61520. Tel. 390-649-0911, fax 309-649-0916, e-mail islma@islma.org.

World Wide Web http://www.islma.org.

## Indiana

Assn. for Indiana Media Educators. Publications. *Focus on Indiana Libraries* (mo.); *Indiana Libraries* (q.).

*Pres.* Robyn Young, Avon H.S., 7575 Oriole Way, Avon 46123. Tel. 317-272-2586 ext. 3015, fax 317-272-4155, e-mail ryoung@avon.k12.in.us; *Pres.-Elect* Jill Youngblood, Adelaide De Vaney Elementary, 1011 S. Brown Ave., Terre Haute 47803. Tel. 812-462-4497, e-mail jey@vigoschools.org; *Secy.* Susie Highley, Creston Middle School, 10925 E. Prospect, Indianapolis 46239. Tel. 812-532-6806, fax 812-532-6891, e-mail shighley@warren.k12.in.us; *Treas.* Kristen Borrelli, Yost Elementary, 100 W. Beam St., Chesterton 46304. Tel. 219-983-3640, e-mail kristen.borrelli@duneland.k12.in.us; *Past Pres.* John McDonald, Connersville Middle

School, 1900 Grand Ave., Connersville 47331-2236. Tel. 765-825-1139, fax 765-827-4346, e-mail mcdonald@fayette.k12.in.us.

Address correspondence to the association, c/o Indiana Lib. Federation, 941 E. 86 St., Suite 260, Indianapolis 46240. Tel. 317-257-2040, fax 317-257-1389, e-mail ilf@indy.net.

World Wide Web http://www.ilfonline. org/AIME.

## Iowa

Iowa Assn. of School Libns. Memb. 192. Term of Office. Jan.–Jan. Publication. *IASL Journal* (online, 4 a year). *Co-Eds.* Karla Krueger. E-mail karla.krueger@uni.edu; Becky Johnson. E-mail bcjohnson@cr.k12.ia.us.

*Chair* Cheryl Carruthers. E-mail ccarruthersa@aea267.k12.ia.us; *V. Chair* Karen Lampe. E-mail klampe@aea14.k12.ia. us; *Secy./Treas.* Diane Brown. E-mail ddbrown @muscatine.k12.ia.us; *Past Pres.* Julie Larson. E-mail larson.julie@iccsd.k12.ia.us.

Address correspondence to the president.

World Wide Web http://www.iasl-ia.org.

## Kansas

Kansas Assn. of School Libns. Memb. 600. Term of Office. Aug. 2008–July 2009. Publication. *KASL News* (online; q.).

*Pres.* Cindy Pfeiffer. Tel. 620-235-3240, e-mail cpfeiffer@usd250.org; *Pres.-Elect* Barb Bahm. Tel. 913-845-2627, e-mail bbahm@ton464.org; *Secy.* Kaylyn Keating. E-mail kaylynk@manhattan.k12.ks.us; *Treas.* Kim Nowak. Tel. 785-735-2870, e-mail knowak@ruraltel.net; *Past Pres.* Laura Soash. Tel. 316-794-4260, e-mail lnsoash @yahoo.com; *Exec. Secy.* Judith Eller, 8517 W. Northridge, Wichita 67205. Tel. 316-773-6723, e-mail judell8517@sbcglobal.net.

Address correspondence to the executive secretary.

World Wide Web http://kasl.typepad.com/ kasl.

## Kentucky

Kentucky School Media Assn. Memb. 600+. Term of Office. Oct. 2008–Oct. 2009. Publication. *KSMA Newsletter* (q.).

*Pres.* Fred Tilsley, Sandgap Elementary. E-mail fred.tilsley@jackson.kyschools.us; *Pres.-Elect* Melissa Gardner. E-mail melissa. gardner@uky.edu; *Past Pres.* Evie Topcik, Louisville Collegiate School, 2427 Glenmary Ave., Louisville 40204. E-mail evtop@ loucol.com.

Address correspondence to the president.

World Wide Web http://www.kysma.org.

## Louisiana

Louisiana Assn. of School Libns. Memb. 250. Term of Office. July 2008–June 2009.

*Pres.* Charlene Picheloup. Tel. 337-229-4701, e-mail chpicheloup@iberia.k12.la.us; *1st V.P.* Annie Miers. Tel. 318-387-0567, e-mail miers@opsb.net; *2nd V.P.* Elizabeth P. Dumas. Tel. 318-396-9693, e-mail dumas@ opsb.net; *Secy.* Janet Lathrop. Tel. 225-635-3898, e-mail lathropj@wfpsb.org.

Address correspondence to the association, c/o Louisiana Lib. Assn., 421 S. 4 St., Eunice 70535. Tel. 337-550-7890, fax 337-550-7846, e-mail office@llaonline.org.

World Wide Web http://www.llaonline. org/sig/lasl.

## Maine

Maine School Lib. Assn. Memb. 210+. Publication. *Maine Entry* (with the Maine Lib. Assn.; q.).

*Pres.* Jeff Small, Cony H.S., Augusta. E-mail jsmall@augustaschools.org; *V.P.* Peggy Becksvoort, Falmouth Middle School. E-mail pbecks@fps.k12.me.us; *Secy.* Joyce Lewis, Winslow H.S. E-mail jlucas@winslowk12. org; *Treas.* Donna Chale, Warsaw Middle School. E-mail dchale@warsaw-ms.sad53. k12.me.us; *Past Pres.* Terri Caouette, Lincoln Middle School. E-mail tcaouette@ yahoo.com; *Exec. Secy.* Edna Comstock. E-mail empoweredna@gwi.net.

Address correspondence to the president.

World Wide Web http://www.maslibraries. org.

## Maryland

Maryland Assn. of School Libns. (formerly Maryland Educational Media Organization). Term of Office. July 2007–June 2009.

*Pres.* Elizabeth Shapiro, Westminster H.S. E-mail enshapi@k12.carr.org; *Pres.-Elect* Michele Forney, High Bridge Elementary. E-mail michele.forney@pgcps.org; *Secy.* Lori M. Carter, Howard County Public Schools. E-mail lori_carter@hcpss.org; *Treas.* Jennifer Harner, Rising Sun Elementary. E-mail jharner@ccps.org; *Past Pres.* Dorothy P. D'Ascanio, Jackson Road Elementary, Silver Spring. E-mail dorothy_p._d'ascanio@fc.mcps.k12.md.us.

Address correspondence to the association, Box 21127, Baltimore 21228.

World Wide Web http://maslmd.org.

## Massachusetts

Massachusetts School Lib. Assn. Memb. 800. Term of Office. June 2008–May 2009. Publication. *Media Forum* (online, q.).

*Pres.* Sandy Kelly, Carlisle Elementary. Tel. 978-369-6550 ext. 314; *Pres.-Elect* Gerri Fegan, West Middle School, Andover. Tel. 978-623-8706; *Secy.* Carol Klatt, Northeast Elementary, Waltham. Tel. 781-314-5647, e-mail klattc@k12.waltham.ma.us; *Treas.* Barbara Andrews, Andrews Consulting. Tel. 617-610-3792, e-mail bandrews4@rcn.com; *Exec. Dir.* Kathy Lowe, Massachusetts School Lib. Assn., P.O. Box 658, Lunenburg 01462. Tel. 978-582-6967, e-mail klowe@maschoollibraries.org.

Address correspondence to the executive director.

World Wide Web http://www.maschoollibraries.org.

## Michigan

Michigan Assn. for Media in Education. Memb. 1,200. Publications. *Media Spectrum* (2 a year); *MAME Newsletter* (4 a year).

*Pres.* Kathleen McBroom, Dearborn Public Schools, 18700 Audette, Dearborn 48124. Tel. 313-827-3078, fax 313-827-3132, e-mail mcbroom@dearborn.k12.mi.us; *Pres.-Elect* Lynn Gordon, Clarkston Community Schools, 6850 Hubbard Rd., Clarkston 48348. Tel. 248-623-5513, fax 248-623-5554, e-mail gordonlm@clarkston.k12.mi.us; *Secy.* Margy Barile, Haslett Public Schools, 5450 Marsh Rd., Haslett 48840. E-mail barilema@haslett.k12.mi.us; *Treas.* Bruce Popejoy, East

Jackson Community Schools, 4340 Walz Rd., Jackson 49201. Tel. 517-764-6010, fax 517-764-6081, e-mail mameexhibits@aol.com; *Past Pres.* Judy Hauser, Oakland Schools, 2111 Pontiac Lake Rd., Waterford 48328. Tel. 248-209-2371, fax 248-209-2538, e-mail judy.hauser@oakland.k12.mi.us; *Exec. Dir.* Roger Ashley, MAME, 1407 Rensen, Suite 3, Lansing 48910. Tel. 517-394-2808, fax 517-394-2096, e-mail ashleymame@aol.com.

Address correspondence to the executive director.

World Wide Web http://www.mame.gen.mi.us.

## Minnesota

Minnesota Educ. Media Organization. Memb. 700. Term of Office. July 2008–July 2009. Publications. *Minnesota Media*; *MEMOrandom*; *MTNews*.

*Pres.* Leslie Yoder, St. Paul Public Schools, 1930 Como Ave., St. Paul 55108. Tel. 651-603-4923, e-mail leslie.yoder@spps.org; *Pres.-Elect* Dawn Nelson, Sandburg Middle School, Golden Valley 55427. Tel. 763-504-8211, e-mail dawn_nelson@rdale.k12.mn.us; *Secy.* Mary Mehsikomer, Region 1/NW-LINKS, P.O. Box 1178, 810 4th Ave. S., Suite 220, Moorhead 56561. Tel. 218-284-3117, e-mail mary@region1.k12.mn.us; *Treas.* Margaret Meyer, 4371 107th Ave., Clear Lake 55319. Tel. 763-261-6324, e-mail mmeyer@becker.k12.mn.us; *Past Pres.* Gary Ganje, Dist. 742 Media Services, 115 13th Ave., South St. Cloud 56301. Tel. 320-252-8770, e-mail gary.ganje@isd742.org; *Admin. Asst.* Deanna Sylte, P.O. Box 130555, Roseville 55113. Tel. 651-771-8672, e-mail admin@memoweb.org.

World Wide Web http://memoweb.org.

## Mississippi

School Section, Mississippi Lib. Assn. Memb. 1,300.

*Co-Chairs* Diane B. Willard, Franklin Junior H.S. Tel. 601-384-2878, e-mail dwillard@fcsd.k12.ms.us; Melissa Moak, Mississippi School of the Arts. Tel. 601-823-1340, e-mail melissa.moak@msa.k12.ms.us; *Exec. Secy.* Mary Julia Anderson.

Address correspondence to School Section, Mississippi Lib. Assn., P.O. Box 13687, Jackson 39236-3687. Tel. 601-981-4586, fax 601-981-4501, e-mail info@misslib.org.

World Wide Web http://www.misslib.org.

## Missouri

Missouri Assn. of School Libns. Memb. 1,000. Term of Office. June 2008–June 2009. Publication. *Connections* (q.).

*Pres.* Gayla Strack. E-mail gayla.strack@raytownschools.org; *1st V.P./Pres.-Elect* Maggie Newbold. E-mail mnewbold@fz.k12. mo.us; *2nd V.P.* Patricia Antrim. E-mail antrim@ucmo.edu; *Secy.* Joyce McMurray. E-mail jmcmurray@fortosage.net; *Treas.* Curtis Clark. E-mail msmediacenter@harrisonville.k12.mo.us; *Past Pres.* Dea Borneman. E-mail deaborneman@missouri state.edu.

Address correspondence to the association, 606 Dix Rd., Jefferson City 65109. Tel. 573-893-4155, fax 573-632-6678, e-mail masl_org@earthlink.net.

World Wide Web http://www.maslonline. org.

## Montana

Montana School Lib. Media Div., Montana Lib. Assn. Memb. 200+. Publication. *FOCUS* (published by Montana Lib. Assn.) (q.).

*Exec. Asst., Montana Lib. Assn.* Debra Kramer, 169 W. River Rock Rd., Belgrade 59714. Tel. 406-670-8446, e-mail debkmla @hotmail.com.

World Wide Web http://www.mtlib.org/ ?q=node/166.

## Nebraska

Nebraska Educational Media Assn. Memb. 370. Term of Office. July 2008–June 2009. Publication. *NEMA News* (q.).

*Pres.* Robin Schrack. E-mail rschrack@esu3.org; *Pres.-Elect* Carrie Turner. E-mail carrieturner@westside66.org; *Treas.* Lynne Wragge. E-mail lynnewragge@hotmail.com; *Past Pres.* Judy A. Henning. E-mail judy. henning@kearneypublic.org; *Exec. Secy.* Jean Hellman. E-mail nemacontact@gmail. com.

Address correspondence to the executive secretary.

World Wide Web http://www.school librariesrock.org.

## Nevada

Nevada School and Children's Libs. Section, Nevada Lib. Assn. Memb. 120.

*Chair* Florica Hagendorn; *Exec. Secy.* Robbie DeBuff. E-mail rjdebuff@hotmail. com.

Address correspondence to the executive secretary.

World Wide Web http://www.nevada libraries.org/publications/handbook/nscls.html.

## New Hampshire

New Hampshire Educ. Media Assn., Box 418, Concord 03302-0418. Memb. 250+. Term of Office. June 2008–June 2009. Publication. *Online News* (fall, winter, spring; online and print).

*Pres.* Sharon Silva, Mastricola Upper Elementary, 26 Baboosic Lake Rd., Merrimack 03054. Tel. 603-424-6221, e-mail sharon. silva@merrimack.k12.nh.us; *V.P.* Kathy Lane, G. H. Hood Middle School, Derry 03038. E-mail klane@derry.k12.nh.us; *Recording Secy.* Melissa Moore, Northwood Elementary, Northwood 03290-6206. Tel. 603-942-5488 ext. 313, e-mail mmoore@northwood.k12.nh.us; *Treas.* Jeff Kent, 43 East Ridge Rd., Merrimack 03054. E-mail jkent@comcast.net; *Past Pres.* Diane Beaman, Laconia 03246. Tel. 603-524-8468, e-mail deaman@metrocast.net.

Address correspondence to the president.

World Wide Web http://www.nhema.net.

## New Jersey

New Jersey Association of School Librarians (NJASL). Memb. 1,100. Term of Office. Aug. 2008–July 2009. Publication. *Bookmark* (mo.).

*Pres.* Angela Crockett Coxen, P.S. 24, The New Roberto Clemente School, 482–507 Market St., Paterson 07501. Tel. 973-321-1000 ext. 22453, fax 973-321-0247, e-mail lmc24@paterson.k12.nj.us; *Pres.-Elect* Pat Massey, South Plainfield H.S., 200 Lake St.,

South Plainfield 07080. Tel. 908-754-4620 ext. 286, fax 908-756-7659, e-mail pmassey @spnet.k12.nj.us; *Corresponding Secy.* Amy Rominiecki, Seneca H.S., 110 Carranza Rd., Tabernacle 08088. Tel. 609-268-4600 ext. 6622, e-mail amyrominiecki@juno.com; *Recording Secy.* Mary Ann Greczek, Dunellen H.S., 411 First St., Dunellen 08812. Tel. 732-968-0885 ext. 17, fax 732-968-3138. e-mail greczekm@dunellenschools.org; *Treas.* Michelle Marhefka, Clearview Middle School, 595 Jefferson Rd., Mullica Hill 08062. Tel. 856-223-2732, fax 856-223-9068, e-mail marhefkami@clearviewregional.edu; *Past Pres.* Leslie Blatt, Dr. William H. Horton School, 291 N. 7 St., Newark 07107. Tel. 973-268-5286, e-mail mrsles@aol.com; *Exec. Dir., New Jersey Lib. Assn.* Pat Tumulty, P.O. Box 1534, Trenton 08607. Tel. 609-394-8032, fax 609-394-8164, e-mail ptumulty@njla.org.

Address correspondence to the president, NJASL, Box 610, Trenton 08607. Tel. 609-394-8032.

World Wide Web http://www.njasl.org.

### New York

School Lib. Media Section, New York Lib. Assn., 252 Hudson St., Albany 12210. Tel. 518-432-6952. Memb. 880. Term of Office. Oct. 2008–Oct. 2009. Publications. *SLMS-Gram* (q.); participates in *NYLA Bulletin* (mo. except July and Aug.).

*Pres.* Carole Kupelian. E-mail carolek@ twcny.rr.com; *Pres.-Elect* Diana Wendell. E-mail dwendell@moboces.org; *V.P. Conferences* Mary Tiedemann. E-mail mtiedemann @wallkillcsd.k12.ny.us; *V.P. Communications* Ellen Rubin. E-mail erubin@ wallkillcsd.k12.ny.us; *Secy.* Pauline Herr. E-mail pherr@acsdny.org; *Treas.* Patty Martire. E-mail pmartire@mtmorriscsd.org; *Past Pres.* Marie Barron. E-mail mbarron@cccsd. org.

World Wide Web http://www.nyla.org

### North Carolina

North Carolina School Lib. Media Assn. Memb. 1,180+. Term of Office. Oct. 2008– Oct. 2009.

*Pres.* Deb Christensen, Union County Public Schools, Central Academy of Technology and Arts, 600 Brewer Drive, Monroe 28112. Tel. 704-296-3088, fax 704-296-3090, e-mail deb.christensen@ucps.k12.nc. us; *V.P./Pres.-Elect* Kelly Brannock, Wake County Public Schools, 3355 Wendell Blvd., Wendell 27591. Tel. 919-365-2660, fax 919-365-2666, e-mail kbrannock@wcpss.net; *Secy.* Walter Carmichael, Vienna Elementary, 1975 Chickasha Rd., Pfafftown 27040. Tel. 336-945-5163, fax 336-945-9506, e-mail wcarmichael1@triad.rr.com; *Treas.* Kathy Cadden, Lake Norman Charter School, 1243 Old Statesville Rd., Huntersville 28078. Tel. 704-948-8600, fax 704-948-8778, e-mail kcadden@lncs.org; *Past Pres.* Trudy Moss, Watauga H.S., 400 High School Drive, Boone 28607. Tel. 828-264-2407, fax 828-264-9030, e-mail mosst@watauga.k12.nc.us.

Address correspondence to the president.

World Wide Web http://www.ncslma.org.

### North Dakota

School Lib. and Youth Services Section, North Dakota Lib. Assn. Memb. 100. Term of Office. Sept. 2008–Sept. 2009. Publication. *The Good Stuff* (q).

*Chair* Kathy Berg, 152 Riverside Park Rd., Bismarck 58504-5332. Tel. 701-323-4561, fax 701-250-4099, e-mail kathy_berg @bismarckschools.org.

Address correspondence to the chairperson.

World Wide Web http://ndlaonline.org.

### Ohio

Ohio Educational Lib. Media Assn. Memb. 1,000. Publications. *OELMA News* (3 a year); *Ohio Media Spectrum* (q.).

*Pres.* Marie Sabol. E-mail sabolm@ hudson.edu; *Secy.* Diane Smith. E-mail smithd@hudson.com; *Treas.* Cynthia Du-Chane. E-mail duchane@infohio.org; *Past Pres.* Kathy Halsey. E-mail khalsey@ canalwin.k12.oh.us; *Dir. of Services* Kate Brunswick, 17 S. High St., Suite 200, Columbus 43215. Tel. 614-221-1900, fax 614-221-1989, e-mail oelma@assnoffices.com.

Address correspondence to the director of services.

World Wide Web http://www.oelma.org.

## Oklahoma

Oklahoma Assn. of School Lib. Media Specialists. Memb. 300+. Term of Office. July 2008–June 2009. Publication. *Oklahoma Librarian.*

*Chair* Sally Rice. E-mail sbratton@ norman.k12.ok.us; *Chair-Elect* Cathy Carlson. E-mail cjcarlson@okcps.org; *Secy.* Carolyn McClure. E-mail mccluca@tulsa schools.org; *Treas.* Tina Ham. E-mail hamti @tulsaschools.org; *Past Pres.* Priscilla Allen. E-mail pdallen@okcps.org.

Address correspondence to the president, c/o Oklahoma Lib. Assn., 300 Hardy Drive, Edmond 73013. Tel. 405-348-0506.

World Wide Web http://www.oklibs.org/ oaslms.

## Oregon

Oregon Educ. Media Assn. Memb. 600. Term of Office. July 2008–June 2009. Publication. *OEMA Newsletter* (online).

*Pres.* Merrie Olson. E-mail lolson43@ msn.com; *Pres.-Elect* Carol Dinges. E-mail carol_dinges@lebanon.k12.or.us; *Secy.* Jenny Takeda. E-mail jenny_takeda@beavton.k12. or.us; *Treas.* Victoria McDonald. E-mail vmcdonald@lshigh.org; *Past Pres.* Gregory Lum. E-mail glum@jesuitportland.org; *Exec. Dir.* Jim Hayden, Box 277, Terrebonne 97760. Tel./fax 541-923-0675, e-mail j23hayden@aol.com.

Address correspondence to the executive director.

World Wide Web http://www.oema.net.

## Pennsylvania

Pennsylvania School Libns. Assn. Memb. 1,400+. Term of Office. July 2008–June 2009. Publication. *Learning and Media* (q.).

*Pres.* Nancy Smith Latanision. E-mail nanka5@ptd.net; *V.P./Pres.-Elect* Doug Francis. E-mail francisd@lasd.k12.pa.us; *Secy.* Beth Ann McGuire; *Treas.* Natalie Hawley. E-mail nhawley@masd.info; *Past*

*Pres.* Margaret Foster. E-mail mfoster@ northallegheny.org.

Address correspondence to the president.

World Wide Web http://www.psla.org.

## Rhode Island

Rhode Island Educ. Media Assn. Memb. 350+. Term of Office. June 2008–May 2009.

*Pres.* Zachary Berger. E-mail zmberger@ gmail.com; *V.P.* Jamie Greene. E-mail greenej@bw.k12.ri.us; *Secy.* Wendy Kirchner. E-mail wkirchner@meetingstreet.org; *Treas.* Jane Vincelette. E-mail jwv@cox.net; *Past Pres.* Jacquelyn Lamoureux. E-mail jackielam@cox.net.

Address correspondence to the association, Box 470, East Greenwich 02818.

World Wide Web http://www.ri.net/ RIEMA.

## South Carolina

South Carolina Assn. of School Libns. Memb. 1,100. Term of Office. June 2008–May 2009. Publication. *Media Center Messenger* (2 print issues a year; 8 online issues a year).

*Pres.* Valerie Byrd Fort. E-mail vfort@ lexington1.net; *V.P./Pres.-Elect* Amanda LeBlanc. E-mail aleblanc@greenville.k12. sc.us; *Secy.* Carole McGrath. E-mail cmcgrath@hampton1.k12.sc.us; *Treas.* Randa Edmunds. E-mail randaedmunds@hotmail. com; *Past Pres.* Kitt Lisenby. E-mail Cynthia. lisenby@kcsdschools.net.

Address correspondence to the president.

World Wide Web http://www.scasl.net.

## South Dakota

South Dakota School Lib. Media Assn., Section of the South Dakota Lib. Assn. and South Dakota Educ. Assn. Memb. 140+. Term of Office. Oct. 2008–Oct. 2009.

*Chair* Kerri Smith, Washington H.S., Sioux Falls. E-mail kerri.smith@k12.sd.us.

## Tennessee

Tennessee Assn. of School Libns. Memb. 450. Term of Office. Jan.–Dec. 2009. Publication. *Footnotes* (q.).

*Pres.* Bruce Hester, Northeast Middle School, 3703 Trenton Rd., Clarksville 37040. E-mail bruce.hester@cmcss.net; *V.P./Pres.-Elect* Becky Jackman, Northeast H.S., 3701 Trenton Rd., Clarksville 37040. E-mail rebecca.jackman@cmcss.net; *Secy.* Paige Eisemann, Woodlawn Elementary, 2250 Woodlawn Rd., Woodlawn 37191. E-mail paige.pickard@cmcss.net; *Treas.* Carol Burr, Goodlettsville Elementary, 514 Donald St., Goodlettsville 37072. E-mail carol.burr@mnps.org; *Past Pres.* Lynn Caruthers, Marvin Wright Elementary, 4717 Derryberry Lane, Spring Hill 37174. E-mail lcaruth@charter.net.

Address correspondence to the president.

World Wide Web http://www.korrnet.org/tasl.

## Texas

Texas Assn. of School Libns. (Div. of Texas Lib. Assn.). Memb. 4,000+. Term of Office. Apr. 2008–Apr. 2009. Publication. *Media Matters* (3 a year).

*Chair* Jackie Chetzron, Richardson ISD. Tel. 469-593-1624, e-mail jackie.chetzron@risd.org; *Chair-Elect* Cindy Buchanan, Aldine ISD. Tel. 281-985-7258, e-mail cbuchanan@aldine.k12.tx.us; *Secy.* Karen Harrel, Spring Branch ISD. Tel. 713-365-5450, e-mail karen.harrell@springbranchisd.com; *Past Chair* MaryJo Humphreys, Round Rock ISD. Tel. 512-424-6102, e-mail maryjohum@yahoo.com.

Address correspondence to Texas Lib. Assn., 3355 Bee Cave Rd., Suite 401, Austin 78746. Tel. 512-328-1518, fax 512-328-8852, e-mail tla@txla.org.

World Wide Web http://www.txla.org/groups/tasl.

## Utah

Utah Educ. Lib. Media Assn. Memb. 512. Term of Office. Mar. 2008–Feb. 2009. Publication. *UELMA Newsletter* (q.).

*Pres.* Debbie Naylor, Lehi H.S., 180 N. 500 E., Lehi 84043. Tel. 801-768-7000 ext. 337, fax 801-768-7007, e-mail dnaylor@alpine.k12.ut.us; *Pres.-Elect* Lanell Rabner, Springville H.S., 1205 E. 900 S., Springville

84663. Tel. 801-489-2870, fax 801-489-2806, e-mail lanell.rabner@nebo.edu; *Secy.* Cathy Keller, Timpanogos H.S., 1450 N. 200 E., Orem 84067. Tel. 801-223-3120, fax 801-223-3120 ext. 377, e-mail kellc786@alpine.k12.ut.us; *Past Pres.* Michael Goodman, Mount Jordan Middle School, 9360 S. 300 E., Sandy 84070. Tel. 801-412-2071, fax 801-412-2055, e-mail mlgcsg@msn.com; *Exec. Dir.* John L. Smith, High Ridge Media, 714 W. 1900 N., Clinton 84015. Tel. 801-776-6829, fax 801-773-8708, e-mail jlsutah@msn.com.

Address correspondence to the executive director.

World Wide Web http://www.uelma.org.

## Vermont

Vermont School Lib. Assn. (formerly Vermont Educ. Media Assn.). Memb. 220+. Term of Office. May 2008–May 2009. Publication. *VSLA News* (q.).

*Pres.* Susan Monmaney, Main Street Middle School, 170 Main St., Montpelier 05602. E-mail susanm@mpsvt.org; *Pres.-Elect* Marsha Middleton, North Country Union H.S., P.O. Box 725, 209 Veterans Ave., Newport 05855. E-mail mmiddleton@ncuhs.org; *Secy.* Dollinda Lund, Lyndon Institute, Lyndon Center 05850. E-mail dollinda.lund@lyndoninstitute.org; *Treas.* Donna Smyth, 4 Homer Ave., Queensbury, NY 12804. E-mail smyth78@gmail.com; *Past Pres.* Jean Fournier, Grace Stuart Orcutt Lib., St. Johnsbury Academy, St. Johnsbury 05819. E-mail jfournier@stjacademy.org.

Address correspondence to the president.

World Wide Web http://vsla.info.

## Virginia

Virginia Educ. Media Assn. Memb. 1,700. Term of Office. (Pres., Pres.-Elect) Nov. 2008–Nov. 2009 (other officers two years in alternating years). Publication. *Mediagram* (q.).

*Pres.* Terrill Britt, G. A. Treakle Elementary, Chesapeake. E-mail britttwe@cps.k12.va.us; *Pres.-Elect* Charlie B. Makela, Arlington Public Schools, Arlington. E-mail cmakela@arlington.k12.va.us; *Secy.* Janice

Raspen, Conway Elementary, Stafford County. E-mail jraspen@staffordschools.net; *Treas.* Frances Reeve, Longwood Univ., Farmville. E-mail reevefm@longwood.edu; *Past Pres.* Nancy Silcox, Samuel W. Tucker Elementary, Alexandria. E-mail nancy.silcox@acps.k12.va.us; *Exec. Dir.* Jean Remler. Tel. 703-764-0719, fax 703-272-3643, e-mail jremler@pen.k12.va.us.

Address correspondence to the association, Box 2743, Fairfax 22031-0743.

World Wide Web http://vema.gen.va.us.

## Washington

Washington Lib. Media Assn. Memb. 1,450+. Term of Office. October–October. Publication. *The Medium* (3 a year).

*Pres.* Dave Sonnen. E-mail wlmadave@gmail.com; *Pres.-Elect* Linda King. E-mail winesapple@aol.com; *V.P.* Gary Simundson. E-mail gsimunds@egreen.wednet.edu; *Secy.* Steve Coker. E-mail cokers@rainier.wednet.edu; *Treas.* Kate Pankiewicz. E-mail kate.pankiewicz@shorelineschools.org; *Past Pres.* Linda Collins. E-mail lcollins@upsd.wednet.edu.

Address correspondence to the association, 10924 Mukilteo Speedway, PMB 142, Mukilteo, WA 98275. E-mail wlma@wlma.org.

World Wide Web http://www.wlma.org.

## West Virginia

School Lib. Div., West Virginia Lib. Assn. Memb. 50. Term of Office. Nov. 2007–Nov. 2009. Publication. *WVLA School Library News* (5 a year).

*Co-Chairs* Karen Figgatt, Bonham Elementary, Rt. 1, Box 425A, Charleston 25312. Tel. 304-348-1912, fax 304-348-1367, e-mail kfiggatt@kcs.kana.k12.wv.us; Celene Seymour, Marshall Univ. Graduate College, 100

Angus E. Peyton Drive, South Charleston 25303-1600. Tel. 304-746-8901, e-mail seymour@marshall.edu.

Address correspondence to the chairpersons.

## Wisconsin

Wisconsin Educational Media and Technology Assn. Memb. 1,100+. Publication. *WEMTA Dispatch* (q.).

*Pres.* Jo Ann Carr E-mail carr@education.wisc.edu; *Pres.-Elect* Keith Schroeder E-mail keitschr@hssd.k12.wi.us; *Secy.* Vicki Santacroce. E-mail vsantacroce@ashwaubenon.k12.wi.us; *Treas.* Sandy Heiden. E-mail sheiden@seymour.k12.wi.us; *Past Pres.* Annette Smith. E-mail arsmith@centurytel.net.

Address correspondence to Courtney Rounds, WEMA Assn. Mgr., P.O. Box 206, Boscobel 53805. Tel. 608-375-6020, e-mail wemtamanager@hughes.net.

World Wide Web http://www.wemaonline.org.

## Wyoming

School Lib. Media Personnel Section, Wyoming Lib. Assn. Memb. 90+. Term of Office. Oct. 2008–Oct. 2009. Publications. *WLA Newsletter*; *SSLMP Newsletter*.

*Chair* Peggy Jording, Newcastle Schools. E-mail jordingp@weston1.k12.wy.us; *Chair-Elect* Barb Osborne, Highland Park Elementary. E-mail osborneb@scsd2.com; *Secy.* Sally Hoover, Newcastle H.S. E-mail hoovers@weston1.k12.wy.us; *Past Pres.* Sheryl Fanning, Cheyenne East H.S., E-mail fannings@laramie1.k12.wy.us.

Address correspondence to the chairperson.

World Wide Web http://www.wyla.org/schools.

# International Library Associations

## International Association of Agricultural Information Specialists

Peter Ballantyne, President
P.O. Box 63, Lexington, KY 40588-0063
E-mail peter.ballantyne@iaald.org
World Wide Web http://www.iaald.org

### Object

The International Association of Agricultural Information Specialists (IAALD) facilitates professional development of and communication among members of the agricultural information community worldwide. Its goal is to enhance access to and use of agriculture-related information resources. To further this mission, IAALD will promote the agricultural information profession, support professional development activities, foster collaboration, and provide a platform for information exchange. Founded 1955.

### Membership

Memb. 3,400+. Dues (Inst.) US$110; (Indiv.) US$50.

### Officers

*Pres.* Peter Ballantyne (Netherlands). E-mail peter.ballantyne@iaald.org; *1st V.P.* Stephen Rudgard (Italy). E-mail stephen.rudgard@iaald.org; *2nd V.P.* Dorothy Mukhebi (Uganda). E-mail dorothy.mukhebi@iaald.org; *Secy.-Treas.* Toni Greider (USA). E-mail toni.greider@iaald.org.

### Publication

*Agricultural Information Worldwide* (memb.).

## International Association of Law Libraries

Jules Winterton, President
c/o Institute of Advanced Legal Studies, 17 Russell Square, London WC1B 5DR, England
World Wide Web http://www.iall.org

### Object

The International Association of Law Libraries (IALL) is a worldwide organization of librarians, libraries, and other persons or institutions concerned with the acquisition and use of legal information emanating from sources other than their jurisdictions and from multinational and international organizations.

IALL's purpose is to facilitate the work of librarians who acquire, process, organize, and provide access to foreign legal materials. IALL has no local chapters but maintains liaison with national law library associations in many countries and regions of the world.

### Membership

More than 800 members in more than 50 countries on five continents.

## Officers

*Pres.* Jules Winterton, Institute of Advanced Legal Studies, Univ. of London, 17 Russell Sq., London WCIB 5DR, England. Tel. 44-20-7862-5884, fax 44-20-7862-5850, e-mail julesw@sas.ac.uk; *1st V.P.* Richard Danner, Duke Univ. School of Law, Box 90361, Durham, NC 27708-0361. Tel. 919-613-7115, fax 919-613-7237, e-mail danner@law.duke.edu; *2nd V.P.* Halvor Kongshavn, Law Lib., Bergen Univ. Lib., N-5020 Bergen, Norway. Tel. 47-55-58-95-25, fax 47-55-58-95-22, e-mail halvor.kongshavn@ub.uib.no; *Secy.* Jennefer Aston, Bar Council of Ireland, P.O. Box 4460, Dublin 7, Ireland. Tel. 353-1-817-5121, fax 353-1-817-5151, e-mail jaston@iol.ie; *Treas.* Ann Morrison, Dalhousie Law School, 6061 University Ave., Halifax, Nova Scotia B3H 4H9, Canada. Tel. 902-494-2640/6301, fax 902-494-6669, e-mail ann.morrison@dal.ca; *Past Pres.* Holger Knudsen, Max-Planck-Institut für Ausländisches und Internationales Privatrecht, Mittelweg 187, D-20148, Hamburg, Germany. Tel. 49-40-41900-226, fax 49-40-41900-288, e-mail knudsen@mpipriv.de.

## Board Members

Amanda Barratt, Brand Van Zyl Law Lib., Univ. of Cape Town, South Africa; Ruth Bird, Bodleian Law Lib., Oxford Univ., England; Barbara Garavaglia, Univ. of Michigan Law Lib.; Ligita Gjortlere, Riga Graduate School of Law Lib., Riga, Latvia; Petal Kinder, High Court of Australia Lib., Canberra; Xinh Luu, Univ. of Virginia Law Lib.; Uma Narayan, Bombay High Court, Mumbai, India; Anita Soboleva, JURIX (Jurists for Constitutional Rights and Freedoms), Moscow, Russia.

## Publication

*International Journal of Legal Information* (3 a year; US$60 indiv.; US$95 institutions).

# International Association of Music Libraries, Archives and Documentation Centres

c/o Roger Flury, IAML Secretary-General
Music Room, National Library of New Zealand
Box 1467, Wellington 6001, New Zealand
Tel. 64-4-474-3039, fax 64-4-474-3035, e-mail secretary@iaml.info
World Wide Web http://www.iaml.info

## Object

The object of the International Association of Music Libraries, Archives and Documentation Centres (IAML) is to promote the activities of music libraries, archives, and documentation centers and to strengthen the cooperation among them; to promote the availability of all publications and documents relating to music and further their bibliographical control; to encourage the development of standards in all areas that concern the association; and to support the protection and preservation of musical documents of the past and the present.

## Membership

Memb. 2,000.

## Board Members

*Pres.* Martie Severt, MCO Muziekbibliotheek, Postbus 125, NL-1200 AC Hilversum, Netherlands. E-mail m.severt@mco.nl; *V.P.s* James P. Cassaro, Theodore M. Finney Music Lib., Univ. of Pittsburgh, B28 Music Bldg., Pittsburgh, PA 15260. Tel. 412-624-4130, fax 412-624-4180, e-mail cassaro+@pitt.edu; Jon Bagues, ERESBIL, Archivo

Vasco de la Música C/ Alfonso XI, 2, Código postal 20100-Errenteria Guipuzcoa, Euskal Herria, Spain. Tel. 34-943-000-868, fax 34-943-529-706, e-mail jbagues@eresbil.com; Aurika Gergeleziu, Fine Arts Information Centre, National Lib. of Estonia, Tönismägi 2, EE15189 Tallinn, Estonia. Tel. 372-6307-159, fax 372-6311-410, e-mail aurika@nlib.ee; Jutta Lambrecht, WDR D&A/Recherche Leitung Musik und Notenarchiv, Appellhofplatz 1, D-50667 Cologne, Germany. Tel. 49-0-221-220-3376, fax 49-0-221-220-9217, e-mail jutta.lambrecht@wdr.de; *Treas.* Kathryn Adamson, Royal Academy of Music, Marylebone Rd., London NW1 5HT, England. Tel. 44-0-20-7873-7321, e-mail k.adamson@ram.ac.uk; *Past Pres.* Massimo Gentili-Tedeschi, Biblioteca Nazionale Braidense, Ufficio Ricerca Fondi Musicali, via Conservatorio 12, I-20122 Milan, Italy. Tel. 39-02-7601-1822, fax 39-02-7600-3097.

## Publication

*Fontes Artis Musicae* (4 a year; memb.). *Ed.*

Maureen Buja, Naxos Digital Services Ltd., Level 11, Cyberport 1, 100 Cyberport Rd., Hong Kong. Tel. 852-2993-5635.

## Professional Branches

Archives and Documentation Centres. Marguerite Sablonnière, Bibliothèque Nationale de France, Département de la Musique, 58 rue de Richelieu, 75002 Paris, France.

Broadcasting and Orchestra Libraries. Angela Escott, Royal College of Music, Prince Consort Rd., London SW7 2BS, England.

Libraries in Music Teaching Institutions. Pia Shekhter, Academy of Music and Drama, Göteborg University, SE-405 30 Göteborg, Sweden.

Public Libraries. Hanneke Kuiper, Public Lib., Oosterdoksstraat 143, 1011 DK Amsterdam, Netherlands.

Research Libraries. Stanislaw Hrabia, Uniwersytet Jagiellonski Instytut Muzykologii Biblioteka, ul. Westerplatte 10 31-033 Krakow, Poland.

# International Association of School Librarianship

Karen Bonanno, Executive Secretary
P.O. Box 83, Zillmere, Qld. 4034, Australia
Fax 617-3633-0570, e-mail iasl@iasl-online.org
World Wide Web http://www.iasl-online.org

## Object

The mission of the International Association of School Librarianship (IASL) is to provide an international forum for those interested in promoting effective school library programs as viable instruments in the educational process. The association provides guidance and advice for the development of school library programs and the school library profession. IASL works in cooperation with other professional associations and agencies.

The objectives of IASL are to advocate the development of school libraries throughout all countries; to encourage the integration of school library programs into the instructional and curriculum development of the school; to promote the professional preparation and continuing education of school library personnel; to foster a sense of community among school librarians in all parts of the world; to foster and extend relationships between school librarians and other professionals connected with children and youth; to foster research in the field of school librarianship and the integration of its conclusions with pertinent knowledge from related fields; to promote the publication and dissemination of information about successful advocacy and program initiatives in school librarianship; to share information about programs and materials for children and youth throughout the international community; and to initiate and coordinate activities, conferences, and other projects in the field of school librarianship and information services. Founded 1971.

## Membership

Approximately 700.

## Officers and Executive Board

*Pres.* James Henri, Hong Kong; *V.P.s* Barbara Combes, Australia; Lesley Farmer, USA; Diljit Singh, Malaysia; *Treas.* Anne Lockwood, Australia; *Dirs.* Busi Dlamini, Africa–Sub-Sahara; Lourense Das, Europe; Marlene Asselin, Canada; Blanche Woolls, USA; June Wall, Oceania; Angel Leung Yuet Ha, East Asia; Ingrid Skirrow, International

Schools; Katharina B. L. Berg, Latin America/Caribbean; Madhu Bhargava, Asia; Michelle Fitzgerald, North Africa/Middle East.

## Publications

Selected papers from proceedings of annual conferences:

32nd Annual Conference, 2003, Durban, South Africa. *School Libraries: Breaking Down Barriers.* US$30.

34th Annual Conference, 2005, Hong Kong. *Information Leadership in a Culture of Change.* US$20.

35th Annual Conference, 2006, Lisbon, Portugal. *The Multiple Faces of Literacy: Reading. Knowing. Doing.* US$20.

36th Annual Conference, 2007, Taipei, Taiwan. *Cyberspace, D-world, E-learning: Giving Libraries and Schools the Cutting Edge.* US$20.

# International Association of Technological University Libraries

President, Maria Heijne, Postbus 98, 2600 MG Delft, Netherlands
World Wide Web http://www.iatul.org

## Object

The object of the International Association of Technological University Libraries (IATUL) is to provide a forum where library directors can meet to exchange views on matters of current significance in the libraries of universities of science and technology. Research projects identified as being of sufficient interest may be followed through by working parties or study groups.

## Membership

Ordinary, associate, sustaining, and honorary. Membership fee 75–150 euros a year, sustaining membership 500 euros a year. Memb. 239 (in 42 countries).

## Officers and Executives

*Pres.* Maria Heijne, Postbus 98, 2600 MG Delft, Netherlands. E-mail M.A.M.Heijne@ library.tudelft.nl; *Secy.* Paul Sheehan, Dublin City Univ. Lib., Dublin 9, Ireland. E-mail paul.sheehan@dcu.ie; *Treas.* Reiner Kallenborn, Munich Technical Univ. Lib., Arcisstrasse 21, Munich 80230, Germany. E-mail kallenborn@ub.tum.de; *Past Pres.* Gaynor Austen, Queensland Univ. Technology Lib., GPO Box 2434, Brisbane, Qld. 4001, Australia. E-mail g.austen@qut.edu.au.

## Publication

*IATUL Proceedings on CD-ROM* (ann.).

# International Council on Archives

David Leitch, Secretary-General
60 rue des Francs-Bourgeois, 75003 Paris, France
Tel. 33-1-40-27-63-06, fax 33-1-42-72-20-65, e-mail ica@ica.org
World Wide Web http://www.ica.org

## Object

The mission of the International Council on Archives (ICA) is to establish, maintain, and strengthen relations among archivists of all lands, and among all professional and other agencies or institutions concerned with the custody, organization, or administration of archives, public or private, wherever located. Established 1948.

## Membership

Memb. Approximately 1,800 (representing about 180 countries and territories).

## Officers

*Secy.-Gen.* David Leitch; *Deputy Secy.-Gen.* Perrine Canavaggio; *Pres.* Ian E. Wilson, Libn. and Archivist of Canada; *V.P.s* Ross Gibbs, National Archives of Australia; Nolda C. Romer-Kenepa, National Archives of the Netherlands Antilles; Tomas Lidman, Na-tional Archives of Sweden; Abdullah A. Kareem El Reyes, National Centre for Documentation and Research, United Arab Emirates; Lew Bellardo, Advisor to the Archivist of the United States; Christine Martinez, Archives de France; Setareki Tale, Government Archives of Fiji; Hans Eyvind Naess, National Archives of Norway.

## Publications

*Comma* (memb.). (CD-ROM only since 2005.)

*Flash* (3 a year; memb.).

*Guide to the Sources of the History of Nations* (Latin American Series, 11 vols. pub.; Africa South of the Sahara Series, 20 vols. pub.; North Africa, Asia, and Oceania Series, 15 vols. pub.).

*Guide to the Sources of Asian History* (English-language series [India, Indonesia, Korea, Nepal, Pakistan, Singapore], 14 vols. pub.; national language series [Indonesia, Korea, Malaysia, Nepal, Thailand], 6 vols. pub.; other guides, 3 vols. pub.).

# International Federation of Film Archives

Secretariat, 1 rue Defacqz, B-1000 Brussels, Belgium
Tel. 32-2-538-3065, fax 32-2-534-4774, e-mail info@fiafnet.org
World Wide Web http://www.fiafnet.org

## Object

Founded in 1938, the International Federation of Film Archives (FIAF) brings together not-for-profit institutions dedicated to rescuing films and any other moving-image elements considered both as cultural heritage and as historical documents.

FIAF is a collaborative association of the world's leading film archives whose purpose has always been to ensure the proper preservation and showing of motion pictures. A total of 141 archives in more than 70 countries collect, restore, and exhibit films and cinema documentation spanning the entire history of film.

FIAF seeks to promote film culture and facilitate historical research, to help create new archives around the world, to foster training and expertise in film preservation, to encourage the collection and preservation of documents and other cinema-related materials, to develop cooperation between archives, and to ensure the international availability of films and cinema documents.

## Officers

*Pres.* Eva Orbanz; *Secy.-Gen.* Meg Labrum; *Treas.* Patrick Loughney; *Membs.* Jan-Erik Billinger, Vittorio Boarini, Sylvia Frank, Luca Giuliani, Lise Gustavson, Eric Le Roy, Carlos Magalhães, Hisashi Okajima, Vladimir Opela, Iván Trujillo Bolio.

Address correspondence to Christian Dimitriu, Senior Administrator, c/o FIAF Secretariat. E-mail c.dimitriu@fiafnet.org.

## Publications

*Journal of Film Preservation.*

*International Index to Film Periodicals.*

*FIAF International Filmarchive* database (OVID).

*FIAF International Index to Film Periodicals* (ProQuest).

For additional FIAF publications, see http://www.fiafnet.org.

# International Federation of Library Associations and Institutions

Jennefer Nicholson, Secretary-General
P.O. Box 95312, 2509 CH The Hague, Netherlands
Tel. 31-70-314-0884, fax 31-70-383-4827
E-mail ifla@ifla.org, World Wide Web http://www.ifla.org

## Object

The object of the International Federation of Library Associations and Institutions (IFLA) is to promote international understanding, cooperation, discussion, research, and development in all fields of library activity, including bibliography, information services, and the education of library personnel, and to provide a body through which librarianship can be represented in matters of international interest. IFLA is the leading international body representing the interests of library and information services and their users. It is the global voice of the library and information profession. Founded 1927.

## Officers and Governing Board

*Pres.* Claudia Lux, Zentral- und Landesbibliothek, Berlin; *Pres.-Elect* Ellen Tise, Univ. of Stellenbosch, South Africa; *Treas.* Gunnar Sahlin, National Lib. of Sweden, Stockholm; *Governing Board* Helena R. Asamoah-Hassan, Kwame Nkrumah Univ. of Science and Technology, Kumasi, Ghana; Barbara J. Ford, Univ. of Illinois at Urbana-Champaign; Premila Gamage, Institute of Policy Studies, Colombo, Sri Lanka; Nancy E. Gwinn, Smithsonian Inst. Lib., Washington, D.C.; Torny Kjekstad, Baerum Bibliotek, Sandvika, Norway; Trine Kolderup Flaten, Bergen Public Lib., Bergen, Norway; Patrice Landry, Swiss National Lib., Bern; Bob McKee, CILIP, London; Danielle Mincio, Bibliothèque Cantonale et Universitaire, Lausanne, Switzerland; Ingrid Parent, Lib. and Archives Canada, Ottawa; Pascal Sanz, Bibliothèque Nationale de France, Paris; Réjean Savard, Univ. de

Montréal-EBSI, Montreal; Barbara Schleihagen, Deutscher Bibliotheksverband e.V., Berlin; Joaquín Selgas Gutiérrez, Biblioteca de Castilla-La Mancha, Toledo, Spain; Lynn F. Sipe, Univ. of Southern California, Los Angeles; Anna Maria Tammaro, Univ. of Parma, Fiesole, Italy; Steve W. Witt, Center for Global Studies, Univ. of Illinois; Zhang Xiaolin, Lib. of Chinese Academy of Sciences, Beijing; *Secy.-Gen.* Jennefer Nicholson; *Coord. Professional Activities* Sjoerd M. J. Koopman.

## Publications

*IFLA Annual Report.*
*IFLA Directory* (bienn.).
*IFLA Journal* (4 a year).
IFLA Professional Reports.
IFLA Publications Series.
IFLA Series on Bibliographic Control.
*International Cataloguing and Bibliographic Control* (q.).
*International Preservation News.*

## American Membership

American Assn. of Law Libs.; American Lib. Assn.; Assn. for Lib. and Info. Science Educ.; Assn. of Research Libs.; Medical Lib. Assn.; Special Libs. Assn. *Institutional Membs.* There are 126 libraries and related institutions that are institutional members or consultative bodies and sponsors of IFLA in the United States (out of a total of 1,119), and 104 personal affiliates (out of a total of 290).

# International Organization for Standardization

Robert Steele, Secretary-General
ISO Central Secretariat, 1 ch. de la Voie-Creuse, Case postale 56, CH-1211 Geneva 20,
Switzerland
41-22-749-01-11, fax 41-22-733-34-30, e-mail central@iso.org
World Wide Web http://www.iso.org

## Object

The International Organization for Standardization (ISO) is a worldwide federation of national standards bodies, founded in 1947, at present comprising 158 members, one in each country. The object of ISO is to promote the development of standardization and related activities in the world with a view to facilitating international exchange of goods and services, and to developing cooperation in the spheres of intellectual, scientific, technological, and economic activity. The scope of ISO covers international standardization in all fields except electrical and electronic engineering standardization, which is the responsibility of the International Electrotechnical Commission (IEC). The results of ISO technical work are published as international standards.

## Officers

*Pres.* Alan Morrison, Australia; *V.P. (Policy)* George Arnold, USA; *V.P. (Technical Management)* Jacob Holmblad, Denmark.

## Technical Work

The technical work of ISO is carried out by 208 technical committees. These include:

*ISO/TC 46–Information and documentation* (Secretariat, Association Française de Normalization, 11 ave. Francis de Pressensé, 93571 Saint-Denis La Plaine, Cedex, France). Scope: Standardization of practices relating to libraries, documentation and information centers, indexing and abstracting services, archives, information science, and publishing.

*ISO/TC 37–Terminology and language and content resources* (Secretariat, INFO-TERM, Aichholzgasse 6/12, 1120 Vienna, Austria, on behalf of Österreichisches Normungsinstitut). Scope: Standardization of principles, methods, and applications relating to terminology and other language and content resources in the contexts of multilingual communication and cultural diversity.

*ISO/IEC JTC 1–Information technology* (Secretariat, American National Standards Institute, 25 W. 43 St., 4th fl., New York, NY 10036). Scope: Standardization in the field of information technology.

## Publications

*ISO Annual Report.*

*ISO CataloguePlus on CD-ROM* (combined catalog of published standards and technical work program) (ann.).

*ISO Focus* (11 a year).

*ISO International Standards.*

*ISO Management Systems* (bi-mo.).

*ISO Memento* (ann.).

*ISO Online* information service on World Wide Web (http://www.iso.org).

# Foreign Library Associations

The following is a list of regional and national library associations around the world. A more complete list can be found in *International Literary Market Place* (Information Today, Inc.).

## Regional

### Africa

Standing Conference of Eastern, Central, and Southern African Lib. and Info. Assns., c/o Zambia Lib. Assn., P.O. Box 32379, Lusaka 10101, Zambia. Tel. 260-966-72-9464, World Wide Web http://www.scecsal.org/ssecret.html. *Chair* Benson Njobvu. E-mail benson.njobvu@gmail.com; *Secy.* Muntinta Beene Nabuyanda.

### The Americas

Asociación de Bibliotecas Universitarias, de Investigación e Institucionales del Caribe (ACURIL) (Assn. of Caribbean Univ., Research, and Institutional Libs.), Box 23317, UPR Sta., San Juan, PR 00931-3317. Tel. 787-790-8054, 787-764-0000, e-mail acuril@uprrp.edu, World Wide Web http://acuril.uprrp.edu/que.htm. *Pres.* Pedro Padilla-Rosa, Biblioteca de Derecho, Universidad de Puerto Rico. E-mail ppadilla@law.upr.edu; *Exec. Secy.* Oneida Rivera de Ortiz, Biblioteca Regional del Caribe y Estudios Latinoamericanos, Sistema de Bibliotecas, Universidad de Puerto Rico, P.O. Box 23317, San Juan 00931. Tel. 787-764-0000 ext. 7916, e-mail acurilsec@yahoo.com.

Seminar on the Acquisition of Latin American Lib. Materials (SALALM), c/o *Exec. Secy.* Hortensia Calvo, SALALM Secretariat, Latin American Lib., 422 Howard Tilton Memorial Lib., 7002 Freret St., New Orleans, LA 70118-5549. Tel. 504-247-1366, fax 504-247-1367, e-mail salalm@tulane.edu, World Wide Web http://www.salalm.org. *Pres.* John Wright. E-mail john_wright@byu.edu.

## Asia

Congress of Southeast Asian Libns. (CONSAL). *Secy.-Gen.* Nguyen Huy Chuong, Dir., Lib. and Info. Center, Hanoi National Univ.; *Secy.* Nguyen Thu Phuong, International Relations Officer, National Lib. of Vietnam, 31 Trang Thi, Hoan Kiem, Hanoi. World Wide Web http://www.consal.org

### The Commonwealth

Commonwealth Lib. Assn., Univ. of the West Indies, Bridgetown Campus, Learning Resources Center, P.O. Box 144, Mona, Kingston 7, Jamaica. Tel. 876-927-0083, fax 876-927-1926, e-mail nkpodo@uwimonal.edu.jm. *Exec. Secy.* Norma Amenu-Kpodo.

Standing Conference on Lib. Materials on Africa (SCOLMA), Social Science Collections and Research, British Lib. St. Pancras, 96 Euston Rd., London NW1 2DB, England. Tel. 020-7412-7567, fax 020-7747-6168, e-mail scolma@hotmail.com, World Wide Web http://www.lse/ac/uk/library/scolma. *Chair* Barbara Spina, School of Oriental and African Studies, Univ. of London, Thornhaugh St., Russell Sq., London WC1H 0XG, England. Tel. 020-7898-4157, fax 020-7898-4159, e-mail bs24@soas.ac.uk.

National and State Libs. Australasia, c/o State Lib. of Victoria, 328 Swanston St., Melbourne, Vic. 3000. Tel. 3-8664-7512, fax 3-9639-4737, e-mail nsla@slv.vic.gov.au, World Wide Web http://www.nsla.org.au. *Chair* Regina Sutton. E-mail library@slv.nsw.gov.au; *Secy.* Kate Irvine. E-mail nsla@slv.vic.gov.au.

## Europe

Ligue des Bibliothèques Européennes de Recherche (LIBER) (Assn. of European Research Libs.), P.O. Box 90153, 5000 LE Tilburg, Netherlands. Tel. 013-466-33-70, fax 013-466-21-46, World Wide Web http://www.libereurope.eu. *Pres.* Hans Geleijnse. E-mail hans.geleijnse@uvt.nl.

# National

## Argentina

Asociación de Bibliotecarios Graduados de la República Argentina (ABGRA) (Assn. of Graduate Libns. of Argentina), Tucumán 1424, 8 piso D, C1050AAB Buenos Aires. Tel. 011-4811-0043, fax 011-4816-2234, e-mail info@abgra.org.ar, World Wide Web http://www.abgra.org.ar. *Pres.* Ana Maria Peruchena Zimmermann; *V.P.* Claudia Ataulfo Rodriguez; *Exec. Secy.* Rosa Emma Monfasani.

## Australia

Australian Lib. and Info. Assn., Box 6335, Kingston, ACT 2604. Tel. 2-6215-8222, fax 2-6282-2249, e-mail enquiry@alia.org. au, World Wide Web http://www.alia.org. au. *Pres.* Roxanne Missingham. E-mail roxanne.missingham@alia.org.au; *V.P.* Derek Whitehead. E-mail derek.whitehead @alia.org.au; *Exec. Dir.* Sue Hutley. E-mail sue.hutley@alia.org.au.

Australian Society of Archivists, P.O. Box 77, Dickson, ACT 2602. Tel. 800-622-251, e-mail ozarch@velocitynet.com.au, World Wide Web http://www.archivists. org.au. *Pres.* Kim Eberhard; *V.P.* Jackie Bettington; *Secy.* Lynda Weller.

## Austria

Österreichische Gesellschaft für Dokumentation und Information (Austrian Society for Documentation and Info.), Lustkandlgasse 4/29, A-1090 Vienna. E-mail office@ oegdi.at, World Wide Web http://www. oegdi.at.

Vereinigung Österreichischer Bibliothekarinnen und Bibliothekare (Assn. of Austrian Libns.), Voralberg State Lib., Fluherstr. 4, 6900 Bregenz. E-mail voeb@mail.ub. tuwien.ac.at, World Wide Web http:// www.univie.ac.at/voeb/php. *Pres.* Harald Weigel; *Secy.* Ortwin Heim.

## Bangladesh

Lib. Assn. of Bangladesh, Central Public Lib. Bldg., Shahbagh, Dhaka 1000. Tel. 2-863-1471, e-mail msik@icddrb.org. *Pres.* M. Abdussattar; *Gen. Secy.* Syed Ali Akbor.

## Barbados

Lib. Assn. of Barbados, P.O. Box 827E, Bridgetown, Saint Michael. E-mail miton @uwichill.edu.bb.

## Belgium

Archief- en Bibliotheekwezen in België (Belgian Assn. of Archivists and Libns.), Keizershaan 4, 1000 Brussels. Tel. 2-519-5393, fax 2-519-5610. *Pres.* Frank Daelemans. E-mail frank.daelemans@kbr.be.

Association Belge de Documentation/ Belgische Vereniging voor Documentatie (Belgian Assn. for Documentation), chaussée de Wavre 1683, B-1160 Brussels. Tel. 2-675-58-62, fax 2-672-74-46, e-mail info@abd-bvd.be, World Wide Web http:// www.abd-bvd.be. *Pres.* Paul Heyvaert; *Secy.* Christopher Boon.

Association Professionnelle des Bibliothécaires et Documentalistes (Assn. of Libns. and Documentation Specialists), Place de la Wallonie, 15 6140 Fontaine-l'Eveque. Tel. 71-52-31-93, fax 71-52-23-07, e-mail biblio.hainaut@ skynet.be, World Wide Web http://www.a-p-b-d.be. *Pres.* Laurence Boulanger; *Secy.* Fabienne Gerard.

Vlaamse Vereniging voor Bibliotheek-, Archief-, en Documentatiewezen (Flemish Assn. of Libns., Archivists, and Documentalists), Statiestraat 179, B-2600 Berchem, Antwerp. Tel. 3-281-44-57, e-mail vvbad @vvbad.be, World Wide Web http://www.

vvbad.be. *Pres.* Geert Puype; *Exec. Dir.* Marc Storms.

## Belize

Belize Lib. Assn., c/o Central Lib., Bliss Inst., P.O. Box 287, Belize City. Tel. 2-7267, fax 2-34246. *Pres.* H. W. Young; *Secy.* Robert Hulse.

## Bolivia

Asociación Boliviana de Bibliotecarios (Bolivian Lib. Assn.), c/o Efrain Virreria Sanchez, Casilla 992, Cochabamba. Tel. 64-1481. *Dir.* Gunnar Mendoza.

Centro Nacional de Documentacion Cientifica y Tecnologica (National Scientific and Technological Documentation Center), Av. Mariscal Santa Cruz 1175, Esquina c Ayacucho, La Paz. Tel. 02-359-583, fax 02-359-586, e-mail iiicndct@huayna. umsa.edu.bo, World Wide Web http:// www.Bolivian.com/industrial/cndct. *Contact* Ruben Valle Vera.

## Bosnia and Herzegovina

Drustvo Bibliotekara Bosne i Hercegovine (Libns. Society of Bosnia and Herzegovina), Zmaja od Bosne 8B, 71000 Sarajevo. Tel. 33-275-301, fax 33-212-435, e-mail nubbih@nub.ba, World Wide Web http:// www.nub.ba. *Pres.* Nevenka Hajdarovic. E-mail nevenka@nub.ba; *Dir.* Ismet Ovcina. E-mail ismet@nub.ba.

## Botswana

Botswana Lib. Assn., Box 1310, Gaborone. Tel. 371-750, fax 371-748, World Wide Web http://www.bla.0catch.com. *Chair* Bobana Badisang; *Secy.* Peter Tshukudu.

## Brazil

Associação dos Arquivistas Brasileiros (Assn. of Brazilian Archivists), Av. Presidente Vargas 1733, Sala 903, 20210-030 Rio de Janiero RJ. Tel. 21-2507-2239, fax 21-3852-2541, e-mail aab@aab.org.br, World Wide Web http://www.aab.org.br.

*Pres.* Lucia Maria Vellosode Oliveira; *Secy.* Isabel Cristina Borges de Oliveira.

## Brunei Darussalam

Persatuan Perpustakaan Kebangsaan Negara Brunei (National Lib. Assn. of Brunei), Perpustakaan Universiti Brunei Darussalam, Jalan Tungku Link Gadong BE 1410. Tel. 2-249-001, fax 2-249-504, e-mail chieflib@lib.ubd.edu.bn, World Wide Web http://www.ppknbd.org.bn. *Pres.* Puan Nellie bte Dato Paduka Haji Sunny.

## Cameroon

Association des Bibliothécaires, Archivistes, Documentalistes et Muséographes du Cameroun (Assn. of Libns., Archivists, Documentalists, and Museum Curators of Cameroon), B.P. 4609, Yaoundé, Nlongkak. Tel. 222-6362, fax 222-4785, e-mail abadcam@yahoo.fr. *Pres.* Hilaire Omokolo.

## Chile

Colegio de Bibliotecarios de Chile AG (Chilean Lib. Assn.), Avda. Diagonal Paraguay 383, Torre 11 of. 122, 6510017 Santiago. Tel. 2-222-56-52, fax 2-635-50-23, e-mail cbc@bibliotecarios.cl, World Wide Web http://www.bibliotecarios.cl. *Pres.* Marcia Marinovic Simunovic.

## China

China Society for Lib. Science, 33 Zhongguancun Nandajie, Beijing 100081. Tel. 10-8854-5141, fax 10-6841-7815, e-mail ztxhmsc@pulicf.nlc.gov.cn, World Wide Web http://www.nlc.gov.cn. *Secy.-Gen.* Gulian Li; *Pres.* Liu Deyou.

## Colombia

Asociación Colombiana de Bibliotecólogos y Documentalistas (Colombian Assn. of Libns. and Documentalists), Cakke 21, No. 6-58, Of. 404, Bogotá. Tel. 1-282-3620, fax 1-282-5487, World Wide Web http://www.ascolbi.org. *Pres.* Carlos Zapata.

## Congo (Republic of)

Direction Générale des Services de Bibliothèques, Archives, et Documentation (Directorate of Libs., Archives, and Documentation Services), Bibliothèque Nationale Populaire, BP 1489, Brazzaville. Tel. 833-485, fax 832-253.

## Costa Rica

Asociación Costarricense de Bibliotecarios (Costa Rican Assn. of Libns.), Apdo. 3308, San José. Tel. 234-9989, e-mail info@cesdepu.com, World Wide Web http://www.cesdepu.com. *Secy.-Gen.* Rodolfo Saborio Valverde.

## Côte d'Ivoire

Association pour le Développement de la Documentation, des Bibliothèques et Archives de la Côte d'Ivoire (Assn. for the Development of Info., Libs., and Archives of Ivory Coast), c/o Bibliothèque Nationale, BPV 180, Abidjan. Tel. 32-38-72. *Secy.-Gen.* Cangah Guy; *Dir.* Ambroise Agnero.

## Croatia

Hrvatsko Knjiznicarsko Drustvo (Croatian Lib. Assn.), c/o Nacionalna i sveucilisna knjiznica, Hrvatske bratske zajednice 4, 10000 Zagreb. Tel./fax 1-615-93-20, e-mail hkd@nsk.hr, World Wide Web http://www.hkdrustvo.hr. *Pres.* Zdenka Sviben. E-mail z.sviben@kqz.hr.

## Cuba

Asociación Cubana de Bibliotecarios (ASCUBI) (Lib. Assn. of Cuba), Biblioteca Nacional Jose Marti, Aranguren y 20 de Mayo, Plaza de la Revolucion, Havana. Tel. 7-870-5680, fax 7-881-2463, e-mail ascubi@bnjm.cu, World Wide Web http://binanet.bnjm.cu/ascubi/grupos.htm. *Pres.* Margarita Bellas Vilarino.

## Cyprus

Kypriakos Synthesmos Vivliothicarion (Lib. Assn. of Cyprus), P.O. Box 1039, 1105 Nicosia. Tel. 22-404-849.

## Czech Republic

Svaz Knihovniku Informachnich Pracovniku Ceske Republiky (Assn. of Lib. and Info. Professionals of the Czech Republic), National Lib., Klementinum 190, 11001 Prague 1. Tel. 221-663-379, fax 221-663-175, e-mail vit.richter@nkp.cz, World Wide Web http://skip.nkp.cz. *Pres.* Vit Richter; *Secy.* Zlata Houskova.

## Denmark

Arkivforeningen (Archives Society), c/o Rigsarkivet, Rigsdagsgarden 9, 1218 Copenhagen. Tel. 3392-3310, fax 3315-3239, World Wide Web http://www.arkivarforeningen.no. *Dir.* Lars-Jorgen Sandberg.

Danmarks Biblioteksforening (Danish Lib. Assn.), Vesterbrogade 20/5, 1620 Copenhagen V. Tel. 3325-0935, fax 3325-7900, e-mail dbf@dbf.dk, World Wide Web http://www.dbf.dk. *Dir.* Winnie Vitzansky.

Danmarks Forskningsbiblioteksforening (Danish Research Lib. Assn.), c/o Statsbiblioteket, Tangen 2, 8200, Århus N. Tel. 8946-2207, fax 8946-2220, e-mail df@statsbiblioteket.dk, World Wide Web http://www.dfdf.dk. *Pres.* Claus Vesterager Pedersen; *Secy.* Hanne Dahl.

Dansk Musikbiblioteksforening (Assn. of Danish Music Libs.), Nordjysk Musikkonservatorium, Ryesgade 52, 9000 Aalborg. World Wide Web http://www.dmbf.nu. *Pres.* Ole Bisbjerg; *Secy.-Gen* Jane Mariegaard.

Kommunernes Skolebiblioteksforening (Assn. of Danish School Libs.), Aboulevard 5, 2 th, DK-1635 Copenhagen. Tel. 33-11-13-91, fax 33-11-13-90, e-mail ksbf@ksbf.dk, World Wide Web http://www.ksbf.dk. *Admin.* Gitte Frausing.

## Dominican Republic

Asociación Dominicana de Bibliotecarios (Dominican Assn. of Libns.), c/o Biblioteca Nacional, Cesar Nicolás Penson 91, Plaza de la Cultura, Pichincha, Santo Domingo. Tel. 809-688-4086, fax 809-688-5841.

## Ecuador

Asociación Ecuatoriana de Bibliotecarios (Ecuadoran Lib. Assn.), c/o Casa de la Cultura Ecuatoriana Benjamin Carrión, Ave. 12 de Octubre 555, Quito. Tel. 2528-840, fax 2223-391, e-mail asoebfp@hotmail.com. *Pres.* Wilson Vega; *Dir.* Laura de Crespo.

## Egypt

Egyptian Assn. for Lib. and Info. Science, c/o Dept. of Archives, Libnship., and Info. Science, Faculty of Arts, Univ. of Cairo, Cairo. Tel. 2-567-6365, fax 2-572-9659. *Pres.* S. Khalifa; *Secy.* Hosam El-Din.

## El Salvador

Asociación de Bibliotecarios de El Salvador (El Salvador Lib. Assn.), Apdo. 2923, San Salvador. Tel. 216-312, fax 225-0278. *Pres.* Carmen Salinas de Salinas.

Asociación de Bibliotecarios Salvadoreños (ABES) (Association of Salvadorian Libns.), Colonia Militar, Pasaje Victor Manuel Guerra Ingles No. 510, San Salvador. Tel./fax 503-237-0875, World Wide Web http://www.ues.edu.sv/abes.

Asociación General de Archivistas de El Salvador (Assn. of Archivists of El Salvador), Edificio Comercial San Fancisco No. 214, Ga. C Ote y 2a Ave. Nte, San Salvador. Tel. 222-94-18, fax 281-58-60, e-mail agnes@agn.gob.sv, World Wide Web http://www.agn.gob.sv.

## Ethiopia

Ye Ethiopia Betemetshaft Serategnoch Mahber (Ethiopian Lib. and Info. Assn.), c/o NCIC, Box 30530, Addis Ababa. Tel. 1-511-344, fax 1-533-368.

## Finland

Suomen Kirjastoseura (Finnish Lib. Assn.), Runeberginkatu 15 A 23, 00100 Helsinki. Tel. 9-6221-340, fax 9-6221-466, e-mail fla@fla.fi, World Wide Web http://kirjastoseura.kaapeli.fi. *Pres.* Tarja Cronberg.

## France

Association des Archivistes Français (Assn. of French Archivists), 9 rue Montcalm, F-75018 Paris. Tel. 1-46-06-39-44, fax 1-46-06-39-52, e-mail secretariat@archivistes. org, World Wide Web http://www. archivistes.org. *Pres.* Christine Martinez; *Secy.* Agnès Dejob.

Association des Bibliothécaires Français (Assn. of French Libns.), 31 rue de Chabrol, F-75010 Paris. Tel. 1-55-33-10-30, fax 1-55-30-10-31, e-mail abf@abf.asso.fr, World Wide Web http://www.abf.asso.fr. *Pres.* Dominique Arot; *Gen. Secy.* Jacques Sauteron.

Association des Professionnels de l'Information et de la Documentation (Assn. of Info. and Documentation Professionals), 25 rue Claude Tillier, F-75012 Paris. Tel. 1-43-72-25-25, fax 1-43-72-30-41, e-mail adbs @adbs.fr, World Wide Web http://www. adbs.fr. *Pres.* Martine Sibertin-Blanc; *Secy.-Gen.* Marie Baudry de Vaux.

## Germany

Arbeitsgemeinschaft der Spezialbibliotheken (Assn. of Special Libs.), c/o Herder-Institute eV, Bibliothek, Gisonenweg 5-7, 35037 Marburg. Tel. 6421-91-78-41, fax 6421-184-139, e-mail geschaeftsstelle@ aspb.de, World Wide Web http://www. aspb.de. *Chair* Juergen Warmbrunn. E-mail warmbrunn@herder-institut.de; *Secy.* Jadwiga Warmbrunn.

Berufsverband Information Bibliothek (Assn. of Info. and Lib. Professionals), Gartenstr. 18, 72764 Reutlingen. Tel. 7121-3491-0, fax 7121-3004-33, e-mail mail@bib-info.de, World Wide Web http://www.bib-info.de. *Pres.* Susanne Riedel. E-mail susanne.riedel@uni-bielefeld.de.

Deutsche Gesellschaft für Informationswissenschaft und Informationspraxis eV (German Society for Info. Science and Practice), Hanauer Landstr. 151-153, 60314 Frankfurt-am-Main 1. Tel. 69-43-03-13, fax 69-490-90-96, e-mail mail@dgi-info. de, World Wide Web http://www.dgd.de. *Pres.* Gabriele Beger.

Deutscher Bibliotheksverband eV (German Lib. Assn.), Strasse des 17 Juni 114, 10623 Berlin. Tel. 30-39-00-14-80, fax 30-

39-00-14-81, e-mail dbv@bibliotheks verband.de, World Wide Web http://www. bibliotheksverband.de. *Pres.* Gudrun Heute-Bluhm; *Chair* Gabriele Beger. E-mail beger@dgi-info.de.

VdA—Verband Deutscher Archivarinnen und Archivare (Assn. of German Archivists), Woerthstr. 3, 36037 Fulda. Tel. 661-29-109-72, fax 661-29-109-74, e-mail info@vda.archiv.net, World Wide Web http://www.vda.archiv.net. *Chair* Robert Kretzschmar.

Verein Deutscher Bibliothekare eV (Society of German Libns.), Universitaetsbibliothek Augsburg, Universitaetsstr. 22, 86159 Augsburg. Tel. 821-598-5300, fax 821-598-5354, e-mail sekr@bibliothek.uni-augsburg.de, World Wide Web http://www.vdb-online.org. *Chair* Ulrich Hohoff.

### Ghana

Ghana Lib. Assn., Knust Lib., Kwame Nkrumah Univ. of Science and Technology, Kumasi. Tel. 51-60133, fax 51-60358, e-mail info@librarygla.org, World Wide Web http://librarygla.org. *Pres.* Valentina J. A. Bannerman. E-mail valnin@yahoo.com.

### Greece

Enosis Hellinon Bibliothekarion (Greek Lib. Assn.), 4 Skoulenion St., 105 61 Athens. Tel. 210-322-6625.

### Guyana

Guyana Lib. Assn., c/o National Lib., 76-77 Church and Main Sts., Georgetown. Tel. 0226-2690, fax 0226-2699, e-mail natlib@sdnp.org.gy, World Wide Web http://www.natlib.gov.gy. *Pres.* Ivor Rodriguez; *Secy.* Gwyneth George.

### Honduras

Asociación de Bibliotecarios y Archiveros de Honduras (Assn. of Libns. and Archivists of Honduras), 11a Calle, 1a y 2a Avdas., No. 105, Comayagüela DC, Tegucigalpa. *Pres.* Francisca de Escoto Espinoza; *Secy.-Gen.* Juan Angel R. Ayes.

### Hong Kong

Hong Kong Lib. Assn., GPO Box 10095, Hong Kong. E-mail hkla@hkla.org, World Wide Web http://www.hklib.org. *Pres.* Michael Robinson. E-mail robinson@ied.edu.hk.

### Hungary

Magyar Könyvtárosok Egyesülete (Assn. of Hungarian Libns.), Hold u 6, H-1054 Budapest. Tel./fax 1-311-8634, e-mail mke@oszk.hu, World Wide Web http://www.mke.oszk.hu. *Pres.* Klara Bakos; *Exec. Secy.* Eva Jaki.

### Iceland

Upplysing—Felag bokasafns-og upplysingafraeoa (Information—The Icelandic Lib. and Info. Science Assn.), Lagmuli 7, 108 Reykjavik. Tel. 553-7290, fax 588-9239, e-mail upplysing@bokis.is, World Wide Web http://www.bokis.is. *Pres.* H. A. Hardarson; *Secy.* A. Agnarsdottir.

### India

Indian Assn. of Academic Libns., c/o Jawaharlal Nehru Univ. Lib., New Mehrauli Rd., New Delhi 110067. Tel. 11-683-1717. *Secy.* M. M. Kashyap.

Indian Assn. of Special Libs. and Info. Centres, P-291, CIT Scheme 6M, Kankurgachi, Kolkata 700054. Tel. 33-2362-9651, e-mail iaslic19@iaslic1955.org, World Wide Web http://www.iaslic1955.org. *Gen. Secy.* Arun Kumar Chakraborty. E-mail akc@bic.boseinst.ernet.in.

Indian Lib. Assn., A/40-41, Flat 201, Ansal Bldg., Dr Mukerjee Nagar, Delhi 110009. Tel./fax 11-2765-1743, e-mail office@ila-india.org, World Wide Web http://www.ila-india.org. *Pres.* Kautilya Shukla; *Gen. Secy.* R. Chandra.

### Indonesia

Ikatan Pustakawan Indonesia (Indonesian Lib. Assn.), Jalan Merdeka Selatan No. 11, 10110 Jakarta, Pusat. Tel./fax 21-385-5729, e-mail mahmudin@lib.itb.ac.id,

World Wide Web http://ipi.pnri.go.id. *Pres.* S. Kartosdono.

## Iraq

Arab Archivists Institute, c/o National Centre of Archives, National Lib. Bldg., P.O. Box 594, Bab-Al-Muaddum, Baghdad. Tel. 1-416-8440. *Dir.* Salim Al-Alousi.

## Ireland

Cumann Leabharlann Na h-Eireann (Lib. Assn. of Ireland), 53 Upper Mount St., Dublin. Tel. 1-6120-2193, fax 1-6121-3090, e-mail president@libraryassociation. ie, World Wide Web http://www.library association.ie. *Pres.* Deirdre Ellis-King.

## Israel

Israel Libns. and Info. Specialists Assn., 9 Beit Hadfus St., Givaat Shaul, Jerusalem. Tel. 2-658-9515, fax 2-625-1628, e-mail icl@icl.org.il, World Wide Web http:// www.icl.org.il. *Pres.* Benjamin Schachter.
Israeli Assn. of Libs. and Info. Centers (ASMI), P.O. Box 3211, 47131 Ramat-Hasharon. Tel. 3-547-2644, fax 3-547-2649, e-mail asmi@asmi.org.il; World Wide Web http://www.asmi.org.il. *Chair* Shoshana Langerman.
Israeli Center for Libs., P.O. Box 801, 51108 Bnei Brak. Tel. 03-618-0151, fax 3-579-8048, e-mail icl@icl.org.il, World Wide Web http://www.icl.org.il. *Chair* Danny Bustin.

## Italy

Associazione Italiana Biblioteche (Italian Lib. Assn.), C.P. 2461, 00185 Rome. Tel. 6-446-3532, fax 6-444-1139, e-mail aib@ aib.it, World Wide Web http://www.aib.it. *Pres.* Mauro Guerrini; *Secy.* Marcello Sardelli.

## Jamaica

Lib. and Info. Assn. of Jamaica., P.O. Box 125, Kingston 5. Tel./fax 876-927-1614, e-mail liajapresident@yahoo.com, World Wide Web http://www.liaja.org.jm. *Pres.* David Drysdale.

## Japan

Joho Kagaku Gijutsu Kyokai (Info. Science and Technology Assn.), Sasaki Bldg., 7 Koisikawa-2, Bunkyo-ku, Tokyo 112-0002. Tel. 3-3813-3791, fax 3-3813-3793, e-mail infosta@infosta.or.jp, World Wide Web http://www.infosta.or.jp. *Pres.* T. Gondoh; *Gen. Mgr.* Yukio Ichikawa.
Nihon Toshokan Kyokai (Japan Lib. Assn.), 1-11-14 Shinkawa, Chuo-ku, Tokyo 104 0033. Tel. 3-3523-0811, fax 3-3523-0841, e-mail info@jla.or.jp, World Wide Web http://www.jla.or.jp. *Secy.-Gen.* Reiko Sakagawa.
Senmon Toshokan Kyogikai (Japan Special Libs. Assn.), c/o Japan Lib. Assn., Bldg. F6, 1-11-14 Shinkawa Chuo-ku, Tokyo 104-0033. Tel. 3-3537-8335, fax 3-3537-8336, e-mail jsla@jsla.or.jp, World Wide Web http://www.jsla.or.jp. *Pres.* Kousaku Inaba; *Exec. Dir.* Fumihisa Nakagawa.

## Jordan

Jordan Lib. Assn., P.O. Box 6289, Amman. Tel./fax 6-462-9412, e-mail info@jorla.org, World Wide Web http://www.jorla.org. *Pres.* Anwar Akroush; *Secy.* Yousra Abu Ajamieh.

## Kenya

Kenya Lib. Assn., P.O. Box 46031, 00100 Nairobi. Tel. 733-732-799, fax 2-811-455, e-mail gitachur@yahoo.com, World Wide Web http://www.klas.or.ke. *Chair* Rosemary Gitachu; *Secy.* Esther K. Obachi.

## Korea (Democratic People's Republic of)

Lib. Assn. of the Democratic People's Republic of Korea, P.O. Box 200, Pyongyang. E-mail kyokoi@jaspul.org.

## Korea (Republic of)

Korean Lib. Assn., San 60-1, Banpo-dong, Seocho-gu, Seoul 137-702. Tel. 2-535-4868, fax 2-535-5616, e-mail klanet@ hitel.net, World Wide Web http://www. korla.or.kr. *Pres.* Ki Nam Shin; *Exec. Dir.* Won Ho Jo.

## Laos

Association des Bibliothécaires Laotiens (Lao Lib. Assn.), c/o Direction de la Bibliothèque Nationale, Ministry of Info. and Culture, B.P. 122, Vientiane. Tel. 21-21-2452, fax 21-21-2408, e-mail bailane@laotel.com.

## Latvia

Lib. Assn. of Latvia, Terbatas iela 75, Riga LV-1001. Tel./fax 6731-2791, e-mail lbb@lbi.lnb.lv, World Wide Web http://www.lnb.lv. *Pres.* Anna Maulina.

## Lebanon

Lebanese Lib. Assn., P.O. Box 13-5053, Beirut 1102 2801. Tel. 1-786-456, World Wide Web http://www.llaweb.org/index.php. *Pres.* Fawz Abdalleh.

## Lesotho

Lesotho Lib. Assn., Private Bag A26, Maseru 100. Tel./fax 340-601, e-mail mmc@doc.isas.nul.ls, World Wide Web http://www.sn.apc.org. *Chair* S. M. Mohai; *Secy.* N. Taole.

## Lithuania

Lietuvos Bibliotekininku Draugija (Lithuanian Libns. Assn.), Sv Ignoto 6-108, 1120 Vilnius. Tel./fax 5-275-0340, e-mail lbd@vpu.lt, World Wide Web http://www.lbd.lt. *Pres.* Vida Garunkstyte.

## Luxembourg

Assn. Luxembourgeoise des Bibliothécaires, Archivistes, et Documentalistes (ALBAD) (Luxembourg Assn. of Libns., Archivists, and Documentalists), c/o National Lib. of Luxembourg, 37 Blvd. Roosevelt, L-2450 Luxembourg. Tel. 352-22-97-55-1, fax 352-47-56-72, World Wide Web http://www.albad.lu. *Pres.* Jean-Marie Reding. E-mail jean-marie.reding@bnl.etat.lu; *Secy.-Gen.* Michel Donven. E-mail michel.donven@bnl.etat.lu.

## Macedonia

Bibliotekarsko Drustvo na Makedonija (Union of Libns.' Assns. of Macedonia), Bul Goce Delcev 6, 1000 Skopje. Tel. 2-3115-177, fax 2-3226-846, e-mail kliment@nubsk.edu.mk, World Wide Web http://www.nubsk.edu.mk. *Pres.* Zorka Cekicevska; *Secy.* Nada Karadzoska.

## Malawi

Malawi Lib. Assn., P.O. Box 429, Zomba. Tel. 50-524-265, fax 50-525-255, e-mail d.b.v.phiri@unima.wn.apc.org. *Chair* Geoffrey F. Salanje; *Secy.-Gen.* Francis F. C. Kachala. E-mail fkachala@chanco.unima.mw.

## Malaysia

Persatuan Perpustakaan Malaysia (Lib. Assn. of Malaysia), P.O. Box 12545, 50782 Kuala Lumpur. Tel./fax 3-2694-7390, e-mail ppm55@po.jaring.my, World Wide Web http://www.ppm55.org.my. *Pres.* Putri Saniah Megat Abdul Rahman. E-mail psaniah@yahoo.com.

## Mali

Association Malienne des Bibliothécaires, Archivistes et Documentalistes (Mali Assn. of Libns., Archivists, and Documentalists), Hamdal Laye Aci 2000, B.P. E4473, Bamako. Tel. 229-9423, fax 229-9396, e-mail dnbd@afribone.net.ml.

## Malta

Malta Lib. and Info. Assn. (MaLIA), c/o Univ. of Malta Lib., Msida MSD 2080. Tel. 2132-2054, e-mail info@malia-malta.org, World Wide Web http://www.malia-malta.org. *Chair* Robert Mizzi.

## Mauritania

Association Mauritanienne des Bibliothécaires, Archivistes et Documentalistes (Mauritanian Assn. of Libns., Archivists, and Documentalists), c/o Bibliothèque Nationale, B.P. 216, Nouakchott. Tel. 525-

18-62, fax 525-18-68, e-mail bibliotheque nationale@yahoo.fr.

## Mauritius

Mauritius Lib. Assn., Ministry of Educ. Public Lib., Moka Rd., Rose Hill. Tel. 403-0200, fax 454-9553, e-mail general. enquiries@mu.britishcouncil.org, World Wide Web http://www.britishcouncil.org/mauritius. *Pres.* K. Appadoo; *Secy.* S. Rughoo.

## Mexico

Asociación Mexicana de Bibliotecarios (Mexican Assn. of Libns.), Apdo. 12-800, Administración Postal Obreto Mundial, 03001 México DF 06760. Tel. 155-5575-3396, fax 155-5575-1135, e-mail correo@ambac.org.mx, World Wide Web http://www.ambac.org.mx. *Pres.* Hortensia Lobato Reyes; *Secy.* Marisela Castro Moreno.

## Myanmar

Myanmar Lib. Assn., c/o National Lib., Government Offices, Kannar Rd., Yangon. Tel. 1-27-2058, fax 01-53-2927. *Pres.* U Khin Maung Tin; *Secy.* U Thein Shwe.

## Nepal

Nepal Lib. Assn., GPO 2773, Kathmandu. Tel. 977-1-441-1318, e-mail info@nla.org. np, World Wide Web http://www.nla.org. np. *Contact* Rudra Prasad Dulal.

## The Netherlands

Nederlandse Vereniging voor Beroepsbeoefenaren in de Bibliotheek-Informatie-en Kennissector (Netherlands Assn. of Libns., Documentalists, and Info. Specialists), Postbus 1466, 3800 BL Amersfoort. Tel. 033-4546-653, fax 033-4546-666, e-mail nvbinfo@wxs.nl, World Wide Web http://www.nvbonline.nl. *Pres.* J. S. M. Savenije.

## New Zealand

New Zealand Lib. Assn. (LIANZA), P.O. Box 12-212, Wellington 6144. Tel. 4-473-5834, fax 4-499-1480, e-mail office@ lianza.org.nz, World Wide Web http://www.lianza.org.nz. *Pres.* Vye Perrone.

## Nicaragua

Asociación Nicaraguense de Bibliotecarios y Profesionales a Fines (Nicaraguan Assn. of Libns.), Bello Horizonte, Tope Sur de la Rotonda 1/2 cuadra abajo, Casa J-11-57, Managua. Tel. 277-4159 ext. 335, e-mail info@anibipa.org.ni, World Wide Web http://www.anibipa.org.ni. *Pres.* Darling Vallecillo.

## Nigeria

Nigerian Lib. Assn., c/o National Lib. of Nigeria, Sanusi Dantata House, Business Central District, Garki District, Abuja 900001. Tel. 8055-365245, fax 9-234-6773, e-mail info@nla-ng.org, World Wide Web http://www.nla-ng.org. *Pres.* A. O. Banjo; *Secy.* D. D. Bwayili.

## Norway

Arkivarforeningen (Assn. of Archivists), Postboks 4015, Ulleval Sta., N-0806 Oslo. Tel. 22-02-26-57, fax 22-23-74-89, e-mail lasa@arkivverket.no, World Wide Web http://www.forskerforbundet.no.

Norsk Bibliotekforening (Norwegian Lib. Assn.), Postboks 6540, 0606 Etterstad. Tel. 23-24-34-30, fax 22-67-23-68, e-mail nbf@norskbibliotekforening.no, World Wide Web http://www.norskbibliotekforening.no. *Dir.* Berit Aaker.

## Pakistan

Pakistan Lib. Assn., c/o National Library of Pakistan, Constitution Ave., Islamabad 44000. Tel. 51-921-4523, fax 51-922-1375, e-mail info@pla.org.pk, World Wide Web http://www.pla.org.pk. *Pres.* Abdul Jalil Khan Bazai; *Secy.-Gen.* Abdur Rahman Qaisafani.

## Panama

Asociación Panameña de Bibliotecarios (Panama Lib. Assn.), c/o Biblioteca Interamericana Simón Bolivar, Estafeta Universitaria, Panama City.

## Paraguay

Asociación de Bibliotecarios Graduados del Paraguay (Assn. of Paraguayan Graduate Libns.), Facultad Politecnica, Universidad Nacional de Asunción, 2160 San Lorenzo. Tel. 21-585-588, e-mail abigrap@pol.una. py, World Wide Web http://www.pol.una. py/abigrap. *Pres.* Margarita Escobar de Morel.

## Peru

Asociación de Archiveros del Perú (Peruvian Assn. of Archivists), Av. Manco Capacc No. 1180, tercer piso, La Victoria. Tel. 1-472-8729, fax 1-472-7408, e-mail contactos@adapperu.com, World Wide Web http://www.adapperu.org. *Pres.* Juan Antonio Espinoza Morante.

Asociación Peruana de Bibliotecarios (Peruvian Assn. of Libns.), Bellavista 561 Miraflores, Apdo. 995, Lima 18. Tel. 1-474-869. *Pres.* Martha Fernandez de Lopez; *Secy.* Luzmila Tello de Medina.

## Philippines

Assn. of Special Libs. of the Philippines, Rm. 301, National Lib. Bldg., T. M. Kalaw St., 2801 Ermita, Manila. Tel. 2-524-4611, World Wide Web http://www.aczafra.com/aslp. *Pres.* Jocelyn L. Ladlad. E-mail ladlad@dlsu.edu.ph; *Secy.* Arlene Y. Gonzales. E-mail goetheinfo@pldtdsl.net.

Bibliographical Society of the Philippines, National Lib. of the Philippines, T. M. Kalaw St., 1000 Ermita, Manila. Tel. 2-583-252, fax 2-502-329, e-mail amb@nlp.gov.ph, World Wide Web http://www.nlp.gov.ph. *Chief* Leticia D. A. Tominez.

Philippine Libns. Assn., Bldg. 3F, Rm. 301, National Lib. of the Philippines, T. M. Kalaw St., 1000 Ermita, Manila. Tel. 2-525-9401, fax 02-525-9401. *Pres.* Susima L. Gonzales.

## Poland

Stowarzyszenie Bibliotekarzy Polskich (Polish Libns. Assn.), al Niepodleglosci 213, 02-086 Warsaw. Tel. 22-825-83-74, fax 22-825-53-49, e-mail biurozgsbp@wp.pl, World Wide Web http://ebib.info. *Pres.*

Elzbieta Stefanczyk; *Secy.-Gen.* Maria Burchard.

## Portugal

Associação Portuguesa de Bibliotecários, Arquivistas e Documentalistas (Portuguese Assn. of Libns., Archivists, and Documentalists), R. Morais Soares, 43C, 1 Dto e Fte, 1900-341 Lisbon. Tel. 21-816-19-80, fax 21-815-45-08, e-mail bad@apbad.pt, World Wide Web http://www.apbad.pt. *Pres.* António José de Pina Falcão.

## Puerto Rico

Sociedad de Bibliotecarios de Puerto Rico (Society of Libns. of Puerto Rico), P.O. Box 22898, Universidad de Puerto Rico, San Juan 00931-2898. Tel./fax 787-764-0000, World Wide Web http://www. sociedadbibliotecarios.org. *Pres.* Maria de los Angeles Lugo; *Secy.* Lourdes Cádiz.

## Russia

Rossiiskaya Bibliotechnaya Assotsiatsiya (Russian Lib. Assn.), 18 Sadovaya St., St. Petersburg 191069. Tel. 812-118-85-36, fax 812-110-58-61, e-mail rba@nlr.ru, World Wide Web http://www.rba.ru. *Pres.* Vladimir N. Zaitsev; *Exec. Secy.* Maya Shaparneva.

## Senegal

Association Sénégalaise des Bibliothécaires, Archivistes et Documentalistes (Senegalese Assn. of Libns., Archivists, and Documentalists), Université Cheikh Anta Diop de Dakar, BP 3252, Dakar. Tel. 221-864-27-73, fax 221-824-23-79, e-mail asbad200@hotmail.com, World Wide Web http://www.ebad.ucad.sn/sites_heberges/asbad/index.htm. *Pres.* Djibril Ndiaye; *V.P.* Khady Kane Touré; *Secy.-Gen.* Bernard Dione.

## Serbia and Montenegro

Jugoslovenski Bibliografsko Informacijski Institut, Terazije 26, 11000 Belgrade. Tel. 11-687-836, fax 11-687-760, e-mail yubin

@jbi.bg.ac.yu, World Wide Web http://www.jbi.bg.ac.yu. *Dir.* Radomir Glavicki.

## Sierra Leone

Sierra Leone Assn. of Archivists, Libns., and Info. Scientists, c/o COMAHS Library New England, Freetown. Tel. 22-22-0758. *V.P.* Oliver Harding.

## Singapore

Lib. Assn. of Singapore, National Lib. Board, 100 Victoria St., No. 14-01, Singapore 188064. Tel. 6749-7990, fax 6749-7480, e-mail lassec@las.org.sg, World Wide Web http://www.las.org.sg. *Pres.* Ngian Lek Choh.

## Slovenia

Zveza Bibliotekarskih Druötev Slovenije (Union of Assns. of Slovene Libns.), Turjaöka 1, 1000 Ljubljana. Tel. 01-20-01-193, fax 01-42-57-293, e-mail zveza-biblio.ds-nuk@quest.arnes.si, World Wide Web http://www.zbds-zveza.si. *Pres.* Melita Ambrožič.

## South Africa

Lib. and Info. Assn. of South Africa, P.O. Box 1598, Pretoria 0001. Tel. 12-337-6129, fax 12-337-6108, e-mail liasa@liasa.org.za, World Wide Web http://www.liasa.org.za. *Pres.* R. More; *Secy.* K. Kitching.

## Spain

Asociación Española de Archiveros, Bibliotecarios, Museólogos y Documentalistas (Spanish Assn. of Archivists, Libns., Curators, and Documentalists), Recoletos 5, 3 izquierda, interior, 28001 Madrid. Tel. 91-575-17-27, fax 91-578-16-15, e-mail anabad@anabad.org, World Wide Web http://www.anabad.org.

## Sri Lanka

Sri Lanka Lib. Assn., Professional Center, 275/75 Bauddhaloka Mawatha, Colombo 7. Tel./fax 11-258-9103, e-mail slla@slltnet.lk, World Wide Web http://www.slla.org.lk. *Pres.* Piyadasa Ranasinge; *Gen. Secy.* D. Daniel.

## Swaziland

Swaziland Lib. Assn., P.O. Box 2309, Mbabane H100. Tel. 404-2633, fax 404-3863, e-mail sdnationalarchives@realnet.co.sz, World Wide Web http://www.swala.sz. *Chair* Faith Mkhonta; *Secy.* Jabulile Dlamini.

## Sweden

Svensk Biblioteksförening (Swedish Lib. Assn.), World Trade Center D5, Box 70380, 107 24 S-Stockholm. Tel. 8-545-132-30, fax 8-545-132-31, e-mail info@biblioteksforeningen.org, World Wide Web http://www.biblioteksforeningen.org. *Secy.-Gen.* Niclas Lindberg.

Svensk Förening för Informationsspecialister (Swedish Society for Info. Specialists), Osquars backe 25, 100 44 Stockholm. Tel. 8-678-23-20, fax 8-678-23-01, e-mail kansliet@sfis.nu, World Wide Web http://www.sfis.nu. *Pres.* Margareta Nelke. E-mail nelke@icatonce.com.

Svenska Arkivsamfundet (Swedish Assn. of Archivists), Stockholms stadsarkiv, Box 22063, 104 22 Stockholm. Tel. 46-197-000, fax 46-197-070, e-mail info@arkivsamfundet.org, World Wide Web http://www.arkivsamfundet.org. *Pres.* Berndt Fredriksson.

## Switzerland

Association des Bibliothèques et Bibliothécaires Suisses/Vereinigung Schweizerischer Bibliothekare/Associazione dei Bibliotecari Svizzeri (Assn. of Swiss Libs. and Libns.), Hallestr. 58, CH-3012 Bern. Tel. 31-382-42-40, fax 31-382-46-48, World Wide Web http://www.bbs.ch. *Gen. Secy.* Barbara Kraeuchi. E-mail b.kraeuchi@bbs.ch.

Schweizerische Vereinigung für Dokumentation/Association Suisse de Documentation (Swiss Assn. of Documentation), Hallestr. 58, CH-3012 Bern. Tel. 31-382-42-40, fax 31-382-46-48. E-mail info@bis.info,

World Wide Web http://www.svd-asd.org. *Gen. Secy.* Barbara Kraeuchi. E-mail b.kraeuchi@bbs.ch.

Verein Schweizer Archivarinnen und Archivare (Assn. of Swiss Archivists), Schweizerisches Bundesarchiv, Brunngasse 60, CH-3003 Bern 8. Tel. 31-312-72-72, fax 31-312-38-01, e-mail vsa-aas@smueller. ch, World Wide Web http://www.vsa-aas.org. *Pres.* Andreas Kellerhals.

## Taiwan

Lib. Assn. of the Republic of China, c/o National Central Lib., 20 Chungshan S. Rd., Taipei 10001. Tel. 2-2331-2675, fax 2-2370-0899. *Secy.-Gen.* Teresa Wang Chang.

## Tanzania

Tanzania Lib. Assn., P.O. Box 33433, Dar es Salaam. Tel./fax 22-277-5411, e-mail tla_tanzania@yahoo.com, World Wide Web http://www.tla.or.tz. *Chair* Alli Mcharazo.

## Thailand

Thai Lib. Assn., 1346 Akarnsongkrau Rd. 5, Klongchan, Bangkapi, 10240 Bangkok. Tel. 02-734-9022, fax 02-734-9021, e-mail tla2497@yahoo.com, World Wide Web http://tla.or.th. *Pres.* Chutima Sacchanand; *Exec. Secy.* Suwadee Vichetpan.

## Trinidad and Tobago

Lib. Assn. of Trinidad and Tobago, Box 1275, Port of Spain. Tel. 868-625-0620, e-mail latt@lycos.com, World Wide Web http://www.latt.org.tt. *Pres.* Lillibeth S. V. Ackbarali; *Secy.* Arlene Dolabaille.

## Tunisia

Association Tunisienne des Documentalistes, Bibliothécaires et Archivistes (Tunisian Assn. of Documentalists, Libns., and Archivists), Centre de Documentation Nationale, 8004 rue Kheredinne Pacha, 1002 Tunis. Tel. 7165-1924. *Pres.* Ahmed Ksibi.

## Turkey

Türk Kütüphaneciler Dernegi (Turkish Libns. Assn.), Necatibey Caddesi Elgun Sok 8/8, Kizilay, Ankara. Tel. 312-230-13-25, fax 312-232-04-53, e-mail tkd.dernek@gmail, World Wide Web http://www.kutuphaneci. org.tr. *Pres.* Ali Fuat Kartal; *Secy.* Håkan Anameric.

## Uganda

Uganda Lib. and Info. Assn., P.O. Box 8147, Kampala. Tel. 141-256-77-467698. *Editor* Matthew Lubuulwa. E-mail nlubuulwa@ yahoo.com.

## Ukraine

Ukrainian Lib. Assn., Lesia Ukrainka Kyiv Public Lib., Turgenivska Str. 83/85, 04050 Kyiv. E-mail pashkovavs@yahoo.com, World Wide Web http://www.uba.org.ua. *Pres.* Valentyna S. Pashkova.

## United Kingdom

ASLIB, the Assn. for Info. Management, Holywell Centre, 1 Phipp St., London EC2A 4PS, England. Tel. 20-7613-3031, fax 20-7613-5080, e-mail aslib@aslib. com, World Wide Web http://www.aslib. co.uk. *Dir.* R. B. Bowes.

Bibliographical Society, Institute of English Studies, Senate House, Rm. 306, Malet St., London WC1E 7HU, England. Tel. 20-7611-7244, fax 20-7611-8703, e-mail secretary@bibsoc.org.uk, World Wide Web http://www.bibsoc.org.uk. *Pres.* John Barnard.

Chartered Inst. of Lib. and Info. Professionals (CILIP) (formerly the Lib. Assn.), 7 Ridgmount St., London WC1E 7AE, England. Tel. 20-7255-0500, fax 20-7255-0561, e-mail info@cilip.org.uk, World Wide Web http://www.cilip.org.uk. *Chief Exec.* Bob McKee.

School Lib. Assn., Unit 2, Lotmead Business Village, Lotmead Farm, Wanborough, Swindon SN4 0UY, England. Tel. 1793-791-787, fax 1793-791-786, e-mail info@ sla.org.uk, World Wide Web http://www. sla.org.uk. *Pres.* Gervase Phinn; *Chief Exec.* Kathy Lemaire.

Scottish Lib. and Info. Council, 1st fl., Bldg. C, Brandon Gate, Leechlee Rd., Hamilton ML3 6AU, Scotland. Tel. 1698-458-888, fax 1698-283-170, e-mail slic@slainte.org. uk, World Wide Web http://www.slainte. org.uk. *Dir.* Elaine Fulton.

Society of Archivists, Prioryfield House, 20 Canon St., Taunton TA1 1SW, England. Tel. 1823-327-030, fax 1823-371-719, e-mail societyofarchivists@archives.org.uk, World Wide Web http://www.archives. org.uk. *Chair* Peter Emmerson; *Hon. Secy.* Jenny Moran.

Society of College, National, and Univ. Libs (SCONUL) (formerly Standing Conference of National and Univ. Libs.), 102 Euston St., London NW1 2HA, England. Tel. 20-7387-0317, fax 20-7383-3197, e-mail info@sconul.ac.uk, World Wide Web http://www.sconul.ac.uk. *Exec. Secy.* Toby Bainton.

Welsh Lib. Assn., Lib., Univ. of Wales, Singleton Park, Swansea SA3 4RJ, Wales. Tel. 1792-295-174, fax 1792-295-851. *Pres.* Andrew Green. E-mail andrew.green @llgc.org.uk.

## Uruguay

Agrupación Bibliotecológica del Uruguay (Uruguayan Lib. and Archive Science Assn.), Cerro Largo 1666, 11200 Montevideo. Tel. 2-400-57-40. *Pres.* Luis Alberto Musso.

Asociación de Bibliotecólogos del Uruguay, Eduardo V. Haedo 2255, 11200 Montevideo. Tel./fax 2-4099-989, e-mail abu@ adinet.com.uy, World Wide Web http:// www.abu.net.uy. *Pres.* Victor Aguirre Negro.

## Vatican City

Biblioteca Apostolica Vaticana, Cortile del Belvedere, 00120 Vatican City, Rome. Tel. 6-6987-9402, fax 6-6988-4795, e-mail bav@vatlib.it, World Wide Web http:// www.vaticanlibrary.vatlib.it. *Prefect* Cesare Pasini.

## Venezuela

Colegio de Bibliotecólogos y Archivólogos de Venezuela (Venezuelan Lib. and Archives Assn.), Apdo. 6283, Caracas. Tel. 212-572-1858. *Pres.* Elsi Jimenez de Diaz.

## Vietnam

Hôi Thu-Vien Viet Nam (Vietnamese Lib. Assn.), National Lib. of Vietnam, 31 Trang Thi, 10000 Hanoi. Tel. 4-8254-927, fax 4-8-253-357, e-mail info@nlv.gov.vn, World Wide Web http://www.nlv.gov.vn.

## Zaire

Association Zaïroise des Archivistes, Bibliothécaires et Documentalistes (Zaire Assn. of Archivists, Libns., and Documentalists), BP 805, Kinshasa X1. Tel. 012-30123. *Exec. Secy.* E. Kabeba-Bangasa.

## Zambia

Zambia Lib. Assn., Great East Rd. Campus, P.O. Box 38636, 10101 Lusaka. Tel. 21-291-381, fax 21-1-292-702. *Chair* Benson Njobvu. E-mail bensonnjobvu@gmail.com.

## Zimbabwe

Zimbabwe Lib. Assn., P.O. Box 3133, Harare. Tel. 4-692-741. *Chair* Driden Kunaka.

# Directory of Book Trade and Related Organizations

## Book Trade Associations, United States and Canada

For more extensive information on the associations listed in this section, see the annual edition of *Literary Market Place* (Information Today, Inc.).

AIGA—The Professional Association for Design (formerly the American Institute of Graphic Arts), 164 Fifth Ave., New York, NY 10010. Tel. 212-807-1990, fax 212-807-1799, e-mail aiga@aiga.org, World Wide Web http://www.aiga.org. *Pres.* Sean Adams, AdamsMorioka, 8484 Wilshire Blvd., Suite 600, Beverly Hills, CA 90211. Tel. 323-966-5990, e-mail sean_a @adamsmorioka.com; *Exec. Dir.* Richard Grefe. E-mail grefe@aiga.org.

American Booksellers Assn., 200 White Plains Rd., Tarrytown, NY 10591. Tel. 800-637-0037, 914-591-2665, fax 914-591-2720, World Wide Web http://www. BookWeb.org. *Pres.* Gayle Shanks, Changing Hands Bookstore, 6428 S. McClintock Dr., Tempe, AZ 85283. Tel. 480-730-1142, fax 480-730-1196, e-mail gayleshanks@msn.com; *V.P./Secy.* Michael Tucker, Books, 1501 Vermont St., San Francisco, CA 94107. Tel. 415-643-3400 ext. 18, fax 415-643-2043, e-mail mtucker @booksinc.net; *CEO* Avin Mark Domnitz. E-mail avin@bookweb.org.

American Literary Translators Assn. (ALTA), Univ. of Texas–Dallas, Box 830688, Mail Sta. JO51, Richardson, TX 75083-0688. Tel. 972-883-2093, fax 972-883-6303, World Wide Web http://www.utdallas.edu/ alta. *Pres.* Jim Kates. *V.P.* Barbara Harshav; *Secy.* Susan Harris; *Admin. Asst.* Lindy Jolly. E-mail lindy.jolly@utdallas. edu.

American Medical Publishers Committee (AMPC), c/o Sara Pinto, Dir., Professional/Scholarly Publishing Div., Assn. of American Publishers, 71 Fifth Ave., New York, NY 10003-3004. Tel. 212-255-0200 ext. 257, fax 212-255-7007, e-mail spinto @publishers.org.

American Printing History Assn., Box 4519, Grand Central Sta., New York, NY 10163-4519. World Wide Web http://www. printinghistory.org. *Pres.* Paul Romaine. *Exec. Secy.* Stephen Crook. E-mail sgcrook@printinghistory.org.

American Society for Indexing, 10200 W. 44 Ave., Suite 304, Wheat Ridge, CO 80033. Tel. 303-463-2887, fax 303-422-8894, e-mail info@asindexing.org, World Wide Web http://www.asindexing.org. *Pres.* Fred Leise. E-mail president@asindexing. org; *V.P./Pres.-Elect* Kate Mertes; *Secy.* Enid Zafran; *Exec. Dir.* Francine Butler.

American Society of Journalists and Authors, 1501 Broadway, Suite 302, New York, NY 10036. Tel. 212-997-0947, fax 212-937-3215, e-mail director@asja.org, World Wide Web http://www.asja.org. *Pres.* Russell Wild. E-mail prez@asja.org; *Exec. Dir.* Alexandra Owens.

American Society of Magazine Editors, 810 Seventh Ave., 24th fl., New York, NY 10019. Tel. 212-872-3735, e-mail asmc@ magazine.org, World Wide Web http:// www.magazine.org. *Pres.* Nina Link. E-mail president@magazine.org; *Exec. Dir.* Marlene Kahan.

American Society of Media Photographers, 150 N. 2 St., Philadelphia, PA 19106. Tel. 215-451-2767, fax 215-451-0880, e-mail mopsik@asmp.org, World Wide Web http://www.asmp.org. *Exec. Dir.* Eugene Mopsik.

American Society of Picture Professionals, 117 S. Saint Asaph St., Alexandria, VA 22314. Tel. 703-299-0219, fax 703-299-9910, e-mail cathy@aspp.com, World Wide Web http://www.aspp.com. *Pres.* Amy Wrynn; *Exec. Dir.* Cathy D.-P. Sachs.

American Translators Assn., 225 Reinekers Lane, Suite 590, Alexandria, VA 22314. Tel. 703-683-6100, fax 703-683-6122, e-mail ata@atanet.org, World Wide Web http://www.atanet.org. *Pres.* Jiri Stejskal; *Pres.-Elect* Nicholas Hartmann; *Secy.* Virginia Perez-Santalla; *Treas.* Peter Krawutschke; *Exec. Dir.* Walter W. Bacak, Jr. E-mail walter@atanet.org.

Antiquarian Booksellers Assn. of America, 20 W. 44 St., 4th fl., New York, NY 10036-6604. Tel. 212-944-8291, fax 212-944-8293, e-mail inquiries@abaa.org, World Wide Web http://www.abaa.org. *Pres.* David Lilburne, Antipodean Books, Maps, and Prints; *V.P.* Stuart Bennett, Stuart Bennett Rare Books; *Exec. Dir.* Susan Benne. E-mail hq@abaa.org.

Assn. of American Publishers, 71 Fifth Ave., New York, NY 10003. Tel. 212-255-0200, fax 212-255-7007. *Washington Office* 50 F St. N.W., Washington, DC 20001-1564. Tel. 202-347-3375, fax 202-347-3690. *Pres./CEO* Tom Allen; *V.P.s* Allan Adler, Tina Jordan; *Dir., Communications and Public Affairs* Judith Platt; *Exec. Dir., School Div.* Jay Diskey; *Exec. Dir., Higher Education* Bruce Hildebrand; *Exec. Dir., International Copyright Enforcement* Patricia Judd; *Chair* Richard Sarnoff, Random House.

Assn. of American Univ. Presses, 71 W. 23 St., Suite 901, New York, NY 10010. Tel. 212-989-1010, e-mail info@aaupnet.org, World Wide Web http://aaupnet.org. *Pres.* Alex Holzman, Temple Univ. Press; *Pres.-Elect* Kathleen Keane, John Hopkins Univ.

Press; *Exec. Dir.* Peter J. Givler. E-mail pgivler@aaupnet.org.

Assn. of Booksellers for Children (ABC), 6538 Collins Ave., No. 168, Miami Beach, FL 33141. Tel. 617-390-7759, fax 617-344-0540, e-mail kristen@abfc.com, World Wide Web http://www.abfc.com. *Exec. Dir.* Kristen McLean.

Assn. of Canadian Publishers, 174 Spadina Ave., Suite 306, Toronto, ON M5T 2C2. Tel. 416-487-6116, fax 416-487-8815, World Wide Web http://www.publishers. ca. *Pres.* Rodger Touchie, Heritage Group, Suite 301, 3555 Outrigger Rd., Nanoose Bay, BC V9P 9K1. Tel. 250-468-5328, fax 250-468-5318, e-mail publisher@heritage house.ca; *V.P.* David Caron, ECW Press, 2120 Queen St. E., Suite 200, Toronto, ON M4E 1E2. Tel. 416-694-3348, fax 416-698-9906, e-mail david@ecwpress.com; *Exec. Dir.* Carolyn Wood. Tel. 416-487-6116 ext. 222, e-mail carolyn_wood@ canbook.org.

Assn. of Educational Publishers (AEP), 510 Heron Dr., Suite 201, Logan Township, NJ 08085. Tel. 856-241-7772, fax 856-241-0709, e-mail mail@aepweb.org, World Wide Web http://www.aepweb.org. *Pres.* Richard Casabonne; *Pres.-Elect* Suzanne I. Barchers; *V.P.* Daniel Caton; *Treas.* Neal Goff; *CEO/Exec. Dir.* Charlene F. Gaynor. E-mail cgaynor@aepweb.org.

Authors Guild, 31 E. 32 St., 7th fl., New York, NY 10016. Tel. 212-563-5904, fax 212-564-5363, e-mail staff@authorsguild. org. *Pres.* Roy Blount, Jr.; *V.P.* Judy Blume; *Treas.* Peter Petre; *Secy.* Pat Cummings.

Book Industry Study Group, 370 Lexington Ave., Suite 900, New York, NY 10017. Tel. 646-336-7141, fax 646-336-6214, e-mail info@bisg.org, World Wide Web http://www.bisg.org. *Co-Chairs* Andrew Weber, Random House; Dominique Raccah, Sourcebooks; *Exec. Dir.* Michael Healy. E-mail michael@bisg.org.

Book Manufacturers' Institute, 2 Armand Beach Drive, Suite 1B, Palm Coast, FL 32137. Tel. 386-986-4552, fax 386-986-4553, e-mail info@bmibook.com, World Wide Web http://www.bmibook.org. *Pres.* James F. Conway III, Courier Corp.;

*V.P./Pres.-Elect* to be announced; *Treas.* John R. Paeglow, I.B.T. Global; *Exec. V.P./Secy.* Bruce W. Smith. Address correspondence to the executive vice president.

Bookbuilders of Boston, 44 Vinal Rd., Scituate, MA 02066. Tel. 781-378-1361, fax 419-821-2171, e-mail office@bbboston. org, World Wide Web http://www. bbboston.org. *Pres.* Marty Rabinowitz; *1st V.P.* Kelly Bower; *2nd V.P.* Ginny Chang; *Treas.* Scott Payne; *Clerk* Gina Choe.

Bookbuilders West, 9328 Elk Grove Blvd., Suite 105-250, Elk Grove, CA 95624. Tel. 415-670-9564, e-mail operations@book builders.org, World Wide Web http:// www.bookbuilders.org. *Pres.* Michele Bisson Savoy, Quebecor World; *V.P./Treas.* Michael O'Brien, Laserwords U.S; *2nd V.P.* David Staloch, McGraw-Hill; *Secy.* Pam Augspurger, Univ. of California Press.

Canadian Booksellers Assn., 789 Don Mills Rd., Suite 700, Toronto, ON M3C 1T5. Tel. 416-467-7883, fax 416-467-7886, e-mail enquiries@cbabook.org, World Wide Web http://www.cbabook.org. *Pres.* Nancy Frater, BookLore, Orangeville, Ontario; *Exec. Dir.* Susan Dayus. E-mail sdayus@ cbabook.org.

Canadian ISBN Agency, c/o Published Heritage, Library and Archives Canada, 395 Wellington St., Ottawa, ON K1A 0N4. Tel. 866-578-7777 (toll-free) or 819-994-6872, fax 819-997-7517, World Wide Web http://www.collectionscanada.ca/isn/index -e.html.

Canadian Printing Industries Association, 151 Slater St., Suite 1110, Ottawa, ON K1P 5H3. Tel. 613-236-7208, fax 613-232-1334, e-mail belliott@cpia-aci.ca, World Wide Web http://www.cpia-aci.ca. *Pres.* Bob Elliott; *Chair* Sean Murray, Advocate Printing and Publishing Co.

Catholic Book Publishers Assn., 11703 Huebner Rd., Suite 106-622, San Antonio, TX 78230. Tel. 210-368-2055, fax 210-368-2601, e-mail cliffk@cbpa.org, World Wide Web http://cbpa.org and http://www. catholicsread.org. *Pres.* Jill Kurtz; *Exec. Dir.* Cliff Knighten.

Chicago Book Clinic, 5443 N. Broadway, Suite 101, Chicago, IL 60640. Tel. 773-561-4150, fax 773-561-1343, e-mail chgobookclinic@aol.com, World Wide Web http://www.chicagobookclinic.org. *Pres.* Dawn Weinfurtner, e-mail dawnw@ friesens.com; *V.P.* Eric Platou. E-mail eric_platou@malloy.com; *Admin.* Kevin G. Boyer. E-mail kgboyer@ix.netcom. com.

Children's Book Council, 12 W. 37 St., 2nd fl., New York, NY 10018-7480. Tel. 212-966-1990, fax 212-966-2073, World Wide Web http://www.cbcbooks.org. *Chair* Suzanne Murphy, Scholastic; *V. Chair* Chip Gibson, Random House Children's Books; *Secy.* Diana Blough, Bloomsbury USA Children's Books.

Copyright Society of the USA, 352 Seventh Ave., Suite 739, New York, NY 10001. World Wide Web http://www.csusa.org. *Pres.* Karen Frank; *V.P./Pres.-Elect* Corey Field; *Secy.* Joseph Salvo; *Treas.* Nancy Mertzel; *Admin.* Amy Nickerson. E-mail amy@csusa.org.

Council of Literary Magazines and Presses, 154 Christopher St., Suite 3C, New York, NY 10014. Tel. 212-741-9110, fax 212-741-9112, e-mail info@clmp.org, World Wide Web http://www.clmp.org. *Pres.* Ira Silverberg; *V.P.* Nicole Dewey; *Exec. Dir.* Jeffrey Lependorf. E-mail jlependorf@ clmp.org.

Educational Paperback Assn., Box 1399, East Hampton, NY 11937. Tel. 631-329-3315, e-mail edupaperback@aol.com, World Wide Web http://www.edupaperback.org. *Pres.* Neil Jaffe; *V.P.* Dan Walsh; *Treas.* Gene Bahlman; *Exec. Secy.* Marilyn Abel.

Evangelical Christian Publishers Assn., 9633 S. 48 St., Suite 140, Phoenix, AZ 85044. Tel. 480-966-3998, fax 480-966-1944, e-mail info@ecpa.org, World Wide Web http://www.ecpa.org. *Pres./CEO* Mark W. Kuyper; *Chair* Mike Hyatt, Thomas Nelson Publishers.

Graphic Artists Guild, 32 Broadway, Suite 1114, New York, NY 10004. Tel. 212-791-3400, fax 212-792-0333, e-mail admin@gag.org, World Wide Web http://www.gag.org. *Pres.* John Schmelzer. E-mail president@gag.org; *Exec. Dir.* Patricia McKiernan. E-mail admin@gag. org.

Great Lakes Independent Booksellers Assn., c/o *Exec. Dir.* Jim Dana, Box 901, 208 Franklin St., Grand Haven, MI 49417. Tel. 616-847-2460, fax 616-842-0051, e-mail info@gliba.org, World Wide Web http://www.gliba.org. *Pres.* Jill Miner. E-mail saturn_booksellers@hotmail.com; *V.P.* Sally Bulthuis. E-mail poohs@iserv.net; *Past Pres.* Carol Besse. E-mail csbesse@bellsouth.net.

Guild of Book Workers, 521 Fifth Ave., New York, NY 10175. Tel. 212-292-4444, e-mail communications@guildofbookworkers.allmail.net, World Wide Web http://palimpsest.stanford.edu/byorg/gbw. *Pres.* James Reid-Cunningham. E-mail president@guildofbookworkers.allmail.net; *V.P.* Andrew Huot. E-mail vice president@guildofbookworkers.allmail.net.

Horror Writers Assn., 244 Fifth Ave., Suite 2767, New York, NY 10001. E-mail hwa@horror.org, World Wide Web http://www.horror.org. *Pres.* Deborah LeBlanc. E-mail president@horror.org; *V.P.* Heather Graham. E-mail vp@horror.org; *Secy.* Vince Liaguno. E-mail secretary@horror.org; *Treas.* Lisa Morton. E-mail treasurer@horror.org.

IAPHC—The Graphic Professional Resource Network (formerly the International Assn. of Printing House Craftsmen), 7042 Brooklyn Blvd., Minneapolis, MN 55429. Tel. 800-466-4274, 763-560-1620, fax 763-560-1350, World Wide Web http://www.iaphc.org. *Pres./CEO* Kevin Keane. E-mail kkeane1069@aol.com.

Independent Book Publishers Association (formerly PMA), 627 Aviation Way, Manhattan Beach, CA 90266. Tel. 310-372-2732, fax 310-374-3342, e-mail info@ibpa-online.org, World Wide Web http://www.ibpa-online.org. *Pres.* Florrie Binford Kichler; *Exec. Dir.* Terry Nathan.

International Standard Book Numbering U.S. Agency, 630 Central Ave., New Providence, NJ 07974. Tel. 877-310-7333, fax 908-219-0188, e-mail isbn-san@bowker.com, World Wide Web http://www.isbn.org. *General Mgr.* Andy Weissberg; *ISBN/SAN Senior Ed.* Louise Timko.

Jewish Book Council, 520 Eighth Ave., Fourth fl., New York, NY 10010. Tel. 212-201-2920, fax 212-532-4952, e-mail jbc@jewishbooks.org, World Wide Web http://www.jewishbookcouncil.org. *Pres.* Lawrence J. Krule; *Exec. Dir.* Carolyn Starman Hessel.

Library Binding Institute, 4300 S. U.S. Hwy. 1, No. 203-296, Jupiter, FL 33477. Tel. 561-745-6821, fax 561-775-0089, e-mail info@lbibinders.org, World Wide Web http://www.lbibinders.org. *Pres.* Gerrit Dykhouse, Wallaceburg Bookbinding. E-mail gdykhouse@wbmbindery.com; *V.P.* Mark Hancock, Utah Bookbinding. E-mail mark@utahbookbinding.com; *Exec. Dir.* Debra Nolan. E-mail dnolan@lbibinders.org.

Magazine Publishers of America, 810 Seventh Ave., 24th fl., New York, NY 10019. Tel. 212-872-3700, e-mail mpa@magazine.org, World Wide Web http://www.magazine.org. *Pres./CEO* Nina Link. Tel. 212-872-3710, e-mail president@magazine.org.

Midwest Independent Publishers Assn., Box 581432, Minneapolis, MN 55458-1432. Tel. 651-917-0021, World Wide Web http://www.mipa.org. *Pres.* Pat Morris, Ricochet Frog Press. E-mail patmorris@comcast.net.

Miniature Book Society. *Pres.* Mark Palkovic. E-mail mark.palkovic@uc.edu; *V.P.* Peter Thomas. E-mail peteranddonna@cruzio.com; *Secy.* Edward Hoyenski. E-mail ehoyensk@library.unt.edu; *Treas.* Karen Nyman. E-mail karennyman@cox.net; *Past Pres.* Julian I. Edison. E-mail jiestl@mac.com. World Wide Web http://www.mbs.org.

Minnesota Book Publishers Roundtable. *Pres.* Steve Deger, Fairview Press, 2450 Riverside Ave., Minneapolis, MN 55454. Tel. 612-672-4774, fax 612-672-4980, e-mail sdeger1@fairview.org; *V.P.* Alison Aten, Minnesota Historical Society Press/Borealis Books, 345 Kellogg Blvd. W., St. Paul, MN 55102. Tel. 651-259-3203, fax 651-297-1345, e-mail alison.aten@mnhs.org. World Wide Web http://www.publishersroundtable.org.

Mountains and Plains Independent Booksellers Assn., 19 Old Town Sq., Suite 238, Fort Collins, CO 80524. Tel. 970-484-

5856, fax 970-407-1479, e-mail info@ mountainsplains.org, World Wide Web http://www.mountainsplains.org.

National Assn. for Printing Leadership, 75 W. Century Rd., Paramus, NJ 07652. Tel. 800-642-6275, 201-634-9600, fax 201-986-2976, e-mail info@napl.org, World Wide Web http://www.napl.org. *Pres./ CEO* Joseph P. Truncale.

National Assn. of College Stores, 500 E. Lorain St., Oberlin, OH 44074-1294. Tel. 800-622-7498, 440-775-7777, fax 440-775-4769, e-mail info@nacs.org, World Wide Web http://www.nacs.org. *CEO* Brian Cartier. E-mail bcartier@nacs.org.

National Coalition Against Censorship (NCAC), 275 Seventh Ave., No. 1504, New York, NY 10001. Tel. 212-807-6222, fax 212-807-6245, e-mail ncac@ncac.org, World Wide Web http://www.ncac.org. *Exec. Dir.* Joan E. Bertin.

New Atlantic Independent Booksellers Assn. (NAIBA), 2667 Hyacinth St., Westbury, NY 11590. Tel. 516-333-0681, fax 516-333-0689, e-mail info@naiba.com. World Wide Web http://www.newatlanticbooks. com. *Pres.* Joe Drabyak, Chester County Book Co., 975 Paoli Pike, West Chester, PA 19380. Tel. 610-696-1661, fax 610-429-9006, e-mail jdrabyak@ccbmc.com; *V.P.* Lucy Kogler. E-mail lucyk@tleaves books.com; *Exec. Dir.* Eileen Dengler.

New England Independent Booksellers Assn., 297 Broadway, Arlington, MA 02474. Tel. 781-316-2988, fax 781-316-2605, e-mail steve@neba.org, World Wide Web http:// www.newenglandbooks.org. *Pres.* Judy Crosby; *V.P.* Mitch Gaslin; *Treas.* Dick Hermans; *Exec. Dir.* Steve Fischer.

New York Center for Independent Publishing (formerly the Small Press Center), 20 W. 44 St., New York, NY 10036. Tel. 212-764-7021, fax 212-840-2046, e-mail contact @smallpress.org, World Wide Web http:// www.nycip.org. *Chair* Lloyd Jassin; *Exec. Dir.* Karin Taylor.

North American Bookdealers Exchange (NABE), Box 606, Cottage Grove, OR 97424. Tel./fax 541-942-7455, e-mail nabe @bookmarketingprofits.com, World Wide Web http://bookmarketingprofits.com. *Dir.* Al Galasso.

Northern California Independent Booksellers Assn., Presidio National Park, 1007 General Kennedy Ave., P.O. Box 29169, San Francisco, CA 94129. Tel. 415-561-7686, fax 415-561-7685, e-mail office@nciba. com, World Wide Web http://www.nciba. com. *Pres.* Nick Setka; *V.P.* Judy Wheeler; *Exec. Dir.* Hut Landon.

Pacific Northwest Booksellers Assn., 214 E. 12 Ave., Eugene, OR 97401-3245. Tel. 541-683-4363, fax 541-683-3910, e-mail info@pnba.org, World Wide Web http:// www.pnba.org. *Pres.* Paul Hanson, Eagle Harbor Book Co. E-mail paulh@eagle harborbooks.com; *Exec. Dir.* Thom Chambliss.

PEN American Center, Div. of International PEN, 588 Broadway, Suite 303, New York, NY 10012. Tel. 212-334-1660, fax 212-334-2181, e-mail pen@pen.org, World Wide Web http://www.pen.org. *Pres.* Francine Prose; *V.P.* Billy Collins; *Exec. Dir.* Michael Roberts. E-mail mroberts@ pen.org.

Periodical and Book Assn. of America, 481 Eighth Ave., Suite 826, New York, NY 10001. Tel. 212-563-6502, fax 212-563-4098, e-mail info@pbaa.net, World Wide Web http://www.pbaa.net. *Pres.* Joe Gallo. E-mail jgallo@ffn.com; *Chair* William Michalopoulos. E-mail wmichalopoulos @hfmus.com; *Exec. Dir.* Lisa W. Scott. E-mail lscott@pbaa.net or lisawscott@ hotmail.com.

Romance Writers of America, 14615 Benfer Rd., Houston, TX 77069. Tel. 832-717-5200, fax 832-717-5201, e-mail info@rwa national.org, World Wide Web http:// www.rwanational.org. *Pres.* Diane Pershing. E-mail president@rwanational.org; *Exec. Dir.* Allison Kelley. E-mail akelley @rwanational.org.

Science Fiction and Fantasy Writers of America, P.O. Box 877, Chestertown, MD 21620. E-mail execdir@sfwa.org, World Wide Web http://www.sfwa.org. *Pres.* Russell Davis. E-mail president@sfwa. org; *V.P.* Elizabeth Moon. E-mail vp@ sfwa.org; *Secy.* Mary Robinette Kowal. E-mail secretary@sfwa.org; *Treas.* Amy Casil. E-mail treasurer@sfwa.org; *Exec. Dir.* Jane Jewell.

Small Publishers Assn. of North America (SPAN), 1618 W. Colorado Ave., Colorado Springs, CO 80904. Tel. 719-475-1726, e-mail info1@spannet.org, World Wide Web http://www.spannet.org. *Exec. Dir.* Scott Flora.

Society of Children's Book Writers and Illustrators (SCBWI), 8271 Beverly Blvd., Los Angeles, CA 90048. Tel. 323-782-1010, fax 323-782-1892, e-mail scbwi@scbwi.org, World Wide Web http://www.scbwi.org. *Pres.* Stephen Mooser. E-mail stephen mooser@scbwi.org; *Exec. Dir.* Lin Oliver.

Society of Illustrators (SI), 128 E. 63 St., New York, NY 10065. Tel. 212-838-2560, fax 212-838-2561, e-mail info@society illustrators.org, World Wide Web http://www.societyillustrators.org.

Society of National Association Publications (SNAP), 1760 Old Meadow Rd., Suite 500, McLean, VA 22102. Tel. 703-506-3285, fax 703-506-3266, e-mail snapinfo @snaponline.org, World Wide Web http://www.snaponline.org. *Pres.* Kathleen Rakestraw; *V.P.* James Vick.

Southern Independent Booksellers Alliance, 3806 Yale Ave., Columbia, SC 29205. Tel. 800-331-9617, 803-779-0118, fax 803-779-0113, e-mail info@sibaweb.com, World Wide Web http://www.sibaweb.com. *Pres.* Karin Wilson.

Technical Assn. of the Pulp and Paper Industry, 15 Technology Pkwy. S., Norcross, GA 30092 (P.O. Box 105113, Atlanta, GA 30348). Tel. 770-446-1400, fax 770-446-6947, World Wide Web http://www.tappi.org. *Pres.* Larry N. Montague; *Chair* Jeffrey J. Siegel; *V. Chair* Norman F. Marsolan.

Western Writers of America, c/o Paul A. Hutton, MSC06 3770, 1 Univ. of New Mexico, Albuquerque, NM 87131-0001. E-mail wwa@unm.edu, World Wide Web http://www.westernwriters.org. *Pres.* Johnny D. Boggs; *V.P.* Robert J. Conley; *Exec. Dir.* Paul A. Hutton.

Women's National Book Assn., c/o Susannah Greenberg Public Relations, P.O. Box 237, FDR Station, New York, NY 10150. Tel./fax 212-208-4629, e-mail publicity@bookbuzz.com, World Wide Web http://www.wnba-books.org. *Pres.* Joan Gelfand; *V.P./Pres.-Elect* Mary Grey James; *Secy.* Ruth Light; *Treas.* Margaret E. Auer.

# International and Foreign Book Trade Associations

For Canadian book trade associations, see the preceding section, "Book Trade Associations, United States and Canada." For a more extensive list of book trade organizations outside the United States and Canada, with more detailed information, consult *International Literary Market Place* (Information Today, Inc.), which also provides extensive lists of major bookstores and publishers in each country.

## International

African Publishers' Network, BP 3429, Abidjan 01, Côte d'Ivoire. Tel. 202-11801, fax 202-11803, e-mail apnetes@yahoo.com, World Wide Web http://www.freewebs.com/africanpublishers. *Chair* Mamadou Aliou Sow; *Exec. Secy.* Akin Fasemore.

Afro-Asian Book Council, 4835/24 Ansari Rd., Daryaganj, New Delhi 110002, India. Tel. 11-2325-8865, fax 11-2326-7437, e-mail afro@aabcouncil.org, World Wide Web http://www.aabcouncil.org. *Secy.-Gen.* Sukumar Das; *Dir.* Saumya Gupta.

Centre Régional pour la Promotion du Livre en Afrique (Regional Center for Book Promotion in Africa), P.O. Box 1646, Yaoundé, Cameroon. Tel./fax 22-4427.

Centro Régional para el Fomento del Libro en América Latina y el Caribe (CERLALC) (Regional Center for Book Promotion in Latin America and the Caribbean), Calle 70, No. 9-52, Bogotá DC, Colombia. Tel. 1-540-2071, fax 1-541-6398, e-mail libro@cerlalc.com, World Wide Web http://www.cerlalc.com. *Dir.* Carmen Barvo.

Federation of European Publishers, rue Montoyer 31, Boîte 8, 1000 Brussels, Belgium. Tel. 2-770-11-10, fax 2-771-20-71, e-mail info@fep-fee.eu, World Wide Web http://www.fep-fee.be. *Pres.* Jonas Modig; *Dir.-Gen.* Anne Bergman-Tahon.

International Assn. of Scientific, Technical, and Medical Publishers (STM), Prama House, 267 Banbury Rd., Oxford OX2 7HT, England. Tel. 44-1865-339-321, fax 44-1865-339-325, e-mail info@stm-assoc.org, World Wide Web http://www.stm-assoc.org. *Chair* Jerry Cowhig; *CEO* Michael Mabe.

International Board on Books for Young People (IBBY), Nonnenweg 12, 4003 Basel, Switzerland. Tel. 61-272-29-17, fax 61-272-27-57, e-mail ibby@ibby.org, World Wide Web http://www.ibby.org. *Admin. Dir.* Elizabeth Page.

International Booksellers Federation (IBF), rue de la Science 10, 1000 Brussels, Belgium. Tel. 2-223-49-40, fax 2-223-49-38, e-mail ibf.booksellers@skynet.be, World Wide Web http://www.ibf-booksellers.org. *Dir.* Françoise Dubruille.

International League of Antiquarian Booksellers (ILAB), Prinsengracht 445, 1016 HN Amsterdam, Netherlands. Tel. 20-627-22-85, fax 20-625-89-70, e-mail info@ilab.org, World Wide Web http://www.ilab.org. *Pres.* Adrian Harrington; *Gen. Secy.* Paul Feain.

International Publishers Assn. (Union Internationale des Editeurs), ave. de Miremont 3, CH-1206 Geneva, Switzerland. Tel. 22-346-3018, fax 22-347-5717, e-mail secretariat@internationalpublishers.org, World Wide Web http://www.ipa-uie.org. *Pres.* Ana Maria Cabanellas; *Secy.-Gen.* Jens Bammel.

## National

### Argentina

Cámara Argentina del Libro (Argentine Book Assn.), Av. Belgrano 1580, 4 piso, C1093AAQ Buenos Aires. Tel. 11-4381-8383, fax 11-4381-9253, e-mail cal@editores.org.ar, World Wide Web http://www.editores.org.ar. *Dir.* Norberto J. Pou.

Fundación El Libro (Book Foundation), Hipolito Yrigoyen 1628, 5 piso, C1089AAF Buenos Aires. Tel. 11-4370-0600, fax 11-

4370-0607, e-mail fundacion@el-libro. com.ar, World Wide Web http://www. el-libro.com.ar. *Pres.* Horacio Garcia; *Dir.* Marta V. Diaz.

## Australia

Australian and New Zealand Assn. of Antiquarian Booksellers, P.O. Box 7127, McMahons Point, NSW 2060. Tel. 2-9966-9926, fax 2-9966-9925, e-mail admin @anzaab.com, World Wide Web http:// www.anzaab.com. *Pres.* Peter Tinslay. E-mail peter@antiquebookshop.com.au.

Australian Booksellers Assn., 828 High St., Unit 9, Kew East, Vic. 3102. Tel. 3-9859-7322, fax 3-9859-7344, e-mail mail@aba. org.au, World Wide Web http://www.aba. org.au. *Pres.* Fiona Stager; *CEO* Barbara Cullen.

Australian Publishers Assn., 60/89 Jones St., Ultimo, NSW 2007. Tel. 2-9281-9788, fax 2-9281-1073, e-mail apa@publishers. asn.au, World Wide Web http://www. publishers.asn.au. *CEO* Maree McCaskill.

## Austria

Hauptverband des Österreichischen Buchhandels (Austrian Publishers and Booksellers Assn.), Grünangergasse 4, A-1010 Vienna. Tel. 1-512-15-35, fax 1-512-84-82, e-mail sekretariat@hvb.at, World Wide Web http:// www.buecher.at. *Mgr.* Inge Kralupper.

Verband der Antiquare Österreichs (Austrian Antiquarian Booksellers Assn.), Grünangergasse 4, A-1010 Vienna. Tel. 1-512-15-35, fax 1-512-84-82, e-mail sekretariat@ hvb.at, World Wide Web http://www. antiquare.at.

## Belarus

National Book Chamber of Belarus, 31a V Khoruzhei Str., 220002 Minsk. Tel. 17-2893-396, fax 17-3347-847, World Wide Web http://www.natbook.org.by. *Dir.* Elena V. Ivanova.

## Belgium

Vlaamse Boekverkopersbond (Flemish Booksellers Assn.), Te Buelaerlei 37, 2140 Borgerhout. Tel. 03-287-66-90, fax 3-281-

22-40, e-mail luc.tessens@boek.be, World Wide Web http://www.boek.be. *Gen. Secy.* Luc Tessens.

## Bolivia

Cámara Boliviana del Libro (Bolivian Booksellers Assn.), Calle Capitan Ravelo No. 2116, 682 La Paz. Tel. 2-244-4239, fax 2-211-3264, e-mail contacto@cabolib.org.bo. *Pres.* Ernesto Martinez Acchini.

## Brazil

Cámara Brasileira do Livro (Brazilian Book Assn.), Rua Cristiano Viana 91, Pinheiros 05411-000 Sao Paulo-SP. Tel./fax 11-3069-1300, e-mail cbl@cbl.org.br, World Wide Web http://www.cbl.org.br. *Pres.* Rosely Boschini; *Dir.* H. Carlos Dias.

Sindicato Nacional dos Editores de Livros (Brazilian Publishers Assn.), Rue da Ajuda 35-18 andar, 20040-000 Rio de Janeiro-RJ. Tel. 21-2533-0399, fax 21-2533-0422, e-mail snel@snel.org.br, World Wide Web http://www.snel.org.br. *Pres.* Paulo Roberto Rocco.

## Chile

Cámara Chilena del Libro AG (Chilean Assn. of Publishers, Distributors, and Booksellers), Av. Libertador Bernardo O'Higgins 1370, Oficina 501, Santiago. Tel. 2-672-0348, fax 2-687-4271, e-mail prolibro @tie.cl, World Wide Web http://www. camlibro.cl. *Pres.* Eduardo Castillo Garcia.

## Colombia

Cámara Colombiana del Libro (Colombian Book Assn.), Calle 35, No. 5A 05, Bogotá. Tel. 1-323-01-11, fax 1-285-10-82, e-mail camlibro@camlibro.com.co, World Wide Web http://www.camlibro.com.co.

## Czech Republic

Svaz českých knihkupců a nakladatelů (Czech Publishers and Booksellers Assn.), P.O. Box 177, 110 01 Prague. Tel. 224-219-944, fax 224-219-942, e-mail sckn@sckn. cz, World Wide Web http://www.sckn.cz. *Pres.* Vladimir Pistorius.

## Denmark

Danske Boghandlerforening (Danish Booksellers Assn.), Langebrogade 6 opgang J, 1 sal, 1411 Copenhagen K. Tel. 3254-2255, fax 3254-0041, e-mail ddb@bogpost.dk, World Wide Web http://www.bogguide. dk. *Pres.* Jesper Moller; *Dir.* Olaf Winslow.

Danske Forlæggerforening (Danish Publishers Assn.), Skindergade 7 st tv, DK 1159 Copenhagen K. Tel. 3315-6688, fax 3315-6588, e-mail danishpublishers@danish publishers.dk, World Wide Web http:// www.danskeforlag.dk. *Chair* Karsten Blauert; *V. Chair* Tine Smedegaard Andersen.

## Ecuador

Cámara Ecuatoriana del Libro, Núcleo de Pichincha, Avda. Eloy Alfaro, N29-61 e Inglaterra Edf. Eloy Al, Quito. Tel. 2-553-311, fax 2-222-150, e-mail celnp@uio. satnet.net, World Wide Web http://celibro. org.ec. *Pres.* Fausto Coba Estrella.

## Egypt

General Egyptian Book Organization, P.O. Box 235, Cornich El-Nil, Ramlat Boulaq, Cairo. Tel. 2-2577-7531, fax 2-2764-276, e-mail info@egyptianbook.org.eg, World Wide Web http://www.egyptianbook.org.eg. *Chair* Nasser El Ansary.

## Estonia

Estonian Publishers Assn., Roosikrantsi 6, 10119 Tallinn. Tel. 644-9866, fax 641-1443, e-mail kirjastusteliit@eki.ee, World Wide Web http://www.estbook.com. *Dir.* Kaidi Urmet.

## Finland

Kirjakauppaliitto Ry (Booksellers Assn. of Finland), Fredrikinkatu 47, 00100 Helsinki. Tel. 9-6859-9110, fax 9-6859-9119, e-mail toimisto@kirjakauppaliitto.fi, World Wide Web http://www.kirjakauppaliitto.fi. *Pres.* Stig-Bjorn Nyberg; *Dir.* Olli Erakivi.

Suomen Kustannusyhdistys (Finnish Book Publishers Assn.), P.O. Box 177, Lönnrotinkatu 11 A, FIN-00121 Helsinki. Tel. 358-9-228-77-250, fax 358-9-612-1226, World Wide Web http://www.publishers. fi/en. *Dir.* Sakari Laiho.

## France

Bureau International de l'Edition Française (BIEF) (International Bureau of French Publishing), 115 blvd. Saint-Germain, F-75006 Paris. Tel. 01-44-41-13-13, fax 01-46-34-63-83, e-mail accueil_bief@bief.org, World Wide Web http://www.bief.org. *CEO* Jean-Guy Boin. *New York Branch* French Publishers Agency, 853 Broadway, Suite 1509, New York, NY 10003-4703. Tel./fax 212-254-4540, World Wide Web http://frenchpubagency.com.

Cercle de la Librairie (Circle of Professionals of the Book Trade), 35 rue Grégoire-de-Tours, F-75006 Paris. Tel. 01-44-41-28-33, fax 01-44-41-28-65, e-mail commercial @electre.com, World Wide Web http:// www.electre.com. *Pres.* Charles Henri Flammarion.

Syndicat de la Librairie Française, 27 rue Bourgon, F-75013 Paris. Tel. 01-53-62-23-10, fax 01-53-62-10-45, e-mail slf@ nerim.fr, World Wide Web http://www. syndicat-librairie.fr. *Pres.* Benoit Bougerol.

Syndicat National de la Librairie Ancienne et Moderne (National Assn. of Antiquarians and Modern Booksellers), 4 rue Gît-le-Coeur, F-75006 Paris. Tel. 1-43-29-46-38, fax 1-43-25-41-63, e-mail slam-livre@ wanadoo.fr, World Wide Web http://www. slam-livre.fr. *Pres.* Alain Marchiset.

Syndicat National de l'Edition (National Union of Publishers), 115 blvd. Saint-Germain, F-75006 Paris. Tel. 1-44-41-40-50, fax 1-44-41-40-77, World Wide Web http:// www.snedition.fr. *Pres.* Serge Eyrolles.

## Germany

Börsenverein des Deutschen Buchhandels e.V. (Stock Exchange of German Booksellers), Grosser Hirschgraben 17-21, 60311 Frankfurt-am-Main. Tel. 069-13-06-0, fax 069-13-06-201, e-mail info@ boev.de, World Wide Web http://www. boersenverein.de. *Gen. Mgr.* Harald Heker.

Verband Deutscher Antiquare e.V. (German Antiquarian Booksellers Assn.), Geschäftsstelle, Norbert Munsch, Seeblick 1, 56459

Elbingen. Tel. 6435-909-147, fax 6435-909-148, e-mail buch@antiquare.de, World Wide Web http://www.antiquare.de. *Pres.* Eberhard Koestler.

## Greece

Hellenic Federation of Publishers and Booksellers, 73 Themistocleous St., 106 83 Athens. Tel. 2103-300-924, fax 2133-301-617, e-mail secretary@poev.gr, World Wide Web http://www.poev.gr. *Pres.* Dimitris Panteleskos, *Secy.-Gen.* Georgios Stefanou.

## Hungary

Magyar Könyvkiadók és Könyvterjesztök Egyesülése (Assn. of Hungarian Publishers and Booksellers), Postfach 130, 1367 Budapest. Tel. 1-343-2540, fax 1-343-2541, e-mail mkke@mkke.hu, World Wide Web http://www.mkke.hu. *Dir.* Peter Laszlo Zentai.

## Iceland

Félag Islenskra Bókaútgefenda (Icelandic Publishers Assn.), Baronsstig 5, 101 Reykjavik. Tel. 511-8020, fax 511-5020, e-mail baekur@simnet.is, World Wide Web http://www.bokatidindi.is.

## India

Federation of Indian Publishers, Federation House, 18/1C Institutional Area, Aruna Asaf Ali Marg, New Delhi 110067. Tel. 11-2696-4847, fax 11-2686-4054, e-mail fip1@satyam.net.in, World Wide Web http://www.fipindia.org. *Pres.* R. C. Govil.

## Indonesia

Ikatan Penerbit Indonesia (Assn. of Indonesian Book Publishers), Jl. Kalipasir 32, Jakarta 10330. Tel. 21-314-1907, fax 21-314-6050, e-mail sekretariat@ikapi.or.id. *Pres.* Arselan Harahap; *Secy.-Gen.* Robinson Rusdi.

## Ireland

CLÉ: The Irish Book Publishers' Assn., 25 Denzille Lane, Dublin 2. Tel. 1-639-4868, e-mail info@publishingireland.com, World Wide Web http://www.publishingireland.com. *Pres.* Seán Ó'Cearnaigh.

## Israel

Book and Printing Center, Israel Export Institute, 29 Hamered St., P.O. Box 50084, Tel Aviv 61500. Tel. 3-514-2868, fax 3-514-2902, e-mail export-institute@export.gov.il, World Wide Web http://www.export.gov.il. *Dir.-Gen.* Yechiel Assia.

Book Publishers' Assn. of Israel, P.O. Box 20123, 61201 Tel Aviv. Tel. 3-561-4121, fax 3-561-1996, e-mail hamol@tbpai.co.il, World Wide Web http://www.tbpai.co.il. *Managing Dir.* Amnon Ben-Shmuel; *Chair* Racheli Edelman.

## Italy

Associazione Italiana Editori (Italian Publishers Assn.), Corso di Porta Romana 108, 20122 Milan. Tel. 2-89-28-0800, fax 2-89-28-0860, e-mail aie@aie.it, World Wide Web http://www.aie.it. *Dir.* Ivan Cecchini.

Associazione Librai Antiquari d'Italia (Antiquarian Booksellers Assn. of Italy), Via Cassia 1020, Rome. Tel. 39-347-64-6-9147, fax 39-06-2332-8979, e-mail alai@alai.it, World Wide Web http://www.alai.it. *Pres.* Umberto Pregliasco.

## Jamaica

Booksellers' Assn. of Jamaica, P.O. Box 80, Kingston. Tel. 876-922-5883, fax 876-922-4743. *Pres.* Keith Shervington.

## Japan

Antiquarian Booksellers Association of Japan, 29 San-ei-cho, Shinjuku-ku, Tokyo 160-0008. Tel. 3-3357-1411, fax 3-3351-5855, e-mail abaj@abaj.gr.jp, World Wide Web http://www.abaj.gr.jp. *Pres.* Yoshio Nakao.

Japan Assn. of International Publications (formerly Japan Book Importers Assn.), Miyako-Bldg 3F, 3-17-3 Kanda-Jimbocho, Chiyoda-ku, Toyko 101-0051. Tel. 3-3264-8791, fax 3-3264-8790, e-mail jaip@poppy.ocn.ne.jp, World Wide Web http://

www.jaip.gr.jp. *Chair* Seishiro Murata; *Secy.-Gen.* Hiroshi Takahashi.

Japan Book Publishers Assn., 6 Fukuro-machi, Shinjuku-ku, Tokyo 162-0828. Tel. 3-3268-1301, fax 3-3268-1196, e-mail rd@jbpa.or.jp, World Wide Web http://www.jbpa.or.jp. *Pres.* Norio Komine; *Exec. Dir.* Tadashi Yamashita.

### Kenya

Kenya Publishers Assn., P.O. Box 42767, Nairobi 00100. Tel. 20-375-2344, fax 20-375-4076, e-mail info@kenyapublishers.org, World Wide Web http://www.kenyapublishers.org. *Chair* Nancy Karimi; *CEO* Robert Obudho.

### Korea (Republic of)

Korean Publishers Assn., 105-2 Sagan-dong, Jongro-gu, Seoul 110-190. Tel. 2-735-2701-4, fax 2-738-5414, e-mail webmaster @kpa21.or.kr, World Wide Web http://www.kpa21.or.kr.

### Latvia

Latvian Publishers' Assn., Brivibas 109-4, LV-1001 Riga. Tel. 7-282-392, fax 7-280-549, e-mail lga@gramatizdeveji.lv, World Wide Web http://www.gramatizdeveji.lv. *Pres.* Tenis Nigulis; *Exec. Dir.* Dace Pugaca.

### Lithuania

Lithuanian Publishers Assn., Ave. Jaksto 22-13, 01105 Vilnius. Tel./fax 5-261-7740, e-mail lla@centras.lt, World Wide Web http://www.lla.lt. *Pres.* Eugenijus Kaziliunas.

### Malaysia

Malaysian Book Publishers' Assn., No. 39 Jl. Nilam 1/2, Subang Sq., Subang High Tech Industrial Park Batu 3, 40000 Shah Alam, Selangor. Tel. 3-5637-9044, fax 3-5637-9043, e-mail inquiry@cerdik.com.my, World Wide Web http://www.mabopa.com.my. *Pres.* Law King Hui.

### Mexico

Cámara Nacional de la Industria Editorial Mexicana (Mexican Publishers' Assn.), Holanda No. 13, CP 04120, Mexico DF. Tel. 155-56-88-20-11, fax 155-56-04-31-47, e-mail difusion@caniem.com, World Wide Web http://www.caniem.com. *Pres.* Juan Luis Arzoz Arbide.

### The Netherlands

KVB—Koninklijke Vereeniging van het Boekenvak (formerly Koninklijke Vereeniging ter Bevordering van de Belangen des Boekhandels) (Royal Dutch Book Trade Assn.), Postbus 15007, 1001 MA Amsterdam. Tel. 20-624-02-12, fax 20-620-88-71, e-mail info@kvb.nl, World Wide Web http://www.kvb.nl. *Exec. Dir.* C. Verberne.

Nederlands Uitgeversverbond (Royal Dutch Publishers Assn.), Postbus 12040, 1100 AA Amsterdam. Tel. 20-43-09-150, fax 20-43-09-179, e-mail info@nuv.nl, World Wide Web http://www.nuv.nl. *Pres.* Henk J. L. Vonhoff.

Nederlandsche Vereeniging van Antiquaren (Netherlands Assn. of Antiquarian Booksellers), Prinsengracht 15, 2512 EW The Hague. Tel. 70-364-98-40, fax 70-364-33-40, e-mail kok@xs4all.nl, World Wide Web http://nvva.nl. *Pres.* Ton Kok.

Nederlandse Boekverkopersbond (Dutch Booksellers Assn.), Postbus 32, 3720 AA Bilhoven. Tel. 30-228-79-56, fax 030-228-45-66, e-mail nbb@boekbond.nl, World Wide Web http://www.boekbond.nl. *Pres.* W. Karssen; *Exec. Secy.* A. C. Doeser.

### New Zealand

Booksellers New Zealand, Box 13-248, Wellington. Tel. 4-478-5511, fax 4-478-5519, e-mail info@booksellers.co.nz, World Wide Web http://www.booksellers.co.nz. *CEO* Linda Henderson.

### Nigeria

Nigerian Publishers Assn., GPO Box 2541, Dugbe, Ibadan. Tel. 2-241-4427, fax 2-241-3396, e-mail nigpa@skannet.com. *Exec. Secy.* Ayoyinka Babatunde.

## Norway

Norske Bokhandlerforening (Norwegian Booksellers Assn.), Øvre Vollgate 15, 0158 Oslo. Tel. 22-39-68-00, fax 22-39-68-10, e-mail firmapost@bokhandler foreningen.no, World Wide Web http://www.bokhandlerforeningen.no. *Dir.* Kristin Cecilie Slordahl.

Norske Forleggerforening (Norwegian Publishers Assn.), Øvre Vollgate 15, 0158 Oslo. Tel. 22-00-75-80, fax 22-33-38-30, e-mail dnf@forleggerforeningen.no, World Wide Web http://www.forleggerforeningen.no. *Contact* Kristin Cecilie Slordahl.

## Peru

Cámara Peruana del Libro (Peruvian Publishers Assn.), Av. Cuba 427, Jesús María, Apdo. 10253, Lima 11. Tel. 511-472-9516, fax 511-265-0735, e-mail cp-libro@amauta.rcp.net.pe, World Wide Web http://www.cpl.org.pe. *Pres.* Gladys Diaz Carrera.

## Philippines

Philippine Educational Publishers Assn., 84 P. Florentino St., Sta. Mesa Heights, Quezon City. Tel. 2-712-4106, fax 2-731-3448, e-mail dbuhain@cnl.net, World Wide Web http://nbdb.gov.ph/publindust.htm. *Pres.* Dominador D. Buhain.

## Poland

Polskie Towarzystwo Wydawców Książek (Polish Society of Book Editors), ul. Świętokrzyska 30, 00-116 Warsaw. Tel. 22-407-77-30, fax 22-850-34-76, e-mail ptwk@wp.pl, World Wide Web http://www.wydawca.com.pl. *Dir.* Maria Kuisz.

Stowarzyszenia Księgarzy Polskich (Assn. of Polish Booksellers), ul. Mazowiecka 2/4, 00-048 Warsaw. Tel. 22-827-93-81, e-mail skp@ksiegarze.org.pl, World Wide Web: http://www.ksiegarze.org.pl. *Pres.* Tadeusz Hussak.

## Portugal

Associação Portuguesa de Editores e Livreiros (Portuguese Assn. of Publishers and Book-

sellers), Av. dos Estados Unidas da America 97, 6 Esq., 1700-167 Lisbon. Tel. 21-843-51-80, fax 21-848-93-77, e-mail apel@apel.pt, World Wide Web http://www.apel.pt. *Pres.* Graca Didier.

## Russia

Assn. of Book Publishers of Russia, ul. B. Nikitskaya 44, 121069 Moscow. Tel. 495-202-1174, fax 495-202-3989, e-mail aski@rol.ru, World Wide Web http://www.aski.ru. *Pres.* Chechenev Constantine Vasilyevich; *Exec. Dir.* Solonenko Vladimir Constantinovich.

Rossiiskaya Knizhnaya Palata (Russian Book Chamber), Kremlin nab, 1/9, 119019 Moscow. Tel. 495-688-96-89, fax 495-688-99-91, e-mail bookch@postman.ru, World Wide Web http://www.bookchamber.ru.

## Serbia and Montenegro

Association of Yugoslav Publishers and Booksellers, P.O. Box 883, 11000 Belgrade. Tel. 11-642-533, fax 11-686-539, e-mail ognjenl@eunet.yu. *Dir.* Zivadin Mitrovic; *Mgr.* Marina Radojicic.

## Singapore

Singapore Book Publishers Assn., c/o Cannon International, Block 86, Marine Parade Central No. 03-213, Singapore 440086. Tel. 6344-7801, fax 6344-0897, e-mail twcsbpa@singnet.com.sg, World Wide Web http://www.publishers-sbpa.org.sg. *Pres.* Tan Wu Cheng.

## Slovenia

Zdruzenie Zaloznikov in Knjigotrzcev Slovenije Gospodarska Zbornica Slovenije (Assn. of Publishers and Booksellers of Slovenia), Dimičeva 13, SI 1504 Ljubljana. Tel. 1-5898-000, fax 1-5898-100, e-mail info@gzs.si, World Wide Web http://www.gzs.si. *Pres.* Milan Matos.

## South Africa

Publishers Assn. of South Africa, P.O. Box 106, Green Point 8051. Tel. 21-425-2721, fax 21-421-3270, e-mail pasa@publishsa.

co.za, World Wide Web http://www. publishsa.co.za. *Exec. Dir.* Dudley Schroeder; *Mgr.* Samantha Faure.

South African Booksellers Assn. (formerly Associated Booksellers of Southern Africa), P.O. Box 870, Bellville 7530. Tel. 21-945-1572, fax 21-945-2169, e-mail saba@ sabooksellers.com, World Wide Web http://sabooksellers.com. *Chair and Pres.* Guru Redhi.

## Spain

Federación de Gremios de Editores de España (Federation of Spanish Publishers Assns.), Cea Bermúdez 44-2 Dcha, 2003 Madrid. Tel. 915-345-195, fax 915-352-625, e-mail fgee@fge.es, World Wide Web http:// www.federacioneditores.org. *Pres.* D. Jordi Ubedai Baulo; *Exec. Dir.* Antonio María Avila.

## Sri Lanka

Sri Lanka Book Publishers Association, 53 Maligakanda Rd., Colombo. E-mail bookpub@sltnet.lk. *Gen. Secy.* Upali Wanigasooriya.

## Sudan

Sudanese Publishers Assn., c/o Institute of African and Asian Studies, Khartoum Univ., P.O. Box 321, Khartoum 11115. Tel. 11-77-0022, fax 11-770-358, e-mail makkawi@sudanmail.net. *Dir.* Abel Rahim Makkawi.

## Sweden

Svenska Förläggareföreningen (Swedish Publishers Assn.), Drottninggatan 97, S-11360 Stockholm. Tel. 8-736-19-40, fax 8-736-19-44, e-mail info@forlaggareforeningen. se, World Wide Web http://www. forlaggare.se. *Dir.* Kristina Ahlinder.

## Switzerland

Association Suisse des Éditeurs de Langue Française (ASELF) (Swiss Assn. of English-Language Publishers), 2 ave. Agassiz, 1001 Lausanne. Tel. 21-319-71-11, fax 21-319-79-10, e-mail aself@centrezational.cl,

World Wide Web http://www.culturactif. ch/editions/asef1.htm. *Secy. Gen.* Philippe Schibli.

Schweizerischer Buchhandler- und Verleger-Verband (Swiss German-Language Booksellers and Publishers Assn.), Alderstr. 40, Postfach, 8034 Zurich. Tel. 044-421-36-00, fax 044-421-36-18, e-mail sbvv@ swissbooks.ch, World Wide Web http:// www.swissbooks.ch. *Exec. Dir.* Martin Jann.

## Thailand

Publishers and Booksellers Assn. of Thailand, 83/156 Moo 6 Ngam Wong Wan Rd., Toong Song Hong, Laksi, Bangkok 10210. Tel. 2-954-9560-4, fax 2-954-9565-6, e-mail info@pubat.or.th, World Wide Web http://www.pubat.or.th.

## Uganda

Uganda Publishers and Booksellers Assn., P.O. Box 7732, Kampala. Tel. 41-270-370, fax 41-251-352, e-mail mbd@infocom. co.ug. *Contact* Martin Okia.

## United Kingdom

Antiquarian Booksellers Assn., Sackville House, 40 Piccadilly, London W1J 0DR, England. Tel. 20-7439-3118, fax 20-7439-3119, e-mail admin@aba.org.uk, World Wide Web http://www.aba.org.uk. *Admin.* Clare Pedder; *Secy.* John Critchley.

Assn. of Learned and Professional Society Publishers, Blenheim House, 120 Church St., Brighton BN1 1AU, England. Tel. 1275-858-837, World Wide Web http:// www.alpsp.org. *Chief Exec.* Ian Russell.

Booktrust, 45 East Hill, Wandsworth, London SW18 2QZ, England. Tel. 20-8516-2977, fax 20-8516-2978, e-mail query@ booktrust.org.uk, World Wide Web http:// www.booktrust.org.uk.

Educational Publishers Council, 29B Montague St., London WC1B 5BW, England. Tel. 20-7691-9191, fax 20-7691-9199, e-mail mail@publishers.org.uk, World Wide Web http://www.publishers.org.uk. *Chair* Paul Shuter; *Dir.* Graham Taylor.

Publishers Assn., 29B Montague St., London WC1B 5BW, England. Tel. 20-7691-9191, fax 20-7691-9199, e-mail mail@publishers.org.uk, World Wide Web http://www.publishers.org.uk. *Pres.* Mike Boswood; *Chief Exec.* Simon Juden.

Scottish Book Trust, Sandeman House, Trunk's Close, 55 High St., Edinburgh EH1 1SR, Scotland. Tel. 131-524-0160, fax 131-524-0161, e-mail info@scottishbooktrust.com, World Wide Web http://www.scottishbooktrust.com. *CEO* Marc Lambert.

Welsh Books Council (Cyngor Llyfrau Cymru), Castell Brychan, Aberystwyth, Ceredigion SY23 2JB, Wales. Tel. 1970-624-151, fax 1970-625-385, e-mail castellbrychan@wbc.org.uk, World Wide Web http://www.cllc.org.uk. *Dir.* Gwerfyl Pierce Jones.

## Uruguay

Cámara Uruguaya del Libro (Uruguayan Publishers Assn.), Colon 1476, Apdo. 102, 11 200 Montevideo. Tel. 82-916-93-74, fax 82-916-76-28, e-mail info@camaradellibro.com.uy, World Wide Web http://www.camaradellibro.com.uy. *Pres.* Alvaro Juan Risso Castellanos.

## Venezuela

Cámara Venezolana del Libro (Venezuelan Publishers Assn.), Av. Andrés Bello, Centro Andrés Bello, Torre Oeste 11, piso 11, of. 112-0, Caracas 1050. Tel. 212-793-1347, fax 212-793-1368, e-mail unegi@cavelibro.org, World Wide Web http://www.cavelibro.org. *Pres.* Leonardo Ramos.

## Zambia

Booksellers and Publishers Assn. of Zambia, P.O. Box 31838, Lusaka. Tel./fax 1-255-166, e-mail bpaz@zamtel.zm, World Wide Web http://africanpublishers.org.

## Zimbabwe

Zimbabwe Book Publishers Assn., P.O. Box 3041, Harare. Tel./fax 4-754-256, e-mail engelbert@collegepress.co.zw.

# National Information Standards
# Organization (NISO) Standards

## Information Retrieval

Z39.2-1994 (R2001)   Information Interchange Format
Z39.47-1993 (R2003)  Extended Latin Alphabet Coded Character Set for
                     Bibliographic Use (ANSEL)
Z39.50-2003          Information Retrieval (Z39.50) Application Service
                     Definition and Protocol Specification
Z39.53-2001          Codes for the Representation of Languages for
                     Information Interchange
Z39.64-1989          (R2002) East Asian Character Code for Bibliographic Use
Z39.76-1996          (R2002) Data Elements for Binding Library Materials
Z39.84-2005          Syntax for the Digital Object Identifier
Z39.88-2004          The OpenURL Framework for Context-Sensitive Services
Z39.89-2003          The U.S. National Z39.50 Profile for Library Applications

## Library Management

Z39.7-2004           Information Services and Use: metrics and statistics for
                     libraries and information providers—Data Dictionary
Z39.20-1999          Criteria for Price Indexes for Print Library Materials
Z39.71-2006          Holdings Statements for Bibliographic Items
Z39.73-1994 (R2001)  Single-Tier Steel Bracket Library Shelving
Z39.83-1-2008        NISO Circulation Interchange Part 1: Protocol (NCIP)
Z39.83-2-2002        NISO Circulation Interchange Protocol (NCIP) Part 2:
                     Implementation Profile 1
Z39.93-2007          The Standardized Usage Statistics Harvesting Initiative
                     (SUSHI) Protocol

## Preservation and Storage

Z39.32-1996 (R2002)  Information on Microfiche Headers
Z39.48-1992 (R2002)  Permanence of Paper for Publications and Documents in
                     Libraries and Archives
Z39.62-2000          Eye-Legible Information on Microfilm Leaders and
                     Trailers and on Containers of Processed Microfilm on
                     Open Reels

Z39.74-1996 (R2002)  Guides to Accompany Microform Sets
Z39.77-2001           Guidelines for Information About Preservation Products
Z39.78-2000 (R2006)  Library Binding
Z39.79-2001           Environmental Conditions for Exhibiting Library and
                      Archival Materials
Z39.87-2006           Data Dictionary—Technical Metadata for Digital Still
                      Images

## Publishing and Information Management

Z39.9-1992 (R2001)   International Standard Serial Numbering (ISSN)
Z39.14-1997 (R2002)  Guidelines for Abstracts
Z39.18-2005           Scientific and Technical Reports—Preparation,
                      Presentation, and Preservation
Z39.19-2005           Guidelines for the Construction, Format, and Management
                      of Monolingual Controlled Vocabularies
Z39.23-1997 (R2002)  Standard Technical Report Number Format and Creation
Z39.26-1997 (R2002)  Micropublishing Product Information
Z39.29-2005           Bibliographic References
Z39.41-1997 (R2002)  Printed Information on Spines
Z39.43-1993 (R2006)  Standard Address Number (SAN) for the Publishing
                      Industry
Z39.56-1996 (R2002)  Serial Item and Contribution Identifier (SICI)
Z39.82-2001           Title Pages for Conference Publications
Z39.85-2001           Dublin Core Metadata Element Set
Z39.86-2005           Specifications for the Digital Talking Book
ANSI/NISO/ISO         Electronic Manuscript Preparation and Markup
12083-1995 (R2002)

## In Development/NISO Initiatives

NISO examines new areas for standardization, reports, and best practices on a continuing basis to support its ongoing standards development program. NISO working groups are exploring these areas:

- Cost of Resource Exchange (CORE)
- DAISY Standard (ANSI/NISO Z39.86 - 2005 Specifications for the Digital Talking Book) Revision
- Exchange of Serial Subscription Information Serials JWP—(NISO and EDItEUR)
- Institutional Identifiers (I2)
- KBART (Knowledge Bases and Releated Tools)-(NISO and UKSG)
- ONIX-PL—(NISO and EDItEUR)
- Metasearch Initiative—Access Management, Collection Description, and Search/Retrieve
- NISO Circulation Interchange Protocol (NCIP) Interest Group

- Standardized Usage Statistics Harvesting Initiative (SUSHI) Standing Committee
- SERU Standing Committee

**NISO Technical Reports, Recommended Practices, and Other Publications**

*Best Practices for Designing Web Services in the Library Context* (RP-2006-01)

*Environmental Guidelines for the Storage of Paper Records* (TR01-1995)

*A Framework of Guidance for Building Good Digital Collections*

*Guidelines for Indexes and Related Information Retrieval Devices* (TR02-1997)

*Guidelines to Alphanumeric Arrangement and Sorting of Numerals and Other Symbols* (TR03-1999)

*Information Standards Quarterly* (*ISQ*) (NISO quarterly magazine)

*Journal Article Versions (JAV): Recommendations of the NISO/ALPSP JAV Technical Working Group* (RP-8-2008)

*Metadata Demystified: A Guide for Publishers*

*Networked Reference Services: Question/Answer Transaction Protocol* (TR04-2006)

*NISO Metasearch XML Gateway Implementers Guide* (RP-2006-02)

*NISO Newsline* (free monthly e-newsletter)

*Ranking of Authentication and Access Methods Available to the Metasearch Environment* (RP-2005-01)

*RFID in U.S. Libraries* (RP-6-2008)

*The RFP Writer's Guide to Standards for Library Systems*

*Search and Retrieval Citation Level Data Elements* (RP-2005-03)

*Search and Retrieval Results Set Metadata* (RP-2005-02)

*SERU: A Shared Electronic Resource Understanding* (RP-7-2008)

*Understanding Metadata*

*Up and Running: Implementing Z39.50—Proceedings of a Symposium Sponsored by the State Library of Iowa*

*Z39.50: A Primer on the Protocol*

*Z39.50 Implementation Experiences*

Workshop reports and white papers are available on the NISO Web site at http://www.niso.org/standards/std_resources.html.

For more information, contact NISO, 1 North Charles St., Baltimore, MD 21201. Tel. 301-654-2512, fax 410-685-5278, e-mail nisohq@niso.org, World Wide Web http://www.niso.org.

# Calendar, 2009–2016

The list below contains information on association meetings or promotional events that are, for the most part, national or international in scope. State and regional library association meetings are also included. To confirm the starting or ending date of a meeting, which may change after the *Library and Book Trade Almanac* has gone to press, contact the association directly. Addresses of library and book trade associations are listed in Part 6 of this volume. For information on additional book trade and promotional events, see *Literary Market Place* and *International Literary Market Place,* published by Information Today, Inc., and other library and book trade publications such as *Library Journal, School Library Journal,* and *Publishers Weekly. American Libraries,* published by the American Library Association, maintains an online calendar at http://www.ala.org/ala/alonline/calendar/calendar.cfm. An Information Today events calendar can be found at http://www.infotoday.com/calendar.shtml.

## 2009

### June

| | | |
|---|---|---|
| 1–4 | International Assn. of Technological University Libraries (IATUL) | Leuven, Belgium |
| 3–4 | Inspiration, Innovation, and Celebration: An Entrepreneurial Conference for Librarians | University of North Carolina, Greensboro |
| 4–7 | North American Serials Group | Asheville, NC |
| 4–8 | Bookfest | Bucharest, Romania |
| 5–7 | London Antiquarian Book Fair | London, England |
| 8–11 | IEEE Intelligence and Security Informatics 2009 | Dallas, TX |
| 8–11 | Search Engine Strategies 2009 | Toronto, ON |
| 10–12 | International Conference on Electronic Publishing (ELPUB 2009) | Milan, Italy |
| 13–16 | Cape Town Book Fair | Cape Town, South Africa |
| 14–16 | Next Library International Unconference | Aarhus, Denmark |
| 14–17 | Special Libraries Assn. | Washington, DC |
| 15–19 | Joint Conference on Digital Libraries (JCDL 2009) | Austin, TX |

**June 2009** *(cont.)*

| | | |
|---|---|---|
| 18–21 | Assn. of American University Presses (AAUP) | Philadelphia, PA |
| 20–25 | Assn. of Seventh-Day Adventist Librarians | Berrien Springs, MI |
| 21–22 | BookExpo Canada | Toronto, ON |
| 22–23 | British Chapter of the International Society for Knowledge Organization | London, England |
| 23–24 | Second International m-Libraries Conference | Vancouver, BC |
| 24–26 | International Conference on Digital Libraries (ICDL 2009) | Paris, France |
| 30–7/3 | LIBER General Conference | Toulouse, France |

**July**

| | | |
|---|---|---|
| 8–10 | International PKP Scholarly Publishing Conference | Vancouver, BC |
| 9–12 | Tokyo International Book Fair | Tokyo, Japan |
| 9–15 | American Library Assn. Annual Conference | Chicago, IL |
| 20–25 | International Conference on Advances in Multimedia (MMEDIA 2009) | Colmar, France |
| 22–28 | Hong Kong Book Fair | Hong Kong, China |

**August**

| | | |
|---|---|---|
| 5–7 | Pacific Northwest Library Assn. | Missoula, MT |
| 6–9 | Americas Conference on Information Systems (AMCIS 2009) | San Francisco, CA |
| 23–27 | IFLA World Library and Information Congress | Milan, Italy |
| 25–28 | American Assn. of Law Libraries | Washington, DC |
| 31–9/1 | Libraries and Society: A Pan-Mediterranean Perspective | Palermo, Italy |
| 31–9/4 | International Congress on Medical Librarianship | Brisbane, Australia |

**September**

| | | |
|---|---|---|
| 2–7 | Moscow International Book Fair (MIBF) | Moscow, Russia |
| 3–4 | European Conference on Knowledge Management (ECKM 2009) | Vicenza, Italy |
| 3–7 | Beijing International Book Fair (BIBF) | Beijing, China |
| 10–13 | Lviv International Book Fair | Lviv, Ukraine |
| 11–13 | Assn. for Rural and Small Libraries | Gaitlinburg, TN |
| 13–15 | WebSearch University | Washington, DC |
| 16–18 | Open Research Society World Summit on the Knowledge Society | Crete, Greece |
| 23–25 | North Dakota Library Assn. | Dickinson |
| 24–27 | Göteborg Book Fair | Göteborg, Sweden |

| | | |
|---|---|---|
| 27–10/2 | European Conference on Digital Libraries | Corfu, Greece |
| 30–10/2 | West Virginia Library Assn. | Snowshoe Mountain |
| 30–10/3 | Idaho Library Assn. | Burley |
| 30–10/3 | Kentucky Library Assn./Kentucky School Media Assn. | Louisville |
| 30–10/3 | Wyoming Library Assn. | Laramie |

**October**

| | | |
|---|---|---|
| 1–3 | LITA National Forum | Salt Lake City, UT |
| 1–4 | National Diversity in Libraries Conference | Louisville, KY |
| 5–8 | International Conference on Academic Libraries | Delhi, India |
| 6–9 | Illinois Library Assn. | Peoria |
| 6–9 | North Carolina Library Assn. | Greenville |
| 7–9 | Assn. of Bookmobiles and Outreach Services | Everett, WA |
| 7–9 | Georgia Library Assn. | Columbus |
| 7–9 | Minnesota Library Assn. | Duluth |
| 7–9 | Missouri Library Assn. | Columbia |
| 7–9 | South Dakota Library Assn. | Aberdeen |
| 7–10 | Nevada Library Assn. | Elko |
| 12–17 | New York Library Assn. | Niagara Falls |
| 14–16 | Minnesota Library Assn. | St. Cloud |
| 14–18 | Frankfurt Book Fair | Frankfurt, Germany |
| 15–16 | Internet Librarian International | London, England |
| 15–18 | ARMA Annual Conference | Orlando, FL |
| 18–20 | Indiana Library Federation | Fort Wayne |
| 18–20 | New England Library Assn. | Hartford, CT |
| 18–21 | Pennsylvania Library Assn. | Harrisburg |
| 20–22 | International Conference on the Knowledge Economy (ICKE2009) | Sandton, South Africa |
| 20–23 | Mississippi Library Assn. | Hattiesburg |
| 20–23 | Wisconsin Library Assn. | Appleton |
| 21–23 | Iowa Library Assn. | Des Moines |
| 21–23 | Ohio Library Council | Cleveland |
| 21–23 | Ohio Educational Library Media Assn. | Columbus |
| 22–24 | Mississippi Library Assn. | Natchez |
| 22–25 | Helsinki Book Fair | Helsinki, Finland |
| 24–27 | Arkansas Library Assn. | Hot Springs |
| 25–27 | International Symposium on Wikis (WikiSym 2009) | Orlando, FL |
| 26–28 | Internet Librarian 2009 | Monterey, CA |
| 28–30 | Nebraska Library Assn. | LaVista |
| 28–30 | South Carolina Library Assn. | Columbia |
| 29–30 | Virginia Library Assn. | Williamsburg |
| 30–11/2 | California Library Assn. | Pasadena |
| 31–11/8 | Istanbul Book Fair | Istanbul, Turkey |

## November 2009

| | | |
|---|---|---|
| 3–6 | Michigan Library Assn. | Lansing |
| 4 | Going Green? Sustainable Publishing | London, England |
| 4–7 | Michigan Library Assn. | Lansing |
| 5–8 | American Assn. of School Librarians | Charlotte, NC |
| 6–11 | ASIS&T Annual Meeting | Vancouver, BC |
| 11–21 | Sharjah International Book Fair | Sharjah, UAE |
| 13–15 | Basel Literature Festival (Buch.09) | Basel, Switzerland |
| 14–18 | American Medical Informatics Assn. | San Francisco |
| 17–19 | KMWorld & Intranets | San José, CA |
| 18–23 | Montreal Book Fair | Montreal, PQ |
| 19–21 | Colorado Assn. of Libraries | Denver |
| 19–21 | Virginia Educational Media Assn. | Roanoke |
| 19–22 | California School Library Association | Ontario |
| 28–12/6 | Guadalajara International Book Fair | Guadalajara, Mexico |

## December

| | | |
|---|---|---|
| 7–9 | Arizona Library Assn. | Glendale |
| 8–12 | Military Librarians Workshop | Monterey, CA |
| 15–18 | International Conference on Information Systems (ICIS 2009) | Phoenix, AZ |

## 2010

### January

| | | |
|---|---|---|
| 15–20 | American Library Assn. Midwinter Meeting | Boston, MA |

### March

| | | |
|---|---|---|
| 23–27 | Public Library Assn. | Portland, OR |

### April

| | | |
|---|---|---|
| 4–6 | Wisconsin Educational Media and Technology Assn. | Wisconsin Dells |
| 7–9 | Kansas Library Assn. | Wichita |
| 13–16 | Texas Library Assn. | San Antonio |
| 18–20 | Missouri Assn. of School Librarians | Osage Beach |
| 19–21 | London Book Fair | London, England |
| 19–21 | Oklahoma Library Assn. | Oklahoma City |

### May

| | | |
|---|---|---|
| 13–14 | Delaware Library Assn. | Dover |

### June

| | | |
|---|---|---|
| 24–30 | American Library Assn. Annual Conference | Washington, DC |

**August**

| | | |
|---|---|---|
| 4–9 | BCALA Conference of African American Librarians | Birmingham, AL |
| 11–13 | Washington Library Assn. | Victoria, BC |

**September**

| | | |
|---|---|---|
| 23–25 | Assn. for Library Service to Children | Atlanta, GA |

**October**

| | | |
|---|---|---|
| 6–8 | Minnesota Library Assn. | Rochester |
| 12–14 | Iowa Library Assn. | Coralville |
| 17–19 | New England Library Assn. | Boxborough, MA |

**November**

| | | |
|---|---|---|
| 4–7 | YALSA Young Adult Literature Symposium | Albuquerque, NM |

# 2011

**January**

| | | |
|---|---|---|
| 7–11 | American Library Assn. Midwinter Meeting | San Diego, CA |

**April**

| | | |
|---|---|---|
| 6–8 | Kansas Library Assn. | Topeka |
| 7–10 | Assn. of College and Research Libraries | Philadelphia, PA |
| 12–15 | Texas Library Assn. | Austin |

**June**

| | | |
|---|---|---|
| 23–28 | American Library Assn. Annual Conference | New Orleans, LA |

**October**

| | | |
|---|---|---|
| 5–7 | Minnesota Library Assn. | Duluth |
| 26–30 | American Assn. of School Librarians | Minneapolis, MN |

# 2012

**January**

| | | |
|---|---|---|
| 20–24 | American Library Assn. Midwinter Meeting | Dallas, TX |

**April**

| | | |
|---|---|---|
| 24–27 | Texas Library Assn. | Houston |

**June**

| | | |
|---|---|---|
| 21–26 | American Library Assn. Annual Conference | Anaheim, CA |

# 2013

**January**

25–29    American Library Assn. Midwinter Meeting    Seattle, WA

**April**

4–7      Assn. of College and Research Libraries     Indianapolis, IN
8–11     Texas Library Assn.                          San Antonio

**June**

27–7/2   American Library Assn. Annual Conference     Chicago, IL

# 2014

**January**

24–29    American Library Assn. Midwinter Meeting    Philadelphia, PA

**April**

8–11     Texas Library Assn.                          Dallas

**June**

26–1/7   American Library Assn. Annual Conference     Las Vegas, NV

# 2015

**January**

23–27    American Library Assn. Midwinter Meeting    Chicago, IL

**April**

10–17    Texas Library Assn.                          Austin

**June**

25–30    American Library Assn. Annual Conference     San Francisco, CA

# 2016

**January**

22–26    American Library Assn. Midwinter Meeting    Boston, MA

**June**

23–28    American Library Assn. Annual Conference     Orlando, FL

# Acronyms

## A

AALL. American Association of Law
Libraries
AAP. Association of American Publishers
AASL. American Association of School
Librarians
ABA. American Booksellers Association
ABFFE. American Booksellers Foundation
for Free Expression
ACAP. ACAP (Automated Content Access
Protocol) Validator
ACRL. Association of College and Research
Libraries
AIC. American Institute for the Conservation
of Historic and Artistic Works
AIIP. Association of Independent
Information Professionals
AILA. American Indian Library Association
AJL. Association of Jewish Libraries
ALA. American Library Association
ALCTS. Association for Library Collections
and Technical Services
ALIC. National Archives and Records
Administration, Archives Library
Information Center
ALISE. Association for Library and
Information Science Education
ALS. National Center for Education
Statistics, Academic Library Survey
ALSC. Association for Library Service to
Children
ALTAFF. Association for Library Trustees,
Advocates, Friends, and Foundations
AMAC. Alternative Media Access Center
AMMLA. American Merchant Marine
Library Association
APA. Allied Professional Association
APALA. Asian/Pacific American Librarians
Association

ARC. National Archives and Records
Administration, Archival Research
Catalog
ARL. Association of Research Libraries
ARLIS/NA. Art Libraries Society of North
America
ASCLA. Association of Specialized and
Cooperative Library Agencies
ASIS&T. American Society for Information
Science and Technology
ATLA. American Theological Library
Association

## B

BCALA. Black Caucus of the American
Library Association
BEA. BookExpo America
BEC. BookExpo Canada
BIG. Conferences and seminars, Blacks in
Government
BSA. Bibliographical Society of America

## C

CACUL. Canadian Association of College
and University Libraries
CAIS. Canadian Association for Information
Science
CALA. Chinese American Librarians
Association
CAP. Canada, Community Access Program
CAPL. Canadian Association of Public
Libraries
CARL. Canadian Association of Research
Libraries
CASL. Canadian Association for School
Libraries
CASLIS. Canadian Association of Special
Libraries and Information Services

CCC. Copyright Clearance Center
CCF. Cultural Community Fund
CD-ROM. Compact Disc Read-Only
    Memory
CDNL. Conference of Directors of National
    Libraries
CERN. European Organization for Nuclear
    Research
*CGP*. Government Printing Office, *Catalog
    of Government Publications*
CIP. Internet/Web, Canadian Internet Project
CITF. Association of American Publishers,
    Critical Issues Task Force
CLA. Canadian Library Association
CLIR. Council on Library and Information
    Resources
CLTA. Canadian Library Trustees
    Association
CMHR. Canadian Museum for Human
    Rights
CNI. Coalition for Networked Information
CNIB. Canadian National Institute for the
    Blind
COLT. Council on Library/Media
    Technicians
COPA. Child Online Protection Act
COSLA. Chief Officers of State Library
    Agencies
CRKN. Networks and networking, Canadian
    Research Knowledge Network
CSLA. Church and Synagogue Library
    Association
CSRL. Center for the Study of Rural
    Librarianship

**D**

DLF. Digital Library Federation
DMCA. Digital Millennium Copyright Act
DRM. Digital rights management
DTIC. Defense Technical Information Center

**E**

EAR. National Technical Information
    Service, Export Administration
    Regulations
EDB. National Technical Information
    Service, Energy Science and
    Technology Database

EMIERT. American Library Association,
    Ethnic and Multicultural Information
    and Exchange Round Table
EPA. Environmental Protection Agency
ERC. European Research Council
ERIC. Educational Resources Information
    Center
ERMI 2. Digital Library Federation,
    Electronic Resources Management
    Initiative

**F**

FAFLRT. American Library Association,
    Federal and Armed Forces Librarians
    Round Table
FAIFE. International Federation of Library
    Associations and Institutions,
    Freedom of Access to Information and
    Freedom of Expression
FAIR. Internet/Web, FAIR (Freely Available
    Institute Resources)
FBI. Federal Bureau of Investigation
FDLP. Government Printing Office, Federal
    Depository Library Program
FDsys. Government Printing Office, Federal
    Digital System
FEDRIP. National Technical Information
    Service, FEDRIP (Federal Research in
    Progress Database)
FIAF. International Federation of Film
    Archives
FISA. Foreign Intelligence Surveillance Act
FLICC. Federal Library and Information
    Center Committee
FOIA. Freedom of Information Act
FOLUSA. Friends of Libraries U.S.A.
FPC. Federal Publishers Committee

**G**

GLBT. American Library Association, Gay,
    Lesbian, Bisexual, and Transgendered
    Round Table
GLIN. Global Legal Information Network
GODORT. American Library Association,
    Government Documents Round Table
GPO. Government Printing Office
GSU. Georgia State University

GWAS. National Center for Biotechnology Information, Genome-Wide Association Studies (GWAS) project

LSP. National Center for Education Statistics, Library Statistics Program

LSTA. Library Services and Technology Act

# I

IAALD. International Association of Agricultural Information Specialists

IACs. Defense Technical Information Center, Information Analysis Centers

IALL. International Association of Law Libraries

IAML. International Association of Music Libraries, Archives, and Documentation Centres

IASL. International Association of School Librarianship

IATUL. International Association of Technological University Libraries

ICA. International Council on Archives

IFLA. International Federation of Library Associations and Institutions

IFRT. American Library Association, Intellectual Freedom Round Table

ILL/DD. Interlibrary loan/document delivery

ILS. Government Printing Office, Integrated Library System

IMLS. Institute of Museum and Library Services

ISBN. International Standard Book Number

ISO. International Organization for Standardization

ISSN. International Standard Serial Number

# L

LAC. Library and Archives Canada

LCDP. Association of Research Libraries, Leadership and Career Development Program

LHRT. American Library Association, Library History Round Table

LIS. Library/information science

LITA. Library and Information Technology Association

*LJ. Library Journal*

LLAMA. Library Leadership and Management Association

LRRT. American Library Association, Library Research Round Table

# M

MAGERT. American Library Association, Map and Geography Round Table

METS. Digital Library Federation, Metadata Encoding and Transmission Standard

MLA. Medical Library Association; Music Library Association

# N

NAGARA. National Association of Government Archives and Records Administrators

NAL. National Agricultural Library

NARA. National Archives and Records Administration

NCBI. National Center for Biotechnology Information

NCES. National Center for Education Statistics

NCLA. National Church Library Association

NCLB. No Child Left Behind

NCLIS. National Commission on Libraries and Information Science

NDIIPP. National Digital Information Infrastructure and Preservation Program

NDNP. Newspapers, National Digital Newspaper Program

NEH. National Endowment for the Humanities

NFAIS. National Federation of Advanced Information Services

NIH. National Institutes of Health

NISO. National Information Standards Organization

NLE. National Library of Education

NLM. National Library of Medicine

NMRT. American Library Association, New Members Round Table

NSL. National Security Letter

NTIS. National Technical Information Service

NTRL. National Technical Information Service, National Technical Reports Library

NVLP. Library of Congress, National Visionary Leadership Project

**O**

OD. Organization development in libraries
OJS. Software programs, Open Journal Systems (OJS) software

**P**

PGC. Portrait Gallery Canada
PLA. Public Library Association
PMC. PubMedCentral
PTDLA. Patent and Trademark Depository Library Association
PTFS. Progressive Technology Federal Systems, Inc.
*PW. Publishers Weekly*

**R**

RIAA. Recording Industry Association of America
RUSA. Reference and User Services Association

**S**

SAA. Society of American Archivists
SAN. Standard Address Number
SHVERA. Satellite Home Viewer Extension and Reauthorization Act
SIIA. Software and Information Industry Association
SLA. Special Libraries Association
SPARC. SPARC (Scholarly Publishing and Academic Resources Coalition)

SRIM. National Technical Information Service, Selected Research in Microfiche
SRRT. American Library Association, Social Responsibilities Round Table
SSP. Society for Scholarly Publishing
StLA. State libraries and library agencies, IMLS State Library Agencies

**T**

TBPA. Taiwan Book Publishers Association
TLA. Theatre Library Association

**U**

ULC. Urban Libraries Council

**V**

VHP. History, Veterans History Project

**W**

WDL. World Digital Library
WLIC. World Library and Information Congress
WNC. World News Connection
WSIS. World Summit on the Information Society

**Y**

YALSA. Young Adult Library Services Association
YPG. Association of American Pubishers, Young to Publishing Group

# Index of Organizations

Please note that many cross-references refer to entries in the Subject Index.

# Subject Index

Please note that many cross-references refer to entries in the Index of Organizations.